FREE AFRICAN AMERICANS

NORTH CAROLINA
VIRGINIA, AND
SOUTH CAROLINA

From the Colonial Period to About 1820

VOLUME I

Winner:
North Carolina Genealogical Society
Award of Excellence in Publishing
and
The American Society of Genealogists'
Donald Lines Jacobus Award

Fifth Edition
by
Paul Heinegg

CLEARFIELD

First Edition, 1992
Second Edition, 1994
Third Edition, 1997
Fourth Edition, 2001
Fifth Edition, 2005

Printed for
Clearfield Company by
Genealogical Publishing Co.
Baltimore, Maryland
2005

Reprinted for
Clearfield Company by
Genealogical Publishing Co.
Baltimore, Maryland
2006, 2007

Volume I ISBN-13: 978-0-8063-5281-7
Volume I ISBN-10: 0-8063-5281-7
Set ISBN-13: 978-0-8063-5280-0
Set ISBN-10: 0-8063-5280-9

Made in the United States of America

Dedicated to the memory of

my mother-in-law,

Katherine Kee Phillips,

a descendant of the
James, Peters, Tann, and Walden Families

CONTENTS

FOREWORD

by
Ira Berlin

If the family is the building block of society, it is also the keystone of historical understanding. Nowhere is this more evident than in the study of black people who were free in the slave societies of the Americas. Often the product of relationships between slaves and free people of various admixtures of African, Native American, and European descent, the free blacks' familial origins and subsequent domestic connections determined their legal status and shaped, in large measure, their social standing. No one has made this point more forcefully than Paul Heinegg, who, during the last twenty years, has meticulously constructed and reconstructed the genealogies of free people of color, first in Maryland and Delaware and then in Virginia and North Carolina. Now, with this expansion of his earlier book on North Carolina and Virginia, Heinegg has extended his work to South Carolina. Taken together, Heinegg provides the fullest discussion of the familial origins of free people of color in the Anglophone colonial South.

Heinegg's work has been of inestimable value to genealogists eager to trace their family roots and to historians equally desirous of mapping the design of colonial society. Indeed, by revealing the ubiquitous domestic connections of people of European, Native American, and African descent, Heinegg has joined the often disparate concerns of genealogists and historians to unearth portions of the long hidden history of Southern free people of color. Along the way, he has noted how free people of color helped define Southern society, for the free people's peculiar place also reveals much about the history of black slaves, white free persons, and Native Americans, both free and slave.

Heinegg's studies of free black families bear with particular force on the period when the South was a society-with-slaves. During those years—prior to the advent of the staple producing plantation, tobacco in the Chesapeake and rice in the Carolinas—the line between freedom and slavery was extraordinarily permeable. Various peoples of European, African, and Native American descent crossed it freely and often. In such socially ill-defined circumstances, white men and women held black and Indian slaves and white servants, and black men and women did like. Peoples of European, African and Native American descent—both free and unfree—worked, played, and even married openly in a manner that would later be condemned by custom and prohibited by law.

Such open relations have long been known to students of the colonial past, but Heinegg's genealogies—by the weight of their number and by their extraordinary detail—make evident their full complexity and expose their extraordinary intimacy. Everywhere whites, blacks, and Indians united in both long-term and casual sexual relations, some coerced and some freely entered. That mixing took place at the top of the social order, where white men of property and standing forced themselves on unwilling servant and slave women, often producing children of mixed racial origins. But Heinegg maintains such relationships produced a scant one percent of the free children of color. Inter-racial sex was far more prevalent at the base of colonial society, where poor and often unfree peoples—mostly slaves and servants of various derivations—lived and worked under common conditions. Indeed, as Heinegg demonstrates, most free people of color had their beginnings in relations between white women (servant and free) and black men (slave, servant, and free). These relations, moreover, often represented long-term and loving commitments. It was precisely the lowly origins of free people of color—outside the ranks of the propertied classes—that condemned free people of color to poverty and excluded them from "respectable" society in the colonial South. The poverty of their parents—particularly their black fathers—denied free children of color the patrimony and the allied connections necessary for social advancement.

Such egalitarian intermingling ended with the advent of the plantation. Legal proscriptions on sexual relations between white and black, particularly between white women and black men accompanied the transformation of the colonial South from a society-with-slaves into a slave society. As Heinegg observes, with the prohibition on inter-racial sexual unions, mixed race children became illegitimate by definition and could be bound out for upwards of thirty years. Their mothers, if servants, received additional terms of servitude. During their captivity, the term of service of both mother and child could be extended for any one of a number of offenses. As a result, free people of color spent a large portion of their lives in the service of others. "In some instances," as Heinegg concludes, "the indenture laws virtually enslaved a person for life."

The punitive prohibitions of inter-racial sexual relations was soon followed by the legislative restriction or outright ban on manumission. As the door slammed shut on black freedom, slaves had their privileges curtailed—most prominently, the right to trade independently. Their inability to trade freely all but eliminated the opportunity to purchase their own freedom and that of family and friends. Likewise, free blacks found their legal rights circumscribed. In various colonies, they were barred from voting, sitting on juries, serving in the militia, carrying guns, owning dogs, or testifying against whites.

Still, the society-with-slaves left its imprint on the slave society that was created in the wake of the Plantation Revolution. "Families like Gowen, Cumbo, and Drigger who were free in the mid seventeenth century," writes Heinegg, already "had several hundred members before the end of the colonial period." These free people of color struggled against the new tide of proscription and disfranchisement. Heinegg's work measures their uneven success.

Many free people pieced together stable, even comfortable lives for their families. The key to their material success, like that of others in the American colonies, was property ownership. Accumulating wealth required years of hard labor and the iron discipline of underconsumption. Even then, free people of color needed assistance. Here Heinegg's work points to the connections of free people of color with kinsmen and neighbors (white and black) who could provide access to property by loaning money, securing bonds, or simply testifying to good character. These linkages often extended outside familial relations, hence often beyond Heinegg's genealogical grasp, but his work provides important suggestions as to where they could be found.

By the middle of the eighteenth century, a small cadre of propertyowning free people of color had emerged in the Southern colonies. Even as slaveholders tightened the noose of proscription and exclusion, these landed, prosperous free men and women made their presence felt. With increasing frequency they appeared in the court, protecting themselves and their property. To assure their legitimacy, many sought out churches to register their marriages and baptize their children, often traveling great distances to do so. While preoccupied with the safety and success of their own families, they sometimes assisted their less fortunate brethren, helping to protect them from unscrupulous men and women who sought to transform free people of color into slaves, either through legal chicanery, illegal subterfuge, or outright force.

Still, most free people of color remained desperately poor, and the prosperity of the propertied minority was fragile and susceptible to rapid erosion. Their marginality, in turn, put all free people at risk and on the move. One of the signal contributions of Heinegg's work is to trace the movement of free people, as they searched for security and opportunity. Heinegg identifies several patterns, the largest of which was the migration from the areas of dense slaveholding settlements—where free people of color originated in the seventeenth century—to the frontiers of the eighteenth-century South. For example, members of the oldest free black families—the Carters, Copes, Driggers, and Johnsons—who had their beginnings in tidewater Virginia, could be found in outlying areas: northeast North Carolina, western Virginia and Maryland, and isolated portions of Delaware. In these recently settled places, Heinegg observes, "Neighbor depended heavily upon neighbor, and whites may have been more concerned with hostile Indians and harsh living conditions than they were with their neighbors' color."

This physical mobility speaks to another less visible migration, the silent escape from the stigma of blackness. Heinegg's genealogical excavations reveal that many free people of color passed as whites—sometimes by choosing ever lighter spouses over succeeding generations. Even more commonly, they claimed Indian ancestry. Some free people of color invented tribal designations out of whole cloth. Here Heinegg, entering into an area of considerable controversy, explodes what he declares the "fantastic" claims of many so-called tri-racial isolates. Yet, only a small portion of the free black population found refuge in either European or Indian ancestry. Many more free people of color, rather than escape blackness, they were engulfed by it as slaveholders usurped their freedom and forced them into slavery.

Whichever direction free people of color migrated or however they maintained their precarious freedom in the American South, Paul Heinegg's work is an indispensable source to understand their travail. Like his earlier books, this expanded edition, Free African American of North Carolina, Virginia and South Carolina, opens yet new avenues to explore the lives of free people of color.

ACKNOWLEDGEMENTS

This project was made possible by the generous policy of the Library of Virginia which loaned me microfilm copies of most of the colonial court order books on interlibrary loan in cooperation with the Montgomery County-Norristown, Pennsylvania Public Library.

The librarians at the North Carolina State Library did hours of research for me--far in excess of what is normally expected.

The Registers of Deeds and County Clerks of dozens of North Carolina and Virginia counties sent me copies of hundreds of deeds and wills. In particular the Northampton County, Virginia court clerk photocopied over 300 pages of the indexes to court records, the court records themselves, and lists of tithables.

The staff of the North Carolina State Archives helped me locate the colonial tax lists. Jonathan Butcher abstracted for me the most important of these, the Bertie and Granville County lists.

I would also like to thank those who have transcribed so many of the microfilm and manuscript records of North Carolina and Virginia: Weynette Parks Haun and Ruth and Sam Sparacio.

Edmund Morgan's book, *American Slavery, American Freedom*, and Joseph Douglas Deal's doctoral thesis, *Race and Class in Colonial Virginia,* most influenced my thinking on colonial Virginia history and made me aware of the possibilities for research in Virginia.

Virginia Easley DeMarce shared with me her extensive references for her work, *Verry Slitly Mixt*, which was published as a series of articles in the *National Genealogical Society Quarterly*.

G.C. Waldrep shared his extensive nineteenth-century research of mixed-race Southside Virginia and North Carolina families.

Robert A. Jackson sent me photocopies of **Pettiford** and **Bibby** family letters and let me use his microfilm copy of North Carolina Marriage Bonds. Roger A. Peterson sent me photocopies of Owen County, Indiana court records, and Coy D. Roberts of Bloomington, Indiana sent me photocopies of Orange County, Indiana free papers. Forest Hazel shared **Jeffries** family court records, and Douglas Paterson shared **Robins** and **Pinn** family records. Doris Stone sent me photocopies of many of the Surry County, Virginia Free Negro records. Scott Wilds shared Darlington District, South Carolina records, and William and Carolyn Adams shared court records for the **Beckett** family.

ABBREVIATIONS AND NOTES ON THE TEXT

CR	Colonial Records in the North Carolina Archives
DB	Deed Book
DOW	Deeds, Orders, Wills, etc.
DW	Deeds, Wills
G.A.	General Assembly Papers at the North Carolina State Archives
JNH	Journal of Negro History
L.P.	Loose Papers at the county courthouse
LVA	The Library of Virginia
M804, 805	Microfilm of the Revolutionary War pension files at the National Archives
Mil. T.R.	Militia Troop Returns at the North Carolina State Archives
PPTL	Personal Property Tax Lists on microfilm at the Library of Virginia
NCGSJ	North Carolina Genealogical Society Journal
NCHR	North Carolina Historical Review
Orders	Order books for the county court of pleas and quarter sessions
OW	Orders, Wills
SS	Secretary of State records at the North Carolina State Archives
T&C	Treasurer and Controller's files at the North Carolina State Archives
VA:, NC:, etc.	Federal census records for the state. Page number is for the printed version in 1790 and the microfilm of the original for all other years
VMHB	Virginia Magazine of History and Biography
WB	Will Book

Sources are referenced in square brackets within the text in abbreviated format. The full citations are in the list of sources at the end of the book.

Arabic numbers indicate the position of each biography within a family history, similar to the Record System. Superscripts after first names indicate the order of birth of individuals with the same first name.

Lower case Roman numerals identify a person's children by birth order. A question mark before the name of a person in a child-list indicates that they are included in the list by best guess based on the available information.

Free African Americans are identified by printing their family names in bold except in their own family history.

The author will answer inquiries on any families.

LIST OF FAMILY NAMES

Abel	Bell	Burden	Cuff	Elmore	Gray
Acre	Bennett	Burke	Cuffee	Epperson	Grayson
Adams	Berry	Burkett	Cumbo	Epps	Gregory
Africa	Beverly	Burnett	Cunningham	Evans	Grice
Ailstock	Bibbens	Burrell	Curle	Fagan	Griffin
Alford	Bibby	Busby	Curtis	Fagggot	Grimes
Allen	Biddie	Bush	Custalow	Farrar	Groom
Allways	Bing	Buss	Cuttillo	Farthing	Groves
Alman	Bingham	Butler	Cypress	Ferrell	Guy
Alvis	Binns	Byrd	Dales	Fielding	Gwinn
Ampey	Bizzell	Cane	Davenport	Fields	Hackett
Ancel	Black	Cannady	Davis	Findley	Hagins
Anderson	Blake	Carter	Day	Finnie	Hailey
Andrews	Blango	Cary	Dean	Fletcher	Haithcock
Angus	Blanks	Case	Deas	Flood	Hall
Archer	Blizzard	Cassidy	Debrix	Flora	Hamilton
Armfield	Blue	Causey	Demery	Flowers	Hamlin
Armstrong	Bolton	Cauther	Dempsey	Fortune	Hammond
Arnold	Bond	Chambers	Dennis	Fox	Hanson
Artis	Boon	Chandler	Dennum	Francis	Harden
Ashberry	Booth	Chapman	Derosario	Francisco	Harmon
Ashby	Bosman	Charity	Dixon	Franklin	Harris
Ashe	Bow	Chavis	Dobbins	Frazier	Harrison
Ashton	Bowden	Church	Dolby	Freeman	Hartless
Ashworth	Bowers	Churchwell	Donathan	Frost	Harvey
Atkins	Bowles	Churton	Douglass	Fry	Hatcher
Aulden	Bowman	Clark	Dove	Fullam	Hatfield
Avery	Bowmer	Cobb	Drake	Fuller	Hatter
Bailey	Bowser	Cockran	Drew	Fuzmore	Hawkins
Baine	Boyd	Cole	Driggers	Gallimore	Hawley
Baker	Brady	Coleman	Dring	Gamby	Haws
Baltrip	Branch	Collins	Driver	Garden	Haynes
Balkham	Brandican	Combess	Drummond	Gardner	Hays
Ball	Brandon	Combs	Drury	Garner	Hearn
Baltrip	Branham	Conner	Duncan	Garnes	Heath
Bannister	Braveboy	Cook	Dungee	George	Hedgepeth
Banks	Braxton	Cooley	Dungill	Gibson	Hewlett
Barber	Britt	Cooper	Dunlop	Gilbert	Hewson
Bartly	Brogdon	Copeland	Dunn	Gillett	Hickman
Bartlett	Brooks	Copes	Dunstan	Godett	Hicks
Barnett	Brown	Corn	Durham	Goff	Hill
Bass	Bruce	Cornet	Dutchfield	Goldman	Hilliard
Bates	Brumejum	Cornish	Eady	Gordon	Hitchens
Battles	Bryan	Cotanch	Easter	Gowen	Hiter
Bazden	Bryant	Cousins	Edgar	Grace	Hobson
Bazmore	Bugg	Cox	Edge	Graham	Hodges
Beavans	Bullard	Coy	Edwards	Grant	Hogg
Beckett	Bunch	Craig	Elliott	Grantum	Hollinger
Bee	Bunday	Crane	Ellis	Graves	Holman

Holmes	Lephew	Month	Pierce	Sampson	Timber
Holt	Lester	Moore	Pinn	Santee	Toney
Honesty	Lett	Mordick	Pittman	Sanderlin	Tootle
Hood	Leviner	Morgan	Pitts	Saunders	Toulson
Hoomes	Lewis	Morris	Plumly	Savoy	Toyer
Horn	Lighty	Mosby	Poe	Sawyer	Travis
Howard	Ligon	Moses	Pompey	Scott	Turner
Howell	Lively	Moss	Portions	Seldon	Tyler
Hubbard	Liverpool	Mozingo	Portiss	Sexton	Tyner
Hughes	Locklear	Muckelroy	Powell	Shaw	Tyre
Hulin	Lockson	Mumford	Powers	Shepherd	Underwood
Humbles	Locus	Munday	Poythress	Shoecraft	Valentine
Hunt	Longo	Muns	Press	Shoemaker	Vaughan
Hunter	Lowry	Murray	Price	Silver	Vena/ Venie
Hurley	Lucas	Murrow	Prichard	Simmons	Verty
Hurst	Lugrove	Nash	Proctor	Simon	Vickory
Ivey	Lynch	Neal	Pryor	Simms	Viers
Jackson	Lyons	Newsom	Pugh	Simpson	Walden
Jacobs	Lytle	Newton	Pursley	Sisco	Walker
James	McCarty	Nicholas	Rains	Skipper	Wallace
Jameson	McCoy	Nickens	Ralls	Slaxton	Warburton
Jarvis	McDaniel	Norman	Randall	Smith	Warrick
Jasper	McGee	Norris	Ranger	Smothers	Waters
Jeffery	McIntosh	Norton	Rann	Sneed	Watkins
Jeffries	Maclin	Norwood	Raper	Snelling	Weaver
Jenkins	Madden	Nutts	Ratcliff	Soleleather	Webb
Johns	Magee	Oats	Rawlinson	Sorrell	Webster
Johnson	Mahorney	Okey	Redcross	Sparrow	Weeks
Joiner	Manly	Oliver	Redman	Spelman	Welch
Jones	Manr	Otter	Reed	Spiller	Wells
Jordan	Manning	Overton	Reeves	Spriddle	West
Jumper	Manuel	Owen	Revell	Spruce	Wharton
Keemer	Marshall	Oxendine	Reynolds	Spurlock	Whistler
Kelly	Martin	Page	Rich	Stafford	White
Kendall	Mason	Pagee	Richardson	Stephens	Whitehurst
Kent	Matthews	Palmer	Rickman	Stewart	Wiggins
Kersey	Mayo	Parker	Ridley	Stringer	Wilkins
Key	Mays	Parr	Roberts	Sunket	Wilkinson
Keyton	Meade	Parrot	Robins	Swan	Williams
King	Mealy	Patrick	Robinson	Sweat	Willis
Kinney	Meekins	Patterson	Rogers	Sweetin	Wilson
Knight	Meggs	Payne	Rollins	Symons	Winborn
Lamb	Melvin	Peacock	Rosario	Taborn	Winn
Landum	Miles	Peavy	Ross	Talbot	Winters
Lang	Miller	Pendarvis	Rouse	Tann	Wise
Lansford	Mills	Pendergrass	Rowe	Tate	Womble
Lantern	Milton	Perkins	Rowland	Taylor	Wood
Lawrence	Mitchell	Peters	Ruff	Teague	Wooten
Laws	Mitchum	Pettiford	Ruffin	Teamer	Worrell
Lawson	Mongom	Phillips	Russell	Thomas	Wright
Lee	Monoggin	Pickett	Sample	Thompson	Young

Virginia
and
North Carolina

Date of Formation of Some Virginia Counties

Albemarle	1744 from Goochland County	
Amelia	1734 from Prince George & Brunswick	
Amherst	1761 from Albemarle	
Augusta	1738 from Orange	
Bedford	1753 from Lunenburg	
Botetourt	1769 from Augusta	
Campbell	1781 from Bedford	
Caroline	1728 from Essex, King & Queen & King Wm	
Charlotte	1764 from Lunenburg	
Chesterfield	1749 from Henrico	
Cumberland	1749 from Goochland	
Dinwiddie	1752 from Prince George	
Fairfax	1742 from Prince William	
Fauqier	1759 from Prince William	
Fluvanna	1777 from Albemarle	
Frederick	1738 from Orange	
Goochland	1728 from Henrico	
Greensville	1780 from Brunswick	
Halifax	1752 from Lunenburg	
Hanover	1720 from New Kent	
Henry	1776 from Pittsylvania	
King George	1720 from Richmond, part of Westmoreland in 1777	
King William	1701 from King & Queen	
Loudoun	1757 from Fairfax	
Louisa	1742 from Hanover	
Lunenburg	1745 from Brunswick	
Madison	1792 from Culpeper	
Mathews	1790 from Gloucester	
Mecklenburg	1764 from Lunenburg	
Nelson	1807 from Amherst	
Nottoway	1788 from Amelia	
Orange	1734 from Spotsylvania	
Patrick	1790 from Henry	
Pittsylvania	1766 from Halifax	
Powhatan	1777 from Cumberland	
Prince Edward	1753 from Amelia	
Prince George	1702 from Charles City	
Prince William	1730 from Stafford and King George	
Rockbridge	1778 from Augusta and Botetourt	
Rockingham	1778 from Augusta	
Southampton	1749 from Isle of Wight	
Sussex	1753 from Surry	

Date of Formation of Some North Carolina Counties

Anson	1750 from Bladen
Ashe	1799 from Wilkes
Bertie	1722 from Chowan
Bladen	1734 from New Hanover
Brunswick	1764 from New Hanover & Bladen
Bute	1764 from Granville. Became Franklin & Warren in 1779
Camden	1777 from Pasquotank
Caswell	1777 from Orange
Chatham	1771 from Orange
Cumberland	1754 from Bladen
Duplin	1750 from New Hanover
Edgecombe	1741 from Bertie
Franklin	1779 from Bute
Gates	1779 from Chowan, Hertford & Perquimans
Granville	1746 from Edgecombe
Guilford	1770 from Rowan & Orange
Halifax	1758 from Edgecombe
Jones	1778 from Craven
Lenoir	1791 from Craven
Martin	1774 from Halifax & Tyrrell
Nash	1777 from Edgecombe
Northampton	1741 from Bertie
Onslow	1734 from New Hanover
Orange	1752 from Bladen, Granville & Johnston
Person	1791 from Caswell
Randolph	1779 from Guilford
Richmond	1779 from Anson
Robeson	1787 from Bladen
Rockingham	1785 from Guilford
Sampson	1784 from Duplin
Stokes	1789 from Surry
Wake	1771 from Cumberland, Johnston & Orange
Warren	1779 from Bute
Wilkes	1778 from Surry

INTRODUCTION

These genealogies, comprising the colonial history of the majority of the free African American families of Virginia and North Carolina, reveal several facets of American colonial history previously overlooked by historians:

- Most families were the descendants of white servant women who had children by slaves or free African Americans.

- Many descended from slaves who were freed before the 1723 Virginia law which required legislative approval for manumissions. Families like **Gowen**, **Cumbo**, and **Driggers** who were free in the mid-seventeenth century had several hundred members before the end of the colonial period.

- Very few free families descended from white slave owners who had children by their slaves, perhaps as low as 1% of the total.

- Many free African American families in colonial North Carolina and Virginia were landowners who were generally accepted by their white neighbors.

- Free Indians blended into the free African American communities. They did not form their own separate communities.

- Some of the light-skinned descendants of free African Americans formed the tri-racial isolates of Virginia, North Carolina, South Carolina, Tennessee, Kentucky, Ohio, and Louisiana.

<u>Virginia Origins</u>
Most of the free African Americans of Virginia and North Carolina originated in Virginia where t! ··y became free in the seventeenth and eighteenth century before chattel slavery and racism fully developed in the United States.

When they arrived in Virginia, Africans joined a society which was divided between master and white servant - a society with such contempt for white servants that masters were not punished for beating them to death [McIlwaine, *Minutes of the Council,* 22-24]. They joined the same households with white servants - working, eating, sleeping, getting drunk, and running away together [Northampton Orders 1664-74, fol.25, p.31 - fol.31; McIlwaine, *Minutes of the Council,* 466-7; Hening, *Statutes at Large,* II:26, 117; Charles City County Orders 1687-95, 468; Westmoreland County Orders 1752-5, 41a].

Some of these first African slaves became free:

- Michael **Gowen**, a "negro" servant, was freed by the 18 January 1654 York County will of Christopher Stafford [DWO 3:16].

- Francis **Payne** of Northampton County paid for his freedom about 1650 by purchasing thi . : white servants for his master's use [DW 1645-51, 14].

- Emanuell Cambow (**Cumbo**), "Negro," was granted 50 acres in James City County on 18 April 1667 [Patent Book 6:39].

- John **Harris**, "negro," was free in 1668 when he purchased 50 acres in York County [Deeds 1664-72, 327].

A number of African Americans living on the Eastern Shore gained their freedom in the seventeenth century. There were at least thirty-three taxable African Americans in Northampton County in the 1670s who were free, later became free, or had free children. They represented one third of the taxable African Americans in the county.[1]

The **Nickens** and **Weaver** families came from Lancaster County where Black Dick (Richard **Nickens**), his wife Chris, and their children were freed in 1690 by the will of John Carter [Wills 1690-1709, 5].

Some free African Americans were beginning to be assimilated into colonial Virginia society in the mid-seventeenth century. Many were the result of mixed race marriages:

- Francis **Payne** was married to a white woman named Amy by September 1656 when he gave her a mare by deed of jointure [DW 1655-68, fol. 19].

- Elizabeth **Key**, a "Mulatto" woman whose father had been free, successfully sued for her freedom in Northumberland County in 1656 and married her white attorney, William Greensted [Record Book 1652-8, 66, 67, 85a, 85b].

- Francis Skiper was married to Ann, an African American woman, before February 1667/8 when they sold land in Norfolk County [W&D E:1666-75; Orders 1666-75, 73].

- Peter **Beckett**, a "Negro" slave taxable from 1671 to 1677 in Northampton County, Virginia, married Sarah Dawson, a white servant [OW 1674-79, 203; OW 1683-89, 59].

- Hester Tate, an English woman servant in Westmoreland County, had several children by her husband James **Tate**, "a Negro slave to Mr. Patrick Spence," before 1690 [Orders 1690-98, 40-41].

As the percentage of African Americans increased, so did tension between free African Americans and slave holders. In 1666 Bastian **Cane**, "Negro," was punished by the Northampton County court for harboring, concealing, and trading with Francis Pigott's "Negro slave" [Orders 1664-74, fol.29]. And as more and more slaves replaced white servants, the Legislature passed a series of laws which designated slavery as the appropriate condition for African Americans:

- In 1670 the Virginia Assembly forbade free African Americans and Indians from owning white servants [Hening, *Statutes at Large*, II:280].

- In 1691 the Assembly prohibited the manumission of slaves unless they were transported out of the colony. It also prohibited interracial marriages and ordered the illegitimate, mixed-race children of white women bound out for thirty years [Hening, *Statutes at Large*, III:86-87].

---

[1]Tithable Heads of Household:

Bastian Cane and his wife Grace, Emanuel Driggers, Basshaw Ferdinando, his wife Susan, and Hannah Carter, John Francisco Negro and Christian Francisco, William Harman and his wife Jane, Anthony Johnson, John Johnston (2), John Kinge, Philip Mongon and his wife, Francis Pane Negro, King Tony and his wife Sarah.

Tithables in White Households:

John Archer Negro, Peter Beckett Negro, Edward and Thomas Carter, Thomas, Frances, and Mary Driggus Negro, Peter and Joan George, Jane Guzell, Ann Harmon, Gabriel and Bab Jacob, and Daniel and Isabell Webb [Order Books 1657-64, p.103, fol.104, 176, 198; 1664-74, fol.14, 15, 19, 42, 54, pp. 15, 42, 54, 55; 1674-79, fol.114, p.191]. In 1677 there were 25 tithable free African Americans and 53 tithable slaves out of a total 467 tithables [1674-79, 189-91].

- In 1705 the Assembly passed a law which all but eliminated the ability of slaves to earn their freedom by ordering that the farm stock of slaves

  shall be seized and sold by the church-wardens of the parish wherein such horses, cattle, or hogs shall be, and the profit thereof applied to the use of the poor of said parish [Hening, *Statutes at Large*, III:459-60].

- In 1712 all fifteen members of the **Anderson** and **Richards** families were freed and given 640 acres in Norfolk County, Virginia, by the will of John Fulcher, creating such a stir that the Legislative Council on 5 March 1712/3 proposed that the Assembly

  provide for a Law against such Manumission of Slaves, which in time by their increase and correspondence with other Slaves may endanger the peace of this Colony [McIlwaine, *Executive Journals of the Council*, III:332].

In an effort to "prevent their correspondence with other slaves" Fulcher's executor, Lewis Conner, by a deed dated 20 March 1712/3, swapped their land in Norfolk County with land on Welshes Creek in Chowan County, North Carolina [Chowan DB B-1:109].

In 1723 the Virginia Assembly prohibited the freeing of slaves except in cases where they had rendered some public service such as foiling a slave revolt. Also in 1723, the Assembly amended the 1705 taxation law to make female free African Americans over the age of sixteen tithable [Hening, *Statutes at Large*, IV:132-3].[2]

Despite the efforts of the legislature, white servant women continued to bear children by African American fathers through the late seventeenth century and well into the eighteenth century. From these genealogies, it appears that they were the primary source of the increase in the free African American population for this period. Over 200 families in this history descended from white women. Many of these women may have been the common-law wives of slaves since they had several mixed-race children.[3]

---

[2]Female free African Americans were made tithable in 1668, but the 1705 law did not include them [Hening, *Statutes at Large*, III:258-9]. Norfolk County officials did not enforce the 1723 amendment until 1735-1736 when female members of the **Anderson, Archer, Bass, Hall, Manley**, and **Price** families were taxed [Wingo, *Norfolk County Tithables, 1730-1750*, 144, 157, 168, 183, 185, 190]. Surry County probably did not enforce the 1723 amendment until 21 November 1758 when the Surry County Court presented thirteen free African Americans for not listing their wives as tithables. They were the **Banks, Barkley, Barlow, Charity, Debrix, Eley, Peters, Simon, Tann, Walden**, and **Wilson** families [Orders 1757-64, 135].

[3]Families descended from white women whose histories are included in this work include the **Allen, Alvis, Ancel, Anderson, Angus, Armstrong, Arnold, Ashby, Baker, Baltrip, Banks, Barber, Barnett, Bazden, Beckett, Bell, Bibbens, Bibby, Boon, Bowles, Boyd, Britt, Brooks, Bryant, Bugg, Bunday, Burke, Burnett, Burkett, Burrell, Buss, Butler, Byrd, Cary, Cassidy, Chambers, Clark, Collins, Combess, Conner, Cook** (two families), **Cooley, Copes, Cousins, Crane, Cunningham, Cuttillo, Davenport, Davis, Day, Dempsey, Dennis, Donathan, Driver, Duncan, Dungee, Dunn, Dunstan, Elliott, Ellis, Faggot, Farrell, Finnie, Fletcher, Flora, Fortune, Fuller, Fullam, Gallimore, Grace, Graham, Grant, Graves, Gray, Grayson, Gregory, Griffin, Grimes, Gwinn, Hall, Hamilton, Hammond, Hanson, Harrison, Haws, Haynes, Heath, Hilliard, Hobson, Hodges, Hogg, Holt, Hood, Howard, Howell, Hubbard, Hughes, Kelly, Kent, King, Lamb, Lang, Lansford, Lawson, Lewis, Ligon, Locus/ Lucas, Lugrove, Lynch, McCarty, McCoy, McIntosh, Madden, Magee, Manly** (two families), **Martin, Mason, Matthews, Mays, Meade, Miles, Mills, Morgan,**

Morris, Murray, Murrow, Nicholas, Norris, Norman, Overton (two families), **Owens, Oxendine,**
Palmer, Parsons, Perkins, Phillips, Pickett, Pierce, Pittman, Pitts, Powell, Price, Proctor, Pursley,
Range, Ratcliff, Redman, Reed, Ridley, Roach, Roberts, Robinson, **Rollins,** Ross, Rowland, **Ruffs,**
Russell, Sample, Sampson, Saunders, Scott, Shepherd (two families), **Simmons, Simms, Simpson,**
Sneed, Sorrell, Sparrow, Stephens, Stewart, Stringer, Swan, **Symons, Tate, Thomas, Timber,**
Toney, Tootle, Toyer, Tyler, Tyner, Tyre, Venie/ Venners, Verty, Viers, Wallace, Warwick, Webb
(two families), **West, Whistler, White** (two families), **Wiggins, Williams,** Wilson, Winn, Wise,
Wood, Wooten and **Worrell** families. Other white women who had mixed-race children were:

- Jane Alexander in 1754 [Prince William County Orders 1754-5, 4, 131]
- Mary Ballard on 29 March 1708 [Northampton County Orders, Wills 1698-1710, 398].
- the mother of Joseph Barham in July 1744 [Charles City County Orders 1737-51, 311]
- Dorothy Bestick, Accomack County in 1687 [W&Co 1682-97, 119a]
- Hannah Boughan in 1714 in Northumberland County [Orders 1713-19, 102].
- Ann Bradger in 1744 [Chamberlayne, *Vestry Book of Stratton Major Parish, King & Queen County*, 56]
- Mary Brady in 1733 [Fouts, *Vestry Minutes of St. Paul's Parish*, 51]
- Mary Breedlove in 1767 [Essex County Orders 1764-7, 415, 469].
- Sarah Bunbury in 1692 [Richmond County Orders 1692-94, 40]
- the mother of Margaret Callahan in 1751 [Frederick County Orders 1751-3, 418].
- Elizabeth Cambridge in 1702 [Essex County Orders 1699-1702, 116]
- Elizabeth Chilmaid in 1706 [York DOW 13:19]
- Margaret Chiswick in 1705 [Richmond County Orders 1704-8, 97].
- Mary Cicile (3 children) in 1702 [Richmond County Orders 1702-04, 157]
- Hannah Clagg in 1695 [Princess Anne County Minutes 1691-1709, 81]
- Mary Collowhough in 1691 [Westmoreland Orders 1690-92, 24]
- Margaret Croney in 1726 [York County DOW 16:70, 387]
- Margaret Davison in 1748 [Frederick County Orders 1745-8, 501, 505]
- Catherine Dennison in 1704 [Lancaster County Orders 1702-13, 107]
- Charlotte Deormond before 1769 [Rowan County, North Carolina Minutes 1766-9, 16].
- Mary Edgar in 1772 [Princess Anne County Minutes 1770-3, 369]
- Eleanor Fielding in York County in 1753 [Judgments & Orders 1752-4, 232].
- Christian Finny in 1736 [Carteret County Minutes 1723-47, fol.33c]
- Margaret Fitzgerald in 1703 [Richmond County Orders 1702-04, 274]
- Isabel Forbess in 1761 and 1764 [Historic Dumfries, *Records of Dettingen Parish*, 114-5]
- Tamer Haislip in 1765 [Chesterfield County Orders 1765-7, 96]
- the mother of Tamer Hastlie in 1761 [Prince Edward County Orders 1759-65, 85].
- Mary Hipsley in 1707 [Westmoreland County Orders 1705-21, 64, 69, 72]
- Isabel Hutton in 1707 [Accomack County Orders 1703-9, 91a, 122]
- Martha Inglish in 1768 [Isle of Wight County Orders 1764-8, 498]
- Dorcas Johnston in 1758 [Caroline County Orders 1755-8, 347].
- Jane Kewmin in 1703 [Richmond County, Va. Orders 1702-04, 154]
- Jane Knox in Augusta County in 1758 [Orders 1757-61, 177, 221, 285].
- Elizabeth Lane in 1691 (two children) [Surry Orders 1682-91, 771, 777]
- Mary Lawhan in 1708 [Middlesex County Orders 1705-10, 177, 181].
- Mary Lawler 30 July 1707 [Westmoreland County Orders 1705-21, 64]
- Isabella Levingston in 1768 [Fairfax County Orders 1768-70, 70, 90].
- Mary Lynn (Robert Hitch) before 1710 [Westmoreland County Orders 1705-21, 144]
- Katherine Mackeel in 1699 [Princess Anne County Minutes 1691-1709, 211, 213, 224]
- Jane Morrison in 1768 and 1770 [Fairfax County Orders 1768-70, 70; 1770-2, 17, 145].
- Mary Ormes in 1697 [Middlesex County Orders 1694-1705, 182].
- the mother of Sarah, a "molotto" in York County in 1694 [OW 9:318]
- Eleanor Poor in 1704 [Lancaster County Orders 1702-13, 70]
- Mary Poore (two children) in 1686 [Surry Orders 1682-91, 529, 630]
- Ann Pullen in 1688 [Henrico Orders 1678-93, 278]
- Eleanor Road in Augusta County in 1747 [Orders 1745-7, 288].

Fifty families descended from freed slaves, twenty-nine from Indians, and nineteen from white men who married or had children by free African American women.[4] It is likely that the majority of the remaining families descended from white women since they first appear in court records in the mid-eighteenth century when slaves could not be freed without legislative approval, and there is no record of legislative approval for their emancipations.

Table 1. Ancestry of Free African American Families in This Genealogy: Virginia and North Carolina	
White servant women	200
Freed slaves	50
Indians	29
White men	19

- Jane Scot in Augusta County in 1749 [Orders 1747-51, 112]
- Ann Screws in 1748 [Isle of Wight County Orders 1746-52, 109]
- Margaret Shaw in 1715 [Prince George County Orders 1714-20, 30],
- Susanna Shelton in 1686 [Surry Orders 1682-91, 508]
- Mary Sherredon in 1736 [Surry DW&c 1730-38, 569]
- Tamer Smith served a six months prison term and paid a 10 pound fine in order to marry Major **Hitchens**, head of a Northampton County, Virginia household of 4 free tithables and 2 slaves in 1737 and 1744 [L.P. 1737, 1744; L.P. #24 (1738) by Deal, *Race and Class*, 216]
- Mary Taggat in 1751 [Lunenburg Orders 2:474]
- Margaret Theloball in 1735 [Princess Ann County Orders 1728-37, 272]
- Ann Tillett in January 1744/5 [Pasquotank County Court Minutes, 1737-53, 141]
- Joan Tinkham in 1687 [Westmoreland County Orders 1675-89, 611]
- Ann Vasper in 1732 [Overwharton, Stafford County Register, 1724-74, 30]
- Mary Vincent in 1664 [Accomack County DW 1664-71, fol. 20]
- Sarah Williamson in July 1716 [Saunders, *Colonial Records of North Carolina*, V:114].
- Catherine Wilson in 1723 [Northampton County, Virginia Orders 18:86].
- Anne Wimball in 1703 [York County DOW 12:80].

[4]Families descended from freed slaves include: **Africa, Anderson, Andrews, Archer, Artis, Black, Blango, Bowser, Braveboy, Brooks, Cane, Carter, Charity, Churton, Cole, Cornish, Cuffee, Cumbo, Demery, Dove, Driggers, Drury, Edwards, Fagan, George, Gowen, Gregory, Harmon, Harris, Jacobs, James, Jeffries, Johnson, Jordan, Leviner, Lewis, Longo, Lytle, Manuel, Mongom, Moore, Mordick, Newton, Nickens, Payne, Roberts, Sisco, Symons, Tann** and **Thompson**. Families descended from Indians who married into the free African American community include: **Bass, Bennett, Bingham, Busby, Cockran, Coleman, Cypress, Findley, Garden, Hatcher, Hatfield, Hiter, Jacob, Jeffery, Jumper, Kinney, Lang, Lawrence, Month, Pinn, Pitman, Pitts, Press, Robins, Teague, Tyler, Vickory, Vaughan** and **Whitehurst**. Families descended from white men who married free African American women include: **Berry, Collins, Combs, Davis, Hailey, Holman, Ivey, Landrum, Lantern, Locklear, Newsom, Marshall, Newsom, Norwood, Pendarvis, Silver, Skipper, Snelling** and **Sweat**.

The replacement of white servants with African slaves, begun in earnest in 1660, continued for more than a century. African slaves had still not completely replaced white servants by 17 October 1773 when the jailer in Prince William County advertised in the *Virginia Gazette* that he had caught a runaway white servant man:

> *Committed to Prince William gaol a certain William Rawlings, who says he is the property of Francis Smith of Chesterfield. The owner is desired to pay charges, and take him away.*

and he advertised in the same edition that he had jailed a runaway white servant woman:

> *Committed to the gaol of Prince William a servant woman about 26 years of age, named Mary Richardson; has on a short printed cotton gown, and striped Virginia cloth petticoat* [Rind edition, p.3, col.3].[5]

Elizabeth Bartlett, an indentured servant from Accomack County, was punished in July 1716 for running away with her mistress' "Negro man named James" [Orders 1714-7, 22]. George Wallis, a white man, and "Negro Dick" were taken up as runaways in Westmoreland County in November 1752 [Orders 1752-5, 41a].

Racial contempt for free African Americans did not fully develop as long as there were white servants in similar circumstances. It was during this period, as late as the end of the eighteenth century, that free African Americans were accepted in some white communities.

Many free African Americans originated in or moved to Surry County, Virginia, where their deeds, marriage bonds, and wills were recorded in the seventeenth and eighteenth century. They were the **Banks**, **Blizzard**, **Byrd**, **Charity**, **Chavis**, **Cornish**, **Debrix**, **Jeffreys**, **Kersey**, **Peters**, **Scott**, **Sweat**, **Tann**, **Valentine**, **Walden**, and **Wilson** families. Descriptions in the Surry County, Virginia, "Registry of Free Negroes" in the late eighteenth and early nineteenth century read:

> *Armstead Peters a Mulatoe man, ...aged about 56 years, born free of a yellowish complexion...* (6 October 1794).

> *James Williams a Mulatto man, pretty dark complexion, born of free parents residents of this county, 35 years old...* (11 May 1797).

> *Joseph Byrd son of Joseph and Nelly Byrd free Mulatto persons & residents of this county 20 years old, 5'5" high, bright complexion, short thick hair, straight & well made* (27 September 1798).

> *William Tan, a mulatto man and son of Jemima Tan, a white woman late of this county. He is of bright complexion, has straight black hair, pretty stout and straight made, aged 21 last September* (3 December 1801) [Back of Guardian Accounts Book 1783-1804, nos. 1, 21, 35, 136].

Since so many free African Americans were light-skinned, many observers assume that they were the offspring of white slave owners who took advantage of their female slaves. Only three of the approximately four hundred families in this history were proven to descend from a white slave owner. They were the children

---

[5]The same advertiser in that edition clearly identified a runaway free African American, Reuben **Dye**, as a "Negro man."

of South Carolina planters: **Collins, Holman,** and **Pendarvis.** Like their fathers, they were wealthy slave owners who were accepted in white society.

In 1782 Virginia relaxed its restrictions on manumission, and thereafter manumitted slaves formed a major part of the free African American population.

By 1790 free African Americans were concentrated on the Eastern Shore of Virginia, the counties below the James River, and the northeastern part of North Carolina [*Heads of Families - Virginia*, 9]. (See Table 2). This was a pattern of settlement similar to that of newly freed white servants. Land was available in Southside Virginia and in the northeastern part of North Carolina at prices former servants could afford [Morgan, *American Slavery*, 227-30].

Table 2. Number of free African Americans in Virginia and North Carolina and their percentage of the total free population in 1790 by county

Virginia		North Carolina	
Charles City	363 (14.8%)	Northampton	458 (8.2%)
York	358 (14.5%)	Hertford	232 (6.6%)
Northampton	464 (12.7%)	Halifax	443 (5.8%)
Surry	368 (11.8%)	Robeson	277 (5.8%)
Henrico	581 (9.4%)	Bertie	378 (5.1%)
Nansemond	480 (9.2%)	Craven	337 (4.9%)
James City	146 (8.8%)	Granville	315 (4.6%)
Dinwiddie	561 (8.5%)		
Powhatan	211 (8.5%)		
Southampton	559 (8.1%)		
Greensville	212 (7.7%)		
Sussex	391 (7.6%)		
Accomack	721 (7.4%)		
Prince George	267 (7.3%)		
Isle of Wight	375 (7.3%)		
Lancaster	143 (6.0%)		
Hardy	411 (5.9%)		
Goochland	257 (5.8%)		
New Kent	148 (5.8%)		
Chesterfield	369 (5.5%)		
Mecklenburg	416 (5.2%)		
Total Virginia:	12,866 (2.8%)	Total North Carolina:	5,041 (1.7%)

Descendants of families which had been free during the colonial period continued to comprise a major part of the free African American population due to natural increase. In 1810 the **Going/ Gowen** family, free since the mid-seventeenth century, headed forty "other free" households with 105 persons in Virginia, sixty-two persons in North Carolina, eleven in South Carolina, and ten in Louisiana. The **Chavis** family, free since the seventeenth century, headed forty-one households containing forty-six persons in Virginia, 159 in North Carolina, and twelve in South Carolina.

Table 3. Number of Persons in the Households of Families who had Been Free During the Colonial Period - 1810 Census

Family Name	Virginia/	North Carolina
Anderson	7	52
Archer	9	51
Artis(t)	86	38
Banks	54	28
Bass	21	80
Battles	25	
Be(a)vans	26	
Beverly	79	
Bunda(y)	70	
Charity	41	
Chavis/ Chavers	46	159
Cousins	52	6
Cuffee	96	
Cumbo		43
Day	46	13
Elliott	43	
Fuller	28	3
Going/ Gowen	105	62
Haithcock	9	70
Hammons		95
Harman	37	
Howell	37	
James		69
Johns	36	
Ligan/ Ligon	39	
Locklear		76
Locus/ Lucas	100	25
Meekins	26	
Moore		65
Nickens	64	6
Overton		58
Oxendine		32
Pin(n)	48	
Reed	12	43
Revell		35
Rich	64	
Richardson		58
Roberts		111
Sample	36	
Sparrow	19	
Valentine	55	7
Vena/ Venie	64	
Walden	24	87
Weaver	64	37

Migration to North Carolina

Several free African Americans voted in the North Carolina General Assembly elections in 1701 [Saunders, *Colonial Records*, I:903]. Jack **Braveboy** was living in Chowan County before 17 July 1716 when he was presented by the court:

> *a negro, Coming into this Government with a woman and do live together as man and wife, it is ordered that the sd. Braveboy produce a Sufficient*

Certificate of their Marryage [Hoffman, *Chowan Precinct North Carolina 1696 to 1723*, 224].

In 1725 John Cotton was indicted for marrying a "Molatto Man to a White woman," and in 1726 the Rev. Mr. John Blacknall was fined fifty pounds for "joyning together in...Matrimony Thomas Spencer and Martha paule a Molatto Woman" [Saunders, *Colonial Records*, II:591, 662].

Many of those who were free in Northampton County, Virginia, settled in Craven County, North Carolina. They were the **Carter, Copes, Driggers, George**, and **Johnston** families. They can be traced directly back to their seventeenth century Virginia ancestors. Those in the early eighteenth century lists of Northampton County, Virginia tithables who immigrated to North Carolina were the **Allen** and **Roberts** families.

The descendants of Nicholas and Bungey **Manuel**, "negro slaves" freed by the 28 October 1718 Elizabeth City County, Virginia will of Edward Myhill, were in the Edgecombe, North Carolina Militia in the 1750s [Elizabeth City County Deeds, Wills 1715-21, 194-5; Clark, *Colonial Soldiers of the South*, 675].

James and Peter **Black** came to Craven County from Essex County, Virginia, where they had been free born. John Heath tried to sell them as slaves to William Handcock, but the Craven County court intervened on their behalf on 21 June 1745.

Moll, Nell, Sue, Sall, and Will **Dove**, "Negroes," came to Craven County, North Carolina, from Maryland with Leonard Thomas who was trying to keep them as his slaves in September 1749, but William Smith travelled to Maryland and proved their claim that they were free born [Haun, *Craven County Court Minutes*, III:465; IV:11-12].

The family histories of over 80% of those counted as "all other free persons" in the 1790-1810 federal census for North Carolina indicate that they were descendants of African Americans who were free in Virginia during the colonial period.

Free African American immigrants were of sufficient number in 1723 that the North Carolina General Assembly received complaints

> *of great Numbers of Free Negroes, Mulattoes, and other persons of mixt Blood, that have lately removed themselves into this Government, and that several of them have intermarried with the white Inhabitants of this Province...* [Clark, *State Records*, XXIII:106-7].

Land Ownership and Relations With Whites
While some North Carolina residents were complaining about the immigration of free African Americans, their white neighbors in Granville, Halifax, Bertie, Craven, Granville, Robeson and Hertford counties welcomed them.

On 9 November 1762 many of the leading residents of Halifax County petitioned the Assembly to repeal the discriminatory tax against free African Americans, and in May 1763 fifty-four of the leading citizens of Granville, Northampton, and Edgecombe counties made a similar petition. They described their "Free Negro & Mulatto" neighbors as

> *persons of Probity & good Demeanor (who) chearfully contribute towards the Discharge of every public Duty injoined them by Law.*

About ten years later a similar petition by seventy-five residents of Granville County included those of a few of the free African Americans of the county: Benjamin, Edward, and Reuben **Bass**, William and Gibea **Chavis**, Lawrence **Pettiford**, and Davie **Mitchell** "(negro)" [Saunders, *Colonial Records*, VI:902, 982; IX:96-97].

During the colonial and early national periods at least one member of most African American families in North Carolina owned land. Land ownership made for closer relations with the white community than with slaves.[6]

The McKinnie family, originally from Isle of Wight County, Virginia, was one of the leading white families in the area around the Roanoke River. Barnaby McKinnie, member of the General Assembly from Edgecombe County in 1735, was witness to many of the early **Bass**, **Bunch**, **Chavis**, and **Gibson** deeds. John McKinnie called Cannon **Cumbo** his friend when he mentioned him in his 28 February 1753 Edgecombe County will. Other leading white settlers who sold them land adjoining theirs and witnessed their deeds were Richard Washington, William and Thomas Bryant, Richard Pace, and William Whitehead. Arthur Williams, member of the General Assembly for Bertie County in 1735, and John Castellaw, (brother?) of James Castellaw, a member of the Assembly from Bertie County, had mixed-race common-law wives, Elizabeth and Martha **Butler** [Saunders, *Colonial Records*, IV:115 and the **Butler** history].

In March 1782 a Continental officer observed a scene in a local tavern at Williamsboro, North Carolina:

> *The first thing I saw on my Entrance was a Free Malatto and a White man seated on the Hearth, foot to foot, Playing all fours by firelight: a Dollar a Game* [Journals of Enos Reeves, March 13, 1782, Manuscript Department, Duke University, cited by Crow, *The Black Experience in Revolutionary North Carolina*, 32].

By 1790 free African Americans represented 1.7% of the free population of North Carolina, concentrated in the counties of Northampton, Halifax, Bertie, Craven, Granville, Robeson, and Hertford where they were about 5% of the free population [*Heads of Families - North Carolina*, 9-10]. In these counties most African American families were landowners, and several did exceptionally well.

The **Bunch**, **Chavis** and **Gibson** families owned slaves and acquired over a thousand acres of land on both sides of the Roanoke River in present-day Northampton and Halifax counties, and the **Chavis** and **Gowen** families acquired over a thousand acres in Granville County. William **Chavis**, a "Negro" listed in the 8 October 1754 muster roll of Colonel William Eaton's Granville County Regiment, owned a thousand acres of land, a lodging house frequented by whites, and eight taxable slaves [Clark, *Colonial Soldiers of the South*, 716]. His son Philip **Chavis** also owned over a thousand acres of land, travelled between Granville, Northampton, and Robeson counties, and lived for a while in Craven County, South Carolina.

---

[6]Goochland County, Virginia, was an example of a location where free African Americans had very limited opportunities to own land, and they had closer relations with slaves. See Reginald Dennin Butler, "Evolution of a Rural Free Black Community: Goochland County, Virginia, 1728-1832," Ph.D. diss., The Johns Hopkins University, 1989. Free African Americans in Maryland also had limited opportunities to own land, and they generally had closer relations with slaves. But in Delaware they had owned land since the seventeenth century, and those who had been free since the colonial period were associated with the white community [Heinegg, *Free African Americans of Maryland and Delaware*].

Edward **Carter** was the fourth largest Dobbs County landowner with 23,292 acres in 1780 [L.P.46.1 in *Journal of N.C. Genealogy* XII:1664]. He was head of a Dobbs County household of 8 "other free," a white woman, and 20 slaves in 1790 [NC:137]. In a most extraordinary move, on 13 February 1773 the Dobbs County court recommended to the General Assembly that Edward **Carter**'s daughters be exempted from the discriminatory tax against female children of African Americans [Saunders, *Colonial Records of North Carolina*, IX:495].

In mid-eighteenth century North Carolina we find wealthy mixed-race families counted in some years by North Carolina tax assessors as "mulatto" and in other years as white. Jeremiah and Henry **Bunch**, Bertie County slave owners, were taxed in Jonathan Standley's 1764 Bertie County list as "free male Molattors" in 1764, but as whites in Standley's 1765 Bertie list, and again as "free Molatoes" in 1766 [CR 10.702.1]. Michael **Going/ Gowen** was taxed in Granville County as white in 1754 and was called "Michael Goin, Mulattoe" in 1759 [CR 44.701.19].

John **Gibson**, Gideon **Gibson** and Gibeon **Chavis**, all married the daughters of prosperous white farmers. Some members of the **Gibson, Chavis, Bunch** and **Gowen** families became resolutely white after several generations.

Relations with Slaves
While some free African Americans owned slaves and were accepted in white society, others married slaves and socialized with slaves. Hester **Anderson**, one of those freed in 1712 in Norfolk County, was the common-law wife of a slave. She was the ancestor of the **Artis** family of Southampton County, Virginia, and several North Carolina counties. James **Revell** of Cumberland County entrusted his executor with the task of making application to the legislature for his wife's freedom [WB C:21].[7]

Abel **Carter** was suspected of aiding a runaway slave. The 14 November 1778 issue of the *North Carolina Gazette of New Bern* advertised a reward for a

negro fellow named Smart...Tis supposed he is harboured about Smith River by one Abel Carter, a free Negro, as he has been seen there several times [Fouts, *NC Gazette of New Bern*, I:83].

However, the majority were small farmers owning a few hundred acres who married other free African Americans. Their marriages can be identified from colonial wills and tax lists, and they were recorded in the county marriage bonds starting in the late eighteenth century.

Discriminatory Taxation
They suffered under the discriminatory North Carolina tax law enacted in 1749 which described taxables as

all and every White Person, Male, of the Age of Sixteen Years, and upwards, all Negroes, Mulattoes, Mustees Male or Female, and all Persons of Mixt Blood, to the Fourth Generation, of the Age of Twelve Years, and upwards, and all white Persons intermarrying with any Negro, mulatto, or Mustee, or other Person of mixt Blood,...shall be deemed Taxables... [Leary & Stirewalt, *North Carolina Research, Genealogy and Local History*, chapter 13].

---

[7]Another member of this family, Hiram **Revels**, first African American to be elected to the U.S. Senate, was born in Fayetteville, Cumberland County, North Carolina in 1822 [*Encyclopedia Britannica, Ready Reference & Index* VIII:538].

Thus, free African American and Indian households can be identified by the taxation of their female family members over twelve years of age. Some light-skinned people would claim to be white to avoid this discriminatory tax, and they would be listed by the tax collector with the notation, "Refuses to list his wife" [Thomas and Michael **Gowin** in the 1761 list of John Pope, CR 44.701.19]. It was in the interest of the tax collector to classify those of doubtful ancestry as "Mulatto" since he received a portion of the tax. However, those with some political and economic influence like the **Bass** and **Bunch** families were often listed as white.

Indentured Apprenticeship
In addition to the discriminatory tax, poor and orphaned African American children were bound out until the age of twenty-one by the county courts just like their poor white counterparts.[8] In July 1733 the General Assembly received complaints from "divers Inhabitants" that

> *divers free People, Negroes, Molattoes residing in this Province were...bound out until they come to 31 years contrary to the consent of the Parties bound out. The said comittee further report that they fear that divers Persons will desert the settlement of those parts ...*

The General Assembly ruled that those illegally bound should be released, the practice of binding out children to thirty-one years of age was to cease, and the children were to be bound out for the same term as white children [Saunders, *Colonial Records*, III:556].[9]

The children were bound as apprentices in various crafts. Some apprentices were bound "to learn the art, trade, and mystery of farming" which may simply have meant working as an unpaid field hand; others were trained as coopers, blacksmiths, cordwainers, or other useful occupations.

The November 1774 Bertie County Court of Pleas and Quarter Sessions ordered eight-year-old Jemima **Wiggins** and ten-year-old Mary Beth **Wiggins**, "bastard Mulattos of Sarah Wiggins," bound to John Skinner. However, this order was reversed in the May 1775 court session when Edward **Wiggins**, the children's father, convinced the court

> *of the said Skinners ill & deceitful Behavior procuring sd Order...* [Haun, *Bertie County Court Minutes*, IV:157].

The courts bound out the children of many free African American women because they were the common-law wives of slaves, but Doll **Burnett** argued against the binding of her daughter Edith in the 28 May 1777 Johnston County court:

---

[8]North Carolina and Virginia enacted apprenticeship laws similar to those in England. In 1646 Virginia passed a law giving justices of the peace at their own discretion the right to bind out children of the poor "to avoyd sloath and idleness wherewith such children are easily corrupted, as also for the relief of such parents whose poverty extends not to give them breeding" [Hening, *Statutes at Large*, XXVII:336].

[9]Carteret County, however, continued the practice of binding mixed-race children until the age of thirty-one at least until 1759 [Minutes, 1747-64, 53]. This attitude of the court may explain why free African Americans made up only 0.3% of the free Carteret County population in 1790. Craven and Granville Counties, on the other hand, bound out free African American girls until the age of eighteen - the same as for white girls, and free African Americans made up almost 5% of the free population of these counties in 1790 (4.6 and 4.9% respectively) [*Heads of families - North Carolina*, 10; Craven Minutes 1764-66, 50d; 1779-84, 79a; 1784-86, 49a; 1786-87, 26b; Granville Minutes, 1792-95, 65, 92].

and the court taking the Conduct Character and Circumstances of the said Doll Burnet into consideration & finding no just reasons to apprehend that the said Edith would become a charge to this County, Ordered her to be returned to the care of her said Mother again [Haun, *Johnston County Court Minutes*, II:260].

In some instances the indenture laws virtually enslaved a person for life. George Cummins had the indenture of his white servant woman named Christian Finny extended by a year and her child bound for thirty-one years by order of the 7 December 1736 Carteret County court because she had a "Mallatto Bastard Child during her service." She may have been the common-law wife of a slave for she was charged with having another "Melato" born 10 July 1739 and another on 20 December 1743. When she applied to the court for her freedom on 9 June 1744, the court ruled that she serve for another five months to pay for the cost of the court suit against her. When she again applied for her freedom six months later, the court ruled that on checking the record she serve another year since she had a "Mullatto Child in the time of her servitude" [Minutes 1723-47, fol.33c, fol.58, 59b-c, 62d, 151-2].

Some unscrupulous masters treated their apprentices like slaves. On 21 September 1742 David Lewis brought John **Russell**, a six-year-old mixed-race boy, into Craven County court, requesting that he be bound to him and promising to

Cause to be learned the sd Boy to Read & Write a Ledgable hand & teach him or cause to be taught the Shoemakers trade...

However, Lewis "made a present of the said boy" to his brother, John Lewis of Chowan County, and his brother sold the boy to Captain Hews of Suffolk County, Virginia [Haun, *Craven County Court Minutes*, III:328, 653].

Between 1759 and 1786 there were sixteen African American apprentices in Craven County who at the completion of their indentures had to petition the court for their freedom. The court ruled in the favor of the petitioners in every case [Minutes 1758-66, 1:22c; 1764-75, 1:50d; 1772-84, 1:49c, 58c-d, 59d, 61c; 2:4b, 34a-b, 49a, 79a; 1784-87, 1:5c, 11c, 33d; 2:26b].[10]

Caleb **Lockalier** was bound apprentice to Stephen Kades who assigned him to Francis Kennaday, who assigned him to James Oneal, who assigned him to Thomas Hadley, who refused to release him from his indenture until ordered to do so by the 27 July 1786 Cumberland County court [Minutes 1784-7, Thursday, 27 July 1786].

John Harris, a white Hyde County carpenter, found guilty of begetting a bastard child by Mary Ba_row, a white spinster, was required by law to support her. However, in June 1756 when the child was about two months old, the court learned that the child was mixed-race. Harris was compensated for his expense by binding the child, a "Molatto Named George," to him for twenty-one years [Haun, *Hyde County Court Minutes*, II:174].[11]

Robert West, Sr., advertised in the *North Carolina Gazette of New Bern* on 13 March 1752 for Thomas **Bowman** as if he were a runaway slave:

---

[10]The Craven County Court also ruled in favor of three African Americans who were born free elsewhere but held in bondage in Craven County between 1770 and 1778 [Minutes 1764-75, 2:147b; 1772-84, 2:38d, 48b, 58c, 69a].

[11]George **Barrow** was head of a Hyde County household of 5 "other free" and a slave in 1800 [NC:363] and 9 "free colored" in 1820 [NC:248].

Ran away from the subscribers on Roanoke River, a Negro fellow named Thomas Boman, a very good blacksmith, near 6 feet high, he can read, write and cyper. Whoever will apprehend him shall be paid 12 Pistoles, besides what the law allows [Fouts, *NC Gazette of New Bern*, I:3].

Almost twenty years later Thomas **Bowman** was a taxable "free Molatto" in John Moore's household in the Bertie County tax list of 1771, 1772, and 1774 [CR 10.702.1, Box 13].

A South Carolinian advertised in the *North Carolina Central and Fayetteville Gazette* on 25 July 1795 for Nancy **Oxendine**, daughter of Charles **Oxendine** of Robeson County:

$10 reward to deliver to the subscriber in Georgetown, a mustie servant woman named Nancy Oxendine, she is a stout wench, of a light complexion about 30 years old. It is supposed she has been ??els away by her brother and sister, the latter lives in Fayetteville [Fouts, *Newspapers of Edenton, Fayetteville, & Hillsborough*, 81].

We also find cases where children were willingly bound by their parents to neighbors, friends, and relatives. Lovey **Bass** bound her illegitimate child Nathan to her neighbor George **Anderson**. George **Anderson** was probably the boy's father. He devised his land to Nathan and his farm animals to Lovey **Bass** but left his wife and children only a shilling each [Original 1771 Granville County will].

Other apprenticeships were simply a way for a person to acknowledge responsibility for a child's support. Mary **Bibby**, a "black" taxable, had a "base born" child named Fanny who was bound out to Amy Ingram in Bute County on 13 May 1772 [Warren County WB A:227]. However, Mary had been living in the Ingram household for at least ten years prior to this. She and a slave named Charles were "black" taxables in Jesse Ingram's household in Gideon Macon's list for Goodwin's District of Granville County in 1761 [CR 44.701.19], and she and Charles were taxables in the Ingram household in the Bute County tax list of William Person in 1771 [CR 015.70001]. Mary was Charles' common-law wife according to a 28 June 1893 letter from a **Bibby** descendant, Narcissa **Rattley**, to her children.[12]

Some masters took the apprenticeships seriously. In Bertie County on 26 September 1768 seven-year-old Frederick **James**, "natural son of Ann James," was bound as an apprentice to John Norwood [CR 10.101.7]. And about fifty years later on 25 February 1817 we find Frederick **James** able to write his own Bertie County will in good handwriting [Original at N.C. Archives].

Sale Into Slavery
    Free African Americans were also in danger of having their children stolen and sold into slavery. In his Revolutionary War pension application on 7 March 1834 Drury **Tann** declared in Southampton County, Virginia, court that

he was stolen from his parents when a small boy by persons unknown to him, who were carrying him to sell him into Slavery, and had gotten with him and other stolen property as far as the Mountains on their way, that his parents made complaint to a Mr. Tanner Alford who was Then a magistrate in the county of Wake State of North Carolina to get me back from Those who had stolen me and he did pursue the Rogues & overtook Them at the mountains and took me from Them.

---

[12]Narcissa Ratley's letter is in the possession of Robert Jackson of Silver Springs, Maryland.

An advertisement in the 10 April 1770 issue of the *North Carolina Gazette of New Bern* describes how the **Driggers** family was victimized in Craven County, North Carolina:

> *broke into the house...under the care of Ann Driggus, a free negro woman, two men in disguise, with marks on their faces, and clubs in their hands, beat and wounded her terribly and carried away four of her children* [Fouts, *NC Gazette of New Bern*, I:65-6].

And John **Scott**, "freeborn negro," testified in Berkeley County, South Carolina, on 17 January 1754 that three men, Joseph Deevit, William Deevit, and Zachariah Martin,

> *entered by force, the house of his daughter, Amy Hawley, and carried her off, with her six children, and he thinks they are taking them north to sell as slaves.*

One of the children was recovered in Orange County, North Carolina, where the county court appointed Thomas **Chavis** to return the child to South Carolina on 12 March 1754 [Haun, *Orange County Court Minutes*, I:70-1].

Stealing free African Americans to sell them into slavery in another state was not a crime in North Carolina until 1779. However, free African Americans were afforded some protection under the law. In 1793 the murderer of John **James** of Northampton County was committed to jail according to the 20 March 1793 issue of the *North Carolina Journal*:

> *Last night Harris Allen, who was committed for the murder of John James, a free mulatto, of Northampton County, made his escape from the gaol of this town. He is a remarkable tall man, and had on a short round jacket* [Fouts, *NC Journal*, I:205].

Service in the Revolutionary War
Many of the families in this history have at least one member who fought in the Revolutionary War. Several moved to South Carolina in the eighteenth century, and their names appear in the musters of the South Carolina Militia in the 1759 Cherokee Expedition [Clark, *Colonial Soldiers of the South*, 701, 883, 892, 894].

This service alongside whites established long lasting friendships. William Bryan, a Justice of the Peace for Johnston County, testified in court for Holiday **Haithcock** in support of his application for a Revolutionary War pension on 21 September 1834 explaining that

> *in the times of our Revolutionary War free negroes and mulattoes mustered in the ranks with white men...This affiant has frequently mustered in company with said free negroes and mulattoes...That class of persons were equally liable to draft - and frequently volunteered in the public Service.*

And H. Thompson Venable wrote for him to the Commissioner of Pensions in Washington,

> *the case of Holliday Hethcock of N.C. has been suspended merely because he was a free man of color. As we understand that several cases of this sort have been admitted, you will oblige us by having it admitted.*

Charles Roberson Kee, a leading citizen of Northampton County, testified that he knew Drury **Walden** for more than twenty years and that

> *no man, not James Polk himself is of better moral character.*"

The Free Negro Code
Many free African American families sold their land in the early nineteenth century and headed west or remained in North Carolina as poor farm laborers. This was probably the consequence of a combination of deteriorating economic conditions and the restrictive "Free Negro Code."

Beginning in 1826 and continuing through the 1850s, North Carolina passed a series of restrictive laws termed the "Free Negro Code" by John Hope Franklin. Free African Americans lost the right to vote and were required to obtain a license to carry a gun. Tensions arising from Nat Turner's slave rebellion in nearby Southampton County, Virginia, played a major role in the passage of these laws.[13] It is also possible that moves against the African American population helped to divert the attention of poor whites from their worsening economic conditions in the 1830s.

With the whole state literally up in arms over Nat Turner's rebellion, delegates to the General Assembly from Newbern called on the Assembly "setting forth the incompetency of free persons of color exercising the privilege of voting." Edmund B. Freeman, editor of the *Roanoke Advocate*, a Halifax County weekly, boldly came to their support in the 5 January 1832 issue:

> *It cannot be denied that free negroes, taken in the mass, are dissolute and abandoned -yet there are some individuals among them, sober, industrious and intelligent - many are good citizens; and that they are sometimes good voters we have the best proofs... We do think that too much prejudice is excited against this class of our population... -but, at the same time, there is a class of white skinned citizens, equally low and abandoned, whose absence whould be little regretted* [N.C. Archives, Microfilm HaRA-2].

If his attitude toward free African Americans was typical of white Halifax County residents, this would help to explain why free African Americans made up over 18% of the free population of the county in 1810 [NC:59]. The editor's back-handed compliment certainly compares well to the sentiments of Robeson County residents:

> *The County of Robeson is cursed with a free-coloured population that migrated originally from the districts round about the Roanoke and Neuse Rivers. They are generally indolent, roguish, improvident, and dissipated* [Franklin, *Free Negro in North Carolina*, 79 (MS in Legislative Papers for 1840-41)].

or a northern paper quoted in the 5 January 1832 issue of the *Roanoke Advocate* complaining about "the evils arising from the immigration of free blacks" from other states into Pennsylvania:

---

[13]Free African Americans arrested in Southampton County after Nat Turner's Rebellion included Arnold **Artist** (**Artis**), Exum **Artes**, Berry **Newsom**, Thomas **Haithcock**, and Isham **Turner**. **Artes**, **Haithcock**, and **Newsom** were sent for further trial [Drewry, *The Southampton County Insurrection*, 195-6].

Overun by an influx of ignorant, indolent & depraved popullation most dangerous to the peace, rights & liberties of our citizens... [N.C. Archives Microfilm HaRA-2, January 5, 1832].

John Hope Franklin recorded a famous case in which Elijah **Newsom** of Cumberland County was prosecuted for carrying his gun in the county [Franklin, *Free Negro in North Carolina*, 77 (State v. Newsom, 27 N.C., 183)]. However, Halifax County and Robeson County appear to have granted gun licenses freely. These licenses were recorded in the county court records from 1841 through 1846.[14]

Many of those who left the state were enumerated in the 1840-1860 censuses of Indiana, Illinois, Ohio, and Michigan. Some went to Canada and a few to Haiti and Liberia. By 1857 when Henry **Chavers (Chavis)** emigrated to Liberia, life for free African Americans in North Carolina must have been truly oppressive. A letter written for him to his friend, Dr. Ellis Malone of Lewisburg in Franklin County, describing Liberia sounds like that of a recently liberated slave:

this Land of Freedom...a nation of free and happy Children of a hitherto downcast and oppressed Race...I now begin to enjoy life as a man should do...did my Coloured Friends only know or could they have seen what I already have seen they would not hesitate a moment to come to this Glorious Country [Ellis Malone Papers, NUCMC, 21-H, William R. Perkins Library, Duke University].[15]

By 1870 many of those who remained behind were living in virtually the same condition as the freed slaves. In the 1870 census for Northampton County, North Carolina, the most common occupation listed for those who were free before 1800 was "farm laborer," the same occupation as the former slaves. Some married former slaves, and by the twentieth century they had no idea their ancestors had been free.

Migration to South Carolina
    Some members of the **Gibson** family moved to South Carolina in 1731 where a member of the Commons House of Assembly complained that "several free colored men with their white wives had immigrated from Virginia." Governor Robert Johnson of South Carolina summoned Gideon **Gibson** and his family to explain their presence there and after meeting him and his family reported,

---

[14]"By petition signed by 5 or more of their respectable neighbors" the 18 August 1845 Halifax Court issued gun licenses to

Lemuel Morgan, Aaron, Arthur and Gabriel Locklear, Matthew Jones, John Smith, Robert Mitchum, Fed Haithcock, Fed Wilkins, Alex Jones, David Reynolds, Julius Flood, Ambrose Hawkins, Simon Purnin, William Jones.

The November 1841 Robeson County Court issued licenses using the form, "Whereas ... a Colored man residing in this County by name ____ doth sustain a good moral Character therefore it is adjudged that the said ____ be permitted to bear fire armes ... & use the same as any other good Citizen of the Community." They were issued to

David, Aaron, and Alexander Oxendine, Ishmael, Ethelred, Nelson, and Willis Roberts, David Scott, William Goings, Henry Sampson, Abraham Jones, George Morgan, Levi and Hector Locklear, and John Blanks.

[15]Bell I. Wiley understandably mistook Chavers for a recently manumitted slave, including this letter in his book, *Slaves No More* (1980), University Press of Kentucky.

*I have had them before me in Council and upon Examination find that
they are not Negroes nor Slaves but Free people, That the Father of them
here is named Gideon Gibson and his Father was also free, I have been
informed by a person who has lived in Virginia that this Gibson has lived
there Several Years in good Repute and by his papers that he has
produced before me that his transactions there have been very regular,
That he has for several years paid Taxes for two tracts of Land and had
several Negroes of his own, That he is a Carpenter by Trade and is come
hither for the support of his Family* [Box 2, bundle: S.C., Minutes of
House of Burgesses (1730-35), 9, Parish Transcripts, N.Y. Hist. Soc. by
Jordan, *White over Black*, 172].

Like the early settlers of the North Carolina frontier Governor Johnson was
more concerned with the **Gibsons'** social class than their race.

Many of the free African Americans who were counted in the census for South
Carolina from 1790 to 1810 originated in Virginia or North Carolina. They were:

**Bass, Berry, Biddie, Bonner, Bowman, Bradley, Braveboy, Bryan,
Bugg, Bunch, Butler, Buzby, Carter, Chavis, Clark, Collins,
Combest/ Cumbess, Cumbo, Demery, Driggers, Ferrell, Gallimore,
Gibson, Gowen, Grooms, Hagan, Haithcock, Harmon, Hatcher,
Hawley/ Holly, Hays, Hazell, Henderson, Hicks, Hilliard, Howard,
Huelin, Hunt, Ivey, Jacobs, Jeffries, Jones, Kersey, Lamb, Locklear,
Lowry, Lucas, Matthews, Mitcham, Mosely, Mumford, Oxendine,
Pavey, Rawlinson, Reed, Rouse, Russell, Scott, Shoecraft,
Shoemaker, Sweat, Tann, Turner, Valentine, Weaver, Webb, Wilson,
and Winn.**

Few colonial South Carolina county court records have survived, so it is difficult
to determine the origin of the other families. However, at least three families were
the descendants of white slave owners who left slaves and plantations to their
mixed-race children: **Collins, Holman,** and **Pendarvis.** James **Pendarvis** expanded
his father's holdings more than fourfold to 4,710 acres and 151 slaves. John
Holman, Jr., established a plantation with fifty-seven slaves on the Santee River
in Georgetown District and then returned to his homeland on the Rio Pongo River
in West Africa to resume the slave trading he learned from his English father
[Koger, *Black Slaveowners*, 104, 108-110, 112-121].

According to Koger, free Indians in Charleston were part of the free African
American community. They married members of the free African American
community and were members of the Brown Fellowship Society, an organization
of "lighter skinned men" which maintained a cemetery, operated a school for the
children of its members, and supported charity and social functions. Proof of
descent from a free Indian allowed free African Americans to avoid the
discriminatory state capitation tax [Koger, *Black Slaveowners*, 16-17; S.C. Dept.
of Archives & History, Public Programs Document Packet No.1]. Free association
of Indians and African Americans is also evident from their family genealogies.
Rachel **Garden,** "a free Mustee," married Robert **Baldwin,** "a free Blackman," in
Charleston on 5 September 1801.

Indian Ancestry
    Indians who adopted English customs became part of the free African
American communities. There were no Indian communities separate and distinct
from the free African American communities. In order to have established a
separate Indian community, Indians would need to have had a strong preference for
marriages and relationships with other Indians. However, no such preference is

evident in the marriages of families with Indian ancestry. They appear to have made no differences between themselves and African Americans.

There were no complete nuclear Indian families (both parents, plus children) among Indian slaves mentioned in seventeenth century Accomack and Northampton County records, while there were many among African slaves [Deal, *Race and Class*, 75]. I did not find any nuclear Indian families in the eighteenth century Virginia and North Carolina tax lists.[16]

Molly Cockran, a free Indian woman from Goochland County, had a child by a slave, "Negro Ben," in August 1765 [Jones, *The Douglas Register*, 348]. The children of Judith Cypress, an Indian woman from Surry County, Virginia, married African Americans. Both families became part of the free African American community.

John Teague was an Indian tenant on land in Accomack County on 8 September 1725 [Orders 1724-31, 37]. His likely descendants were Robert **Teague**, a "Mulato" taxable on himself and a horse in Northampton County, Virginia, in 1787 [Schreiner-Yantis, *1787 Census*, 1260] and Sacker **Teague** who registered as a "free Negro" in Accomack County: *born July 1785, a light Black, 5 feet 10-1/2 Inches, Born free* [Register of Free Negroes, no.3].

William **Press**, an Indian "born...of the body of a free Negro called Priscilla," was fined for failing to list himself as a taxable in Northampton County, Virginia, in 1730 [Mihalyka, *Loose Papers 1628-1731*, 239].

The descendants of David Pinn, an Indian taxed in Benjamin George's Christ Church Parish, Lancaster County household in 1745 and 1746, were so much a part of the African American community by 1785 that a descendant left his estate to his wife with the proviso that she not marry a slave. Otherwise, it was to go to his sister who had married a member of the free African American **Nickens** family [Library of Virginia Microfilm, Lancaster Tithables 1745-95, 1, 6; *Northumberland County Wills and Administrations*, 80].

Archer Bowmer, son of an Indian woman, registered in Halifax County, Virginia, on 20 May 1827: *a dark mulatto man about 64 years of age...grey wooly hair, was born free* [Registers of Free Negroes, 1802-1831, no. 114].

---

[16] The slave population of some Virginia counties may have had a fair amount of Indian ancestry in the early eighteenth century. Daniel Jenifer's "negro Slave called old Daniel" had a child by his Indian slave, Nanny, before 15 April 1687 when Jenifer made his Accomack County will. Their child Annis was called a "mustie" young woman in a 9 December 1697 Accomack County Court case [Orders 1697-1703, 8]. Mary Scarburgh's slave, Songo, had an Indian wife named Molo when Scarburgh made her 19 December 1691 Accomack County will [Orders 1682-97, 216, 228a]. I count thirty-two Indian children brought to court to have their ages adjudged in Charles City County Court between 1687 and 1695, a similar number in Henrico County between 1683 and 1687 and another thirty children in Henrico County between 1691 and 1712 [Charles City Orders 1687-95, 144, 180, 244, 263, 295, 314, 332, 349, 351, 353, 385, 409, 415, 421, 458, 461, 474, 482, 505, 507, 535; Henrico Orders 1678-93, 139-41, 146-7, 150, 157-8, 161, 163, 177, 210, 241, 391, 430; 1694-1701, 40, 71, 80, 82, 112, 117, 149, 169, 200, 210, 211, 213, 218, 229-31, 235, 237; 1707-9, 29; 1710-4, 134, 161]. The Henrico County Court bound out as an apprentice "Joe a Mollatto the Son of Nan an Indian Woman" in November 1740 [Orders 1737-46, 128]. And "Tom a Mulatto or Mustee" petitioned the Henrico County Court for his freedom in January 1737/8, testifying that he was the grandson of a white woman but was held as a slave by Alexander Trent [Orders 1737-46, 20]. In June 1722 "Peg a Mulattoe woman Servant ... whose mother was an Indian" was ordered by the Henrico County Court to serve her master until the age of thirty years [Orders 1719-24, 182].

It appears that some Indians with English surnames took their names from African American parents. Solomon **Bartlett** (born about 1727), a "free Mulatto" living in Bertie County in 1772, was probably the ancestor of Solomon and Fanny **Bartlett** (born about 1800) who were counted in the 1808 Nottoway Indian census [Executive Papers, June 21-July 22, 1808, Gov. William H. Cabell, box 154a, LVA].

John **Dungee**, a "free Mulatto," received thirty lashes in July 1755 when he was convicted of the attempted rape of a white woman in Brunswick County, Virginia [Orders 1753-6, 451, 498]. He was probably the grandfather of John **Dungee**, a Pamunkey Indian "descended from the aborigines of this dominion," who petitioned the Virginia Legislature to allow his wife, the daughter of a slave and her slaveowner, to remain in Virginia in 1825 [King William County Legislative Petition, 19 December 1825, LVA].

Francis Skiper was married to Ann, an African American woman, before 2 February 1667/8 when they sold 100 acres of land in Norfolk County [W&D E:28; Orders 1666-75, 73]. They may have been the ancestors of George Skiper, one of the Nottoway Indians who sold land in Southampton County on 2 February 1749 [DB 1:98].

The history of the **Bass** family, a mixed-race Nansemond and English family, illustrates the position of culturally-English Indians in Virginia and North Carolina. Their ancestor, John Bass of Norfolk County, Virginia, married an Indian woman in 1638. There is no evidence that the family ever adopted any Indian customs.

John's son, William[1] **Bass**, purchased land in Norfolk County in 1729. William's son, Edward Bass, purchased land there in 1699 and had normal dealings in the county court [DB 6, no.2, fols. 36, 170, 255; Orders 1708-10, 124; 1710-17, 14, 136]. William[1]'s daughter, Mary Bass, was the mistress of two white children who were bound to her by the Norfolk County court on 8 June 1714 [DB 6:189].

William[1] Bass obtained a certificate from the Norfolk County court Clerk in 1727:

> *An Inquest p'taining to possession & use of Cleared & Swamplands...William Bass, Senr. & his kinsmen...are persons of English and Nansemun Indian descent with no Admixture of negor, Ethiopic blood.*

William[1] Bass' son by the same name, William[2] **Bass**, described as tall and swarthy, also obtained a certificate of Indian ancestry from the Norfolk County Clerk on 20 September 1742 [Bell, *Bass Families of the South*, 15]. His descendants were at least as much African as Indian since he married Sarah **Lovina**, the "Molatto" daughter of a "Negro Woman" named Judith **Lovina** in 1729 [Norfolk WB 6:fol.96; DB 12:188; 18:41-2]. About seventy years later on 27 May 1797 their <u>grandson</u> obtained a certificate from the Norfolk County Clerk stating that he was

> *of English and Indian descent and is not a Negroe nor y[t] a Mulattoe as by some falsely and malitiously stated.*

and that he was the <u>son</u> of Sarah **Lovina**,

a vertious woman of Indian descent [LVA accession no.26371].[17]

William[2] Bass' brothers came to North Carolina in the early eighteenth century, and their descendants settled in Northampton, Bertie, and Granville counties. Those who settled in Northampton and Bertie counties prospered and were among the larger landowners in the county. They married whites and most were considered white after a few generations. The Granville branch of the family were relatively small landowners who married free African Americans and were considered African American after a few generations.

One of the Granville County descendants, William **Bass**, was called "free negro" in an undated Granville County court presentation [CR 44.289.19]. Another William **Bass** was the foster son of a slave in Marlboro District, South Carolina. His extraordinary case illustrates both the extent which the family intermarried with African Americans and the degree of repression suffered by free African Americans in the mid-nineteenth century. On 14 December 1859 he petitioned the legislature to become the slave of Philip W. Pledger explaining that

> *his position as a free person of color, a negro, is more degrading and involves more suffering in this State, than that of a slave...he is preyed upon by every sharper with whom he comes in contact...and is charged with and punished for every offence guilty or not, committed in the neighborhood...and lives a thousand times harder, and in more destitution, than the slaves of many planters* [Henry, *Police Control of the Slave in South Carolina*, 196-7 (*Charleston Courier*, 20 December 1859)].[18]

Tri-racial, "Portuguese," and "Indian" Communities

Some of the lighter-skinned descendants of these families formed their own distinct communities which have been the subject of anthropological research. Those in Robeson County, North Carolina, are called "Lumbee Indians," in Halifax and Warren counties: "Haliwa-Saponi," in South Carolina: "Brass Ankles" and "Turks," in Tennessee and Kentucky: "Melungeons" and "Portuguese," and in Ohio: "Carmel Indians." Several fantastic theories on their origin have been suggested. One is that they were from Raleigh's lost colony at Roanoke and another that they were an amalgamation of the Siouan-speaking tribes in North and South Carolina [Blu, *The Lumbee Problem*, 36-41].

Documents from a court case held in Johnson County, Tennessee in 1858 provide a detailed description of one such family. They illustrate the extent to which the family was accepted by the white community and the extent to which the family history was already clouded by myths in 1858. Joshua **Perkins**, born about 1732 in Accomack County, Virginia, was the "Mulatto" son of a white woman [Orders 1731-36, 133]. He owned land in Robeson County, North Carolina, in 1761, moved to Liberty County, South Carolina, and in 1785 moved to what later became Washington County, Tennessee [Bladen County DB 23:80, 121, 104-5, 424-5, 147-8; Philbeck, *Bladen County Land Entries*, no. 1210]. Along the way, succeeding generations of his family married light-skinned or white people. They owned a ferry, race horses, and an iron ore mine; ran the local school house, and were election officials. However, conditions had changed drastically just prior to

---

[17]Other free African American families (**Anderson, Weaver, Perkins, Bright, Newton,** and **Price**) were issued certificates of Nansemond Indian ancestry by the Norfolk Court on 15 and 20 July 1833 [Bell, *Bass Families of the South*, chapter on Nansemond Indian Ancestry of Some Bass Families, 1, 8].

[18]Philip Pledger may have been related to Morris **Pledger**, head of an Anson County, North Carolina household of 6 "other free" in 1800 [NC:203].

the Civil War in 1858 when Jacob F. **Perkins**, great-grandson of Joshua **Perkins**, brought an unsuccessful suit against one of his neighbors in the Circuit Court of Johnson County for slander because he called him a "free Negro" [The Perkins File in the T.A.R. Nelson Papers in the Calvin M. McClung Collection at the East Tennessee Historical Center].

More than fifty witnesses made depositions or testified at the trial. Many of the deponents had known three generations of the family in North Carolina, South Carolina, or Tennessee. Sixteen of twenty-two elderly witnesses who had actually seen Joshua **Perkins** testified that he was a "Negro," describing him as a

dark skinned man with sheeps wool and flat nose...[Ibid., deposition of Nancy Lipps].

black man, hair nappy...Some called Jacob (his son) a Portuguese and some a negro [Ibid., deposition of John Nave, 88 years old].

Knew old Jock (Joshua) in North Carolina on Peedee...right black or nearly so. Hair kinky...like a common negro [Ibid., deposition of Abner Duncan, 86 years old].

However, eighteen witnesses for Perkins testified that Joshua **Perkins** was something other than "Negro" - Portuguese or Indian.[19] They said little about his physical characteristics and those of his descendants. Instead, they argued that he could not have been a "Negro" and been so totally accepted by his community:

dark skinned man...resembled an Indian more than a negro. He was generally called a Portuguese. Living well...Kept company with everybody. Kept race horses and John Watson rode them [Ibid., deposition of Thomas Cook, 75 years old].

mixed blooded and not white. His wife fair skinned...They had the same privileges [Ibid., deposition of Catherine Roller, 80 years old].

Hair bushy & long - not kinky. Associated with white people...Associated with...the most respectable persons. Some would call them negroes and some Portuguese [Ibid., deposition of John J. Wilson, about 70 years old].

He was known of the Portuguese race...Four of his sons served in the Revolution...Jacob and George drafted against Indians...they came from and kept a ferry in South Carolina [Ibid., deposition of Anna Graves, 77 years old].

They kept company with decent white people and had many visitors [Ibid., deposition of Elizabeth Cook, about 71].

I taught school at Perkins school house...they were Portuguese...associated white peoples, clerked at elections and voted and had all privileges [Ibid., deposition of David R. Kinnick, aged 77].

---

[19]The use of the term "Portuguese" for a mixed-race person accepted as white was used as early as October 1812 when the Marion District, South Carolina Court of Common Pleas ruled that Thomas **Hagans** did not have to pay the levy on "Free Negros" because he was Portuguese [*NCGSJ* IX:259]. Thomas was the son of Zachariah **Hagins**, a "Mulatto" bound out in Johnston County, North Carolina Court in October 1760 [Haun, *Johnston County Court Minutes*, I:46].

Some who testified in favor of the Perkins family had never seen Joshua **Perkins** and seemed to be genuinely confused about the family's ancestry:

I was well acquainted with Jacob Perkins (a second generation Perkins). *A yellow man - said to be Portuguese. They do not look like negroes. I have been about his house a great deal and nursed for his wife. She was a little yellow and called the same race. Had blue eyes and black hair. Was visited by white folks* [Ibid., deposition of Mary Wilson].

One of the deponents, seventy-seven-year-old Daniel Stout, explained very simply how people of African descent could have been treated well by their white neighbors:

Never heard him called a negro. People in those days said nothing about such things [Ibid., deposition of Daniel Stout].

Many of these light-skinned communities were isolated from both the white and former slave populations after the Civil War. Mobile **Hobson** was the descendant of Ann Hobson, a white woman of Elizabeth City County, and a slave. He was a very old man when interviewed by the Virginia Writers Project which described him as "Grecian featured with skin as white as a white man's." He described events in Poquoson, Virginia, after the Civil War:

We used to go to de white churches fo' de war; an' arter dey started schools dey say we was Injuns. Well, we was, too, partly. But we wasn't no Negroes. First dey say we couldn't go in de white church no more. Well, we stopped goin'. Den when dey start de schools, dey say we couldn't go to de white schoolhouse. Some wouldn't go to de colored schoolhouse, an' some would. My dad wouldn't let us go to school wid de Negroes, so we didn't git no schoolin. When it come to marryin' we was in a worse fix. Couldn't marry white an' we wasn't aimin to marry colored. Started in to marryin' each other an' we been marryin' close cousins ever since [WPA, *The Negro in Virginia*, 36]. (The forward to the 1994 printing warns that a thicker dialect was added in some interviews).

And a study in 1886 described these groups and their relations with the newly freed slaves:

The line of demarcation between the Old and New "Ishy" is not only still plainly visible, but bids fair long to continue so. Associating but little with each other, intermarriage is not common. A free Negro who marries a freed one almost invariably loses caste and is disowned by his people.

In their habits, manner, and dress, the free negroes still resemble, as they always did, the poorest class of whites much closer than they do the freedman [Dodge, "Free Negroes of North Carolina," *Atlantic Monthly* 57 (January 1886):20-30].[20]

Mixed-race families from Virginia were among the earliest settlers of Bladen County, North Carolina, from which Robeson County was formed in 1787. They were described in a report to the colonial governor of North Carolina in 1754:

---

[20]"Old" and "new issue" were terms used to distinguish African Americans free before and after the Civil War. The term probably referred to the new monetary currency issued after the war.

50 families a mixt Crew, a lawless People, possess the Lands without patent or paying quit rents; shot a Surveyor for coming to view vacant lands being inclosed in great swamps.

... No Indians...in the county [Saunders, *Colonial Records*, V:161].

The colonial tax lists for Bladen County listed the following mixed-race families as "Mulattoes" from 1768 to 1770: **Braveboy, Carter, Chavis, Clark, Cox, Cumbo, Dimry, Doyal (Dial), Drake, Evans, Goin, Groom, Hammons, Hayes, Hunt, Ivey, James, Johnston, Jones, Kersey, Lamb, Locklear, Lowery, Overton, Oxendine, Perkins, Phillips, Russell, Skipper, Sweat, Sweeting, Walden, Wharton, Wilkins**, and **Wilson**. One person was called an Indian: Thomas Britt [Byrd, William L., III, *Bladen County Tax Lists, 1768-1774*, I: 4-9, 14-17, 24-46, 50].

A complaint of 13 October 1773 listed "free Negors and Mullatus living upon the Kings land...Raitously Assembled together" in Bladen County: Captain James **Ivey**, Joseph **Ivey**, Ephraim **Sweat**, William **Chavours Clark**, Bengman **Dees**, William **Sweat**, George **Sweat**, William **Groom**, Sen', William **Groom**, Jun', Gidion **Grant**, Thomas **Groom**, James **Frace**, Isaac **Vaun**, Sol. **Stableton**, Edward **Locklear**, Tiely **Locklear**, Major **Locklear**, Recher **Groom**, and Ester **Carsey** [G.A. 73, Box 7].

And a representation from Bladen County to the House of Assembly on 18 December 1773 complained of

the number of free negroes and mulattoes who infest that county and annoy its Inhabitants [Saunders, *Colonial Records*, IX:768].

Most of the families listed in the 1790 and 1800 Robeson County census as "other free" are traced in this history back to persons referred to as "Negroes" or "Mulattos" in Virginia or North Carolina. These are the **Branch, Braveboy, Brooks, Carter, Chavis, Cumbo, Dunn, Evans, Gowen, Hammond, Hogg, Hunt, Jacobs, James, Johnston, Kersey, Locklear, Manuel, Newsom, Oxendine, Revell, Roberts, Sweat** and **Wilkins** families.

It appears from court records that free African Americans in Robeson County were at times accepted by the white population. They attended white schools and churches, voted, and mustered with whites. On 1 April 1805 the Robeson County court appointed James **Lowery** overseer of a road, a position usually reserved for whites [Minutes I:321]. However, they lost many of their rights with the passage of North Carolina's "Free Negro Codes" from about 1826 to 1850. Charles **Oxendine** was indicted by the Robeson County court for assault and battery and fined fifteen dollars. When he failed to pay his fine, the court ordered the sheriff to hire him out since he was a "free Negro." Oxendine appealed the ruling to the supreme court of North Carolina in 1837 on the basis that the law unconstitutionally discriminated against free persons of color.

During the Civil War, two cousins of the **Lowery** family of Robeson County were murdered while absent from fortification duty. The white man suspected of their murder was himself murdered shortly afterwards. A few months later in March 1865 a grandson of James **Lowery**, Allen **Lowery**, and his son William were murdered by the White Home Guard on the suspicion they were aiding escaped Union prisoners. The following month Hector **Oxendine** was murdered on the suspicion he helped General Sherman when he marched through Robeson County.

In response to these acts Henry Berry **Lowery**, a son of Allen **Lowery**, led a band of armed men who killed or drove from the county those who were involved in the murders. The band remained at large for nearly ten years despite the determined efforts of the White Home Guard, federal troops, and huge rewards for bounty hunters [Blu, *The Lumbee Problem*, 50-65].

The New York Herald sent journalist Alfred Townsend to the county to report on the band. He described the area where most of the former free persons of color were living as

Scuffletown...The Mulatto Capital...spreads besides three or four miles on both sides of the (Rutherford Railway) track and is surrounded on three sides with swamps, a tract of several miles, covered at wide intervals with hills and log cabins of the rudest and simplest construction, sometimes a half dozen of these huts being proximate. The people have few or no horses, but often keep a kind of stunted ox to haul their short, rickety carts... and a little old lever-well of the crudest mechanism. The cabin is found built of hewn logs, morticed at the ends, the chinks stopped with mud, the chimney built against one gable on the outside of logs and clay, with sticks and clay above where it narrows to the smoke hole. There is beside the large chimney place, a half barrel, sawed off, to make lye from the wood ashes, and the other half of the barrel is seen to serve the uses of a washtub. The mongrel dog is always a feature of the establishment. The two or three acres of the lot are generally ploughed or planted in potatoes or maize...The bed is made on the floor, there are two or three stools; only one apartment comprising the whole establishment. Just such a place as the above is the house of Henry Berry Lowery, the outlaw chief, except that, being a carpenter he has nailed weather strips over the interstices, between the logs and made himself a sort of bedstead and some chairs. His cabin has two doors, opposite each other. The Scuffletowners go out to work as ditchers for the neighboring farmers who pay them magnanimous wages of $6 a month. The above picture while true of the majority of Scuffletowners, is not justly descriptive of all. The Oxendines are all well to do, or were before this bloody feud began, and the Lowerys were industrious carpenters, whose handiwork is seen at Lumberton, Shoe Heel and all round that region...The whites hated the settlement because it was a bad example to the negroes. But most people were Baptists or Methodists, and nearly all owned their own homesteads [Townsend, *The Swamp Outlaws*, 42-5].

He described Henry Berry **Lowery** as "a yellow fellow, Indian-looking...of mixed Tuscarora, mulatto, and white blood...has straight black hair, like an Indian...one of the handsomest mulattoes you ever saw." And stated that the **Lowery**s "and their blood relatives showed Indian traces while Scuffletown at large is mainly plain, unromantic mulatto." He described the predominantly-white county seat of Lumberton as

wholly built of unpainted planks or logs which have become nearly black with weather stains. The streets are sandy and without pavements of either brick or wood [Townsend, *The Swamp Outlaws*, 39, 42-6].

Though started for the purpose of exacting revenge for the murders of members of the **Lowery** family, the band also demonstrated that the community could not be intimidated by whites. Much of the white community was in fear of the band, but their leader was quoted as saying,

We don't kill anybody but the Ku Klux [Townsend, *Swamp Outlaws*, 26-7].

The end of the band came in 1874 with the death of Steve **Lowery**, but the establishment of a self defence force helped their community maintain some political power at a time when white aggression prevented many African Americans from exercising their political rights.

After the Civil War the former free persons of color voted for the same party as the former slaves: Republican. This made for an almost equal division between the Democrats and the Republicans in Robeson County (and in North Carolina as a whole) [Blu, *The Lumbee Problem*, 20, 61, 73]. However, those who had been free before the Civil War objected to the arrangement whereby the schools were divided between white and "Colored" districts. Their settlements were included in twelve of Robeson County's "Colored" districts.

In 1885 North Carolina passed a law sponsored by Hamilton McMillan, a Democrat from Robeson County, creating separate school districts for the former free persons of color of the county. McMillan invented the name "Croatan Indians" and theorized that they had descended from a friendly tribe of Indians on the Roanoke River in eastern North Carolina who had mixed with the whites in Sir Walter Raleigh's lost colony in 1587 [Blu, *The Lumbee Problem*, 62]. Twelve "Croatan Indian" districts were created from districts which had formerly been "Colored" [Minutes, County Board of Education, 1885-1911, 1-4]. This swung many of their votes to the Democrats.

Thus, in the early part of the Jim Crow era, the Democrats solidified their position in the legislature and solved the problem of drawing racial lines in a county where they had been blurred. In 1900 when the former slaves were disenfranchised by Jim Crow laws and "Red Shirt" violence, the "Croatan Indians" lost much of their political influence since the Republicans were no longer a factor in politics.

The 1885 law did not confer any benefits, just made a division that created three castes in Robeson County: white, Colored and "Croatan Indian." Later, there would be three sets of water fountains, seating areas, rest rooms, etc. [Blu, *The Lumbee Problem*, 23, 62-3]. The change of name from "mulattoes" to "Croatan Indians" did not change white attitudes toward them. Whites shortened the name to the pejorative "Crows." The name was changed to "Cherokee Indians of Robeson County" in 1913, "Siouan Indians of Lumber River" in 1934-1935, and they were recognized by the U.S. Congress as Lumbee Indians in 1956.

The 1885 North Carolina bill changed the history of Indians in the Southeast. Anthropologist James Mooney included the Croatan Indians and other mixed-race communities in adjoining North and South Carolina counties in his studies of the Indian tribes of the Southeast in 1907, and Frank G. Speck travelled throughout the Southeast "discovering" lost tribes [Blu, The *Lumbee Problem*, 41].

Person County granted a group called "old issue negroes" their own separate school on 2 February 1887. It was discontinued about 1896 but reestablished on 4 January 1901: listed as "Mongolian" through 1906, "Cuban" from 6 April 1908 through 1911, and listed as for "the Indian race" in October 1912 [Person County School Board Minutes cited by G.C. Waldrep, III, personal communication, 20 April 2000]. Other invented North Carolina Indian tribes followed: the Sampson County Coharie Indians, Columbus County Waccamaw-Siouan Indians, and Halifax County Haliwa-Saponi Indians. Virginia recognized the former free-person-of-color community of Norfolk County as Nansemond Indians and the community in Amherst county as Monacan Indians.

A study in 1920 described the group in Halifax County:

Probably the largest group of free Negroes to be found in North Carolina was the exclusive "old issue" settlement known far and wide as the Meadows, near Ransom's Bridge on Fishing Creek in Halifax County. The group still bears the appellation "old issue" and are heartily detested by the well-to-do Negroes in the adjoining counties [Taylor, R. H., *The Free Negro in North Carolina* (James Sprunt Historical Publications) v. 17, no.1, p.23].

Indian Reservations

Indians living on Virginia reservations during the colonial and early national periods made little distinction between themselves and African Americans.

In 1811 Thomas Jefferson described the remaining members of the Mattopony tribe as being "three or four men only and they have more Negro than Indian blood [Johnston, *Race Relations in Virginia*, 281].

A number of free African American families joined the Pamunkey reservation during the colonial and early national period. A Pamunkey petition to the governor of Virginia in 1836 included the names: Isaac **Miles**, Jr. (one of the "headmen"), Anderson **Holt**, William **Holt**, Ben **Holt**, Archia **Miles**, Sylvanus **Miles**, Pleasant **Miles**, William **Sweat**, Abram **Sweat** and Allen **Sweat** [Rountree, *Pocahontas's People*, 344]. One hundred and forty-three whites in Prince William County, Virginia, petitioned the legislature in 1843 concerning the Pamunkey Tribe saying

Now the Pamunkys form only a small remnant of the population, having so largely mingled with the negro race as to have obliterated all striking features of Indian extraction. Their land is now inhabited by two unincorporated bands of free mulattoes in the midst of a large slave holding community.

The Pamunkey submitted a counter-petition in which they claimed that they were generally of at least half Indian extraction [LVA, Legislative Petitions, King William County, 1843, B-1207, B-1208, cited by Russell, *Free Negro of Virginia*, 129].

The Gingaskin Indians of Northampton County, Virginia, said to be as numerous as all other tribes in the county put together, numbered only thirty persons by 1769. In 1813 their descendants were described as a heterogeneous mixture of Indian, Negro, and white [Whitelaw, *Virginia's Eastern Shore*, 30, 284]. Their land was divided among the heads of families, and in 1828 the clerk of Northampton County court stated that their descendants were respectable free Negro landowners [Johnston, *Race Relations in Virginia*, 280-1].

The nearest thing to a census of the reservations is provided by the deeds by which Indians living on tribal lands sold or leased their land. The deeds were signed by the "chief men" (and women) of the tribe.

The principal members of the Nottoway and Nansemond living in present-day Southampton County were:

King Edmunds, James Harrison, Ned, Peter, Robert Scoller, Sam, Wanoke Robin, William Hines, Frank, Wanoke Robin, Jr., Cockarons Tom, and *Cockarons Will* (in 1735).

Sam, Frank, Jack Will, John Turner, Wat Bailey, and *George Skiper* (in 1750).

John Turner, and Celia Rogers (a Nansemond Indian) and *Suky Turner* (in 1795) [Surry County DB 8:550; Southampton County DB 1:98; 7:714].

Between 1734 and 1756 the Nottoway had been so reduced by "the want of the common necessaries of life, sickness, and other casualties" that the Virginia Legislature allowed them to sell a total of 18,000 acres of their land in Southampton County [Hening, *Statutes at Large*, IV:459; V:170; VI:211; *VMHB* V:339]. They used land sales and leases to support themselves. There were only six adults and eleven children in the census taken in 1808:

adults: *Littleton Scholar, Tom Turner, Jemmy Wineoak, Edy Turner, Nancy Turner, and Betsy Step*

children: *Tom Step, Henry Turner, Alexander Rogers, John Woodson, Winny Woodson, Anny Woodson, Polly Woodson, Fanny Bartlett, Solomon Bartlett, Billy Woodson, and Jenny Woodson* [Executive Papers June 21- July 22, 1808, Gov. William H. Cabell, Box 154a, LVA].

No adult Indian was married to or sharing a household with any other adult Indian [Roundtree, "The Termination and Dispersal of the Nottoway Indians of Virginia," *VMHB* 95:193-214].

A legislative petition from Southampton County in 1818 reported that

Their husbands and wives are chiefly free negroes [Legislative Petition, Southampton County, December 16, 1818, LVA].

Some of the names of the members of the Chowan Tribe were recorded in Chowan County deeds by which they sold their land on Bennett's Creek in 1734 in what was later Gates County. They were

Charles Beasley, James Bennett, Thos Hoyter, Jeremiah Pushin, John Reading, John Robins, & Nuce Will [Chowan DB W-1, 215-216, 237-239, 247-253].

By 1790 the surviving members of the tribe were described as

a parcel of Indian women, which has mixed with Negroes, and now there is several freemen and women of Mixed blood as aforesaid which has descended from the sd Indians.

when they sold the last 400 acres of the original patent for 11,360 acres [General Assembly Session Records, Nov-Dec 1790, Box 2; Gates County DB 2:273, 274; A-2:33].

About 300 Tuscarora men, women, and children were living on 40,000 acres in Bertie County between 1752 and 1761 [Saunders, *Colonial Records*, V:161-2, 320-1]. The tribe never gave up its Indian customs. Their numbers had been reduced to 260 in 1766 when they leased part of their land. 155 members of the tribe moved to the state of New York after the 1766 lease, and the remainder joined them in 1802 [Swanton, *Indian Tribes of North America*, 87].

Since they left the Southeast, it is difficult to determine the extent to which they mixed with the free African American population of Bertie County. Many of their names were recorded in the deeds of 1766 and 1777 by which they leased over 8,000 acres of the land in the southwest corner of Bertie County between the Roanoke River and Roquist Pocosin to the Attorney General:

James Allen, Sarah Basket, Thomas Basket, William Basket, Betty Blount, Billy Blount, Sr., Billy Blount, Jr., Edward Blount, George Blount, Sarah Blount, Thomas Blount, Bille Blunt, Jr, Samuel Bridgers, William Cain, John Cain, Molly Cain, Wineoak Charles, Jr., Wineoak Charles, Sr., Bille Cornelius, Charles Cornelius, Isaac Cornelius, Billy Denis, Sarah Dennis, Billy George, Snipnose George, Watt Gibson, James Hicks, John Hicks, Sarah Hicks, Senicar Thomas Howell, Tom Jack, Capt. Joe, John Litewood, Isaac Miller, James Mitchell, Bille Mitchell, Bille Netof, Bille Owens, John Owens, Nane Owens, William Pugh, John Randel, Billy Roberts, Tom Roberts, Jr., John Rogers, Harry Samuel, John Senicar, Thomas Senicar, Ben Smith, John Smith, Molly Smith, Thomas Smith, Bille Sockey, William Taylor, Bridgers Thomas, Tom Thomas, Lewis Tuffdick, West Whitmel Tufdick, Whitmel Tuffdick, Isaac Whealer, James Wiggians, John Wiggins, Molly Wineoak and Bette Yollone [DB L-2:56; M:314-9].

The names of the Piscataway Indians living in Richmond County, Virginia were mentioned in a court case in September 1704:

Young Toby, Long Tom, Jack the Fidler, Old Mr. Thomas, Bearded Jack, Jemmy, Harry Capoos, and Bearded Jack [Orders 1702-1704, 361].

Members of the Sapony in Orange County, Virginia, were mentioned in a court case in 1742-1743 in which they were charged with stealing a hog and burning the woods:

Alex Machartion, John Bowling, Manissa, Caft Tom, Isaac Harry, Blind Tom, Foolish Jack, Charles Gibb, John Collins, and Little Jack [*VMHB* III:190].

The Cherokee lived in the mountainous regions of North Carolina and East Tennessee and had little contact with the colonists.

ABEL FAMILY

1. Elizabeth[1] Abel, born say 1710, was a white woman living in Chowan County in July 1737 when she was charged in court with keeping a "Lew'd and disorderly Tippleing house Contrary to the Law" and "Entertaing peoples Servants" [Haun, *Chowan County Court Minutes*, II:74, 76]. She was probably the mother of
   2. i. Bethiah, born say 1737.
   3. ii. Serenah, born say 1745.
   4. iii. Nanny, born say 1750.

2. Bethiah Abel, born say 1737, was living in Bertie County in March 1770 when her "Mulatto" orphan, Betty, was bound to William Bryan [Haun, *Bertie County court Minutes*, III:893, 896; IV:74]. Her children were
   5. i. Elizabeth[2], born about 1758.
   ii. ?Zedekiah, born about 1760, a fourteen-year-old orphan bound to Edward Skull to be a carpenter in 1774, no parent named.
   6. iii. ?Ginny, born say 1762.
   iv. Solomon, born say 1764, orphan of Bethiah, no age or race mentioned when he was bound to William Bryan to be a shoemaker on 28 March 1770.

3. Serenah[1] Abel, born say 1745, was living in Bertie County on 30 March 1767 when the court ordered her "Mulatto" children bound out. She complained to the May 1788 Bertie court about the indenture of her daughter Sall to John Bosman [Haun, *Bertie County court Minutes* III:765; IV:225, 274; VI:225, 721, 733]. Her children were
   i. Betty[3], born about 1762, eight-year-old orphan of Serenah bound to Keder Harrell on 25 March 1770.
   ii. James, born about 1763, four-year-old "Mulatto" bastard of Serenah, bound to Jacob Jernegan on 30 March 1767, about fifteen years old in May 1777 when he was bound to Thomas Pugh, Sr.
   iii. Hardy, born about 1765, two-year-old "Mulatto" bastard of Serenah, bound to William Bryan to be a shoemaker on 30 March 1767.
   iv. Jacob, born about 1772, "Mulatto" bastard of Serenah, six years old in November 1778 when he was ordered bound to James Gardner to be a shoemaker. He was sixteen in February 1789 when he and Huel Abel were bound to William Pugh to be shoemakers. Jacob was head of a Bertie County household of 3 "other free" in 1810 [NC:177].
   v. ?Huel, born about 1777, twelve years old in February 1789 when he and Jacob Abel were bound to William Pugh to be shoemakers.
   vi. Sall, born say 1780, bound to John Bosman in 1788.

4. Nanny Abel, born say 1750, was the mother of a three-year-old "Mulatto" child, Allen, who was bound apprentice in Bertie County in 1777 [Haun, *Bertie County court Minutes* VI:797]. She was the mother of
   i. Allen, born about 1774, three years old in Christmas 1777, bastard "Mulatto" of Nanny, ordered by the November 1777 court bound to Ezekiel Wimberly to be a cordwainer. He was bound to Lewis Wimberly to be a shoemaker on 7 November 1791.

5. Elizabeth[2] Abel, born about 1758, was the twelve-year-old "Mulatto" of Bethiah Abel bound to William Bryan in Bertie County on 28 March 1770 [Haun, *Bertie County court Minutes* III:896; IV:70, 243; V:454, 497]. She was the mother of
   i. Andrew, born about 1771, six-year-old "Mulatto" bastard of Betty ordered bound to William Bryan to be a shoemaker in August 1777.

    ii.   Jean, born about 1772, two-year-old son of Elizabeth ordered bound to William Bryan in May 1774.

    iii. Lemuel, born about September 1772, twenty-month-old son of Elizabeth ordered bound to William Bryan in May 1774.

    iv. Serenah[2], born about January 1774, four-month-old daughter of Elizabeth ordered bound to William Bryan in May 1774, eight years old on 13 May 1783 when she was bound to Ann Gliston.

    v.   Anthony, born about 1775, two-year-old "Mulatto" bastard of Betty bound to William Bryan to be a shoemaker in August 1777.

    vi. ?John, born say 1778, no age or parent named when he was bound to Joseph Horn to be a cooper on 10 August 1784.

6.   Ginny Abel, born say 1762, was ordered bound to William Bryan for six years in August 1777. The same court ordered the indenture of her child,

    i.   Edy, born about January 1776, a one and one-half-year-old "Mulatto" bastard of Ginney Abel bound to William Bryan by the August 1777 court.

A member of the family registered in Norfolk County, Virginia on 10 July 1812:
Margaret Abel, 4 feet 11 In. & a half, 22 years of age of a yellowish complexion... Born free [Register of Free Negros & Mulattos, no. 73].

ACRE FAMILY

1.   Jane Acre, born say 1738, was living in Truro Parish on 16 May 1759 when she was indicted by the Fairfax County court for having a "Molatto" child. She failed to appear for her trial, so the court fined her 50 shillings [Orders 1756-63, 342, 368]. She may have been related to Benjamin Acres, a "mulatto" boy listed in the 26 March 1718 Westmoreland County inventory of Joseph Bailey [DW 6:272]. Jane was apparently the mother of

    i.   Rodham, born say 1759, a bastard child bound ordered bound by the churchwardens of Truro Parish to James Moore on 19 June 1759 [Orders 1756-63, 342, 368].

ADAMS FAMILY

Members of the Adams family of Richmond County, Virginia, may have descended from the Adams family of St. Mary's County, Maryland, since Harriet Adams's husband Cornelius **Lawrence** came from St. Mary's County and there were five "other free" Adams families in the 1790 St. Mary's County census. Members of the Adams family in Virginia were

    i.   John, head of a Rockingham County household of 7 "other free" in 1810 [VA:14].

    ii.   John, head of a Richmond County household of 4 "other free" in 1810 [VA:411].

    iii. Humphrey, head of a Rockingham County household of 3 "other free" in 1810 [VA:15].

    iv. Milly, head of an Essex County household of 3 "other free" in 1810 [VA:208].

1   v.   Phillis, born about 1789.

    vi. Harriet **Lawrence**, born about 1799, registered in Essex County on 17 November 1828: *wife of Cornelius Lawrence formerly Harriet Adams, born free, dark Mulattoe, 29 years of age, 5 feet one and a half inches* [Register of Free Negroes 1810-43, p.54, no.130]. Her husband Cornelius obtained a certificate of freedom in St. Mary's County, Maryland, on 28 November 1816: *aged nineteen years...light complexion...born free* [Certificates of Freedom 1806-64, 37] and registered in Essex County on 21 June 1824: *born free by certificate of St. Mary's County, Maryland, 27 years of age* [Register of Free Negroes 1810-43, p.46, no. 115].

1. Phillis Adams, born about 1789, registered in Essex County on 18 March 1839: *born free by certificate of the clk. of Richmond County, black, about 50 years of age, 5 feet 3 inches.* She was the mother of
   i. Polly, born about 1816, registered in Essex County on 18 March 1839: *daughter of Phillis Adams, born free, dark Brown, about 23 years of age, 5 feet 2-2/8 inches.*
   ii. Robert, born about 1816, registered in Essex County on 28 July 1829: *son of Phillis Adams, born free, Black, about 13 years of age, 5 feet 2-2/8 inches* [Register of Free Negroes 1810-43, pp.34, 62 nos.88, 143, 144].

AFRICA FAMILY

1. Meshack Africa, born say 1735, and his wife Nell were taxable "negroes" in James Wilson's household in Edmunds Bridge District of Norfolk County from 1751 to 1759, called "Africa and Nell" [Wingo, *Norfolk County Tithables, 1751-1765*, 27, 38, 59, 99, 108, 153]. Wilson set them free by his Norfolk County will with the approval of the governor and Council of Virginia in 1761 [McIlwaine, *Executive Journals*, IV:188]. He was called "Affrica, a free Negro," on 18 August 1768 when the Norfolk County court ordered him to post bond of 50 pounds to keep the peace for six months because John Coats swore the peace against him [Orders 1768-71, 12]. Meshack and his wife Nell were taxable "free negroes" in Edmunds Bridge District from 1767 to 1780. He was taxable on 50 acres from 1767 to 1770. He was called "Free Africa" in 1772, "FN Africa" in 1773, "Meshack Africa" in 1774 and 1780 [Wingo, *Norfolk County Tithables 1766-1780*, 26, 51, 92, 128, 181, 191, 222, 247, 280]. He was taxable in St. Brides Parish, Norfolk County, from 1783 to 1796: taxable on his son Meshack in 1787, charged with 2 tithes in 1790 and from 1792 to 1795 [PPTL, 1782-91, frames 412, 447, 587, 601, 658, 697; 1791-1812, frames 3, 48, 63, 117, 153, 186]. Meshack was the father of
   i. Meshack[2], born say 1766, taxable on a free poll in Norfolk County in 1787 and 1789, his tax charged to his father Meshack Africa. He married Hannah **Fuller**, 4 April 1789 Princess Anne County bond, Beriah Butt surety, 19 April marriage. He may have been identical to Meshack **Fuller** who was taxable in Norfolk County in 1794 and was a "free Negro" taxable in St. Brides Parish from 1803 to 1811 [PPTL, 1791-1812, frames 103, 456, 548, 609, 674].
   ii. ?Kader, head of a Norfolk County household of 7 "other free" in 1810 [VA:802], a "free Negro" taxable in St. Bride's Parish from 1814 to 1817 [PPTL, 1813-24, frames 67, 71, 167, 201]. He purchased land in Norfolk County by deed proved in 1817 [DB 47:168].
   iii. ?Sally, head of Norfolk County household of 5 "other free" in 1810 [VA:802]. She was counted in the list of "free Negroes" in St. Brides Parish with 3 male tithables and 3 cattle in 1815 and was taxable on a free male in 1817 [PPTL, 1813-24, frames 71, 201].
   iv. Trimagin, taxable in St. Brides Parish, Norfolk County, from 1794 to 1799 [PPTL, 1791-1812, frames 117, 186, 313, 204, 313].
   v. ?Wright, born about 1775, taxable in St. Brides Parish, Norfolk County, from 1796 to 1800, counted in the lists of "free Negroes" from 1801 to 1817, taxable on 2 tithes and 3 horses in 1814 [PPTL, 1791-1812, frames 186, 204, 313, 400, 456, 548, 636, 716, 802; 1813-24, frames 167, 201]. He registered as a "free Negro" in Norfolk County on 17 December 1810: *5 feet 11 Inches, 35 years of age, light complexion, Born free* [Register of Free Negros & Mulattos, no. 41].

He purchased 60 acres of land in Norfolk County on 24 February 1810 for $250 and purchased three more tracts by deeds proved in 1816, 1817, and 1823 [DB 45:48; 46:63; 47:351; 50:422].

vi.   ?Wilson, listed as a "free Negro" in St. Brides Parish in 1816 and 1817 [PPTL, 1813-24, frames 167, 201].

AILSTOCK FAMILY

1.   Michael[1] Ailstock, born say 1725, was sued in Caroline County, Virginia court in a suit which was dismissed on 14 June 1746. He was also involved in several minor court cases in Caroline County in September 1751, June 1762, March 1763, and May 1773 [Orders 1740-6, 606; 1746-54, 275; 1759-63, 317, 393; 1772-6, 242]. He purchased 353 acres in Trinity Parish, Louisa County, on 8 May 1764 [DB C:16-18]. He was involved in a number of Louisa County law suits. On 9 May 1768 the court awarded John Collins, executor of James Collins, deceased, an attachment against his estate for 15 pounds which was executed on an old gun. James Overton sued him on 11 August 1766. Thomas Knighton sued him for 100 pounds currency on 8 August 1768 and another 5 pounds on 15 September 1772. And Knighton was awarded 8 pounds, 10 shillings in his suit against him for slander on 13 June 1769, but the court was of the opinion that the damages were excessive and a new jury awarded Knighton 5 shillings on 9 April 1770. William and Ann Knighton of Caroline County were his witnesses against Thomas Knighton. He sued John Clark's executors on 13 April 1772. On 11 May 1772 the court ordered his suit against Samuel Winston's executors referred to arbitration. David Cosby attended twenty-eight days as his witness against Winston's executors. On 11 May 1772 he was awarded 6 pounds, 8 shillings damages in his suit against William Clasby for trespass, assault and battery [Orders 1760-74, 14; 1766-74, 1, 6, 9, 26-7, 43, 45, 53, 76, 118; 1766-72, 1, 6, 9, 26, 82, 98, 134-5, 169, 195, 199, 297, 327, 363, 364, 408, 426, 484, 486, 487, 491]. On 8 March 1773 Micajah Davis accused him of stealing ten shillings worth of leather, but the court found him not guilty. David Smith was his witness in a suit against Colonel Johnson for which he was awarded 2 pounds, 9 shillings [Orders 1773, 12, 20, 28]. He and his wife Rebecca sold their 353 acres in Trinity Parish to Moses **Going** on 13 January 1777 [DB E:127-8]. He was living in Louisa County on 25 December 1777 when he sold two plots of 54 acres each in Louisa County, one on both sides of Gibson's Creek and Anderson's line and the other on both sides of Gibson's Creek [Unrecorded Deeds of Louisa County 1762-1803, 1-2]. On 2 June 1777 the Amherst County court ordered that he post bond of sixty pounds security for his appearance at the next court to answer Mary McCabe for a breach of the peace. He owned land in Amherst County by 5 January 1778 when he and James **Hartless** were among the freeholders ordered to work on a new road from Irish Creek Gap down Pedlar River to Campbell's Road [Orders 1773-82, 187, 211-2]. He sold property by deed proved in Louisa County court on 11 May 1778, 8 June 1778 and on 8 October 1781. The Louisa County court exempted him from paying county levies (due to old age) on 10 April 1780 [Orders 1774-82, 192, 197, 298, 335]. He was taxable on a horse and 5 cattle in Louisa County from 1782 to 1784 but free from personal tax [PPTL, 1782-1814]. His 6 September 1791 Louisa County will, proved 13 April 1795, named his wife Rebecca; children Joseph, Michael, Absalom, Mary, Elizabeth, Susanna, and granddaughter Rebecca [WB 3:597]. His widow Rebecca was included in a list of free "mulattoes" in Louisa County about 1802 [Abercrombie, *Free Blacks of Louisa County*, 21]. Michael was the father of

i.   the parent of Rebecca. Rebecca was listed as a free Negro in Louisa County about 1802 with her two children and her grandmother: *Rebecca Ailstock and her 2 children to wit: Robert and Polley and Rebecca the Elder* [Abercrombie, *Free Blacks of Louisa County*, 21].

ii. Michael[2], born say 1750, called Michael Ailstock, Junr., on 9 March 1773 when his suit against William Johnson, Gent., was dismissed by the Louisa County court. On 11 May 1773 the court awarded him 2 pounds, 4 shillings in the same suit, but granted Johnson a leave to make discounts at the next court. On 8 November 1773 the court attached his goods in the hands of Ann Pulliam worth 1 pound, 17 shillings for a debt he owed James Twopence [Orders 1766-74, 92, 97, 115, 177]. He was taxable in Amherst County in 1782 [PPTL 1782-1803, frame 9], taxable in Louisa County from 1783 to 1794 [PPTL, 1782-1814] and was taxable in Albemarle County from 1795 to 1807, probably related to Patience Alstock who was counted in a "list of Free Negroes & Mulattoes" in Albemarle County in 1813 [PPTL, 1782-1799, frames 445, 477, 584; 1800-1813, frames 22, 66, 111, 135, 154, 200, 290, 337, 553]. On 6 January 1800 he was ordered to remain in the Albemarle County jail for a breach of the peace until he posted bond of $100 and his securities James **Going** and Shadrack **Battles** posted bond of $50 each for his good behavior. He sold property by indenture proved in court on 6 July 1801 [Orders 1798-1800, 380, 393].

2   iii. Joseph, born say 1752.
3   iv. Absalom[1], born about 1762.
     v. Mary.
    vi. ?William[1], born say 1764, taxable in Henrico County in 1785 [PPTL 1782-1814, frame 78].
   vii. Elizabeth, married Thomas **Mason** in Louisa County in April 1791.
4 viii. Susanna, born say 1768.

2. Joseph Ailstock, born say 1752, was awarded 2 pounds, 9 shillings in his Louisa County suit against William Johnson, Gent., on 13 April 1773 [Orders 1766-74]. He was taxable in Louisa County in 1783, 1786, 1793, 1794, 1795 (listed with 3 tithables), and 1796 [PPTL, 1782-1814]. He was taxable on a horse in Fredericksville Parish, Albemarle County, in 1787 [PPTL, 1782-1799, frame 109]. He was taxable in Lexington Parish, Amherst County, in 1789 [PPTL 1782-1803, 165] and was ordered to work on the road from the Blue Ridge at Irish Creek Gap to the three forks of the Pedlar River in Amherst County on 4 November 1789 [Orders 1787-90, 590]. He was taxable in Fredericksville Parish, Albemarle County, from 1798 to 1800 [PPTL, 1782-1799, frames 549, 584; 1800-1813, frame 22]. Duncan **Holmes** sued him in Albemarle County court for trespass, assault and battery on 7 May 1799, and he sued Jacob Burress for the same on 7 August 1799. The suit was dismissed on agreement of the parties on 6 August 1800 [Orders 1798-1800, 215, 267; 1800-1, 116]. He was a "fn" taxable in the upper district of Henrico County from 1803 to 1814: taxable on 12 acres which was transferred to him by Drury Wood in 1803; listed with his unnamed wife as "Blacks Free" in 1813 [PPTL 1782-1814, frames 488, 534, 594, 638, 724, 758, 823; Land Tax List 1799-1816]. On 13 January 1805 he sold 12 acres on the side of the stage road in Henrico County to Waddy Turner of Richmond for 40 pounds [DB 7:186]. He was head of a Henrico County household of 4 "other free" in 1810 [VA:987]. He was the father of

    i. ?Absalom[2], born about 1780, a "fn" taxable in the upper district of Henrico County in the same list as Joseph Hailstock from 1803 to 1809 [PPTL 1782-1814, frames 487, 534, 594; Land Tax List 1799-1816]. He registered in Rockingham County, Virginia, on 5 September 1831: *51 years of Age (A Mulatto Man) and Six Feet high...Free Born as appears by the affidavit of Mary Davis.* (His wife?) Sally Ailstock registered the same day: *a Mulatto Woman 50 Years of Age...Free Born as appears by the affidavit of Mary Davis* [Boyd-Rush, *Register of Free Blacks, Rockingham County*, 64].

    ii. ?John, born say 1782, taxable on a horse in Fredericksville Parish, Albemarle County, in 1800 and 1801 [PPTL, 1800-1813, frames 22, 66], a "fn" taxable in the upper district of Henrico County in 1803, 1804, 1805, 1807, 1812, and 1813 [PPTL 1782-1814, frames 488, 534, 724, 758; Land Tax List 1799-1816].

    iii. ?Robert, born say 1786, a "free Negro" taxable in the upper district of Henrico County from 1803 to 1814 [PPTL 1782-1814, frames 434, 488, 594, 638, 723, 758, 823; Land Tax List 1799-1816].

    iv. Sally, born say 1788, "daughter of Joseph Ailstock," married Reuben **Jones**, 24 October 1807 Henrico County bond, Absalom Ailstock surety.

3. Absalom[1] Ailstock, born about 1762 in Louisa County, was seventy years old when he applied for a pension for his services in the Revolution while residing in Rockbridge County on 1 October 1832. He was called a ninety-four-year-old "colored freeman" on 29 September 1849 when he applied for increased payments of his pension. He remained in Louisa County about twelve or thirteen years after the Revolution when he moved to Rockbridge County [Dorman, *Virginia Revolutionary Pension Applications*, 1:34-35]. He was taxable in Louisa County from 1785 to 1799 and from 1809 to 1814, in a list of "free Negroes & Mulattoes" in 1813 [PPTL, 1782-1814]. He was a "Mulatto" carpenter with his children on Robert Gillespy's land in "A List of Free Negroes & Mulattoes in the District of John Holloway, Commissioner, in Botetourt County for the Year 1802" and again in 1803 [Orders 1800-04, Loose Papers, nos. 30-36, 51-58]. His wife was probably white or considered white since she was not listed with him, and his son James was apparently born between the 1802 and 1803 census. He was head of a Botetourt County household of 9 "other free" in 1810 [VA:604] and was also counted in Bath County in 1810, head of a household of 8 "other free" and a white woman [VA:446]. His children were

    i. ?Jenny, born say 1780, married Jesse **Going**, 2 December 1799 Albemarle County bond.

    ii. Rebecca, born say 1782, a "Labourer & Spinster" in 1802, perhaps the Becky Ailstock who James **Going** was supposed to marry by 2 December 1799 Albemarle County bond.

    iii. Caty, born say 1783, a "Labourer & Spinster" in 1802.

    iv. Polly, born say 1785, counted in 1803 but not in 1802.

    v. Elizabeth[2]/ Betsy, born say 1787, a "labourer & Spinster" in 1802.

    vi. William, born say 1792, a "Small" boy in 1802.

    vii. Absalom[3], born say 1794, a "Small" boy in 1802.

    viii. Thomas, born say 1798, a "Small" boy in 1802.

    ix. James, born 1802-03.

4. Susanna Ailstock, born say 1768, was counted in a List of "free Negroes and Mulattoes" with her children Salley, Ursula, Betsey, Lewis, William and Kitty near Trinity Church in Louisa County in the district of Peter Crawford (no date but probably about 1801-3) [Abercrombie, *Free Blacks of Louisa County*, 20]. She and (her children) Sarah, Ursley, Kitty and Elizabeth L. Ailstock were included in a list of "free Negroes & Mulattoes" above the age of sixteen in 1813 [PPTL, 1782-1814]. She was the mother of

    i. Sally, born say 1785.

    ii. Ursula, born say 1787.

    iii. Betsey, born say 1789.

    iv. Lewis[2], born say 1791

    v. William, born say 1793, taxable on a horse in Louisa County in 1814.

    vi. Kitty, born say 1795.

Other members of the family in Virginia were

    i.   Reuben, born say 1752, living in Caroline County on 12 August 1756 when the court ordered the churchwardens of St. Mary's Parish to bind him to Thomas Roy, Gentleman [Orders 1755-8, 191]. He was a "Free Negro & Mulatto" above the age of sixteen in Essex County in the same list with Francis and John Halestock in 1814, listed with Frank and Kitt Halestock in 1816 and 1819 [PPTL, 1782-1819, frames 541, 629, 630, 776].

    ii.   Lewis[1], born say 1754, living in Caroline County on 12 August 1756 when the court ordered the churchwardens of St. Mary's Parish to bind him to Thomas Roy, Gentleman [Orders 1755-8, 191].

5   iii.   Kezor, born say 1760.

    iv.   Charles, born say 1770, indicted in King George County on 4 August 1796 for retailing liquor without a license [Orders 1790-9, 473]. He was taxable in King George County from 1787 to 1797 [PPTL, 1782-1830, frames 40, 87, 117, 153] and head of a King George County household of 2 "other free" in 1810 [VA:203].

    v.   Elce, an illegitimate child bound by the Amherst County court to William Leigh on 15 October 1792 [Orders 1790-4, 455].

    vi.   Michael[3], born about 1792, registered as a free Negro in Augusta County on 28 June 1819: *a man of colour, aged about twenty seven years, five feet eight inches and a quarter high, black complexion, long black whiskers...declared to be a free man, as appears from a certificate of the Clerk of Albemarle County* [Register of Free Negroes, no.25].

    vii. Patsey, born about 1801, registered as a free Negro in Augusta County on 27 March 1827: *a woman of colour aged 26 years of dark complexion 4 feet 11 inches high...entitled to her freedom as appears from the Clerk of Albemarle County* [Register of Free Negroes, no.89].

5.   Kezor Ailstock/ Hailstock, born say 1760, was taxable on 2 horses in Mecklenburg County, Virginia, in 1784 and taxable in the lower district of the county from 1787 to 1795, called Dekezer Ailstocks in 1793 [PPTL, 1782-1805, frames 69, 195, 242, 420, 475, 495, 575]. He may have been the husband of Martha Hailstock who was counted in a list of "free Negroes & Mulattoes in the lower District of Lunenburg County" in 1802 and 1803 with her children Milly, Betsy and Sally, living near Harper's Bridge [Lunenburg County Free Negro and Slave Records, 1802-3, LVA]. She was counted as a free "Mulatto" in Mecklenburg County in 1813 [PPTL, 1806-28, frame 341]. She was the mother of

    i.   ?Mary Hailestock, born say 1787, married William **Thompson**, 19 February 1808 Mecklenburg County bond, Abel **Stewart** security.

    ii.   Milly, born say 1793.

    iii.   Sally, born say 1795.

    iv.   Betsy, born say 1797, called Betsy Haystack when she was counted as a free "Mulatto" over the age of 16 years in Mecklenburg County in 1813 [PPTL, 1806-28, frame 345].

    v.   ?Nancy, born say 1800, bound by the Mecklenburg County court to John Bradley on 12 April 1802 (no parent named) [Orders 1801-3, 193].

    vi.   ?William, born say 1802, bound by the Mecklenburg County court to John Bradley on 12 April 1802 (no parent named) [Orders 1801-3, 201], registered in Mecklenburg County, Virginia, on 17 December 1827: *a man of yellow complexion about twenty three years of age, Six feet and one half inch high...born of a free woman in this County* [Free Person of Color, no. 50, p.39].

ALFORD FAMILY

1.   Rachel Alford, born say 1745, was a "free Christian white woman" living in Hamilton Parish, Fauquier County, Virginia, on 28 August 1769 when the court ordered the churchwardens to bind her "last child" to Armistead Churchill and to bind her "Mulatto" son George to George Crump [Minutes 1768-73, 130, 133]. She was the mother of
   i.   George, born say 1766.
   ii.   ?James, ordered bound by the churchwardens of Hamilton Parish on 23 March 1772.
   iii. ?Jesse, ordered bound by the churchwardens of Hamilton Parish on 23 March 1772 [Minutes 1768-73, 371].
   iv.   ?Sally, "Free Negroe" head of a Fauquier County household of 7 "other free" in 1810 [VA:358].

ALLEN FAMILY

The Allen family of Virginia may have originated in Northampton or York County, Virginia, because several members were living in those counties in the early eighteenth century. They were
1   i.   Jane, born say 1690.
     ii.   John[1], born say 1703, a "negro" taxable in Edward Miflin's Northampton County, Virginia household in Ralph Pigot's list for 1721 [L.P. 1721-31].
     iii. Elizabeth, born say 1706, a "Mulatto" tithable in William Stakes' Northampton County, Virginia household from 1724 to 1731 [L.P. 1721-31].
     iv.   Sarah, born say 1708, a tithable in Nathaniel Andress's Northampton County, Virginia household in 1725 [L.P. 1721-31]. Sarah was a "Mullattoe" who was charged in Accomack County court on 1 December 1730 with having a bastard child [Orders 1724-31, 217].

1.   Jane Allen, born say 1690, was presented by the York County court on 16 November 1761 for failing to list herself as a tithable but discharged from paying levies at the next court on 21 December 1761 when she was described as a "poor old woman" [Judgments & Orders 1759-63, 298, 313]. She may have been the mother of
2   i.   Joseph[1], born say 1710.
     ii.   Samuel[1], born about 1713, a "Mulatto" bound until the age of twenty-one, eleven years old on 2 September 1724 when he was listed in the inventory of the York County estate of Joseph Walker, Esq. [DOW 16, pt. 2, 329].
3   iii. Elizabeth, born say 1724.
4   iv.   Sarah, born say 1730.

2.   Joseph[1] Allen, born say 1710, was presented by the York County court on 15 November 1735 for not listing his "Molatto" wife as a tithable [OW 18:237]. He purchased 100 acres in Isle of Wight County on the south side of the Nottoway River and east side of Whitewood Swamp on 21 January 1745/6 with William Bynum as witness [DB 7:292]. He sued Roger Brooks for trespass, assault and battery in Isle of Wight County court on 13 November 1747, but he died before the case came to trial. On 12 May 1748 Mary Allen petitioned the court for administration of his estate [Orders 1746-52, 62, 96, 97]. Purchasers at the 5 December 1751 sale of his estate included James Allen, Thomas **Tabour** (**Taborn**), and Judy **Tabour**, late Allen. The account of the estate, recorded on 15 May 1752, included a slave in the possession of William Bynum who was guardian of the heirs and security for administration of the estate. His daughter Mary **Booth**, "late Allen," signed (by mark) the

estate appraisal [WB 5:391-2; 6:5]. Mary, her husband Lewis **Booth**, Judith **Taborn**, and Joseph Allen (by his guardian Lewis **Booth**) brought a chancery suit against William Bynum and William Allen on 11 July 1754, claiming that William had sold slaves belonging to the estate valued at 80 pounds [Orders 1749-54, 511; LVA Chancery file 1757-003]. Joseph's children were

    i.   Mary, born say 1728, wife of Lewis **Booth**.

    ii.   Judy[1], born say 1730, married William **Taborn** in Northampton County, North Carolina, according to the Revolutionary War pension application of their son William [M804-2335, frame 0798]. See further the **Taborn** history.

    iii. ?James, a buyer at the 5 December 1751 sale of the estate of Joseph Allen.

5   iv.   Sarah[2], born say 1733.

6   v.   William[1], born say 1735.

    vi.   Joseph[2], born say 1736, an infant orphan of Joseph Allen ordered bound out as an apprentice by the court in Southampton County on 14 December 1749. On 14 July 1757 he brought a chancery suit in Southampton County against William Bynum, administrator of his father's estate. The suit was dismissed on 10 July 1761 due to Bynum's death [Orders 1749-54, 34; 1754-9, 363; 1759-63, 122]. On 6 August 1762 he was sued in Isle of Wight County by Benjamin Baker for a debt of 12 pounds which was charged to (his brother) William Allen who was his security [Orders 1759-63, 347, 505-6]. He left a 20 October 1764 Isle of Wight County will, proved 7 August 1766, leaving all his estate to his sister Sarah Allen who he named executor [WB 6:431]. When the will was proved, the court ordered the sheriff to summon Jesse Allen, brother and heir at law of Joseph Allen, to contest the will [Orders 1764-8, 267]. Perhaps the court meant William Allen.

3.   Sarah[1] Allen, born say 1730, was presented by the York County court on 16 November 1761 for failing to list herself as a tithable. The case was dismissed on 21 December 1761 when she paid her tax [Judgments & Orders 1759-63, 298, 312]. She may have been the mother of

    i.   Mary, born say 1748, taxable in Elizabeth River Parish, Norfolk County, in 1768 [Wingo, *Norfolk County Tithables, 1766-80*, 80].

7   ii.   Judy[2], born say 1750.

8   iii. John[3], born say 1755.

4.   Elizabeth Allen, born say 1724, was living in York County on 19 August 1765 when the court ordered the churchwardens of Yorkhampton Parish to bind out her children "unless she shew good cause to the contrary" [Orders 1763-5, 450]. She was taxable in James City County on a free male tithable in 1806 and 1807 and head of a household of 2 female "Free Persons of Colour above 16 years" in 1813 [PPTL, 1800-15]. She may have been the mother of

9   i.   John[2], born about 1744.

10   ii.   Mary, born say 1750.

11   iii. Martha/ Patty, born say 1760.

5.   Sarah[2] Allen, born say 1733, was living in Southampton County, Virginia, on 9 August 1750 when her son Arthur (no age or race mentioned) was bound apprentice [Orders 1749-54, 80]. She was the executor and only heir of her brother Joseph Allen's 20 October 1764 Southampton County will, proved 7 August 1766 [WB 6:431]. She was the mother of

12   i.   Arthur[1], born say 1749.

6.   William[1] Allen, born say 1735, was an infant orphan of Joseph Allen in September 1751 when the Southampton County court allowed his guardian

William Bynum additional time to make a return of his estate to court. The sheriff reported that he had removed himself from the county or was avoiding a summons on 13 October 1757 when Henry Crafford obtained an attachment against his estate for 3 pounds, 17 shillings [Orders 1749-54, 167; 1754-9, 391]. He was living in Northampton County on 13 January 1759 when he sold by Southampton County deed 100 acres on the north side of the Meherrin River and east side of Whitewood Swamp (which was the land his father Joseph Allen purchased 21 January 1745/6) [DB 2:16-17]. He sued William Bynum, the executor of his father's estate, in a chancery case in Southampton County on 14 August 1760, saying he was of age and wanted his part of his father's estate. The court ordered the defendant to make an account of the estate and ordered a commission to make a final decree [Orders 1759-63, 59; LVA, chancery case 1761-008]. He was security for a debt (his brother) Joseph Allen owed Benjamin Baker of Isle of Wight County on 6 August 1762 [Orders 1759-63, 347, 505-6]. He was one of the "Black" members of the undated colonial muster roll of Captain James Fason's Northampton County, North Carolina Company [Troop Returns, 1-3].[21] He was taxable in Granville County in the list of Philip Pryor for 1767 with (his wife?) Ann Allen, Joseph Allen, and Mary Allen "Mollatoes" [Tax List 1767-1809]. He was called William Allen "Mulatto" in Granville County on 5 March 1770 when he bound his daughter Nancy as an apprentice to James Knott [Owen, *Granville County Notes*, vol.II]. His children were

    i.   Joseph[3], born about 1755, a "Mullatto" taxable in William Allen's household in 1767, a twenty-two-year-old "mullatto" planter listed in the 1778 Granville County Militia Returns [Mil. TR 4-40 by *The North Carolinian* VI:726].

    ii.   Mary, a "Mullatto" taxable in William Allen's household in 1767.

   iii.   Nancy, born 5 July 1757, twelve years old on 5 July 1769, according to her indenture in Granville County court on 5 March 1770.

7.   Judy[2] Allen, born say 1750, was a "mulatto" living in Norfolk County on 16 July 1772 when the court ordered the churchwardens of Elizabeth River Parish to bind her daughter Jenny to Jacob Williams. She was called a "free negro" on 18 March 1774 when the court ordered her daughters Jenny and Betty bound to John Ransberg [Orders 1771-3, 92; 1773-5, 32]. She was the mother of

    i.   Jenny, born say 1770.

    ii.   Elizabeth, born say 1772.

8.   John[3] Allen, born say 1755, was a "Mulatto" shoemaker apprenticed for two years to John Muirhead of Norfolk County when he ran away on 10 June 1769 according to the 23 November 1769 issue of the *Virginia Gazette* [Headley, *18th Century Newspapers*, 4]. He was called "a free man of mixed blood" in 1787 when the North Carolina General Assembly emancipated his "mulatto" wife Betty and their child Mary, who he had purchased [Clark, *State Records*, XXIV:930]. He died before December 1799 when (his brother?) Arthur Allen recorded the account of sales of his Northampton County, North Carolina estate [Gammon, *Records of Estates, Northampton County*, I:110]. His wife was probably the Betsy Allen who was head of a Northampton County household of 5 "other free" in 1810 [NC:710]. His children were

    i.   Mary, born say 1780.

    ii.   ?Arthur[2], married Patience **Hawley**, 14 January 1813 Northampton County bond, no bondsman named.

---

[21]James Fason lived in the Corduroy Swamp area of Northampton County [DB 4:65-6].

9. John[2] Allen, born about 1744 in Williamsburg, registered in Petersburg on 16 July 1810: *a brown Mulatto man, five feet eight 1/4 inches high, about sixty six years old, born free in Wmsburg.* His wife Polly **Jasper** registered the same day: *a light brown Mulatto woman, five feet one half inches high, fifty years old, born free in Chesterfield County, wife to John Allen* [Register of Free Negroes 1794-1819, no. 635-6]. They were the parents of

    i. ?Sally, born about 1777, registered in Petersburg on 11 July 1810: *a light brown Mulatto woman, five feet two inches high, thirty three years old, born free & raised in the Town of Petersburg* [Register of Free Negroes 1794-1819, no. 633].

    ii. Eliza, born about 1777, registered in Petersburg on 25 August 1795: *(daughter of John Allen a free Mulatto) a dark brown Mulatto girl, four feet eleven inches high, eighteen years old, & raised in the Town of Petersburg* [Register of Free Negroes 1794-1819, no. 103].

    iii. Jane, born about 1778, registered in Petersburg on 31 December 1794: *a light brown, Mulatto woman, five feet three inches high, sixteen years old, daughter of John Allen, a free Mulatto, born free & raised in the neighborhood of Petersburg & by the request of her father registered* [Register of Free Negroes 1794-1819, no. 97]. She was head of a Petersburg household of 2 "other free" and a slave in 1810 [VA:118b].

    iv. ?Dicy, head of a Petersburg household of 1 "other free" and a slave in 1810 [VA:118b].

    v. ?Jerry, born about 1785, registered in Petersburg on 13 August 1806: *a light brown Free Negro man, five feet six inches high, twenty one years old, born free & raised in the Town of Petersburg* [Register of Free Negroes 1794-1819, no. 392].

10. Mary Allen, born say 1750, was taxable on a horse and 4 cattle in James City County in 1782 [PPTL, 1782-99]. She may have been the mother of

    i. Joseph[4], born say 1771, taxable in James City County from 1792 to 1814: taxable on a horse in 1792 and 1793, taxable on 2 free male tithes from 1801 to 1804, called a "mulatto" in 1810 and 1813 [PPTL, 1782-99; 1800-15].

    ii. Samuel[2], Sr., born about 1773, registered in York County on 19 September 1831: *5 feet 3 1/2 inches high, tawny complexion, about 58 years of age, large eyebrows, high cheek bones, bony face...Born free* [Free Negroes Register 1831-50, no. 289].

    iii. James, born say 1784, a "Mulatto" taxable in James City County from 1805 to 1814 [PPTL, 1800-15].

11. Martha Allen, born say 1760, was head of a York County household of 6 "other free" in 1810 [VA:887]. She was taxable in York County on a free tithe and a horse from 1810 to 1812, head of a household of 2 "free Negro or mulattos over 16" in 1813 and taxable on a head of cattle in 1815 [PPTL, 1782-1841, frames 350, 373, 384, 419]. She was probably the mother of

    i. Thomas, born about 1784, registered as a free Negro in York County on 18 October 1813: *black fellow abt 29 yrs. of age, 5 feet 4-1/2 Inches high, long visage...Born free in the parish of Yorkhampton* [Register of Free Negroes 1798-1831, no.72].

    ii. William[3], born about 1790, taxable in York County on his own tithe and a horse in 1814 [PPTL, 1788-1841, frames 402, 419]. He registered as a free Negro in York County on 21 February 1814: *of dark complexion abt. 23 years of age, 5 feet four Inches high...large eyebrows & short hair. Born of a free woman* [Register of Free Negroes 1798-1831, no. 76].

12. Arthur[1] Allen, born say 1749, was ordered bound apprentice in Southampton County on 9 August 1750. He was living in Southampton County when he,

John **Byrd**, Jr., Hardy Beal, Arthur **Allen**, Arthur **Byrd** and James **Byrd** were sued by Jesse Watkins in a case that was dismissed at their costs on 11 February 1773 [Orders 1768-72, 83; 1772-7, 107]. Arthur was head of a household of 2 "Black" persons 12-50 years old and 4 "Black" persons less than 12 or over 50 years old in Captain Dupree's District of Northampton County in 1786 for the North Carolina state census. He was head of a Northampton County household of 9 "other free" in 1790 [NC:74] and 10 in 1810 [NC:710]. He purchased 171 acres in Northampton County from Giles and Sarah Cook of Southampton County for 45 pounds on 24 November 1775 and purchased the same land from them eighteen years later on 26 March 1793 for the same price. Arthur and his wife Amy sold it soon afterwards to Nathaniel Edwards for 77 pounds by an undated deed proved June the same year [DB 6:100; 10:42, 48]. He died before 5 June 1815 when his estate was administered by William **Hawley**. His wife at that time, Esther, received one year's provisions on 8 June 1815 [Minutes 1813-21]. His children were

- i. ?William[2], born say 1780, married Elizabeth **Booth**, 12 December 1804 Nash County bond, William Pilgrim bondsman. William Allen was head of a Franklin County household of 7 "other free" in 1810 [NC:825].
- ii. ?Amy, head of a Northampton County household of 6 "free colored" in 1820 [NC:212]. She had a bastardy suit against Anthony **Wells** on 7 June 1820 and against John **Chavers** (**Chavis**) on 6 June 1822 in the Northampton County court [Minutes 1817-21, 281; 1821-25, 110].
- iii. Green, son of Arthur Allen and Esther **Williams**, born in Northampton County on 7 February 1807 and died on 7 August 1879 in Cass County, Michigan [Cass County Death Certificate], married Angelina **Wade**, daughter of John **Wade**, 14 October 1829 Northampton County bond, Anthony Deberry bondsman. Green Allen was head of a Northampton County household of 5 "free colored" in 1830.

Three mixed-race Allen children were bound apprentices in Cumberland County, North Carolina, by order of the court in February 1764. They were

- i. Rachel, born about 1754, a "Mullattoe Girl ten years old" in February 1764.
- ii. Benjamin, born about 1756, an "orphan Mullattoe Boy".
- iii. Juda[3], born about 1760, an "Orphan Mullattoe Girl" [Minutes 1759-65, 102, 108].

Other members of the Allen family were

- i. Richard, (a white man) presented by the Westmoreland County, Virginia court on 29 March 1733 for living in adultery with Ann, a "Mulato woman." The presentment was dismissed because they had married in Maryland [Orders 1731-9, 75a]. She may have been the Ann Allen of Cople Parish, Westmoreland County, who was presented by the grand jury on 28 November 1738 for having a "Mulatto" child [Orders 1731-9, 296, 302].
- ii. William, a "Mulatto" who acknowledged an indenture to Christian Allen in Henrico County court in February 1767 [Orders 1763-7, 676].
- iii. William, a "milato" taxable in the household of James Hemphil in Rowan County, North Carolina, in 1768. "Jude a millata" was also taxable in Hemphil's household [*NCGSJ* VIII:40].
- iv. Simon, head of a Frederick County household of 8 "other free" in 1810 [VA:595].
- v. John, "free negro" head of a Fairfax County household of 10 "other free" in 1810 [VA:232].
- vi. Saunders, head of a Goochland County household of 4 "other free" in 1810 [VA:682].

vii. Exum, born about 1781, registered in Southampton County on 21 February 1804: *age 23, bright mulatto, 5 feet 8 inches high, free Born* [Register of Free Negroes 1794-1832, no. 302].

ALMAN/ ALMOND FAMILY

Members of the Alman/ Almond family were

i. Sally, taxable on 2 cattle in Gloucester County, Virginia, in 1788 and 1789 [PPTL, 1782-99].

ii. Jenny[1], head of a Gloucester County, Virginia household of 10 "other free" in 1810 [VA:399].

iii. Edward, born say 1769, taxable in Gloucester County on a free tithe from 1790 to 1797 [PPTL, 1782-99; 1800-20], a "mul°" taxable from 1809 to 1820 [PPTL, 1800-20].

iv. James, born say 1769, taxable in Gloucester County in 1790 and 1791 [PPTL, 1782-99], a mul° taxable in 1813 and 1814 [PPTL, 1800-20]. He was a "FN" taxable in New Kent County from 1805 to 1809 [PPTL 1791-1828, frames 404, 417, 428, 440].

v. Zachariah, born say 1775, taxable in Gloucester County in 1796 and 1797 [PPTL, 1782-99].

vi. Jenny[2], "the younger," head of a Gloucester County household of 10 "other free" in 1810 [VA:399].

vii. Mildred, head of a Gloucester County household of 8 "other free" in 1810 [VA:399], taxable on a slave from 1817 to 1820 [PPTL, 1800-20].

viii. Alice, head of a Gloucester County household of 6 "other free" in 1810 [VA:399].

ix. Lewis, born say 1783, a "mulatto" taxable living in Guinea Quarter of Gloucester County in 1804 and 1805 [PPTL, 1800-20].

x. Easter, head of a Norfolk Borough, Virginia household of 3 "other free" in 1810 [VA:886], listed as a "mul°" in Gloucester County in 1813 [PPTL, 1800-20].

xi. Kitt Allmand, a "free Negro" taxable in Nansemond County on 2 cattle, 16 horses and 3 slaves in 1815 [Yantis, *Supplement to the 1810 Census of Virginia*, S-14]. He was head of a Nansemond County household of 8 "free colored" in 1820 [VA:80a].

xii. Grace Almonds, head of a Washington, D.C. household of 4 "other free" in 1800.

Isle of Wight County

1. Martha Allmond, born say 1760, was presented by the Isle of Wight County court on 4 May 1780 of having an illegitimate "mulato" child [Orders 1780-83, 3]. She was the mother of

i. Randall, born say 1780, son of Patty Allmond, ordered bound apprentice to John Anthony by the Isle of Wight County court on 4 January 1796 [Orders 1795-7, 269]. He was a "F.N." taxable on a horse in Isle of Wight County in 1806 [PPTL 1782-1810, frames 732].

ALVIS FAMILY

1. Katherine Alvis, born say 1720, was the mother of a nine-year-old "free Negro" boy named William Alvis who was bound apprentice to Robert Crawley of York County on 21 May 1750 [Deeds 1741-54, 350]. She was the mother of

2 i. William[1], born about 1741.

3 ii. ?Israel[1], born say 1743.

iii.   ?Patience, born say 1745, paid as a witness for John **Poe** in his York County suit against Anthony and Jasper **Peters** on 18 March 1765 [Judgments & Orders 1763-5, 358].

4   iv.   ?Emmanuel[1], born say 1747.

2.   William[1] Alvis, born about 1741, was bound apprentice to Robert Crawley of York County on 21 May 1750. He ran away on 28 February 1751, and Crawley placed an ad in the 14 November 1751 issue of the *Virginia Gazette*, describing him as a twelve-year-old "Negroe" who was "said to live at Brunswick" [Windley, *Runaway Slave Advertisements*, 1:24]. He registered in Petersburg on 14 August 1800: *a dark brown free Mulatto man, five feet six and a half inches high, sixty years old, born free & raised in the County of York* [Register of Free Negroes 1794-1819, no. 155]. He was the father of
   i.   ?Ann, born say 1772, the mother of William Alvis who registered in Petersburg on 24 February 1812: *a brown Mulatto man or lad, five feet five and a half inches high, seventeen years old, born free and raised in the County of Chesterfield, son of Ann Alvis a free woman* [Register of Free Negroes 1794-1819, no. 692].
   ii.   Nancy, born about 1774, registered in Petersburg on 14 August 1800: *a dark brown Mulatto woman, five feet six and a half inches high, spare made with short bushy hair, twenty six years old, daughter of Wm Alvis, born free & raised in the County of Chesterfield* [Register of Free Negroes 1794-1819, no. 156].
   iii.   Elizabeth[2], born about 1778, registered in Petersburg on 14 August 1800: *a dark brown Mulatto woman, five feet four and a half inches high, twenty two years old, short bushy hair, daughter of Wm Alvis* [Register of Free Negroes 1794-1819, no. 157].

3.   Israel[1] Alvis, born say 1743, had a child named William **Always** by Martha **Armfield** in Bruton Parish on 26 April 1765. He (called Israel **Allways**) and his wife Martha, "free Mulattas," were married by 13 March 1767 when their daughter Elizabeth **Allways** was born [Bruton Parish Register, 29, 31]. He was presented by the York County court on 19 November 1770 for selling rum without a license and was one of forty people presented by the York County court on 15 November 1773 for absenting himself from his parish church [Judgments & Orders 1770-2, 105; 1772-4, 438]. On 15 November 1779 he was presented for failing to list his tithables [Orders 1774-84, 240]. He was taxable in York County on 8 cattle in 1782, 9 cattle and 3 horses in 1784 and taxable on a slave in 1796 and 1797 [PPTL, 1782-1841, frames 69, 91, 106, 218, 227, 235]. He was the father of
   i.   William[2], born 26 April 1765, a 16-21 year old tithable in the household of Israel Alvis in 1785 and taxable in his own household until 1802 [PPTL 1782-1841, frames 106, 138, 190, 253, 263, 274].
   ii.   Elizabeth[1], born 13 March 1767 in Bruton Parish, married William **Davenport**, 7 July 1796 York County bond.
   iii.   Emmanuel[2], born say 1774, taxable in York County from 1795 to 1797 (called Emmanuel, Jr.) [PPTL, 1782-1841, frames 209, 218, 227] and a "free Negro" taxable in Richmond City in 1814 [Waldrep, *1813 Tax List*].

4.   Emmanuel[1] Alvis, born say 1747, was a soldier serving in the Revolution on 15 June 1778 and 21 June 1779 when the York County court allowed his wife Mildred Alvis pay for her subsistence [Orders 1774-84, 163, 219]. He was taxable in York County on 4 cattle in 1785, taxable on 2 tithes in 1797, 1798, 1802, 1803, 1805, and a tithe in 1806 and 1807. Perhaps Mildred was the Milly Alvis who was head of a household of 1 "free Negro & mulattoes over 16" in 1813 [PPTL, 1782-1841, frames 106, 180, 199, 209, 227, 235, 274, 284, 304, 314, 325, 384]. He may have been the father of

i. Israel[2], born say 1771, called Israel Alvis, Jr., when he was taxable in York County in 1792. He was head of a household of 2 "free Negroes & mulattoes over 16," one of whom was tithable in 1813 [PPTL 1782-1841, 180, 199, 384, 402] and head of a York County household of 2 "other free" in 1810 [VA:870].

ii. Nancy, born about 1779, obtained a certificate of freedom in Chesterfield County on 8 September 1806 (and 13 September 1819): *dark mulatto complexion, twenty seven years old, spare made, short bushy hair, born free* [Register of Free Negroes 1804-53, no. 35, 346].

iii. John, born about 1782, registered in York County on 15 October 1804: *a dark Mulatto man about five feet seven and a quarter Inches high, 22 years of age, he has a thick nose...short woolly hair...born of free parents in the Parish of Bruton & County of York* [Register of Free Negroes 1798-1831, no. 27]. He was head of a York County household of 6 "other free" in 1810 [VA:870] and head of a household of 4 "free Negroes & mulattoes over 16," two of whom were tithable in 1813 [PPTL, 1782-1841, frames 384, 402].

iv. Samuel, born about 1791, registered in York County on 16 December 1822: *a dark mulatto about 31 years of age 5 feet 9-3/4 inches high* [Register of Free Negroes 1798-1831, no.167]. He was taxable in York County in 1809 and head of a household of 2 "free Negroes & mulattoes over 16," one of whom was tithable in 1813 [PPTL, 1782-1841, frames 337, 384, 402].

v. William[3], born about 1795, registered in York County on 16 December 1822: *a dark Mulatto about 27 years of old 5 feet 10-1/2 Inches high...Born free* [Register of Free Negroes 1798-1831, no.167].

Other members of the family were

i. William[3], born about 1778, called William Alvis, Jr., when he was taxable in York County in 1799 [PPTL, 1782-1841, frames 243, 253, 263, 274], registered in York County on 15 October 1804: *yellowish complexion about 26 years of age 5 feet 8 Inches high...born free in the parish of Bruton* [Register of Free Negroes 1798-1831, no.25].

ii. Adam, born say 1786, taxable in York County in 1807 [PPTL, 1782-1841, frame 325], head of a York County household of 5 "other free" in 1810 [VA:870].

iii. James, head of a York County household of 3 "other free" in 1810 [VA:887].

iv. Fanny, born about 1789, registered in York County on 16 December 1822: *a very fat Mulatto about 33 years of age...she has long hair...fierce eyes...born free* [Register of Free Negroes 1798-1831, no. 191].

v. Sally, born about 1793, registered in York County on 16 December 1822: *about 29 years of age...short curly hair...born free* [Register of Free Negroes 1798-1831, no. 158].

vi. Elizabeth[3], born about 1806, registered as a free Negro in York County on 1 November 1831: *tawny complexion about 25 years of age, 3 feet 5-1/4 inches high...long face, large nose, thick pouting lips & long hair which she wears plaited* [Free Negroes Register 1831-50, no. 331].

vii. Mariah, born about 1810, registered in York County on 17 October 1831: *a mulatto woman about 21 or 22 years old, 5 feet 4-1/4 inches high...straight black hair* [Register, no. 310].

AMPEY FAMILY

The Ampey family may have been related to the Impey family of Maryland who descended from a white woman in Anne Arundel County. Members of the Ampey family in Virginia were

i.   William, born say 1755, head of an Amherst County household of 5 persons in 1783 [VA:48]. In October 1782 John **Redcross** sued him in Amherst County court for slander, and William countersued **Redcross** for trespass. Both cases were dismissed because they failed to appear. He and John **Redcross** were sued for a debt of 40 pounds on 3 May 1786 [Orders 1782-4, 49-50; Orders 1784-7, 510]. He was taxable in Amherst County from 1782 to 1786 [PPTL 1782-1803, 9, 43, 70]. He was a "free" taxable head of household with William Ampy, Jr., and 2 horses in Dinwiddie County in the list of Braddock Goodwin in 1797, 1798 and 1799 [PPTL, 1791-99 (1797 B, p.1), (1798 A, p.1), (1799 A, p.1)]. He may have been the William Ampy who was head of a Shenandoah County household of 2 "other free" in 1810 [VA:17].

ii.   Hannah, born about 1781, registered in Petersburg on 15 July 1805: *dark brown Mulatto woman, five feet two and a half inches high, twenty four years old, born free in Charles City County* [Register of Free Negroes 1794-1819, no. 340].

iii. Nancy, born about 1784, registered in Petersburg on 9 July 1805: *a light Mulatto woman, five feet five inches high, twenty one years old, little freckles under her eyes, born free & raised in Dinwiddie County* [Register of Free Negroes 1794-1819, no. 312]. She was head of a Richmond City household of 1 "other free" in 1810 [VA:370].

iv.   Betty, "Persons of Color" head of a Cumberland County, Virginia household of 4 "other free" in 1810 [VA:103].

ANCEL/ HANSEL FAMILY

1.   Mary Ancell, born say 1695, was the servant of William Livingston on 20 February 1720 when the York County court ordered that she serve him additional time for having a bastard child and running away for seven weeks. She was probably the mother of a "mulatto boy" named James Hancell who was listed in the York County inventory of the estate of James Goodwin which was recorded in court on 15 February 1719/20 [OW 15:554; 16:10]. She was probably the ancestor of

i.   James, born say 1713, a "mulatto boy" on 15 February 1719/20.

ii.   Henry, head of a Northampton County, North Carolina household of 4 "other free" in 1810, called Henry Ansel [NC:710] and 14 "free colored" in Halifax County in 1820, called Henry Hansel [NC:139].

ANDERSON FAMILY

The Anderson family was freed by the 29 October 1712 will of John Fulcher in Norfolk County, Virginia. He appointed Lewis Conner executor and granted his

Negroes men and women and Children there freedom...

And he left them 640 acres of land on Sewall's Point in Norfolk County [WB 9:223]. The freeing of these fifteen slaves prompted the Council on 5 March 1712/3 to recommend that the General Assembly

provide by a law against such manumission of slaves, which may in time by their increase and correspondence with other slaves may endanger the peace of this Colony [McIlwaine, *Executive Journals of the Council,* III:332].

Probably in an effort to "prevent their correspondence with other slaves" Fulcher's executor, Lewis Conner, by a deed dated 20 October 1715, swapped their land in Norfolk County with 640 acres of land on Welshes Creek in the part of Chowan County, North Carolina, which later became Martin and Washington Counties [Chowan DB B#1:109]. On 30 March 1712/3 the Andersons confirmed this exchange for an additional 300 acres of land by a deed of confirmation which identified them by name:

> *Robert Richards, Maria Richards, Kate Anderson, Hester Anderson, Betty Anderson, Lewis Anderson, Sarah Anderson...and our Children to witt - Peter Anderson, George Anderson, Dinah Anderson, Nedd Anderson, Rachell Anderson, Mingo: Anderson, Tony Anderson, and Susan Anderson Infants* [Norfolk DB 9:240].

Although the deed of exchange for the land was acknowledged and recorded in Chowan County, North Carolina, in September 1715 [DB B#1:109], it appears that the Andersons never took possession of the land. And there is no record of the Andersons ever selling the land in North Carolina.

On 20 May 1715 Lewis Conner sued the Anderson family to get the Chowan County deed admitted into the Norfolk County record and thus reclaim his bond as administrator of Fulcher's estate, but the Anderson family refused. The case was postponed, alternately at the request of plaintiff and defendants for two years, until 21 June 1717 when a Norfolk County jury found in favor of the Andersons that Conner had not fulfilled his obligations [Orders 1710-17, 191]. Lewis Conner appealed to the court at Williamsburg which ruled in his favor on 22 October 1717 [Orders 1710-17, 119, 191; The Williamsburg court ruling is referred to in Norfolk Orders 1734-36, 1, 10-11].

In 1718 the **Richards** and Anderson families brought suit against Lewis Conners for debt, but the case, "not being prosecuted," was dismissed [Orders 1718-19, 1].

On 11 August 1714 Robert **Richards** was called "a free Negro man" when the Norfolk County court ordered him to stand trial at the General Court in Williamsburg for receiving stolen cloth from John Chichester's slave. Kate Anderson, who was not charged, was found making a shirt for **Richards** from three yards of the material [Orders 1710-17, 90, 91].

It appears that some white residents of Norfolk County were disturbed by the manumission of so many slaves in their community. On 11 November 1714 the Norfolk County Grand Jury entered a presentment against "the free Negroes," but it was dismissed the next month because there was no reason for the presentment stated [Orders 1710-7, 103, 105]. And on 18 December 1715 Lewis Conner charged George, a slave of Margaret Willoughby, with attacking him when he met George and Kate Anderson on the "King's Road" [Orders 1710-7, 103, 105, 137].

On 20 December 1734 Edward/ Ned Anderson, one of the children freed by Fulcher's will, sued Lewis Conner's heirs over "Whether there be deed or no deed relating to the land in Bath County in Carolina." The court ruled against Edward, referring to the 22 October 1717 suit at Williamsburg [Orders 1734-36, 1, 10-11].

1. Kate[1] Anderson, born say 1670, may have been the mother of Hester, Betty, Lewis, and Sarah Anderson, the other adults listed after her in the above mentioned Norfolk County deed [Norfolk DB 9:240] since the 17 March 1717/8 Norfolk County court case referred to the family as "Kate Anderson and all the free Negroes" [DB 1710-17, 191]. Her son Edward was called "son Born of the Body of Kate a Negro woman set free by the will of said Fulcher"

on 20 December 1734 in Norfolk County court [Orders 1734-36, 10-11]. Her children were

    i.   ?Hester[1] Anderson **Artis**, born say 1687, ancestor of the **Artis** family of North Carolina and Southampton County, Virginia.

2   ii.   ?Elizabeth[1]/ Betty Anderson, born say 1688.

    iii.   ?Lewis[1], born say 1690 since he was an adult when John Fulcher wrote his 1712 will. He was tithable in his own household in the 1730 Norfolk County List of Tithables, adjacent to Peter Anderson [Wingo, *Norfolk County Tithables 1730-50*, 47]. Perhaps they were identical to "Lewis" and "Peter" (no last name) who were presented by the Norfolk County court on 16 November 1744 for not listing their wives as tithables [Orders 1742-6, 108]. He married Katherine **Bass** before 25 July 1748 when her father Edward **Bass** made his Northampton County, North Carolina will [Original at N.C. Archives]. By this will Katherine received 50 acres near Urahaw Swamp in Northampton County which she and Lewis sold on 12 November 1757 [DB 2:424].

3   iv.   ?Sarah[1], born say 1691.

4   v.   Edward/Ned, born say 1702.

    vi.   ?Abraham, born say 1703, a "free negro" sued in Princess Anne County court on 2 December 1729 by Alexander Jameson for killing his mare. The court found Abraham guilty and ordered that he pay Jameson two pounds. The same court fined him 2,000 pounds of tobacco for concealing two tithables (one of whom was probably his wife) [Minutes 1728-37, 43, 44].

According to the 20 March 1712/3 release for the land in Norfolk County the children of Kate, Hester, Betty, Lewis, and Sarah were

5   i.   Peter[1], born say 1694.

6   ii.   George[1], born say 1696.

    iii.   Dinah, born say 1698.

    iv.   Rachel, born say 1700.

    v.   Mingo, born say 1705.

    vi.   Tony, born say 1707.

    vii.   Susan, born say 1710.

2.   Elizabeth[1] Anderson was probably born about 1688 since she was an adult when John Fulcher wrote his 1712 will. She may have been the "Betty Anderson (Free)" who was taxable in Norfolk County in Tanners Creek District in 1735 [Wingo, *Norfolk County Tithables 1730-50*, 144]. She was a "Free Negro" who sued Susannah Flurry on 21 January 1743/4 and William Mansfield on 18 April 1746 in Norfolk County court [Orders 1742-46, 65, 70, 112, 115, 119]. She may have been protesting the treatment of her children bound apprentices to them. She was awarded 40 shillings in her suit of trespass, assault and battery against Susannah Flurry on 16 November 1746 and the same court presented her for not listing her tithables [Orders 1742-46, 108]. Her children may have been

7   i.   Lewis[2], born say 1713.

8   ii.   Margaret[1], born say 1730.

3.   Sarah[1] Anderson, born say 1691, was living in Norfolk County on 19 July 1753 when the court ordered the churchwardens of Elizabeth River Parish to bind her daughter Cate to John Standhope. She was deceased by 18 April 1754 when the Norfolk County court ordered the churchwardens of Elizabeth River Parish to bind out her daughter Nanny to Mereck Meech [Orders 1753-55, 40, 183]. Her children were

    i.   Kate[2], born say 1738, bound apprentice to John Standhope in July 1753. She was called a "free Negro" on 17 October 1755 when the court ordered the churchwardens of Elizabeth River Parish to bind her son Charles Anderson to James Ashley [Orders 1755-9, 18].

ii.   Ann, born say 1740, bound apprentice in 1754, taxable on the west side of Church Street in Norfolk Borough in 1767 [Wingo, *Norfolk County Tithables, 1766-80*, 32]. She may have been the mother of Samuel Anderson, a "free negro" living in Elizabeth River Parish on 15 December 1774 when the court ordered the churchwardens to bind him to Francis **Jordan** (who also lived in Norfolk Borough) [Orders 1773-5, 65].

4.   Edward/ Ned Anderson was probably born about 1702 since he was still a child in 1712 when he was freed by Fulcher's will. He was bound as an apprentice tanner to John Jameson on 3 February 1720 in Princess Anne County, the county adjoining Norfolk [Minutes 1717-28, 64] and taxable in Tanners Creek district of Norfolk County in 1733 [Wingo, *Norfolk County Tithables 1730-50*, 105]. He was called the "son Born of the Body of Kate a Negro woman set free by the will of said Fulcher" when he sued Lewis Conner's heirs in Norfolk County court on 20 December 1734 [Orders 1734-36, 10-11]. He may have been the father of

9   i.   Martha, born say 1733.
10   ii.   Marshall, born say 1740.
11   iii.   Dempsey/ Demce, born say 1752.

5.   Peter[1] Anderson, born say 1694, was a minor when John Fulcher made his will in 1712. He sued James Chapman in Princess Anne County court for trespass on 3 February 1724/5. Henry Holmes and William Easter were his witnesses [Minutes 1717-28, 219, 220]. He was a taxable in Tanners Creek District of Norfolk County in 1731 adjacent to Lewis Anderson and taxable a second time in the same list: "Peter Anderson & 2 more" [Wingo, *Norfolk County Tithables, 1730-50*, 47, 49]. He may have been the father of

i.   Joyce, born before 1746, taxable in Town Bridge District of Norfolk County in 1761 and 1765 and in the district of the Town of Portsmouth and the Southern Branch in 1767 [Wingo, *Norfolk County Tithables, 1751-65*, 182, 216; *1766-80*, 44].

ii.   Juda, born before 1746, taxable in the June 1761 list for Town Bridge District of Norfolk County, perhaps the Judith Anderson whose "Mulatto" daughter, Sally Anderson, was bound apprentice to John Coones in Edgecombe County, North Carolina, in April 1763 [Minutes 1759-64, 59].

iii.   Effia/ Affiar, born say 1748, a taxable "free negro" in Western Branch District of Norfolk County in 1765 and in the east division of the Borough of Norfolk in 1767 [Wingo, *Norfolk County Tithables, 1751-65*, 211; *1766-80*, 37].

6.   George[1] Anderson, born say 1696, was the ancestor of the North Carolina branch of the Anderson family. On 13 January 1738 he bought 260 acres of land on the south side of Bear Swamp where he was then living in Bertie County, North Carolina, for "2 pounds silver money" from John **Bass** [DB E:530]. This land became part of Northampton County when it was formed in 1741. In February 1738 he appeared in Bertie court to apprentice a child to Daniel Oquin. This child was identified in the minutes of the 10 November 1741 Bertie court as "Laurance Anderson a Negro servant" [Haun, *Bertie County Court Minutes*, I:217, 255, II:341]. George sold his 260 acres in Northampton County on 1 March 1745, and about 1746-48 he was taxed on two tithes in Granville County, North Carolina, in the list of Jonathan White adjacent to Lewis Anderson. He was listed with his wife and children in the 1752 list of Robert Harris:

Anderson, George his wife and sons George, Jermiah and Daughter Kate
5 black tithes [CR 044.701.19]

On 3 June 1755 he bought 240 acres in Granville from Jonathan White. He sold 200 acres of this land to his son Jeremiah on 22 December 1762 and on the same day sold 100 acres adjoining this land to Edward **Bass** [DB B:458; F:280-1]. On 3 August 1768 Nathan **Bass**, the illegitimate son of Love **Bass**, was bound to him as an apprentice. However, Nathan was already living in George's house, taxable in his household in the 1767 list of Stephen Jett [CR 44.701.19]. George's will was proved in Granville County in May 1771. Lovey **Bass** was probably his mistress since he gave his plantation to her son Nathan **Bass** and gave her two cows and calves. He gave only one shilling to his wife Mary and children: Jerry Anderson, Kate **Harris**, and Betty **Smith** [Original in Granville County, not recorded]. At his death he owed 17 pounds, 8 shillings to Young, Miller & Company of Granville County, British merchants, who listed him in their claims after the Revolutionary War. The claim mentioned George Anderson's executor, John Whicker [*NCGSJ* XVIII:41]. His children were

12   i.   ?Lawrence, born say 1730.

        ii. Betty **Smith**, mentioned in her father's 1771 will, perhaps related to "Sarah Smith (Malato) 1 Black tithe" who was head of her own household in the 1768 Granville Tax List of Len Henley Bullock and the free African American **Smith** family of Norfolk County, Virginia.

       iii. George[2], born circa 1735, listed as George's son in the 1751 list of Jonathan White. He was in his own household in 1753, taxable on a "Black" tithe in the list of Robert Harris adjacent to his father.

13   iv. Jeremiah, born before 1740.

       v. Katherine, born say 1737, taxable in her parents household in 1751. She was listed in her parents household in 1757 but was not listed with them in 1761. She was probably the "Wife Cathrine" in George **Harris**' Oxford District household in 1761.

       vi. ?Ruth, born say 1738, never taxable in George's household. She was a "Mulatto Servant woman" belonging to Colonel William Eaton, on 5 September 1755 when her two-year-old "Mulatto Girl," Priscilla, born December 1752, was bound to Eaton and his wife Mary [Owen, *Granville County Notes,* vol. II].

       vii. Nehemiah, born before 1746 since he was over sixteen years old in 1761 when he was a "black" male taxable in his father's household in the list for Oxford District. He was taxable in his father's household in the 1767 list of Stephen Jett but not in his 1768 list, and he was not mentioned in his father's 1771 will.

7.   Lewis[2] Anderson was probably born about 1713 since he was not mentioned in John Fulcher's 1712 Norfolk County will. There is no indication of who his parents were, but he may have been the son of Elizabeth[1] Anderson. He married Sarah **Bass**, the daughter of John[2] **Bass**, before 18 January 1732 when **Bass** made his 18 January 1732 Bertie County will. Lewis was taxable in all the extant colonial Granville County, North Carolina Tax Lists, on himself in the first list circa 1746-48 by Jonathan White adjacent to George[1] Anderson, and with his wife and children in the remaining lists [CR 44.701.19]. On 1 August 1750 he paid George Morris 50 pounds for 200 acres on both sides of Fishing Creek in Granville [DB A:320]. He was number 87 in the 8 October 1754 Muster Roll of the regiment of Colonel William Eaton, Granville County, Captain John Sallis's Company [Clark, *Colonial Soldiers of the South,* 723]. On 10 November 1755 Lewis Anderson (signing), his wife Sarah and son Shadrack, all of Granville County, sold (for 31 gallons of brandy to Jethra **Bass** of Northampton County) 100 acres in Northampton County on the north side of Urahaw Swamp "being all the land bequeathed the sd Sarah Anderson

by the will of her father John Bass dec'd" [DB 2:233]. Jethra (Jethro) **Bass** was the son of Sarah's brother John[3] **Bass**. On 3 April 1762 Lewis bought a further 96 acres on the north side of Fishing Creek in Granville County [DB E:361]. In 1782 he was taxable in Oxford District on 296 acres, a horse, and 5 cattle. His 20 January 1783 Granville County will was proved in May 1785 [WB 1:439]. On 10 March 1784 in confirmation of this will he made a deed of gift to his son Lewis Anderson, Jr., for 200 acres on both sides of Fishing Creek [DB O:299]. We can determine Lewis and Sarah's children from the early Granville County tax lists and Lewis' 1783 will:

    i.   Shadrack, born before 1739, taxable in his father's Granville household in 1751. His father left him 100 acres but appointed his brother Lewis Jr., as his guardian, so perhaps he was disabled.

14   ii.   Leshea/ Lisha, born before 1739.

    iii.   Mary, born about 1739, taxable in her father's Granville household in 1751 in the tax list of Jonathan White. In 1762 she was taxable with her parents in the list of Saml. Benton for Oxford District & Fishing Creek but not with them in Samuel Benton's 1764 list, so she was probably the "wife Mary" with Reuben **Bass** who was also in Samuel Benton's 1764 list. She was the daughter, "Mary **Bass**," mentioned in her father's 1783 will.

    iv.   Tamer, born about 1742, taxable in 1754 with her parents in John Sallis' tax list. She was also taxable with them in 1755 but not in the next extant list of 1757. She was probably the "wife Tamer" listed with Edward **Bass** in the Oxford District Tax List of 1761. She was the daughter, Tamer **Bass**, named in her father's will.

    v.   Sarah **Tyler**, born about 1745, first taxable in the 1757 list of Richard Harris. She was listed in her father's household in the 1765 list of Samuel Benton but was not listed with him in Stephen Jett's 1767 list. She may have married Bartlett **Tyler** who was taxed with "his Wife and Sister Jane" in Robert Harris' 1768 list.

15   vi.   Lewis[3], born about 1745.

8.   Margaret[1] Anderson, born say 1730, petitioned the Norfolk County court against Nathaniel Adams on 18 October 1753 [Orders 1750-53, 205]. She, called "Peg Anderson free negro," was tithable in Tanners Creek district of Norfolk County in 1759 and a "free negro" tithable in the Southern Branch District in 1766 [Wingo, *Norfolk County Tithables 1751-65*, 141; *1766-80*, 6]. Her children may have been

    i.   Harry, born say 1750, son of "free Pegg" (no family name mentioned), bound to Nathaniel Adams on 22 May 1752 [Orders 1750-53, 87]. And he was called "Harry Son of Pegg a free Negro" on 19 July 1754 when Richard Scott petitioned the court on his behalf against Nathaniel Adams [Orders 1753-5, 69].

    ii.   Isaac[1], born say 1752, called "Son of free Peg" on 20 March 1755 when the Norfolk County court ordered the churchwardens of Elizabeth River Parish to bind him to Richard Lewelling [Orders 1753-5, 122] and called a "free negro" on 15 November 1757 when the Princess Anne County court ordered him bound until the age of twenty-one to Abigail Lewling to be a wheelwright. On 26 April 1782 the Princess Anne County court paid him 12 shillings for fodder he had provided to the Revolution [Minutes 1753-62, 310; 1773-82, 546]. He married Hester **Jordan**, 11 December 1781 Princess Anne County bond, Marshall Anderson surety.

    iii.   Nathaniel[1], born say 1754, a "free negro" ordered bound by the churchwardens of Elizabeth River Parish to John Dennis in Norfolk County on 16 January 1755 [Orders 1753-5, 105]. He was a "free Negro" head of a household of 3 "Black" persons in Blackwater Precinct, Princess Anne County, in 1783 [VA:60], taxable on a tithe and a horse in 1787 [Schreiner-Yantis, *1787 Census*, 1156]. He served as a seaman in the Revolution [Jackson, *Virginia Negro Soldiers*, 29]. He was a "N"(egro) taxable in Portsmouth and Elizabeth River Parishes in Norfolk County in 1804 and 1805 [PPTL, 1791-1812, frames 478, 554].

    iv.   Margaret[2], a "Mullatto" bound by the Princess Anne County court to Amy Burford to read, sew and knit on 19 December 1758 [Minutes 1753-62, 339].

9. Martha Anderson, born say 1733, was living in Lynhaven Parish, Princess Anne County, on 18 May 1762 when the court ordered her sons Joseph and Peter Anderson bound as apprentices to Talbert Thompson [Minutes 1753-62, 488]. Her children were

    i.   ?Sarah, born say 1750, called "Sarah a free Negro daughter of ____ " when the Princess Anne County court bound her to Benjamin Jenkins to learn to read and sew. The court called her a "free Mullatto" when it bound her to Mary Jenkins to read, sew, and knit on 18 March 1760 [Minutes 1753-62, 367, 376]. She was a "free negro" taxable in her own household on the north side of Tanners Creek in Norfolk County in 1766, taxable in the household of her husband William[1] **Fuller** in 1767 and 1768 in the same district [Wingo, *Norfolk County Tithables, 1766-80*, 5, 49, 73].

    ii. Joseph, born 17 April 1751, son of Martha Anderson (no race mentioned), bound to Talbert Thompson to be a sailmaker in Princess Anne County on 18 May 1762 [Minutes 1753-62, 488]. He was called a "free Negro" when he was bound by the churchwardens of Elizabeth River Parish to John Wilson in Norfolk County on 21 October 1762 [Orders 1759-63, 210] and a "Mulatto" when he was bound as an apprentice shoemaker to William Stephenson in Norfolk County on 18 June 1772 [DB 25:fol.247].

16   iii. Peter[2], son of Martha, born 24 May 1754.

    iv. ?Easter[2], a "Free Mulatto" bound to Tamer Griffin by the Princess Anne County court on 14 April 1774 [Minutes 1773-82, 39].

    v. James, born in September 1768, a nine-year-old "free Negro" bound as an apprentice ropemaker to Lemuel Roberts by the Norfolk County court on 19 December 1777 [Orders 1776-9, n.p.].

10. Marshall Anderson, born say 1740, was sued for a debt of three pounds, nineteen shillings in Princess Anne County court on 4 December 1767, and he was sued for a debt of four pounds by James **Whitehurst** on 10 May 1782. Isaac Anderson testified against him. On 15 August 1783 the court fined him 1,000 pounds of tobacco for committing adultery with Susanna Pebworth (a white woman) [Minutes 1762-9, 429; 1782-4, 67, 135, 157]. He was a "free negro" head of a household of 8 "Blacs" in Blackwater Precinct, Princess Anne County in 1783 [VA:60], a "free Negro" taxable on himself, Jacob **Mills** and (his son?) Marvel Anderson in 1784 [*Virginia Genealogical Society Quarterly* 27:267], and taxable on himself and one other person, 2 horses, and 10 cattle in 1787 [Schreiner-Yantis, *1787 Census*, 1156]. He may have been the father of

    i.   Marvel, born say 1762, taxable in Marshall Anderson's household in 1784. He married Nancy **Whitehurst**, 7 January 1791 Princess Anne County bond, Charles **Whitehurst** surety.

    ii. Sally, born say 1767, married Charles **Whitehurst** 8 February 1788 Princess Anne County bond, Joseph **Whitehurst** surety.

    iii. Betsy, born say 1770, married John **Sparrow**, 26 March 1791 Princess Anne County bond, Marshall Anderson surety.

    iv. Demce, Jr., married Betsy **Weaver**, 4 January 1796 Princess Anne County bond, Thomas **Weaver** surety, 5 January marriage.

11. Dempsey/ Demce Anderson, born say 1752, was paid one pound by the Princess Anne County court on 26 April 1782 for corn he had provided to the Revolution [Minutes 1773-82, 546]. He was a "free Negro" head of a household of 6 "Black" persons in Blackwater Precinct, Princess Anne County, in 1783 [VA:60], a "free Negro" taxable on himself and "Negro Jack" (a slave) in 1784 [*Virginia Genealogical Society Quarterly* 27:267], and taxable on 2 horses and 6 cattle in 1787 [Schreiner-Yantis, *1787 Census*, 1156]. His 11 May 1807 Princess Anne County will, proved 5 October the same year, named his wife Rose and daughter Elizabeth **Carter** and son Joshua Anderson who was living away from home when his father made his will. His estate included a slave who belonged to Jacomine N. Thorogood [WB 2:319]. Dempsey and Rose were the parents of

   i. Elizabeth[2], married Stephen **Carter**, 1 January 1796 Princess Anne County bond, Dempsey Anderson surety.

   ii. Joshua.

12. Lawrence Anderson, born say 1730, may have been George Anderson's son since George indentured him as an apprentice in Bertie County in 1738. Perhaps he was the Lawrence Anderson who was in the muster roll of Captain Thomas Goldsmith's Company of Independent Foot, on duty in South Carolina and Georgia from August 25, 1756 to October 24, 1756 [Clark, *Colonial Soldiers of the South*, 979]. The free Andersons counted in the 1790 South Carolina census may have been his descendants:

   i. John, head of a household of 1 "other free" in Charleston, Berkeley County, St. John's Parish.

   ii. William, head of a household of 1 "other free" in Charleston District, St. James Santee Parish.

13. Jeremiah Anderson was born before 1740 since he was taxable in 1751 in his father's Granville County household in Jonathan White's list. He purchased 200 acres for 5 pounds from his father on 22 December 1762 and sold this land on 10 April 1768 [DB F:280; H:415]. By 1764 he was in his own household, taxable with his wife Margaret and (his brother-in-law?) David **Mitchell** in Samuel Benton's list and was taxable on two tithes in the 1766 summary list. He may have been the Jeremiah Anderson who purchased 108 acres on Jacket Swamp in Halifax County, North Carolina, from Thomas Bull on 5 February 1763 and sold it on 22 August 1775 [DB 13:738]. In 1780 he was taxable in adjoining Northampton County on an assessment of 100 pounds [GA 46.1]. He was head of a Northampton County household of a "Black" person 12-50 years old and 4 "Black" persons less than 12 or over 50 years old in Dupree's District in 1786 for the state census (called Jerry Andrews). He purchased 100 acres in Northampton County on the road in Henry Hart's line on 3 September 1790 [DB 9:11] and was head of a Northampton County household of 7 "other free" in 1790 [NC:73]. He may have been the husband of Milla **Stewart** who was mentioned in the 6 June 1789 Northampton County will of her mother Margaret **Roberts**, proved September 1794, with Jeremiah Anderson executor [WB 2:54]. Jeremiah died before 1 January 1794 when his 100 acres was released to Mille Anderson, administratrix of his estate. Milly and George Anderson sold this land on 27 August 1798 [DB 10:83, 399]. Two of his children may have been

   i. George[3], who sold Jeremiah's land on 27 August 1798. He may have been the George Anderson (45 years and older) who was head of a Richmond County, North Carolina household of 10 "free colored" in 1820 [NC:204].

17   ii. Charles, born about 1774.

14. Leshea/ Lisha Anderson, born before 1739, was taxable in her father's Granville household in 1751. She had an illegitimate daughter Liddy, born

about 1763, who was bound apprentice to Lewis Anderson, Sr., on 3 August 1768. George[1] Anderson mentioned Lisha and her daughter in his May 1771 Granville County will. She later married William **Tabourn**. Her child was

    i. Liddy, born about 1763, married Morris **Evans**, 8 December 1784 Granville County bond with Burwell **Evans** bondsman.

15. Lewis[3] Anderson was born about 1743 since he was first taxable in 1755 in the Granville County list of Richard Harris. He was still in his father's household in 1768 in the list of Stephen Jett. He married Winnie about 1769. She was probably Winnie **Bass** who was taxable in the household of her parents, Benjamin and Mary **Bass**, adjacent to the Andersons in the 1768 list of Stephen Jett. Her illegitimate son, Jacob, was bound to Lewis on 3 August 1768 [CR 044.101.2-7]. Lewis purchased 265 acres on Beaverdam Swamp on 4 March 1769, purchased 75 acres on the north side of Fishing Creek on 4 January 1777, and sold the 265 acres on Beaver Dam for 60 pounds on 6 February 1777 [DB H:531, L:69, 127]. In 1777 his taxable property in Oxford District was evaluated at a little over 96 pounds, and by 1782 he was taxable on 75 acres, 2 horses, and 9 cattle. As mentioned above he received a further 200 acres by deed of gift from his father on 10 March 1784. He was taxed on 371 acres in 1785 and 571 acres in 1791. He sold 100 acres adjoining **Bass** to his son Peter on 8 May 1798 and another 7-1/2 acres to Peter on 14 June 1804 [DB Q:159; R:378]. He was head of a Granville County household of 6 "other free" in 1800 [NC:542]. His 29 June 1804 will was proved in May 1805, and his wife Winny made a nuncupative will in Granville County on 31 December 1809 [WB 7:108]. A full list of Lewis' children is given in a refunding bond dated 2 July 1814 in the Granville County estate papers:

    i. Jacob, born about 1765, three years old on 3 August 1768 when he was bound to Lewis Anderson, Junior. He was taxed on 100 acres in Oxford District from 1788 to 1803, 386 acres in 1806, and 150 acres on Cattail Creek from 1817-27. He was head of a Granville County household of 6 "other free" in 1800 [NC:543], 6 in 1810 [NC:904], 9 "free colored" in 1820 [NC:3], and 4 in 1830 [NC:28].

    ii. Peter[3], born prior to 1775, purchased 100 acres from his father on 8 May 1798. On 20 August 1814 Peter sold 43 acres on Fishing Creek to his younger brother Thomas Anderson, and on 31 March 1820 he sold 64 acres to Thomas Hunt [DB Q:159; Y:155; Z:35]. He was head of a Granville County household of 6 "other free" in 1800 [NC:582], 10 in 1810 [NC:904], 6 "free colored" in 1820 [NC:3], and 4 in 1830 [NC:19].

    iii. Abel, born before 1775, taxable on a free poll in Tabbs Creek District in 1796 and taxable in 1809 [Tax List 1796-1802, 341]. He married Susannah **Evans**, 23 May 1804 Granville County bond, Benjamin **Mitchell** bondsman. He was head of a Granville County household of 6 "other free" in 1810 [NC:914]. He and Jeremiah Anderson owned 240 acres in Vigo County, Indiana [Wright, "Negro Rural Communities," *Southern Workman* 37:165-66].

    iv. George[4], born about 1775/6, married Sarah **Evans**, 14 October 1800 Granville County bond, William **Pettiford** bondsman. He was taxed on 93-1/2 acres in Oxford District in 1808 [Tax List 1803-09, 289], and was head of a Granville County household of 4 "other free" in 1810 [NC:904], 5 "free colored" in 1820 [NC:3], and 3 in 1830 [NC:19].

    v. Isaac[2], born about 1775, married Melethan **Hines**, 28 September 1800 Granville County bond, Peter **Chaves** bondsman. Isaac was taxed on 220 acres in Oxford District in 1796. He made a deed of trust for 220 acres to Randal Minor on 10 November 1815 [DB X:201]. He sold 50 acres on Cattail on 14 March 1818 [DB Y:4] and made further sales between 1821 and 1835 [DB 1:84, 6:555, 6:556]. He was head of a Granville County household of 4 "other free" in 1800 [NC:545], 4 in

1810 [NC:904], 4 "free colored" in 1820 [NC:3], and 3 in 1830 [NC:29]. His wife Melethan was living at the age of seventy-five in the household of William **Evans** in 1850 [NC:104].

vi. Augustine, born about 1776, married Patient **Reaves**, 19 December 1796 Granville County bond, Abel Anderson bondsman. He was taxed on a free poll in 1797 in Epping Forest District and on 131 acres in Tabbs Creek District from 1798 to 1806. He sold this land on 30 January 1808 [DB T:425]. He was head of a Granville County household of 2 "other free" in 1800 [NC:561], 2 in 1810 [NC:908], and 2 "free colored" in 1820 [NC:11]. His estate was administered in 1827 by Lewis Parham. His wife made a 12 September 1842 will.

vii. Rhody, married Darling **Bass**, 31 January 1796 Granville County bond, Wm. **Mitchell** bondsman. His 10 November 1839 Granville County will mentioned Henry **Anderson** who was Rhody's son by Jesse **Chavis** before her marriage to Darling [WB 16:334].

viii. Rebecca, head of a Granville County household of 2 "other free" in 1800 [NC:583]. She married Edward **Going**, 31 October 1807 Granville County bond, her brother George Anderson bondsman.

ix. Joyce, married Zachariah **Mitchell**.

x. Winnifred, married Benjamin **Mitchell**, 19 December 1803 Granville County bond with her brother George Anderson bondsman.

xi. Abraham, born about 1789, head of a Granville household of 6 "free colored" in 1830 [NC:77] and living in Granville in 1850 [NC:126]. He sold 3 acres on the east side of Fishing Creek on 2 April 1816 and later that year on 31 August traded the land he was left by his father to William M. Sneed [DB X:59, 267]. He made a deed of trust to Isaiah M. Paschal about 1840 [DB 9:513].

xii. Benjamin, born about 1790, sold 75 acres on the east side of Harris' Creek and Fishing Creek, bequeathed "by my father Lewis Anderson dec.," on 3 August 1816 [DB X:90]. He was living in Granville County in 1850 [NC:126].

xiii. Wright, born after 1793.

xiv. Lewis[4], born about 1799-1800, living in Granville County in 1850 [NC:109]. He married Mary **Houze** (**House**), 1 January 1822 Granville County, George Anderson bondsman.

xv. John, born after 1793, taxable on a free poll in 1806 and on 60 acres on Hatcher's Run in Oxford District in 1817-27. He sold this land to Lithy and Eliza Anderson on 16 May 1835 [DB 6:506]. He was head of a Granville household of 1 "other free" in 1810 [NC:898] and 4 "free colored" in 1820 [NC:3].

xvi. Thomas, born after 1793, purchased 43 acres from his older brother Peter Anderson on 20 August 1814 [DB Y:155]. He was head of a Granville household of 1 "other free" in 1810 [NC:898], 7 "free colored" in 1820 [NC:3], and 6 in 1830 [NC:31].

xvii. Sarah, born after 1793, married John **Chavis**, 8 June 1815 Granville County bond, Abraham Anderson bondsman, W.M. Sneed witness.

16. Peter[2] Anderson, born 24 May 1754, son of Martha Anderson, was bound as an apprentice sailmaker to Talbert Thompson in Princess Anne County on 18 May 1762 [Minutes 1753-62, 488]. He was taxable in Norfolk County on the east side of Church Street in 1774 [Wingo, *Norfolk County Tithables 1766-80*, 230]. His children may have been

i. Sally, born about 1774, registered in Petersburg on 27 February 1806: *Sally Scott alias Anderson, a dark negro woman, four feet ten inches high, thirty two years old, born free in Norfolk County & raised in the City of Richmond* [Register of Free Negroes 1794-1819, no. 372]. She may have been the Sally Anderson who was head of a Petersburg household of 2 "other free" in 1810 [VA:334b].

    ii.   Wilson, born say 1778, head of a Norfolk Borough, Norfolk County household of 5 "other free" in 1810 [VA:887], perhaps the Wilson Anderson who was head of a Richmond City household of 5 "other free" the same year [VA:343]. He may have been named for John Wilson to whom Joseph Anderson was bound an apprentice in October 1762 [Orders 1759-63, 210].

    iii. Nathaniel[2], born say 1780, "a free mulatto man," married Mourning **Reid**, "a mulatto woman," 5 February 1803 Norfolk County bond, Pliny Skipwith surety.

    iv. Hetty, born say 1790, head of a Norfolk Borough, Norfolk County household of 2 "other free" in 1810 [VA:886].

17. Charles Anderson, born about 1774, was head of a Northampton County, North Carolina household of 2 "other free" in 1800 [NC:424]. He may have been the Charles Anderson who registered in Norfolk County on 20 May 1811: *5 feet 8 In., 47 years of age of a Dark Complexion blind in the right Eye pitted with the Small pox with a Sink in the right cheek, Born free.* His wife Mary Anderson, *wife of Chas. Anderson* registered on the 2 May 1811: *36 years of age light complexion 5 feet 4 1/2 Inches high, Born free* [Register of Free Negros & Mulattos, nos. 54, 50]. Their children may have been

    i.   William, born about 1791, registered in Norfolk County on 20 May 1811: *5 feet 10 In., 20 years of age of a yellowish Complexion, Born free* [Register, no. 52].

    ii. Nisum (Newsom?), born about 1794, registered on 20 May 1811: *5 feet 8 In., 17 years of age of a Yellow Complexion freckled on the face, Born free* [Register, no. 53].

    iii. Richard, born say 1800, married Mary **Newton** (free blacks), 4 December 1824 Norfolk County bond, Isaac **Fuller** security.

Northampton County, Virginia

1. Catherine Anderson, born say 1720, was a "Negro" tithable head of her own household in John Savage's list for Northampton County in 1742, 1743, and 1744 (adjacent to Ann **McKinnie**) [L.P. 1742-44]. Her children bound apprentice in Northampton County were

    i.   Patience, born about 1738, "daughter of Katherine," bound apprentice in October 1742 [Orders 1732-42, 484].

    ii. James, born about 1740, "free Negro" orphan of Catherine Anderson, nine years old in February 1748/9 when he was bound apprentice with his mother's approval [Orders 1748-51, 34; L.P. #34, Catherine Anderson's petition].

    iii. ?Sarah, born about 1742, a six-year-old "Negro" bound apprentice on 14 October 1748 [Orders 1748-51, 26].

    iv. Solomon, born about 1748, twelve-year-old son of "free Negro Catherine Anderson," bound apprentice on 14 May 1760 [Minutes 1754-61, 230].

Another Anderson family not related to the Norfolk County family

1. Jane[1] Anderson, born say 1715, was a white indentured servant living in Prince George County on 14 November 1738 when she sued William Eaton for her freedom dues. On 13 March 1738/9 the churchwardens of Bristol Parish bound out her "Mulatto" daughter Jane Anderson to William Eaton [Orders 1737-40, 209, 241]. She was the mother of

2   i.   ?Sarah, born say 1735.

3   ii. Jane[2], born say 1738.

    iii. ?John, born say 1742, petitioned the Augusta County court against Rev. John Craig on 22 June 1763 for detaining him as a slave. The court ordered him released on the deposition of Joel Barker that he was the son of a free white woman and was bound out by the churchwardens of Brunswick County, Virginia, until the age of twenty-one [Orders 1763-4, 122].

2. Sarah Anderson, born say 1735, was living in Southampton County on 10 February 1757 when the court ordered the churchwardens to bind out her unnamed "Mullatto" child. And on 10 November 1757 the court ordered the churchwardens to bind out her "mulatto" children Amos and Fanny [Orders 1754-9, 333, 395]. She may have been the Sarah Anderson who was living in Southam Parish, Cumberland County, Virginia, on 23 January 1764 when the court ordered the churchwardens to bind her "Mulatto" child Jane to Edward Mosby. On 23 November 1772 the Cumberland County court ordered the churchwardens to bind out her "mulattoe" children Jane, Jeffrey and Fan to Peter Bondur [Orders 1762-4, 375; 1772-4, 49]. She was the mother of

    i.   Amos, born say 1755.

4   ii. Fanny, born say 1757.

    iii. Jane[3], born say 1762.

    iv. Jeffrey, born say 1765, a "mulattoe orphan" living in Cumberland County, Virginia, on 28 August 1769 when the court ordered the churchwardens of Southam Parish to bind him to Thomas Walton. He was bound to Peter Bondur on 23 November 1772 [Orders 1767-70, 414]. He was a "Mulatto" taxable in Buckingham County from 1795 to 1801 [PPTL 1782-97; 1797-1803].

    v. Diana, orphan of Sarah Anderson living in Cumberland County on 28 February 1785 when the court ordered the churchwardens of Littleton Parish to bind her to John Lipsford [Orders 1774-8, 204].

3. Jane[2] Anderson, born say 1738, the "Mulatto" daughter of Jane Anderson, was living in Prince George County on 13 March 1738/9 when the court ordered the churchwardens of Bristol Parish to bind her to William Eaton [Orders 1737-40, 209, 241]. She may have been the mother of

    i.   John, born about 1757, registered in Petersburg on 20 August 1794: *a dark brown Mulatto man, five feet three inches high, thirty seven years old, born free & brought up as a Turner in the City of Richmond* [Register of Free Negroes 1794-1819, no. 78]. He was head of a Petersburg household of 3 "other free" in 1810 [VA:331].

    ii. Clay, head of a Prince George County household of 3 "other free" in 1810 [VA:545].

    iii. Hall, head of a Charles City County household of 1 "other free" in 1810 [VA:942].

    iv. Maria, head of a Henrico County household of 6 "other free" in 1810 [VA:996].

4. Fanny Anderson, born say 1757, was living in Cumberland County, Virginia, on 27 January 1777 when the court ordered the churchwardens of Southam Parish to bind out her daughter Anne Anderson (no race indicated) to John Jude [Orders 1774-8, 392]. She was the mother of

    i.   Anne, born say 1775, bound out on 27 January 1777.

    ii. ?Dicy, a "Mulatto" bound to Thomas Walton in Littleton Parish, Cumberland County on 26 April 1785 [Orders 1774-8, 321].

Indiana

Obadiah Anderson was one of the first "colored families" to settle in Randolph County, Indiana, soon after 1825 [Historical & Genealogical Society of Randolph County, *History of Randolph County*, 134].

ANDREWS FAMILY

1. Tom[1], born say 1700, a "negro" slave, was freed by the 28 November 1720 Surry County, Virginia will of Bartholomew Andrews after the death of Andrews' wife Elizabeth. The will was proved on 18 May 1726 [DW 8:637]. Tom may have been the ancestor of the free Andrews family:

2   i.   Thomas[2], born say 1770.
   ii. Charles, born about 1771, listed as William **Cypress**'s tithable in Surry County in 1794 [PPTL, 1782-90, frame 548]. He registered in Petersburg on 18 August 1794: *a light yellow Mulatto man, five feet five and a half inches high, twenty three years old, born free & raised in the county of Chesterfield*. He registered again on 19 January 1798: *a light yellow Mulatto man, five feet five and a half inches high, twenty six years old, short bushy hair, square well made* [Register of Free Negroes 1794-1819, no. 44, 125]. And he registered in Surry County on 24 July 1799: *a bright mulatto man about 5'6" high, 26 years, has curled hair, by profession a Shoe-maker* [Hudgins, *Register of Free Negroes*, 51, 88].
   iii. Hannah, head of a Richmond City household of 4 "other free" in 1810 [VA:362].

2. Thomas[2] Andrews, born say 1770, married Rebecca **Charity**, 26 April 1791 Surry County, Virginia bond, Joseph **Byrd** surety, 11 May marriage by Rev. Samuel Butler, rector of Southwark Parish Episcopal Church. He was a "Mulatto" taxable in Cabin Point district of Surry County in 1793 and 1794. Becky was taxable on a male "free Negro & Mulatto" in 1814 [PPTL, 1791-1816, frames 103, 154, 768]. He may have been the father of

   i.   Patsy, born say 1791, "dau of Beckey Andrews," married Grayham **Scott**, 20 April 1810 Surry County bond, David **Charity**, surety, 22 April marriage by Rev. James Hill.
   ii. Archer, born about 1793, registered in Surry County on 25 January 1814: *Archer Anders, a very bright Mulattoe man, born of free parents, has long straight hair, very well made, about 21 years of age, and is 5'8-1/2" high*. He registered as Archer Andrews on 22 February 1830 [Hudgins, *Register of Free Negroes*, 51, 88].
   iii. Thomas[3], born about 1794, registered in Surry County on 25 January 1814: *a very bright Mulattoe man born of free parents...about 20 years of age, well made, and is 5'7-1/2" high* [Hudgins, *Register of Free Negroes*, 51]. He married Faithy **Walden**, daughter of Drewry **Walden**, 20 February 1815 Surry County bond, Nicholas **Scott** surety, 22 February marriage by Rev James Warren, Methodist.

ANGUS FAMILY

1. Isabell Angus, born say 1695, had a "mollatto" child before 4 June 1718 when John Cornick (her master?) agreed to pay the churchwardens of Princess Anne County 15 pounds out of Isabell's estate which was in his hands [Minutes 1717-28, 17]. She was probably the ancestor of
   i.   Abraham, head of a Petersburg Town household of 6 "other free" and 3 slaves in 1810 [VA:334b].

ARCHER FAMILY

1. John[1] Archer, born say 1647, was one of the first Africans freed in Northampton County, Virginia. He was in the List of Tithables: "John Archer negro" in Mrs. Grace Robins' household with her white servants in 1665, 1666, 1671, 1675, and 1677 [Orders 1664-74, fol.14, 29, fol. 114; 1674-79, 74, 190]. Perhaps he was the "Jno" who was listed among the slaves of Major

John Robins in the 1664 List of Tithables [Orders 1657-64, 198]. On 28 February 1697 he bound his son Thomas Archer as an apprentice in Northampton County court:

> *Thomas Archer the son of John Archer voluntarily and of his own free will and with his said Fathers consent was bound by this court to Major John Robins till twenty one years of age he being eleven years of age the 20 day of this Instant month of February* ...[Orders 1689-98, 461].

On 30 May 1699 William Ronan sued him in court for a ten-foot horse-mill wheel he had failed to deliver [Orders 1698-1710, 9]. John's son was

2   i. Thomas[1], born 20 February 1686/7.

2. Thomas[1] Archer, born 20 February 1686/7, was taxable in the Great Bridge District of Norfolk County, Virginia, more than forty years later in 1730:

1730	*Thomas Archey -1*
1731	*Thomas Archey & his son*
1732	*Thomas Archer & John, his son & Wm. Weaver -3*
1733	*Thomas Archer & John, his son & Wm. Weaver -3*
1734	*Duglis Grimes & Ann Archey, a mulato -2*
	Thos: Archer & his wife & John Archer -3
1735	*Thos. Archer, Son Jno., wife Mary & Daughter Ann*

[Wingo, *Norfolk County Tithables 1730-50*, 2, 29, 55, 78, 127, 159, 168, 172].

Thomas and his family moved to Bertie County, North Carolina, where he signed as witness to a February 1741 deed to William **Weaver**, a tithable in his 1735 Norfolk household [DB F:319]. On 1 May 1744 he was called Thomas Archer, labourer, when he bought 200 acres near Chinkapin Neck for "the sum of one whole years work already paid" [DB F:526], and on 6 July 1750 he paid 100 pounds for a further 340 acres adjoining Thomas Johnson [DB G:395]. This land was located in the southeast corner of present-day Hertford County near the Bertie County line. He was taxable as a "free Mulatto" with his wife Mary and children in the 1751 Bertie Tax List [CCR 190] and the lists from 1753 until 1759 when Hertford County was formed from Bertie [CR 10.702.1]. In 1758 he was taxable in the list of John Brickell with his wife Mary, but in 1759 he was taxable in the list of Henry Hill with his wife Nancy. Perhaps she was related to Thomas **Harrell** who was listed in his household that year.[22] We lose track of most of the family at this point because the early records for Hertford County were burned in a court house fire. However, Hertford County probate returns filed with the State Government have survived, and there we find a return for Thomas Archer in October 1761 [SS 883, Returns of Probates of Wills, by *NCGSJ* XIV:102]. The administratrix of his estate was Elizabeth Archer who was probably the wife of one of his three sons who were all married to an Elizabeth: Thomas[2], William, and Baker Archer. We can identify his children from the Norfolk and Bertie County tax lists:

3   i. ?Mary, born say 1712.
4   ii. John[2], born before 1715.
      iii. Ann, born before 1719 since she was taxable in Norfolk County in 1734. She was probably the Ann Archer who was taxable in the 1751 Bertie County household of Abel **Manly**, called his wife Ann in the 1757 tax list of William Wynns.

---

[22]Thomas **Herrill** was a "Mulatto" living in Northampton County, Virginia, on 30 April 1723 when he petitioned the county court [Packet no.5, Thomas Herrill's petition].

    iv.   Thomas² Jr., born say 1730, head of his own household of two tithes in 1754. He was taxable with his wife Eliza. in the 1759 list of John Brickell in the constable's list of Edward Williams. He was taxable in Hertford County on four persons in 1768, on five persons in 1770 [Fouts, *Tax Receipt Book*, 58], and on 200 acres, 5 cattle, and 2 horses in District 5 of Hertford County in 1779 [GA 30.1]. He was head of a Hertford County household of 5 "other free" in 1790 [NC:26] and 8 in 1800.

    v.   William, born say 1732, taxable in the 1757 list of John Brickell on himself, his wife Eliza, and James **Weaver**. He was head of a Hertford County household of 5 "other free" and a white woman in 1790 [NC:26] and 6 "other free" in 1800.

    vi.   Baker, born say 1734, taxable in 1751 in his father's Bertie County household [CCR 190]. He was married to Elizabeth by 1757 when he was taxed with her in John Brickell's list. He was taxable in Hertford on 3 persons in 1770 [Fouts, *Tax Receipt Book*,11] and taxable on a horse and 3 cattle in District 3 of Hertford County in 1779 [GA 30.1].

    vii.   Abel, born say 1735, taxable in 1751 in his father's Bertie County household [CCR 190]. He was taxable on a married poll in District 3 of Hertford County in 1779 [GA 30.1].

    viii.   ?Armstrong, born say 1736, listed in his own Bertie County household in the 1756 constable's list of Edward Williams and an insolvent taxpayer in 1757. He mustered with Captain Benjamin Lane's Edgecombe County Militia in the 1750's [Clark, *Colonial Soldiers of the South,* 674]. He was taxable in Norfolk County from 1782 to 1788 and from 1807 to 1811: taxable on his son Thomas in 1786 [PPTL, 1782-91, frames 392, 412, 447, 546, 587, 601, 621, 637, 675; 1791-1812, frames 641, 683, 737]. He was head of a Hertford County household of 4 "other free" in 1790 [NC:25], 3 "other free" and a white woman in 1800, 6 "other free" in 1810 [NC:105], and 9 "free colored" in 1820 [NC:186].

    ix.   Hancock, born say 1738, taxable in his father's household in the 1757 list of John Brickell. His father made a deed of gift to him of 340 acres in Bertie County on 29 March 1755 [DB H:157].

5   x.   Jacob², born say 1745.

3.   Mary Archer, born say 1712, was taxable in Norfolk County in 1735 in the district above Great Bridge (the same district as Thomas Archer) in John Pinkerton's household, perhaps the same Mary Archer who was counted in James Wilson, Jr.'s household that same year [Wingo, *Norfolk County Tithables 1730-50*, 167, 168]. She may have been identical to Mary Archer who was taxable on two persons in Hertford County in 1770 [Fouts, *Tax Receipt Book*, 67], and she may have been the mother of

6   i.   Jacob¹, born say 1732.

4.   John² Archer was born before 1715 since he was taxable in 1730 in Norfolk County, Virginia. On 6 March 1741/2 he paid 40 pounds for 200 acres in Bertie County near "Hot House" on Edward **Carter**'s line [DB F:352]. In 1751 he and his wife Frances were "free Mulatto" taxables in Bertie County [CCR 190], and in 1757 he was in the Bertie County List of John Brickell with his wife and two children, Ann and Jeremiah [CR 10.702.1, box 1]. He was still listed in the Bertie Tax Lists after 1759 when Hertford County was separated from Bertie, so his land was probably on the Bertie side of the Hertford County line. He and his wife Frances and their son Jeremiah were taxables in the 1775 list of Thomas Ward [CR 10.702.1]. He purchased 100 acres in Bertie County near Luson Swamp on 2 October 1777 [DB M:381] and was taxable on this land and 7 cattle in 1779 in Wynn's and King's district. The February 1787 Bertie court exempted him from paying poll tax, probably

because of his old age [Haun, *Bertie County Court Minutes*, V:635]. His children were

  i.   Ann, born circa 1744 since she was taxable in her father's household in the 1757 list of John Brickell.
 ii.   Jeremiah, born circa 1745 since he was taxable in his father's household in 1757.
iii.   ?Ezekiel, born say 1747, not taxed in Bertie County, taxable in Hertford County in District 5 on 3 cattle and 2 horses [GA 30.1]. He was head of a Hertford County household of 7 "other free" and 3 slaves in 1800.
 iv.   Zachariah, born say 1750, taxed in Jonathan Stanley's 1766 Bertie Tax List. In 1772 he was head of a household with Sarah Archer, possibly his wife, in the list of Thomas Ward adjacent to John Archer. Zachariah was one of the freeholders ordered to work on a road over Loosing Swamp, and he was a juror in the 22 September 1772 term of the Bertie County court [Haun, *Bertie County Court Minutes*, IV:15, 30]. By 1779 he was in Martin County with a tax assessed on 456 pounds in the Tax List filed with the State Government [GA 30.1]. He was granted 150 acres on the Cypress Swamp in Martin County on 1 March 1780 [Grant Book 36:40; N.C. Archives, SS call no. S.108.824, location 1-5]. In the 1787 State Census for Martin County he had 8 persons in his District 7 household. He was head of a Martin County household of 6 "other free" and a white woman in 1790 [NC:68], 1 "other free" and a white woman in 1800 [NC:383], and 2 "other free" in Edgecombe County in 1810 [NC:771]. By his 14 December 1817 Edgecombe County will, proved February 1818, he left land and his "mansion" to his wife Joanna and mentioned his brothers John and Jeremiah.
7 v.   John[3], born say 1753.
 vi.   ?Caleb, born after 1747 since he was not taxed in Bertie County in 1759. He was head of a Hertford County household of 5 "other free" in 1790 [NC:26] and 9 in 1800 in Captain Lewis' District. He was allowed 26 pounds pay for service in the Revolution from 10 November 1777 to 10 August 1778 [Haun, *Revolutionary Army Accounts*, vol.II, Book 2, 280]. On 7 June 1792 he appointed James Carraway of Cumberland County his attorney to receive his payment for services in the Continental line in 1778 and 1779 [*NCGSJ* VIII:98].

5. Jacob[2] Archer, born say 1745, was taxable in 1758 in his father's household in the Bertie County list of John Brickell, taxable on two tithes in Hertford County in 1770 [Fouts, *Tax Receipt Book*, 42] and taxable on 125 acres in District 2 of Hertford County in 1779 [GA 30.1, p.19]. He was head of a Hertford County household of 8 "other free" in 1790 [NC:26] and 7 in Captain Langston's district in 1800. He later moved to Sumner County, Tennessee, where his undated will was recorded about 1807. He left land in Hertford County, North Carolina, to his son Jacob and $40 each to his oldest son Josiah and second son Hezekiah. The will also mentioned his wife Sarah and other unnamed children [WB 1:121]. His three children named in his will were

  i.   Josiah, head of a Hertford County household of 2 "other free" in 1800.
 ii.   Hezekiah, head of a Hertford County household of 4 "other free" in 1800.
iii.   Jacob[3].

6. Jacob[1] Archer, born say 1730, was taxable in his own household in the Western Branch District of Norfolk County from 1750 to 1778 [Wingo, *Norfolk County Tithables, 1730-50*, 202; *1751-65*, 43, 61, 86, 105, 136, 168] and taxable on 5 cattle in Norfolk County in 1782 [PPTL, 1782-91, frame 394]. His children may have been

      i.   John, born say 1750, taxable in John Lelloe's Norfolk County household in 1766 and in the household of (his father?) Jacob Archer in 1771. His Norfolk County tax was charged to Lucy **Shoecraft** in 1770 [Wingo, *Norfolk County Tithables 1766-80*, 46, 132, 151, 263].

8   ii.   Evans, born about 1754.

9   iii. Thomas[3], born say 1758.

    iv.   Oliff, head of a Norfolk County household of 3 "other free" in 1810 [VA:794].

7.   John[3] Archer, born say 1753, was a "free Mulatto" taxable in the household of John Sholer, Jr., in an untitled Bertie tax list for 1765. In 1766 he was taxable in William Whealer's household, and in 1767 he was in Henry **Bunch**'s household in Jonathan Standley's list [CR 10.702.1]. By 1779 he was in Martin County where he was taxable as a married man [GA 30.1]. He may have been the John Archer who sold 50 acres in Halifax County, North Carolina, joining Reedy Branch on 16 December 1783 [DB 15:206]. He was head of a Halifax County household of 9 "other free" in 1790 [NC:63], and 5 "other free" and a white woman in 1810 [NC:3]. He was probably deceased by 4 December 1817 when his children (unnamed) were mentioned in the will of his brother Zachariah. Prudence Archy, eighty-eight years old in 1850, a "Mulatto" born in North Carolina and living with Polly **Murray** in the Wilson County, Tennessee census, may have been his widow or sister. The **Murray** family lived in both Martin and Halifax counties about 1790. His children were

      i.   ?Polly, charged Jesse **Brooks** in Halifax County court on 20 February 1800 with begetting her bastard child [Minutes 1799-1802, 96].

    ii.   ?Reddick, head of a Halifax County household of 3 "other free" in 1800 [NC:286] and 6 in Edgecombe County in 1810 [NC:726].

   iii. ?Jonathan, head of an Edgecombe County household of 4 "other free" in 1810 [NC:768].

    iv.   Norfleet, born about 1785, the sixteen-year-old son of John Archer ordered bound to Elijah Wilkins to be an apprentice blacksmith by the Halifax County court on 16 February 1801. He was head of a Halifax County household of 2 "other free" in 1810 [NC:4] and 5 "free colored" in 1820 [NC:138].

     v.   ?Penny, head of a Halifax County household of 2 "other free" in 1810 [NC:4] and 6 "free colored" in Hertford County in 1820 [NC:186].

    vi.   ?David, head of a Halifax County household of 4 "free colored" in 1820 [NC:138].

8.   Evans Archer, born about 1754, was taxable in Norfolk County, Virginia, in 1786 and 1787 [PPTL, 1782-91, frames 525, 558]. He was head of a Hertford County household of 3 "other free" in 1790 [NC:25], 3 in 1800, and 3 "free colored" in 1820 [NC:186]. He was sixty-nine years old on 27 September 1823 when he applied for a Revolutionary War pension in Hertford County court, stating that he enlisted in Portsmouth, Virginia, for eighteen months until January 1782. He lived with his daughter Margaret, a single woman with a four-year-old child. Martin **Bizzell** testified for him [M805-25, frame 0001]. In 1835 he was listed as a Revolutionary War pensioner in a report to Congress [Clark, *State Records of North Carolina*, XXII:571]. One of his children was

      i.   Margaret, counted in a list of "free Negroes and Mulattoes" in St. Brides Parish, Norfolk County, in 1814, a "free Negro" taxable on a free male tithable in 1816 [PPTL, 1813-24, frames 67, 167].

9.   Thomas[3] Archer, born say 1758, purchased 25 acres at the head of the Western Branch of the Elizabeth River in Norfolk County for 50 pounds on 10 May 1780 [DB 30:64]. He was taxable in Norfolk County in 1776 [Wingo,

Norfolk County Tithables 1766-80, 203], head of a household of 7 persons in 1785 [VA:93], taxable on a horse in Portsmouth and Elizabeth River Parishes from 1783 to 1817: taxable on 2 free males in 1791, 1792, and 1794, a planter on Western Branch in 1801 when he was counted in a list of "free Negroes and Mulattoes," called a "M"(ulatto) in 1802 and 1803, charged with Thomas Archer, Jr.'s tithe in 1805, a "B.M" (Black Man) taxable on a horse and 6 cattle in Portsmouth from 1815 to 1817 [PPTL, 1782-1791, frames 430, 466, 525, 637; 1791-1812, frames 17, 77, 383, 426, 554, 641, 720; 1813-24, frames 94, 121, 271]. He was head of a Norfolk County household of 6 "other free" in 1810 [VA:819]. Perhaps his wife was Eunice Archer, born about 1756, who registered in Norfolk County on 20 August 1810: *4 feet 11 Inc., 54 Years, of age Yellow Complexion* [A Register of Free Negros & Mulattos in the County of Norfolk, #32]. He sold 4 acres at the head of Western Branch to Jesse **Weaver** on 5 March 1817, and on 20 October 1812 he made a Norfolk County deed of gift of all his personal estate to his daughter Elizabeth **Weaver** [DB 47:163; 48:85]. His children were

    i.   Elizabeth, married **Weaver**.
    ii.   ?Sally **Weaver**, sold for $200 her inheritance from (her father?) Thomas Archer, consisting of a tract of land at the head of the Western Branch adjoining Adam **Perkins**, by deed proved in Norfolk County in 1819 [DB 48:107-8].

Another member of the Archer family was
10   i.   Thomas[4], born before 1776.

10. Thomas[4] Archer, born before 1776, was head of an Orange County, North Carolina household of 5 "free colored" in 1820 [NC:352]. He was identified as a Revolutionary War soldier and father of Nancy, wife of Elias **Roberts**, in Elias' Chatham County free papers. The papers stated that Thomas **Archie** had resided in Chatham County for twenty-three years but was living in Orange County, North Carolina, when the papers were issued on 10 February 1823 [Orange County, Indiana DB D:432]. He was the father of

    i.   ?Jesse[1], married Pattie **Heathcock** (**Haithcock**), 24 October 1807 Orange County bond, Holiday **Heathcock** bondsman. He was head of an Orange County household of 5 "free colored" in 1820 [Book A, 420].
    ii. ?Moses, married Polley **Roberts**, 23 April 1813 Orange County bond, Mathias **Milton** & Moses **Bass** bondsmen. Moses Archie was head of a Chatham County household of 4 "other free" in 1820 [NC:192].
    iii. ?Sally, married Benjamin **Roberts**, 30 June 1817 Orange County bond, Jesse Archer bondsman.
    iv. Nancy, wife of Elias **Roberts**.

Southampton County
1. Luke Archer, born say 1750, was a "Negro" taxable in St. Luke's Parish, Southampton County, on 2 slaves above 16, 2 slaves 12-16 and 2 horses in 1788, taxable on a slave and 3 horses in 1789, a slave and a horse in 1790, 2 free male tithables in 1792, taxable on 2 slaves over the age of 16 in 1793, taxable (called Luke **Artis**) on a horse in 1794, taxable on a slave aged 12-16 in 1797, 2 slaves over 16 in 1798, and taxable on his own tithe and a horse from 1799 to 1804 [PPTL 1782-92, frames 654, 704, 754, 811, 868; 1792-1806, frames 45, 72, 258, 308, 369, 404, 505, 542, 612, 681, 796, 833]. He married Honour **Artis**, daughter of Lewis **Artis**, 26 January 1792 Southampton County bond. He registered in Southampton County on 1 June 1802: *age 55, Mulatto, 5 feet 8-1/4 inches, freed by Joshua Vick Southampton County deed* [Register of Free Negroes 1794-1832, no. 228]. (His widow) Hannah Archer was taxable on a horse in 1805 and 1806. On 21 April 1807 the Southampton County court summoned the administrators of his estate George **Artis** and wife

Hannah to give supplemental security for the administration of the estate [Minutes 1804-7, 276]. He may have been the father of

    i.   Eley, born about 1790, registered in Southampton County on 17 February 1827: *age 37, very bright complected, 5 feet 11-1/2 inches, free born* [Register of Free Negroes 1794-1832, no. 1605]. He was a "f.n." taxable in the St. Luke's Parish, Southampton County household of Thomas Barnes in 1817 [PPTL 1807-21, frame 571].

2   ii. Lemuel[1], born say 1795.

    iii. Reuben, born about 1799, registered in Southampton County on 15 March 1827: *age 28, rather light complection, 5 feet 11 inches, free born* [Register of Free Negroes 1794-1832, no. 1612]. He was a "f.n." taxable in Evans Pope's St. Luke's Parish, Southampton County household in 1812 [PPTL 1807-21, frame 297].

    iv. Burwell, born about 1802, registered in Southampton County on 12 April 1827: *age 25, light complected, 5 feet 11 1/4 inches, free born* [Register of Free Negroes 1794-1832, no. 1633].

    v. Rebecca, born about 1804, registered in Southampton County on 15 March 1827: *age 23, rather light complection, 5 feet 8 inches, free born* [Register of Free Negroes 1794-1832, no. 1613].

2.   Lemuel[1] Archer, born say 1795, was a "f.n." taxable in St. Luke's Parish, Southampton County, in Reuben **Haithcock**'s household in 1814, in the household of Bryant Davis in 1817 [PPTL 1807-21, frames 293, 572] and head of a Northampton County, North Carolina household of 4 "free colored" in 1820 [NC:212]. He and his wife Dolly and their six children obtained free papers in Northampton County on 23 March 1831 and recorded them on 22 October 1838 in Logan County, Ohio [Turpin, *Register of Black, Mulatto, and Poor Persons*, 11]. Dolly (Dorothy) was devised land in Logan County, Ohio, by the 31 July 1835 Northampton County will of her father Nathaniel **Newsom** [WB 4:137]. Nathaniel **Newsom** owned land on the Roanoke River in Northampton County adjoining Halifax County [Northampton County DB 10:463, 479; WB 2:297]. Lemuel and Dorothy's children were

    i.   Jesse[2], born about 1815, counted in the 1860 Logan County census in Jefferson Township, Zanesfield Post Office, with 7 children born in Ohio [Census, p.135].

    ii. Tabitha.

    iii. Anny.

    iv. Eady.

    v. Bedfort.

    vi. Lemuel[2].

ARMFIELD FAMILY

1.   Daniel[1] Armfield, born say 1715, was the "Mullatto" servant of Robert Stubblefield on 21 February 1738 when his master brought him before the Essex County court for absenting himself from his service for one year and fifteen days [Orders 1736-8, 217]. He was in York County by 20 June 1743 when he sued Ambrose Jackson for debt. The parties reached agreement before the case came to trial. And he sued Edward Fuller for trespass, assault and battery on 17 February 1745/6. The court found in Daniel's favor and awarded him 40 shillings damages after hearing testimony from Joseph Lark who travelled twenty-one miles to testify and Pearson Picket who travelled twenty-five miles [W&I 19:197, 417, 423, 439]. He, a "free negro," and his wife Elizabeth registered the birth of their son Matthew in Bruton Parish, James City County, in 1746 [Bruton Parish Register, 6]. On 19 January 1746/7 the court presented him for not listing his wife as a tithable [W&I 19:486]. Peter **Gillett**'s suit against him was dismissed in York County court on 22 September 1747 because both parties were in agreement. On 15 August 1748

he sued the executors of John Crawley for debt, but the case was dismissed at his expense. Peter **Gillett** was an evidence against him. On 20 February he brought a second suit against Crawley's executors for a debt due by account, and the court ruled against him again. He sued Peter **Gillett** for trespass, assault and battery on 10 September 1760, and the court ordered Peter to pay him 6 pence. Daniel's witnesses were Thomas Blassingame, William Lyon, and David **Bartley**. He sued William Lyon, Jr., for trespass, assault and battery on 19 December 1763 and was awarded 40 shillings. On 17 December 1764 the court presented him for not listing his daughters Betty and Martha as tithables [Judgments & Orders 1746-52, 39, 123, 158-9, 177, 187; 1759-63, 184, 222, 321; 1763-5, 126, 171, 362]. Daniel and Elizabeth were the parents of

> i. Martha, born say 1740, sued by Anne **Gwinn** and her "next friend" Jane **Savy** (**Savoy**) in York County for trespass, assault and battery on 16 May 1763. She was found not guilty [Judgments & Orders 1763-5, 14, 37]. She was called "a free mulatto" when the birth of her bastard child William **Allways** was recorded in Bruton Parish in 1765. She and Israel **Allways** (**Alvis**), "free Mulattas," were married by 13 March 1767 when their daughter Elizabeth **Allways** was born [Bruton Parish Register, 29, 31].

2   ii. Elizabeth, born say 1742.

> iii. Matthew[1], born 26 February 1746.
>
> iv. ?Mary, taxable in the upper district of York County on a free tithable, a horse and 4 cattle in 1783 [PPTL, 1782-1841, frame 72].

2. Elizabeth Armfield, born say 1742, was sued for trespass, assault and battery in York County by Anne **Gwinn** and her "next friend" Jane **Savy** (**Savoy**) on 16 May 1763. She was found guilty and ordered to pay 20 shillings [Judgments & Orders 1763-5, 14, 37]. She was called "a free mulatto" when she registered the birth of her son James in Bruton Parish in 1766. She was taxable on her property in York County from 1782 to 1803: on 13 cattle in 1782, on 1-2 slaves from 1792 to 1797, on 2 free tithables in 1802, called Betty **Lyons** in 1790, 1791 and 1793 [PPTL, 1782-41, frames 69, 72, 106, 138, 147, 163, 173, 180, 193, 199, 209, 218, 227, 274, 284]. She was head of a York County household of 7 "other free" in 1810 [VA:870]. Her children were

> i. ?Milly, born say 1760, a "Poor orphan" ordered bound out by the churchwardens of Bruton Parish on 19 May 1760 [Judgments & Orders 1759-63, 143].
>
> ii. James, born 16 March 1766, "Bastard son of Elizabeth Armfield," called James **Lyons** when he was taxable in York County in 1788 [PPTL, 1782-1841, frame 141].
>
> iii. Daniel[2], born 15 February 1768, baptized 3 April [Bruton Parish Register, 27, 32, 35], called Daniel **Lyons** when he was taxable in York County from 1788 to 1814, taxable on a slave from 1795 onwards [PPTL, 1782-1841, frames 141, 152, 163, 211, 221, 230, 238, 245, 256, 266, 277, 287, 297, 307, 328, 391, 408].

3   iv. ?Matthew[2], born about 1779.

> v. ?Warren, born say 1781, taxable in York County in 1803 and 1805 [PPTL, 1782-1841, 284, 304].
>
> vi. John **Lyons**, born 22 January 1783, baptized 26 March 1783, son of Betty Armfield.
>
> vii. ?William **Lyons**, born about 1787, registered in York County on 16 December 1822: *a bright Mulatto about 35 years of age...has short hair...born free.* When William renewed his registration nine years later on 28 September 1831, the clerk added the notation: *since the above has become bald, wears whiskers, grey Beard & much the appearance of an Indian* [Free Negro Register, 1798-1831, no. 194].

     viii. ?Nancy **Lyons**, head of a Richmond City household of 1 "other free" in 1810 [VA:340].

3. Matthew² Armfield, born about 1779, was taxable on his own tithe in 1803 and taxable on a slave and a horse in 1805 [PPTL 1782-1841, frames 284, 304, 325, 362, 384, 402]. He registered as a "free Negro" in York County on 16 December 1822: *about 43 years old 5 feet 7-1/4 Inches high* [York County Register, no.189]. His wife Nancy Armfield born about 1787, registered on 19 September 1831: *wife of Matt a person of light complexion about 43 or 44 years of age, 5 feet 1-1/2 inches high black eyes long thin face, high cheek bones*. He was head of a York County household of 5 "other free" in 1810 [VA:870]. He was the father of

     i. Betsy, born about 1808, registered in York County on 19 September 1831: *daughter of Matt, light complexion, 23 years of age, four feet 9 inches high, full face, black eyes, fine long black hair...Dutch made & pouting lips* [York County Free Negroes Register, 1831-50, nos. 283-4].

ARMSTRONG FAMILY

1. Frances Armstrong, born say 1735, was probably the mother of Pegg Armstrong (no age or race mentioned) who was bound apprentice to William McPhersons in Norfolk County on 17 April 1760 [Orders 1759-63, 25]. She was living in the adjoining county of Henrico on 3 May 1762 and 2 June 1766 when the court ordered her "Mulatto" children: Thomas, Adam, Rachel, Judith, and Tobias bound out by the churchwardens of Henrico Parish [Orders 1755-62, 585; 1763-67, 577]. In July 1777 she was living in the adjoining county of Goochland when her son Bob Armstrong, "a Mulatto boy," was ordered bound out by the churchwardens of St. James Northam Parish [Orders 1771-78, 498]. Her children were

     i. ?Margaret/ Pegg, born say 1752, bound apprentice in Norfolk County on 17 April 1760 [Orders 1759-63, 25].

     ii. Thomas, born say 1753, a "mulatto" who ran away from John Jude of Cumberland County, Virginia, according to the 13 October 1768 issue of the *Virginia Gazette* (Rind).

     iii. Adam, born say 1755, a Revolutionary War soldier from Henrico County [Jackson, *Virginia Negro Soldiers*, 29]. He married Mary **Scott**, 18 November 1796 Henrico County bond, Benjamin **Scott** security. He was taxable in the lower district of Henrico County from 1787 to 1809 [PPTL 1782-1814, frames 119, 137, 508, 549, 571].

     iv. Rachel, born say 1757, head of a Campbell County household of 8 "other free" in 1810 [VA:848].

     v. Judith¹, born say 1759.

     vi. Tobias, born say 1761.

     vii. ?Frank, a "mulattoe" orphan bound by the churchwardens of Southam Parish to John Dean by order of the Cumberland County court on 26 June 1777 [Orders 1774-8, 405]. He was a "Mulatto" taxable in Chesterfield County in 1791 [PPTL, 1786-1811, frames 98].

     viii. Robert, born say 1777, bound apprentice in Goochland County in July 1777 [Orders 1771-78, 498]. He was a "FN" taxable in the northern district of Campbell County from 1792 to 1798 [PPTL, 1785-1814, frames 225, 299, 328, 385, 417]. He was living in Lynchburg on 16 February 1799 when he who received a certificate from George Jude of Campbell County stating that he had served his time from childhood to the age of twenty-one with trust and fidelity at which time he gave him his freedom [Headley, *18th Century Newspapers*, 10]. He was a "Mᵒ" taxable in Powhatan County from 1804 to 1810 [PPTL, 1787-1825, frames 275, 290, 337, 377].

ix. ?William, born about 1778, a "M°" taxable in Powhatan County from 1800 to 1815, listed with 2 "free negroes & mulattoes over the age of 16" in 1813 [PPTL, 1787-1825, frames 203, 220, 252, 275, 290, 337, 377, 417, 435, 476]. He married Nancy **Coy**, twenty-one years of age, "Free Negroes," 13 July 1809 Powhatan County bond, Charles **Coy** surety. He registered in Powhatan County on 19 December 1822: *Age: 44; Color: Yellow; Stature: 5'9-1/2"; Born Free* [Register of Free Negroes, no. 83].

x. James, a "M°" taxable in Powhatan County in 1804 and 1805 [PPTL, 1787-1825, frames 275, 290].

2. Milly Armstrong, born about 1753, registered as a "Free Negro" in Campbell County on 9 August 1803: *5 Feet 1-1/2 Inches; Years of Age: 50; Colour: black; born free in Hanover County* [A Register of Free Negroes and Mulattoes, 3]. She may have been the mother of

3   i. Benjamin, born say 1769.

ii. William, a "free Negro" counted in Campbell County with a female over the age of sixteen in his household [PPTL 1785-1814, frame 892].

iii. Lucy, born say 1780, head of a Richmond City household of 4 "other free" in 1810 [VA:339].

iv. Judith[2], born about 1780, registered as a "Free Negro" in Campbell County on 20 January 1802: *Age: 22; 5 Feet 6 Inches; Colour: black; born free.*

v. Sally, born about 1785, registered in Campbell County on 9 August 1803: *5 feet 5 Inches, Age: 18; Colour: Yellowish; born free in Hanover County* [A Register of Free Negroes and Mulattoes, 2].

3. Benjamin Armstrong, born say 1769, was a "F.N." taxable in Campbell County from 1804 to 1814: taxable on 2 males in 1804 and 1811, listed with a woman over the age of sixteen in 1813 [PPTL, 1785-1814, frames 592, 691, 892, 922] and head of a Campbell County household of 10 "other free" in 1810 [VA:880]. He was the father of

i. Fanny, born say 1790, daughter of Benjamin Armstrong, married Peter **Moss**, 27 December 1809 Campbell County bond, Peter **Moss** and Benjamin Armstrong bondsmen.

ii. ?David, a "F.N." taxable in Campbell County in 1807 [PPTL, 1785-1814, frame 691].

ARNOLD FAMILY

1. Mary Arnold, born say 1720, was living in Carteret County, North Carolina, on 4 June 1751 when the county court ordered her "Mulatto" daughter Margaret bound to Jabez Weeks [Minutes 1747-64, fol. 18a]. Her children were

2   i. ?Moses, born say 1740.

ii. Margaret, born about 1744, seven years old when she was bound apprentice on 4 June 1751.

2. Moses Arnold, born say 1740, and his wife Mary were taxables in the Western District of Norfolk County, Virginia, from 1761 to 1768, and he was a "free Mulatto" taxable in the district on the south side of Tanners Creek until 1780 [Wingo, *Norfolk County Tithables 1751-65*, 165, 211; *1766-80*, 37, 64, 110, 163, 166, 271]. He was taxable in Norfolk County from 1783 to 1791: taxable on a slave under the age of sixteen named Bess in 1783; called a "free mulato" in 1788 [PPTL, 1782-91, frames 410, 558, 621, 637, 675; 1791-1812, frame 17]. He may have been the father of

3   i. Robert, born say 1770.

3. Robert Arnold, born say 1770, was a "free Negro" taxable in St. Ann's Parish, Albemarle County, in 1789 and from 1798 to 1801 [PPTL, 1782-1799, frames 194, 528, 567; 1800-1813, frames 3, 45]. He was head of a Nelson County household of 5 "other free" in 1810 [VA:676]. His wife Doratha Arnold, born about 1787, registered as a "free Negro" in Amherst County on 8 November 1843: *wife of Robert Arnold, a bright mulatto - about 56 years of age - 5 feet 6 Inches high - Born free.* They were the parents of

    i.   Jonathan, registered in Amherst County on 8 November 1843: *born on the 12th of March 1804...a brown mulatto...son of Robert & Doshia Arnold.*
    ii. Drury, registered in Amherst Cocunty on 8 November 1843: *born 15th August 1809...dark mulatto...son of Robert & Doshia Arnold.*
    iii. Elizabeth, daughter of Robert Arnold, married Edward **Winters** in Amherst County in 1839. Elizabeth registered in Amherst County on 15 November 1843: *wife of Edward Winters bright mulatto...24 years old...born free.*
    iv. ?Elvira Ann, married Thomas **Winters** in Amherst County in 1833. Elvira registered in Amherst County on 18 March 1844: *wife of Thomas Winters, free woman of colour 29 years old bright mulatto, born free* [McLeroy, *Strangers in their Midst*, 62, 64, 65, 67, 112].

Another member of the Arnold family was

    i.   Joseph, a "Mulatto" taxable in King William County in 1813 [PPTL 1812-50].

ARTIS FAMILY

1. Hester[1] (Easter) Artis, alias **Anderson**, born say 1687, was one of the slaves freed by the 29 October 1712 will of John Fulcher of Norfolk County, Virginia [WB 9:223]. The August 1733 Bertie County court described her as "a free Negroe woman living in Virga." when her attorney, Richard Washington, asked the court to bind "her Son, a Negroe boy named Robin Artis," as an apprentice. The court ordered that Robin,

    > *adjudged by the court to be 12 years,...be bound to John Hodgson Gent. of this Precinct and the Court...knowing this sd boy's father to be a slave...*[Haun, *Bertie County Court Minutes*, I:93].

Robin was probably named for Robin **Richards**, another slave that Fulcher freed with the **Andersons**. Hester's children were

    i.   Robin, born about 1721.
2   ii. ?John[1], born say 1723.
3   iii. ?Abraham[1], born say 1724.
4   iv. ?Martha[1], born say 1731.
5   v.   ?Lewis[1], born say 1733.
    vi. ?Edward[1], born say 1736, sued Joseph Newsom in Southampton County on 10 March 1757 for trespass, assault and battery. The court permitted Edward a continuance to take the deposition of William Shuffle, and on 12 August that year Newsom was found guilty and ordered to pay Edward 5 shillings [Orders 1754-9, 342, 363, 377-8].

2. John[1] Artis, born say 1723, sold a horse and household goods to Albridgton Jones in Isle of Wight County on 12 August 1746 [DB 7:448]. He was granted land in Johnston County, North Carolina, on 20 June 1749 and sold this land on 18 October 1756 [Haun, *Johnston County Deed Book*, II:137]. He was called a "negro" in Southampton County on 12 October 1752 when he asked the court to add his wife Sarah to the list of tithables. He was sued in Southampton County court by James Jordan Scott on 8 January 1756 and by

John Pope on 14 July 1757, but the case was dismissed when the parties agreed. On 13 October 1758 Temble and Fisher sued him for a debt of 10 pounds which he failed to pay, so the sheriff sold his effects: a tar kiln, heap of lightwood, three sows, thirteen shoats, gourds, three bushels of corn, a cider hogshead, two stools, a washing tub, table, shoe lasts, a couch frame, three benches, a field of growing corn, potatoes, peas, and cotton. He was sued for a debt of 2 pounds, 6 shillings by Albridgton Jones on 13 November 1760. Since he had left the county, the sheriff attached part of his estate which was in the hands of Matthew Charles. On 8 February 1776 the court ordered the churchwardens of St. Luke's Parish to bind out his "poor children" Martha, Joyce, Mildred, Milbra, Hester, Tempe, and Hardy H. [Orders 1749-54, 169, 260, 283; 1754-9, 361, 465, 484; 1759-63, 75; 1772-7, 428; Minutes 1775-8]. He was the father of

<table>
<tr><td>6</td><td>i.</td><td>?John², Jr., born say 1744.</td></tr>
<tr><td>7</td><td>ii.</td><td>?Archibald, born say 1753.</td></tr>
<tr><td></td><td>iii.</td><td>?Lauer, born say 1755, head of an Edgecombe County, North Carolina household of 5 "other free" in 1790 [NC:54].</td></tr>
<tr><td></td><td>iv.</td><td>?William¹, born say 1745, died before 11 June 1772 when the inventory of his estate was returned to Southampton County court [Orders 1772-7, 8].</td></tr>
<tr><td></td><td>v.</td><td>Martha², born about 1770, called Patsy Artis when she registered in Southampton County on 12 June 1794: about 28 years old, a free woman born of free parents in Southampton, black. She was a plaintiff in a suit against a member of the Bryant family which abated in Southampton County court on 8 January 1795 [Minutes 1793-9, 137]. She may have been the Patty Artis who married Robert Clements, 22 January 1801 Southampton County bond, 23 January marriage. Patt Clements was head of a Southampton County household of 5 "other free" in 1810 [VA:87]. She was about 40 years old when she registered in Southampton County on 30 July 1810: Martha Clements, age 40, Blk., 5 feet 5-3/4 inches, free born [Register of Free Negroes 1794-1832, nos. 28, 729].</td></tr>
<tr><td></td><td>vi.</td><td>Joyce.</td></tr>
<tr><td></td><td>vii.</td><td>Mildred¹, born say 1772, mother of James Artis who was ordered bound out in Southampton County on 10 July 1794. Her suit against a member of the Bryant family abated on 8 January 1795 [Minutes 1793-9, 100, 137]. James was taxable in St. Luke's Parish, Southampton County, in 1809 and 1810 [PPTL 1807-21, frames 66, 163].</td></tr>
<tr><td>8</td><td>viii.</td><td>Milbry, born about 1765.</td></tr>
<tr><td></td><td>ix.</td><td>Hester/ Esther, married Simon Vick, 8 March 1792 Southampton County bond, Giles Vick surety. Simon was head of a Southampton County household of 10 "other free" in 1810 [VA:54].</td></tr>
<tr><td>9</td><td>x.</td><td>Tempy¹, born say 1768.</td></tr>
<tr><td></td><td>xi.</td><td>Hardy, born say 1770, taxable in St. Luke's Parish, Southampton County, from 1796 to 1798 [PPTL 1792-1806, frames 181, 259, 309]. He married Elizabeth Howard, 25 June 1799 Granville County, North Carolina bond, and was head of a Warrenton, Warren County, North Carolina household of 5 "other free" in 1800 [NC:785].</td></tr>
</table>

3. Abraham¹ Artis, born say 1724, purchased 50 acres in Nottoway Parish, Isle of Wight County, adjoining John Vick on 24 March 1745 [DB 7:274]. On 13 June 1754 he was one of fourteen heads of household who were sued in Southampton County court for failing to pay the discriminatory tax on free

African American and Indian women.[23] He pled not guilty at first but withdrew his plea and confessed when Francis **Locust**, James **Brooks**, James **Brooks**, Jr., John **Byrd** and John **Byrd**, Jr., were found guilty. He was fined 500 pounds of tobacco [Orders 1749-54, 501, 512; 1754-9, 25, 38]. Richard Vick sued him for a debt on 14 March 1755, but the case was dismissed when they agreed, and the court awarded him 3 pounds, 8 shillings for a debt due to him by account from Vick [Orders 1754-9, 64, 67]. He died before 18 April 1772 when his Southampton County estate was appraised [WB 2:492]. He may have been the ancestor of

10 i. Lydia, born say 1748.

  ii. Edward[2], born say 1750, fined 500 pounds of tobacco on 10 January 1771 for not listing himself as a tithable [Orders 1768-72, 345]. He was called Ned Artis in 1772 when he was paid 12 shillings by the estate of Abram Artis, deceased [WB 3:51-2]. He was taxable in St. Luke's Parish, Southampton County, on 2 slaves and a horse in 1782 and taxèd on his own tithe from 1783 to 1809, called a "free Negro" from 1804 to 1806 [PPTL 1782-92, frames 507, 543, 555, 584, 613, 632, 654, 704, 754, 868, 891; 1792-1806, frames 72, 154, 180, 308, 404, 505, 542, 612, 795, 833; 1807-21, frames 44, 66]. He was head of a Southampton County household of 5 "other free" in 1810 [VA:54].

11 iii. Absolem[1], born say 1755.

12 iv. Ann[1], born say 1760.

13 v. George[1], born say 1760.

  vi. John[3], born say 1761, taxable in Southampton County from 1782 to 1802: his tax charged to James Magget in 1787; taxable in 1789 and 1790; taxable on his own tithe and 16-21 year-old Simon **Vick** in 1796; called John Artis, Sr., from 1799 to 1801 [PPTL 1782-92, frames 508, 513; 704; 1792-1806, frames 369, 404, 508, 513, 740, 754]. He married Pherbe **Caton**, 10 September 1800 Southampton County bond, Nathan Worrell surety.

  vii. Burwell, born say 1762, a free man of color from Southampton County who was listed in the size roll of troops who enlisted at Chesterfield Court House [The Chesterfield Supplement cited by NSDAR, *African American Patriots*, 147; Jackson, *Virginia Negro Soldiers*, 29]. He married Angey **Hurst**, 21 August 1783 Southampton County marriage [Minister's Returns, 633]. He was taxable in Southampton County from 1785 to 1792, taxable in John Jackson's household in 1789 [PPTL 1782-92, frames 555, 584, 632, 704, 713, 754, 811, 868].

  viii. Miriam[1], born about 1770, married Reuben **Haithcock**, 10 February 1791 Southampton County bond, Charles Birdsong security, 17 February marriage. She registered in Southampton County on 31 July 1810: *Miriam Hathcock, age 40, Dark Mulatto, 5 feet 3-1/2 inches, free born* [Register of Free Negroes 1794-1832, no. 772].

  ix. Ainge, married Sampson **Cary**, 5 March 1796 Southampton County bond, Micajah **Johnson** surety.

  x. John[4], born about 1775, taxable in Southampton County in 1792 and from 1798 to 1820: taxable with Joseph Artis in Joel Newsum's household in 1792; called John Artis, Jr., from 1798 to 1804 [PPTL, 1782-1792, frame 881; 1792-1806, frames 309, 506, 513, 543, 612, 681, 796; 1807-11, frames 44, 66, 163, 184]. He married Blytha **Powell**, 15 February 1802 Southampton County bond, John Pope surety, Evans Pope witness. He registered in Southampton County on 1 August 1810: *age 35, Blk., 5 feet 10 inches, free born*. Tabitha, who

---

[23]The other householders were John **Porteus**, John **Demery**, Isaac **Young**, Thomas **Wilkins**, Francis **Locust**, James **Brooks**, Jr. and Sr., John **Byrd**, Jr. and Sr., Lewis **Artis**, William **Brooks**, Ann **Brooks**, and William **Tabor**.

was apparently his wife, registered the same day: *age 35, Blk., 5 feet 1-1/2 inches, free born* [Register of Free Negroes 1794-1832, nos. 800, 801]. He was head of a Southampton County household of 8 "other free" in 1810 [VA:58]. He and his wife Tabitha were living on Thomas Newsum's land in 1812; he and his unnamed wife and daughter Lucy were living on Newsum's land in 1813; they were taxable on a horse in 1814; his wife was called Faithy when they were planters living on Thomas Newsum's land in 1815; he was taxable with son Cordy in 1820 [PPTL [PPTL, 1807-21, frames 283, 311, 411, 435, 780]. Faith, born about 1794, registered in Southampton County on 13 July 1821: *age 27, rather of a bright complection, 4 feet 10 1/2 inches, free born.* Cordall registered in Southampton County on 8 August 1821: *age 22, rather bright complection, 5 feet 3-1/4 inches, Cert. by Jno. Pope free born* [Register of Free Negroes 1794-1832, nos. 1282, 1286].

xi. Joseph, born about 1782, registered in Southampton County on 16 August 1810: *age 28, Blk., 5 feet 5-1/2 inches, free born* and registered again on 16 June 1831. His wife was apparently identical to Ona Artis who registered on 7 August 1810: *age 27, Mulatto, 5 feet 3 inches, free born* and registered again on 16 June 1831: *age 48, yellow, 5 feet 3 inches, free born, see no. 837* [Register of Free Negroes 1794-1832, nos. 833, 837, 1846, 1847]. Joseph was head of a Southampton County household of 5 "other free" in 1810 [VA:76]. He was taxable in St. Luke's Parish, Southampton County, from 1801 to 1804; taxable in the household of Joseph Barnes in 1805; a hatter living with his wife Oney on Henry Person's land in 1813; listed with wife Onny in 1815; on Aggy **Kersey**'s land in 1817 [PPTL 1792-1806, frames 506, 543, 612, 681, 796, 833; 1807-21, frames 44, 163, 184, 311, 411, 435, 571].

4. Martha[1]/ Pat Artis, born say 1731, was living in Southampton County on 13 October 1758 when the court ordered the churchwardens to bind out her children Lucretia, Elvin and Alderman [Orders 1754-9, 463]. She was the mother of

    i. Lucretia, born say 1753.
    ii. Elvin, born say 1755.
    iii. Alderman, born say 1757.
14 iv. ?Priscilla, born about 1761.

5. Lewis[1] Artist, born say 1733, was sued in Southampton County court on 14 December 1752 by Thomas Jarrell. The court awarded Jarrell 20 shillings according to the act of assembly in that case provided. On 13 June 1754 he was one of fourteen heads of household who were sued in Southampton County court for failing to pay the discriminatory tax on free African American and Indian women [Orders 1749-54, 299, 321-2, 354, 501, 512; 1754-9, 25, 38]. He sued William Lane in court on 9 July 1761, and the court ordered a commission to take the deposition of several witnesses in Carolina. The suit was decided in Artis' favor when Lane failed to appear [Orders 1759-63, 116, 138, 145]. He was listed in the undated colonial Northampton County, North Carolina Muster Roll of Captain James Fason's Company [Mil. T.R. 1-3]. He was sued for debt in Southampton County by James Jordan Scott on 12 September 1771 and was added to William Blunt's list of tithables on 12 September 1776. He was taxable in Southampton County on 2 horses and 5 cattle in 1782, 2 horses and 8 cattle in 1783 and taxable in St. Luke's Parish until 1793 when his name was crossed off the list of tithables [PPTL 1782-92, 508, 513, 555, 584, 868; 1792-1806, frame 45]. His suit for debt against William Vicks was submitted for arbitration on 9 July 1784. The court awarded him an attachment against Richard **Demery**'s property on 9 December 1784 to satisfy a debt of 4,000 pounds of tobacco. He and Abraham Artis were

sued for a debt of 4 pounds on 11 May 1787 [Orders 1768-72, 449; 1772-7, 445; 1778-84, 464; 1784-9, 7, 272]. He was tithable in Southampton County in 1782. His children were

15 i. ?Abraham[2], born say 1765.

 ii. ?Mary, a Black person 12-50 years old living alone in Dupree's District of Northampton County for the 1786 State Census. The parish wardens of St. George Parish, Northampton County, paid Peter **Steward** for keeping her from 1 January to 1 April 1800 [CR 71.927.1].

 iii. Honour, born say 1773, "daughter of Lewis Artis," married Luke **Archer**, 26 January 1792 Southampton County bond, Newit Vick surety, 27 January marriage. Luke registered in Southampton County on 1 June 1802: *age 55, Mulatto, 5 feet 8-1/4 inches high, emancipated by Joshua Vick, So. deed* [Register of Free Negroes 1794-1832, no. 228]. His widow Hannah **Archer** was taxable in Southampton County on a horse in 1805 and 1806 [PPTL 1792-1806, frame 796]. On 21 April 1807 the Southampton County court summoned George Artis and wife Hannah, the administrators of Luke **Archer**'s estate, to give supplemental security for the administration of the estate [Minutes 1804-7, 276]. Hannah Artis registered in Southampton County on 30 July 1810: *age 35, Blk., 5 feet 6 inches, free born* [Register of Free Negroes 1794-1819, no. 721].

 iv. ?Benjamin, born about 1783, registered in Petersburg on 13 October 1806: *a brown free Negro man, five feet six inches high, twenty three years old, born free & raised in Northampton County* [Register of Free Negroes 1794-1819, no. 398]. He may have been the Benjamin Artis who complained to the Southampton County court against his master John Day on 17 August 1801 [Minutes 1799-1803, 207].

6. John[2] Artis Jr., born say 1744, purchased land in Edgecombe County on the south side of Toisnot Swamp near Mill Branch on 10 June 1765 [DB C:369]. Perhaps this was the John Artis who enlisted in 1781 in Abraham Shepard's Tenth Regiment, Colonel Hall's Company. He and John Godwin were imprisoned for robbery in Halifax on 15 August 1781. He left the service on 1 November 1782 [Clark, *State Records of North Carolina*, 17:190, 16:1007, 15:609; *N.C. Historical & Genealogical Register*, II:128]. On 21 December 1782 he sold his Edgecombe County land [DB E:256]. He and Lauer Artis were probably the ancestors of

 i. Lewis[2], born before 1776, head of an Edgecombe County household of 6 "other free" in 1810 [NC:731] and 4 "free colored" in 1820 [NC:731]. Perhaps his wife was Elizabeth Artis, the only heir of Edward **Griffith**, deceased, who received a land warrant of 1,000 acres for service in the North Carolina Line [*N. C. Genealogy* XVI:2582]. He may have been identical to Edward **Griffin**, a "Mulatto" head of a Edgecombe County household of 1 "other free" in 1790 and 1800 [NC:202] who served in the Revolution.

 ii. Edy, born 1775, a "base born" child ordered by the 26 August 1776 Edgecombe County court bound as an apprentice to Joseph Sims and his wife Charity [Minutes 1772-84, n.p.].

 iii. John[5], born before 1776, head of an Orange County, North Carolina household of 5 "free colored" in 1820 [NC:354]. He was a buyer at the 2 March 1803 Edgecombe County sale of estate of Robert Peale [Watson, *Estate Records of Edgecombe County*, 201].

 iv. Mary, born before 1776, head of an Edgecombe County household of 5 "free colored" in 1820 [NC:102]. She was a buyer at the 2 March 1803 Edgecombe County sale of estate of Robert Peale [Watson, *Estate Records of Edgecombe County*, 201].

    v. Absalom[2], born before 1776, head of an Edgecombe County household of 2 "free colored" in 1820 [NC:102].

    vi. Richard[1], born 1779, a "Mulatto" boy apprenticed as a cooper to John Norwood by the 25 November 1782 Edgecombe County court [Minutes 1772-84, n.p.]. He was a buyer at the 2 March 1803 Edgecombe County sale of estate of Robert Peale [Watson, *Estate Records of Edgecombe County*, 201].

    vii. William[2], born say 1780, a "Mulatto" head of an Edgecombe County household of 2 "other free" in 1800 [NC:179] and 3 in 1810 [NC:731].

    viii. Winney, born 1781, a "Mulatto" child ordered bound by the Edgecombe County court on 25 November 1782 [Minutes 1772-84], head of an Edgecombe County household of 4 "other free" in 1810 [NC:732].

    ix. Ann, born say 1782, head of an Edgecombe County household of 6 "other free" in 1810 [NC:732]. She was a buyer at the 2 March 1803 Edgecombe County sale of estate of Robert Peale [Watson, *Estate Records of Edgecombe County*, 201].

    x. Champion, born about 1790, head of an Edgecombe County household of 2 "other free" in 1810 [NC:731] and 6 "free colored" in Cumberland County, North Carolina, in 1820 [NC:154].

7. Archibald Artis, born say 1753, died before November 1782 when Stephen **Powell** was granted administration of his estate in Johnston County on a bond of 200 pounds. The account of sales of the estate totalled a little over 43 pounds [Haun, *Johnston County Court Minutes*, III:232]. He was mentioned in the Revolutionary War pension application of Holiday **Haithcock** which had a testimonial by William Bryan, a Justice of the Peace:

> *... that in the times of our Revolutionary War free negroes and mulattoes mustered in the ranks with white men in said State ..This affiant has frequently mustered in company with said free negroes and mulattoes ...That class of persons were equally liable to draft - and frequently volunteered in the public Service. This affiant was in the army a short time at Wilmington at the time Craig was near that place and remembers that one mulatto was in his company as a common soldier whose name Archibald Artis - Sworn to and subscribed this 21 day November 1834.*

Since he served in the Revolutionary War and died about 1782, he may have died while in the service. Delilah Artis, who was taxable on 60 acres in Johnston County in 1784, was probably his widow [GA 64.1]. In May 1786 the Johnston County sheriff was ordered to bring two of his orphans (unnamed) into court to be bound out [Haun, *Johnston County Court Minutes*, III:325]. Delila was head of a "free colored" Wayne County household in 1820 [NC:457]. Perhaps Archibald and Delila's children were

    i. Luke, born 1776-94, head of a Johnston County household of 7 "free colored" in 1820 [NC:260].

    ii. Joseph, born 1776-94, head of a Wayne County household of 4 "free colored" in 1820 [NC:457]. In 1840 he was over fifty-five years old, head of a household of 3 "free colored" in Harrison Township, Vigo County, Indiana.

8. Milbry Artis, born about 1765, daughter of John Artis, was bound apprentice by the churchwardens of St. Luke's Parish, Southampton County, on 8 February 1776 [Orders 1772-7, 428; Minutes 1775-8]. She was the mother of Amy and Polly Artis who were ordered bound out in Southampton County on 10 July 1794 [Minutes 1793-9, 100]. She registered in Southampton County on 28 July 1810: *age 45, blk., 5 feet 6 inches, free born* [Register of Free Negroes 1794-1832, no. 710]. She was taxable on a horse in St. Luke's

Parish, Southampton County, from 1809 to 1811; taxable on a free male tithable in 1810; listed with her son Isham, daughters Polly, Amey, and Matildar on Jacob Barrett's land in 1812; a spinner living with her daughter Matilda on William Farguson's land in 1813; listed with son Israel in 1817 [PPTL 1807-21, frames 284, 311, 571]. She was the mother of

 i. Amy, born about 1785, registered in Southampton County on 28 July 1810: *age 25, Blk., 5 feet 5-3/4 inches, free born* [Register of Free Negroes 1794-1832, no. 711]. She had an illegitimate child by Solomon **Hurst** before 19 March 1804 [Minutes 1803-4, unpaged].

 ii. Polly, born about 1788, registered in Southampton County on 28 July 1810: *age 22, Blk., 5 feet 6 inches, free born* [Register of Free Negroes 1794-1832, no. 712].

 iii. Isham, listed as a taxable in his mother's household in 1812.

 iv. Matilda, listed in her mother's household in 1812.

 v. Israel[2], listed in his mother's household in 1817.

9. Tempy[1] Artis, born say 1768, poor child of John Artis, was ordered bound out by the churchwardens of St. Luke's Parish on 8 February 1776 [Orders 1772-7, 428]. She was the mother of Norborn and Edwin Artis who were ordered bound out by the overseers of the poor of Nottoway Parish, Southampton County, on 15 October 1804 [Minutes 1803-4, unpaged]. She was the mother of

 i. Norborn, born about 1794, ordered bound out on 15 October 1804. He registered in Southampton County on 7 January 1816: *age 22, blk., 5 feet 6 inches, free born* [Register of Free Negroes 1794-1832, no. 995].

 ii. Edwin.

10. Lydia Artis, born say 1748, was living in Southampton County on 10 August 1769 when her son Jacob was bound out by the churchwardens of St. Luke's Parish [Orders 1768-72, 182]. She was taxable in St. Luke's Parish, Southampton County, on her son Isham in 1794 and 1796 [PPTL 1792-1806, frame 72, 180]. She was head of a Southampton County household of 6 "other free" in 1810 [VA:86]. Her children were

 i. Mildred[2], a "poor" child of Lydia Artis bound out by the churchwardens of St. Luke's Parish on 14 August 1777 [Orders 1772-7, 492]. She was head of a Southampton County household of 12 "other free" in 1810 [VA:67].

16 ii. Jacob[1], born say 1766.

 iii. Jordan, born about 1767, a "poor child" of Lid Artis ordered bound out by the Southampton County court on 11 July 1776 [Orders 1772-7, 437]. He was taxable in St. Luke's Parish, Southampton County, in William Pope's household in 1789 and taxable in his own household from 1791 to 1796 [PPTL 1782-92, frames 717, 811, 868; 1792-1806, frames 45, 72, 154, 180]. He registered in Southampton County on 3 September 1797: *age 30, Black man 5 8-1/2 inches, Free born* [Register of Free Negroes 1794-1832, no. 117].

 iv. Isham, born say 1774, son of Lydia Artis, bound out in Southampton County on 14 September 1780 [Orders 1778-84, 132]. He was taxable in his mother's household in 1794 and taxable in his own household from 1795 to 1804. He and his wife Lydia were listed in Southampton County in 1814 [PPTL 1792-1806, frames 154, 180, 258, 308, 369, 404, 542, 612; 1807-21, frame 411].

11. Absolem[1] Artis, born about 1745, was living in Southampton County on 12 September 1771 when James Jordan Scott's suit against him was dismissed at his costs [Orders 1768-72, 447]. He was taxable in St. Luke's Parish, Southampton County, from 1782 to 1813: taxable on a free male tithable aged 16-21 and a horse in 1787, taxable on his unnamed son in 1805, taxable on 3

persons in 1807, 2 in 1809, 2 in 1811, living on Blaney's land with his wife Creacy and daughter Vilet in 1813 [PPTL 1782-92, frames 513, 555, 584, 613, 632, 654, 704, 754, 811; 1792-1806, frames 45, 154, 180, 258, 308, 369, 404, 505, 542, 612, 681, 795, 833; 1807-21, frames 44, 66, 163, 184]. He was head of a Southampton County household of 7 "other free" in 1810 [VA:57]. He registered in Southampton County on 2 August 1810: *age 65, Blk, 5 feet 7 inches, free born*. His wife Creesy registered the same day: *age 60, yellow, 5 feet 2 inches, free born* [Register of Free Negroes 1794-1832, no. 816, 817]. His children were

i. ?Joshua, born about 1770, registered in Southampton County on 1 August 1810: *age 40, Blk., 5 feet 11 inches, free born*. Jemima, who was apparently his wife, registered the same day: *age 30, Blk., 5 feet 5 inches, free born* [Register of Free Negroes 1794-1832, nos. 809, 810]. He was taxable in St. Luke's Parish, Southampton County, in William Pope's household in 1790, taxable in Isaac Pope's household in 1791, in Joel Newsum's household in 1793, listed with his wife Jemima and daughter Pris on Thomas Newsom's land in 1813, listed with his son Henry in 1820 [PPTL 1782-92, frame 767, 821; 1792-1806, frames 59, 72, 154, 180, 258, 308, 369, 404, 505, 542, 612, 795, 833; 1807-21, frames 44, 163, 311, 411, 571, 780], head of a Southampton County household of 7 "other free" in 1810 [VA:60].

ii. ?Abraham[3], born about 1774, registered in Southampton County on 8 August 1800: *age 26, Black, 5 feet 8 3/4 inches, born of free parents 1800* [Register of Free Negroes 1794-1832, no. 148]. He registered the certificate in Norfolk County [Freed Negro loose papers, Chesapeake County Courthouse]. He was taxable on a horse in St. Luke's Parish, Southampton County, in 1802 and 1803. He and his wife Cyntha were "fn's" living on William Simmons's land in 1813, taxable on a horse in 1814 [PPTL 1792-1806, frame 543, 612; 1807-21, frames 311, 411].

iii. ?Israel[1], born about 1776, registered in Southampton County on 28 March 1798: *age 22, blackman, 5 feet 6 inches, free born, renewed March 6 1801* [Register of Free Negroes 1794-1832, no. 122]. He was taxable in Southampton County in Buxton Barnes' household from 1794 to 1796, listed in his own household from 1797 to 1800 [PPTL 1792-1806, frames 73, 155, 182, 259, 309, 370, 404].

iv. Levinia (Viney), married Artis **Powell**, with Absolem Artist's consent, 23 July 1800 Southampton County bond, Hanson Pope security, 18 August marriage.

v. ?Charles, born about 1783, married Mason **Powell**, 30 December 1801 Southampton County bond, Evans Pope, surety. He registered in Southampton County on 2 August 1810 (the same day as Absolem and Creasy Artis): *age 27, Blk., 5 feet 4 inches, free born*. (His wife) Mason registered the same day: *age 25, yellow, 5 feet 2 inches, free born* [Register of Free Negroes 1794-1832, nos. 815, 818]. He was head of a Southampton County household of 6 "other free" in 1810 [VA:60]. He was taxable in St. Luke's Parish, Southampton County, from 1801 to 1803, taxable in Jonas Bryant's household in 1805, charged with his own tax from 1806 to 1811, taxable with his wife Mason on Ben Worrell's land in 1812 and on Isaac Pope's land in 1813, living on Burwell Bryant's land in 1817 [PPTL 1792-1806, frames 506, 543, 612, 795, 833; 1807-21, frames 44, 163, 311, 411, 571].

vi. Violet.

12. Ann[1] Artis, born say 1760, was the mother of Elizabeth and Tempy Artis, poor children ordered bound out in Southampton County on 14 October 1784. Her daughter Mason was ordered bound out on 12 July 1786 [Orders 1778-84,

507; 1784-9, 187]. She was head of a Southampton County household of 7 "other free" in 1810 [VA:54]. She was taxable in Southampton County on a horse in 1803, listed with her unnamed daughter on Joel Newsom's land in 1813 [PPTL 1792-1806, frame 648; 1807-21, frame 311]. She was the mother of

  i. Elizabeth, a poor child bound out on 14 October 1784.
  ii. Tempy[2], a poor child bound out on 14 October 1784.
  iii. Mason, born about 1779, registered in Southampton County on 7 April 1824: *age 45, Mulatto, free born* [Register of Free Negroes 1794-1832, no. 1452].

13. George[1] Artis, born say 1760, was head of a Northampton County, North Carolina household of 3 "other free" in 1790 [NC:74], 5 in 1810 [NC:710] (and 5 "other free" in Southampton County in 1810 [VA:53]), and 3 "free colored" in Northampton County, North Carolina, in 1820 [NC:212]. Moses **Newsom** bequeathed him one silver dollar by his 17 September 1805 Northampton County will. His first wife was apparently Martha **Newsom**, daughter of Moses **Newsom** [WB 2:297]. He had apparently married the widow of Luke **Archer** by 21 April 1807 when the Southampton County court summoned him and his wife Hannah, administrators of the estate of Luke **Archer**, deceased, to give supplemental security for the administration of the estate [Minutes 1804-7, 276]. On 15 January 1810 he purchased 4 acres on the south side of the Nottoway River in Southampton County for $2 dollars [DB 12:99], and he and his wife Hannah sold this land for $30 on 12 March 1823 [DB 19:164]. He was a "f.n." taxable on a horse in St. Luke's Parish, Southampton County, from 1803 to 1811, listed with his wife Hannah as "f.n." planters from 1812 to 1814, living on John Whitfield's land in 1817 [PPTL 1792-1806, frames 612, 682, 796, 833; 1807-21, frames 44, 66, 163, 184, 283, 311, 411, 571]. His 30 December 1819 Northampton County will was proved in March 1824 [WB 3:296]. He had two young women, 14-26 years old, in his Northampton County household in 1820, but his will mentioned only his unnamed wife and two sons. His children were

  i. Newsom, born before 1776, head of a Northampton County household of 7 "free colored" in 1820 [NC:212]. His father left him tools and "reading books."
  ii. Kinchen, born 1790, was in the Third Northampton County Regiment in the War of 1812 with (his brother?) Collin Artis [N.C. Adjutant General, *Muster Rolls of the War of 1812,* 20]. By 1850 he was in household no. 630 in the census for Cass County, Michigan: 60 years old, Mulatto, born in North Carolina, $400 personal estate, with Idna, 48 years old, Mulatto, born in Virginia. Their children Kinchen and Diana were born in Ohio. He and Newsome Artist were named in a Champaign County, Ohio suit for partition of James **Newsom**'s land in 1832.
17 iii. ?Collin, born about 1783.

14. Priscilla Artis, born about 1761, a "poor" child, was bound apprentice in St. Luke's Parish, Southampton County, on 13 June 1771, no parent named [Orders 1768-72, 420]. She was taxable in Southampton County on 2 free male tithes in 1801 [PPTL 1792-1806, frame 506]. She registered in Southampton County on 2 December 1801: *age 40, Black, 5 feet 4 1/2 inches, free born* [Register of Free Negroes 1794-1832, no. 220]. She registered in Petersburg on 6 September 1805: *a black free Negro woman, five feet four and a half inches high, forty four years old, formerly of Southampton County & Register no. 220* [Register of Free Negroes 1794-1819, no. 356]. She was the mother of

  i. Matthew, born about 1782, registered in Southampton County on 12 December 1801: *age 19, Black, 5 feet 9-1/4, Free born, lives with*

Pris^a Artis his mother [Register of Free Negroes 1794-1832, no. 222].
registered in Petersburg on 5 September 1805: *a dark brown, near black Negro man, five feet nine inches high, twenty three years old, born free in Southampton County p. certificate of Register* [Register of Free Negroes 1794-1819, no. 360]. He was administrator of the estate of Nancy Artis on 18 November 1806 when the Southampton County court summoned him to give additional security [Minutes 1804-7, 236]. He was head of a Southampton County household of 4 "other free" in 1810 [VA:75]. He was a "F.N." taxable in Southampton County in Saint Luke's Parish in 1800, in Nottoway Parish in 1804 and 1805, in St. Luke's Parish from 1809 to 1811, living with his wife Polly on John Blow's land in 1813 and 1817 [PPTL 1792-1806, frames 405, 717, 755; 1807-21, frames 163, 184, 311, 411, 571]. He registered again in Southampton County on 31 July 1810: *age 28, Blk., 5 feet 9-1/2 inches, free born* [Register of Free Negroes 1794-1832, no. 794].

ii. William, born about 1783, registered in Southampton County on 2 December 1801: *age 18, Black, 5 feet 8-1/4, Free born, lives with Pris^a Artis his mother* [Register of Free Negroes 1794-1832, no. 221]. He registered in Petersburg on 5 September 1805: *a dark brown, near black Negro man, five feet eight and a half inches high, twenty two years old, born free in Southampton County per Register* [Register of Free Negroes 1794-1819, no. 361].

15. Abraham^2 Artis, born say 1765, married Elizabeth **Tabour** (**Taborn**) with the consent of her mother Judy **Tabour**, 11 October 1788 Greensville County, Virginia bond, Peter Pelham security, Tempy **Tabour** witness. He was taxable on a horse in Greensville County in 1795 and 1798 [PPTL 1782-1850, frames 185, 228]. He was a buyer at the 1788 Northampton County, North Carolina sale of the estate of Martha Lewis [Gammon, *Records of Estates, Northampton County*, I:70]. He was head of a Northampton County household of 2 "other free" in 1790 [NC:73] and 6 in Halifax County, North Carolina, in 1800 [NC:3]. Perhaps his children were

18   i. Willie, born about 1783.
      ii. Berry, who was jailed for a minor offense by the 19 and 21 May 1834 Halifax County, North Carolina court [Minutes 1832-46].

16. Jacob^1 Artis, born say 1766, son of Lydia Artis, was bound apprentice in Southampton County on 10 August 1769. He was taxable in St. Luke's Parish, Southampton County, in William Pope's household in 1784, in Robert Williams, Sr.'s household in 1788, charged with his own tithe from 1789 to 1800 [PPTL 1782-92, frames 551, 650, 704, 754, 868; 1792-1806, frames 72, 154, 308, 369, 404]. He died at his house on the evening of 30 July 1800 according to testimony in Southampton County court on 8 August 1800 which charged a "Mulatto man" named Allen **Demmory** (**Demery**) and a white man named James Porter with his murder. The court heard from five white witnesses and (Jacob's widow) Rebecca **Artis** and sent the prisoners to Suffolk for trial. On 17 August 1801 the court ordered the overseers of the poor to bind out his orphans Delila, Bowling, Jacob, Jenny, and Lotty Artis [Minutes 1799-1803, 109-10, 123, 204, 213]. He was the father of

      i. Delilah Artis **Roberts**, born about 1794. She and her husband Henry **Roberts** obtained free papers in Northampton County on 30 April 1834 and registered in Logan County, Ohio, on 11 January 1839. The papers describe her as having a yellow complexion, aged about forty years, 5 feet 4 inches tall. Their children named in the papers were Darius and Ailsey T. Roberts [Turpin, *Register of Black, Mulatto, and Poor Persons*, 11].
      ii. Bowling.

    iii.   Jacob, called a poor "free negro" child of Rebecca Artis when he was ordered bound out on 15 July 1805 [Minutes 1804-7].

    iv.   Jenny, called a poor "free negro" child of Rebecca Artis when she was ordered bound out on 15 July 1805 [Minutes 1804-7].

17. Collin/ Cullen Artis, born about 1783, was in the Third Northampton County Regiment in the War of 1812 [N.C. Adjutant General, *Muster Rolls of the War of 1812*, 20]. His 24 April 1843 Northampton County "free papers," recorded in Ross County, Ohio, described him as "a man of colour, aged about sixty years, his wife Milly as "aged about 53 years" and named their children and grandchildren [Turpin, *Register of Black, Mulatto, and Poor Persons*, 33]:

    i.   Patsy, born about 1813, (and her children Nancy, Hamet, Angey, George, Zachariah, and Isehiah).

    ii.   Olif, (and son John).

    iii. Milly, born about 1826.

    iv. Cherry, born about 1829.

18. Willie Artis, born about 1783, registered in Southampton County on 19 March 1806: *age 23, 6 feet 1 inch, free born* [Register of Free Negroes 1794-1832, no. 345]. He was head of a Greensville County household of 9 "free colored" in 1820 [VA:259]. He registered in Greensville County on 2 April 1827 and again on 7 February 1832: *born of free parents as appears from a register of the Clerk of Southampton County, of a black complexion, about forty nine years of age, six feet 2 & 1/2 inches high, by occupation a farmer.* Thena Artis, who was probably his wife, registered on 3 April 1827 and on 7 February 1832: *born free, of a yellow complexion, about forty five years of age, five feet four & 1/2 inches high.* She was called "Thena Artis, formerly Day" when her son Henry **Day** registered the same day [Register of Free Negroes, 1805-1832, nos. 158, 159, 190, 192, 195]. Thena was the mother of

    i.   Henry **Day**, registered in Greensville County on 7 February 1832: *son of Thena Artis, formerly Day, born free of a dark complexion, about twenty two years of age, five feet seven inches high...by occupation a farmer* [Register of Free Negroes, 1805-1832, no. 195].

    ii.   Earrick Artis, born about 1810, registered in Greensville County on 7 February 1832: *son of Thena Artis, of a black complexion, about twenty two years of age, five feet ten & 1/2 inches high...by occupation a farmer* [Register of Free Negroes, 1805-1832, no.194].

19. George[3] Artis, born about 1815, a carpenter, built the frame structure of the Chain Lake Missionary Baptist Church in Calvin Township, Cass County, Michigan [Lucas, *History of Chain Lake Missionary Baptist Church*]. He was in household no. 1594 in Cass County in 1860: George W. Artis, 45 years old, "Mulatto," carpenter, $150 real estate, $25 personal, with wife S., 34 years old. Their oldest child was born in Ohio in 1843, and their youngest was born in Michigan in 1850.

Other members of the Artis family in Southampton County were

    i.   Phebe, born say 1760, paid by the Southampton County court for the maintenance of her unnamed son on 9 March 1787 [Orders 1784-9, 262].

    ii.   Patience, born about 1765, registered in Southampton County on 1 August 1810: *age 45, Blk., 5 feet 5-1/2 inches, free born* [Register of Free Negroes 1794-1832, no. 798]. She was head of a Southampton County household of 4 "other free" in 1810 [VA:86]. She was taxable on a free male tithable in Southampton County in 1801, listed with no property in 1805; she and her daughter Tabitha were living on Ann Pope's land in 1813, and she and her son Tom were taxable on John

Underwood's land in 1820 [PPTL 1792-1806, frames 506, 543, 795; 1807-21, frame 311, 780].

iii. Elizabeth, born say 1768, mother of Michael Artis, a "poor child" ordered bound apprentice in Southampton County to George Gurley on 11 September 1789 and ordered bound out again on 8 April 1790 [Minutes 1786-90, n.p.].

iv. Sally, born say 1768, married Jacob **Freeman**, 4 February 1789 Southampton County bond.

v. Edmund, born about 1774, ordered bound apprentice by the overseers of the poor of St. Luke's Parish on 11 September 1788 [Orders 1784-9, 437]. He registered in Southampton County on 12 July 1810: *age 36, Blk., 5 feet 9 inches, free born* [Register of Free Negroes 1794-1832, no. 586]. He was taxable in St. Luke's Parish, Southampton County, in Jonas Bryant's household from 1797 to 1799, taxable in Thomas Newsom's household in 1795, and a "free Negro" taxable in Nottoway Parish from 1802 to 1811 [PPTL 1792-1806, frames 167, 580, 717; 1807-21, frames 4, 87, 126, 209]. He married Nanny **Evans**, 23 February 1796 Southampton County bond. He was head of a Southampton County household of 8 "other free" in 1810 [VA:74].

vi. William, born say 1775, a 16-21 year-old taxable in St. Luke's Parish, Southampton County, in Nathan Bryant's household in 1792, listed in his own household in 1793 and 1800 [PPTL 1782-92, frame 812; 1792-1806, frame 45, 405].

vii. Charlotte, born say 1777, ordered bound apprentice by the overseers of the poor of St. Luke's Parish on 11 September 1788 [Orders 1784-9, 437].

viii. Dempsey, born about 1778, ordered bound out by the overseers of the poor in the upper district of St. Luke's Parish to Newit Edwards on 12 February 1789 [Orders 1784-9, 481]. He registered in Southampton County on 31 July 1810: *age 32, Blk., 5 feet 8 inches, free born* [Register of Free Negroes 1794-1832, no. 789]. He was taxable in St. Luke's Parish, Southampton County, from 1791 to 1817: a 16-21 year-old taxable in Newit Edwards' household from 1791 to 1794, a "f.n." taxable in 1805, charged with his own tax after 1800, listed with his wife Nancy on Lewis Worrell's land in 1812, listed with Nancy **Bowing** as "Free Negroes" in 1814, living on M. Gwaltney's land in 1817 [PPTL 1782-92, frames 815, 873; 1792-1806, frames 78, 506, 543, 612, 796, 833; 1807-21, frames 66, 163, 184, 283, 411, 571].

ix. Ann, born about 1778, registered in Southampton County on 30 July 1810: *age 32, Blk., 4 feet 11 inches, free born* [Register of Free Negroes 1794-1832, no. 764].

x. ?Richard[2], born say 1780, married Rebecca **Banks**, 30 December 1801 Southampton County bond, Evans Pope surety. He was taxable in St. Luke's Parish, Southampton County, in 1788, his tax charged to Simon Everitt from 1792 to 1796, charged with his own tax in 1801, his tax charged to William Newton in 1805, charged with his own tax in 1810 and 1811 [PPTL 1782-92, frame 873; 1792-1806, frames 51, 78, 185, 506, 796; 1807-21, frames 163, 184]. He was head of a Southampton County household of 2 "other free" in 1810 [VA:64].

xi. Miriam[2], born say 1780, married Aaron **Norfleet**, 12 March 1808 Southampton County bond, Barnes Bolling surety. Aaron registered in Southampton County on 18 September 1798: *age 42, blackman, 5 feet 8 1/2 inches, set free by Jno. Norfleet, Southampton Co. Deed* [Register of Free Negroes 1794-1832, no. 125].

xii. Drew, born about 1783, registered in Southampton County on 27 June 1804: *age 21, blk, 5 feet 5-1/2 inches high, free born* [Register of Free Negroes 1794-1832, no. 309].

xiii.   Phereby, born say 1784, mother of a poor child named Arthur who was ordered bound apprentice in Southampton County on 15 July 1805 [Minutes 1804-7]. Ferebe married Moses **Browne**, 24 February 1810 Southampton County bond, Benjamin **Whitfield** surety. Moses was head of a Southampton County household of 5 "other free" in 1810 [VA:66].

xiv.   George[2], born about 1784, registered in Southampton County on 30 July 1810: *age 26, Blk., 5 feet 5-1/2 inches, free born* [Register of Free Negroes 1794-1832, no. 734].

xv.   Exum, born say 1785, taxable in St. Luke's Parish, Southampton County, from 1802 to 1806, a "f.n." listed with wife Clary in 1813 and 1814, living on John Rochell's land in 1817 [PPTL 1792-1806, frame 543, 612, 833; 1807-21, frames 283, 311, 411, 571].

xvi.   Tempy[3], born about 1787, registered in Southampton County on 1 August 1810: *age 23, Blk., 5 feet 1 inch, free born* [Register of Free Negroes 1794-1832, no. 799].

xvii.   Evans, born about 1792, received one of the "Certificates Granted to Free Negroes & Mulattoes" in Sussex County on 2 November 1826: *free born, light complexion, 5'10", aged 34* [Certificates Granted to Free Negroes & Mulattoes 1800-50, no. 531].

ASHBERRY FAMILY

1.   Martha Ashberry, born say 1740, was the servant of Gideon Patterson on 26 July 1762 when he was summoned to appear in Cumberland County, Virginia court to show cause why he detained her in service [Orders 1762-4, 3]. She was probably the mother of

i.   Milly, a "Mulatto" orphan bound by the Cumberland County court to Gideon Patterson on 24 May 1762 [Orders 1758-62, 477].

ASHBY FAMILY

1.   Mary Ashbye, born say 1705, was a white servant listed in the York County estate of James Shields with her "Mulatto" sons Matthew and John on 21 August 1727 [OW 16, pt. 2, 509]. She was the mother of

2   i.   Matthew[1], born say 1723.
3   ii.   John[1], born say 1725.
4   iii.   ?Roseanna, born say 1732.

2.   Matthew[1] Ashby, born say 1723, was indicted for assault and battery in York County on 19 November 1759. He pled guilty and was fined 30 shillings [Judgments & Orders 1759-63, 90, 107, 113-4]. Matthew and his wife Ann registered the birth of their daughter Mary in Bruton Parish, James City County, in 1764. In November 1765 his slaves Harry and John were among thirty-four slaves who were attending the "Negro School" in Williamsburg which had been established by Dr. Bray's Associates, and his free children John and Mary Ashby were among twenty-nine attending the school on 16 February 1769 [Stephenson, *Notes on the Negro School in Williamsburg, 1760-1774*, Colonial Williamsburg Foundation (1963), Appendix no. 1, iv, citing Manuscripts of Dr. Bray's Associates, American Papers, 1735-1774, S.P.G. Archives, London]. He purchased his wife and two children from Samuel Spurr for 150 pounds and was called a "free Mulatto" on 27 November 1769 when he successfully petitioned the governor and Council of Virginia to allow him to free his wife Ann and their children John and Mary [Hillman, *Executive Journals*, VI:334-5]. On 25 October 1770 there was an ad in the *Virginia Gazette* which claimed that a slave named Sam, who had run away from Matthew Mayes of Amelia County, was being harbored by Matthew Ashby [Windley, *Runaway Slave Advertisements*, 1:87]. His 25 November 1769 York

County will, proved 15 April 1771, named his wife Ann and their children John and Mary. He left his estate to his good friend John Blair, Esq., who was to see to the support of his wife and education of his children. However, Blair refused the executorship, so it was granted to his widow Anne [Wills & Inventories Book 22:25-6; Orders 1770-2, 229]. They were the parents of

- i. ?Harry/ Henry, born say 1758, attending the school in Williamsburg in November 1765. He married Susanna **Jones**, 23 January 1796 York County bond. He was taxable in James City County from 1795 to 1801. Susanna Ashby was taxable in James City County on a horse in 1807 and head of a household of a "Free Person of Colour above 16 years" in 1813 [PPTL 1782-99; 1800-15].

- ii. John², born say 1760, taxable in the upper district of York County in 1782, taxable on his own tithe and a horse from 1791 to 1794, taxable on a slave and a horse in 1796, taxable on two tithes in 1812 and head of a household of 2 "free Negroes & mulattoes over 16" in 1813 [PPTL, 1782-1841, frames 69, 91, 106, 147, 170, 190, 218, 227, 253, 304, 373, 384]. He was head of a York County household of 6 "other free" in 1810 [VA:870].

- iii. Mary, born 24 October 1764, a "free Mulatta" [Bruton Parish Register, 26], perhaps identical to Polly Ashby who was listed in York County among the "free Negroes & mulattoes over 16" in 1813 [PPTL, 1782-1841, frame 384].

3. John¹ Ashby, born say 1725, was a "servant man" valued at 16 pounds in the 1 October 1750 inventory of the York County estate of Thomas Cobbs [W&I 20:192]. He was married to Sarah Ashby, "Free Mulattoes," in 1765 when the birth and baptism of their children Matthew and Philemon were recorded in Bruton Parish, James City County [Bruton Parish Register, 26, 32]. He was presented by the York County court on 19 November 1770 for failing to list himself as a tithable [Judgments & Orders 1770-2, 105, 337]. He died before 21 October 1776 when the York County court ordered the churchwardens of Bruton Parish to bind out his unnamed orphans and also (his son) Matt Ashby. On 15 June 1778 the court allowed (his widow) Sally Ashby, "wife of ___ Ashby" 12 pounds for the subsistence allowed wives, children and aged parents of poor soldiers serving in the Revolution. She was called the mother of a soldier when she received an allowance on 21 June 1779 and 17 July 1780 [Orders 1774-84, 127, 163, 219, 273]. Their children were

- i. ?James, born say 1763, paid as a witness on 19 July 1785 in a suit against Peter **Gillett** in York County court [Orders 1784-7, 185], taxable in York County from 1786 to 1813, taxable on two tithables and a horse from 1809 to 1811 [PPTL, 1782-1841, frames 128, 180, 199, 218, 227, 243, 304, 337, 350, 362, 384]. He was head of a York County household of 10 "other free" in 1810 [VA:870].

- ii. Matthew², born 18 July 1765, baptized 6 October 1765, ordered bound out by the churchwardens of Bruton Parish, York County, on 21 October 1776 [Orders 1774-84, 127], a taxable "Mulatto" in Warwick County in 1789 [PPTL, p.1], taxable in York County from 1794 to 1810 [PPTL, 1782-1841, frames 199, 218, 227, 253, 274, 304, 337, 350] and head of a York County household of 11 "other free" in 1810 [VA:887]. Perhaps his widow was Elizabeth Ashby who was taxable on a free male tithable in York County in 1811 [PPTL, 1782-1841, frame 362].

- iii. Philemon², born 16 September 1767, "son of John and Sarah Ashby his Wife free mulattoes."

- iv. ?Richard, born about 1775, registered in York County on 15 October 1810: *a dark Mulatto about 35 years of age 5 feet 8-1/4 Inches high - is a sturdy well made fellow...Born free* [Free Negro Register 1798-1831, no.57]. He was head of a York County household of 11 "other free" in 1810 [VA:887]. He was taxable in York County from 1795 to 1812. He died before 1814 when his estate was taxable on 2 horses [PPTL, 1782-1841, frames 209, 235, 253, 274, 294, 337, 350, 384, 402].

    v.   ?Thomas, born about 1792, registered as a "free Negro" in York County on 19 September 1831: *about 39 years of age, 5 feet 6-1/4 inches high, decayed front teeth, whiskers* [Free Negroes Register, 1831-50, no. 305].

4.   Roseanna Ashby, "a mulatto wench," born say 1732, was bound apprentice to Thomas Whitworth by the churchwardens of St. John's Parish, King William County. In February 1763 she was living in Amelia County when she completed her indenture and successfully petitioned the court to release her and her children Daniel and Phil from Thomas Whitworth [Orders 1763, fols. 20, 83, 85-6]. Her children were

    i.   Daniel, born say 1758.
    ii. Phil¹, born say 1761.

ASHE FAMILY

Five members of the Ash family, probably brothers and sisters, were living in Southside Virginia and North Carolina about 1750. They were

1   i.   Thomas, born say 1730.
2   ii. Rachel, born say 1735.
3   iii. Sarah, born say 1740.
4   iv. Nancy, born say 1742.
5   v.   Moses¹, born say 1745.

1.   Thomas Ash, born say 1730, was taxable in Granville County in the list of Lemuel Lanier in 1750 [CR 44.701.23] and was living with his wife Abigail in Granville County in 1755 where they were taxable on two "Black" tithes [CR 44.701]. On 19 March 1759 he was sued in Granville County court by Leonard Henly Bullock for concealing a tithable [Minutes 1754-70, 55]. They may have been the parents of

6   i.   Charles¹, born say 1755.

2.   Rachel Ash, born say 1735, was presented by the grand jury of Isle of Wight County on 3 May 1759 for having a bastard child, but the case was dismissed on 3 Jan 1760 because she was not then residing in the county [Orders 1759-63, 3, 93]. She was living in Isle of Wight County on 4 April 1764 when her children Lazarus, Chloe and Lydia Ash were bound apprentices [Orders 1764-68, 11]. She was a "free Molletto" living in Saint Brides Parish on 18 August 1768 when the Norfolk County court ordered the churchwardens to bind out her children Peter and Judith Ash to John Pasteur [Orders 1768-71, 11]. Her children were

    i.   Lazarus, born say 1755, a "son of Rachel Ash" ordered bound out to Thomas Applewhite, Jr., in Isle of Wight County in 1756 [Orders 1755-57, 131].
    ii. Chloe, born say 1759, "orphan of Rachel" bound apprentice in Isle of Wight County on 4 April 1764 [Orders 1764-68, 11]. She was head of an Isle of Wight County household of 3 persons in 1782 [VA:29].
    iii. James², born about 1761, "orphan of Rachel" bound apprentice in Norfolk County on 4 April 1764 [Orders 1764-68, 11], perhaps the James Ash who was head of a Nansemond County household of 5 persons in Buxton's list for 1783 [VA:57] and a "Mulatto" head of a Nansemond County household in Buxton's list for 1784 [VA:74]. He was taxable in Isle of Wight County in 1784 [PPTL 1782-1810, frame 55]. In 1784 he was called James Ash of Isle of Wight County when

he petitioned the Virginia Legislature for payment due him for eighteen months service as a Continental soldier in one of the Isle of Wight County divisions [Virginia State Library Legislative Petitions, 23 November 1784]. He registered in Petersburg on 20 August 1794: *a dark brown Mulatto Man, five feet high, thirty three years old, born free & raised in Isle of Wight County* [Register of Free Negroes 1794-1819, no. 71]. He was taxable in the lower parish of Nansemond County in 1815 [Waldrep, *1813 Tax List*].

iv. Lydia, born say 1763, "a Molatto the Child of Rachell Ash" ordered bound apprentice by the churchwardens of Newport Parish in Isle of Wight County on 5 July 1764 [Orders 1764-68, 77].

v. Peter^2, born say 1765, ordered bound apprentice to John Pasteur in Norfolk County on 18 August 1768 [Orders 1768-71, 11].

vi. Judith, born say 1767, ordered bound apprentice to John Pasteur in Norfolk County on 18 August 1768 [Orders 1768-71, 11].

vii. ?Sam, born say 1771, a "F.N." taxable in Isle of Wight County in 1792 and from 1795 to 1802 [PPTL 1782-1810, frame 240, 360, 374, 403, 442, 538, 556].

viii. ?Henry, born say 1775, a "F.N." taxable in Isle of Wight County from 1798 to 1805: taxable on a slave in 1798 and 1799, 2 slaves in 1801 and 1802, just his own tithe in 1803 and 1804 [PPTL 1791-1828, frames 427, 472, 521, 575, 595, 651, 671].

3. Sarah Ash, born say 1740, was living in Isle of Wight County, Virginia, on 2 June 1763 when the court ordered her children Sandy, James and Peter Ash bound out as apprentices [Orders 1759-63, 441]. She was living in Norfolk County two years later on 15 August 1765 when the court ordered the churchwardens of Portsmouth Parish to bind out her "free Negro" sons Sandy and James Ash to Solomon Deans [Orders 1763-65, 254]. On 1 April 1773 she complained to the Isle of Wight County court that William Bagnal was misusing her son Peter Ash who was bound apprentice to Bagnal. The court ordered him bound out to someone else. On 7 August 1777 and 5 March 1779 she complained to the Isle of Wight County court against Sharp Reynolds. This or another case brought by her against Reynolds was still pending on 1 May 1783 [Orders 1772-80, 110, 396, 427, 463; 1780-3, 201]. She was head of an Isle of Wight County household of 7 persons in 1782 [VA:29], 5 "other free" in Halifax County, North Carolina, in 1800 [NC:286], and 4 in 1810 [NC:4]. Her children were

    i. Sandy, born say 1758, bound an apprentice to Solomon Deans in Norfolk County on 15 August 1765 [Orders 1763-65, 254].

7   ii. James^1, born say 1760.

    iii. Peter^1, born say 1762, a "Molatto Child of Sarah Ash" ordered bound apprentice by the churchwardens of Newport Parish in Isle of Wight County on 2 June 1763 and ordered bound out again on 1 April 1773 [Orders 1759-63, 441; 1772-80, 110].

8   iv. Jesse^1, born say 1763.

    v. ?Simon, born say 1767, a "poor free Negro" (no parent named) ordered bound apprentice in Isle of Wight County on 2 March 1775 [Orders 1772-80, 322], a "mulatto" head of a Nansemond County household in 1784 [VA:74] and taxable at Knott's Neck in Nansemond County in 1815 [Yantis, *Supplement to the 1810 Census of Virginia*, s-14]. He was head of a Nansemond County household of 3 "free colored" in 1820 [VA:87].

    vi. Charles^2, born say 1769, a "poor mulatto" orphan of Sarah Ash, bound apprentice in Isle of Wight County on 7 October 1779 [Orders 1772-80, 490]. He was a "F.N." taxable in Isle of Wight County from 1792 to 1810 [PPTL 1782-1810, frames 240, 270, 330, 374, 403, 442, 538, 556, 615, 633, 691, 732, 750, 808, 826].

    vii.   ?Kitt/ Christopher, born say 1772, head of a Halifax County, North Carolina household of 5 "other free" in 1800 [NC:286] and 7 in 1810 [NC:4].

   viii.   ?Mourning, born about 1778, registered in Petersburg on 18 August 1800: *a strait made, brown Mulatto woman, five feet six inches high, twenty two years old, long bushy hair, born free & raised in Isle of Wight County* [Register of Free Negroes 1794-1819, no. 191].

    ix.   ?Charity, born about 1779, registered in Petersburg on 6 May 1809: *a dark brown negro woman, five feet, thirty years old, born free & raised in Isle of Wight County p. Registry* [Register of Free Negroes 1794-1819, no. 464].

4.   Nancy Ash, born say 1742, was called "an Indian and Free born" by her daughter Jenny in February 1785 when Jenny petitioned the Bertie County court saying that she and her two children were being held in slavery by John Gardner. Gardner asserted that Jenny was a "Mustee, and a slave" who he received by the will of Samuel Cotton at the age of about ten years and that she had been in his possession for about fourteen years. The court called her "Jenny Ash, a Mulatto Woman" when it ordered Gardner to appear in court to answer her petition [Byrd, *In Full Force and Virtue*, 1-2]. Nancy was the mother of

9   i.   Jenny[1], born about 1761.

     ii.   Jesse[2], born in December 1776, registered in Petersburg on 26 January 1796: *a Black Negro Lad, five feet six and a half inches high, short knotty hair (and by the affidavit of Jonathan Curtis is son of Nancy Ash a Free woman and was born Free in the County of Princess Anne and nineteen years old Dec. last* [Register of Free Negroes 1794-1819, no. 107].

5.   Moses[1] Ash, born say 1745, was a "Mulatto" head of a Nansemond County household in 1784 [VA:74]. His widow may have been Suckey Ash, a "Free Negro" taxable on 2 horses in Nansemond County in 1815 [Yantis, *Supplement to the 1810 Census of Virginia*, S-14]. She was head of a Nansemond County household of 5 "free colored" in 1820 [VA:81B]. Their children may have been

     i.   Moses[2], born about 1771, a nine-year-old boy bound to Jethro Sumner in Warren County, North Carolina, in September 1780 to learn to read and write and husbandry [Minutes 1780-3, 51]. He was called Moses Ash **Bowser** on his Warren County indenture [WB 3:155].

     ii.   Patty, born about 1762, registered in Petersburg on 14 August 1800, *a light brown Mulatto woman, five feet one inches high, thirty eight years old, thin made with thick bushy hair, born free & raised in Nansemond County* [Register of Free Negroes 1794-1819, no. 165].

    iii.   William, born about 1778, registered in Petersburg on 23 June 1810: *a yellow brown Mulatto man, five feet three 3/4 inches high, thirty two years old, born free in Nansemond County* [Register of Free Negroes 1794-1819, no. 619]. He was called Billey Ash in 1810 when he was head of a Petersburg household of 3 slaves (probably should have been entered in the "other free" column) [VA:117b]. He may have been the Bill Ash who was a "Free Negro" taxable on a head of cattle and 2 horses at Knott's Neck in Nansemond County in 1815. He registered in York County on 20 January 1823: *a yellow brown Mulatto about 44 or 45 years of age 5 feet 3-3/4 Inches high - a little bald on top of his head, bushy hair with whiskers...some small freckles over his face...has the appearance of a French Negro or Mul[o] on first view - Born free as appears by Register of his freedom signed by J. Grammer, Clk of Hustings Ct. of Petersburg on 23 June 1810, no. 619* [Register of Free Negroes 1798-1831, no.203].

iv. Levina, born about 1779, registered in Petersburg on 14 August 1800: *a light brown Mulatto woman, five feet three and a half inches high, twenty one, with short bushy hair, born free & raised in Nansemond County* [Register of Free Negroes 1794-1819, no. 162]. She was head of a Petersburg household of 3 "other free" in 1810 [VA:121b]. She married Griffin **Scott**, 21 June 1817 Petersburg Hustings Court marriage.

v. Nathaniel, taxable in Norfolk County from 1793 to 1817: a "free Negro" fisherman on Western Branch in 1801, counted with Jim Ash in Portsmouth as "B.M." (Black Men) in 1815 [PPTL, 1791-1812, frames 77, 132, 294, 384, 460, 554, 641, 720; 1813-24, frames 94, 121, 263].

vi. Oliver, born say 1790, a "Free Negro" taxable at Knott's Neck in Nansemond County in 1815.

vii. James[4], born say 1792, taxable in Isle of Wight County in 1809 and 1810 [PPTL 1782-1810, frames 790, 845]. He may have been the James Ash, "a free man of colour," who married Priscilla **Hall**, "a free woman of colour," 31 December 1814 Norfolk County bond, Nathan Mathews security. He was a "Free Negro" taxable at Knott's Neck in Nansemond County in 1815 [Yantis, *Supplement to the 1810 Census of Virginia*, S-14].

6. Charles[1] Ash, born say 1755, was living in Caswell County prior to 18 May 1778 when a land entry mentioned his improvements sold to William Noyal Norsworthy [Pruitt, *Land Entries: Caswell County*, 15]. He was counted in Halifax County, North Carolina, in the state census of 1786 in District 13 with 7 free males and 3 free females in his household. He was head of a Halifax County household of 11 "other free" in 1790 [NC:64], 8 in 1800 [NC:286], and 9 in 1810 [NC:2]. His child may have been

    i. Levi, born 1776-94, head of a Halifax County household of 7 "free colored" in 1820 and 10 in 1830.

7. James[1] Ashe, born say 1760, son of Sarah Ash, was ordered bound an apprentice to Solomon Deans in Norfolk County on 15 August 1765 [Orders 1763-65, 254]. He was head of a Bertie County household of 6 "other free" and a white woman in 1790 [NC:11], 4 "other free" in Halifax in 1800 [NC:3], and 4 "free colored" in Edgecombe County in 1820 [NC:123]. He was in the First Company detached from the Halifax County, North Carolina Regiment in the War of 1812, listed with Halvin Ash (his son? Elvin) [N.C. Adjutant General, *Muster Rolls of the War of 1812*, 19]. Perhaps his children were

    i. Elvin, born before 1776, head of a Halifax County household of 1 "other free" in 1810 [NC:3] and 1 "free colored" in 1830.

    ii. James[3], born say 1780, head of a Halifax County household of 4 "other free" in 1810 [NC:4].

    iii. Henry, born 1776-94, a "Negro" head of a Guilford County household of 6 "free colored" in 1830.

8. Jesse[1] Ash, born say 1763, a "mulato bastard child of Sarah," was bound apprentice in Isle of Wight County on 4 December 1766 and was "a free Mulatto" (no parent named) bound apprentice on 4 March 1773 [Orders 1764-68, 328; 1772-80, 89]. He was taxable in Nottoway Parish, Southampton County, in the household of John **Williams** in 1784 and in his own household in 1786 [PPTL 1782-92, frame 554, 584]. The 4 March 1794 Northampton County, North Carolina court charged him with begetting a bastard child by Mary **Scott** [Minutes 1792-96, 103]. He was head of a Northampton County household of 3 "other free" in 1800 [NC:424], 4 in 1810 [NC:710], 9 "free colored" in 1820 [NC:212], and 9 in 1830. His wife may have been Mary

Ashe who was mentioned in the 2 January 1807 Northampton County will of Moses **Byrd** [WB 2:362]. One of his children may have been

    i. Ballus, born 1776-94, head of a Northampton County household of 4 "other free" in 1810 [NC:710] and 8 "free colored" in 1820.

9. Jenny[1] Ashe, born about 1761, was a "Mulatto woman" living in Bertie County in February 1785 when the court ordered John Gardner, Sr., to bring her to the next court and give bond not to convey her or any of her children out of the state so as to prevent their attendance in court [Haun, *Bertie County Court Minutes,* V:522-3]. Perhaps it was her children who were bound apprentices in Bertie County as follows:

    i. Nancy[2], born about 1787, a nine-year-old bound an apprentice in Bertie County on 14 November 1796.

    ii. Elizabeth, born about 1789, bound to Frederick Lawrence on 13 August 1798.

    iii. Patsy, born about 1790, bound to Edmond Dunston on 14 November 1796 [*NCGSJ* XV:167].

    iv. Isom, born about 1794, bound to Edmond Dunston as an apprentice farmer on 16 May 1807.

    v. Abner, born about 1796, bound to Edmond Dunston as an apprentice farmer on 16 May 1807 [*NCGSJ* XVI:153].

    vi. Theophilus, born 1801, bound to Amos Rayner as an apprentice cooper on 9 February 1807 [*NCGSJ* XVI:154].

    vii. Jenny[2], born 1806, a four-year-old "orphan of colour" bound to James Warren on 14 November 1810 [*NCGSJ* XVII:42].

ASHTON/ ASTEN FAMILY

Burdett and Richard **Lucast** were taxable in the lower district of Westmoreland County from 1795 to 1798. Burdett was called Burdett A. **Lucas** in 1797 and Richard was called Richard A. **Locust** in 1798. They were called Burdett and Richard Ashton in the tax lists from 1799 to 1815, and Burdett was again called **Lucus** in the 1810 Westmoreland County census. They may have been related to the slaves who were taxable in the Westmoreland County estate of Burdett Ashton in 1787 [PPTL, 1782-1815, frames 314, 433, 461, 476]. Members of the Ashton family were

1   i. Jemima, born say 1760.

2   ii. Lawrence, born say 1765.

    iii. Sally, born say 1768, living in Westmoreland County on 26 March 1793 when the court ordered the churchwardens of Cople Parish to bind out her children but rescinded the order the following day [Orders 1790-5, 236, 239, 253].

    iv. Burdett, a "free Mulatto" farmer living on James Kelly's land in Westmoreland County in 1801 [*Virginia Genealogist* 31:41], called Burditt **Lucus** when he was head of a Westmoreland County household of 6 "other free" in 1810 [VA:777].

3   v. Winny, born about 1776.

4   vi. Richard, born say 1777.

    vii. Peggy, born say 1785, married Edmond **Tate**, 12 December 1806 Westmoreland County bond, Joseph **Tate** security.

    viii. William, a "free Negro" farmer living on Johnson Wright's land in Westmoreland County in 1801 [*Virginia Genealogist* 31:45].

    ix. Jacob, head of a Westmoreland County household of 6 "other free" in 1810.

    x. Delpha, head of a Westmoreland County household of 6 "free colored" in 1830. She registered in Westmoreland County in September 1831: *a black woman, 5'1-1/2" high, about 33 years of age, born free* [Register of Free Negroes, 1828-1849, no.109].

xi. Susan, born about 1797, head of a Westmoreland County household of 5 "free colored" in 1830. She registered in Westmoreland County in May 1842: *bright Mulatto, 5 feet 7-1/2 inches high, about 45 years old, free born* [Register of Free Negroes, 1828-1849, no.339].

1. Jemima Ashton, born say 1760, was a "free Mulatto" farmer living on James Kelley's land with children Blane, Ludwell, Betsey, Meredith and Kelsick Ashton in 1801 [*Virginia Genealogist* 31:41]. She was head of a Westmoreland County household of 5 "other free" in 1810. She was the mother of

   i. Blain, born about 1787, registered in Westmoreland County in September 1821: *a Black Boy about 34 years of age, five feet eleven inches high, son of Mima Asten who was free born* [Free Negro Register, 1819-1826, p.8]. He was head of a Westmoreland County household of 8 "free colored" in 1830.

   ii. Ludwell, head of a Westmoreland County household of 4 "free colored" in 1830.

   iii. Betsey, born about 1788, registered in Westmoreland County in October 1831: *a mulatto woman, 5'6" high, about 43 years of age, born free* [Register of Free Negroes, 1828-1849, no. 120].

   iv. Meredith, head of a Westmoreland County household of 5 "free colored" in 1830.

   v. Kelsick, registered in Westmoreland County in September 1821: *a Black Boy about five feet eleven inches high, son of Mima Ashton who was free born* [Free Negro Register, 1819-1826, p.7].

2. Lawrence[1] Ashton, born say 1765, married Elizabeth **Scott**, 14 April 1788 Fairfax County bond and 14 April 1788 Fauquier County bond. He was taxable in the lower district of Westmoreland County from 1794 to 1815: called Lawrence **Locust/ Lucas** from 1796 to 1798, counted in the list of "free Negroes & Mulattoes" in 1813 [PPTL, 1782-1815, frames 406, 447, 461, 476, 562, 593, 642, 765, 831]. He and Elizabeth Ashton were counted as "free Mulattoes" living on James Kelley's land in Westmoreland County in 1801 with children Rodham, Fanney, John, Hulley and Lotty [*Virginia Genealogist* 31:40]. He was head of a Westmoreland County household of 9 "other free" in 1810 [VA:766] and 6 "free colored" in 1830. They were apparently the parents of

   i. Rodham, born about 1796, head of a Westmoreland County household of 7 "free colored" in 1830. He registered in Westmoreland County on 28 September 1835: *a Mulatto man about 39 years old, 5 feet 11" high, black eyes, Born free* [Register of Free Negroes, 1828-1849, p.25, no.219].

   ii. Fanny.

   iii. John.

   iv. Hulley.

   v. Lotty, married Samuel **Day**, 7 January 1818 Westmoreland County bond, Samuel **Tate** security.

3. Winny Ashton, born about 1776, was a "free Mulatto" farmer living on William Ball's land in Westmoreland County with children Lawrence, Fanny, Mealey, Meteldea and Barbary Ashton in 1801 [*Virginia Genealogist* 31:41]. She was head of a Westmoreland County household of 6 "other free" in 1810 (called Winney Asten, Sen.). She registered in Westmoreland County in May 1832: *a black woman, 5 feet high about 56 years of age, free born* [Register of Free Negroes, 1828-1849, p.20, no.177]. She was probably the mother of

   i. Lawrence[2].

   ii. Fanny.

   iii. Mealey.

iv. Meteldea/ Matilda, a "FN" above the age of sixteen when she was listed in Westmoreland County in 1813 [PPTL, 1782-1815].
v. Barbary.

4. Richard Ashton, born say 1777, was taxable in the lower district of Westmoreland County from 1795 to 1814: called Richard **Lucust** in 1795 and 1796, Richard A. **Locust** in 1797, counted in the list of "free Negroes & Mulattoes" in 1813 [PPTL, 1782-1815, frames 433, 461, 476, 539, 642, 765, 800]. He married Jenny **Lawrence**, 23 December 1797 Westmoreland County bond. He and his wife Jenney were "free Mulattoes" living on Murphey's land in Westmoreland County with child Fleet Ashton in 1801 [*Virginia Genealogist* 31:40] and he was head of a Westmoreland County household of 3 "free colored" in 1830. They were the parents of
i. Fleet, born say 1799.

ASHWORTH FAMILY

1. James Ashworth, born say 1740, was in Captain James Leslie's Company of South Carolina Militia in the expedition against the Cherokees in 1759 [Clark, *Colonial Soldiers of the South*, 905]. He was described as a "tall, lusty man, of a swarthy complexion, and short black hair" who lived in the "Back Country" of South Carolina in the 1760s [Brown, *South Carolina Regulators*, 31]. He was head of an Opelousas, Louisiana household of 11 "other free" in 1810 and 6 "free colored" in St. Landry Parish in 1820 [LA:306, 101]. He married Keziah **Dial** according to the Opelousas marriage licenses of his children. James and Keziah were the parents of
i. Jesse, born say 1785, "of South Carolina," son of James Ashworth, Sr., and Keziah **Dial**, married Sarah **Perkins**, daughter of Joshua **Perkins** and Mary Mixon, on 3 October 1810 in Opelousas [Opelousas license nos.14, 17]. Jesse was head of a St. Landry Parish household of 7 "free colored" in 1820 [LA:101]. Sarah Ashworth was a fifty-nine-year-old "Mulatto" counted in the 1850 Calcaisieu Parish, Louisiana census.
ii. Polly, born say 1792, daughter of James Ashworth and Keziah **Dial** of South Carolina, married George **Perkins**, by 4 December 1810 Opelousas license. George was head of a St. Landry Parish household of 5 "free colored" in 1820 and 10 in 1830 [LA:107, 27].
iii. James, born say 1789, son of James and Keziah Ashworth, married Mary **Perkins**, daughter of Joshua and Mary **Perkins**, on 23 September 1811 in St. Landry's Parish, Louisiana [Opelousas license no.13]. He was head of a St. Landry Parish household of 6 "free colored" in 1820 [LA:101] and 5 in 1830 [LA:26].
iv. Moses, born say 1791, "of South Carolina," married Anna **Bunch** by 23 November 1821 Opelousas license [License no. 58]. He was head of a St. Landry Parish household of 6 "free colored" in 1830 [LA:26].
v. Aaron, son of James Ashworth and Keziah **Dial**, married Mary **Bunch** 16 September 1829 Opelousas marriage [License no. 58].

ATKINS FAMILY

Members of the Atkins family were
1   i. John, born say 1780.
ii. Milly, head of an Essex County household of 3 "other free" in 1810 [VA:208].
iii. Frank, head of a Free Town, Brunswick County, Virginia household of 1 "other free" in 1810 [VA:770].

iv. Betsy, born about 1791, registered in Charles City County on 16 September 1824: *a bright mulatto woman aged 33 years, born free in this county* [Minutes 1823-9, 77].

1. John Atkins, born say 1780, received 9 pounds for (his wife) Eliza Atkins as her share of the Charles City County estate of her father Edward **Bradby** in 1802 [WB 1:591]. They were the parents of
    i. Edward, born 16 December 1812, obtained a certificate of freedom in Charles City County on 15 September 1831: *son of John Atkins, eighteen years old the 16th December last, bright mulatto, born free in this county* [Minutes 1830-7, 75].

ALDEN/ AULDEN FAMILY

1. Mary Aulden, born about 1741, was living in Chesterfield County on 7 May 1779 when the court ordered the churchwardens of Dale Parish to bind out her daughter Nancy [Orders 1774-84, 227]. Mary Alden registered in Petersburg on 18 August 1794: *a light brown stout Mulatto woman, five feet two inches high, about fifty three years old, free born & raised in Chesterfield County* [Register of Free Negroes 1794-1819, no. 26]. She was the mother of
    i. Nancy, born before 7 May 1779.
    ii. ?Mary Alden, apprenticed to Frederick Traylor in May 1782 when he complained about her to the court and agreed that she should be bound by the churchwardens of Dale Parish to someone else [Orders 1774-84, 352].

AVERY FAMILY

Members of the Avery family of South Carolina and Louisiana were
    i. Joseph Ivery, born say 1770, head of a Greenville County, South Carolina household of 6 "other free" in 1800 (counted next to William **Sweat**) [SC:31].
    ii. Amos, born before 1776, married Sarah **Sweat**, 25 January 1819 Wilkinson County, Mississippi bond [Book B:137]. He was head of a St. Landry Parish, Louisiana household of 6 "free colored" in 1820 [LA:107]. He may have been identical to Amos Ivey who was head of a Marlboro District, South Carolina household of 7 "other free" in 1800 [SC:54a].

Mecklenburg County, Virginia
1. Dicy Avery, born say 1770, was head of a Mecklenburg County household of a white woman over the age of forty-five in 1820 [VA:148b]. She was the mother of an illegitimate child named Henry Avory who was bound apprentice by the Mecklenburg County, Virginia court to Dudley Haile, blacksmith, on 12 December 1803 [Orders 1803-5, 85]. She was the mother of
    i. Henry, born about 1790, registered as a free Negro in Mecklenburg County, Virginia, on 28 October 1826: *a free Mulattoe about thirty six years old...born of a free Woman in this County* [Register, p.21, no.17]. On 21 November 1828 he purchased 125 acres in Mecklenburg County adjoining the lands of William **Stewart**, deceased, from Joseph **Stewart** [DB 23:512].

BAILEY FAMILY

1. Ann Bailey, born say 1725, was called a "free Negro" on 18 July 1754 when she sued William Freeman in Norfolk County court for taking her daughter Sue outside the colony. She was called a "free Molatto" on 17 January 1755 when the court bound her daughter Sue to Lewis Stanford. She was the "free

negro" mother of James Bailey who complained to the Norfolk County court on 17 December 1772 about the treatment he was receiving from his master John Lewelling [Orders 1753-5, 64a, 96, 110; 1771-3, 140]. She was the mother of

    i. Sue, born say 1745, ordered bound apprentice to Lewis Stanford by the churchwardens of Elizabeth River Parish in Norfolk County on 17 January 1755.

2   ii. ?Amy, born say 1750.

    iii. ?William, taxable in District 1 of Hertford County, North Carolina, on 76 acres, a slave 50-60 years old, 3 horses, and 9 cattle in 1779 [GA 30.1, p.5], head of a Hertford County household of 6 "other free" and a white woman in 1790 [NC:25] and 3 "other free," a white woman, and a slave in 1800, perhaps the William Bailey who was head of a Norfolk County household of 1 "other free" in 1810 [VA:889]. He may have been the father of Sue Bailey, married William **Webb**, 18 December 1792 Norfolk County bond, James Williams surety.

    iv. ?Thomas, married Rebecca **Harmon**, 24 December 1771 Norfolk County bond, William Bayley surety.

    v. James, born say 1760, complained to the court against his master John Lewelling. His case was dismissed on 23 January 1773 [Orders 1771-3, 147].

    vi. ?Lemuel, (no race indicated) ordered bound to Francis **Jordan** by the Norfolk County court on 19 March 1774 [Orders 1773-5, 33], perhaps identical to Samuel Bailey, head of a Norfolk County household of 8 "other free" and a slave in 1810 [VA:816].

    vii. ?Priscilla, head of a Petersburg Town household of 4 "other free" in 1810 [VA:124b].

2. Amy Bailey, born say 1750, was a "free negro" living in Norfolk County on 17 August 1775 when the court ordered the churchwardens of Elizabeth River Parish to bind her daughter Frances to Thomas Marshall [Orders 1773-5, 78]. She was the mother of

    i. Frances, born say 1775.

BAINE FAMILY

1. Betty Baines, born say 1730, was a "free woman" living in Gloucester County and married to a fifty-two or fifty-three-year-old "mulatto man" (slave) named Gabriel on 20 January 1776 when his master John Hudson of Albemarle County placed an ad in the Virginia Gazette offering a reward for his return. Gabriel had formerly been the property of a Mrs. Thornton at the mouth of Queen's Creek in York County [*Virginia Gazette* (Pinkney)]. Betty may have been the mother of

    i. Humphrey Baine, born say 1760, a soldier from Henrico County who served in the Revolution [Jackson, *Virginia Negro Soldiers*, 29].

    ii. Nancy Baine, head of a Richmond City household of 3 "other free" in 1810 [VA:361].

BAKER FAMILY

1. John[1] Baker, born say 1755, was called "a Mulatto by a White Woman" when the York County, Virginia court ordered the churchwardens of Yorkhampton Parish to bind him out as an apprentice on 21 February 1763. On 20 October 1766 he was a "Mulatto boy" who the court ordered bound to someone else because he was greatly misused by his master Cuthbert Hubberd [Judgments & Orders 1759-63, 391, 470; Orders 1765-8, 147]. He may have been the brother of Barbara Baker, a seven-year-old "Mulata Girl born of a white woman" who petitioned the New Hanover County, North Carolina court on 2

September 1761 to be bound apprentice to James Gregg [Minutes 1738-69, 199]. He was taxable in New Kent County from 1787 to 1814: called a "molatto" from 1791 to 1796 and from 1805 to 1814; taxable on 2 tithes in 1799, 1801, 1812; listed in 1813 with his unnamed son who was called John, Jr., in 1814 [PPTL 1782-1800, frames 93, 109, 141, 159, 180, 202; 1791-1828, frames 264, 279, 293, 304, 317, 328, 341, 353, 367, 405, 417, 428, 441, 452, 462, 491, 503]. He was head of a New Kent County household of 8 "other free" in 1810 [VA:745]. His children were

   i.   ?Henry, born say 1782, a "M"(ulatto) New Kent County taxable from 1807 to 1810 [PPTL 1791-1828, frames 429, 441, 452].

   ii.   John^2, born say 1795, taxable in his father's New Kent County household in 1813 and 1814.

   iii.   ?Prisilla, head of a Richmond City household of 3 "other free" and a slave in 1810 [VA:321].

Northumberland County:

1. Alice Baker, born say 1665, the servant of John Taylor, was convicted by the Northumberland County court in April 1683 for having "a bastard Child by a Negro man" [Orders 1678-98, 175]. She may have been the ancestor of

   i.   William, born say 1743, a "runaway mulatto boy," the servant of John Billups, who was caught before 5 September 1758 when Thomas Sullinger was paid by the Caroline County court for returning him. He ran away again in 1761. He was called a "mulatto servant" on 13 May 1763 when the court charged him with stealing goods from John Baylor, Esq. There was insufficient evidence to try him before the Court of Oyer and Terminer, but the court convicted him of a misdemeanor and ordered that he receive thirty-nine lashes [Orders 1755-8, 388; 1759-63, 143, 419].

Other members of a Baker family were

   i.   John, "a free man of colour," married Lilly **Walker**, a "free woman of colour," 24 November 1803 Norfolk County bond, perhaps the John Baker who was head of a Goochland County household of 6 "other free" in 1810 [VA:683].

   ii.   Eliza, born before 1776, head of a Halifax County, North Carolina household of 4 "free colored" in 1820 [NC:142].

BALKHAM FAMILY

1. Thomas Baulkham, born about 1714, was a "Mulattoe" who petitioned the Orange County court for his freedom from his master Arjalon Price in September 1739. The case was dismissed in March 1740 when Thomas admitted that he was bound until the age of thirty-one but was only about twenty-six at the time [Orders 1739-41, 68, 87, 116, 137]. On 22 June 1758 the court ordered that he be paid as a witness for William Minor in the Orange County suit of Reuben **Lantor**. On 23 November 1758 he and Ann **Rustin** were indicted for fornication. He pled not guilty and the case was dismissed on 23 August 1759, probably because they married [Orders 1754-63, 404, 479, 491]. Ann was probably identical to Ann **Rustin**, born say 1715, who petitioned the Prince George's County, Maryland court together with her sister Alice on 24 August 1736 saying that they were the children of Elizabeth **Riston** by a white man and asked that the constable where they lived be ordered to remove them from the list of taxables. The court granted their request [Court Record 1736-8, 151]. Thomas was taxable on a tithe in Orange County in 1752 (called Thomas Backhum) and on 2 tithes from 1755 to 1769 (called Thomas Balcam/ Balkom/ Balkham). He was overseer for Elijah Morton in 1756 [Little, *Orange County Tithables*, 28, 36, 42, 64, 76, 82, 92, 96, 109].

BALL FAMILY

1. Elizabeth Ball, born say 1765, was a weaver counted in the list of "Free Molattoes" living on William Edward's land with her children George and Clarisa in Westmoreland County in 1801 [*Virginia Genealogist* 31:40]. She was the mother of
    i.   George.
    ii. Clarisa, head of a Westmoreland County household of 5 "other free" in 1810 and taxable on two "Mo." persons in 1813 [PPTL 1782-1815, frame 766].

Other members of the Ball family in Virginia were
    i.   Jane, a "Mulatto" child living in Loudoun County on 8 February 1779 when the court ordered the churchwardens of Cameron Parish to bind her to William Evans [Orders 1776-83, 150].
    ii. Robert, head of a Loudoun County household of 4 "other free" in 1810 [VA:288].
    iii. Sally, head of a Richmond City household of 4 "other free" and a slave in 1810 [VA:341].

BALTRIP FAMILY

1. Ann Baltrip, born say 1740, was living in Halifax County, Virginia, in June 1761 when the churchwardens of Antrim Parish were ordered to bind out her "Mulatto" child Frank to John Middleton [Pleas 3:254]. On 12 April 1765 she was sued for debt by the churchwardens of Cornwall Parish, Lunenburg County (for having an illegitimate child?) [Orders 1764-5, 53]. She was the servant of Edmond Denney of Rowan County, North Carolina, on 10 May 1770 when the court bound her children to her master, her "Melatto" daughter Hannah until the age of thirty-one and her white son John until the age of twenty-one [Minutes 1769-72, 30, 35 (abstract pp. 207, 212)]. She was the mother of
    i.   ?James, born about 1759 in Virginia, one of the Continental soldiers from Bute County who enlisted on 3 September 1778: *5 feet 4" high, 20 years old, dark hair, dark eyes* (listed next to Edward **Going** in the same list as Charles **Rowe**) [NCAr:Troop Returns by *NCGSJ* XV:109].
2   ii. Hannah, born about March 1759.
    iii. Frank, born say 1761, bound out in Halifax County, Virginia, on June 1761 [Pleas 3:254].
    iv. John, born about March 1763, a white boy who was seven years and two months old on 10 May 1770 when he was bound out in Rowan County.

2. Hannah Baltrip, born about March 1759, was nine years and two months old on 10 May 1770 when the Rowan County court bound her to Edmond Denney. She was taxable in the Surry County, North Carolina household of Edmund Denny in 1775 [Absher, *Some Pioneers from Wilkes County,* 188]. She was probably thirty years old on 26 October 1791 when the Wilkes County court ordered that she be set free "from this time hinceforth & forevermore" [Absher, *Wilkes County Court Minutes,* III:18]. On 27 January 1791 the Wilkes County court ordered that Edmond Denny have a hearing in court about her orphan children [Absher, *Some Pioneers from Wilkes County,* 83]. She was head of a Wilkes County household of 4 "other free" in 1800 [NC:29]. The children bound to Edmund Denny were
    i.   Sarah Baltrip, alias **Roe**, born about 1778, bound in Wilkes County to Charles Gordon on 28 October 1790 [Absher, *Wilkes County Court*

Minutes, III:19] and to Edmund Denny at the age of fourteen years on 3 August 1792 [Absher, *Wilkes County Will Books* 1:33].

    ii. Milly, born about 1781, a ten-year-old bound to Edmond Denny on 28 October 1791, to receive a horse at the age of eighteen years [Absher, *Wilkes County Court Minutes,* III:19].

BANKS FAMILY

1. Elizabeth[1] Banks, born say 1665, was the white servant of Major James Goodwin on 20 June 1683 when she was presented by the York County court for "fornication and Bastardy with a negroe slave." She was given thirty nine lashes, and the term of her indenture was extended [DOW 6:498]. She was the apparently the mother of

2   i. Mary[1], born in 1683.
3   ii. Anne[1], born say 1685.

2. Mary[1] Banks, born in 1683, was called the "Mallatto" servant of Martin Goodwin in York County court on 24 November 1702 when she agreed to serve him an additional year for having an illegitimate child and bound her "Mallato" daughter Hannah Banks to Peter Goodwin until the age of twenty-one years. Peter Goodwin was to provide her with three barrels of corn and clothing at the completion of her indenture according to law. On 23 February 1703/4 she indentured her three or four-month-old "Mollatto" daughter Elizabeth to Martin Goodwin and agreed to serve him an extra year for paying her fine [DOW 12:67, 181, 188]. She was the mother of

4   i. Hannah[1], born say 1702.
5   ii. Elizabeth[2], born about November 1703.
6   iii. ?William[1], born say 1705.
7   iv. ?John[1], born say 1708.

3. Anne[1] Banks, born say 1685, was presented by the York County court on 24 September 1706 for fornication [DOW 13:17]. She may have been the mother of

8   i. Ann[2], born say 1706.

4. Hannah[1] Banks, born say 1702, daughter of Mary Banks, was a "Mulatto" bound until the age of twenty-one years to Peter Goodwin on 24 November 1702 in York County [DOW 12:67]. She may have been the mother of

9   i. Mary[3]/ Moll, born say 1725.

5. Elizabeth[2] Banks, born about November 1703, was the "Mollatto" daughter of Mary Banks of York County. She was listed in the 20 December 1722 inventory of the York County estate of Mary Reade: a "mulatto Girle" valued at 7 pounds [OW 16, pt. 1, 209]. She may have been the mother of

10   i. Mary[2]/ Moll Banks, born say 1724.
11   ii. Elizabeth[3] Banks, born say 1727.

6. William[1] Banks, born say 1705, was a "mulatto Boy" listed in the 20 December 1722 inventory of the York County estate of Mary Reade, valued at 8 pounds. Mary Read gave him to her son Samuel Read by her 7 December 1722 York County will: "one Mulatto Boy _____ ks" [OW 16, pt. 1, 165, 209]. He was living in Southampton County on 12 September 1752 when he was sued for a 2 pound, 5 pence debt due by account. He and his wife Frances were exempted from paying levies in Southampton County on 14 July 1757. He, or perhaps a son by that name, was sued by James **Brooks** for a 5 pound, 5 shilling debt, but on 10 July 1761 the sheriff reported that he was no longer an inhabitant of the county [Orders 1749-54, 269; 1754-9, 372; 1759-63, 128]. William and Frances may have been the ancestors of

12   i.   Edith, born about 1753.
13   ii. William[2], born say 1755.
      iii. Priscilla, born say 1760, mother of Charlotte Banks, a poor child
           bound out in Southampton County on 15 July 1799 [Minutes 1799-
           1803, 25]. Prissy registered in Southampton County on 1 August 1810:
           age 50, Blk., 5 feet 3 inches, free born [Register of Free Negroes
           1794-1832, no. 804]. She was listed in Ned **Whitfield**'s household on
           William Newton's land in St. Luke's Parish, Southampton County in
           1812 and 1814 [PPTL 1807-21, frame 305, 428].
14   iv. Silas, born say 1761.

7. John[1] Banks, born say 1708, was a "Mulatto Servant by Indenture" valued at
    12 pounds in the 9 September 1725 inventory of the Surry County estate of
    Bartlett Morland. He was called a "Mallatto fellow" who lately belonged to
    Bartlett Morland, deceased, on 17 June 1727 when his value was reappraised
    at 6 pounds by order of the court [DW 7:603, 741, 972]. He may have been
    identical to the John Banks who was presented by the York County court on
    15 December 1735 for not listing his "Molatto" wife as a tithable. His wife
    may have been Sarah, the daughter of Mary **Roberts**, who was named in her
    mother's 19 September 1749 York County will [OW 18:245; W&I 20:163].
    John purchased 100 acres on the east side of Cypress Swamp in Surry County
    on 21 September 1756 [DB 7:276]. On 21 November 1758 the Surry County
    court issued a presentment against him and (his son) John Banks, Jr., for "not
    listing their wife's according to law supposing the said persons to be
    Mulattoes" [Orders 1757-64, 135]. His 3 September 1780 Surry County will,
    proved 26 December the same year, left his plantation to his son Matthew
    Banks and mentioned other unnamed children [*Virginia Genealogist* 13:52].
    Matthew died before 22 February 1796 when his heirs (brother and sisters)
    sold their share of his land [Deeds 1792-99, 344-6]. John[1] was the father of
15   i.   John[2], Jr., born say 1735.
      ii. Matthew, born say 1748, named in his father's will. He was head of
           a Surry County household of 1 free person in 1784 [VA:78], and in
           1787 he was taxable on the 100 acres he inherited from his father. He
           sold this land to William Kea in 1795 and purchased 75 acres in Surry
           County on 1 February 1795 from Sampson **Walden** [Property Tax
           Alterations, 1796; Deeds 1792-99, 296-7]. He was taxable on his
           personal property from 1783 to 1794 [PPTL, 1782-90, frames 369,
           399, 490, 565; 1791-1816, frames 75, 176]. He died before 22
           February 1796 when his heirs (brother and sisters: John Banks, Judy
           Charity, Susanna **Howell**, and Hannah **Roberts**) sold this 75 acres to
           Howell **Deberix** [Deeds, 1792-99, 344-6].
      iii. Judy[1], born say 1750, married Henry **Charity**, head of a Surry County
           household of 9 persons in 1782 [VA:43].
      iv. Susanna, born say 1752, married ____ **Howell**.
      v.   Hannah[3], born say 1755, married Joseph **Roberts**.

8. Ann[2] Banks, born say 1706, was presented by the York County court on 20
    December 1731 for having a bastard child on information of the
    churchwardens of Yorkhampton Parish. She apprenticed her "Mulatto"
    daughter Hannah to Patrick Matthews in York County on 18 November 1745.
    Eliza Banks was witness to the indenture [OW 17:248, 273, 308, 338; W&I
    18:5; 19:397; Deeds 1741-54, 152]. She was living in Southampton County
    on 12 July 1759 when the court ordered that she be exempt from paying
    levies. The court dismissed James **Brooks**' suit against her on 11 September
    1761 when he failed to prosecute, and his suit against her abated on 13 August
    1762 when the sheriff reported that she was no longer an inhabitant of the
    county. On 10 December 1762 **Brooks** was fined 5 shillings for assaulting her
    [Orders 1754-9, 516; 1759-63, 151, 234, 272]. She was the mother of

16   i.   Hannah[2], born say 1731.
17   ii.   ?Elizabeth[4]/ Betty, born about 1744.
      iii.   ?Caelea, a "poor child" living in Southampton County on 14 May 1761 when the court ordered the churchwardens to bind her out [Orders 1759-63, 102, 183].

9.   Mary[3]/ Moll Banks, born say 1725, was a "Mulatto Woman" presented by the York County court on 20 November 1749 for not listing herself as a tithable [Judgments & Orders 1746-52, 256, 277, 284]. She was probably identical to "M____s" (damaged order book page), a "free Mulatto" whose son Jimmy was ordered bound to Patrick Matthews by the York County court on 19 August 1751. She was the mother of
      i.   Peter, born say 1741, Moll's "Mulatto" son living in Crab Neck on 16 July 1753 when he bound himself as an apprentice planter to Thomas Wooten, Jr., in York County on 16 July 1753 [Deeds, Bonds 1741-54, 551-2]. He was presented by the court on 16 November 1772 and 15 November 1773 for not listing himself as a tithable [Judgments & Orders 1772-4, 151, 437].
18   ii.   James, born about 1749.
19   iii.   ?William[3], born about 1767.

10.   Mary[2]/ Moll Banks, born say 1724, was the mother of Jane Banks, an orphan (no parent or race mentioned) who was bound apprentice to Walter Leak in Goochland County in September 1744 and called a child of Mary Banks when she was bound to Judith Leak in September 1760 [Orders 1741-44, 132; 1757-61, 365].[24] She was a "free Mulatto" taxable in Walter Leake's Goochland County household in 1746 [List of Tithables]. She was living in Goochland County in May 1757 when her children were bound apprentices [Orders 1750-57, 646; 1757-61, 180]. She was the mother of
      i.   ?Gideon[1], born say 1742, an "orphan boy" (no parent or race mentioned) bound to William Leak in Goochland County in October 1742 [Orders 1741-44, 132].
20   ii.   Jane[1], born about 1744.
21   iii.   Louisa, born say 1746.
22   iv.   John[3], born 25 February 1749.
      v.   Judith[2], born say 1751, an orphan ordered bound out by the churchwardens of St. James Northam Parish in Goochland County in May 1757 (no parent named) and called child of Mary when she was bound to Judith Leak in February 1759 [Orders 1750-7, 646; 1757-61, 180].
23   vi.   Jacob[1], born in August 1754.
      vii.   Agnes, born say 1756, an orphan ordered bound out by the churchwardens of St. James Northam Parish in Goochland County in May 1757 (no parent named) [Orders 1750-57, 646] and called child of Mary when she was bound to Judith Leak in February 1759 [Orders 1757-61, 180]. She was probably the same as Agnes, daughter of "Mary Begs a Negroe w Wal: Leek," who was born January 1756 and baptized 13 June 1756 by Rev. William Douglas [Jones, *Douglas Register*, 348].
      viii.   ?Mary[4], born say 1758, married James **Johnson** (in Goochland County), "both of this parish & Mulattoes," on 7 November 1776 [Jones, *Douglas Register*, 347]. He may have been the James **Johnson**

---

[24]Perhaps Moll Banks was identical to "Moll a Mulatto Girl" who was ordered bound by the churchwardens of St. James Parish to John Williams by the November 1731 Goochland County court [Orders 1731-5, 46].

who was head of a Buckingham County household of 17 "other free" in 1810 [VA:799].

11. Elizabeth[3] Banks, born say 1727, may have been identical to "Mulatto Betty" who was living in Warwick County on 6 July 1749 when the court ordered the churchwardens to bind her son Malicai to Thomas Hobday to be a planter [Minutes 1748-62, 43 (p.30 of transcript)]. She may have been the ancestor of

    24   i.   Malachi[1], born say 1749.

    25   ii.   Elizabeth[5], born say 1762.

          iii. Mary[7]/ Molly, born about 1769, registered in York County on 18 December 1809: *a Mulatto woman about 40 years of age, 5 feet & an half Inch high, her face a little pitted with the small pox, has very large nostrils, pouting thick lips and is a low well set woman - was born of free parents in the Cy of Warwick but has been residing in this Cy for the last 10 Years.* She was head of a Yorktown, York County household of 2 "other free" in 1810 [VA:870].

          iv. William[4], born say 1770, a 16-21 year-old taxable in Warwick County in 1789 and a "Mulatto" taxable there in 1798 [1789 PPTL, p.1; 1798, p.1]. He was taxable in York County from 1793 to 1813 [PPTL, 1782-1841, frames 191, 200, 209, 219, 227, 254, 263, 304, 373]. He was head of a York County household of 4 "free colored" in 1820 (called William Banks, Jr.) [VA:157].

          v.   Thomas[1], born say 1772, a 16-21 year-old taxable in Warwick County in 1789 and a "Mulatto" taxable there in 1798 [1789 PPTL, p.1; 1798, p.1]. He was taxable in York County from 1801 to 1807 [PPTL, 1782-1841, frames 263, 275, 304, 315, 325] and head of a York County household of 5 "other free" in 1810 [VA:871] and 4 "free colored" in 1820 [VA:155].

          vi. Joshua, born say 1780, taxable in York County from 1801 to 1805 [PPTL, 1782-1841, frames 263, 275, 284, 304], head of a Warwick County household of 5 "other free" in 1810 [VA:681].

          vii. William[5], born say 1782, a "Mulatto" over the age of sixteen in 1798 when he was listed in Warwick County, called William Banks, Jr. [PPTL, p.1].

12. William[2] Banks, born say 1755, was head of a Northampton County, North Carolina household of 3 "Black" persons 12-50 years old and 4 "Black" persons less than 12 or over 50 years old in Captain Dupree's district for the 1786 state census. He was permitted to take the oath of insolvent debtor in the 23 August 1798 session of the Halifax County, North Carolina court. Perhaps his widow was Oney Banks, head of a Northampton County household of 5 "free colored" in 1820 [NC:218]. He may have been the father of

          i.   Brittain, born say 1785, ordered bound to Philip Brittle to be a planter by the 3 December 1792 Northampton County court [Minutes 1792-96, 40]. Brittain was head of a Hertford County household of 4 "other free" in 1810 [NC:101].

          ii.   Temperance, born say 1786, head of a Halifax County household of 5 "other free" in 1810 [NC:9] and 4 "free colored" in Northampton County in 1820 [NC:214].

          iii. Elizabeth[9], bound an apprentice farmer to Jesse Smith, Sr., by the 5 December 1814 Northampton County court [Minutes 1813-21], perhaps the Betsy Banks who married Randall **Tann**, 5 July 1816 Northampton County bond, John Priden bondsman.

          iv. Nancy[1], head of a Northampton County household of a "free colored" woman in 1820 [NC:220].

13. Edith Banks, born about 1753, was living in Southampton County on 9 May 1783 when the court ordered the churchwardens of St. Luke's Parish to bind

out her children Jacob and Rebecca Banks [Orders 1778-84, 314]. She registered in Southampton County on 8 April 1808: *age 55, yellow (Colour), 5 feet 3-1/2 inches high, free born* [Register of Free Negroes 1794-1832, nos. 424]. She was a "free Negro" spinner living on Stith Nicholson's land in Southampton County in 1812 and 1813 [PPTL 1807-21, frames 297, 313]. She was the mother of

    i.   Jacob[3], born about 1775, registered in Southampton County on 21 February 1798: *age 23, Blackman, 6 feet 5/8 inches, free born.* He registered again on 12 March 1817 at the age of forty-five [Register of Free Negroes 1794-1832, nos. 121, 1048]. He was taxable in St. Luke's Parish, Southampton County, in John Applewhite's household from 1791 to 1794, a "f.n." with no fixed residence in 1817 [PPTL 1782-92, frames 811, 868; 1792-1806, frame 45, 72; 1807-21, frame 573].

    ii.   Rebecca, born say 1780, married Richard **Artis**, 30 December 1801 Southampton County bond, Evans Pope surety.

    iii.   ?William, taxable in Nottoway Parish, Southampton County, in 1801 (no race indicated) [PPTL 1792-1806, frame 473].

14.   Silas Banks, born say 1761, was taxable in the Southampton County household of William Drewry in 1788 [PPTL 1782-92, frame 658], head of a Northampton County, North Carolina household of 3 "other free" in 1790 [NC:74], 7 in 1800 [NC:429], and 4 "free colored" in Halifax County in 1820 [NC:142]. He was probably outside the county of Northampton in 1810 when (his wife) Omey Banks was head of a household of 5 "other free" in 1810 [NC:715]. He (called Cyrus Banks) and his wife Naomi were named in the 20 September 1832 Champaign County, Ohio petition of Henry **Newsome** for partition of 200 acres in Rush County, Ohio [Champaign County Court of Common Pleas, Thursday, September 1832]. Naomi was apparently identical to Ona Banks who was living with (her son?) Everitt Banks in the Northampton County household of (her son-in-law) Thomas **Smith** in 1850. Silas and Naomi were the parents of

    i.   ?William[8], born about 1791, a poor child bound out in Southampton County on 19 May 1800 [Minutes 1799-1803, 87]. He registered in Southampton County on 20 December 1817: *age 26, 5 feet 9 inches, rather bright (Colour), free born* [Register of Free Negroes 1794-1832, no. 1132]. He married Maria **Pompey**, 9 August 1825 Northampton County bond, Silas Banks bondsman.

    ii.   Everitt, born about 1802, married Rebecca **Artis**, 2 March 1824 Northampton County bond, Everitt Stancell bondsman. He was named as executor of the 25 May 1840 Northampton County will of his uncle Moses **Newsom** [WB 5:48]. He and Ona Banks (born about 1765) were living in the household of (his brother-in-law?) Thomas **Smith** in 1850. He married second, Cherry **Tann**, 6 December 1852 Northampton County bond, January 1853 marriage by Green Stancell.

    iii.   Nancy[4], born about 1808, married Thomas **Smith**, 9 September 1822 Northampton county bond, Everitt Banks bondsman. In 1850 Thomas was head of a Northampton County household with Nancy **Smith** and (Nancy's brother and mother?) Everitt and Ona Banks.

15.   John[2] Banks, Jr., born say 1735, was married before 21 November 1758 when he was presented by the Surry County court for not paying tax on his wife. In 1782 he was head of a Surry County household of 7 persons [VA:43]. He was taxable in Surry County from 1782 to 1800: taxable on 3 horses and 19 cattle in 1782; taxable on Benjamin Banks in 1787; taxable on Nathan Banks in 1788; taxable on Nathan Banks from 1788 to 1790; taxable on a slave named Tab in 1789; taxable on Jacob **Tann**'s tithe in 1797 and 1798 [PPTL, 1782-90, frames 364, 383, 403, 411, 488, 519, 564; 1791-1816, 26, 127, 205, 284,

319, 400]. His estate was settled in Surry County in 1802 [WB 1:580-581]. His children were

    i. ?Jeremiah, born say 1760, head of a Surry County household of no whites in the 1784 list of William Boyce [VA:78]. He was taxable in Surry County from 1783 to 1813: taxable on slaves Joe and Tab, 2 horses and 8 cattle in 1787; taxable on slaves Jo and Aggy in 1788; taxable on slaves Lydia, Harry, Aggy, Fanny in 1789; taxable on slaves Lydia, Harry and Dadan in 1791; taxable on William **Clark**'s tithe and slaves Harry, Liddia, Moses, and Jem in 1800; taxable on 4 free males and 2 slaves in 1809; a "free Negro & Mulatto" taxable on 2 slaves in 1813 [PPTL, 1782-90, frames 372, 403, 411, 488, 519; 1791-1816, 26, 127, 205, 284, 362, 400, 475, 516, 556, 610, 648, 685, 726]. He married Hannah Copeland Price, 15 March 1788 Surry County bond, Edmund Bennett surety. He was head of a Surry County household of 5 "other free" and 2 slaves in 1810 [VA:598].

    ii. Priscilla, born say 1762, "daughter of John Banks," married William **Walden**, 2 February 1778 Surry County bond.

26   iii. Benjamin, born about 1765.

    iv. Faithy, born say 1768, "daughter of John Banks," married James **Wilson**, 31 May 1786 Surry County bond, Joseph **Roberts** surety, 1 June 1786 Isle of Wight marriage.

    v. ?John[4], born say 1769, taxable in Surry County from 1788 to 1790, called John Banks, Jr. [PPTL, 1782-90, frames 488, 519, 564]. He married Mildred **Valentine**, 29 May 1789 Surry County bond, Sampson **Walden** surety, 31 May marriage in Southampton County [Minister's Returns, 642].

    vi. Nathan, born about 1771, taxable in Surry County from 1788 to 1795: listed in his father's household from 1788 to 1790 [PPTL, 1782-90, frames 488, 564; 1791-1816, frames 26, 205]. He registered in Surry County on 3 September 1795: *son of John Banks, a mulattoe man aged 24 years pretty stout made about 5' 10 or 11" high, born of free parents* [Back of Guardian Accounts Book 1783-1804, no. 6]. He was a "free Negro" taxable in Isle of Wight County from 1799 to 1810 [PPTL 1782-1810, frames 459, 508, 540, 557, 617, 634, 692, 733, 751, 809, 828].

27   vii. ?Anthony, born about 1776.

    viii. ?William, a "free Negro" taxable in Isle of Wight County in 1804 and 1805 [PPTL 1782-1810, frames 634, 693].

    ix. ?Clara, married Davis **Jones**, 5 June 1795 Isle of Wight County bond, Francis Young surety, 6 June marriage.

16. Hannah[2] Banks, born say 1731, daughter of Ann Banks, bound herself as an apprentice to Patrick Matthews in York County on 18 November 1745 until the age of twenty-one years [Deeds, Bonds 1741-54, 152]. She was presented by the York County court on 17 November 1766 for not listing herself as a tithable [Orders 1765-68, 161, 206]. She may have been the mother of

    i. Judith[3], born about 1767, registered in York County on 11 February 1803: *a free negro, 36 years of age, five feet 3/4 Inches High of a yellowish complexion, flat nose, wide mouth & black eyes with a dimple in her right cheek when she smiles* [Free Negro Register 1798-1831, no. 21]. She may have been the Judy Banks who was taxable on a slave in York County in 1804 [PPTL, 1782-1841, frame 295].

17. Elizabeth[4]/ Betty Banks, born about 1744, registered in Petersburg on 13 October 1794: *a dark brown Mulatto woman, five feet one inches high, supposed about fifty years old, born free & raised in the County of Richmond* [Register of Free Negroes 1794-1819, no. 93]. She was the mother of

i. Sally, born about 1771, registered in Petersburg on 13 October 1794: *a light Mulatto woman, five feet six inches high, twenty three years old, daughter of Betty & born free* [Register of Free Negroes 1794-1819, no. 94].

18. James Banks, born about 1749, was the son of M___s (damaged order book page), a free Mulatto" living in York County on 19 August 1751 when the court ordered the churchwardens of Yorkhampton Parish to bind out her son Jimmy. James was called a "poor orphan" on 21 February 1763 when the court ordered the churchwardens of Yorkhampton Parish to bind him to James Anderson and called a "Mulatto" in the indenture bond which bound him as an apprentice blacksmith for seven years [Judgments & Orders 1749-53, 451; Deeds 1755-63, 497]. He was taxable in York County from 1784 to 1812 and head of a household of 2 "free Negroes & mulattoes over 16" in 1813 [PPTL, 1782-1841, frames 91, 139, 148, 171, 180, 227, 362, 373, 385]. He may have been the father of
    i. Critty, born about 1781, registered in York County on 16 December 1822: *a very light Mulatto about 41 years of age, 5 feet 4 Inches high*.

19. William[3] Banks, born about 1766, married Patty **Maclin**, 8 September 1787 York County marriage by Rev. John Davenport [*VMHB* XXV:300]. He was taxable in York County from 1788 to 1812, called William Banks "of Poquoson" from 1805 to 1811 and in 1812 when he was taxable on a slave [PPTL, 1782-1841, frames 139, 148, 181, 190, 209, 263, 275, 284, 304, 315, 325, 351, 362, 373]. He was head of a York County household of 8 "other free" in 1810 [VA:870] and 4 "free colored" in 1820 [VA:155]. He registered in York County on 16 December 1822: *a Mulatto about 55 years of age, 5 feet 8-1/2 inches high* [Free Negro Register 1798-1831, no.149]. He was a "free man of colour" who died about 1843-1847 according to a chancery suit over division of his land among his ten children, all of whom were of full age in 1853: William, Fanny (wife of John **Morris**), Milly (married Henry **Wallace**), Christian, Godfrey, Sally (married John **Wallace**), Mary, James, Thomas and Betsy [LVA chancery case 1853-012]. His children were
    i. William[7], born say 1788.
    ii. Fanny, (described as a "lunatic" in 1853) married John **Morris**, plaintiff in the chancery suit.
    iii. Milly, born before 1798, head of a York County household of 1 "free Negroes & mulattoes over 16" in 1813 [PPTL, 1782-1841, frame 385], called Milly **Hunley** of Bruton Parish on 2 December 1846 when she married Henry **Wallace** by York County bond.
    iv. Christian.
    v. Godfrey.
    vi. Sally, married John **Wallace**, 18 December 1848 York County bond.
    vii. Mary.
    viii. James.
    ix. Thomas[3].
    x. Betsy.

20. Jane[1] Banks, born about 1744, was bound to William Leak in Goochland County in September 1744 (no parent or race mentioned) and was called a child of Mary when she was bound to Judith Leak in September 1760. She sued Judith Leak in Goochland County court in June 1762 for her freedom dues [Orders 1741-4, 490; 1756-61, 365; 1761-65, 63, 208]. She died before 22 October 1770 when the Cumberland County court ordered the churchwardens of Southam Parish to bind her "mulattoe" daughter Mary Banks to Edmund Clements. On 25 April 1774 Mary was called the orphan of Jane Banks (no race indicated) when the court ordered her bound to Joseph Leek [Orders 1770-2, 107; 1774-8, 156]. She was the mother of

     i. Mary[5], born say 1765, bound out in Cumberland County in 1770.

21. Louisa Banks, born say 1746, was bound to Walter Leak in Goochland County in November 1749. She was called a child of Mary Banks when she was bound to Judith Leak in September 1760 [Orders 1744-9, 561; 1757-61, 365]. She was the mother of
     i. Mary[6], born say 1766, "infant of Louisa Banks" (no age or race mentioned) bound to Shadrack Mimms in April 1767 [Orders 1765-70, 15]. She married Henry **Isaacs**, 4 November 1787 Goochland County bond, Josiah Leake surety. She was called Molly **Isaacs** in October 1804 when her children Peyton and Austin **Isaacs** (nine and eleven years old) were bound to William Clarke [Goochland County Miscellaneous Court Papers 1728-1840, LVA cited by Butler, *Evolution of a Rural Free Black Community*, 224]. Molly was head of a Goochland County household of 6 "other free" in 1810 [VA:699].
    ii. Gideon[2], child of Louisa, a "free Negro," bound to Shadrack Mimms in Goochland in November 1768 [Orders 1765-70, 277].

22. John[3] Banks, born 25 February 1749, was an orphan ordered bound out by the churchwardens of St. James Northam Parish in Goochland County in May 1757 and was called the child of Mary when he was bound to Judith Leak in February 1759 [Orders 1750-7, 646; 1757-61, 180]. He was taxable in the upper district of Goochland County from 1787 to 1813: charged with James Banks' tithe from 1795 to 1798, a "Mulatto" planter near James Wares' land in 1804, living near James Holman from 1805 to 1813, charged with John Banks, Jr.'s tithe in 1811, listed with his wife Sally, John, Judy and Nancy Banks in 1813 [PPTL, 1782-1809, frames 149, 217, 278, 338, 387, 419, 478, 523, 614, 736, 820; 1810-32, frames 3, 156]. He was head of a Goochland County household of 11 "other free" in 1810 [VA:684]. He registered as a free Negro in Goochland County on 3 September 1823: *a man of colour, was 74 years of age the 25th day of last February, about six feet high* [Register of Free Negroes, p.152]. He enlisted in Goochland County about 1779, served for two years, and was discharged at the barracks in Albemarle County. On 22 May 1822 when he applied for a pension, his family consisted of his wife Sally, his thirteen-year-old niece Mary Banks and his twelve-year-old nephew John **Brown**. He died before 19 August 1845 when his wife applied for and was granted a widow's pension. She stated that she was born about 1756 and that they were married about the spring of 1772 by Parson McLaerin in the Episcopal Church of Cumberland County, Virginia. On 6 February 1846 Walter D. Leake of Henrico County testified that Sally had a daughter living who was at least seventy years old [National Archives Pension File W.5763; Dorman, *Virginia Revolutionary Pension Applications*, IV:51]. He was the father of
     i. Sally, born 2 July 1779, "son of John Banks," married Thomas **Lynch**, 29 July 1801 Goochland County bond, Edward **Fuzmore** surety, 29 July marriage [Minister's Returns, 78].
    ii. Judith[4], born about 1794, twenty-one-year-old daughter of John Banks, married Elijah **Day**, 28 December 1815 Goochland County bond, Jacob **Martin** surety [Ministers' Returns, 127].
   iii. Jane[3], born say 1785, "daughter of John Banks," married Dick **Adams**, 5 December 1803 Goochland County bond, Josiah Leaks surety, 5 December marriage [Ministers' Returns, 85]. Richard **Adams** was head

of a Goochland County household of 4 "other free" in 1810 [VA:682].[25]

23. Jacob[1] Banks, born in August 1754 according to his pension application, was an orphan ordered bound out by the churchwardens of St. James Northam Parish in Goochland County in May 1757 (no parent named) and called child of Mary Banks when he was bound to Judith Leak in February 1759. In December 1772 he sued Elisha Leak whom he was bound to as an apprentice, and the court bound him instead to Peter Pollock to learn the trade of carpenter [Orders 1750-57, 646; 1757-61, 180; 1771-78, 263]. He married Susannah **Jones**, "Mulattoes both," on 29 August 1775 in Goochland County [Jones, *The Douglas Register*, 347]. He was taxable in the upper district of Goochland County from 1782 to 1813: taxable on a horse and 2 cattle in 1782, charged with John **Lynch**'s tithe in 1789, listed as a "Mulatto" carpenter on Thomas E. Randolph's land in 1804, charged with Martin and Elisha Banks' tithes in 1806, a "Mulatto" farmer living on Jesse Sanders's land when he was charged with Elisha Banks' tithe in 1809, charged with John Banks' tithe from 1810 to 1813, listed with wife Sucky in 1813 [PPTL, 1782-1809, frames 15, 42, 72, 131, 175, 217, 278, 356, 419, 478, 614, 685, 777, 863; 1810-32, frames 4, 69, 155]. He was head of a Goochland County household of 7 "other free" in 1810 [VA:684]. He registered as a "free Negro" in Goochland County on 21 September 1818: *a free man of color aged 64 years about five feet Six inches high* [Register of Free Negroes, p.106, no.221]. He was living in Goochland County on 17 September 1832 when he made a declaration to obtain a pension for his Revolutionary War services. He was a "free man of Color" who served eighteen months as a wagoner. He died 5 January 1835 [Dorman, *Virginia Revolutionary Pension Applications*, IV:51]. Jacob's children were

   i.   Elizabeth[6], born say 1776, "daughter of Jacob Banks," married Drury **Farrar**, 2 December 1792 Goochland County bond, 3 December marriage by Rev. Lewis Chaudoin.

   ii.   ?William[5], born say 1780, taxable in Goochland County in 1798 [PPTL, 1782-1809, frames 478], married Nancy **Martin**, 16 February 1808 Goochland County bond, John **Martin** surety.

   iii.   Polly, born say 1781, daughter of Jacob **Banks**, married John **Tiler** (**Tyler**), 23 December 1797 Goochland County bond, Francis **Tiler** surety.

   iv.   Martin, born about 1787, married Betsy Ann **Howell**, daughter of Charles **Howell**, 11 March 1812 Goochland County bond, William **Howell** surety. He registered in Goochland County on 22 August 1810: *a free man of color, about twenty three years of age, five feet seven inches & an half high* [Register of Free Negroes, p.39, no.79].

   v.   Elisha, born about 1788, registered in Goochland County on 22 August 1810: *five feet seven inches an half high, about twenty two years of age, yellow complexion, hair inclining to bushy* [Register of Free Negroes, p.39, no.80]. He married Nancy **Lynch**, daughter of Polly **Lynch**, "people of color," 10 March 1813 Goochland County bond, 11 March marriage, Robert **Lynch** surety. He was a "Mulatto" taxable in 1813 with his wife Nancy, farming land owned by Rice Innes.

   vi.   Nancy[2], born say 1790, "daughter of Jacob Banks," married William **Cooper**, 29 August 1809 Goochland County bond, 1 September marriage, Jacob **Martin** surety.

---

[25]Richard **Adams** purchased his freedom from James Holman in 1803 [DB 18:618]. For details on Richard **Adams** and other Goochland County free African Americans see Reginald Butler's doctoral thesis, "Evolution of a rural free black community: Goochland County, Virginia, 1728-1832."

vii. John, born say 1792, taxable in Jacob Banks' household from 1810 to 1813.

24. Malachi[1] Banks, born say 1749, was taxable in York County on 19 May 1783 when the court presented Elizabeth Pescud for not listing him as a tithable [Orders 1774-84, 324, 334]. And he was taxable on his own tithe from 1784 to 1814 [PPTL, 1782-1841, frames 83, 97, 170, 181, 190, 227, 275, 325, 337, 362, 373, 385, 403]. On 21 January 1793 the York County court discharged him from his recognizance on the complaint of Elizabeth **Cuttillo** and Mary **Hopson** for a breach of the peace [Orders 1788-95, 507]. He may have been the father of

    i. Godfrey, taxable in York County in 1791 [PPTL, 1782-1841, frame 170], head of a York County household of 5 "other free" in 1810 [VA:871].

    ii. Lucy, head of a York County household of 3 "other free" in 1810 [VA:871].

    iii. Malachi[2], born about 1792, registered in York County on 19 February 1810: *a slim fellow of yellow complexion 5 feet 6 Inches high abt 18 years of age, short thick hair, large flat nose...Born of a free Woman in the parish of York Hampton*. On 15 July 1833 he and his wife Judith registered their daughter Lucy: *a small Girl about 10 years of age, a little cross Eyed...a wide gap between her Teeth (she and her Brother, now at the Breast, are children of Malachi & Judith Banks, free persons of colour* [Free Negro Register 1798-1831, nos. 39, 147, 42; 1831-50, no. 298].

25. Elizabeth[5] Banks, born say 1762, was called a "Free Mulatto" on 2 March 1783 when her son John was baptized in Bruton Parish, York and James City counties [Bruton Parish Register, 35]. She was taxable in York County on a horse in 1800, on a free tithable and a slave in 1801, 2 tithables from 1802 to 1804, 2 horses in 1805, 2 tithables and 2 horses in 1806 and taxable on a horse in 1807 [PPTL, 1782-1841, frames 254, 263, 275, 285, 295, 304, 315, 325], head of a York County household of 4 "other free" in 1810 [VA:887] and 3 "free colored" in 1820 [VA:157]. She was the mother of

    i. John, baptized in Bruton Parish on 2 March 1783. He was taxable in York County in 1805 and 1807, taxable on 2 tithes in 1809, taxable on a slave in 1810, taxable on a tithe and a horse in 1811 and 1812 [PPTL, 1782-1841, frames 304, 325, 337, 351, 362, 373] and head of a York County household of 6 "other free" and a slave in 1810 [VA:887].

26. Benjamin Banks, born about 1765, was taxable in Surry County from 1787 to 1816: taxable in John Banks' household in 1787; taxable on 2 tithes in 1805; 3 in 1807; 4 "free Negroes & Mulattoes above the age of 16," 3 of whom were male tithables in 1813 [PPTL, 1782-90, frames 411, 519; 1791-1816, 26, 177, 252, 319, 400, 475, 556, 589, 628, 666, 704, 726, 848]. He was twenty-three years old when he married Mary **Valentine**, 12 December 1788 Surry County bond, John Banks surety. He registered as a "free Negro" in Surry County on 5 September 1798: *...son of John Banks ...a Mulatto man bright complexion aged about 30 years, has bushy hair, about five feet eight inches high, pretty well made, by profession a planter* [Back of Guardian Accounts Book 1783-1804, no.32]. He married, second, Lucy **Bruce**, daughter of Elizabeth **Bruce**, 22 January 1803 Surry County bond, 19 February marriage, James **Roberts** surety. Benjamin was head of a Surry County household of 9 "other free" in 1810 [VA:601] and 12 "free colored" in 1830. The inventory of his Surry County estate was taken in 1832 [WB 6:303-4]. His wife Lucy was called "widow and relict of Benjamin Banks" in her 25 September 1841

Surry County will, proved 24 February 1845, which named her children Parthenia and Dawson and many of her grandchildren. Their children were

    i.   William[6], born about 1787, registered in Surry County on 2 June 1809: *a Mulatto Man aged about 22 years a son of Benjamin Banks of Surry County, thick lips has a large Nose, yellow complexion, his hair grows low in his forehead...and is 5'6" high* [Hudgins, *Surry County Register of Free Negroes*, 38].

    ii. Sampson, born about 1789, registered in Surry County on 28 March 1831: *a mulatto man, son of Benjamin Banks...has curley hair, a pleasant countenance, of a bright complexion, stout made, is about 42 years of age and is 5'8-1/2" high* [Hudgins, *Surry County Register of Free Negroes*, 91].

   iii. Parthenia, married Elias **Francis**.

   iv. Dawson, born about September 1803, registered in Surry County on 26 December 1825: *a son of Benjamin Banks, a free Mulato Man of Surry County...aged 22 years, some time in Sept. 1825 is 5'9-3/4" high, of a bright complexion, pretty stout & straight made* [Hudgins, *Surry County Register of Free Negroes*, 81]. He was a "free Negro" fisherman on Dawson Davis' land in 1841.

    v. Elizabeth[7]/ Betsy, born say 1786, the mother of Benjamin's grandson John Banks who registered as a "free Negro" in Surry County on 23 May 1834: *The bearer John Banks son of Betsy Banks was born Nov 14th 1816 in the above named county within two miles of my House and lived with his Grandfather Benjamin Banks at the above named place until the year 1832. The above named John Banks was free born and his connections for three generations past. James Wilson.*

27. Anthony Banks, born about 1776, was a "FN" taxable in Sussex County from 1804 to 1809 [PPTL 1782-1812, frames 610, 646, 675, 699, 747]. He was taxable in Greensville County from 1810 to 1814: listed with Nancy in 1813, "Mulattos," called Anthony Miles Banks in 1814 when he was taxable on 2 free tithes and 2 horses [PPTL 1782-1850, frames 400, 413, 430, 445, 460]. He and his wife Nancy were the heirs of Thomas and Lucretia **Stewart**. On 12 December 1807 he and Nancy, Henry **Stewart**, and Peyton **Stewart** sold 114 acres in Greensville County on the south side of Fountain Creek and both sides of Jordan's Road which they received by Thomas **Stewart**'s will, and on 8 May 1809 Anthony and Nancy purchased 30 acres adjoining this land in Greensville County from James and Sarah **Watkins**. This was James and Sarah's allotment from the estate of Lucretia **Byrd**, widow of Thomas **Stewart** [DB 3:520; 4:117]. On 12 February 1810 the Greensville County court granted him a license to keep an ordinary at his house [Orders 1806-10, 429]. He received a certificate of freedom in Sussex County on 1 September 1814. He was described as a *free born, brown skin man, 5'9-1/2" tall, aged 26* [Register of Free Negroes, no.244]. His wife Nancy Banks registered as a "Free Negro" in Greensville County, Virginia, on 14 September 1814: *wife of Anthony Banks, born free, of a black Complexion, aged twenty six years...five feet 4-1/2 Inches high in shoes* [Register of Free Negroes, no.46]. Anthony and Nancy were living in Perry Township, Logan County, Ohio, in 1850 [Census p.206]. Two of their children were

    i. Ewing S., born about 1807, forty-five years old when he registered in Logan County, Ohio, on 11 June 1852: *5'10" tall, dark brown complexion...son of Anthony & Nancy Banks.*

    ii. Eaton Wilkison, born about 1813, twenty-one years old when he registered in Logan County on 24 June 1834: *5'10" tall, dark brown complexion...son of Anthony & Nancy Banks* [Turpin, *Register of Black, Mulatto, and Poor Persons*, 13, 10].

Other York County descendants were

i. Thomas[2], born about 1788, registered in York County on 18 November 1822: *a Mulatto fellow about 34 years of age 5 feet 6-1/4 inches high, has a very rough face* [Free Negro Register 1798-1831, no.132]. He was taxable in York County from 1812 to 1814, head of a household of 2 "free Negroes & mulattoes over 16" in 1813 (probably himself and his wife) [PPTL, 1782-1841, frames 373, 385, 403].

ii. Elizabeth[8]/ Betsy, born about 1788, registered in York County on 16 December 1822: *a dark Mulatto 34 years of age 5 feet 8-/12 inches high* [Register, no.183]. She was head of a York County household of 4 "other free" in 1810 [VA:871].

iii. Hannah[4], born about 1804, registered in York County on 19 September 1831, *a woman about 27 years old, 5 feet 5-3/4 inches high, quite black...broad face, high cheek bones* [Register, no.352].

iv. Lavinia, born about 1806, registered in York County on 16 January 1832: *a woman of tawny complexion, about 26 years of age, 5 feet 5 and a half high, high cheek bones, sunken or hollow eyes, flat nose* [Register, no.327].

v. William[9], born about 1807, registered in York County on 19 September 1831: *alias Stump, a dark fellow 5 feet 4-3/4 inches high twenty four years old, has...a stump toe. Born free* [Register, no.291].

vi. William[10], born about 1808, registered in York County on 19 September 1831: *a bright mulatto about 23 years of age 5 feet 7-3/4 inches high...short hair, little or no beard and a high nose* [Register, no.299].

vii. Martha, born about 1810, registered in York County on 17 October 1831: *a woman of Tawney complexion about 20 or 21 years of age 5 feet 3-1/2 Inches high...high forehead & large eye brows. Born free* [Register, no.308].

viii. Matilda, born about 1815, registered in York County on 15 July 1833: *light complexion, about 18 years of age, 5 feet 5-1/4 Inches high, light yellow Eyes - high cheek bones...Has the scar of vaccination for Kine or smallpox on her left arm* [Register, no.351].

Other descendants in North Carolina were

i. Jane[2], born say 1765, head of an Edenton Town, Chowan County, North Carolina household of 2 "other free" in 1790 [NC:19], 3 in 1800 [NC:116], and 4 in 1810 [NC:533].

ii. Jacob[2], born before 1776, head of a Craven County, North Carolina household of 4 "free colored" in 1820 [NC:77]. He married Phebe **Moore**, 13 August 1821 Craven County bond.

iii. Lettice, born 1776-94, head of a Chowan County household of 3 "free colored" in 1820 [NC:129].

iv. Sarah, born 1794-1806, head of an Edenton household of 2 "free colored" in 1820 [NC:130].

v. Washington, born 1794-1806, head of an Edenton household of 1 "free colored" in 1820 [NC:130].

vi. Nancy[3], born 1794-1806, head of a Chowan County household of 2 "free colored" in 1820 [NC:129].

vii. Mary[8], born 1794-1806, head of an Edenton household of 1 "free colored" in 1820 [NC:130].

BANNISTER FAMILY

1. Isabella, born say 1730, a "Mulatto woman," was the mother of James, Oliver, Frank, and Cate who were named in Caleb Sesson's 21 June 1771 Orange County, Virginia will, proved 22 August 1771. Sesson asked that his sons and executors William, Caleb, and George Sesson have the children legally bound to them and that they be divided equally according to valuation

[WB 2:436-7].[26] They were valued in the 13 November 1771 inventory of his estate:

James a Negro man 30 pounds, Oliver a Lad 30 pounds, Frank a Negro boy 25 pounds, Cate a Negro boy 15 pounds [WB 2:442].

Isabella may have been related to Sarah Banister, head of a Queen Anne's County, Maryland household of 7 "other free" in 1790. And they may have been related to Mary Bannister who was sued for debt by the churchwardens of Caroline County, Virginia, in 1740 (for having a bastard child?) [Orders 1740-43]. Isabella's children were

	i.	James, born say 1752.
2	ii.	Oliver, born say 1755.
3	iii.	Francis, born say 1758.
	iv.	Catherine, born say 1761.
	v.	?Arthur, born say 1771, died before 27 January 1794 when (his brother?) Oliver Banister was granted administration on his estate on 1,000 pounds security in Orange County, Virginia [Minute Book 1789-97, 205].
4	vi.	?Henry, born before 1776.
5	vii.	?Esther, born say 1776.

2. Oliver[1] Bannister, born say 1755, was called a "Mullatto Claim'd by Wm Sesson" on 28 March 1782 when he petitioned the Orange County court for his freedom (from his indenture?) [Minutes 1774-89, 171]. On 27 January 1794 he was granted administration on the Orange County estate of (his brother?) Arther Bannister [Minutes 1789-97, 205]. He was a "Free Negro" head of a Culpeper County household of 5 "other free" in 1810 [VA:7]. He may have been the father of

i.	Oliver[2], born say 1790, a "Mulatto" bound as an apprentice tailor to James M. Early in Botetourt County on 14 June 1796 [Gill, *Apprentices of Virginia*, 15]. He was head of a Rockbridge County household of 4 "other free" in 1810 [VA:284].
ii.	Elijah, born 1776-94, head of a Botetourt County household of 1 "free colored" and a white woman in 1820.
iii.	Winn, born 1776-94, head of a Mecklenburg County, Virginia household of 6 "free colored" in 1820.
iv.	Thomas, born say 1780, a "free Negro & mulatto" taxable living with his wife and five children in Chesterfield County in 1811 [PPTL, 1786-1811, frame 824].

3. Francis[1] Bannister, born say 1758, was counted in the "List of Free Negroes & Mulattoes" for Botetourt County in 1802. He was listed as a cooper living on James Lackey's land in John Holloway's District with his wife Lucy and children and in George Rowland's District for 1803 [A List of Free Negroes & Mulattors within the District of James Tunor Commissioner of Botetourt for the Year 1802, no.51; 1803, no.1]. He was head of a Botetourt County household of 11 "free colored" in 1820. His children were

i.	?Eleanor, born say 1783, married Samuel **Day**, 26 December 1801 Botetourt County bond, Francis Bannister surety.
ii.	Becky, born say 1786.
iii.	Nancy, born say 1787.
iv.	Isbell, born say 1789.
v.	Rachel, born about 1791, eleven years old in the 1802 Botetourt list.
vi.	James[2], born about 1792, ten years old in 1802.
vii.	Jenkins, born about 1793, nine years old in 1802. He registered as a "free Negro" in Botetourt County in July 1819: *Jenkin Bannister son*

---

[26]He also left four pounds currency annually for five years to Sarah **Lantor**.

of Francis, 25 years old, yellow colour 5'7" Born Free [Free Negroes &c Registered in the Clerks office of Botetourt County, no.23].

viii. Alexander, born about 1796, six years old in 1802, head of a Botetourt County household of a "free colored" man in 1820.

ix. Francis[2], born about 1798, four years old in 1802.

x. William, born about 1800, two and one-half years old in 1802.

xi. John, born about 1803, counted in the 1803 Botetourt list.

4. Henry Bannister, born before 1776, was head of a Botetourt County household of 6 "free colored" in 1820. He may have been the father of

i. Simon, born about 1810, twenty-one years old when he registered as a "free Negro" in Botetourt County in November 1831: *Bright Black, 5'6" or 7" high* [Register, no.73].

ii. Eliza, born about 1818, eighteen years old when she registered in March 1836: *Bright Mulatto, 5'2" high* [Register, no.89].

5. Esther Bannister, born say 1776, was the mother of

i. Christopher, born about 1796, twenty-four years old on 13 June 1820 when he registered in Botetourt County: *Ch[s] Banister, son of Esther Banister, Dark Yellow, 5'8", born free by information from Ch[s] Beale Esqr* [Register, no.33a]. He married Maria **Madden** sometime after 11 June 1823 when he acknowledged paternity of her daughter Sally [Madden, *We Were Always Free*, 49, 53, 54, 206].

BARBER FAMILY

1. Jane Barbers, born say 1727, was living in Chesterfield County, Virginia, on 5 July 1754 when the court ordered the churchwardens of Dale Parish to bind out her "Mulatto" child Nanny. Her daughter was called Ann Barber in April 1755 when the court ordered the churchwardens to bind her out to a trade [Orders 1749-54, 510; 1754-9, 61]. She was the mother of

2 i. ?William[1], born 17 May 1745.

3 ii. ?Thomas, born about 1748.

4 iii. Nanny/ Nancy, born before 5 July 1754.

2. William[1] Barber, born on 17 May 1745 in Dinwiddie County, was living in Surry County, North Carolina, on 2 January 1833 when he made a declaration in court to obtain a Revolutionary War pension. He stated that he was living in Halifax County, Virginia, when called into the service and moved to Surry County about 1805. His widow was Amey or Noama Barber [M805-48]. He was taxable in the southern district of Halifax County, Virginia, from 1782 to 1803: called a "Mulatto" starting in 1792, listed with 2 tithables in 1795 and 1796; 3 in 1798, 3 in 1800 when he was called "Senr." [PPTL, 1782-1799, frames 5, 127, 185, 259, 412, 434, 533, 598, 671, 808; 1800-12, 49, 175, 304]. He was head of a Surry County, North Carolina household of 8 "other free" in 1810 [NC:697] and 6 "free colored" in 1820 [NC:670]. He was probably the father of

i. William[2], Jr., born about 1773 in Virginia, a "Mulatto" taxable in Halifax County from 1801 to 1803 [PPTL, 1800-12, frames 120, 175, 304], head of a Surry County, North Carolina household of 3 "other free" in 1810 [NC:697], listed in the 1850 census as a Mulatto farmer with a white wife Mary.

ii. Matthew[1], born say 1775, a "FN" taxable in Halifax County in 1803 [PPTL, 1800-12, frame 304].

iii. Sally, married Richard **Lawrence**, 23 September 1817 Surry County, North Carolina bond.

3. Thomas Barber, born about 1748, a "Mullatto" servant, complained to the Chesterfield County court against his master the Rev. Mr. William Leigh. Leigh agreed to discharge him from further servitude on 5 November 1779. His suit for assault and battery against John Coates and Robert Burton was dismissed on agreement of the parties in June 1784 [Orders 1774-84, 264, 552]. He was taxable in Chesterfield County from 1791 to 1799 [PPTL, 1786-1811, frames 80, 293, 227, 366]. He registered in Petersburg on 18 August 1794: *a light brown Mulatto man, five feet 5 & a half inches high & thin made, about forty six years old, free born* [Register of Free Negroes 1794-1819, no. 23]. He was listed as a "F.N." tithable in the upper district of Henrico County in 1803 [Land Tax List, 1799-1816 (includes Personal Property Tax lists)]. His widow Juday registered in Petersburg on 24 January 1803: *(widow of Thos. Barber a free man) a light brown Mulatto woman, five feet four inches high, forty years old, born free, freckles in her face* [Register of Free Negroes 1794-1819, no. 249]. She was head of a Petersburg Town household of 7 "other free" in 1810 [VA:122a]. They were the parents of

    i.   John[2], born 27 July 1780, registered in Petersburg on 18 June 1807: *a brown Mulatto man, five feet seven and a half inches high, nineteen years old 27 July next, son of Judah Barber, a free woman* [Register of Free Negroes 1794-1819, no. 409].

    ii.   ?William[3], born about 1785, registered in Petersburg on 13 August 1806: *Billy Barber, a light brown free negro man, five feet seven inches high, twenty one years old, a shoemaker by trade, born free & raised in the Town of Petersburg* [Register of Free Negroes 1794-1819, no. 394]. He was taxable in Chesterfield County from 1802 to 1807 [PPTL, 1786-1811, frames 480, 518, 556, 689].

    iii.   Matthew[2], born September 1790, registered in Petersburg on 29 January 1811: *a yellow brown Mulatto man, five feet six 3/4 inches high, twenty one years old Sept. next, son of Judah Barber a free Mulatto woman* [Register of Free Negroes 1794-1819, no. 654].

4. Nancy Barber, born about 1752, obtained a certificate of freedom in Chesterfield County on 14 September 1807: *fifty five years old, yellow complexion, born free* [Register of Free Negroes 1804-53, no. 46]. She was called Nanny Barber when she was taxable on 1-2 horses in Chesterfield County from 1793 to 1804, taxable on a tithe from 1796 to 1801, a "Mulatto living on her own land in 1809 [PPTL 1786-1811, 156, 227, 262, 293, 329, 368, 443, 480, 518, 556, 738]. She may have been the mother of

    i.   John[1], born about 1770, taxable in Chesterfield County from 1791 to 1811 when he was living on James Scott's land [PPTL, 1786-1811, frames 80, 227, 441, 556, 782]. He obtained a certificate of freedom in Chesterfield County on 9 January 1809: *thirty nine years old, yellow complexion, born free* [Register of Free Negroes 1804-53, no. 98]. His wife Priscilla registered in Petersburg on 3 January 1809: *yellow brown free negro woman, five feet two inches high, thirty six years old, wife of John Barber, born free & raised in the Town of Petersburg* [Register of Free Negroes 1794-1819, no. 445].

    ii.   Aggy, born about 1773, obtained a certificate of freedom in Chesterfield County on 13 June 1808: *thirty five years old, yellow complexion, born free* [Register of Free Negroes 1804-53, no. 72, 455]. She was a "Mulatto" living in Chesterfield County with her five children in 1811 [PPTL 1786-1811, frame 824].

    iii.   Suckey, born about 1779, obtained a certificate of freedom in Chesterfield County on 14 September 1807: *twenty eight years old, brown complexion, born free* [Register of Free Negroes 1804-53, no. 47]. She was a "Mulatto" taxable on a horse and living on William Varner's land in Chesterfield County in 1809 [PPTL, frame 738]. She was called Sucky **Harris** on 3 July 1812 when she registered in

Petersburg: *(formerly Barber) a yellow brown Mulatto woman, five feet three 3/4 inches high, thirty three years old, born free and raised in the County of Chesterfield* [Register of Free Negroes 1794-1819, no. 708].
  iv. Jinsey, born about 1782, obtained a certificate of freedom in Chesterfield County on 13 June 1808: *twenty six years old, yellow complexion, born free* [Register of Free Negroes 1804-53, no. 73].
  v. Phebe W., born about 1787, obtained a certificate of freedom in Chesterfield County on 14 September 1807: *twenty years old, yellow complexion, born free* [Register of Free Negroes 1804-53, no. 48, 151].

Other members of the family were:
  i. John, head of a Frederick County, Virginia household of 7 "other free" in 1810 [VA:563].
  ii. Elizabeth, born before 1776, head of a Hyde County, North Carolina household of 5 "free colored" in 1820 [NC:248].
  iii. Jenny, born before 1776, head of a Hyde County household of 5 "free colored" in 1820 [NC:248].
  iv. Sarah, married Peter **Godett**, 26 April 1797 Craven County, North Carolina bond, William Tignor bondsman. Peter was head of a Craven County household of 1 "other free" in 1790 [NC:130].
  v. Harry, head of a Stafford County household of 3 "other free" in 1810 [VA:126].
  vi. Aaron, an Indian wheelwright living on Connelly Mullins' land in Goochland County from 1809 to 1811 [PPTL, 1782-1809, frame 862; 1810-32, frames 4, 69], counted in a list of "free Negroes & Mulattoes" in Fluvanna County in 1813 and 1814 [PPTL, 1809-50, frames 503, 526].
  vii. Samuel, head of a Norfolk County household of 1 "other free" and a slave in 1810 [VA:887].
  viii. Marina **Mackey**/ Barber, born say 1820, a "free woman of Colour," presented by the Spring 1843 session of the Hyde County court for unlawfully marrying a slave named Riley who was owned by R.U.S. Moore. Marina was probably related to Robert **Mackey**, head of a Hyde County household of 2 "other free" and a white woman in 1800 [NC:372].

BARTLETT/ BARTLEY FAMILY

Mixed-race members of the Bartley/ Bartlett family born before 1750 were
1   i. Solomon[1], born about 1727.
2   ii. Joseph, born say 1735.
3   iii. Miriam Bartlett, born say 1738.
4   iv. David, born say 1740.

1. Solomon[1] Bartlett/ Bartley, born about 1727, was living in Southampton County (called Solomon Bartlett) on 13 April 1758 when John Powell sued him for trespass, assault and battery. The case was dismissed on agreement of the parties [Orders 1754-9, 431]. He was exempted from paying taxes by the Bertie County court in 1777 [Haun, *Bertie County Court Minutes*, IV:246]. He and his wife Amy were "free Mulattows" taxed in the 1770 Bertie list of James Moore and in James Churchwell's 1772 tax list [CR 010.702.1].[27] He probably died before August 1781 when the Bertie court ordered his children

---

[27]He was called Bartlet in the 1770 and 1772 tax lists and in the court records, but he was called Bartly in the tax lists from 1772-1775. His children were called Bartlett in 1790, Bartley in 1800, and Bartlet in 1810 and 1820.

bound out as apprentices. They were called children of Amey Bartlet in November 1782. In August 1783 the court ordered that John Johnston have administration of his estate on 400 pounds security [Haun, *Bertie County Court Minutes*, V:393, 435, 468, 465, 496]. His children were

    i.   ?Hall, head of a Bertie County household of 4 "other free" in 1790 [NC:11]. Rebecca Bartley (his widow?) was head of Bertie County household of 2 "other free" in 1800 [NC:34].

    ii.   Henry[2], born about 1769, fourteen years old in 1783 when the Bertie court ordered him bound as an apprentice shoemaker. He was head of a Bertie County household of 2 "other free" in 1800 [NC:34]. He married Edith **Butler**, 1 June 1804 Bertie County bond.

    iii.   Benjamin[2], born about 1771, ten years old in August 1781 when the Bertie court ordered him bound as an apprentice cooper [Haun, *Bertie County Court Minutes*, V:398].

    iv.   Solomon[2], born about 1772, eleven years old in 1783 when the Bertie court ordered him bound as an apprentice shoemaker. He was head of an Edgecombe County household of 1 "other free" and a slave in 1800 [NC:186], 4 "other free" in 1810 [NC:740], and 6 "free colored" and a slave in 1820 [NC:119].

2.   Joseph Bartley, born say 1735, was called Joseph Barkley, a "Mulatto," on 21 November 1758 when the Surry County, Virginia court presented him for not listing his wife as a tithable [Orders 1757-64, 135].[28] And he was called Joseph Barkley the following year on 19 November 1759 when the York County court presented him for not listing himself as a tithable. The case was dismissed when he paid his tax. He was called Joseph Bartlett on 20 August 1764 when he sued Christiana Kemp for debt in York County court in a case that was dismissed on agreement of the parties. On 17 December 1764 he was called Joseph Bartley when the court ordered him to pay the parish of Bruton 500 pounds of tobacco for not listing his wife as a tithable [Judgments & Orders 1759-63, 281, 308, 320, 90]. He and his wife Elizabeth, "Boath free mulattoes," registered the birth of their son James in Bruton Parish, James City County in 1768 [Bruton Parish Register, 33]. And he and his wife Elizabeth sued William **Wilson** in court for trespass, assault and battery on 18 June 1770 [Orders 1768-70, 508; 1770-2, 25]. He may have been identical to Josias Bartley who was taxable in York County from 1792 to 1795, taxable on two slaves and a horse in 1793 [PPTL, 1782-1841, frames 180, 191, 199, 209]. He was a "M"(ulatto) tavern keeper with Mary Bartlet on Tanner's Creek in Norfolk County from 1800 to 1802 [PPTL, 1791-1812, frames 351, 371, 383, 427]. Joseph and Elizabeth were the parents of

5   i.   James, born 8 July 1768.

    ii.   ?Matthew, born 25 January 1783, son of Elizabeth Bartlett, a Free mulatto" [Bruton Parish Register, 35].

    iii.   ?Benjamin[5], born about 1786, registered in Norfolk County on 17 November 1811: *5 feet 9 In. 25 years of age of a Yellowish Complexion, Born free* [Register of Free Negros & Mulattos, no. 65].

3.   Miriam Bartlett, born say 1738, was living in Southampton County, Virginia, on 8 February 1759 when her "mulatto" son Henry[1] Bartlett was bound apprentice [Orders 1754-59, 487]. She may have been the Mary Bartley who lived on land in Surry County, Virginia, on each side of Tarapin Swamp which was described on 16 November 1770 by Joseph Hargrave as "the land whereon Mary Bartley formerly lived" [DB 10:119; Hopkins, *Surry County Deeds and Estate Accounts, 1756-1787*, 52]. One of her descendants may have lived with the Nottoway Indians for a while since Solomon[3] Bartlett (born about 1800)

---

[28]Others from Bruton Parish presented by the Surry Court were the **Peters** and **Tann** families.

and Fanny Bartlett (born about 1798) were listed in an 1808 Nottoway Indian census [LVA, Box 154a, Executive Papers June 21-July 22 1808, pp.4-5]. Solomon registered in Southampton County on 29 November 1821: *5 feet 9 1/4 inches high Brown complection, one of the Nottoway Tribe of Indians* [Register of Free Negroes 1794-1832, no. 1298]. Miriam was the mother of

i. ?Benjamin[1], born about 1755, a "poor child" bound apprentice in Southampton County on 14 November 1771. He may have been related to a member of the **Byrd** family because his apprenticeship to Nathan Bryant was vacated and he was bound instead to John **Byrd** "for reasons appearing to the court" on 14 May 1772 [Orders 1768-72, 470, 532]. He registered as a free Negro in Southampton County on 12 June 1794: *Age 39, Colour Black, born of free parents in Southampton* [Register of Free Negroes 1794-1832, no. 27]. He was a "M"(ulatto) taxable in St. Luke's Parish, Southampton County, from 1806 to 1810 but not taxable there in 1811 [PPTL 1792-1806, frame 838; 1807-21, frames 47, 69, 166].

ii. Henry[1], born say 1758, apparently identical to Henry Barclay who complained to the Southampton County court against his master Simon Vick on 13 February 1777 [Minutes 1775-8, n.p.].

4. David Bartley, born say 1740, was paid as a witness for Daniel **Armfield** in his York County suit against Peter **Gillett** on 16 March 1761. He was sued for a 6 pound debt in York County court on 19 July 1762 [Judgments & Orders 1759-63, 222, 398]. He and his wife Lucretia, "free mulattoes," registered the birth of their son Godfrey **Macklin** in Bruton Parish, James City County. Lucretia was probably the daughter of Godfrey **Maclin**. David may have been deceased by 1782 when a Lucretia McLin was counted in the 1782 census for Richmond, Virginia [VA:111]. David and Lucretia were the parents of

i. Godfrey **Macklin**, born 29 November 1764 [Bruton Parish Register, 27].

5. James Bartley, born 8 July 1768, was baptized 14 August 1768 in Bruton Parish [Bruton Parish Register, 33]. He (called James Bartlett) was charged with murdering John **Gillett** and sent by the York County court for further trial in Williamsburg on 21 December 1796. Reuben **Gillett** was a witness against him [Orders 1795-1803, 141]. James was taxable in York County from 1789 to 1813 (called James Bartlett in 1792, 1793, 1806, 1809, and 1810). He was taxable on 3 slaves in 1806 and head of a household of 2 "free Negroes & mulattoes over 16" and a slave in 1813 [PPTL, 1782-1841, frames 148, 180, 191, 199, 264, 284, 304, 314, 351, 363, 385]. He was head of a York County household of 3 "other free," a slave and a white woman 16-26 years old in 1810 [VA:871]. He registered as a "free Negro" in York County on 18 November 1822: *a light Mulatto about 61 years of age 5 feet 9-3/4 Inches high, has long grey hair.* And his wife Nancy registered the same day: *a bright Mulatto about 52 years of age 5 feet 2-3/4 Inches high, has short wooly hair which is grey, flat nose...broad mouth* [York County Register, nos. 143, 144]. He may have been the father of

i. William Bartlett, born say 1791, taxable in York County in 1812 and 1814, called William Bartly in 1815 [PPTL, 1782-1841, frames 374, 402, 419].

A member of the Bartlett family probably had children by a slave. Lucy and Sarah Bartlett were emancipated by letter from Elizabeth Harrison proved in York County court on 16 April 1787 [Orders 1784-7, 440].

Others members of the family in Virginia were

i. Patty Bartlett, head of a Prince Edward County household of 8 "other free" in 1810 [VA:556].

ii. Cary Bartlett, head of a Richmond City household of 3 "other free" in 1810 [VA:333].
iii. Benjamin[3] Bartley, born about 1783, registered in Southampton County on 25 August 1806: *Blk., 5 feet 5 1/2 inches high, Free born* [Register of Free Negroes 1794-1832, no. 394].
iv. Benjamin[4] Bartlett, a "fn" taxable in Charlotte County in 1806, 1807, 1809 (adjoining Samuel Bartlett), 1812, taxable on horse in 1813 [PPTL 1782-1813, frames 688, 722, 755, 851, 893], a "F.N." head of a Charlotte County household of 1 "other free" in 1810 [VA:68].
v.   Edward Bartlett, a "mulatto" taxable in Gloucester County in 1812 [PPTL, 1800-20].

BASS FAMILY

The Bass family descended from John[1] Bass of Norfolk County, Virginia, who married Keziah Elizabeth Tucker, an Indian. Most of their children married whites and became part of the white community. However, many descendants of their son William[1] Bass married African Americans and became part of that community. William[1] Bass's son, William[2] Bass, remained in Norfolk County and married an African American. Two other sons, Edward[1] and John[2] Bass, moved to North Carolina and probably married African Americans as did most of their descendants.

1. John[1] Bass, an early settler of Norfolk County, Virginia, was born on 7 September 1616. On 14 August 1638 he married Keziah Elizabeth Tucker, daughter of

    Robin the Elder of ye Nansimuns kingdom, a Baptized Xtian[29]

    His children were
    i.   Nathaniel[1], born 29 May 1640, d. 1652.
    ii.   Keziah[1], born 4 September 1643.
    iii. Elizabeth[1], born 12 July 1645.
    iv.   Jordan, born 27 June 1648, d. 1651.
    v.   Samuel[1], born 23 March 1653.
2   vi.   William[1], born 29 March 1654, d. 13 August 1741.
    vii. Richard[1], born 2 August 1658, died in Norfolk County in 1722.[30]
    viii. John, born 14 March 1661, died the same day.

2. William[1] Bass, born 29 March 1654, married Catherine Lanier who died 17 February 1691/2. He was called William Bass, Sr., on 13 October 1715 when he admitted in Norfolk County court that he owed John Hodgson 50 pounds of tobacco [Orders 1710-17, 169]. On 17 March 1726/7 he claimed to have cleared lands near the Dismal Swamp which "hath been used by his and Their forebears since & before English governance in Virginia." He received a

---

[29]Transcripts of the Bass family vital records and certificates signed by Norfolk County court clerks are contained in Albert D. Bell's, *Bass Families of the South*, Chapter on Nansemond Indian Ancestry of Some Bass Families, pp. 11-16 (Rocky Mount, N.C. 1961). The Bass family bible in the Virginia State Library gives Keziah's name as Elizabeth Tucker [Library of Virginia Accession no.26371].

[30]Richard[1] Bass' son, Andrew, born 9 June 1698, received patents for 550 acres in Craven County, North Carolina, on 7 March 1736/7 and 630 acres in Johnston County on 1 June 1739 and another 709 acres in Johnston County a few years later [Hoffman, *Land Patents*, I:324, 353, 356]. He and his brother, Richard[2] Bass, were wealthy Dobbs County slave owners [*NCGSJ* XV:73, 74]. Richard[1]'s son, Alexander, born 27 July 1702, was probably the Alexander Bass who was head of a Chesterfield County, Virginia household of 11 whites in 1783 [VA:51]. Perhaps Alexander's neighbor, Thomas Bass, head of a household of 8 whites and 16 slaves, was his brother (born 5 July 1719) or son [VA:51].

certificate from the Norfolk County Clerk confirming his rightful possession of the land and further stating that

> *William Bass, Senr. &...his sons Wm. Bass, Thomas Bass and Joseph Bass, & spinster daughter Mary Bass are persons of English and Nansemun Indian descent with no Admixture of negor, Ethiopic blood*

He was called William Bass, Senr., and was living in Western Branch District of Norfolk County on 6 January 1729 when he purchased 103 acres in Norfolk County at the mouth of Deep Branch for 25 pounds [DB G:fol.35 (p.183)]. He was taxable with his son Thomas in the Western Branch District of Norfolk County in 1730, 1731 (called William Bass, Sr.), 1732 (with William Horse/Horsey in his household), and 1733-36 living near Richard and Eliza **Price** and William **Price** whose wife was taxable in 1736 [Wingo, *Norfolk County Tithables, 1730-50*, 20, 38, 73, 94, 138, 183]. He was probably in debt when he made his 1 October 1740 will since he left his land to his daughter Mary, "if she can Save it." The will, proved 17 September 1742 in Norfolk County, mentioned his children William, Edward, Joseph, Thomas, and Mary (executrix), and grandson William Bass [WB H:8]. The record of his death on 13 August 1741 is in the Bass family papers which also record that his son John and his daughter Keziah, Jr., predeceased him [Bell, *Bass Families of the South*, 12]. His children were

3	i.	Edward[1], born 19 October 1672.
4	ii.	John[2], born 4 December 1673.
	iii.	Keziah[2], born 30 October 1675, died 1704.
5	iv.	William[2], born 28 October 1676.
	v.	Joseph[1], born 21 December 1679.
	vi.	Mary[1], born 15 June 1681, sued ___ Mux in Norfolk County Orphans Court on 15 May 1700. The Norfolk County court bound two-year-old Sarah Crawley and nine-year-old Elizabeth Johnson to her as apprentices on 18 June 1714. Sarah was probably the daughter of Jane Crawley who sued John Nichols in court on the same day [DB 6:189; Orders 1710-7, 84].
	vii.	Thomas[1], born 13 November 1687, married Martha Willis 22 June 1724, married second, Tamer Spivey 2 May 1729. He was taxable in the household of his father William[1] Bass from 1730 to 1736. Thomas and his wife Tamer may have left the county sometime between 1736 and 1750 since they were not included in the tax lists from 1750 to 1766. They sold land in Norfolk County on 17 June 1756 [Bell, *Bass Families of the South*, 52].

3. Edward[1] Bass, born 19 October 1672, was living in Norfolk County on 16 November 1699 when he purchased 15 acres of land on the Western Branch of Elizabeth River from John Fulsher who was the slave owner who freed the **Anderson** family by his Norfolk County will in 1712. Edward appeared in Norfolk County court on 17 November 1698 and admitted that he owed Hugh Campbell 500 pounds of tobacco, in June 1702 he admitted that he owed Thomas Whinfield 70 pounds of tobacco for goods he purchased at the sale of the estate of William Whitehurst, and on 15 February 1709 he sued Henry Lawley for a 3 pound debt. On 20 July 1711 he was presented by the Norfolk County court for retailing liquor without a license but the presentment was dismissed at his cost when he convinced the court that it was a mistake. On 16 December 1715 he sued Joseph Muns, Jr., for 20 pounds damages for riding his mare [DB 6, no.2, fols. 36, 170, 255; Orders 1708-10, 124; 1710-17, 14, 136]. On 30 January 1720/1 he was called "Edward Bass of Norfolk County, Virginia, Parish of Elizabeth" when he purchased 100 acres adjacent to his brother John, near the head of Horsepool Swamp in Chowan Precinct, North Carolina [DB C-1:113]. On 26 March 1723 he was granted 200 acres on

Urahaw Swamp in what became Northampton County after 1741 [Hoffman, *Province of North Carolina Land Patents*, 192]. He and his wife Love sold their land in Chowan County by deed of 28 March 1726 [DB C-1:609].[31]

Between 12 August 1728 and 15 May 1744 he purchased another 615 acres adjoining his land [Bertie DB C:135, Northampton DB 1:40, 89, 129]. His 25 July 1748 Northampton County will was proved in August 1750 and left over 525 acres to his children with the remainder to be sold to discharge debts [Original at N.C. Archives]. He left his wife Lovewell 100 acres during her life. More than ten years later on 7 May 1761 she and her heirs, Lucy Jones and Thomas Cugley, sold this land for 75 pounds to Jethro Bass, her deceased husband's grand nephew [DB 3:121]. Their children named in Edward's will were

6   i.   John[4], born say 1716.

     ii. Katherine **Anderson,** born say 1718, married to Lewis **Anderson** when her father made his 25 July 1748 Northampton County will. She received 50 acres in Northampton County which she and Lewis sold on 12 November 1757 [DB 2:424].

   iii. Dinah, born say 1720, perhaps the wife of John **Pone**, "black" taxables in the 1755 Granville County summary list and taxables in the 1754 list of Robert Harris along with the **Andersons, Pettifords**, and William Bass [CR 44.701.19].[32]

7   iv. Benjamin[1], born say 1722, died about 1798.

     v. Joseph[2], born say 1724. He sold the 50 acres in Northampton County which he received by his father's will on 18 August 1757 and a further 50 acres in Northampton while a resident of Granville County on 2 September the same year [DB 2:399, 489]. On 30 March 1758 he bought 50 acres in Granville County on a branch of Fishing Creek and sold it on 26 February 1765 [DB E:50; G:355]. He was taxable in Granville County on a tithe in the 1758 list of Thomas Person and taxable with his wife Jane in 1762 and 1764 in Samuel Benton's list for Oxford and Fishing Creek Districts, listed as insolvent in 1764, perhaps the Joseph Bass who was head of a Chesterfield County, South Carolina household of 6 "other free" in 1800 [SC:100].

8   vi. Sampson/ Samuel[2], born say 1726.

9   vii. Edward[3], born say 1728, died before November 1800.

  viii. James[1], born say 1730, taxable with his brother Benjamin in Oxford District, Granville County, in 1761. On 10 November 1764 he sold 50 acres in Northampton County by deed proved in Granville County [DB H:63].

   ix. Kesiah[3], born say 1732.

    x. Mary[3], born say 1734.

   xi. Reuben[1], born say 1736, bequeathed his father's manor plantation of 100 acres in Northampton County after the death of his mother. He sold this 100 acres on 5 May 1761 [DB 3:96], and in 1764 he was taxed in Granville County with his wife Mary, probably Mary **Anderson**. He purchased 50 acres in Granville from Lawrence **Pettiford** on 20 October 1768 [DB H:473]. On 16 February 1777 he sold 50 acres in Granville on Beaverdam Creek [DB L:315], and in 1782 he was taxable on 2 horses. He was taxable on one poll in 1785,

---

[31]The marriage of a Love Harris and <u>John</u> Bas, both of "Nanse Mum" County, on 8 January 1696 was recorded in Perquimans Precinct, North Carolina [See John[2] Bass].

[32]David **Pone** was head of a New Hanover County household of 5 "free colored" in 1820 [NC:235].

and he had 2 males and 4 females in his household in Fishing Creek in 1786 for the state census.

4.   John[2] Bass (William[1], John[1]), born 4 December 1673, was living in Norfolk County on 15 October 1701 when a case against him brought by Thomas Hodges, Surveyor, for being delinquent "from the high wayes" was dismissed on his paying costs [DB 6:220]. He was not mentioned in his father's will because he predeceased him. His marriage was recorded in Perquimans Precinct, North Carolina:

> *John Bas and Love Harris was Married ye 8th day of Janewary 1696 both of Nanse Mum County and Nanse Mum Parresh by Mager Samuel Swann Esqr.* [Haun, *Old Albemarle County North Carolina,* 62].

Love Harris was living in Norfolk County on 19 May 1693 when the court acquitted Ann Harris, Love Harris, and Elizabeth Jennett of any wilful neglect in the death of a 5 week old child of Ann Harris. This was probably the same Ann Harris, widow of Richard Harris, who bound her daughter Jean Harris to Malachy Thruston in Norfolk County court that same day. Four days prior to this she bound her son John Harris to James Lowry, and two months later on 18 July 1693 she presented an inventory of "what little estate Richard Harris died seized of" in Norfolk County court [DB 5, pt. 2, 287, 292-3, 298]. On 30 January 1720/1 John Bass bought 200 acres in Chowan Precinct near the head of Horsepool Swamp [DB C-1:115]. A year later on 16 July 1722 he was in that part of Bertie County which became Northampton County where he bought 200 acres adjoining Urahaw Swamp [DB A:105]. Between 1722 and 1729 he purchased 5 tracts of land including a patent for 460 acres, accumulating a total of 1,060 acres adjoining Urahaw Swamp [DB A:129; C:126, 135; Hoffman, *Province of North Carolina Land Patents,* 225]. His 18 January 1732 Bertie County will named his children, gave his wife Mary "the liberty of the plantation...for bringing up my small children," referred to "my sd last wife's children," and left 50 acres to his friend, Daniel Wharten Burbegg [SS 876/3:305]. Norfolk County Bass family papers record his death in the year 1732 at the age of fifty-eight. Mary remarried and as "Mary Staples widow and relict of John Bass, Sr." she sold her one third interest in the plantation where she was living on 21 November 1748 [Northampton DB 1:356]. John Bass's children named in the will were

10   i.   John[3], born say 1700.
     ii. Judith **Cannady**, born say 1702, wife of William **Cannady** of Edgecombe County. She received 100 acres by her father's will. She and husband William sold this land on 7 April 1744 [Northampton DB 1:175].
     iii. Sarah[2] **Anderson**, born say 1704, wife of Lewis **Anderson**, received 100 acres in Northampton County by her father's will. She and her husband Lewis sold this land on 10 November 1757 [DB 2:233].
     iv. Ann[1] Johnston, born say 1706, mother of Aaron Johnston who received 100 acres by her father's will. While living in Orange County, North Carolina, on 9 February 1758 he sold this 100 acres in Northampton County [DB 2:455]. He may have been the Aron Johnson who was counted as white in Wake County in 1790 [NC:104].
11   v.   Edward[2], born say 1710.
12   vi. William[3], born say 1712, living in Bute County in 1771.
13   vii. Lovey Bass, born say 1720.
     viii. Mary[2], born say 1722, received 100 acres on the north side of Urahaw Swamp by her father's will.
     ix. Aaron, born say 1724, received his father's plantation on the south side of Bear Swamp. There was an Aaron Bass who was taxable on one poll in Dobbs County in 1769 [*NCGSJ* XV:74] and taxable on one poll in

Johnston County in 1784 [GA 64.1]. There was also an Aaron Bass who was counted as white in Chatham County, head of a household of a male and 3 females in 1790 [NC:87] and head of a Chatham County household of 3 "other free" in 1800.

x.   Patience, born say 1726.[33] Her father left her his plantation on the south side of Bear Swamp.

xi.   Moses, born say 1728, received land on the north side of Bear Swamp by his father's will. He entered 100 acres on the west side of the Northwest River about 3/4 mile from Raft Swamp including his improvements on 21 November 1752. He was living near "the drains of Drowning Creek" on 1 February 1754 when Robert Carver entered 100 acres there [Philbeck, *Bladen County Land Entries*, nos. 677, 934]. He was taxable on 3 "white" tithes in Cumberland County, North Carolina, in 1755 [T&C 1], and he received a grant for 100 acres on Raft Swamp in Cumberland County on 21 October 1758 [Hoffman, *Land Patents*, I:474]. On 19 August 1761 the Cumberland County court granted permission for the mill he had erected on Raft Swamp to be designated a public grist mill, and the court granted him a license to keep an ordinary [Minutes 1759-65, 70].[34] In May 1762 he posted bond not to leave the county before the next court to answer a suit by the governor and James Simpson, but he was not mentioned again in the Cumberland County court Minutes. His estate was settled in Prince George Parish, Georgetown District, South Carolina, on 28 February 1777. His estate mentioned his cousins, Jeremiah and Wright Bass, and Mourning, Sarah, Elizabeth, and Ann **Going**, children of Jacob **Going** [South Carolina DB S-5:283, 284]. His estate settlement did not mention any children, but he was probably related to William Bass, head of a Fayetteville, Cumberland County household of 5 "other free" and 1 white woman in 1790 [NC:42]. He may have been the "William Bass a free negro" who was presented by the Granville County court for living together in fornication and adultery with Patsy **House** [CR.44.289.19, no date].[35]

xii.   Elizabeth[2], not mentioned in her father's will but called the "now wife of Edward Taylor" whose son John Taylor was given a deed of gift of 100 acres on the south side of Hunting Quarter Swamp in Northampton County on 6 November 1747 by her brother John Bass [DB 1:321].

5.   William[2] Bass (William[1], John[1]), born 28 October 1676, was sued by Elizabeth Price in Norfolk County court on 20 November 1713, and he sued Thomas Cretcher for a 1 pound, 12 shilling debt on 20 August 1714 [Orders 1710-7, 73, 94]. He married Sarah **Lovina/ Leviner** on 20 April 1729 [Bell, *Bass Families of the South*, Chapter on Nansemond Indian Ancestry of Some Bass Families, 15]. Sarah was the "Molatto" daughter of John Nicholls' "Negro" slave, Jean **Lovina**. She received 200 acres on Western Branch of Elizabeth River by her master's 11 November 1696 Norfolk County will, proved 17 May 1697 [WB 6, fol.95a-96]. William purchased 150 acres adjoining his

---

[33]A Patience Bass was the wife of Philip **Pettiford**. However, Philip's pension application stated that his wife was born about 1736 (eighty-four years old in 1820) [Philip's pension application and a 28 June 1893 letter from Narcissa Rattley in the possession of Robert Jackson of Silver Spring, Maryland].

[34]This land was considered to be part of Bladen County according to a 12 November 1766 Bladen County deed [DB 1738-1779, 326]. Raft Swamp is in present day Hoke County near the Robeson County line.

[35]Patsy **House** may have been related to Nicholas **House**, a fourteen-year-old "Mulatto" bound to Maurice Cock by the Middlesex County, Virginia Court on 2 July 1694 [Orders 1680-94, 700].

wife's land from her nephew William **Lovina** on 12 November 1728 [DB G:110]. He was taxable in the Southern Branch District of Norfolk County near Deep Creek from 1730 to 1732 (with John Staple in his household), from 1733 to 1736, and in 1750 with his unnamed wife and son John Bass [Wingo, *Norfolk County Tithables, 1730-50*, 11, 30, 64, 97, 133, 163, 190].[36] On 18 March 1736/7 William and Sarah sold 48 acres on the Southern Branch of the Elizabeth River to Thomas Deal, explaining in the deed that it was land "that Major Nichols gave unto the said Sarah Bass before her marriage to the sd. Wm. Bass" [DB 12:188]. He appeared before the county clerk on 20 September 1742, three days after his father's will was proved, and obtained a certificate similar to the one obtained by his father:

> *William Bass, the Bearer, tall, swarthy, dark eyes, weight abt. 13 stone, scar on back of left hand, is of English & Indian descent with no admixture of negro blood, numbered as a Nansemun by his own Choosing. The sd. Bass dwells in this County and hath a good name for his industry and honesty.*

William[2] died 20 October 1751 [Bell, *Bass Families of the South*, 15, 13]. Administration on his estate was granted to John Bass on 17 April 1752, and the appraisal of his estate was recorded in Norfolk County on 19 July 1756 [Orders 1750-3, 82; 1755-59, 77]. On 14 March 1757 Sarah Bass and John Bass ("Son of Sarah") and his wife Elizabeth sold another 50 acres of her land on the north side of the head of Deep Creek, the southern branch of the Elizabeth River adjoining John Bass's line, "being part of a Tract of two hundred Acres of Land given the Above mentiond Sarah Bass by Will of Maj[r] Nichols" [DB 18:41-2b]. Sarah's death on 2 October 1762 at the age of eighty years and the births of William and Sarah's children were recorded in the Bass family papers [Bell, *Bass Families of the South*, 13]. William and Sarah's children were

   i.   Sarah[1], born say 1727, taxable in May 1743. Her father William Bass petitioned the Norfolk County court on 20 May 1743 to exempt her from the tax on free African American and Indian women because of her weak constitution, and the court agreed to exempt her during her indisposition [Orders 1742-46, 37].

14   ii.   John[6], born 20 February 1731.
15   iii. William[4], born say 1733.
16   iv.   Joseph[3], born say 1738.
     v.   Thomas[3], born say 1740, taxable in Norfolk County with (his brother) Joseph Bass in 1778 and 1780 [Wingo, *Norfolk County Tithables, 1766-80*, 267, 284]. He married Sally **Butler**, 14 March 1796 Norfolk County bond, Thomas Deal surety, March 1796 marriage by Rev. Arthur Emmerson. He was taxable in Norfolk County from 1783 to 1790 [PPTL, 1782-91, frames 430, 466, 525, 561, 638, 678]. He may have been the father of Jacob Bass (born about 1778) who registered in Petersburg on 23 September 1800: *a light brown Mulatto man, five feet four inches high, twenty two years old, short brown hair & much pitted with the small pox - born free in Norfolk County & raised in Prince George County* [Register of Free Negroes 1794-1819, no. 208].

6.   John[4] Bass (Edward[1], John[1]), born say 1716, died before his father's will was written on 17 July 1748. Elijah may have been his son since his grandfather gave him "land where my late son John dwelt." His son was probably

---

[36]Perhaps John Staples was the husband of Mary Staples, widow of John[2] Bass, who died in Northampton County in 1732. A Mary Staples was taxable on her son John Staples in Norfolk County in 1757 [Wingo, *Norfolk County Tithables 1751-1765*, 104].

17   i.   Elijah[1], born say 1743.

7.   Benjamin[1] Bass (Edward[1], John[1]), born say 1722, was the executor of his father's Northampton County will by which he received 125 acres where his father was living on Quarter Swamp in Northampton County [Original at N.C. Archives]. He moved to Granville County where he bought 103 acres on Fishing Creek on 7 March 1758 [DB C-2:429]. On 4 April 1758 he sold 50 acres of his Northampton County land and a month later on 22 May 1758 bought 50 acres adjoining his land in Northampton from his brother Samuel [DB 2:460, 461]. In addition to the 125 acres he received by his father's will he had title to another 150 acres since on 10 February 1759 he sold 275 acres of his land in Northampton County which his father had purchased in 1743 and 1744 [DB 3:53].

In 1761 he was taxable in Oxford District, Granville County, with his wife Mary and brother James on 3 "Black polls," and he and his wife and children were taxable in the remaining colonial tax lists for Oxford District. On 10 November 1764 he purchased 50 acres in Northampton County near the Maple Spring Hills from his brother James [Granville DB H:63]. On 19 November 1772 Rodey Bass, a five-year-old orphan, was bound as an apprentice to him [CR 044.101.2-7]. Perhaps she was his grandchild. In 1780 he was taxed on an assessment of 607 pounds in Oxford District, Granville County. In 1782 he was taxable on 103 acres, 2 horses, and 3 cattle. On 5 August 1782 he purchased an additional 480 acres in Granville for which he paid 1,000 pounds. He sold 100 acres of this to his son Benjamin Bass, Jr., for 5 pounds on 18 August 1783, sold 21 acres on 3 November 1794, sold 20 acres on 14 December 1797, and sold the remainder on 14 May 1798 [DB O:197, 331; P:100; Q:115, 199]. He and his wife Mary sold 100 acres in Northampton County at Urahaw Swamp on 26 July 1784 [DB 7:267]. He was head of a Tar River household of 7 males and 4 females in the state census of 1786. His son Absalom was charged with his tax in Tar River District in 1797 and 1798 [Tax List 1796-1802, 132]. He purchased 119 acres on Falling Creek in Halifax County, North Carolina, from John **Richardson** on 22 April 1799 [DB 18:460]. His children can be identified from the Granville County tax lists. They were

i.   Selah, born about 1750 since she was first taxable in 1762 in Samuel Benton's list for Oxford and Fishing Creek Districts. She was probably the Sealia **Mitchell**, wife of Archibald **Mitchell**, who was taxed in his household in the 1767 list of Stephen Jett.

ii.   Sally, born about 1752 since she was first taxable in 1764 in Samuel Benton's list. She was called Cary Bass in the 24 November 1801 Halifax County deed by which she sold 17 acres "which had belonged to her father Benjamin Bass" to John **Richardson**, Jr. She was called Sarah Bass (daughter of Benjamin Bass) in her 22 March 1802 Granville County marriage bond to John **Richardson**, Absolem Bass bondsman.

iii.   Winney, born about 1752 since she was first taxable in 1764 in Samuel Benton's list. Her bastard child Jacob was bound to Lewis **Anderson, Junior**, who she married about 1767 [CR 044.101.2].

iv.   Hardy, born about 1755 since he was first taxable in the summary list for 1767. On 23 December 1788 he married Nancy **Hines**, Granville County bond with Reuben Bass bondsman. In 1790 he was taxable on 100 acres and one poll in Oxford District, and in 1797 he was taxable on only poll tax. He was head of a Granville County household of 4 "other free" in 1800.

v.   Benjamin[3], Jr., born about 1756 since he was first taxable in the 1768 list of Stephen Jett. He married Milley **Pettiford**, 3 January 1781 Granville County bond with Reuben Bass bondsman. He bought 100 acres in Tar River District from his father in 1783 [DB O:331]. He was taxable in Granville County in Tar River District on one poll and his 100 acres in 1785 and in 1798 [Tax List 1796-1802, 132]. He was head of a Granville County household of 2 "other free" in 1800. Perhaps one of his ancestors was the Benjamin Bass who was counted in the 1850 Indiana census in Marion Township, Owen County: a forty-seven-year-old "Mulatto" with $1,000 personal estate, living with Delila Bass, both born in North Carolina [household #187].

- vi.   Morning, born about 1756 since she was first taxable in 1768.
- vii.   Absalom, born say 1760, not mentioned in the early tax records but taxable in Granville County in 1787 on his father's land. He married Patsy **Haynes**, 15 January 1794 Granville County bond with Benjamin Bass surety. He was head of a Granville County household of 7 "other free" in 1800.
- 18   viii. ?Reuben[2], born say 1761.
- ix.   ?Prissy, born say 1764, married Jesse **Day**, 6 November 1782 Granville County bond, Solomon Walker bondsman.
- x.   ?Milly, who had an unnamed "base born child" by Jesse **Chavers**. Benjamin and Absalom Bass were her security in November 1794 Granville County court [Minutes 1792-95, 197-8], and Clement **Bunch** posted bond in December 1798 for a bastard child he had by her [Camin, *N.C. Bastardy Bonds*, 87].

8. Sampson/ Samuel[2] Bass (Edward[1], John[1]), born say 1724, sold the 50 acres he inherited from his father to his brother Benjamin on 22 May 1758 [Northampton DB 2:460]. He was taxable in Granville County in Nathaniel Harris's list in 1758 and in John Pope's list for Bare Swamp District in 1762, called Sampson Bass. This part of Granville County became Bute County in 1764 and Sampson bought 100 acres in Bute County on the south side of Cedar Creek on Beaverdam Branch from William Bass on 26 January 1771 [Warren County DB 3:224]. He was a resident of Brunswick County, Virginia, on 2 April 1765 when he gave 270 acres in Northampton County near the Virginia border to his son Burwell Bass of Northampton County [DB 4:463]. He was taxed on 2,062 pounds property and 12 slaves in Northampton County in 1780 [LP 46.1]. He was called Samuel, Sr., when he bought 200 acres near the Virginia border on 4 June 1784 [DB 7:276]. His 13 August 1787 Northampton County will was proved in December 1790 [WB 1:408]. He left land and six slaves to his wife Sarah and children, most of whom were considered white. They were

- i.   Ann[2].
- ii.   Herod.
- iii.   Susanna Snipes.
- iv.   Matthew.
- v.   Samuel[3], who received a slave by a Halifax County deed of gift from his father on 14 June 1790, "1 negro man Nat, now in possession of my grandson Burgess Bass which sd negro I lent my son Burrell Bass some years ago" [DB 17:213]. He was head of a Halifax County household of 7 "other free" and a slave in 1810 [NC:4].
- vi.   Burwell.
- vii.   Lucy Peebles.
- viii. Phebe Jordan.

9. Edward[3] Bass (Edward[1], John[1]), born say 1728, received 50 acres in Northampton County by his father's will. He sold this and another 20 acres in Northampton County on 15 May 1758 [DB 2:462]. By 1761 he was taxable in the Granville County list for Oxford District with wife Tamer--probably Tamer **Anderson**, daughter of his neighbor Lewis **Anderson**, a taxable in her father's household in John Sallis' 1754 tax list. She was also taxed with her father in

1755, but did not appear in his household in the next extant list of 1757 [CR 44.701.19]. On 22 December 1762 Edward purchased 100 acres in Granville County from George **Anderson** [DB F:281]. On 8 April 1767 he purchased 200 acres at the head of Fishing Creek in Bute County [Warren County DB 1:304] and sold this land twelve years later on 7 May 1779 [Warren DB 7:230]. In 1782 he was taxable in Granville on 100 acres, a horse, and 14 cattle. He had 11 persons in his Raglands District, Granville County household in the 1786 state census. On 9 November 1792 he bought an additional 206 acres on Boling's Creek in Granville for 75 pounds and a month later on 10 December 1792 sold his 100 acres on the north prong of Fishing Creek for 100 pounds [DB N:165; P:77]. His 17 March 179_ will was proved in Granville County court in November 1800 [WB 5:116]. He mentioned his wife Tamer and his children:

   i.   Stephen, born about 1758, probably the third person taxable in his father's household in the 1771 summary list. He was taxable on one poll in Granville in 1785, 1790 and 1791, and in Oxford District in 1801 [Tax List 1796-1802, 284].

   ii.   Lewis, taxable on one poll in Oxford District in 1804 and 1806 [Tax List 1803-1809, 79, 177].

   iii.   Truateny(?). Perhaps this was the Truenty Bass who was paid 3 pounds, 8 shillings for her attendance in the suit brought by Hardy Bass against William **Taborn** in Granville County court on 11 August 1786 [Minutes 1786-87].

   iv.   Darling, married Rhoda **Anderson**, 7 July 1797 Granville County bond with William **Mitchell** bondsman. He was head of a Granville County household of 2 "other free" in 1800, 3 in 1810 [NC:904], and 3 "free colored" in 1820 [NC:1]. He was taxed on one poll in Oxford District in 1800, 260 acres in 1801, and he was taxable on poll tax for himself and Jason Bass in 1803 [Tax List 1796-1802, 230, 284; 341; 1803-09, 31]. From 1809 to 1820 he was taxable on 109 acres on Bolings Creek in Oxford District. His 10 November 1839 Granville County will was proved in August 1845. He lent all his property to his wife Rodey and after her death, to Henry **Anderson** who was her son by Jesse **Chavis** before her marriage to Darling [WB 16:334].

19   v.   Prudence, born say 1768.

   vi.   Mary Ann, perhaps the Mariah Bass who married Edward **Mitchell**, 5 January 1795 Granville County bond.

   vii.   Tamer, married John **Roe**, 2 December 1801 Granville County bond with George **Pettiford** bondsman. John **Rowe** married second, Sally **Pendergrass**, 2 March 1802 Person County bond.

   viii.   Mordecai, neglected to give in his list of tithables in Wake County in 1794 [MFCR 099.701.1, frame 212], married first, Nancy Askew, 31 October 1799 Wake County bond with Lewis **Pettiford** bondsman, and second, Nancy **Chavis**, 13 December 1803 Granville County bond with George **Pettiford** bondsman. He was taxable on 1 poll in Oxford District in 1806 [Tax List 1803-09, 177]. He was a "Negro" head of a Guilford County household of 4 "free colored" in 1830.

   ix.   Dempsey, married Phoebe **Day**, 4 October 1808 Granville County bond, Reuben **Day** bondsman. He was head of a Granville County household of 4 "other free" in 1800, 6 in 1810 [NC:858], and 3 "free colored" in Ledge Neck District in 1820 [NC:17]. His 4 December 1827 Granville County will was proved in February 1828. He left all his estate to his wife Phereba [WB 10:405].

   x.   Justina(?).

   xi.   Jason.

10. John[3] Bass (John[2], William[1], John[1]), born say 1700, purchased 200 acres on 10 April 1722 near Urahaw Swamp in the part of Bertie County which became

Northampton County in 1742. He purchased 100 acres on Plaquet Branch of Antonkey Marsh, 150 acres on 17 January 1727, and received a patent for 410 acres south of Bear Swamp on 2 August 1727 [DB A:108; B:348, 360]. On 7 February 1736 the Bertie County court fined him for selling brandy without a license [Haun, *Bertie County Court Minutes*, I:199]. He was the executor of his father's 1732 will. On 16 August 1736 he bought 200 acres at the mouth of Beech Swamp in Edgecombe County [DB 1:164].[37] He sold 410 acres of his land in Northampton County to George **Anderson** on 13 January 1738 [Bertie DB E:530]. He bought 150 acres in Edgecombe on 16 December 1740 [DB F:190] and sold another 400 acres in Northampton by deeds of 2 October and 30 December 1742 [DB 1:40,56]. He was a slave owner by August 1742 when he proved rights on five "whites" and 3 "blacks" in Northampton County [SS 906 by *North Carolina Genealogy*, 1825]. He voted for Joseph Sikes in the Northampton County election of 1762 [SS 837 by *NCGSJ* XII:170]. His 14 June 1777 Northampton County will was proved in September 1777. He left 16 slaves and 600 acres to his children [WB 1:292-4]. Most of his children, who were very prosperous, married whites and were considered white. His children were

20 i. Thomas[2], born say 1723.

  ii. John[5], born say 1726, executor of his father's will. His 4 October 1786 Halifax County will was proved November the same year. He left land and slaves to his wife Ann which was to revert to his brothers, Jacob and Isaac, at her death [WB 3:116].

21 iii. Jacob[1], born say 1728.

22 iv. Isaac, born before 1745.

  v. Abraham, purchased 700 acres in Edgecombe County on the south side of Betty's Branch on 16 October 1765 [DB O:163]. On 8 February 1779 while residing in Nash County he sold 240 acres in Bute and Nash counties. This was part of 549 acres he was granted in Edgecombe County on 9 December 1761. Jean Bass witnessed the deed [Franklin County DB 1:20].

23 vi. Jethro[1], born say 1734.

  vii. Drury.

  viii. Alice Earp, named her grandchildren and left the residue of her estate to Ruth **Byrd** by her 13 October 1796 Northampton County will, Elizabeth **Walden**, John Earp, and William Earp witnesses [WB 2:133]. The Earp family of Northampton County was considered white.

  ix. Uridice.

  x. Elizabeth[3] Brittle/ Bittle, wife of John Bittle whose children were named in his 12 January 1787 Northampton County will [WB 1:377]. William **Bittle** was head of a Northampton County household of 5 "other free" in 1790 [NC:74].

11. Edward[2] Bass (John[2], William[1], John[1]), born say 1710, received the "manor Plantation" by his father's will. He purchased land by deeds proved in Dobbs County April 1750 to April 1754 [DB 2:409] and January 1777 to April 1779 [DB 11:311].[38] His eldest child was

  i. Wright[1], born say 1730, purchased land by deed proved in Dobbs County between April 1765 and April 1769 [DB 7:437] and by a deed from Arthur Bass proved in Dobbs County between 1746 and 1810 [DB

---

[37]This part of Edgecombe became Halifax County in 1758.

[38]Only the index for these Dobbs County deeds has survived [Microfilm Grantee Index 1746-1880, M.F.95]. Other members of the Bass family whose deeds were registered in Dobbs County were Andrew [DB 4:72, April 1755-April 1758], Richard [DB 5:05, April 1758-April 1761], Thomas [DB 7:466, April 1765-April 1769], Matthew [DB 7:494, April 1765-April 1769], and Andrew, Jr. [DB 7:105].

22:442]. He was a Dobbs County taxable in 1769 [SS 837, p.5A, by *NCGSJ* XV:74]. He was counted as white in the 1790 census for Georgetown District, Prince Georges Parish, South Carolina. He was described in the 29 June 1786 court record of the estate of his uncle Moses as "eldest son of Edward Bass, dec., who was the eldest brother of Moses Bass [South Carolina DB S-5:283, 284].

12. William[3] Bass (John[2], William[1], John[1]), born say 1712, sold the land he inherited in Northampton County to John Bass on 30 December 1742 [DB 2:185]. He was one of the first members of the Bass family in Granville County where he was taxed in the list of Jonathan White in 1749. In 1761 he was taxable with his son Thomas in Oxford District. On 19 November 1762 he purchased 200 acres on the south side of Cedar Creek near the Beaver Dam Branch from Thomas **Huland** (Huelin) [DB F:441]. He was a "Black" taxable in Granville County in John Pope's list for St. John's Parish, Bare Swamp District, in 1762. Bute County was formed from this part of Granville County in 1764, and in 1771 he was a Bute County taxable in the list of Philemon Hawkins on 5 "Black" tithes: himself, his wife, daughter "Honner," and sons Ben and John [CR 015.70001, p.12]. He may have been the William Bass who appeared in Granville County court on 7 April 1770 as the "next Friend" of Olive Bass when she sued Jean **Tylor**, alias **Mitchell** [Minutes 1754-70, 202]. William sold 100 acres on the south side of Cedar Creek to Sampson Bass on 26 January 1771 and another 100 acres adjoining this on 17 September 1771 [Warren County DB 3:224; 4:263]. His children were

    i. ?Simon[1], not identified as William's son, but listed adjacent to him in Philemon Hawkins' Bute County list of taxables, taxed on 4 "Black" tithes for himself, his unnamed wife, son James, and (daughter?) Elizabeth.

    ii. Thomas[4], born about 1749 since he was taxable in 1761 in his father's Oxford District household. He was an overseer, taxable in Nathan Thomas's household in the 1771 Bute County list of Philemon Hawkins [CR 015.70001, p.4].

24   iii. ?Frederick[1], born say 1750.

    iv. Honor[1], born say 1752, taxable in 1771 in Bute County.

    v. Benjamin[2], born say 1754, taxable in 1771 in Bute County.

    vi. John[8], born before 1760, taxable in 1771 in Bute County.

13. Lovey Bass (John[2], William[1], John[1]), born say 1720, had three illegitimate children bound to George **Anderson** in Granville County [CR 044.101.2]. She may have been George's mistress. He gave her two cows and calves by his May 1771 Granville County will and gave his plantation to her son Nathan who was living in his household. He gave his wife and children only one shilling apiece [Original in County, not recorded]. Lovey's children were

25   i. Nathan[2], born in 1752.

    ii. Margaret, born about 1756, twelve years old when she was bound apprentice to George **Anderson** on 3 August 1768. He gave her a young mare by his May 1771 Granville County will.

    iii. ?Wright[2], born say 1758, married Tabathy **Snelling**, 12 November 1781 Granville County bond, Drury **Pettiford** bondsman. On 8 May 1783 he bought 35 acres in Granville County joining Nathaniel Bass and **Tabor** and another 35 acres on 14 April 1794 [DB N:177; P:53]. He was taxed on 80 acres and one poll in Fishing Creek District next to Nathan Bass in 1796 [Tax List 1796-1802, 11]. He was head of a Granville County household of 9 "other free" in 1800. He was taxed on his 70 acres in Fishing Creek in 1804 and taxed in Fort Creek District on 222-1/2 acres, 2 free polls, and 2 slaves in 1805 [Tax List 1803-9, 55, 115]. He may have been the Wright Bass who was head of a Wilkes County household of 6 "free colored" in 1820 [NC:545].

    iv. Dicey[1], born about 1766, a four-year-old "base born mulatto child of Lovey Bass" bound to Mary **Anderson**, wife of George **Anderson**, on 18 July 1770 [CR 44.101.2-7]. She may have been Lovey Bass's unnamed bastard child charged to Bartlet **Tyler** on 13 January 1767 [Camin, *N.C. Bastardy Bonds*, 87]. She married Drury **Pettiford**, 12 November 1781 Granville County bond.

14. John[6] Bass (William[2], William[1], John[1]), born 20 February 1731, purchased 50 acres on 8 July 1742 in Southern Branch Precinct of Norfolk County which was land "Thomas Deall bought of William Bass, the Father of John Bass" [DB 13:17a-18a]. John was sued in Norfolk County court by Richard Freeman on 15 November 1753, but the case was dismissed when both parties reached an agreement [Orders 1753-55, 2]. From 1751 to 1761 he was head of his own household in Colonel Craford's list of tithables for the Southern Branch District of Norfolk County from Batcheldor's Mill to Portsmouth near his brother William Bass.[39] In 1752 John Murer was in his household; in 1756 and 1757 John **Price** was in his household; in 1761 John Bass was in his household, and in 1761 and 1765 he shared a household with his brother William [Wingo, *Norfolk County Tithables, 1751-65*, 18, 41, 54, 88, 100, 115, 138, 174, 205]. He and Robert Kinder received a patent for 181 acres in Norfolk County near the head of Deep Creek adjoining Bass's own land on 30 August 1763, and he and his wife Elizabeth of Portsmouth Parish sold their 90 acre share of this land to Ebenezer **Hall** on 14 May 1764. And they sold a 50 acre tract adjoining this land to Ebenezer **Hall** on 14 May 1764 [DB 35:362: 21:86B, 200A]. John and his brother William[4] Bass were sued for debt in Norfolk County court by Solomon Hodges on 16 November 1764 [Orders 1763-65, 162].[40] John and his wife Elizabeth and (his brother) Joseph Bass were taxable on 100 acres of land in the list for Portsmouth to New Mill Creek in 1766, 1767, with (John's daughter?) Sarah Bass in 1768, and by himself in 1770. On 19 April 1770 he appeared in court and declared that he had six or seven barrels of corn belonging to John Smith who was indebted to John Ivy [Orders 1768-71, 150, 158, 167]. He died 11 March 1771, and Elizabeth was taxable that year on a tithe and 100 acres and taxable in 1772 with (their son?) William Bass. She was charged with the tax for William in 1774 and for him and (her son?) John Bass in 1778 [Wingo, *Norfolk County Tithables, 1766-80*, 6, 44, 75, 121, 155, 186, 236, 266]. They were the parents of

    i. Sarah[3], born 13 October 1751. Her birth was also recorded in the register of Southern Branch Parish [*WMQ* 1:160].

26 ii. William[5], born 23 June 1755.

    iii. Mille, born 12 January 1758.

    iv. John[9], born 22 December 1763, taxable in Norfolk County in 1782 and 1783 but not in the subsequent lists [PPTL, 1782-90, frame 383, 427].

    v. Giles, born 29 January 1764.

    vi. Joshua[1], born 21 March 1767, taxable in Norfolk County in 1787 and from 1791 to 1796 [PPTL, 1782-90, frame 561; 1791-1812, frames 18, 35, 78, 98, 133].

---

[39]William Crafford entered the marriage dates for Thomas[1] Bass and the birth dates of his children in the Bass family records on 21 January 1745 [Bell, *Bass Families of the South*, Chapter on Nansemond Indian Ancestry of Some Bass Families, p.14].

[40]Solomon Hodges was probably a descendant of the Solomon Hodges whose birth in 1702 and death in 1730 are the first entries in the Bass family bible which was printed in England in 1725. The first Bass family entry is for the birth of Sarah Bass, daughter of John[6] Bass, on 13 October 1751 [*Bass Families of the South*, Chapter on Nansemond Indian Ancestry of Some Bass Families, p.13]. The Hodges family were Norfolk County slave owners.

15. William[4] Bass (William[2], William[1], John[1]), born say 1733, received a gun by his grandfather's 1 October 1740 Norfolk County will [WB H:8]. He was a taxable in the Norfolk County list for the Southern Branch District from Batcheldor's Mill to Portsmouth in the household of his father William Bass in 1751, in his own household from 1752 to 1754, in the household of his mother Sarah Bass, in 1756 and 1757, and in his own household in 1759. He was living with his brother John in 1761 and was head of a household with his wife Naomi and (his brother?) John Bass in 1765, taxable on three tithes and 100 acres in the district from Portsmouth to New Mill Creek with his wife Naomy from 1766 to 1768 [Wingo, *Norfolk County Tithables, 1751-65*, 18, 41, 55, 88, 100, 115, 138, 174, 205; 1766-80, 6, 44, 75]. Naomy may have been the daughter of Joseph **Hall** who lived in Norfolk County in 1735 [Wingo, *Norfolk County Tithables 1730-1750*, 157]. Naomy **Hall**, born say 1743, was taxable in her father's Bertie County, North Carolina household in 1757 [CR 10.702.1, box 1]. William and his brother John[6] Bass and John's wife Elizabeth sold 50 acres on the main road to Suffolk adjoining William's own land on 17 May 1764, and he and his wife Naomy sold 30 acres adjoining John Bass on the west side of Deep Creek beginning at the main road on 16 May 1771 [DB 21:238; 25:100]. John Ballentine sued him for a 4 pound, 10 shilling debt on 22 March 1771 [Orders 1768-71, 236]. He was taxable on a tithe and 100 acres in 1770 and a tithe and 70 acres in 1771 but may have been deceased by 10 June 1772 when Naomy was taxable in the household of her brother-in-law Joseph Bass [Wingo, *Norfolk County Tithables, 1766-80*, 121, 155, 186]. William and Naomy may have been the parents of

27   i.   James[2], born in August 1760.
28   ii.   Willis, born say 1763.

16. Joseph[3] Bass (William[2], William[1], John[1]), born say 1738, was tithable in the Norfolk County household of (his brother) John Bass from 1766 to 1768, with Ebenezer **Hall** in 1770, in his own household in 1771 [Wingo, *Norfolk County Tithables, 1766-80*, 6, 44, 75, 105, 155]. He was taxable in Norfolk County from 1782 to 1813: called a "M"(ulatto) in 1799, 1801, 1802 and 1807; living on Deep Creek in 1801 when he was counted in a "List of Free Negroes and Mulattoes" with (his deceased brother William's wife?) Naomy and (his wife?) Lydia and (daughters?) Julia and Polly Bass [PPTL, 1782-91, frames 383, 431, 467, 483, 525, 562, 638; 1791-1812, 295, 371, 427, 642; 1813-24, frame 16] and head of a Norfolk County household of 4 "other free" in 1810 [VA:822]. He was surety for the 7 May 1792 Norfolk County marriage of (his daughter?) Elizabeth Bass and Joseph **Hall**. He may have been the father of

   i.   Elizabeth, married Joseph **Hall**, 7 May 1792 Norfolk County bond, Joseph Bass surety.
  ii.   Julia, listed in Joseph Bass's household in 1801.
iii.   Polly, listed in Joseph Bass's household in 1801.

17. Elijah[1] Bass (John[4], Edward[1], John[1]), born say 1743, was still living in Northampton County on 4 April 1758 when he was mentioned in a Bass family deed [DB 2:461]. He married Mary Bass, 13 February 1777 Bute County bond, Richard Scott bondsman. According to her application for his pension, they were married the following day. In 1780 he was living in Granville County where he was taxed on an assessment of 108 pounds in Oxford District. He enlisted in the Tenth Regiment of the North Carolina Line on 10 February 1781 as a substitute for Ebenezar Riggan and was killed in the battle of Eutaw Springs on 8 September 1781 [M804-2038, frames 533, 528]. His children were called orphans of Elijah Bass on 4 February 1781 when the court bound them out to Benjamin Bass [Owen, *Granville County Notes*, vol. V]. After his death his wife Mary married Benjamin **Richardson** on 14 February 1783 with Philip **Pettiford** as bondsman [M804-2038, frame 531]. Elijah's children bound out on 4 February 1781 were

    i.   John[11], born about 1772, married Olive **Richardson**, 8 December 1798 Granville County bond, Absalom Bass bondsman.

    ii. Phatha, born about 1775.

    iii. Sarah[4], born about 1777, married John **Richardson**, 22 March 1802 Granville County bond, Absalom Bass bondsman.

    iv. David, born about 1779.

18. Reuben[2] Bass (Benjamin[1], Edward[1], John[1]), born say 1761, may have been one of seven males in Benjamin Bass, Sr.'s Granville County household in the 1786 state census. He married Polly **Hines**, 23 December 1788 Granville County bond with Hardy Bass bondsman. He was head of a Wake County household of 7 "other free" in 1800 [NC:753]. He was called a "free man of color" when he and his daughter Lydia **Pettiford** petitioned the Wake County court on 15 April 1815 to bind her children to him. His child was

    i.   Lydia, born say 1779, married Lewis[2] **Pettiford**. She had two children before her marriage, Thomas born about 1796, and Ned born about 1797. She asked the Wake County court to apprentice them to her father because her husband was hiring them out against her will [CR 099.101.1].

19. Prudence Bass (Edward[3], Edward[1], John[1]), born say 1768, posted her own Granville County bastardy bond in April 1791, and in January 1794 Edward Bass and Jacob **Anderson** paid the bond for a child she had by Jesse **Day** [Camin, *N.C. Bastardy Bonds,* 87]. She bound her children Jethro and Cullen to her brother Jason in 1801 [Bell, *Bass Families of the South,* 159]. Her children were

    i.   Jethro[4], born April 1787, married Polly **Mitchell**, 3 April 1809 Granville County bond, Henry **Anderson** bondsman. Jethro and Polly were living in household #874 of Harrison Township, Vigo County, Indiana in 1850.

    ii. Cullen, born May 1795.

20. Thomas[2] Bass (John[3], John[2], William[1], John[1]), born say 1723, was not mentioned in his father's will because he predeceased him. He purchased 240 acres in Bertie County near Amos Grant's patent line on 24 December 1741 and sold this land on 29 November 1746 [DB F:28; G:6]. In 1751 he was taxable on himself and a slave, Nan, in the Bertie County summary list filed with the central government [CCR 190]. In 1757 he and (his brother?) Isaac Bass were taxables in the list of John Hill, Esqr. On 20 May 1763 he purchased an additional 100 acres adjacent to his land near the Cashie River in Bertie County [DB K:328]. And he and his son John were taxed as "Free Mulattos" that year in the Bertie tax list of John Hill [CR 10.702.1, box 2]. His 20 March 1764 Bertie County will, proved in May 1764, named his wife Thomason and his children: John, Jacob, Mary, and Isbell. Jeremiah and Embry **Bunch** were executors [WB A:68]. Thomason was probably "Tamerson Bass" who was mentioned in the 21 April 1775 Bertie will of her father Henry **Bunch**. Thomason was listed as white in the 1769 Bertie County tax list of David Standley, but was a "free Malletor" in Jonathan Standley's 1770 list and David Standley's 1771 list [CR 10.702.1, box 2]. Their children were counted as white in the 1790 census and thereafter. They were

    i.   John[7], born say 1746, taxable in his father's household in 1763.

    ii. Jacob[2].

    iii. Mary[4].

    iv. Isbell.

    v.   Sally, called "orphan" of Thomas Bass in the inventory of Thomas Bass's estate by Tomason Bass [Gammon, *Record of Estates, Bertie County* II, 8].

21. Jacob[1] Bass (John[3], John[2], William[1], John[1]), born say 1725, purchased 100 acres near Urahaw Swamp in Northampton County on 6 February 1746 and sold this land two years later on 4 March 1748 [DB 1:284, 342]. He purchased 150 acres in Granville County on the north side of Swift Creek on 7 March 1757 [DB C:202]. On 20 February 1748 he purchased 200 acres on Tumbling Creek in the part of Edgecombe County which became Nash County in 1777, and he and his wife Ann sold this land on 19 January 1761 [DB 3:319; OO:212]. A few weeks later on 8 February 1761 he purchased 50 acres on the north side of Sandy Creek in Granville County and another 140 acres in the same area a year later on 8 February 1762 [DB E:94; D:94]. He was taxable in 1762 in Goodwins District with son Alexander and slave Dick. This part of Granville County became Bute County in 1764, and Jacob purchased 120 acres on Sandy Creek in Bute County on 3 September 1770 and 125 acres on both sides of Sandy Creek on 1 February 1772. He gave 2 acres of this land to the Baptist Society of Sandy Creek on 16 October 1770 and he and his wife Ann sold another 245 acres on Carraway Branch on 10 May 1775 [Warren County DB 3:6, 526; 5:83, 246]. He was taxable in William Person's 1771 Bute County tax list with son Theophilus and slaves Dick, Bob, and Mollin(?) [CR 015.70001]. In 1771 he and Francis Wells were paid 13 pounds, 10 shillings for building the bridge over Sandy Creek [Bute County Minutes 1767-76, 161]. He was head of a Franklin County household of 7 whites and 10 slaves in 1790 [NC:58]. His children were
    i.   Alexander, born about 1750, since he was taxable in 1762.
    ii. Theophilus, born before 1760, since he was taxable in 1771. He was head of a Franklin County household of 11 whites and 5 slaves in 1790 [NC:58].
    iii. ?Jacob[3], Jr., head of a Franklin County household of 6 whites and 3 slaves in 1790 [NC:58].
    iv. ?Riddick, head of a Franklin County household of 4 whites and 3 slaves in 1790 [NC:58].

22. Isaac Bass (John[3], John[2], William[1], John[1]), born say 1738, was taxed in his own Bertie County household in the constable's list of Michael Collins in 1756. He married Nancy **Bunch**, Thomason Bass's sister. He purchased 181 acres in the fork of Peachtree and Back Swamp on 18 February 1754 in what was then Edgecombe County near the present Nash-Franklin County border [DB 4:559]. His 27 December 1800 Nash County will, proved February 1801, left nine slaves and land to his wife Nancy and children who were considered white [WB 1:136]. His children were
    i.   Cader, the major beneficiary of the 1775 will of his grandfather Henry **Bunch**. He would not have been mentioned in Isaac's 1800 Nash County will since he predeceased him in Bertie County in 1791. He was taxed on 450 acres and a slave in the 1779 Bertie tax list of Wynn's and King's District [CR 10.702.1, box 2]. He posted bond for a bastard child he had by Sarah **Farmer** in August 1787 [Camin, *N.C. Bastardy Bonds*, 8]. Sarah was the daughter of Joseph **Farmer**, a "free Mulatto" taxable in his own household in the 1763 Bertie list of John Hill.[41]
    ii. Jethro[2], who received 150 acres by his father's will.
    iii. Jesse.
    iv. Isaac.
    v.   John[10].
    vi. Augustine.
    vii. a daughter, married ___ Davenport.

---

[41]Joseph **Farmer** was head of a white Bertie County household of 6 males and 6 females in 1790 [NC:12]. Sarah was one of his children mentioned in his November 1796 Bertie County will.

viii.   Nise Rogers.
ix.   Louicy Lawrence.

23.   Jethro[1] Bass (John[3], John[2], William[1], John[1]), born say 1734, received a deed of gift of 200 acres on the north side of Urahaw Swamp in Northampton County from his father John[3] Bass on 24 February 1755 [DB 2:185]. He purchased a total of 740 acres of land in the same area between 1761 and 1777 [DB 4:121, 127, 128, 179; 5:11; 6:125, 326]. He and his wife Susannah sold 50 acres of this land on 12 February 1773 [DB 5:265]. He was head of a Northampton County household of 8 "other free" and 3 slaves in 1790 [NC:74]. His 27 September 1794 Northampton County will, proved March 1795, left land and slaves to his children, but left his wife Elizabeth only the labor of one slave until son Jethro became twenty-one [WB 2:73]. Elizabeth challenged the will in Northampton court when it was proved on 2 March 1795 [Minutes 1792-96, 147, 166]. His children named in his will were

    i.   Council, born say 1760, married Patty Griffin, 4 May 1782 Bertie County bond, Cader Bass bondsman. Council was head of a Northampton County household of 7 "other free" and 2 slaves in 1790 [NC:74] and counted as white in 1810 with 8 slaves [NC:715]. His 2 September 1830 Northampton County will, proved December the same year, left twenty-two slaves to his heirs [WB 4:74].

    ii.   John Redick, probably born after 1770, was to receive schooling according to his father's 1794 will. He received land on the road adjoining John Pinner and the Urahaw Swamp by the division of the estate of his brother Burwell Bass in March 1798 [Gammon, *Record of Estates Northampton County*, I:24]. John was head of a Northampton County household of 4 "other free" in 1810 [NC:715] and 9 "free colored" and 2 slaves in 1820 [NC:218]. His 9 April 1828 Northampton County will named his wife Rhody and children: Uriah, Peggy, Sterling, Lovel, Mary, Martha, James[3], John[12], Gideon, and William[6]. He stipulated that after moving to Indiana the following Fall, Dolphin and James **Roberts** were to sell his horses and divide the proceeds among his children [WB 4:40].

    iii.   Burwell, born after 1774 since he was still a minor in 1795. He died before the March 1798 session of the Northampton County court when the land he received by his father's will was divided among his sister Merica and brothers John Redick and Jethro [Gammon, *Record of Estates Northampton County*, I:24].

    iv.   Jethro[3], born after 1774 since he was still a minor in 1795. He was head of a white Northampton County household with 20 slaves in 1810 [NC:715].

    v.   Maria/ Merica.

24.   Frederick[1] Bass (William[3], John[2], William[1], John[1]), born say 1750, and his wife Olive sold 200 acres on the southwest side of the Pee Dee River on the Flat Fork of Brown Creek in Anson County on 11 August 1777 and purchased 30 acres in the same area on 5 August 1778 [DB 7:196; 4:24]. Olive appeared in Granville County court on 7 April 1770 with (her father-in-law?) William Bass who was called her "next Friend" when she sued Jean **Tylor**, alias **Mitchell**. Olive was awarded damages of one penny [Minutes 1754-70, 202]. Frederick was a buyer at the sale of the Anson County estate of Jesse Ivy on 29 January 1785 [Holcomb, *Anson County, North Carolina*, 138]. He sold 150 acres on the Pee Dee River to (his son?) Frederick Bass, Jr., on 28 February 1797 and 100 acres to (his son?) Simon Bass later that year on 30 September [DB F&G:51, 74]. He was head of an Anson County household of 9 "other free" in 1790 [NC:37], 8 in 1800 [NC:204] and 10 in 1810 [NC:33]. His children were probably

    i.   Frederick^2, Jr., born say 1770, head of an Anson County household of 3 "other free" in 1790 [NC:35] and counted a second time in Anson, head of a household of two "other free" and a white female [NC:36]. He and his wife Nancy sold their land on the Pee Dee River on 9 August 1799 [DB F&G:39].

    ii. Simon^2, born before 1776, head of an Anson County household of 6 "other free" in 1800 [NC:204] and 9 "free colored" in 1820 [NC:12]. He purchased 20 acres adjoining Frederick, Jr., from Letitia Bass on 17 January 1800 and sold this land on 17 August 1801 [DB H-2:177].

29   iii. Elijah^2, born say 1775.

    iv. Letitia, who sold 20 acres of land adjoining Frederick Bass, Jr., to Simon Bass on 17 January 1800 [DB F&G:66].

    v. Olive, head of an Anson County household of 2 "other free" in 1800 [NC:204].

25. Nathan^2 Bass (Lovey, John^2, William^1, John^1), born in 1752, was probably the illegitimate son of Lovey Bass and George **Anderson**. He was bound apprentice to George **Anderson** on 3 August 1768. However, he had already been in George's household in 1767, taxable in Stephen Jett's list [CR 44.701.19]. George gave him his plantation by his Granville County will, proved May 1771. In 1771 he was head of his own household of 3 taxables. On 1 February 1779 Thornton **Pettiford** was bound to him as an apprentice planter, and the following day he married Sarah Bass, Granville County bond with Hardy Bass bondsman. In 1782 he was taxable on 95 acres, 4 horses and 3 cattle in Oxford District, and in 1786 he had 4 males and 5 females in his household in Raglands District. On 9 October 1787 he bought 170 acres on Fishing Creek adjoining Hugh **Snelling** for 50 pounds from Lawrence **Pettiford**. On 16 April 1796 he sold 50 acres on Fishing Creek to John **Tyner** [DB O:537; P:284]. **Tyner** may have been his brother-in-law since Nathan paid his tax for him in 1808 and 1817 [Tax List 1803-09, 275]. He was head of Granville County household of 9 "other free" in 1800 and 10 "free colored" in 1820 [NC:9]. He married, second, Martha Bass, 19 June 1806 Granville County bond, Jesse Bass bondsman. His Granville County will, probated in 1837, mentioned his wife Martha, children, son-in-law Lewis **Pettiford** ("who married my daughter Dinah"), and grandchild Lemuel **Valentine** [WB 14:20]. His estate papers list children: Warner, Dolly/ Polley, Dicy/ Dinah, Honor, Jesse, Sally, and Patsy [CR 044.508.8]. His children were

    i.   Warner.

    ii. Dolly, married Elijah **Valentine**, 28 June 1806 Granville County bond, Benjamin **Mitchell** bondsman.

    iii. Dinah/Disey^2, born about 1793, married Lewis **Pettiford**, 23 December 1809 Granville County bond, Elijah **Valentine** bondsman. Dicy was a fifty-seven-year-old woman listed with Lewis **Anderson** in the 1850 Granville County Census.

    iv. Honor^2, married Major **Jones**, 25 August 1814 Granville County bond, Elijah **Valentine** bondsman.

    v. Jesse.

    vi. Sally **Pettiford**.

    vii. Patsy, married Henry **Taborn**.

26. William^5 Bass (John^6, William^2, William^1, John^1) born 23 June 1755, was taxable in Norfolk County in the household of his mother Elizabeth Bass in 1772 and 1774, in his own household in 1780 [Wingo, *Norfolk County Tithables, 1766-80*, 155, 186, 284] and taxable in Norfolk County from 1782 to 1810: taxable on a slave, a horse and 9 cattle in 1787; a planter on Deep Creek in a "List of Free Negroes and Mulattoes" and head of a household with males John, Andrew and William Bass and females (his wife) Lucy and Betsey Bass in 1801; taxable on 2 tithes in 1801, 3 in 1803, 4 from 1804 to 1807

[PPTL, 1782-90, frames 383, 431, 484, 525, 561, 622, 638, 678; 1791-1812, frames 371, 427, 461, 479, 555, 574, 674, 684, 720, 738]. He was head of a Norfolk County household of 7 persons in 1785 [VA:93] and 8 "other free" in 1810 (called William Bass, Sr.) [VA:822]. On 27 May 1797 he recorded a certificate of Indian descent in Norfolk County which is obviously incorrect and conflicts with nearly all earlier Bass family documents:

> *This doth certify that William Bass, son of John Bass and grandson of William Bass, is of English and Indian descent and is not a Negroe nor y^t a Mulattoe as by some falsely and malitiously stated. His late Mother Sarah Ann Bass was a vertious woman of Indian descent, a daughter of Symon Lovina and Joan Tucker lawfully begotten. Sd Joan Tucker was a sister of Robin Tucker a Christian Indian of ye Nansemund nation. The sd. William Bass, the elder, was a son of Mary Bass and William Senr. Mary was a daughter of Great Peter, King of ye Nansemunds. These are ___mon (common?) knowledge. All the Basses of this County descend from $Capt^n$ Nathaniell Basse, as satisfactorily proved by the records preserved. May y^e 17, 1797. Test: Wm. Portlock Junr.* [Library of Virginia Accession no.26371].[42]

William and his wife Lucy recorded the births of their children John and William in the Bass family bible [Bell, *Bass Families of the South*, 13]. He made a Norfolk County deed of gift to Willis Bass for 30 acres adjoining Willis Bass and John Gibbs on 19 July 1798 [DB 45:1]. William and Lucy's children were

    i.   John[12], born 1 August 1782, "son of William Bass and Lucy his wife." He was called John Gibbs Bass, "free man of colour," on 18 August 1812 when he married Salley **Price**, "free woman of colour," 18 August 1812 Norfolk County bond, William Bass surety. He purchased 17 acres adjoining his land in Portsmouth Parish on 28 March 1814, and he and his wife Sally sold 20 acres on the north side of Deep Creek and the head of the Southern Branch on 5 July 1814 [DB 46:160, 250].

    ii.   William[6], born 4 April 1784, married Elizabeth **Perkins**, 2 November 1812 Norfolk County bond, Adam **Perkins** surety.

    iii. Andrew, married (his cousin?) Leviney Bass, 1 February 1812 Norfolk County bond, Willis Bass surety. He was taxable in Norfolk County from 1809 to 1817: a "B.M." listed in Norfolk County as a "Free Negro" over the age of 16 living near Willis Bass in D.C (Deep Creek) from 1815 to 1817 [PPTL, 1791-1812, frames 684, 720, 738; 1813-24, frames 96, 125, 242]. (Bell also lists an Andrew Bass, born 9 April 1799(?), "son of Willis Bass and Jemima his mother.")

27. James[2] Bass (William[4], William[2], William[1], John[1]), born in August 1760 in Norfolk County according to his pension application, was taxable on a free tithe in Norfolk County in 1787 and from 1798 to 1810: a labourer in a "List of Free Negroes and Mulattoes" on Deep Creek and head of a household with males (sons?) John and Willis Bass and females (his wife?) Lott, (daughters?) Lane, Sarah and Lovy Bass in 1801; taxable on a slave in 1810 [PPTL, 1782-90, frame 562; 1791-1812, frames 243, 295, 351, 427, 461, 479, 555, 572, 674, 720]. He leased 5 acres in Norfolk County on the road to the canal for five years on 10 March 1814 [DB 46:121]. He was a "B.M." (Black Man) who was taxable as a "Free Negro" in Norfolk County from 1813 to 1817 [PPTL, 1813-24, frames 15, 56, 96, 125, 242]. He moved to Bedford County,

---

[42]Sarah Ann Bass was William's grandmother, not his mother. She was the "Molatto" daughter of Jean/ Joan **Lovina**, a "Negro Woman," who was freed by the will of John Nichols.

Tennessee, about 1819 and received a pension for his services as a private in the Virginia Militia [National Archives File S1745]. He was the father of

    i.   John, born say 1790, a "B.M." taxable as a "Free Negro" in Deep Creek, Norfolk County from 1810 to 1817: called "son Jas" (son of James) in 1810 and 1813 [PPTL, 1791-1812, frame 720; 1813-24, frames 15, 56, 96, 126, 242].

    ii. Lane, listed in James Bass's household in 1801.

    iii. Willis, listed in James Bass's household in 1801.

    iv. Sarah, listed in James Bass's household in 1801.

    v.   Lovy, listed in James Bass's household in 1801.

28. Willis Bass (William[4], William[2], William[1], John[1]), born say 1763, was taxable in Norfolk County from 1784 to 1787 but not taxable again in Norfolk County until 1796 [PPTL, 1782-91, frames 466, 525, 562], so he was apparently the Willis Bass who was head of a Hertford County, North Carolina household of 4 "other free" in 1790 [NC:26]. He was taxable in Norfolk County from 1796 to 1817: called a "B.M." (Black Man) when he was a "Free Negro" taxable in Norfolk County from 1814 to 1817: a labourer living on Deep Creek in a "List of Free Negroes and Mulattoes," head of a household with males (his sons?) Wilson and Willis Bass and females (his wife) Jemima, (his daughters?) Viney, Lovy, and Irstellor(?) Bass in 1801; listed with 3 "Free Negroes and Mulattoes" in 1814, and 2 in 1816 and 1817 [PPTL, 1791-1812, frames 168, 222, 295, 351, 371, 383, 427, 479, 555, 574, 642, 684, 720, 738; 1813-24, frames 56, 96, 125, 242]. He was head of a Norfolk County household of 6 "other free" in 1810 [VA:822]. He and his wife Jemima recorded the births of their children in the Bass family bible [Bell, *Bass Families of the South*, 13]. Jemima was sixty-six years old on 10 April 1835 when she deposed that she was the only child of James **Nickens** who served as a seaman in the Revolution [Hopkins, *Virginia Revolutionary War Land Grant Claims*, 166]. Willis was deceased on 19 May 1834 when the Norfolk County court certified that Jamima Bass was the widow of Willis Bass, deceased, and only heir of her father James **Nickens** and his brother Nathaniel **Nickens** [Minutes 24:139]. Willis and Jemima's children were

    i.   Wilson, listed in Willis's household in 1801, a "B.M." (Black Male) taxable a "free Negro" tithe on Deep Creek in 1815 and 1817, perhaps identical to Nelson Bass who was a "B.M." tithable on a "free Negro" tithe on Deep Creek in 1816 [PPTL, 1813-24, frames 96, 135, 242]. Nelson married Nancy **Price**, 9 December 1817 Norfolk County bond, James **Price** surety.

    ii. Willis, born say 1792, a "free Negro" tithable in 1817 [PPTL, 1813-24, frame 242].

    iii. Viney, married Andrew Bass, 1 February 1812 Norfolk County bond, Willis Bass surety.

    iv. Lovy, listed in Willis's household in 1801.

    v.   Irstelllor(?), listed in Willis's household in 1801.

    vi. ?Lemuel, born say 1798, a "B.M." taxable as a "Free Negro" in Deep Creek, Norfolk County, from 1815 to 1817 [PPTL, 1813-24, frames 96, 126, 242].

    vii. Joshua[2], born 14 July 1804 [Bell, *Bass Families of the South*, 13]

29. Elijah[2] Bass (Frederick[1], William[3], John[2], William[1], John[1]), born say 1775, was head of an Anson County household of 3 "other free" in 1800 [NC:204]. He may have been the Elijah Bass who was counted in Robeson County that same year, head of a household of 5 "other free" in 1800 [NC:362] and 6 in Robeson County in 1810 [NC:237]. He was granted administration on the Robeson County estate of (his brother?) Frederick Bass on 200 pounds security on 9 April 1801 [Minutes 1797-1806, 149]. He was one of the freeholders of Robeson County ordered to work on a road with Breton Barnes on the first

Monday in July 1807 [Minutes 1806-13, 38] but was not mentioned again in Robeson County records. He may have been the same Elijah Bass who was head of a Kershaw District, South Carolina household of 6 "other free" and 2 slaves in 1810 [SC:433]. He wrote a 28 December 1839 Kershaw County will, recorded on 16 June 1854, describing himself as a "freeman of Color." He mentioned but did not name his children and lent his wife Milbury Eliza 500 acres "on waters of Beaver Dam and Bell Branch, waters of Twenty Five mile Creek of the Wateree river in Kershaw" which was conveyed to him on 10 February 1809. And he suggested that "my wife may desire to return to North Carolina. Elijah Bass" (signing) [WB A:231].[43] In August 1846 a grandchild of Elijah Bass named Mrs. White sued a South Carolina tax collector for attempting to collect from her the "free Negro" capitation tax. She testified that her grandmother was a "mulatto," her grandfather a Revolutionary soldier, her father Elijah Bass a "dark quadroon if he was one," and her brother an "ordinary white sandhill boy" [Catterall, *Judicial Cases Concerning American Slavery*, II:400-1]. Elijah may have been the father of

    i.   Frederick[3], born say 1795, purchased 103 acres in Robeson County on the east side of Bay Branch on 6 May 1820 [DB S:275].

    ii.   Joseph[4], born after 1776, head of a Robeson County household of 7 "free colored" in 1820 [NC:300].

BATES FAMILY

1.   Benjamin Bates, born say 1731, was a "Mullatto Bastard Child" who the Charles County, Maryland court sold to Peter Harrant on 9 November 1731 [Court Record 1731-4, 41]. He may have been the ancestor of the members of the Bates family who were living in nearby Prince William County, Virginia, in 1810:

    i.   John, head of a Prince William County household of 9 "other free" in 1810 [VA:508]. He may have been the husband of Sophia Bates whose seventeen-year-old daughter registered as a free Negro in Washington, D.C. on 26 July 1827: *a mulatto woman...daughter of Sophia Bates of Dumfries, Virginia, who was born free* [Provine, *District of Columbia Free Negro Registers*, 96-6].

    ii.   Cyrus, head of a Prince William County household of 5 "other free" in 1810 [VA:508].

Prince George and Charles City counties
1.   William Bates, born say 1744, the son of Mary **Cumbo**, was bound out by the Charles City County court in August 1744 [Orders 1737-51, 319]. He may have been the ancestor of

    i.   Fanny, head of a Prince George County, Virginia household of 7 "other free" in 1810 [VA:545].

    ii.   Hetty, head of a Prince George County, Virginia household of 7 "other free" in 1810 [VA:545].

    iii. Archibald, head of a Prince George County, Virginia household of 1 "other free" in 1810 [VA:545].

---

[43]Elijah was probably related to Molly Bass, born perhaps 1770, whose Kershaw County, South Carolina will was written 14 February 1829 and proved 14 July the same year. She left land, three slaves, and $600 to her son Elijah, grandchildren Fanny Jackson, Josiah, Ely, Elijah, and Martha Bass, and great granddaughters Levisa Jackson and Mary Bass [DB O:274].

BATTLES FAMILY

Members of the Battles family were

      i.   Hannah, born say 1716, sued Noble Ladd for trespass viet armis in Albemarle County, Virginia court on 14 May 1747. When the case came to trial on 9 July 1747, Ladd produced a writing signed by Hannah (her mark) on 25 May 1747 by which she acknowledged receiving full satisfaction from him for all damages recovered against him in an action of assault and battery in Albemarle County court. However, the court ruled that it was not valid since she was still under his influence. He appealed to the General Court, but the judgment was confirmed. On 13 August 1748 the case was dismissed when Ladd agreed to pay Hannah all the costs provided Hannah would endeavor to recover them against William Battersby and repay Ladd if she was successful [Orders 1744-8, 280, 300, 388, 414, 415].

1   ii. Sarah, born say 1725.

1.   Sarah Battle, born say 1725, was living in Goochland County on 16 June 1762 when the court ordered the churchwardens of St. James Northam Parish to bind out her son Shadrack to learn the trade of blacksmith [Orders 1761-5, 16]. She was the mother of

2   i.   Shadrack[1], born about 1746.
3   ii. ?Robert, born say 1755.
4   iii. ?Jane, born say 1760.
      iv. ?Elizabeth[1], head of a Henrico County household of 6 "other free" in 1810 [VA:980], a "fn" taxable on a slave over the age of sixteen in the upper district of Henrico County in 1811, perhaps the mother of Milly Battles who was a "fn" taxable on a slave and 2 horses in the same district in 1812 [PPTL 1782-1813, frames 658, 717].

2.   Shadrack[1] Battles, born about 1746, complained about John Crouch to the Goochland County court in August 1762, and the court cancelled its order to bind him to Crouch [Orders 1761-5, 78]. He married Dolly **Moss** in Louisa County on 25 July 1780 [Jones, *The Douglas Register*]. He was taxable in Fredericksville Parish, Albemarle County, from 1782 to 1813: taxable on 2 tithables in 1788, 1799 and 1801; taxable on a slave in 1797 and 1798; taxable on 3 tithes in 1802, listed in St. Ann's Parish from 1805 to 1811; taxable on his unnamed son from 1805 to 1810; called a "F. Molatto" in 1806, a "free negro" in 1810 (also listed as a "Mulatto" in the town of Fredericksville in 1810); a "Mulatto" from 1811 to 1813; taxable on 3 tithes in 1813 [PPTL, 1782-1799, frames 11, 26, 55, 72, 110, 148, 195, 244, 292, 342, 382, 445, 477, 511, 551, 585; 1800-1813, frames 24, 68, 112, 156, 201, 227, 269, 318, 410, 456, 517, 562]. Robert Murray sued him for assault and battery in a case that was continued in Albemarle County from 10 June 1784 past 10 June 1785. Jane Battles sued him for trespass, assault and battery in court on 10 August 1793, but the case was dismissed. Thomas Carr, Jr., sued him for a 2 pound, 12 shilling debt on 13 September 1793; Joice Shiflet sued him for a 1 pound, 10 shilling debt on 7 June 1796 and for a 5 pound debt on 4 April 1797. Jesse White sued him for 5 pounds due by bill on 3 October 1798. He and James **Going** were security for Michael **Ailstock**'s bond of 6 January 1800 to keep the peace in Albemarle County. He, William Battles, Bartlett **Bowles**, Zachariah **Bowles**, Thomas **Farrow**, and Griffin **Butler** were among the male laboring tithables ordered to work on the Albemarle County road whereof John F. Hawkins was surveyor on 2 December 1800 [Orders 1783-5, 216, 274, 364, 507; 1791-3, 477, 502; 1795-8, 116, 282, 359; 1798-1800, 133, 382; 1800-1, 250]. He was "a man of colour" who was about seventy-four years old on 11 October 1820 when he appeared in Albemarle County court to apply for a pension for his services in the Revolution. He testified that he enlisted while

resident in Amherst County in 1777 and served for three years. He was a carpenter but was no longer able to support himself and his sixty-year-old wife. He owned 200 acres on the Hardware River in Amherst County which he sold in 1775 [M805-63, frames 183-9]. He was bondsman for the 21 October 1786 Albemarle County marriage of Jonathan **Tyre** and Usly **Gowing**. Shadrack was head of an Albemarle County household of 6 "other free" in 1810 [VA:151]. He was probably the father of

    i.   Shadrack[2], Jr., taxable in Fredericksville Parish, Albemarle County, from 1810 to 1813 [PPTL, 1800-1813, frames 410, 456, 472, 517, 562], registered as a free Negro with his father in Amherst County in 1810 [McLeRoy, *Strangers in Their Midst*, 113].

5   ii.   Elizabeth, born say 1770.

    iii.   Polly, born say 1784, married John **Spinner**, 2 April 1805 Albemarle County bond. John was probably related to Richard **Spinner**, head of an Albemarle County household of 9 "other free" in 1810 [VA:173] and a "mulatto" with 3 persons in his household over the age of sixteen in 1813; and Keziah and Patty **Spinner**, each listed as a "mulatto" in Fredericksville Parish, Albemarle County, in 1813 [PPTL, 1800-1813, frames 575, 576].

    iv.   Lucy, born about 1787, registered as a free Negro in the Corporation of Staunton, Virginia, on 25 August 1810: *about 23 years of age, yellow complexion, slender made, free born, as appears from her indentures of Apprenticeship* [Register of Free Negroes, no. 5].

    v.   Edward, taxable in Fredericksville Parish, Albemarle County, in 1803, a "Mulatto" taxable in 1813 [PPTL, 1800-1813, frames 156, 562].

    vi.   William, taxable in Fredericksville Parish, Albemarle County, from 1800 to 1806 and in 1810 [PPTL, 1782-1799, frames; 1800-1813, frames 23, 156, 201, 246, 269, 410].

3.   Robert Battles, born say 1755, married Nancy **Bowls (Bowles)**, 12 December 1793 Albemarle County bond, Charles **Barnett** bondsman. Daniel **Bowles** (his foster son?) sued him in Albemarle County on 14 August 1794, and the court ordered that Robert show cause why he unlawfully beat and misused Daniel. The court ordered him to post bond of $100 to keep the peace on 8 January 1795 when he was accused of assaulting Lucy **Barnett** [Orders 1793-5, 202, 298]. He was taxable in Fredericksville Parish, Albemarle County, from 1793 to 1813: taxable on a slave in 1798 and 1805; called a "Mulatto from 1805; taxable on 3 tithes and 3 horses in 1813 [PPTL, 1782-1799, frames 382, 415, 445, 478, 511, 551, 585; 1800-1813, frames 67, 112, 156, 201, 246, 291, 339, 382, 429, 473, 517, 562]. He was head of an Albemarle County household of 7 "other free" in 1810 [VA:185]. He may have been the father of

    i.   Alexander, born about 1802, registered in Augusta County, Virginia, on 28 October 1823: *a free man of a mulatto complexion aged twenty one years in April and was born free in the County of Albemarle* [Register of Free Negroes, no.61].

4.   Jane Battles, born say 1760, sued Shadrack Battles for trespass, assault and battery in Albemarle County on 10 August 1793, but the court dismissed the case. On 5 April 1796 the court ordered the overseers of the poor of the southwestern district to bind her illegitimate child Betty Battels to Dixon Dedman until the age of eighteen [Orders 1791-3, 477; 1795-8, 39]. She was probably the Juanna Battle who was head of a Richmond City household of 1 "other free" in 1810 [VA:330]. She was the mother of

    i.   Elizabeth[3], born say 1786, bound to Dixon Dedman on 5 April 1796.

5.   Elizabeth[2] Battles, born say 1770, was a "FN" taxable in St. Ann's Parish, Albemarle County, on a horse in 1805, a "Free Molato" taxable on a horse in

1806, a "FN" taxable on her unnamed son in 1807, a "Mulatto" taxable on a horse in 1812 and 1813 [PPTL, 1800-1813, frames 227, 269, 318, 499, 541]. She was head of an Albemarle County household of 2 "other free" in 1810 [VA:180]. She may have been the mother of

    i.   Turner, a "Mulatto" taxable in St. Ann's Parish, Albemarle County, from 1810 to 1812 [PPTL, 1800-1813, frames 410, 456, 499], head of an Albemarle County household of 3 "other free" in 1810 [VA:180].

BAZDEN FAMILY

1. Martha Basden, born about 12 July 1732, was a white child living in Isle of Wight County in 1742 when her brother Joseph died and left her a legacy of eight pounds. On February 1749/50 she released her claim to the legacy to her father. She lived with her father until he died intestate on 20 July 1770. Between 1771 and 1773 she brought a chancery suit in Southampton County against her brother James Basden and the executor of her father's estate because they refused to give her any part of his estate. She argued that she was entitled to eight pounds with interest as well as something for the "care and affectionate behaviour" she rendered to her father in his later years. Her brother James argued that she had been a burden to her father: *on Account of her having had two Bastard Children of such a Complexion as almost induced the said James her Father to expose her to the Blame and contempt of the world* [Chancery Court Papers 1771-1788; LVA chancery file 1773-007]. On 9 August 1770 the court ordered her "Malatto" son Lewis bound until the age of twenty-one [Orders 1768-72, 309]. One of her children was

    i.   Lewis, born about 1760, taxable in Sussex County in 1787 his tax charged to Thomas Pretlow, his tax charged to Samuel Cornwell in 1788 [PPTL 1782-1812, frames 214, 220], a "F.N." taxable in Isle of Wight County from 1790 to 1794 [PPTL 1782-1810, frames 194, 213, 257, 286, 310]. He was taxable in Surry County from 1796 to 1815: taxable on a slave in 1798; a slave named Daphney in 1799 [PPTL, 1791-1816, frames 251, 320, 363, 442, 517, 589, 628, 666, 728, 804]. He married Sarah **Tann**, "25 years old," 27 October 1803 Southampton County bond, Mat **Williams** surety, 28 October marriage. He was called Lewis Baseden when he registered as a "free Negro" in Surry County on 16 August 1800: *a mulatto, grey headed, light complexion, 5' 6 1/2 inches high, 40 years old, born of a free woman resident of Southampton County* [Back of Guardian Accounts Book, 1783-1804, no.61], and he was called Louis Bazden in 1810, head of a Surry County household of 4 "other free" [VA:601]. His wife Sally registered in Surry County on 15 February 1812: *Sally Bazden late Sally Tann a daughter of John and Susanna Tann decd. free mulattoes of Southampton county, of a bright complexion, aged about thirty four years of age...is 4'11-1/4" high* [Hudgins, *Surry County Register of Free Negroes*, 47]. Sally apparently died not long after registering because Lewis married Ava **Dunkins**, 6 June 1817 Southampton County bond.

BAZMORE FAMILY

1. Elizabeth Bazmore, born say 1695, was taxable on her son John in 1730 in Norfolk County, Virginia [Wingo, *Norfolk County Tithables 1730-50*, 36]. Eight years later the Bazmore family was in Bertie County, North Carolina, where John purchased 317 acres on the "Looseing Swamp" on 21 January 1737/8 [DB E:264]. He proved his rights in Bertie court on 10 November 1742:

John Bazemore, Mary Basemore, Elizabeth ~~Basemore~~ Edwards, Mary ~~Basemore~~ Edwards, Jesse Basemore, Thomas Basemore, John Basemore, Sarah Basemore [Haun, *Bertie County Court Minutes*, II::381].

The family was taxed as "free Mulattos" in the 1761 tax list of William Gray, the 1763 list of John Hill, the 1764 list of Jonathan Standley, the summary list for 1765 and 1766, the 1768 list of Jonathan Standley, and David Standley's list for 1769, 1770, and 1771 [CR 10.702.1]. However, they were counted as white in David Standley's list for 1772 and 1774, and they were counted as white in the 1790 Bertie County census [NC:11]. Elizabeth was likely born before 1700 since the 13 October 1761 session of the Bertie County court excused her from paying taxes because she was "very aged and infirm" [Haun, *Bertie County Court Minutes*, II:559]. Her children were

    i.   John, born say 1714, taxable in Norfolk County, Virginia, in 1730 [Wingo, *Norfolk County Tithables, 1730-50*, 36]. His 4 December 1748 Bertie County deed of sale of 450 acres on Ahoskie Swamp was witnessed by Joseph **Hall**, another "free Mulatto" from Norfolk County [DB G:271]. In 1763 he was taxed on his son Thomas and 2 slaves in John Hill's list. By 1779 he and his sons were taxable on 9 slaves and 1,826 acres of land in Bertie County for Wynn's and King's District. His 10 July 1789 Bertie County will was proved in May term 1790 and named his children who were all considered white in the 1790 census: John, Jr., Thomas, James, William, Tamer Sowell, Sarah Thomas, and Elizabeth White [WB 2:328].

    ii.   ?Jesse, born say 1720, one of John Bazemore's head rights in 1742 [Haun, *Bertie County Court Minutes*, II:381]. He was taxable in the 1756 summary list for Bertie County. He and his wife Frances were "free Mulattos" in the 1761 Bertie tax list of William Gray. He bought land from his brother John [DB K:297]. He was taxed on 503 acres in the 1779 list of Wynn's and King's District and purchased another 8 tracts of land between 1786 and 1796 [DB N:266; O:21-2, 342: P:85; Q:128, 137; S:56]. He was head of a white Bertie County household with 14 slaves in 1790 [NC:11]. His 17 June 1800 Bertie County will was proved in February 1809, and mentioned his wife Frances and his children: Jesse, Turner, Zilpha, Mary, Susanna, Esther Griffin, and Dicey Thomas.

BECKETT FAMILY

1.   Peter[1] Beckett, born say 1655, was a "Negro" slave who was taxable with Thomas **Driggers** from 1671 to 1677 in the Northampton County, Virginia household of John Eyres:

> *Mjr. Eyres*
>   *Tho: Driggus }*
>   *Peter Beckett }*
>   *Mary Crew   } Neg 4* [Orders 1664-74, fol.114; 1674-79, 75, 191].

Sarah Dawson, a white servant, was another member of Eyre's household. She was born about 1661 since her age was adjudged to be sixteen years when Eyre brought her into Northampton County court on 26 November 1677 [OW 1674-79, 203]. Seven years later in 1684 she was given twenty-one lashes and ordered to serve Eyre another six years for having "three bastard Maletto Children by her said Masters Negro slave Peter." On 30 May 1687 and 28 May 1688 she was presented for bastard bearing and the following year on 29 July 1689 was called "Sarah the wife of Peter Beckett slave to Major John Eyre" when the court ordered one of her children released to her, "Shee findinge sufficient security to save the parish harmelesse from the said Childe"

[OW 1683-89, 59, 280, 292, 358, 442-3]. On 28 July 1702 she consented to the indenture of their daughter Ann, "daughter of Sarah Beckett," to Mrs. Ann Eyre until the age of eighteen [OW 1698-1710, 96]. Peter was free by 30 November 1703 when "Peter Beckett and Sarah his wife" successfully sued John Morrine for debt in Northampton County court. John Robins brought an action upon the case against him, but neither party appeared when it came for trial on 21 January 1717/8 [OW&c 1698-1710, 176; Orders 1710-6, 55]. Peter and Sarah's children were

2   i.   Rebecca[1]/ Beck, born say 1690.
3   ii. Ann, born 10 December 1697.
4   iii. Jean, born say 1700.
5   iv. Elizabeth[1]/ Betty[1], born say 1705.

2. Rebecca Beckett, born say 1690, was summoned to the Northampton County court on 12 January 1724/5 to show cause why her son William should not be bound to John Robins, and summoned the following month on 11 February to answer Mark Freshwater's petition to have her son Mark bound to him because he had been living with him for five years. In the petition Freshwater also called Mark Beckett the "free Negro" son of Peter Beckett [Orders 1722-9, 149, 155, Mihalyka, *Loose Papers I:*81]. However, Mark was more likely the grandson of Peter since there is no record of a Peter Beckett in the eighteenth century Northampton County lists of tithables which begin in 1720. On 10 March 1724/5 John Robins attested to a note from Rebecca informing the court that she consented to her son Mark's indenture to Freshwater at the age of twenty-one [Orders 1722-9, 172]. Rebecca was a "melatto" taxable in Jonathan Stott's household in 1724 and 1725, tithable in the household of John **Drighouse** in 1726, in Berry Floyd's household in 1728, and in Joachim Michael's household from 1729 to 1743 [Bell, *Northampton County Tithables*, 77, 155, 168, 262, 274, 289, 308, 326, 330, 353]. She was presented by the court on 13 May 1735 for bastard bearing and was granted levy-free status by the court on 12 June 1744 due to an infirmity [Orders 1732-42, 155, 163; 1742-8, 163]. Her children were

6   i.   Mark, born say 1711.
      ii. William[1], born 10 December 1714, ten-year-old son of Rebecca Beckett bound apprentice to John Robins on 10 February 1724/5 until the age of twenty-one [Orders 1722-9, 161]. He was a 10-16 year old boy in the Northampton County household of John Robins from 1724 to 1730 [Bell, *Northampton County Tithables*, 58, 76, 104, 113, 118, 167, 201]. On 14 May 1734 Elishe **Webb** charged him with being the father of her illegitimate child. He was still the servant of John Robins at the time, so the court ordered the sheriff to take him into custody after his term of servitude expired [Orders 1732-42, 97, 103, 107].
      iii. Rachel, born about 1718, twelve-year-old daughter of Rebecca Beckett, bound apprentice to Thomas Marshall on 10 November 1730 [Orders 1729-32, 53]. She was presented on 13 November 1739 for bastard bearing [Orders 1732-42, 372].
7   iv. Isaac[1], born in April 1724.
8   v. ?Solomon[1], born say 1727.

3. Ann Beckett, born 10 December 1697, the four-year-old "daughter of Sarah Beckett," was bound apprentice to Mrs. Ann Eyre by the Northampton County court on 28 July 1702 until the age of eighteen years with her mother's consent [OW 1698-1710, 96]. Ann received twenty-five lashes on 20 June 1716 for having a bastard child by John **Drighouse** (**Driggers**). She was called a "Mallato" in July 1718 when she was again punished for having a bastard child [Orders 1710-16, 244, 252; 1716-8, 120]. She was a taxable "melatto" in Richard Carue's household in 1724 and 1725 [Bell, *Northampton County Tithables*, 54, 79]. She may have been the mother of

i. Nancy, born say 1715, taxable in Esther Map's household in 1731 [Bell, *Northampton County Tithables*, 226].

9 ii. ?Sarah[1], born say 1718.

4. Jean Beckett, born say 1700, a "free negro woman," was taxable in the Northampton County household of William Cowdry in 1724, taxable in the household of Thomas Savage, Sr., in 1725, and taxable in the household of Thomas[2] **Driggers** in the list of Matthew Harmonson for 1727, 1729 and 1731. She was his common-law wife, called Jane **Drighouse** when she was taxable in his household in 1737 and in 1744 with her daughter Esther **Drighouse** [Bell, *Northampton County Tithables*, 66, 93, 127, 136, 194, 198, 226]. Thomas **Drighouse**, a "free Negro," left a 21 April 1757 Northampton County will, proved 14 June 1757, by which he made Jane Beckett his executor and left all he had to her and her three daughters: Hester, Betty, and Lydia Beckett [WB 21:281]. Jean's children were

i. Sarah[2] Beckett, born say 1721, called the daughter of Jean **Drighouse** when the sheriff took her mother into custody as bond for her appearance in court for bastard bearing. She received twenty-five lashes on 8 April 1740 [Orders 1732-42, 394; Mihalyka, *Loose Papers*, II:124]. She was taxable in Thomas **Drighouse**'s household from 1737 to 1739, called Sarah Becket in 1737 and 1738, called Sarah in 1739, and called Sarah **Drighouse** when she was taxable in Mark Beckett's household in 1740 [Bell, *Northampton County Tithables*, 266, 272, 285, 305]. She married Isaiah **Drighouse** (**Driggers**).

ii. ?Comfort[1] Beckett, born say 1723, tithable in Thomas **Drighouse**'s household in 1739 and 1740 [Bell, *Northampton County Tithables*, 285, 308]. She married Jacob **Morris** by 1743.

iii. Hester Beckett, born say 1727, a tithable in her parents' household in 1744.

iv. Elizabeth[2]/ Betty.

v. Lydia Beckett.

5. Elizabeth[1] Beckett, born say 1705, was called Betty **Drighouse** when she was tithable in John **Drighouse**'s Northampton County household from 1724 to 1727, but called Betty Beckett in 1727. John married Lydia **Carter** before June 1728 when she was tithable in his household as Lydia **Drighouse**. Elizabeth was tithable in her own household in 1728 adjacent to ___ **Mongon**, but she was again a tithable, "not employed in crop," in John and Lydia **Drighouse**'s household in 1729. She was tithable in James Forse's household in 1731, in Thomas Cable's in 1737, and in Norly Ellegood's household from 1739 to 1744 [L.P. 1729; Bell, *Northampton County Tithables*, 54, 78, 105, 127, 145. 147, 172, 229, 264, 283, 310, 321, 338, 356]. She was presented for bastard bearing on 14 June 1732 (her fine paid by Major James Forse) and presented on 10 May 1737 (her fine paid by Thomas Cable) [Orders 1732-42, 8, 261, 269]. She was the mother of

i. ?Sarah[3], born about 1732, eight-year-old orphan bound to Benjamin Dunton on 8 April 1740 [Orders 1732-42, 396], perhaps the Sarah Backit who was taxable in the household of John Wilkins in 1766 [Bell, *Northampton County Tithables*, 380]

ii. ?Peter[2], born in February 1734/5, a three-year-old bound apprentice in Northampton County to Samuel **Church** and his wife Elizabeth on 11 October 1737 (no parent named) [Orders 1732-42, 279], taxable in John Bowdoin's household in 1766 and 1769 [Bell, *Northampton County Tithables*, 380, 392].

iii. ?William[2], born 6 August 1742, a seven-year-old orphan "Negro" bound apprentice to Eleanor Ellegood on 13 September 1749 [Orders 1748-51, 130].

iv. Isaac[2], born 25 November 1746, "son of Betty Beckett," bound apprentice in Northampton County in 1760 [Minutes 1754-61, 230]. He was about thirteen when he was bound to Thomas Bell on 12 August 1760 [Minutes 1754-61, 230]. He registered as a "free Negro" in Northampton County on 11 June 1794 [Orders 1789-95, 354]. He was taxable in Northampton County from 1798 to 1813 [PPTL, 1782-1823, frames 243, 304, 529].

v. ?Joshua, born 5 December 1748, a six-year-old "Negro" bound apprentice to Ralph Batson in Northampton County on 6 December 1754 [Orders 1753-58, 172, 219-20], said to be about fourteen years old on 13 March 1764 when he was bound to Sarah Batson [Minutes 1761-5, 108]. On 14 November 1770 Isaac Clegg was presented by the grand jury for not listing Joshua as a tithable [Minutes 1765-71, 399]. He was taxable in Northampton County from 1783 to 1813 [PPTL, 1782-1823, frames 21, 63, 79, 189, 304, 529]. He married Sally **Stevens**, 21 May 1803 Northampton County bond, Jacob **Thompson** security. He was head of a Northampton County household of 7 "free colored" in 1820 [VA:219].

6. Mark Beckett, born say 1711, had been living with Mark Freshwater for five years when he was bound to him by the Northampton County court on 10 March 1724/5 [Orders 1722-9, 172]. He was a "malatto" boy 10-16 years of age in Mark Freshwater's Northampton County household in the list of John Robins for 1725, a tithable in Freshwater's household from 1727 to 1729, and tithable in Ann Dod's household in the list of John Robins for 1737 and 1738 [Bell, *Northampton County Tithables*, 119, 144, 167, 255, 277]. He married Margaret **Drighouse**, widow of Azaricum **Drighouse (Driggers)**. As guardian of Jacob **Drighouse** he presented an inventory of the orphan's estate in court on 12 April 1743 [Orders 1742-48, 33, 45, 56, 69]. He and his wife Pegg Beckett were taxable in their own household with Sarah **Drighouse** (Jean Beckett's daughter) from 1740 to 1743, taxable in 1744 with Jacob **Drighouse** (Peggy's son), and he and Peggy were taxables in 1765 and in 1769 [Bell, *Northampton County Tithables*, 305, 328, 334, 350, 360, 375, 387]. On 22 November 1750 he was paid 490 pounds of tobacco for services to the county, perhaps for work done on the courthouse [Orders 1748-51, 299]. In February 1771 the court bound Levin Beckett to him as an apprentice [Minutes 1771-5, 251]. He was taxable in Northampton County in 1783 [PPTL, 1782-1823, frame 18]. He was the father of

i. ?Solomon[2], born say 1760, a "Mulatto" taxable in Northampton County from 1782 to 1789 [PPTL, 1782-1823, frames 3, 73, 94]. He served in the Revolution from Northampton County [NSDAR, *African American Patriots*, 147]. There were three marriages for persons named Solomon Beckett in Northampton County: to Sarah **Liverpool**, bond of July 1800; to Adah **Liverpool**, bond of 7 July 1801, Josiah **Liverpool** security; and to Abigail **Stevens**, bond of 19 February 1803, Jacob **Thompson** security. And a Solomon Beckett, born before 1776, was head of a Northampton County household of 5 "free colored" in 1820 [VA:217A].

ii. Isaiah, born in November 1773, twelve-year-old son of Mark Beckett, bound apprentice in Northampton County to Peter Bowdoin on 14 December 1785. He registered as a "free Negro" in Northampton County on 11 June 1794 [Orders 1783-7, 379; 1789-95, 354].

iii. Peter[4], born 6 January 1775, son of Mark Becket, bound apprentice to Peter Bowdoin on 11 September 1787 [Orders 1787-9, 45]. He may have been the Peter Beckett who married Ariena **Nutt**, 10 January 1800 Accomack County bond, Babel Major, surety. She may have been the Arena Becket who married Thomas **Bibbins**, 2 August 1800 Accomack County bond, Peter **Bibbins** surety.

Mark may have been the grandfather of
  i.   Levin, born in February 1771, bound to Mark Beckett in Northampton
       County on 10 May 1774 [Minutes 1771-5, 251].
  ii. Diana[2], born say 1773, "ward of Mark Becket," married Ezekiel
       Moses, 22 August 1791 Northampton County bond, William Stith
       security. Ezekiel was head of a Northampton County household of 4
       "free colored" in 1820 [VA:216A].

7. Isaac[1] Beckett, born in April 1724, son of Rebecca Becket, was bound to
    Thomas Marshall on 10 November 1730 [Orders 1729-32, 53]. He was taxable
    in William Stott's Northampton County household in 1743, a taxable head of
    a household of himself and (his wife?) Mason Beckett in 1765 [Bell,
    Northampton County Tithables, 371], and a "Mulatto" taxable in 1787 [PPTL,
    1782-1823, frames 73]. His wife may have been Mason **Stephens**, born say
    1728, a tithable in her parents' Northampton County household in 1744.
    Between 1793 and 1803 he acknowledged that he was indebted to the British
    Merchants, Atchison, Hay, and Company, but could not pay since he had been
    insolvent since 1793 [*Virginia Genealogist*, v.17, no.3]. He may have been the
    father of
  i.   Elizabeth/ Betty[3], born in March 1750, a sixteen-year-old, no parent or
       race mentioned, bound apprentice in Northampton County to Thomas
       John Marshall, Gent., on 10 June 1766 [Minutes 1765-71, 46]. She
       may have been the Betty Beckett who was head of Occohanock, St.
       George Parish, Accomack County household of 5 "other free" in 1800
       [*Virginia Genealogist* 2:86] or the one who was head of a Machipungo,
       St. George Parish, Accomack County household of 6 "other free" in
       1800, living near William Roberts [*Virginia Genealogist* 2:128].
  ii. Peter[3], born in August 1752, fourteen years old when he was bound
       apprentice in Northampton County to Thomas John Marshall, Gent.,
       on 10 June 1766 (no parent named) [Minutes 1765-71, 46]. On 8 June
       1779 he and Mary **Jeffery** were witnesses for Abraham **Collins** in his
       suit against Scarburgh **Bingham** [Minutes 1777-83, 167]. He was a
       delinquent Northampton County taxable in 1786 [*Virginia Genealogist*
       20:269] and was taxable from 1787 to 1801, called Peter Beckett, Sr.,
       starting in 1800 [PPTL, 1782-1823, frames 63, 114, 304]. Between
       1775 and 1803 he admitted that he was indebted to British Merchants,
       Atchison, Hays, and Company. He reported that (his brother?) William
       Beckett sailed to the West Indies just before the Revolution, was
       pressed aboard a British armed ship, and had lived in Dublin since then
       [*Virginia Genealogist* 17:259-60].
  iii. Mary, born say 1765, married Mark **Moses**, 13 December 1785
       Northampton County bond, Isaac Becket security.
  iv. Kesiah, married Henry **Liverpool**, 17 March 1799 Northampton
       County bond, Solomon **Liverpool** security.
  v.   Sukey, married Patrick **Collins**, 14 November 1807 Northampton
       County bond, William **Drigus** security.

8. Solomon[1] Beckett, born say 1727, was a tithable in Joachim Michael's
    Northampton County household in 1744, a tithable with (his wife?) Peggy
    Beckett in 1765 [Bell, *Northampton County Tithables*, 362, 371], and a "free
    Negro" taxable in Accomack County from 1783 to 1800, called Solomon, Sr.
    [PPTL 1782-1814, frames 39, 238, 441]. He was head of a St. George Parish,
    Accomack County household of 7 "other free" in 1800, living near Jo.
    Stringer's [*Virginia Genealogist* 2:129]. He may have been the father of
  i.   George, born say 1753, sued in Northampton County court for a 4
       pounds, 8 shilling debt on 13 April 1774 [Minutes 1771-5, 247]. He
       was a seaman from Accomack County who served in the Revolution
       and died intestate leaving no children. His estate was divided in

Accomack County among his four sisters, Nancy, Betty, Rebecca, and Mason [Orders 1832-36, 251].

ii. Nancy **Beavans**, born say 1762, deceased by 24 February 1834 when George Beckett's estate was divided among her five children. The same court order referred to her as "the said Mary" [Orders 1832-6, 251]. Her children named in the court order were Solomon, Thomas, Peter, Mary, and John **Beavans**.

iii. Betty[3], born say 1764, deceased by 24 February 1834 when George Beckett's estate was divided among her four children Peter, Rachel, Rosey, and Nanny. Perhaps her daughter was the Rosey Beckett who registered in Accomack County on 26 June 1832: *born about 1783, a Black, 5'2-1/4", born free in Accomack County* [Register of Free Negroes, 1785-1863, no. 575].

iv. Rebecca[2], born say 1766, registered as a "free Negro" in Northampton County on 12 June 1794 [Orders 1789-95, 358]. She died before 24 February 1834 when George Beckett's Accomack County estate was divided among her three children: Rosey, Solomon, and William.

v. Mason, born say 1770, head of a Machipungo, St. George Parish, Accomack County household of 2 "other free" in 1800 [*Virginia Genealogist* 2:129].

9. Sarah[2] Beckett, born say 1718, was a tithable in Jonathan Bell's Northampton County household in 1737, tithable in Peter Dowty's household in 1738, in Daniel Fisher's in 1739, in Roland Dowty's household in 1740, and in Arthur Downing's household in 1743 [Bell, *Northampton County Tithables*, 274, 289, 348]. She received twenty-five lashes on 8 April 1740 for bastard bearing and was presented on 7 November 1743 for bastard bearing [Orders 1732-42, 394; 1742-8, 131]. She was a "free Negro" who petitioned the Northampton County court on 13 November 1749 to bind her "Negro Child Spencer" to William Bradford of Accomack County [Orders 1748-51, 139-40]. Her children were

i. Rachel, born 25 May 1743, a three-year-old daughter of Sarah Beckett, bound apprentice to Posthumus Core in Northampton County in 1746 [Orders 1742-48, 344], perhaps the Rachel Beckett who was head of an Accomack County household of 5 "other free" in 1810 [VA:12].

ii. Dinah[1], born say 1745, daughter of Sarah Beckett, bound to Posthumus Core on 8 October 1745, whipped for bastard bearing on 13 May 1766 [Orders 1742-8, 255; Minutes 1765-71, 39, 59]. She registered as a "free Negro" in Northampton County on 12 June 1794 [Orders 1789-95, 358].

iii. Spencer, born 17 October 1749, "Negro Child" of Sarah Beckett bound apprentice to William Bradford of Accomack County on 13 November 1749 [Orders 1758-51, 139; L.P. #35, Sarah Beckett's Petition]. He was a "Mulatto" or "Negro" Northampton County taxable from 1787 to 1805 [PPTL, 1782-1823, frames 73, 94, 190, 243, 304, 387].

10   iv. ?Comfort[2], born in December 1753.

v. John[1], born September 1756, "negro son of Sarah Becket," bound apprentice to Zerobabell Downing in Northampton County on 18 November 1759 [Minutes 1754-61, 205]. A suit brought against him by John Michael, Sr., was dismissed by the Northampton County court on 8 June 1784 [Orders 1783-7, 116]. He was taxable in Northampton County from 1793 [PPTL, 1782-1823, frames 152]. He was head of a St. George Parish, Accomack County household of 5 "other free" in 1800 [*Virginia Genealogist* 2:129].

11   vi. Adah, born say 1760.

10. Comfort[2] Beckett, born in December 1753, was a four-year-old "Negro orphan" bound apprentice to Caleb Scott in Northampton County on 14 February 1758 [Orders 1753-58, 477]. She was the mother of

    i.   Abraham², born about 1782, son of Comfort Becket, twelve years old in July 1794 when the Northampton County court ordered the Overseers of the Poor to bind him to Ephraim **Stevens** [Orders 1789-95, 369]. He was head of a Northampton County household of 7 "free colored" in 1820, called Abram Becket, Jr. [VA:218].

11. Adah Beckett, born say 1760, was presented by the grand jury of Northampton County on 9 May 1780 for bastard bearing [Minutes 1777-83, 237]. She was a "Negro" taxable on a free male in 1804 and 1805 [PPTL, 1782-1823, frame 365, 387]. She was the mother of

    i.   Peter⁵, born about 1780, son of Adah Beckett, eleven years old on 13 April 1791 when the Northampton County court ordered the Overseers of the Poor to bind him to Hezekiah James [Orders 1789-95, 133]. He was taxable in Northampton County from 1798 to 1805: called Peter Beckett, Junr., from 1798 to 1801; called "Negro son of Adah" in 1802 [PPTL, 1782-1823, frames 242, 305, 325, 387].

Other Beckett descendants were

    i.   Rosey, registered in Accomack County: *born about 1764, a Black, born free in Accomack County* [Register of Free Negroes, 1785-1863, no. 821].

    ii. Solomon³, born say 1765, a "free Negro" taxable in Accomack County from 1787 to 1810: called "Solomon Junr." in 1787, taxable on a slave over the age of sixteen in 1800 and 1810 [PPTL 1782-1814, frames 129, 356, 443, 526, 723], head of a St. George Parish, Accomack County household of 3 "other free" and 4 slaves in 1800 [*Virginia Genealogist* 2:128].

    iii. Nancy, born before 1776, head of a Northampton County household of 6 "free colored" in 1820 [VA:217A].

    iv. Abraham¹, born say 1776, taxable in Northampton County from 1793 to 1813 [PPTL, 1782-1823, frames 152, 190, 304, 529]. He married Sarah **Thompson**, 26 October 1797 Northampton County bond, Jacob **Thompson** security.

    v. Anthony, head of an Accomack Parish, Accomack County household of 6 "other free" in 1800 [*Virginia Genealogist* 1:103].

    vi. Sarah⁴, head of an Accomack County household of 3 "other free" in 1810 [VA:60].

    vii. Peter, registered in Accomack County: *born about 1783, yellow complexioned, 5'9-1/2", born free in Accomack County* [Register of Free Negroes, 1785-1863, no. 750].

    viii. John², born in December 1784, registered in Accomack County on 29 September 1807: *Black, rather light, 5 feet 6-1/8 Inches...Born free* [Register of Free Negroes, 1785-1863, no. 6].

    ix. Harry, born 17 September 1785, registered in Accomack County: *Black, 5 feet 3-3/4 Inches...Born Free* [Register of Free Negroes, 1785-1863, no. 9].

    x.   John³, born in Spring 1790, registered in Accomack County on 29 September 1807: *light Black, 5 feet 4 Inches, Born free* [Register of Free Negroes, 1785-1863, no. 28].

    xi. Edmund, born about 1785, registered in Accomack County: *Black, 5 feet 8-1/2 Inches...Born free* [Register of Free Negroes, 1785-1863, no. 30]. He was taxable in Northampton County from 1811 to 1813, living on Caleb Downing's land [PPTL, 1782-1823, frames 486, 529].

    xii. Isaac³, born in December 1793, registered in Accomack County on 29 September 1807: *a light black, 5 feet 9 Inches, Born free* [Register of Free Negroes, 1785-1863, no. 77].

BEE FAMILY

1. Cleopatra Bee, born say 1720, was presented by the churchwardens of Bruton Parish in York County on 20 July 1741 for having a "Molatto" bastard child [OW 19:45, 79, 89]. She was fined 50 shillings by the churchwardens of Chesterfield County on 7 February 1753, probably for having an illegitimate child [Orders 1749-54, 428]. She may have been the ancestor of

   i. Francis, born about 1753, taxable on 9 cattle in Northumberland County in 1787 [Schreiner-Yantis, *1787 Census*, 1261]. He married Elizabeth Dikes, 12 April 1796 Northumberland County bond; and second, Sally **Evens**, 21 February 1798 Northumberland County bond, William Corbell security. He was taxable in Lancaster County from 1803 to to 1814 [PPTL, 1782-1839, frames 237, 385, 390] and head of a Lancaster County household of 10 "other free" in 1810 [VA:337]. He registered in Lancaster County on 17 August 1812: *Age 59, Color dark mulatto...was an indented servant until 31 years of age.* Sally, born about 1774, registered on 15 July 1811: *Age abt. 37, Color dark mulatto...born free* [Burkett, *Lancaster County Register of Free Negroes*, 5, 6].

   ii. Isaac, born about 1755, an eighteen-nineteen-year-old "mulatto" whose "father was a freeman," ran away from Lewis Burwell of Mecklenburg County according to the 8 September 1774 issue of the *Virginia Gazette* (Purdie & Dixon).

   iii. Gabriel, born say 1780, married Nelly **Toulson**, 29 September 1802 Northumberland County bond, James **Toulson** security. Gabriel was a "free mulatto" head of a Northumberland County household of 2 "other free" in 1810 [VA:973]. He registered as a "free Negro" in Northumberland County on 30 July 1814: *black man, about ___ age, 5 feet ___, Born of free parents in North^d County* [Register, no.71].

   iv. Massy, head of a Lancaster County household of 4 "other free" in 1810 [VA:339].

BELL FAMILY

1. Jane^1 Bell, born say 1662, was a Surry County, Virginia taxable in Thomas Davis' household in 1689 [*Magazine of Virginia Genealogy*, vol.23, 3:56]. She may have been the ancestor of

   i. Jane^2, born say 1720, living in Surry County on 16 June 1742 when the churchwardens of Albemarle Parish were ordered to bind out her child (no race mentioned) [Orders 1741-44, 32].

2 ii. Samuel, born in Surry County, Virginia, in 1749.

3 iii. Graham^1, born say 1750.

   iv. Hardy, born about 1800, a "Boy of Color" bound to Samuel Bell by order of the 27 August 1810 Robeson County court [Minutes II:214]. He was head of a Robeson County household of 5 "free colored" in 1820 [NC:310].

   v. Zadock, born say 1775, purchased 13 acres on Little Fishing Creek in Halifax County, North Carolina, on 6 November 1797 [DB 18:303]. He was head of a Halifax County household of 5 "other free" in 1800 [NC:290] and 5 in 1810 [NC:7]. He was probably the husband of Lucy Bell who was mentioned in the 3 December 1808 Halifax County will of her father Austin **Curtis Jones** [WB C:484]. Her mother was probably Ann **Curtis**.

4 vi. Jane^3/ Jenny Bell, born say 1776.

2. Samuel Bell was born in Surry County, Virginia, in May 1749. He was living in Sampson County, North Carolina, in February 1782 when he volunteered in Captain Coleman's Company under Major Griffith McRae and Colonel

Lytle. He marched to Wilmington, to Georgetown, and to Charleston, but was never in any engagement. After the war, he lived in Sampson County until about 1807 when he moved to Robeson County where he applied for and was granted a pension on 31 August 1832 [M804-0207, frame 0489]. He was head of a Sampson County household of 10 "other free" in 1790, 15 in 1800 [NC:509], 5 in Robeson County in 1810 [NC:234], and 2 "free colored" in Robeson County in 1820 [NC:309]. His children were probably

   i.   Joshua, born 1776-94, a bricklayer, head of a Cumberland County, North Carolina household of 3 "free colored" in 1820 [NC:154].

   ii.   Rebecca, married Ephraim **Hammonds**, 26 February 1812 Cumberland County bond, Thomas **Sampson** bondsman.

   iii.   Hetty, a "free female child," bound to Elizabeth Howell by the New Hanover County court on 23 September 1795 [Minutes 1792-98, 152].

3.   Graham^1 Bell, born say 1750, appeared in Greensville County court on 19 May 1804 to post his property as a $500 bond for the appearance of his son Graham Bell, Jr., who was charged with forging a bond of $333 to himself from Sterling Edmond of Brunswick County. Asa **Byrd** was one of the witnesses who testified against Graham, Jr. [Orders 1799-1806, 387-8]. Graham, Sr., was the father of

   i.   Graham^2, born about 1780, registered in Petersburg on 11 April 1814: *a light brown Mulatto man, five feet nine and a half inches high, thirty four years old January last, a shoe maker, born free & raised in the Town of Petersburg* [Register of Free Negroes 1794-1819, no. 748]. He was probably the Graham **Bird** Bell who was living in Sussex County on 16 July 1778 when the court ordered the churchwardens to bind him out [Orders 1777-82, 47].

4.   Jane^3/ Jenny Bell, born say 1776, was head of a Bertie County household of 3 "other free" in 1800 [NC:35]. She may have been the mother of the following children indentured in Bertie County, no parent indicated:

   i.   David, born 5 March 1794, no race indicated, bound to Benjamin Wimberley as an apprentice shoemaker on 12 August 1799 [CR 10.101.8, by *NCGSJ* XV:169].

   ii.   Reuben, born May 1796, no race indicated, bound as a shoemaker to Benjamin Wimberley on 12 August 1799 [*NCGSJ* XV:170].

   iii.   Winifred, born 1798, no race indicated, bound to Ebenezer Smith on 10 August 1807 [CR 10.101.9 by *NCGSJ* XVI:154].

   iv.   Solomon, born about 1800, seven-years-old when he was bound to Ebenezer Smith on 10 November 1807 and called "an orphan of colour Six years of age" when he was bound to Richard Veale to be a shoemaker on 15 August 1809 [*NCGSJ* XVII:40].

   v.   Joseph, born about 1801, "an orphan of colour," bound to Ebenezer Smith to learn shoemaking on 15 August 1809.

   vi.   Nancy, born about 1803, "an orphan of colour" bound to Richard Veale on 15 August 1809.

Lancaster County

1.   Elizabeth Bell, born say 1688, was a white servant who ran away and absented herself from the service of her master, William Chapman of Lancaster County, for twenty-one days. On 12 May 1703 the court ordered that she receive twenty lashes at the county whipping post, serve her master an additional forty-two days, and serve another eighteen months to pay the expense of her recovery. She was the servant of George Flower on 14 June 1704 when she was ordered to serve an additional five years for having a "Bastard child by a negroe" [Orders 1702-13, 32, 75]. She was probably the mother of

2   i.   Jane, born about June 1704.

ii. Will, born about April 1709, the "Molatto" servant of John Carter, Esq., in February 1737/8 when he petitioned the Charles City County court for his freedom. In April 1738 the court examined a record of the Lancaster County court and ruled that he serve another two years [Orders 1737-51, 34, 39].

2. Jane Bell, born about June 1704, was a "mulatto servant" living in Lancaster County, Virginia, on 13 June 1733 when she agreed to serve her master John Hubbard until Christmas that year and then to serve Charles Lee an additional year in return for Lee's buying her time from her former master and allowing her to live with her husband who was Lee's slave [Orders 1729-43, 85]. She was probably the ancestor of

   3   i. Elias, born say 1740.

        ii. Dorcas, born about 1754, married John **Weaver**, 10 June 1789 Lancaster County bond. She registered as a "free Negro" in Lancaster County on 18 July 1803: *wf/o John, Age 49, Color dark, Served till 31 years of age* [Burkett, *Lancaster County Register of Free Negroes*, 1].

       iii. James, born about 1754, registered in Southampton County on 11 May 1808: *age 54, Black, 5 feet 9 inches, free born from Richd. City per certificate*. He registered again on 1 October 1812: *age 58, Blk., 5 feet 7-1/2 inches, free born, see certificate Lancaster County*. And he registered again on 12 May 1815: *age 61, Blk., 5 feet 8 inches, free born* [Register of Free Negroes 1794-1832, nos. 425, 904, 954].

       iv. Sarah, born about 1755, registered as a "free Negro" in Lancaster County on 17 October 1803: *Age 48, Color dark...born free* [Burkett, *Lancaster County Register of Free Negroes*, 1].

3. Elias Bell, born say 1740, died before 25 April 1789 when his daughter Betty Bell was married in Lancaster County. His children were

        i. Betty, born say 1770, "daughter of Elias Bell, decd.," married Benjamin **Pinn**, 25 April 1789 Lancaster County marriage.

       ii. ?Betsy, head of a Norfolk County household of 9 "other free" in 1810 [VA:822].

      iii. ?John, born about 1777, registered in Norfolk County on 20 July 1812: *5 feet 6 inches 35 years of age, light complexion, Born free* [Register of Free Negros & Mulattos, #79]. He may have been the husband of Nancy Bell, sole heir of James **Thomas**, a Revolutionary seaman from Norfolk County. She registered in Norfolk County on 20 July 1812: *5 feet 3 In. 32 Years of age of a dark Complexion, Born free as appears by the oath of James Pretlow* [Register, #76].

      iv. ?Lurana, born about 1779, registered as a "free Negro" in Norfolk County on 17 July 1810: *5 feet 4 Inc., 31 years of age, of a light Complexion* [Register, #26]. She was head of a Norfolk County household of 8 "other free" in 1810 [VA:817].

       v. ?Coleman, born about 1782, registered as a "free Negro" in Lancaster County on 17 September 1805: *Age 23, Color black...born free* [Burkett, *Lancaster County Register of Free Negroes*, 2]. He married Agge **Weaver**, 26 December 1806 Lancaster County marriage. He was head of a Lancaster County household of 5 "other free" in 1810 [VA:338]. On 23 June 1834 he was in Northumberland County when he gave his consent and was security for the marriage of (his son?) James Bell, "colored," to marry Eliza **Jones**, widow.

      vi. ?Thorton, born about 1783, head of a Westmoreland County household of 7 "other free" in 1810 [VA:768], called William Thornton Bell when he registered in Westmoreland County in May 1832: *a man of light complexion, 5 feet 10 inches high, about 49 years of age* [Register of Free Negroes, 1828-1849, no.149].

vii.   ?Sally, born about 1793, registered in Norfolk County on 20 July 1812: *5 feet 4 1/2 inches 19 years of age light complexion, Born free* [Register of Free Negros & Mulattos, #80].

BENNETT FAMILY

1.   James Bennett, born say 1700, was one of the Chowan County Indians who sold their land on Bennett's Creek in 1734 in the part of Chowan County which later became Gates County:

> *James Bennett, Thos Hoyter, Charles Beasley, Jeremiah Pushin, John Robins, John Reading & Nuce Will Cheif men of the Chowan Indians...* [Chowan DB W:250].

He and John Robins were also called chief men of the Chowan Indians on 19 November 1758 when they sold 300 acres of Indian land by deed proved in Gates County [DB 2:101]. He, James Bennett, Jr., and Amos Bennett were called "Bennett's Creek Indians" in October 1763 when they sold land by deed acknowledged in Chowan County court. And a deed from him and John Robins was proved in Chowan County in October 1765 [Minutes 1761-6, 164, 273]. His descendants were probably

   i.   George, born about 1768, a thirteen-year-old "Indian Boy" ordered by the Gates County court to be bound as an apprentice shoemaker to Edward Brisco in February 1781 [Fouts, *Minutes of Gates County Court 1779-86*, 29]. He was head of a Gates County household of 1 "other free" in 1790 [NC:23], 4 in 1800 [NC:262], 5 in 1810 [NC:842] and 4 "free colored" in 1820 [NC:143]. He and (his brother?) Joseph Bennett and James and Benjamin Robins were called "chief men and representatives of the Chowan Indian Nation" on 12 April 1790 when they sold for $100 four hundred acres of land which was part of the original Indian patent of 24 April 1724 [DB A-2:153].

   ii.   Joseph, born about 1769, a twelve-year-old "Indian Boy" called Josiah Bennett in February 1781 when the Gates County court ordered him bound as an apprentice cooper to Henry Booth [Fouts, *Minutes of Gates County Court 1779-86*, 29]. He was head of a Gates County household of 1 "other free" in 1790 [NC:23] and an insolvent Gates County taxpayer in 1794 [Fouts, *Minutes of Gates County Court*, I:17].

   iii.   Nancy, born before 1776, head of an Edenton, Chowan County household of 2 "free colored" women in 1820 [NC:130].

   iv.   Rachel, head of a Currituck County household of 4 "other free" in 1800 [NC:138].

   v.   Esther, head of an "other free" Chowan County household in 1810 [NC:532].

BERRY FAMILY

1.   John[1] Berry, born say 1660, was a white man living in York County, Virginia, in September 1693 when he had a son by Mary **Jewell/ Cuttillo**, "a mollotto." She was living in the lower precincts of Poquoson Parish on 24 May 1694 when she was presented by the court for having a child by him [DOW 10:341; Richter, *A Community and its Neighborhoods*, 343; Bell, *Charles Parish Registers*, 61]. John Berry and Mary **Cuttillo** were the parents of

2   i.   James[1] **Cattilla**, born 16 September 1693.

2.   James[1] Berry, born 16 September 1693, son of Mary **Cattilla**, was called James **Cattilla** when his birth was registered in Charles Parish, York County (no father named). He was called James Berry and married to a woman named Mary in Elizabeth City County on 2 October 1719 when the birth of their son

James was registered in Charles Parish [Bell, *Charles Parish Registers*, 50].
He was presented by the Elizabeth City County court on 20 November 1728
for not coming to church [Orders 1723-30, 285, 295]. He was called James
Berry, Sr., on 2 November 1761 when the Elizabeth City County court
granted him and Charles **Hopson (Hobson)** a certificate for taking up a
runaway slave named Daniel belonging to Thomas Whiting. On 7 December
1762 the court ordered that he be levy free [Court Records 1760-9, 46, 114].
He was called "Old James Berry" in 1765 when the Elizabeth City Parish
vestry paid Edward **Cuttillo** for boarding him [von Doenhoff, *Vestry Book of
Elizabeth City Parish*, 163]. He died before 15 January 1779 when the
inventory of his York County estate was taken. His children were

3 i. James², born 2 October 1719.
  ii. ?Ann, born say 1734, taxable in Sarah **Cuttillo**'s York County
   household on 19 November 1750. She married Edward **Cuttillo**.
  iii. ?Samuel, born say 1750, a "Mulatto" man, a shoemaker, who ran away
   from Judith Harbert of Hampton according to an ad she placed in the
   18 July 1771 issue of the *Virginia Gazette* [Windley, *Runaway Slave
   Advertisements*, 1:313].

3. James² Berry, born 2 October 1719, was baptized on 6 December 1719 in
 Charles Parish [Bell, *Charles Parish Registers*, 50]. He was a resident of
 Elizabeth City County on 7 December 1762 when he was granted
 administration on the estate of John George, deceased. On 7 November 1764
 the court ordered that his wife be added to the list of tithables [Court Orders
 1760-9, 114, 262]. He was married to Mary by 14 May 1769 when their son
 James was born [Bell, *Charles Parish Registers*, 50]. The York County court
 presented him on 16 November 1772 for not listing Charles **Hopson** as a
 tithable [Judgments & Orders 1772-4, 151]. In August 1771 he purchased land
 in Elizabeth City County called Finches Dam tract from Martha Armistead.
 James transferred this land to his son Edward by early 1780. In March of that
 year Callowhill Mennis petitioned the York County court for permission to
 clear a road from his plantation through Edward Berry's land to the main
 county road [Richter, *A Community and its Neighborhoods*, 359]. He rented
 a slave from Anthony Robinson in January 1778 according to the account of
 Robinson's York County estate [WI 22:405]. His wife Mary died on 8 October
 1784 [Bell, *Charles Parish Registers*, 203]. He was taxable in the lower
 precinct of Charles Parish, York County, in 1784 [PPTL, 1782-1841, frame
 83]. His 5 February 1800 Elizabeth City County will was proved on 27
 February 1800. He left his estate to his wife Ann and named his son James
 Berry and Elizabeth Davis executors [DW 34:522]. He was the father of

4 i. Edward¹, say 1750.
  ii. Elizabeth², married Thomas **Epps** according to a York County court
   suit she and her husband brought in chancery against the heirs of her
   brother Edward Berry. She may have been living in Lunenburg County
   about 1779 when her father's estate was settled [LVA, chancery case
   1798-002].
  iii. James³, born 14 May, baptized 18 June 1769 [Bell, *Charles Parish
   Registers*, 50].
  iv. Frances, born 5 September, baptized 21 December 1777.

4. Edward¹ Berry, born say 1750, was married to Martha and living in Charles
 Parish by 9 July 1775 when their son James was born, and he was married to
 Elizabeth by 4 March 1783 when their daughter Sally was born. His son
 Edward was identified as a "Mulatto" when he was baptized on 12 March
 1786 in Charles Parish [Bell, *Charles Parish Registers*, 50-1]. He was taxable
 in Elizabeth City County on a free tithe in 1782 [Fothergill, *Virginia Tax
 Payers*, 9]; taxable in York County on a free tithe and slaves Peter, Dinah,
 Joe, Lucy, and Dinah in 1784; taxable on 3 tithes, 2 slaves over the age of 16,

6 horses and 14 cattle in 1785; taxable on a slave in 1790 and 1799 and taxable on 100 acres in York County in 1791 and 1800 [Personal Tax List, 1782-1841, frames 76, 98, 160, 244; Land Tax List, 1791, p.1; 1800, p.1]. He was also taxable in Elizabeth City County on a 12-16 year-old slave in 1790 [PPTL, p.1]. Edward and his sister Elizabeth were identified as the heirs of James Berry in a 1798 York County chancery case in which Edward's sister brought a successful suit against Edward's heirs [LVA, Chancery case 1798-002]. The inventory of Edward's estate, valued at 202 pounds, was taken in York County in October 1790. It included a slave woman and three children. His wife remarried and was called Elizabeth **Cotillo** (**Cuttillo**) on 21 December 1791 when she returned an account of his estate. The 19 October 1803 division of his estate assigned 40 acres and the dwelling house to Elizabeth's husband Edward **Cattilla**, and the remaining 105 acres was divided among Edward's children James, Edward, Sarah, Mary, and Elizabeth [WI 23:450-2, 634; Orders 1803-14, 140-1]. Edward was the father of

- i. James[4], born 5 June, baptized 9 July 1775, son of Edward and Martha [Bell, *Charles Parish Registers*, 50], taxable in York County in 1803 and 1804 [PPTL, 1782-1841].
- ii. Martha, born 23 April, baptized 14 June 1778, daughter of Edward and Martha [Bell, *Charles Parish Registers*, 50].
- iii. Sally, born 4 March 1783, baptized 18 May, "dau. of Edw[d] and Eliz[a] __[a] City" (of Elizabeth City) [Bell, *Charles Parish Registers*, 51].

5   iv. Edward[2], born 26 December 1785.

- v. Mary, born say 1787.
- vi. Elizabeth[3], married Charles **Hopson** (**Hobson**), 20 June 1808 York County bond, Abraham **Hopson** bondsman.

5. Edward[2] Berry, born 26 December 1785, "a Mulatto," was baptized on 12 March 1786 in Charles Parish, York County [Bell, *Charles Parish Registers*, 50]. He was taxable in York County from 1806 to 1820 [PPTL, 1782-1841, frames 315, 351, 363, 385, 403, 468, 480]. He owned 25 acres of land in 1852 when his widow Elizabeth **Hopson** (who married James **Hopson**) brought a successful chancery suit against their children James, Thomas, Elizabeth, Abraham, Mary, Edward, Martha and Rebecca in order to have the land sold [LVA chancery suit 1852-004]. Edward and Elizabeth were the parents of

- i. James, born say 1807, died before the 1852 chancery suit was filed leaving a widow without issue who married John **Epps Hopson**.
- ii. Thomas, born about 1809, registered in York County on 19 September 1831: *a bright mulatto, nearly 22 years of age, 5 feet 9-1/4 inches high, tolerably long curly hair, hazle eyes...Born free* [Free Negroes Register 1831-50, no.295]. He died before 1852 leaving one unnamed child.
- iii. Elizabeth, born say 1811, married to John **Cotillo** before 1852.
- iv. Abraham, born say 1813, died without issue before 1852.
- v. Mary Ann, born about 1814, registered in York County on 19 September 1831: *a girl of very light Complexion, nearly 17 years old, 5 feet 5 inches high...a scar on the left arm in Consequence of being vaccinated, full black eyes...Born free* [Register, no.292]. He married Michael **Hall** and died leaving one child before 1852.
- vi. Edward[3], born about 1817, registered in York County on 16 February 1835: *a bright Mulatto about 18 years of age 5 feet 8 Inches high...broad face, long curly hair, flat nose...Born of free parents in York County* [Register, no.387].
- vii. Martha, born say 1819, married Edward **White** before 1852.
- viii. Rebecca, born say 1821, married Topping **Brown** before 1852.

Other members of a Berry family were

1   i. Elizabeth[1], born say 1726.

2 ii. Ann, born say 1728.
3 iii. Margaret, born say 1735.

1. Elizabeth[1] Berry, born say 1726, was the "Mulatto" servant of Drury Stith in August 1747 and 28 March 1750 when the Brunswick County, Virginia court bound her son James Berry and daughter Mary Berry as apprentices to her master [Orders 1745-49, 244; 1749-50, 53]. She was the mother of
4 i. James[1], born about 1747.
5 ii. Mary, born say 1748.

2. Ann Berry, born say 1728, a "free Mulatto Woman," was living in Spotsylvania County on 6 August 1754 when she bound her three-year-old daughter Mary Berry to Roger Dixon until the age of eighteen years to learn to knit, spin and other household business [WB B:209-10]. She was the mother of
   i. Mary, born 20 March 1751, head of a Fredericksburg, Spotsylvania County household of 4 "other free" in 1810 [VA:107b].
   ii. ?James[2], a "Mulatto Bastard" bound apprentice until the age of twenty-one by the Orange County, Virginia court on 25 March 1768 [Orders 1763-9, 480].

3. Margaret Berry, born say 1735, was the mother of Anthony Berry, "a mulatto" who was bound apprentice to Tim. Cleven in Anson County and brought before the Cumberland County, North Carolina court on 20 January 1757 when Cleven's request for an indenture was rejected by the court. On 17 January 1758 she brought her orphan son John Berry into court to be bound apprentice to Michael Blocker. He was bound instead to William Dawson, Esq., on 18 January 1758 when Margaret confessed to the court that Anthony was born while she was a servant [Minutes 1755-9, 18, 32]. She was probably related to Henry Berry who, according to tradition, was one of the first free African Americans to come to Robeson County with James **Lowry** [Blu, *The Lumbee Problem*, 36]. James **Lowry**'s grandson, Henry Berry **Lowry**, was named for him. Margaret's children who were bound apprentices in Cumberland County were
   i. Anthony, born about 1754, bound apprentice to Tim. Cleven in Anson County and then to William Dawson, Esq., of Cumberland County, North Carolina on 18 January 1758 [Minutes 1755-59, 32].
   ii. John, born say 1756, bound apprentice to Michael Blocker on 17 January 1758.
   iii. Thomas, born say 1757, a child brought into court by Margaret Berry, bound to Michael Block by order of the 20 July 1758 Cumberland County court, no race or parent named [Minutes 1755-9, 38].

4. James[1] Berry, born about 1747, was one of the members of Captain Joseph Spencer's 7th Virginia Regiment who did not return from furlough in Gloucester Town. Spencer advertised a reward for their return in the 8 August 1777 issue of the *Virginia Gazette*, describing James as

a mulatto fellow, about 30 years old, 5 feet 8 or 9 inches high; enlisted in Fredericksburg but served his time with Mr. Thomas Bell of Orange County [*Virginia Gazette*, Purdie edition, p.4, col. 3].

He may have been the James Berry who was taxable in Dinwiddie County in the household of Dr. Thomas **Stewart** in 1785 and a "free" taxable in 1793 and 1799 [PPTL, 1782-90 (1785 B, p.23); 1791-9 (1793 A, p.2), (1799 B, p.2)], and he may have been the ancestor of
   i. Nancy, a "F.N." taxable in Henrico County on a slave above the age of 16 years from 1801 to 1804 [PPTL B, p.2] and on 1 acre of land in

1802 [Land Tax List A, p.3]. She married Adam **Floyd**, 31 March 1806, "both free people of color," Henrico County bond, Samuel Cole surety.

ii.   Lucy, married Dempsey **Stewart**, 4 February 1786 Greensville County, Virginia bond, Cannon **Cumbo** bondsman, Thomas and Barney **Steward** witnesses.

iii. Lucinda, head of a Richmond City household of 3 "other free" in 1810 [VA:331].

iv.   Polly, head of a Southampton County household of 1 "other free" and a slave in 1810.

v.   Thomas, born about 1785, registered in Petersburg on 26 December 1806: *a light brown free Mulatto man, five feet nine and a half inches high, spare made, twenty one years old, shoe maker, registered by desire of his father* [Register of Free Negroes 1794-1819, no. 403].

5.   Mary Berry, born say 1748, was bound by the Brunswick County, Virginia court to Drury Stith, Gentleman, on 28 March 1750. On 25 September 1775 the Brunswick County court ordered the churchwardens of St. Andrew's Parish to bind out her "Mulattoe" son Thomas Berry. She was called Molly Berry (no race indicated) on 28 October 1782 when the court ordered the churchwardens of St. Andrew's Parish to bind out her children Thomas, Betty and Sylvia [Orders 1749-50, 53; 1774-82, 92, 115; 487]. She was the mother of

i.   Thomas, perhaps the Thomas Berry who was taxable in Norfolk County from 1799 to 1816: a labourer in a "List of Free Negroes and Mulattoes" at Gosport in 1801, a "free Negro" in Portsmouth in 1813 and 1816 [PPTL, 1791-1812, frames 295, 383, 479, 738, 770; 1813-24, frames 16, 126].

6   ii.   Betty, born about 1765.

iii. Sylvia.

6.   Betsy Berry, born about 1765, registered in Petersburg on 9 January 1811: *a brown Mulatto woman, five feet 3/4 inches high, forty six years old, long bushy hair, born free & raised in the County of Prince George* [Register of Free Negroes 1794-1819, no. 653?]. She was the mother of

i.   ?Julius, taxable in the upper district of Henrico County in 1802 [Land Tax List, 1799-1816] head of a Petersburg Town household of 3 "other free" in 1810 [VA:121b].

ii.   ?Sarah, head of a Richmond City household of 3 "other free" in 1810 [VA:336].

iii. ?Polly, born 31 December 1788, registered in Petersburg on 21 December 1809: *a light brown Mulatto woman, five feet two inches high, twenty one years old 31st instant, born free & raised in Dinwiddie County* [Register of Free Negroes 1794-1819, no. 501].

iv.   ?Betsy, born about 1791, registered in Petersburg on 8 June 1810: *a brown Mulatto woman, five feet high, nineteen years old, long bushy hair, born free in Dinwiddie County* [Register of Free Negroes 1794-1819, no. 552].

v.   Nancy, born about 1795, registered in Petersburg on 8 June 1810: *a brown Mulatto girl, five feet one and a half inches high, long bushy hair, fifteen years old, daughter of Betsy Berry a free woman residing in Dinwiddie County* [Register of Free Negroes 1794-1819, no. 553].

Other members of the Berry family were

i.   Nancy, head of a Jefferson County, Virginia household of 6 "other free" in 1810 [VA:102].

ii.   Naney, head of a Barnwell District, South Carolina household of 3 "other free" in 1800 [SC:53].

BEVERLY FAMILY

Mixed-race members of the Beverly family, probably born before 1750, were
1   i.   Barsheba, born say 1740.
2   ii.   Sylvester, born about 1742.

1. Barsheba Beverly, born say 1740, was a "Mulato" taxable in Pittsylvania
County in John Wilson's list for 1767. She may have been the mother of
    i.   Priscilla, taxable in Buckingham County on a horse and 3 cattle from
1782 to 1794: a "Mulatto" taxable from 1783 to 1785, a "Mulatto"
taxable on a slave in 1787 and 1788 [PPTL 1782-97]. She was head of
a Buckingham County household of 1 "other free" in 1810 [VA:823].
She was listed in the Land Tax Summaries for Buckingham County
between 1788 and 1814, called a "mulatto" from 1788 to 1791, living
on land on Hatcher's Creek [Ward, *Buckingham County Land Tax
Summaries*, 32].
    ii. Jean, taxable in Buckingham County on a horse and 3 cattle from 1782
to 1786: a Mulatto taxable from 1783 to 1785 [PPTL 1782-97]. She
was head of a Buckingham County household of 12 "other free" in
1810 [VA:776].
    iii. Betty, head of a Buckingham County household of 14 "other free" in
1810 [VA:775a], perhaps the Betty Beverly who sued Thomas Gibson
for false imprisonment in Culpeper County on 23 July 1763 [Minutes
1763-4, 404, 423].
    iv. William, taxable in Buckingham County in 1782, a "Mul°" taxable in
1789, taxable on a horse from 1797 to 1803, a "Mul°" taxable in 1798,
[PPTL 1782-97; 1798-1803]. He was head of a Buckingham County
household of 15 "other free" in 1810 [VA:775a]. He married Edy **Pinn**
in Amherst County in November 1800 [Sweeny, *Marriage Records of
Amherst County*].

2. Sylvester Beverly, born about 1742, was a Revolutionary War soldier from
Franklin County, Virginia, who enlisted in 1776 and served until the end of
the War. He was eighty years old and owned 126 acres of land in 1822 when
he petitioned the Legislature for a state pension [Jackson, *Virginia Negro
Soldiers*, 30]. Perhaps he was the Silvanus Beverly who was taxable in
Buckingham County on a horse and 4 cattle in 1782, a "Mulatto" taxable in
1783 and 1784 [PPTL 1782-97]. Sill Beverly was taxable in Franklin County
in 1799, head of a Fluvanna County household of 7 "other free" in 1810
[VA:493] and listed as a "free negro" in Franklin County in 1813 [PPTL,
1786-1803; Waldrep, *1813 Tax List*]. He was probably the father of
    i.   Anna, married Benjamin **Chavers**, 24 August 1801 Franklin County
bond, Silvester Beverly surety.
    ii. Herod, married Lucy **Freeman**, "Negro, freed slave of John Early,
dec'd," 23 February 1808 Franklin County bond. He was head of a
Fluvanna County household of 3 "other free" in 1810 [VA:480].
    iii. Rebecca, married Jesse **Shavers**, 16 December 1805 Franklin County
bond, Harod Beverly surety.
    iv. Elizabeth, married George **Marrs**, 23 February 1808 Franklin County
bond, Harod Beverly surety.
    v. Polly, married Martin **Couzens**, 31 March 1814 Franklin County bond,
Benjamin **Chavis** surety.

Other members of the Beverly family were
    i.   Reuben, taxable in Buckingham County in 1787, taxable on a horse in
1791, taxable with George Beverly in 1798 [PPTL 1782-97; 1798-
1803].

ii.   Jonathan, a "Mul°" taxable in Buckingham County in 1798 and from 1804 to 1809, taxable on a horse from 1799 to 1803 [PPTL 1798-1803; 1804-9], head of a Buckingham County household of 3 "other free" in 1810 [VA:820]. He registered as a free Negro in Amherst County in July 1847: *aged about 62 years, 5 feet 10 inches high, dark complexion* [McLeRoy, *Strangers in Their Midst*, 72].

iii. Susannah, charged with the Buckingham County tax of William and F. Beverly in 1798 [PPTL 1798-1803].

iv.   Francis, a "bachelor," married Mary **Williams**, a "spinster," 29 November 1792 Amherst County bond with the consent of her mother Nancy **Williams**, Rolley **Penn** surety. He received a grant for 10 acres in Buckingham County on both sides of Booring Bridge on 1 May 1818 [Grants 67:242].

v.   Charles, taxable in Buckingham County in 1801 [PPTL 1798-1803], head of a Buckingham County household of 12 "other free" in 1810 [VA:775a], perhaps the Charles Beverly who married Mary **Johns**, 29 March 1827 Amherst County bond, James **Johns** security.

vi.   Major, head of a Rockbridge County household of 10 "other free" in 1810 [VA:290].

vii. Lucy, head of a Fredericksburg, Spotsylvania County household of 2 "other free" and a slave in 1810 [VA:111a].

viii. Samuel, born about 1797, married Rhoda **Terry** on 12 March 1819 in Amherst County, William **Terry** witness [Sweeny, *Marriage Records of Amherst County*]. Samuel and Rhoda registered as free Negroes in Amherst County on 19 December 1850: *Samuel Beverly Bright mulatto - Strait hair, somewhat grey - Five feet, Six Inches & Half - Fifty three years old*; *Rhoda Beverly wife of Saml Beverly - Bright mulatto - Strait hair - Five feet three & half Inches high - Fifty three years of age* [McLeRoy, *Strangers in their Midst*, 73]. William **Terry** was head of an Amherst County household of 7 "other free" in 1810 [VA:287].

ix.   James, married Polly **Redcross**, in Amherst County in 1820.

BIBBENS/ BEAVENS FAMILY

1.   Mary Bibens, born say 1700, was presented by the grand jury of Accomack County on 4 November 1718 for having a "Mallatto" bastard child in Accomack Parish [Orders 1717-19, 23, 28]. She was called a white Christian woman on 1 September 1719 when she was ordered to be put in prison for the same offense, but the order was reversed when Captain Edward Scarborough agreed to pay her fine. At first, she refused to name the father, then named "one Hille an Indian" on 2 September 1719, and later that same day admitted that the father was "one Negro Slave named Jack belonging to Mr. Edmd. Scarburgh." She was presented again for having a bastard child on 4 October 1721 and on 7 May 1723 when she was called Mary Bivens [Orders 1719-24, 5, 5b, 6, 36, 59]. And on 2 September 1729 she was accused of having two more "Mullato" bastard children. On 8 December 1730 her two-year-old "Mullattoe Boy" Talflett Bibbens was ordered bound to Edmund Scarborough [Orders 1724-31, 168, 201]. She was called Mary Bibbins, otherwise Bevins, in adjoining Northampton County on 12 March 1733/4 when she was presented for having another "Mulatto" bastard child. She was sold for five years [Orders 1732-42, 97, 102]. She died before 8 August 1749 possessed of so small an estate that the Northampton County court ordered the sheriff to dispose of it [Orders 1748-51, 115, 135]. She was the mother of

2   i.   Taflett, born about 1728.
3   ii.   ?Elizabeth, born say February 1733/4.

2.   Taflett Bibbens, born about 1728, was a two-year-old "Mullattoe" boy bound apprentice in Accomack County on 8 December 1730. He was called Taffley

Beavans when he was a "Mullatto" taxable in Accomack County from 1783 to 1788: taxable on 2 tithables and 2 horses in 1784, taxable on a free male tithable but free from taxation on his own tithe in 1788 [PPTL, 1782-1814, frames 39, 129, 262]. The Accomack County court exempted him from taxation due to age and infirmity on 29 May 1792 [Orders 1790-6, 379]. Perhaps his widow was Ann Beavans who was a "fn" taxable on 2 free males and 3 horses in Accomack County in 1798 and 1799 [PPTL 1782-1814, frames 356, 394], perhaps identical to Nancy Bibbens, sister of George **Beckett**, a Revolutionary War veteran from Accomack County. Nancy was head of a St. George Parish, Accomack County household of 4 "other free" in 1800 [*Virginia Genealogist*, v.2, no.3, 129]. Taffley may have been the father of

    i.   Solomon Bevans, a "fn" taxable in Accomack County from 1799 to 1810 [PPTL, 1782-1814, frames 395, 592, 723], head of an Accomack County household of 5 "other free" in 1810 [VA:9].

    ii.   Peter Bevans, head of an Accomack County household of 8 "other free" in 1810 [VA:9]. He registered in Accomack County: *born about 1767, a light yellow, 5'4", born free in Accomack County* [Register of Free Negroes, 1785-1863, no. 738].

    iii. Thomas Bibbins, born about 1770, married Arena **Becket**, 2 August 1800 Accomack County bond, Peter Bibbins surety. Thomas Bevans was head of an Accomack County household of 5 "other free" in 1810 [VA:10]. Tom Beavan registered in Accomack County: *born about 1770, yellow complexioned, 5'6-1/2", born free in Accomack County* [Register of Free Negroes, 1785-1863, no. 729]. His wife was called Tinney Beavans when she was counted in his household in 1813 [PPTL, 1782-1814, frame 833].

    iv. Lot Bevans, head of a Accomack Parish, Accomack County household of 2 "other free" in 1800 [*Virginia Genealogist*, v.1, no.3, 103].

    v.   Catherine Beavans, head of an Accomack County household of 3 "other free" in 1810 [VA:12].

    vi. Mary, married Edmund **Nutts**, 18 June 1800 Northampton County bond, Southy **Collins** surety, with the consent of Nanny Bibbins.

3.   Elizabeth Bibbens, born say February 1733/4, was probably the illegitimate "Mulatto" child born to Mary Bibbins in Northampton County before 12 March 1733/4. On 14 May 1751 she was presented for bastard bearing. She was the mother of Thomas Bibbins, a "Mulatto" who was bound to Holloway Bunting in Northampton County on 12 March 1750/1 [Orders 1732-42, 97, 102; 1748-51, 345, 376, 398]. She was the mother of

    i.   Thomas, born before 12 March 1750/1, bound to Holloway Bunting. He was called "Thomas Bevans free Negro" on 12 April 1774 when the court ruled that he should serve his master Edmund Scarbrough until the age of thirty-one [Minutes 1771-7, 225, 240].

4   ii.   Mary, born about 1754.

4.   Mary Bibbens, born about 1754, "child of Betty Beavans Negro," was ten years old when she was bound to Robinson Savage, Jr., in Northampton County on 11 September 1764 [Minutes 1761-5, 132]. She was called Mary Beavans when she registered as a "free Negro" in Northampton County on 10 June 1794 [Orders 1789-95, 354]. She was a "Negro" taxable on a free male in Northampton County in 1802 and 1803 [PPTL, 1782-1823, frames 325, 345]. She was the mother of

    i.   Samuel, born in December 1764, son of Mary Bibbins, bound to Thomas Bullock on 12 November 1783 [Orders 1783-7, 51]. He was called Samuel Beavans when he registered as a "free Negro" in Northampton County on 12 June 1794 [Orders 1789-95, 358]. He was a "free Negro" taxable in Northampton County in 1796 and 1797

[PPTL, 1782-1823, frame 206]. He was head of a Northampton County household of 2 "free colored" in 1820 [VA:218].

ii. ?Moses Beavans, registered as a "free Negro" in Northampton County on 12 June 1794 [Orders 1789-95, 358]. He married Nancy **West**, ____ 1807 Northampton County bond and was a "free negro" man living with a "free negro" woman on Harrison's land in Northampton County in 1813 [PPTL 1782-1823, frame 529]. He was head of a Northampton County household of 7 "free colored" in 1820 [VA:218].

iii. ?Reavel, head of a Northampton County household of 5 "free colored" in 1820 [VA:217A].

iv. John Bevans, a "free Negro" taxable in Northampton County in 1797 [PPTL, 1782-1823, frame 224].

BIBBY FAMILY

1. Mary Bibby was a "Mulatto" born before 24 July 1727 when the churchwardens of Bristol Parish, Virginia, ordered her bound to William Matt [Chamberlayne, *Register of Bristol Parish,* 36].[44] On 22 March 1759 she was in Granville County where she successfully sued William Laneer for release from her servitude [Owen, *Granville County Notes,* Vol I]. In 1761 Mary was a taxable "free black" in the Granville County household of Jesse Ingram in the list of Gideon Macon for Goodwin's District:

> *Jesse Ingram*
> *Richd Ingram*
> *moll Beb*   *1 free black*
> *Charles*   *1 male slave over 16 years*   [CR 44.701.19].

She was called Mary Bibbey in Jesse Ingram's household in 1762 [*NCGSJ* XIII:26]. In 1771 she was taxable in Joshua Ingram's household in William Person's list for Bute County:

> *Joshua Ingram List Edmond Biby Mary biby Negr. Chales* [CR 015.70001].

She was the wife of Ingram's slave Charles [28 June 1893 letter from Narcissa Rattley].[45] In November 1771 the Bute County court ordered her "base born" children bound as apprentices [Minutes 1767-76, 194; WB A:218, 226, 227, 232, 233]. Perhaps they were ordered indentured because Joshua Ingram had become infirm. His will was presented in February 1772 Bute County court [Minutes 1767-76, 211]. Her children were

i. Edmund, born about 1758, taxable in 1771. He was ordered bound to John Pinnion in November 1771 [Minutes 1767-76, 194; WB A:218]. He was listed among the Continental soldiers from Bute County who enlisted for nine months on 3 September 1778: *Edmon Bibby, Place of Abode Bute County, born N.C., 5'4", 20 years old, Dark Fair, Dark Eyes* [NCAr:Troop Returns, Box 4, by *NCGSJ* XV:109].

ii. Fanny, born about 1759, twelve years old in November 1771 when the Bute County court ordered her bound an apprentice [WB A:232]. She married William **Dunstan**, 11 July 1778 Bute County bond.

2 iii. ?Thomas, born say 1761.

---

[44]The abstract of the minutes states that the churchwardens were to "bind out to Godfrey Ragsdail two Mullatto Children by name Dol and bidde as the law directs. It is that a Child be bound to Wm Matt as the law Directs by name Mary bibby.

[45]Narcissa Rattley's letter is in the possession of Robert Jackson of Silver Spring, Maryland.

iv. Solomon, born about 1764, seven years old in November 1771 when the Bute County court ordered him bound an apprentice planter to Peter Goodwin [WB A:233]. He received a pension for his Revolutionary War service as a private in the Tenth Regiment, Yarborough's Company, of the North Carolina Continental Line in 1781. He was living near Sandy Creek in the part of Franklin County which was formed from Bute County when he volunteered. He was called a "free person of Color" on 18 June 1841 when he applied for a pension while living in Franklin County [M805-85, frame 0047]. He married Charity **Young**, 25 December 1789 Franklin County bond.[46] He was head of a Franklin County household of 4 "other free" in 1790 [NC:58] and 7 in 1810 [NC:825].

v. Absolem, born about 1764, seven years old in November 1771 when the Bute County court ordered him bound an apprentice planter to John Pinnion [WB A:227]. He enlisted in the Tenth Regiment, Dixon's Company, of the N.C. Continental Line on 18 May 1781 for one year and was discharged on 21 May 1782 [*N.C. Historical & Genealogical Register* II:185]. He was head of a Franklin County household of 4 "other free" in 1790 [NC:58] and 1 "other free" in 1810 [NC:825].

vi. William, born about 1766, five years old in November 1771 when the Bute County court ordered him bound an apprentice planter to John Pinnion [WB A:226].

2. Thomas[1] Bibby, born say 1761, enlisted as a private in Ballard's Company in the Tenth Regiment of the North Carolina Continental Line on 29 June 1779 for nine months and was discharged 1 December 1779. He was living in Burke County when he made a declaration in the county court to obtain a pension [T&C, Box 14 by *The North Carolinian* VI:753]. He may have been the Thomas Bibby, "F.N.," who married Phebe **Ligon**, 22 September 1806 Chesterfield County, Virginia bond with John **Ligon** bondsman. His children were

i. ?Betsy, head of a Petersburg household of 3 "other free" in 1810 [VA:118b].

ii. Polly (F.N.), born say 1788, "daughter of Thomas Bibby (F.N.), married Embry **Tomkins**, 30 December 1806 Chesterfield County bond. Embry was head of a Richmond City household of 3 "other free" and six slaves in 1810 [VA:329].

iii. ?Ned, born about 1793, obtained a certificate of freedom in Chesterfield County on 13 September 1813: *twenty three years old, bright yellow complexion, born free* [Register of Free Negroes 1804-53, no. 191]. He married Elizabeth **Ligon**, born about 1789 ("24 years old") 13 September 1813 Chesterfield County, Virginia bond.

iv. ?Thomas[2], born about 1813, obtained a certificate of freedom in Chesterfield County on 11 June 1827 (and on 13 June 1836): *fourteen years old, Mulatto complexion, born free* [Register of Free Negroes 1804-53, nos. 572, 1117].

There were also members of the Bibby family who were apprenticed in Cumberland County, North Carolina, no parent named:

i. Hannah, born about 1746, twelve-year-old "Malatoe girl late in possession of Mary Jones," bound to Stephen Phillips on 21 January 1758 [Minutes 1755-9, 33].

ii. Edward, born about 1753, a "Malatoe Child late in the possession of Mary Jones Decd," bound apprentice to Colonel Thomas Armstrong in

---

[46]Narcissa Rattley mentioned Solomon Bibby's 25 December 1789 marriage to Charity **Young** in her 28 June 1893 letter.

Cumberland County on 21 January 1758 [Minutes 1755-9, 33]. He was head of a Cumberland County household of 1 "other free" in 1810, called Ned Beebe [NC:565].

BIDDIE/ BIDDEY FAMILY

Members of the Biddie family living in Lunenburg County, Virginia, about 1760-1770 were

1   i.   Thomas, born say 1740.
     ii. Edward, born say 1742, taxable in Lunenburg County on 4 tithes and 300 acres in 1764 [Bell, *Sunlight on the Southside*, 247]. This may have been the land which Thomas Biddie purchased in 1761. He sued Edward Ragsdale in Lunenburg County court on 11 April 1771. The case was discontinued because Biddy failed to prosecute it further [Orders 1769-77, 109]. He was head of a Ninety-Six District, Union County, South Carolina household of a white male over 16 years of age, 2 under 16, and 4 females in 1790 [SC:92] and a Union District household of 4 "other free" in 1800 [SC:229].
     iii. Peter, born say 1750, successfully petitioned the Lunenburg County court on 14 March 1771 for his freedom from his master, Edward Ragsdale [Orders 1769-77, 108, 122]. He was head of a Ninety-Six District, Union County, South Carolina household of a white male over 16 years of age, 1 under 16, and 2 females in 1790 [SC:92].

1.   Thomas Biddie, born say 1740, purchased for 60 pounds 400 acres on the head branches of Flat Rock Creek in Lunenburg County jointly with John **Evans** (alias **Epps**) on 6 October 1761 [DB 6:473]. He and his wife Susannah Biddie sold their half of this land to **Evans** on 10 January 1771 [DB 11:434]. He was taxable on two tithes and 200 acres in Lunenburg County in 1769 [Bell, *Sunlight on the Southside*, 282]. He purchased 400 acres on Flat Rock Creek jointly with John **Epps**, and he and his wife Susannah sold their half to **Epps** on 8 January 1771 [DB 11:433]. A number of suits against him were dismissed by the Lunenburg County court: Isaac Reeves' on 11 June 1767, John Ross' on 10 December 1767, John Milleson's on 14 February 1771, and John Tabb's on 12 March 1772. He sued Joseph Williams, the former sheriff, on 13 April 1769 and Jonathan Patteson, one of the justices, on 16 Nov 1771 [Orders 1766-69, fol. 67, 120, p. 140; 1769-77, 93, 166, 177, 178, fol. 206]. On 17 December 1771 a plat for 100 acres on the Tiger River, Craven County, South Carolina was surveyed for him, and on 22 May 1772 David Hopkins recorded a plat for land adjoining his in Berkeley County [S.C. Archives series S213197, item 72; S213184, vol. 17:66]. He was head of a Ninety-Six District, Union County, South Carolina household of 4 white males over 16 years of age, 2 under 16, and 3 females in 1790 [SC:92] and 9 "other free" in Union District in 1800 [SC:229]. He may have been the father of
     i.   Edmon, head of a Union District, South Carolina household of 5 "other free" and a white woman in 1800 [SC:232A].
     ii. Mary, head of a Union District, South Carolina household of 7 "other free" in 1800 [SC:231].
     iii. John, born 17 July 1762, head of a Union District household of 4 "other free" in 1800 [SC:230]. He made a declaration in Union District court on 30 October 1832 to obtain a pension for his service in the Revolution. He stated that he was born in Lunenburg County on 17 July 1762 and lived in Union District when he volunteered. He moved to Marshall County, Alabama, by 26 December 1837 when he applied to have his pension paid there. His widow Sarah applied for a survivor's pension on 5 November 1842. Elizabeth Lee testified for her, stating that they were married in Union District at the house of

Presley Williams, Esq., and that John died on 14 October 1841 [M805-85, frame 0372].

Other members of the Biddie family were

    i. Patt, born say 1742, complained to the Surry County, Virginia court against her mistress Elizabeth Stith on 19 April 1763. She was called Patt Buddie a month later on 17 May when the court determined that she was unjustly detained and set her free [Orders 1757-63, 359, 368].

    ii. Hester Buddie, born say 1744, petitioned the Surry County court against Hartwell Hart on 21 June 1763, but the case was dismissed. Joseph Hill was her witness [Orders 1757-63, 371-2].

BING FAMILY

Members of the Bing family were

    i. Matthew, head of a Beaufort District, South Carolina household of 5 "other free" in 1790 and 8 in 1800 [SC:104].

    ii. John, head of a Beaufort District, South Carolina household of 5 "other free" in 1790 [SC:11].

    iii. Isaac, head of a Barnwell District, South Carolina household of 5 "other free" in 1800 [SC:65].

    iv. William, a "free Negro" taxable in Winton County, South Carolina, in 1800 [Tax Returns 1787-1800, S.C. Archives Microfilm AD 942, frame 313].

BINGHAM FAMILY

1. Elizabeth Bingham, born say 1718, was presented by the Northampton County, Virginia court on 13 November 1739 for bastard bearing, but the court ordered the presentment dismissed on 11 December 1739 because she was an "Indian" [Orders 1732-42, 372, 378]. She was the mother of

    i. ?Mary, born about 1738, a six-year-old orphan bound by the Northampton County court to Richard Parrimore on 12 June 1744 [Orders 1742-8, 163].

    ii. ?Southy[1], born about 1742, a two-year-old orphan bound by the Northampton County court to Richard Parrimore on 12 June 1744 [Orders 1742-8, 163]. He was sued by John Evans in Northampton County court for 1 pound, 10 shillings on 13 December 1785. Ephraim **Stevens** was his security [Orders 1783-7, 370, 421, 542]. The court dismissed his suit against the administrator of Harmonson Joyne, deceased, on 17 August 1787, ruling that the plaintiff had not suffered any damages. On 11 November 1788 and 14 March 1792 he was presented for tending crops on the Indians' lands [Orders 1787-9, 20; 1789-95, 193]. He was taxable in Northampton County from 1785 to 1797, called a "free Negro" in 1797 and 1802 [PPTL, 1782-1823, frames 44, 171, 224, 325, 387].

    iii. Daniel, born in December 1743, child of Elizabeth Bingham, seven years old on 12 March 1750/1 when the Northampton County court ordered the churchwardens to bind him to Thomas Grice [Orders 1748-51, 348].

    iv. Elishe, born in August 1746, four-year-old orphan bound to Jacob Abdell on 12 March 1750/1 [Orders 1748-51, 349].

    v. ?Lucretia, born say 1748, complained against her master John Waterfield, Sr., and Honour Mapp for ill usage on 15 May 1765. The case was dismissed in August when the parties agreed [Minutes 1761-5, 172; 1765-71, 6]. She was head of a Northampton County household of 3 "free colored" in 1820 [VA:218].

2   vi. ?Scarburgh, born 1 January 1750.

vii.   ?Elizabeth[2], born in August 1751, bound to William Scott, Sr., on 9 September 1766 [Minutes 1765-71, 64]. She married Nathan **Drighouse**, 23 January 1794 Northampton County bond.

2.   Scarburgh Bingham, born 1 January 1750, was an orphan bound by the Northampton County court to Rev. Henry Barlow on 12 August 1760 and a twelve-year-old "Indian" bound to Savage Cowdry 12 January 1762. Abraham **Collins** won a case against him for 10 pounds on 8 June 1779, and Mary **Jeffery** won a case against him for 30 pounds on 11 July 1780 [Minutes 1754-61, 230; 1761-1765, 4; 1777-83, 167, 252]. His suit against William Dixon abated on 14 August 1793 by his death [Orders 1789-95, 302]. Scarbrough was the parent of

    i.   Southy[2], born in November 1774, son of Scarbrough bound by the Northampton County court to John Elliott on 13 September 1780 [Minutes 1777-83, 278].

    ii.   ?Henry, registered as a "free Negro" in Northampton County on 10 June 1794 [Orders 1789-95, 354]. He married Ritter **Collins**, 13 June 1794 Northampton County bond, Ralph **Collins** surety. He was taxable in Northampton County in 1793 [PPTL, 1782-1823, frame 171].

    iii.   ?Littleton, born about 1782, a thirteen-year-old bound to Hillary Stringer on 11 February 1795 [Orders 1789-95, 412]. He married Rosey **Beckett**, 18 September 1804 Northampton County bond, Moses Bingham security. He was taxable in Northampton County in 1803 [PPTL, 1782-1823, frame 345].

    iv.   ?Moses, born 28 December 1773, bound to Spencer Wilson on 8 September 1778 [Minutes 1777-83, 102]. He was taxable in Northampton County from 1795 to 1805: called a "Negro" in 1805 [PPTL, 1782-1823, frames 189, 386]. He married Esther **Collins**, twenty-five-year-old daughter of Rafe **Collins**, 24 November 1819 Northampton County bond.

They were the ancestors of

    i.   Tinsey, born say 1776, married William **Gardner**, 25 November 1797 Northampton County bond, Isaac **Stevens** security. William was taxable in Northampton County in 1800 and Tinsey was a "N"(egro) listed there in 1813 [PPTL 1782-1823, frames 286, 536].

    ii.   Tamar, registered as a "free Negro" in Northampton County on 12 June 1794 [Orders 1789-95, 358], married Ralph **Collins**, 20 December 1799 Northampton County bond, John Simkins security.

    iii.   Jenny, married Isaac **Gustin**, 13 November 1804 Northampton County bond, Jacob Floyd security.

    iv.   Betsy, married Thomas **Baker**, 5 December 1805 Northampton County bond, Nathan **Drighouse** security.

    v.   Lucy, married Abraham **Nedab**, 29 December 1813 Northampton County bond, with consent of Tinsey **Weeks**, mother of Lucy.

    vi.   Polly, married William **Jeffery**, 26 January 1803 Northampton County bond, Samuel **Beavans** security.

BINNS FAMILY

1.   Jeremiah[1] Binns, born say 1750, was head of a New Kent County household of 7 whites (free persons) in 1785 [VA:92]. He was taxable in the lower end of Saint Peter's Parish in New Kent County from 1782 to 1811: taxable on a horse and 3 cattle from 1782 to 1800; taxable on Jeremiah Binns, Jr.'s tithe in 1789 and 1790; taxable on Jeremiah, Jr., and Reuben Binns' tithe in 1792; 2 horses in 1802; 2 tithes and a horse in 1803; listed as a "M"(ulatto) in 1807, 1810, and 1811 [Personal Property Tax List 1782-1800, frame 9, 19, 48, 81, 93, 109, 125, 144, 159, 180, 237a; 1791-1828, frames 225, 264, 279, 293,

304, 316, 328, 353, 367, 379, 417, 429, 441, 452, 462]. He was head of a New Kent County household of 1 "other free" in 1810 [VA:744]. He was probably the father of

    i.   Jeremiah[2], Jr., born say 1772, taxable in New Kent County from 1789 to 1820: 16-21 years of age when he was listed as Jeremiah Binns' tithable in 1789, 1791 and 1792; taxable on a horse from 1801 to 1803; taxable on a slave and a horse in 1806 and 1809; listed as a "M"(ulatto) in 1807 and thereafter [Personal Property Tax List 1791-1828, frames 353, 367, 379, 417, 429, 441, 462, 473, 484, 491, 496, 509, 573], head of a New Kent County household of 6 "other free" and a white woman aged 26-45 in 1810 [VA:746].

    ii.   Reuben, born say 1775, taxable in New Kent County from 1792 to 1807: 16-21 years of age when he was listed as Jeremiah Binn's tithable in 1792; taxable on a horse in 1802; taxed on 2 free tithables in 1806; listed as a "M"(ulatto) in 1807 [Personal Property Tax List 1791-1828, frames 353, 367].

    iii.   John, a "M" taxable in New Kent County in 1801, 1802 and 1804 [Personal Property Tax List 1791-1828, frames 353, 367, 392].

BIZZELL FAMILY

Members of the Bizzell family of North Carolina were

    i.   David, born say 1735, taxable in Hertford County on two persons from 1768 to 1770, taxable on a horse and two cattle in District 4 of Hertford County in 1779, and taxable on 60 acres and one poll in Nathan Harrel's List for 1784 [Fouts, *Tax Receipt Book*, 15; GA 30.1; LP 64.1]. He was head of a Hertford County household of 3 "other free" in 1800.

1   ii.   Solomon[1], born say 1740.

1.   Solomon[1] Bizzell, born say 1740, was taxed on 40 acres, 20 cattle, and 30 pounds cash in District 3 of Hertford County in 1779 and was taxed on 260 acres and one poll in Nathan Harrel's List for 1784 [G.A. 30.1, 64.1]. He was head of a Hertford County household of 11 "other free" in 1790 [NC:26] and 11 in 1800. The eighteenth and early nineteenth-century records for Hertford County were destroyed in courthouse fires, so we can only guess that his children may have been

    i.   John, born before 1776, head of a Hertford County household of 1 "other free" in 1800 and 13 "free colored" in 1820 [NC:188]. He was one of the "Sundry persons of Colour of Hertford County" who petitioned the General Assembly in November- December 1822 to repeal the act which declared slaves to be competent witnesses against free African Americans [*NCGSJ* XI:252].

    ii.   Noah, head of a Hertford County household of 4 "other free" in 1810 [NC:98].

    iii.   Solomon[2], head of a Hertford County household of 10 "free colored" in 1820 [NC:188].

    iv.   William Bussell, head of a Robeson County household of 5 "other free" in 1790 [NC:48]. He was probably related to John Buzzel, a "Mulatto," whose son Willie Abel **Hammond** had a guardian, William Vines, appointed for him in Beaufort County court in September 1809 on a bond of 1,000 pounds. In December 1810 Vines was permitted to sell the perishable part of the estate of Margaret **Hammond** [Beaufort County court Minutes, 1809-14, n.p.].

BLACK FAMILY

James Black and Peter Black were in Craven County, North Carolina, on 21 June 1745 when they complained to the county court that

> *they were free born person[s] of the County of Essex in Virginia, & brought into this Province by Jno. Heath & by sd. Jno. Heath sold to Wm. Handcock as Slaves...*

The court ruled that they were free men [Haun, *Craven County Court Minutes,* III:465]. Perhaps they were brothers. Members of the Black family of Essex County were

1   i.   James, born say 1715.
2   ii. Peter, born say 1720.
3   iii. Peggy, born say 1722.

1.   James Black, born say 1715, was called "James Black free Negro" in the muster roll of Abner Neale's Craven County Company in 1754 and 1755 [Clark, *Colonial Soldiers of the South,* 708]. His probable descendants were

4   i.   Martin^1, born in 1751.
5   ii. Lettice^1, born about 1752.

2.   Peter Black, born say 1720, complained to the 21 June 1745 Craven County court that he was held as a slave [Haun, *Craven County Court Minutes,* III:365]. Perhaps his widow was Betty Black, born say 1730, taxable on a female "Black" tithe in Craven County in 1769 [SS 837]. On 14 September 1770 the Craven County court ordered the clerk to issue her a certificate that she was insolvent and no longer liable to be taxed [Minutes 1767-75, 158b]. Her children were probably those who were bound out six months after this court order:

6   i.   Lettice^2, born 15 September 1761.
     ii. James^2, born 15 March 1764, bound to Thomas Heath to be taught farming by the 12 September 1771 Craven County court.
     iii. David, born 10 March 1766, ordered bound to Thomas Heath to be taught farming by the 12 September 1771 Craven County court, married Peggy **Clear**, 7 January 1806 Craven County bond.
     iv. Dozey, born 2 August 1768, bound to Thomas Heath to be taught farming by the 12 September 1771 Craven County court.
     v.   Martin^2, born 1 January 1770, bound to Thomas Heath to be taught farming by the 12 September 1771 Craven County court. He complained to the March 1811 Craven County court that his children, who were born "in lawful wedlock," were bound out by the court without his knowledge or consent [Franklin, *Free Negro in North Carolina,* 127].

3.   Peggy Black, born say 1722, the daughter of an Indian, was the mother of a "free yellow woman" named Judy whose daughter Mary claimed to be free born in Essex County about 1766 according to the 13 May 1789 issue of the *Virginia Independent Chronicle* [Headley, *18th Century Newspapers,* 28]. Peggy was the mother of

7   i.   Judy, born say 1745.

4.   Martin^1 Black, born in 1751, sold 90 acres on the east side of Hancock's Creek on Cahoque Creek in Craven County to William **Dove** on 6 February 1775 [DB 22:73]. He enlisted for three years in Stevenson's Company of the North Carolina Continental Line on 16 May 1777. He was in Valley Forge and West Point and reenlisted for eighteen months in Evans Company in 1782 [M805-92, frame 0147]. He was head of a Carteret County household of 2

"other free" in 1790 [NC:128] and an Onslow County household of 4 "other free" in 1800 [NC:143]. He married Ann **Moore**, 12 April 1784 Craven County bond with George **Perkins** bondsman. His 16 September 1821 Carteret County will was proved in November 1821 and executed by his son-in-law, Samuel **Martin**. He gave his Revolutionary War pension to Samuel **Martin** and $10 to his son William. His children were

    i. Keziah, married Samuel **Martin**, 4 June 1819 Carteret County bond.

    ii. William.

5. Lettice[1] Black, born about 1752, was an eleven-year-old "free Negro" bound apprentice to Samuel Griffith in Craven County in July 1763. William Herritage applied to the court on her behalf to have her bound instead to Patrick Gordon [Minutes 1762-4, 27d]. She was head of a Craven County household of 3 "other free" in 1790 [NC:130]. Perhaps her children were

    i. Dinah, born about 1771, "a free Negroe Girl aged 13," bound apprentice until the age of eighteen to Ann Banks by the 16 Sept 1784 Craven County court [Minutes 1772-84, 2:79a].

    ii. Edward, born about 1777, a six-year-old "free negroe" bound apprentice to Thomas Heath on 12 September 1783 to be a shoemaker [Minutes 1772-84, 2:59c].

6. Lettice[2] Black, born 15 September 1761, was a ten-year-old "Free Born Negroe Girl" who was bound apprentice to Mary Heath on 12 September 1771 [Minutes 1766-75, 179a]. She was head of a Craven County household of 3 "other free" in 1790 [NC:134]. Perhaps she was the mother of

    i. Hagar, born in May 1781, a "free Negroe Child" bound to Mary Heath until the age of eighteen by the 17 September 1784 Craven County court [Minutes 1784-86, 5c].

    ii. Sally, born say 1792, married Kelsey **Braddock**, 7 February 1810 Craven County bond, Elijah **George** bondsman. Kelsey was probably the son of Peter **Braddock**, head of a Carteret County household of 8 "other free" in 1790 [NC:129].

7. Judy Black, born say 1745, was said to have been a "yellow woman" and the mother of

    i. Mary, born about 1766, twenty-three years old on 13 May 1789 when she claimed to have been free born in Essex County [Headley, *18th Century Newspapers*, 28].

Other members of the family in North Carolina were

    i. Sary, born say 1753, a "molatto" taxable in the 1766 Bertie County list of John Crickett [CR 10.702.1].

    ii. Caroline, head of a Carteret County household of 5 "other free" in 1810 [NC:450].

    iii. Jacob, head of an Orange County household of 3 "other free" in 1800 [NC:513].

    iv. Sarah, head of a Rutherford County household of 1 "free colored" in 1820 [NC:397].

Other members of the Black family in Virginia were

    i. John, head of a Prince William County household of 5 "other free" in 1810 [VA:508].

    ii. Simon, head of a Frederick County household of 6 "other free" in 1810 [VA:514].

    iii. Sally, head of an Augusta County household of 4 "other free" in 1810 [VA:322].

    iv. Nancy, head of a Petersburg Town household of 2 "other free" in 1810 [VA:327].

BLAKE FAMILY

The Blake family of Virginia may have descended from Faith Blake whose orphan Sarah Blake was bound by the Amelia County court to John Roberts on 27 September 1759. She was sued by the churchwardens for debt (for having an illegitimate child?) on 27 March 1760 [Orders 1757-60, 240, 279]. Members of the family were

    i.   Martin, born say 1770, a "free Mulatto" living in Amelia County on 24 September 1772 when the court ordered the churchwardens of Raleigh Parish to bind him to Will Jones [Minutes 1769-72, n. p.].

    ii. Betsy, born about 1781, registered in Bedford County on 29 November 1831: *a mulatto, aged 50, 5 feet 1 inch high, free born.* She may have been the mother of Polly, Harbert, Betsy and Sally Blake who registered the same day [Register of Free Negroes 1820-60, p.17].

BLANGO FAMILY

1.   Tom[1] Blanco, born say 1673, a "Negroe" belonging to Madam Porter of Bristol, petitioned the Kent County, Maryland court for his freedom on 11 December 1694. His Excellency the Governor informed the Justices about the case, but they ruled that "the said Negro offered several false suggestions to the Court" and ordered that he receive twelve lashes [Court Record 1694-8, 493]. He may have been the father or grandfather of Thomas, Rachel, and Sarah Blango who were taxables in Beaufort County, North Carolina, in 1755 [SS 837]:

2   i.   Thomas[2], born say 1710.
3   ii. Rachel, born say 1720.
4   iii. Sarah[1], born say 1730.

2.   Thomas[2] Blango, born say 1710, was a "free Negro" head of a Beaufort County household with Sarah and Betty Blango in 1755:

    Blango, Tom Sar. Blango Betty Blango (Free Negroes)   *3*   [SS 837].

He was called "Thomas Blango free negro" in June 1757 Beaufort County court when he was a defendant in a case brought by Thomas Pearce [Minutes 1756-61, 1:32a (docket no.22)]. He was one of the superannuated and invalid members of the Beaufort County Militia under the command of Colonel William Brown prior to 1765 [Clark, *Colonial Soldiers of the South,* 781]. His children may have been

5   i.   Thomas[3], born say 1730.
       ii. Betty, born say 1735, taxable in Tom Blango's Beaufort County household in 1755 [SS 837].

3.   Rachel Blango, born say 1720, was a "free Negro" head of a Beaufort County household in 1755:

    Blango, Rachel Sar. Blango Sarah Blango Junr
    Dinah Blango (Free Negroes)   *4*   [SS 837].

In June 1758 the Beaufort County court ordered that: *a free Negroe Woman named Rachel Blango, another named Sarah Blango the younger, another named Dinah Blango and a Man named Gabe, and another Negroe Woman named Bett Moore, another Mary Moore ____, and Keziah Moore be Summoned to appear at next court to produce a Master for their Children in order they may be bound out as the law directs* [Minutes 1756-61, 2:46c]. Perhaps she was the Rachel, "Free Negro," taxable in the household of John,

"Free Negro," (no family name mentioned) in the Beaufort County Tax List in 1764 [SS 837]. John may have been John Punch **Moore**, and she may have been the Rachel **Moore** who was head of a Beaufort County household of 2 "other free" in 1800 [NC:15]. See further the **Moore** history. Rachel's children may have been

6   i.   Sarah², Jr., born say 1738.
7   ii.   Dinah¹, born say 1740.

4.   Sarah¹ Blango, born say 1730, was taxable in Rachel Blango's Beaufort County household in 1755 [SS 837]. She was sued for debt by James Calef in the June 1756 session of the Beaufort County court, and the June 1761 session ordered her to pay him 16 pounds [Minutes 1756-61, 1:9c (Docket no.23); 2:41d]. She was taxed in Beaufort County on an assessment of 240 pounds in 1779 [*NCGSJ* XV:142]. She purchased 200 acres on the east side of Nevill's Creek from Thomas Blango (Jr.?) on 9 June 1789 [DB 6:125] and swapped 100 acres of this land with John Gray Blount for land nearby by deed of 4 March 1801 [DB 1:457, 459]. She was head of a Beaufort County household of 5 "other free" in 1790 [NC:125]. She may have been the mother of

   i.   Benjamin, born say 1758, a deceased soldier of Beaufort County whose estate was administered before June 1792 by Sarah Blango.
   ii.   Moses¹, born say 1760, a deceased soldier of Beaufort County whose estate was administered before June 1792 by Sarah Blango [*NCGSJ* XVIII:72].

5.   Thomas³ Blango, born say 1730, was called Thomas Blango, Jr., when he was sued for debt by James Calef in the June 1756 Beaufort County court in a case which was declared a non-suit in the June 1761 session [Minutes 1756-61, 1:9c (docket no.23); 2:44a]. He purchased 640 acres in Beaufort on the east side of Nevill's Creek at the mouth of Bridge Branch from John Benston by an unrecorded deed and sold this land by deeds of 2 April 1774, 10 April 1777, 20 January 1788 by the sheriff for debt, 5 June 1788 by the sheriff for debt, and 9 June 1789 to Sarah Blango [DB 5:20, 307; 6:125, 324, 341]. He was called "Nasowman" in the 10 April 1777 deed, perhaps claiming that his family was from Nassau. In 1779 he was taxed in Beaufort County on an assessment of 320 pounds [LP 30.1, by *NCGSJ* XV:142]. He was head of a Beaufort County household of 10 "other free" in 1790 [NC:125]. His children may have been

   i.   Isaac, born before 1776, head of a Beaufort County household 5 "other free" in 1800 [NC:2], 10 in 1810 [NC:114], and 8 "free colored" in 1820 [NC:7]. He was called Isaac Blango Moore in the March 1814 session of Beaufort County court when Solomon Blango was bound to him as an apprentice cooper [Minutes 1809-14, n.p.]. By his 2 January 1836 Beaufort County will, proved June 1842, he lent his plantation and land to his sister Nancy, then to Patsy **Moore**, wife of Charles **Moore**, and lent 20 acres to his brother's child Hannah, wife of John **Moore** [WB D:281].
8   ii.   Margaret, born say 1773.
9   iii.   Solomon¹, born say 1775.
10   iv.   Sarah³, born 1776-94.
   v.   Patsy **Moore**.
   vi.   Nancy.

6.   Sarah² Blango, born say 1738, was a "Free Negro" taxable in Rachel Blango's household in 1755 (called Sarah Blango, Jr.) [SS 837]. In June 1758 she was called "Sarah Blango the younger" when she was ordered to produce a master for her child to be bound apprentice to [Minutes 1756-61, 1:46d]. Perhaps she was the "Sarah Blango Moore (free negro)" whose plight was advertised in the 9 October 1778 issue of the North Carolina Gazette of New Bern:

...that she was last night robbed of two of her own children, by three men in disguise; one a boy about six years old named Ambrose, the other a girl named Rose, of the same age, they being twins... [Fouts, *NC Gazette of New Bern*, I:80-1].

The **Moore** family was the largest free African American family in Beaufort and Craven Counties. She may have been the Sall Blango who was head of a Beaufort County household of 11 "other free" in 1800 [NC:2] and 8 in 1810 [NC:115]. She was the mother of

    i.   John/ Jack, born about 1797, the seventeen-year-old son of Sally Blango, bound by the Beaufort County court to James Meredith to be a cooper in March 1814 [Minutes 1809-14, n.p.].

    ii. ?Dorcas Blango, born about 1757, successfully petitioned the 9 June 1778 Craven County court for freedom from her indenture to Isaac Patridge [Minutes 1772-84, 1:61c].

    iii. Ambrose **Moore**, born 1772, married Polly **Carter**, 29 December 1804 Craven County bond, Jacob **Moore** bondsman. He was head of a Craven County household of 2 "free colored" in 1820 [NC:67]. On 4 November 1821 he and his wife Polly sold land in Craven County which she inherited from her father George **Carter** [DB 43:82].

    iv. Rose, born 1772, perhaps the Rose **Carter**, born 1776-94, who was head of a Carteret County household of 3 "free colored" in 1820 [NC:123].

7.   Dinah[1] Blango, born say 1743, was a "Free Negro" taxable in Rachel Blango's Beaufort County household in 1755 [SS 837]. The June 1758 Beaufort County court called her a "free Negroe Woman" when it ordered her to produce a master in court for her children to be bound to. Perhaps she was the wife of Gabe, a "free Negroe Man," who was listed after her in the court order [Minutes 1756-61, 2:46c]. She was head of a Beaufort County household of 6 "other free" in 1790 [NC:125]. One of her children may have been

    i.   Gabriel, born before 1776, head of a Beaufort County household of 7 "other free" in 1800 [NC:2], 9 in 1810 [NC:113], and 8 "free colored" in 1820 [NC:7].

8.   Margaret Blango, born say 1773, was head of a Beaufort County household of 5 "other free" in 1800 [NC:2]. She was called Margaret M. Blango in the March 1814 session of the Beaufort County court when her son Willie **Moore** Blango was bound as an apprentice [Minutes 1809-14, n.p.]. She was the mother of

    i.   Willie **Moore** Blango, born about 1800, a fourteen-year-old "free person of Color, son of Margaret M. Blango," bound an apprentice shoemaker to William Orell in March 1814.

    ii. Winnie M. Blango, born about October 1802, eleven years and six months old in March 1814 when she was bound to William Orell in Beaufort County court.

9.   Solomon[1] Blango, born say 1775, was head of a Beaufort County household of 1 "other free" in 1790 [NC:126]. He may have been deceased by March 1814 when the Beaufort County court bound his fourteen-year-old son Moses Blango to Joseph Trippe [Minutes 1809-14, n.p.]. He was the father of

    i.   Moses[2], born about 1800, bound an apprentice cooper to Joseph Trippe in March 1814.

    ii. ?Isaac[2], born about 1802, a twelve-year-old free Boy of Color, no parent named, bound an apprentice cooper to Nathan Archibell by the March 1814 Beaufort County court.

iii. ?Dinah[2], born about 1805, a nine-year-old free girl of Color, no parent named, bound apprentice to Nathan Archibell by the March 1814 Beaufort County court.

iv. ?Solomon[2], born about 1806, an eight-year-old free Boy of Color, no parent named, bound as an apprentice cooper to Isaac Blango Moore by the March 1814 Beaufort County court [Minutes 1809-14, n.p.].

10. Sarah[3] Blango, born 1776-94, was head of a Beaufort County household of 5 "other free" in 1810 [NC:114] and 5 "free colored" in 1820 [NC:7]. She was the mother of

i. ?Phebe, born about 1801, a thirteen-year-old free girl of Color, no parent named, bound an apprentice housekeeper to Joseph B. Hinton by the March 1814 Beaufort County court.

ii. Patsy July Blount Blango, born about 1802, daughter of Sarah Blango, bound apprentice to Joseph Shute by the March 1814 Beaufort County court.

iii. ?Harman, born about 1804, a ten-year-old free Boy of Color, no parent named, bound an apprentice shoemaker to Isaac Smith [Minutes 1809-14, n.p.].

BLANKS FAMILY

1. John Blanks, born say 1754, was a white taxable in James Ellis' Bladen County household in 1770 and a "Mixt Blood" taxable in his own household in 1774, a "Black" taxable in 1775, taxable on 100 acres, 3 horses and 5 cattle in 1779, and head of a household of 2 Blacks 12-50 years old and 4 over 50 or under 12 in 1786 [Byrd, *Bladen County Tax Lists*, I:29, 124; II:36, 142, 169, 202]. He was head of Bladen County household of 8 "other free" in 1790 [NC:188]. He was living in Robeson County on 14 January 1797 when he sold 100 acres in Bladen County in the fork of Slapass and Fryer Swamps [DB 7:210]. He may have been the father of

i. Alfred, born about 1783, a "free Mulatto boy" about twelve years old in June 1795 when he was bound as an apprentice by the New Hanover County court [Minutes 1792-8, 143]. He was head of a Bladen County household of 9 "free colored" in 1820 [NC:146].

ii. Munford, (probably named for the **Mumford** family), head of a New Hanover County household of 4 "free colored" in 1820 [NC:221].

iii. Esther, head of a New Hanover County household of 4 "free colored" in 1820 [NC:221].

BLIZZARD FAMILY

Members of the Blizzard family were

1   i. Charles[1], born say 1730.
2   ii. Ann, born say 1736.
3   iii. Samuel[1], born say 1738.
4   iv. Sarah[1], born say 1739.
5   v. Edward, born say 1740.
    vi. William[1], born say 1745, sued by William Parham in Sussex County court for a 3 pound, 19 shilling debt on 19 March 1767 [Orders 1766-70, 65].
6   vii. Hezekiah[1], born say 1749.
   viii. Hezekiah[2], born say 1770, taxable on a slave named Cyrus in Surry County, Virginia, in 1799 [PPTL, 1791-1816, frame 363].
   ix. Burwell, taxable on a horse in Brunswick County, Virginia, from 1785 to 1807 [PPTL, 1782-98, frames 315, 355, 391, 488, 534; 1799-1815, frames 84, 132, 251, 288, 341, 432].

1. Charles[1] Blizzard, born say 1730, baptized his children Charles and Hannah
    Blizzard in Albemarle Parish, Sussex and Surry counties in 1758 and 1759
    [Richards, *Register of Albemarle Parish*, 18, 102]. On 18 August 1758 the
    Sussex County court ordered him to work on the road from the High Hills to
    Spring Swamp Chappel. A suit brought by Charles and his wife Ann against
    James Bell for trespass, assault and battery was discontinued in Sussex County
    court on 18 March 1762 on agreement between the parties. He was sued for
    debt in Sussex County on 17 March 1768 [Orders 1757-9, 192; 1761-4, 63,
    79; 1766-70, 219]. He and his wife Anne were Joseph **Kennedy**'s (**Cannady**)
    godparents when he was christened in Albemarle Parish on 3 July 1768
    [Richards, *Register of Albemarle Parish*, 145]. The inventory of his Sussex
    County estate totaled 38 pounds and was returned to court on 20 May 1773
    [WB C:43-4]. His children were

    i.   Charles[2], born 24 July 1756, son of Charles and Anne Blizzard,
         baptized in Albemarle Parish, Sussex and Surry counties on 4 February
         1759. He was taxable in Surry County from 1786 to 1789. He died
         before 1790 when his estate was listed. Perhaps his widow Ann was the
         Anne Blizzard who was listed in Surry County as a "free Negro &
         Mulatto above the age of 16" in 1813 [PPTL, 1782-90, frames 397,
         444, 469, 595; 1791-1816, frame 728].
    ii. Hannah, born 19 May 1758, daughter of Charles and Anne Blizzard,
         baptized 19 May 1758 in Albemarle Parish, Sussex and Surry counties
         [Richards, *Register of Albemarle Parish*, 18].
    iii. ?Mazy, born say 1765, married William **Santee**, 7 February 1786
         Sussex County bond.
    iv. ?Milly, born say 1766, married Thomas **Edwards**, 3 August 1787
         Sussex County bond. Thomas **Edwards** was a "FN" taxable in Sussex
         County in 1793 and 1804 [PPTL 1782-1812, frames 369, 624].

2. Ann Blizzard, born say 1736, was living in Surry County, Virginia, in October
    1750 when the churchwardens of Albemarle Parish sued her for debt (for
    having an illegitimate child?) [Orders 1749-51, 156]. She may have been the
    mother of

7   i.   William[2], born about 1766.
    ii. Mason, born say 1770, a "poor child" living in Brunswick County,
         Virginia, on 25 June 1770 when the court ordered the churchwardens
         of St. Andrew's Parish to bind her and William **Dungill** as apprentices
         [Orders 1768-72, 289]. She married Jack **Wooton**, 19 November 1802
         Sussex County bond, Abraham **James** surety. Jack **Wooton** and
         Abraham **James** were "FN" taxables in Sussex County in 1804 [PPTL
         1782-1812, frames 625, 629]. Jack registered in Sussex County on 7
         August 1812: *brown complexion, 5 feet 7 inches, age 37, freed by deed
         of Edward Wooton on 5 February 1789* [Register of Free Negroes,
         1800-50, no. 147].
    iii. Elizabeth, born say 1774, married Armstead **Peters**, 26 April 1792
         Surry County, Virginia bond.

3. Samuel[1] Blizzard, born say 1738, and his wife Sarah baptized their daughter
    Lucy Blizzard in Albemarle Parish, Sussex and Surry counties, on 16 May
    1762. Aaron **Peters**, Lydia Blizzard and Selah Flood were the godparents
    [Richards, *Register of Albemarle Parish*, 214]. Samuel was head of a Sussex
    County household of 8 free persons in 1782 [VA:44], taxable in Sussex
    County from 1782 to 1795: taxable on 2 horses and 5 cattle in 1782; charged
    with his son Samuel's tithe in 1783; taxable on a free male 16-21 in 1792
    [PPTL 1782-1812, frames 71, 92, 112, 169, 194, 210, 220, 239, 272, 296,
    319, 331, 367, 380]. He was the father of

i. Randolph, born 24 February 1760, son of Samuel and Sarah Blizzard, baptized 8 July 1764, godparents Aaron **Peters**, ___ Blizzard, and Lucy **Peters** [Richards, *Register of Albemarle Parish,* 228].

ii. Lucy, born 21 January 1761, baptized 16 May 1762 [Richards, *Register of Albemarle Parish,* 214].

iii. William[2], born 23 December 1762, son of Samuel and Sarah Blizzard, baptized 10 June 1763 [Richards, *Register of Albemarle Parish,* 265].

iv. Samuel[2], Jr., born say 1762, taxable in Sussex County from 1783 to 1795: called son of Samuel Blizzard in 1783; his tax charged to Robert Lamb in 1786; charged with his own tax in 1789 and 1790; listed with Joseph **Canada** in Mary Andrews' household in 1791; charged with his own tax from 1792 to 1795 [PPTL 1782-1812, frames 92, 196, 240, 272, 296, 319, 331, 366, 380]. He was a "Mulatto" taxable in Prince George County from 1801 to 1809 [PPTL, 1782-1811, frames 530, 549, 575, 624, 649, 698].

v. ?John, born about 1773, taxable in Surry County in 1791 and 1807 [PPTL, 1791-1816, frames 26, 628] and taxable in Sussex County in 1795, 1797 and 1803 [PPTL 1782-1812, frames 380, 431, 585]. He registered in Surry County on 20 October 1800: *a free born mulattoe Man a resident of Surry County aged about 27 years, 5'7-1/2" high, bushy hair, pretty well formed of a bright complexion has a large nose and by trade a planter* [Back of Guardian Accounts Book 1783-1804, Register of Free Negroes, no.81]. He married Polly **Byrd**, 22 June 1803 Sussex County bond, Drewry Taylor surety, 23 June marriage.

4. Sarah[1] Blizzard, born say 1739, was the mother of orphans Susanna and Peter Blizzard who were ordered bound out by the churchwardens in Surry County on 17 September 1765. Peter was called a "poor Mulatto" on 21 January 1772 when the court issued the same order. On 23 February 1779 he and (his brothers?) James and Samuel Blizzard, apprentices to William Rae, complained to the Surry County court that Rae was ill treating them [Orders 1764-74, 81, 276; 1775-85, 80]. On 19 November 1779 and 21 October 1779 the Sussex County court ordered the churchwardens to bind out her orphan children Samuel, James and Sarah [Orders 1777-82, 81, 87]. She was the mother of

8   i. Susanna, born say 1759.

9   ii. Peter, born say 1761.

     iii. James, born say 1768, an apprentice of William Rae on 23 February 1779.

     iv. Samuel[3], born say 1770, an apprentice of William Rae on 23 February 1779. He was taxable in Cabin Point district of Surry County in 1787 and 1788 and from 1806 to 1816: listed with 2 "free Negroes & Mulattoes" in 1813 [PPTL, 1782-90, frames 444, 469; 1791-1816, frames 611, 648, 685, 704, 728, 849].

10   v. Sarah[2], born before 1776.

5. Edward Blizzard, born say 1740, was living in Sussex County in June 1764 when he was charged with breach of the peace on Barbara Emerson who confessed to the court that she had lived in adultery with Edward for the previous ten years. He was discharged because it appeared to the court that she was a person of such ill fame that they could not admit her as a witness. On 21 December 1780 the court ordered his son Armstead bound out as an apprentice, "it appearing to the court that his father neglects his education" [Orders 1764-6, 70; 1777-82, 113]. He was the father of

i. Armstead, born say 1760, son of Edward Blizzard, ordered bound out by the Sussex County court on 21 December 1780. He was taxable in Sussex County from 1790 to 1796: listed with Thomas Clary in 1791 [PPTL 1782-1812, frames 273, 297, 331, 366, 380, 420].

6. Hezekiah[1] Blizzard, born say 1749, was taxed on an assessment of 16 pounds in the 1783 Duplin County, North Carolina List of Captains Ward, Hubbard, and Whitehead (called Ezekiel Blizzard) [*N.C. Genealogy* XVIII:2781]. He married Leah **Cartey (Carter)**, 19 December 1782 Duplin County bond and was bondsman for the 15 November 1789 Duplin County marriage bond of Emmanuel **Carter**. He was among several light-skinned African Americans counted as white in Duplin County in 1790, head of a household of 1 male and 5 females [NC:190]. Perhaps his children were

    i.   John, born say 1775, head of a Duplin County household of 6 "other free" in 1800. He purchased 207 acres near Goshen Swamp in Duplin County by three deeds signed 1 October 1810 and 17 September 1812 [DB 4A:407, 408, 409]

    ii. Keziah, married Jonathan **Nickens**, 18 January 1783 Duplin County bond.

7. William[3] Blizzard, born about 1766, was living in Brunswick County, Virginia, on 20 January 1773 when he and Rebecca **Dungeon (Dungee)** were ordered to be let out to the lowest bidder [Hopkins, *St. Andrew's Parish Vestry Book*, 92]. He was taxable in Surry County in 1786 [PPTL, 1782-90, frame 397]. He registered as a "free Negro" in Surry County on 6 October 1794: *a mulattoe man, born free in the County aforesaid, aged about 28 years of a yellowish complexion, about 5'10" high of a thin visage and slender made* [Back of Guardian Accounts Book 1783-1804, no.2]. He may have been the father of

    i.   Betsy, alias Betsy Blizzard, of lawful age, married James **Ruff**, 23 May 1823 Surry County bond, William Blizzard surety.

8. Susan Blizzard, born say 1759, was head of a Surry County household of 8 "other free" in 1810 [VA:601]. She was the mother of

    i.   Samuel[4], born about 1786, registered in Surry County on 26 August 1822: *the son of Susan Blizzard aged 36 years is 5'7-3/4" high, was born free, is of bright complexion*. He married Caty **Williams**, daughter of James **Williams**, 28 December 1807 Surry County bond, David **Charity** surety, 7 January 1808 marriage.

9. Peter Blizzard, born say 1761, was called the orphan of Sarah Blizzard on 17 September 1765 when the Surry County court ordered the churchwardens to bind him out and called a "poor Mulatto" on 21 January 1772 when the court issued the same order. On 23 February 1779 he, James, and Samuel Blizzard, apprentices to William Rae, complained to the court that Rae was ill treating them [Orders 1764-74, 81, 276; 1775-85, 80]. He was called Peter Blizzard of Surry County on 29 October 1788 when he sold 100 acres in Prince George County which Edward Newell had sold to him in the year 1782 for serving as a soldier in the Continental Service for eighteen months in place of John Newell [DB 1787-92, 232]. He was taxable in Surry County from 1788 to 1816: listed with 4 "free Negroes & Mulattoes above the age of 16" in 1813; taxable on 2 free tithes in 1812 and 1813, 3 in 1815, and 2 in 1816 [PPTL, 1782-90, frames 469, 594; 1791-1816, 105, 232, 282, 361, 439, 514, 588, 628, 666, 704, 726, 847]. Peter married Mary **Charity**, 30 September 1791 Surry County bond, and was head of a Surry County household of 2 "free colored" in 1830. They were the parents of

    i.   ?Carter, born say 1796, taxable in Surry County in 1816 [PPTL, 1791-1816, frame 847].

    ii. William Evans, born about 1802, registered in Surry County on 20 November 1822: *son of Peter and Mary Blizzard of this County, aged 20 years is 5'7" high, streight and well made*.

    iii. Sherrard, born about 1813, registered in Surry County on 20 July 1833: *son of Peter Blizzard & Mary his wife...about 20 years of age rather of a dark complexion...and is 5'8-1/4" high and of a slender make* [Hudgins, *Surry County, Virginia, Register of Free Negroes*, 76, 112].

10. Sarah[2] Blizzard, born before 1776, was head of a Surry County household of 8 "free colored" in 1830. Her Surry County estate was settled in 1839 [Wills, Etc. 7:663-5]. She was the mother of

   i. Champion, born in February 1801, registered in Surry County on 20 August 1822: *son of Sally Blizzard, he was born free, is of a bright complexion, has a flat Nose...5'6" high, pretty straight made was 21 years old last February.*

   ii. Willis, born about 1806, registered in Surry County on 22 March 1828: *son of Sally Blizzard a free woman of Surry County...of a dark complexion stout make, large flat nose, thick lips, is 5'5-1/4" high and about 22 years of age.*

   iii. Charles[3], born 20 June 1807, registered in Surry County on 23 June 1828: *son of Sally Blizzard a free black woman of Surry County...of a dark complexion, flat nose, is 5'6" high, well made, and was 21 years of age the 20th day of the present month* [Hudgins, *Surry County Register of Free Negroes*, 75, 86].

BLUE FAMILY

Members of the Blue family were

   i. Stepney, born say 1750, a slave who ran away from his owner, Nathan Yancy of York County, in 1774 with his wife Esther **Roberts**, "a free Negro woman" [*Virginia Gazette* of 29 September and 2 November 1774].

   ii. Mary, a "free Molatto" bound to Mary Scott of Elizabeth River Parish on 20 June 1771 by order of the Norfolk County court [Orders 1771-3, 1].

   iii. William[1], a "Negro" jailed in Norfolk Borough according to the 12 January 1797 issue of the Norfolk Herald and Public Advertiser [Headley, *18th Century Newspapers*]

   iv. William[2], born about 1787, registered in Petersburg on 14 January 1809: *a light brown free Mulatto man, six feet inches high, twenty one - twenty two years old, rather thin & straight made, short hair, a black smith, born free & raised in the City of Richmond* [Register of Free Negroes 1794-1819, no. 453].

BOLTON FAMILY

1. Lettice Bolton, born say 1700, was the mother of Charles, a "bastard Mulatto boy...by a Negro or Mulatto man slave," who was bound out by the churchwardens of Cople Parish, Westmoreland County, Virginia, to William Keene of Northumberland County on 24 October 1720 [Westmoreland Deeds & Wills 7:68-9]. She was the ancestor of

   i. Charles, born before 24 October 1720.

   ii. ?Solomon, head of a Georgetown District, Prince George's Parish, South Carolina household of 8 "other free" in 1790.

   iii. ?Spencer, head of a Georgetown District, Prince George's Parish, South Carolina household of 8 "other free" in 1790.

BOND FAMILY

1. Elizabeth Bond, born say 1705, was "a mulatto woman" listed in the 20 February 1726/7 inventory of the Essex County estate of John Gilby with her

"mulatto children" Eleanor Bond (four years old) and Sarah Bound (two years old) [Dorman, *Wills, Bonds, Inventories 1722-30*, 52]. She was the mother of

    i.   Eleanor, born about 1723.

    ii.   Sarah, born about 1725.

    iii. Anna, born say 1730, a "Runaway Molatto servant" belonging to John Stone of King and Queen County who was taken up by Benjamin Rhodes before 7 February 1752 when he proved his claim in Middlesex County court [Orders 1745-52, 380].

BOON FAMILY

Members of the Boon family in North Carolina and Virginia and were

1   i.   Patt, born say 1742.

2   ii.   James[1], born say 1745.

3   iii. Daniel, born say 1760.

    iv. Jacob, born say 1760, a "yellow" complexioned soldier from Isle of Wight County listed in the size roll of troops who enlisted at Chesterfield Courthouse [The Chesterfield Supplement cited by NSDAR, *African American Patriots*, 147].

    v.   Milly, "free negro" head of a Fairfax County household of 7 "other free" in 1810 [VA:238].

    vi. John, head of a Hyde County, North Carolina household of 1 "other free" in 1810 [NC:138], probably related to Hannah Boon, born 1776-1794, head of a Craven County household of 4 "free colored" in 1820 [NC:72].

1.   Patt Boon, born say 1742, was living in Bertie County in August 1774 when the court ordered her "bastard Mulatto" children: Lewis, Katie, Judah, and Arthur bound apprentices to James Brown [Haun, *Bertie County Court Minutes*, II:92]. Her children were

4   i.   Rachel[1], born say 1760.

    ii.   Lewis, born about 1763, "bastard Mulatto of Patt Boon," bound apprentice in 1774. He was head of a Northampton County, North Carolina household of 9 "other free" in 1800 [NC:429], 5 in Halifax County in 1810 [NC:5], and 5 "free colored" in Halifax in 1820 [NC:142]. He purchased 35 acres adjoining Jesse **Richardson** on Falling Creek in Halifax County from Hardy **Richardson** on 1 March 1822 [DB 25:590].

    iii. Katie, born about 1765, the nine-year-old "bastard Mulatto of Patt" ordered bound to James Brown by the August 1774 session of the Bertie County court.

5   iv. Rebecca, born say 1768.

    v.   Judah/ Judith, born about 1768, six-year-old "bastard Mulatto of Patt" bound to James Brown by the August 1774 session of the Bertie County court, head of a Hertford County household of 4 "other free" in 1810 [NC:107].

    vi. Arthur, born about 1773, one-year-old "bastard Mulatto of Patt" bound by the Bertie County court to James Brown in August 1774, head of a Hertford County household of 6 "other free" in 1790 [NC:25].

    vii. ?Cader, born before 1776, head of a Bertie County household of 1 "other free" in 1810 [NC:160] and 16 "free colored" in 1820 [NC:54].

    viii. ?James[3], born say 1780, married Jincey **Tann**, 5 June 1826 Northampton County bond. On 18 August 1835 Mima Boon petitioned the Halifax County court to bind her children Lewis and Lam Boon to their uncle James because the children's father was insane. He may have been the James W. Boon, "Male Mulatto," who was eighty years old in 1860 in Halifax County, household number 1513. He owned

$652 real estate and was living with Caroline who was forty-nine years old.

ix. ?Patsy, head of a Hertford County household of 2 "other free" in 1810 [NC:107] and 2 "free colored" in 1820 [NC:206].

x. ?Ruth, born before 1776, head of a Northampton County household of 7 "free colored" females in 1820 [NC:218].

2. James[1] Boon, born say 1745, was a "Mixt. Blood" taxable in Hertford County in 1770 [Fouts, *Tax Receipt Book*, 31] and head of a Gates County household of 1 "other free" in 1790 [NC:23]. In February 1790 the Gates County court ordered his twelve-year-old "orphan" son Thomas Boon bound an apprentice shoemaker to Thomas Marshall. The inventory of his estate was recorded in Gates County court on 20 February 1794 [Fouts, *Minutes of County Court of Pleas and Quarter Sessions 1787-93*, 8, 14]. He was the father of

i. ?James[2], born before 1776, head of a Halifax County household of 8 "free colored" in 1820 [NC:142].

ii. ?Moses, born before 1776, head of a Gates County household of 8 "free colored" in 1820 [NC:144].

iii. ?David, born before 1776, head of a Northampton County household of 1 "other free" in 1810 [NC:714] and 10 "free colored" in Hertford County in 1820 [NC:182]. He was in the Northampton County Regiment in the War of 1812.

iv. ?Elias, born before 1776, head of a Halifax County household of 6 "free colored" in 1820 [NC:142].

v. ?Elisha, born before 1776, head of a Northampton County household of 4 "free colored" in 1820 [NC:218]. He was in the Northampton County Regiment in the War of 1812.

vi. ?William, head of a Halifax County household of 6 "free colored" in 1820 [NC:142].

vii. Thomas, born about 1778, a twelve-year-old bound apprentice in Gates County in 1790.

3. Daniel Boon, born say 1760, was a "negro" head of a Nansemond County household of 1 black person in 1783 [VA:56]. He may have been the father of

i. Sarah, born about 1787, registered in Petersburg on 30 December 1808: *a yellowish brown free negro woman, five feet three inches high, twenty one years old, born free in Nansemond County p. Certificate of Prince George County* [Register of Free Negroes 1794-1819, no. 439]. She was head of a Petersburg Town household of 4 "other free" in 1810 [VA:127b].

ii. James[4]/ Jim, born about 1792, registered in Petersburg on 1 December 1818: *a free man of Colour, five feet six inches high, twenty six years old, dark complection, born free in Isle of Wight County* [Register of Free Negroes 1794-1819, no. 940]. He may have been identical to the James Boon who was a "Free Negro" taxable in Nansemond County in 1815 [Yantis, *Supplement to the 1810 Census of Virginia*, S-14].

iii. Jesse, born about 1796, received one of the "Certificates granted to Free negroes & mulattoes from October 1800" in Sussex County on 28 February 1820: *brown complexion, 5'10", free born, 24 years old* [Certificate no.383].

4. Rachel[1] Boon, born say 1760, was a "Molatter" taxable in 1772 in James Purvis' household in the Bertie County List of Reddick Rutland [CR 10.702.1]. She was head of a Bertie County household of 3 "other free" in 1800 [NC:34]. Her children were

i. ?Sarah, born about 1776, ordered bound to Thomas Pugh, Junior, by the Bertie court in February 1789 (no parent named) [Haun, *Bertie*

County Court Minutes, VI:728]. She was head of a Bertie County household of 2 "other free" in 1810 [NC:166].

ii.   ?Rachel[2], born about 1779, four years old on 14 May 1783 when she was bound apprentice in Bertie County (no parent named) [Haun, *Bertie County Court Minutes,* XIV:160].

iii. Willis, born about 1782, son of Rachel, bound an apprentice shoemaker to Richard Veal on 16 May 1791 [*NCGSJ* XIV:165], head of a Chowan County household of 2 "free colored" in 1820 [NC:118].

iv.   Hill, born about 1783, son of Rachel, bound an apprentice shoemaker to Richard Veal on 16 May 1791 [*NCGSJ* XIV:165], head of a Bertie County household of 15 "other free" in 1820 [NC:54].

5. Rebecca Boon, born say 1768, was living in Bertie County on 7 May 1792 when her seven-year-old son Cary was bound to Richard Veal to be a shoemaker [*NCGSJ* XIV:166]. She was head of a Northampton County household of 8 "free colored" in 1820 [NC:218]. Her children were

i.   Cary, born about 1784.

ii.   ?Benjamin, head of a Bertie County household of 3 "other free" in 1810 [NC:166].

iii. ?Robert, born about 1795, bound an apprentice cartwheel maker to William Sowell on 13 May 1799 (no parent identified) [*NCGSJ* XIV:169].

Other members of the Boon family were

i.   Isaac, born about 1775, registered in Southampton County on 26 August 1816: *age 41, Mulatto, 5 feet 5-1/4 inches, free born* [Register of Free Negroes 1794-1832, no. 1025].

BOOTH FAMILY

1. James Booth, born say 1685, a "free Negro," was living in Isle of Wight County on 27 March 1709 when he was convicted of being part of a conspiracy involving "great numbers of Negro and Indian" slaves in James City, Surry and Isle of Wight counties. He was found guilty of having (prior) knowledge of the conspiracy and of entertaining several of the conspirators at his house. He received twenty-nine lashes [Colonial Papers, VSL microfilm reel 610, folder 20, nos. 11-14, cited by Brown, *Good Wives, Nasty Wenches,* 216]. He may have descended from Elizabeth Booth, daughter of Elizabeth **Kay**/ **Key** of Northumberland County [Northumberland County Record Book 1652-58, 66, 67, 85a, 85b; 1658-66, 27, 43, 44]. He may have been the father of

2   i.   Lewis[1], born say 1720.

2. Lewis[1] Booth, born say 1720, was married to Mary **Allen**, daughter of Joseph **Allen**, on 5 December 1751 when she signed (by mark) the appraisal of her deceased father's Isle of Wight County estate. On 11 July 1754 Lewis, Mary, her sister Judith **Taborn**, and brother Joseph Allen (by Lewis Booth his guardian) sued their brother William **Allen** claiming he had sold slaves belonging to their father's estate valued at 80 pounds [WB 5:391-2; Orders 1749-54, 511; LVA Chancery file 1757-003]. They may have been the parents of

3   i.   Priscilla, born say 1745.
4   ii.   Jesse[1], born say 1750.

3. Priscilla Booth, born say 1745, was the mother of two "base begotten" children Jesse and Sylvia Booth who were ordered bound as apprentices by the Nash County, North Carolina court in April 1778 [Bradley, *Nash County Court Minutes* I:5]. She may have been identical to Priscilla **Tann** who was

married to Benjamin **Tann** when he made his 11 September 1806 Nash County will. Jesse Booth was executor of the will and a neighbor of the **Tann** family [WB 4:42]. Her children were

 i. Jesse[2], born say 1762, perhaps identical to Jesse **Tann**.
 ii. Sylvia, born say 1764.

4. Jesse[1] Booth, born say 1750, was granted two tracts of land in Nash County on 13 March 1780, one for 300 acres on Cooper's Creek adjoining Lammon and another for 137 acres on the south side of the Tar River adjoining Lammon [DB 3:276-7]. He purchased 10 acres of land from his neighbor, Benjamin **Tann**, on 10 February 1804 and was executor of Benjamin's 11 September 1806 Nash County will, proved November 1806 [DB 7:215; WB 4:42]. On 14 August 1809 the Nash County court bound Berry and Elijah **Locus**, orphans of James **Locus**, to him as apprentices [Rackley, *Nash County Court Minutes* VI:71]. He was head of a Nash County household of 8 "other free" in 1800 [NC:90], 6 in 1810 [NC:668], and 7 "free colored" in 1820 [NC:441]. On 20 June 1821 he made a deposition in Nash County that Hannah **Tann** was the daughter of Jesse **Tann** and rightful heir of James **Tann**, a soldier who died while serving in the Revolution [SS 460.2]. He may have been the father of

 i. Lewis[2], head of a Nash County household of 3 "other free" in 1800 [NC:90].
 ii. Archel, head of a Nash County household of 4 "other free" in 1810 [NC:669].
 iii. Rebecca, head of a Nash County household of 3 "free colored" in 1820 [NC:442].

BOSMAN/ BOZMAN FAMILY

1. James[1] Bozman, born say 1745, and his wife Susannah were the parents of Susannah Bozman whose 3 February 1771 birth was registered in St. Peter's Parish, New Kent County. He may have been the son of Lucy Boastman whose illegitimate daughter Sherwood's 5 January 1755 birth was recorded in St. Peter's Parish [NSCDA, *Parish Register of St. Peter's*, 148, 146]. He was head of a New Kent County household of 8 "mulattoes" in 1783 [VA:36], 8 "whites" and a dwelling in 1785 [VA:92] and 7 "other free" in 1810 [VA:745]. He was taxable on 2 horses and 4 cattle in the lower end of Saint Peter's Parish, New Kent County from 1782 to 1801: taxable on a slave in 1796; taxable on 2 free tithables and 2 horses in 1801 and 1802. He apparently died about 1803 since Susannah Bosman was taxable on a free male tithable from 1803 to 1806 [PPTL 1782-1800, frames 9, 87, 93, 109, 142, 159, 180, 202; 1791-1828, frames 264, 279, 293, 304, 317, 328, 341, 353, 367, 380, 392, 405, 417]. He was the father of

 i. ?Harman, born say 1765, taxable on a horse in New Kent County in 1787 and 1788, taxable on his own tithe from 1787 to 1796 and from 1801 to 1803 [PPTL 1782-1800, frames 93, 109, 142, 202; 1791-1828, frame 264, 279, 293, 353, 380].
 ii. ?James[2], Jr., born say 1766, taxable in New Kent County from 1787 to 1820: called James, Jr., from 1787 to 1802; taxable on a slave and 2 horses in 1803; listed as a "M"(ulatto) in 1807 and thereafter; listed with his unnamed wife in 1813; taxable on 2 tithes and a horse in 1820 [PPTL 1782-1800, frames 93, 109, 142, 159, 180, 202; 1791-1828, frames 225, 264, 279, 293, 304, 317, 328, 341, 353, 367, 380, 392, 405, 417, 428, 452, 462, 473, 491, 503, 573].
 iii. Susannah, born 3 February 1771.
 iv. Sarah, born 22 March 1773, "of James and Susannah Bosman" [NSCDA, *Parish Register of St. Peter's*, 148].
2 v. ?John, born say 1782.

    vi. ?Benakin, a "Mulatto" taxable in New Kent County from 1809 to 1820, listed with his unnamed wife in 1813 [PPTL 1791-1828, frames 441, 452, 462, 473, 491, 503, 573], head of a New Kent County household of 4 "other free" in 1810 [VA:746].

2.   John Boasman, born say 1782, was taxable in New Kent County from 1798 to 1802 [PPTL 1791-1828, frames 317, 341, 367], called John Bowsman in 1810, head of a Richmond City household of 6 "other free" [VA:330]. He and his unnamed wife were listed as "Blacks free" in the upper district of Henrico County in 1813 [PPTL 1782-1814, frame 757]. They were probably the parents of

    i.   James, born about 1812, registered in Henrico County on 7 September 1839: *about 27 years of age, a light mulatto man, 5 feet 8 inches, Born free as appears by a certificate of his register from the clerk of the Richmond Hustings Court.* His wife Caroline Boasman registered the same day: *formerly Caroline Ferrell, about 25 years of age, a mulatto woman, 5 feet 2 inches, wife of d° *[Register of Free Negroes and Mulattoes, 1831-1844, p.34, nos. 937, 938].

BOW FAMILY

1.   Sarah **Overton**, born say 1713, was a "Mallatto Woman" freed from her indenture to Edmund Chancey after being allowed by the October 1745 Pasquotank County court to "go up the river to see for her age in a Bible there." She was the mother of three "Mallatto Children," Bob, Jack Spaniard, and Spanial Bow, who were bound to Edmund Chancey until the age of twenty-one years by the Pasquotank County court on 12 July 1738 [Haun, *Pasquotank County Court Minutes 1737-46*, 32, 179, 186].[47] Chancey left a Pasquotank County will on 15 March 1753 by which he bequeathed the remainder of the service of "Jack Spanyerd boe and Spanyoll Boe" to his son Daniel Chancey and left the remainder of the service of Bob Boe, Rachel Boe, and Frank Boe, and her two children to his daughter-in-law Rachel Chancey [Grimes, *Abstract of North Carolina Wills*, 114-7]. Sarah's children were

2   i.   Robert/Bob Bow, born 10 December 1729(?).
3   ii. Frank Bow, born say 1731.
      iii. Rachel, born say 1733.
      iv. Jack Spaniard Bow, born November 1734.
      v.   Spanial Bow, born May 1738.

2.   Robert[1] Bow, born 10 December 1729(?), was the son of Sarah **Overton**, the "Mallatto" servant of Edmund Chancey. He was bound to Edmund Chancey until the age of twenty-one by order of the Pasquotank County court on 12 July 1738. He petitioned the Pasquotank County court for his freedom in October 1760 and won his case on testimony from Jonathan Reding and Lodwick Gray [Minutes 1758-60, Wednesday, October Court, n.p]. In 1769 he was a "Mulatto" taxable in Pasquotank County [SS 837]. He was head of a Pasquotank County household of 5 "other free" in 1790 [NC:27]. He may have been the ancestor of

4   i.   Tully, born say 1765.
      ii. Ephraim L. Bough, born before 1776, head of a Pasquotank County household of 2 "free colored" in 1820 [NC:285].

---

[47]The 12 July 1738 minutes read, "Sarah _____ Mallatto Woman now in the P___ of Ed__ Chancey Vizt: Bob Bow Born ~~March~~ December the 10th. 1729(?) ..." And the court minutes of October 1745 and January 1745/6 record the successful petition of Sarah **Overton** for her release from servitude from Edmund Chancey after the completion of her indenture [Minutes 1737-46, 179, 186].

iii. Joshua, born say 1780, head of a Pasquotank County household of 6 "other free" in 1810 [NC:886].

iv. Henry, born say 1780, called a "free man of Colour" on 10 November 1832 when he purchased 2-1/3 acres of land which had once belonged to Mederit **Nixon**, a "free man of colour." Henry sold this land on 4 April 1834 [DB AA:30; CC:83].

v. Nancy, born say 1790, married James **Overton**, 19 January 1809 Pasquotank County bond, William Spence bondsman.

vi. Levi, born say 1805, purchased 40 acres in Pasquotank County on 25 February 1830 for $360, 33 acres by a deed recorded 13 September 1838, and 90 acres on Little River by deed recorded the same day [Z:333; CC:429, 431]. He married Mary **Mitchell** ("colored"), 3 August 1853 Pasquotank County bond.

vii. Ephraim Bough, head of a Pasquotank County household of 5 "free colored" and 4 slaves in 1820 [NC:285].

3. Frank Bow, born say 1731, was a "Negro ~~Serv~~ Mullatto" servant of Edmund Chancey in July 1748 when the Pasquotank County court bound her "Mullatto" daughter Sue to her master [Haun, *Pasquotank County Court Minutes 1747-53*, 45]. Chancey left the remainder of her service and that of her two unnamed children to Rachel Chancey by his 15 March 1753 Pasquotank County will [Grimes, *Abstract of North Carolina Wills*, 114-7]. She was a "Mullatto Woman" taxable in 1769 in Pasquotank County [SS 837]. She was the mother of

i. Sue, a "Mullatto Daughter," born 1 February 1747/8, ordered bound to Edmund Chancey by the July 1748 Pasquotank County court.

ii. ?Sarah, born about 1751, a three-year-old "Mallatto" girl bound by the Pasquotank County court to Rachel Chancey in October 1754 [Minutes 1754-5, n.p.]. She was head of a Pasquotank County household of 8 "other free" in 1810 [NC:888].

4. Tully[1] Bowe, born say 1765, was head of a Pasquotank County household of 3 "other free" in 1790 [NC:27]. His 31 October 1827 Pasquotank County will, proved in December 1827, gave his land and oxen to his wife Elizabeth and named his children: Robert, Jemima, Timothy, David, Amos, and Tully and grandchild Lacell. His children were

i. Robert[2], born say 1790. His wife Rhoda as the heir of Lemuel **Hall**, received one-fifth part of 29-8/10 acres on Big Flatty Creek. They sold this land on 3 July 1822 [DB W:273].

ii. Jemima.

iii. Timothy.

iv. David, married Sophia Hybert, 1 April 1818 Cumberland County, North Carolina bond, Wily Mask bondsman.

v. Amos.

vi. Abby, identified as the wife of John **Overton** and daughter of Tully and Betty Bowe on 26 October 1830 when she registered as a free person in Pasquotank County [Byrd, *In Full Force and Virtue*, 192].

vii. Tully[2].

BOWDEN FAMILY

1. Mary Bowden, born say 1730, was the "Mulatto Servant" of Augustine Washington on 26 May 1752 when the Westmoreland County court ordered her to serve him an additional year after the completion of her indenture for running away for five months. She may have been living in the household of Robert Sibbalds who was sued by Augustine Washington on 21 February 1752 for detaining his "Mulatto Woman." Sibbalds was acquitted of any wrongdoing on 27 July 1752 [Orders 1750-2, 109, 124]. Mary ran away again and was

called the "Mulatto" servant of Augustine Washington on 19 October 1756 when the Essex County court ordered that she be conveyed from constable to constable to her master's house in Westmoreland County [Essex County Orders 1754-7, 272]. She apparently escaped because on 29 August 1758 the Westmoreland County court ruled that she had stayed away for two years and ordered that she serve Augustine Washington an additional four years and six months [Westmoreland County Orders 1758-61, 1a]. She was apparently identical to "Mol" who was listed in the Westmoreland County estate of Augustine Washington, recorded 30 November 1762:

Mol a Woman age unknown free at 31 years old __
Pat free at 31 years old 25 pounds
Nan a Mulatto free at 31 years old and title Disputable __
[Inventories of Estates no. 4, 1756-67, 180].

Mary was the mother of

  i.   Martha, born say 1750, "Mulatto" daughter of Mary Bowden bound apprentice by the churchwardens of Washington Parish, Westmoreland County, to Augustine Washington on 29 January 1750/1 [Orders 1750-2, 31].
  ii. ?Mary, head of a Spotsylvania County household of 8 "other free" in 1810 [VA:103b].

BOWERS FAMILY

1. Elizabeth Bowers, born say 1712, was a "Mulatto" whose son James Bowers was bound apprentice in Brunswick County, Virginia, on 2 August 1739 and whose unnamed daughter was bound to Thomas Powell in Brunswick County in June 1742 [Orders 1732-41, 254; 1741-83, 118]. She was the mother of

  2   i.   ?Sarah, born say 1733.
  3   ii. ?Mary, born say 1735.
       iii. James, born before 2 August 1739. He may have been identical to James **Shoemaker**. See the **Shoemaker** history. There was also a James Bowers who was head of a Kent County, Maryland household of 4 "other free" and a slave in 1800 [MD:169].
  4   iv. ?Lucy, born say 1754.

2. Sarah **Shoemaker**, born say 1733, was living in Craven County, North Carolina, in May 1754 when the court issued a summons for her to show cause why her child John Bowers should not be bound out [Haun, *Craven County Court Minutes*, IV:231]. She was the mother of

  i.   John Bowers, born before May 1754.
  ii. ?Saul Bowers, born say 1760, head of a Craven County household of 3 "other free" in 1790 [NC:131], perhaps identical to Paul Bowers, head of a Kent County, Maryland household of 4 "other free" in 1800 [MD:157].
  iii. ?Solomon Bowers, bondsman for the 2 April 1803 Craven County marriage of William **Powers** and Lucretia **Lewis**.

3. Mary Bowers, born say 1735, was sued for a debt of 15 pounds currency in Southampton County court by the churchwardens of Nottoway Parish on 9 January 1756, probably for having an illegitimate child. On 10 September 1761 the court ordered the churchwardens to bind out her son Giles Bowers, a poor child [Orders 1754-9, 204, 226; 1759-63, 139]. She was the mother of

  5   i.   Giles, born say 1755.

4. Lucy Bowers, born say 1754, was living in Brunswick County, Virginia, on 22 December 1777 when the court ordered the churchwardens of Meherrin Parish to bind out her "natural son" Balaam [Orders 1774-82, 178]. She was called the mother of Burwell Bowers on 12 September 1782 when he

complained to the Southampton County court against his master Joshua Harris [Orders 1778-84, 251, 254]. Her son Benjamin registered as a "free Negro" in Southampton County in 1794. Lucy was a "Mulatto" taxable on a free male tithable in St. Luke's Parish, Southampton County, in 1803 and 1804 [PPTL 1792-1806, frames 617, 686]. Her children were

    i.   Balaam, bound apprentice in Brunswick County on 22 December 1777.

   ii.   Burwell, born say 1770, complained to the Southampton County court against his master Joshua Harris on 12 September 1782.

  iii.   Benjamin, born about 1774, registered as a "free Negro" in Southampton County on 28 November 1794: *reputed son of Lucy Bowers a free woman of this County abt. 20 years old 5 feet 6 inches high, a Mulattoe* [Register of Free Negroes 1794-1832, no. 92].

5.   Giles Bowers, born say 1755, was taxable in Isle of Wight County from 1782 to 1809, listed as a "F.N." in 1792 and thereafter, called Jiles Bowser from 1804 to 1806 [PPTL 1782-1810, frames 4, 27, 45, 60, 74, 89, 242, 271, 346, 390, 428, 473, 491, 652, 673, 715, 771, 791]. He may have been the father of

    i.   James[2], born say 1790, a "F.N." taxable in Isle of Wight County from 1807 to 1810 [PPTL 1782-1810, frames 771, 790, 846].

BOWLES FAMILY

1.   Amy Bowles, born say 1725, was an illegitimate "Free Mulatto" who was bound by the churchwardens of St. Martin's Parish, Hanover County, to serve John Williams and his wife Mary until the age of thirty-one. Her daughter Jane Bowles sued for her freedom in Louisa County in 1778 [Orders 1774-82, 239]. They may have been the descendants of Ann Bowles who was indicted for fornication in York County on 24 June 1687. Her case was continued, but the outcome was not recorded [DOW 7:347; 8:3]. Amy was taxable on 2 horses and 8 cattle in Albemarle County in 1782 [PPTL, 1782-1799, frame 6]. Amy's was the mother of

    i.   Jane, born about 1750, sued for her freedom from the executors of James Michie, deceased, in Louisa County court on 11 May 1778. The court determined that she was the daughter of Amy Bowles, a "Mulatto Bastard child," who was bound by the churchwardens of St. Martin's Parish to John Williams and his wife Mary. Williams' descendants sold Jane to James Michie. Jane was about twenty-nine years old on 10 May 1779 when the court ordered her released from servitude because she had never been indentured [Orders 1774-82, 194, 197, 213, 229, 239]. She was taxable on a horse in Fredericksville Parish, Albemarle County, from 1802 to 1804 [PPTL, 1800-1813, frames 113, 156, 202].

   ii.   ?Zachariah, born about 1754, taxable in Fredericksville Parish, Albemarle County, from 1791 to 1813: taxable on a horse in 1795; taxable on a horse and stud horse in 1810; listed as a "Mulatto" in 1812 and 1813 [PPTL, 1782-1799, frames 292, 343, 382, 446, 477, 512, 550, 585; 1800-1813, frames 24, 68, 113, 156, 202, 245, 291, 339, 382, 429, 473, 517, 562]. He sold property by indenture to Samuel Carr in Albemarle County court on 1 December 1800 and Carr proved an indenture to him on the same date [Orders 1800-1, 243-4]. He was head of an Albemarle County household of 2 "other free" in 1810 [VA:185]. He was sixty-five years old on 30 March 1819 when he appeared in Henrico County court to apply for a pension for his services in the Revolution. He stated that he enlisted on 19 January 1777 in Hanover County. He was a rough carpenter with a large family, 45 acres of very poor land, a work horse, cow and a few hogs and household furniture. His wife was fifty years old and they had three unnamed sons residing with them: twenty-four years old, twenty-two years old, and seventeen years old. He was placed on the Virginia Roll on 26 February 1819 [M850-109, frames 460-3].

2   iii. ?Susanna, born say 1758.

      iv. ?Bartlett, born say 1762, taxable in Louisa County in 1782 and 1785 [PPTL, 1782-1814] and taxable in Fredericksville Parish, Albemarle County, from 1793 to 1813: taxable on 2 horses in 1793, listed as a "Mulatto" in 1812 and 1813 [PPTL, 1782-1799, frames 382, 446, 477, 512, 550, 585; 1800-1813, frames 24, 68, 113, 156, 202, 245, 291, 339, 382, 429, 473, 517, 562]. He was head of an Albemarle County household of 2 "free colored" in 1820.

      v. ?Stephen, say 1763, served in the Revolution from Albemarle County [Jackson, *Virginia Negro Soldiers,* 31].

      vi. ?Lucy[1], born say 1764, married Charles **Barnett**, 7 September 1785 Albemarle County bond, George **Mann** bondsman.

      vii. ?John, born say 1767, said to have eloped with a "mulatto" woman named Ursula and her nine-year-old daughter Rachel "or more probably were married off from Benjamin D. Willis by a black freeman" according to the 8 November 1797 issue of the *Virginia Gazette & General Advertiser.* The ad went on to say that John had been a waterman and they were presumed to be in the neighborhood of Milton or Charlottesville as it was said Bowles' mother lived near Charlottesville. John was a "free Negro" taxable in St. Ann's Parish, Albemarle County, from 1799 to 1813: called a "Mulatto" from 1810 to 1813 [PPTL, 1782-1799, frame 585; 1800-1813, frames 4, 46, 93, 136, 178, 227, 269, 363, 410, 456, 499, 541] and head of an Albemarle County household of 6 "other free" in 1810 [VA:182].

      viii. ?Martha, born say 1768, spinster, married Griffin **Butler**, 24 October 1790 Albemarle County bond, Zachariah Bowles bondsman. Griffin was head of an Albemarle County household of 10 "other free" and a slave in 1810 [VA:186].

      ix. ?Nancy, born say 1772, married Robert **Battles**, 12 December 1793 Albemarle County bond, Charles **Barnett** bondsman.

2.   Susanna Bowles, born say 1758, was taxable on a horse in Fredericksville Parish, Albemarle County, from 1791 to 1813: taxable on 1 free male tithe from 1801 to 1803, 2 in 1805 and 1806, 3 in 1813; called a "Mulatto" from 1805 to 1807 and in 1813 [PPTL, 1800-1813, frames 68, 113, 156, 202, 245, 291, 339, 382, 429, 473, 517, 562]. She was the mother of

      i. ?Francis, born say 1776, taxable in Fredericksville Parish, Albemarle County, from 1802 to 1813: called a "Mulatto" from 1810 to 1813 [PPTL, 1800-1813, frames 113, 155, 382, 456, 473, 518, 541].

      ii. ?David, born say 1782, a "free Negro" taxable in St. Ann's Parish, Albemarle County, from 1801 to 1803 [PPTL, 1800-1813, frames 46, 93, 136].

      iii. Jacob, born say 1785, taxable in Fredericksville Parish, Albemarle County, in 1806 and 1813: called "Suca son" in 1806; called a "Mulatto from 1810 to 1813 [PPTL, 1800-1813, frames 291, 381, 428, 472, 517].

      iv. ?James, born say 1787, a "Mulatto" taxable in Fredericksville Parish, Albemarle County, from 1809 to 1813 [PPTL, 1800-1813, frames 381, 428, 456, 472].

      v. ?Peter, born say 1790, taxable in Fredericksville Parish, Albemarle County, in 1809, 1812, and 1813: called a "Mulatto" in 1812 and 1813 [PPTL, 1800-1813, frames 382, 518, 561]. He was head of an Albemarle County household of 2 "free colored" in 1820.

Other members of the Bowles family were

    i.   William Bolls, born say 1753, a "Negro shoemaker" who was jailed in Middlesex County according to the 21 September 1775 issue of the *Virginia Gazette*.

    ii.   Lucy[2], head of an Albemarle County household of 6 "other free" in 1810 [VA:185].

    iii.   Caty, head of an Albemarle County household of 4 "other free" in 1810 [VA:185].

    iv.   Sophia, born about 1796, registered as a free Negro in Goochland County on 18 January 1819: *about 23d year, of light yellow Complexion, about 5 feet four inches high...free born* [Register of Free Negroes, no.228].

    v.   Thomas, taxable in Fredericksville Parish, Albemarle County, in 1801 [PPTL, 1800-1813, frame 69], a "free Negro" living in Dumfries on 15 August 1806 when he was listed among a group of whites and free African Americans who were accused of uniting for the purpose of stealing, plundering, etc. [Johnston, *Race Relations*, 57].

BOWMAN FAMILY

Members of the Bowman family were

    i.   Thomas, born say 1730, living in North Carolina on 13 March 1752 when Robert West, Sr., placed a notice in the North Carolina Gazette of New Bern:

        Ran away from the subscribers, on Roanoke River, a Negro fellow, named Thomas Boman, a very good blacksmith, near 6 feet high, he can read, write and cyper, Whoever will apprehend him shall be paid 12 Pistoles, besides what the law allows [Fouts, *NC Gazette of New Bern*, I:3].

        About twenty years later Thomas Boman was a taxable "free Molatto" in John Moore's household in the Bertie County tax list of 1771, 1772, and 1774 [CR 10.702.1, Box 13].

    ii.   Robert, born say 1735, "a molato" taxable in Andrew Duche's household in Colonel William Craford's 1756 list of tithables in Norfolk County, Virginia [Wingo, *Norfolk County Tithables, 1751-65*, 100].

1   iii.   William, born say 1740.

    iv.   James[1], a soldier in the Virginia Line who died before 6 October 1783 when an affidavit by Betty **Morris**, a "free Mulatto woman," that William Bowman was his brother and only surviving heir was certified by the Henrico County court [Orders 1781-4, 439].

    v.   Charles[1], born say 1762, taxable in Henrico County on a horse and 2 cattle in 1783 [PPTL 1782-1814, frame 21], taxable in Chesterfield County on a horse in 1786 [PPTL, 1786-1811, frame 3], taxable in Henrico County in 1794 [PPTL 1782-1814, frame 315] and taxable in Chesterfield County on 3 tithes in a list of "Mulattoes and free Negroes" in 1809 and 1810 [PPTL, 1786-1811, frames 753, 799].

2   vi.   Edward[1], born say 1764.

3   vii.   Francis[1], born say 1767.

    viii.   James[3], a "F.N." taxable in Isle of Wight County in 1790 and 1791: his tax charged to Francis Boykin in 1790 [PPTL 1782-1810, frames 194, 212] and taxable in adjoining Surry County from 1794 to 1816: called a "free Negro" in 1794, 1796 and 1811; listed with 4 "free Negroes & Mulattoes above the age of 16" in 1813 [PPTL, 1791-1816, frames 177, 253, 397, 438, 518, 610, 647, 685, 725, 848].

    ix.   Polly, head of a Henrico County household of 7 "other free" in 1810 [VA:1008].

1. William[1] Bowman, born say 1740, a "Mulatto," was charged with felony in Chesterfield County on 10 October 1767. His case was referred to the General Court [Orders 4:146]. Betty **Morris**, a "free Mulatto woman," appeared before the mayor of Richmond, John Beckley, and made oath that William Bowman was the only surviving brother and heir at law of James Bowman, deceased, late a soldier in the Virginia Line. The affidavit was certified in Henrico County court on 6 October 1783 [Orders 1781-4, 439]. He may have been the ancestor of

    i.   James[2], born say 1760, taxable in Henrico County on a horse and 6 cattle from 1783 to 1785 [PPTL 1782-1814, frames 21, 43, 69], taxable in Charles City County on a tithe, a horse and 6 cattle from 1786 to 1800 [PPTL, 1788-1814]. He was living in Henrico County on 20 June 1804 when he sold 30 acres in Charles City County where William Day was then living for 31 pounds [DB 5:56].

    ii.   John, born say 1764, taxable in Charles City County in 1785, taxable on 2 tithes in 1798 and 1799 and 1 in 1800 [PPTL, 1788-1814]. He may have been the husband of Peggy Bowman, illegitimate daughter of Dixon **Brown** who gave her 10 acres of land where she was then living by his 24 January 1811 Charles City County will which was proved 18 January 1821 [WB 2:471]. In October 1826 she and other heirs of her sister Susannah **Harris** appointed James **Brown** to sell Susannah's land [DB 7:371].

4   iii. William[2], born say 1768.

    iv.   Nelson, born say 1775, taxable in Charles City County in 1799, a "Mulattoe" taxable in 1814 [PPTL, 1788-1814]. He was head of a Charles City County household of 5 "free colored" in 1820 [VA:10].

5   v.   Wiley, born say 1778.

6   vi.   Richard, born say 1780.

    vii. William[3], born say 1781, taxable in Charles City County from 1805 to 1810 (called William Bowman, Jr.) [PPTL, 1788-1814].

7   viii. Samuel, born say 1785.

    ix.   Oliver, born say 1787, a "free mulatto" declared exempt from taxes by the Charles City County court on 15 June 1837 [Minutes 1830-7, 322].

8   x.   Edward[2], born say 1792.

2. Edward[1] Bowman, born say 1764, was presented by the Henrico County court on 3 May 1785 for failing to list his tithables [Orders 1784-7, 170]. He married Catherine **Scott**, "daughter of Robert and Catherine Scott," 28 December 1786 Henrico County, Virginia bond, John and Andrew **Scott** surety. He was taxable on a horse in the lower district of Henrico County from 1787 to 1814: called a "free Negro starting in 1806, a "Mulatto" in 1809 [PPTL 1782-1814, frames 100, 158, 174, 231, 249, 289, 302, 315, 327, 340, 351, 387, 420, 431, 460, 509, 550, 571, 611, 679, 765, 783]. He and Francis Bowman were taxed jointly on 55 acres in the lower district of Henrico County from 1802 to 1816, called "free Mulattos" in 1803 and 1805 [Land Tax List 1799-1816]. He was head of a Henrico County household of 10 "other free" in 1810 [VA:1008]. His children may have been

    i.   Martin, born about 1792, obtained a certificate of freedom in Chesterfield County on 8 February 1813: *twenty one years old, bright yellow complexion, born free* [Register of Free Negroes 1804-53, no. 182].

    ii.   Samuel, born about 1793, obtained a certificate of freedom in Chesterfield County on 12 September 1814: *twenty one years old, bright mulatto complexion, born free* [Register of Free Negroes 1804-53, no. 228].

    iii. Edward[3]/ Ned, born say 1794, married Betsey **Otter**, "free persons of colour," 7 March 1815 Chesterfield County bond, Martin Bowman security.

3. Francis[1] Bowman, born say 1767, was taxable in the lower district of Henrico County from 1785 to 1807: called a "free Negro" starting in 1806 when he was listed with son Charles [PPTL 1782-1814, frames 77, 82, 100, 158, 174, 249, 289, 302, 315, 327, 340, 351, 387, 420, 431, 460, 509, 551]. On 7 August 1790 the Henrico County court dismissed his suit against Johnson **Smith** because his attorney had not been instructed on the premises, and the same court ordered that he receive 25 lashes for hog stealing [Orders 1789-91, 368]. He and Francis Bowman were taxed jointly on 55 acres in the lower district of Henrico County from 1802 to 1816, called "free Mulattos" in 1803 and 1805 [Land Tax List 1782-1816]. He was head of a Charles City County household of 4 "other free" in 1810 [VA:98] and a "Mulattoe" taxable in 1813 [PPTL, 1788-1814]. On 17 June 1824 his son Champion Bowman chose him as his guardian in Charles City County court [Minutes 1823-9, 60]. He was the father of

    i.   Charles, born say 1790, taxable in his father's Henrico County household in 1806.

    ii. Champion, chose his father Francis Bowman as his guardian in 1824.

4. William[2] Bowman, born say 1768, was taxable in Charles City County in 1789 [PPTL, 1783-7] and taxable in the lower district of Henrico County in 1794 [PPTL 1782-1814, frame 315]. He was taxable in Charles City County on 3 tithes in 1798, 2 in 1799 and 1800, 3 in 1801 (called William Bowman, Sr.), and was a "Mulattoe" taxable in 1813 [PPTL, 1788-1814]. He was head of a Charles City County household of 7 "free colored" in 1820 [VA:4]. His wife Eliza registered in Charles City County on 20 October 1831: *wife of Wm Bowman, of bright complexion, 45 years old, born free in this county* [Minutes 1830-7, 80]. He was the father of

    i.   Catherine, born about 1805, obtained a certificate of freedom in Charles City County on 19 July 1827: *daughter of Wm Bowman, now Catherine Green, a mulatto woman, about twenty two years of age, 5 feet 2-1/2 inches, born free in this county* [Minutes 1823-9, 239; Register of Free Negroes 1835-64, p.6, no. 202].

    ii. Archer, born about 1811, registered in Charles City County on 20 October 1831: *son of William Bowman, a bright mulatto lad, 20 years old, born free in this county* [Minutes 1830-7, 80].

5. Wiley Bowman, born say 1778, was taxable in Charles City County in 1799, a "Mulattoe" taxable in 1814 [PPTL, 1788-1814] and head of a Charles City County household of 3 "other free" in 1810 [VA:957]. He was the father of

    i.   Edward[4], born about 1810, registered in Charles City County on 16 August 1832: *son of Wilie Bowman, a mulatto man, twenty two years old, born free in this county* [Minutes 1830-7, 117].

    ii. Fanny, born 8 March 1815, registered in Charles City County on 16 August 1832: *daughter of said Wilie, seventeen years old 8 March 1832, born free in this county* [Minutes 1830-7, 117].

    iii. Nancy, born 28 May 1817, registered in Charles City County on 16 August 1832: *daughter of said Wilie, fifteen years old 28 May 1832, mulatto girl, born free in this county* [Minutes 1830-7, 117].

    iv. Maria, born 18 March 1819, registered in Charles City County on 16 August 1832: *son of said Wilie, thirteen years old 18 March 1832, born free in this county* [Minutes 1830-7, 117].

    v.   Charles[2], born 18 March 1819, registered in Charles City County on 16 August 1832: *son of said Wilie, thirteen years old 18 March 1832, born free in this county* [Minutes 1830-7, 117].

    vi. Christiana, born 18 October 1823, registered in Charles City County on 16 August 1832: *daughter of said Wilie, eight years old 18 October 1831, mulatto girl, born free in this county* [Minutes 1830-7, 117].

6. Richard[1] Bowman, born say 1780, was taxable in Charles City County in
    1802, a "Mulattoe" taxable in 1813 and 1814 [PPTL, 1788-1814] and head of
    a Charles City County household of 7 "free colored" in 1820 [VA:5]. He was
    paid 4 shillings on 18 June 1807 for digging the grave of John Blanks of
    Charles City County [WB 2:59]. He was the father of
    i.   Susanna, born 28 October 1803, obtained a certificate of freedom in
         Charles City County on 19 July 1832: *daughter of Richard Bowman,
         Sr., bright mulatto woman, 28 years old 28 October last* [Minutes
         1830-7, 43].
    ii. Francis[2]/ Frank, born 15 June 1806, obtained a certificate of freedom
         in Charles City County on 21 July 1825: *son of Richard Bowman, of
         bright complexion, nineteen years old 15th of last month, 5 feet 5-1/8
         inches, born free in this county* [Minutes 1823-9, 127].
    iii. Richard[2], born in September 1811, obtained a certificate of freedom in
         Charles City County on 21 July 1831: *son of Dick Bowman, 19 years
         of age last September, bright mulatto* [Minutes 1830-7, 69].
    iv. Frances T., born in April 1815, obtained a certificate of freedom in
         Charles City County on 20 October 1831: *daughter of Richard
         Bowman, Sr., a bright mulatto girl, sixteen years of age last April*
         [Minutes 1830-7, 79].

7. Samuel Bowman, born say 1784, was taxable in Charles City County in 1805
    and a "Mulattoe" taxable in 1813 [PPTL, 1788-1814]. He was the father of
    i.   John, born about 1806, registered in Charles City County on 17
         November 1831: *son of Sam Bowman, a mulatto man about 25 years
         old, born free in this county.* His wife Nancy registered on 20
         September 1832 [Minutes 1830-7, 80, 123].

8. Edward[2] Bowman, born say 1792, was a "Mulattoe" taxable in Charles City
    County in 1813 [PPTL, 1788-1814] and head of a Charles City County
    household of 5 "free colored" in 1820 [VA:4]. He was married to Catherine
    Brown by 13 June 1825 when he was paid $20 as her legacy of a bed and
    furniture [WB 3:115]. He was granted administration on the estate of Mary
    Harris, deceased, on 17 May 1832 [Minutes 1830-7, 107]. He, John Bowman,
    and Abraham **Brown** were buyers at the sale of the estate [WB 4:29-30].
    James **Brown** (son of Dixon) and others brought a chancery suit against
    Edward's children Erasmus, Susan, Rebecca, and Elizabeth on 19 February
    1835 [Minutes 1830-7, 223]. He was the father of
    i.   Erasmus, born February 1815, registered in Charles City County on 17
         November 1831: *son of Edward Bowman, yellowish complexion, 16
         years old February last* [Minutes 1830-9, 83].
    ii. Susan M., born 28 December 1817, registered in Charles City County
         on 17 November 1831: *daughter of Edward Bowman, a mulato girl, 13
         years old 28 December last* [Minutes 1830-9, 84].
    iii. Rebecca M., born 20 July 1820, registered in Charles City County on
         17 November 1831: *daughter of Edward Bowman, a mulato girl, 11
         years old 20 July last* [Minutes 1830-9, 84].
    iv. Delly F., born 5 April 1823, registered in Charles City County on 17
         November 1831: *daughter of Edward Bowman, yellowish complexion,
         8 years old 5 April last* [Minutes 1830-9, 84].
    v.   Betty **Byrd**, born 7 August 1827, registered in Charles City County on
         17 November 1831: *daughter of Edward Bowman, yellowish
         complexion, 4 years old 7 August last* [Minutes 1830-9, 84].

BOWMER FAMILY

1. An unnamed Indian woman, born say 1730, was the mother of three children living in Antrim Parish in September 1765 when the Halifax County, Virginia court ordered them bound to William Thompson [Orders 1764-6, 226]. She was the mother of
2   i.   Fanny, born about 1756.
       ii.   Veice, born say 1760.
3   iii.   Archer, born about 1763.

2. Fanny Bomar, born about 1756, was living in Halifax County, Virginia, in June 1787 when the court bound out her illegitimate children Philip, Abram, William and Samuel Bomar to Colonel William Thompson [Pleas 1786-8, 171]. Her children were
       i.   ?Pat, born say 1772, mother of Herbert Bomar who was bound to William Thompson in Halifax County in December 1807 [Pleas 1806-7, 478]. He registered in Halifax County on 26 June 1824: *Herbert Bowman, aged about 34 years, five feet six and a half inches high, of a yellow complexion...born of a free woman of Colour* [Registers of Free Negroes, 1802-1831, no. 74].
       ii.   Mary, born say 1774, "Bastard child of Fanny Bomar," bound by the Halifax County court to Elizabeth Moody on 21 June 1787 [Pleas 1786-8, 172], perhaps identical to Massey Bowman, who registered in Halifax County in 1834. Her son Phil Bomar was bound by the court to John W. Scott in August 1816. He registered in Halifax County on 27 January 1823: *aged about 23 years six feet two inches high, of a yellow complexion* [Registers of Free Negroes, 1802-1831, no. 67].
       iii.   Philip[1] Bomer, an "Indian" taxable in the northern district of Halifax County, Virginia, in 1798 [PPTL, 1782-1799, frame 765].
       iv.   Samuel, born about 1786, registered in Halifax County on 1 October 1814: *Samuel Bowman, aged twenty eight years, about six feet and six eighths of an inch high, yellow complexion and was born of a free woman...registered as a free Mulatto* [Registers of Free Negroes, 1802-1831, no. 50].
       v.   ?Elijah, born about 1786, registered in Halifax County on 32 February 1822: *Elijah Bowman, aged 36 years five feet 11 inches high of a yellow complexion... born of a free woman* [Registers of Free Negroes, 1802-1831, no. 64].

3. Archer Bowmer, born about 1763, was taxable in the northern district of Halifax County, Virginia, from 1791 to 1799, called a "FN" in 1795 [PPTL, 1782-1799, frames 368, 391, 557]. He married Nancy **Bird**, 17 August 1804 Halifax County bond. He registered in Halifax County on 20 May 1827: *Archer Boman, Sr., a dark mulatto man about 64 years of age, five feet 6-1/2 inches high, grey wooly hair, was born free.* Nancy registered the same day: *a dark mulatto woman about 40 years of age, five feet 3 inches high, black bushy hair, born free.* They were probably the parents of Drunilla and Cinderrilla Boman who registered the same day:
       i.   Drunilla, born about 1804, registered on 20 May 1827: *light mulatto woman, five feet one inch high, black wooly hair* [Registers of Free Negroes, 1802-1831, nos. 114-117].
       ii.   Cinderella, born about 1804, registered on 20 May 1827: *light mulatto woman, five feet one inch high, black wooly hair* [Registers of Free Negroes, 1802-1831, nos. 114-117].

BOWSER FAMILY

1. Anthony[1] Bowser, born say 1650, was called "Tony Bowze Negro late Servt to Major Gennll Bennett Deceased" when he petitioned the Virginia General Court in March 1676 for his freedom which was granted on his payment of 800 pounds of tobacco yearly [Catterall, *Judicial Cases Concerning American Slavery* I:81]. He was probably the ancestor of
    - i.   Anthony[2], petitioned the Isle of Wight County court on 11 August 1748 for his freedom from Martha Parker. His petition was rejected on hearing the arguments of both parties [Orders 1746-52, 120].
2 - ii. Mary, born say 1731.
3 - iii. Sarah, born say 1740.
4 - iv. Thomas[1], born say 1745.
5 - v.   Pat, born say 1747.
6 - vi. James[1], born say 1750.
    - vii. James[2], born say 1763, head of a Fayette District, Moore County, North Carolina household of 1 "other free," 1 white female, and 1 white male under sixteen years of age in 1790 [NC:44].

2. Mary Bowzer, born say 1731, had been the servant of Henry Best prior to 25 January 1762 according to the Vestry minutes of Suffolk Parish, Nansemond County [Hopkins, *Suffolk Parish Vestry Book 1749-84*, 24]. She may have been the mother of
7 - i.   Olive, born say 1760.

3. Sarah Bowser, born say 1740, was living in Isle of Wight County on 7 February 1760 when her child Betty Tale (no race mentioned) was bound apprentice, perhaps the same "Betty a Negro Girl, a child of Sarah a Free Negro," who was ordered bound out two months earlier on 6 December 1759 [Orders 1759-63, 114, 98]. Her children were
    - i.   ?Richard[1], born say 1757, listed in the 1778 tax list for Isle of Wight as a recusant who declined or neglected to take the oath of allegiance to the state and was thus subject to double taxation [*WMQ* 25:170]. He was taxable on 2 horses in Southampton County in 1782 [PPTL 1782-92, frame 507] and taxable in Isle of Wight County from 1782 to 1806: taxable on a horse in 1782 when he was listed as a "free Mulatto;" listed as a "F.N." in 1790 and thereafter; taxable on a horse and 2 cattle in 1785; taxable on a horse from 1786 to 1794 [PPTL 1782-1810, frames 4, 56, 75, 89, 146, 226, 271, 346, 418, 473, 523, 652, 715].
    - ii. Betty Tale, born say 1759, daughter of Sarah Bowzer.
8 - iii. ?Philip, born say 1760.
    - iv. ?Dorothy, born say 1768, a "poor Mulato," no parent named, ordered bound out in Isle of Wight County on 1 May 1783. She was called Dolly Bowzer when she married Sampson **Bones**, 1 June 1787 Isle of Wight County bond, Scott Hollowell surety, 2 June marriage. Sampson **Bones** was head of an Isle of Wight County household of 10 "other free" in 1810 [VA:36].
    - v.   ?Charity, a "poor Mulato," no parent named, ordered bound out in Isle of Wight County on 1 May 1783 [Orders 1780-3, 178].
    - vi. ?Martha, a "poor Mulato," no parent named, ordered bound out in Isle of Wight County on 1 May 1783 [Orders 1780-3, 178].
    - vii. ?Ann, a "poor Mulato," no parent named, ordered bound out in Isle of Wight County on 1 May 1783 [Orders 1780-3, 178].
    - viii. Jeremiah, orphan of Sarah Bowzer ordered bound out in Isle of Wight County on 6 August 1778 [Orders 1772-1780, 431].

ix. Willis, born say 1785, a "poor Mulatto child of Sarah Bowzer," ordered bound apprentice to Anthony Holladay in Isle of Wight County on 6 January 1795 [Orders 1795-97, 15].

4. Thomas[1] Bowser, born say 1745, was taxable in Hertford County on 2 persons in 1768, 3 in 1769, and taxed on a mare and a cow in District 3 of Hertford County in 1779 [Fouts, *Tax Receipt Book*, 58; GA 30.1]. He was head of a Hertford County household of 9 "other free" in 1790 [NC:26]. On 11 December 1792 Peter Bird placed a notice in the North Carolina Central and Fayetteville Gazette accusing Thomas of stealing his horse:

    Stolen from the subscriber at Wake Court House a bright bay horse by a free mulatto man of the name Thomas Bowser, a blacksmith [Fouts, *Newspapers of Edenton, Fayetteville, and Hillsborough*, 64].

    He married (second?) Ann **Milton**, 28 December 1792 Southampton County, Virginia bond, Randolph **Milton** surety. Ann was the daughter of Elisha **Milton** who mentioned her in his 1 December 1788 Southampton County will, proved 21 August 1797 [WB 5:2]. She was called "Ann Milton, alias Ann Bowser," in a codicil to the 20 February 1791 Southampton County will of Ethelred Taylor, recorded 14 July 1791. The will also mentioned Patsey **Milton**, "so called daughter of Ann Milton, Jr." [WB 5:437]. Thomas was appointed guardian of Patsey **Milton**, orphan of Ann **Milton**, by the Southampton County court on 15 January 1798 [Minutes 1793-9, 321]. He was head of a Halifax County, North Carolina household of 4 in 1800 [NC:288], 7 in 1810 [NC:7], and 9 "free colored" in 1820 [NC:142]. His children may have been

    i. Randal, head of an "other free" household in Moore's District of Hertford County in 1800.
9   ii. James[3], born say 1775.
    iii. Charles, born say 1780, head of a Halifax County, North Carolina household of 7 "other free" in 1810 [NC:7].
    iv. Patsey, mentioned in the 1788 Southampton County will of her grandfather Elisha **Milton** [WB 5:2].
    v. Isaac, head of a Halifax County, North Carolina household of 6 "free colored" in 1820 [NC:142].

5. Pat Bowser, born say 1748, was living in Isle of Wight County on 4 December 1777 and 6 June 1782 when her son Adam Bowzer was bound apprentice. On 7 February 1782 the court ordered the churchwardens to bind out her "poor mulatto" children Jack, Bett, Fan, Harrison, Patt, Wilson and Eady Bowzer [Orders 1772-80, 417; 1780-3, 42, 62]. Her children were

    i. Adam, born say 1767, "a poor Mulattoe" bound apprentice in Isle of Wight County on 5 March 1778 and called "son of Pat" when he was again ordered bound out on 6 June 1782 [Orders 1772-80, 417; 1780-83, 62]. He was a "F.N." taxable in Isle of Wight County from 1788 to 1802 [PPTL 1782-1810, frames 114, 195, 212, 257, 286, 310, 361, 404, 455, 508, 558], and a "free Negro" taxable in Nottoway Parish, Southampton, from 1803 to 1812, listed his wife Tricy and taxable on 2 horses in 1813 [PPTL 1792-1806, frames 648; 1807-21, frames 9, 90, 130, 248, 337]. He was head of a Southampton County household of 7 "other free" in 1810 [VA:74]. On 16 February 1818 the Southampton County court rescinded the order of the previous court to bind out his son Merix Bowser [Minutes 1816-9, unpaged].
    ii. Jack, born say 1769, ordered bound out on 7 February 1782.
    iii. Bett, born say 1771, ordered bound out on 7 February 1782.
    iv. Fan, born say 1773, ordered bound out on 7 February 1782.
    v. Harrison, born say 1775, ordered bound out on 7 February 1782.

    vi.   Patt, born say 1777, ordered bound out on 7 February 1782.

   vii.   Wilson, born say 1779, ordered bound out on 7 February 1782.

  viii.   Eady, born say 1780, a "poor mulatto" child of Pat ordered bound apprentice on 7 February 1782.

6.   James[1] Bowser, born say 1750, was a Norfolk County, Virginia tithable in 1767 and was living in Benjamin Hodges' Norfolk County household in Great Bridge District in 1770 [Wingo, *Norfolk County Tithables, 1766-80*, 3, 100]. He was listed in the 1778 tax list for Isle of Wight as a recusant who declined or neglected to take the oath of allegiance to the state and was thus subject to double taxation [*WMQ* 25:170]. He was head of his own household, living alone in Isle of Wight County in 1782 [VA:32] and taxable there from 1782 to 1800: a "free Mulatto" taxable on 2 horses in 1782; taxable on slaves Bridget (over the age of 16), Judith and Nan (age 12-16) in 1785; taxable on Bridget, Judith, Nancy and Hannah in 1786; taxable on a slave over the age of 16 and 3 slaves aged 12-16 in 1787 (called James Bowers); a "F.N." taxable on a slave above aged 16 and a slave aged 12-16 in 1793 and 1794; a "F.N." taxable on a slave over the age of 16 in 1795; taxable on 2 slaves above the age 16 and a slave aged 12-16 in 1798 [PPTL 1782-1810, frames 4, 61, 89, 135, 181, 241, 331, 346, 418, 428, 491]. He was a "yellow" complexioned soldier born in Charles City County who was living in Nansemond County when he was listed in the size roll of troops who enlisted at Chesterfield Courthouse [The Chesterfield Supplement cited by NSDAR, *African American Patriots*, 148]. He made a nuncupative Isle of Wight County will on 5 September 1800 leaving his whole estate to his wife Bridget Bowzer [WB 11:284]. Bridget was a "F.N." taxable in Isle of Wight County from 1801 to 1813: taxable on 2 slaves in 1801; 3 in 1802; 2 in 1803; 3 in 1804, 2 in 1805 and 1806, listed with Philip Bowser in 1809 when they were taxable on a slave [PPTL 1782-1810, frames 523, 577, 595, 652, 673, 715, 791]. Nathaniel and Thomas Bowser testified on 17 October 1833 that Nathaniel Bowser, Thomas Bowser, and Betsy Bowser, Moses **Ash**, Caroline **Ash**, Lydia **Ash**, Thomas **Ash**, and Curtis **Ash** were the only heirs of James Bowser who had served in the Revolution in 1782. In 1835 they received bounty land scrip for his service [M804-306, frame 0123]. His children may have been

    i.   Nathaniel, born say 1768, a plaintiff with (his brother?) Thomas Bowser against James Buxton, executor of Edward A. Best, in Nansemond County court in 1798 [Watson, *Nansemond County Clerks' Fee Books*, 28], taxable on a lot with $20 annual rent in Nansemond County in 1802 [1802 PPTL B, p.3].

   ii.   James[3], born before 1771, a "Free Negro" over the age of 45 in 1815 when he was taxable on a slave, 2 cattle, and 17 horses in "S. Hole" in Nansemond County in 1815 [Waldrep, *1813 Tax List*].

  iii.   Thomas[2], born say 1771, recorded a deed of emancipation for (his wife?) Nancy in Nansemond County in 1792 [Watson, *Nansemond County Clerks' Fee Books*, 29], taxable on a lot with $20 annual rent in Nansemond County in 1802 [1802 Land Tax List B, p.2], a "Free Negro" taxable on a head of cattle and 3 horses at "P.P." in Nansemond County in 1815 [Yantis, *A Supplement to the 1810 Census of Virginia*, S-14].

   iv.   Betsy.

    v.   perhaps a daughter, the mother of Moses, Caroline, Lydia, Thomas, and Curtis **Ash**, heirs of James Bowser. Perhaps Moses Ash was identical to Moses **Ash** Bowser, born about 1771, a nine-year-old boy called Moses Ash when the court ordered him bound to Jethro Sumner in Warren County, North Carolina, in September 1780 to learn to read and write and husbandry [Minutes 1780-3, 51]. He was called Moses Ash **Bowser** on his Warren County indenture [WB 3:155].

7. Olive Bowser, born say 1760, was living in Isle of Wight County on 6 February 1783 when the court ordered the churchwardens to bind out her daughter Louisa [Orders 1780-3, 124]. She was a resident of Surry County, Virginia, by 3 October 1801 when her daughter Nancy registered as a "free Negro" [Back of Guardian Accounts Book 1783-1804, no. 135]. Her children were

10 i. Nancy, born Christmas 1780.
  ii. Louisa, ordered bound out in Isle of Wight County on 6 February 1783.

8. Philip Bowzer, born say 1760, was head of an Isle of Wight County household of 1 white (free) person in 1782 [VA:29]. He was taxable on a horse in Isle of Wight County from 1782 to 1810: listed as a "F.N." in 1790 and thereafter; taxable on slaves Sarah, Rose and Olive, and 2 cattle in 1784; taxable on slaves Sarah, Olive, Rose and Davey in 1785; taxable on a slave in 1786; taxable on 4 slaves and 2 cattle in 1787; a slave in 1788 and 1789; a slave in 1790; 2 slaves in 1791 and 1792; 3 slaves in 1793; taxable on his own tithe, Dick Bowzer, Jr.'s tithe and 2 slaves in 1794; a free tithable aged 16-21 and 4 slaves in 1795; taxable on a slave in 1802, 1805 and 1807. Bridget Bowser and her taxables were listed with him in 1809 [PPTL 1782-1810, frames 4, 45, 60, 74, 89, 134, 181, 226, 242, 271, 331, 346, 418, 429, 491, 521, 575, 595, 652, 673, 715, 771, 791, 846]. He was a "free Negro" head of an Isle of Wight household of 4 "other free" and a slave in 1810 [VA:15]. He may have been the father of
  i. Richard[2], born say 1773, taxable in Philip Bowzer's Isle of Wight County household in 1794 [PPTL 1782-1810, frame 331]. He was aged 16-45 when he was listed in Nansemond County in 1813 [Waldrep, *1813 Tax List*].

9. James[3] Bowser, born say 1775, was an insolvent taxpayer in Halifax County, North Carolina, in 1799. He may have been the father of
  i. Drury, born Christmas 1795, ordered bound an apprentice to James Cooley by the 19 August 1800 Halifax County court [Minutes 1799-1802, 125].
  ii. Susanna, born about 1799, two years old when she was ordered bound an apprentice by the 19 August 1801 Halifax County court.
  iii. Macon, born about 1800, ten months old when he was ordered bound an apprentice to James Wright by the 19 August 1801 Halifax County court.

10. Nancy Bowser, born Christmas 1780, registered as a "free Negro" in Surry County, Virginia, on 3 October 1801: *a negro woman of a bright complexion, aged 21 yrs next Christmas, 5'2" high, has bushy hair daughter of Olive alias Olive Bowser a free negro late a resident of this county* [Back of Guardian Accounts Book 1783-1804, no. 135]. She was living in York County on 17 October 1831 when her daughter Sally **Roberts** registered. Her children were
  i. ?Lucy, born about 1810, registered in York County on 18 November 1833: *a bright Mulatto about 23 years of age, 5 feet 3 Inches high...broad flat face, very Black Eyes and long hair* [Free Negroes Register, 1831-50, no.356].
  ii. Sally **Roberts**, born about 1816, registered in York County on 17 October 1831: *daughter of Nancy Bowser, a bright mulatto girl about 15 years of age, 5 feet 4-3/4 inches high...full head of hair, large nose* [Register, no.314].

Other members of the Bowser family were
  i. Kinchen, born about 1791, registered as a "free Negro" in Brunswick County, Virginia, on 26 June 1826: *a free man of yellow Complexion*

about five feet three Inches high thirty years of age was born free as appears from the Evidence of John D Wilkins and has no scars or marks perceivable and by Occupation a Ditcher [Wynne, *Register of Free Negroes*, 85].

ii.   James, a "F.N." taxable in Nottoway Parish, Southampton County, in 1813 [PPTL 1807-21, frame 337].

BOYD FAMILY

1.   Elizabeth Boyd, born say 1742, the servant of Charles Chaddock of Dettingen Parish, Prince William County, was free from her indenture by 2 August 1773 when her "mulatto bastard" Hannah Boyd was bound to Chaddock [*Historic Dumfries Virginia, Records of Dettingen Parish*, 118]. Her children were

2   i.   ?Augustine, born say 1760.
  ii.   Hannah, born 17 February 1768 according to her indenture.
  iii.   ?Anthony, born before 1776, head of a Botetourt County household of 3 "free colored" in 1820 [VA:49].

2.   Augustine Boyd, born say 1760, was among a group of Revolutionary seamen who deserted and for whom a reward was offered in the 11 September 1779 issue of the *Virginia Gazette* [Jackson, *Virginia Negro Soldiers*, 31]. He was taxable in Northumberland County in 1787 [Schreiner-Yantis, *1787 Census*, 1261]. He married Grace **Sorrell**, 24 July 1795 Northumberland County bond, Thomas Pollard security, and was a "free mulatto" head of a Northumberland County household of 7 "other free" in 1810 [VA:973]. He was the father of

  i.   Frances, "daughter of Augustine Boyd," married James **Sorrell**, 4 March 1811 Northumberland County bond, William Boyd security.
  ii.   Sally, married William **Toulson**, 22 February 1802 Northumberland County bond, Joseph **Toulson** security, with the consent of Augustine Boyd for Sally.
  iii. ?William[2], born about 1787, married Polly **Toulson**, 13 March 1809 Northumberland bond, Jerry **Toulson** security. That same day William and Polly registered as "free Negroes" in Northumberland County: *Wm Boyd, bright mulatto, 22 yrs, 5 feet 11 inches high. Polly Toulson, bright mulatto, about 18, 5 feet 2 Inches high* [Northumberland County courthouse Register, nos. 40-1].
  iv.   ?Lewis, married Patty **Evans**, 9 February 1802 Northumberland County bond, John **Evans** security.
  v.   ?Peggy, married Hancock **Carpenter**, 12 December 1811 Northumberland County bond, Presly Coleman security. Hancock was probably the son of James **Carpenter**, "free Mulatto" head of a Northumberland County household in 1810 [VA:974].
  vi.   ?James, born about 1787, registered as a "free Negro" in Northumberland County on 10 March 1806: *bright mulatto, about 19 years old, 5 feet 5 Inches high, Born free* [Northumberland County courthouse Register, no.21].

BRADBY FAMILY

1.   Richard[1] Bragby, born say 1710, and his wife Elizabeth were living in Charles City County in April 1738 when the court ordered that they appear at the next court to show cause why their children should not be bound out because Benjamin Harrison, Gentleman, informed the court that they were "not bringing up their children in an honest way of Liveing as well as in ye fear of God" [Orders 1737-51, 39]. They may have been the parents of

  i.   James Bradberry, born say 1746, taxable in St. David's Parish, King William County, from 1782 to 1787: taxable on 2 horses in 1782 and 1783 [PPTL 1782-1811]. He may have been identical to James Bradby, an Indian who attended William and Mary College in 1754 [Rountree, *Pocahantas's People*, 172].

2   ii.   Edward[1], born say 1748.
3   iii. Richard[1], born say 1750.

2.   Edward[1] Bradby, born say 1748, was called Edward Bragby when he was bound to Jonathan V____ (Vaughan?) in Charles City County on 6 July 1757 [Orders 1751-7]. He was called Edward Bradby when he was taxable in Charles City County on his own tithe and 2 horses in 1784, taxable on 2-3 tithes from 1787 to 1801 (called Edward Bradby, Sr.) [PPTL, 1783-7; 1788-1814], and taxable on 100 acres from 1782 to 1802 [Land Tax List, 1782-1830]. He died before 1802 when his widow Susannah Bradby administered his Charles City County estate. She allotted 9 pounds each to Mary Bradby, John **Fields**, Eliza **Atkins**, Susannah Bradby and Edward Bradby, and allotted herself 51 pounds as her one-third share. The remainder of the estate was appraised at about 88 pounds and included beds, furniture, three guns, three plows, farm animals, a looking glass, two spinning wheels, a pair of spectacles and a parcel of books [WB 1:591, 601]. Edward was probably the father of
i.   Edward[2], born say 1771, taxable in Charles City County from 1792 to 1796 (called Edward Bradby, Jr.) and taxable from 1803 to 1805 [PPTL, 1788-1814]. He was probably identical to Edward Bradberry who was taxable in New Kent County from 1798 to 1800 [PPTL 1782-1800]. He was head of a James City County household of 6 "free colored" in 1820 [VA:118].
ii. Mary, born say 1775.
iii. John[1], born say 1777, taxable in Charles City County in 1798 [PPTL, 1788-1814].
iv. ____, wife of John **Fields**.
v.   Eliza **Atkins**, born say 1780.
vi. Susannah.

3.   Richard[2] Bradby, born say 1750, was taxable in Charles City County in 1797 [PPTL, 1788-1814] and taxable in King William County from 1798 to 1813: taxable on his own tithe and a horse while residing in the Pamunkey Indian town in 1798, taxable on a slave over the age of sixteen in the Indian town in 1800 and 1802 (but not subject to tax on his own tithe), taxable on a free male tithable and a horse in 1803 (called "Richard Bradberry UP" to differentiate him from another Richard Bradberry who was taxable on his own tithe, a slave, and a horse), taxable on a horse but not taxable on his own tithe in 1804, taxable on a free male tithable in 1805, taxable on a horse but not on his own tithe in 1807, 1809, 1811 and 1812, listed as a "Mulatto" taxable on 2 horses in 1813 [PPTL 1782-1811; 1812-50]. He may have been the father of
i.   Patrick, taxable in the Pamunkey Indian town in King William County from 1797 to 1799: taxable on his own tithe and a slave in 1797, taxable on his own tithe and a horse in 1797 and 1798, called Patrick Bradberry when he was taxable in King William County on his own tithe and a horse in 1803 [PPTL 1782-1811]. He was a "free Negro" taxable in the upper district of Henrico County in 1814 [PPTL 1782-1814, frame 823].

Other members of the Bradby family were
i.   Edward[3], born say 1773, taxable in Chesterfield County from 1794 to 1796, 1803 to 1805, a "Mulatto" taxable in 1810, and a "free Negro" with a male and 4 females over the age of sixteen in his household in 1813 (called Edward Bradbery) [PPTL, 1786-1811, frames 213, 246, 280, 538, 577, 614, 799]. He was a "free Negro" taxable on 2 horses

horses in the lower district of Henrico County in 1812 [PPTL 1782-1814, frame 697].

4   ii.   John², born say 1779.
5   iii. Smallwood¹, born say 1782.
      iv. Bolling, born say 1784, taxable in Charles City County in 1805, a "Mulattoe" taxable in 1813 and 1814 [PPTL, 1788-1814].
      v.   Burwell, born say 1800, purchased 50 acres from Peter Crew by deed acknowledged in Charles City County court on 17 January 1833. He complained to the Charles City County court on 20 July 1837 for a breach of the peace against him by a "man of color" named Lot **Griffin** [Minutes 1830-7, 141, 327].
      vi. Alexander, born about 1805, obtained a certificate of freedom in Charles City County on 20 January 1825: *a man of bright complexion, twenty years of age, 5 feet 7 inches, born free in this county* [Minutes 1823-9, 91].
      vii. John³, born 2 February 1809, obtained a certificate of freedom in Charles City County on 15 July 1830 on testimony of Peter Crew: *a mulatto man, twenty one years old on 2 February 1830* [Minutes 1830-7, 23].

4.   Smallwood¹ Bradby, born say 1782, was taxable in Charles City County in 1805 and a "Mulattoe" taxable in 1813 [PPTL, 1788-1814]. He renewed his certificate of freedom in Charles City County on 17 November 1831 explaining that his former certificate had been destroyed by the burning of his house [Minutes 1823-9, 86]. His wife Rebecca (born about 1786) registered on 15 September 1831: *wife of Smallwood Bradby, a very bright mulatto woman about forty five years old, born free in this county* [Minutes 1823-9, 188; 1830-7, 75-6]. He may have been the father of
      i.   Smallwood², Jr., born about 1806, obtained a certificate of freedom in Charles City County on 21 September 1826 on testimony of John Folkes: *a bright mulatto born free in this county* [Minutes 1823-9, 188]

5.   John² Bradby, born say 1779, was taxable in Charles City County in 1800 (called John Bradby, Jr.) and taxable from 1802 to 1805 [PPTL, 1788-1814]. He died before March 1832 when the administrator of his Charles City County estate paid John **Adkins** his bill of 88 cents [WB 4:57]. He was the father of
      i.   Littleberry, born about 1811, registered on 15 December 1831: *son of John Bradby, deced., a mulatto man, about 20 years old, born free in this county* [Minutes 1830-7, 105].
      ii. Sally, born 18 January 1817, obtained a certificate of freedom in Charles City County on 16 August 1832: *(testimony of W. Christian) daughter of John Bradby, a mulatto girl, aged fifteen the 18 January last* [Minutes 1830-7, 117].

BRANCH FAMILY

1.   Randall Branch was listed among the "Black" members of the undated colonial muster of Captain James Fason's Northampton County, North Carolina Militia [Mil. T.R. 1-3]. In 1769 he was taxable in Dobbs County [SS 837 by *NCGSJ* XV:74], and in 1790 he was head of a Robeson County household of 11 "other free" [NC:49]. He sold land in Robeson County by deed proved on 7 April 1801 [Minutes 1797-1806, 144]. His children were most likely
      i.   Moses, head of a Robeson County household of 1 "other free" in 1800 [NC:363] and 1 "free colored" in 1820 [NC:297].
      ii. Mary, head of a Robeson County household of 5 "free colored" in 1820 [NC:316].
      iii. William, head of a Halifax County, North Carolina household of 6 "free colored" in 1820 [NC:142].

Members of the family in Virginia were
  i. Peter, "F.N.," head of an Isle of Wight County household of 6 "other free" in 1810 [VA:40].
  ii. Jesse, head of a Southampton County household of 7 "other free" in 1810 [VA:75].

BRANDICAN FAMILY

Members of the Brandican family were
  i. Reuben, born about 1755, registered in King George County in 1801: *Reuben Brannican, alias Gammon, a mulatto man aged about forty six years, about six feet high, long curley hair and at this time large & muscular...was born in this County of free parents* [Register of Free Negroes, no.39]. He was head of a King George County household of 6 "other free" in 1810 [VA:192]. He was taxable in King George County from 1788 to 1815: called Reuben Gammon in 1788, listed as a "mulatto" in 1813 [PPTL, 1782-1830, frames 55, 125, 143, 262, 302, 367].
  ii. Henry, taxable in King George County from 1789 to 1815: called Henry Gammon in 1788, listed as a "mulatto" from 1813 to 1815 [PPTL, 1782-1830, frames 59, 64, 104, 153, 237, 338, 367].
  iii. Aden, a "mulatto" taxable in King George County from 1797 to 1813: listed as a "mulatto" in 1813 and 1814 [PPTL, 1782-1830, frames 153, 176, 276, 338, 367].

BRANDOM/ BRANNON FAMILY

Mixed-race members of the Brannum/ Branham family, born about 1720, were probably the children of a servant of Godfrey and Elizabeth Ragsdale since several mixed-race Brannum/ Brandon children were born in their household between 1720 and 1730: Margaret "a Mollatto belonging to Godfry & Eliz: Ragsdale" (called Margaret Brannum when she was bound to Ragsdale in 1722), and Ned (no last name) "a Mulatto" born in Godfrey Ragsdale's household in Bristol Parish [Chamberlayne, *Register of Bristol Parish*, 11, 50, 305]. They may have been related to Jemmy Brandon who was listed among the "Negros &c At the Home House" in the 15 July 1728 Surry County estate of Nathaniel Harrison, Esq. [DW 1715-30, 843]. Mixed-race members of the Brandon family were

1   i. Peter[1], born say 1715.
2   ii. Mary[1], born say 1718.
3   iii. Margaret[1], born 7 November 1720.
4   iv. Benjamin[1] Branham, born say 1721.
5   v. Doll, born say 1723.
      vi. Ann, born say 1725, listed in the 6 June 1755 inventory of the Chesterfield County estate of Godfrey Ragsdale (with her brother Ned?): *Ned Mulatto to be free in three years - 18 pounds, Nan ditto - 5 pounds* [WB 1:178-9]. And she was probably identical to "Nann a Mulatto" who successfully sued Mary Ragsdale for her freedom on 1 August 1755 [Orders 1749-54, 117].
      vii. Frances[1] Brannum, "alias Harris," born say 1726, living in Chesterfield County on 7 February 1752 when the court ordered the churchwardens of Dale Parish to bind out her unnamed children [Orders 1749-54, 171].
      viii. Edward[1], born about 1727, a "Mulatto Child by name Ned" (no surname) born in Godfrey Ragsdale's house before 9 July 1730 when he was bound to Ragsdale [Chamberlayne, *Register of Bristol Parish*, 50]. He was called Ned Brandom in 1751 when he was taxable in Thomas Bevill's Amelia County household in the district between Flatt and Deep Creeks [1751 Tax List]. He was listed in the 6 June 1755

inventory of the Chesterfield County estate of Godfrey Ragsdale: *Ned Mulatto to be free in three years* [WB 1:178-9].

6   ix.   Eleanor, born say 1728.
7   x.   Mary[2], born say 1729.
8   xi.   Edward[3] Branham/ Brannum, born say 1760.

1.   Peter[1] Brannan, born say 1715, was living in Henrico County in May 1741 when the court ordered the churchwardens of Dale Parish to bind out his "Mulatto" children: Sarah, George, Will, and Aggy [Orders 1737-46, 143]. His children were
     i.   Sarah, born say 1733.
     ii.   George[1], born say 1735.
     iii.   William[1], born say 1738.
     iv.   Aggy, born say 1740.

2.   Mary[1] Brandom, born say 1718, was living in Bristol Parish on 12 June 1743 when her children John and Charles Brandom were baptized. She was the mother of
     i.   John[1], son of Mary Brandom, born 22 October 1740, baptized 12 June 1743 [Chamberlayne, *Register of Bristol Parish*, 293].
     ii.   Charles[1], born 1 March 1742/3, baptized 12 June 1743 in Bristol Parish, son of Mary Brandom [Chamberlayne, *Register of Bristol Parish*, 293].

3.   Margaret[1] Brannum, born 7 November 1720, baptized 28 May 1721, was called "Margaret a Mollatto belonging unto Godfrey and Elizabeth Ragsdale" when her birth and baptism were recorded in Bristol Parish (Henrico, Prince George, and Dinwiddie counties). She was two years old on 10 October 1722, called Margaret Brannum (no race mentioned), when she was bound to Godfrey Ragsdale [Chamberlayne, *Register of Bristol Parish*, 305, 11]. She was called Peg Brannum on 7 February 1752 when the Chesterfield County court ordered the churchwardens of Dale Parish to bind out her unnamed children [Orders 1749-54, 171]. She may have been the ancestor of
     i.   Jinny, born about 1766, registered in Petersburg on 18 August 1794: *a stout made light brown Mulatto woman, five feet six and a half inches high, twenty eight years old, born free in County of Prince George* [Register of Free Negroes 1794-1819, no. 46].
     ii.   William[3], born about 1769, registered in Petersburg on 19 August 1794: *a brown Mulatto man, five feet six and a half inches high, twenty five years old, born free in Dinwiddie County*. Renewed 28 August 1816 [Register of Free Negroes 1794-1819, no. 51, 812].
     iii.   Shadrack, born about 1771, registered in Petersburg on 16 March 1796: *a stout well made dark brown Mulatto man, five feet seven and a half inches high, short wooly hair, twenty five years old, & raised in the Town of Petersburg* [Register of Free Negroes 1794-1819, no. 110]. He married Frances Brown, 17 March 1794 Hustings Court, Petersburg marriage. (His wife?) Frances Brandon (born about 1771) registered in Petersburg on 18 August 1794: *a dark brown Mulatto woman, five feet two inches high, twenty three born free in County of Prince George* [Register of Free Negroes 1794-1819, no. 47]. He was head of a Petersburg household of 2 "other free" in 1810 [VA:121b].
     iv.   Moses[3], born about 1773, taxable in Petersburg in 1799 [1799 PPTL, p.2] and registered in Petersburg on 14 January 1807: *a brown free negro man, five feet seven inches high, thirty four years old, born free & raised in the Town of Petersburg* [Register of Free Negroes 1794-1819, no. 404]. He was head of a Petersburg household of 4 "other free" in 1810 [VA:121b]. His wife Obedience registered on 7 June 1810: *wife of Moses Brandon, a dark brown free woman of Colour, five*

feet five and a half inches high, thirty six years old, spare & strait made, born free & raised in the Town of Petersburg [Register of Free Negroes 1794-1819, no. 404, 511].

   v. Daniel, born about 1779, registered in Petersburg on 28 June 1806: *a brown free negro man, five feet eleven and a half inches high, twenty seven years old, born free & raised in the Town of Petersburg* [Register of Free Negroes 1794-1819, no. 385]. He was head of a Petersburg household of 7 "other free" in 1810 [VA:121b].

4.   Benjamin[1] Branham, born say 1721, was living in Louisa County on 28 May 1745 when he, William **Hall**, Thomas **Collins**, Samuel **Collins**, William **Collins**, George **Gibson**, Thomas **Gibson**, William **Donathan**, and Samuel **Bunch** were presented by the court for failing to list a tithable (probably their wives) [Orders 1742-8, 152, 157, 172]. He and his wife Frances **Gibson** were lent the plantation they were then living on by the 18 December 1756 Louisa County deed of her father Gilbert **Gibson**. On 27 August 1772 he made a Louisa County deed of trust for 209 acres which was proved on 11 October 1773, and on 17 April 1784 he and Frances sold 4 acres of their home tract on the waters of Peters Creek [DB B:140-2; D1/2:537; H:373-4]. On 8 May 1780 the Louisa County court exempted him from paying county levies (due to old age) [Orders 1774-82, 303]. He was taxable on a horse in Louisa County from 1782 to 1794, taxable on an unnamed son in 1791 and 1794 [PPTL, 1782-1814]. He left a 24 August 1794 Louisa County will, proved 13 April 1795, naming his children Nathaniel, Benjamin, Jr., Susanna, Sally, Annis (wife of John Lemay), Mary (wife of John **Dalton**) and Peggy (wife of Kimbrough Sanders) [WB 3:600]. He was the father of

   i.   Nathaniel, married Patty Napper, 26 March 1795 Louisa County bond, John **Dalton** surety. He was taxable in Louisa County from 1782 to 1814, listed as a "free Negro & Mulatto" in 1813 and 1814 [PPTL, 1782-1814].

   ii. Benjamin[2], Jr., taxable in Louisa County from 1782 to 1814, listed as a "free Negro & Mulatto" in 1813 and 1814 [PPTL, 1782-1814].

   iii. Susanna, mother of Ambrose Branham and Malachia Branham. Malachia was taxable in Louisa County from 1795 to 1814, listed as a "free Negro & Mulatto" in 1813 and 1814 [PPTL, 1782-1814].

   iv. Sally.

   v. Annis, wife of John Lemay (stepson of Gilbert **Gibson**).

   vi. Mary, wife of John **Dalton**.

   vii. Peggy, wife of Kimbrough Sanders.

5.   Doll/ Dorothy Brandon, born say 1723, was probably the "Mullatto" Child named Dol (no surname) bound to Godfrey Ragsdale in Bristol Parish on 24 July 1727 [Chamberlayne, *Register of Bristol Parish*, 36]. She was the mother of Charles and Moses Brandon (no race indicated) who were bound out by the Sussex County court in November 1756. The court repeated the order on 18 December 1767 and also included her son Andrew [Orders 1754-6, 426; 1766-70, 203]. Her children were

   i.   Charles[2], born about 1754, bound out in Sussex County in November 1756. He may have been the Charles Brandum who was sued by Wood **Lawrence** for 8 pounds, 8 shillings in Brunswick County, Virginia court on 30 November 1786 [Orders 1784-8, 432, 475]. He registered in Petersburg on 19 August 1794: *a brown Mulatto man, five feet high, forty years old, born free in the County of Sussex* [Register of Free Negroes 1794-1819, no. 59]. He was taxable in Chesterfield County in 1791, 1792 (with Plato Brandom), 1807 and 1809 [PPTL, 1786-1811, frames 81, 117, 689, 738].

   ii. Moses[1], born say 1756, taxable in St. Andrew's Parish, Brunswick County, Virginia, in 1787 and 1788: taxable on 2 slaves above the age of sixteen and 2 aged twelve to sixteen in 1787, two slaves above sixteen in 1788 [PPTL 1782-98, frames 184, 212].

   iii.   Andrew.

6.   Eleanor Branham/ Brandom, born say 1728, was living in Brunswick County, Virginia, on 24 July 1753 when the court ordered the churchwardens to bind out her children Thomas and Molly Branham. And on 29 January 1755 the court ordered the churchwardens to bind out her children Thomas, Molly and Vines Brannum [Orders 1753-6, 9, 340]. On 12 May 1763 the Lunenburg County court ordered the churchwardens of St. James Parish to bind out her son Thomas Brandom [Orders 1763-64, 35]. She was the mother of

9	i.	Mary[3]/ Molly, born say 1744.
10	ii.	Thomas[1], born about 1746.
11	iii.	Vines/ Viney, born say 1754.
	iv.	?William[2], born say 1755, head of a Mecklenburg County, Virginia household of 5 persons in 1782 [VA:34]. He was presented by the court on 14 October 1782 for failing to list himself as a tithable, and he was listed as a tithable in Mecklenburg County in 1783 [Orders 1779-84, 236, 257; PPTL, 1782-1805, frame 50]. He was a "melatto" taxable in the northern district of Campbell County in 1789, listed on the same day as William Brannom, Jr. [PPTL, 1785-1814, frame 123].

7.   Mary[2] Brandom, born say 1729, was the mother of orphans Edward and Ann Brandom who were living in Chesterfield County on 6 August 1750 when the court ordered the churchwardens of Dale Parish to bind them out [Orders 1749-54, 66]. She registered the birth of her children Elizabeth, John, Aaron, Judith, Peter and Gabriel in Bristol Parish [Chamberlayne, *Register of Bristol Parish*, 293]. She was the mother of

12	i.	Ann[2], born say 1747.
	ii.	Edward[2], born about 1749, registered in Petersburg on 18 August 1794: *a dark brown Mulatto man, five feet one inches high, forty five years old, born free in the County of Dinwiddie* [Register of Free Negroes 1794-1819, no. 28]. He was taxable in Dinwiddie County in 1787 and 1788 [PPTL, 1782-90 (1787 A, p.2), (1788 A, p.2)].
	iii.	?Jacob, taxable in Dinwiddie County from 1787 to 1789 [PPTL, 1782-90 (1787 A, p.2), (1788 A, p.2), (1789 A, p.3)].
	iv.	Elizabeth, born 11 April 1758 [Chamberlayne, *Register of Bristol Parish*, 289], registered in Petersburg on 22 July 1799: *a dark brown Mulatto woman, five feet and a half inches high, with short matted hair, forty years old, born free in Prince George County & raised in the Town of Petersburg* [Register of Free Negroes 1794-1819, no. 146].
	v.	John[2], son of Mary Brandom, born 4 October 1760.
	vi.	Aaron, born 1 August 1762 [Chamberlayne, *Register of Bristol Parish*, 293], registered in Petersburg on 2 October 1802: *a dark brown Mulatto man, five feet nine inches high, forty two years old, short bushy hair, born free & raised in the Town of Petersburg*. His wife Sylvia, born about 1756, registered on 21 December 1809: *a dark brown, near black, free woman of colour (wife of Aaron Brandon) fifty three years old, born free & raised in Prince George County* [Register of Free Negroes 1794-1819, nos. 53, 244, 524]. He was called Aaron Brander in 1810, head of a Petersburg household of 7 "other free" [VA:122a].
	vii.	Judith, born 16 July 1764 [Chamberlayne, *Register of Bristol Parish*, 293], registered in Petersburg on 18 August 1794: *a dark Mulatto woman, four feet eleven and a half inches high, twenty six years old, born free & raised in the Town of Petersburg* [Register of Free Negroes 1794-1819, no. 40].

viii. Peter[2], born 16 January 1766 [Chamberlayne, *Register of Bristol Parish*, 293], head of a Petersburg Town household of 2 "other free" in 1810 [VA:126b].

ix. Gabriel, born 2 October 1767, registered in Petersburg on 30 June 1794: *a dark Mulatto man about Twenty seven years old five & a half feet high, born in the county of Prince George of a free woman & raised in the Town of Petersburg* [Register of Free Negroes 1794-1819, no. 6].

8. Edward[3] Branham/ Brannum, born say 1760, was head of an Amherst County household of 1 free person in 1783 [VA:48] and 3 free persons in 1785 [VA:85]. He was taxable in Amherst County from 1783 to 1788 and from 1799 to 1805, a "man of color" in 1811, 1815 and 1817, in a list of "Free Negroes & Mulattoes" in 1814, 1818, and 1819 [PPTL 1782-1803, frames 25, 39, 96, 135, 449, 478, 549, 584; 1804-23, frames 20, 61, 208, 284, 298, 436, 489, 528]. He married Nancy **Evans**, 6 December 1790 Amherst County bond, Charles Christian security. He was one of the freeholders ordered to work on the road from Oransby's cabin to the fork of Megginson's road in Amherst County on 17 February 1794 [Orders 1790-4, 707]. He was the father of

i. ?Creasy, born 1776-94, head of an Amherst County household of 5 "free colored" in 1830.

ii. Polly, born say 1793, daughter of Edward and Nancy Branham, married James **Johns** in Amherst County in 1810.

iii. Levi, born about 1795, registered in Amherst County in 1830: *son of Edward Branham free born aged thirty five a Bright Mulatto 5 feet six inches high* [Register, no. 44].

iv. Judith, born about 1808, registered on 28 December 1833: *daughter of Edward and Nancey Branham born free - aged about twenty five years a bright mulatto straight hair five feet one inch high* [Register, no. 69].

9. Thomas[1] Brandon/ Brandom, born about 1746, "Son of Elenor Brandon, was ordered bound apprentice to Hutchings Burton by the churchwardens of St. James Parish, Lunenburg County, on 12 May 1763. He may have been identical to Thomas Branham (no parent named) who was ordered bound out in Brunswick County on 22 September 1760 [Orders 1760-84, 96]. He was taxable in Burton's Lunenburg County household in the 1764 list for St. James Parish [Bell, *Sunlight on the Southside*, 247]. He complained to the court that Burton was mistreating him, and the court bound him instead to Jacob **Chavis** on 13 July 1764 [Orders 1763-4, 35, 91; 1764-5, 108]. He purchased 130 acres on Middle Bluestone Creek in Mecklenburg County, Virginia, for 30 pounds on 11 July 1778 [DB 5:283-4]. He was head of a Mecklenburg County household of 6 "free colored" in 1820. He was living in Mecklenburg County, Virginia, on 15 June 1833 when he applied for a pension for his services in the Revolution, stating that he was born in Hanover County and was about eighty-seven years old. On 19 October 1840 his widow Margaret **Walden** Brandom, born about 1753, made a deposition in order to obtain a survivor's pension for his services. She testified that they were married on 3 January 1771 and he died 17 December 1834. Her application included a copy of a book containing the family register which was provided by William J.B. Bedford of the Charlotte County courthouse [Dorman, *Virginia Revolutionary Pension Applications*, 9:74-75]. She was identified as the daughter of Thomas **Evans**, wife of Thomas Brandom, in a Mecklenburg County Chancery Suit in 1819 [LVA 1819-006]. Perhaps she was Thomas **Evans'** illegitimate child by a member of the **Walden** family, or perhaps **Walden** was his wife's maiden name. The family register identified Thomas and Margaret Brandon's children:

i. Nancy, born 2 September 1771, called Nancy Brannom in the 22 May 1787 Mecklenburg County will of her grandfather Thomas **Evans** [WB

2:250]. She married Frederick **Graves**, 20 December 1800 Mecklenburg County bond, Ephraim **Drew** security. They were probably the parents of Hugh **Graves**, head of a Mecklenburg County household of 3 "free colored" in 1820.

ii.   Agnes, born 2 June 1773.

iii. Walden, born 5 July 1775, head of a Mecklenburg County, Virginia household of 6 "free colored" in 1820.

iv.   Suckey, born 12 September 1777.

v.   Edward[4], born 10 November 1779, married Betsy **Chavis**, 1806 Mecklenburg County bond. He was a "f. negro" wheelwright taxable in Charlotte County in 1802, taxable with Jacob **Chavis** in 1803 [PPTL 1782-1813, frames 533, 542, 588]. He was head of a Mecklenburg County household of 6 "free colored" in 1820.

vi.   Elizabeth, born 3 February 1782, perhaps the Elizabeth Brandom who married Archer **Stewart**, 1818 Mecklenburg County bond, Ned Brandom security.

vii. Thomas[2], born 30 August 1786, registered in Mecklenburg County on 19 December 1815: *a man of Colour five feet seven Inches high, slender made, dark complexion, 24 years old, free born in the County* [Register, no. 12, p.7]. He purchased property by indenture proved in Mecklenburg County court on 21 December 1812, and he and his wife Sally sold it by indenture of bargain and sale proved on 17 January 1814. His wife Sarah was identified as the daughter of Elizabeth **Chavous** (widow of Jacob **Chavous**) on 20 June 1814 when Thomas **Evans** brought a suit in chancery against Elizabeth's children [Orders 1811-13, 386; 1813-15, 86, 210].

viii. Margaret[2], born 22 January 1790, married John **Garnes**, 8 September 1823 Warren County bond, Benjamin **Durom** (**Durham**) bondsman.

ix.   John, born 30 September 1792.

x.   Jesse, born 7 May 1796, married Parthena **Drew**, 2 July 1822 Warren County bond, William **Carsey** (**Kersey**) bondsman.

10. Mary[3] Brandom, born say 1744, was the mother of Rhode Brandom who was bound out in Mecklenburg County on 11 August 1766 [Orders 1765-8, 195]. She was the mother of

13   i.   Rhode, born say 1762.

14   ii. ?Moses[2], born say 1772.

11. Viney Brandom, born say 1754, was presented by the grand jury of Mecklenburg County, Virginia, on 14 March 1791 for living in adultery with Thomas Dison (a white man) on the plantation of William Cleaton. They were each fined 1,000 pounds of tobacco. She purchased land from Thomas G. Taylor by deeds proved in court on 14 November 1796 and 11 June 1804 [Orders 1787-92, 565, 597; 1795-8, 165; 1803-5, 181]. She was taxable in Mecklenburg County on her son John in 1805 and taxable on a horse from 1807 to 1815: taxable on a free male tithable in 1807, called Mrs. Viney Brandom in 1811, listed as a "Mulatto" in 1813. Perhaps her son was John **Dyson** who was a "Mulattoe" taxable in 1816 [PPTL, 1782-1805, frame 1049; 1806-28, frames 55, 157, 230, 326, 380, 497, 536]. He was about 70 years old when he was counted in the 1850 Mecklenburg County census [VA:62b]. Viney was taxable on 100 acres from 1804 until 1817. She left an 1818 Mecklenburg County will naming her children Sally, Mason, Frederick, David Chapman, John and Nancy. In 1818 fifty acres of her land were transferred to Mason Brandom and her estate transferred another fifty acres to Sally Brandom in 1819 [Land Tax Lists 1782-1811A, 1811B-1824A, B lists]. Viney was the mother of

i.   ?Mary[5], born say 1778, married Frederick **Goen**, 29 December 1800 Mecklenburg County bond.

ii. ?William[4], born say 1785, taxable in the lower district of Mecklenburg County in 1802 [PPTL, 1782-1805, frame 915].

iii. Mason, born say 1786, over the age of sixteen in 1802 when he was listed in the lower district of Mecklenburg County in 1802, a "Mulatto" not yet twenty-one in 1806 when he was taxable on a horse, listed as a tithable in 1809 [PPTL, 1782-1805, 915, 1018; 1806-28, frames 27, 128, 157, 230, 326].

iv. Sally, listed as a "Mulatto" over the age of sixteen in Mecklenburg County in 1813, received 50 acres from Viney Brandom's estate in 1819 [PPTL, 1806-28, frame 327].

v. John, born say 1789, over the age of sixteen when he was listed in Viney Brandom's Mecklenburg County household in 1805, a "Mulatto" taxable from 1813 to 1820 [PPTL, 1806-28, frame 326, 700]. He may have been the John Brandum who married Mary **Chavis**, 20 November 1824 Granville County bond, George **Anderson** bondsman.

vi. David **Chapman**, a "Free" Mecklenburg County taxable in 1806, taxable on 2 horses in 1809 and 1810 [PPTL, 1806-28, frames 27, 128, 157].

vii. Frederick, taxable in the lower district of Mecklenburg County in 1802 [PPTL, 1782-1805, frames 915, 1018].

12. Anne Brannum, born say 1740, daughter of Mary Brandon, was bound out with her brother Ned by the Chesterfield County court on 6 August 1750 [Orders 1749-54, 66]. She was a free "Mulatto" living in Goochland County in May 1763 when the churchwardens of St. James Northam were ordered to bind out her children: Jane, Patsy, and Siller to John Payne [Orders 1761-65, 183]. Her children were

i. Jane, born say 1758.

ii. Patsey, born say 1760.

iii. Siller, born about 1762, registered as a free Negro in Goochland County on 21 October 1822: *Siller Cooper formerly Siller Branam, a woman of color about sixty years old, about five feet one inch high, of yellow complexion and was free born* [Register of Free Negroes, p.136, no.287].

13. Rhode Brandom, born say 1762, was called the son of Mary Brandom when he was bound out by the churchwardens of Mecklenburg County, Virginia, to Isaac Holmes on 11 August 1766 and called a "Molotto Boy" on 12 October 1772 when the court ordered him bound to John Ballard, Jr. He was sued for debt in Mecklenburg County on 13 May 1783 [Orders 1765-8, 195; 1771-3, 329; 1779-84, 315]. He acted as the next friend of his infant daughter Elizabeth Brandom in a Mecklenburg County suit for trespass, assault and battery against Daniel Brown on 11 March 1800. The parties submitted the case to arbitration by Samuel Holmes, Jr., and John Northington [Orders 1798-1801, 310, 353]. Rodnom/ Rhode was taxable in the lower district of Mecklenburg County from 1784 to 1802 and was taxable in the upper district with his son Charles in 1804 and with sons Charles and Burwell in 1805 [PPTL, 1782-1805, frames 65, 95, 135, 395, 591, 793, 915, 994, 1080]. His widow may have been the Elizabeth Brandom who purchased 45 acres in Mecklenburg County adjoining William **Stewart** on Mill Creek from James **Stewart** on 10 September 1811 [DB 14:461]. She was head of a Mecklenburg County household of a tithable "free Negro and Mulatto" male and female over the age of sixteen years in 1813 [PPTL, 1782-1805, frame 306]. She died intestate before February 1839 leaving a 40 acre tract and children Charles, Peter, George, and Mary Brandom [LVA, chancery case 1839-012]. She was the mother of

i. Charles[4], born say 1787, over the age of sixteen in 1804 when he was listed in his father's Mecklenburg County household, listed as "free

Negro & Mulatto" in 1813 [PPTL, 1782-1805, frame 305]. He was head of an Abrams Plains, Granville County, North Carolina household of 6 "free colored" in 1820 [NC:23].

ii.   Burwell, born say 1789, over the age of sixteen in 1805 when he was listed in his father's Mecklenburg County household, head of a household of a male and female "free Negro & Mulatto" in 1813 [PPTL, 1782-1805, frame 306].

iii. Elizabeth, born say 1791, an infant in 1800, perhaps the Elizabeth Brandom who received fifteen lashes by order of the Mecklenburg County court for stealing clothes worth $4 from Robert Carter's house on 26 December 1803 [Orders 1803-5, 101, 121, 135].

iv.   Peter[3], born 30 June 1784, registered in Mecklenburg County on 19 December 1815: *a man of Colour 29 years of age five feet six inches high...dark complexion inclined to be fleshy was free born in the County* [Register of Free Negroes, no.13, p.7].

v.   George, born 1776-1794, head of a Mecklenburg County household of 6 "free colored" in 1820.

vi.   Mary, married Robert **Mayo** but was no longer his wife when her mother's estate was divided in February 1839. Robert was head of a Mecklenburg County household of 5 "free colored" in 1820.

vii. Hannah.

14.   Moses[2] Brandon, born say 1772, married Alley **Jackson**, 3 January 1794 Charlotte County bond, John **Chavus** surety. He was taxable in Charlotte County from 1794 to 1813: a "f. negro" taxable on a horse in 1799, a planter listed with his children Jimmy, Polly and Alley in 1802; a "fm" carpenter listed with wife Abby, 2 male and 2 female children in 1807; taxable on 2 free males in 1809 and 1810, a "free Negro" head of a household of 2 males and 2 females in 1813 [PPTL 1782-1813, frames 288, 314, 365, 397, 431, 464, 496, 533, 542, 638, 648, 688, 707, 717, 740, 751, 772, 835, 846, 869]. His wife may have been identical to Abby Brandon whose children registered as "free Negroes" in Charlotte County. Abby Brandon was the mother of

i.   James, born about 1792, a "fm" taxable on a horse in Charlotte County in 1813 [PPTL 1782-1813, frame 869]. He registered in Charlotte County on 11 November 1826: *son of Abby Brandon, a free woman, Dark looking complexion, aged 34, born free* [Ailsworth, *Charlotte County--Rich Indeed*, 487].

ii.   Polly, born about 1795, registered in Charlotte County on 17 June 1826: *daughter of Abbey Brandon, Dark somewhat bright complexion, aged 31, born free* [Ailsworth, *Charlotte County--Rich Indeed*, 487].

Other members of the family were

i.   Mary[4] Brandon, born say 1765, head of a Rowan County, North Carolina household of 4 "other free" in 1790 [NC:170].

ii.   Mary[4], born about 1768, registered in Petersburg on 30 January 1798: *Mary Brondon, a dark brown Mulatto woman, five feet three inches high, short bushy hair, thirty years old, born free & raised in the Town of Petersburg* [Register of Free Negroes 1794-1819, no. 131].

iii. Bolivo(?) Branton, born before 1776, head of a Wilkes County household of 2 "free colored" in 1820 [NC:494].

iv.   Charles[3], born say 1778, taxable in Prince George County from 1799 to 1811: called a "dark man" in 1799, a "Mulatto" in 1801 and 1802, a "free negro" in 1803 and "free" in 1810 [PPTL, 1782-1811, frames 505, 530, 549, 575, 599, 623, 649, 699, 719, 739].

v.   Charles[5], born about 1788, registered in Petersburg on 8 June 1810: *a free man of colour, nearly black, five feet five and a half inches high, born free p. certificate from clerk of Sussex County (no age). Reentered*

29 December 1814, 26 years old [Register of Free Negroes 1794-1819, no. 565].

BRAVEBOY FAMILY

1. John[1] Braveboy, born before 1700, was tithable in Beaufort Precinct, North Carolina, on 25 December 1712:

   Att Mackoys Garrison Wm Read, Jno Braborn? & francis Gibson & 1 Negro of Mr. Mackoys - 5 [Haun, *Old Albemarle County Miscellaneous Records*, 181].

   He was the slave of James Ward on 26 August 1713 according to a suit brought in the General Court of North Carolina by Patience Speller, widow of Stephen Swaine, who claimed that John failed to repay her for purchasing his freedom [Byrd, *In Full Force and Virtue*, 11]. He was addressed by the Chowan County court on 17 July 1716:

   Jack Braveboy, a negro, Coming into this Government with a woman and do live together as man and wife, it is ordered that the sd. Braveboy produce a Sufficient Certificate of their Marryage [Hoffman, *Chowan Precinct 1696 to 1723*, 224].

   In March 1721 he was sued in the General Court of North Carolina by Havett and his wife, executors of the last will of Thomas Clark [Saunders, *Colonial Records of North Carolina*, V:231]. On 13 April 1725 he purchased 50 acres in Chowan County on the Southwest side of the Yeopim River near the mouth of Darby's Creek, and he sold this land seven years later on 14 November 1732 [DB C-1:442, 694]. His probable descendants were

   2　i. David, born say 1730, died about 1787.
   　　ii. John[2], born say 1732, a "Black" tithable in Tyrrell County in 1755 [T.O. 105, box 1], head of a Beaufort County household of 1 "other free" and 6 slaves in 1790 [NC:127], 1 "other free" in 1800 [NC:4], and 1 in 1810 [NC:116]. He was probably the John Brayboy who volunteered as a soldier in Carteret County in 1778 [*The North Carolinian* VI:728]. He enlisted on 27 August 1778 for three years in Captain Ballard's Company in the North Carolina Continental Line but was listed as a deserter a little over a year later on 29 October 1779 [Clark, *State Records*, XVI:1020].
   3　iii. Mary, born say 1734.
   4　iv. Joshua, born say 1740.
   　　v. Sukey, born say 1745, a buyer at the November 1774 sale of the Bertie County estate of James Pearce [Gammon, *Record of Estates, Bertie County* II, 76]
   　　vi. Nancy, born before 1750, a "free Mulatto" taxable in the 1761 Bertie County tax list of William Gray in the household of (her sister?) Mary Braveboy [CR 10.702.1, box 1]. Perhaps she was the Ann Braveboy who was listed with Mary Braveboy as buyers at the sale of the Bertie County estate of Joseph Wimberly which was recorded on 27 February 1767 [Gammon, *Record of Estates, Bertie County* II, 110].

2. David Braveboy, born say 1730, entered 100 acres in Bladen County east of Five Mile Swamp on 10 April 1761 [Philbeck, *Bladen County Land Entries*, no.1188]. He was head of a Bladen County household of 3 "white" polls in 1763, a taxable "Mulato" in 1769, taxable with his wife in 1772, a "Mixt Blood" taxable on himself, his wife and daughter in 1774, a "Molato" taxable in 1776, and taxable on 1 poll and 250 acres in 1784 [Byrd, *Bladen County Tax Lists*, I:16, 43, 71, 80, 93, 123, 134; II:67, 74; Bladen County Tax List

(1763, 1784)]. In his 20 October 1787 will he mentioned his wife Lydia and his children [WB 1:10]. Lydia was head of a Robeson County household of 7 "other free" in 1790 [NC:48]. Administration of her estate was granted to her son Stephen on 5 October 1797 on a bond of 50 pounds with Thomas **Ivey** and Ishmael **Roberts** securities [Minutes 1797-1806, 17]. Their children were

  i.   ?Jacob², born say 1747, not mentioned in his father's will but may have been the eldest son. Perhaps he was the member of the Braveboy family taxable in Bladen County in 1763: "Jas. Blunt & Braveboy 2 "white (free) polls." He was a "Mulato" Bladen County taxable in Solomon **Johnston**'s household in 1769 and a "Molato" taxable in Richard **Wharton**'s household in 1771 [Byrd, *Bladen County Tax Lists*, I:17, 45, 62]. He was head of a Robeson County household of 5 "other free" in 1800 [NC:367] and 5 in Cumberland County, North Carolina, in 1810 [NC:575].
  ii.   Patience **Hammons**, perhaps the wife of Horatio **Hammonds**.
  iii. Nancy **Carter**.
  iv.   Patty Braveboy, born say 1752, perhaps the Patty Braveboy who was head of a Cheraw District household of 2 female "other free" persons in 1790, living next to Sam Braveboy, head of a Cheraw District household of 1 "other free" male over the age of 16, 1 male "other free" under 16, and 1 female "other free" [SC:380].
  v.   Milly Braveboy.
  vi.   Stephen, born about 1759. He received his father's plantation of 150 acres. He sold land by deed proved in Robeson County on 8 April 1800 and purchased land by deed proved on 6 April 1801 [Minutes 1797-1806, 104, 142]. He was head of a Robeson County household of 1 "other free" in 1800 [NC:366]. He was probably over fifty years old in 1809 when the Robeson County court excused him from paying poll taxes [Minutes 1806-13].
  vii. Levy, who was probably the "L. Brave Boys" who was head of Cumberland County household of 2 "other free" in 1810 [NC:622].

3. Mary Braveboy, born say 1734, was a "free Mulatto" taxable in the 1761 Bertie tax list of William Gray. She was tithable with her son John in an untitled 1766 Bertie tax list, and she was tithed on her son only in 1771 [CR 10.702.1]. She was counted as white in the household of her son John in the 1790 census for Martin County [NC:68]. Her children were

  i.   John³, born about 1754, tithable in 1766. In 1770 he was a "free Mulatto" in Abraham Sullivent's household in the Bertie tax list of David Standley, and he was taxable with his mother in Standley's 1771 list [CR 10.702.1, box 2]. In 1774 he was a "Negro" head of his own household in David Standley's list. In 1779 he was taxable on an assessment of 243 pounds in District 6, Martin County [GA 30.1]. In 1790 he was head of a Martin County household of 7 "other free" and a white woman: John Braveboy & mother [NC:68].
  ii.   ?Jacob¹, born about 1759, called a "bastard Mulattoe aged about 15" by the May 1774 Bertie County court when it ordered him bound as an apprentice bricklayer [Haun, *Bertie County Court Minutes*, IV:74]. In 1774 he was taxable in Benjamin Stiles household in David Standley's Bertie tax list. He enlisted for two and one-half years as a private in Fifth Regiment, William's Company of the N.C. Continental Line on 9 May 1776 and was discharged 10 November 1778 [*N.C. Historical & Genealogical Register*, II:181]. He was head of a Martin County household of 3 free males and 3 free females in William Barden's District no. 5 for the state census in 1787 and head of a Martin County household of 10 "other free" in 1800 [NC:387].

4. Joshua Braveboy, born say 1740, was called as a witness but failed to appear in the Cumberland County, North Carolina suit of the Governor and James Simpson vs. Moses **Bass** on 17 October 1758 [Minutes 1755-79, 39]. He held land in Cumberland County before 26 October 1767 [Patents, 12:143]. He was a taxable "Mulato" in Bladen County with his son Lewis in 1768 [Byrd, *Bladen County Tax Lists*, I:8]. He moved to Craven County, South Carolina, where he received a grant for 150 acres on Lynches Creek on 4 March 1772 [S.C. Archives series S213019, vol. 25:215]. He was taxable in Prince Frederick Parish, South Carolina, in 1786 [S.C. Tax Returns 1783-1800, frame 118] and head of a Georgetown District, South Carolina household of 5 "other free" in 1790. He was the father of
    i.   Lewis, recorded a plat for 118 acres on Crackers Neck near the Savannah River in Orangeburgh District, South Carolina, on 9 December 1784 [S.C. Archives series S213190, vol. 2:187]. He was head of a household of 5 "other free" in South Orangeburg District, South Carolina, in 1790 [SC:99], taxable on 300 acres and a "free Negro" in Winton, South Carolina, in 1800 [S.C. Tax Returns 1783-1800, frame 301, 313].
    ii. ?Morris, taxed in South Carolina on 1,000 acres and 8 slaves on 22 April 1825 [S.C. Archives Index 0015 052 1824 03420]. His 3 June 1843 Williamsburg District will was recorded 7 August 1843. He divided his land and slaves between his wife Drusiler and children: Morris Murphey Braveboy, Elizabeth Braveboy, Moses Murphey Braveboy, Margaret Thomas, and Annis E. Matthews [WB vol.I, D:394].

BRAXTON FAMILY

Members of the Braxton family in Virginia were
    i.   Gilbert, born about 1769, a "Free Person of Colour" living on Dandriges' land in Berkeley County (present-day West Virginia) in 1813 [Waldrep, *1813 Tax List*], registered as a free Negro in Essex County on 10 August 1829: *born free by cert. of Ro: Pollard, Clerk of King & Queen County, colour: black, about 60 years of age, 5 feet 9 & 3/8 inches* [Register of Free Negroes 1810-43, p.75, no. 170].
    ii. Abram, head of a New Kent County household of 5 "other free" in 1810 [VA:744].
    iii. Samson, born about 1783, registered as a free Negro in Essex County on 15 December 1810: *born free by statement of John P. Lee in person, dark Mulattoe, about 27 years of age, five feet 8-1/4 Inches* [Register of Free Negroes 1810-43, p.17, no. 40].

BRITT FAMILY

1. Thomas[1] Britt, born say 1685, had by Sue **Puccum (Puckham)** an illegitimate child who was baptized in St. Anne's Parish, Anne Arundel County, Maryland, on 28 February 1719/20 [Wright, *Anne Arundel County Church Records*, 86]. They may have been the parents of
2   i.   Frances, born say 1728.
3   ii. Amy, born say 1730.
    iii. Thomas[2], an "Indian" taxable in Bladen County in 1768 [Byrd, *Bladen County Tax Lists*, I:6], perhaps the father of John Britt who was married to Mary **Cox** on 29 June 1810 when she was left land and slaves by the 29 June 1810 Robeson County will of her father Gilbert **Cox**.

2. Frances Britt, born say 1728, was the servant of James Parish of Brunswick County, Virginia, in March 1747 when the churchwardens of St. Andrew's

Parish were ordered to bind her "Mulatto" son Reuben Britt to her master [Orders 1745-49, 345]. She was the mother of

    i.   Reuben, born say 1747.

    ii.   ?Amos Brite, born say 1749, a "Free Mulatto" taxable in William Sholer's household in Bertie County, North Carolina, from 1765 to 1767. He was called Amos Britt in 1800, head of a Spartanburg County, South Carolina household of 7 "other free" [SC:188].

3.   Amy Britt, born say 1730, was living in Brunswick County, Virginia, on 24 September 1759 when the churchwardens of St. Andrew's Parish were ordered to bind out her "Mulatto" daughter Faith [Orders 1757-9, 400]. She was the mother of

    i.   Faith, born say 1748, perhaps the Faithy Britt whose illegitimate child Sarah was bound out by the Sussex County court on 17 March 1768 [Orders 1766-70, 214].

BROGDON FAMILY

Members of the Brogdon family were

1   i.   ____, born say 1747.
2   ii.   William, born about 1756.
3   iii.   Mary, born say 1760.

1.   ____ Brogdon, born say 1747, may have been the first husband of Fanny **Harris**. Fanny was the mother of

    i.   ?Molly **Harris** Brogdon, born say 1768, married William **Flood**, 12 November 1785 Mecklenburg County bond, William Brogdon consenting. She was probably the Molly **Flood** who was a "Free Negro" head of a Charlotte County household of 9 "other free" [VA:1010].

    ii.   Nancy Braughton (Brogdon?), born about 1775, registered in Petersburg on 8 July 1805: *Nancy Braughton, a very light Mulatto woman, five feet two inches high, thirty years old, long curled hair, holes in her ears, born free and raised in the County of Chesterfield, daughter of Fanny Harris* [Register of Free Negroes 1794-1819, no. 294].

2.   William Brogdon, born about 1756, was head of a Mecklenburg County, Virginia household of 4 persons in 1782 [VA:34] and was taxable in Mecklenburg County in 1782 and 1787 [PPTL, 1782-1805, frames 14, 188]. He married Caty **Carter** (daughter of Peggy **Carter**), 31 August 1786 Mecklenburg County bond. His step-daughter Polly **Carter** married William **Bird (Byrd)**, 19 November 1796 Charlotte County bond, John **Chavus** surety. Polly **Carter** was probably related to Henry **Carter**, head of a Charlotte County household of 5 "other free" in 1810 [VA:46]. William was taxable in Charlotte County from 1789 to 1813: a "free negroe" in 1799; a "f. Mulattoe" in 1801; a shoemaker listed with wife Caty and six children Henry, Harrison, Sterling, Betsy, Catey, and Patsy in 1802 and 1803; listed as a ditcher in 1805, 1807 and 1810; listed as a shoemaker from 1811 to 1813 [PPTL 1782-1813, frames 174, 189, 216, 240, 264, 313, 337, 381, 397, 431, 464, 496, 533, 542, 580, 648, 682, 751, 784, 814, 846, 886]. He was a "F.N." head of a Charlotte County household of 6 "other free" in 1810 [VA:44]. He registered in Charlotte County on 11 November 1826: *Mulatto complexion, aged 70, born free.* Caty registered the same day: *(daughter of Peggy Carter, a free woman) legally married to Wm. Brogdon, Mulatto complexion, aged 60, born free.* She registered again on 7 November 1831: *Yellow complexion, aged 70, born free* [Ailsworth, *Charlotte County--Rich Indeed*, 487, 490]. William and Caty were the parents of

    i.   Sterling, born about 1788, registered in Charlotte County on 1 December 1828: *son of Caty Brogdon, Bright complexion, aged 30, free born* [Ailsworth, *Charlotte County--Rich Indeed*, 488]. He was a sixty-year-old "Black" carpenter counted in the 1850 census for Charlotte County [VA:12a]

    ii.   Henry, born say 1789.

    iii.   Harrison, born about 1791, registered in Charlotte County on 6 June 1831: *son of William Brogdon and Caty Brogdon, free people, Bright complexion, aged 40, born free* [Ailsworth, *Charlotte County--Rich Indeed*, 488].

    iv.   Catey, born say 1795.

    v.   Betsy, born about 1800, a fifty-four-year-old "Black" woman counted in the 1850 census for Charlotte County [VA:11a].

    vi.   Patsey **Brandon**, born about 1802, registered in Charlotte County on 11 November 1826: *wife of James Brandon and a daughter of Wm. Brogden & Caty his wife, free people, Mulatto complexion, aged 24, born free* [Ailsworth, *Charlotte County--Rich Indeed*, 487].

    vii.   ?Amey, born about 1806, registered in Charlotte County on 7 November 1831: *Bright complexion, aged 25, born free* [Ailsworth, *Charlotte County--Rich Indeed*, 490].

3.   Mary Brogdon, born say 1760, was listed as a midwife in "A list of Free Negroes and Mulattoes for the Year 1802" in Lunenburg County [Clerk of Court's Office, Lunenburg County]. She may have been the mother of

    i.   Billy Brogden **Valentine**, born about 1804, registered in Mecklenburg County in 1826: *a Free Mulatto about 22 years of age six feet one Inch high* [Register of Free Negroes, no.18, p.21].

BROOKS FAMILY

1.   Richard[1] Brooks, born about February 1661/2, was the white servant of Madam Elizabeth Reade on 10 February 1677/8 when the York County court adjudged him to be sixteen years of age and ordered him to serve his mistress until the age of twenty-four. He was probably the father of a "Mollatto boy named Dick" the son of "Black Betty" who were slaves which Madam Reade left to her son Robert Reade by her 10 February 1685/6 York County will [DOW 6:35; 7:257]. Richard was probably the father of

2   i.   ?James[1], born say 1679.

    ii.   Richard[2], born say 1682, a "Malatto Man named Dick Brookes" who was willed by Robert Reade to his son Thomas Reade in 1712. His two free children by a white woman named Mary Hanson were listed in the 7 April 1713 inventory of Robert Reade's estate: "James & Richard Hanson indented Mulattoes" [DOW 14:241, 251-3]. Mary identified "Dick Broo_ a Malatto slave belonging to Robert Read" as the father of her illegitimate child when she appeared in court on 2 July 1706 [DOW 12:414, 424]. Richard **Hanson** may have been identical to the Richard Hanson whose suit for debt against John Cooper was dismissed by the Southampton County court at the defendant's costs on 13 August 1762 [Orders 1759-63, 233].

2.   James[1] Brooks, born say 1679, had property of (his son?) William Brooks valued at 3 pounds currency on 17 January 1731/2 when the York County court ordered an attachment on the property to pay a debt William owed John **Byrd**. The court called James the "slave" of John Buckner when Buckner was ordered to bring him into court [OW 17:256, 262]. On 13 June 1754 he (called James Brooks, Sr.) was one of fourteen heads of household who were sued in Southampton County court by William Bynum (informer) for failing to pay the

discriminatory tax on free African American and Indian women.[48] He died before 8 March 1759 when a writing purporting to be his last will was presented to the Southampton County court for proof but was ordered to be lodged in the office because James Brooks (Jr.) entered a caveat against it. On 13 March 1760 the court ruled that the will was not valid because at the time he made it, he was the slave of his son James Brooks, Jr. The court based its ruling on the York County bill of sale by which James Brooks, Jr., purchased his father from John Buckner on 9 March 1733/4; the deposition of Young Moreland who testified that James Brooks, Sr., "mullattoe," was once a slave of Major John Buckner of York County but was purchased by his son James Brooks in exchange for a "negroe" slave named David; and the deposition of Charles Hansford, Sr., of York County who testified that he knew a "mullattoe called Jemmy Brookes" who lived as a servant or slave with Mr. John Buckner of Yorktown but left those parts and was said to have been freed by his son [Orders 1749-54, 500, 512; 1754-9, 24-5, 34-5, 502; 1759-63, 24]. James was the father of

3   i.   ?William[1], born say 1705.
4   ii. James[2], born say 1707.
5   iii. Mary, born say 1709.

3.   William[1] Brooks, born say 1705, was presented by the York County court on 20 November 1727 for failing to list his "Mulatto" sister Mary as a tithable. On 17 January 1731/2 John **Byrd** sued him in York County court for a three pound currency debt for which the sheriff attached his estate in the hands of (his father?) James Brooks [OW 16:489; 17:256, 262]. He received a patent for 190 acres on the south side of the Nottoway River in Isle of Wight County adjoining land of William Killygrew on 20 May 1742 [Patents 20:280]. He sued William Bittle in Isle of Wight County on 11 June 1747 [Orders 1746-52, 23, 24]. He was living in Southampton County on 13 June 1754 when he was one of fourteen heads of household who were sued by William Bynum (informer) for failing to pay the discriminatory tax on free African American and Indian women. The court dismissed the suit against him on 13 February 1755, perhaps due to his old age. On 11 August 1757 he was among the freeholders who were ordered to work on a road in Southampton County for which Joseph Delk was surveyor [Orders 1754-9, 25, 38, 372]. In Isle of Wight County he was sued by Charles Jones on 3 September 1761 and sued for 22 pounds, 19 shillings by Archibald Dunlop and David Ralston on 4 March 1762 [Orders 1759-63, 257, 283, 328, 330, 347]. He was witness to the Southampton County will of John **Byrd**, proved 12 April 1781 [WB 3:322]. On 14 October 1784 the court presented him for failing to list a tithable and exempted him from paying taxes on 12 May 1785 [Orders 1778-84, 513; 1784-9, 67]. He was taxable in St. Luke's Parish, Southampton County, from 1782 to 1788: taxable on 4 horses and 16 cattle in 1782 [PPTL 1782-92, frames 504, 515, 544, 559, 638, 656]. He was living in St. Luke's Parish when he made his 9 May 1788 Southampton County will, proved 9 October 1788. He gave ten pounds to his daughter Ann **Dunkin**, five pounds and half his plantation to his wife Hannah **Swett** during her lifetime, and the remainder to his son William **Swett** "begotten of the body of Hannah Swett" [WB 4:276]. Hannah Brooks was taxable on a horse from 1799 to 1812. Bill **Hunt** and his wife Lucy were living on her land in 1813 [PPTL 1792-1806, frames 373, 407, 838; 1807-21, 47, 68, 166, 187, 287, 319]. Hannah's will was proved in Southampton County on 21 July 1817 [Minutes 1816-9, unpaged]. William was the father of

---

[48]The other householders were John **Porteus**, John **Demery**, Isaac **Young**, Thomas **Wilkins**, Francis **Locust**, James **Brooks**, Jr., John **Byrd**, Jr. and Sr., Abraham **Artis**, Lewis **Artis**, William **Brooks**, Ann **Brooks**, and William **Tabor**.

i. Ann **Dunkin (Duncan)**, perhaps identical to Ann Brooks who was granted a patent in Isle of Wight County for 150 acres on the north side of the Meherrin River adjoining James Brooks' land near Brook's Branch on 1 April 1749 [Patents 28:543]. She was fined 500 pounds of tobacco in Southampton County on 13 February 1755 for failing to list herself as a tithable. She pled not guilty at first but changed her plea when both James Brooks, Jr., and James Brooks, Sr., were found guilty [Orders 1749-54, 501, 513; 1754-9, 25, 39]. She and William Brooks paid 5 shillings to the Southampton County estate of James Powell on 9 December 1773 [WB 3:88].

ii. ?Jesse[1], born say 1740, sued in Southampton County for a debt of 7 pounds, 14 shillings which he owed Joseph Delk from 9 April 1767. He had left the county or was avoiding a summons on 8 March 1770 when the court attached his goods that were said to have been in the hands of (his father?) William Brooks [Orders 1768-72, 257, 276]. He was a "Mix Blood" taxable on himself and Daniel **Dolvin** in Bladen County, North Carolina, in 1774 [Byrd, *Bladen County Tax Lists*, I:123, 134].

iii. William **Swett**, probably identical to William S. Brooks who was taxable in Southampton County in 1789 [PPTL 1782-9, frames 704, 754].

4. James[2] Brooks, born say 1707, purchased his father from Major John Buckner by a 9 March 1733/4 York County bill of sale [Southampton County Orders 1759-63, 24]. He was called James Brooks, Jr., when he was granted 200 acres in Isle of Wight County on the north side of the Meherrin River by the side of Pine Pole Branch on 12 January 1746 [Patents 24:620]. He sued Richard Taylor, Jr., in Southampton County on 8 March 1753 for a 6 pound, 9 shilling debt. And on 11 January 1754 Richard Taylor, Jr., sued him for trespass, assault and battery. The case was dismissed on agreement of the parties. On 13 June 1754 he (called James Brooks, Jr.) was one of fourteen heads of household who were sued in Southampton County court by William Bynum (informer) for failing to pay the discriminatory tax on free African American and Indian women. Samuel Kindred testified against him. On 14 July 1757 he was ordered to pay William and Thomas Francis as witnesses for him in his suit against Hollowell Denson. He sued William **Banks** for 5 pounds, 5 shillings on 10 July 1761, sued Ann **Banks** on 11 September 1761, and on 10 December 1762 was fined 5 shillings for assaulting Ann **Banks**. He was sued by Thomas **Tabor** for trespass, assault and battery on 13 May 1762 and ordered to pay **Tabor** 20 shillings. His suit against James **Byrd** was dismissed on agreement between the parties on 9 September 1762 [Orders 1749-54, 333, 355, 500, 512; 1754-9, 24-5, 34-5, 40, 370; 1759-63, 128, 151, 219, 221, 234, 238, 272, 284]. He (signing) and his wife Martha sold 200 acres adjoining Brooks Branch and Sweathouse Swamp in Southampton County on 12 November 1761 [DB 3:98]. He was taxable in St. Luke's Parish, Southampton County, on a horse in 1786 and 2 horses from 1787 to 1797, taxable on John Brooks' tithe and 3 horses in 1794 and 1795 [PPTL 1782-92, frames 586, 632, 655, 705, 755, 870; 1792-1806, frames 47, 74, 156, 184, 261]. By his 5 February 1798 Southampton County will he lent half his land on the east side of the county road to his wife Hannah during her lifetime, and gave the other half on the same side of the road to his grandson John **Chavos**, "commonly called John Brocks, son of Elizabeth Brocks." His land on the east side of the county road was to be sold by his daughter Sarah **Reed** who was executor of the will [WB 5:58].[49] Hannah Brooks was taxable in Southampton County on a horse from 1798 to 1800 [PPTL 1792-1806,

---

[49]The name appears like Brocks in some parts of the will. The signature (signing) could be Brooks.

frames 261, 312, 373, 407]. She was head of a Southampton County household of 11 "other free" in 1810 [VA:88]. James was the father of

6   i.   Elizabeth, born say 1730.
    ii.   Sarah, married John **Reed** and was mentioned in his 23 August 1790 Southampton County will [WB 4:395].

5.   Mary Brooks, born say 1709, was a "Mulatto" tithable in York County on 20 November 1727. On 16 March 1740/1 she was presented by the court for having a bastard child on the information of Ellyson Armistead, one of the churchwardens of Yorkhampton Parish, and she confessed to the offense on 18 May 1741. John Cornelius was security for payment of her fine. She may have been the mother of John Brookes who was ordered bound apprentice to Thomas Dulaney of Charles Parish on 19 January 1746/7. The court made the indenture official when Richard **Limas** complained that Dulaney was harboring John Brookes. **Limas** had been presented for not listing his wife as a tithable, but when he appeared in that same session of the court he was ordered to pay the taxes for his sons [OW 16:489; W&I 19:12, 486-7]. Mary was probably the mother of

    i.   John[1], born before 16 March 1740/1, living in Southampton County on 13 May 1762 when he and Ed **Heathcock** (**Haithcock**) were sued by Samuel Sands for debt. The sheriff reported that he was no longer an inhabitant of the county when he and John **Reed** were sued by John Wilkinson for 9 pounds, 17 shillings on 9 September 1762 [Orders 1759-63, 219, 239].

6.   Elizabeth Brooks, born say 1730, sued John Brooks in a Southampton County chancery case on 14 May 1773 [Orders 1772-7, 181]. She was probably the common-law wife of a member of the **Chavis** family since her son was called "John Chavos commonly called John Brocks" in his grandfather's 1798 Southampton County will. Elizabeth may have been the Betty Brooks who was head of a Robeson County, North Carolina household of 4 "other free" in 1790 [NC:48] and the Elizabeth Brooks who was head of a Duplin County household of 2 "other free" in 1800. Her children were

    i.   John Brooks, born say 1752, called John Brooks when he was taxable in Southampton County in 1789 and 1790, taxable on a horse in 1799 [PPTL 1782-92, frames 707, 756; 1792-1806, frame 370].

They were probably the ancestors of the Brooks family of North Carolina:

    i.   John[2], born about 1758, a Revolutionary War pensioner [Clark, *State Records of North Carolina*, XXII:571], head of a Robeson County household of 5 "other free" in 1800 [NC:367] and 7 in 1810 [NC:147]. He claimed to be ninety-five or ninety-six years old on 30 May 1853 when he applied for a pension for service in the Revolution and was still living in Robeson County on 22 March 1858 when he applied for (and received) bounty land [Pension File S-6732].
    ii.   John[3]/ Jack, born about 1772, a twelve-year-old "Mulatto boy" apprenticed to George Logan in New Hanover County on 9 January 1784.
    iii. Solomon, born about 1774, a ten-year-old "Mulatto boy" bound apprentice to William Ewans in New Hanover County on 9 January 1784 [Minutes 1779-92, 116].
    iv.   James[3], head of an Edgecombe County household of 2 "other free" in 1810 [NC:715] and 4 "free colored" in 1820 [NC:117].
    v.   Major, born before 1776, head of an Orange County household of 4 "other free" in 1810 [NC:831] and 7 "free colored" in 1820 [NC:352].
    vi.   Mary[2], born before 1776, head of a Hyde County household of 7 "other free" in 1810 [NC:114] and 7 "free colored" in 1820 [NC:244].

vii. Jesse[2], born before 1776, charged with begetting a bastard child by Polly **Archer** in Halifax County, North Carolina, on 20 February 1800 [Minutes 1799-1802, 96]. He was head of a Washington County household of 4 "other free" in 1810 [NC:790] and 7 "free colored" in 1820 [NC:405].

viii. Bartley, head of a Bertie County household of 2 "other free" and a 26-forty-five-year-old white woman in 1810 [NC:172].

<u>Essex County</u>
1. Elizabeth Brooks, born say 1685, appeared in Essex County court on 22 January 1712/3 to bind her daughter Frances, "a Mulato Child," to Edward Hudson until the age of thirty-one [W&D 1711-4, 103]. She was the mother of
   i. Frances, born say 1712.

<u>Henrico County</u>
1. Penelopy Brooks, born say 1702, petitioned the Henrico County court in 1741 on behalf of her son William against Henry Royall. In January 1741/2 the court ordered Royall to discharge her son James Brooks [Orders 1737-46]. Her son William may have been identical to "Moll." William who was born in Henry Royall's house and bound to him by the churchwardens of Bristol Parish on 9 October 1724 [Chamberlayne, *Register of Bristol Parish*, 18-19]. Penelopy was the mother of
   i. William, born say 1720.
   ii. James, born say 1722.

They may have been the ancestors of
   i. John, born say 1758, taxable on a horse in Fredericksville Parish, Albemarle County, in 1788 and 1789: taxable on 2 tithes in 1788 [PPTL, 1782-1799, frames 149, 194; 1800-1813, frames].
2 ii. William, born say 1760.

2. William Brooks, born say 1758, was taxable in Fredericksville Parish, Albemarle County, from 1788 to 1801: taxable on 2 tithes and a horse in 1789 [PPTL, 1782-1799, frames 149, 194, 244, 292, 343, 383, 416, 446, 478, 512, 551, 586; 1800-1813, frames 24, 68]. Perhaps his widow was Mary Brock who was taxable in Fredericksville Parish, Albemarle County, from 1802 to 1813: taxable on her unnamed son and a horse in 1803; called a "Mulatto" starting in 1805; taxable on a free male tithable in 1813 [PPTL, 1800-1813, frames 113, 155, 246, 291, 427, 472, 518, 560]. She was head of an Albemarle County household of 7 "other free" in 1810 [VA:186]. They may have been the parents of
   i. William Brocks, born say 1786, taxable on a horse in Fredericksville Parish, Albemarle County, from 1804 to 1810; called a "Mulatto" from 1806 to 1808 [PPTL, 1800-1813, frames 201, 292, 339, 382, 429]. He married Milly **Tyree** 5 January 1807 Albemarle County bond, with the consent of Jonathan **Tyree**. He was head of an Albemarle County household of 4 "other free" in 1810 [VA:187].
   ii. John Brocks, born say 1789, a Mulatto" taxable in Fredericksville Parish, Albemarle County, from 1807 to 1811 [PPTL, 1800-1813, frames 340, 382, 428, 472, 518]. He married Nancy **Tyree**, 6 January 1807 Albemarle County bond, William Brock bondsman. He was head of an Albemarle County household of 4 "other free" in 1810 [VA:186].
   iii. Olly Brock, a "Mulatto" taxable in Fredericksville Parish, Albemarle County, in 1813 [PPTL, 1782-1799, frames; 1800-1813, frame 560].

Other members of the Brooks family in Virginia were

    i.   William, "marriner," counted in the 1800 census for Alexandria, Virginia, with his wife Mary, "both Free Negroes," in 1800 [*Virginia Genealogist* 4:55]

    ii.   Sam[1], head of a Frederick County household of 3 "other free" in 1810 [VA:562].

    iii. Sam[2], head of a New Kent County household of 1 "other free" and a slave in 1810 [VA:744].

    iv. William, head of a Petersburg Town household of 2 "other free" in 1810 [VA:119a].

BROWN FAMILY

1.   William[1] Brown, born say 1670, was called "William Brown Negro" on 28 April 1715 when he was security for "William Brown Mulatto" and on 31 July 1718 when he admitted in Westmoreland County, Virginia court that he owed Henry Roe 225 pounds of tobacco. He was called "William Brown Negro the next of kin to William Brown Mulatto decd." on 30 March 1726 when he testified in Westmoreland County court that (his son?) William died without leaving a will. He was appointed administrator of the estate. The appraisers, William Brown Wroe and Original Wroe, found an old chest, 6 plates and some old cooper's, joiner's and carpenter's tools at William Brown "Negroe's" (house). As administrator, William sued Richard Morton for a debt of 1,300 pounds of tobacco on 28 August 1729. The inventory of the estate of William Brown (Senior) was taken by Original Brown on court order of 24 February 1740 and included 3 horses, a feather bed, cows, 11 barrels of corn, shoes, a gun and candlesticks [Orders 1705-21, 266, 353a; 1721-31, 113, 293; Estate Settlements 1723-46, 26, 243]. He was probably the father of

2   i.   William[2], born say 1690.

2.   William[2] Brown, born say 1690, was called "William Brown Mulatto" when he was sued in Westmoreland County court for a debt of 1,820 pounds of tobacco on 28 April 1715. He died before 30 March 1726 when "William Brown Negro" was granted administration on his Westmoreland County estate [Orders 1705-21, 266; 1721-31, 113, 266, 312, 341, 344a, 359a]. He was the father of

    i.   Abraham[1], born about 1718, a "Mulato Lad (Son of Wm Brown Mulato decd.)" bound as an apprentice goldsmith to Allin Horton in Westmoreland County for the term of five years on 27 August 1729 [Orders 1721-31, 287a]. He may have been the Abraham Brown, Sr., who Abraham Brown, Jr., called his uncle in his 11 July 1789 Charles City County will. Abraham, Jr., directed that Abraham, Sr., should be maintained by his estate [WB 1:16-7].

    ii.   William[3], born about 1719, a ten-year-old "Mulatto boy,...Son of Wm Brown Decd.," bound as an apprentice farmer to Sarah Monroe until the age of twenty-one by the Westmoreland County court on 26 February 1728/9 [Orders 1721-31, 246].

3   iii. ?Elizabeth, born say 1722.

    iv.   Susanna, born about 1724, "an orphan Child of Wm Brown Malato decd....adjudged Six years old," who was bound as an apprentice to John Binks until the age of eighteen years by the Westmoreland County court on 25 February 1729/30 [Orders 1721-31, 307a].

3.   Elizabeth Brown, born say 1722, was living in Charles City County in February 1743/4 when the court ordered the churchwardens to bind out her sons John and Abraham, no race indicated, to Jacob Danzee. She was called "a Molatto" in May 1744 when the court ordered the churchwardens of Westover Parish to bind her son Will Brown to John Jacob Danzee [Orders 1737-51, 288, 299]. She was the mother of

      i.   John[1], born say 1739.

4   ii. Abraham[2], born say 1741.

5   iii. ?Edward[1], born say 1742.

      iv. William[4], born say 1743, son of Elizabeth, bound out in May 1744, perhaps the William Brown who was paid 1 pound on 28 June 1787 for acting as crier at the sale of the Charles City County estate of Thomas Cowles, deceased [WB 1:173].

6   v. ?Dixon[1], Sr., born say 1745.

      vi. ?Freeman[1], born say 1748, paid 2 pounds by the Charles City County estate of John Gregory, Jr., for looking after a slave named Savery and her children during the year 1778 [WB 1:342-3]. He was taxable in Charles City County from 1784 to 1807 [PPTL 1783-7; 1788-1814], taxable on 40 acres in 1782 [Land Tax List, 1790, p.1; 1800, p.1], and head of a household of 5 "other free" in 1810 [VA:959]. He was a man of color from Charles City County who served in the Revolution [*Charles City County historical Society Newsletter* 6:10-14 cited by NSDAR, *African American Patriots*, 148]. On 3 December 1811 he sold 1 acre on the cross road leading from the courthouse road to Swineyard's Road for $1 to Ishmael **Carter** "to have and to hold provided he leaves lawful issue." He sold 40 acres in Charles City County bounded by George Hubbard, Nancy Smith and Bowling Gills to Terrell Crew on 20 January 1831 [DB 5:560; 7:489].

7   vii. ?Benjamin, born say 1755.

8   viii. ?Isaac, born about 1760.

4.   Abraham[2] Brown, born say 1741, purchased 156 acres in Westover Parish, Charles City County, from William Tyree and John Wayles on 27 September 1769 for 96 pounds currency. And he purchased two slaves named Sarah and Phillis for 60 pounds on 8 December 1770 [DW 1766-74, 155-6, 274]. He was taxable in Charles City County on slaves Silvey and Isaac, 5 horses and 15 cattle in 1784 and taxable on slaves Silvey, Isaac and Jane in 1785 [PPTL, 1783-7]. He was paid 12 pounds, 15 shillings by the Charles City County estate of Samuel Harwood on 15 June 1778 and 13 pounds, 11 shillings by the estate of William Merry, deceased, in 1784 [WB 1:177, 355]. He called himself Abraham Brown, Jr., in his 11 July 1789 will which was proved 17 June 1790. He left his wife Sarah Brown 25 pounds specie, son John Brown 118 acres he had purchased from Samuel Riddlehurst, left daughter Mary Brown a slave named Jany, left sons Abraham and William all his remaining land which he had purchased from William Tyree to be divided between them when they came of age, left daughter Elizabeth Brown a slave named Sall and divided the remainder of his estate equally among his wife Sarah and children John, Mary, Abraham, William and Elizabeth Brown, ordered that his uncle Abraham Brown, Sr., should be maintained out of his estate and allowed Elizabeth **Syldom** the use of the house and garden on his land during her lifetime [WB 1:16-17]. His wife Sarah left a 1 June 1791 Charles City County will which was proved 15 December 1791. She left a slave named Silvy and a horse to her son Abram, left a slave girl named Mary to her son William, left a feather bed to her youngest daughter Elizabeth and divided the remainder among her surviving children. Elizabeth **Seldon**, Benjamin Brown and Frances **Harris** were witnesses [WB 1:70]. Abraham was the father of

9   i. John, born say 1764.

      ii. Mary, "daughter of Abram Brown deceased," married Abram **Thomas** (alias **Cumbo**) by marriage agreement of 13 April 1791 proved in Charles City County court on 15 December 1791 by which he recognized her right to slaves Isaac and Jane, two feather beds, and some stock of cattle and hogs which were in her possession [DB 4:66]. Administration on her estate was granted to Abraham Brown on 17

March 1836 with Morris **Harris** providing $90 security [Minutes 1830-7, 270].

10   iii.   Abraham[2], born say 1769.

iv.   William[6], born say 1772, taxable in Charles City County in 1793 [PPTL 1788-1814] and taxable on two tracts of land in 1790 and 1800, one of 92-1/2 acres and the other of 30 acres [Land Tax List, 1790, p.1; 1800, p.1]. On 17 July 1800 he (signing) swapped 125-1/2 acres with 115-1/2 acres which his brother Abraham Brown received by the will of their father. That same day he sold 20 acres in Westover Parish on the dividing line between his land and John Brown's to Abraham **Thomas** (alias **Cumbo**) [DB 4:514, 516, 520]. He and his wife Lucy (both signing) sold 41-1/2 acres he received by his father's will to Abraham **Thomas** for 65 pounds on 20 February 1806 [DB 5:118]. He was head of a household of 8 "other free" in 1810 [VA:958]. He was called William Brown, Sr., "a man of colour," on 1 August 1817 when he made a deed of trust for 80 acres to secure a debt of $38 he owed William F. Walker. He and his wife Lucy (both signing) sold 20 acres bounded by his own land, the land of John Brown, and the land of George **Jones** to George **Jones** for $150 on 8 May 1821 [DB 6:91, 458]. He may have been the William Brown, Sr., who made a deed of trust for a horse on 20 October 1830 [DB 7:472]. He was head of a head of a Charles City County household of 13 "free colored" in 1820 [VA:4].

v.   Elizabeth, born before 1776, head of a Charles City County household of 5 "other free" in 1810 [VA:953] and 6 "free colored" in 1820 [VA:8]. She may have been the mother of Sally Brown who registered in Charles City County on 20 October 1836: *daughter of Betsy Brown the midwife, brown complexioned, twenty-seven the 9 December last* [Minutes 1830-7, 297].

5.   Edward[1] Brown, born say 1742, was taxable in Charles City County from 1784 to 1794 [PPTL 1783-7; 1788-1814] and taxable on 200 acres from 1782 to 1793 [Land Tax List, 1782-1830]. He was the father of

i.   Edward[3], born say 1763, called Edward, Jr., when he was taxable in the household of Edward Brown in 1784 and called "son of Ned" in 1809 when he was taxable on 2 tithes [PPTL, 1783-7; 1788-1814]. He may have been the Edward Brown whose wife Rebecca was named in the 12 November 1803 Charles City County will of Frances **Harris** [WB 1:650]. He was head of a Charles City County household of 8 "other free" in 1810 [VA:957] and was a man of color from Charles City County who served in the Revolution [*Charles City County historical Society Newsletter* 6:10-14 cited by NSDAR, *African American Patriots*, 148].

ii.   William[5], born say 1765, taxable in Charles City County in 1787, called "son of Ned" when he was taxable in 1804 and 1806 [PPTL 1783-7; 1788-1814].

iii.   Freeman[2], born say 1767, taxable on a horse in 1787 and taxable on his own tithe and a horse in 1788, called "son of Ned" when he was taxable in 1806 [PPTL, 1783-7, 1788-1814].

iv.   James[1], born say 1771, taxable in Charles City County (called James Brown, Jr.) from 1792 to 1799 [PPTL, 1788-1814].

v.   John, born say 1789, called "son of Ned" when he was taxable in 1810 [PPTL 1788-1814].

6.   Dixon[1] Brown, Sr., born say 1745, was taxable in Charles City County on 100 acres in 1782 [Land Tax List 1782-1830] and taxable on his own tithe, (his son) Edward Brown, two horses and 11 cattle in 1784 [PPTL 1783-7]. He was witness to the 29 July 1784 Charles City County will of James **Harris** [WB

1:55]. He purchased 50 acres on the road leading from Soans's Bridge to the Charles City courthouse joining his own land for 50 pounds on 11 September 1790 and another 72 acres in the same area for 90 pounds on 2 February 1797. He purchased 70 acres at the mouth of Lennard's Mill Run adjoining Isabella Lennard and Soans's line on 19 December 1796 for 77 pounds, and he and his wife Susannah (making their marks) sold this land on 2 February 1797 for 80 pounds [DB 4:28, 323, 331, 332]. His wife Susanna was named in the 12 November 1803 Charles City County will of her mother Frances **Harris** [WB 1:650]. He was taxable on 220 acres near the Charity School from 1797 to 1821 [Land Tax List 1782-1830] and head of a household of 4 "other free" in 1810 [VA:938]. He made a 24 January 1811 Charles City County will, proved 18 January 1821. He left 40 acres to be divided between his son Dixon Brown and daughter Susannah **Harris** (wife of Chavis **Harris**) which was the land they were then living on; left his house and 75 acres to be divided among his daughter Catherine Brown, son James Brown and son Peter Brown; left 30 acres to his illegitimate children Polly **Harris**, Susannah **Harris** (wife of James **Harris**), and Peggy **Bowman** which was the land they were then living on; left 10 acres each to his daughters Elizabeth and Milly Brown; left 10 acres to his son Edward Brown's children Polly, Lucy and Rachel Brown; left 10 acres to be divided between his daughter Sally Brown's children Betsey **Harris**, Cornelius Brown, Polly Brown, Sabrina Brown, Lucy Brown, Reuben Brown and Elizabeth Brown; 10 acres to be divided among his daughter Lucy Brown's children Dancy, Locey, Henry, Edward and Eliza Brown; a bed and furniture to his daughter Catherine and appointed his son Dixon Brown and Henry C. **Harris** his executors. James **Harris**, Peter Brown, Edward **Bowman**, James Brown, Jr., Billy Brown, Milly Brown and Dixon Brown posted 500 pounds security for Henry C. **Harris**'s administration of the estate [WB 2:471]. He was the father of

    i.   Edward², born say 1763, taxable in the Charles City County household of Dixon Brown in 1783, called "son of Dixon" in 1790 and 1793 [PPTL, 1783-7; 1788-1814]. He was probably deceased by 24 January 1811 when his children Polly, Lucy and Rachel were left 10 acres by the will of their grandfather Dixon Brown.

11   ii.   Dixon², Jr., born say 1766.

12   iii.   Sally, born say 1768.

    iv.   James², born say 1770, taxable in Charles City County in 1791, called James Brown, Sr., when he was taxable from 1792 to 1799, a "Mulattoe" taxable on 2 tithes and 3 horses in 1812 [PPTL, 1788-1814]. He was head of a Charles City County household of 5 "other free" in 1810 [VA:959] and 4 "free colored" in 1820 [VA:13].

    v.   Lucy, mother of Dancy, Locey, Henry, Edward, and Eliza Brown. Dancy was living in Albemarle County on 31 December 1821 when he sold his part of Dixon Brown's estate to Locky **Goin** (wife of David) for $10 [DB 6:501].

    vi.   Catherine, married to Edward **Bowman** by 13 June 1825 when he was paid $20 as her legacy of a bed and furniture [WB 3:115].

13   vii.   Elizabeth, born say 1785.

    viii.   Milly, born say 1788, head of a Charles City County household of 4 "other free" in 1810 [VA:953]. She made a 14 September 1827 Charles City County will, proved 17 July 1834, leaving 10 acres she was living on to her brother Dixon during his lifetime and then to be divided between her niece Patsey **Harris** and Cyrus Brown [WB 4:80].

14   ix.   Peter, born about 1797.

And he was the father of illegitimate children which he recognized:

    i.   Polly **Harris**.

    ii.   Susannah **Harris**, illegitimate daughter of Dixon Brown and wife of James **Harris**, received 10 acres of land by the 24 January 1811

Charles City County will of her father. She died intestate without a living child before October 1826 when Polly Harris, Morris Harris and Patsy his wife, Pegg **Bowman**, James Brown, Jr. ("son of Dixon"), and his wife Sally, and Peter Brown and his wife Susan appointed James Brown to sell the land. Edward Brown was the highest bidder at $32 [DB 7:371].

iii.   Peggy **Bowman**.

7.   Benjamin Brown, born say 1755, was taxable on his own tithe and a horse in Waynoke Precinct of Charles City County in 1784 [PPTL, 1783-7]. He was paid 10 shillings for shoes he provided Elizabeth Christian in 1782 [WB 1:79]. He was witness to the 1 June 1791 Charles City County will of Sarah Brown [WB 1:70] and head of a household of 3 "other free" in 1810 [VA:958]. He was the father of

i.   William[7], born say 1784, called "son of Ben" when he was taxable in 1805 and 1807 [PPTL 1788-1814].

8.   Isaac Brown, born about 1760, was taxable in Lower Westover Precinct of Charles City County in 1786 [PPTL, 1783-7], and head of a Charles City County household of 10 "other free" in 1810 [VA:959] and 4 "free colored" in 1820 [VA:13]. He purchased 75 acres in Charles City County from Peter Ladd for $200 on 15 February 1804 [DB 5:34]. He applied for a pension in Charles City County at the age of sixty-nine on 19 May 1829 when he was living on his 70 acres of land with his unnamed wife, twenty-year-old son, twenty-one year-old daughter and her four-year-old child. He stated that he enlisted in Charles City County in 1780 and served eighteen months [M804-366]. He made a deed of trust (making his mark) for 75 acres of land adjoining Peter Ladd and the Cellar Run as well as all his personal estate for the benefit of Peter Ladd, Jr., on 22 January 1829 [DB 7:366]. He made a 10 April 1830 Charles City County will, which was proved 19 August 1830. He left one third his estate to his wife Sarah, to be divided among his children at her decease, left the remaining two thirds to son Micajah and daughter Sally Ann Brown, noted that his sons Carver and Travis were able to get their own living since they were able bodied unlike their brother Micajah, and noted that his daughters Maria and Clarissa were married and had already been provided for [WB 3:407-8]. He was the father of

i.   Maria.
ii.   Clarissa.
15   iii.   Carver, born about 1791.
iv.   Travis, born about 1793, taxable in Charles City County in 1814 [PPTL 1788-1814].
v.   Sally Ann, born about 1807, twenty-one years old on 29 January 1829.
vi.   Micajah, born about 1809, twenty years old on 29 January 1829. His sister Sally Ann sold land to him by deed proved in Charles City County on 19 December 1833, and he sold 7 acres by deed proved on 16 April 1835 [Minutes 1830-9, 149, 230].

9.   John Brown, born say 1764, was taxable in the Charles City County household of (his father) Abraham Brown in 1785 [PPTL, 1783-7], taxable on 118 acres in 1790 and 1800 [Land Tax List, 1790, p.1; 1800, p.1], and head of a household of 5 "other free" in 1810 [VA:958]. He was the father of Rebecca Brown, granddaughter of Frances **Harris** who left her a spinning wheel by her 12 November 1803 Charles City County will [WB 1:650]. On 6 October 1804 he (signing) made a deed of trust to Wyatt Walker for 118 acres which he received by the will of his father Abraham Brown to secure a bond which Dixon Brown had posted for him to satisfy an execution against his estate by Thomas Blanks [DB 5:65]. He was a "man of colour" who made a deed of trust (signing) on 28 May 1817 for 80 acres which was all the land he was

then living on which descended to him by the will of his father Abraham. He and his wife Priscilla (both signing) sold 16 acres adjoining his land and Abraham Brown's to George **Jones** for $96 on 8 May 1821 [DB 6:92]. The account of his Charles City County estate was taken by Abraham Brown and had its first entry on 1 November 1825. Abraham distributed about $11 to James Brown, Sr., and Carver Brown who was also paid $1.62 for accommodations furnished the appraisers of the estate [WB 3:236]. John was the father of

    i.   James, born say 1785, taxable in Charles City County in 1806, called "son of John" in 1810 [PPTL, 1788-1814].

    ii.   Rebecca, granddaughter of Frances **Harris** who left her a spinning wheel in 1804.

10. Abraham² Brown, born say 1769, "son of Abraham," was taxable in Charles City County in 1790, a "Mulattoe" taxable in 1813 [PPTL, 1788-1814], taxable on two tracts of land, one of 92-1/2 acres and the other of 30 acres in 1790 and 1800 [Land Tax List, 1790, p.1; 1800, p.1], and head of a Charles City County household of 10 "other free" and 3 slaves in 1810 [VA:957] and 9 "free colored" in 1820 [VA:3]. He was a man of color from Charles City County who served in the Revolution [*Charles City County historical Society Newsletter* 6:10-14 cited by NSDAR, *African American Patriots*, 148]. On 17 July 1800 he and his wife Susannah (both signing) swapped the 115-1/2 acres he received by his father's will with 125-1/2 acres which his brother William received by the will [DB 4:514, 516]. He and his wife Susanna made a deed of gift to Cornelius Brown, John Brown, Henry C. **Harris** and Dixon Brown, Jr., as trustees for a tract of land adjoining John Brown upon which a meeting house known as "Elam" was to be set apart expressly for the use of the Baptist Church on 20 November 1818 ("but when unoccupied by the baptist to be free for any minister of the Gospel to preach us") [DB 6:214]. He was granted administration on the Charles City County estate of his brother John Brown, Sr., on 20 October 1825 [Minutes 1823-9, 141]. He left a 12 April 1836 Charles City County will (signing), proved 19 November 1840. He left his son Christopher the house where Christopher then lived and 20 acres of land on the north side of his plantation, left the remainder of his land to his three sons Allen, Abraham James, and Samuel Brown, and left the remainder of his estate to his children Allen, Abraham James, Christopher and Samuel Brown, Patsy **Thompson**, Polly Brown, Susanna Brown, and his grandson Robert Brown, son of his daughter Nancy **Jones** [WB 4:375]. He died in Charles City in August 1840 [Register of Free Negroes, 1835-64, no. 11]. His children were

    i.   Allen.

    ii.   Abraham James, called James A. Brown in the settlement of his father's estate [WB 4:423].

    iii. Christopher.

    iv. Samuel.

    v. Patsy **Thompson**.

    vi. Polly.

    vii. Susanna.

    viii. Nancy **Jones**, mother of Robert Brown.

11. Dixon² Brown, born say 1766, was head of a Charles City County household of 5 "other free" in 1810 [VA:938] and 2 "free colored" in 1820 [VA:8]. He died before 21 February 1833 when (his son?) James Brown was granted administration on his estate [Minutes 1830-7, 144]. His widow Lucy Brown sold the land she was allotted from his estate to James Brown by deed acknowledged on 19 July 1836 [Minutes 1830-7, 284]. He was the father of

16   i.   ?Dixon³, born say 1792.

ii. James, born 2 July 1794, registered as a "free Negro" in Charles City County about 1810 and renewed his registration in 1842 and 1859: *son of old Dixon, brown complexion, 48 the 2 July 1842* [Register of Free Negroes, 1835-64, no. 51]. He married Sally **Stewart** ("colored"), 11 March 1816 Charles City County bond [*Wm & Mary Quarterly Historical Papers* Vol. 8, No.3, p.194]. He was head of a Charles City County household of 4 "free colored" in 1820 [VA:7]. He ("son of Dixon"), William T. Brown and Will Brown ware called "people of color" on 21 February 1828 when the Charles City County court allowed them to keep a gun [Minutes 1823-9, 284]. He (called James Brown, Jr.) and Edward **Bowman** were attorneys for Elizabeth Brown's sale of 10 acres of land she received by the will of her father Dixon Brown. She was living in Liberia on 18 December 1828 when they paid $20 to her son Richard B. Brown who was living in Petersburg. James purchased the land on the same day from the buyer for $20 [DB 7:359, 360]. He sold 7 acres adjoining his land and land of Peter Brown to Peter Brown on 15 May 1828 [DB 7:291]. He was called son of Dixon Brown on 17 July 1834 when he was granted administration on the estate of Milly Brown with Reuben Brown, Jr., as his security. He and others brought a suit in chancery against Edward **Bowman**'s children on 19 February 1835. On 16 April 1835 he was granted administration on the estate of Thomas **Harris** with Abraham Brown and Edward **Bowman** as his securities [Minutes 1830-7, 223, 234].

12. Sally Brown, born say 1768, was head of a Charles City County household of 5 "free colored" in 1820 [VA:11]. She was named in the 24 January 1811 Charles City County will of her father Dixon Brown which was proved 18 January 1821 [WB 2:471]. According to the will, she was the mother of

i. Reuben, born say 1785, taxable in Charles City County in 1806 [PPTL, 1788-1814]. He obtained a certificate of freedom in Charles City County (no date): *dark brown* (at a later date): *dead* [Register of Free Negroes 1835-64, no.71]. He made an 11 February 1839 Charles City County will, proved 21 March 1839, leaving a walnut table to his sister Lucy's daughter Airanna Brown and dividing the remainder of his estate between his "kinsman" Mitchel **Harris** and friend Barnet **Harris** who he named executors. Ned **Bowman** was paid for digging the grave and Jesse Brown was paid $4 for making the coffin [WB 4:333, 363].

ii. Cornelius, born say 1787, taxable in Charles City County in 1809 [PPTL 1788-1814], head of a household of 1 "other free" in 1810 [VA:940]. He purchased 50 acres in Charles City County for $200 on 20 March 1819, and he and his wife Polly Brown (both making their mark) sold 3-1/3 acres in Charles City County known as "Binns" bounded by Henry Adams and Chavis **Harris** (devised to Cornelius by Dixon Brown) to Chavis **Harris** for $11 on 4 January 1825 [DB 6:246; 7:41]. He was living in Africa (Liberia) when he was taxable on 50 acres on Wilcox's Mill Road, Charles City County, from 1826 to 1830 [Land Tax List 1782-1830].

iii. Betsey **Harris**, born say 1788.

iv. Polly. She, Elizabeth Brown, and Edward **Bowman** were attorneys in fact for a deed from Cornelius Brown to Reuben Brown proved in court on 20 December 1832 [Minutes 1830-9, 136].

v. Sabrina.

vi. Lucy, mother of Arianna Brown who registered in Charles City County on 16 June 1831: *daughter of Lucy S. Brown, Mulatto girl, eleven years old 3d last month* [Minutes 1830-7, 59].

vii. Elizabeth.

13. Elizabeth Brown, born say 1785, daughter of Dixon Brown, made James Brown, Jr., and (her brother-in-law) Edward **Bowman** her attorneys to sell 10 acres of land she received by the will of her father Dixon Brown. She was living in Liberia on 18 December 1828 when they paid $20 from the sale of the land to her son Richard B. Brown who was living in Petersburg [DB 1:359]. She was the mother of

    i. Richard B., born say 1805, living in Petersburg on 18 December 1828. He was probably the Richard Brown whose account of sales was recorded in Charles City County on 3 March 1832 and included buyers Oliver **Bowman**, Molly Brown, Valentine **Harris**, Daniel **Harris**, James Brown, Peter Brown, Ed **Bowman**, James Brown, Jr., Burwell **Harris**, Mitchel **Harris**, Austin Brown and Reuben Brown [WB 3:467]. On 16 February 1832 the court appointed James Brown guardian to his orphans Pleasant and Cyrus Brown [Minutes 1830-7, 91]. However, Cyrus and Pleasant were called children of Dixon Brown, Jr., when they registered in Charles City County on 19 January 1832 [Minutes 1830-9, 89].

14. Peter Brown, born about 1797, received one-third part of 75 acres by his father Dixon Brown's 24 January 1811 Charles City County will which was proved 18 January 1821 [WB 2:471]. In October 1826 he and his wife Susan appointed James Brown to sell their rights to 10 acres which Susannah **Harris**, deceased, received by Dixon's will [DB 7:371]. He purchased 7 acres adjoining his land from (his brother) James Brown on 15 May 1828 [DB 7:291]. He obtained a certificate of freedom in Charles City County on 18 August 1814 and renewed it in August 1832: *aged thirty five, born free in this county, died 1842* [Register of Free Negroes 1835-64, p.2, no.70]. He made a 1 November 1841 Charles City County will, proved 15 December 1842. He left 10 acres which he received by the will of his father Dixon Brown as well as $30 to his daughter Harriet **Harris** but noted that her husband Valentine **Harris** was to have no other control over the land than to live on it and cultivate it during her lifetime. He left a heifer to Harriet's son James **Harris**, left a horse and cart to his son Albert Brown, left his wife Sarah one third of the balance of the estate and the remainder to his son Albert who he named as executor [WB 4:447]. He was the father of

    i. Harriet, born 17 November 1819, obtained a certificate of freedom in Charles City County on 17 November 1831: *daughter of Peter Brown, yellow complexion, twelve years old 4th April last* [Minutes 1830-7, 83]. She married Valentine **Harris**.

    ii. Albert, born 22 November 1821, obtained a certificate of freedom in Charles City County on 17 November 1831: *yellow complexion, son of Peter Brown, ten years old 22nd November* [Minutes 1830-7, 83].

15. Carver Brown, born about 1791, obtained a certificate of freedom in Charles City County on 20 November 1817 and renewed it on 20 June 1825: *bright Mulatto, aged thirty four, born free in this county* [Register of Free Negroes 1835-64, no.101]. He was head of a Charles City County household of 6 "free colored" in 1820 [VA:10]. He was named in the 10 April 1830 Charles City County will of his father Isaac Brown. He was the father of

    i. Walker, born 9 April 1813, registered in Charles City County on 16 March 1835: *son of Carver Brown, brown complexion, aged twenty one 9 April last* [Minutes 1830-9, 222].

    ii. Pryor, born about 1818, registered in Charles City County on 16 March 1835: *son of Carver Brown, brown complexion, aged seventeen* [Minutes 1830-9, 222].

16. Dixon[3] Brown, born say 1792, was head of a Charles City County household of 5 "free colored" in 1820 (called Dixon Brown, Jr.) [VA:8]. He was the father of

   i.   Cyrus, born 24 July 1816, obtained a certificate of freedom in Charles City County on 19 January 1832: *son of Dixon Brown, Jr., brown complexion, fifteen years old 24th July last, born free in this county* [Minutes 1830-7, 89].

   ii. Pleasant, born 17 April 1821, obtained a certificate of freedom in Charles City County on 19 January 1832: *son of Dixon Brown, Jr., yellowish complexion, ten years old 17th April last, born free in this county* [Minutes 1830-7, 89].

Other members of the Brown family in Charles City County were

   i.   Samuel, born about 1770, registered in Petersburg on 19 June 1810: *a dark brown Mulatto man, five feet four inches high, forty years old, born free in Charles City County* [Register of Free Negroes 1794-1819, no. 614].

   ii. Cranston, born say 1782, taxable in Charles City County in 1803 and a "Mulattoe" taxable in 1814 [PPTL, 1788-1814]. He was head of a Charles City County household of 6 "free colored" in 1820 [VA:11].

Other members of the Brown family in Virginia were

   i.   Sarah, born say 1725, "Mulatto" mother of Elizabeth Brown who was born 28 March 1745 in Bristol Parish [Chamberlayne, *Register of Bristol Parish*, 290].

   ii. Elizabeth, born about 1752, registered in Petersburg on 21 May 1802: *a dark brown Mulatto woman, five feet four inches high, fifty years old, born free & raised in the Town of Petersburg* [Register of Free Negroes 1794-1819, no. 232]. She was head of a Petersburg Town household of 2 "other free" in 1810 [VA:125a].

   iii. Charles, born about 1764, registered in Petersburg on 30 June 1804: *a dark brown Mulatto man, five feet seven inches high, forty years old, straight and well made, born free & raised in the County of Prince George* [Register of Free Negroes 1794-1819, no. 276].

   iv. John, born say 1768, head of a Chesterfield County household of 8 "other free" in 1810 [VA:1062]. He may have been identical to Jack Brown, husband of Nancy Brown who registered in Petersburg on 26 January 1798: *a light brown Mulatto woman, short bushy hair, five feet high, twenty seven years old the 9 Dec. 1797, daughter of Elizabeth Muns of this town a free woman & now wife of Jack Brown a free man* [Register of Free Negroes 1794-1819, no. 128].

   v.   Sally, born about 1781, registered in Petersburg on 15 August 1800: *a brown Mulatto woman...five feet seven inches high with bushy hair, nineteen years old, born free & raised in the County of Prince George* [Register of Free Negroes 1794-1819, no. 184].

   vi. James, born about 1787, registered as a "Free Negro" in Greensville County, Virginia, on 1 April 1825: *free born of a yellow Complexion about 38 years old 5'6-3/4 Inches high (in shoes)...a hatter & planter*, and his wife Temperance registered on 7 April 1825: *(wife of James Brown) free born of yellowish Complexion, Thirty Six years old, feet 5 Inches high in Shoes...& her 5 children viz. Berry, Dixon, & Wm Green boys & Arrian, Delina, & Francis Ann daughters* [Register of Free Persons of Colour, nos.139, 144].

Bertie County, North Carolina

1. Francis Brown, born say 1720, was a witness (with Benjamin Wynn) to the 1742 deed by which Gabriel **Manly** purchased 100 acres of land in Bertie County [DB F:339]. Francis was head of a Bertie County household in 1758

and 1759, counted with Moses **Manly** as two "Black" taxables in the list of John Brickell [CR 10.702.1]. In 1759 this part of Bertie County became Hertford County which lost most of its early records in courthouse fires of 1830 and 1862. However, a 1779 Tax List filed with the central government has survived, and he may have been the Francis Brown who was taxable in District 4 of this list on 140 acres and a horse [G.A.30.1, p.71].[50] His descendants may have been

  i. John, born say 1750, perhaps the John Brown who was taxable on one poll in Hertford County in 1779 (adjacent to Francis Brown). He received a patent for 260 acres on Hardy Pace's Mill Swamp in Northampton County, North Carolina, on 29 October 1782 [DB 7:154] and purchased 30 acres adjoining this on Urahaw Swamp in October 1798 [DB 10:393]. He was head of a Northampton County household of 5 "other free" in 1790 [NC:72].

 ii. Robert, born say 1755, head of a Northampton County household of 7 "other free" in 1790 [NC:72] and 3 in 1800 [NC:430]. Perhaps his widow was Mary Brown, born before 1776, head of a Northampton County household of 6 "other free" in 1810 [NC:712] and 4 in Halifax County, North Carolina, in 1830. On 3 March 1818 the Northampton County court ordered her to show cause why (her children?) Aaron and Allen Brown should not be bound apprentices [Minutes 1813-21].

iii. Beverly, born say 1760, married Hannah **Parham**, 15 November 1785 Greensville County, Virginia bond, William Batte security.[51] They were married 20 November by Rev. William Andrews, a Methodist minister. Beverly was living in Greensville County on 27 March 1788 when the sheriff credited him for overcharging tax on five more horses than he owned in 1787 [Orders 1781-9, 356]. He was head of a Northampton County, North Carolina household of 6 "other free" in 1810 [NC:712]. The 7 June 1812 session of the Northampton County court ordered John and Fanny **Dungill**, children of color, bound to him to be a blacksmith and spinster respectively. William **Walden** provided security of 500 pounds for the indenture. He was declared an insolvent debtor in District 6 of Halifax County on 15 August 1842 [Minutes 1832-46].

 iv. William, born before 1776, head of a Hertford County household of 9 "free colored" in 1820 [NC:188].

  v. John, born say 1770, head of a Pasquotank County household of 2 "other free" in 1790 [NC:27], 3 in 1800, and 7 "other free" and 1 slave in 1810 [NC:883].

BRUCE FAMILY

1. James[1] Bruce, born say 1728, purchased 100 acres on Clay's Branch in Southwarke Parish, Surry County, Virginia, on 18 July 1749 and purchased another 50 acres adjoining this land on 1 December 1760 [DB 5:431; 8:64]. This adjoined land of the **Banks** family [Hopkins, *Surry County Deeds, 1756-1787*, 91 (DB 12:219)]. He was head of a Surry County household of 8 whites

---

[50]The land Francis Brown was taxable on in 1779 may have been the same 140 acres Gabriel **Manley** purchased from Joseph Wynns on 23 February 1746/7 near the Holley Swamp [Bertie DB G:347, 236].

[51]The **Parham** family were probably the freed slaves of the white Parham family of Sussex County. Caesar **Parham**, born about 1762, was head of a Sussex County household of 11 "other free" in 1810. He received a certificate in Sussex County on 9 June 1810: *Cezar (no last name), dark brown complexion, 5'4-1/4", 48 years old, freed by July 1784 deed of Steth Parham* [Certificates granted to Free negroes & mulattoes from October 1800, #84].

(free persons) in 1782 and 9 in 1784 [VA:43, 78]. He was taxable in Surry County from 1783 to 1802: charged with Sampson **Walden**'s tithe, a slave named Isaac, 2 horses and 8 cattle in 1787; charged with Jacob Bruce's tithe in 1794; charged with Jacob and James Bruce, Jr.'s tithes in 1797 [PPTL, 1782-90, frames 371, 402, 409, 517; 1791-1816, 76, 175, 284, 361, 440, 475]. He was taxable on 120 acres in Surry County in 1790 [1790 Land Tax List, p.3]. His will, recorded in Surry County on 25 January 1803, named his children Jemima, Lucy, Jacob, Sarah, James, and John Bruce. He left land on the east side of John Cocke's and Nathaniel Savedge's lines to his son James, left land on the west side of those lines to his son John, and left the remainder of his estate to his wife Elizabeth. His son James was executor [WB 1:583-5]. Elizabeth was taxable from 1803 to 1815: taxable on (her son) James Bruce's tithe in 1803 and 1804; listed as a "free Negro & Mulatto" in 1813; taxable on a free male and 2 cattle in 1815 [PPTL, 1791-1816, 514, 555, 610, 648, 666, 726, 804] and head of a Surry County household of 5 "other free" in 1810 [VA:601]. They were the parents of

 i. Jemima, listed as a "free Negro & Mulatto" in Surry County in 1813 [PPTL, 1791-1816, frame 726].

 ii. Jacob, born say 1778, taxable in Surry County from 1794 to 1816: listed with (his father) James Bruce in 1794 and 1797; charged with his own tax from 1798; listed as a "free Negro" in 1815 [PPTL, 1791-1816, frames 175, 284, 318, 399, 475, 555, 610, 648, 685, 807, 847].

 iii. James[2], born say 1780, taxable in Surry County from 1797 to 1805: listed with (his father) James Bruce from 1797 to 1802; listed with (his mother) Elizabeth Bruce in 1803 and 1804; taxable on 2 tithes in 1805 [PPTL, 1791-1816, frames 284, 318, 399, 475, 514, 588]. His Surry County will was witnessed by Saeca **Cypress** and Edith **Thompson** and was proved 24 April 1806. He left ten dollars to Benjamin Bailey Bruce and the remainder of his estate to Robert Bailey Bruce [WB 2:98].

 iv. Lucy, born say 1782, daughter of Elizabeth Bruce, married Benjamin **Banks**, 22 January 1803 Surry County bond, 19 February marriage, James **Roberts** surety.

 v. John, born say 1790, taxable in Surry County from 1809 to 1816: listed with 2 "free Negroes & Mulattoes above the age of 16" in 1813; taxable on a slave and 2 horses in 1815 [PPTL, 1791-1816, 648, 685, 726, 807, 848]. He married Elizabeth **Cypress**, 24 December 1812 Surry County bond, Benjamin **Banks** surety, Samuel **Blizzard** witness. Their son William Bruce registered in Surry County on 23 December 1842: *a mullatoe boy, son of Betsy Cypress...is a spare make, bushy hair...aged about 24 years and is 5'8-1/4" high* [Hudgins, *Surry County Register of Free Negroes*, 106, 164].

 vi. Sarah.

BRUMEJUM/ BRUMAGEN FAMILY

1. Eliza Brumejum, born say 1692, was presented by the court in Anne Arundel County, Maryland, in August 1712 for having a "Mallato" bastard child. She confessed that "a Negroe man called James belonging to Stephen Warman" was the father of the child, and the court ordered that she be sold for seven years and bound her unnamed son to her master for thirty-one years [Judgment Records 1712-15, Liber TB, no. 3, p.5]. She was probably the ancestor of

2 i. James, born say 1712.

  ii. R. Brumager, head of a Baltimore City household of 1 "other free" in 1810 [MD:75].

2. James Brumigem, born say 1712, was tried by the Frederick County, Virginia court on 24 January 1746/7 for breaking into the house of Captain John Hite

and taking some gunpowder. He was found not guilty of felony but found guilty of petty larceny and given thirty-one lashes, made to stand in the pillory and ordered to post bond of 40 pounds currency for his good behavior. He was called a "Mulatto" on 5 March 1746/7 when the court ordered that he receive twenty-five lashes for abusing Lawrence Stevens in a very ill manner. On 6 March 1746/7 the court ordered that the sheriff sell James' goods: a horse, saddle, bridle, coat jacket, leather jacket, rifle, gun powder horn, silver buckles, silver clasps, three axes, a cross-cut saw, and a hand saw for a debt of about 8 pounds he owed Jost Hite, John Hite and Lewis Stephens. His estate was attached for debt again on 7 August 1747, 7 June 1748 and 3 August 1748. He died before 6 September 1748 when the court granted administration of his estate to Peter Tostee, his greatest creditor [Orders 1745-8, 201, 213, 224, 301-2, 435, 462, 488]. He may have been the ancestor of

3   i.   Thomas Brumagen, born say 1740.

3.   Thomas Brumagen, born say 1740, was indicted with Jane Clark for fornication by the Frederick County, Virginia court on 7 September 1762. Jane was discharged but Thomas was ordered to pay a fine of 500 pounds of tobacco. Richard Pearis, Gent., undertook to pay his fine. He was sued by William and Jane Phillips on 5 November 1762, but the case was agreed before coming to trial. He was convicted of stealing a steer belonging to John Shearer on 2 September 1766 and chose to receive 39 lashes corporal punishment rather than be tried at the General court. Seth Dungen sued him for 3 pounds, 10 shillings on 8 October 1766 [Orders 1762-3, 156, 393; 1765-7, 172, 224]. He may have been the father of

       i.   George Brumagam, born say 1760, taxable in Frederick County, Virginia, in 1787. He enlisted as a soldier in the Revolution from Virginia: *George Brumma, yellow complexioned, born in Australia* [NSDAR, *African American Patriots*, 148].

BRYAN FAMILY

Joan Bryan, born say 1683, was the servant of Mary Dudley of Cople Parish, Westmoreland County, on 30 June 1703 when she confessed to the court that she had a "mulatto" child. And on 25 July 1705 she confessed to having a child by a white man [Orders 1698-1705, 194, 269a, 270].

Mary Bryan, born say 1687, was the servant of John Sergenton on 24 May 1707 when she confessed to the York County court that she had a "Mulato" child. The court ordered the churchwardens of Bruton Parish to sell her for five years when she completed her service to her master [DOW 13:66].

Their descendants may have been

1   i.   William[1], born about 1748.
      ii.   Sarah, head of a Currituck County, North Carolina household of 4 "other free" in 1790 [NC:20].
     iii.   Bridgett, "Free Colored" living alone in Tyrrell County, North Carolina, in 1790 [NC:34].

1.   William[1] Bryan, Jr., born about 1748, was a taxable "Malletor Servant" in Thomason **Bass**'s household in the 1769 Bertie County tax list of David Standley, and in John Standley's 1770 tax list [CR 10.702.1]. He was head of a Charleston District, St. Bartholomew's Parish, South Carolina household of 5 "other free" in 1790. His children may have been

       i.   Kedar, perhaps named for Thomasin **Bass**' son Cader. He married Mary **Evans**, 1 May 1817 Cumberland County, North Carolina bond. He was head of a Fayetteville household of 4 "other free" in 1790 (Kedar Bryant) [NC:42], 4 in New Hanover County in 1800 (Cato

Bryan) [NC:311], and 7 "free colored" in Fayetteville in 1820 (Cader Briant) [NC:189]. He and Curtis Chesnutt were found not guilty of unspecified charges in Cumberland County court on 5 September 1828. He was acquitted of petty larceny in Cumberland County court on 6 March 1829, but his codefendant, a slave named Moses, was found guilty. On 3 June 1829 he was ordered to bring his sons Jesse **Parker** and Luke Bryant to court and show cause why they should not be bound out [Minutes 1827-31, n.p.]

    ii.   Andrew, who established what would become the First African Baptist Church of Savannah [Berlin, *Slaves Without Masters*, 70].

BRYANT FAMILY

1.   Martha Bryant, born say 1730, confessed to the churchwardens of St. Stephens Parish in Northumberland County, Virginia court on 14 February 1748 that she had a bastard child which was a "Mulatto" [Orders 1743-49, 421]. She may have been the ancestor of

    i.   Samuel, "F. Negro" head of a Culpeper County household of 6 "other free" in 1810 [VA:7].

    ii.   Sylvana, head of a New Hanover County, North Carolina household of 4 "free colored" in 1820.

    iii.   Sally, head of a Halifax County, North Carolina household of 7 in "free colored" in 1830.

BUGG FAMILY

1.   Betty Bugg, alias Doss, born say 1726, was the daughter of a white woman and a "negro" slave according to a case heard before the Halifax County, Virginia court. Betty had a son Silvester during her term of indenture to Robert Turner. Her children were

    i.   Silvester, born about 1743, twenty-six years old in June 1769 when he petitioned the Halifax County, Virginia court for release from his indenture to George Hoomes Gwyn. He won his case in Halifax County court, but he lost the appeal in the General Court of Williamsburg. He had to serve five more years to complete his full thirty-one year indenture before he was released [Halifax County Pleas 6:378-9; Catterall, *Judicial Cases Concerning American Slavery,* I:88-90].

    ii.   ?Frank, born say 1768, "free Negro" head of a 96 District, Edgefield County, South Carolina household of 1 "other free" in 1790 [SC:65] and 2 in Newberry District in 1810 [SC:122a].

    iii.   ?Samuel, born say 1770, head of a 96 District, Newberry County, South Carolina household of 6 "other free" in 1790 [SC:65] and 8 in Edgefield County in 1810 [SC:788].

    iv.   ?Benjamin, born say 1784, married Tabitha **Walden**, 3 May 1805 Mecklenburg County, Virginia bond, James Noel security.

    v.   ?Tony, "free Negro" head of a Sussex County household in 1810.

    vi.   ?Pleasant, born say 1785, "free Negro" head of a Brunswick County, Virginia household of 5 "other free" in 1810 [VA:707] and 7 "free colored" in 1820 [VA:594].

    vii.   ?Bats, a "free Negro" head of a Newberry District, South Carolina household of 2 "other free" in 1810 [SC:122].

BULLARD FAMILY

1.   John Bullard, born say 1745, was taxable in Bladen County, North Carolina, in the same household with Gutridge **Locklear** ("Molatoes") in 1770 [Byrd, *Bladen County Tax Lists*, I:33]. He may have been the ancestor of

    i.   Jordan, born about 1791, a twelve-year-old "boy of colour" who was bound apprentice to William McNeill by the Robeson County court on 3 January 1803 [Minutes 1797-1806, 231].

BUNCH FAMILY

The Bunch family probably descended from John Bunch, born say 1630, who received a patent for 450 acres in New Kent County on 18 March 1662 [Patents 5:152]. He may have been the ancestor of several mixed-race members of the family:

1	i.	Paul[1], born say 1675.
2	ii.	John[1]. born say 1684.
3	iii.	Henry[1], born say 1690.

1.   Paul[1] Bunch, born say 1675, received a patent for 265 acres in North Carolina on the south side of the Roanoke River joining Quankey Pocosin and Gideon **Gibson** on 1 January 1725, and he bought a further 300 acres joining this land [Halifax DB 8:283]. He may have been the same Paul Bunch who was listed in the King William County, Virginia Rent Roll in 1704.

His Chowan County will was written on 16 November 1726 and probated on 10 March 1726/7 [SS 876, 3:138-9]. He left his land and eight slaves to his son John and to Fortune Holdbee and her daughters Keziah and Jemima. Elizabeth Bunch (no relationship stated) and his daughter Russell received only one shilling each. He did not mention a wife nor did he mention his relationship to Fortune Holdbee. She may have been his common-law wife since he gave her one slave as long as she remained single.[52]

The May 1734 Bertie court minutes referred to Keziah as "an orphan Child Entitled to a considerable Estate...(by the will of Paul Bunch) bound to Capt. Thos. Bryant till the age of Thirty one contrary to law," and the August 1735 Bertie County court Minutes referred to the estate of "a Mulatto woman, ~~Keziah Holdebee~~, and three children [Haun, *Bertie County Court Minutes,* I:135, 154]. Paul[1] Bunch had the following children:

4	i.	John[2], born say 1692.
	ii.	Russell, a daughter, received one shilling by her father's will.
	iii.	?Keziah Holdebee.
	iv.	?Jemima Holdebee.

2.   John[1] Bunch, born say 1684, "a Mulatto," and Sarah Slayden, a white woman, petitioned the Council of Virginia on 16 August 1705 to allow them to marry because the Minister of Blisland Parish (in New Kent and James City counties) had refused to marry them. The Council was undecided on the issue since "the intent of the Law (was) to prevent Negros and White Persons intermarrying," and John Bunch was a "Mulatto." The matter was referred to the court to decide [McIlwaine, *Executive Journals of the Council,* III:28, 31].[53] He was

---

[52]Fortune sold this land, "plantation where I now live ... formerly Paul Bunches," on 5 July 1727 [Bertie DB B:276], and received a patent for 640 acres in New Hanover County in August 1735 [Saunders, *Colonial Records of North Carolina*, III:52].

[53]A runaway "Mallatto Man Slave" named Jack, who belonged to Samuel Harwood, Jr., of Charles City County, apparently knew of John Bunch since he went by his name when he was living in South Carolina. George Rives, who had lived on Harwood's plantation, stated in a deposition recorded in Prince George County court on 8 September 1719 that he had met Jack while trading in South Carolina in April 1719 and that Jack had been in the company of a trader from Prince George County named

called John Bunch, Jr., when he received a patent for 400 acres in Hanover County on the upper side of Taylor's Creek on 18 February 1722 and called John Bunch on 2 July 1724 when he received a patent for another 400 acres adjoining his land. He patented another 400 acres adjoining his land on 17 August 1725 and another 400 acres on both sides of the Southana River on 28 September 1728 [Patents 11:162; 343; 12:244; 14:3]. He may have been the father of

    i.   Samuel, born say 1720, living in Louisa County on 28 May 1745 when he, Thomas **Collins**, Samuel **Collins**, William **Collins**, George **Gibson**, Thomas **Gibson**, William **Donathan**, and Benjamin **Branham** were presented by the court for failing to list a tithable (probably their wives) [Orders 1742-8, 152, 157, 172]. He received a patent for 400 acres in Louisa County on the Newfound Branch of Camp Creek on 8 April 1767 [Patents 36:1037].

3.   Henry[1] Bunch Sr., probably born about 1690, was a resident of Chowan County on 18 December 1727 when he purchased 200 acres in Bertie County on Reedy Branch. On 30 May 1729 he purchased 640 acres in Bertie on Conaritsat Swamp from Thomas Pollock [DB C:21, 266]. He was taxed on himself and two slaves in the 1750 Bertie County summary tax list and was a "Free Mulatto" taxable with two slaves in John Hill's 1763 Bertie tax list. Henry made a will in Bertie on 21 April 1775, proved in August 1775. He had already deeded 840 acres of land on Conaritsat and Mulberry to his grandson Jeremiah, Jr., in 1765, and in his will left most of the remainder of his land to his grandson Cader **Bass** [WB B:34-7]. Henry Sr. named as heirs the following children:

5   i.   Jeremiah[1], Sr., born say 1715.
     ii.   Tamerson, married Thomas **Bass**.
     iii. Susannah, married Lazarus **Summerlin**.
     iv. Rachel, married Joseph **Collins**.
     v.   Nancy, married Isaac **Bass**.
6   vi. Embrey, born say 1730/35.

4.   John[2] Bunch, born say 1692, owned land adjoining Gideon **Gibson**'s land, and he probably named his son Gideon for him. He sold the land that "my father Paul Bunch bought of James Kelly on Occaneche" on 28 August 1728 and purchased 100 acres in Bertie County on the south side of the Roanoke River near Tuckahoe Marsh on 12 May 1729. He purchased 270 acres in Bertie on the south side of the river on 8 February 1728/9, and another 50 acres on the south side of the river, and sold these two plots as one parcel of 320 acres on 4 November 1732 [Bertie DB C:21, 142, 146, 288; Edgecombe DB 1:19]. Like the **Gibson**s he moved to Berkeley County, South Carolina, where he recorded a Plat for 350 acres northeast of the Santee River and lot 177 in Amelia Township on 15 November 1735 [Colonial Plats 13:425]. He recorded a plat for a further 100 acres on the Santee River and a half-acre town lot in Amelia Township a month later on 13 December 1735 [Colonial Plats 2:461]. On 15 December 1755 he and his wife Mary made a deed of gift of half this land to their son John, Junior [Charleston DB Q-Q:193-4]. Their children were

7   i.   Gideon, born say 1713.
     ii.   John[3], Jr., received half his father's land on 15 December 1755.
     iii. ?Jacob, who recorded a plat for 200 acres in St. Matthew's Parish on 2 June 1772 which was land adjoining Gideon and John Bunch [Colonial Plats 13:425].
     iv. ?James, who lived on land adjoining John Bunch in St. Matthew's Parish, Berkeley County [Colonial Plats 13:425].

Robert Hix [Deeds, Wills, Etc. 1713-28, 350].

v. ?Naomy, married John Joyner, Junr., 23 December 1754 (both of Amelia Township) [*History of Orangeburg, S.C.*, 137].

5. Jeremiah[1] Bunch, Sr., born say 1715, made a will in Bertie on 8 Mar. 1797, proved a few days later. It did not identify his wife, who predeceased him, but named his children:

    i. William, probably born about 1740, but did not marry until middle age, bond 23 December 1785 Mary Bunch, with Frederick Bunch bondsman. He left a will in Bertie in 1816.

8   ii. Henry[2], born say 1743.

    iii. Jeremiah[2], born about 1745, married, bond 14 January 1765 Judah Hill, Micajah Bunch bondsman. He died intestate in Bertie in 1809.

    iv. Nehemiah, left a will in Bertie County in 1815.

    v. Frederick, born about 1745/8, left a will in Bertie County in 1810.

    vi. Nanny, married **Collins**.

6. Embrey Bunch, born say 1730/35, made a will in Bertie County on 20 July 1780, proved May 1789. He left a wife Elizabeth and children:

    i. Micajah[2] Sr., born circa 1760/65, married bond 8 April 1791 Levinia Holder, with Elisha Holder bondsman, and secondly, bond 17 November 1801 Teletha Smith, with Micajah Bunch Jr. bondsman. He moved to Christian County, Kentucky about 1803.

    ii. Mary, married _____ Williams.

    iii. Zadock, born before 1775. Unmarried, made his will 30 January 1801, proved May 1801.

    iv. Nanny, married Rigdon **Pritchard**, 29 February 1792 Bertie County bond.

    v. Milley, unmarried in 1801.

7. Gideon Bunch, born say 1713, was probably John[2] Bunch's son since he sold the land John inherited. He was living in Brunswick County, Virginia, in 1740 [Orders 1732-41, 253; 1737-44, 41, 64]. He was a defendant in a June 1747 Lunenburg County, Virginia court case [Orders 1746-48, 209] and was taxable in Lunenburg County on himself and Cage Bunch (his son Micajah?) in 1749 [Bell, *Sunlight on the Southside*, 114]. He was taxed as "Gibion" Bunch on 2 polls in the 1750 Granville County, North Carolina tax list of Samuel Henderson [CR 44.701.19]. He was taxable on one black poll in 1755 in Orange County, North Carolina:

Bunch, Gideon a Molata 0/1 [T&C Box 1, p.4].

Members of the **Gibson** family were also taxed as "Molatas" in Orange County in 1755. He was indebted to Samuel Benton of Orange County for 3 pounds, 11 shillings in June 1756 [Haun, *Orange County Court Minutes*, I:171]. He recorded a plat for 100 acres on the northeast side of Four Hole Swamp in Berkeley County, South Carolina on 5 December 1758 [Colonial Plats 8:30], and he was listed with (son?) Ephraim Bunch in the Berkeley County Detachment under command of Captain Benjamin Elliot: drafted 8 November 1759 and discharged 8 January 1760 [Clark, *Colonial Soldiers of the South*, 938]. He and his son William were "Black" taxables in Fishing Creek District, Granville County, in 1761 and in 1762 with the notation, *Refs. to list his wife &c.*

On 15 March 1763 while a resident of Berkeley County he sold 565 acres in Halifax County, North Carolina, of which 265 acres had been patented to Paul Bunch on 1 Jan 1725, the remaining acreage having been purchased by Paul Bunch from Thomas Wilkins on the south side of the Roanoke River joining

Quankey Pocoson, Sims, and Gideon **Gibson**. William and Temperance Bunch were witnesses to the deed [DB 8:283].

On 26 June 1765 he recorded a memorial for 100 acres on Four Hole Swamp in Berkeley County [S.C. Archives series S111001, vol. 6:455]. He was the plaintiff in a suit in Granville County, North Carolina, on 11 August 1765 in which he accused William Bowling of trespass, but Gideon did not appear [Minutes 1754-70, 138]. On 2 March 1773 he recorded a plat for 200 acres in St. Matthew's Parish, Berkeley County on a branch of Four Holes called Target, adjoining Jacob and John Bunch [Colonial Plats, 13:424]. Perhaps he was the Gidian Bunch whose 17 March 1804 St. James, Goose Creek, Charleston County, South Carolina will was proved 7 May the same year [WB 29:629]. His children were

9   i.   Micajah[1], born say 1733.
      ii.   ?Ephraim, born say 1738, in the Berkeley County, South Carolina detachment under command of Captain Benjamin Elliot: drafted 8 November 1759, discharged 8 January 1760 [Clark, *Colonial Soldiers of the South*, 938]. He married Lydia Crier, daughter of Thomas Crier/Cryer and Elizabeth Powell. Ephraim and Lydia had three children according to testimony in Charleston District on 26 August 1813: *Elizabeth Powell married Thomas Crier and they Begat a Daughter by name Lydia Crier who married Ephraim Bunch and they begat two daughters and a son, that is now living by name Martha, Deborah and Elisha Bunch, the deponents say that Elizabeth Powell before mentioned and all their family were white people clear of any mixt blood and that neither of them ever heard any reflections Cast on their Colour or Blood, William (X) Kennedy, Jesse Joyner* [South Carolina Archives, Miscellaneous Records (Main Series), Volume 4-G, p. 207, cited by *The South Carolina Magazine of Ancestral Research* XVI:27].
      iii. William, born say 1740, an over sixteen-year-old taxable in his father's household in the 1762 list for Fishing Creek District: "Son William." A 7 November 1763 Granville County deed of sale for land from Henry Fuller to William **Chavers** refers to land on the north side of Tar River adjoining **Chavis** and William Bunch, and in 1764 he was a "Black" taxable in Henry Fuller's household in the Granville County list of Samuel Benton. He may have been the William Bunch who witnessed Gideon Bunch's sale of land in Halifax County on 15 March 1763 and owned land in St. Matthew's, Berkeley County, South Carolina, on 2 June 1772 [Colonial Plats, 13:425].
      iv.   ?Liddy, born before 1743, taxable in the 1754 Granville County tax list of Gideon Macon with (her brother?) Micajah Bunch in John Stroud's household.
      v.   ?Fanny, born about 1745-49, a 12-16 year-old taxable in the Fishing Creek District, Granville County household of John **Griffin** and his wife Miles **Griffin** in 1761.

Gideon's children named in the South Carolina will were
      vi.   Jeremiah, who purchased land from John Bunch by deed recorded in Charleston District between 1800 and 1801 [Lucas, *Index to Deeds of South Carolina*, D-7:224].
      vii. Hester Chern.
      viii. Mary Chamberlain.
      ix.   Daniel, head of a white Charleston County household of 10 persons in 1800 [SC:60].
      x.   David.

8.   Henry[2] Bunch, born say 1743, was taxed as a "Free Mulatto" in his father's Bertie County household in the 1763 list of John Hill. He married Eleanor

Bayson, 29 February 1764 Bertie County bond with Thomas **Bass** bondsman. In 1764 he was taxed on himself in his own household in Jonathan Standley's list, in 1767 on a slave, and he was taxed for the last time in Bertie County in 1769 in the household of Abraham Moses. He moved to Orange County by 1780 when he was taxable on a 2,179 pounds assessment in St. Mary's District [CR 073.701.1 by *NCGSJ* XI:155]. He was head of an Orange County household of 3 "other free," 1 white woman, and 3 slaves in 1800 [NC:550] and 5 "other free" and 1 slave in 1810 [NC:953]. He may have been the father of

    i.   Thomas, head of an Orange County household of 3 "other free" and 1 white woman in 1800 [NC:550].

    ii.   Eleanor, married John Perry on 2 March 1797, (her brother?) Thomas Bunch bondsman. She obtained a divorce from the General Assembly in December 1798. In her petition she claimed that John Perry took to card playing, wasting his property, and abusing her soon after they married. She and her child moved to her father's house [*NCGSJ* XVII:206].

9.   Micajah[1] Bunch, born say 1733, was probably identical to Cage Bunch who was taxable in Gideon Bunch's Lunenburg County household in 1749 [Bell, *Sunlight on the Southside*, 114]. He was taxable in 1754 in the Granville County list of Gideon Macon in John Stroud's household [CR 44.702.19]. He was called "Micager Bunch Molata" when he was taxed on 1 "Black" tithe in Orange County in 1755 [T&C Box, p.19]. He was a defendant for debt in Halifax County, Virginia, in June 1764, and in June 1769 the Halifax County court ordered that an attachment against his estate be dismissed [Pleas 4:312; 6:341]. He may have been the Micajah Bunch who was a delinquent taxpayer on "Indian Land" in Fincastle County, Virginia, in 1773. This meant that he was living in present-day Tennessee [*Magazine of Virginia Genealogy* 34:10]. He was taxable on an estate of 42 pounds in present-day Ashe County in 1778 [*NCGSJ* X:15-18]. He may have been the father of

    i.   Clement, born say 1770, an orphan boy bound to Anthony Cozart by the Orange County court on 25 November 1777. He was surrendered to the Granville County court by his bondsman, John Wilburn, on 1 November 1790 [Minutes 1789-91]. In December 1798 he posted a bastardy bond in Granville County for a child he had by Mildred **Bass** [Camin, *N.C. Bastardy Bonds*, 87].

Others in South Carolina

    i.   Lovet, head of a South Orangeburg District household of 8 "other free" in 1790 [SC:99]. He lived for a while in Robeson County, North Carolina, since "Lovec Bunches old field" was mentioned in the 1 March 1811 will of John **Hammons** [WB 1:125].

    ii.   Gib., a taxable "free negro" in the District between Broad and Catawba River, South Carolina, in 1784 [South Carolina Tax List 1783-1800, frame 37].

    iii.   Paul[2], head of a Union District, South Carolina household of 6 "other free" in 1800 [SC:241].

    iv.   Henry[3], head of a Newberry District, South Carolina household of 2 "other free" in 1800 [SC:66].

    v.   Ralph J., Nobel Peace Prize winner in 1950, probably descended from the South Carolina branch of the family, but this has not been proved. He was born in Detroit, Michigan, on 7 August 1904, son of Fred and Olive Bunche. The 1900 and 1910 census for Detroit lists several members of the Bunch family who were born in South Carolina, but Fred Bunch was not among them.

BUNDAY FAMILY

1. Ann[1] Bunday, born say 1703, was the servant of John Perry of Essex County on 18 July 1721 when she was ordered to serve her master an additional year for having a "Mulatto Child" [Orders 1716-23, 104]. She may have been the mother or grandmother of

2   i.   James, born about 1744.
      ii. Francis, born about 1758, living in Essex County on 16 January 1786 when he and Henry **Cook**, "free Mulattoes," were accused of entering the lumber house of Lott and Higby Merchants in the City of Richmond on 21 December 1785 and stealing a large quantity of cloth valued at over 200 pounds currency. James Higbee testified that he had found part of the goods in the possession of the defendants, and Richard Covington testified that he had purchased about five yards of material from Francis Bunday. Other remnants were found on or purchased from Mary Bunday, Lucy Bunday and Cenn Bunday; and Sukey Bunday purchased a remnant from Mary Bunday. The defendants were sent to Richmond for further trial [Orders 1784-7, 177-8]. He was taxable in King and Queen County in 1791 and 1792 [PPTL, 1782-1803] and taxable in Essex County from 1794 to 1803 [PPTL, 1782-1819, frames 256, 260, 272, 285, 297, 308, 357] and a "Free Negro" head of a Culpeper County household of 5 "other free" in 1810 [VA:7]. He was a sixty-year-old resident of Culpeper County on 21 April 1818 when he applied for a pension for his services in the Revolution. According to his deposition of 17 October 1820 he was a sixty-seven or sixty-eight-year-old painter whose only family was a boy of about twelve or thirteen years [M805-139, frames 554-7].

2. James Bunday, born about 1744, was a "mulatto man" with about twelve or thirteen more years to serve when he was listed in the 18 March 1763 Essex County estate of Humphrey Brooke [Dorman, *Culpeper County Will Books. Will Book A: 1749-1770*, 102]. On 17 May 1784 the Essex County court presented him for failing to list his tithables, and on 16 May 1785 the court presented him for failing to list (his sons?) Henry and David as tithables [Orders 1784-7, 9, 85]. He was head of an Essex County household of 7 "Black" persons in 1783 [VA:52] and was taxable in Essex County from 1783 to 1803: taxable on 2 free persons, 2 horses and 2 cattle in 1783 [PPTL, 1782-1819, frames 40, 74, 155, 210, 234, 246, 297, 308, 343, 357]. He may have been the father of
      i.   William, born say 1761, taxable on a tithe and a horse in Essex County in 1787 (called Willm. Bond) and taxable in Essex County from 1809 to 1816 [PPTL, 1782-1819, frames 155, 425, 510, 528, 616]. He was a Revolutionary soldier who lived in Culpeper County [Jackson, *Virginia Negro Soldiers*, 32]. He was a "Free Mulatto" head of a Culpeper County household of 5 "other free" in 1810 (called William Bunda) [VA:8].
      ii. John, born say 1763, head of an Essex County household of 1 "Black" person in 1783 [VA:52]. The Essex County court presented him on 17 May 1784 for failing to list his tithables, and the court ordered that he be listed on the tax list of Muscoe Livingston, Gent., on 18 October 1785 [Orders 1784-7, 9, 56]. He was taxable in Essex County from 1783 to 1803: his tax charged to Abner Cox in 1787, taxable on a horse in 1790 and taxable in Essex County from 1809 to 1813: called "John Bunday Senr." in 1811, "John Bunday Yellow" in 1812, listed with a male and female "free Negro" over the age of sixteen in 1813 [PPTL, 1782-1819, frames 40, 74, 195, 210, 234, 246, 273, 285, 297, 308, 343, 425, 439, 510]. He was head of an Essex County household of 4 "other free" in 1810 [VA:202].

iii. David, born say 1764, taxable in Essex County from 1785 to 1800 [PPTL, 1782-1819, frames 75, 210, 234, 246, 260, 273, 285, 297, 308].

iv. Harry[1], born say 1765, a "Mulatto" bound by one of the churchwardens of St. Ann's Parish, Essex County, to William Thomas. On 20 January 1772 the court ruled that he and (his sister?) Cate should not be detained as servants by the executors of Thomas' estate because the indenture was illegal [Orders 1770-3, 224]. Henry was taxable in St. Ann's Parish, Essex County, in 1802, 1811 and 1812 [PPTL, 1782-1819, frames 357, 460, 480]. Harry was called Harry Bunday, Sr., in 1810, head of an Essex County household of 3 "other free" [VA:202].

v. Catherine[1]/ Cate, a "Mulatto" indentured to William Thomas on 20 January 1772 when the Essex County court ruled that the indenture was illegal [Orders 1770-3, 224]. She may have been the Catherine Bunday who was head of an Essex County household of 2 "other free" in 1810 [VA:202].

vi. James, Jr., taxable in Essex County in 1802 and 1803 [PPTL, 1782-1819, frames 343, 357].

Other members of the Bunday family were

i. Violet, taxable in Essex County on a slave above the age of 16 and 2 horses in 1809 [PPTL, 1782-1819, frames 425].

ii. Sarah, head of an Essex County household of 7 "other free" in 1810 [VA:202].

iii. Qisler, head of an Essex County household of 5 "other free" in 1810 [VA:202].

iv. Harry[2], Jr., taxable in Essex County from 1811 to 1819, listed with a "free Negro" male and female over the age of sixteen and a horse in St. Ann's Parish in 1813 [PPTL, 1782-1819, frames 460, 480, 528, 616, 769], head of an Essex County household of 5 "other free" in 1810 [VA:202].

v. Polly, head of an Essex County household of 4 "other free" in 1810 [VA:202].

vi. Christian, born about 1780, registered in Petersburg on 5 August 1812: *a brown Mulatto woman, five feet four inches high, thirty two years old, born free in the County of Essex* [Register of Free Negroes 1794-1819, no. 716].

vii. Catherine[2], born about 1781, registered in Petersburg on 10 August 1805: *a brown Mulatto woman, five feet four inches high, twenty four years old, holes in her ears, born free per certificate of Registry from the County of Essex* [Register of Free Negroes 1794-1819, no. 352]. And she registered in Chesterfield County on 8 September 1806 [Register of Free Negroes 1804-53, 36].

viii. Nelson, taxable in St. Ann's Parish, Essex County, from 1811 to 1819: taxable on a male and female "free Negro" over the age of sixteen in 1813 [PPTL, 1782-1819, frames 460, 480, 510, 528, 617, 769], head of an Essex County household of 3 "other free" in 1810 [VA:202].

ix. Lewis, taxable in St. Ann's Parish, Essex County, from 1811 to 1814: taxable on a male and female "free Negro" over the age of sixteen and a horse in 1813 [PPTL, 1782-1819, frames 460, 480, 510, 528], head of an Essex County household of 3 "other free" in 1810 [VA:202].

x. Ann[2], head of an Essex County household of 3 "other free" in 1810 [VA:202].

xi. Sylvia, head of a Spotsylvania County household of 7 "other free" in 1810 [VA:113a].

xii. Betty, head of a Spotsylvania County household of 7 "other free" in 1810 [VA:113a].

xiii.   Nancy Bunda, "Free Negro" head of Culpeper County household of 2 "other free" in 1810 [VA:8].
xiv.   Sally Bunda, "Free Molatto" head of a Culpeper County household of 3 "other free" in 1810 [VA:8].
xv.   Thomas Bunda, "Free Negro" head of a Culpeper County household of 1 "other free" in 1810 [VA:14].
xvi.   William Bunda, "Free Negro" head of a Culpeper County household of 1 "other free" in 1810 [VA:9].
xvii.   Samuel[2], born 1776-94, head of a Guilford County, North Carolina household of 11 "free colored" in 1830.

BURDEN/ BURDINE FAMILY

1.   Priscilla **Timbers**, born 19 March 1757, a "mollato girl," was the daughter of Sarah Timbers of Overwharton Parish, Stafford County, Virginia [Overwharton Parish Register, 1724-1774, 189]. On 3 July 1805 a Mrs. Mary McCalanahan appeared in Greenville County, South Carolina court and testified that Sarah Timbers and her daughter Priscilla had lived with her in Virginia and that Priscilla was the mother of David, Thomas, Lewis, James, John, Patsy, and Charlotte **Burden/ Burdin** [DB R:162]. Priscilla was the mother of

i.   David, counted as a "free colored" head of a Pendleton District, South Carolina household with a slave in 1820.
ii.   Thomas.
iii.   Lewis. His biography was published in Randolph County, Indiana, in 1882 [Tucker, *History of Randolph County*].
iv.   James.
v.   John, born 1785-1804, head of a Wayne Township, Wayne County, Indiana household of 11 "free colored" in 1840.
vi.   Patsy.
vii.   Charlotte.

BURKE FAMILY

Members of the Burke family in Virginia and Maryland were
i.   John, born about 1686, a "Mollatto" servant of Mrs. Elizabeth Hawkins, who was twenty-one years old on 10 June 1707 when the Charles County, Maryland court ordered that he be set free. Mary Elliott, wife of William Elliott, testified that he had been sold to Henry Hawkins by her former husband Henry Brawner [Court Record 1704-10, 326].
1   ii.   Ann[1], born say 1688.

1.   Ann[1] Burk, born say 1688, a "Mulatto" servant of Burditt Ashton, Gent., petitioned the Westmoreland County, Virginia court for her freedom on 28 October 1709. The court ruled that she should serve until the age of thirty-one, but it reconsidered the case on 28 June 1711 and decided that she should be free because she was born before the law was passed which bound mixed-race children until the age of thirty-one [Orders 1705-21, 132a, 143a, 162a]. She may have been the mother of
i.   Ann[2], born say 1713, indicted by the Westmoreland County court on 28 May 1734 for having an illegitimate child (no race indicated) [Orders 1731-9, 137a, 146].

Other members of the Burke family were
2   i.   Judah, born say 1734.

ii. Rachel, born say 1767, a "mulatto" living in Hamilton Parish, Fauquier County, on 25 May 1767 when the court ordered the churchwardens to bind him to George Neavil [Orders 1764-8, 268].

iii. Ben, born about January 1774, a "Mulatto of six months" living in Hamilton Parish, Fauquier County, on 27 June 1774 when the court ordered the churchwardens to bind him to Lucy Jones [Minutes 1773-80, 198].

iv. Enoch, head of a Loudoun County household of 5 "other free" in 1810 [VA:308].

v. Polly, head of a Prince William County household of 6 "other free" in 1810 [VA:507].

2. Judah Burke, born say 1734, was called "Juda a Molatta woman" and was the servant of Joseph Herron, Esq., in January 1756 when the Chowan County court bound her "Mollatta" son Frank to serve her master until the age of thirty-one. In January 1764 Frank and (his brother) Jacob and (sister) Lucy were called "Mulatto" children of "___ a free wench" when they were bound to Lydia Herron. She was called "Mulatto" Judy on 29 January when the court bound her "Free Mulatto" daughter Lucy to Richard Brownrigg, Esq., until the age of twenty-one. And she was called "Judah Burke a Mulattoe Woman" on 21 March 1771 when she petitioned the court to be discharged from the service of William Boyd, Esq. The court granted her petition but ordered her to bring her children into court to be bound out, and the court bound her "Negroe" sons Frank and Jacob to Samuel and William Topping to be house carpenters and joiners [Minutes 1755-61, 26; 1761-6, 193; 1766-72, 318; 591, 594, 605]. She was head of an Edenton, Chowan County, North Carolina household of 5 "other free" in 1800 [NC:116]. She was the mother of

i. Frank, born 5 July 1755, bound apprentice in Chowan County in January 1756 and bound to Lydia Herron to be a sawyer in January 1764. He was sixteen years old on 29 January 1771 when the court bound him to Samuel Topping to be a house carpenter and joiner [Minutes 1755-61, 26; 1761-6, 193; 1766-72, 605].

ii. Jacob, born about 1759, a four-year-old "Free Mulatto" boy bound by the Chowan County court to Lydia Herron to be a sawyer in January 1764. He was twelve years old on 29 January 1771 when the court bound him to William Topping to be a house carpenter and joiner [Minutes 1755-61, 26; 1761-6, 193; 1766-72, 605].

iii. Lucy, born about July 1763, a one-year-old "Free Mulatto" bound by the Chowan County court to Lydia Herron to learn to spin and weave in January 1764. She was called "Lucy a Free Mulatto child born of the body of Mulatto Judy" on 29 January 1767 when the court bound her to Richard Brownrigg, Esq., until the age of twenty-one, "now three years & six months of age" [Minutes 1761-6, 193; 1766-72, 318]. She was head of an Edenton, Chowan County household of 1 "free colored" in 1820 [NC:130].

iv. Patrick, born about 1765, one year and six months old on 29 January 1767 when the Chowan County court bound him to Richard Brownrigg to be a planter [Minutes 1766-72, 318].

Their descendants were

i. Thomas, born 1776-1794, head of an Edenton household of 3 "free colored" in 1820 [NC:130].

ii. Nancy, head of a Chowan County, North Carolina household of 3 "other free" in 1810 [NC:534].

iii. Ephy Birk, born about 1784, a five-year-old "base born mulatto" daughter of Catherine **Bush**, who was bound apprentice to Neill Leech in Cumberland County, North Carolina, on 31 January 1789 [Minutes 1787-91, Friday minutes].

    iv. Henry, born 1794-1806, head of an Edenton, Chowan County household of 4 "free colored" in 1820 with a woman over forty-five years of age [NC:130].

    v. Hager, born 1794-1806, head of a Chowan County household of 1 "free colored" in 1820 [NC:129].

BURKETT FAMILY

1. Joan Burkett, born say 1684, was the servant of John Jones on 7 May 1702 when she confessed in Richmond County, Virginia court that her illegitimate child "was gott by a Negro" [Orders 1702-04, 164]. She was probably the ancestor of

    i. Solomon, born say 1750, taxable on two "mulattos" in Bertie County in 1770 in the list of James Moore [CR 10.702.1].

2   ii. Peggy, born say 1755.

3   iii. Elizabeth, born say 1765.

2. Peggy Burkett, born say 1755, was head of a Nansemond County household of 5 "black" persons in 1783 [VA:57]. She may have been the mother of

    i. Jim, a "free Negro" taxable on two horses in Nansemond County in 1815.

    ii. Gibson, a "free Negro" taxable in Nansemond County in 1815.

    iii. Willis, a "free Negro" taxable in Nansemond County in 1815 [Yantis, *Supplement to the 1810 Census of Virginia*, S-14].

3. Elizabeth Burkett, born say 1765, was the mother of Nelson Burkett, a five-year-old "Molatto Child son of Elizabeth Burkett" who was bound an apprentice shoemaker to Edward Brisco by the Gates County court in August 1790 [Fouts, *Minutes of County Court of Pleas and Quarter Sessions 1787-93*, 70]. She was head of a Gates County household of 9 "free colored" in 1820 [NC:144]. Her children were

    i. Nelson, born about 1785, bound apprentice in 1790.

    ii. ?Christopher, born 1776-1794, head of a Chowan County household of 5 "free colored" (with a woman born before 1776) in 1820 [NC:114]. He purchased his wife and children who were slaves, and in October 1825 the Chowan County court gave him permission to manumit them. His wife Charity was about fifty or sixty years old at that time, his daughter Peggy about fourteen years old, and his daughter Nancy about seven years old [Byrd, *In Full Force and Virtue*, 26-7].

BARNETT/ BURNETT FAMILY

1. Mary Barnett, born say 1710, was the white servant of Edwin Hickman of Spotsylvania County, Virginia, on 5 September 1728 when she confessed to the churchwardens of St. George Parish that she had a "Mulatto bastard by a Negroe man." And she confessed to having a second child by a "Negro" man before 4 November 1730 [Orders 1724-30, 262, 270; 1730-32, 5, 9, 14]. She may have been the mother of Dinah, Cloe, Sawny and Doll Burnett, "mulatto children" ordered bound out by the churchwardens of St. Margaret's Parish in Caroline County on 12 April 1751. On 12 July 1759 the court ordered that Charles Noden be arrested for removing Dinah, Peter, Sawney, Doll, Sarah and Scilla Burnetts out of the county [Orders 1746-54, 251; 1759-63, 53]. The children named in the court orders were

2   i. Dinah, born say 1738.

    ii. Cloe, born say 1740.

    iii. Peter[1], born say 1742.

3   iv. Sawney/ Sanders[1], born say 1745.

4   v. Doll, born say 1748.

vi. Sarah, born say 1751, taxable on a horse in St. Ann's Parish, Albemarle County, from 1789 to 1792: taxable on her unnamed son in 1791 [PPTL, 1782-1799, frames 170, 221, 269, 319]. She may have been the Sally Barnett who was head of a Richmond City household of 5 "other free" in 1810 [VA:329].

vii. Scilla, born say 1754.

2. Dinah Burnett, born say 1738, sued her master Charles Noden in Caroline County court on 12 June 1759 but Noden failed to appear. When the court moved on 10 September 1762 to attach his estate, Richard Woolfolk reported that he had nothing in his hands belonging to Noden [Orders 1759-63, 91, 369]. She may have been the mother of

    i. William[1], born about 1755, head of a Dobbs County, North Carolina household of 5 "other free" in 1790 [NC:137]. He may have been the William Barnett who was a Dobbs County taxable with Thomas Davis in 1769 [SS 837 by *NCGSJ* XV:74]. He was twenty-three years old in 1778 when he was listed in the Militia Returns for Dobbs County [*The North Carolinian* VI:730]. He was a "Mulatto" who enlisted with the 10th Regiment in 1780 and was said to have died without heirs [Crow, *Black Experience in Revolutionary North Carolina*, 98].

5   ii. Frankly, born say 1756.

6   iii. Charles, born about 1764.

7   iv. Angela, born say 1765.

    v. Edith, no age mentioned when she registered as a "Free Negro" in Campbell County on 20 January 1802: *5 Feet 2-1/2 Inches, darkish Colour, born free* [A Register of Free Negroes and Mulattoes, p.2].

    vi. Jenny, born about 1776, registered in Campbell County on 20 January 1802: *Age: 25; 5 Feet 4-1/2 Inches; Colour: darkish; Where set Free: Albemarle; by Whom set free: blank*.

    vii. David[2], taxable in Albemarle County from 1796 to 1803: called a "Free Negro" in 1803 [PPTL, 1782-99, frames 477, 585; 1800-1813, frames 23, 68, 93, 136, 156]. He married Judy **Brown**, 14 November 1807 Henrico County bond, Jacob **Brown** surety. Jacob **Brown** was head of a Henrico County household of 3 "other free" in 1810 [VA:978]. David was a "free Negro" taxable in Henrico County in 1806 [PPTL 1782-1814, frame 482]. Perhaps Judy was the Judah Barnett who was head of a Henrico County household of 2 "other free" in 1810 [VA:978] and 8 "free colored" in Albemarle County in 1820.

3. Sawney/ Sanders[1] Burnett, born say 1745, was ordered bound out by the churchwardens of St. Margaret's Parish in Caroline County on 12 April 1751. He purchased 150 acres from Joseph Boon on the north side of the Neuse River in Johnston County, North Carolina, on 10 December 1770 [Haun, *Johnston County Deed Abstracts*, Tr-1:116]. He sold this land about seven years later by a deed proved in the Johnston County court in 1777, and he sold another tract of land by deed proved in May 1777 Johnston County court [Haun, *Johnston County Court Minutes*, II:206, 251]. He was head of a Johnston County household of 5 free males and 7 free females in 1787 for the state census, 12 "other free" in 1790 [NC:140], 11 "other free" in 1800 [NC:544] and 10 in 1810 [NC:956]. His children may have been

    i. Aaron, born before 1776, head of an Orange County household of 6 "other free" in 1810 [NC:831] and 12 "free colored" in 1820 [NC:354].

    ii. David[1], born say 1760, described as a "man of color" who served as a soldier in Blount's Company [Crow, *Black Experience in Revolutionary North Carolina*, 98]. He enlisted on 2 April 1776 but was omitted from Blount's Company in 1778 [*N.C. Historical &*

Genealogical Register II:181]. He died without heirs and his land warrant was escheated.

4. Doll Burnett, born say 1750, was ordered bound out by the churchwardens of St. Margaret's Parish in Caroline County on 12 April 1751. She was living in Johnston County, North Carolina, on 28 May 1777 when her daughter Edith was brought before the county court to be bound out:

> *and the court taking the Conduct Character and Circumstances of the said Doll Burnet into consideration & finding no just reasons to apprehend that the said Edith would become a charge to this County, Ordered her to be returned to the care of her said Mother again* [Haun, *Johnston County Court Minutes*, II:260].

In February 1786 she bound William Burnett to William Bulls by indenture proved in Johnston County court [Haun, *Johnston County Court Minutes*, III:306]. Doll was head of a Johnston County household of a female and 2 males in J. Boon's list in 1787 for the state census and head of a Johnston County household of 5 "other free" in 1790 [NC:140]. Her children were

      i.   Edith, born say 1770, bound to Jeremiah Powell in 1782 [Haun, *Johnston County Court Minutes*, III:213, 238]. She was head of a Wayne County household of 8 "free colored" in 1820 [NC:456].

8   ii.   Jesse, born say 1772.

     iii. Sanders[2], born about 1774, eighteen years old when he was bound an apprentice to Nathan Powell in May 1792.

     iv. Lotte, born about 1776, sixteen years old when she was bound to Nathan Powell in May 1792.

9   v.   William[3], born say 1778.

10   vi. ?Rebecca, born about 1786.

11   vii. ?Patience perhaps 1790.

5. Franky, born say 1756, a free "Negroe" woman (no last name indicated), had a child named Lucy Barnet who was born 13 June 1778 and baptized 17 June 1779 [Jones, *The Douglas Register*, 348]. She was called Franky Barnett in Goochland County in 1795 when her children Roger, Tarlton and Hailey Barnett were bound to David Ross [Orders 20:155 cited by Butler, *Evolution of a Rural Free Black Community*, 208]. She was counted in a list of "Free Negroes & Mulattoes" in Fluvanna County in 1813 and was taxable on a horse from to 1818 [PPTL 1782-1826, frames 503, 562, 584, 609]. Her children were

      i.   Lucy, counted in a list of "Free Negroes & Mulattoes" in Fluvanna County in 1813, taxable on a horse in 1817 [PPTL 1782-1826, frames 503, 585].

     ii.   ?Roda, counted in a list of "Free Negroes & Mulattoes" in Fluvanna County in 1813 [PPTL 1782-1826, frame 503].

     iii. Roger.

     iv. Tarlton, taxable in Fluvanna County in 1817 [PPTL 1782-1826, frames 585].

     v.   Hailey.

6. Charles Barnett was born about 1764 in Albemarle County, Virginia, and lived there until 1800. According to his Revolutionary War Pension application he was a "mulatto" who enlisted in Charlottesville in the 7th Virginia Regiment. Sharod **Going** testified that he was with him at Chesterfield Courthouse. In 1800 he moved to Carter County, Tennessee, then to Georgia, and to Granville County, North Carolina, about 1808 [Dorman, *Virginia Revolutionary Pension Applications*, IV:87]. He obtained a certificate of freedom in Albemarle County on 2 August 1796: *a Dark mullatto man aged about thirty years, of a*

yellow complexion, five feet seven and three quarter inches high, having proved to the satisfaction of this Court that he was born a free man within this County [Orders 1795-8, 137]. He married Lucy **Bowles**, 7 September 1785 Albemarle County bond. He was bondsman for the 12 December 1793 Albemarle County marriage of Robert **Battles** and Nancy **Bowles**. He and his wife Lucy sued Robert **Battles** for trespass, assault and battery on 5 May 1796, and he and his wife Lucy sold property by deed proved in Albemarle County on 6 June 1796 [Orders 1795-8, 86, 108, 144]. He was taxable in Fredericksville Parish, Albemarle County, from 1787 to 1791. His tax was charged to William Clarkson in 1798. (His wife) Lucy was head of an Albemarle County household of 7 "other free" in 1810 [VA:185], a "Mulatto" taxable on a horse in 1812 and 2 free male tithables and a horse in 1813 [PPTL, 1782-1799, frames 110, 149, 244, 291, 342, 382, 415, 445, 478, 530; 1800-1813, frames 518, 562]. Charles was head of a "free colored" household in Granville County, North Carolina, in 1830. According to his pension application, he was back in Albemarle County on 28 December 1840 and received his last pension payment on 4 September 1848. His pension application file includes a 31 July 1849 letter from Thomas Peace of Granville County who wrote to the Albemarle County Clerk that Charles Barnett, "a man of color...left a widow and a parcel of children in a very distressed condition." He may have been the father of

   i.   James, a "Mulatto" taxable in St. Ann's Parish, Albemarle County, in 1812 and 1813 [PPTL, 1800-1813, frame 499, 541].

   ii.   Peter[2], born about 1790, a "Mulatto" taxable in Albemarle County, in 1809, 1812 and 1813 [PPTL, 1800-1813, frames 363, 518, 541], registered in Albemarle County on 9 August 1815 and in Augusta County on 28 October 1823: *a free man of dark mulatto complexion* [R e g i s t e r o f A u g u s t a C o u n t y , n o . 5 6 , http://jefferson.village.virginia.edu/vshadow2/].

  iii. Elizabeth, head of an Albemarle County household of 3 "other free" in 1810 [VA:151].

  iv. Elizabeth, head of an Albemarle County household of 2 "other free" in 1810 [VA:150].

   v.   Ally, born say 1790, the mother of Mary Barnett who registered in Fluvanna County on January 1857: *a Renewal of her Register granted by the County Court of said County on the 24th Day of February 1834...about Forty years of age, about five feet high, yellow Complexion* [Order Book p.7, no. 94].

7.   Angela Barnett, born day 1765, was in the Henrico County jail with Nathan **Fry** and William **Anthony** on 7 February 1791 for a breach of the peace and were ordered to remain there until they gave security of 40 pounds each for their good behavior for a year. While she was in jail, the court ordered that her child be restored to her and supported at the expense of the county [Orders 1789-91, 428]. On 29 September 1792 Angela was charged in Henrico County court with murdering a white man named Peter Franklin. Jesse Carpenter testified that

> *in the night of the third instant he accompanied the deceased to the House of a certain William Anthony in this County (with whom the prisoner lived) in search of some runaway negroes which they suspected were harboured at the said House, and for the taking of whom a reward was offered in the Virginia Gazette. That in their search they apprehended a small boy at the said House, whom they carried away as a runaway, he answering the description of one of the runaways described in the said Advertisement. That in consequence of information received from the said Boy, they went to the same house the following evening about eleven O'clock at night to apprehend two other runaways, and upon knocking at the door, it was*

opened by the said Will Anthony, to whom they communicated their suspicions and went in (There being very little light in the house). That upon their entering the house, they were abused by the prisoner in the most indecent manner, in Consequence of which the decedent threatened the prisoner that if she persisted in her abuse, he would correct her. That in a few minutes afterwards the prisoner was discovered by the deceased searching behind a trunk upon which the decedent made a seeming disposition to strike the prisoner with a small cowhide which he held in his hand. That the deponent did not see any stroke given by the deceased to the prisoner, but at the same instant the prisoner struck the deceased and knocked him down, upon which the deponent caught hold of the Weapon with which the blow was given, and it seemed to him to be a square piece of Wood, but did not get it out of the hands of the prisoner. That in the Scuffle the deponent was pushed out of the door and as he went out, he got hold of the deceased and dragged him out also, who appeared to be much hurt, he complaining of being badly cut. That the deponent so soon as he could get the deceased upon his horse conveyed him home the distance being about four miles, in effecting which he was obliged to hold him on his horse the greater part of the way, during which the decedent appeared out of his senses. That the said Franklin after lingering a few days departed this life and this deponent believes died of the said Wound given him by the prisoner [Orders 1791-4, 278-9].

The court ordered that she be sent to Richmond for trial. Angelina Barnett was taxable in the upper district of Henrico County on the tithe of (her son?) Allen Barnett, a slave and a horse in 1804 and taxable on Allen Barnett and a horse in 1805. She was taxable on 2 lots in 1806, 1810 and 1811 [Land Tax List, 1799-1816]. She may have been the mother of

    i.   Allen, born say 1786, married Lucretia **Wood**, "free people of color," 7 December 1807 Henrico County bond, Elijah **Wood** surety. He was a "free Negro" taxable in the upper district of Henrico County from 1803 to 1811; taxable on 30 acres in Henrico County in 1813 [PPTL 1782-1814, frames 482, 528, 657; Land Tax List 1799-1816]. He was head of a Henrico County household of 10 "other free" in 1810 [VA:996].

8.   Jesse Burnett, born say 1772, was bound an apprentice to Jeremiah Powell in Johnston County in 1782 [Haun, *Johnston County Court Minutes*, III:238]. He was head of a Cumberland County, North Carolina household of 9 "free colored" in 1820 [NC:208]. On 23 January 1830 he purchased 50 acres in Cumberland County on Middle Creek between Bones Creek and Little Rockfish Creek from Absalom **Hammons** [DB 39:459]. He and his wife Elizabeth were mentioned in their son Needham's free papers on 5 September 1842 in Cumberland County [Minutes 1842-44]. Their children were

12   i.   ?Betsy, born say 1807.

    ii.   Needham, born 20 September 1812, according to Daniel Baker, Esq., and Duncan Gillie Rae who testified on his behalf in Cumberland County court on 5 September 1842. They stated that he was a "free man of colour" born in Cumberland County of free parents, Jesse and Elizabeth Burnett. The 6 June 1842 Cumberland County court permitted him to take the oath of insolvency when he was sued by Thomas B. Wooten [Minutes 1842-44, n.p.].

    iii.   ?Peter[3], born 6 December 1815. James Bowden testified in Cumberland County court that Peter Burnett, born of a free mother in Duplin County, was bound apprentice to him and completed his indenture on 6 December 1836 at the age of twenty-one years. The 10 December 1836 court described him as being: *of Slender Frame about six feet high of a dark mulatto complexion bushy hair* [Minutes 1836-8, n.p.].

iv. David[3], born say 1816, received a deed of gift from (his father?) Jesse Burnett which was proved in Cumberland County on 8 December 1837. The 8 December 1841 Cumberland County court issued him a license to carry a gun in the county.

v. ?Calvin, born about 1825, nineteen years old on 8 March 1844 when he was bound to John McLowin.

vi. ?Margaret, born about 1826, a sixteen-year-old "free girl of colour" bound to George McMillan in Cumberland County on 5 December 1842.

vii. ?Sarah A., born about 1832, ten years old when she was bound to Amos Jessup on 7 December 1842.

9. William[3] Burnett, born say 1778, was indentured to William Bulls by Doll Burnett in Johnston County in February 1786 [Haun, *Johnston County Court Minutes*, IV:200; III:306]. He was head of a Cumberland County, North Carolina household of 7 "other free" in 1810 [NC:608] and 10 "free colored" in 1820 [NC:152]. He may have been the father of

i. Nathan, born about 1800, obtained free papers in Cumberland County in 1819: *a bright mulatto, born about 1800, 5'10-3/8"*... and registered them in Perry County, Mississippi in 1822 [Probate Records A:316-7].

10. Rebecca Burnett, born about 1786, was a two-year-old "mulatoe" when she and (her younger sister?) Lid Burnet were bound apprentices to James Campbell by the Cumberland County, North Carolina court on 31 July 1788 [Minutes 1787-91]. Rebecca was the mother of

i. ?James, born about 1802, five-year-old "boy of Colour," bound to Michael Blocker by the 16 September 1807 Cumberland County court [Minutes 1805-08]. He may have been the James Burnett who owed tax on an improved lot in Fayetteville in 1821 [5 June 1822 Minutes].

ii. ?Rachel, born about 1802, a five-year-old "Mullatto" girl bound to Richard Dudley by the 16 September 1807 Cumberland County court [Minutes 1805-08].

iii. ?Rose, a two-year-old "Mullatto" girl bound to Richard Dudley by the 16 September 1807 Cumberland County court.

iv. Jane, born about 1809. On 10 March 1838 in Cumberland County court she produced a copy of her November 1815 Moore County indenture to Cornelius Dowd which stated that she was about six years old.[54] She also had a record of the completion of her indenture in November 1829. She appeared in Cumberland County court again on 4 March 1841 when she proved to the court that she was the daughter of Rebecca Burnett and was a free born resident of the town of Fayetteville. She was described as being: *of a dark Mulatto complexion, five feet four and a half inches high stout in person her uper fore teeth nearly all decayed* [Minutes 1835-44].

11. Patience Burnett, born say 1790, was head of a Cumberland County, North Carolina household of 3 "free colored" in 1820 [NC:216]. She was the mother of two "Coloured" children bound to Duncan Campbell of Cumberland County until the age of eighteen. They were

i. Sarah, born about 1814, eleven years old on 11 March 1825 [Minutes 1823-27].

ii. Eliza, born about 1818, seven years old on 11 March 1825.

12. Betsy Burnett, born say 1807, was living in Cumberland County, North Carolina, in December 1837 when her children were apprenticed. They were

---

[54]Moore County was formed from Cumberland County in 1784.

    i.   William Henry, born in December 1825, twelve years old when he was bound to Anson Bailey of Cumberland County to be a farmer on 8 September 1837 [Minutes 1836-38].

    ii. ?Louisa, born about 1827, no parent named on 8 September 1837 when she was a ten-year-old "free girl of colour" bound to Stephen Hollingsworth. She was bound to Alfred Jackson on 7 December 1840 [Minutes 1838-40].

    iii. ?George, born about 1828, no parent named, a nine-year-old "free boy of colour" bound to Stephen Hollingsworth to be a farmer on 8 September 1837. He was bound to Alfred Jackson on 7 December 1837.

    iv. Candie, born about 1833, a four-year-old "free girl of colour" bound to Alfred Jackson on 7 December 1837.

    v. ?Nancy, born about 1836, no parent named, bound to Alfred Jackson on 7 December 1837 [Minutes 1836-38].

Other members of the family in Virginia were

    i. Susanna Burnett, born say 1743, added to Thomas John's list of tithables for Loudoun County, Virginia, on 13 November 1759 [Orders 1757-62, 298].

    ii. Michael Barnet, a "Mulatto" ordered bound by the churchwardens of Augusta County to Peter Hog, Gentleman, on 23 August 1766, perhaps the child of Pat Barnett whose son Thomas was ordered bound to Jacob Miller on 22 March 1768, no race indicated [Orders 1765-7, 240; 1768, 127].

    iii. William[2], born say 1772, married Judith **Thomason**, 10 January 1793 Mecklenburg County, Virginia bond. He was head of an Albemarle County household of 4 "other free" in 1810 [VA:151].

BURRELL FAMILY

1. Susannah[1] Burrell, born say 1719, a "free Molatto," was the mother of several "free Negro" children born in North Farnham Parish, Richmond County, Virginia. She was probably a sister of Barbara Burrell, "a free Molatto," whose daughter Winifred was born 7 December 1740 [King, *The Register of North Farnham Parish 1663-1814*, 28]. Susannah's children were

    i. ?Winey Burwell, born say 1735, a "mulatto Servant Girl" who complained to the Orange County, Virginia court on 28 June 1753 that her master, Andrew Mannon, was misusing her [Orders 5:456].

    ii. Lucy, born 25 March 1737, daughter of Susanna Burrell."

    iii. Sam[1], born 25 May 1739, "a free Negro son of Susanna Burrel."

    iv. Sam[2], born 15 August 1742, "son of Sue a free Molatto."

    v. Susanna[2], born 26 January 1753, "daughter of Susanna Burrell, a free Negro."

Their descendants may have been

    i. Elisa Burrell, head of a Westmoreland County household of 12 "other free" in 1810.

    ii. Winnie Charity Burwell, born about 1772, registered in Middlesex County on 15 March 1802: *born free; 30 years of age; 5'0"; yellow complexion* [Register of Free Negroes 1800-60, p.15].

    iii. Clarissa Burwell, head of a Petersburg Town household of 3 "other free" in 1810 [VA:121b].

    iv. Hanna Burwell, head of a Prince George County household of 4 "other free" in 1810 [VA:549].

    v. Patty Burwell, head of a Henrico County household of 2 "other free" in 1810 [VA:996].

BUSBY/ BUZBY FAMILY

1. Thomas Busby, born about 1674, was an "Indyan boy" servant to Mr. Robert Caufield of Surry County, Virginia, in July 1684 when his age was adjudged at ten years (in order to know when he was tithable) [Haun, *Surry County Court Records, 1682-91*, 444]. His descendants may have been related to the **Hawley/ Holly** and **Scott** families of North and South Carolina. On 12 March 1754 a "mulatto boy Busby alias John Scott" was recovered in Orange County, North Carolina, after being stolen from his mother. He was the son of Amy **Hawley** and grandson of John **Scott** of South Carolina. The Orange County court appointed Thomas **Chavis** to return the child to his family in South Carolina [Haun, *Orange County Court Minutes*, I:70, 71]. White members of the Busby family were taxables in Bladen County, North Carolina, from 1768 to 1789 [Byrd, *Bladen County Tax Lists*, I:2, 68; II:44, 45, 72, 206].

Members of the family in South Carolina were

   i. Mary Buzby, head of a Beaufort District household of 10 "other free" in 1790 [SC:11] and 5 "other free" in 1800 [SC:104]. In 1790 Mary was living in the same district as Moses **Scott**, head of a Beaufort District household of 8 "other free" [SC:11].

   ii. John Busby, born before 1776, head of a Barnwell District household of 2 "other free" in 1800 [SC:62] and 2 "free colored" in 1820 [SC:3a]. He was a man of color who served in the Revolution [Moss, *Roster of South Carolina Patriots*, 127; NSDAR, *African American Patriots*, 181].

BUSS/ BUSH FAMILY

1. Edward Buss, born say 1671, was called a "Mulatto slave or servt. to Mr. James Vaulx" when the Westmoreland County court ordered Vaulx to appear in court to answer his complaint. On 30 September 1702 Edward testified that he was the son of an "English or white woman." He was free by 24 February 1708/9 when he brought a successful suit for 402 pounds of tobacco against the estate of Philip Brown in Westmoreland County court. On 28 June 1710 he was presented by the court for failing to attend his parish church, and on 24 June 1713 he and Margaret Redley were convicted of fornication and cohabiting together [Orders 1698-1705, 169a, 172a; 1705-21, 116, 145a, 217]. On 29 June 1721 he won a suit for 1,600 pounds of tobacco against the estate of Nathaniel Pope [Orders 1721-31, 4]. He may have been the ancestor of

   i. Edward Bush, born say 1713, called "Edward Bush alias Ridly, carpenter, born on the Body of Margaret Ridly" on 25 October 1742 when he sold (signing) 80 acres in Westmoreland County at the head of Pope's Creek while residing in St. Mark's Parish, Orange County [Westmoreland D&W 1738-44, 256].

   ii. William Bush, born say 1731, a "Melato" with two years to serve on 28 August 1750 when he was listed in the inventory of the Westmoreland County estate of William Strother [Records & Inventories 1746-52, 134b].

Other members of the Bush family were

2   i. Jane, born about 1777.

   ii. Sally, head of an Augusta County household of 5 "other free" in 1810 [VA:398].

   iii. Charlotte, head of a Richmond City household of 2 "other free" in 1810 [VA:349].

   iv. Catherine, born say 1763, mother of Ephy **Birk**, a five-year-old "base born mulatto child" bound apprentice to Neil Leech on 31 January 1789

by order of the Cumberland County, North Carolina court [Minutes 1787-1791, no page].
    v.   William, born 1776-1794, head of Caswell County, North Carolina household of 5 "free colored" in 1820 [NC:42].
   vi.   Frances, head of a Johnston County, North Carolina household of 8 "free colored" in 1820 [NC:259].
  vii.   Rachel, head of a Lenoir County, North Carolina household of 7 "other free" and 4 slaves in 1810 [NC:297].

2.   Jane Bush, born about 1777, registered as a free Negro in Essex County on 21 September 1829: *born free by certificate of Bailee Spindle, Esq., bright Mulattoe, 52 years of age, 5 feet 5 inches* [Register of Free Negroes 1810-43, p.110, no. 240]. She was the mother of
      i.   ?Elizabeth, born about 1798, married Lawrence **Bird (Byrd)**, 7 April 1817 Essex County bond. She registered in Essex County on 19 August 1829: *Elizabeth Bird who was Elizabeth Bush, appearing by marriage bond born free, Mulatto, 31 years of age, 5 feet 7-3/4"*.
    ii.   ?Sandy, born about 1803, registered in Essex County on 21 March 1825: *born free by evidence of Richard Rowzee in open court, bright Mulattoe, 22 years of age, 5 feet 9-1/8 inches.* He registered again on 21 September 1829.
   iii.   Nancy, born about 1806, registered in Essex County on 21 September 1829: *daughter of Jane Bush, a free born woman, bright Mulattoe, 23 years of age, 5 feet 5-5/8 inches.*
   iv.   Jane, Jr., born about 1807, registered in Essex County on 21 September 1829: *daughter of Jane Bush, a free born woman, bright Mulattoe, 22 years of age, 5 feet 6-5/8 inches.*
    v.   Dandridge, born about 1810, registered in Essex County on 21 September 1829: *son of Jane Bush, a free born woman, bright Mulattoe, 22 years of age, 5 feet 6-5/8 inches* [Register of Free Negroes 1810-43, pp.48, 106, 111, 112; nos. 118, 232, 241-4].

BUTLER FAMILY

1.   Ann Butler, born say 1670, was the servant of Samuel Hersey on 15 January 1690 when she admitted in Somerset County, Maryland court that she had a "Molatta" child by "Emanuel Negro" a slave of William Coulborne. She promised to pay Hersey 1,200 pounds of tobacco for his expenses in raising the child. Emanuel was given 39 lashes on 10 June 1690 when he was convicted of stealing a hog [Judicial Records 1689-90, 36, 57, 60a, 106, 200]. She may have been the ancestor of the members of the Butler family who were in North Carolina by 1751:

2   i.   Margaret, born say 1722.
3   ii.   Elizabeth, born say 1730.
4   iii.   Martha, born say 1734.
      iv.   Robert, born say 1735, listed in the Summary List of the Bertie County Tax List for 1751 filed with the central government [CCR 190]. In 1755 he posted bastardy bonds for two unnamed children he had by Jane **Mitchell** [Camin, *N.C. Bastardy Bonds*, 8]. In 1757 he was taxable on a tithe in the list of John Hill, Esqr., and in 1763 he was a "Free Mulatto Male" taxable in his own household in John Hill's list [CR 10.702.1, box 1]. In 1764 he and (his son?) John **Mitchell**, "2 free molattos," were listed in the Bertie County Summary Tax List, and in 1766 he was taxed in his own household in the list of John Crickett. In 1770 he was one of the freeholders who were ordered by the September Bertie County court to work on the road to Cashie Bridge under Arthur Williams, overseer [Haun, *Bertie County Court Minutes*, IV:375]. He purchased 100 acres on the south side of Cypress Swamp

in Bertie County on 29 February 1780 and sold it on 16 February 1785 [DB M:476, 720]. He was head of a Bertie household of 4 persons for the 1787 North Carolina State census. He died before May 1790 when Amos Turner returned an inventory of his estate in Bertie County court [Haun, *Bertie County Court Minutes*, VI:813].

v.   Rachel, born say 1746, taxable in Granville County in 1762 in Samuel Benton's list for Oxford District & Fishing Creek in the household of (her brother-in-law?) George **Pettiford** [CR 44.701.23].

2.   Margaret Butler, born say 1722, was head of a household of herself and "free Mulatto" Isaac Butler in the 1761 Bertie tax list of John Hill. On 15 July 1768 her brother James Currey informed the court that she (a "Singlewoman") had been delivered of a bastard child [N.C. Archives, Bertie County Bastardy Bonds 1740-1815, folder for 1766-1770]. And in September 1768 she brought John Castellaw and Edward MGloghan to court as securities "for her keeping Harmless and indemnifying the Parish of this County from Charge" [Haun, *Bertie County Court Minutes*, III:831]. Margaret may have been the daughter of Thomas Corrie of Bertie County who named children James, David, John Margaret, Janet and Jacob in his 12 January 1750 Bertie County will which was proved in May 1754 [Gammon, *Abstracts of Wills, Bertie County*, p. 14, no. 53]. And she may have been the mother of

i.   Isaac, born say 1738, taxable in Bertie County in 1751 [CCR 190] and a "Free Mulatto Male" taxable in the list of John Hill in Margaret Butler's household in 1761.

ii. William[1], born say 1745, taxable head of a Bertie household of 2 "free molattos" in the 1763 summary list.

iii. Abigail[1], born before 1750, taxable in her own Bertie household with (her brother?) William Butler in the 1761 list of John Hill.

5   iv. John, born about 1755.

3.   Elizabeth Butler, born say 1730, was a "Free Mulatto Female" taxed in the 1761 and 1763 Bertie County Tax List of John Hill in the household of Arthur Williams along with David **James** and seven slaves. Arthur Williams was a member of the North Carolina General Assembly for Bertie County in 1735 [Saunders, *Colonial Records of North Carolina*, IV:115].[55] She was Arthur William's common-law wife and the mother of his two sons Isaac and Elisha who were taxed as white servants in 1767 in his household in the list of John Crickett and as "Mollatoes" in 1768:

Masters	White Servants	Mulattoes	Male Slaves	Female Slaves
Arthur Williams	Constant Reddit	Isaac Williams	Gye	Grace
	John Sawkil	Elisha Williams	Sezer	Bess
		Wm. James	Robin	Joan
		Elizth. Butler	Treser	
		Elizth. James		
		Mary James	[CR 10.702.1]	

Arthur left a 28 January 1775 Bertie County will, proved May 1775, leaving slaves Guy, Cesar, Grace and Joan to Elizabeth Butler "now living with me" and naming Elizabeth's children Isaac, Elisha, Ann, Cathoran, Joab, and Arthur. He also named Sarah, wife of Josiah Reddit [WB B:30-4]. In the undated Bertie County List of Humphrey Hardy, Elizabeth was head of a

---

[55]Arthur Williams also proved the 28 October 1730 Bertie County will of Thomas **Kersey** [SS Wills 1730-1733, Thomas Ceorsie, North Carolina Archives].

household of 5 taxables: slaves Gye, Cezar, Grace, Joan and herself (not identified by race). The children of Elizabeth Butler and Arthur Williams were

 i. ?Sarah, born say 1746, married Josiah Redditt, 14 May 1767 Bertie County bond.

 ii. Isaac Williams, born say 1748, counted as white in 1771 and thereafter. He married Nancy **Bunch**, 7 December 1769 Bertie County bond with Jeremiah and Henry **Bunch**, Jr., bondsmen.

 iii. Elisha Williams, counted as white in 1771 and thereafter, married Sarah Josey, 24 March 1775 Bertie County bond.

 iv. Ann, wife of Joseph Simons.

 v. Catherine.

 vi. Joab.

 vii. Arthur.

4. Martha Butler, born say 1734, was a "Free Mulatto Female" taxable in 1761 and 1763 in John Castellaw's household in the Bertie County list of John Hill and was taxable in Castellaw's household in the lists for 1766 through 1772. She was apparently John Castellaw's common-law wife since in 1771 William Castellaw was taxed in the Bertie County list of Humphrey Nichols as a "free Molattoe," and in 1771 John made a deed of gift to "William Castellaw son of Martha Butler" [DB L:283]. The deed was proved in Bertie County by the oath of Arthur Williams who was probably the common-law husband of Elizabeth Butler. Martha was head of a Gates County household of 10 "free colored" in 1820 [NC:143]. Her son was

 i. William **Castellaw**, born say 1755.

5. John Butler, born about 1755, was a taxable "Mollato" in William Butler's household in the 1774 list of Humphrey Nichols. He married Keziah **Prichard**, 27 December 1797 Bertie County bond with her brother Christopher **Prichard** bondsman. He was living in Bertie County on 17 November 1820 when he applied for a pension for his services in the Revolution, stating that he enlisted in May 1776 at Windsor, Bertie County, in the North Carolina Line. He was sixty-six years old and owned 220 acres of poor land that he lived on with his wife Milly, fifty years old, and four children [*NCGSJ* XI:22]. They were

 i. Temperance, born about 1802.

 ii. Sucky, born about 1803.

 iii. William[3], born about 1804.

 iv. Abigail[2], born about 1812.

Other members of the family were

 i. James, born in March 1759, a twelve-year-old "Mulatto" boy living in Loudoun County on 9 September 1771 when the court ordered the churchwardens of Cameron parish to bind him to Hardage Lane, Gentleman. He came into court on 14 September 1778 and agreed to serve Lane until 25 December 1779 to complete all his service including runaway time [Orders 1770-3, 213; 1776-83, 120]. He may have been the James Butler who was head of a Campbell County household of 10 "other free" in 1810 [VA:879].

 ii. Jack Butlers, born say 1760, a "mulatto" who was listed among seven deserters, drafted out of Prince George County, Virginia, for whom a reward was offered in the 28 November 1777 issue of the *Virginia Gazette* [Purdie edition, p.3, col. 3], perhaps the "Buttlers Jack" who was head of a Martin County, North Carolina household of 2 "other free" in 1790 [NC:68].

 iii. Christopher, head of a Stafford County, Virginia household of 7 "other free" in 1810.

iv. Lurany, born about 1788, registered in Sussex County, Virginia, on 23 September 1814: *yellow complexion, 5'4", free born, 26 years old* [Certificates granted to Free negroes & Mulattos, no.249].

BYRD FAMILY

1. Margaret Bird, born say 1682, was the servant of Orlando Jones of York County on 24 June 1703 when he reported to the court that she had a bastard child by a "Negroe" and asked that she be punished. Later that year on 5 November he decided not to prosecute and the charges were dismissed [DOW 12:123, 157]. She was the mother of

2   i.   John[1], probably born 24 December 1696.
3   ii.   ?Elizabeth, born say 1720.

2. John[1] Byrd, probably born 24 December 1696, was a "Mallatto Servant" who was listed with "Mallatto Servant man" William **Cannady** in the York County estate of Orlando Jones on 15 December 1719. John was valued at 20 pounds, and William was valued at 15 pounds currency, so they probably still had several years to serve. On 16 January 1726/7 he petitioned the York County court setting forth that Graves Pack, Gent., was keeping him as a servant although he was of age and free. The court ordered him discharged from Pack's service on 24 December 1727. On 21 February 1731/2 he obtained an attachment against the estate of William **Brooks** for three pounds currency which was in the hands of James **Brooks**. In December 1735 he was presented by the York County court for failing to list his "Molatto" wife as a tithable [OW 16, pt. 2, 427, 433; 17:256, 262; 18:245]. He purchased 150 acres on the north side of the Meherrin River adjoining Buckhorn Swamp and Farrows Branch in Isle of Wight County on 16 July 1744 [DB 7:3]. He and his wife Susannah sold this land adjoining Tarraran Swamp by Southampton County deed on 12 March 1755 [DB 2:62]. On 13 June 1754 he was one of fourteen heads of household who were sued in Southampton County court by William Bynum (informer) for failing to pay the discriminatory tax on free African American and Indian women.[56] Absolem Joyner testified against him. He was sued by William Bynum again on 14 August 1760, this time for trover, but he was found not guilty. He and Joshua **Hunt** were sued for a 2 pound debt on 11 March 1763. John paid the debt when Joshua failed to appear [Orders 1749-54, 495-6, 500-1, 512; 1754-9, 25, 36-7, 41; 1759-63, 59, 68-9, 290]. He purchased 286 acres in Southampton County on 11 June 1767, part of it on the north side of the Meherrin River near Jacob's Branch of Buckhorn Swamp, and the other on the north side of Dawson's Mill Pond [DB 4:19]. On 8 September 1768 he made a motion in court to have himself and his sons Arthur and Nathan added to William Persons' list of tithables. On 9 April 1772 he and (his sons) James Byrd and John Byrd were sued for a 36 pound, 12 shillings debt they owed Cordall Norfleet. On 14 May 1772 the court bound Benjamin **Bartlett** to him as an apprentice, and on 13 August 1772 the court exempted him from paying levies. He transferred land to Nathan Byrd by deed proved in Southampton County court by Arthur Byrd on 12 November 1778 [Orders 1768-72, 68-9, 521, 532; 1772-7, 30, 78; Orders 1778-84, 43]. His undated will was proved in Southampton County on 12 April 1781. He gave his plantation and most of his livestock to his son Arthur, a heifer to Arthur's daughter Susannah, a cow and calf to (his son-in-law?) Joshua **Hunt**, and gave five shillings to each of his other sons John, James, Charles, Philip, Moses and Nathan, most of whom were then living in North Carolina where

---

[56]The other householders were John **Porteus**, John **Demery**, Isaac **Young**, Thomas **Wilkins**, Francis **Locust**, James **Brooks**, Jr. and Sr., John **Byrd**, Jr., Abraham **Artis**, Lewis **Artis**, William **Brooks**, Ann **Brooks**, and William **Tabor**.

they were counted as "other free" in the 1790 Northampton County census. John **Wood**, Elizabeth Williams, and William **Brooks** were witnesses [WB 3:322].[57] His children were

4   i.   John[2], born say 1727.
5   ii.   Arthur, born say 1729, executor of his father's will.
6   iii.   James[1], born say 1732.
7   iv.   Charles, born say 1735.
        v.   perhaps a daughter who may have married Joshua **Hunt**.
        vi.   Philip, living in Northampton County before 1774 when he was listed among the "Black" members of the undated colonial muster roll of Captain James Fason's Company [Mil. T.R. 1-3]. He and (his common-law wife?) Jane **Young** jointly purchased 50 acres on the road leading to Halifax Town between his own land and Samuel Low's on 16 March 1778. On 29 October 1782 he was granted 11 acres near Isaac Edward's line which was near the land of his brother Charles [DB 6:262; 7:132]. He was head of a Northampton County household of 2 free males and 2 free females in Captain Winborne's District for the 1786 North Carolina State Census, 5 "other free" in 1790 [NC:76], and 7 in 1800 [NC:425]. His 9 January 1807 Northampton County will was proved in March of that year [WB 2:363]. He left his land to his niece Tamer Byrd and mentioned Harriet **Walden**. Harwood **Walden** was executor and William **Walden** was a witness.
8   vii.   Moses, born say 1745.
       viii. Nathan, added to William Person's list of tithables for Southampton County with his father and brother Arthur Byrd on 8 September 1768. He sued Joshua Savory, with William Bynum as security, for trespass in Southampton County on 9 January 1772. The court found Savory guilty of killing his mare. His father transferred land to him by deed proved in Southampton County court on 12 November 1778, and he and his wife Martha sold land by deed proved in court on 12 August 1779. He and Arthur were sued in Southampton County court for a debt of 65 pounds, but he was ruled to be "no inhabitant" when the case was called for trial in May 1784 [Orders 1768-72, 83, 484, 534, 536; 1772-7, 50; 1778-84, 43, 88, 429]. He probably came to Northampton County after the death of his father. He was granted a patent on 43 acres in Northampton County on 29 October 1782. He bought a further 150 acres adjoining this land on 22 February 1784 and sold all this land on 1 January 1788 [DB 7:128, 139; 8:136]. He was head of a Northampton County household of 8 "other free" in 1790 [NC:76].
       ix.   ?Martha, head of a household of 4 "Black" persons 12-50 years old and 4 "Black" persons less than 12 or over 50 years old in Dupree's District, Northampton County, for the 1786 North Carolina state census.

3.   Elizabeth Bird, born say 1720, was a "molatto woman" whose daughter Moll was ordered bound out by the churchwardens of Bristol Parish, Virginia, on 9 December 1740 [Chamberlayne, *Register of Bristol Parish*, 102]. She was a "Mulatto" living in Amelia County on 24 November 1757 when she sued Alexander Bolling for her freedom [Orders 1757-60, 36]. She was the mother of

9   i.   Moll, born say 1738.
10   ii.   ?Joseph[1], born say 1739.

---

[57]William **Brooks** was also presented by the York County Court in December 1735 for failing to list his "Molatto" wife as a tithable [OW 18:245].

iii. ?John[3], born say 1741, bound himself as an apprentice to Trustram Hex in York County on 15 January 1759 until 15 October 1762. He was sued for debt in York County on 15 August 1763 by John **Pow (Poe)**. On 15 July 1765 the court ordered Edward Bowcock to pay him as a witness in the suit of Tristram Hix [DB 6:175; Judgments & Orders 1759-63, 7; 1763-5, 63, 429].

iv. ?Robert[2], born about 1759, called a "free Mulatto" on 26 February 1767 when the Amelia County court ordered the churchwardens of Nottoway Parish to bind him to Moses Hurt, Jr. [Orders 1766-9, 36]. He was head of a Pittsylvania County household of 6 "free colored" in 1820 [VA:781]. He registered in Pittsylvania County on 11 September 1822: *a bright Mulatto Man about sixty three years of age about five feet three inches high, he has black hair nearly straight somewhat mixed with grey hairs* [Register of Free Negroes, no. 35, pp. 12-13].

4. John[2] Byrd, born say 1727, was presented by the York County court on 19 January 1746/7 for not listing himself as a tithable [W&I 19:486]. He was living in Southampton County on 13 June 1754 (called John Byrd, Jr.) when he was sued by William Bynum (informer) for failing to pay the discriminatory tax on free African American and Indian women [Orders 1749-54, 501, 512; 1754-9, 25, 37]. He was added to William Person's list of tithables for Southampton County on 8 September 1768. He deposed that he rented a plantation belonging to Beale for 11 pounds when he was summoned by the Southampton County court as garnishee on 12 March 1772. He, Hardy Beal, Arthur **Allen**, Arthur Byrd and James Byrd were sued by Jesse Watkins in a case that was dismissed at their costs on 11 February 1773 [Orders 1768-72, 83; 1772-7, 107; Minutes 1771-2]. He received 5 shillings by the 12 April 1781 Southampton County will of his father John[1] Byrd. He was taxable in Southampton County from 1782 to 1786: taxable on 3 slaves, 3 horses and 11 cattle in 1782; 4 horses and 16 cattle in 1783; 3 horses and 6 cattle in 1786 [PPTL 1782-92, frames 503, 515, 544, 559, 586]. He may have been the father of

i. Sophia, born about 1756, registered in Southampton County on 28 March 1827: *age 71, Mulatto, 5 feet 5-1/8 inches, free born* [Register of Free Negroes 1794-1832, no. 1629].

ii. Charlotte, born say 1765, married Abraham **Reid/ Reed**, 27 February 1786 Southampton County bond.

iii. Aaron, born about 1781, married Aira **Taylor** (nee **Williams**), 19 February 1803 Southampton County bond, Burwell **Gardner** surety. He was a "free Negro" Southampton County taxable in Nottoway Parish in 1802 and 1803, taxable in St. Luke's Parish from 1807 to 1815 and living in Nottoway Parish in 1817 [PPTL 1792-1806, frames 581, 648; 1807-21, frames 46, 163, 185, 313, 414, 438, 573] and head of a Southampton County household of 3 "other free" in 1810 [VA:60]. In 1808 Aaron and Aira sued Lemuel **Clark**, the executor of the estate of Aira's father John **Williams**, over her part of her father's estate [LVA Chancery suit 1814-017]. He registered in Southampton County on 21 July 1807: *age 26, yellow, 6 feet 1/4 inch high* [Register of Free Negroes 1794-1832, no. 414].

iv. William, born say 1783, registered in Southampton County on 2 October 1801: *no age, Black rather yellow, 5 feet 7 1/2 inches, free born*, perhaps identical to Billy Byrd who registered on 17 August 1810: *age 27, yellow, 5 feet 6 inches, free born* [Register of Free Negroes 1794-1832, no. 219, 838]. He was taxable in St. Luke's Parish in 1803 [PPTL 1792-1806, frame 617], head of a Southampton County household of 2 "other free" in 1810 [VA:56].

5. Arthur Byrd, born say 1729, was added to William Person's list of tithables for Southampton County with his father and brother Nathan on 8 September 1768 [Orders 1768-72, 83]. He and his wife Tabitha sold property by deed proved in Southampton County on 10 July 1780. He and his brother Nathan Byrd were sued in Southampton County for a 65 pound debt in May 1784, and Arthur won a suit against Joel Newsum for 52 pounds, 10 shillings in paper money on 14 October 1784. Arthur, John and James Byrd were sued for a debt of 2,050 pounds currency of the year 1780 on 13 May 1785, but the suit abated against Arthur because he was ruled to be not an inhabitant of the county [Orders 1778-84, 339, 429, 448, 497; 1784-9, 73]. He was taxable in Southampton County in 1782 on his own tithe, a slave, a horse and 15 head of cattle, taxable in James Byrd's household in 1788, taxable in Jacob Byrd's household in 1789, taxable on a horse in his own household in 1790, head of a household with David Byrd in 1791, and a "Negro" taxable on a horse in 1792. He had "removed" from the county when the tax list was prepared for 1793 [PPTL 1782-92, frames 507, 655, 707, 754, 811, 869; 1792-1806, frame 46]. He was head of a Northampton County household of 4 Black persons 12-50 years old and 2 Black persons less than 12 years or more than 50 years old in Dupree's District for the 1786 North Carolina state census. He was in Northampton County on 16 February 1788 when Abram Lubley and his wife Lucy gave him a bond for their one third share of land adjoining Ann Taylor and William Deloatch which he endorsed to Henry Suter on 19 March 1788 [Gammon, *Record of Estates Northampton County*, I:6]. He married Ann Byrd, 8 October 1789 Southampton County, Virginia bond, James Byrd surety, 10 October marriage [Minister's Returns, 62]. He was head of a Northampton County household of 5 "other free" in 1790 [NC:74]. Administration of his estate was granted to Jacob Turner on 5 March 1792 on a bond of 200 pounds in Northampton County court [Minutes 1792-76, 4]. His children were

    i.   Susannah[1], mentioned in her grandfather's 1781 Southampton County will. She purchased 30 acres near Marsh Swamp in Halifax County, North Carolina, for 55 silver dollars on 16 August 1785 [DB 15:426] and was head of a Halifax County household of 8 "other free" in 1800 [NC:292].

11 ii. ?Richard, born say 1765.

    iii. ?Peggy, born say 1768, head of a Halifax County household of 4 "other free" in 1790 [NC:66].

    iv. ?Edward/ Edmund[1], born say 1770, head of a Halifax County household of 2 "other free" in 1800 [NC:292], 7 in 1810 [NC:7], and 11 "free colored" in 1820 [NC:141].

    v.   ?David[1], born about 1773, registered in Southampton County on 20 January 1795: *age 22, (blank) complexion, 5 feet 6 inches high, Free born* and registered again on 31 July 1810: *age 38, yellow, 5 feet 7 inches, free born.* (His wife) Didah Byrd registered the same day: *age 25, Mulatto, 5 feet 5 inches, free born* [Register of Free Negroes 1794-1832, nos. 99, 783, 784]. He was taxable in Southampton County from 1791 to 1814: taxable in Arthur Byrd's household in 1791, in John Robertson's household in 1792 (with Shadrack **Demery**), called a "M"(ulatto) in 1805, living with his wife Diddy **Taylor** on John Drake's land from 1812 to 1814 [PPTL 1782-92, frames 811, 883; 1792-1806, frame 796; 1807-21, frames 44, 284, 312, 414]. He was head of a Southampton County household of 6 "other free" in 1810 [VA:58].

12 vi. ?Jesse, born say 1775.

6. James[1] Byrd, born say 1732, purchased 150 acres in Southampton County on Buckhorn Swamp from Thomas Harris on 10 January 1760. This was the land which John Byrd sold Harris five years earlier on 12 March 1755 [DB 2:62,

311]. John Green's suit against him for 2 pounds, 11 shillings was dismissed on 9 July 1761, and James **Brooks'** petition against him was dismissed on 9 September on agreement of the parties [Orders 1759-63, 116, 238]. He was added to William Person's list of tithables for Southampton County on 8 September 1768. He sued John Powell on 8 November 1770 in a case that was dismissed on agreement of the parties [Orders 1768-72, 83, 334, 353]. He was taxable in Southampton County from 1782 to 1789: taxable on 4 horses and 15 cattle in 1782, 3 horses and 15 cattle in 1785, 2 free males aged 16-21 in 1787, taxable on Arthur Byrd in 1788, and taxable on his own tithe, another James Byrd and a slave in 1789 [PPTL 1782-92, frames 508, 539, 634, 655, 705]. The inventory of his Southampton County estate, taken on 28 October 1790, included nineteen head of cattle. The account of the estate allowed his unnamed sons 10 shillings for his coffin [WB 5:82, 88-9]. He may have been the father of

13   i.   James², born about 1763.
14   ii.   Jacob, born say 1768.
      iii. Asa, born about 1765, taxable in James Byrd's household in 1784 (called Else Bird), called Asea Byrd in Moses Byrd's Southampton County household in 1788, taxable in Francis Branch's household in 1794, in Henry Smith's household in 1795, charged with his own tax in 1796 [PPTL 1782-92, frames 545, 655, 705; 1792-1806, frames 75, 170, 184]. He registered in Southampton County on 17 March 1806: *age 41, yellow, 5 feet 7 3/4 inches, free born* [Register of Free Negroes 1794-1832, no. 342]. He was taxable on the south side of the Meherrin River in Greensville County from 1795 to 1814: taxable on a slave in 1795, listed as a "Mulatto" in 1813 and 1814 [PPTL 1782-1850, frames 300, 318, 335, 351, 370, 385, 400, 413, 445, 460]. On 19 May 1804 he was a witness in Greensville County court for the Commonwealth against Graham **Bell**, Jr., who was charged with forging a bond to himself for $333 from Sterling Edmond of Brunswick County. Asa gave bond to appear as a witness in the District Court in Brunswick County [Orders 1799-1806, 387-8]. On 13 August 1804 the grand jury presented him for retailing liquor without a license and for disturbing religious worship at Round Hill Meeting House, but he was found not guilty of both charges [Orders 1799-1806, 3909, 408, 410, 411, 423, 433, 452; 1806-10, 26, 27, 170].[58] He gave his consent for the Greensville County marriage of (his daughter?) the unnamed bride of Peyton **Stewart**, 12 May 1806 Greensville County bond [Marriage Bonds, 58]. On 18 September 1806 he purchased a crop of corn and peas, a bed, furniture, and two hogs in Greensville County for 16 pounds from Peyton **Stewart**. He married Lucretia **Stewart**, widow of Thomas **Stewart**, before 10 October 1806 when they and her children Henry **Stewart** and Peyton **Stewart** and his wife Vicey sold 114 acres which they received by Thomas **Stewart**'s will [DB 3:511, 520]. On 16 January 1808 he was examined in court but found not guilty of his wife's murder. He made a deed of gift to (his stepdaughter?) Viney G. Stewart which was proved in Greensville County court on 9 May 1808 [Orders 1806-10, 204, 231]. On 12 June 1809 the court presented Buckner Brewer for swearing two oaths at him [Orders 1806-10, 359]. He made a deed of trust for land for the use of John **Hathcock** proved in Northampton County court on 4 March 1822 [Minutes 1821-25, 70]. Asa was head of a Halifax County, North Carolina household of 5 "free colored" in 1830 and 4 "free colored" in Rush County, Indiana, in 1840.

---

[58]There was a similar case on 11 March 1807 when the Greensville County court indicted a white man named Robert Morris for disturbing religious service at Bethel [Orders 1806-10, 104].

15   iv.   Pherebe/ Phebe, born about 1765-1770.
        v.   Sally, born about 1776, registered in Southampton County on 17 March
               1806: *age 30, blk., 5 feet 4 inches, free born* [Register of Free Negroes
               1794-1832, no. 343]. She registered in Petersburg on 9 June 1806: *a
               yellow brown free Negro woman, five feet four and a half inches high,
               thirty years old, born free in the County of Southampton p. certificate
               of the Register in Southampton* [Register of Free Negroes 1794-1819,
               no. 381]. She was head of a Petersburg Town household of 5 "other
               free" and a slave in 1810 [VA:124a].
        vi.   Peter, born about 1779, registered in Southampton County on 29 June
               1801: *age 22, Black rather yellow, 5 feet 6 3/4 inches high, free born*
               [Register of Free Negroes 1794-1832, no. 214].
        vii.   Susannah[2], born about 1782, registered in Southampton County on 10
               February 1832: *age 50, yellow, 5 feet 3-1/2 inches, free born* [Register
               of Free Negroes 1794-1832, no. 1967].

7.   Charles Byrd, born say 1735, purchased 150 acres on Little Swamp in
        Northampton County, North Carolina, on 12 July 1760 [DB 3:84]. He voted
        for Joseph Sikes in the Northampton County election of 1762 [SS 837 by
        NCGSJ XII:170]. He sold part of his land on 25 November 1771 and bought
        a further 100 acres for 100 pounds near his land on the north side of Little
        Swamp on 4 October 1778. He sold 2 acres of the land he bought in 1760 on
        4 December 1779 [DB 5:133; 6:283; 7:18]. He was head of a Northampton
        County household of 2 free males and 2 free females in Captain Winborne's
        District for the 1786 state census. The inventory of his estate was proved in
        Northampton County by John **Walden** in December 1788 [Gammon, *Record
        of Estates, Northampton County*, I:58]. His widow was probably Ruth Byrd
        who was head of a Northampton County household of 5 "other free" in 1790
        [NC:76]. She was a buyer at the sale of the estate of Solomon Byrd on 12
        March 1790 and was devised the residue of the estate of Alice Earp (nee **Bass**)
        by Alice's 13 October 1796 Northampton County will [WB 2:133]. Their
        children may have been
        i.   Solomon, born say 1755, bought 100 acres in Northampton County for
               400 pounds on 19 February 1780 and sold 50 acres of this land on 1
               December 1780 [DB 7:51, 63]. He was head of a Northampton County
               household of 5 Black males, 4 white females and a white male in
               Captain Winborne's District for the 1786 state census. The account of
               sales for his estate was recorded in Northampton County on 12 March
               1790 by the administrator, John **Walden** [Gammon, *Record of Estates,
               Northampton County*, I:71].
        ii.   James[3], born about 1780, registered as a "Free Negro" in Greensville
               County on 21 November 1811: *Born free of a Yellow Complexion, aged
               about thirty one years...five feet eight & 1/2 Inches high* [Register,
               no.21].

8.   Moses Byrd, born say 1745, enlisted as a musician in Lewis' Company of the
        North Carolina Continental Line in Halifax County in 1776 and was omitted
        in January 1778 [N.C. DAR, *Roster of Soldiers from N.C. in the Revolution*,
        112]. He was taxable in Southampton County from 1782 to 1803: taxable on
        a horse and 4 cattle from 1782 to 1787, taxable on Asa Byrd in 1788, taxable
        on Thomas Byrd in 1795, called a "Mulatto" in 1802 [PPTL 1782-92; frames
        508, 544, 634, 655, 705, 755, 812, 869; 1792-1806, frames 156, 183, 261,
        311, 373, 407, 509, 546, 615]. He was living in Northampton County, North
        Carolina, before 2 January 1807 when he made his Northampton County will,
        proved March 1808 [WB 2:362]. He left most of his estate to his wife
        (unnamed) and after her death to Willie Thomas and Mary **Ash**. James, Sarah,
        and Elisha Byrd were witnesses. He was the father of

i. ?Thomas, born say 1778, taxable in Southampton County from 1795 to 1817: taxable in Moses Byrd's household in 1795, taxable on a horse in his own household in 1801, called a "M"(ulatto) or "f.n." after 1802, living with his wife Lottie on William Vick's land in 1813 [PPTL 1792-1806, frames 183, 508, 614, 684, 798; 1807-21, frames 164, 284, 413, 572]. He was head of a Southampton County household of 10 "other free" in 1810 [VA:59].

ii. Willie, born 1776-94, executor of his father's will, head of a Northampton County household of 6 "free colored" in 1820 [NC:214].

9. Moll Bird, born say 1738, the daughter of a "molatto woman" named Elizabeth Bird, was ordered bound out by the churchwardens of Bristol Parish, Virginia, on 9 December 1740 [Chamberlayne, *Register of Bristol Parish*, 102]. She may have been the Mary Bird who was living in Brunswick County, Virginia, on 28 February 1780 when the court ordered the churchwardens of Meherrin Parish to bind out her illegitimate "Mulattoe" children Joe and Peter [Orders 1774-82, 331]. She was the mother of

i. ?Prissy, born 23 December 1752, registered in Petersburg on 27 January 1798: *a light brown Mulatto woman, five feet three inches high, forty five years old the 23 Dec. 1797, born free & raised in the Town of Petersburg* [Register of Free Negroes 1794-1819, no. 130].

16 ii. Robert[1], born say 1755.

iii. Joseph[2], born say 1765, ordered bound apprentice in Brunswick County on 28 February 1780 [Orders 1774-82, 331]. He married Nettie **Jackson**, 20 August 1790 Charlotte County bond, Burwell **Jackson** surety.

iv. Peter, born say 1767, ordered bound apprentice in Brunswick County on 28 February 1780 [Orders 1774-82, 331].

17 v. Catherine **Jackson**, born about 1769.

18 vi. ?Peggy, born say 1770.

19 vii. ?William, born about 1775.

10. Joseph[1] Byrd, born about 1739, was living in Surry County, Virginia, on 22 June 1773 when the court ordered him to pay 3 pounds per annum support for an illegitimate child he had by Ann **Charity** [Orders 1764-74, 380]. He purchased 50 acres in Surry County on the east side of Washington's Road on 6 June 1780 [DB 11:363] and was head of a Surry County household of 6 persons in 1782 [VA:42]. He was taxable in Cabin Point district of Surry County from 1782 to 1807: taxable on Walden Bird's tithe in 1794 and 1795; taxable on Joseph Byrd, Jr.'s tithe from 1797 to 1799; taxable on Willis Byrd's tithe in 1800 [PPTL, 1782-90, frames 351, 378, 399, 468, 594; 1791-1816, 55, 156, 250, 283, 315, 359, 473, 554, 610]. He registered as a free Negro in Surry County on 22 February 1797: *a mulattoe man of a bright complexion born of free parents...aged about 58 years, pretty square made, very bald, & 5'7" tall* [Back of Guardian Accounts Book 1783-1804, no.23]. Two of his children, described as sons of Joseph and Nelly Byrd, registered as "free Negro" residents of Surry County. He may have been the Joseph Bird who was head of an Orange County, North Carolina household of 8 "other free" in 1800 [NC:547]. His will was proved in Surry County, Virginia, in 1808 [Wills, Etc. 2:206-7]. Nelly was head of a Surry County household of 4 "other free" in 1810 [VA:601] and 6 "free colored" in 1830. Their children were

i. William, born about 1777, registered on 27 September 1798: *son of Joseph and Nelly his Wife free persons and residents of said County, aged about 21 years old, about 5'10-1/4" high, of a bright complection short thick hair straight and well made by profession a planter.*

ii. ?Cyrus, born say 1778, taxable in Surry County in 1796 and 1797 [PPTL, 1791-1816, frames 251, 282].

- iii. Joseph[3], born about 1780, registered on 8 October 1798: *son of Joseph and Nelly his wife...aged about 20 years, 5'5" high, of a bright complexion, short thick hair, straight and well made, by profession a planter* [Back of Guardian Accounts Book 1783-1804, nos .34, 35]. He married Betsy **Andrews**, daughter of Thomas **Jones**, 23 December 1816 Surry County bond, John **Charity** security.
- iv. ?Willis, born about 1781, registered in Petersburg on February 4, 1801: *a brown Mulatto man, five feet six inches high, twenty years of age, appears by affidavit of Benja. Bilbro & Coleman Harrison of the County of Surry have been born free & raised in the County of Surry* [Register of Free Negroes 1794-1819, no. 214].
- v. ?Henry, born about 1783, received one of the "Certificates granted to Free negroes & mulattoes from October 1800" in Sussex County on 8 March 1813: *yellow complexion, 5'10", free born, 30 years old* [Register of Free Negroes, no. 203].
- vi. Sally, born say 1786, "daughter of Joseph Byrd," married Wright **Walden**, 30 March 1804 Surry County bond, surety James **Williams**.
- vii. ?Betsy, born say 1789, married James **Ruffin**, 20 January 1810 Surry County bond, Wright **Walden** surety. James was probably related to Thomas **Ruffin**, head of a Southampton County household of 5 "other free" in 1810 [VA:79].
- viii. ?Rebecca, born say 1792, married James **Cypress**, 26 January 1818 Surry County bond, John **Charity** surety [Marriage Bonds, 107].

11. Richard Byrd, born say 1765, was head of a Halifax County, North Carolina household of 2 "other free" in 1790 [NC:66], 10 "other free" and a slave in 1810 [NC:9], and 12 "free colored" in 1830 (supposedly 100 years old). His 12 February 1835 Halifax County will, proved August the same year mentioned his unnamed wife and six children [WB 4:122]. His children were
    - i. Henry, born 1794-1806, head of a Halifax County household of 4 "free colored" in 1830.
    - ii. Susan **Turner**.
    - iii. Thomas.
    - iv. William.
    - v. Margaret.
    - vi. Elisha[2].

12. Jesse Byrd, born say 1775, was head of a Halifax County, North Carolina household of 6 "other free" in 1810 [NC:9]. Administration of his estate was granted to James H. Grant in Northampton County court on 3 June 1816 on a bond of 500 pounds. His children were
    - i. Edmund[3], born say 1803, a "boy of color" bound apprentice to James H. Grant to learn to be a farmer by order of the 3 June 1816 Northampton County court. He was identified as the orphan of Jesse when Grant recorded his apprenticeship bond in Northampton County court on 8 March 1825 [Minutes 1821-25, 363].
    - ii. David[2], born say 1805, bound apprentice to Drury **Walden** by order of the 2 March 1818 Northampton County court. David was identified as the son of Jesse in the 5 June 1822 session of the Northampton County court when Drury **Walden** renewed his $500 apprenticeship bond with Sterling **Hathcock** and William **Walden** sureties [Minutes 1821-25, 105]. David mortgaged his livestock to James **Hathcock** by 12 May 1837 Northampton County deed [DB 28:62].
    - iii. ?Angelina, a "free girl of color" bound apprentice to James C. Harrison by order of the 4 June 1822 Northampton County court.

13. James[2] Byrd, born about 1763, married Sarah **Hathcock**, 30 August 1789 Southampton County marriage [Ministers' Returns, 646]. She was called Sarah

Bird on 12 October 1786 when the court bound out her "poor child" Michael **Heathcock** [Orders 1784-9, 215]. James was taxable in Southampton County in the household of (his father?) James Byrd in 1789, taxable in his own household from 1790 to 1804: taxable on Peter Byrd in 1794, taxable on 2 tithables in 1797, called a "Mulatto" in 1802 [PPTL 1782-92, frames 705, 755, 813, 871; 1792-1806, frames 48, 74, 156, 183, 261, 407, 509, 546, 615, 684]. He registered in Southampton County on 20 November 1810: *age 47, Blk., 5 feet 10 inches, free born* [Register of Free Negroes 1794-1832, no. 852]. He was a witness to the 2 January 1807 Northampton County will of Moses Byrd and was head of a Northampton County household of 10 "other free" in 1810 [NC:714]. Administration on his Northampton County estate was granted to his son Elisha on 3 June 1816 on a surety of 250 pounds provided by Elias **Roberts** and Stephen **Walden**. Elisha petitioned the court on 2 March 1819 for partition of James' land among his heirs [Minutes 1813-21, 166]. His child was

    i.   Elisha[1], born 1776-94, living with his wife Disey, "fn," on J. Bailey's land in Southampton County in 1813 [PPTL 1807-21, frame 314]. He was head of a Northampton County household of 6 "free colored" in 1820 [NC:218]. He registered in Southampton County on 23 January 1823: *age 33, mulatto man, 5 feet 6-1/4 inches high, free born* [Register of Free Negroes 1794-1832, no. 1355].

14. Jacob Byrd, born say 1768, was taxable in Southampton County from 1789 to 1807: charged with Arthur Byrd's tithe in 1789, charged with Josiah Byrd's tithe in 1805, taxable on 2 tithables aged 16-21 in 1806 and 3 in 1807, called a "Mulatto" from 1802 to 1806 [PPTL 1782-92, frames 707, 756, 813, 870; 1792-1806, 156, 183, 261, 311, 373, 4-8. 509, 615, 684, 799, 835; 1807-21, frame 44]. He may have been the father of

    i.   Josiah, born say 1782, taxable in Jacob Byrd's Southampton County household in 1805, head of a Northampton County household of 6 "other free" in 1810 [NC:715]. He was taxable on 100 acres and a free poll in Chatham County in Captain Bynum's District in 1815, and he purchased land by deed proved in the Thursday, February 1825 session of the Chatham County court. He was head of a Chatham County household of 8 "free colored" in 1820 [NC:211]. Administration of his estate was granted to Frederick Rolens in the Wednesday, May 1836 session of the court.

15. Pherebe Byrd, born about 1765, registered in Southampton County on 22 June 1810: *age 45, Blk rather yellow, 5 feet 5 1/2 inches high, free born* [Register of Free Negroes 1794-1832, no. 484]. She may have been identical to Phebe Byrd who registered in Petersburg on 3 July 1810: *a dark brown Mulatto woman, five feet six inches high, forty years old, born free in Southampton County p. certificate of Registry* [Register of Free Negroes 1794-1819, no. 634]. She was the mother of

    i.   ?John[4], born about 1787, registered in Southampton County on 31 July 1810: *age 23, Mulatto, 6 feet 1/2 inch, born free* [Register of Free Negroes 1794-1832, no. 791]. He was a "Mulatto" taxable in St. Luke's Parish, Southampton County, in 1812, a "f.n." laborer living on the Indian Reservation in Southampton County from 1815 to 1818 [PPTL 1807-21, frames 284, 436, 574, 784].

    ii.   Priscilla, born about 1794, registered in Petersburg on 9 October 1810: *a light coloured Mulatto girl (daughter of Phebe Byrd) a free woman, five feet three inches high, sixteen - seventeen years old, born free & raised in the County of Southampton* [Register of Free Negroes 1794-1819, no. 643].

16. Robert[1] Bird, born say 1755, died before 16 August 1800 when his widow
     Patty Bird (born about 1758) registered in Petersburg: *widow of Bob Bird,
     decd., a brown Mulatto woman, five feet three inches high, forty two years
     old, long bushy hair, born free and raised in the County of Chesterfield*
     [Register of Free Negroes 1794-1819, no. 192]. They were the parents of
         i.   ?Betsy, born about 1775, registered in Petersburg on 3 August 1805:
             *a brown Mulatto woman, five feet two inches high, thirty years old,
             bushy hair, born free & raised in Dinwiddie County* [Register of Free
             Negroes 1794-1819, no. 347].

20   ii. ?Martha, born 1 October 1780.
         iii. Robert[3]/ Bob, born 9 September 1781, registered in Petersburg on 16
             August 1800: *son of Bob Bird, decd., & Patty Bird his wife who were
             free Mulattos, a brown Mulatto lad, eighteen years old 9 September
             last, near five feet high, short bushy hair* [Register of Free Negroes
             1794-1819, no. 193].
         iv. ?Peggy, born 28 June 1784, registered in Petersburg on 29 July 1803:
             *a dark brown Mulatto woman, five feet eleven and a half inches high,
             nineteen years old the 28 June last, long Bushy hair, born free &
             raised in the Town of Petersburg* [Register of Free Negroes 1794-1819,
             no. 254].

17. Catherine Byrd, born about 1769, married Isaac **Jackson**, 22 September 1797
     Lunenburg County bond. She was called Catherine **Jackson** when she
     registered in Charlotte County on 16 October 1819: *formerly the wife of Isaac
     Jackson, daughter of Mary Bird, Mulatto complexion, aged 50, born free*
     [Ailsworth, *Charlotte County--Rich Indeed*, 486]. She was the mother of
         i.   James[2], born about 1797, registered in Charlotte County on 6
             November 1827: *James Bird, Junr., son of Caty Bird, a free woman,
             aged 30, born free* [Ailsworth, *Charlotte County--Rich Indeed*, 487].

18. Peggy Byrd, born say 1770, was a "fm" planter listed in Charlotte County
     with 2 female and 2 male children in 1803, listed with 4 female children, a
     male child and 2 horses in 1805 and 1806, listed by herself in 1810, listed
     with 5 females and 3 horses in her household from 1811 to 1813 [PPTL 1782-
     1813, frames 580, 641, 648, 682, 751, 783, 803, 814, 846, 886]. She was a
     "Free Negro" head of a Charlotte County household of 6 "other free" in 1810
     [VA:44]. She was the mother of
         i.   ?Edmund[2], born say 1790, a "fm" listed with a female member of his
             family in his household in Charlotte County in 1811 and 1812, a
             ditcher listed with a male and 2 females in his household in 1813
             [PPTL 1782-1813, frames 814, 836, 846, 869, 886].
         ii. ?James, born say 1792, a "fm" taxable on a horse in Charlotte County
             in 1813 [PPTL 1782-1813, frame 868].
         iii. Peyton, born about 1802, registered in Charlotte County on 2 July
             1832: *son of Peggy Bird, Mulatto complexion, aged 30, born free*
             [Ailsworth, *Charlotte County--Rich Indeed*, 490].

19. William Byrd, born about 1775, married Polly **Carter**, "dau. in law" (step
     daughter) of William **Brogdon**, 19 November 1796 Charlotte County bond,
     John **Chavus** surety, 22 November marriage. He was taxable in Charlotte
     County from 1795 to 1813: called a "free negroe" in 1799, a ditcher listed
     with sons Graybird and Washington Byrd in 1802 and 1803, listed with wife
     Polly, 2 male children and a female child in 1805 and 1806, 3 male and 3
     female children from 1811 to 1812, a total of 5 males and 3 females in his
     household in 1813 [PPTL 1782-1813, frames 314, 352, 381, 431, 542, 580,
     648, 682, 803, 814, 846, 886]. He was a "F.N." head of a Charlotte County
     household of 11 "other free" in 1810 [VA:44]. He registered in Charlotte
     County on 3 February 1809: *Mulatto complexion, aged 34, born free*. Polly

registered on 7 November 1831: *Yellow complexion, aged 52, born free* [Ailsworth, *Charlotte County--Rich Indeed*, 485, 490]. He and Polly were the parents of

    i.   Gray, born about 1799, registered in Charlotte County on 6 November 1827: *son of William and Polly Bird, free people, Mulatto complexion, aged 28, born free* [Ailsworth, *Charlotte County--Rich Indeed*, 487].

    ii. Washington, born about 1801, registered in Charlotte County on 6 November 1827: *son of William and Polly Bird, Mulatto complexion, aged 26, born free* [Ailsworth, *Charlotte County--Rich Indeed*, 487].

20. Martha Bird, born 1 October 1780, registered in Petersburg on 29 July 1803: *a light Mulatto woman, five feet two and a half inches high, twenty two years old the 1st of last Oct., born free & raised in the Town of Petersburg* [Register of Free Negroes 1794-1819, no. 253]. She was the mother of

    i.   Sally, born about 1797, registered in Petersburg on 16 November 1814: *a brown Mulatto girl, five feet two inches high, seventeen years old 26 October last, daughter of Martha Bird, decd., a free woman of colour, born free & raised in the Town of Petersburg, Registered by desire of Patty Bird her Grandmother* [Register of Free Negroes 1794-1819, no. 759].

Essex County

1. Molly Bird, born say 1740, was a "Mulatto" woman whose son John Bird was ordered bound out by the churchwardens of St. Ann's Parish in Essex County on 18 March 1771. She may have been the mother of "free Negroes" Reuben and James (no family name) who were bound out by the churchwardens of St. Ann's Parish on 20 August 1766 [Orders 1770-3, 33; 1764-7, 405]. She was taxable on a horse in St. Ann's Parish, Essex County, in 1799 [PPTL, 1782-1819, frame 308]. She was the mother of

    i.   ?Reuben[1], born about 1764, applied for a pension in Powhatan County on 15 June 1820 at the age of fifty-six years. He testified that he enlisted in Hillsborough, North Carolina, and served in Captain James Gunn's regiment of dragoons. Benjamin Sublett testified that he met Reuben, a sixteen or seventeen-year-old "Mulatto boy," while serving in the Revolution in May 1780. Gabriel Gray testified that Reuben served as "Boman" for his brother Lieutenant William Gray. In 1820 Reuben's family consisted of his 37 year-old wife and a seven-year-old girl [M804-243, frame 0362]. He was head of a Petersburg household of 5 "other free" in 1810 [VA:121b]. He registered in Petersburg on 9 June 1810: *a brown Mulatto man, five feet seven inches high, forty seven years old, born free in Essex County, a stone mason* [Register of Free Negroes 1794-1819, no. 576].

    ii. ?James, taxable in St. Ann's Parish, Essex County, from 1796 to 1814: taxable on 2 male "Free Negroes" in 1813 [PPTL, 1782-1819, frames 272, 297, 308, 332, 343, 357, 382, 393, 409, 459, 510, 528], head of an Essex County household of 6 "other free" and a white woman over 45 years old in 1810 [VA:201].

    iii. ?Jesse, born about 1766, a "free" taxable in Dinwiddie County from 1793 to 1798 [PPTL, 1791-9 (1793 A, p.2), (1794 B, p.2), (1795 A, p.2), (1796 A, p.2), (1798 B, p.2)]. He registered in Petersburg on 29 August 1800: *a light brown Mulatto man, thirty four years old, five feet nine inches high, born free in the County of Essex as appears from an affidavit of Walker Halls of the sd County* [Register of Free Negroes 1794-1819, no. 199]. He was head of a Petersburg Town household of 9 "other free" in 1810 [VA:118a].

    iv. John, born about 1769, taxable in St. Ann's Parish, Essex County, from 1790 to 1814: listed with a male and female "Free Negro" over the age of sixteen in 1813; not charged as a tithable in 1814 but taxable on a horse [PPTL, 1782-1819, frames 196, 210, 223, 260, 272, 343, 357, 382, 393, 409, 425, 439, 459, 480, 510, 528], head of an Essex County household of 11 "other free" in 1810 [VA:199]. He was called John Bird, Sr., when he registered in Essex County on 15 August 1829: *born free by certificate of John P. Lee, former Clerk of this Court, about 60 years of age, dark Mulattoe, 6 feet 7 eights of an inch.* His wife was apparently Sally Bird, Sr., who registered the same day: *born free by statement of Richard Rowzee in writing, about 56 years of age, bright Mulattoe, 5 feet 4-1/8 inches* [Register of Free Negroes 1810-43, pp.85-6, nos. 189, 191]. She was named in the 29 January 1820 Essex County will of her father Humphrey **Fortune**'s 29 January 1820 Essex County will which John Bird opposed when it was offered for proof in March court 1820 [WB 19:92].

   v.   ?Reuben[2], born 17 May 1777, registered in Petersburg on 29 August 1800: *(by a copy of the Registry from John P. Lee Clerk of County Court of Essex County) twenty two years one month & 18 days old, a shade lighter than black, 5'8-1/4" & free born 5 July 1799. The bearer thereof appears to answer to said register* [Register of Free Negroes 1794-1819, no. 198]. He was taxable in Petersburg in 1799 [1799 PPTL B, p.2], taxable in Chesterfield County in 1806 (called Reubin Bride "Mulato"), taxable in 1807 (called Reubin Bird), taxable on 2 horses while living on Mrs. Claiborne's land in 1809, and taxable on a tithe and 3 horses in 1810 [PPTL, 1786-1811, frames 632, 689, 738, 782].

   vi.   ?Nancy, born say 1782, mother of Edward Bird who registered in Essex County on 16 June 1823: *son of Nancy Bird, born free by statement of John Beazey, 24 years of age, 5 feet 6 & 3/4 inches* [Register of Free Negroes 1810-43, p.43, no. 109].

Other members of the Byrd family in Virginia were

   i.   Samuel, a "Mulato" taxable in Hanover County from 1786 to 1814: taxable on a slave named Lucy over the age of sixteen in 1786; on 2 free males, a slave over 16, and three horses in 1789 [PPTL, 1782-91, pp.151, 177, 207, 247; 1792-1803, pp. 10, 62, 92, 148, 249; 1804-24], taxable on a lot in Hanover Town in 1800 [Land Tax List, 28] and a "free" head of a Hanover County household of 7 "other free" and a slave in 1810 [VA:893]. He was arrested on suspicion of being involved in Gabriel's slave rebellion in Richmond in 1803 but released for want of evidence because slaves could not give testimony against him. However, his son, a slave, was executed [Russell, *Free Negro in Virginia*, 65].

CANE FAMILY

1.   Sebastian Cane, born say 1632, was a free resident of Dorchester in New England, who had visited Northampton County, Virginia, in 1652 and 1654 as a seaman when he made a deposition in court about a tobacco cargo [DW 1654-55, 73]. Back in Dorchester in 1656 he entered into bond (with his house and land, including 4-1/2 acres planted in wheat as his security) with Mrs. Ann Keayne to purchase the freedom of (his sister?) Angola, one of the family's African slaves. Angola was freed a week after Sebastian signed the agreement. He lived in Dorchester for at least ten years from 1652 to 1662 when he sold his whole estate to a friend, Francis Vernon. His estate consisted of a one third share in a 10-14 ton vessel, the Hopewell (later sold for 12 pounds), and one barrel each of liquor, sugar, mackerel, and codfish [Suffolk Deeds, Liber II (Boston: Rockwell and Churchill, 1883), 297 by Deal, *Race and Class*, 374-379].

He moved to Northampton County, Virginia, where he was head of a household with King **Tony** in 1664, and from 1665 to 1668 he was tithable with his wife Grace-Susanna [Orders 1657-64, fol.198; Orders 1764-74, 15, fol.29, fol.42, fol.54]. She was most likely the twenty-year-old former slave of Stephen Charlton. Charlton sold a three-year-old girl named Grace-Susanna to Richard Vaughan on 19 March 1647, stipulating that she was to be free at the age of thirty years [DW 1645-51, 150, 152].[59]

In 1666 Bastian received ten lashes for harboring a runaway slave of Francis Pigot, and he was imprisoned for a month for trading with another of Pigot's slaves (perhaps Thomas **Carter**, Peter **George**, or John **Archer**) [Orders 1664-74, fol.29, p.44]. His 1670 will, witnessed by his neighbor, John **Francisco**, mentioned only his wife Grace [Orders 1664-74, fol.89].

CANNADY/ KENNEDY FAMILY

Members of the Cannady family, probably descendants of a white woman, were
1   i.   William[1], born say 1695.
2   ii. Joseph[1], born say 1710.
      iii. Ann/ Nanny, born say 1715, presented by the York County court on 15 May 1738 for not listing herself as a tithable [OW 18:414, 434].
3   iv. William[2], born say 1716.

1. William[1] Cannady, born say 1695, was a "Mallatto Servant man" who was listed with "Mallatto Servant" John **Bird** in the York County estate of Orlando Jones on 15 December 1719. William was valued at 15 pounds, and John **Byrd** was valued at 20 pounds, so they probably still had a few years to serve. William was free from his indenture before 19 December 1726 when Robert Laughton sued him in York County court for a debt of 1 pound, 13 shillings. Matthew Hawkins was William's security [OW 15, pt. 2, 531; 16, pt. 2, 420, 426, 439]. He married Judith **Bass** sometime before her father John **Bass** made his 18 January 1732 Bertie County, North Carolina will. Her father left her 100 acres on the south side of Urahaw Swamp which became part of Northampton County in 1741 [SS 876/3:305].[60] William was living in Edgecombe County on 7 April 1744 when he and Judith sold this land in Northampton County [DB 1:175]. They were living in Guilford County on 27 January 1779 when they sold two parcels of 50 acres each in Northampton County on Urahaw Swamp [DB 6:326, 332]. They may have been the ancestors of
    i.   Judith, mother of Willie Cannady (born about 1786) who was bound an apprentice by the Edgecombe County court on 21 May 1791.
    ii. Jacob, born before 1776, head of a Halifax County, North Carolina household of 6 "free colored" in 1830 [NC:329]. The 11 October 1832 issue of the Roanoke Advocate advertised that there was a letter for him at the Halifax Post Office.
    iii. Mary, head of a Halifax County household of 3 "other free" in 1810 [NC:3].

2. Joseph[1] Cannady/ Kannady, born say 1710, was presented by the York County court on 15 December 1735 for not listing his "Molatto" wife Betty as a tithable. On 24 November 1741 Betty received 10 shillings for Mary **Roberts**

---

[59]See Deal, *Race and Class* for more details of the life of Grace-Susanna and nearly all the other mid-seventeenth century African American residents of Northampton County, Virginia.

[60]Others free African American families of York County who later lived in or near Northampton County, North Carolina, were the **Allen**, **Banks**, **Brooks**, **Byrd**, and **Roberts** families [OW 18:245].

from Francis Hewitt according to the account of his York County estate. Betty was Mary **Roberts'** daughter, named in Mary's 20 November 1749 York County will. On 19 November 1744 Joseph was again presented for not listing his wife as a tithable, and he was ordered to pay tithes on all his tithables when he appeared in court on 17 December 1744. A suit brought against him by George **Jones** for trespass, assault and battery was dismissed on 19 May 1746 when neither party appeared. John **Rollison (Rawlinson)** sued him for debt on 20 November 1752 but the case was discontinued because **Rawlinson** did not prosecute. Joseph paid 14 shillings to the estate of Ann Keith which was returned to court on 17 June 1754. Elizabeth was paid 1 pound, 4 shillings by the estate of Simon Whitaker on 6 August 1769 [W&I 18:237, 245; 19:250, 314, 332, 432; 20:163-4, 329; 22:8; Judgments & Orders 1752-4, 153, 168]. Joseph and Betty may have been the parents of

4   i.   Hugh^1, born say 1735.
5   ii.   Joseph^2, born about 1739.
       iii. Jane, living in York County on 17 December 1764 when a grand jury presentment against her was dismissed [Judgments & Orders 1759-63, 320].

3.   William^2 Cannady, born say 1716, was paid 1 pound, 6 shillings by the York County estate of Pluny Ward. He paid about the same amount to the estate which was settled on 12 September 1738. He was presented by the York County court on 19 November 1744 and 1746 for not listing his wife as a tithable [W&I 18:450-1; 19:314, 332, 472, 486]. He was probably the father of

       i.   William^3, born say 1740, presented for not listing his wife as a tithable in York County on 21 November 1765. On 17 July 1769 he was sued for a 40 shilling debt due by account. He was a soldier in the Revolution on 17 August 1778 and 21 June 1779 when the York County court allowed his wife Frances Kennedy a subsistence payment [Judgments & Orders 1763-5, 90, 126; 1768-70, 299; Orders 1774-84, 170, 219].
6   ii.   James^1, born say 1750.

4.   Hugh/ Uriah Cannady, born say 1735, was sued in Sussex County by John Montgomery for a 3 pound, 15 shilling debt on 18 June 1767 [Orders 1766-70, 120]. He and his wife Anne baptized their son Joseph on 3 July 1768 in Albemarle Parish, Sussex and Surry counties. The godparents were Timothy Santee and Samuel and Sarah **Blizzard** [Richards, *Register of Albemarle Parish*, 145]. Hugh died before 16 November 1775 when the Sussex County, Virginia court ordered the churchwardens to bind out his unnamed orphan children [Orders 1770-76]. He was the father of

7   i.   ?Hugh^2, born say 1757.
       ii.   ?John, born say 1761, taxable in Sussex County in Huriah Cannady/ Kennedy's household in 1782 and 1783, a "free man" whose tax was charged to Stephen Andrew in 1784 [PPTL 1782-1812, frames 69, 83, 112]. He married Susannah **Tann**, 27 December 1786 Southampton County, Virginia bond, John **Tann** surety, 22 January 1787 marriage. The executors of John Lamb sued him and Richard Andrews in Sussex County court in December 1788 [Orders 1786-91, 434]. He was taxable in Nottoway Parish, Southampton County (no race indicated) from 1787 to 1792, taxable on 2 horses in 1792 [PPTL 1782-92, 619, 680, 732, 782; 1792-1806, frames 6, 28]. He was taxable in Sussex County from 1794 to 1800 and from 1802 to 1812 [PPTL 1782-1812, frames 112, 368, 381, 431, 472, 486, 526, 574, 734, 766, 801, 855]. He was a "FN" taxable in Henrico County in 1801 [PPTL 1782-1814, frame 448]. He married, second, Creesy **Chavis**, 9 December 1806 Sussex County marriage [Minister's Returns, 283]. He was a "Free

Negro" head of a Sussex County household of 6 "other free" in 1810 [VA:632] and was over fifty-five years old when he was head of a Sussex County household of 5 "free colored" in 1830.

iii. Joseph³, born 3 July 1768 [Richards, *Register of Albemarle Parish*, 145], taxable in Sussex County from 1789 to 1792: his tax charged to Mary Andrews in 1791 [PPTL 1782-1812, frames 241, 274, 296, 320]. He married Tabitha **Scott**, 23 December 1797 Surry County bond, William **Scott** surety. He was taxable in Surry County in 1799 [PPTL, 1791-1816, frame 367]. He married, second, Patty **Jones**, 26 February 1804 Sussex County bond, John **Jones** surety, 29 February marriage.

5. Joseph² Canada, born about 1739, registered as a "free Negro" in Southampton County on 11 September 1794: *Joseph Canada a free mulattoe 55 years old 5 feet 6-1/2 inches high has resided in Southampton 15 or 20 years .... born of free parents in Jas. City* [Register of Free Negroes 1794-1832, no. 121 (located between nos. 90 and 91)]. He may have been the father of

i. James³, taxable in the St. Luke's Parish, Southampton County household of Molly **Chavis** in 1805 [PPTL 1792-1806, frame 803], married Elizabeth **Scott**, 20 February 1808 Sussex County bond, Jordan Cannady surety, 21 February marriage. He was taxable in Sussex County in 1810 and 1812 [PPTL 1782-1812, frames 766, 855].

6. James¹ Cannady, born say 1750, was taxable in James City County from 1782 to 1813: taxable on 4 horses and 18 cattle in 1782, a "Mulatto" taxable on 3 horses and 16 cattle in 1785, 2 slaves and 3 horses in 1788, 2 free tithables from 1794 to 1796, a slave in 1809 and 1810, 2 free tithables in 1811 and 1812, and had 5 female "Free Persons of Colour" over the age of sixteen in his household in 1813 [PPTL, 1782-99; 1800-24]. He was taxable on 45 acres in 1790 and taxable on one tract of 45 acres and another of 78 acres in 1800 [1790 Land Tax List, p.2; 1800 Land Tax List, p.2]. He was living in James City County on 19 December 1811 when he made a Charles County deed of gift of a cow and two calves to his grandson Walker **Cumbo**, son of Turner **Cumbo** and his wife Rebecca of Charles City County [DB 5:405-6]. He was the father of

i. ?Sally, born say 1770, taxable in James City County on a slave and a horse in 1792, a "mulatto" over the age of sixteen in James City County in 1813 [PPTL, 1782-99; 1800-24].

ii. ?James², Jr., born say 1773, taxable in James City County from 1797 to 1812, a "mulatto" taxable with 2 female "Free Persons of Colour" over the age of sixteen in his James City County household in 1813 [PPTL, 1782-99; 1800-24].

iii. Rebecca, married Turner **Cumbo** before 19 December 1811.

7. Hugh2 Cannady, born say 1757, was taxable in Sussex County from 1782 to 1800: called Uriah Kennedy from 1782 to 1784; charged with John Kennedy's tithe in 1782; taxable on slave Beck in 1784; charged with Joseph Cannady's tithe in 1789; charged with Jones Canada's tithe in 1791; taxable on 2 tithes in 1795 and 1797 [PPTL 1782-1812, frames 69, 83, 118, 167, 192, 211, 221, 241, 274, 298, 320, 368, 381, 431, 472, 486, 526]. He was head of a Monongalia County household of 11 "other free" in 1810 [VA:514] and taxable again in Sussex County in 1811 [PPTL 1782-1812, frame 801]. His children were

8 i. ?Jones, born say 1778.

ii. Silvey, born say 1780, married Major Debrick (**Debrix**) of Surry County, "consent of Hew Cannady," 7 February 1797 Sussex County bond, Joseph Cannady surety, 9 February marriage.

    iii. Mary, born say 1782, "daughter of Hew Cannaday," married Edward **Chavers**, 21 December 1799 Sussex County bond, John Cannida surety, 22 December marriage.

    iv. ?Eady, born say 1788, married John **Walden**, 9 August 1809 Surry County bond, 10 August marriage.

    v. ?Jordan, born about 1789, received one of the "Certificates granted to Free negroes & mulattoes from October 1800" in Sussex County on 10 March 1815: *bright complexion, 5'9", 26 years old* [Register of Free Negroes, no. 256].

8. Jones Cannady, born say 1778, was taxable in Sussex County in 1790, 1791, and 1799 [PPTL 1782-1812, frames 274, 298, 486]. He married Fanny **Scott**, 20 February 1799 Surry County bond, William **Scott** surety. He was surety for the 17 August 1799 Sussex County marriage bond of David **Charity** ("of Surry County") and Nancy **Debberick** (**Debrix**). He was taxable in Surry County from 1801 to 1816: listed with 2 "free Negroes & Mulattoes above the age of 16" in 1813 [PPTL, 1791-1816, frames 445, 521, 590, 629, 667, 706, 733, 852]. His Surry County will was proved in 1833 [WB 6:563-5]. Jones and Fanny's children were

    i. William[4], born about 1801, registered in Surry County on 25 November 1822: *son of Fanny Canada, a free woman of colour, aged 21 years is 5'11-1/4" high of bright complexion has long hair and grey eyes.*

    ii. Nancy Ann, born say 1803, registered in Surry County on 26 April 1824: *daughter of Jones and Frances Canady, free Mulatto persons of Surry County she is bright Mulatto...she has pretty straight hair, small Eyes, her features are rather handsome than otherways, & is 5'5" high* [Hudgins, *Surry County Register of Free Negroes*, 75, 79].

Other members of the Cannady family were

    i. Behethland, born say 1758, married Luke **Hughes**, 10 July 1779 at St. Paul's Parish, King George County [St. Paul's Parish Register, 223].

    ii. Thomas, born before 1780, a taxable "Mulatto" in Culpeper County in 1800 [*Virginia Genealogist* 16:186].

CARTER FAMILY

1. Paul[1] Carter, born say 1620, was imported as a slave by Nathaniel Littleton of Northampton County, Virginia, in 1640 [Orders 1640-45, 42]. He was mentioned without a surname in the 1656 will of Littleton's wife Anne who left him to her son Edward. Edward Littleton mentioned Paul, his wife Hannah and their children Edward and Mary Carter by their surnames in his 1663 will to his wife Frances who later married Francis Pigot [*VMHB* 75:17-21; DW 1657-66, 168]. Paul Carter and his wife were taxable in 1664 in Frances Littleton's household in Northampton County, Virginia:

    Mr. Littletons Family
    Wm Clements
    peter George Negro
    Paull Carter & wife
    Ould Jack Negro   5   [Orders 1657-64, fol.198].

He probably died shortly afterwards since he was not mentioned again in the lists of tithables. His wife Hannah was freed by their then master, Francis Pigot, in May 1665. Francis **Paine** and Emmanuel **Driggus** promised Pigot that they would support her if necessary [DW 1665-68, pt.2, 15]. Hannah lived in the household of Bashaw **Fernando** and his wife where she was a taxable in 1668, 1671, 1675 and 1677 [Orders 1664-74, 55, fol.114; 1674-79,

75, 191]. Francis Pigot gave "Negroes" James Carter, Paul Carter and Anthony George to his son Ralph Pigot and gave "Negroes" Peter George and Edward Carter to his son Thomas Pigot by his 27 March 1684 will [OW 1683-9, 119-20]. Some of Paul and Hannah's children were freed and were the ancestors of the Carter family of Delaware, Maryland, North Carolina, and Virginia. Others remained slaves.[61] Their children mentioned in the wills of their masters were

  i. Elizabeth, born about 1640, a taxable "Nigro" in John Robins' household in 1665 [Orders 1664-74, 15].
2 ii. Edward[1], born say 1642.
  iii. Paul[2], born say 1643.
  iv. Mary, born say 1645.
3 v. Thomas[1], born about 1647.
  vi. James[1], born about 1649, taxable in Francis Pigot's household in 1677 [OW 1674-1679, 191], probably remained a slave, a fifty-six-year-old man listed in Ralph Pigot's 1705 estate inventory [DW 1692-1707, 417].

2. Edward[1] Carter, born say 1642, was first taxable in Francis Pigot's Northampton County household in 1677 [Orders 1674-79, 191]. Pigot bequeathed him to his son Thomas Pigot in 1684 [OW 1683-9, 119-123]. He was called the "Negro slave to Mr. Thomas Pigot" on 29 September 1687 when he received thirty lashes for insolently abusing and striking a white woman named Elizabeth Sterling [OW 1683-89, 299-300, 309]. In 1714 he and William Whitehead posted bond for the maintenance of his grandchild, the child of his "mulatto" daughter Hannah [Orders 1711-16, 149]. The inventory of his Northampton County estate was recorded on 13 February 1727/8 [Wills, Deeds 1725-33, 104-5]. His children were

4 i. ?Edward[2], born say 1680.
5 ii. Hannah[1], born say 1690.

3. Thomas[1] Carter, born about 1647, was a sixteen-year-old slave in 1663 [DW 1657-66, 168]. In 1665 and 1666 he and Peter **George** were taxed in Pigott's Northampton County household as "Negroes" Peter and Thomas, and in 1666 Captain Pigott charged free "Negro" Bastian **Cane** with harboring, concealing, and trading with them [Orders 1664-74, 15, fol.29]. He was a taxable "Negro" in Francis Pigot's household in 1667-1677 [Orders 1664-74, fol.42, p.55, fol.114; 1674-79, 75, 191]. In 1684 he, his wife Ellenor, and their two daughters Elizabeth and Mary were freed by the will of their master, Francis Pigot, with the proviso that they pay his heirs 1,000 pounds of tobacco a year for ten years. Two years later in 1686, Pigot's heirs released them from these payments [OW 1683-89, 119-123]. On 28 September 1692 he was called "Thomas Carter Negro" when he successfully sued John Wescott for a 1 pound, 6 shilling debt in Northampton County court [OW&c 1689-98, 194]. In 1693 he apprenticed his children Elizabeth, Thomas, and Margaret to "his loving friend" William Gelding from the time of his own death until they reached the age of nineteen years. Gelding agreed to teach them to read and provide them with freedom dues [OW&c 1689-98, 250]. He died before 1699 when his wife Eleanor was called a widow [OW&c 1698-1710, 8]. Their children were

6 i. Elizabeth, born about 1678.
7 ii. Mary, born say 1681.
8 iii. Thomas[2], born say 1686.

---

[61]Frank and Elijah Carter, "freed by Thomas Parramore," were taxable in Northampton County in the 1790s [PPTL 1782-1823, frames 161A, 225, 265].

iv.   Margaret[1], born say 1688, apprenticed in 1693. She may have been the Margaret Carter who was living with John Crew when he gave her all his estate by his nuncupative Northampton County will. On 28 February 1709/10 Jean Grimes and James Sanders testified that Crew had changed his mind before his death, but the court ruled against them [OW&c 1698-1710, 517].

9   v.   ?Edward[3], born say 1690.

4.   Edward[2] Carter (Edward[1]), born say 1680, was tithable on himself and a slave in the 1712 tax list for Beaufort Precinct, North Carolina. In 1716 he was taxed in Beaufort Precinct on 301 acres which he held by patent granted that same year [Haun, *Old Albemarle County Records*, 264]. By his 23 March 1735/6 New Hanover County will, proved 10 May 1736, he set his slave, Peter, free for sixty years and left land on the east side of the Northeast Branch of Cape Fear River to his grandchildren: William, Edward, Solomon, and Thomasin Carter [SS 877/142].[62] His children were not named in his will, but one of them was

10   i.   the unnamed parent of Edward[2]'s grandchildren, born say 1695.

5.   Hannah[1] Carter (Edward[1]), born say 1690, was called the daughter of Edward Carter in Northampton County court in 1714 when he and William Whitehead paid her fine for bearing an illegitimate child [Orders 1710-16, 149]. William Brumfield, a white resident of Northampton County, swore in court in December 1721 that he was never "concerned carnally" with her [Orders 1719-22, 150]. She was a tithable "mulatto" in Ralph Pigot's household in 1724 and 1725, in William Waterson's household from 1726 to 1730, in Ralph Pigot's household in 1731, in Muns Bishop's household from 1737 to 1739, and in her own household in 1740 and 1741 [Bell, *Northampton County Tithables*, 293]. She petitioned the court to release her son Thomas from his indenture to William Satchell because he was not teaching him a trade or giving him schooling and was planning to remove him from the county [L.P. #14 (1728 II)]. She died before November 1741 when Ralph Pigot, Gent., was granted administration on her Northampton County estate [Orders 1732-42, 461, 467]. Her children were

11   i.   Thomas[3], born 7 December 1712.
12   ii.   ?Elizabeth, born say 1714.
    iii.   Luke, born 8 February 1715/6, bound by his mother to Absolem Satchell on 20 June 1716 with the consent of the court [Orders 1710-16, 244, 252].
    iv.   William[2], born about 1721, an illegitimate child for whom Hannah was fined 500 pounds of tobacco in December 1721. William **Harmon**, "Negro," paid the fine and indemnified the parish of any charges [Orders 1719-22, 144, 146]. On 8 April 1740 John Wilson complained to the court that he had maintained "William Carter a "Mulatto" from the age of two only to have him taken away by his mother Hannah when he was "upwards of sixteen." The court ordered William bound to John Wilson [Orders 1732-42, 395].
    v.   Southy, perhaps the illegitimate child Hannah was presented for on 11 May 1725. Captain Ralph Pigot paid her fine and indemnified the parish. On 10 November 1741 the court bound him to Munge Bishop [Orders 1722-9, 181, 190; 1732-42, 462]. Administration on his Northampton County estate was granted to Jacob Shores on 9 January 1753 on 20 pounds security [Orders 1751-3, 214-5, 225-6].

---

[62]He may have been the "Free Peter" who paid one shilling to the estate of John Smith, recorded 7 March 1758 Hyde County Court [Haun, *Hyde County Court Minutes*, II:186].

vi.   an illegitimate child, born about 1729, for whose birth Hannah was presented in May 1729. Colonel John Robins paid her fine and indemnified the parish [Orders 1722-29, 382, 384, 387].

6.   Elizabeth Carter (Thomas¹), born about 1678, was a twenty-seven-year-old woman listed in the Northampton County inventory of Ralph Pigot's slaves in 1705. She and her children apparently remained slaves since they were listed with her in the inventory. They were

i.   Edward⁴ (Ned), born about 1695, a ten-year-old in 1705. He was taxable with his sister Sarah in Culpepper Pigot's household from 1720 to 1722, and in Jacob Stringer's household in 1723. He and Paul Carter, "negros," were taxable in John Waterson's household in 1726, called "Paule, Ned negros" in 1725 and 1727-1739. And an Edward Carter, "Negro," died in 1716 when Edward Mifflin petitioned the Northampton County court for administration on his estate. However, Matthew Moor convinced the court that Edward was his slave [Orders 1716-8, 4].

ii.   Hannah², born about 1698, a seven-year-old in 1705.

iii.   Sarah, born about 1701, a four-year-old in 1705.

iv.   Dinah, born about 1703, a two-year-old in 1705, perhaps the "Dinah Negro," taxable in John Pigot's household in 1720.

7.   Mary Carter (Thomas¹), born say 1681, "Daughter of Ellenor Carter widow," was free in Northampton County by 30 May 1699 when she was presented for bearing an unnamed illegitimate child by Daniel, a slave belonging to Daniel Benthall. She was again presented for bastardy in 1703 [OW&c 1698-1710, 8, 18, 165]. Her illegitimate children may have been

i.   Jacob, born say 1699, tithable in Jacob Waterfield's Northampton County household in 1720, a "negro" tithable in John **Drighouse**'s household in 1722, a "mulatto" tithable with his wife Tabitha **Copes** in Azaricum's **Drighouse**'s household in 1727, and tithable with his wife Tabitha in his own household from 1728 to 1731 [Bell, *Northampton County Tithables*, 3, 26, 121, 161, 172, 190, 229].

ii.   Lydia, probably born about 1703, presented by the grand jury of Northampton County on 11 May 1725 for having a bastard child which died before 8 June 1725 when Thomas Costin paid her fine [Orders 1722-29, 181, 190]. She was a "Malatto" taxable in Thomas Costin's household in 1725 and taxable in her own household in Ralph Pigot's list for the lower precinct of Northampton County. She married John **Driggers** by 1728 when she was a taxable in his household. He died in 1729, and she was called Lydia **Drighouse** on 11 May 1731 she was presented for having a bastard child [Orders 1729-32, 84].

8.   Thomas² Carter (Thomas¹), born say 1686, was bound by his father as an apprentice to William Gelding of Magotha Bay, Northampton County, in 1693 [OW 1689-98, 250]. On 20 June 1716 he was sued in Northampton County court by Daniel **Jacobs** who was granted an attachment against his estate for 1,100 pounds of tobacco [Orders 1711-16, 255]. He was a taxable in Daniel **Jacob**'s Northampton County household in 1720 and taxable in his own household from 1721 to 1723, taxable with his wife Elizabeth from 1724 to 1733, and taxable with their son Moses in 1727 [Bell, *Northampton County Tithables*, 17, 24, 37, 51, 68, 73, 87, 94, 109, 122, 156, 185, 210, 232]. He was called a "Mulatto man," about thirty years of age, in Northampton County court on 8 October 1724 when he and Alice Cormack (a white woman) were whipped for harboring a slave named Caesar, belonging to John Armistead of Gloucester County, who was hanged for stealing goods from the store of John Robins [Orders 1722-29, 145-6; Mihalyka, *Loose Papers II:*95]. He may have been the Thomas Carter "Mullattoe" who petitioned the Cumberland County,

North Carolina court on 19 January 1758 to remove his grandchildren: Abraham, Penney, Moses, Samuel, and Elizabeth Carter from the possession of James Wright who was illegally detaining them. The court bound Abraham as an apprentice to Plunkett Ballard, and then the 18 April 1758 Cumberland County court returned them all to the care of their mother Mary Carter. The 18 January 1759 court reversed the earlier court decision and returned them to James Wright [Minutes 1755-59, 32, 34, 45]. Thomas' children were

13   i.   ?John², born say 1714.

       ii.   Moses¹, born about 1717, a 12-16 year old tithable in his father's household in 1729.

      iii. ?Isaac¹, born say 1720, sold 149 acres on the north side of Eagle Swamp in Craven County, North Carolina, by an undated deed, 30 October ____, about 1745-49 [DB 2:82]. He was number 61 in the 25 October 1754 Muster Roll of Lewis Bryan's Craven County Company (not identified by race) [Clark, *Colonial Soldiers of the South*, 703]. He received a patent for 164 acres in Craven on the south side of the Great Contentnea in October 1755 [Hoffman, *Land Patents*, I:61].

14   iv. ?Mary, born say 1730.

15   v.   ?Margaret³, born say 1732.

16   vi. ?James², born say 1734.

9.   Edward³ Carter (Thomas¹), born say 1690, chose Daniel **Jacobs** "Negrow" as his guardian in Northampton County, Virginia, in 1707 [OW&c 1698-1710, 320]. He was a "Negro" tithable in his own household in Northampton County from 1720 to 1723, tithable with his wife Margaret and his two boys John and Edward in 1724 and 1725, but was not tithable again in Northampton County [Bell, *Northampton County Tithables*, 1, 13, 24, 36, 51, 68, 73, 95]. He purchased 300 acres in Bertie County, North Carolina, on the Potecasi Branch and the Indian Path in August 1730 [DB C:291]. This land was on the east side of Potecasi Creek in what was then Society Parish, Bertie County, and became Hertford County in 1759. On 10 May 1750 he and his wife Margaret made deeds of gift of 200 acres to two of their children, Margaret and Mary, who were taxed as "free Mulattos" in the 1751 Bertie tax list filed with the central government [CCR 190]. In 1757 he was taxed in the list of John Brickell adjacent to his daughter Margaret and her husband James **Nicken** [C.R. 010.702.1, Box 1]. Administration of his estate was granted John Carter for 400 pounds surety on 22 January 1760 [Haun, *Bertie County Court Minutes* II:502]. Edward and Margaret's children were:

17   i.   John¹, born say 1712.

       ii.   Edward⁵, born say 1714, a taxable 10-16 year old in Northampton County, Virginia, in 1724 and 1725.

      iii. Mary, born say 1728, married Henry **Best**. On 10 May 1750 she was called wife of Henry **Best** in her parents' deed of gift of 200 acres on the east side of Potecasi Creek in what was then Society Parish, Bertie County [DB G:354]. She and Henry were taxed as "free Mulatoes" in the 1751 Bertie County tax list filed with the central government [CCR 190], and they were taxed in the 1757 list of John Brickell with their slave, "Negro Santey." Perhaps he was the Henry Best who sold land by four deeds proved in the part of Johnston County which later became Dobbs County between November 1746 and April 1754 [DB 1:34, 1:287, 2:235, 2:422]. He may have been living near Edward⁶ Carter of Dobbs County. In 1757 Henry and Mary were taxed in the list of John Brickell with a slave, "Negro Santey," and in 1758 they were taxed in the list of John Brown [CR 10.702.1, box 1]. There are few surviving colonial Hertford County records, so there is no further record of them. However, a Mary Best was head of a Hertford County household of 3 white females and 3 slaves in 1790 [NC:26].

iv. Margaret[2], born say 1730, married James **Nicken**. On 10 May 1750 she was called wife of James **Nicken** in her parents' deed of gift to her for 200 acres in Society Parish, Bertie County [DB G:356]. James and Margaret were taxed as "fr. Muls." in the 1750 Bertie County tax summary filed with the central government [CCR 190], and they were taxable in the 1757 list of John Brickell [CR 10.702.1 Box 1].

10. The unnamed child of Edward[2] Carter (Edward[2], Edward[1]), born say 1695, was the parent of Edward[1] Carter's grandchildren who were mentioned in his 23 March 1735/6 New Hanover County will. They were

    i. William[1], born say 1715. He was to receive his share of his grandfather's estate immediately since he was the oldest grandson. He and William Gray, executor of his father's estate, were granted 640 acres in Onslow County "in trust for the Grand Child of Edw[d] Carter dece[d]" on 19 June 1736 [Saunders, *Colonial Records of North Carolina* IV:221]. He may have been the William Carter who was number 11 in the 27 November 1752 New Hanover County Muster Roll of the Wilmington Company commanded by Captain George Merrick [Clark, *Colonial Soldiers of the South,* 683].

18   ii. Edward[6], born say 1720.
19   iii. Solomon, born say 1725.
    iv. Thomasin.

11. Thomas[3] Carter, born 7 December 1712, a "Malato," was four years old on 20 August 1717 when his mother Hannah Carter, a "Mallatto," bound him to Thomas Costin in Northampton County, Virginia [Orders 1716-18, 34]. He was a "malotto" taxable in William Satchell's household in 1731 and a taxable in the household of his mother Hannah in 1739 [Bell, *Northampton County Tithables,* 222, 293]. On 10 July 1733 his mother petitioned the court, complaining that his then-master William Satchell was not educating him. He had completed his indenture by 12 March 1733/4 when Satchell was ordered to pay him his freedom dues [Orders 1732-42, 68, 71, 95-6]. On 11 July 1738 he was called a "Mulatto planter" when he sued Francis Stokely for trespass, assault and battery and was awarded 15 shillings damages ("the Battery being proved"), and he was awarded 20 shillings on 14 November 1738 in his suit against Stephen Odeer for trespass, assault and battery ("the Battery being proved") [Orders 1732-42, 325, 326, 330, 334, 338]. He was a witness for Sarah Carter in her suit against John Hall, Jr., for 50 bushels of corn on 10 March 1741/2 [Orders 1732-42, 472]. He may have been the Thomas Carter who was a witness for Humphrey **Jones** in his 19 March 1753 York County, Virginia suit against John **Rollison** (**Rawlinson**). The parties by their counsel agreed that they were "Mulattos" [Judgments & Orders 1752-4, 196]. Thomas was fined 500 pounds of tobacco in Charles City County on 6 September 1758 for failing to list his wife as a tithable [Orders 1758-62, 57]. He may have been the ancestor of

    i. Sally, a "free" head of a Williamsburg City household of 1 "black" person in 1782 [VA:45].
    ii. Ishmael, married Elvey **Martin**, 20 June 1809 Charles City County bond [*Wm & Mary Quarterly Historical Papers* Vol. 8, No.3, p.193]. On 3 December 1811 Freeman **Brown** sold him 1 acre in Charles City County on the cross road leading from the courthouse road to Swineyard's Road for $1 "to have and to hold provided he leaves lawful issue" [DB 5:560]. He was taxable on a horse in Charles City County in 1811 and was a "Mulattoe" taxable there in 1813 [PPTL 1807-23].
    iii. Littleton, taxable in York County from 1813 to 1820: taxable on a male and a female in a "list of free Negroes & Mulattoes over the age of 16" in 1813 [PPTL 1782-1841, frames 386, 404, 468, 480].

12. Elizabeth Carter (Edward, Hannah), born say 1714, a "Negroe," made oath in Northampton County, Virginia court on 8 October 1734 that William **Roberts** was the father of her illegitimate child. John Kendall paid her fine [Orders 1732-42, 136]. She was presented by the court on 8 May 1750 and 11 June 1755 for having other illegitimate children. She was charged with felony on 24 November 1775 but found not guilty [Orders 1748-51, 207, 230; 1753-8, 219; 1771-7, 303-5]. She was probably the mother of

    i.   Henry, born in June 1755, bound to John Storpe to learn the tailor's trade on 10 July 1765 [Minutes 1761-5, 179].

    ii. Isaiah, born in March 1758, twelve years old on 12 June 1770 when he was bound to Thomas Bullock [Minutes 1765-71, 372]. He was taxable in Northampton County from 1787 to 1813: taxable on 2 free males and a horse in 1802, a "Negro" living in the Indian Town from 1811 to 1813 [PPTL, 1782-1823, frames 64, 207, 326, 388, 487, 531]. He registered as a "free Negro" in Northampton County on 10 June 1794 [Orders 1789-95, 354].

    iii. James[5], born 15 February 1759, a six-year-old "negro" bound to Thomas Pettit on 14 August 1765 and bound to Anne Pettit, widow, on 13 January 1778 [Minutes 1765-71, 8, 33]. He was a soldier in the Revolution who enlisted in Northampton County, Virginia, and applied for a pension while living there [Jackson, *Virginia Negro Soldiers*, 32]. He was a "Mulatto" or "free Negro" taxable in Northampton County from 1787 to 1805, free from taxation in 1806, living in the Indian town of Northampton County in 1809 and 1810 [PPTL, 1782-1823, frames 64, 125, 207, 345, 408, 447, 467, 530]. He registered as a "free Negro" in Northampton County on 10 June 1794 [Orders 1789-95, 354]. James Carter, Sr., was head of a Northampton County household of 4 "free colored" in 1820 [VA:217].

13. John[2] Carter (Thomas[2], Thomas[1]), born say 1712, was a boy over ten and under sixteen years of age in the Northampton County, Virginia household of his father Edward Carter in 1725 and was tithable in Azaricum **Drighouse**'s household in 1730 [Bell, *Northampton County Tithables*, 73, 213]. He was a "free Negro," listed in the 4 October 1754 and 4 October 1755 Muster Roll of Craven County, North Carolina, for the district between the head of Slocumb's Creek and the head of Turnagain Bay. This is near the Craven - Carteret County line. Listed in this same muster roll were "free Negro" Peter **George**, and Jacob **Copes** who were also from Northampton County, Virginia. John may have been the same John Carter who two years earlier was in New Hanover County in the 27 November 1752 Muster Roll of the Wilmington Company commanded by Captain George Merrick (no race mentioned) [Clark, *Colonial Soldiers of the South*, 708, 683]. Perhaps his children were

19   i.   Abel, born say 1732.

    ii. Tabitha[1], born say 1750, whose daughter Jane, born 1766, was ordered bound apprentice to Thomas Shine by the 11 March 1772 Craven County court [Minutes 1766-75, 191a]. Jenny was head of a Craven County household of 1 "other free" in 1790 [NC:134].

13. Mary Carter (Thomas[2], Thomas[1]), born say 1732, was the mother of five "Mullatoe" children mentioned in her father's 19 January 1758 Cumberland County petition [Minutes 1755-59, 32]. They were

    i.   Abraham, born about 1750.

    ii. Penney, born about 1752.

    iii. Moses[2], born about 1754, about three years old on 18 April 1758 when the Cumberland County court ordered him bound to James Wright. He was a "man of color" who enlisted as a private in Captain Joseph Rhodes' 1st Regiment on 19 July 1782 until 1 July 1783. He made a declaration to obtain a pension in Sampson County on 25 October 1820

[M805-167, frame 0077]. He purchased 100 acres on the west side of Six Runs and Rowan Swamp in Sampson County on 13 May 1788 [DB 9:175]. He was head of a Sampson County household of 9 "other free" in 1790 [NC:52], 8 in 1800 [NC:515], counted as white in 1810 along with several other Sampson County free African Americans, head of a household of 4 males and 5 females [NC:485], and head of a household of 6 "free colored" in 1820 [NC:278]. His wife may have been Susanna Carter, the executrix of the 1807 Sampson County will of her father Abraham **Jacobs**, who also owned land near Rowan Swamp.

    iv. Samuel, born about 1755.

    v. Elizabeth, born about 1757.

14. Margaret[3] Carter (Thomas[2], Thomas[1]), born say 1732, was a "free Mustee Woman" living in Cumberland County, North Carolina, on 22 June 1759 when the court bound her two-year-old child Henry Carter an apprentice to James Wright [Minutes 1755-59, 50]. Her son was

    i. Henry, born about 1757, two years old when he was bound an apprentice to James Wright on 22 June 1759 in Cumberland County. He was head of a Sampson County household of 8 "other free" in 1790 [NC:52], 8 in 1800 [NC:515], counted as white in 1810, head of a Sampson County household of four males and three females [NC:485], and 10 "free colored" in 1820 [NC:278].

15. James[2] Carter, born say 1734, was a taxable "Mulato" in Bladen County, North Carolina, with his son Isaac in 1768. He was head of a Bladen County household of a white male 21 to 60, 4 white males under 21 or over 60, and 6 white females in 1786 [Byrd, *Bladen County Tax Lists*, I:5, 34, 81, 94, 103, 134; II:68, 76, 182, 183, 184]. He purchased 200 acres in Bladen County on Hogg Swamp east of Tadpole from his son Isaac on 7 March 1783 [DB 1:32]. He was the father of

    i. Isaac[2], born say 1754, a "Molato" taxable in his father's Bladen County household from 1768 to 1776, head of a Bladen County household of one white male 21 to 60, two under 21 or over 60 and three white females in 1786. He was granted 200 acres in Bladen County on Hogg Swamp east of Tadpole on 11 March 1775 and sold this land to his father on 7 March 1783 [DB 1:32].

    ii. James[4], a "Molato" taxable in the Bladen County household of his father James Carter, Sr., in 1770, taxable head of his own Bladen County household in 1776, head of a household of one white male 21 to 60, one under 21 or over 60 and five white females in 1786.

    iii. ?Mark, a "Molato" taxable in the Bladen County household of (his father?) James Carter in 1776, head of a Bladen County household of one white male from 21 to 60 and two white females in 1786. He was taxable on 200 acres in Bladen County in Captain Regan's District in 1784 and head of a Robeson County household of 4 "other free" in 1800. He sold land in Robeson County by deed proved on 9 July 1800 and purchased land by deed proved on 6 October 1801 [Minutes 1797-1806, 120, 171].

    iv. ?Emmanuel, born say 1765, entered 100 acres in Robeson County on Poplar Bay near Jacobs Swamp on 22 September 1789 [Pruitt, *Land Entries: Robeson County*, I:28]. He purchased 50 acres in Robeson on Ashpole Swamp from James **Lowery** by deed proved in 1797 [DB G:142] and sold land in Robeson County by deed proved on 7 April 1800 [Minutes 1797-1806, 99]. He was head of a Robeson County household of 5 "other free" in 1790 [NC:50]. His wife may have been Nancy Carter who was mentioned in the 20 October 1787 Robeson County will of her father David **Braveboy** [WB 1:10].

16. John[1] Carter (Edward[3], Thomas[1]), born say 1712, was a 10 to 16 year old taxable in his father's Northampton County, Virginia household in 1724 and 1725. He was granted administration of Edward Carter's Bertie County estate on 22 January 1760 [Haun, *Bertie County Court Minutes*, II:502]. He bought 360 acres on the east side of Potecasi Creek in Bertie County on 11 February 1746, and he and his wife Ann, "late of Society Parish," sold this land four years later on 25 February 1750 [DB G:370]. He was taxed on himself, his wife Ann, and two slaves, Dick and Pat, from 1757 to 1759 in the Bertie County Tax List of John Brickell [CR 010.702.1, Box 1]. He bought 230 acres on the north side of Ahoskie Swamp near Jackson's Ferry on the Chowan River and Bonner Bridge in what was then Bertie County but became Hertford County after 1759 [DB H:405]. His children may have been

    i.   "Winifred Carter orphan of John Carter," (no race indicated) born about 1756, bound apprentice to Miles Mason Shehan and his wife in Bertie court on 30 August 1764 [*NCGSJ* XIV:29].

20   ii.   Charles, born say 1758.

17. Edward[6] Carter (____, Edward[2], Edward[1]), born say 1720, was not yet twenty-one years old when his grandfather Edward[2] Carter made his 23 March 1735/6 New Hanover County will. He patented 330 acres on the south side of the Neuse River and west side of Panther Creek on 12 April 1745 [Hoffman, *Land Patents*, I:253]. He was residing in New Hanover County on 31 August that same year when he purchased 170 acres adjoining this land in what was then Craven County but later became Dobbs County [Craven DB 2:554]. On 5 September 1764 he successfully sued James Farr for a little over 8 pounds in New Hanover County court [Minutes 1738-69, 221]. He acquired land in Dobbs, Duplin, and Craven counties, holding a total of 1,870 acres by 11 December 1770.[63] In addition to these 1,870 acres there were twenty-two grantee deeds registered to him in Dobbs County between 1750 and 1799. Only the deed index to these deeds has survived.[64] Most other Dobbs County records were lost in a courthouse fire. Edward was taxable in 1769 in Dobbs County with (his wife?) Elizabeth and eight slaves:

---

[63] 12 Apr 1745 330 acres in Craven County south of Neuse River [Hoffman, *Land Patents*, I:253].

31 Aug 1745 170 acres in Craven County south of Neuse River [DB 2:554].

03 Jul 1751 200 acres in Duplin County, by Anthony Williams' will [SS/Wills/DRB2:547].

01 Jul 1758 140 acres in Craven County south of Neuse River.

22 Apr 1763 100 acres in Duplin County north east of Cape Fear.

22 Apr 1763 50 acres in Dobbs County on Mill Marsh, his line.

26 Sep 1766 350 acres in Dobbs County south of Neuse River.

11 Dec 1770 170 acres in Dobbs County south of Neuse River.

26 Oct 1767 40 acres in Dobbs County south of Neuse River.

24 May 1773 80 acres in Dobbs County south of Neuse River [Hoffman, *Land Patents*, I:83, 461-2; II:77, 197, 464, 347].

08 Oct 1784 300 acres in Duplin County north of Buck Marsh [DB 1A:133].

[64] The index entries for his deeds are

Grantee: DB 2:300; 3:254; 5:497, 580; 7:123; 8:276, 310; 10:209, 235, 308, 442; 11:311, 418; 12:337, 447, 518; 13:114, 124; 14:327, 603; 17:217; 18:300; 22:365.

Grantor deeds: DB 7:123; 11:315; 13:195; 14:159, 212, 337, 377 [Microfilm Grantee Index to Dobbs County Deeds, M.F.95]. Dobbs County was formed from part of Johnston County in 1758 and Lenoir County was formed from Dobbs in 1791.

Edward Carter, Elizabeth, John Clemmons, "Couzuns" Bib and Bush;
Negroes Jack, Frank, Cudjo, Dinah, Cate, Violet, Pat and Dinah 5 white
polls and 8 black polls [SS 837, p.7, by *NCGSJ* XV:75].[65]

Edward was number 55 (and his brother Solomon, number 56) in an undated
colonial muster roll of a company of foot soldiers in the Dobbs County militia
of Captain William Whitfield [Clark, *Colonial Soldiers of the South*, 641-2].
He was one of the inhabitants of Dobbs County whose firelock was pressed
into service during the 1771 expedition against the insurgents [Clark, *State
Records of North Carolina*, XXII:413]. While residing in Dobbs County on 12
October 1772 he sold 100 acres on the northeast side of Cape Fear and east
side of Cypress Swamp in what was then Duplin County to his brother
Solomon Carter [DB 3:437]. This was land Edward purchased on 22 April
1763 and was part of New Hanover County when their grandfather made his
will [DB 15:506]. A month later on 27 November 1772 while still a resident
of Dobbs County he sold 85 acres of his Craven County land on the north side
of Trent River [DB 20:164].

In a most extraordinary move, on 13 February 1773 the Dobbs County court
recommended to the General Assembly that Edward's daughters be exempted
from the discriminatory tax against female children of African Americans. The
court named his daughters: Tamer Deaver, Margaret, Rachel, Ann, Sally,
Patience, and Elizabeth Carter [Saunders, *Colonial Records of North Carolina*,
IX:495]. In 1778 he entered a total of 958 acres in Dobbs County [Entries
139-40, 337-39, 362]. He was the fourth largest Dobbs County landowner with
23,292 acres in 1780 in the district south of the Neuse River near Kinston
[L.P. 46.1 in *Journal of N.C. Genealogy* XII:1664]. On 8 October 1784 he
was called "Edward Carter of Dobbs" when he bought 300 acres in Duplin
County on the north side of the Northeast Cape Fear River and in the fork of
Buck Marsh and Poley Bridge Branch with Solomon Carter as witness [DB
1A:133]. He was head of a Dobbs County household of 8 "other free," one
white woman who may have been his wife, and 20 slaves in 1790 [NC:137].
His children were

    i. ?George[1], born say 1745, sold land by deed registered in Dobbs
        County between April 1765 and April 1769 [DB 7:77].

    ii. Tamer Deaver, perhaps the wife of John Dever, a Dobbs County
        taxable in 1769 [SS 837, p.7, by *NCGSJ* XV:75].

    iii. Margaret[4], who was granted land by her father by deed registered in
        Dobbs between April 1789 and April 1792 [DB 14:212]. She was head
        of a Lenoir household of 5 "other free" in 1800 [NC:31] and 2 "other
        free" in 1810 [NC:305].

    iv. Rachel **Bush**, born say 1750, perhaps the wife of Bibby Bush, taxable
        in Dobbs County in 1769 [SS 837, p.5, by *NCGSJ* XV:74], and taxed
        on 2,138 acres in 1780 [L.P.46.1]. Fourteen Dobbs County grantee
        deeds to him were registered between 1784 and 1803 [DB 8:106, 145,
        11:315 (from Edward Carter), 13:114 (from Edward Carter), 14:547,
        17:324, 18:116, 18:223 (from Edward Carter); 19:123, 151, 173 (from
        Chelly Carter); 20:71 (from Henry Carter), 97 (from John Carter), 72].
        Rachel sold land to Barnabas McKinnie by deed registered in Dobbs
        County between 1805 and August 1810 [DB 23:104]. She was head of
        a Lenoir County household of 7 "other free" and four slaves in 1810
        [NC:297].

---

[65]"Couzens" Bib & Bush may have been related to Bibby Bush, a 1769 Dobbs County taxable who
may have been the husband of Edward Carter's daughter, Rachel. A Bibby Bush was a surveyor of roads
in Essex County in 1742 [Orders 1742-3, 39] and a Bush Beebe was head of a Rhode Island household
of 5 "other free" in 1790 [RI:20].

v. ?James[3], born say 1752, taxable in Dobbs County in 1769 (in the household of Robert Crawford) [SS 837]. He was head of a Lenoir County household of 2 "other free" and one white woman in 1800 [NC:31] and 5 "other free" in 1810 [NC:305]. He purchased land from Margaret Carter by deed registered in Dobbs County between 1796 and 1798 [DB 17:278], purchased land by deed registered between 1799 and 1801 [DB 19:156], and by five deeds registered between 1810 and 1819 [DB 24:169, 211, 323, 338, and 352].

vi. Ann.

vii. Sally.

viii. Patience, who was granted land by her father by deed registered in Dobbs County between April 1789 and April 1792 [DB 14:159].

ix. Elizabeth.

x. ?John[4], married Elizabeth Johnston, 5 __ 1780 Duplin County bond, (his brother-in-law?) Bebe Bush witness. John was taxable on 1,942 acres in 1780 [L.P. 46.1]. (His father?) Edward Carter conveyed land to him by deed registered in Dobbs County between April 1789 and April 1792 [DB 14:377]. John was head of a Lenoir County household of 4 "other free" and one white woman in 1800 [NC:30].

xi. ?Henry, head of a Lenoir County household of 3 "other free," one white woman, and one slave in 1800 [NC:30] and 4 "other free" in 1810 [NC:286]. He sold land by deeds registered in Dobbs from 1799-1801 [DB 19:283], 1802 to 1803 [DB 20:71], and 1823-28 [DB 26:57].

xii. ?Nancy, granted land by (her father?) Edward Carter by deed registered in Dobbs between April 1789 and April 1792 [DB 14:337].

18. Solomon Carter (____, Edward[2], Edward[1]), born say 1725, was not yet twenty-one years old when his grandfather Edward Carter made his 23 March 1735/6 New Hanover County will. He was a resident of Duplin County on 6 May 1758 when he purchased 300 acres in Craven County near the Duplin County line on the north side of Tuckahoe Creek known by the name of Springs [DB 2:208]. He sold this land on 12 September 1763 while a resident of Duplin County [DB 11:283]. He received patents for 300 acres in Dobbs County on the north side of Tuckahoe Creek on 27 April 1767 and 360 acres in Duplin County on the Northeast Branch of Cape Fear River on both sides of Matthew's Branch on 29 April 1768 [Hoffman, *Land Patents,* II:347, 437]. He was in Dobbs County with his brother Edward, listed in the undated Muster Roll of foot soldiers in Captain William Whitfield's Company [Clark, *Colonial Soldiers of the South,* 642] and bought land from Edward in Duplin County on 12 October 1772 [DB 3:437]. He sold land by a deed registered in Dobbs County between April 1771 and April 1773 [DB 9:132] and purchased land by deeds proved in Dobbs from 1799-1801 [DB 19:204] and 1805-10 [DB 23:6, 143, 154]. He was counted as white in the 1790 Duplin County census, head of a household of two males, one female, and 3 slaves [NC:190] and counted as "other free" in Duplin County in 1800, head of a household of 4 "other free" and 3 slaves. He transferred his land to his sons by deeds which were apparently not recorded. On 30 January 1806 he was allowed the use of the plantation where he was living for the remainder of his life by a deed from his son David [DB 4A:4]. Constant Carter was probably his wife. On 29 August 1809 she sold to (her son?) Alexander Carter of Duplin County 26 cattle "in consideration of a bond for maintaining sd Constant during her natural lifetime." Their children were

i. David, born say 1760, counted as white in 1790, head of a Duplin county household of 5 males and 1 female [NC:191], and head of a Duplin County household of 9 "other free" in 1800. He sold 235 acres in Duplin County, land which had been Solomon Carter's, on 30 January 1806 with the proviso that his father have use of part of the plantation until his death [DB 4A:4].

21   ii.   ?Edward[7], born circa 1765.
      iii.   ?Leah Cartey, born say 1765, married Ezekiah **Blizzard**, 19 December 1782 Duplin County bond. On 27 December 1811 Alexander Carter sold Leah Carter of Lenoir County 146 acres of land in Duplin County [DB 4A:392].
      iv.   Manuel, born say 1770, married Fereba Alberson, 15 November 1789 Duplin County bond, Solomon Carter bondsman. He was head of a "white" Duplin household of 1 male and 1 female in 1790 [NC:191] and head of a Duplin household of 6 "other free" in 1800. He was probably Solomon's son since he sold land which had belonged to Solomon.[66] In 1810 he was counted as white in Duplin County, head of a household of 7 males, two of them over forty-five years old, one woman over forty-five years old, and one slave [NC:690].
      v.   Alexander, born say 1775, married Sarah Herring, 6 June 1795 Duplin County bond, Solomon Carter bondsman. He was head of a Duplin County household of 4 "other free" in 1800. On 5 December 1806 he sold 100 acres in Duplin which previously belonged to Solomon Carter, and on 29 August 1809 he made a deed with Constant Carter, probably his mother, to maintain her for life [DB 3A:550; 4A:79]. He made 10 purchases and sales of land in Duplin County between 1806 and 1813 [DB 3A:306, 550, 556; 4:284, 392, 393, 394, 396, 402, 462]. One was for land at the head of Carter's Mill Pond and Juniper Branch adjacent to Jonathan **Nickens**, a relative of James **Nickens**, who married Margaret Carter of Hertford County.

19. Abel Carter (John[2], Thomas[2], Thomas[1]), born say 1732, was "a Molatto" accused by the March 1750 Session of the Craven County court of concealing his taxables [Haun, *Craven County Court Minutes*, IV:31]. He was not penalized because the court accepted his defense that he was living with his father who was never legally warned by the Constable. He was listed as a "free Negro" with John Carter in Abner Neale's 1754 and 1755 Craven Muster Roll [Clark, *Colonial Soldiers of the South*, 708]. In 1769 Abel was taxable in Craven County on 2 Black males and 3 Black females [SS 837]. On 14 November 1778 an advertisement in the North Carolina Gazette of New Bern accused him of harboring a runaway slave:

> *negro fellow named Smart...Tis supposed he is harboured about Smith River by one Abel Carter, a free Negro, as he has been seen there several times* [Fouts, *NC Gazette of New Bern*, I:83].

He was head of a Craven County household of 7 "other free" persons in 1790 [NC:130]. His children may have been
      i.   John[3], born 1754, enlisted in Captain Quinn's Tenth Regiment. He was engaged in skirmishes near West Point and Kings Ferry. He made a declaration in September Term 1820 Craven County court to obtain a pension. He was a cooper, living with his sister Margaret **Fenner** when he made his declaration in 1820. Asa **Spelman** testified on his behalf. He died before 30 July 1821 [M805-166, frame 497]. He may have been one of two John Carters, heads of "other free" Carteret County households in 1790 [NC:128, 129].
22   ii.   George[2], born about 1755.
23   iii.   Isaac[3], born about 1760.

---

[66]He sold 250 acres on the east side of the fork of Northeast & Matthews Branch in Duplin County on 6 March 1804 for $450 [DB 3A:536], sold 150 acres on the great branch across Beaverdam on 7 July 1807 for $150 [DB 4A:306], and sold a further 100 acres in Duplin on Northeast Swamp and the south side of Matthews Branch on 9 February 1808 for $100 [DB 3A:513].

iv.   Margaret[5] **Fenner**, sister of John[3] Carter. She was called Margaret **Moore** in June 1797 when she petitioned the Craven County for permission to manumit her "negro man slave" named Jack **Fennel** who was her husband by whom she had had a number of children. Through his industry they had acquired a 200 acre plantation stocked with cattle and hogs [Byrd, *In Full Force and Virtue*, 41]. John **Fenner**, Sr., was head of a Craven County household of 5 "free colored" in 1820 [NC:65].

v.   Joshua, head of a Craven County household of 4 "other free" in 1790 [NC:130]. He received 4 pounds pay for forty days service in the Craven County Militia under Major John Tillman in an expedition to Wilmington [Haun, *Revolutionary Army Accounts, Journal "A"*, 141].

vi.   Solomon, born about 1773, a "Free Negro Boy Aged Five Years," apprenticed as a cooper to Richard Neale by the 13 March 1778 Craven County court [Minutes 1772-84, vol. 1, p.70c].

vii.   Mary, petitioned the Craven County court about 1800 for permission to free her husband Anthony who was her slave [Byrd, *In Full Force and Virtue*, 45].

viii.   Tabitha[2], born say 1785, married William **Howard**, 9 June 1807 Craven County bond, James **Godett** bondsman. William **Howard**, born before 1776, was head of Craven County household of 6 "free colored" in 1820 [NC:65].

20.   Charles Carter (John[1], Edward[3], Thomas[1]), born say 1758, purchased 50 acres in Halifax County, North Carolina, joining Rosser, Carter, Johnson, and Cymons branch on 24 August 1779 from John Carter [DB 14:287]. Perhaps John was the one who was counted as one "free colored" in Rowan County in 1820 [NC:348]. Charles was head of a Halifax County household of 5 "other free" in 1790 [NC:61]. He may have been the father of

i.   Randol, head of a Halifax County household of one "other free" in 1790, adjacent to Charles Carter [NC:61].

ii.   Frederick, head of a Halifax County household of one "other free" in 1790, adjacent to Randol Carter [NC:61].

iii.   Samuel, head of a Halifax County household of one "other free" in 1800 [NC:298], six in 1810 [NC:9], and 11 "free colored" in 1820 [NC:144].

iv.   William[3], born say 1775, head of a Halifax County household of one "other free" in 1800 [NC:298].

21.   Edward[7] Carter (Solomon, _____, Edward[2], Edward[1]), born say 1765, was head of a Duplin County household of 2 males and one female counted as white in 1790 [NC:190] and head of a household of 5 "other free" in Duplin County in 1800. He and his son Elisha Carter, "son of Edward & Rachel his wife," received a deed of gift of 150 acres in Duplin County from Solomon Carter on 18 September 1797 [DB 3A:425]. His child was

i.   Elisha, born 19 April 1792, moved to Washington County, Virginia, where on 20 April 1813 he sold the 150 acres in Duplin County deeded to him and his father in 1797. His mother Rachel testified that he was then twenty-one years old [Duplin DB 4A:462].

22.   George[2] Carter (Abel, John[2], Thomas[2], Thomas[1]), born say 1755, was head of a Carteret County household of 10 "other free" in 1790 [NC:129]. He purchased land in Craven County on 5 November 1809 [mentioned in DB 43:82]. He married (second?) Sarah **Kelly**, 8 September 1818 Craven County bond, Peter **George** bondsman. His 21 March 1820 Craven County will, proved June the same year, left 30 acres to his son Theophilus, and divided the remainder between his wife Sarah and his children [WB C:191]. His children were named in a 4 November 1821 deed by which his heirs sold land

on the south side of the Neuse River near the head of Adams Creek [DB 43:82]. His children were

    i.   Theophilus, born 1776-94, head of a Craven County household of 7 "free colored" in 1820 [NC:65], perhaps named for Theophilus **Norwood** of Carteret County. He married Betsy **George**, 16 November 1804 Craven County bond with George Carter bondsman.

    ii. Hannah[3], wife of Peter **George**.

    iii. William[4], born 1794-1806, head of a Craven County household of 7 "free colored" in 1820 [NC:65]. His wife was named Nancy according to the 4 November 1821 deed by which he sold his father's land.

    iv. Charity, wife of Jacob **Dove**.

    v.   Elizabeth, wife of Abel **Moore**.

    vi. Polly, wife of Ambrose **Moore**.

    vii. Elsey, wife of John **Moore**.

23. Isaac[3] Carter (Abel, John[2], Thomas[2], Thomas[1]), born about 1760, was called a "Mulatto" in his Revolutionary War pension application. He enlisted in the 8th North Carolina Regiment on 1 September 1777, was taken prisoner, and was discharged on 20 February 1780 [Crow, *Black Experience in Revolutionary North Carolina*, 98]. He married Sarah **Perkins**, 3 February 1786 Craven County bond, George **Perkins** bondsman. Isaac was head of a Craven County household of 5 "other free" in 1790 [NC:131]. His children were bound apprentices with his consent to William Physioc in Craven County on 11 March 1811. They were also mentioned in the Craven County will of their uncle Isaac **Perkins** [WB C:326]. They were

    i.   William[5], born about 1797, fourteen years old when he was bound apprentice on 11 March 1811.

    ii. Sarah, born about 1801, ten years old when she was bound apprentice on 11 March 1811.

    iii. Mehetabel/ Hetty, born about 1802, nine years old when she was bound apprentice on 11 March 1811.

    iv. Isaac[4], born about 1806, five years old when he was bound apprentice on 11 March 1811.

Members of the family who remained on the Eastern Shore of Virginia were

    i.   Mitta, head of a St. George's Parish, Accomack County household of 2 "other free" and 1 slave in 1800 [*Virginia Genealogist* 2:131].

    ii. Ben, head of an Accomack County household of 3 "other free" in 1800 [*Virginia Genealogist* 1:105].

    iii. Ezekiel, born before 1776, "Brick layer," head of a Northampton County household of 6 "free colored" in 1820 [VA:216A].

    iv. Hannah, born before 1776, head of a Northampton County household of 8 "free colored" in 1820 [VA:217A].

    v.   Grace, born before 1776, head of a Northampton County household of 8 "free colored" in 1820 [VA:217A].

    vi. Eliza, born before 1776, head of a Northampton County household of 5 "free colored" in 1820 [VA:217A].

    vii. Judy, born before 1776, head of a Northampton County household of 7 "free colored" in 1820 [VA:217].

    viii. Major, born before 1776, head of a Northampton County household of 2 "free colored" in 1820 [VA:217].

CARY FAMILY

1. Mary Cary, born say 1699, complained to the York County court on 20 July 1719 that she had bound a "Mulatto" boy to Nathaniel Hook as a carpenter, but Hook was not teaching him that trade. The court dismissed her suit. She was probably identical to a white woman named Mary Cary who still had three

years to serve when she was listed in the 4 July 1719 York County inventory of the estate of Edward Powers [OW 15, pt. 2, 455, 466, 471]. She may have been the ancestor of

2   i.   Robert, born say 1745.

       ii.   Thomas, head of a Spotsylvania County household of 11 "other free" in 1810.

     iii.   William, head of a Petersburg Town household of 5 "other free" in 1810 [VA:119a].

     iv.   Benjamin, head of a Petersburg Town household of 2 "other free" and a white woman 16-26 years old in 1810 [VA:121a].

      v.   Jack, head of a Petersburg Town household of 2 "other free" in 1810 [VA:127a].

     vi.   Edy, head of a Petersburg Town household of 2 "other free" in 1810 [VA:127a].

   vii.   Christopher, head of a Frederick County household of 3 "other free" in 1810 [VA:595].

  viii.   Nancy, head of a Frederick County household of 6 "other free" in 1810 [VA:340].

2.   Robert[1] Cary, born say 1745, was taxable on a horse in Charles City County in 1790 and taxable on a horse and 150 acres in 1800 [1790 PPTL, p.4; 1800, p.4; 1800 Land Tax List, p.4] He made a 20 October 1800 Charles City County will, proved 20 November 1800. He left his son David land on the north side of the road leading from the east run to James Ladd's adjoining Hubbard's, left 10 pounds to his daughter Frances Cary and left the remainder of the land he was living on to his grandson Robert Cary, son of David Cary. He left his granddaughter Elizabeth Cary, son of David, a cow and his grandson Robert 3 barrels of corn for sundry services. And he directed that the remainder of his estate was to be divided among all his surviving children except David and Frances [WB 1:508]. He was the father of

       i.   David, born say 1770.

      ii.   Frances, born say 1772, perhaps identical to Frs. Cary, "F. Negro" head of a Culpeper County household of 1 "other free" in 1810 [VA:22].

     iii.   Bartlet, paid 6 pounds, 12 shillings by the estate of Robert Cary, deceased, "for money lent his father" [DB 1:578], perhaps identical to Cary Bartlet, head of a Richmond City household of 3 "other free" in 1810 [VA:333].

3.   David[1] Cary, born say 1770, was taxable in Charles City County in 1800 [1800 PPTL, p.5] and head of a Charles City County household of 10 "other free" in 1810 [VA:959]. He made a 3 April 1823 Charles City County will which was proved 13 September 1823. He left two cows, a horse and cart and his land on the south side of the road to his wife and directed that his land on the north side of the road be rented out for the use of his children Polly, David, Nancy, Ebed, and Zachariah and the children of his two daughters Cretty and Betty who were deceased [WB 2:563-4]. His widow Amey registered in Charles City County on 16 November 1826: *a woman of yellowish complexion, about 60 years old, 4 feet 11-1/2 inches high, short nose, large nostrils, was born free in this county* [Minutes 1823-9, 196]. He was the father of

       i.   Robert[2], named in his grandfather's 20 October 1800 will.

      ii.   Cretty.

     iii.   Betty, named in her grandfather's 20 October 1800 will.

     iv.   Polly Frances, born about 1783, registered in Petersburg on 9 July 1805: *a dark brown Negro woman, five feet one half inches high, twenty two years old, born free in Charles City County* [Register of Free Negroes 1794-1819, no. 304].

v. David[1].
vi. Nancy, head of a Richmond City household of 3 "other free" in 1810 [VA:340].
vii. Ebed.
viii. Zachariah.

CASE FAMILY

1. Roger Case, born about 1674, was called "Roger a Mollatto Servant" in Surry County, Virginia court in 1694 when he still had one year to serve Thomas Drew of Surry County [Haun, *Surry County Court Records*, V:112]. He was called Roger Case when he was taxable in Thomas Drew's Lawnes Creek Parish, Surry County household in 1695 through 1701, called Roger in 1700, and abstracted as Robt. Case in 1701. He was taxable in his own household in 1703 [*Magazine of Virginia Genealogy* vol.23, no.3, 71, 75, 77; vol. 24, 70, 71, 73, 79, 81]. He brought a successful suit against John Sugar in Surry County court in May 1705 for payment for two sows he sold to Sugar for 20 shillings. Evan Humphreys and John **Kecotan (Tann)** were his witnesses [Haun, *Surry County Court Records*, VI:57]. In 1721 he was taxable in Chowan County next to Hubbard **Gibson**, Jr. [Haun, *Old Albemarle County Miscellaneous Records*, 331], and he purchased land in the part of Chowan County which later became Northampton County, North Carolina [Hoffman, *Chowan Precinct 1696-1723*, no. 1391]. On 10 November 1740 he sold 100 acres adjoining his lands in Occoneechee Neck, Northampton County [Northampton DB 1:57]. He may have been the father of

  2   i. John, born say 1710.
       ii. William, born say 1715, a "Mulatto" taxable on two "Black" polls in Currituck County in 1755 [T&C 1].

2. John Case, born say 1710, named his children in his Currituck County will, proved in 1763:
       i. Cornelius.
      ii. Elizabeth.
     iii. Hall.
  3   iv. Jonathan, born say 1737.

3. Jonathan Case, born say 1737, served in the Revolution in Alexander Whitehall's Company of North Carolina Militia commanded by Colonel Samuel Jarvis [Saunders, *Colonial and State Records*, XVII:1054]. He was living in Currituck County on 2 June 1791 when he applied for a pension for eighteen months service as a Continental soldier [*NCGSJ* VIII:213]. He was head of a Currituck County household of 4 "other free" in 1790 [NC:21] and 10 in 1800 [NC:138]. His son may have been
  4   i. Joseph, born about 1755.

4. Joseph Case, born about 1755, was counted as white in 1790, head of a Currituck County household of 1 white male over 16, 2 under 16, and 3 females [NC:21]. He was head of a Currituck County household of 6 "other free" in 1800 [NC:138]. He made a declaration in Currituck County court on 10 May 1820 to obtain a pension for his services in the Revolutionary War. He claimed to be about sixty-five years of age and that all his possessions were worth only $32.50. He had a fifty-five-year-old wife and twenty-two-year-old son Grundy [M805-168, S41472]. His son was
       i. Grundy, born about 1798.

Case Family of Accomack County, Virginia
1. Mary Case, born say 1683, was the servant of John West on 3 December 1701 when the churchwardens of Accomack County Parish presented her for having

a "Mullatto Bastard Child." She was presented for having another child on 6 April 1703 [Orders 1697-1703, 122a, 126a, 144]. She was probably the ancestor of

   i.   Elizabeth, head of a St. George Parish, Accomack County household of 3 "other free" and one slave in 1800 [*Virginia Genealogist* 2:130].

   ii.   Major, head of an Accomack Parish, Accomack County household of 3 "other free" in 1800 [*Virginia Genealogist* 1:105].

   iii.   Bridget, head of an Accomack County household of 5 "other free" in 1810 [VA:17].

   iv.   George, head of an Accomack County household of 2 "other free" in 1810 [VA:16].

CASSIDY FAMILY

1.   Catherine Cassity, born say 1685, a white servant of John Hutchins, confessed in Lancaster County court on 12 May 1703 that she had a "Mallatoe" child [Orders 1702-13, 32]. Her descendants were

   i.   Ann, head of a Lancaster County household of 5 "white" (free) persons and a dwelling in 1784 [VA:74]. She married John **Pinn**, 12 September 1785 Northumberland County bond.

   ii.   Betty, a "free mulatto" head of a Northumberland County household of 4 "other free" in 1810 [VA:973].

   iii.   James, born about 1786, registered as a "free Negro" in Lancaster County on 19 September 1808: *Age 22, Color yellow...born free* [Burkett, *Lancaster County Register of Free Negroes*, 4]. He was head of a Lancaster County household of 4 "other free" in 1810 [VA:341]. He registered in Middlesex County on 24 October 1827: *born free; 45 years of age; 5'5"; yellow complexion*. His wife was probably Lucy Ann Casity who registered in Middlesex County on 21 October 1827: *born free; 37 years of age; 5'5"; yellow complexion* [Register of Free Negroes 1827-60, p.1].

   iv.   Patty, a "free mulatto" head of a Northumberland County household of 9 "other free" in 1810 [VA:975].

   v.   Patty Ann, married Moses **Blundon**, widower, 28 October 1834 Lancaster County bond, John **Cassity** security.

   vi.   Samuel, married Mary **Spriddle**, daughter of Nancy **Spriddle**, 15 December 1819 Lancaster County bond, James **Spriddle** security.

   vii.   William, born about 1757, taxable in York County in 1784 [Fothergill, *Virginia Taxpayers*, 23], taxable in Norfolk County in 1801 and 1803, counted in a list of "free Negroes and Mulattoes" on Tanner's Creek in Norfolk County in 1801 with (his son?) John Cassedy, (his wife?) Sarah Cassedy, Eliza Gilleat (**Gillett**) and a female named "Ren'" [PPTL, 1791-1812, frames 383, 462]. He registered in York County on 16 December 1822: *a dark mulatto about 65 years of age 5 feet four Inches high...born free* [Register of Free Negroes 1798-1831, no.163].

   viii.   Milly, born about 1783, registered in York County on 16 December 1822: *a dark mulatto about 38 years of age 5 feet 2-1/4 Inches high very black* [Register of Free Negroes 1798-1831, no.179].

CAUSEY FAMILY

1.   Judith[1] Causey, born say 1730, was head of a Northumberland County household of 5 "Blacks" in 1782 [VA:37]. She was most likely the mother of

2   i.   William[1], born about 1747.

3   ii.   Abel, born say 1755.

4   iii.   James, born say 1762.

   iv.   Thomas, born say 1765, his Northumberland County tax paid by Abel Causey in 1787 [Schreiner-Yantis, *1787 Census*, 1262].

2. William[1] Causey, born about 1747, enlisted in the Revolution for three years and was discharged on 16 February 1780 by the captain of the ship *Dragon* [Jackson, *Virginia Negro Soldiers*, 32]. He registered as a "free Negro" in Northumberland County on 12 January 1807: *Mulatto, about 60 years old, 5 feet 9-1/4 Inches, Born free* [Northumberland County Courthouse Register, no.27]. He was a "free mulatto" head of a Northumberland County household of 9 "other free" in 1810 [VA:975]. He married (second?) Rachel **Barr**, 23 April 1810 Northumberland County bond, John Causey security. Rachel Causey, born about 1755, registered as a "free Negro" in Northumberland County on 9 March 1807: *dark Mulatto, about 52 years old, 5 feet 2 inches, Emancipated by the will of John Bar* [Register, no.30]. He was the father of
   i.   Philip **Sprittle**, born 29 December 1770 in Northumberland County, "Son of William Causse & Elizabeth Sprittle" [Fleet, *Northumberland County Record of Births*, 107]. Betty **Spriddle** was a "Mulatto" head of a Northumberland County household in 1810 [VA:994].
   ii. ?Polly, born say 1775, a "Mulatto" living in Northumberland County on 10 June 1799 when the county court certified that she was born free [Orders 1793-1800, 80].
   iii. Elizabeth, born say 1782, a "Mulatto" living in Northumberland County on 10 June 1799 when the county court certified that she was born free [Orders 1793-1800, 80]. She was called the "daughter of William Causey" when she married A. **Nickens**, 5 July 1800 Northumberland County bond, Joseph Mott security.
   iv. Nancy, married Joseph **Weaver**, 6 May 1810 Northumberland County bond, Amos **Nicken** security, with permission of William Causey.

3. Abel Causey, born say 1755, was head of a Northumberland County household with no whites in 1784 [VA:75] and was taxable on 8 cattle in 1787 [Schreiner-Yantis, *1787 Census*, 1262]. He was a "free mulatto" head of a Northumberland County household of 5 "other free" in 1810 [VA:975]. He may have been the father of
   i.   Susan, born say 1786, married Anthony **Weaver**, 30 May 1807 Northumberland County bond, James **Toulson** security.

4. James Causey, born say 1762, was a seaman from Northumberland County who served in the Revolution [Jackson, *Virginia Negro Soldiers*, 32]. He was a "free mulatto" head of a Northumberland County household of 3 "other free" in 1810 [VA:975]. He was probably the father of
   i.   Judith[2], married George **Credit**, widower, 2 May 1821 Northumberland County bond, James Causey security. George was a "free mulatto" head of a Northumberland County household of 4 "other free" in 1810 [VA:976]. Judith married, second, James **Sorrell** and was listed with him and their children in the 1850 Northumberland County census.

CAUTHER/ CATHER FAMILY

1. Jane Cauther, born say 1745, was the mother of Rose Cauther, a "Molatto Bastard" who was ordered by the Augusta County court to be bound to John Campbell on 17 May 1768. On 27 June 1769 she was fined 500 pounds of tobacco for having a bastard child, no race indicated [Orders 1768, 143; 1768-9, 315]. She was the mother of
   i.   Rose, born say 1768.
   ii. ?Sarah, born say 1770, a "Mulatto" child ordered bound to Nep Hansberger by the Augusta County court on 11 April 1772 [Orders 1769-73, 365]. She was called Sarah Cather, a "mulatto," when she was bound by the churchwardens of Augusta Parish to Stewart Hunsberger on 19 September 1772.

    iii. ?Betty, born say 1772, a bastard (no race indicated) ordered bound to Jacob Miller by the Augusta County court on 11 April 1772 [Orders 1769-73, 365], called a "mulatto" when the churchwardens of Augusta Parish bound her to Jacob Millar on 19 September 1772 [Augusta Co. Vestry Book 1746-1779, p.506, 509 by Gill, *Apprentices of Virginia*, 42].

CHAMBERS FAMILY

1.   Elizabeth Chambers, born say 1726, was the servant of Elliott Benger, Esqr., on 1 July 1746 when she confessed to the Spotsylvania County court that she had an illegitimate "Mulatto" child by William **Scroghams**, a "Servant Negro man" of John Spotswood, Gent. [Orders 1738-49, 380]. She was probably the ancestor of

    i. John, born say 1750, a "free Molatto" who testified on 8 June 1775 at the trial of Will, a Negro slave belonging to the estate of Francis Taliaferro. Will was charged in Caroline County, Virginia court with breaking and entering the house of Thomas Cason of King George County and stealing sundry articles which belonged to Chambers [Orders 1772-6, 601]. John was head of a Spotsylvania County household of 7 "other free" and a white woman aged 26-45 in 1810 [VA:102b].

    ii. Polly, head of a Spotsylvania County, Virginia household of 3 "other free" in 1810 [VA:103b].

CHANDLER FAMILY

Several mixed-race members of the Chandler family were living in Westmoreland County, Virginia, from 1741 to 1755:

1   i.   Francis, born say 1715.
2   ii. John, born say 1720.

1.   Francis Chandler, born say 1715, was living in Westmoreland County on 1 April 1741 when the churchwardens of Cople Parish presented him and Rebecca **Paine** for cohabiting together. The same court described Francis' wife Margaret Chandler as a "Mulatto" and ordered her to appear to answer the presentment of the grand jury for living in adultery with George Henson [Orders 1739-43, 100]. He may have been the father of

    i. Elizabeth, born say 1738, a "melatto" listed (with "melatto" Stephen **Jones**) in the Lunenburg County, Virginia inventory of the estate of Thomas Blank on 20 August 1753. Elizabeth and Stephen were apparently his indentured servants because no slaves were listed in his will [WB 1:74, 107].

3   ii. Tabitha, born say 1742.

2.   John Chandler, born say 1720, a "Mulatto," was sued in Westmoreland County, Virginia court for a 2 pound debt on 30 September 1755 [Orders 1755-8, 7a]. His wife was probably Sarah Chandler, daughter of Edward **Mozingo**, who was mentioned in her father's 10 November 1753 Richmond County, Virginia will [Wills 1753-67]. He may have been the father of

4   i. William^1, born say 1740.

3.   Tabitha Chandler, born say 1742, had a "mulatto" child named Ann who was ordered bound out by the Henrico County court in April 1760 [Orders 1755-62, 409]. She may have been related to Mary Chandler (no race indicated) who was bound out to Matthew Talbert in Amelia County on 12 November 1736 [Orders 1:14]. Tabitha was the mother of

    i. Ann, born say 1760.

4. William[1] Chandler, born say 1740, was living in Halifax County, Virginia, in May 1765 when the court presented him, Shadrack **Gowin**, Peter **Rickman**, and Philip **Dennum** for concealing a tithable. The tithables were probably their wives. He purchased land by deed proved in Halifax County court in March 1768 [Pleas 5:46; 6:58]. William was probably the father of
    i.   William[2], born say 1767, bondsman for the 25 February 1797 Mecklenburg County, Virginia marriage of Siller **Walden** and Matthew **Stewart**. He was head of a Randolph County, North Carolina household of 4 "other free" [NC:64]. He may have been the father of William Chandler (born about 1795) who obtained free papers in Randolph County on 23 September 1833 and recorded them in Owen County, Indiana, on 18 June 1834 [DB 4:153 by Peterson, *Owen County Records*, 30].
    ii. Samuel, born say 1769, married Sinai **Stewart**, 23 December 1793 Mecklenburg County, Virginia bond, William Chandler bondsman. He was head of a Randolph County household of 11 "other free" in 1810 [NC:64].
    iii. Jean, married George **Stewart**, 27 December 1797 Mecklenburg County, Virginia bond, Moses **Stewart** security.

Another member of the Chandler family was
    i.   Thornton, born about 1776, counted in a "List of Free Negroes in the Parish of St. Ann's" in Essex County with a male and female above the age of sixteen in 1813 [PPTL, 1782-1819, frame 510], registered as a free Negro in Essex County on 15 August 1829: *born free by statement in writing of Richd Rowzee, dark Mulattoe, 53 years of age.* He married Catherine **Fortune** [Register of Free Negroes 1810-43, nos. 190, 192].

CHAPMAN FAMILY

1. Betty Chapman, born say 1756, sued Frezill McTeir for her freedom in Lunenburg County court on 11 September 1777. He was called Frizell Martin on 13 May 1779 when the court ordered her discharged from his service. On 10 July 1800 the court summoned Henry Freeman to show cause why he was detaining her children Lizzy and Mary Chapman who were suggested to the court to be entitled to their freedom [Orders 1777-84, 3, 28; 1799-1801, fol. 84]. She was living on Flat Rock Creek, Lunenburg County in 1802 and 1803 when she was counted in a "List of free Negroes & Mulattoes" with her children: Nancy, Winny, Lucy, Charlotte, Henry, and Biddy [LVA, Lunenburg County, Free Negro & Slave Records, 1802-1803]. She was the mother of
    i.   Robert, born say 1779, child of Betty Chapman, ordered bound apprentice by the 10 February 1780 session of the Lunenburg County court [Orders 1777-84, fol. 50].
    ii. Nancy, born say 1780, living in her mother's household in 1802 and 1803 with her children Betsy and John Chapman.
    iii. Winny, born say 1782, living in her mother's household in 1802 and with her daughter Lucy in 1803.
    iv. Eliza, living at Stony Creek, Lunenburg County with her daughter Patsey in 1802 and 1803.
    v.   ?Milly, living at Thomas Scarborough's in Lunenburg County in 1802 with her daughter Lily and a child not yet named.
    vi. Lucy, living in her mother's household in Lunenburg County in 1802 and 1803, head of a Campbell County household of 1 "other free" in 1810 [VA:854].
    vii. Charlotte[1], living in her mother's household in 1802, 1803, and 1814 [*Magazine of Virginia Genealogy* 33:266].

    viii.   Henry[2].

    ix.   Biddy.

Other members of the Chapman family were

    i.   Jesse, a "free Negro" taxable in Surry County from 1796 to 1816, listed in 1813 with 5 "free Negroes & Mulattoes above the age of 16," 3 of whom were male tithables [PPTL, 1791-1816, frames 256, 367, 521, 611, 649, 731, 851].

    ii.   Saul, head of a Prince William County household of 6 "other free" in 1810 [VA:502].

    iii.   Henry[1], born about 1778, registered in Middlesex County, Virginia, on 23 June 1800: *born free; 22 years old; 5'5-1/4"; yellow complexion* [Register of Free Negroes, 1800-60, p.15].

    iv.   James, "Free man of color," head of a Washington County, Virginia household of 2 "other free" in 1810 [VA:201a].

    v.   Richard, a "free negro" taxable in Pittsylvania County in 1810 [Yantis, *A Supplement to the 1810 Census of Virginia*, D-17].

    vi.   Mary, head of an Albemarle County household of 1 "other free" in 1810 [VA:182].

    vii.   Sally, born about 1793, registered in Halifax County, Virginia, on 21 May 1831: *about 38 years of age, five feet five inches high, of a yellow complexion* [Registers of Free Negroes, 1802-1831, no. 144].

    viii.   Charlotte[2], born about 1796, registered in Lunenburg County on 12 October 1846: *yellow Colour, born free about 50 years of age, about 5 feet 3 inches high* [WB 5, after page 89, no.129]. She was counted in Lunenburg County in 1814 with her daughter Eliza [*Magazine of Virginia Genealogy* 33:266].

CHARITY FAMILY

1.   Charity, born say 1660, was a "Negro girle" tithable in Arthur Jordan's household in the 1677 list for Surry County, Virginia, and a "Negro woman" in his household in the 1678 list [*Magazine of Virginia Genealogy,* vol.22, 3:60]. She was a "Negro woman" slave of Arthur Jordan freed by his 24 September 1698 will [DW 5:160]. She may have been the daughter of a "Negro Woman Judith" who was to be free seven years after George Jordan's decease according to his 25 February 1677/8 Surry County will, proved 5 November 1678 [DW 1671-84, 192]. Judith was probably the slave by that name who was taxable in Mr. Thomas Jordan's household in Surry County from 1679 to 1685 [*Magazine of Virginia Genealogy,* vol.22, 3:65; 4:48, 51; vol. 23, 1:44, 47]. Charity was called a free "negro woman" when she was presented by the Surry County court in May 1702 for having a bastard child. On 20 August 1712 she brought suit for 30 pounds sterling damages against George Jordan, Jr., for an assault and "other Enormitys" on her daughter Jane **Mingo**. Jane would have been about ten years old at that time if she was the child Charity was presented for in 1702. Jordan delayed the case until 17 December 1712 when the jury found that he took her away by force from her mother and detained her in his service for several days before the assault took place. They also found that Charity was born in Virginia, freed by Arthur Jordan's will in 1698, and had Jane **Mingo** in Surry County after she was freed. After hearing evidence from Thomas and William Hux, the jury found in Jane's favor for only one shilling damages, and only if the court ruled that Jane was legally a free person. The court ruled so later in that session [Orders 1701-13, 17, 399, 401, 403, 407, 410]. Charity's was the mother of

    i.   Jane **Mingo**, probably born before May 1702 when her mother was presented for having a bastard child. She may have been the mother of Mary **Mingo** whose "Molatto Son" Shadrack **Mingo** was ordered bound to Doctor John Ramsey in Norfolk County on 16 August 1754 [Orders

1753-55, 73]. Perhaps another descendant was William **Mingo**, head of a Southampton County household of 9 "other free" in 1810.

Their descendants were apparently the Charity family of Surry County:
    i. John[1], sued for a 2 pound/ 1 shilling debt in Surry County on 17 September 1753, died insolvent before 16 March 1762 according to the account of the Surry County estate of Martha Bryan [Orders 1753-7, 290; DW&c 10:274].

2   ii. William, born say 1720.
3   iii. Sarah[1], born say 1722.
4   iv. Jeffrey[1], born say 1725.
5   v. Mary[1], born say 1735.
    vi. Hannah, born say 1738, complained to the Surry County court on 19 February 1760 that her master William Mooring was detaining her past her indented time of service. The court ordered her discharged from his service [Orders 1757-63, 228, 233].

2. William Charity, born say 1720, was among fourteen free African Americans of Surry County, Virginia, who were presented by the court on 21 November 1758 for failing to pay tax on their wives, "supposing the said persons to be Mulattoes" [Orders 1757-64, 135]. He proved a claim in Surry County court on 23 October 1764 for taking up a runaway [Orders 1764-74]. He died before 27 October 1778 when the Surry County court ordered his estate appraised [Orders 1775-85, 70]. His children may have been

6   i. Henry[1], born say 1741.
7   ii. David[1], born say 1749.
8   iii. Elizabeth[1], born say 1751.
    iv. Benjamin[1], born say 1758, presented in Surry County on 26 February 1783 for not listing his taxable property [Orders 1775-85, 201]. He was head of a Surry County household of 5 "whites" in 1784 [VA:78] and was a freeholder in Governor's Road Precinct on 26 July 1785 when he, David Charity, Nicholas **Scott**, John **Debereax**, Armstead **Peters** and several white freeholders were ordered to maintain the road in their area [Orders 1775-85, 443]. He married Sarah **Stephens**, 5 September 1803 Surry County bond, William **Scott** surety. He was taxable in Cabin Point district of Surry County from 1783 to 1807 [PPTL, 1782-90, frames 367, 399, 470, 596; 1791-1816, frames 57, 126, 234, 287, 445, 559, 611, 629].

9   v. Sterling, born about 1768.
    vi. Jeffrey[2], born say 1774, a "poor infant" of Southwark Parish bound apprentice on 24 March 1778 [Orders 1775-85, 53].

3. Sarah[1] Charity, born say 1722, was living in Southwarke Parish, Surry County, on 20 May 1755 when the court ordered the churchwardens to bind out her son Sharrard [Orders 1753-7, 212]. She was the mother of

10   i. Sherwood[1] (Sherod), born say 1747.

4. Jeffrey[1] Charity, born say 1725, was a defendant in a Surry County suit for debt in January 1748/9 and 26 February 1754 when the court ruled that Jeffrey was "not an inhabitant of this County" [Orders 1744-9, 530; 1753-57, 116]. He was listed in the 16 November 1756 account of the Surry County estate of John Simmons [DW 10:76]. On 19 June 1759 the court ordered the churchwardens to bind out his son Hartwell Charity because he had left the county without making provision for his child [Orders 1756-63, 194]. He was the father of

    i. Hartwell, born say 1760, taxable in Cabin Point District of Surry County from 1783 to 1807 [PPTL, 1782-90, frames 367, 399, 447, 549; 1791-1816, frames 58, 158, 287, 404, 519, 590, 629]. He was surety for the 17 October 1809 Isle of Wight County marriage bond of Randall **Wilson** and Milly Charity. Perhaps Hartwell's widow was Cherry Charity who was called the relict of H. Charity when she was counted as a "free Negro & Mulatto" in Surry County in 1813 [PPTL, 1791-1816, frame 732].

5. Mary[1] Charity, born say 1735, was bound out by the churchwardens of Southwarke Parish in Surry County on 15 April 1747 [Orders 1744-49, 300]. She was called Mary Chariott, a "Molatto woman," on 15 August 1758 when the Surry County court ordered the churchwardens to bind out her children Ann, Robert, Charles, and Jane. On 16 December 1766 the court ordered the churchwardens to bind out "poor Mulattos" Nanny, Robert, Charles, Jenny, Thomas, Cherry, and Sarah Charity [Orders 1757-63, 123; 1764-74, 102-3]. She was the mother of

11   i.   Ann, born say 1753.
        ii.   Robert, born say 1755.
        iii. Charles, born say 1756, a "yellow" complexioned soldier born in Surry County who enlisted in the Revolution in Dinwiddie County and later moved to Cumberland County, Virginia [NSDAR, *African American Patriots*, 148].
12   iv.   Jane, born say 1758.
        v.   Thomas, born say 1760, head of a Surry County household of 3 "whites" (free persons) in 1784 [VA:78]. He and Hartwell Charity were listed among the freeholders who were ordered to maintain the road in Galloway's Precinct on 28 December 1785 [Orders 1774-84, 473].
        vi.   Cherry, born say 1762, listed as a "free Negro & Mulatto" in Surry County in 1813 [PPTL, 1791-1816, frame 732].
        vii. Sarah[2], born say 1764.

6. Henry[1] Charity, born say 1741, was sued for a 3 pound, 6 shilling debt in Surry County on 15 June 1762 [Orders 1757-63, 335]. He purchased 125 acres in Southwark Parish on the east side of Great Branch on 19 August 1766. He and his wife Sacugoth Charity sold 50 acres of this land to Peter **Valentine** on 12 January 1768 and he sold the remaining 75 acres on 15 August 1769 [DB 8:315, 374, 431]. He and William **Walden** were sued for debt on 19 July 1768 [Orders 1764-74, 159]. He was head of a Surry County household of 9 persons in 1782 [VA:43] and 10 in 1784 [VA:78]. He was taxable in Surry County from 1782 to 1800: taxable on a horse and 9 cattle in 1782; taxable on 2 tithes in 1786; taxable on Squire and Henry Charity's tithes in 1787; taxable on John Charity's tithe in 1799 and 1800 [PPTL, 1782-90, frames 358, 379, 397, 449, 549; 1791-1816, frames 281, 323, 404]. On 4 June 1787 he purchased 50 acres in Southwark Parish adjoining William **Walden** from Nanny and Sarah **Simon** which was land descended to them from Thomas **Simon**, a Surry County resident presented by the court for failing to pay tax on his wife on 21 November 1758 [Orders 1757-64, 135]. Henry was married to Judy **Banks** by 22 February 1796 when they sold her part of her rights to land descended to her from her brother Matthew **Banks** [Deeds 1792-9, 344-6]. His will was proved in 1801 [Wills, etc. 1:466-7] and the transfer of his land (to his wife and children) was recorded in the Surry County Tax Alterations: 50 acres to Judith Charity, 54 acres to Elijah Charity, and 12 acres to John Charity. His children were

13   i.   Wilson, born about 1770.
        ii.   ?Henry[2], born say 1771, a 16-21-year-old taxable in the household of (his father?) Henry Charity in 1787, called Henry Charity, Jr., when he was taxable in Henry Charity, Sr.'s household in 1797 and 1798, not mentioned again in Surry County records [PPTL, 1782-90, frames 449; 1791-1816, 323, 366].

iii. Elijah, born about 1774, taxable in Surry County from 1791 to 1816: his tax charged to Charity from 1791 to 1794; charged with his own tax from 1795; listed with 2 "free Negroes & Mulattoes" in 1813 [PPTL, 1791-1816, frame 8, 57, 108, 158, 235, 286, 364, 442, 518, 589, 629, 666, 706, 730, 850]. He registered as a "free Negro in Surry County on 9 January 1796: *son of Henry Charity a resident of this County, a dark mulattoe man, aged about 22 years, pretty well made, short hair, 5'11" high, born of free parents* [Back of Guardian Accounts Book 1783-1804, no.16]. He married Charlotte Charity (of lawful age), 29 January 1803 Surry County bond, Joseph **Roberts** surety. Elijah was head of a Surry County household of 8 "other free" in 1810 [VA:604] and 12 "free colored" in 1830.

iv. Keziah, born about 1780, twenty-four-year-old "daughter of Judith Charity," married Nicholas Scott **Valentine**, 28 May 1804 Surry County bond, Wright **Walden** surety.

v. Sarah[3], born say 1790, "daughter of Judith Charity who consents," married David **Fulks**, 23 March 1807 Surry County bond, David **Debrix** surety. David **Folks** registered in Surry County on 26 June 1818: *a free Negroe Man of bright complexion, aged about 36 years next January who is 5'5-1/4" high...was born free as appears by a Certificate from Edenton North Carolina produced by him* [Hudgins, *Surry County Register of Free Negroes*, 69].

vi. John[3], born say 1781, taxable in Henry Charity's household in 1799 and 1800, taxable in Judy Charity's household from 1801 to 1804, called "son of Judith" from 1805 to 1812 [PPTL, 1791-1816, frames 366, 404, 444, 479, 519, 558, 590, 611, 649, 686, 706]. He may have been the John Charity who was ordered by the Surry County court on 23 June 1807 to pay support for his illegitimate female child by Mary **Walden**. He married Mason Charity, daughter of Mary **Blizzard**, 28 June 1808 Surry County bond, Peter **Blizzard** surety. He was head of a Surry County household of 6 "other free" in 1810 [VA:604] and 11 "free colored" in 1830. His son Acquilla Charity registered in Surry County on 26 November 1831: *son of John Charity & Mason his wife...of a dark complexion, spare made...about 21 years of age and is 5'8-1/2" high* [Hudgins, *Surry County Register of Free Negroes*, 103].

7. David[1] Charity, born say 1749, was presented by the Surry County court on 15 May 1770 for not listing his tithables [Orders 1764-74, 213]. He was head of a Surry County household of 4 persons in 1782 [VA:43], 4 in 1784 [VA:78], and 10 "other free" in 1810 [VA:604]. He was taxable in Surry County from 1784 to 1812: taxable on a horse and 2 cattle in 1784; charged with Tom **Stephens**' tithe in 1797 and 1798; taxable on a horse in 1816 [PPTL, 1782-90, frames 379, 448, 549; 1791-1816, frames 8, 106, 158, 234, 287, 323, 365, 444, 519, 558, 611, 649, 667, 706]. And he was taxable on 60 acres from 1795 to 1814 [1795 Property Tax Alterations; Land Tax Lists]. His children were

i. Elsey, born say 1782, "daughter of David Charity," married Aaron **Taylor** 23 December 1799 Surry County bond [Ministers Returns, 54].

ii. Elizabeth[2], born about 1783, "daughter of David Charity," married Joseph **Roberts**, 17 May 1802 Surry County bond, David Charity surety, married by Rev. James Warren of the Methodist Church [Ministers Returns, 61]. She registered in Surry County on 26 March 1805: *a woman of a bright complexion aged about 22 years, short hair...5'3" high* [Hudgins, *Surry County Register of Free Negroes*, 25].

iii. ?John[4], Jr., born say 1786, married Lucretia Charity, "daughter of Rebecca **Andrews**," 2 September 1807 Surry County bond, David Charity surety. Lucretia was Rebecca Charity's daughter, born before her 20 April 1791 marriage to Thomas **Andrews**. She may have been the Lucretia Charity who was counted as a "free Negro & Mulatto" in 1813 [PPTL, 1791-1816, 733].

8.   Elizabeth[1] Charity, born say 1751, was the mother of Alexander and David Charity who were bound out by the Surry County court on 28 January 1783 [Orders 1775-85, 192]. She consented to the 28 December 1792 marriage of her daughter Edy Charity. Her children were

    i.   Alexander/ Elick, born say 1770, a "poor Mulatto infant" bound apprentice in Surry County on 27 July 1779 [Orders 1775-85, 88]. He was taxable in Surry County from 1787 to 1816: a 16-21-year-old Surry County tithable in 1787, his tax charged to John Ellis; charged with his own tax from 1791 to 1794; listed with William **Scott** in 1795; charged with his own tithe from 1796; listed in 1813 with 2 "free Negroes & Mulattoes" [PPTL, 1782-90, frames 416; 1791-1816, frames 7, 107, 243, 325, 406, 590, 629, 667, 706, 733, 850]. He married Polly **Debrix**, daughter of John **Debrix**, 12 June 1800 Surry County bond, Aaron **Taylor** surety.

    ii.   Nanny, born say 1771, "daughter of Betty Charity," bound out by the Surry County court on 25 May 1784 [Orders 1775-85, 298]. She married Peter **Newby**, 14 April 1792 Southampton County bond. Peter was a "free Negro" taxable in Sussex County in 1784 [PPTL 1782-1812, frame 114], head of a Randolph County, North Carolina household of 4 "other free" in 1800 [NC:350] and a Southampton County household of 9 "other free" in 1810.[67]

    iii.   David[2], Jr., born about 1776, tithable in Cabin Point District of Surry County from 1793 to 1801: called David Charity, Jr. [PPTL, 1791-1816, frames 108, 234, 287, 366, 404, 444]. He married Nancy **Debberick (Debrix)**, 17 August 1799, Sussex County bond, Jones **Cannada** surety. He registered as a "free Negro" in Surry County on 20 September 1800: *son of Elizabeth Charity coloured mulattoe man - aged about 24 years, pretty well made, bushy hair, 5'6-1/2" high, born of a free parent* [Back of Guardian Accounts Book 1783-1804, no.65].

    iv.   Edy, born say 1776, daughter of Elizabeth Charity, married William **Scott**, 28 December 1792 Surry County bond, Major **Debrix** security. Her son John Charity, "son of Edith," was taxable in Surry County in 1810 and 1811 [PPTL, 1791-1816, frames 668, 687].

    v.   ?John[3], born say 1781, taxable in William **Scott**'s Surry County household from 1799 to 1802 [PPTL, 1791-1816, frames 385, 426, 463, 500].

    vi.   Sherod/Sherwood[2], born 23 March 1782, taxable in Surry County from 1800 to 1807: listed in the household of Constable Samuel Carrel in 1800; listed with Micajah Coggins in 1801; charged with his own tax from 1805 to 1807 [PPTL, 1791-1816, frames 404, 444, 591, 611, 630]. He married Ariana **Stephens**, daughter of Lucy **Stephens**, 27 May 1806 Surry County bond, Major **Debrix** security. He registered

---

[67]Other members of the Newby family were Moses **Newby**, born about 1782, sixteen years old when he was apprenticed to John Bullock of Orange County as a potter in 1798. He was a potter in 1805 when the Guilford County Court ruled that he was free because his parents had been emancipated by Quakers. George **Newby**, born about 1801, was twelve years old in 1813 when he was apprenticed as a potter to William Dennis of Randolph County [NCGSJ May 1985, p.93]. He was head of a Jackson Township, Wayne County, Indiana household of 5 "free colored" in 1840. Joseph **Newby** was head of a Sussex County household of 7 "other free" in 1810, also counted in Isle of Wight County, "free Negro" head of a household of 4 "other free" in 1810 [VA:20]. Harry, Aaron, Tony, and Edmond **Newby** were "free Negro" taxables in Nansemond County in 1815 [*Supplement to the 1810 Census of Virginia*, S-14].

in Surry County on 1 October 1804: *a mulatto man of a bright complexion aged about 22 years 23 day of March last, who is 5'8" high, pretty straight and well made, very short hair...was born of free parents of this county* [Hudgins, *Surry County Register of Free Negroes*, 23].

9. Sterling Charity, born about 1768, was ordered bound an apprentice with Jeffrey Charity, "poor infants," on 26 May 1778 [Orders 1775-85, 53]. He was taxable in Surry County from 1787 to 1802: his tax charged to Samuel Cocke in 1787 and 1788; charged with his own tax from 1791; charged with Wright **Walden**'s tithe in 1798 [PPTL, 1782-90, frames 449, 471; 1791-1816, frames 7, 106, 253, 325, 405, 480]. He married Elizabeth **Jones**, 13 March 1793 Surry County bond, Davis Charity witness, Sampson **Walden** surety, 14 March marriage by Rev. Nathaniel Berriman, Deacon of the Methodist Church [Marriage Returns, 36]. Sterling was a Mulatto" taxable in Prince George County from 1803 to 1811, taxable on slave and 2 horses in 1809 [PPTL, 1782-1811, frames 576, 600, 650, 698, 721, 741] and head of a Prince George County household of 6 "other free" in 1810 [VA:546]. He registered in Surry County on 28 September 1818: *a free-born Man of colour, aged 50 years who is of a bright complexion, much pitted with the small pox, 5'3-3/4" high, pretty stout & square made...has round & distended Nostrils* [Hudgins, *Surry County Register of Free Negroes*, 69]. His children were
    i. Nancy, "daughter of Sterling Charity," married Archer **Lowery**, 8 April 1812 Surry County bond, Joseph **Roberts** security.
    ii. Elizabeth[3], born 4 November 1797, registered in Surry County on 27 September 1819: *a mulatto Woman the daughter of Sterling Charity and Betsy his wife free persons of Colour of this County aged 22 years the 4th day of November next is 5'1" high* [Hudgins, *Surry County Register of Free Negroes*, 71].

10. Sherwood[1] Charity, born say 1747, was called an infant (no parent or race mentioned) when he was ordered bound an apprentice by the churchwardens of Southwarke Parish in Surry County, Virginia, on 19 November 1751 [Orders 1751-53, 18]. The court called him the son of Sarah Charity when he was ordered bound out on 20 May 1755. On 19 February 1760 the court ordered John Angus to appear to show cause why Sherrard should not be removed from his service [Orders 1757-63, 228]. He purchased 100 acres on the south side of "Johnshehawkin" swamp on 27 April 1779 [DW 11:48]. He died before 25 June 1782 when Sarah Charity, "widow and relict of Sherwood Charity decd.," was summoned to take the inventory of her husband's estate [Orders 1775-85, 151]. She recorded the inventory on 10 August 1782 [DW 11:298]. The 27 September 1785 Surry County court appointed her guardian to her children: "Rebecca, Mary Ann, Clary, Wilmouth, and Anna Charity, orphans of Sherwood Charity decd" [Orders 1775-85, 453]. The transfer of Sherod's 100 acres to Sarah was recorded in the property tax alterations for Surry County in 1783, and she was taxable on this land through 1807 [Land Tax Lists]. She was head of a Surry County household of 7 "whites" in 1782 [VA:43] and 0 whites in 1784 [VA:78]. She was taxable on a horse in Surry County from 1782 to 1816: taxable on 5 cattle in 1787; taxable on slave Fanny in 1803; taxable on 2 slaves in 1809 [PPTL, 1782-90, frames 352, 397, 470; 1791-1816, frames 7, 107, 256, 324, 405, 520, 590, 629, 649, 686, 733, 851]. Sally was head of a Surry County household of 2 "other free" and a white woman over forty-five years of age in 1810 [VA:603]. Sherwood and Sarah's children were
    i. ?Harwood, born say 1768, "not 25" years old on 2 April 1792 when he and Queen Charlotte Charity were mentioned in the Surry County will of Archibald Dunlop. He was taxable in Surry County from 1791 to 1816: his tax charged to Archibald Dunlop from 1791 to 1793;

charged with his own tax in 1799; called Harwood C. Charity starting in 1805; taxable on 2 slaves from 1805 to 1813; listed with 1 "free Negro & Mulatto" in 1813 [PPTL, 1791-1816, frames 10, 59, 108, 367, 480, 559, 590, 629, 667, 706, 731]. Harrod was head of a Surry County household of 1 "free colored" in 1830.

   ii.   Rebecca, born say 1773, married Thomas **Andrews** 26 April 1791 Surry County bond, Joseph **Byrd** surety, 11 May marriage.

14   iii.   Mary^2, born say 1775.

   iv.   Clary, married Wilson Charity, 9 February 1796 Surry County bond, Sampson Granthum surety.

   v.   Wilmouth.

   vi.   Anne, "daughter of Sarah Charity, married Moses **Debrix** 30 December 1800 Surry County bond, Davis (David?) Charity surety.

   vii.   Bolling, orphan of Sherwood Charity, deceased, bound apprentice in Surry County on 28 January 1783 [Orders 1775-85, 192].

11. Ann Charity, born say 1753, had an illegitimate child by Joseph **Byrd** before 22 June 1774 when the Surry County court ordered him to pay 3 pounds per annum in child support [Orders 1764-74, 380]. She was the mother of

15   i.   Squire^1, born 8 September 1768.

   ii.   ?William, born say 1776, taxable in Cabin Point District of Surry County from 1793 to 1802: his tax charged to William **Cypress** in 1793; listed with Squire Charity in 1802 [PPTL, 1791-1816, frame 107, 478], a "F.N." taxable in Isle of Wight County from 1803 to 1806 [PPTL 1782-1810, frames 618, 635, 694, 735].

   iii.   ?Joseph, born say 1780, a "F.N." taxable in Isle of Wight County from 1798 to 1800 [PPTL 1782-1810, frames 444, 509].

12. Jane Charity, born say 1758, a "poor Mulatto" daughter of Mary Charity, was ordered bound out in Surry County on 15 August 1758 and 16 December 1766 [Orders 1757-63, 123; 1764-74, 102-3]. She was the mother of

   i.   Nancy, born about 1780, registered as a "free Negro" in Surry County on 27 January 1802: *daughter of Jane Charity who was late resident of this county of a dark complexion, has a white spot on her left cheek, 5' high has short hair - aged about 22 years* [Back of Guardian Accounts Book 1783-1804, no.136]. She was over fifty-five years of age in 1830, head of a Surry County household of 3 "free colored" in 1830.

13. Wilson Charity, born about 1770, was taxable in the Cabin Point district of Surry County from 1787 to 1813: his tax charged to Henry Charity in 1790; charged with his own tax starting in 1791; listed with Henry Charity in 1794; charged with his own tax from 1795 to 1804; taxable on 2 tithes in 1805, 1806 and 1807; listed with 3 "free Negroes & Mulattoes" above the age of sixteen in 1813 [PPTL, 1782-90, frames 446, 596; 1791-1816, frames 8, 158, 234, 287, 366, 444, 519, 590, 611, 629, 649, 733]. He married Susanna **Monroe**, 27 December 1787 Surry County bond, William **Walden** surety. On 9 January 1796 he registered as a "free Negro" in Surry County: *son of Henry Charity a resident of this County, a bright mulattoe man aged about 25 years, pretty well made, short hair, 5'10" high, born of free parents* [Back of Guardian Accounts Book 1783-1804, no.15]. He married second, Clary Charity, 9 February 1796 Surry County bond, Sampson Granthum surety. He was the father of

16   i.   James, born about 1788.

14. Mary^2 Charity, born say 1775, married Peter **Blizzard**, 30 September 1791 Surry County bond, William C. Partain surety. Her child born before her marriage was

i. Mason Charity, born say 1790, "daughter of Mary Blizzard," married John Charity, 28 June 1808 Surry County bond, Peter **Blizzard** bondsman.

15. Squire[1] Charity, born 8 September 1768, "orphan of Ann Charity decd.," was ordered bound an apprentice by the Surry County court on 23 July 1782 [Orders 1775-85, 157]. He was taxable in Surry County from 1787 to 1813: a 16-21-year-old taxable in the household of (his brother?) Henry Charity in 1787; charged with his own tax in 1791; charged with William Charity's tax in 1802; taxable on a slave named Dolly over the age of sixteen in 1803; taxable on 2 slaves in 1805 and 1806; 4 slaves in 1807; 2 free males, 2 slaves and 2 horses in 1809 and 1810; 3 free males and 2 slaves in 1811 and 1812; 4 free males and 5 "free Negroes & Mulattoes" in 1813 [PPTL, 1782-90, frames 449, 471, 549, 596; 1791-1816, frame 8, 77, 128, 208, 254, 286, 322, 365, 403, 443, 478, 519, 558, 611, 629, 649, 667, 686, 706, 732]. He married Lucy **Elliott**, 25 April 1791 Surry County bond, Henry Charity surety, 26 April marriage by Rev. Samuel Butler, Rector of Southwark Parish, Episcopal Church [Ministers' Returns, 32]. He was head of a Surry County household of 9 "other free" and a slave in 1810 [VA:603], taxable that year on 67 acres in Surry County [Property Tax Alterations]. He registered in Surry County on 24 December 1821: *a free man of Colour aged 53 years the 8th day of September last, is 5'6-3/4" high of yellow Complexion* [Hudgins, *Surry County Register of Free Negroes*, 74]. The inventory of his estate was recorded in Surry County in 1838 [Wills, Etc. 7:478-480]. He and Lucy were the parents of
   i. Squire[2], born in January 1796, registered in Surry County on 21 December 1817: *a son of Squire Charity and Lucy, his wife of Surry County, free people of Colour the said Squire Charity is about 22 years old next January 1818 is of a bright Complexion, has a large nose, tolerable straight and Stout made and has straight hair...is 5'3-3/8" high.*
   ii. Park, born 6 August 1797, registered in Surry County on 24 August 1818: *a Mulattoe Man, the son of Squire Charity and Lucy his wife free person of Colour of this County, aged 21 years the 6th day of August instant is 5'9-1/4" high, of bright complexion streight and well made, thin Visage, and prominent lips.*
   iii. Hamlin, born 8 October 1804, registered in Surry County on 26 December 1825: *a Son of Squire Charity, was born free, aged 21 years, the 8 October 1825, of a bright complexion, straight hair, 5'7-1/4" high.*
   iv. Henry[3], born 25 January 1792, registered in Surry County on 26 January 1813: *son of Squire Charity & Lucy, his Wife of Surry County, free people of Colour...is said by his Father to have been 21 years old the 25th this Instant (Ja^y) is of a bright complexion, has a flat Nose, tolerable straight & long hair, for one of colour...is stout made & rather knock-knee'd - is 5'7" high* [Hudgins, *Surry County Register of Free Negroes*, 49, 68, 69, 81].

16. James Charity, born about 1788, registered in Surry County on 24 February 1812: *son of Wilson Charity a free Mulattoe man of Surry County, aged about 24 years, or there abouts, is 5'8-3/4" high, very long hair, long pekid face, (sharp) nose, his hair grows low in his fore head* [Hudgins, *Surry County Register of Free Negroes*, 48]. He was taxable in Charles City County in 1809 and a "Mulattoe" taxable there in 1813 and 1814 [PPTL 1809-23]. He purchased ten barrels of corn for $43 at the sale of the Charles City County estate of John Royall on 10 February 1823 [WB 2:551, 552]. He was the father of

    i.   Archer, born 18 September 1814, registered in Charles City County on 17 December 1835: *son of James Charity, a mulatto man, 21 years of age ye 18 September 1835* [Orders 1830-9, 257].

    ii. Littleton, born 19 April 1816, registered in Charles City County on 21 December 1837: *son of James Charity, 21 years of age 19 April last, mulatto man* [Orders 1830-9, 337].

    iii. Walker, born in August 1818, registered in Charles City County on 21 December 1837: *son of James Charity, 19 years of age August last, mulatto man* [Orders 1830-9, 337].

CHAVIS FAMILY

1.   Thomas[1] Chivers, born say 1627, was appointed to a jury of twelve men in Isle of Wight County on 28 July 1658 to determine whether 900 acres belonged to Major Nicholas Hill or to John Snollock [*VMHB* V:406]. He purchased 1,100 acres of land at the head of Sunken Marsh near Chipoakes Creek in Surry County, Virginia, on 20 May 1659 for two cows, payment of 4,000 pounds of tobacco in October that year, and payment of 4,000 pounds of tobacco in October 1660. He died sometime before 13 April 1664 when his daughter Elizabeth was bound out until she came of age [DW 1:151; Haun, *Surry County Court Records*, I:149; II:232]. His children were

    i.   Elizabeth[1], born say 1648, bound apprentice to Robert Cartwright on 13 April 1664. Cartwright agreed to pay the securities for the indenture, Thomas Flood and Ben Harrison, one three-year-old mare at the conclusion of the apprenticeship. She was probably the ancestor of the **Gibson** family. She was called Elizabeth Chavis on 28 March 1672 when she made a successful petition to the General Court of Virginia to release her son Gibson **Gibson** who had been unlawfully bound by Berr. Mercer to Thomas Barber who had gone to England leaving the boy with Samuel Austin [Minutes of the Council 1670-76, 106, Virginia Historical Society Mss 4V81935a2; McIlwaine, *Minutes of the Council*, 302-3]. She died before 6 August 1681 according to the Surry County deed by which her brother sold land which descended to them by their father's will [DW 2:297].

    ii. _____, born say 1650, another sister of William who was said to have died before 6 August 1681 when William sold land descended to them by their father's will [DW 2:297].

2   iii. William[1], born say 1654.

2.   William[1] Chivers (Thomas[1]), born say 1654, was called "orphan of Thomas Chivers" on 14 July 1672 when he chose William Carpenter for his guardian in the Surry County court [Haun, *Surry County Court Records*, III:127]. Sometime in 1675 or 1676 the executor of the estate of Robert Cartwright, deceased, paid William Carpenter 600 pounds of tobacco to discharge the claims of the "Chivers" orphans against the estate. In 1677 he was a tithable in William Carpenter's household in the upper end of Southwarke Parish [DW 2:222, 264], and in 1679 and 1680 he was listed as a tithable in Carpenter's Sunken Marsh household:

Wm Carpenter Wm Knot Wm Shivers Saml Pawlett & Eliz Blyth 5

and by 1681 he was taxable in his own household [DW 2:346, 416, 453]. He was called William Shivers, planter, on 6 August 1681 when he sold 200 acres in Surry County, explaining in the deed that the land descended to him and his sisters by his father's will, that his sisters had since died and that he was living on a plantation of 400 acres. Between 1682 and 1691 he sold the remainder of the 1,100 acres he had inherited by his father's 8 February 1663 will (which has not survived). He had married Elizabeth by 5 September 1682 when she released her dower rights to the land which was located in Southwarke Parish about a mile from James River on Sunken Marsh [DW 2:297, 310-2, 330, 342-3; 3:29; 4:254; Haun, *Surry County Court Records*, III:383; IV:412, 425, 485]. Elizabeth may have been Elizabeth **Blyth**, a taxable in Carpenter's 1679 household. William was a head of household in Sunken Marsh District of Surry County, taxable on one tithe in 1689 [*Magazine of Virginia Genealogy*, vol. 23, no.3, 54]. He was reported to have left the county by 8 August 1690 when William Norwood was required to deliver what he had of his estate to the sheriff to pay William's debts [Haun, *Surry County Court Records* IV:766, 767]. On 26 August 1690 Benjamin Harrison complained that William Chivers was indebted to him [D&W 4:153]. William was called William Shivers of Southwarke Parish (Surry County) on 6 October 1691 when he sold Benjamin Harrison the last 60 acres of the land willed to him by his father [D&W 4:254, 309]. He may have been the father of

3   i.   Thomas² Shivers, born say 1682.
4   ii.   ?Bartholomew¹, born say 1685.
     iii.   ?___, born say 1700, mother of John Chavis **Walden** whose estate inventory was presented in Brunswick County, Virginia, on 2 September 1761 [WB 4:265]. See the **Walden** history.

3.   Thomas² Shivers (William¹, Thomas¹), born say 1682, was a taxable in John Griffin's Surry County household in the upper precinct of Southwarke Parish from 1700 to 1702 [*Magazine of Virginia Genealogy*, vol.24, no.2, 81, no.3, 68, 74]. He may have been the father or grandfather of

5   i.   William³, born say 1709.
6   ii.   Amy, born say 1710.
7   iii.   Thomason, born say 1720.
8   iv.   Frances¹, born say 1720.
9   v.   Rebecca¹, born say 1721.
10   vi.   George¹, born say 1728.
11   vii.   Menoah, born say 1730.
12   viii.   Sarah, born say 1732.
13   ix.   Catherine, born say 1734.
14   x.   Henry¹, born say 1735.
     xi.   Gilbert, born say 1738, "a mulatto bastard boy," no parent named when he was bound apprentice to John Simmons in Prince George County on 9 May 1738 [Orders 1737-40, 105]. He was taxable in Prince George County from 1799 to 1802, called Gibb Chavis a "dark man" in 1800 and a "Mulatto" in 1801 and 1802 [PPTL, 1782-1811, frames 485, 507, 530, 551].

4.   Bartholomew¹ Chavis (William¹, Thomas¹), born say 1685, was living in Henrico County on 1 March 1707 when he recorded his cattle mark in court. On 2 September 1708 he sued Francis **Scott** for trespass, and on 1 October 1708 Thomas **Evans** sued him for a 6 pound debt. He had left the county by 1 November 1708 when Evans attached his estate which consisted of a stallion branded "BC," a bed blanket and some corn in the field [Orders 1707-9, 28, 74, 92]. He was sued for trespass by Ruth Parker in Surry County, Virginia court on 15 October 1712. The suit was dismissed when neither party appeared at the next session on 29 November 1712, and on the same day a suit against him for debt by Robert Rogers was dismissed when neither party appeared [Orders 1701-13, 405-6, 408]. And neither party appeared again in 1714 when he was sued for debt in Surry County court by Arthur Kavanaugh [Orders 1713-18, 32]. He was in North Carolina on 1 March 1719/20 when he received a patent for 300 acres on the north side of the Roanoke River near Urahaw Swamp in what was then Chowan County but became Bertie County in 1722 and Northampton County in 1741 [Hoffman, *Province of North Carolina Land Patents*, 281]. On 1 September 1721 he bought another tract

of land adjacent to his own between Wheeler's Mill and Urahaw Swamp. This land was near the **Bass** and **Gibson** families. He and his wife Martha sold 100 acres of their land near Urahaw Swamp on 30 March 1722/3 [DB C-1:1482]. By 30 July 1726 he had accumulated over one thousand acres on the north side of the Roanoke and another 630 acres on the south side in what later became Halifax County.[68]

In 1727 he made a deed of gift of land on the south side of the Roanoke to his son William [Bertie DB B:289]. He was one of the "Gentlemen of Edgecombe Precinct" who signed a petition to alter the seat of government from Edenton to present-day Raleigh [Saunders, *Colonial Records of North Carolina*, VII:298-9]. He was still living in Northampton County in 1743 when a deed mentioned land adjoining Bat Chavers [DB 1:127]. He died before 25 February 1750 when his son William sold his 630 acres on Quankey Pocosin, "a grant to Barth Chavers late of Albemarle County" [Edgecombe DB 3:36]. His children were

15	i.	William[2], born say 1706.
16	ii.	?Jacob[1] Shives, born say 1710.
17	iii.	?John[1], born say 1712.
	iv.	?Matthew[1], born say 1715, applied for a warrant for 300 acres in South Carolina in 1752 explaining that he was a "free negro" and had been in the province for twelve years [*JNH* V:74].
18	v.	?Thomas[3], born say 1718.
19	vi.	?Richard, born say 1724.
20	vii.	?Joseph[1] Cheavers, born say 1726.
21	viii.	?Bartholomew[2], born say 1730.
	ix.	?Gideon[1], born say 1732, "a free Negroe Man Called Gideon" who was sentenced to receive thirty-nine lashes at the whipping post in Chowan County in July 1753 for assaulting Constable John Ross "in the Execution of his office." He was called Gideon Chavers in January and April 1754 in his Chowan County court suit against John Perry [Haun, *Chowan County Court Minutes*, III:207, 232, 243]. He died before September court, 1769 when Jane Marshall was granted administration on his Chowan County estate. He was probably related to a seven-year-old "base born Mulatoe" named Betty Chavers who was bound out by the court to William Halsey on 19 March 1772 [Minutes 1766-72, 476-7, 488, 508, 655]. And he may have been the father of Drury Chavers who enlisted as a soldier in Bailey's Company of the North Carolina Line in Edenton on 25 May 1781 and left the service on 25 May 1782 [N.C. DAR, *Roster of Soldiers from N.C. in the Revolution*, 115-6].

5.   William[3] Chavis (Thomas[2], William[1], Thomas[1]), born say 1709, was a "Free Mulatto," who still had two years of service to complete his indenture on 15

---

[68]Grantee Deeds:

1 Mar 1719 300 acres north of Roanoke.

9 Sep 1722 540 acres north of Roanoke [Hoffman, *Province of N.C. Land Patents*, 281, 180].

1 Sep 1721   north of Roanoke [Chowan DB C-1:154].

1 Sep 1721 640 acres north of Roanoke [DB C-1:1383].

30 Jul 1726 630 acres south of Roanoke [mentioned in Bertie DB B:289].

Grantor Deeds:

4 Nov 1726 430 acres south of Roanoke [Bertie DB B:312].

     1727 200 acres south of Roanoke [Bertie DB:289].

30 Mar 1722 100 acres north of Roanoke [Chowan DB C-1:1482].

10 May 1728 100 acres north of Roanoke [Bertie DB B:423].

1 Nov 1730 200 acres north of Roanoke [Bertie DB C:293].

July 1728 when he was listed in the inventory of the Surry County estate of Nathaniel Harrison [DW 7:850]. (His father?) Thomas Shivers was a neighbor of Nathaniel Harrison in the list of tithables for the upper precincts of Surry County in 1701 [*Magazine of Virginia Genealogy*, vol.24, 3:68]. He may have been the William Chaver who married Rebecca **Gillet** on 8 July 1730 in Christ Church Parish, Middlesex County [NSCDA, *Parish Register of Christ Church*, 167]. And he may have been the William Chavis who was a plaintiff in a 22 July 1758 suit in Sussex County court for a 50 shillings debt [Orders 1757-61, 188]. He owned some property in Brunswick County, Virginia, on 27 May 1760 when it was attached to pay a debt he owed Gray Briggs [Orders 1760-84, 42, 43]. He may have been the father of

22   i.   John[3], born say 1740.

6. Amy Chavis (Thomas[2], William[1], Thomas[1]), born say 1710, was presented by the Surry County court on 21 May 1729 for having a bastard child. She was living in Southwarke Parish, Surry County, between 16 May 1749 and 20 June 1749 when she was fined 50 shillings and given twenty-five lashes for having a bastard child [DW 1715-30, 928; Orders 1744-49, 543, 559]. She may have been the same Amy Chavers who was subpoenaed for the plaintiff in the suit of the King vs. John McWilliams in the January 1766 Halifax County, North Carolina court [Gammon, *Record of Estates* II:2]. And she may have been the mother of

        i.   Benjamin[1], born say 1729, owed Richard Vick a debt of 3 pounds due by account in Southampton County on 14 March 1755 [Orders 1754-9, 68], listed in the Edgecombe County, North Carolina muster of militia in the 1750s [N.C. Archives Troop Returns, box 1, folder 12, last page], taxable with his wife Jane in the 1757 Granville County list of Robert Harris and an insolvent taxpayer that year.

        ii.   William[4], born say 1739, ran away from his master Thomas Burgess and was ordered by the Southampton County court to serve him an additional sixteen weeks on 11 December 1755 [Orders 1754-9, 166].

23   iii.   Mary, born say 1745.

       iv.   Winny, born say 1755, mother of Milly Chavis who sued for her freedom in February 1828 claiming that she was stolen from her mother in Brunswick County about forty or fifty years before when she was six or seven years old [Catterall, *Judicial Cases Concerning American Slavery*, I:151]. James Arthur released Milly and her daughter Nancy from slavery in Pittsylvania County on 16 January 1829 [Griffith, *Pittsylvania County Register*, 246].

7. Frances[1] Chavis (Thomas[2], William[1], Thomas[1]), born say 1720, was living in Charles City County on 5 February 1755 when the court ordered the churchwardens of Westover Parish to bind out her son William. She may also have been the mother of ___ Chavis who William Hudson petitioned the churchwardens to bind apprentice to him in June 1742 [Orders 1737-51, 217; 1751-7, 178]. Her children were

24   i.   ?Jacob[2], born about 1736.

25   ii.   ?Susannah[1], born about 1740.

26 iii.   ?Margaret, born say 1742.

       iv.   William[6], born say 1747, bound apprentice in Charles City County in February 1755.

8. Thomason[1] Chavis (Thomas[2], William[1], Thomas[1]), born say 1720, was living in Lunenburg County, Virginia, in June 1752 when the churchwardens of Cumberland Parish were ordered to bind out her "Base born children" Elizabeth, Abraham, James, and Peter [Orders 1752-3, 56]. Her children were

        i.   ?Isaac[1], born say 1737, sued John Ashwell for a 2 pound debt in Lunenburg County in July 1764 [Orders 1764-5, 103].

      ii. ?Findwell, born say 1739, mother of Nancy Chavis who was bound to Samuel Manning by the churchwardens of St. James Parish in Mecklenburg County, Virginia, on 18 September 1766 [Orders 1765-8, 212]. She may have been the Nancy Chavous who married Charles **Voluntine** (**Valentine**), 28 November 1785 Mecklenburg County bond, Thomas **Maclin** security.

27   iii. ?Susannah², born say 1740.

28   iv. Elizabeth², born say 1742.

      v. Abraham, born say 1743.

29   vi. James¹, born say 1745.

     vii. Peter¹, born say 1750.

9.   Rebecca¹ Chaves (Thomas², William¹, Thomas¹), born say 1721, was a resident of Bristol Parish, Prince George County, on 11 November 1734 (no race or parent indicated) when she was bound out to John West and (her sister?) Sarah Chaves was bound to William Macewen [Chamberlayne, *Register of Bristol Parish,* 71]. Amelia County was formed in 1734 from the part of Prince George County where John West and William Macewen were living, and John West, Sr., was a tithable there in the list of tithables below Deep Creek adjacent to John West, Sr., in 1736 [Tax List, Amelia County Courthouse]. In 1740 she was tithable in West's household, called Beck Chivers [1736 and 1740 Tax List, Amelia County Courthouse], and on 19 September 1740 the churchwardens of Raleigh Parish, Amelia County, were ordered to bind out her son Adam Chaves (no race mentioned). On 26 August 1756 the Amelia County court ordered the churchwardens of Nottoway Parish to bind out her children Betty and Pat; on 22 March 1759 the court ordered the churchwardens to bind out her unnamed children, and on 28 August 1760 she was called a "Free Negro" when the court ordered the churchwardens of Nottoway Parish to bind out her children James, Ned, Patt, and Rebecca [Orders 1735-46, 125; 1754-8, n.p.; 1757-60, 195; 1760-3, 44]. A few months later in December 1760 the Lunenburg County court ordered the churchwardens of Cumberland Parish to bind out her son Ned [Orders 1759-60, 211]. The Amelia County court ordered the churchwardens of Nottoway Parish to bind out her children Cain and Sherred on 24 March 1763, ordered her children Patt, Beck, and Molly bound out in 1764, and ordered her unnamed children bound out on 29 April 1768 [Orders 1763, 30; 1764-5, 87, 289, 325; 1766-9, 149]. Her children were

      i. Adam, born say 1738, "Child of Rebecca Chavis," ordered bound out by the Amelia County court on 19 September 1740, ordered bound out by the churchwardens of Nottoway Parish on 26 July 1754, no parent named, and ordered bound to Richard Rogers on 27 November 1755 [Orders 1735-46, 125; 1751-5, 185; 1754-8, n.p.].

     ii. ?Lydia¹, born say 1739, ordered bound out in Amelia County on 19 March 1741 (no parent named). She was living in Nottoway Parish, Amelia County, on 24 March 1763 when the court ordered the churchwardens to bind out her son David [Orders 1735-46, 96; 1763, 30]. The Mecklenburg County court ordered the churchwardens of St. James Parish to bind David (no parent named) to John M. Luce on 10 October 1768 [Orders 1768-71, 129].

     iii. Kate, born say 1746, daughter of Rebecca Chaves (no race indicated), ordered bound apprentice by the churchwardens of Raleigh Parish, Amelia County, in January 1746/7 on the motion of David Ellington. She was called "Cate Chavis a poor child" on 28 July 1763 when the court ordered the churchwardens of Nottoway Parish to bind her out [Orders 1746-51, 29; 1763, fol. 102].

     iv. Lucy, born before November 1747, "Daughter of Rebecca Chavis" (no race indicated), bound apprentice in Amelia County in November 1747. She was called "Lucy Chavis a Free Negro" on 26 June 1760 when the

Amelia County court ordered the churchwardens of Nottoway Parish to remove her from her former master David Ellington and bind her instead to William Hilsman [Orders 1746-51, 57; 1760-3, 16].

30   v.   James[2], born say 1749.

        vi.   Edward[1]/ Ned, born before January 1749/50, bound by the churchwardens of Nottoway Parish, Amelia County, in January 1749/50 (no parent or race indicated). On 24 November 1757 the Amelia County court summoned David Ellington to answer the complaint of Ned and Lucy Chavis, "poor orphans" who were bound to him, and on 22 December 1757 he was called "Ned Chavis a free Negro Boy" when the court bound him instead to William Hardy. He was called the child of Rebecca Chavis on 28 August 1760 when the court ordered the churchwardens of Amelia County to bind him out [Orders 1746-51, 192; 1757-60, 36, 45; 1760-3, 44]. A few months later in December 1760, he was living in adjoining Lunenburg County when he was ordered bound out by the churchwardens of Cumberland Parish [Orders 1759-60, 211]. He was bound out again on 13 December 1764 to Michael McKie (no parent named) [Orders 1764-65, 199]. He served in the Revolution [Eckenrode, *List of the Revolutionary Soldiers of Virginia*, 324]. He was tithable in Charlotte County in 1783 [PPTL 1782-1813, frame 20] and tithable in Mecklenburg County, Virginia, from 1786 to 1799 [PPTL 1782-1805, frames 122, 368, 411, 634].

31   vii.   Elizabeth[3], born say 1751.

    viii.   Pat, born say 1754, a child of Rebecca Chavis, ordered bound out on in Amelia County on 28 August 1760, called a "free Negro" on 23 March 1764 when the court ordered the churchwardens of Nottoway Parish to bind her out [Orders 1760-3, 44; 1764-5, 87].

      ix.   Rebecca[2], born say 1756, a child of Rebecca Chavis, ordered bound out in Amelia County on 28 August 1760, called a "free Negro" on 23 March 1764 when the court ordered the churchwardens of Nottoway Parish to bind her out, and called an orphan of Beck Chavis on 22 November 1764 when the court ordered her bound to Henry Clay [Orders 1760-3, 44; 1764-5, 87, 289, 325]. She may have been the Rebecca Chavis who sued John for trespass, assault, and battery in Mecklenburg County, Virginia, on 14 March 1786 [Orders 1784-87, 496, 595, 699].

       x.   Molly, born say 1758, called an orphan of Beck Chavis on 22 November 1764 when the Amelia County court ordered her bound to Henry Clay [Orders 1764-5, 289, 325].

      xi.   ?Tammy, born say 1760, living in Amelia County on 28 August 1760 when the court ordered the churchwardens of Nottoway Parish to bind her to John Clark [Orders 1760-3, 55].

     xii.   Cain, born say 1761, son of Beck Chavis ordered bound by the churchwardens of Nottoway Parish in Amelia County on 24 March 1763 [Orders 1763, 30].

    xiii.   Sherwood, born say 1763, son of Beck Chavis ordered bound by the churchwardens of Nottoway Parish in Amelia County on 24 March 1763 [Orders 1763, 30]. No parent was named when he was ordered bound out by the churchwardens of St. James Parish to John M. Luce in Mecklenburg County on 10 October 1768 [Orders 1768-71, 129].

10.   George[1] Chavers (Thomas[2], William[1], Thomas[1]), born say 1728, was a taxable in the 1752 Lunenburg County list of Field Jefferson in his own household adjoining Robert Hudson [Tax List 1748-52, Virginia State Library Accession no.20094, p.2] and taxable in Ephraim Drew's household in the 1775 list [Bell, *Sunlight on the Southside*, 353]. He was one of the freeholders of Lunenburg County who were ordered to clear and maintain a road in their area

in September 1756 [Orders 1755-57, 187]. He and George Carter received a patent for 354 acres in Brunswick County on 20 August 1760 [Patents 34:698]. The 1 November 1766 session of the Brunswick County, Virginia court recorded payment to him of 150 pounds of tobacco from the public levy for providing 75 ells of cloth [Orders 1765-8, 190]. While a resident of Mecklenburg County on 22 December 1781 he sold 100 acres in "the upper end" of Brunswick County, Virginia, on Jeryes Creek [Brunswick WB 2:228]. He was taxable in Mecklenburg County on 8 cattle in 1784, taxable on a horse and 9 cattle in 1787 and 1788. His estate was taxable on 2 horses in 1789 [PPTL 1782-1805, frames 90, 95, 189, 235, 285]. His children may have been

    i.   Milden, born say 1751, purchased 50 acres adjoining James Bowen in Mecklenburg County on 14 June 1779 and sold this land for 50 pounds on 25 March 1785 [DB 5:451; 6:503]. He was sued for a debt of 1,000 pounds of tobacco in Mecklenburg County court on 16 March 1787 [Orders 1784-87, 703]. He was head of a Mecklenburg County household of 7 persons in 1782 [VA:34], taxable in Mecklenburg County on 2 horses from 1783 to 1794 [PPTL 1782-1805, frames 45, 95, 398, 498]. The attachment of Henry Chavis against Milden abated on 12 November 1798 by Henry's death [Orders 1798-1801, 61].

32   ii.   John[5], born say 1755.

33   iii.   Anthony, born say 1757.

    iv.   ____, a sister of John Chavis, married Charles **Watts** according to the testimony of Thomas **Evans** [Mecklenburg County Legislative Petitions of 14 December 1820 and 19 January 1836, LVA]. Charles registered in Petersburg on 16 August 1794: *a light Mulatto man, forty five years old, five feet seven inches high, born free in the county of Prince George* [Register of Free Negroes 1794-1819, no. 7]. He was taxable in Petersburg on two slaves and three horses in 1799 [1799 PPTL, B p.12]. He was probably related to Daniel **Watts**, head of a Norfolk County household of 7 "other free" in 1810 [VA:814].

    v.   Thomas[5], born say 1765, married Nancy **Thaxton**, 27 January 1786 Charlotte County bond, William Dabbs surety, 3 February marriage by Rev. Thomas Johnston [Minister's Returns, 90]. He was taxable in Charlotte County from 1787 to 1795 and from 1801 to 1813: taxable on a horse in 1789, listed as a "fn" planter in 1805 and 1806 [PPTL 1782-1813, frames 93, 126, 159, 190, 216, 240, 264, 288, 327, 516, 550, 586, 621, 648, 654, 682, 756, 788, 821, 852, 895]. He was taxable on 2 horses in Halifax County, Virginia, in 1798 [PPTL, 1782-1799, frame 769] and a "Free Negro" head of a Charlotte County household of 5 "other free" in 1810 [VA:68]. His wife Nancy was probably the Nancy Chavous who registered in Charlotte County on 2 August 1824: *Bright complexion, aged 60, born free* [Ailsworth, *Charlotte County--Rich Indeed*, 489].

11. Menoah/ Noah Chavis (Thomas[2], William[1], Thomas[1]), born say 1730, was taxable in Henry County from 1783 to 1788 [PPTL, 1782-1830, frames 30, 77, 147, 265, 279]. In his 19 January 1789 Henry County will, proved 30 November 1789, he mentioned David **Going** and left 100 acres to his children [WB 1:180]:

    i.   Patty **Earl**, perhaps the Martha Chavers who was taxable on a horse in Henry County in 1790 [PPTL, 1782-1830, frame 338].

    ii.   Nancy Bigers **Earl**.

12. Sarah Chaves (Thomas[2], William[1], Thomas[1]), born say 1732, was bound to William Macewen of Prince George County in November 1734 [Chamberlayne, *Register of Bristol Parish,* 71]. She may have been identical to Sarah Chavers who was head of a Charlotte County household of 1 "other free" in 1810 [VA:46]. She was called Sally Chavus in her 17 May 1811

Charlotte County will, proved 3 December 1811, by which she left furniture, a flax wheel and a spinning wheel to her granddaughter Betsey Chavus, a dutch oven to her son Bartlett Chavus's unnamed wife, and the remainder to her friends John Fennell and Thomas Friend. She asked that Fennell and Friend let "her old man and husband" Simon enjoy his liberty as a free man and allow him to keep together all the remainder of her estate. At Simon's death, the remainder was to be sold with one-third to go to Simon's daughter Amy and two-thirds to her son Bartlett "or his children if he be dead" [WB 3:184]. She was the mother of

    i. Bartlett[2], one of two Bartlett Chavuses taxable in the southern district of Halifax County, Virginia, from 1801 to 1806, perhaps the one who married Betsy **Talbot**, 11 July 1803 Halifax County bond.

13. Catherine Chavis (Thomas[2], William[1], Thomas[1]), born say 1734, was a "Mullatto Girl" bound apprentice in Henrico County, Virginia, in July 1740 (no parent named) [Orders 1737-46, 113]. She was probably the same Catherine Chavis who was living in Lunenburg County in October 1756 when the churchwardens of Cumberland Perish were ordered to bind out her children Sam, Lucy, and Ann Chavus. In November 1757 the churchwardens of Cornwall Parish were ordered to bind her children Nan and Lucy to Philip Jones [Orders 1755-57, 223; 1757-9, 3]. Her children were

    i. Samuel, born say 1751, a "Melatto boy" (no parent named) bound apprentice to Philip Jones by the churchwardens of Cumberland Parish in Lunenburg County in April 1751 [Orders 1748-52, 396]. On 13 October 1783 the Mecklenburg County, Virginia court ordered his male laboring tithables to work on a road [Orders 1779-84, 437]. He was head of a Mecklenburg County household of 7 white (free) persons in 1782 [VA:34] and taxable in Mecklenburg County in 1788 [PPTL 1782-1805, frame 211]. On 20 May 1788 he was tried in the Mecklenburg County court for entering the smoke house of David Ross at night and taking a quantity of bacon valued at 10 shillings but found not guilty [Orders 1787-92, 232-6]. In 1789 he was taxable in the Dinwiddie County household of Matthew **Stewart** and taxable in his own Dinwiddie County household in 1790, 1800, a "free Negro" taxable who followed "cropping" and lived near David Browder in 1801 and a "free" taxable in 1802 [PPTL, 1790 A, p.3; 1790 A, p.3; 1801 B, p.25; 1802 A, p.4]. He was taxable in Lunenburg County in 1798 [PPTL 1782-1806] and counted in the "list of free Negroes and Mulattoes" in Mecklenburg County from 1813 to 1815 [PPTL, 1806-28, frames 307, 417, 435].

    ii. Lucy, born say 1753, perhaps the Lucy Chavers who married Robert **Cole**, "both black persons," according to the deposition of Mary Belcher of Charlotte County, Virginia, taken on 27 April 1808. Belcher testified on Lucy's behalf when she challenged the nuncupative Wake County will of her nephew John **Jackson** Chavis, son of her sister Betty Chavis [N.C. Stack File C.R. 099.928.11 by *NCGSJ* III:21]. Lucy was living in Mecklenburg County when she gave power of attorney to "friend and relation" John Chavis of Raleigh to challenge the will. She challenged the will herself in Wake County court in May 1808. Frederick **Ivey** and Peter Chavis also testified on her behalf [Haun, *Wake County Court Minutes* VII:67-8, 151]. Lucy proved the account of his Wake County estate in February 1809 [N.C. Stack File C.R. 099.928.11 by *NCGSJ* III:21].

    iii. Ann, born say 1755.

34   iv. ?Elizabeth[4], born say 1757.

14. Henry[1] Chavers (Thomas[2], William[1], Thomas[1]), born say 1735, was a Lunenburg County taxable in the list of Hugh Lawson in 1752 (called Henry

Cheffers) [Tax List 1748-52, 2] and taxable in 1764 adjacent to Jacob Chavis [Bell, *Sunlight on the Southside*, 248]. He was sued for debt by Richard Hanson in Lunenburg County court on 9 June 1768, but the suit was dismissed because he was not living in the county [Orders 1766-69, 151]. And he was sued in Brunswick County, Virginia court on 29 September 1772, but the suit was dismissed for the same reason [Orders 1772-74, 117]. He mortgaged eight head of cattle, eleven pigs, a mare, and his furniture for 25 pounds he owed to Dinwiddie Crawford, & Co., merchants of Glasgow, in Mecklenburg County on 9 April 1774 [DB 4:319; Orders 1774-9, 191]. He was head of a Mecklenburg County household of 8 persons in 1782 [VA:33] and was taxable there on 2 horses and 3-5 head of cattle from 1782 to 1798 [PPTL 1782-1805, frames 14, 45, 95, 236, 288, 341, 570, 681]. His 25 May 1798 will was proved 10 September 1798. He lent 50 acres to his wife Elender and their daughter Rebecca, to revert to his son Boling at their deaths and left the remainder of his land to his son Henry [WB 4:40]. Elender, Boling, and (Boling's wife) Susan Chavous mortgaged this 50 acres to Thomas Organ on 10 January 1804 for a 29 pound debt they owed Benjamin Lewis [DB 12:181]. Elender was a "mulatto" taxable on a horse in Mecklenburg County in 1810 [PPTL, 1806-28, frame 159]. Henry[1]'s children were

    i.   Henry[3], Jr., born say 1766, taxable in Mecklenburg County from 1786 to 1803: taxable on his son Burton in 1803 [PPTL 1782-1805, frames 136, 189, 399, 479, 570, 681, 942]. His daughter Sine was mentioned in her grandfather's will. She married Buckner **Valentine**, 21 December 1802 Mecklenburg County bond, Boling Chavous security. Henry received the balance of his father's land. On 21 November 1799 he brought a suit in chancery to enjoin Ellender, Rebecca and Boling Chavis from cutting down any more of the lands or committing waste on the land they received by Henry, Sr.'s will [Orders 1798-1801, 269]. Henry, Jr.'s own 5 January 1806 Mecklenburg County will, proved 8 September the same year, lent his land and property to his wife Luviecie and then to her son Wyatt **Singleton** [WB 5:443]. A deed from Lucretia Chavers, Wyatt **Singleton** and Anne Chisman(?) his wife was proved in Mecklenburg County court on 17 June 1811 [Orders 1809-11, 469].

    ii.   Rebecca[5].

35   iii.   Boling, born say 1772.

    iv.   Susannah/Suckee, born say 1773, married Frederick **Goen**, 9 March 1789 Mecklenburg County bond with a note from her father Henry Chavers, Sr., Belar (Boling) Chavous, and Robert Singleton witnesses.[69]

15.   William[2] Chavis (Bartholomew[1], William[1], Thomas[1]), born say 1706, received a deed of gift from his father in 1727 for land in Bertie County on the south side of the Roanoke River near the Quankey Pocosin in what became Edgecombe County in 1741 and Halifax County in 1758 [DB B:289]. He proved his rights for 15 "Blacks" in Edgecombe County in February 1742 [SS 906 by *N.C. Genealogy* XIII:1825] and received a patent for 400 acres near Nutbush Creek in Edgecombe County on 3 March 1743 [Hoffman, *Land Patents,* I:223]. In 1746 this part of Edgecombe became Granville County where he accumulated more than twelve hundred acres of land by 14 May 1751. On 29 November 1748 he was granted a license to keep an ordinary at his dwelling house in Granville County. He was mentioned in the 30 May 1753 Granville County court case of Rex vs. Samuel Harden. Complainant

---

[69]Robert **Singleton** may have been identical to the one who was head of a Prince Edward County household of 4 persons in 1782 [VA:42], and a Robert **Singleton** married Polly **Thomason**, 30 December 1795 Mecklenburg County bond.

Henry Webb stated that Chavis, the owner of a lodging house, kept part of Webb's money in his desk for safe keeping, but Samuel Harden stole the remainder of his money from him. When Webb asked Chavers to help search Harden for the money, Chavers told him

> *I am a Black man & don't care to undertake such a thing* [Owen, *Granville County Notes*, vols. I, III].

In 1753 William was taxable in Granville County on himself, his 2 children, and 7 slaves in the list of John Brantly, and in 1754 he was taxable on 13 persons including his wife Frances in the list of Edward Moore:

> *Wm. Chavis Francis Gibeon William Jur. Lettis Geiser*
> *Francis Sons & Wife and Daughters   Negroes Gordin Peter*
> *Nune Frank Alice mol   13* [CR 44.701.19].

In March 1754 he brought the theft of Amy **Hawley**'s son Busby to the attention of the Orange County, North Carolina court. The child was stolen from South Carolina and recovered in Orange County. The court ordered Thomas Chavis to return him to his mother [Haun, *Orange County Court Minutes*, I:70-71]. He was called "William Chavers, Negro" in the 8 October 1754 Muster Roll of the Granville County Regiment of Colonel William Eaton [Clark, *Colonial Soldiers of the South*, 716]. His wife Frances was probably light skinned since in the same list his sons were called "William Chavers, jun., Mulatto," and "Gilbert Chavers, Mulatto." On 4 February 1755 William purchased 320 acres in Orange County and sold this on 27 August 1768 [DB 1:40; 2:549]. By 7 November 1763 he had acquired over 2,900 acres in Granville, Orange, and Edgecombe Counties.[70] On 10 May 1770 he appeared in court in Bute County complaining that he was afraid Asa **Tyner** planned to

---

[70]Grantee Deeds:

Aug 1727 200 acres South of Roanoke [Bertie DB B:289]
8 Mar 1743 400 acres Nutbush Creek [Hoffman, *Land Patents*, I:233]
15 Aug 1748 300 acres North of Tar River [Granville DB A:82]
14 May 1751 640 acres Sides of Tabbs Cr. [Granville DB B:409]
9 Nov 1751 335 acres West of Tabbs Cr. [Granville DB B:408]
4 Feb 1755 320 acres South of Flat R. [Orange DB 1:40]
9 May 1755 449 acres South Tabbs Creek [Granville]
24 Oct 1761 270 acres Sides of Collins Cr. [Granville DB E:396]
12 Nov 1761 276 acres North of Tar River [Granville DB E:329]
12 May 1762 647 acres Sides of Buffalo Cr [Granville DB E:323]
12 Aug 1762 700 acres South of Tar River [Granville DB E:401]
7 Nov 1762 170 acres North of Tar River [Granville DB F:507]

Grantor Deeds:

8 Feb 1745 400 acres Nutbush Creek [Edgecombe 5:452]
29 Nov 1748 200 acres North of Tabbs Cr [Granville DB A:66]
4 Mar 1752 300 acres North of Tar River [Granville DB B:47]
6 Sep 1756 340 acres North of Tabbs Cr. [Granville DB C:73]
20 Feb 1760 449 acres South of Tabbs Cr. [Granville DB D:25,26]
13 May 1762 237 acres North of Tar River [Granville DB E:322]
27 Aug 1768 320 acres South of Flat R. [Orange DB 2:549]
25 Oct 1770 300 acres east side of Buffulo Cr. [Warren DB 3:203]
30 Mar 1774 347 acres Sides of Buffalo Cr. [Warren DB 5:183]

do him some bodily harm or damage his estate.[71] This was the start of a series of court cases between him and **Tyner**. Asa **Tyner** also appeared as a witness against him in a case for John Smith [Minutes 1767-79, 128, 239]. Asa was William Chavis' son-in-law who married his daughter Keziah about 1765. She was taxable in her father's household in 1764 but not in 1766. Asa and "Cuzzah" **Tyner** sold 700 acres adjoining William Chavis, deceased, on the Granville-Bute County line on 11 August 1777 [Warren County DB 6:198].[72] Asa **Tyner** was a buyer at the sale of William's estate.

The inventory of William Chavis' estate was settled by his son Philip on 5 February 1778 in Granville County and included 11 slaves, 39 cattle, 6 horses, and 21 head of sheep [WB 1:164]. His wife Frances was taxable on a 2,551 pounds assessment in 1780 in Epping Forest District, and her estate was settled in May court 1781 by John Smith, her son by her first marriage.[73] He claimed his right to six slaves which were due him from his father after his mother's death. Frances' estate, which included a bible and slaves, was sold for 6,350 pounds [WB 1:303]. Frances was apparently the daughter of Gibby **Gibson** who left his daughter Frances Smith a girl slave named Verity by his 3 March 1726/7 Charles City County will [DW 1724-31, 161-2]. William's children were

36 i. Philip[1], born say 1726.

  ii. Sarah **Harris**, born before 1735, taxable in 1750 in the Granville County household of her husband Edward **Harris**. On 6 September 1756 her father William made a deed of gift to her and her husband of 340 acres on the north side of Tabbs Creek [DB C:73].

37 iii. Gideon[2]/ Gibeon, born say 1737.

  iv. William[5], Jr., born say 1741, taxable in 1753 in his father's Granville County household in the list of Edward Moore. In 1761 he was head of his own household with "Slave Gorden" in Fishing Creek. He purchased 170 acres on the north side of the Tarr River on 7 November 1763 and sold this land as William Chavers, Junr., on 19 October 1767 to Edward **Silvey** [DB F:507; L:327]. In 1764-67 he was in the list of Stephen Jett with wife Ellender, but was taxed on only himself in the 1769 summary list. In 1771 he was a "Black" tithable overseer of slave, Gordin, in Major **Evans'** Bute County household in the list of Philemon Hawkins [CR.015.70001, p.12 of pamphlet]. He was charged with assault in February 1769 and felony in February 1773 in Granville County court [Dockets 1773-83]. He may have been the "William Chavous Clark Commonly Called Boson Chavers" who was one of the "free Negors and Mulattus...Raitously Assembled together in Bladen Countey October 13 1773" [G.A. 1773, Box 7]. Bosen Cheves owned land near Gum Swamp and Long Branch in Richmond County, North Carolina, before 24 January 1780 [Pruitt, *Land Entries: Richmond Co.*, 3, 12]. As William Chavis he was taxable on 150 acres in Bladen County in 1784 with (his older brother?) Philip. A deed of sale for debt of his land in Robeson County on the east side of Parsimon Branch

---

[71]Bute County was formed from Granville County in 1764.

[72]Their marriage was further confirmed by a 3 September 1767 letter from Anthony Armistead of Northampton County to Col. Samuel Benton, Clerk of Granville County. Armistead wrote, "Mathew Ran ... is got with old William Chavers, or one Asa Tiner that Married his daughter... Whether old Chavers Lives in Granville or Bute County, I can't tell ..." [CR 44.928.8 by *NCGSJ* XI:35].

[73]He was probably the John Smith who was found guilty of having a bastard child by Rachel Chavis in Edgecombe County in August 1756 [Haun, *Edgecombe County Court Minutes*, I:131-2].

joining the state line was proved in the April 1797 Robeson County court [DB G:47].
- v. Lettice, born about 1742, taxable in her father's household in the 1754 list of Edward Moore. She most likely married Aquilla **Snelling**.
- vi. Keziah, born about 1742, called "Geiser" when she was taxable in her father's household in the 1754 list of Edward Moore, and called Keziah when she was taxable in her father's Epping Forest District household in 1761. She was taxable in her father's household in 1764 but not in 1766, about the time she married Asa **Tyner**.
- vii. Fanny, born before 1750, taxable in her father's Epping Forest District household in 1761.

16. Jacob[1] Chavis (Bartholomew[1], William[1], Thomas[1]), born say 1710, was granted a patent for 100 acres in Bladen Precinct "joining the river down to a Creek ...commonly Called Ichebe" on 15 May 1735 [Hoffman, *Land Patents*, I:347]. This was east of present-day Fayetteville in Cumberland County near Locks Creek and the Cape Fear River. He was called John Jacob Shives when he received a Bladen County land warrant for 220 acres on the southwest side of the Northwest River and the upper side of his own land about 3 miles above Rock Fish Creek on 13 September 1737. He was no longer on this land on 26 February 1753 when Samuel Baker entered land adjoining a line "formerly called John Jacob Shieves Survey" [Philbeck, *Bladen County Land Entries*, nos. 200, 845]. Perhaps he was deceased by 1755 when (his son?) John Chavis was head of a Cumberland County household of 6 "mulatto" taxables in 1755 with (Jacob's widow?) Misses Chavis:

Chivis, Jno ffredk Jo: Jac[b] Miss[es] Chavis & Richd do 0/6 [T&C, Box 1].

Jacob's descendants may have been
- i. John[2], born say 1730, taxable in Cumberland County in 1755. He was taxable with his unnamed wife in Bladen County in 1776 ("Molatoes") and taxable on 150 acres in 1789 [Byrd, *Bladen County Tax Lists*, II:64, 75, 200].
- ii. Joel Chivers, born say 1740, perhaps the "Jo:" taxable in John Chavis' 1755 Cumberland County household. He was taxed in the Anson County household of Edward Black in 1763. On 26 October 1767 he patented 50 acres in Anson County on Lanes Creek [Hoffman, *Land Patents*, II:423]. Administration on his Anson County estate was granted to (his wife?) Sarah Chivers who gave bond of 150 pounds on 11 October 1775 [Minutes 1771-7, 166]. Perhaps his son was Joseph Chavis, head of a Rowan County household of 4 "other free" in 1800 [NC:399], called Joel Shavers in 1810, head of a Rowan County household of 4 "other free" [NC:320].
- iii. John[7] Chavers, born say 1760, sold land by deed proved in Cumberland County on 24 October 1787 [Minutes 1787-91; the deed has not survived]. He was head of a Richmond County, North Carolina household of 7 "other free" in 1790 [NC:46]. Duncan McFarland sued him in the April 1795 Richmond County court. The jury found for McFarland for 20 pounds, but the court arrested judgment and found for the defendant because the action was grounded on an attachment with no bond or affidavit as required by law. He was called Jonathan Chavis when he was charged by the July 1797 Richmond County court with begetting a bastard child by Poll Pettis who was probably white. Thomas Pettis, "child of Colour," ordered bound out by the June 1802 Richmond County court, was probably their son. Jonathan Chavis was one of the freeholders of Richmond County ordered by the July 1800

court to work on the road from Rockingham to Hitchcock Creek [Minutes 1793-1804, 291-3, 346, 520, 560].

iv. Richard[2] Chavers, taxable in Cumberland County in 1755, head of a Richmond County household of 5 "other free" in 1790 [NC:46] and as "Bud" Chavers, a taxable "Molato" in Archibald McKissak's Bladen County household in 1776 [Byrd, *Bladen County Tax Lists*, II:68], head of an Anson County household of 8 "other free" in 1800 [NC:224].

v. Thomas Chivers, patented 200 acres in Anson County on Lanes Creek on 18 April 1771 [Hoffman, *Land Patents*, II]. He and Joel Chivers were on an Anson County jury to lay out a road from the Province line to the new road that ran from the Cheraws on 10 September 1771 [Minutes 1771-7, 61].

vi. Susanna[4] Chavers, head of a Richmond County household of 3 "other free" in 1790 [NC:46].

vii. Richmond, born about 1771, released from his indenture in New Hanover County court on 25 February 1793 after faithful service to Joseph Gautier [Minutes 1792-98, 42]. He was head of a Brunswick County, North Carolina household of 8 "other free" in 1800 [NC:13] and was probably the R. Chavius who was head of a Brunswick County household of 4 "other free" in 1810 [NC:232].

17. John[1] Chavis (Bartholomew[1], William[1], Thomas[1]), born say 1712, was tithable in the earliest Granville County, North Carolina list of Jonathan White, circa 1748 [CR 44.701.1] but not taxed again in Granville County. In 1751 he was in South Carolina where he was called "John Chevis a free negro carpenter from Virginia" when he applied for rights to land for himself, wife, nine children and a foundling infant, saying he had begun improvements on Stevens Creek [*JNH* V:74]. He sold 600 acres in Granville County, South Carolina, to John **Scott** by deed proved in 1753 [DB N-N:446]. He was called "John Cheves (Free Brazile)" on 18 July 1764 when Henry Brazile recorded a memorial for 200 acres on Long Cane Creek near the Savannah River adjoining his land [South Carolina Archives series S111001, 6:289]. He may have been the father of

i. Major, born say 1734, recorded a plat for 300 acres on the Savannah River in Granville County, South Carolina, on 21 July 1766 [South Carolina Archives series S213184, 16:286].

ii. Ann, born say 1737, recorded a grant for 50 acres in Granville County on 8 May 1758 [South Carolina Archives series S213019, 8:273]. She may have been the Anes Chavos who was head of a Barnwell District household of 5 "other free" in 1800 [SC:54].

iii. Frederick, recorded a plat for 100 acres in Colleton County on Goodland Swamp near the Edisto River on 30 January 1770 [South Carolina Archives series S213184, 15:258]. He may have been the ancestor of Frederick Chavis who petitioned the South Carolina Legislature with Lewis Chavis, Durany Chavis, James **Jones**, Bartley **Jones**, Mary **Jones**, Jonathan **Williams** and Polly **Dunn** on 9 December 1859 inquiring if persons of Indian descent were considered to be free persons of color and liable to pay the poll tax [South Carolina Archives series S165015, year 1859, item 12].

iv. John, born say 1748, recorded a memorial for 100 acres on Neds Branch and Steel Creek near the Savannah River in Granville County, South Carolina, on 3 January 1771 [South Carolina Archives series S111001, 10:294]. He may have been the John Chavis, "a free black" who petitioned the South Carolina Legislature for a pension in 1823 based on the wounds he had received in the Revolutionary War [South Carolina Archives series S108092, reel 22, frames 125, 128].

v. Hannah, head of a 96 District, Edgefield County household of 6 "other free" in 1790 and 10 "other free" in Barnwell District in 1800 [SC:58].

vi. Lazarus, born about 1756, enlisted with Captain Moon in South Carolina for fourteen months in 1778 under General Andrew Williamson. He was in the battles of Stono and Savannah. He applied for and received a pension in Orangeburg on 4 March 1835. A lawyer contacted the pension office in Washington on 12 November 1859 stating that it was highly important to prove that Lazarus Chavis received a pension [M805, reel 180, frame 153]. He was head of an Orangeburg District household of 6 "other free" in 1790 [SC:100]. He owned land in the fork of the Edisto River near Rockey Swamp in Orangeburg District on 13 July 1802 [South Carolina Archives series S213192 39:6].

vii. Elijah, recorded a plat for 50 acres on Dunn Swamp, Colleton County, in 1784 based on a survey of 1 June 1775 [South Carolina Archives series S213190, 2:198]. He was head of an Orangeburg District, South Carolina household of 8 "other free" in 1790 [SC:100].

viii. Lettice, head of a South Orangeburg District household of 6 "other free" in 1790 [SC:100].

ix. Joseph, taxable on 90 acres in Winton, South Carolina, in 1800 [S.C. Tax Returns 1783-1800, frame 304].

x. Richard, recorded a plat for 100 acres on Crackers Neck near Rocky Branch and the Savannah River in Orangeburg District on 25 August 1784 [South Carolina Archives series S213190, 2:129].

xi. Mary, recorded a plat for 84 acres on Tinkers Creek in Orangeburgh District on 15 March 1786 [South Carolina Archives series 213190 3:233].

18. Thomas[3] Cheaves (Bartholomew[1], William[1], Thomas[1]), born say 1718, was appointed by the Orange County, North Carolina court to return Amy **Hawley**'s child to her in Berkeley County, South Carolina, on 12 March 1754 [Haun, *Orange County Court Minutes*, I:70-71]. He may have been the father of

38   i. Thomas[4], born say 1742.

19. Richard[1] Chavis (Bartholomew[1], William[1], Thomas[1]), born say 1724, was head of a household of two taxables in Jonathan White's 1750 Granville County list. In 1753 he was in the list of Robert Harris: *Richard Chavers negro 1 "white" tithe*. On 12 August 1760 he and his wife Luraina were charged with trespass by William Chavers. They were found guilty and paid 39 shillings [Minutes 1754-70, 57]. In 1762 he was listed with his wife and children in the "Bare Swamp" District of Granville County:

Richard Chavers & wife Lucrese & son John &
Daughter Mille 4 free blacks

Richard was an insolvent taxpayer in 1763. On 8 November 1763 he and his wife charged Philip Chavis in the Granville County court with trespass and assault and battery. Philip was found guilty and paid a 2 pound fine. On 13 November 1765 he won a judgment for trespass against William Eaves for 5 pounds [Minutes 1754-70, 87, 108-9]. He probably died about this time for in 1766 his wife "Luraner" was listed as a head of household with 3 taxables in the summary list [CR 44.701.20]. Several of their children probably moved to Sumter District, South Carolina, before 1810. Their children were

i. John[4], born say 1747, taxable in his father's Bear Swamp District household in 1762, perhaps the John Chavers who was head of a Marlboro County, South Carolina household of 6 "other free" in 1800 [SC:59] and a Sumter District household of 3 "other free" in 1810 [SC:220].

ii. Milly, born say 1749, taxable in her father's Bear Swamp District household in 1762. She may have married Edward **Silver**.

iii. Lurany, born about 1751, taxable in her father's Bear Swamp District household in 1763.

iv. Suffiah, born about 1751, taxable in her father's Bear Swamp District household in 1763.

v.   Robert, born about 1755, taxable in his mother's household in the 1767 list of Stephen Jett, head of a Sumter District, South Carolina household of 3 "other free" in 1810 [SC:220a].

vi. Charity, born about 1755, taxable in her mother's household in the 1767 list of Stephen Jett.

20. Joseph[1] Cheavers (Bartholomew[1], William[1], Thomas[1]), born say 1726, was listed in the undated 1750's Edgecombe County muster of Captain William Haywood, the last person on the list after Cannon **Cumber** (**Cumbo**) and John **Sweet** (**Sweat**) [Clark, *Colonial Soldiers of the South*, 677]. He was probably living in the part of Edgecombe County which became Halifax County in 1758. Administration on his Halifax County estate was granted to Nicholas Long on 24 February 1785 on 500 pounds security [Minutes 1784-87, 49]. His children may have been

39   i.   Isham[1], born say 1746.

ii. Caesar, born say 1750, received pay for his services in the Revolution [Haun, *Revolutionary Army Accounts*, vol.II, Book 2:280], head of a Bertie County household of 7 "other free" in 1790 (Cezar Chevat) [NC:12].

iii. John[6], born say 1757, indentured servant of James Milner mentioned in his 1773 Halifax County inventory. He was one of the buyers in the account of the sale of the Halifax County estate of Francis Morelan which was recorded in February 1778 [Gammon, *Record of Estates* II:30]. He was taxable on one free poll in District 9 of Halifax County in 1782. John's land adjoining Hazelnut Branch in Halifax County was mentioned in an 8 April 1786 deed [DB 16:171], and he was taxable on 575 acres in District 12 of Halifax County in 1790. He wrote his name as John Chavous on 6 July 1803 when he bound himself to marry Betsy **Carsey** (**Kersey**) in Warren County, Hutchings **Mayo** bondsman (also signing). Administration on his Halifax County estate was granted to Elizabeth Chavis on 18 November 1824 on $1,000 security [Minutes 1822-24].

iv. Penny Cavus, head of a Halifax County household of 3 "other free" in 1800 [NC:300].

v.   Sarah, head of a Halifax County household of 5 "other free" in 1810 [NC:12].

vi. Martha, head of a Halifax County household of 5 "other free" in 1810 [NC:12].

21. Bartholomew[2] Chavis (Bartholomew[1], William[1], Thomas[1]), born say 1730, was taxable in Jonathan White's 1749 tax list for Granville County [CR 44.701.19]. He and Aaron **Haithcock** sold their household goods to John **Walden** in Northampton County, North Carolina, on 1 January 1796 [DB 11:42], and he was a buyer at the sale of John **Walden**'s Northampton County estate between August 1797 and June 1800 [Gammon, *Record of Estates, Northampton County*, I:112]. He was head of a Northampton County household of 6 "other free" and 2 slaves in 1800 [NC:431]. William Bell of Northampton County allowed him to remain in possession of the place where he was living for six years by his 22 January 1801 will [WB 2:488]. He was one of the heirs of Jackson **Hull**, a Continental soldier who died at Valley

Forge [*NCGSJ* I:160].[74] In 1803 Bartholomew was issued a grant of 640 acres for his services [*N.C. Genealogy* IX:1127]. He was a witness to the 6 November 1806 Northampton County will of Mike **Walden** [WB 2:330]. In 1810 he was head of a Halifax County household of 13 "other free" [NC:13]. His descendants may have been

40   i.   Isham[2], born say 1758.

       ii.   Henry[2], born say 1760, taxable on 170 acres and one poll in Hertford County in Nathan Harrel's List for 1784 [LP 64.1]. He was a soldier who served in the Revolution from November 1778 to August 1779. His widow Peggy made a deposition in Hertford County on 14 July 1792 to obtain his pay. William **Manly** attested to her statement [*NCGSJ* VIII:214].

       iii.   Uriah, head of a Halifax County household of 5 "other free" in 1810 [NC:13].

       iv.   Solomon, born say 1761, taxable on one free poll in Halifax County in 1782 and head of a Halifax County household of 2 "other free" in 1810 [NC:13]. He received Continental Army pay [Clark, *State Records of North Carolina*, XVII:198].

       v.   Robert, head of a Halifax County household of 2 "other free" in 1810 [NC:13].

       vi.   Matthew[2], head of a Halifax County household of 1 "other free" in 1810 [NC:13].

22.   John[3] Chavis (William[3], Thomas[2], William[1], Thomas[1]), born say 1740, was sued by Henry Westbrooke for debt in Southampton County on 12 May 1763 [Orders 1759-63, 309]. He was called John Cheaves and was of full age on 15 October 1763 when he signed a deposition in the Southampton County chancery suit of Drury Lundy against Isham Lundy [Chancery Court Papers 1750-70, frame 0472]. He was called John Chavis when he was paid 5 shillings by James Stewart for making a coffin for Robert Hancock of Brunswick County, Virginia, in September 1765 [DB 3:435-6]. He was granted an attachment against the estate of John Gholson in Brunswick County, Virginia court for a 1 pound, 12 shilling debt in April 1771. On 9 November 1772 he was tried at a court of Oyer and Terminer in Brunswick County for killing John Anderson. Moody Harris testified that Anderson was drunk when he came to the storehouse of Daniel Call & Company, challenged Chavis to wrestle him, and then became abusive when Chavis refused. Anderson then attacked Chavis striking him twice, and Chavis countered by hitting Anderson on the side of his head with a four inch square piece of timber. Anderson fell to the ground and died three days later. The Brunswick County court ordered that Chavis be tried in Williamsburg where he was acquitted of manslaughter [Orders 1768-72, 339; 1772-4, 151, 152; *Virginia Gazette*, Rind edition, p.2, col. 3]. On February 1786 he sold a wagon and five horses for ten pounds by Brunswick County, Virginia deed. He signed the deed, making his mark, and acknowledged the deed as his in court as John Chavus on 27 March 1786, but he was called "I the said John Chavus Walden" in the deed when he defended the buyer from any claims [DB 14:183-4]. On 24 May 1784 the Brunswick County court presented him for retailing liquor without a license, but the case was dismissed on 20 June 1784. He was sued in court for debt on 26 April 1785, on 27 June 1785 (for 5 pounds), 25 July 1785, 28 February 1786 (for 35 pounds), 28 August 1786 (for 42 pounds), 28 March 1787 (5 pounds), 28 August 1787 (4 pounds), and 28 July 1788 (3 pounds). He sued William Crook on 28 February 1786 and sued Joseph Hill on 25 November 1788 [Orders

---

[74]Jackson **Hull** was probably related to Judith Hull who died before 8 September 1756 when her "Mulatto natural daughter" Anne **Hull** was apprenticed to Robert Jones in Granville County [Owens, *Granville County Notes*, vol. I].

1760-84, 405, 434; 1784-8, 113, 138, 181, 237, 295, 310, 319, 453, 472, 563; 1788-92, 39, 95]. He may have been the common-law husband of Elizabeth **Brooks** whose son John Chavos was mentioned in the 5 February 1798 Southampton County will of her father James **Brooks** [WB 5:58]. John may have been the father of

    i.   John, born say 1762, taxable in Moses Foster's St. Luke's Parish, Southampton County household in 1790, charged with his own tax from 1807 to 1811, living on Ch. Westbrook's land in 1817 [PPTL 1782-92, frame 760; 1807-21, frames 47, 70, 189, 576]. He was called John Shivers on 16 November 1818 when he made a declaration in Southampton County court setting forth that he was a soldier in the Revolutionary War by voluntary enlistment [Minutes 1816-9, unpaged]. He was called Jack Chavis in 1810 when he was head of a Southampton County household of 3 "other free" [VA:77].

23.   Mary Chavis (Amy, Thomas², William¹, Thomas¹), born say 1745, was called Moll Chavis when her illegitimate child Lucretia Chavis was ordered bound out by the Southampton County court on 11 November 1773. She purchased 10 acres in Southampton County on the north side of Three Creeks adjoining Joseph Markes for 5 pounds on 9 August 1782 [Orders 1772-8, 283; DB 6:59]. She was taxable in St. Luke's Parish, Southampton County, on a horse from 1794 to 1807: taxable on a free male tithable in 1801 and 1802, called a "Mulatto" in 1804, charged with John Chavis's tithe in 1805, taxable on a free male tithable and a horse in 1806 and 1807 [PPTL 1792-1806, frames 76, 158, 185, 264, 314, 375, 409, 511, 549, 618, 686, 802, 838; 1807-21, frame 47]. She may have been the mother of

41   i.   Frances²/Fanny, born say 1765.

    ii. Edward²/ Ned, born about 1767, registered in Southampton County on 12 May 1794: *a free man born in Sussex of free parents, a yellowish black complexion, 27 years of age lives in Southampton County & works at the trade of wheelwright* [Register of Free Negroes 1794-1832, no. 30]. He married Mary **Cannady**, 21 December 1799 Sussex County bond. He was a "Mulatto" taxable in St. Luke's Parish, Southampton County, on a horse from 1795 to 1804: taxable on 2 free male tithables and a horse in 1802 and 1804 [PPTL 1792-1806, frames 157, 185, 263, 313, 375, 409, 511, 618, 686]. Perhaps his widow was Molly Chavis, a "f.n." taxable in Southampton County on a horse and James **Cannada**'s tithe in 1805, taxable on a free male tithable and a horse in 1806 [PPTL 1792-1806, frames 803, 839].

   iii. Lucretia, bound out in Southampton County on 11 November 1773 [Orders 1772-8, 283].

   iv. Milly, born about 1774, registered in Sussex County on 16 October 1812: *light Complexion, 5 feet 4-1/2 inches, age 38, free born* [Certificates Granted to Free Negroes & Mulattoes 1800-50, no. 188].

    v. Jacob, born say 1775, a poor child bound out by the Southampton County court on 10 June 1784 [Orders 1778-84, 444]. He was taxable in Moses Foster's St. Luke's Parish, Southampton County household in 1791 and 1792 [PPTL 1782-92, frame 815, 874].

   vi. Samuel, born about 1777, a poor child bound out by the Southampton County court on 10 June 1784 [Orders 1778-84, 444]. He was taxable in St. Luke's Parish, Southampton County, in Moses Foster's household from 1791 to 1795, a "Mulatto" taxable on a slave aged 12-16 and a horse in 1802, taxable on a horse in 1803 [PPTL 1782-92, frame 815, 874; 1792-1806, frames 52, 79, 160, 550, 619]. He registered in Southampton County in December 1804: *age 27, blk., 5 feet 9 inches high, free born* [Register of Free Negroes 1794-1832, no. 316].

vii. Betsy, born about 1777, registered in Southampton County on 11 July 1810: *age 33, Mulatto, 5 feet 5 inches, born free* [Register of Free Negroes 1794-1832, no. 582].

viii. Henry, born about 1779, registered in Southampton County in August 1801: *age 22, Black, 5 feet 11-1/8, free born* [Register of Free Negroes 1794-1832, no. 217]. He was taxable in St. Luke's Parish, Southampton County, in 1798, a "Mulatto" taxable in 1804 and 1805 [PPTL 1792-1806, frames 313, 375, 688, 803].

ix. Mary, taxable in Southampton County on a free male tithable and a horse in 1807 [PPTL 1807-21, frame 47].

x. Lucretia, born about 1786, registered in Sussex County on 1 December 1831: *free born, light complexion, 5'4-5/8", aged 45* [Certificates Granted to Free Negroes & Mulattoes 1800-50, no. 531].

xi. John, born about 1788, registered in Southampton County on 22 April 1809: *age 22, Mulatto, 5 feet 9 inches, free born.* He registered again on 16 March 1816 [Register of Free Negroes 1794-1832, no. 844, 1000].

24. Jacob[2] Chavis (Frances, Thomas[2], William[1], Thomas[1]), born about 1736, purchased 100 acres in Lunenburg County on the south side of Little Bluestone Creek adjoining Hudson on 6 October 1761 [DB 6:475]. The Lunenburg County court ordered the churchwardens to bind James Chavis to him in June 1762 [Orders 1761-62, 32], and he was taxable with James Chavis on 100 acres in the Lunenburg County list of Edmund Taylor in 1764 [Bell, *Sunlight on the Southside,* 248]. On 13 May 1763 he was among seven residents of Lunenburg County who were sued for minor debts by Starling, Thornton, and Company, and the same day Hugh McVay's suit against him was dismissed on the recommendation of David Christopher and Matthew Marable, Gentlemen, who investigated the matter and reported to the court. On 10 May 1764 he was one of six residents of St. James Parish, Lunenburg County, who were presented for unlawful gaming (gambling) at David Christopher's ordinary [Orders 1763-4, 42, 59; 1764-5, fol. 2]. On 10 May 1764 he provided security for Henry Chavis' Lunenburg County court case, and on 11 May 1764 his suit against John Ragsdale was dismissed by the Lunenburg County court. On 13 July 1764 the court ordered the churchwardens of St. James Parish to remove Thomas **Brandon** from Hutchings Burton and bind him instead to Jacob [Orders 1764-5, fol.5, pp.11, 108]. By 14 February 1774 he owned over 1,000 acres of land in the part of Lunenburg County which became Mecklenburg County in 1765. He received a patent for 287 acres in Mecklenburg County at the head of Reedy Branch on 15 June 1773 [Patent Book 41:315], purchased 148 acres on 18 May 1772 from the executors of Thomas Hawkins, deceased, for 5 shillings, and purchased 200 acres on the head branches of Little Creek adjoining Stith from William **Donathan** on 16 July 1773. Chaves Creek, located between Stiths Creek and Stony Creek in the northwest corner of Mecklenburg County, was probably named for him [DB 3:417; 4:144; Ludwig Bucholtz Map, LVA]. He purchased 340 acres on Middle Bluestone Creek on 14 February 1774, and purchased 150 acres adjoining John Hudson and Benjamin Pulliam on 4 March 1779 [DB 4:243; 5:398-9]. On 9 December 1777 the Mecklenburg County court allowed the sheriff, Jacob, and two white men 3 pounds each for taking prisoner Thomas Green to Williamsburg to be tried for murder, and the court allowed Jacob 6 pounds for "bringing up the Laws" (probably transporting a copy of the law books from Williamsburg) [Orders 1773-9, 350, 387; 1779-84, 6]. He was taxable in the upper district of Mecklenburg County on 712 acres from 1782 to 1787, taxable on 430 acres from 1793 to 1798 and taxable on 330 acres until 1809 [Land Tax List 1782-1811A, A lists]. He assigned his right to a grant of 362 acres on Sandy Creek in Mecklenburg County, based on a survey of 17 May 1783, to Thomas **Stewart** of Dinwiddie County [Land Grants

L:614]. He was arrested for counterfeiting by order of the Governor on 4 December 1778 but found not guilty by the York County court on 2 January 1779 [McIlwaine, *Journals of the Council of the State of Virginia*, II:229, 246; York County Orders 1774-84, 199]. He was head of a Mecklenburg County household of 13 "whites" (free persons) and 2 slaves adjoining William Hudson in 1782 [VA:34], taxable on 2 slaves (Cork and Bess), 24 cattle, and 8 horses in 1782, on slaves Cork and Bess, 18 cattle and 8 horses in 1783 and on a slave, 17 cattle, and 7 horses in 1787 [PPTL 1782-1805, frames 4, 24]. He sold 200 acres in Mecklenburg County on the head branches of Little Creek to William **Stewart** on 8 March 1779 [DB 5:399]. On 29 July 1797 he mortgaged 430 acres where he was then living on Bluestone Creek adjoining Thomas **Brandom** and mortgaged his slave Cork, 3 horses, 8 cattle, 6 featherbeds and other household effects to James Hester, Thomas Vaughan, and David Stokes for an execution against his estate in the suit of George Purdie, and on 14 September 1787 he mortgaged two tracts of land, one of 142 acres called cabin point and the other of 182 acres on Sandy Creek for a debt of 198 pounds he owed Field & Murray, Merchants. On 8 June 1789 and 26 August 1789 he and his wife Elizabeth sold these two tracts near the ferry road on Little Bluestone Creek for 500 pounds [DB 7:187, 362, 505-6, 589; 8:123]. He sued Thomas **Evans** and William **Stewart** in Mecklenburg County on 13 Feb 1786 [Orders 1784-87, 461]. On 13 September 1790 Henry Chavis, Sr., Henry Chavis, Jr., and James **Stewart** testified in Mecklenburg County court that they were indebted to William **Stewart** and could help pay his debt to Jacob Chavis [Orders 1787-92, 536]. He sold his slave Cork, 5 cattle, a mare and 5 feather beds on 11 February 1792 (making his mark J.C.) for a debt of 100 pounds he owed Robert Smith [DB 8:123]. He was sued for debt in Dinwiddie County in November 1789 [Orders 1789-91, 129]. A group of Glasgow merchants won a suit against him for a 136 pound debt in Mecklenburg County court on 16 May 1798 [Orders 1795-8, 458]. In December 1799 James Hester, Thomas Vaughan and David Stokes released him from the bond they held on the property he mortgaged in 1788 [DB 10:46-7]. On 13 November 1800 his assignee Jacob Shelor sued Thomas **Epps Hobson** and William **Epps** in Lunenburg County court for a debt of 7 pounds [Orders 1799-1801, 112]. He registered in Mecklenburg County on 15 March 1803:

> On the application of Jacob Chavous It is ordered that the said Jacob aged sixty seven, born free, Black, stature about six feet high, be registered as a free man and that a certificate of the same be granted him [Orders 1801-3, 388].

On 11 July 1806 in Mecklenburg County he gave power of attorney to (his son?) John Chavis of North Carolina to recover a debt from William **Stewart** of North Carolina [DB 13:1-2]. His 26 April 1805 Mecklenburg County will, proved 11 July 1808, lent his lands and personal estate to his unnamed wife, after her death gave 5 shillings apiece to his unnamed sons and divided the land among his unnamed daughters [WB 6:104]. His widow Elizabeth gave permission for her daughter Elizabeth to marry Arvy **Scott** by 9 January 1809 Mecklenburg County bond. Elizabeth (Sr.) apparently died before 16 May 1814 when her brother Thomas **Evans** brought a Mecklenburg County chancery suit against the heirs of (their father) Thomas **Evans**, deceased. He named Elizabeth's children then living: John, Isaac, Jacob, William, Susannah, Elizabeth, Patsey (wife of Arva **Scott**), Sarah (wife of Thomas **Brandom**), and Peter Chavous [Orders 1813-15, 187, 210]. He also stated in his suit that (his father) Thomas **Evans** died in 1787 and that his land passed to his widow who held possession "about thirteen years until her Death, after which Jacob Chaves who married one of the daughters of said Thomas Evans...rented the land to Elizabeth Naish (**Nash**) and put her in possession" [LVA chancery file 1819-006]. Jacob and Elizabeth's children were

42   i.   John[8], born say 1764.

      ii.   Isaac[2], born say 1766, over sixteen years of age in 1788 when he was counted in the Mecklenburg County property tax list of his father Jacob Chavous [PPTL 1782-1805, frame 211]. He married Elizabeth **Evans**, 6 September 1800 Granville County, North Carolina bond, Peter Chavis bondsman. He was taxable on one poll in Abrams Plains District of Granville County in 1791 and on two "black" polls in Napp of Reed District in 1796, taxable on one free poll and one slave poll in Abrams Plains in 1799, and one poll and 100 acres in 1800 [Tax List 1796-1802, 25, 187, 244]. He purchased 150 acres in Granville County on Island Creek on 5 February 1802 [DB O:522]. He was head of a Granville County household of 3 "other free" in 1800, 3 "other free" and one white woman in 1810 [NC:858], and 1 "free colored" in Mecklenburg County in 1820. He died intestate "without having any children or the issue of such but having a widow Elizabeth Chavus & several Brothers and Sisters of whom John Chavus is one" according to a Granville County quit claim deed which John Chavis made to Isaac's widow Elizabeth Chavis on 8 July 1831, relinquishing any part of his estate [DB 7:253]. He was a "free man of color of Charlotte County" who enlisted in the 14th Virginia Regiment in March 1777 according to his heirs Jacob Chavos, William Chavos, Sally **Brandom**, and Patsy **Scott** who applied for a land grant on 1 May 1837 for his services in the Revolution [Hopkins, *Virginia Revolutionary War Land Grant Claims,* 48].

43   iii.   Jacob[3], Jr., born say 1772.

      iv.   William[9], born 22 February 1776, the son of Jacob Chavis, married Priscilla **Drew** in January 1806, and died in Virginia in January 1848 according to the biography of his son James M. Chavis [*Buck Township, Ohio, Biographical Sketches,* 1038-9].[75] William was also identified as Jacob's son in 1796 when he was taxable in his father's Mecklenburg County household and taxable in his own household in 1797 [PPTL 1782-1805, frame 610, 634]. He may have been the William Chavis who was taxable in Dinwiddie County in 1804: *Chavis, Wm (free) school master* [PPTL 1800-1809, 1804 List of Braddock Goodwyn, p.4]. According to the Mecklenburg County marriage bonds, William Chavous married Priscilla **Drew**, 29 ___ 1806 bond, Benjamin Lewis and Richard Russell securities. He was also identified as the son of Jacob when he and a female over the age of sixteen (probably his wife) were counted in the list of free Negroes and Mulattos for Mecklenburg County in 1813 [PPTL 1806-28, frame 307]. Priscilla was listed as a seventy-year-old "Mulatto" in Mecklenburg County in the 1850 census with Martha, Polly, Betsy, Susan and Emily Chavious [VA:141b].

      v.   Susannah, perhaps the Susannah Chavis, a "fn" weaver, who was taxable on a horse in Charlotte County from 1810 to 1812 [PPTL 1782-1813, frames 773, 783, 804, 814, 846].

      vi.   Elizabeth[9], born say 1791, married Arva **Scott**, 9 January 1809 Mecklenburg County bond, with a note from Elizabeth Chavis "mother of Elizabeth," Frederick **Ivy** security. She did not marry Arva; her sister Martha did. She may have been the Betty Chavus who was listed as a weaver in Charlotte County with a male child in her household in

---

[75]The marriage date of James M. Chavis and his wife Nancy **Stewart** (daughter of Archer and Jane **Stewart**), stated in the biography (15 December 1835) was the same as the date recorded in the Mecklenburg County marriage bonds.

1809 and 1810, listed with John **Cousins** and his children in 1811 and 1812 [PPTL 1782-1813, frames 751, 783, 814, 846].

vii. Martha/ Patsy, married Arva **Scott**. He and his wife Martha **Scott** released their rights to land due to her from the estate of her father Jacob Chavis, Sr., to her brother Jacob Chavis, Jr., of Charlotte County by deed proved in Mecklenburg County on 10 July 1809 [DB 14-107, 308].

viii. Peter[2], born about 1775, a sixteen-year-old taxable in his father's Mecklenburg County household in 1791 [PPTL 1782-1805, frame 369]. He purchased 100 acres in Granville County on Island Creek on 1 February 1798 and sold this land on 2 August 1813 [DB Q:230; W:119]. He married Rachel **Locklear**, 29 April 1807 Wake County bond, Irby Philips bondsman. He was taxable on 27 acres in Houses Creek District of Wake County from 1809 to 1813 and sold land to Curtis **Snelling** in 1814. He died in 1819 when his widow Rachel petitioned the Wake County court to assign her his perishable estate [N.C. Archives CR 099.508.66].

ix. Sarah, married Thomas **Brandom**.

25. Susannah[1] Chavis (Frances, Thomas[2], William[1], Thomas[1]), born about 1740, a "free Negro," had a daughter Elizabeth whose 19 November 1764 birth was registered in Bruton Parish, James City County [Bruton Parish Register, 28]. She registered in Petersburg on 14 August 1800: *Sucky Chavis, a brown Mulatto woman, five feet three inches high, thin made about sixty years old, born free & raised in the City of Williamsburg* [Register of Free Negroes 1794-1819, no. 169]. She was the mother of

i. Elizabeth[5], born 19 November 1764, "Daughter of Sukey Chavis a free Negro" [Bruton Parish Register, 28].

ii. ?Thomason[2], born about 1765, registered in Petersburg on 18 August 1794: *a dark brown, well made Mulatto woman, five feet two inches high, about twenty nine years old, born of a free woman in the City of Williamsburg* [Register of Free Negroes 1794-1819, no. 21]

44   iii. Susannah[3], born 21 June 1767.

iv. ?Elizabeth[6], born about 1775, registered in Petersburg on 15 August 1800: *a light brown Mulatto woman, five feet five inches high, twenty five years old, with short bushy hair, born free & raised in the City of Williamsburg* [Register of Free Negroes 1794-1819, no. 173].

26. Margaret Chaves (Frances, Thomas[2], William[1], Thomas[1]), born say 1742, was a "Mullatto Girl" living in Charles City County on 1 August 1750 when the court ordered the churchwardens to bind her to Richard Hailes. On 1 July 1761 the court ordered the churchwardens of Westover Parish to bind out her son George, and on 2 September 1761 the court bound out her daughter Rebecca [Orders 1737-51, 574; 1758-62, 302, 313]. Her children were

i. George[2], born say 1759.

ii. Rebecca[4], born say 1760, orphan of Margaret Chavis, bound out by the Charles City County court in September 1761.

27. Susannah[2] Chavis (Thomason[1], Thomas[2], William[1], Thomas[1]), born say 1740, was living in Mecklenburg County, Virginia, when the court ordered the churchwardens to bind out her son John Chavis to Jacob Chavis. She may have been the mother of Nanny Chavous, "orphan of Frederick Chavous," who the court ordered bound to Samuel Manning on 8 September 1766 [Orders 1765-8, 170, 212]. The churchwardens of St. James Parish sued her for debt in August 1768, perhaps for having a bastard child. On 13 September 1768 the court allowed her to take the deposition of the wife of Samuel Manning, and on 9 July 1771 the churchwardens discontinued their suit and were ordered to pay Susannah her costs. She and her son Yarborough sued Benjamin Pennington,

Jr., perhaps the master he was apprenticed to, in Mecklenburg County on 8 September 1783. James King obtained an attachment on her estate for a 40 pound debt due by note of hand for arrears of rent. On 15 March 1787 the sheriff reported that he had attached six head of cattle, a colt, a basket, two spinning wheels, three water pails, three basins, a box, a candlestick, a pot and a cow hide [Orders 1768-71, 38-9, 91, 126; 1771-73, 54; 1779-84, 425, 485; 1784-7, 701]. She probably had a child by a member of the Manning family since was called the mother of Polly **Manning** when she sent a note approving Polly's 9 December 1794 Mecklenburg County marriage. She was the mother of

    i.   John, born say 1764.

    ii. ?Ann/ Nanny, called "orphan of Frederick Chavous" when the court ordered the churchwardens to bind her to Samuel Manning on 8 September 1766 [Orders 1765-8, 212].

    iii. Yarborough, born say 1769. He and "Susannah Chavous his Mother & next friend" sued Benjamin Pennington, Jr., in Mecklenburg County on 8 September 1783 [Orders 1779-84, 425, 485]. He was a 16-21 year old taxable in Mecklenburg County in 1787, called Earby Chavious in 1799 [PPTL 1782-1805, frames 190, 756]. He was called Earby Chavis when he married Fanny **McLin**, 9 March 1797 Mecklenburg County bond, Thomas **McLin** surety.

    iv. ?Benjamin **Manning**, born say 1774, married Fanny **Guy**, 5 May 1796 Mecklenburg County bond, Earbe (Yarborough) **Chavis** security.

    v. Polly **Manning**, born say 1776, married John Ginnet **Stewart**, 9 December 1794 Mecklenburg County bond, Earbe Chavis security, "with a note from Susanna Chavous, mother of Polly."

28. Elizabeth[2] Chavis (Thomason[1], Thomas[2], William[1], Thomas[1]), born say 1740, was called "Betty Chavis a Malato" on 23 April 1752 when the Amelia County court ordered the churchwardens of Nottoway Parish to bind her out as an apprentice [Orders 1751-5, 37]. She was living in Lunenburg County in October 1759 when the court ordered the churchwardens of Cumberland Parish to bind her to French Haggard. On 11 May 1769 the court ordered her children Rebecca and Benjamin also bound to Haggard. She complained to the court on 11 April 1771 that Pleasant Meredith was holding them in servitude, and the court ordered them bound out to someone else on 10 December 1772 [Orders 1767-69, 214; 1769-77, 112, 183, 267]. However, they were all in Cumberland County five months later on 24 May 1773 when the court ordered the churchwardens of Littleton Parish to bind out her "mulattoe" children Beck and Ben Chavers to Pleasant Meredith [Orders 1772-4, 216]. She was the mother of

    i.   Rebecca[3], born say 1767, perhaps the Rebecca Chavers who registered in Bedford County on March 1812: *aged 45, Black Colour, 5 feet 6-3/4" inches high, Born free* [Register of Free Negroes 1820-60, p.16]. Beck was called a free Mulatto woman when the Cumberland County court bound her son Jesse to John Wright on 26 October 1789 [Orders 1788-92, 174, 209]. He may have been the Jesse Chavis who was called the son of Betty Chavis on 22 December 1800 when the Cumberland County court ordered him bound to John Jackson instead of his former master William Meredith [Orders 1797-1801, 432].

    ii. Benjamin[2], born say 1769, a "free Mulatto" charged in Cumberland County with burning down the jail, sent to the district court in Prince Edward County for trial [Orders 1792-7, 657].

    iii. ?James[3], born about 1775, a farmer and shoemaker living on Zachariah Davis' land in the lower district of Lunenburg County in 1814 when he was counted with his wife Lucy, members of the **Kelly** family and Becky Chavers in the "List of Free Negroes and Mulattoes" [*Magazine of Virginia Genealogy* 33:266]. He registered in Lunenburg County on

14 November 1837: *about 62 years of age, black complexion, His eyes rather Red, His hair a little grey* [WB 5, after page 89, no. 87].

 iv. ?Aaron, bound by the Cumberland County court to Archibald Anglea on 25 January 1790 [Orders 1788-92, 203].

29. James[1] Chaves (Thomason[1], Thomas[2], William[1], Thomas[1]), born say 1744, was one of the children of Thomason Chavis who was ordered bound out by the churchwardens of Cumberland Parish in Lunenburg County, Virginia, in June 1752 [Orders 1752-53, 56]. He was ordered bound out by the churchwardens of Mecklenburg County to Jacob Chavis in June 1762 [Orders 1761-62, 32] and was a taxable in Jacob Chaves' household in the Lunenburg County list of Edmund Taylor in 1764 [Bell, *Sunlight on the Southside*, 248]. He purchased 100 acres in Mecklenburg County adjoining Christopher Hudson on 9 November 1767 and sold this land to John Hudson on 13 July 1772 [DB 1:521; 3:426]. He was head of a Mecklenburg County household of 3 in 1782, listed adjacent to Henry Chavous [VA:33]. He and his wife Jane **Evans** were mentioned in the 22 May 1787 Mecklenburg County will of her father Thomas **Evans** [WB 2:250]. He was probably the James Chavis who was head of a Granville County household of 5 free males and 3 free females in 1786 for the state census. He was taxable in Granville on 2 polls in 1788 and 4 polls in 1789 [Tax List, 1786-91]. In May 1791 he mortgaged 12 head of cattle, 2 bulls, 40 hogs, and other items in Granville County [WB 1:241]. On 6 August 1794 he sold 220 acres on Grassy Creek in Granville County to (his brother-in-law) Thomas **Evans** of Mecklenburg County, and on 8 November 1796 he purchased another 200 acres in Granville County on Grassy Creek [DB P:90; Q:37]. He married, second, Betsey **Smith**, 4 July 1799 Granville County bond, Thomas **Wilson** bondsman.[76] He was head of a Granville County household of 3 "other free" in 1800. He was taxable on 183 acres and no polls (over fifty years old) in Country Line District in 1804 [Tax List 1803-09, 62]. His children were

 i. ?Kinchen, born say 1760, a Mecklenburg County taxable from 1787 to 1804 [PPTL 1782-1805, frames 189, 236, 287, 498, 795, 916, 1021]. He married Milly Chavous, 22 December 1788 Mecklenburg County bond, and he was bondsman for the 6 April 1804 Mecklenburg County marriage of John **Walden**. Kinchen was head of an Orange County, North Carolina household of 5 "other free" in 1810 [NC:818] and 5 "free colored" in 1820 [Book A:410].

 ii. Evans, born say 1770, called the son of James and Jane Chavis in Thomas **Evans**' 1787 Mecklenburg County will. He was a "free Negro" taxable in the 1798 tax list for Country Line District, Granville County, and taxable on one free poll and one slave in Abrams Plains in 1799 [Tax List 1796-1802, 139, 187]. He married Lucy **Smith**, 21 April 1802 Granville County bond, Charles Chavis bondsman; and second, Ciller **Smith**, 29 July 1805 Granville County bond, H. Hutchings bondsman. On 25 December 1821 he mortgaged his land and household goods in Granville County for a $62 debt he owed [DB I:109]. He was head of a Granville County household of 4 "free colored" males and 3 female slaves in Country Line District in 1820 [NC:35]. He was taxable in Country Line District in 1818 but was exempt from poll tax by 1823 when he was taxable on 30 acres. He was not named in the chancery case in Mecklenburg County in 1819.

30. James[2] Chavis (Rebecca[1], Thomas[2], William[1], Thomas[1]), born say 1749, was ordered bound out by the churchwardens in Amelia County on 12 March 1753 (no parent named) and called son of "Rebecca Chavis a Free Negro" when he

---

[76]Thomas **Wilson** was head of a Granville County household of 2 "other free" in 1810 [NC:861].

was bound out in Amelia County on 28 August 1760 [Orders 1751-5, 149; 1760-3, 44]. He was taxable in Mecklenburg County from 1782 to 1820: taxable on a horse and 2 cattle in 1782, a "Mulatto" taxable with his unnamed wife in 1813, over the age of forty-five when he was taxable in 1815 [PPTL 1782-1805, frames 14, 45, 141, 234, 478, 681, 1021, 1051; 1806-28, frames 160, 232, 257, 333, 386, 502, 702]. On 14 May 1800 the Mecklenburg County court ordered Frederick **Gowen** to pay James and his wife Fanny Chavous $1.06 as witnesses for him in the suit of John George [Orders 1798-1801, 367, 424]. He purchased land in Mecklenburg County by deed recorded on 25 January 1817 and sold land by deed recorded 5 April 1823 [DB 16:401; 20:285]. He was head of a Mecklenburg County household of 10 "free colored" in 1820. His estate was settled in Mecklenburg County in 1824 [WB 10:85]. A chancery suit in Mecklenburg County in 1832 named his children [LVA chancery file 1832-026]. They were

 i. James[4], born say 1777, taxable in Mecklenburg County on a horse in 1798, 1800, 1804 and 1805 [PPTL 1782-1805, frames 682, 795, 1021, 1051], perhaps the James Chavous who married Luvina **Nash**, 24 February 1829 Mecklenburg County bond, Edward **Brandon** security.

 ii. Lydia[2], born say 1780, married Jeremiah **Harris**, 13 November 1797 Mecklenburg County bond, James **Chavis** security.

 iii. Jincy, born say 1788, married Archer **Stewart**, 14 August 1809 Mecklenburg County bond, Edward **Brandon** security. Archer, born 1775-1794, was head of a Mecklenburg County household of 8 "free colored" in 1820. The chancery suit named their children Fanny, Nancy, Dabney, Pettus and William who was administrator of his father's estate.

 iv. William[10], born say 1789, a "Mulattoe" taxable in Mecklenburg County from 1812 to 1814, called "son of Js." [PPTL, 1806-28, 285, 307, 417]. He married Elizabeth **Ivy**, 6 March 1819 Mecklenburg County bond, Edward **Brandon** surety.

 v. Thomas[6], born say 1791, a "Mulattoe" taxable over the age of sixteen in Mecklenburg County in 1815 [PPTL, 1806-28, 502].

 vi. Ann, wife of Drury **Wilson**.

 vii. Pleasant, born about 1795, married Dicey **Singleton**, 28 December 1821 Mecklenburg County bond, Henry **Stewart** security. He was a fifty-five-year-old shoemaker counted in Mecklenburg County with his wife Harriet in 1850 [VA:128].

 viii. Henry[4], born about 1798, a "Mulattoe" taxable over the age of sixteen in Mecklenburg County in 1815 [PPTL, 1806-28, 502], a fifty-two-year-old counted in the 1850 census with his wife Betsy [VA:88b].

 ix. Ellison, bought land by deed proved in Mecklenburg County on 21 June 1824. He and Susan Chavous sold land by deeds proved on 22 May and 6 August 1827 [DB 21:37; 22:416; 476].

 x. Elizabeth[6], married Edward **Brandon**, 10 March 1806 Mecklenburg County bond, Frederick **Ivey** security. Her husband was called Nathaniel **Brandon** in the chancery suit.

31. Elizabeth[3] Chavis (Rebecca[1], Thomas[2], William[1], Thomas[1]), born say 1751, was called the daughter of Rebecca Chavis on 26 August 1756 when the Amelia County court ordered the churchwardens of Nottoway Parish to bind her out [Orders 1754-8, n.p]. She was living in Lunenburg County in September 1760 when she successfully sued Hutchings Burton for her freedom dues [Orders 1759-61, 32, 159, 170]. She may have been the Betty Chavus who was head of a Halifax County, Virginia household of 2 persons in 1782 [VA:24]. She was called Liza Chavers on 17 June 1784 when the Halifax County court ordered her to show cause why her illegitimate son Barltett should not be bound out [Pleas 1783-6, 78]. She was the mother of

    i.   Jesse, born say 1766, "child of Elizabeth Chavious," bound out by the churchwardens of St. James Parish, Mecklenburg County, on 13 November 1769 [Orders 1768-71, 278]. He was taxable in Granville County in the undated (perhaps 1787) list of John Dickerson for Fishing Creek in Hugh **Snelling**'s household and in his own household in 1790. Benjamin and Absalom **Bass** were his securities in August 1794 Granville County court when he was charged with having an illegitimate child by Nelly **Bass** [Minutes 1792-95, 197-8]. He was called Jesse Chavers of Petersburg on 8 April 1798 when he sold 8 head of cattle in Granville County for 20 pounds [WB 5:276] and was taxable on 140 acres in Oxford District in 1802 [Tax List 1796-1802, 337]. He was head of a Granville County household of 6 "other free" in 1810 [NC:912] and 9 "free colored" in 1820 [NC:9]. He married Nancy **Mitchell**, 2 May 1812 Granville County bond, Darling **Bass** bondsman.

    ii. Bartlett[1], born about 1776, bound apprentice in Halifax County, Virginia, on 17 March 1785 to John Nobles and bound out to John Hughes on 18 October 1787 [Pleas 11:253; 12:270]. He registered as a "free Negro" in Halifax County on 11 October 1802: *Bartlet Chavus (Batteau) aged about twenty six years, five feet five and half Inches high, between a Black and a yellow Colour* [Register, no. 22]. He married Elizabeth **Mathis** (**Matthews**), 10 February 1803 Halifax County bond. He was taxable in the southern district of Halifax County in 1798 and 1800, and there were two Bartlett Chavuses who were "Mulatto" taxables in Halifax County from 1801 to 1806: one called "Batteau" in 1803 who may also have been the one called "Sr." in 1801 and 1805. Both were counted as planters in the list of "free Negroes & Mulattoes" in 1801: one living on "P.C." (P. Creek) and the other on "UR" (the Upper Road) [PPTL, 1782-99, frame 810; 1800-12, frames 50, 158, 178, 308, 363, 508, 615].

32. John[5] Chavis (George, Thomas[2], William[1], Thomas[1]) born say 1755, enlisted in the Fifth Virginia Regiment in December 1778 and served for three years. Captain Mayo Carrington, in a bounty warrant written in March 1783, certified that Chavis had "faithfully fulfilled [his duties] and is thereby entitled to all immunities granted to three year soldiers" [Mecklenburg County Legislative Petition of 14 December 1820]. He and Anthony Chavis brought a suit against Robert Taylor which was dismissed by the Henrico County court by agreement of the parties on 13 March 1784 [Orders 1781-4, 477]. He was taxable in Mecklenburg County on his own tithe in 1785 and a tithe and 3 horses in 1786 [PPTL 1782-1805, frames 99, 127, 211]. He was deceased by 11 June 1787 when the Mecklenburg County court ordered the overseers of the poor to bind out his orphans Charles, John, Mary and Randol Chavous [Orders 1787-92, 32]. On 20 April 1818 his sons John, Charles, and Randolph Chavis of Mecklenburg County gave their power of attorney to Melchizedek Roffe to collect money due to them from the State Treasurer for their father's service in the Revolution [*Virginia Genealogist*, p.153; Mecklenburg County DB 17:218-9]. William O. Goode, former member of the General Assembly from Mecklenburg County, wrote a letter on 12 January 1836 in support of the petition to the Legislature made by his son Randall. Goode stated that John and his brother Anthony Chavis were wagoners in the Revolution who were issued certificates of public debt at the end of the war, about 21 pounds for Anthony (signed by Captain Young) and 89 pounds for John (signed by Captain Carrington). These certificates were burnt in a fire in the Petersburg home of Charles **Watts** who was John Chavers' brother-in-law according to the testimony of Thomas **Evans** who had been a resident of Petersburg at the time of the fire [Mecklenburg County Legislative Petitions of 14 December 1820 and 19 January 1836, LVA]. John's children were

i. John[10], born say 1780, married Sally **Blair**, 27 July 1801 Mecklenburg County bond, Thomas **Cypress** security. He may have been the John Chavis who was head of a Petersburg Town household of 8 "other free" in 1810 [VA:122a].

ii. Charles[2], a "Hireling" living in the lower district of Lunenburg County on Hounds Creek in 1802 when he was counted in a "List of free Negroes & Mulattoes" [LVA, Lunenburg County, Free Negro & Slave Records, 1802-1803]. He married Lucy **Chapman**, 20 December 1810 Lunenburg County bond. He was a "Mulatto" taxable in Mecklenburg County in 1813 [PPTL, 1806-28, 333].

iii. Mary.

iv. Randolph/ Randol, say 1785, registered in Mecklenburg County on 21 March 1815: *Randill Chavis a free man of yellowish Complection, about twenty four years old, about five feet six inches high.* He was called Randolph Chavis when he registered again in February court 1818 and on 18 August 1823 when his date of birth was estimated as 1785 [Free Person of Color, pp.6, 10, 17]. He was head of a Mecklenburg County household of 6 "free colored" in 1820. He made a deed of release in Mecklenburg County which was proved in November 1832 [DB 25:246].

33. Anthony Chavis (George, Thomas[2], William[1], Thomas[1]), born say 1757, was identified as a brother of John Chavis in the Mecklenburg County, Virginia petition of John's son, Randal Chavis [Mecklenburg Petition of 19 January 1836, LVA]. He bought 101 acres in Mecklenburg County from William Avery for 3,000 pounds of tobacco on 11 November 1780 and sold this land adjoining Henry Avery and Thomas **Stewart** for 20 pounds on 10 March 1792 [DB 6:103; 8:220]. He was head of a Mecklenburg County household of 3 persons in 1782 [VA:33]. He and John Chavis brought a suit against Robert Taylor which was dismissed by the Henrico County court on agreement of the parties on 13 March 1784 [Orders 1781-4, 477]. He was taxable on a tithe, 2 horses, and 2 cattle in Mecklenburg County in 1786 and a tithe in 1791 [PPTL 1782-1805, frames 122, 368]. He married Rebecca **Stewart**, 10 September 1792 Mecklenburg County bond. He was a taxable "Blackman" in Island Creek District, Granville County in 1803 [Tax List 1803-09, 42]. In 1810 he was head of a Granville County household of 7 "other free" [NC:858]. He died in Granville County in May 1831 according to the survivor's pension application of his son Peter [M805, reel 180, frame 145]. His children were

i. Peter[3], born about 1778, married Maron **Bird**, 4 November 1800 Granville County bond, Charles **Evans** bondsman. He was bondsman for the 29 December 1812 Chatham County marriage of James Chavis and Nancy **Bird**. He was one of the freeholders of Chatham County who were ordered by the court to work on the road from New Hope Bridge to William Goodwin's in February 1814 [Minutes 1811-18, 147]. He was head of a Chatham County household of 6 "other free" in 1810 (adjacent to Charles **Evans** and Jacob **Bird**) [NC:193], living in Chatham County on 13 January 1840 when he applied for his father's pension [M805-180, frame 145].

ii. ?Miles, head of a Chatham County household of 5 "other free" in 1800.

iii. ?Washington, head of a Chatham County household of 7 "other free" in 1810 [NC:208].

iv. ?Garrison, born say 1785, an insolvent taxpayer in Chatham County in Captain Marsh's district in 1806 [Minutes 1805-10, 158] and taxable on one free poll in Captain B. Jones' 1815 list for Chatham County. He was head of a Moore County household of 5 "free colored" in 1820 [NC:312].

   v.   ?James[5], born say 1786, married Nancy **Bird**, 29 December 1812
        Chatham County bond, Peter Chavis bondsman. He and John Chavis
        were among the freeholders of Chatham County ordered by the court
        to work on the road from White Oak Bridge to Polly Leavin's in
        November 1814 and from New Hope to the big falls in Cape Fear in
        February 1818 [Minutes 1811-18, 180; 1816-22, 101]. There is no
        record of his purchasing land in Chatham County, but he was taxable
        on 75 acres and one free poll in the 1815 list of Ed Farrar.

45 vi.   Elizabeth[8], born say 1789.
   vii.   ?Banister, born 1776-94, one of the freeholders of Chatham County
        who were ordered by the court to work on the road from New Hope
        Bridge to William Goodwin's (with Peter Chavous) in February 1814
        [Minutes 1811-18, 147]. He married Milly **Walden**, 29 December 1819
        Mecklenburg County, Virginia bond, John **Stewart** surety, married by
        Minister Alexander M. Cowan. He was head of a Mecklenburg County
        household of 4 "free colored" in 1820 [VA:148b].

34. Elizabeth[4] Chavis (Catherine, Thomas[2], William[1], Thomas[1]), born say 1757,
     was living in Lunenburg County in May 1761 when the court ordered the
     churchwardens of Cornwall Parish to bind her as an apprentice to Philip Jones
     [Orders 1761-2, 17]. She may have been the Elizabeth Chavis whose son John
     Jackson Chavis was bound as an apprentice to William **Stewart** in
     Mecklenburg County. **Stewart** moved to Wake County, North Carolina, about
     1790, and John **Jackson** went with him and died there about 1808 when
     Stewart tried to prove his nuncupative Wake County will. Elizabeth's sister
     Lucy, wife of Robert **Cole**, challenged the will by presenting a deposition
     taken from Mary Belcher of Charlotte County, Virginia, on 27 April 1808 that
     John **Jackson** Chavis was christened in her home and that Lucy was his only
     living relative [N.C. Stack File C.R. 099.928.11 by *NCGSJ* III:21; Haun,
     Wake County Court Minutes VII:67-8, 151]. Elizabeth was the mother of
      i.   John **Jackson**, bound as an apprentice blacksmith to William **Stewart**
           in Mecklenburg County, Virginia, died in Wake County about 1808.

35. Bolling Chavis (Henry[1], Thomas[2], William[1], Thomas[1]), born say 1772, was
     taxable in the Mecklenburg County household of (his father) Henry Chavis
     from 1790 to 1793 and taxable in Mecklenburg County in 1800 and 1803
     [PPTL 1782-1805, frames 341, 423, 479, 794, 943]. He first married Nancy
     Thomerson, 14 June 1793 Warren County bond with Eaton **Walden** security;
     and second, Suckey **Thomason**, "daughter of Amy Thomason," 25 January
     1798 Mecklenburg County, Virginia bond, Banister **Thomason** surety.[77]
     Bolling, his mother Ellender and his sister Rebecca brought suit in
     Mecklenburg County against his brother Henry over a dividing line in their
     land on the Meherrin River which they received by their father's will. Boling
     died before 24 March 1804 when Henry and the others reached agreement
     [Mecklenburg County unrecorded deed 1804, LVA]. On 12 March 1806 the
     Mecklenburg County court ordered the sheriff to dispose of his estate since no
     one would administer it and appointed Jabez Northington as guardian of
     Bolling's orphan Edwin Chavous [Orders 1805-6, 124]. Bolling was the father
     of
      i.   Edwin, born say 1794, perhaps the Edward Chavous who was a
           "Mulatto" taxable in Mecklenburg County from 1815 to 1819 [PPTL,
           1806-28, frames 500, 534, 652].

---

[77]William **Thompson**, born 1776-1794, was head of a Mecklenburg County household of 10 "free
colored" in 1820 [VA:159b].

36. Philip[1] Chavis (William[2], Bartholomew[1], William[1], Thomas[1]), born say 1726, bought 100 acres of land in Northampton County, North Carolina, on 25 February 1752 and purchased another 108 acres a few days later on 4 March 1752 from Edith Booth "for a valuable consideration" [DB 2:62, 68]. This was land adjacent to his own land in the northeast corner of Northampton County near the Meherrin River, part of an island on the "old county line." His father gave him 300 acres in Granville County on the north side of the Tar River at the mouth of Collins Creek on 4 March 1752 [DB B:47], and he was taxable on one tithe in Granville County in the list of Lemuel Lanier adjacent to his father in 1753. On 27 May 1756 he and wife Selah sold the 108 acres in Northampton County [DB 2:267]. In 1757 he had three persons in his household in the list of Samuel Henderson adjacent to his father, and in the 1758-9 undated list of Phil. Hawkins he was listed with wife Selah and slave "Jordin" [CR 044.701.19]. By 29 July 1761 he had accumulated 1,350 acres of land, most of it on Buffalo Creek in Granville County [DB B:47; E:43, 178; Northampton DB 2:62]. His land in Craven County, South Carolina, near Wassoo Creek was mentioned in an estate sale advertised in the 26 July to 2 August 1760 South Carolina Gazette [Warren, *South Carolina Newspapers*, 34]. In 1761 he was taxable on 2 "free black" tithes for himself and his wife "Celea" and black tithes for 2 female slaves, "Peg and Parrott," in Granville County. He had two illegitimate children by Hannah **Francis** of Johnston County about 1760 [Haun, *Johnston County Court Minutes*, I:86, 89].

He was called "Free negroe Planter" on 12 August 1763 when he sold the 300 acres in Granville County which his father gave him on 4 March 1752 [DB G:209]. On 13 August 1764 he sold an unstated number of acres of his land in Bute County on the north side of the Tar River to his father [Warren DB 1:102]. He was sued in Granville County court by William Hamilton & Company in November 1765 for a ten pound debt which John Williams, Jr., confessed to by power of attorney [Minutes 1754-70, 123]. The sheriff sold 700 acres of Philip's land in Granville County to pay this debt on 5 August 1766 [DB H:172]. He was a resident of South Carolina on 3 December 1766 when he sold his father 400 acres in Bute County on both sides of Buffalo Creek adjoining his father's Granville County land [DB 1:266]. He also resided in Bladen County, North Carolina, where he bought land on the east side of Wilkinson's Swamp, which is in present-day Robeson County on the South Carolina border. This was land formerly owned by Robert **Sweat**. Philip and his wife "Sele" sold this land on 21 November 1768 [DB 23:104].

He was a resident of Craven County, South Carolina, on 15 June 1772 when he sold 100 acres of his land in Northampton County [DB 5:246].[78] On 22 July 1772 he repurchased the same 100 acres he had sold in Bladen County in 1768 [DB 23:424].

On 5 February 1778 he was back in Granville County where he settled the inventory of the estate of his father in Granville County court. According to the account of sales Philip bought 2 slaves, 39 head of cattle, 22 sheep, and many other items [WB 1:164-5]. He was called Philip Cheaves of South Carolina on 3 March 1778 when he sold a tract of land of unstated acreage in the part of Bute County which became Franklin County in 1769 [DB 1:9]. About a month later on 7 May 1778 he entered 100 acres on the Franklin County border with Granville County "near the Buffuloe Race paths" joining his deceased father's land [DB O:85]. He was residing in Georgetown District, South Carolina, on 20 November 1778 when he sold land in Granville County to Hugh **Snelling** [DB O:3]. The 2 November 1779 Granville County, North

---

[78]This deed was signed "John Chavis" without a dower release.

Carolina court called him "Phillip Chavers an Inhabitant of another State" when it subjected him to fourfold tax because his property was not inventoried. He was called Philip Chavis of Bladen County on 16 February 1780 when he sold his 100 acres in Granville County "near the Buffuloe Race paths" and another 500 acres on the Franklin-Granville County lines south of the Tar River to Major **Evans** for 3,000 pounds [Franklin DB 1:140]. In 1780 he was assessed tax on 4,260 pounds property in Granville County's Fishing Creek District in the list of Col. Dickerson, and was taxable in Granville County on 1,060 acres, 4 slaves, and 8 cattle in 1782. He was charged with felony in Granville County in 1782, but there is no record of a trial taking place or its outcome [Minutes 1773-83, November 1782 Dockets]. He and his wife Celia sold land in Granville County on 28 December 1782 [DB O:236].

On 8 March 1783 he purchased 200 acres in Bladen County, 160 acres of which was the land he had sold in 1768 [DB 1:95], and in 1784 he was taxable in Bladen County tax on 750 acres, 3 free polls, and a slave. He was called "Philip Chaves, Senr." on 2 September 1785 when he sold two tracts of land of about 200 acres each in what was by then Robeson County. On 25 June 1786 he sold a tract of 100 acres on Shoe Heel Swamp in Robeson and as "Philip Chavers" (no Senior) he sold 300 acres on both sides of the Lower Ashpole on 8 December 1793 [DB A:83; B:160; D:227]. His children were

46 i. ?Ishmael, born say 1747.
   ii. Philip[2], born say 1758, "alias Philip Frances," was Philip[1]'s illegitimate son who was bound an apprentice by the Johnston County court in January 1762 shortly after the death of his mother Hannah **Francis** [Haun, *Johnston County Court Minutes*, I:89]. Perhaps his will is the one written by "Philip Shaver" in Little River, Camden District, South Carolina, on 18 July 1793 and proved on 9 September 1793 [WB 2:95]. He lent his wife "Maria Margaret Shaver" plantations of 250 acres and 450 acres as well as 5 slaves, which at her death were to go to his daughters Maria Margaret Polick and Mary Scott.
   iii. ?Charles[1], born in October 1760, three years old in October 1763, "son of Hannah Chavis," bound as an apprentice shoemaker by the May 1763 session of the Orange County, North Carolina court [Haun, *Orange County Court Minutes*, II:586]. Perhaps Hannah Chavis was identical to Hannah **Francis** whose son Philip was bound apprentice in Johnston County court in 1762. Charles was taxable on one poll in Abrams Plains District of Granville County in 1788. He married Nancy **Taborn**, 4 November 1795 Granville County bond with Benjamin **Bass** bondsman and was head of a Granville County household of 4 "other free" in 1800 and 11 in 1810 [NC:858].
47 iv. ?Erasmus, born say 1768.

37. Gibeon[2] Chavis (William[2], Bartholomew[1], William[1], Thomas[1]), born say 1737, was taxable in 1753 in his father's household in the Granville County list of Robert Harris. He and Gideon[1] **Bunch** were probably named for Gideon **Gibson** who was living on the south side of the Roanoke in the same area as Gibeon's father in 1727. He married Ann Priddy who was the "daughter Anne, wife of Gibby Chavers," mentioned in the 2 July 1759 Granville County will of her father Robert Priddy, proved December 1759 [Owen, *Granville County Notes*, vol.I]. Robert Priddy was a white Granville County farmer. On 1 June 1755 Gibeon's father made a deed of gift to him for 400 acres on Little Creek on the north side of Tar River [DB C:73], and in 1757 he was taxable on one tithe in his own household in the list of John Martin. By 1761 he had married and was listed in Fishing Creek taxable on himself and his wife Nanny [CR 44.701.19]. He was charged with trespass, assault, and battery by John Babtist Marr in Granville County court on 11 August 1765 but was found not guilty [Minutes 1754-70, 147]. In 1769 he was taxable on 3 persons, and in 1771 he

had 6 taxables in his household. He left a 4 January 1777 Granville County will (signing), proved in May 1777, which mentioned only his wife and son William. Aquilla **Snelling** (signing) and Elender Chavis (making her mark) were witnesses. His estate inventory listed 5 horses, 17 cattle, and 53 hogs [WB 1:158]. Part of his land was sold and 150 acres assigned to his wife Ann by her right of dower [WB 1:143, 166]. She was assessed 2,000 pounds property tax in Fishing Creek in Colonel Dickerson's District in 1780. Their children were

  i. Patience, born say 1755, called "daughter of Anne Priddy, daughter of testator," in Robert Priddy's will. She married John Jackson, a white man, and was living with him in Rowan County on 16 September 1771 when they sold the land she inherited from her grandfather [Granville DB I:309].

  ii. Susanna[2], born say 1756, called "daughter of Anne Priddy, daughter of testator" in Robert Priddy's will. She married Andrew Ingram, a white man, and was living with him in Cumberland County, North Carolina, on 1 December 1772 when they sold the land she inherited from her grandfather [Granville DB K:202].

  iii. William[7], born about 1757, probably the third person taxed in his father's 1769 household. His father left him his land and plantation. In 1780 he was still under the care of a guardian, his uncle George Priddy, who paid his tax on an assessment of 2,362 pounds in Fort Creek. On 13 March 1785 he sold 400 acres on both sides of Little Creek in Granville County on the north side of the Tar River for 543 pounds, purchased land in Granville County on 13 October 1786 and sold 20 acres adjoining his own land and **Snelling** on 10 February 1788 [DB O:376, 575, 585]. He may have been the William Chavis who married Sarah **Kersey**, 13 March 1790 Granville County bond. He was head of a Wake County household of 6 "other free" in 1800 [NC:757].

38. Thomas[4] Cheaves (Thomas[3], Bartholomew[1], William[1], Thomas[1]), born say 1742, may have been the Thomas Chevas who was listed as a deserter from the Cherokee Expedition, Captain John Hitchcock's Company of the South Carolina Militia on 15 November 1759 [Clark, *Colonial Soldiers of the South*, 930]. In 1763 he was in Granville County, taxable in William Eaves' Bare Swamp District household. This part of Granville County became Bute County in 1764 and Thomas was a "black" taxable in William Mackbie's household in the 1771 Bute County list of Philimon Hawkins [CR.015.70001, p.5 of pamphlet]. He may have been the Thomas Chavis who was head of a Granville County household of 10 "other free" and one slave in 1810 [NC:866], and he may have been the father of

  i. Jordan[2], born say 1775, purchased 25 acres in Wake County on the east side of Mine Creek adjoining Hugh **Snelling** on 21 June 1800 and sold this land to John Chavis on 25 July 1805 [DB Q:429; U:433]. He married (his second cousin?) the daughter of Aquilla and Lettice **Snelling** (nee Chavis) and was mentioned in Lettice's 2 April 1814 Wake County will. He was head of a Wake County household of 2 "other free" and 4 slaves in 1800 [NC:756]. His Wake County tax was paid by Reuben **Evans** in 1820 [CR 99.252]. He purchased 300 acres on lower Long Branch, north of the Yadkin River and on the waters of Mulberry Creek, in Wilkes County in 1813 and purchased another 100 acres adjoining this in 1814. He was head of a Wilkes County household of 6 "free colored" in 1820 [NC:519]. In 1829 he sold 85 acres of his land to (his mother-in-law) Mary **Mitchell** [DB GH:469, 505; M:206]. He had married Lucy **Harris**, daughter of Molly **Mitchell**, sometime before he was mentioned in her 20 August 1833 Wilkes County will.

39. Isam/ Isham[1] Chavis (Joseph[1], Bartholomew[1], William[1], Thomas[1]), born say 1746, was sued by Abner Nash in Halifax County, North Carolina court in November 1768 [Gammon, *Record of Estates* II:12]. He was head of a Cumberland County, North Carolina household of 8 "other free" in 1790 [NC:38]. He entered 110 acres bordering his own land and John Walker's in Cumberland County on 16 May 1786 [Pruitt, *Land Entries: Cumberland County*, 60]. He was a carpenter who was granted 200 acres in Cumberland on the south side of Campbell's Creek on 21 December 1787. He and his wife Rachel sold this land on 27 February 1794, and he sold 400 acres in Cumberland on Jones' Creek and Upper Little River on 16 July 1795 [DB 14:168; 16:49]. He died before 14 April 1796 when (his son?) William Chavis was granted administration on his estate on 100 pounds security [Minutes 1791-97, Thursday, 14 April 1796]. Later that year William sold land which Isham was granted in 1789 [DB 16:372]. His children were probably

    i.   William[8], born say 1775. On 8 July 1796 he sold 100 acres in Cumberland County on Upper Little River and the next day sold 170 acres in Cumberland County on MacDougald's Branch which was granted to Isham Chavis on 16 March 1789 [DB 16:372; 18:196]. He was head of a Cumberland County household of 4 "other free" in 1810 [NC:584].
    ii. Azekiel(?), head of a Cumberland County household of 4 "free colored" in 1820 [NC:191].

40. Isham[2] Chavis (Bartholomew[2], Bartholomew[1], William[1], Thomas[1]), born say 1758, was taxable in Dinwiddie County from 1782 to 1804: called Isham Walding in 1782 and 1784, called Isham Chavis in 1787 and 1788, called Isham **Walden** from 1789 to 1800 and in 1801 when he was counted as a "free Negro" and called "free" Isham Chavis when he taxable in 1804 [PPTL, 1782-90 (1782 A, p.18), (1784, p.25), (1787 B, p.2) (1788 B, p.5), (1789 A, p.21); 1791-9, (1791 A, pp. 4, 20), (1795 B, p.21), (1797 B, p.20), (1798 A, p.18), (1799 A, p.19); 1800-9, (1800 B, p.23), (1801 B, p.25), (1804 a, p.4)]. He may have been the member of the Chavis family who married Milly **Stewart**. Milly, born about 1762, registered in Petersburg on 24 December 1808: *Milly Chavis, formerly Stewart, a light brown Mulatto woman, forty six years old, born free & raised in the County of Prince George p. certificate of Registry from Clk. of Dinwiddie County. Reentered 2 March 1820 tho not a light brown ditto* [Register of Free Negroes 1794-1819, no. 433]. She was the mother of

    i.   ?Stephen, born about 1778, registered in Petersburg on 15 August 1799: *a dark brown Mulatto man, five feet eight inches high, with short bushy hair, twenty one years old in March last, born free & raised by Wm Scott in the County of Dinwiddie* [Register of Free Negroes 1794-1819, no. 149].
    ii. Ezekiel, born about 1789, registered in Petersburg on 24 December 1808: *a light brown Mulatto man, five feet seven inches high, nineteen years old, born free & raised in the Town of Petersburg. Registered by desire of his mother Milly Chavis. Reentered 13 June 1810 by name Ezekiel Stewart (by desire)* [Register of Free Negroes 1794-1819, no. 432]. Ezekiel Chaves was taxable on Vinet Claiborne's land in Chesterfield County with his unnamed wife in 1811 [PPTL, 1786-1811, frame 824].
    iii. Caty, born about 1798, registered in Petersburg on 7 August 1811: *Caty Steward, a brown Mulatto girl, thirteen years old 26 November last, daughter of Milly Chavis* [Register of Free Negroes 1794-1819, no. 667].
    iv. Polly, born about 1802, registered in Petersburg on 7 August 1811: *Polly Steward, a dark brown Mulatto girl, four feet eleven inches high, nine years old 9 April last. born free & raised in the Town of*

Petersburg, daughter of Milly Chavis [Register of Free Negroes 1794-
1819, no. 668].

41. Frances[2]/ Fanny Chavis (Mary, Amy, Thomas[2], William[1], Thomas[1]), born say
1765, was head of a Southampton County household of 5 "other free" in 1810
[VA:71]. She was a "f.n." taxable in Southampton County from 1801 to 1820:
taxable on a free male tithable and a horse from 1801 to 1804, taxable on
Benjamin Chavis's tithe and a horse in 1805, taxable on a horse in 1806 and
1807, taxable on 2 slaves and a free male tithable from 1809 to 1812, listed
with her son Ellick and daughters Polly and Milly in 1813, living on her own
land in 1820 [PPTL 1792-1806, frame 512, 549, 802; 1807-21, frames 47, 70,
166, 189, 288, 316, 415, 576, 661, 689, 786]. On 17 March 1817 the
Southampton County court exempted her from paying taxes on her slave Toney
because he was aged and infirm [Minutes 1816-9, unpaged]. She was the
mother of
    i. ?Mason, born about 1784, a witness against Sam **Rand (Rann)**, a
        "Mullatto boy" accused in Southampton County court on 20 January
        1806 of stealing $5 from a boy slave named Burwell belonging to
        James Crichlow [Minutes 1799-1803, 85]. Mason registered in
        Southampton County on 30 August 1811: *Mason Shavers, age 27, Blk.,*
        5 feet 4-1/2 inches high, free born [Register of Free Negroes 1794-
        1832, no. 595].
    ii. ?Benjamin, born about 1785, taxable on a horse in St. Luke's Parish,
        Southampton County, from 1807 to 1811 [PPTL 1807-21, frames 48,
        70, 167, 189]. He registered in Southampton County on 27 March
        1816: *age 31, Blk, 5'6", free born* [Register of Free Negroes 1794-
        1832, no. 1003].
   iii. ?Temperance, born about 1786, registered in Southampton County on
        31 July 1810, 20 May 1817 and again on 3 March 1821: *age 35, black*
        woman who has daughter named Ann Eliza aged 15 Martha Ann aged
        12 years & Frances aged 8 years 5 feet 1/2 inch high, free born
        [Register of Free Negroes 1794-1832, nos. 792, 1089, 1259].
    iv. ?Isaac, born about 1789, ordered bound apprentice in St. Luke's
        Parish, Southampton County, on 11 December 1795 [Minutes 1793-9,
        163], taxable in St. Luke's Parish in 1811 [PPTL 1807-21, frame 189].
        He registered in Southampton County 28 January 1811; *age 22, Blk.,*
        free born, 6 feet high [Register of Free Negroes 1794-1832, no. 585].
    v. Polly, born about 1789, registered in Southampton County on 1 April
        1814: *age 25, mulatto, 5'5-1/2", free born* [Register of Free Negroes
        1794-1832, no. 832].
    vi. Alexander, born about 1794, registered in Southampton County on 29
        July 1815: *age 21, 5'10-3/4", free born, yellow complection* [Register
        of Free Negroes 1794-1832, nos. 970, 1491, 2004].
   vii. Milly, born about 1796, registered in Southampton County on 1 April
        1814: *age 18, Mulatto, 5'5-1/4", free born* [Register of Free Negroes
        1794-1832, no. 833].
  viii. ?James, ordered bound apprentice in St. Luke's Parish, Southampton
        County, on 11 December 1795 [Minutes 1793-9, 163].

42. John[8] Chavis (Jacob[2], Frances, Thomas[2], William[1], Thomas[1]), born say 1764,
was called John Chavis, Junior, in 1786 when he was taxable on one tithe and
a horse in Mecklenburg County, Virginia [PPTL 1782-1805, frame 122]. He
was a grandson of Thomas **Evans** who named him in his 22 May 1787
Mecklenburg County, Virginia will [WB 2:250] and was one of the heirs of
Jacob Chavis who were named in a Mecklenburg County chancery case in
1819. He attended Washington Academy which later became Washington and

Lee University [*North Carolina Historical Review*, VII:333].[79] He was introduced to the Presbytery of Lexington, Virginia, at their meeting from 15 to 19 October 1799. According to the minutes of the meeting he was personally known to most of the members. The following year the General Assembly of the Presbyterian Church of the United States in Philadelphia ruled that

> *John Chavis, a black man of prudence and piety, who has been educated and licensed to preach by the Presbytery of Lexington in Virginia, be employed as a missionary among people of his own colour*

On 9 June 1801 he delivered a discourse to the Lexington Presbytery at Rocky Springs Meetinghouse, and the Presbytery agreed to his request to join the Hanover Presbytery, recommending him as

> *a man of exemplary piety, & possessed of many qualifications which merit their respectful attention* [Acts and Proceedings, 15, by *NCHR.*, VII:331, 333].

On 6 April 1802 he recorded his free papers in Rockbridge County:

> *Rev. John Chavis, a black man...has been known to the court for several years past...has been a student at Washington Acadmy where they believe he went through a regular course of Academical Studies* [Orders 6:10].

He moved to Chatham County where he purchased 100 acres on Weaver's Creek on 9 November 1804 [DB O:70]. His conversation with an educated African American woman in Chatham County was reported in *The Association Missionary Magazine of Evangelical Intelligence* [vol. I (August, 1805), 49 by *JNH*, 142-155]. On 15 May 1806 he was residing in Wake County when he purchased 233 acres adjoining Mine Creek and Haw Branch in Wake County for $700 from Joshua Eastland of Chatham County [DB T:268]. (His father?) Jacob Chavis of Mecklenburg County, Virginia, gave him power of attorney to recover a debt from William **Stewart** of North Carolina on 11 July 1806 [Mecklenburg DB 13:1-2]. He had established a school before 26 August 1808 when he announced in the *Raleigh Register* that

> *the present quarter of his school will end the 15th of September, and the next will commence on the 19th. He will, at the same time, open an evening school for the purpose of instructing children of colour, as he intends, for the accommodation of some of his employers, to exclude all children of colour from his day school* [*NCHR*, 339].

He was said to have joined the Orange Presbytery in 1809 and preached in Granville, Orange, and Wake Counties for the next twenty years or so [*NCHR*, 335]. He purchased another 100 acres on Weaver's Creek in Chatham County on 23 July 1811 and sold this second tract of 100 acres for 100 pounds on the 28 April 1817 and the remaining 100 acres for $650 on 7 March 1818 (signing both deeds) [DB T:237; V:106; X:343]. In the November 1814 session of the

---

[79] According to the editor of *The Princeton Alumni Weekly* of 29 March 1935, "it is almost certain" that he attended Princeton University under Dr. Witherspoon. He further reported that the Princeton trustees' minutes for 26 September 1792 state: *Mr. John Todd Henry of Virginia and John Chavis a free Black Man of that State was recommended by the Revd. John B. Smith to be received into this fund* (the Leslie Fund *for the education of poor and pious youths with a view to the ministry of the Gospel in the Presbyterian Church.)*

Chatham County court, he and Cary Chavis were found guilty of an unnamed offense, but were granted an appeal [Minutes 1811-18, 183]. On 28 June 1815 he was living in Wake County when he purchased 111 acres on the south side of the Neuse River on Laurel Creek [DB 3:336]. He was head of a Chatham County household of 5 "other free" in 1810 (adjacent to Charles **Evans** and Peter Chavers) [NC:193] and 9 "free colored" in 1820 [NC:211]. Senator Willie P. Magnum and his brother Priestly Magnum, Governor Charles Manly, and Congressman Abraham Rencher were probably his students since he referred to each of them as "my son" in his letters to the senator [*NCHR*, 326, 341, 345]. On 13 December 1827 he wrote to his friend Senator Mangum about a deed of trust for land adjoining Tignal Jones and Job Rogers in Wake County which was given to him and his wife Frances during their lifetimes. And three days later on 18 December 1827 he wrote to the senator inviting him to attend the next examination at his school in Wake County at Revises Crossroads [State Department of Archives and History, The Mangum Papers, 316-318]. On 22 April 1830 Joseph Gales, editor of the *Raleigh Register*, reported that he had recently attended an examination "of the free children of color" at the school and "seldom received more gratification from any exhibition of a similar character" [*NCHR*, 340]. He made a quit claim deed in Granville County on 8 July 1831 relinquishing any right to the estate of his brother Isaac Chavis [DB 7:253]. In a letter to Mangum on 10 March 1832 he wrote, "If I am Black, I am free born American and a revolutionary soldier." However, there is no record that he ever served in the Revolution. Reverend John Chavis died 15 June 1838 [*Watchman of the South*, Obituary Notice by *Virginia Genealogical Society Quarterly* 19:123]. He may have been the father of

  i. Thomas[7], born say 1801, an insolvent taxpayer for the year 1822, reported in the Wednesday, August 1823 session of the Chatham County court. He was one of the freeholders of Chatham County who were ordered to work on the road from the Randolph County line to the branch below Rebecca Evans in the Monday, November 1827 session of the court.

  ii. William[12], born say 1805, one of the freeholders of Chatham County who were ordered to work on the road from William Ragland's to John Dorsett's by the Monday, February 1836 session of the court.

43. Jacob[3] Chavis, born say 1772, was over sixteen years of age in 1788 when he was counted in the Mecklenburg County property tax list tax of his father Jacob Chavous [PPTL 1782-1805, frame 211]. He married Phoebe **Scott**, daughter of Betsey **Scott**, 24 December 1800 Charlotte County bond and 8 December 1800 Mecklenburg County bond, Thomas A. Jones & James Wilson security, with a note from James Wayne. He was called a wheelwright when the Mecklenburg County court bound Willie and Archibald / **Nash** to him on 12 October 1807 and 12 September 1808 [Orders 1807-9, 239, 467]. He was a "free negroe" taxable in Charlotte County from 1795 to 1813: taxable on a slave in 1796; taxable on 2 free males in 1801; listed as a "free negroe" wheelwright with his wife Pheby and son Martin in 1802; taxable on 2 free males, 3 slaves, 2 horses, and 2 cart wheels in 1806; taxable on 2 free males and 2 slaves in 1807; taxable on 3 free males and a slave in 1810; and a "fn" wheelwright listed with 5 males (two of whom were tithable) and 3 females in list of free Negroes and Mulattoes in 1813 [PPTL 1782-1813, frames 314, 339, 367, 398, 433, 465, 502, 534, 542, 671, 707, 717, 751, 773, 814, 886]. (His brother-in-law and sister) Arvy and Martha **Scott** released their right to land which was due to her from the estate of her father Jacob Chavis, Sr., to Jacob by deed proved in Mecklenburg County on 10 July 1809 [DB 14:107, 308]. He was a "Free Negro" head of a Charlotte County household of 10 "other free" in 1810 [VA:45]. Jacob's widow Phoebe was one of the buyers

at the sale of his 15 December 1842 Charlotte County estate [WB 10:23-4].
Jacob and Phebe were the parents of

    i.   Abraham Martin, born about 1802, registered in Charlotte County on
7 May 1827: *son of Jacob Chavous and Phoebe his wife, Yellow
complexion, aged 25, born free* [Ailsworth, *Charlotte County--Rich
Indeed*, 487].

    ii.   Mack, born about 1803, registered in Charlotte County on 4 April
1831: son of Jacob and Phobe Chavous, free persons, Bright
complexion, aged 28 [Ailsworth, *Charlotte County--Rich Indeed*, 488].

    iii.   William, born about 1805, registered in Charlotte County on 1 october
1827: *son of Jacob Chavous and Phoebe his wife, free people of
Colour, Yellow complexion, aged 21, born free* [Ailsworth, *Charlotte
County--Rich Indeed*, 487].

    iv.   Mary, born about 1809, registered in Charlotte County on 3 October
1836: *daughter of Jacob Chavous & Phoebe his wife, Dark brown
complexion, aged 27* [Ailsworth, *Charlotte County--Rich Indeed*, 491].

    v.   Jacob, born about 1816, registered in Charlotte County on 4 December
1837: *son of Jacob Chavous and Phoebe his wife, free persons, Dark
Mulatto, aged 21* [Ailsworth, *Charlotte County--Rich Indeed*, 491].

44. Susannah[3] Chavis, born 21 June 1767, was the daughter of Sucky Chavis, "a
free mulatto" of Bruton Parish, James City County [Bruton Parish Register,
31]. She registered in Petersburg on 30 December 1808: *Sucky Chavis, a
yellowish brown free negro woman, five feet seven and a half inches high,
forty [overwritten] years old, born free & raised in Wmsburg* [Register of Free
Negroes 1794-1819, no. 441]. She was the mother of

    i.   ?Edward, born about 1783, registered in Petersburg on 28 December
1808: *a dark brown, near black man, five feet ten and a half inches
high, straight & spare made, twenty five years old, born free & raised
in York County* [Register of Free Negroes 1794-1819, no. 436].

    ii.   John[14], born about 1789, registered in Petersburg on 30 December
1808: *a dark brown free Negro man, five feet eight and a half inches
high, nineteen years old, son of Sucky Chavis a free woman* [Register
of Free Negroes 1794-1819, no. 440].

    iii.   William[11], born say 1792, "bastard of Susannah Chavous," bound by
the Overseers of the Poor of Mecklenburg County to Samuel Holmes,
Jr., on 18 January 1800 [Orders 1798-1801, 289].

    iv.   ?Jeronias(?), born say 1794, bound by the Overseers of the Poor of
Mecklenburg County to William Puryear on 14 June 1802 (no parent
named) [Orders 1801-3, 251].

    v.   ?Sarah, born say 1796, bound by the Overseers of the Poor of
Mecklenburg County to William Puryear on 14 June 1802 (no parent
named) [Orders 1801-3, 251].

45. Elizabeth[8] Chavis (Anthony, George, Thomas[2], William[1], Thomas[1]), born say
1789, "a woman of Colour," was ordered brought before the Monday,
February 1821 session of the Chatham County court so that her children could
be bound out as apprentices [Minutes 1816-22]. She was listed as a sixty-year-
old "Mulatto" woman in Chatham County in 1850 [NC:370 A&B]. She may
have been the daughter of Anthony Chavis who was living in Mecklenburg
County about 1858 when descendants of Thomas **Stewart** filed a chancery suit
[LVA Chancery file 1872-008]. Her children were

    i.   Nancy, "a Girl of Colour," born 25 December 1807, bound apprentice
to Brooks Brantly by the Monday, May 1821 session of the Chatham
County court and bound instead to Hezekiah Dorsett in the Wednesday
session.

ii.   Polly, born about 1811, "a Girl of Colour" bound apprentice to George Rogers to read, write, and cypher by the Monday, May 1821 session of the Chatham County court.
iii. William[13], born 10 December 1814, bound to John Dorsett as an apprentice farmer and to be taught to read and write by the Monday May 1821 session of the court.
iv.   ?Caty, born about 1819, bound apprentice to David Justice by the Tuesday, May 1826 session of the court, no parent named [Minutes 1822-27].
v.   ?Elizabeth[10], born about 1819, a nine-year-old "Coloured Girl" bound apprentice to Hezekiah Dorsett by the Tuesday, May 1828 session of the court, no parent named [Minutes 1828-33].
vi.   ?Clary, born about 1825, an eleven-year-old "Coloured girl" bound apprentice to Daniel Marsh by the Monday, 8 February 1836 session of the court, no parent named.

46. Ishmael Chavis (Philip[1], William[2], Bartholomew[1], William[1], Thomas[1]), born say 1747, was taxable in Bladen County with his unnamed wife ("Mulatoes") from 1768 to 1774 [Byrd, *Bladen County Tax Lists*, I:5, 14, 44, 60, 82, 95, 124, 134]. He patented 100 acres in Bladen County on the lower side of Long Swamp, northeast of Drowning Creek, on 14 May 1772 [Hoffman, *Land Patents*, II:265]. He and his wife Reigel sold this land on 20 December 1774 [DB 23:501]. He was taxable in Bladen County on 100 acres and one poll in Captain Cades' District in 1784. He sold another 100 acres on the south side of Long Swamp on 22 January 1788 in what was then Robeson County and sold 100 ares on the west side of Drowning Creek on 26 December 1795. He bought 100 acres on the north side of Back Swamp in 1796 and sold it eight years later to Thomas **Lowry** on 17 May 1804 [DB A:189; E:402; F:93; O:163]. He was head of a Robeson County household of 10 "other free" in 1790 [NC:48], and 8 in 1800 [NC:371]. Perhaps his children were
    i.   John[9], born say 1774, head of a Robeson County household of 6 "other free" and one white woman in 1800 [NC:370] and 5 "other free" in 1810 [NC:222].
    ii. Albert, head of a Robeson County household of 5 "other free" in 1800 [NC:370].
    iii. Joseph[3], born say 1785, head of a Robeson County household of 4 "other free" in 1810 [NC:218].

47. Erasmus Chavis (Philip[1], William[2], Bartholomew[1], William[1], Thomas[1]), born say 1768, was head of a Bladen County household of 3 "other free" in 1790 [NC:188], 9 in 1800, 14 in 1810 [NC:195], and 12 "free colored" in 1820 [NC:136]. He was the father of
    i.   Rachel **Carter**, who on 25 May 1839 appointed (her brother?) Eliah Chavis of Robeson County her attorney to sell her share of her father's land [DB X:224].
    ii. Eliah.
    iii. ?Stephen, born about 1777, a "Mulatto Boy" who was stolen in Bladen County and returned to his mother Elizabeth Cheaves in Surry County, North Carolina, on 17 February 1782 [Absher, *Surry County, North Carolina, Court Minutes*, 40].

48. Henry[5] Chavers, born say 1832, emigrated to Liberia on 3 July 1857 [American Colonization Society Papers, microfilm, reel 314, by Bell I. Wiley]. He dictated a letter from Liberia to Dr. Ellis Malone of Louisburg in Franklin County, North Carolina, on 2 August 1857 describing his great pleasure in being in the: *Land of Freedom...a nation of free and happy Children of a hitherto downcast and oppresed Race...Tell them I now begin to enjoy life as a man should do...did my Coloured Friends only know or could*

they have seen what I already have seen they would not hesitate a moment to come to this Glorious Country. He asked Dr. Malone to give his respects to: *All my relations at Dunsans up Tar River* (and to) *tell Hilray Dunsans to come and bring all his tools* [Wiley, *Slaves No More*, 272-3].[80]

Other members of the family living in South Carolina were

    i.   Jordan[1], "Mulatoe" head of a Cheraw District, South Carolina household of an "other free" male over the age of 16 and 4 "other free" females in 1790 [SC:358].

    ii.   Elizabeth[7], head of a Richland District household of 3 "other free" in 1810 [SC:177a].

    iii.   John[13], born say 1788, head of a Richland District household of 3 "other free" in 1810 [SC:175a].

Members of the family living in Louisiana were

    i.   John[12] Chavers, born say 1785, head of a St. Landry Parish, Louisiana household of 6 "free colored" in 1820 [LA:41] and 10 "free colored" in 1840, probably the ancestor of John Chavis, constable for St. Landry's Parish on 27 July 1868 [Bonds Book 4:164].

    ii.   Zedekiah Chavers, born about 1775 in South Carolina, a "free colored" man living alone in Barnwell District, South Carolina in 1830 [SC:190], a seventy-five-year-old "Black" man living alone in Washington Parish, Louisiana, in 1850 [LA:456].

    iii.   Joseph[2] Chavers, born about 1784, head of a Washington Parish, Louisiana household of a "free colored" man and 3 white females in 1830 [LA:20], listed as a white man born in South Carolina in the household of a white woman named Mary Hoffman in Washington Parish, Louisiana, in 1850 [LA:456].

A member of the Chavis family living in Alabama was

    i.   William[14], a constable who tried to arrest a white man named Heath. In June 1859 Heath convinced the court that William Chavis could not be a witness against him by showing that "the great grandfather and great grandmother of .. Chavis were .. each .. the progeny of a full-blooded negro and a white person." Some of the witnesses testified that his great grandparents "claimed to be of Indian, and not of negro blood," but the court ruled in Heath's favor [Catterall, *Judicial Cases Concerning American Slavery,* III:232].

CHURCH FAMILY

Members of the Church family on the Eastern Shore of Virginia were

    i.   Susanna, born say 1674, a "Molatto" presented by the Accomack County court on 16 November 1692 for having an illegitimate child [Orders 1690-7, 81a].

1   ii.   Samuel[1], born say 1677.

    iii.   Stephen[1], a tithable in Northampton County, Virginia, in 1720, a "negro" tithable in the household of Tamer Mapp in 1737, a tithable in John Haggoman's household in 1738, and a tithable in Adam Fisher's household in 1739 [Bell, *Northampton County Tithables*, 26, 79, 259, 281, 287]. He was sued on 12 February 1724/5 for assault by John Coffin and put in the stocks for an hour for misbehavior towards the court [Orders 1722-9, 164, 174]. He was sued by Godfrey Pole for a 4 pounds debt which was executed against his security Elizabeth

---

[80]See further the **Dunstan** history. The Ellis Malone Papers are at the William R. Perkins Library at Duke University [NUCMC, 21-H].

Church on 9 October 1728 [Orders 1722-9, 354]. On 10 November 1730 he was presented for incontinent living with Elizabeth Church but was discharged because the case was insufficiently proved. However, the case against Elizabeth was proved and she was fined 50 pounds of tobacco and ordered to give security of 10 pounds not to cohabit with him. Stephen was presented again on 9 November 1731 for incontinent living with Elizabeth Church and the case was again discharged for insufficient evidence at his costs [Orders 1729-32, 50, 57, 66, 74, 116-7, 124]. Elias Roberts sued him for debt on 13 February 1733/4 [Orders 1732-42, 94].

1. Samuel[1] Church, born say 1677, was tithable in Northampton County, Virginia, in 1720 and tithable with his wife Elizabeth from 1725 to 1742. John Lunn, probably a white man, was a tithable in his household from 1724 to 1728 [Bell, *Northampton County Tithables*, 22, 39, 63, 77, 106, 128, 144, 193, 226, 247, 249, 264, 278, 283, 310, 322, 339]. Elizabeth, or perhaps a sister-in-law by the same name, presented for bastard bearing on 17 November 1719. Samuel and his wife Elizabeth were sued in Northampton County in December 1722 for verbally abusing Josiah Cowdrey. Samuel sued John **Drighouse**, "Negro," for assault and battery, but the case was dismissed on 13 March 1722/3 when neither party appeared. Elizabeth brought an action upon the case against John Haggoman on 12 March 1724/5 and a case of assault and battery against Elias Roberts in July 1725. On 15 June 1726 Samuel and his wife Elizabeth acknowledged a deed for land to John Marshall. He and his wife Elizabeth were granted levy-free status due to their old age and poor circumstances on 13 November 1742 [Orders 1719-21, 44; 1722-9, 41, 58, 175, 194, 245; 1742-8, 31]. They may have been the parents of
   i. Thomas, born say 1710, a 10-16 year old tithable in the household of Ezekiel Church in 1724 and tithable in Samuel Church's household from 1728 to 1731. He was sued for trespass on 10 August 1731, and on 13 March 1733/4 he was presented for living incontinently with Elizabeth Monk, wife of William Monk. Elizabeth Church, wife of Samuel Church, was summoned as a witness. The court ruled that there was too great a familiarity between them and Thomas was ordered to post bond of 20 pounds not to cohabit with Elizabeth Monk [Orders 1732-42, 99, 103, 109, 113]. He and his wife Susannah Church were tithables from 1739 to 1744 [Bell, *Northampton County Tithables*, 56, 283, 310, 322, 338, 356, 357]. On 12 May 1747 Susannah was called Susannah Johnson alias Church when she was presented for "intermarrying or cohabiting with Thomas Church, a mulato." However, the following month on 10 June the King's attorney discontinued the suit, and granted his wife tax-free status, "it appearing to the court that the said Thomas is a white person." He was sued for swearing on 12 April 1749 [Orders 1742-8, 402-3, 422; 1748-51, 53, 95].
   ii. Samuel[2], Jr., born say 1712, a 10-16 year old tithable in Ezekiel Church's household in 1724, a 12-16 year old tithable in Samuel Church's household in 1728.

Their descendants on the Eastern Shore of Virginia were
   i. James, born say 1750, head of a Machipingo, St. George's Parish, Accomack County household of 7 "other free" in 1800 [*Virginia Genealogist* 2:131] and 8 in 1810 [VA:15].
   ii. Stephen[2], head of an Accomack County household of 8 "other free" in 1810 [VA:88].
   iii. Charity, head of an Accomack County household of 7 "other free" in 1810 [VA:88].

    iv. Stephen³, head of an Accomack County household of 6 "other free" in 1810 [VA:15].

    v. Abram, born in 1769, registered in Accomack County: *yellow complexion, 5 feet 8 inches high, Emancipated by Zororbabel Ames's last will & Testament of record in Accomack County court* [Register of Free Negroes, no. 48], head of a Northampton County household of "free colored" in 1820 [VA:216A].

    vi. Solomon, born before 1776, head of a Northampton County household of 8 "free colored" in 1820 [VA:217A].

Other members of the Church family were

    i. Sarah, born say 1722, presented by the Amelia County court on 21 November 1740 for having a "Mulatto Child" [Orders 1:132].

CHURCHWELL FAMILY

1. Mary Churchwell, born say 1742, was head of a Buxton's District, Nansemond County household of 4 whites (free persons) in 1783 [VA:57]. She was probably the mother of

    i. Charles, born say 1760, a "Mulatto" head of a household of no whites and one dwelling in Buxton's District of Nansemond County in 1784 [VA:74].

2   ii. Samuel, born say 1762.

    iii. Liddy, born about 1769, registered in Petersburg on 11 July 1805: *a brown Mulatto woman, five feet four inches high, bushy brown, rather fine, rather thin long hair, thirty six years old, born free in Nansemond County* [Register of Free Negroes 1794-1819, no. 337]. She was head of a Petersburg Town household of 10 "other free" in 1810 [VA:118a].

2. Samuel Churchwell, born say 1762, was a "Mulatto" head of a household of no whites, 1 dwelling, and 2 other dwellings in Buxton's District of Nansemond County in 1784 [VA:74] and a "Free Negro" living in Nansemond County in 1815 [Yantis, *A Supplement to the 1810 Census of Virginia*, S-14]. He may have been the father of

    i. Polly, born about 1787, twenty-five years of age on 20 July 1812 when she registered as a "free Negro" in Norfolk County: *5 feet 4 In. of a Yellowish Complexion. Born free as appears by the Oath of John Price* [Register of Free Negros & Mulattos, #75].

CHURTON FAMILY

1. Joseph Churton, born say 1750, was called "Negroe Joe late the property of Mr. William Churton of this County deceased and sett free by the last Will and Testament of the said William Churton for meritorious services" on 17 March 1768 when the Chowan County court approved the manumission [Minutes 1766-72, 366]. He was a "black" taxable in William Boyd's list for the town of Edenton in 1769 [CR 024.701.2]. He was head of a Chowan County household of one "other free" in 1790 [NC:19] and was still living in Chowan County in 1800 [NC:114]. He was probably the father of

    i. Alfred, born before 1776, a Chowan County taxable in the town of Edenton in an undated list, taxed on one free poll and 1-1/2 town lots [CR 024.701.2]. He was taxable on one free poll in a 1797 list of Edenton tithables and taxed on one free and one slave poll in 1799 [*NCGSJ* XVI:219; XVII:225]. He was head of a Chowan County household of 1 "other free" and two slaves in 1800 [NC:114], 2 "other free" and 2 slaves in 1810 [NC:528], and 2 "free colored" in 1820 [NC:130].

ii. Mariann, taxable on one poll and 1-1/2 town lots in Edenton in an undated Chowan County tax list [CR 24.701.2].

CLARK FAMILY

1. Judeth Clarke, the servant of Joshua Slade of York Parish, York County, Virginia, confessed in court on 24 August 1694 that she committed the "sinn of fornication with a Negro" [DOW 10:3, 28]. She may have been the ancestor of

    i. ___, husband of Mary who was named in the 19 September 1749 York County will of her mother Mary **Roberts** [W&I 20:163]. They may have been the parents of John Clarke, a "free Mulatto" who was living in York County on 19 May 1760 when the court ordered him bound by the churchwardens of Charles Parish to Merritt Moore [Judgments & Orders 1759-63, 143].

    ii. James[1], born say 1740, taxable with his wife in Bladen County, North Carolina, in 1768 ("Mulatoes") [Byrd, *Bladen County Tax Lists*, I:5], head of a Marlboro County, South Carolina household 7 "other free" in 1800 [SC:59].

    iii. Cooper, born say 1743, taxable with his wife in Bladen County, North Carolina, in 1768 ("Mulatoes") [Byrd, *Bladen County Tax Lists*, I:5], head of a Marlboro County household of 2 "other free" in 1800 [SC:59].

    iv. Joseph, a "Mulato" taxable in Bladen County in 1770 and 1772 [Byrd, *Bladen County Tax Lists*, I:44, 94].

    v. James[2], head of Sumter County, South Carolina household of 11 "other free" in 1800 [SC:935], probably related to Azana Clark, head a Sumter County household of 9 "other free" in 1810 [SC:215a], and Mary Clark, head of a Sumter household of 4 "other free" in 1810 [SC:215a]. He may have been identical to James Clark, Sr., who purchased 300 acres on the mouth of Cow Branch of Drowning Creek, Bladen County, North Carolina, jointly with John Stack on 30 September 1755. He assigned all his rights to the plantation he was living on to John Stack on 26 April 1757 [Philbeck, *Bladen County Land Entries*, no. 1058; Campbell, *Bladen County Wills*, 2].

2   vi. William[1], born say 1755.
3   vii. William[2], born about 1760.

    viii. George[1], born say 1762, married Levisay **Evans**, daughter of Hannah **Evans**, 13 May 1795 Amherst County bond, Leonard Clark security. He was taxable in Amherst County from 1783 to 1801. His estate was taxable on a horse in 1804 [PPTL 1782-1803, frames 23, 44, 97, 102, 166, 195, 225, 326, 393, 449, 515; 1804-23, frame 21]. He and William Clark purchased land on Mill and Porridge Creeks in Amherst County from Rawley **Pinn** on 18 March 1800 [DB I:161]. His widow Loisa Clark married Charles **Johns** of Bedford County by 10 October 1805 Amherst County bond, Lewis Martin security, Susannah Clark witness.

4   ix. Fanny, born say 1763.
5   x. James[3], born say 1764.
6   xi. John[1], born say 1765.

    xii. William[3], born say 1770, a "Mulatto Boy" bound apprentice in Surry County on 28 June 1774 [Orders 1764-74, 451].

    xiii. Thomas, born say 1773, married Hannah **Ash**, 30 June 1794 Southampton County bond, John Clark surety. He was head of a Northampton County, North Carolina household of 5 "other free" in 1800 [NC:431] and head of an Anson County household of 2 "free colored" in 1820 [NC:12].

xiv. Lemuel, born say 1774, taxable in Nottoway Parish, Southampton
County, in 1797, a "Mulatto" taxable in 1799, a "free Negro" taxable
on a horse from 1800 to 1812, taxable on 2 free male tithables in 1812
[PPTL 1792-1806, frames 241, 343, 443, 478, 586, 658, 723, 762,
872; 1807-21, frames 11, 94, 132, 250], head of a Southampton
County household of 4 "other free" in 1810 [VA:75]. He married Mary
Williams, 29 January 1795 Isle of Wight bond, David Jones surety. In
1814 he brought a Southampton County chancery suit against Aaron
Byrd and his wife over his wife Mary's part of the estate of her father
John **Williams** [LVA Chancery file 1814-017].

xv.   Wilson, taxable in Nottoway Parish, Southampton County, called a
"Mulatto" in 1796, a "f.n." from 1804 to 1812 [PPTL 1792-1806,
frames 218, 724, 873; 1807-21, frames 11, 94, 133, 250].

xvi. John/ Jack, born about 1772, registered in Southampton County on 18
September 1798: *age 26, yellow man, 5 feet 9 inches, free born*
[Register of Free Negroes 1794-1832, no. 123]. He was called John
Clark, Jr., a "Mulatto" taxable in Nottoway Parish, Southampton
County, in 1796, perhaps the John Clark, "free Negro," who was
taxable there in 1800 [PPTL 1792-1806, frames 218, 443].

xvii. Nancy, born say 1775, head of a Southampton County household of 5
"other free" in 1810 [VA:78].

xviii. Edmond, a "Mulatto" ordered bound out by the churchwardens of St.
Ann's Parish in Essex County on 20 January 1772 [Orders 1770-2,
226].

2. William[2] Clark, born say 1755, was granted 72 acres on the head branches of
Pedlar River in Amherst County on 20 July 1780 [Patents E, 1780-1, 282]. He
was head of an Amherst County household of 7 whites (free persons) in 1783
[VA:48] and 8 in 1785 [VA:85]. On 3 May 1785 the Amherst County court
ordered that he, George Clark and William **Ampey** work on the road from
Irish Creek Gap to Mill Creek, and on 6 October 1789 he, Peter **Hartless**,
George Clarke, Leonard Clark, James Clark and Joseph **Ailstock** were ordered
to work on the road from Blue Ridge at Irish Creek Gap to the three forks of
Pedlar River [Orders 1784-7, 131; 1787-90, 590]. He was taxable in Amherst
County from 1782 to 1820: with "CM" after his name in 1800, "Blue Ridge"
from 1801-3, a "man of color" in 1811, 1812, and 1815, a "Mulatto" in 1813,
a planter over the age of 45 in a list of "Free Negroes & Mulattoes" in 1816
and 1818. He was taxable on 2 tithes in 1794, 3 from 1795-1798, 4 from
1799-1803, 3 from 1804-7, 4 from 1809-10, and 5 from 1811-12 [PPTL 1782-
1803, frames 9, 23, 44, 54, 70, 97, 136, 195, 225, 257, 326, 347, 370, 393,
419, 450, 479; 1804-23, frames 21, 62, 103, 144, 165, 188, 209, 230, 253,
326, 403, 537, 551, 584]. He married (second?) Nancy **Williams**, spinster, 3
September 1794 Amherst County bond, Leonard Clark surety. He and George
Clark purchased land in Amherst County on Mill and Porridge Creeks from
Rawley **Pinn** for 100 pounds on 18 March 1800 [DB I:161]. He was head of
an Amherst County household of 9 "other free" in 1810 [VA:258]. He may
have been the father of

i.   ?Leonard, born say 1772, taxable in Amherst County from 1791 to
1807 [PPTL 1782-1803, frames 225, 347, 370, 419, 450; 1804-23,
frames 21, 63, 144]. He married Sally **Williams**, 12 March 1796
Amherst County bond, William Clarke surety. He was head of a
Rockingham County household of 5 "other free" in 1810 [VA:290].

ii. ?Jane, born say 1780, married Henry **Heartless**, 25 June 1798 Amherst
County bond, William Clarke surety.

iii. ?John[2], born say 1780, taxable in Amherst County from 1805 to 1815:
called a "man of color" in 1811, 1812, 1815, a "Mulatto" in 1813
[PPTL 1804-23, frames 62, 208, 230, 253, 326] and head of an
Amherst County household of 4 "other free" in 1810 [VA:299]. He

married Mary **Hartless**, and he and Mary Clark were among members of the **Hartless** family who sold land on Pedlar River on 8 August 1818. They were living in Ohio on 8 April 1823 when they sold an additional 141 acres on Pedlar River to Reuben **Peters** [DB R:39].

iv. Nancy, daughter of William Clark, married James Clark in Amherst County on 20 September 1809 [Marriage Register, 217].

v. ?William, Jr., born say 1795, a "Mulatto" taxable in Amherst County in 1813 [PPTL 1804-23, frame 253].

vi. ?George[2], a "Mulatto" taxable in 1813, a "man of color" taxable in Amherst County in 1815 [PPTL 1804-23, frame 326].

vii. ?Henry, a "man of color" taxable in Amherst County in 1815 [PPTL 1804-23, frame 326].

3. William[2] Clark, born about 1760, married Hannah **Peters**, 19 March 1785 Stafford County bond, William **Peters** surety [Madden, *We Were Always Free*, 195]. He was "a Free Mulatto" head of a Culpeper County household of 7 "other free" in 1810 [VA:18]. On 7 December 1816 he obtained "free papers" in Culpeper County which were recorded later in Ross County, Ohio: *William Clerke, a Mulatto man, 50 or 60, 5'7", served in the Revolutionary War in 1780 and 1781...is a free man, who has a wife and several children, and wishes to visit his mother in law in Frederick Co., at Charles Carter's place.* On 12 December 1816 Sally **Peters**, "a free woman of color," made oath in Rockingham County, Virginia, that Coleman, eighteen years old, and Nicholas, thirteen years old, were the sons of William and Hannah Clerk and were free born in Culpeper County [Turpin, *Register of Black, Mulatto and Poor Persons*, 20-21]. William (Sr.) was sixty-four years old on 22 August 1820 when he appeared in Culpeper County court to apply for a pension for his services in the Revolution. According to his pension records, he died on 8 December 1827 and his children were Willis Clark, William Clark, Kitty **Madden** (wife of Willis **Madden**), and Nicholas Clark [Madden, *We Were Always Free*, 191-199]. William and Hannah's children were

i. Coleman, born about 1798 (perhaps the same person as Willis Clark).

ii. Kitty, born about 1800, registered as a "free Negro" in Culpeper County on 23 September 1822: *a bright Mulatto Woman above the age of twenty one years five feet two inches high.* She married Willis **Madden** [Madden, *We Were Always Free*, 64].

iii. William[4], born about 1803.

iv. Nicholas.

4. Fanny Clark, born say 1760, was living in Cumberland County, Virginia, on 22 May 1780 when the court ordered the churchwardens of Littleton Parish to bind her "mulattoe" son Harry Clark to Tucker Baughan [Orders 1779-84, 118]. She was the mother of

i. Harry, born say 1779, a "M°" taxable in Powhatan County from 1803 to 1814, probably married in 1813 when he was listed with 2 "free Negroes & Mulattos" over the age of 16 in 1813 [PPTL 1787-1825, frames 254, 293, 397, 437, 456].

ii. Peter, born say 1782, "mulatto" son of Fanny ordered bound to Tucker Baughan on 24 May 1784 [Orders 1784-6, 22].

5. James[3] Clark, born say 1764, was head of an Amherst County household of 9 "other free" in 1810 [VA:298]. He and his wife Anny sold land to Henry **Hartless** by deed proved in Amherst County on 19 July 1802 [Orders 1801-2, 217]. He was taxable in Amherst County from 1789 to 1820: taxable on 2 tithables from 1803 to 1806, 1810 and 1811, 3 in 1812, called a "man of color" in 1811, 1812, and 1815, a "Mulatto" in 1813, in a list of "Free Mulattoes & Negroes with his unnamed son in 1814 and in 1816 when he was over the age of 45, living on his own plantation, and taxable on 3 tithables

[PPTL 1782-1803, frames 166, 225, 348, 419, 584; 1804-23, frames 21, 62, 103, 144, 165, 187, 209, 230, 252, 284, 326, 403, 503, 537, 549]. He married (second) Nancy Clark in Amherst County on 20 September 1809 [Marriage Register, 217]. He was the father of

    i.   Micajah, born say 1785, taxable in Amherst County from 1809 (called son of Jas.) a "man of color" in 1811, a "Mulatto" in 1813, in a list of "Free Mulattoes & Negroes in 1814 [PPTL 1804-23, frames 209, 252, 284, 328, 403]. He married Sally **Duncan**, on 15 November 1809 in Amherst County with the consent of Sally's parents, Ambrose and Jane Ambrose [Marriage Register, 218, 240]. Ambrose was called Ambrose **Evans** when he was head of an Amherst County household of 6 "other free" in 1810 [VA:302]. Micajah was head of an Amherst County household of 3 "other free" in 1810 [VA:302]. He and Charles **Evans** were witnesses to the 7 May 1817 Amherst County marriage of Lydia **Evans**, daughter of Ambrose **Evans**, to John Gulliver [Marriage Register, 247].

    ii.   ?Nelson, born about 1793, applied to the Amherst County court in April 1851 for a certificate that he was a white man but registered as a "Free Negro" in Amherst County on 12 July 1860: *brown complexion, 67 years of age, 5 feet 11 1/2 inches high, born in Bedford* [Register of Free Negroes, no.339; McLeRoy, *Strangers in Their Midst*, 101, 136].

    iii.   ?Benjamin H., born about 1800, registered in Amherst County on 22 August 1822: *a free man of colour aged twenty two years five feet eight inches high of a bright yellow complection grey eyes with a natural mark on his right cheek and was born free & by occupation a waterman* [Register of Free Negroes, no. 10].

    iv.   ?James[4], born about 1801, registered on 12 July 1860: *dark brown complexion, 59 years of age...born in Amherst* [Register of Free Negroes, no.338].

6.   John[1] Clark, born say 1765, was a "Mulatto" taxable in Nottoway Parish, Southampton County, in 1796 [PPTL 1792-1806, frame 218]. He was surety for the Southampton County marriage bond of (his brother?) Thomas Clark and Hannah **Ash** on 30 June 1794. He was head of a Halifax County, North Carolina household of 6 "other free" in 1810 [NC:12]. Perhaps his children were

    i.   Anthony, born about 1790, head of a Halifax County household of 6 "free colored" in 1820 [NC:143] and 10 in 1830. He may have been the Anthony Clark who was head of a Richmond City, Wayne County, Indiana, household of 12 "free colored" in 1840.

    ii.   Reuben, born about 1809, described as a "child of color" when he was ordered bound out by the 20 May 1822 Halifax County court.

Another Clark family:

1.   Rachel Clark, born say 1730, was a "Widow Woman" who was summoned by the Craven County, North Carolina court on 10 May 1759 to bring her children to the next court to have them bound apprentices [Minutes 1758-61, 28a]. She died before 10 October 1767 when Edward Franck of Craven County was ordered by the court to receive her "Molatto Orphans" in his care until they could be indentured by the next court [Minutes 1767-75, 52a]. Her children named in the court order were

    i.   Joseph, born say 1755.

    ii.   Moses, born say 1758.

    iii.   ?Mariah, head of a Craven County household of 2 "free colored" in 1820 [NC:77].

COBB FAMILY

1. John Cobb, born about 1690, was not yet fourteen on 29 December 1702 when he asked the Northampton County, Virginia court to appoint someone to take care of him and his estate until he was of age to choose a guardian. He chose his guardian on 28 November 1704 [OW 1698-1710, 165, 212]. He was taxable in Northampton County from 1720 to 1744, called a "mul" in 1726 [Bell, *Northampton County Tithables*, 11, 22, 31, 45, 63, 113, 175, 220, 242, 245, 274, 289, 312, 347, 364]. On 12 February 1729/30 a Northampton County jury awarded him 17 shillings in his case against Isaac Mu___ for assault, and on 11 August 1730 he sued Daniel Eshon for assault and battery but the case was dismissed on agreement of the parties [Orders 1729-32, 8, 36, 43]. On 11 October 1748 he sued Henry Stott for damaging his ability to prove his debts or give evidence in a hearing by declaring, "you are a mulatto and I will prove it." John argued that he could not have been a "mulatto" because he collected debts, gave evidence in controversies "between other white persons and free subjects," and possessed the good will and esteem of his neighbors [*John Cobb v. Henry Stott*, Northampton County Loose Papers, 1748, cited by Deal, *A Constricted World*]. The case was discontinued when both parties agreed [Orders 1748-51, 24, 37]. John's wife was apparently white since she was never tithable in his household. He sold land by deed proved in Northampton County on 12 September 1758 [Minutes 1754-61, 166]. He left a 20 August 1766 Northampton County will, proved 12 November 1766, by which he left three slaves to his son Joshua, a slave to his son Southy, and divided the remainder among his wife Rachel and daughters Susanna, Elishe, Sarah and Rachel Cobb. He left a shilling to his grandson John Cobb, son of Stratton Cobb [Wills & Inventories 24:42-3]. He was the father of

    i.   Stratton, born say 1714, taxable in John Cobb's Northampton County household in 1731, 1738 and 1743 and listed as a taxable adjoining John Cobb in 1744 [Bell, *Northampton County Tithables*, 220, 274, 347, 364]. He was probably deceased in 1766 when his son John Cobb received a shilling by his grandfather's Northampton County will. A John Cobb was a Continental soldier who died before 8 December 1778 when the Northampton County court authorized the vestry of Hungar's Parish to support his widow [Minutes 1777-83, 125].

    ii.   ?Southy[1], born say 1720, taxable in John Cobb's Northampton County household in 1737, 1739, 1740 and 1743 and taxable in Richard Brazer's household in 1744 [Bell, *Northampton County Tithables*, 263, 289, 347, 364].

    iii.   Susanna.

    iv.   Elishe.

    v.   Sarah.

    vi.   Rachel.

    vii.   Joshua, born in May 1755, eleven years and four months old on 20 August 1766 when his father made his will.

    viii. Southy[2], born about June 1761, an orphan bound by the Northampton County court to Thomas Rose on 9 May 1770 [Minutes 1765-71, 370].

They were probably related to John Cobb of Bertie County, North Carolina:

1. John Cobb, born say 1733, was a "molattor" Bertie County, North Carolina taxable in Edward **Wilson**'s household in the list of Jonathan Standley in 1764 and a "free Mulattor" taxable in **Wilson**'s household in 1767 [CR 10.702.1, box 2]. He was the father of

    i.   Lewis, born about 1754, fifteen-year-old "orphan of John Cobb," bound to John Barnes to be a shoemaker on 27 September 1769 in Bertie County.

2   ii.   Nathan, born about 1754.

iii.   ?Becky, head of a Sampson County household of 3 "other free" in 1790 [NC:53].

2.   Nathan Cobb, born about 1754, the sixteen-year-old "orphan of John Cobb," was bound to James **Prichard** to be a cooper on 29 March 1770 [CR 10.101.7 by *NCGSJ* XIV:34, 35]. He was a "Malletor" taxable in James **Prichard**'s household in 1770. He married Winney **Mitchell**, 9 August 1779 Bertie County bond, Jesse **Prichard** bondsman. He gave security in Bertie County court in May 1787 for a bastard child he had by Christian **Kale** [Haun, *Bertie County Court Minutes*, V:646]. She was probably the daughter of Mary **Cales**, a "Mulatto" taxable head of a Bertie County household with (her son?) Moses **Cale** in the 1761 list of John Hill. Nathan was counted as white in Bertie County, head of a household of 4 females, 4 males, and a slave in 1790 [NC:12]. His 27 April 1812 Bertie County will named his wife Cateth and his children Elisha, Thomas, William, Christian Mires, Mary **Hogard**, Winnifred **Hogard**, Elisabeth, Peneth, and John [C.R. 10.801.2, p.56 by *Journal of N. C. Genealogy* (1965) 11:1516]. He was the father of
   i.   Elisha, married Sarah Lucas, 1 April 1801 Bertie County bond.
   ii.   Thomas.
   iii.   William.
   iv.   Christian Mires.
   v.   Mary **Hogard**.
   vi.   Winnifred, married Elisha **Hogard**, 3 September 1804 Bertie County bond.
   vii.   Elisabeth.
   viii.   Peneth.
   ix.   John.

COCKRAN FAMILY

1.   Molly Cockran, born say 1745, was a "free Indian" living in Goochland County in August 1765 when her children John and Henry were ordered bound out by the churchwardens of St. James Northam Parish [Orders 1765-67, 51]. Her daughter Betsy, by "Negroe Ben," was born on 31 October 1765 [Jones, *The Douglas Register*, 348]. Their children married free African Americans and became part of the free African American community of Goochland County. Molly was taxable in the upper district of Goochland County on a free male tithable and a horse in 1793 and taxable on a horse in 1794 [PPTL, 1782-1809, frames 339, 357]. Her children were
   i.   John, born say 1761, married Sally **Johns**, 30 April 1790 Goochland County bond, 2 May marriage [DB 15:386]. He was taxable in the upper district of Goochland County from 1787 to 1803 [PPTL, 1782-1809, frames 164, 175, 339, 464, 525, 666], a "FN" taxable in the northern district of Campbell County in 1807 [PPTL, 1785-1814, frame 693], and head of a Campbell County household of 1 "other free" in 1810 [VA:853].
2   ii.   Henry, born say 1763.
   iii.   Elizabeth, born 31 October 1765, baptized 19 January 1766 in Goochland County [Jones, *The Douglas Register*, 72]. She married Benjamin **Farrar**, 10 March 1784 Goochland County bond, (her mother) Mary Cockran surety. Perhaps she was the Betsy **Farrar** who was head of a Nelson County household of 3 "other free" in 1810 [VA:691].

2.   Henry Cockran, born say 1763, son of Mary Cockran, was ordered bound apprentice in Goochland County in August 1765 [Orders 1765-67, 51]. He was taxable in Goochland County from 1787 to 1816: a "Mulatto" living near Duval Carroll's in 1804, charged with James Cockran's tithe in 1807, listed

in 1813 on William Richardson's land with wife Polly and Ruth Cockran (whose name was partially erased), charged with Henry Cockran, Jr.'s tithe in 1816 [PPTL, 1782-1809, frames 163, 175, 279, 357, 479, 616, 686, 738, 821; 1810-32, frames 5, 71, 97, 158, 281]. He was head of a Goochland County household of 8 "other free" in 1810 [VA:689]. He registered as a "free Negro" in Goochland County on 12 August 1815: *a free man of color of Yellow complexion about five feet eight inches high, about fifty three years old, short black curled hair...free born* [Register of Free Negroes, p.89, no.171]. His children were

    i.   ?James, born say 1788, who had "resided on the plantation of Jo. Woodson for 20 years," married Elizabeth **Wood** (of age), 13 August 1811 Goochland County bond, Joseph **Scott** surety. He was taxable in the upper district of Goochland County from 1807 to 1815: a "Mulatto" ditcher with wife Eliza on Joseph Woodson's land in 1813 [PPTL, 1810-32, frames 159, 189]. James was surety for the 5 June 1815 Goochland County marriage of Nancey **George**, alias **Cooper**, "an orphan," and Benjamin **McDonald**, a "free man of color."

    ii.   Elizabeth, born say 1795, "daughter of Henry Cockran," married Bartlet **Hoomes**, 4 August 1812 Goochland County bond, Jacob **Martin** surety, 6 August marriage.

    iii.   Polly, born say 1797, "daughter of Henry Cockran," married Randolph **Cooper**, 13 December 1813 Goochland County bond, 16 December marriage.

    iv.   Ruth, born say 1798, "daughter of Henry Cockran," married Roger **Cooper**, Jr., 31 October 1814 Goochland County bond, 3 November marriage.

COLE FAMILY

1.   Benedict Cole, born say 1665, was the "Negro (baptized)" slave of Richard Cole. Thomas Kirton married Richard Cole's widow and declared in Westmoreland County court on 28 August 1678 that "the Negro boy called Benedict Cole" was to be free at Kirton's death or departure from the country and to serve "but till the adge of twenty and no more." Kirton died before 27 July 1692 when Benedict successfully sued for his freedom in Westmoreland County court [Orders 1675-1689, 130; 1698-1705, 68a]. He may have been the ancestor of the Cole family of Fairfax and Prince William Counties, Virginia. They were probably related to the Cole family of St. Mary's County, Maryland. Members of the family in Virginia were

2   i.   Elizabeth, born say 1730.
3   ii.   Phebe, born say 1732.
    iii.   Robert[1], born say 1735, a "free Negro" of Truro Parish, Fairfax County, presented by the grand jury on 22 May 1760 for living in fornication with ___ wood (probably a white woman) by the information of William Moler [Orders 1756-63, pt. 1, 463].

2.   Elizabeth Cole, born say 1730, was living in Fairfax County, Virginia, on 29 March 1751 when she (no race indicated) petitioned the court setting forth that she was unjustly detained as a servant by Francis Summers. The court ruled that she was free and ordered her discharged from his service [Orders 1749-54, 143]. She was the mother of

    i.   ?William, born say 1755, a "Molato" living in George Dent's household on 21 November 1771 when the Fairfax County court presented Dent for failing to list him as a tithable [Orders 1770-2, 319]. He was taxable in the lower district of Prince William County in 1787, 1792, from 1794 to 1797, and from 1803 to 1810, called "Black" in 1804, 1806 and 1809 [PPTL, 1782-1810, frames 95, 203,

254, 309, 385, 523, 571, 704, 732], head of a Prince William County household of 10 "other free" in 1810 [VA:508].

ii.   Betty **Handless**, born about 1756, registered in the District of Columbia court in Alexandria on 31 August 1809: *Tawny colour...about fifty three years old...Know her mother Betty Cole, both born free in Fairfax County, Virginia, Wm. Rhodes* [Arlington County Register of Free Negroes, 1797-1861, pp. 19-20].

3.   Phebe Cole, born say 1732, was living Fairfax County on 20 December 1752 when she was presented by the churchwardens of Truro Parish. The presentment was dismissed on 22 February 1755 [Orders 1749-54, 269; 1754-6, 183, 266]. She was a "free negro" living in Dettingen Parish, Prince William County, on 7 August 1767 when her children Robert, Catherine, Thomas, Joseph, Eleanor, and Sarah were bound apprentices [Orders 1766-69, 56]. Thomas and Robert were bound to William Bennett on 10 June 1768, and Catherine and Joseph were bound to him on 7 September the same year [Historic Dumfries, *Records of Dettingen Parish*, 56-59]. She was taxable in Prince William County on a free male in 1795 and taxable on a horse in 1796 and 1797 [PPTL, 1782-1810, frames 267, 309, 335]. Her children were

4   i.   Robert^2, born say 1753.
5   ii. Catherine, born about 1755.
         iii. Thomas, born say 1757, bound an apprentice carpenter to William Bennett on 10 June 1768. He was listed among seven deserters from Thomas W. Ewell's Company of State Troops in a 20 June 1777 advertisement in the *Virginia Gazette*, described as: *a dark mulatto, about 5 feet 7 inches high living in Prince William County* [Purdie edition, p.1, col. 3]. He was taxable in the lower district of Prince William County in 1786, 1787, 1792, and from 1794 to 1798, called a "free Black" in 1798 [PPTL, 1782-1810, frames 71, 95, 203, 254, 309, 362].
         iv. Joseph, born say 1760, bound an apprentice carpenter to William Bennett on 7 September 1768. He was taxable in Prince William County in 1787 and 1796 [PPTL, 1782-1810, frames 95, 309].
         v.   Eleanor/ Nelly, born about 1765, a "free Black" taxable in the lower district of Prince William County on a horse in 1798, a free male tithe in 1803, 2 free tithes in 1804, a "B" taxable on a free male and a horse in 1806, a "Black" taxable on a horse in 1809 [PPTL, 1782-1810, frames 362, 523, 638, 732], head of a Prince William County household of 2 "other free" in 1810 [VA:508]. She registered in Prince William County on 5 June 1815 and produced her papers in the District of Columbia court in Alexandria on 11 June 1815: *a free black woman about fifty years of age...was born free* [Arlington County Register of Free Negroes, 1797-1861, pp. 19-20].
         vi. Sarah, a "B" taxable on a horse in the lower district of Prince William County in 1806 [PPTL, 1782-1810, frame 639], head of a Prince William County household of 4 "other free" in 1810 [VA:508].
         vii. ?Henry, taxable in Prince William County from 1794 to 1798 and from 1803 to 1810, listed as a "free Black" in 1798 [PPTL, 1782-1810, frames 254, 266, 309, 362, 523, 638, 704], head of a Prince William County household of 10 "other free" in 1810 [VA:508].

4.   Robert^2 Cole, born say 1753, was bound an apprentice shoemaker to William Bennett in Dettingen Parish on 10 June 1768 [Historic Dumfries, *Records of Dettingen Parish*, 56]. He married Lucy **Chavers**/ **Chavis**, "both black persons" according to the Charlotte County deposition of Mary Belcher [N.C. Stack File C.R. 099.928.11 by *NCGSJ* III:21]. Robert apparently died before 9 February 1784 when the Mecklenburg County court ordered the churchwardens to bind out Lucy's orphan son Robert Cole [Orders 1779-84,

515]. Lucy's nephew John **Jackson Chavis**, son of her sister Betty **Chavis**, was bound as an apprentice to William **Stewart** in Mecklenburg County; **Stewart** moved to Wake County, North Carolina, about 1790; and John **Jackson** went with him and died there about 1808 when **Stewart** tried to prove his nuncupative Wake County will. Lucy challenged the will by presenting a deposition taken on 27 April 1808 from Mary Belcher of Charlotte County that John **Jackson Chavis** was christened in her home and that Lucy was his only living relative [N.C. Stack File C.R. 099.928.11 by *NCGSJ* III:21; Haun, *Wake County Court Minutes* VII:67-8, 151]. Lucy recorded the inventory of John **Jackson Chavis**'s estate in Wake County in February 1809 [Wynne, *Record of Wills, Inventories*, II:107]. She was head of a Mecklenburg County household of 2 "free Negro" or "Mulatto" females over the age of sixteen in 1813 [PPTL 1806-21, frame 307], a "free colored" woman with a "free colored" boy under the age of fourteen in 1820 [VA:144a], and was counted in the 1850 Mecklenburg County census as a 100-year-old Black woman who was blind, listed with Susan and Peter **Brandom** in the household next to Israel **Cole**, a forty-five-year-old Black carpenter [VA:104b]. Robert and Lucy were the parents of

   i.   Robert^3, born about 1774, taxable in William **Stewart**'s Mecklenburg County household, responsible for his own tithe in 1794 [PPTL 1782-1805, frames 451, 516]. He married Mary **Stewart**, 31 December 1802 Mecklenburg County bond, Martin **Cousins** security. Robert was security for the Mecklenburg County marriage of Martin **Cousins** and Elizabeth **Brandon** of the same date. On 10 October 1803 he was ordered to work on a road in Mecklenburg County with Robert **Brannum**, Thomas **Spence**, William **Stewart**, Humphrey **Wilson**, Joseph **Stewart**, Frederick **Ivey**, Pompey **Mayo**, and Richard **Dunston** [Orders 1803-5, 45]. He registered in Mecklenburg County on 14 November 1803: *Ordered that it be certified that Robert Cole, planter, is a free man, that he is the age of twenty nine years, about five feet ten Inches high and of dark complexion* [Orders 1803-5, 52].

   ii.   Jincey, married Martin **Cousins**, 31 December 1802 Mecklenburg County bond, Robert **Cole** security.

Lucy's children were

   i.   Burwell, son of Lucy **Cole**, bound by the Mecklenburg County court to Ellyson Crew to be a planter on 8 October 1798 [Orders 1798-1801, 39].

   ii.   ?Caty, bound by the Mecklenburg County court to Ellyson Crew on 9 December 1799, no parent named [Orders 1798-1801, 280].

   iii.   ?Thomas, a "Malatto" bound by the Mecklenburg County court as an apprentice to Jacob Garrot, wheelwright, on 9 September 1805 [Orders 1803-5, 461].

5.   Catherine **Cole**, born about 1755, was bound apprentice to William Bennett in Prince William County on 7 September 1768. She was taxable on a horse in the lower district of Prince William County in 1797 [PPTL, 1782-1810, frame 336]. She registered in Prince William County on 22 May 1810 and produced her papers in the District of Columbia court in Alexandria on 8 June 1815: *was at that time fifty five years of age, born free in the County aforesaid* [Arlington County Register of Free Negroes, 1797-1861, p.28]. She was the mother of

   i.   John, born about 1773, taxable in Prince William County from 1794 to 1798, listed as "Black" in 1795 [PPTL, 1782-1810, frames 254, 267, 309, 362], registered in Prince William County on 24 March 1806 and produced his papers in the District of Columbia court in Alexandria: *a free black man, son of Katy Cole, a free black woman...thirty three years of age* [Arlington County Register of Free

Negroes, 1797-1861, no. 25, p.24]. He was a "free negro" head of a Fairfax County household of 3 in 1810 [VA:243].

ii.   ?Samuel, head of a Prince William County household of 3 "other free" in 1810 [VA:508].

iii. ?David, taxable in Prince William County from 1795 to 1797 and from 1803 to 1810, called a "Blackman" in 1795 and 1803 and 1809 [PPTL, 1782-1810, frames 267, 523, 638, 703], head of a head of a Prince William County household of 1 "other free" in 1810 [VA:508].

iv.   ?Frances, a "Mulatto" taxable on a horse in Prince William County in 1802 [PPTL, 1782-1810, frame 503].

Prince Edward County

1.   Mary Cole, born say 1745, was the mother of an "orphan" Abigail Cole who was bound apprentice to John Owen until the age of thirty-one in Prince Edward County in November 1757 [Orders 1754-8, 133]. She was the mother of

i.   Abigail, born say 1755.

ii.   ?Robin, born about 1784, registered in Halifax County, Virginia, on 26 October 1812: *aged 28 years about five feet eight inches high of a dark colour and who it appears was born of a free Woman is hereby registered as a free negroe* [Register, no.36].

South Carolina

1.   Jonathan Cole, born say 1705, was living in Wadmalaw, South Carolina, when the birth of his "Mulatto" son Thomas was recorded in the register of St. Philip's Parish, Charleston, South Carolina. He was the father of

2   i.   Thomas, born 14 April 1729.

ii.   Susanna, married William **Raper** [Koger, *Black Slaveowners*, 15].

2.   Thomas[1] Cole, born 14 April 1729, was the "Mulatto" son of Jonathan Cole of Charleston, South Carolina. He was called "an Adult mulatto" on 5 June 1754 when he was baptized in St. Philip's Parish [Salley, *Register of St. Philip's Parish, 1720-58*, 100, 145]. He called himself a bricklayer in his 21 October 1771 Charleston will, proved 8 November the same year. He directed his executors to sell his house in Beresford's Alley and slaves Prince, Will, and Carolina and to divide the proceeds among his children: Thomas, Barbara, William, Elizabeth, and John Cole, and to sell his house and land on Meeting Street and divide the proceeds among his wife Ruth and children when his youngest child came of age. He named his friend Thomas Lotan Smith, Esq., and brother-in-law William **Raper** executors [WB 14:109-10]. His wife Ruth was a "Free" head of a St. Philips & Michaels Parish, South Carolina household of 4 "other free" and 3 slaves in 1790 and head of a Newberry District household of 3 "other free" in 1800 [SC:68] and a "free Negro" head of a Newberry District household of 6 "other free" in 1810 [SC:117a]. She called herself the sister of William **Raper** on 12 October 1788 when she and her daughter Barbara petitioned the legislature to be appointed administrators of his widow Susanna **Raper**, "a free woman of color" [Schweninger, *Race, Slavery and Free Black Petitions*, no. 11378801]. She was the sponsor for the baptism of her granddaughter Ruth **Raper Garden** at St. Philip's Parish on 13 March 1812 [Koger, *Black Slaveowners*, 166]. Her 31 January 1817 Charleston will was proved on 15 August the same year. She left her house and lot in Federal Street, a slave named Amey (daughter of Flora), and her pew in St. Philip's Church to her daughter Barbara Maria **Bampfield**, wife of George **Bampfield**, and after her death to her four grandchildren: Thomas Cole, John Cole, Eliza Cole, and Eliza Maria **Jones**. She left the house where she was residing in Guignard Street to her grandchildren John and Eliza Cole and directed that her slave Flora with her daughters Lucinda and Belinda be sold and the proceeds divided among her four grandchildren. And she left the

lot and premises adjoining her house in Guignard Street to her daughter Magdalen **Brown**. She appointed her nephew-in-law John **Garden** executor [WB 33:1276-7]. Thomas and Ruth were the parents of

    i.   Thomas^2, "free" head of a St. Philip's and Michael's Parish, South Carolina household of 5 "other free" in 1790 and a "free colored" head of a Charleston household with one slave in 1840.

    ii.   Barbara Maria **Bampfield**, died about 1832 when her executor, Jehu **Jones**, Jr., sold her slave Fatima for $200 and divided the proceeds among Sarah **Cole** and Elizabeth Maria **Jones**.

    iii.   William.

    iv.   Elizabeth.

    v.   Magdalen **Brown**.

    vi.   John, married Sarah.

Other members of the Cole family in South Carolina were

    i.   John, head of a Union District household of 5 "other free" in 1800 [SC:241].

    ii.   Sarah, head of a Newberry District household of 5 "other free" in 1800 [SC:68].

    iii.   Mary, head of a Newberry District household of 7 "other free" in 1800 [SC:69].

    iv.   Joseph, head of a Kershaw District household of 8 "other free" in 1810 [SC:410].

COLEMAN FAMILY

1.   Judith, born say 1700, was an Indian or the descendant of an Indian brought into Virginia by Francis Coleman sometime after the year 1705 and held as a slave for her lifetime. Her descendants Dick and Pat, who were held as slaves by Coleman's descendants, sued for and won their freedom in a case which was affirmed on appeal in the Fall of the year 1793 [Catterall, *Judicial Cases*, I:101-2]. Other descendants won their freedom from Robert Hall of Dinwiddie County before 1 July 1789, from John Hardaway of Dinwiddie County before 16 August 1794, from Joseph Hardaway of Dinwiddie County in November 1797 and from John Wyche of Brunswick County in 1819. Judith was the ancestor of

2   i.   Sarah, born say 1740.

    ii.   David^1, born about 1744, registered in Petersburg on 15 August 1800: *a dark brown stout, well made Mulatto Man, five feet eight inches high, fifty six years old, with short bushy hair, formerly held as a slave by Joseph Hardaway but obtained his freedom by a Judgment of the Gen'l Court in November 1797* [Register of Free Negroes 1794-1819, no. 170].

    iii.   Cuffee, born about 1748, registered in Southampton County on 30 March 1805: *age 57, blk., 5 feet 10 inches high, Sued his freedom, Dinwidy* [Register of Free Negroes 1794-1832, no. 322].

    iv.   Daniel, born about 1752, registered in Petersburg on 10 February 1798: *a dark Brown Free Negro, or Indian, six feet two inches high, about forty six years old, short bushy hair, a little grey, formerly held as a slave by Joseph Hardaway but obtained his freedom by a judgment of the Gen'l Court in Nov. 1797* [Register of Free Negroes 1794-1819, no. 132]. He was a ditcher living near George May when he was counted as a "free Negro and Mulatto" taxable in Dinwiddie County in 1801 [PPTL, 1800-9, B list, p.25]. He may have been the Daniel Coleman who was head of a Halifax County, North Carolina household of 6 "free colored" in 1820 [NC:143].

    v.   Dick, orphan of Judy Coleman, deceased, ordered bound out by William Foushee, overseer of the poor for the third district of Henrico

County, to William Waddell on 3 September 1787 [Orders 1787-9, 131]. He was head of a Richmond County, Virginia household of 10 "other free" in 1810 [VA:401].

vi. Pat, won her freedom from the Coleman family in 1793.

vii. Betty[1], born about 1767, registered in Petersburg on 18 August 1794: *a dark brown woman, five feet six & a half inches height, twenty seven years old, liberated by a judgment of Gen'l Court from John Hardaway of Dinwiddie County being a descendant of an Indian woman* [Register of Free Negroes 1794-1819, no. 32].

viii. Nancy, born about 1767, registered in Petersburg on 18 August 1794: *a dark brown, well made Mulatto woman, five feet one and a half inches high, twenty seven years old, freed by Judgment of the Gen'l Court of John Hardaway of Dinwiddie County being a descendant of an Indian* [Register of Free Negroes 1794-1819, no. 37].

ix. Tempe, born about 1768, registered in Petersburg on 18 August 1794: *a dark brown, well made woman, five feet two inches high, twenty six years old, liberated by a Judgment of the Gen'l Court of John Hardaway of Dinwiddie County as being a descendant of an Indian. Renewed 25 Sept. 1799, 14 Oct. 1800, 20 Sept. 1803* [Register of Free Negroes 1794-1819, no. 33].

x. Charles, born about 1769, registered in Petersburg on 16 August 1794: *a dark Mulatto man, near five feet eight inches high, about twenty five years old, was born in the Possession of John Hardaway of Dinwiddie County from whom he obtained his freedom by judgment of the Gen'l Court being the descendant of an Indian & served as an apprentice with Robert Armstead in the Town of Petersburg* [Register of Free Negroes 1794-1819, no. 11].

xi. Betty[2], born about 1777, registered in Petersburg on 27 May 1805: *a dark brown negro woman, five feet four and a half inches high, twenty eight years old, formerly held as a slave by John Hardaway of Dinwiddie County & liberated by a Judgment of the Gen'l Court as descended of an Indian* [Register of Free Negroes 1794-1819, no. 290].

3 xii. Caty, born about 1779.

xiii. Jemima, born about 1780, registered in Petersburg on 11 July 1805: *a dark brown Mulatto woman, five feet two inches high, twenty five years old, born free & raised in the County of Prince George* [Register of Free Negroes 1794-1819, no. 333].

xiv. Hannah, born about 1781, registered in Petersburg on 17 September 1802: *a dark brown Mulatto woman, five feet four inches high, twenty one years old, born free & raised in the Town of Petersburg* [Register of Free Negroes 1794-1819, no. 240].

xv. Betty[3], born about 1782, registered in Petersburg on 18 September 1803: *a free Negro woman, dark brown, five feet two and a half inches high, twenty one years old, born free & raised in the Town of Petersburg* [Register of Free Negroes 1794-1819, no. 260].

xvi. Rachel, born about 1785, registered in Petersburg on 9 July 1805: *a dark brown Negro woman, four feet eleven inches high, twenty years old, born free & raised in the Town of Petersburg* [Register of Free Negroes 1794-1819, no. 310]. She was head of a Petersburg Town household of 5 "other free" in 1810 [VA:124a].

xvii. Lucy, born about 1787, registered in Petersburg on 31 December 1808: *a dark brown free Negro woman, five feet three and a half inches high, twenty one years old, born free & raised in the Town of Petersburg* [Register of Free Negroes 1794-1819, no. 443]. She was head of a Petersburg Town household of 2 "other free" in 1810 [VA:118a].

xviii. Bob, head of a Prince George County household of 3 "other free" in 1810 [VA:550].

xix. Aggy, head of a Petersburg Town household of 2 "other free" in 1810 [VA:120a].

2. Sarah Coleman, born say 1740, won her freedom from Robert Hall of Dinwiddie County. She was free before 19 August 1794 when her daughter Susannah registered in Petersburg and she was probably free before 1 July 1789 when her son David Coleman was bound as an apprentice in Petersburg. She was the mother of

    i. Susannah, born about 1768, registered in Petersburg on 19 August 1794: *a dark brown woman, five feet three and a half inches high, about twenty six years old, stout made, the daughter of Sarah Coleman who obtained her freedom of Robert Hall by a suit in the Gen'l Court & the said Susannah has been allowed to pass as free by the sd Robert Hall of Dinwiddie County to whom she belonged by her mother's obtaining her freedom* [Register of Free Negroes 1794-1819, no. 58].

    ii. David[2], born about 1779, a "mulatto" (no age or parent named), bound as an apprentice cabinetmaker to John McCloud in Petersburg on 1 July 1789 [Petersburg Hustings Court Minutes 1784-91, 286]. He registered in Petersburg on 25 April 1801: *a stout, well-made dark brown Negro man, five feet five inches high, nineteen years old, short knotty hair, a son of Sally Coleman who formerly was held by Robert Hall of the County of Dinwiddie & obtained her freedom by a Judgment of the Gen'l Court* [Register of Free Negroes 1794-1819, no. 215].

    iii. Disey, orphan of Sarah Coleman, ordered bound out by William Foushee, overseer of the poor for the third district of Henrico County, to William Waddell on 3 September 1787 [Orders 1787-9, 131].

3. Caty, born about 1779, registered in Brunswick County, Virginia, on 27 September 1819: *Caty, a woman about Forty years of age, light complexion, Five feet one & a half Inches high...recovered her freedom in Brunswick Superior Court at September term 1819 of John Wyche.* She was the mother of

    i. Fanny Coleman, born about 1807, registered in Brunswick County on 28 September 1829: *a free woman of light complexion, five feet four inches high, about twenty two years of age...is one of the children of Caty who recovered her freedom from John Wyche in...1819* [Wynne, *Register of Free Negroes*, 29, 104].

    ii. Green Coleman, born about 1809, registered in Brunswick County on 26 September 1831: *of dark complexion, about twenty one years old, five feet seven inches and a quarter high...one of the children of Caty who recovered her freedom from John Wyche...in 1819* [Wynne, *Register of Free Negroes*, 119].

Other members of a Coleman family were

    i. Thomas, born about 1703, a "small negro man, aged about fifty years," who presented the deposition of John Binum to the Halifax County, Virginia court on 14 June 1753. Binum stated that Coleman was free born and that his family lived in Surry County, Virginia. The court ruled that he should be freed [Pleas 1752-5, pt.1, 162].

    ii. Ned, a "Free Negro" living with (his wife?) Rose Coleman on a lot in Leedstown, Westmoreland County, where he sold bread [*Virginia Genealogist* 31:46]. He was head of a Westmoreland County household of 2 "other free" in 1810.

COLLINS FAMILY

The Collins and **Bunch** families were taxable "Molatas" in Orange County, North Carolina, in 1755 [T&C, box 1]. They were also associated with the **Gibson** family. Lucrecy Collins witnessed the 1775 Orange County, North Carolina will of George **Gibson** [WB A:195]. They probably came to Orange County from Louisa County, Virginia. George **Gibson**, Thomas **Gibson**, Thomas **Collins**, Samuel **Collins**, William **Collins**, and Samuel **Bunch** were living in Louisa County on 28 May 1745 when they were presented by the court for failing to list a tithable (probably their wives) [Orders 1742-8, 152, 157, 172]. Some members of the family moved to Wilkes County with the **Gibsons** and like the **Gibsons**, they were counted there as white in 1790. This part of Wilkes County became Ashe County in 1799, and both families were counted there as "other free" in 1800.

1. Catherine McCollins, born say 1687, was a white woman servant of Elias Edmonds on 12 August 1705 when she confessed in Lancaster County court that she had a "mulattoe Child born of her body begotten by a Negroe" [Orders 1702-13, 127]. Her children may have been

     i. Catherine, born say 1705, a "free mulatto woman" of North Farnham Parish presented by the Richmond County, Virginia court in November 1725 for having an illegitimate child [Orders 1721-32, 248, 267].

2   ii. Thomas, born say 1708.

2. Thomas[1] Collins, born say 1708, was presented by the Louisa County court on 28 May 1745 for failing to list a tithable who was probably his wife and on 26 November 1745 he was presented for profane swearing [Orders 1742-8, 152, 157, 172, 174, 179]. He was a taxable in the 1750 Granville County list of John Wade [CR 44.701.23]. This part of Granville County became Orange County in 1752, and Thomas was a "Molata" taxable there on 3 "Black" tithes in 1755 [T&C, box 1, p.19]. He owned land on Flat River adjoining George **Gibson** and Moses **Ridley** [*Orange County Loose Papers*, vol. V, no. 131; vol. VI, no. 579]. He may have been the father of

3   i. George[1], born about 1728.

    ii. Thomas[2], Jr., born say 1734, an Orange County taxable listed nearby Thomas Collins in 1755 [T&C, box 1, p.19]. He may have been the Thomas Collins, Sr., who was head of a white Moore County household of 1 male over 16, 2 females, and a slave in 1790 [NC:44], and there was a Thomas Collins, Jr., head of a white Moore County household of 2 males under 16, 3 over 16, and 4 females in 1790 [NC:43]. He was head of an Ashe County household of 7 "other free" in 1800 [NC:74].

   iii. John, born say 1736, a "Molata" taxable in Orange County, taxed on 1 Black tithe in 1755 [T&C, box 1, p.15].

3. George[1] Collins, born about 1728, purchased 100 acres in Anson County, North Carolina, on 14 June 1764 [DB 3:268]. This part of Anson County became Richmond County in 1779, and his land was mentioned in a 2 February 1780 Richmond County land entry [Pruitt, *Richmond County Land Entries*, 10, 58]. He sold land by deed proved in the March 1783 session of Richmond County court. In December 1783 he and Arthur Dees were security for (his sons?) Thomas and George Collins, Jr., in a Richmond County court case [Minutes 1780-95, 33, 47]. The Richmond County court excused him from paying poll tax in 1788 because he was sixty years old. He was head of a Georgetown District, Prince George's Parish, South Carolina household of 7 "other free" in 1790 [SC:54]. He may have been the father of

    i. Thomas[3], born say 1760, a defendant in Richmond County, North Carolina court in December 1783 [Minutes 1780-95, 47].

ii. Charles[2], born say 1765, ordered by the January 1787 Richmond County, North Carolina court to receive twenty lashes for larceny committed in 1783 [Minutes 1780-95, 50, 111].

iii. George[3], Jr., born say 1767, head of a Richmond County household of 4 "other free" in 1790 [NC:45]. He entered 50 acres in Richmond County on Mayners Creek of Hitchcock Creek on 12 June 1794 [Pruitt, *Richmond County Land Entries*, nos. 169, 1013] and was taxed on 160 acres in 1795. He purchased 100 acres by deed proved in the January 1796 session of the Richmond County court and sold 50 acres to (his brother?) Elisha Collins by deed proved in the same session [Minutes 1793-1804, 312-3].

iv. Elisha, born say 1770, one of the freeholders ordered by the October 1794 session of the Richmond County court to work on the road to Catfish Road [Minutes 1793-1804, 282]. He was taxable on 250 acres in 1795. He purchased 50 acres from (his father?) George Collins by deed proved in Richmond County in January 1796 [Minutes 1793-1804, 313].

v. David[2], head of an Anson County household of 4 "other free" in 1800 [NC:203].

4. Samuel Collins, born say 1724, was presented by the Louisa County court on 28 May 1745 for failing to list a tithable who was probably his wife. On 25 November 1746 Richard Vernon sued him for 16 pounds, 9 shillings and fourteen pounds of deer skins, and on 24 February 1746/7 he and William Collins were presented for fishing and hunting on the Sabbath [Orders 1742-8, 152, 157, 172, 215, 227, 233]. He was a "Molata" taxable in Orange County on 2 Black tithes in 1755 [T&C, box 1, p.19]. He may have been the Samuel Collins who was head of a Wilkes County household of 1 male 21-60 and 1 female in the 1787 state census.

Wilkes and Ashe County, North Carolina descendants were

i. George[2], one of the hunters who had a cabin in present-day Ashe County when the first land grants were issued in the 1780s. He was taxable there on a 26 pound estate in 1778 [*NCGSJ* X:11, 14]. He was head of a Wilkes County household of 1 male 21-60, 3 males under 21 or over 60, and 3 free females for the 1787 state census and o1 white male over 16, 3 white males under 16, and 4 females [NC:123].

ii. David[1], taxable on an estate of 41 pounds in present-day Ashe County in 1778 [*NCGSJ* X:17]. He was head of a Tenth Company, Wilkes County household of 3 males over 16, 2 under 16, and 6 females in 1790 [NC:123].

iii. Martin, head of a Tenth Company, Wilkes County household of 1 male over 16, 3 under 16, and 4 females in 1790 [NC:123].

iv. Valentine, head of a Tenth Company, Wilkes County household of 1 male over 16 and 2 females in 1790 (abstracted as Vol) [NC:123] and head of an Ashe County household of 6 "other free" in 1800 [NC:75].

v. Vadery, perhaps the "Hardy" Collins who was head of a Wilkes County household of 1 male over 16, 2 under 16, and 4 females in 1790 [NC:123]. He was called Vadery in 1800, head of an Ashe County household of 4 "other free" in 1800. The 26 January 1791 Wilkes County court referred to a road near Sandy Island Ford and Vardie Collens [Absher, *Wilkes County Court Minutes 1789-97*, 20].

vi. Ambrose, taxable on an estate of 20 pounds in present-day Ashe County in 1778 [*NCGSJ* X:17]. He was head of a Tenth Company, Wilkes County household of 1 male over 16, 2 under 16, and 2 females in 1790 [NC:123]. He was head of an Ashe County household of 4 "other free" in 1800 [NC:76].

vii.   Charles[1], taxable in present-day Ashe County on an estate of 44 pounds in 1778 [*NCGSJ* X:17].

Northampton County, Virginia

1.   Susan Collins, born say 1707, consented to the indenture of her "Mulatto" daughter Rebecca to Thomas Jenkins in Northampton County court on 12 February 1729/30. She was presented for bastardy on 14 May 1734, 9 November 1736 and on 14 February 1737/8. On 12 August 1740 she agreed to serve Elishe Stringer for twenty years on condition that she be allowed to marry Stringer's "Negroe fellow" Caesar and "live with him until she shall be parted by death" [Orders 1729-32, 10; 1732-42, 107, 114, 255, 260, 296, 301, 408]. She was a "Negro" taxable in Digby Semore's Northampton County household in 1737, called "Sue, negro" in 1738, taxable in Elishe Stringer's household in 1740 and 1741 but was not listed in Stringer's household in 1744 [Bell, *Northampton County Tithables*, 260, 281]. She was the mother of

2   i.   Rebecca, born 17 August 1729.
     ii. Rachel, born say 1734, "Negroe" daughter of Susanna Collins, bound to Michael Christian on 10 December 1734 [Orders 1732-42, 142].
3   iii. Ann, born say 1737.

2.   Rebecca[1] Collins, born 17 August ___ (left blank in the record, say 1729), was bound to Thomas Jenkins on 12 February 1729/30. She was a "Negroe girl" listed in the inventory of the Northampton County estate of Thomas Jenkins in 1735 [W&I 18, part 2, 208]. She sued Alderton Gilding for her freedom on 10 September 1751, but the court ordered her to serve until 1 August 1752 according to the indenture produced in court [Orders 1729-32, 10; Orders 1751-3, 7, 35]. She was the mother of

     i.   Susanna[2], born 31 July 1758, daughter of Rebecca Collins, bound to Robert Warren on 13 January 1772 [Minutes 1771-7, 27]. Sue's son Thomas, born in May 1785, was bound by the Northampton County court to John Evans on 9 January 1793 [Orders 1789-95, 271].

3.   Ann Collins, born say 1737, was living in Northampton County on 13 February 1771 when her nine-year-old daughter Jane Collins was bound out. She may have been the A. Collins who won a suit for ten pounds against Scarburgh **Bingham** on 8 June 1779. Peter **Beckett** and Mary **Jeffery** were witnesses for her [Minutes 1765-71, 433; 1777-83, 167]. She was probably the Nanny Collins who registered as a "free Negro" in Northampton County on 12 June 1794 [Orders 1789-95, 358]. She was the mother of

     i.   Jane, born 15 March 1762, bound to Eyre Stockley on 13 February 1771. She registered as a "free Negro" in Northampton County on 12 June 1794 [Orders 1789-95, 358].
     ii. ?Rebecca[2], born say 1764, mother of Sue Collins who was seven years old when she was bound to John Evans by the Northampton County court on 14 May 1788 [Minutes 1787-9, 144]. Rebecca registered as a "free Negro" in Northampton County on 13 June 1794 [Orders 1789-95, 364].
     iii. ?Betty, registered as a "free Negro" in Northampton County on 12 June 1794 [Orders 1789-95, 358].
     iv. ?Ritter, registered as a "free Negro" in Northampton County on 13 June 1794 [Orders 1789-95, 364].

Other members of the Collins family in Northampton County were

     i.   John, bound to Guy Grimes on 12 January 1768 [Minutes 1765-71, 154]. He was taxable in Northampton County in 1787, 1795, 1796, and taxable on a slave in 1800 and 1801 [PPTL, 1782-1823, frames 64, 191, 206, 284, 305]. He registered as a "free Negro" in Northampton County on 13 June 1794 [Orders 1789-95, 364]. He married Betsy

Jeffries, 3 February 1803 Northampton County bond, Samuel **Beavans** security. Perhaps Betsy was the Betty Collins who was head of a Northampton County household of 5 "free colored" in 1820 [VA:216A].

ii. Lighty, born 30 July 1767, a "free negro" bound to John Tyler on 13 August 1771 [Minutes 1771-7, 3]. He was taxable in Northampton County from 1791 to 1803 [PPTL, 1782-1823, frames 129, 172, 225, 346]. He married Lear **Drighouse**, 3 January 1794 Northampton County bond, Thomas Lewis security.

iii. Ralph, born say 1772, taxable in Northampton County from 1791 to 1813 [PPTL, 1782-1823, frames 129, 243, 326, 388, 531], security for the 2 July 1793 Northampton County bond of Betty **Stephens** and Isaac **Reed**. He registered as a "free Negro" in Northampton County on 10 June 1794 [Orders 1789-95, 354]. He married Tamar **Bingham**, 20 December 1799 Northampton County bond, John Simkins security. He was head of a Northampton County household of 8 "free colored" in 1820 [VA:217]. His twenty-five-year-old daughter Esther Collins married Moses **Bingham**, 24 November 1819 Northampton County bond.

iv. Sarah, born about 1778, registered in Petersburg on 11 September 1805: *a brown Mulatto woman, five feet two an a half inches high, a little pitted with small pocks, twenty seven years old, born free in the County of Northampton, Virga. & Registry of that County* [Register of Free Negroes 1794-1819, no. 359].

v. Mack, married Betsey **Shepherd**, 27 November 1809 Northampton County bond, Abraham **Lang** security. He was head of a Northampton County household of 3 "free colored" in 1820 [VA:217].

vi. Nathaniel, married Salley **Stockley**, 6 October 1807 Northampton County bond; and second, Molly **Sample**, 16 August 1810 Northampton County bond, Isaiah **Carter** security.

Members of the Collins family in King William and King and Queen counties, Virginia, were

i. John, born say 1750, taxable in King William County on 198 acres in 1782 and 1783, taxable on 28 acres in 1787 but not subject to land tax in the following years. He was taxable in King William County on a free male tithable from 1787 to 1799 and from 1802 to 1814: listed as a "Mulatto" in 1813 and 1814 [PPTL 1782-1811; Land Tax List 1782-1832].

1 ii. Mason[1], born about 1758.

2 iii. William[1], born say 1765.

1. Mason[1] Collins, born about 1758, was taxable in King William County from 1787 to 1796 and from 1799 to 1802: taxable on 27 acres, a horse and 4 cattle in 1787 [PPTL 1782-1811; Land Tax List 1782-1832]. He was living in King William County on 2 January 1794 when he sold two cows, a yearling and a sow to Thomas Jones for 4 pounds, 11 shillings [Record Book 3:48]. He was taxable in King and Queen County from 1804 to 1820: taxable on 2 tithables from 1807 to 1812, called a "Mulatto" in 1807, a "free Negro" from 1809 to 1812, listed with 4 "Mulattos" (male and female) over age sixteen in 1813, over the age of forty-five in 1815 [PPTL, 1804-23]. He was about sixty years old on 15 May 1818 when he made a declaration in King and Queen County court to obtain a pension for his services in the 11th Virginia Regiment. He declared that he had travelled north as bowman to an officer named Holt Richeson in 1777 and enlisted while in the state of Pennsylvania. He called himself an "illiterate Mulatto" on 11 December 1820 when he stated that he had a life estate in 85 acres and that his family consisted of a twenty-year-old

woman named Maneroy, seventeen-year-old Mason, fifteen-year-old Mary and eleven-year-old Eliza. He was probably the father of

  i.   Elijah, a "free Negro" or "Mulatto" taxable in King & Queen County from 1811 to 1815 [PPTL, 1804-23].
  ii.   Thomas, a "free Negro" taxable in King and Queen County from 1814 to 1816 [PPTL, 1804-23].
  iii. Rily, a "free Negro" taxable in King and Queen County in 1816 [PPTL, 1804-23].
  iv.   Maneroy, born about 1800.
  v.   Mason², born about 1803.
  vi.   Mary, born about 1805.
  vii. Eliza, born about 1809.

2. William¹ Collins, born say 1765, was taxable in King William County from 1787 to 1818: taxable on a horse in 1798, taxable on 2 free males in 1802 and 1810, listed as a "Mulatto" in 1813. David Pannell transferred 25 acres to him in 1786 and William was taxable on the land from 1787 to 1811 [PPTL 1782-1811; Land Tax List 1782-1832]. On 24 June 1793 he purchased 25 acres in the parish of St. Johns in King William County adjoining Thomas Pollard, David Pannell and his own land for 25 pounds [Record Book 3:17]. He became a charter member of the Lower College Baptist Church with his wife Jane. Jane may have had Pamunkey Indian ancestry since in 1836 a Richard Collins was called "a descendant of the Indian Tribe" when he became a member of the same church [Colosse Baptist Church Minute Book 1814-1834; 1814-1870, 20 cited by Rountree, *Pocahantas's People*, 341]. He may have been the father of

  i.   William², Jr., taxable in King William County from 1811 to 1820: listed as a "Mulatto" in 1813, a "Free Negro" in the years following [PPTL 1782-1811; 1812-50].

A member of the Collins family in Bertie County, North Carolina, was

  i.   Josiah, born say 1750, a "free Molatto" taxable in his own Bertie County household in the 1771 list of Jonathan Standley [CR 10.702.1, box 2]. Perhaps he was the same Josiah Collins who was appointed a Bertie County constable in February 1777 [Haun, *Bertie County Court Minutes*, IV:212]. His family was associated with the Henry **Bunch** family of Bertie County. He was probably related to Lucy Collins, head of a Bertie County household of 4 "other free" in 1800 [NC:36].

Hyde County, North Carolina
1. Cate Collings, born say 1744, was called an "Indian Woman" servant of William Gibbs when she was summoned by the March 1765 Hyde County court [Minutes II:113]. Perhaps her descendants were

  i.   Susannah, born before 1776, head of a Hyde County household of 2 "free colored" in 1820 [NC:248].
  ii.   Charity, born 1794-1806, head of a Hyde County household of 6 "free colored" in 1820 [NC:246].
  iii. Horatio, a "free man of color" who had "taken up with" a slave named Winney, property of Henry Lucas, in Hyde County on 1 April 1843 [CR 053.928.2].
  iv.   Nancy, a "free woman of color" who had "taken up with" a slave named Ellick, property of Ananias Sadler, in Hyde County on 1 October 1842 [CR 053.928.2].

South Carolina
Members of the Collins family who were counted as "other free" in South Carolina were

    i.   Cary, head of a South Orangeburg District, South Carolina household of 6 "other free" in 1790.

    ii. Reason, head of a Fairfield District household of 5 "other free" in 1810 [SC:606].

An unrelated South Carolina family:

1.   Robert Collins, born say 1720, was a white plantation owner in St. Thomas and Dennis Parish, Charleston District. He left a will which left 545 acres to his African-American wife Susannah Collins and their children: Nelly, Esther, Rachel, Charlotte, Rebecca, Gasham, Elias, Robert, and Jonathan Collins [Koger, *Black Slaveowners*, 119-121]. His children were

    i.   Nelly.
    ii.   Esther.
    iii. Rachel.
    iv. Charlotte.
    v.   Rebecca.
    vi. Gasham.
    vii. Elias, married Elizabeth **Holman**. He was head of a Winyan County household of 5 "other free" and 68 slaves in 1800 [SC:760] and 6 "other free" and 16 slaves in Georgetown in 1810 [SC:219].
    viii. Robert[2], married Margaret **Holman**. He was head of a St. Dennis Parish, Berkeley County household of 2 "other free" and 10 slaves in 1810 [SC:442].
    ix. Jonathan, head of a St. Dennis, Berkeley County household of 1 "other free" and 2 slaves in 1810 [SC:442].

COMBESS/ CUMBEST FAMILY

1.   John[1] Combess/ Combest, born say 1670, was taxable in Spesutia Hundred, Baltimore County, Maryland, in 1695 (present-day Harford County) [Wright, *Inhabitants of Baltimore County*, 7]. He was the father of

    i.   Sarah, born 17 January 1693, "d/o John Combest," in St. George's Parish, Baltimore County. She married William Robinson on 8 December 1713 at St. George's Parish.
2   ii.   Ketturah, born 10 October 1695.
    iii. Mary, born 20 April 1698, "d/o of John Combest," at Swan Creek, St. George's Parish.
3   iv. Martha, born 9 September 1700.

2.   Ketturah Combest was born 10 October 1695, "d/o John Combest," in St. George's Parish, Baltimore County. She was head of a household and taxable on herself and (her son?) John Combess on two tithes in Spesutia Lower Hundred, Baltimore County, in 1737. He was probably identical to John Combest, a "Mulatto," aged eleven years and six months in June 1716 when he was bound to George Wells by the Baltimore County court [Proceedings 1715-8, 12]. Ketturah was probably the mother of

    i.   John[2], born about December 1704.

3.   Martha Combest was born 9 September 1700, "d/o John Combest," at the head of Collats Creek, St. George's Parish, Baltimore County [Reamy, *St. George's Parish Register, 1689-1773*, 1, 3, 7, 16, 21]. She was head of a household, taxable on herself and her son Jacob Combess on two tithes in Spesutia Lower Hundred, Baltimore County, in 1737 [Wright, *Inhabitants of Baltimore County*, 16]. She was the mother of

    i.   Jacob, born 10 November 1718, "son of Martha Combest" in St. George's Parish. He was taxable on 46-3/4 acres in Spesutia Hundred, Harford County, in 1783 [MSA S1161-6-10, p.124].

Some of their descendants were in South Carolina in 1770:

    i.   Josiah[1] and Penelope, witnesses in a murder case against William Fust and Christopher Davis in the South Carolina Court of General Sessions on 19 January 1770 [Journal of the S.C. Court, p.41].

4 ii. Winna, born say 1752.

4.   Winna Combest, born say 1752, was a "Mulatto" head of a Cheraw District, South Carolina household of 3 "other free" in 1790. She may have been the mother of

    i.   Josiah[2], born about 1770, a twelve-year-old "poor Boy" bound to Joseph Booth until the age of twenty-one on 3 August 1782 in St. David's Parish, South Carolina.

    ii. Mary, born about 1776, a six-year-old girl bound to Thomas Lankford in St. David's Parish on 3 August 1782.

    iii. Joans, born about 1777, a five-year-old girl bound to Francis Robertson in St. David's Parish, South Carolina, on 3 August 1782 [Holcolm, *Saint David's Parish Vestry*, 24, 25].

    iv. John[3], head of an Edgefield District, South Carolina household of 4 "other free" in 1810 [SC:766].

COMBS FAMILY

1.   John[1] Combs, born say 1675, (apparently a white man) and Sarah **Whiting** were living in Charles Parish, York County, when their children were born. Sarah **Whiting** may have been identical to "Sarah, a molatto servant...the daughter of an English woman," who sued her master Thomas Harwood in York County court for her freedom on 26 March 1694, claiming that she was twenty-one years old. She was called "Sarah Whiting a mulatto" when the 16 April 1694 birth of her daughter Mary was recorded in the Charles Parish Register. She was living in Charles Parish on 24 February 1701/2 when she was indicted by the York County court for fornication. John was sued again a year later on 24 February 1702/2 for 500 pounds due by bill for Sarah Whiting's fine [DOW 9:318; 11:554, 580; 12:94, 117]. She was probably the sister of Ann **Whiting**, a "mulatto," who had a daughter named Ann on 14 December 1701 [Bell, *Charles Parish Registers*, 193]. They were apparently treated as a married couple by 24 July 1705 when John Comes and his wife Sarah were paid as witnesses for Captain Thomas Cheasman in his suit against Denis Obrion. And the birth of their son John Combs was recorded in Charles Parish as if they were married. However, he was called John Combs of Charles Parish on 24 July 1707 when he confessed in court to the charge of fornication. And he was cited for fornication again on 25 February 1707/8. On 16 May 1720 he was called John Cooms when he complained to the York County court that two of his children who were bound to Edmund Sweeney were not being educated. On 16 March 1723/4 he sued James Faison in a disagreement over his account which Edward Tabb, Gent., resolved. On 21 September 1730 Francis Hayward, Gent., informed the court that John's son and granddaughter were not receiving due care [OW 12:344; 13:73, 83, 120; 15:584; 16:262, 277; 17:110]. John and Sarah registered the birth of their children in Charles Parish between 1705 and 1712, and Sarah's death on 16 January 1752 was registered in Charles Parish [Bell, *Charles Parish Registers*, 68, 194-5]. They were the parents of

    i.   ?Mary, born 16 April 1694, "daughter of Sarah Whiting a mulatto."

    ii. ?Ann, born say 1703, living in Charles Parish on 20 February 1720/1 when she was presented by the York County court for bastardy. She was whipped in York County on 16 February 1740/1 because she could not pay her fine [OW 16:38, 76; W&I 18:677].

    iii. Catherine, born 14 February 1704/5, "daughter of Sarah Whiting by John Combs."

    iv. John[2], son of John Combs by Sarah, born in 1707.

    v. Sarah, daughter of John and Sarah, born 10 January 1712, may have married Matthew[2] **Cuttillo**.

    vi. ?William[1], born about 1718, a thirty-nine-year-old James City County "Mulatto" planter, 5 feet 6 inches tall, listed in the August 1757 Size Roll of Captain Thomas Waggener's Company at Fort Holland [Clark, *Colonial Soldiers of the South*, 463].

2   vii. ?Thomas[1], born say 1720.

2. **Thomas**[1] Combs, born say 1720, and Frances Combs were living in Charles Parish on 17 February 1742 when their son William was born (no race mentioned) [Bell, *Charles Parish Registers*, 68]. On 17 December 1744 the York County court ordered that he pay taxes on his "Molatto" wife [W&I 19:314, 332]. On 18 May 1752 the court presented him for not listing himself as a tithable and fined him 1,000 pounds of tobacco. On 19 January 1761 the court ordered the churchwardens of Charles Parish to bind out his children because he was unable to provide for them. He was presented by the court on 21 November 1763 for not listing (his niece?) Martha Cattilla (**Cuttillo**) as a tithable. He had apparently established a common-law marriage with Anne **Wilson** by 17 November 1766 when he was presented by the York County court for not listing her as a tithable [Judgments & Orders 1752-4, 18, 58; 1759-63, 90, 128, 199, 204, 246; 1765-68, 161, 206]. His 29 June 1777 York County will, proved 15 September 1777, left a heifer to each of his "old" children: William, Thomas, Edmund, and George Combs and left Ann **Wilson** and her children "had by me" the remainder of his estate [W&I 22:374-5]. Ann died before 15 September 1777 when Mead Wood was granted administration on the estate, "Ann Wilson the executrix being dead and William Combs refusing (to be) the Executor" [Orders 1774-84, 151]. Thomas and Frances were the parents of

3   i. William[2], born 17 February 1742.

    ii. Thomas[2], born 4 May 1744, son of Thomas and Frances Combs [Bell, *Charles Parish Registers*, 67, 68]. He may have been the Thomas Combs who was taxable in Nottoway County, Southampton County, from 1783 to 1790, called a "Mulatto" in 1785, a "free Negro" in 1789 [PPTL 1782-92, frames 517, 534, 563, 587, 609, 731, 783]. And he may have been the father of Sally Combs who registered in Southampton County on 31 August 1797: *age 18, Mulatto, 5 feet 5 inches-3/4 height, free born* [Register of Free Negroes 1794-1832, no. 116].

    iii. James, born 19 November 1745, baptized 18 December 1745, son of Thomas and Frances.

4   iv. Edmund[1], born 5 January 1747.

    v. John[3], baptized 16 September 1750, son of Thomas and Frances.

    vi. George, born say 1752.

Thomas and Anne had

    vii. Sally Wilson, born 24 June, baptized 28 July 1765, daughter of Thomas Combs and Anne Wilson.

    viii. Anne Combs, born 22 April 1769, baptized 25 June, daughter of Thomas and Anne Combs.

    ix. Martha Combs, daughter of Thomas and Anne, born 17 February, baptized 22 March 1772.

    x. Willis Combs, son of Thomas and Anne born 4 May 1774, baptized 12 June. On 15 January 1787 the York County court bound him to Abraham **Francis**, shoemaker, because his father's estate was insufficient to maintain him [Orders 1784-7, 402].

    xi. Frances[1], daughter of Thomas and Anne, born 17 March 1776, baptized 14 April [Bell, *Charles Parish Registers*, 67, 68].

3.   William[2] Combs, born 17 February 1742, baptized 20 March, was the son of Thomas and Frances Combs. He had an account with the estate of Anthony Robinson which included his rent for 1776 and 1777 and clothes he cut for the estate in 1778 [W&I 22:483-6]. He and his wife Mary were living in Charles Parish, York County, on 15 August 1781 when their "Mulatto" daughter Elizabeth was born [Bell, *Charles Parish Registers*, 68, 67]. He was taxable in York County from 1784 to 1799 [PPTL, 1782-1841, frames 89, 95, 161, 181, 200, 228, 243]. William and Mary were the parents of

    i.   John, son of William and Mary, born 27 December 1776, baptized 16 February. He may have been the John Combs, alias John Fry, who married Alice **Ware**, ("free persons of color") "former servant of the late John Lear and daughter of Elzey **Ware**, deceased," 11 December 1816 Fredericksburg bond, surety R.S. Chew.
    ii.   Anne, daughter of William and Mary Combs, born 14 December 1778, baptized 14 February 1779 [Bell, *Charles Parish Registers*, 68].
    iii. Elizabeth, born 15 August 1781, baptized 4 November. She may have been the Betsy Combs who was head of a York County household of 9 "other free" in 1810 [VA:873].
    iv.   Mary, daughter of William and Mary, born 11 July 1783, baptized 14 September.

4.   Edmund[1] Combs, born 5 January 1747, baptized 5 January 1747, was the son of Thomas and Frances Combs. He and his wife Mary were living in Charles Parish, York County, when they registered the birth of their "Mulatto" son Gideon **Pickett** Combs on 5 December 1778 and their "Mulatto" son Abraham on 8 April 1782. Mary was probably related to John and Elizabeth **Pickett** whose "Mulatto" son William was born on 7 August 1784 [Bell, *Charles Parish Registers*, 67-68, 152]. Edmund was taxable in York County from 1784 to 1805: on 2 tithes in 1796, 1801 and 1804 [PPTL, 1782-1841, frames 89, 95, 161, 181, 219, 264, 295, 305]. Their children were

    i.   John[4], son of Edmund and Mary, born 17 October 1774, baptized 28 November 1774, married Elizabeth **Huson (Hewson)** ("spinster" of Charles Parish), 22 December 1800 York County bond. He was head of a York County household of 5 "other free" in 1810 [VA:873].
    ii.   William[3], born 14 February 1776, son of Edmund and Mary, baptized 14 April 1776, probably died young.
    iii. Frances[2], daughter of Edmund and Mary, born 25 July 1777, baptized 8 March 1778.
    iv.   Gdo. **Pickett** Combs, born 5 December 1778, "Mulatto" son of Edmund and Mary.
    v.   William[4], born 27 February 1780, son of Edmund and Mary, baptized 16 April 1780. He was taxable in York County from 1809 to 1812 [PPTL, 1782-1841, frames 339, 363, 374] and head of a York County household of 4 "other free" and a slave in 1810 [VA:873].
    vi.   Abraham, born 8 March 1782, "Mulatto" son of Edmund and Mary, baptized 28 April 1782, taxable in York County in 1811 [PPTL, 1782-1841, frame 363].
    vii. Jane, born 6 February 1784, "Mulatto daughter of Edmund and Mary," baptized 2 May.

Other descendants were

5   i.   Thomas[3] Combs, born say 1760.
     ii.   Mary, born about 1800, registered in York County on 20 January 1823: *a bright mulatto about 23 years of age...has a thin head of hair* [Register of Free Negroes 1798-1831, no.197].
     iii. William[5], born about 1808, registered in York County on 19 September 1831: *23 years of age, 5 feet 10-1/2 inches high, light curly hair, very white and clear skin* [Free Negroes Register 1831-50, no.297].

5. Thomas[3] Combs, born say 1760, was a "poor orphan" ordered bound out by the churchwardens of Charles Parish, York County, on 19 March 1764 [Judgments & Orders 1763-5, 176]. He was taxable in York County from 1784 to 1789 [PPTL, 1782-1841, frames 89, 95, 139, 149]. He and his wife Mary were living in Charles Parish, York County, on 2 March 1786 when their "Mulatto" daughter Hebe was born [Bell, *Charles Parish Registers*, 68]. Their child was

    i. Hebe, born 2 March 1786, baptized 10 June.

CONNER FAMILY

1. Elizabeth Connors, born say 1690, was a "white Christian Woman" who was bound out for five years by the churchwardens of Charles Parish, York County, on 24 November 1710 for "having a mulatto Bastard Child the sd Cunnears appeared & acknowledged the fact" [OW 14:41]. She was probably the mother of

2   i. Lewis, born say 1720.
3   ii. Mark, born say 1722.
4   iii. James, born say 1725.

2. Lewis Conner, born say 1720, purchased 100 acres in Craven County, North Carolina, on the north side of the Trent River joining Edward Frank and the White Oak Pocosin near Chinquapin Creek on 10 April 1760. Fifty acres of this land was sold by (his brother?) James Conner on 4 June 1768 [DB 2:526; 15:126].[81] Lewis was head of a household of one "Black" male and one "Black" female taxable in Craven County in 1769 [SS 837]. Perhaps his widow was Merion Conner, head of a Beaufort County household of 3 "other free" in 1790 [NC:125]. Their children may have been

5   i. John[1], born say 1757.
    ii. Isaac, born about 1767, a twelve-year-old "Mulatto" ordered bound to George Parris until the age of thirty-one years in Tryon County on 18 January 1779 [Minutes of Court of Pleas and Quarter Sessions].
    iii. Michael, head of a Robeson County household of 5 "other free" in 1800 [NC:373] and 4 in 1810 [NC:242].
6   iv. Rachel C___er (Conner), born say 1775.
    v. Edward, head of a Lenoir County household of 6 "other free" and 8 slaves in 1810 [NC:301].

3. Mark Conner, born say 1722, received a patent for 100 acres joining Lewis Conner on 28 October 1765 on the north side of Chinquapin Creek in the part of Craven County which became Jones County in 1790 [Hoffman, *Land Patents*, II:19]. He was a head of a Craven County household of one "Black" male and one "Black" female taxable in 1769 [SS 837] and was head of a Jones County household of 9 "other free" in 1790 [NC:144]. Perhaps he was the father of

    i. John[2], (Senr), head of a Jones County household of 4 "other free" in 1810 [NC:256].
    ii. Ephram, head of a Jones County household of 6 "other free" in 1810 [NC:256].
    iii. Zilphy, head of a Greene County household of 7 "free colored" in 1820 [NC:245].

4. James Conner, born say 1725, sold fifty acres of land on the north side of the Trent River near Chinquapin Creek in Craven County on 4 June 1768. This was land purchased by (his brother?) Lewis Conner on 10 April 1760 [DB

---

[81]This part of Craven County became Jones County in 1779.

2:526; 15:126]. James was head of a household of one "Black" male and one "Black" female taxable in Craven County in 1769 [SS 837]. He was probably the James Conner who was listed among the superannuated members of the Beaufort County Militia under the command of Colonel William Brown prior to 1765, listed after Thomas **Blango** [Clark, *Colonial Soldiers of the South*, 781]. He was taxable in Beaufort County in 1779 on an assessment of 361 pounds, in the same district as Thomas **Blango** (the district of Jesse Blount, Robert Williams, and Jacob Shute) [*NCGSJ* XV:142]. He was head of a New Hanover County household of 5 "other free" in 1800 [NC:311]. Perhaps his children were those counted in New Hanover County:

    i. Moses, head of a household of 2 "other free" in 1800 [NC:311].

    ii. William, born before 1776, head of a household of 9 "free colored" in the town of Wilmington in 1820 [NC:205].

    iii. Polly, born before 1776, head of a household of 4 "free colored" in 1820 [NC:224].

    iv. John⁴, born 1776-94, head of a household of 9 "free colored" in the town of Wilmington in 1820 [NC:205].

5. John¹ Conner, born say 1757, was head of a Jones County household of 13 "other free" in 1790 [NC:144]. His August 1798 Jones County will named his wife Rebecca and four children. Rebecca was head of a Jones County household of 7 "other free" in 1810 [NC:256]. Their children were

    i. John³, head of a Jones County household of 6 "other free" in 1810 [NC:256].

    ii. Jesse, head of a Lenoir County household of 5 "other free" and one white woman in 1810 [NC:301].

    iii. Silas.

    iv. Daniel.

6. Rachel C___er (Conner), born say 1775, was head of a Beaufort County household of 3 "other free" in 1800 [NC:5]. She was probably the mother of

    i. Churchill, born about 1801, "a free Boy of Color," bound apprentice to Isaac Smith by the March 1814 Beaufort County court (no parent named).

    ii. Keziah, born about 1803, a ten-year-old "free Girl of Color, ordered bound an apprentice seamstress to Joseph B. Hinton by the March 1813 Beaufort County court.

    iii. Chappel, born about 1803, "a free Boy of Color" bound apprentice to W. Smaw by the March 1814 Beaufort County court (no parent named) [Minutes 1809-14, n.p.].

COOK FAMILY

1. Sarah Cooke, born about 1673, was a servant who petitioned the York County court for her freedom on 26 February 1693/4 stating that she was the daughter of an English woman named Mary Cooke and that she had served her master for twenty-one years. The result of her petition was not recorded [DOW 9:297, 352]. She may have been the ancestor of

    i. Robert, born say 1740, a "free Negro" tithable in Bertie County, North Carolina, in the list of H. Nichols in 1774 with (his wife?) Peney Cook and tithable on 3 tithes in the 1775 summary list [CR 10.702]. Administration on his Bertie County estate was granted to Cesar Cook on 15 February 1780 [Gammon, *Record of Estates, Bertie County* II, 23].

2   ii. Henry, born about 1746.

2. Henry Cook, born about 1746, a "free Negro born in Gloucester County," indentured himself for five years in order to get cured of "a pox." He was

about 5 feet 10 or 11 inches high and twenty-four years of age in April 1770 when he ran away from the master to whom he was indentured. He was described further as being

> *lusty and very well made, of a good black complexion, and thick lips; his clothing mean, being an old brown cloth waistcoat and breeches much patched with green cloth, osnabrug shirt, yarn stockings, very bad shoes, though he took leather with him ready cut for another pair. He understands a little of the carpenter business, and has likewise followed the water. He took with him a Negro fellow belonging to William Tate...took with them a yawl of 28 feet...*[*Virginia Gazette*, Purdie & Dixon's edition, p. 3, col. 2].

He was living in Essex County on 16 January 1786 when he and Francis **Bunday**, "free Mulattoes," were accused of entering the lumber house of Lott and Higby Merchants in the City of Richmond on 21 December 1785 and stealing a large quantity of cloth valued at over 200 pounds currency. The defendants were sent to Richmond for further trial [Orders 1784-7, 177-8]. He may have been the father of

    i.   Charles, born say 1768, taxable in Gloucester County in 1789, from 1797 to 1800, listed as a "Mulatto" from 1804 to 1817, over the age of forty-five in 1815 [PPTL 1782-99; 1800-20]. He was a "free negro" head of a Gloucester County household of 5 "other free" in 1810 [VA:402A].

    ii. William, a "Mulatto" taxable in Gloucester County from 1804 to 1817 [PPTL 1800-20], a "free negro" head of a Gloucester County household of 3 "other free" in 1810 [VA:402A].

    iii. John, a "Mulatto" taxable in Gloucester County from 1805 to 1815 [PPTL 1800-20], a "free negro" head of a Gloucester County household of 1 "other free" and 2 slaves in 1810 [VA:402A].

    iv. Richard, head of a Mathews County household of 3 "other free" in 1810 [VA:453].

Spotsylvania County

1.   Sarah Cook, born say 1734, was the servant of Joseph Allen on 7 March 1758 when she acknowledged in Spotsylvania County court that she had a "Molatto" child in her master's house. The court ordered that she serve her master an additional year for his trouble and that she be sold by the churchwardens for another five years when she completed her service to her master. The court issued the same order on 6 August 1759, perhaps for a second child [Orders 1755-65, 65, 142]. She may have been the ancestor of

2   i.   George[1], born about 1751.

    ii. Peter, a "M^a" taxable on one tithe and a horse in Culpeper County in 1800 [*Virginia Genealogist* 16:186], called Peter Kook in 1810, a "free Negro" head of a Culpeper County household of 7 "other free" in 1810 [VA:52].

    iii. Winney, a "free Negro" head of a Culpeper County household of 3 "other free" in 1810 [VA:51].

    iv. Alyce, head of a Fredericksburg, Spotsylvania County household of 2 "other free" in 1810 [VA:113b].

2.   George[1] Cook, born about 1751, was about twenty-six years old and had five more years of his indenture to serve William Knox of Culpeper County when he ran away. Knox offered a reward for his return in the 11 April 1777 issue of the *Virginia Gazette*, describing him as

> *a very dark servant mulatto man...a likely stout made fellow...clothed in homespun woolen and linen.*

The ad also stated that he had applied to a recruiting officer to enlist as a soldier in order to free himself of his indenture [Purdie's edition, p. 3, col. 3]. He was a "free Negroe" taxable on a tithe and a horse in Culpeper County in 1800 [*Virginia Genealogist* 16:186]. He may have been the father of

    i.   Ama, head of a Goochland County household of 5 "other free" in 1810 [VA:687].

    ii.   James, "free Negro" head of a Charlotte County household of 3 "other free" in 1810 [VA:68].

Other Members of the family were

1   i.   Nancy, born about 1762.

    ii.   Roger, born about 1770, a twenty-eight-year-old "mulatto" who ran away from Francis Eppes of Prince George County according to the 3 July 1798 issue of the *Virginia Gazette*.

    iii.   Mary, head of an Elizabeth City County household of 8 "other free" and 1 slave in 1810 [VA:183].

    iv.   Sucky, born say 1770, mother of Frank Cook (born in January 1791) who registered in Petersburg on 27 June 1811: *a brown man of colour, five feet three 3/4 inches high, twenty years old January last, born free and raised in the County of Chesterfield, son of Sucky Cook a free woman* [Register of Free Negroes 1794-1819, no. 666].

    v.   Jincy, head of a Petersburg Town household of 2 "other free" in 1810 [VA:123a].

    vi.   Judy, head of a Petersburg Town household of 2 "other free" in 1810 [VA:121b].

    vii.   Charlotte, born about 1784, registered in Petersburg on 1 November 1802: *a dark brown Mulatto woman, five feet four inches high, eighteen years old, short knotty hair, born free & raised in Charlotte County* [Register of Free Negroes 1794-1819, no. 245]. She was head of a Petersburg Town household of 2 "other free" in 1810 [VA:121a].

1.   Nancy Cook, born about 1762, registered in Petersburg on 15 August 1800: *a light brown Mulatto woman, five feet one and a half inches high, thirty eight years old, bushy head of hair, appears from the certificate produced to have been born free in the County of King & Queen & party raised in Charlotte County* [Register of Free Negroes 1794-1819, no. 181]. She was head of a Petersburg Town household of 3 "other free" in 1810 [VA:123a]. She may have been the mother of

2   i.   Rhoda, born about 1784.

2.   Rhoda Cook, born about 1784, registered in Petersburg on 7 June 1810: *a light brown free woman of Colour, five feet five inches high, twenty six years old, born free & raised in Charlotte County* [Register of Free Negroes 1794-1819, no. 513]. She was the mother of

    i.   George[2], born about 1799, registered in Petersburg on 6 January 1818: *a free lad of Colour, nineteen and a half years old, five feet seven 3/4 inches high, dark brown Complection, son of Rhoda Cook, a free woman* [Register of Free Negroes 1794-1819, no. 892].

    ii.   John, born about 1802, registered in Petersburg on 6 January 1818: *sixteen years old, five feet seven inches high, dark brown Complection, son of Rhoda Cook, a free woman* [Register of Free Negroes 1794-1819, no. 893].

COOLEY/ COLLEY FAMILY

1.   Ann Colley, born say 1704, was the servant of Margaret Blagg of Westmoreland County on 28 March 1722 when the churchwardens of Washington Parish ordered her sold for five years after her indenture was

completed for having a "Mulatto bastard Child" [Orders 1721-31, 15]. She may have been the ancestor of

    i.   George[1], presented by the grand jury of Charles City County on 6 September 1758 for concealing a tithable. George, Charles, Thomas, and George Coley, Jr., pleaded not guilty, but the court decided that they were required to list their wives as tithables because they were "Mulatto" and fined them 500 pounds of tobacco each. George made an indenture of bargain and sale to Gabriel Coley which he acknowledged in court on 4 November 1761 [Orders 1758-62, 56, 78, 325]. He may have been identical to George Coley who was head of Montgomery County, North Carolina household of 7 white persons in 1790 [NC:165].

    ii.   Charles, a "Mulatto" convicted for failing to list his wife as a tithable in Charles City County in 1758 [Orders 1758-62, 56, 78], perhaps the Charles Coley who was head of a Halifax County, North Carolina household of 1 white male over 16, 1 under 16, and 3 white females in 1790 [NC:48].

    iii.   Thomas, a "Mulatto" convicted of failing to list his wife as a tithable in Charles City County in 1758 [Orders 1758-62, 56, 78], perhaps the Thomas Colly who was head of a Robeson County, North Carolina household of 1 white male over 16 and 1 white female in 1790 [NC:48].

    iv.   George[2], a "Mulatto" convicted of not listing his wife as a tithable in Charles City County in 1758 [Orders 1758-62, 56, 78].

    v.   Martin Colley, "F.N." head of a Rockingham County, Virginia household of 9 "other free" in 1810 [VA:13]. He registered in Rockingham County on 20 October 1819: *(a free man of Colour) about 45 years of age...a Bright Mullettoe...free born as appears by the affidavit of Abner Yates of this county* [Boyd-Rush, *Register of Free Blacks, Rockingham County*, 20].

    vi.   Robert Cooley, head of a Richmond City, Virginia household of 8 "other free" and 2 slaves in 1810 [VA:374]. He served the nobility at Williamsburg and was later an attendant in the council chambers and courts of justice in Richmond [Mordecai, *Richmond in By-gone Days*, 312-3].

    vii.   Robin Cooley, born before 1776, head of a Halifax County, North Carolina household of 6 "free colored" in 1830. The 25 February 1842 session of the Halifax County court allowed him to use his gun in the county.

    viii.   John Colley, head of a Richmond City, Virginia household of 3 "other free" and a slave in 1810 [VA:367].

    ix.   William Coley, married Tabitha **Peters**, 25 April 1818 Halifax County, North Carolina bond. She may have been identical to Tobby Cooley who married Henry **Peters**, 8 November 1826 Halifax County bond.

COOPER FAMILY

1.   Daniel[1] Cooper, born say 1725, was listed as Mrs. Anne Scott's tithable in Goochland County in 1746 [List of Tithables] and was taxable in the upper district of Goochland County on his own tithe and a horse in 1782 [PPTL, 1782-1809, frame 8]. He may have been the father of

2   i.   Joseph, born say 1745.

       ii.   Margaret, born say 1747, a "free negro" head of a Norfolk County household in Elizabeth River Parish in 1768 [Wingo, *Norfolk County Tithables, 1766-80*, 80].

3   iii.   Ann, born say 1750.

4   iv.   James, born about 1750.

5   v.   ?Rachel, born say 1753.

vi.   William[1], born say 1754, a taxable overseer on the Goochland County plantation of the Reverend William Douglas in 1775 [List of Tithables].

2.   Joseph Cooper, born say 1745, a "free mulatto," and his wife Lydia registered the birth of their son William in Bruton Parish, James City County, on 9 March 1768 [Bruton Parish Register, 32]. He was one of a long list of residents of Bruton Parish, York County, who were presented by the court on 15 November 1773 for failing to list themselves as tithables [Orders 1772-4, 436, 442]. He and Lydia were the parents of
      i.   William[2], born 9 March 1768.

3.   Ann Cooper, born say 1750, was living in Goochland County in November 1770 when the churchwardens of St. James Northam Parish were ordered to bind out her children Roger and Daniel, no race mentioned, to William Michell [Orders 1767-70, 502]. Her children were

6   i.   Roger[1], born say 1768.
     ii. Daniel[2], born say 1770, bound out in Goochland County in November 1770 [Orders 1767-70, 502]. He was taxable in the upper district of Goochland County from 1799 to 1814: a "Mulatto" carpenter living near Edward Bolling's in 1804, a "free born carpenter" on George S. Smith's land from 1805 to 1813, listed with wife Nancy in 1813 [PPTL, 1782-1809, frames 525, 543, 596, 666, 686, 738, 778, 821, 864; 1810-32, frames 5, 97, 158, 190]. He married Nancy **Cooper** (who James Quigg testified was at "a distance from her parents"), 16 December 1803 Goochland County bond, George **Tyler** surety. Daniel was head of a Goochland County household of 5 "other free" in 1810 [VA:689]. His Goochland County estate was assessed at $239 on 12 March 1817 [DB 22:354]. Nancy registered as a free Negro in Goochland County on 20 September 1819: *widow of Daniel Cooper decd. aged about thirty four years, about five feet seven inches high, of yellow complexion...free born* [Register of Free Negroes, p.111].
     iii. ?Isham, born about 1781, registered in Goochland County on 19 September 1808: *five feet seven inches & an half high, about twenty seven years of age, light yellow complexion...free born* [Register of free Negroes, p.23].
     iv. ?William[3], born say 1785, a "Mulatto" farmer living on M.V. Woodson's land in the upper district of Goochland County in 1811, a waterman in 1812, [PPTL, 1810-32, frames 70, 97, 113]. He married Nancy **Banks**, 29 August 1809 Goochland County bond, Jacob **Martin** surety, 1 September marriage.

4.   James Cooper, born about 1750, was taxable in the upper district of Goochland County from 1789 to 1800, taxable on a slave under the age of 12 in 1790 [PPTL, 1782-1809, frames 219, 236, 280, 420, 479, 525, 545]. He was a seventy-year-old "free man of color when he applied for a pension while residing in Augusta County, Virginia, on 26 June 1820. He stated that he had enlisted in Goochland County and that his family consisted of himself and Lukey **Orchard**, a free woman of color upwards of fifty years old, who lived with him. He owned a horse and was renting 4-5 acres. His application included a certificate dated October 1787 from a justice of the peace in Goochland County, describing him as a "molatto Free man," which was to be used as a pass to travel to North Carolina and Georgia [Dorman, *Virginia Revolutionary Pension Applications,* 20:76-7]. His common-law wife, a white woman named Lilly Anne Craddock, had a child who was either stillborn or died shortly after birth in Goochland County in 1787 [Orders 1787, 429-436]. He was head of an Augusta County household of 2 "other free" and a white woman over 45 in 1810 [VA:371]. Lukey **Orchard** was head of an Augusta County household of 5 "other free" in 1810 [VA:371]. James and Pleasant

Cooper were listed as "people of color" in the first district of Augusta County in 1813 [Waldrep, *1813 Tax List*]. He was the father of

    i. Pleasant, received a warrant for bounty land for his father's services [Jackson, *Virginia Negro Soldiers*, 33].

5. Rachel Cooper, born say 1753, apprenticed her sons Daniel and David to Japheth Fowler for five years. In April 1783 she complained to the Goochland County court that he was ill-treating her sons and intended to remove them from the county [Orders 1779-83, 173]. She married Squire **Caesar**, "Free Negroes," 13 March 1800 Goochland County bond, Thomas F. Bates surety, 16 March marriage. Squire was head of a Goochland County household of 4 "other free" in 1810 [VA:689] and was living with his wife Rachel near John Lewis in 1813 [PPTL, 1810-32, frame 159]. Rachel was the mother of

    i. David, born say 1772, taxable in the upper district of Goochland County from 1798 to 1805: a "Black Free man" shoemaker at William Humber's in 1804, a "free born" shoemaker living on William Britt's land in 1805 [PPTL, 1782-1809, frames 480, 525, 615, 666, 686, 738].

    ii. Daniel[2], born say 1773, taxable in the upper district of Goochland County in 1799, his tax charged to David Ross in 1799 [PPTL, 1782-1809, frames 533].

6. Roger[1] Cooper, born say 1768, was taxable in the upper district of Goochland County from 1786 to 1815: a "Mulatto" farmer living near William George's in 1804, listed with (wife?) Patsey on William M. Richardson's land in 1813, over the age of forty-five in 1815 [PPTL, 1782-1809, frames 140, 150, 175, 279, 387, 464, 525, 543, 615, 687, 738, 778, 822, 864; 1810-32, frames 5, 76, 159, 189, 258]. He was head of a Goochland County household of 10 "other free" in 1810 [VA:688]. He may have been the father of

    i. Randolph, born say 1790, married Polly **Cockran**, "daughter of Henry **Cockran**," 13 December 1813 Goochland County bond, 16 December marriage. He was a "Mulatto" carpenter living at Squire **Caesar**'s in 1813 [PPTL, 1810-32, frame 159, 190].

    ii. Francis, born say 1792, a "Mulatto Waterman" living at Roger Cooper's in 1813, a "Mulatto Ditcher" at Roger Cooper's in 1814 [PPTL, 1810-32, frames 159, 189, 258].

    iii. Roger[2], Jr., born say 1793, married Ruth **Cockran**, "daughter of Henry **Cockran**," 31 October 1814 Goochland County bond, 3 November marriage. He was a sawyer living at Squire **Caesar**'s in 1814 [PPTL, 1810-32, frames 190].

COPELAND FAMILY

Members of the Copeland family in Virginia were

    i. Michael, head of a New Kent County household of 6 "other free" and a slave in 1810 [VA:747].

    ii. Richard, head of a Henrico County household of 8 "other free" in 1810 [VA:980], perhaps the Richard Copeland who married Elizabeth **Roach**, 29 November 1797 Loudoun County bond.

    iii. Exum, born about 1790, registered in Norfolk County on 21 October 1811: *5 feet 6 1/2 In. 21 years of age dark Complexion...Born free* [Register of Free Negros & Mulattos, #64].

    iv. David, a "Free Negro" taxable at Allen's Mill in Nansemond County in 1815.

    v. Allen, a "Free Negro" taxable at N. Milner's in Nansemond County in 1815.

    vi. George, a "Free Negro" taxable at McClenney's in Nansemond County in 1815 [Yantis, *Supplement to the 1810 Census of Virginia*, S-14].

Members of the family in North Carolina were
  i.   Isaac, head of a Wake County household of 4 "other free" in 1790
       [NC:105]. He purchased 200 acres in Wake County on the east side of
       a road adjoining Clifton and John Lewis on 26 November 1793, sold
       this land on 22 March 1799, and purchased 100 acres in Wake County
       on the waters of Middle Creek and both sides of Buffalo Swamp on 26
       November 1799 [DB Q:154, 439]. He was probably the father of
       Thomas Copeland, born about 1790, who was head of a Wake County
       household of 6 "free colored" in 1840 and a "Mulatto" household in
       1860 which included (his mother?) Nancy **Harris** Copeland, a
       "Mulatto" aged ninety.
  ii. Cato, born about 1758, head of a Craven County household of 1 "other
       free" in 1790 [NC:134] and 2 in Halifax County in 1810 [NC:12].
       While a resident of Halifax County he applied for and was granted a
       pension for three years service in the 2nd North Carolina Regiment.
       According to the pension application he married Nancy **Mitchell**, 11
       December 1778 Halifax County bond, 16 December 1778 marriage.
       Cato died in 1827 and his wife Nancy Copeland applied for a
       survivor's pension on 21 November 1842 [M805-219, frame 0072].
  iii. Benjamin, born before 1776, head of a Hertford County household of
       3 "free colored" men in 1820 [NC:182]. Benjamin, James and Donnel
       Copeland were among "Sundry persons of Colour of Hertford County"
       who petitioned the General Assembly in 1822 to repeal the act which
       declared slaves to be competent witnesses against free African
       Americans [*NCGSJ* XI:252].

COPES FAMILY

1. Margaret[1] Copes, born say 1681, was presented by the churchwardens of
   Hungers Parish, Northampton County, Virginia, on 29 December 1699 for
   having a "Maletto Barstard child" but was discharged because her child was
   not born in the county. On 19 April 1701 she indentured her year-and-two-
   month-old daughter Tabitha to Richard Smith until the age of eighteen. She
   and John Harper proved the will of Captain Isaac Foxcroft in court on 8
   November 1702 [OW&c 1698-1710, 36, 83, 106]. She was the mother of
2.   i.   Tabitha, born about December 1699.
     ii. Margaret[2], born say 1705, married Azaricum **Drighouse (Driggers)**.

2. Tabitha Copes, born before December 1699, was a "Mulato" presented by the
   Northampton County, Virginia court for bastardy on 11 May 1725 [Orders
   1722-29, 181]. She was tithable in the Northampton County household of
   Azaricum and Margaret **Drighouse** in 1726 and was called Tabitha **Carter** in
   their household in 1727 with her husband Jacob **Carter**. They were taxable in
   their own household from 1728 to 1731 [L.P. 1726-31]. Her children were
     i.   Elishe, born about September 1719, thirteen-month-old "daughter of
          Tabitha Copes" bound apprentice by her mother to John Marshall on
          10 October 1720 [Orders 1719-22, 95]. Elishe may have been the
          ancestor of Daniel Copes, head of an Accomack Parish, Accomack
          County household of 6 "other free" in 1800 [*Virginia Genealogist*
          1:104] and 6 in 1810 [VA:87].
3.   ii. Jacob, perhaps the bastard child Tabitha was presented for in 1725 (son
          of Jacob **Carter**?).

3. Jacob Copes, born before 11 May 1725, was a "free Negro" listed in the
   muster roll of Abner Neale's Craven County, North Carolina Company
   between the head of Slocomb's Creek and Turnagain Bay on 4 October 1754

and 1755 [Clark, *Colonial Soldiers of the South*, 708].[82] A petition in Craven County court on behalf of him and his wife and children was postponed on 13 September 1768 to the next court, but the matter of the petition and the outcome were not recorded [Minutes 1767-75, 93b]. He was a taxable head of a Craven County household of a Black male and 3 Black females in 1769 [SS 837], taxable as a married man in the list for the District of Captains Adam Tooley and John Nelson in 1779 [LP 30.1], and was head of Craven County household of 16 "other free" in 1790 [NC:130]. His children were

<ol type="i">
<li>Mary, born say 1755, called the daughter of Jacob Copes when she was deemed an insolvent person because of "her infirmity" by the 10 June 1772 Craven County court. On 8 September 1772 this decision was reversed on unstated evidence by the sheriff [Minutes 1772-84, vol.1, p.3a, p.6c]. She was head of a Craven County household of 5 "free colored" in 1820 [NC:65].</li>
<li>?Nancy, born 1776-94, head of a Craven County household of 3 "free colored" in 1820 [NC:76].</li>
<li>?Catherine, born 1794-1806, head of a Craven County household of 4 "free colored" in 1820 [NC:72].</li>
<li>?Elsey, born 1794-1806, head of a Craven County household of one "free colored" in 1820 [NC:77].</li>
</ol>

CORN FAMILY

1. Rebecca Corney, born say 1668, was the servant of John Baxter in August 1689 when she was fined by the Charles City County court for having an illegitimate "Mulatto" child [Orders 1687-95, 225]. She may have been the ancestor of

<ol type="i">
<li>Lucy[1] Corn, born say 1740.</li>
<li>Robert Corn, born say 1745.</li>
</ol>

2. Lucy[1] Corn, born say 1740, was living in Chesterfield County on 4 December 1778 when the court ordered the churchwardens to bind out her daughter Phebe. She was the ancestor of

<ol type="i">
<li>?Lucy[2], born about 1758, registered in Petersburg on 19 August 1794: *a dark brown, stout made Mulatto woman, with bushy black hair, five feet one inches high, thirty six years old, born free & raised in Chesterfield County* [Register of Free Negroes 1794-1819, no. 56]. She may have been the Lucy Corn whose daughter Lucy Corn was bound out in Dale Parish by order of the Chesterfield County court on 5 February 1779 [Orders 1774-84, 202].</li>
<li>?Bess, born say 1762, a "poor child" bound apprentice in Chesterfield County on 4 February 1763 [Orders 1759-67, 386].</li>
<li>?Joe, born about 1764, registered in Petersburg on 25 August 1794: *a dark brown Mulatto man, five feet six inches high, thirty years old, born free and raised in Chesterfield County* [Register of Free Negroes 1794-1819, no. 88]. He was taxable in Chesterfield County from 1791 to 1805 [PPTL, 1786-1811, frames 82, 444, 482, 519, 557, 596].</li>
<li>Phebe, born about 1768, daughter of Lucy Corn, bound apprentice in Chesterfield County on 4 December 1778. She was apprenticed to John Stewart Redford on 6 December 1782 when he was ordered to appear in court to answer her complaint [Orders 1774-84, 197, 388]. She registered in Petersburg on 19 August 1794: *a brown Mulatto woman, five feet one and a half inches high, twenty six years old, born free and*</li>
</ol>

---

raised in Chesterfield County [Register of Free Negroes 1794-1819, no. 65].

v. ?Robert[2], born say 1770, a "poor child" bound apprentice with (his brother?) Matthew Corn in Dale Parish by order of the Chesterfield County court on 7 October 1774. The court again ordered him bound out on 5 July 1775 [Orders 1774-84, 56, 87].

vi. ?Matthew, born say 1772, a "poor child" bound apprentice in Dale Parish by order of the Chesterfield County court on 5 August 1774 and ordered bound out with (his brother?) Robert Corn on 7 October 1774. He was probably identical to Matt C<u>am</u>, child of Lucy C<u>am</u>, who was ordered bound out by the churchwardens of Dale Parish in November 1781. He was called Matthew Corn when he was bound out again on 10 March 1787 [Orders 1774-84, 48, 56, 331; 1784-7, 463]. He was taxable in Chesterfield County from 1795 to 1805 [PPTL, 1786-1811, frames 229, 297, 330, 369, 444, 482, 519, 558, 596].

vii. ?Ritter, born about 1775, registered in Petersburg on 15 August 1800: *a short well made, dark brown Mulatto woman, five feet one inches high, twenty five years old, short thick hair, born free & raised in the County of Surry* [Register of Free Negroes 1794-1819, no. 171].

viii. ?Roland, bound apprentice in Chesterfield County on 5 March 1779 [Orders 1774-84, 207].

ix. Pegg, bound apprentice in Chesterfield County on 6 September 1782 [Orders 1774-84, 372].

x. ?Mary, born about 1783, registered in Petersburg on 11 July 1804: *a small made, yellow brown Mulatto woman, five feet high, twenty one years old, born free & raised in the Town of Petersburg* [Register of Free Negroes 1794-1819, no. 328]. She was head of a Petersburg household in 1810 [VA:121b].

xi. ?Sally[1], born say 1788, head of a Petersburg Town, Virginia household of 3 "other free" in 1810 [VA:335].

xii. ?John, born about 1793, registered in Chesterfield County on 26 February 1816: *yellow complexioned, twenty-two to twenty-three years old, born free* [Register of Free Negroes 1804-53, no. 252].

xiii. ?Sally[2], born about 1805, registered in Petersburg on 3 August 1807: *an infant daughter of Judah Harrison, a free woman, two years old Oct. next, of a dark brown complexion* [Register of Free Negroes 1794-1819, no. 415].

3. Robert[1] Corn, born say 1745, was taxable in the St. James Parish, Lunenburg County household of Hutchings Burton in 1764 [Bell, *Sunlight on the Southside*, 247]. He was living in Mecklenburg County, Virginia, on 8 May 1780 when he applied for bounty land in court stating on oath that he was recruited as a soldier in the French and Indian War before 7 October 1763 [Orders 1779-84, 36]. He was taxable on a free tithe and 2 horses in Mecklenburg County from 1782 to 1789 [PPTL, 1782-1805, frames 14, 41, 79, 287]. He was security for Richard **Evans** when he was sued for debt in Mecklenburg County court on 10 May 1784 [Orders 1784-7, 6, 49, 107, 338]. On 6 March 1789 he made a deed of trust in Mecklenburg County of his household furniture, his working tools, 2 horses, and 14 hogs for a debt of 1,335 pounds of tobacco and 10 pounds he owed William Baskerville and George Hunt Baskerville [DB 7:550]. He was head of a Wake County household of 3 "other free" in 1790 [NC:106] and one in 1800 [NC:756]. He was taxable on 200 acres in Wake County in 1792 [Haun, *Wake County Court Minutes*, II:635]. He married Prisey **Wiggins**, 12 December 1802 Wake County bond, Josiah **Mitchell** bondsman. Prissey was probably the widow of Matthew **Wiggins**. Robert's 1 June 1816 Wake County will, proved August the same year, named only his wife Priscilla and his son Robert Brooks Corn.

Mary **Locus** was a witness, and Lawrence **Pettiford** was a witness and executor of the will [CR 099.801.16]. His children were

4   i.   Julius, born about 1763.

       ii.   ?Hissey, born say 1765, married William **Stuard**, 21 ___ (no month or year but probably before 1790) Mecklenburg County marriage bond, Robert Corn surety.

      iii.   ?Justin, born say 1770, head of a Wake County household of 3 "other free" in 1790 [NC:106]. Perhaps his widow was Jane Corne, born before 1776, head of an Orange County, North Carolina household of 6 "free colored" in 1820 [NC:370].

5   iv.   Robert Brooks, born about 1772.

       v.   ?Rebecca, married Josiah **Mitchell**, 23 February 1798 Wake County bond, David Valentine bondsman.

4.   Julius Corn, born about 1763, was listed in the Mecklenburg County household of (his father?) Robert Corn in 1784, was taxable in his own household in 1787 and 1788 [Personal Tax List 1782-1805, frames 79, 189, 235] and was also taxable on a free tithe and a horse in Brunswick County, Virginia, in 1787 [Schreiner-Yantis, *1787 Census*, 537]. He was head of a Wake County household of 3 "other free" in 1790 [NC:104] and 7 in 1800 [NC:756]. In June 1791 the Wake County court charged him with having an illegitimate child by Tempy **Taborn** [Haun, *Wake County Court Minutes*, II:499]. He was taxable on 200 acres in Wake County in 1793 and 1794, 200 acres and 2 free polls in 1799, and 100 acres and 2 free polls in 1802: listed with Robert Corn who was taxable on 100 acres and Robert B. Corn who was taxable on 38 acres and 1 poll [MFCR 099.701.1, frames 36, 151, 227, 253]. He died before 12 April 1817 when his estate papers were filed. His heirs were John Corn, Henry Corn, Willis **Taborn**, and minors: Caty, Terrell, Berry and Peggy Corn [CR 099.508.75]. His children were

       i.   John.

       ii.   Henry, born 1794-1806, head of an Orange County household of 5 "free colored" in 1820 (with a woman born before 1776) [NC:304].

      iii.   Willis **Taborn**.

      iv.   Caty.

       v.   Berry, married Fanny **Curtis Anderson**, 11 May 1837 Guilford County bond, Lewis **Jeffers** bondsman.

      vi.   Peggy, married Barnabus **Scott**, 21 March 1829 Wake County bond, Gilford **Scott** bondsman.

5.   Robert Brooks Corn, born about 1772, was listed in the Mecklenburg County household of (his father?) Robert Corn in 1788 and was listed in the household of John C. **Walden** in 1791 [PPTL 1782-1805, frames 235, 416]. He was surety for the 29 September 1794 Greensville County, Virginia marriage bond of Mark **Going** and Sarah **Jones**. He married Ginsy **Jeffers**, "over 21 years of age," 26 March 1795 Greensville County bond, Drury **Going** surety, and was head of a Wake County household of 4 "other free" in 1800 [NC:756] and 9 in Orange County in 1810 [NC:816]. His widow Jincey Corne, born before 1776, was head of an Orange County household of 9 "free colored" in 1820 [NC:312]. He bought land in Orange County before his death but did not complete the payments. Richardson Corn (his son) purchased the land from the sheriff on 24 May 1830 and identified Robert's children: Dixon, Dickerson, Eaton, Richard, Anderson, Polly, Jane, and Ann Corn [DB 17:149; 24:94]. Their children were

       i.   ?James, married Tempy **Hammon**, 18 November 1816 Wake County bond, John Williams bondsman.

       ii.   Dixon, head of an Orange County household of 2 "free colored" in 1820 [Book A:412]. He married Tempe **Jeffers**, 5 February 1821 Orange County bond, Lewis **Jeffers** bondsman.

   iii.   Dickerson.
   iv.   Eaton, ("white") married Elizabeth **Chavis** (colored), 7 January 1832
        Guilford County bond.
   v.   Richard.
   vi.   Anderson.
   vii.   Polly.
   viii.   Jane.
   ix.   Ann.

CORNET FAMILY

Members of the Cornet family were
1   i.   Byrd, born say 1760.
    ii.   Sarah, born say 1762, head of a Northampton County, North Carolina
        household of 1 "Black" person 12-50 years old in the 1786 state census
        in Elisha Webb's District.
    iii.   Parthena, born about 1767, registered in Petersburg on 18 August
        1794: *a yellow Mulatto woman, five feet six & a half inches high,*
        twenty seven years old, born in the County of Northampton, No. Ca.,
        born free [Register of Free Negroes 1794-1819, no. 20].
    iv.   Jonas, born about 1771, registered in Petersburg on 23 August 1794:
        a brown Mulatto man, five feet eight inches high, twenty three years
        old, from a certificate of Lawrence Smith appears to have been born &
        raised in Northampton County, N. Carolina [Register of Free Negroes
        1794-1819, no. 80].
    v.   Joseph, born say 1784, head of a Stafford County, Virginia household
        of 3 "other free" in 1810.

1.   Byrd Cornet, born say 1760, enlisted in the North Carolina Continental Line
on 20 July 1778 [*N.C. Historical & Genealogical Register* II:581]. He was
living in Northampton County, North Carolina, between 24 June 1783 and
September 1790 when he was paid money by the estate of Thomas Deloatch
[Gammon, *Records of Estates, Northampton County*, I:72], and he paid 1
pound to the St. George Parish, Northampton County wardens on 4 June 1798
[CR 71.927.1, fol. 34]. Byrd was head of a Northampton County household
of 8 "other free" and 3 slaves in 1790 [NC:75] and was counted as "other
free" in the Chatham County census in 1800, called "Hew Bird Cornet"
[NC:196]. On 14 June 1819 he married Betsy Skippey (**Skipper**), Cumberland
County, North Carolina bond, Daniel Munroe bondsman. He may have been
the father of
    i.   Ned, head of a Pasquotank County household of 2 "other free" and one
        slave in 1810 [NC:892].

CORNISH FAMILY

1.   Margaret[1] Cornish, born say 1610, was probably the unnamed mother of
"robt. Cornish & his Mother" mentioned in an April 1663 billing account
recorded in Surry County, Virginia court [Haun, *Surry Court Records*, II:245].
Robert Cornish may have been the son of Robert **Sweat** who was made to do
penance during divine service at James City Church on 17 October 1640
because he *hath begotten with Child a negro woman servant belonging unto*
Lieutenant Sheppard [McIlwaine, *Minutes of the Council*, 477]. She was
witness to the 2 February 1666 Surry County indenture of Dorothy **Thorne** to

serve Charles Barham and his wife for six years.[83] She was taxable on two tithes in the list for Lawns Creek Parish on Hog Island in 1668 and one in 1669 and 1670 [Haun, *Surry Court Records*, II:340, 314, 372; *Magazine of Virginia Genealogy*, vol.22, no.2, 20, 21]. On 10 October 1670 the General Court of Virginia called her a "negro woman" when it exempted her from paying taxes because of her poverty and old age [McIlwaine, *Minutes of the Council*, 225]. Her children were probably

    i.   Robert[1], born say 1640, mentioned with his unnamed mother in an April 1663 billing account recorded in Surry County court.

    ii.   William **Sweat**, born about 1642.

2   iii.   Anthony, born say 1645.

2.   Anthony Cornish, born say 1645, was a taxable head of a household on Hog Island in Lawnes Creek Parish from 1673 to 1702, with (his son?) Robert Cornish in 1693 and 1694 and with John Prime (Prince?) in 1702 [Haun, *Surry Court Records*, III:37; *Magazine of Virginia Genealogy*, vol. 22, no.2, 42, 44, 49; no. 3, 56, 63, 68; no.4, 52, 57; vol. 23, no.1, 38, 43, 50; no.2, 65, 69; no.3, 61, 65, 73]. On 5 March 1677 the Surry County court granted Edward Travis an attachment against his estate for 1,056 pounds of tobacco, and on 5 July 1681 he and his wife were fined 50 pounds for not going to church. He was listed among the Surry County householders and freeholders on 3 January 1687. In September 1696 he and William **Sweat** were security for Margaret **Sweat**'s administration on the estate of Robert **Sweat**. Perhaps his (first) wife was Katherine Cornish who was mentioned in a Surry County court case on 11 January 1685/6 [DW 2:285; Haun, *Surry Court Records*, III:193, 344; IV:622; V:168, 494]. And he may have married Margaret **Shaw** who was taxable in his household in 1698 [*Magazine of Virginia Genealogy*, vol. 24, no.2, p.73], perhaps the Margaret Cornish who was taxable in John Hencock's Lawns Creek Parish household in 1703 [DW 5:291]. Anthony was a defendant in a March 1702/3 Surry County court case for which the plaintiff failed to appear [Haun, *Surry Court Records*, VI:31]. His children were probably

    i.   Robert[2], born say 1677, taxable in Anthony Cornish's household in 1693 and 1694 [*Magazine of Virginia Genealogy*, vol.24, 65, 73]. He was a defendant in a November 1699 Surry County court case for which the plaintiff failed to appear [Haun, *Surry Court Records*, V:235].

    ii.   Elizabeth, born say 1685, taxable in 1701 in the household of James Ely, a neighbor of Anthony Cornish [*Magazine of Virginia Genealogy*, vol.24, no.3, p.71]. She may have been the Elizabeth Cornish who was living in the lower parish of Surry County on 20 January 1730/1 when she was presented by the court for having a bastard child [DW 8:69].

COTANCE/ COTANCH FAMILY

1.   Jack Cotance, born say 1726, was a "Mullatto" who brought an unsuccessful suit for his freedom from Simon Whitehurst in Princess Anne County, Virginia court on 21 July 1747 [Minutes 1744-53, 98, 105]. He was probably the John Cotanch who was listed in Child's Company of soldiers in the North Carolina Continental Line on 20 July 1778, listed as dead in Lytle's Company in 1782 [*Hathaway's Register* 1:582]. He may have been the father of

    i.   Willie, head of a Martin County, North Carolina household of 1 "other free" in 1790 [NC:67] and 7 in 1810 [NC:451]. Perhaps he was out of

---

[83]Dorothy **Thorne** was probably the ancestor of Thomas **Thorn** who was presented by the Surry Court for failing to list his "Mulatto" wife as a taxable but excused the same day "for reasons Appearing to the Court" [Orders 1757-64, 135].

the county in 1800 when (his wife?) Dollee Cottanch was head of a Martin County household of 3 "other free" [NC:391].

COUSINS FAMILY

1. Elizabeth Cousins, born say 1700, died before 23 February 1756 when James Holman was granted administration on her Cumberland County, Virginia estate. The following day the court ordered the churchwardens of King William Parish to bind out her orphans. She was probably the mother or grandmother of "Poor Orphans" Rocco, Jack, and Jane Couzens who were ordered bound out by the churchwardens of King William Parish on 28 July 1755 [Orders 1752-8, 284, 355, 369]. She may have been the mother of

   i.   Elizabeth[2], born say 1721, sued Anne Daniel in Goochland County court on 15 March 1742/3 for her freedom dues [Orders 1741-4, 194].

2 ii. Pat, born say 1724.
3 iii. Mary[1], born say 1729.

   iv. John[1], born say 1733, called Jack Cousins, a "Poor Orphan" bound by out in Cumberland County on 28 July 1755 [Orders 1752-8, 284]. He was a "free Negro" who had to post bond in Goochland County court for his good behavior in March 1755 when he was accused of threatening to beat Charles Bates. William Pledge was his security [Orders 1750-7, 512]. John was listed as an overseer in William Pledge's Goochland County household in the list of tithables for 1755 [List of Tithables]. He may have been the John Cousens who was sued for 3 pounds, 8 shillings by Robert Pleasants in Cumberland County on 22 August 1785 [Orders 1784-6, 399, 476].

4 v.   Francis[1], born say 1735.
5 vi. Frances[1], born say 1737.

2. Pat[1] Cousins, born say 1724, was most likely identical to "Pat an Indented servant" (no last name or race mentioned) whose daughter "Margaret a Mulatto Girl" was bound apprentice to John Woodson, Jr., of Goochland County in June 1745 [Orders 1744-49, 75]. Margaret Cousins' children were later bound out to John Woodson in June 1759 [Orders 1757-61, 218]. Pat was probably the mother of

6 i.   Margaret[1], born say 1741.
7 ii. Elizabeth[3], born say 1744.

3. Mary[1] Cousins, born say 1729, may have been identical to "Moll a Mulatto girl" of Goochland County who was bound by the churchwardens of St. James Parish to John Williams in November 1731 [Orders 1730-1, 46]. She was called Mary Cousins when she brought a complaint in Goochland County court against John Williams on 21 July 1748 and on 22 August 1750 when she sued Williams for her freedom dues. She was awarded 3 pounds, 10 shillings by the court in August 1751. She was called "Mary Cousins a free Negro" in April 1764 when the court summoned her to show cause why her children Nan and Sam should not be bound out. She did not appear, and the court bound them to Richard Davis Hines [Orders 1744-9, 457; 1750-7, 25, 85, 1761-65, 292, 320]. She was the mother of

   i.   Abraham, "a Mulatto being Son of Moll Servant to John Williams," bound by the churchwardens of St. James Northam Parish to John Williams in August 1745 [Orders 1744-9, p.99].

   ii. Ann, born say 1760, bound apprentice in Goochland County in May 1764.

   iii. Samuel, born about 1762, bound apprentice in Goochland County in May 1764 and called a "Mulatto" child of Mary Cousins when he was bound out again in September 1779 [Orders 1778-79, 232]. He was a "Mulatto" taxable in Goochland County from 1786 to 1788 [PPTL,

1782-1809, frames 112, 154, 180] and a "M" taxable on a horse in Powhatan County in 1789 [PPTL, 1787-1825, frame 31]. He was taxable in Chesterfield County from 1790 to 1793 and a "F. Negroe" taxable there from 1802 to 1810 [PPTL, 1786-1811, frames 61, 137, 178, 502, 578, 615, 657, 1717, 799]. He registered as a free Negro in Goochland County on 20 September 1808: *five feet five inches high, supposed to be forty five or fifty years of age, short curled hair, dark complexion* [Register of Free Negroes, p.25, no.52] and registered in Chesterfield County on 8 November 1819: *fifty seven years old, brown complexion, born free* [Register of Free Negroes 1804-53, no. 369].

  iv.   James[2], born say 1764, an infant of Mary Cousins ordered bound to John Woodson in Goochland County in March 1764 [Orders 1761-65, 282].

  v.   Frances[2], born say 1765, a child of Mary Cousins bound to William Blunkall in Goochland County in February 1767 [Orders 1767-71, 9].

  vi.   Jacob[2], born say 1766, "mulatto" son of Mary Couzens, ordered bound out by the churchwardens of King William Parish to Jane Holeman by the Cumberland County court on 23 November 1767 [Orders 1767-70, 63].

  vii.   Nancy, born say 1775, a "Mulatto" child of Mary Cousins bound out in Goochland County in September 1779 [Orders 1778-79, 232].

4.   Francis[1] Cousins, born say 1735, was a "Free Mulatto" charged with the felonious intent of poisoning Obediah and Mary Smith in Goochland County in March 1754. Paul Michaux and James Holman posted fifty pounds bond for him [Orders 1750-57, 364-5, 381, 383, 489]. He married Mary **Martin** in Goochland County on 15 December 1759:

> *Francis Cousins & Mary Martin Mulattoes both of Manikin town* [Jones, *The Douglas Register*, 4].

He enlisted in the Revolution from Goochland County [Jackson, *Virginia Negro Soldiers*, 33]. He was living in adjoining Cumberland County on 9 April 1763 when he sued James Bryant for trespass, assault and battery. He was called Francis **Smith** Cousins on 26 January 1767 when he sued Samuel **Goff** for 4 pounds due by note. On 28 November 1774 the court presented him for failing to list Charles **Howell** as a tithable in his household [Orders 1762-4, 166; 1764-7, 386; 1774-8, 300, 441]. He was taxable in Powhatan County on 2 horses from 1787 to 1788, a "M" taxable in 1789, and a "M°" taxable in 1793 [PPTL, 1787-1825, frames 4, 17, 31, 90]. He was head of a Goochland County household of 8 "other free" in 1810 [VA:687]. He had a daughter Ridley, a slave who had three children: Frank, William, and Lucy Ann. He purchased them from Robert Pleasants and set them free on 18 March 1816 by his Goochland County deed [DB 22:191]. He was the father of

  i.   ?Abbey, born say 1778, married Tom **Mayo**, 2 July 1799 Goochland County bond, Joseph **Attkisson** surety.

  ii.   Francis[2] (Frank), married Chloe Cousins, 16 April 1806 Goochland County bond, Edward **Fuzmore** surety. Chloe registered as a free Negro in Goochland County on 15 January 1823: *about Fifty six years old, about five feet two inches high...emancipated by a decree of the court of Appeals in vertue of the wills of John & Jonathan Pleasants* [Register of Free Negroes, p.140]. Francis left a 3 December 1842 Goochland County will, proved 18 November 1844 leaving his estate to his wife Cloa during her lifetime and naming children Sam, Frederick, Henry, Watt and invalid daughter Milly. John Copeland brought a chancery suit against the estate claiming that Francis had agreed to sell a 10 acre tract to him but had never made out a formal deed [LVA Chancery case 1848-022].

iii.   Ridley, emancipated on 18 March 1816.

5.   Frances[1]/ Fanny Cousins, born say 1737, petitioned for her freedom from further service to James Holeman in Cumberland County on 25 September 1758. Her case was dismissed when she failed to prosecute [Orders 1758-62, 25, 85]. On 16 August 1763 the Goochland County court ordered the churchwardens of St. James Northam Parish to bind out her children James, William, and Elizabeth [Orders 1761-65, 210], and on 26 September 1763 the Cumberland County court ordered the churchwardens of King William Parish to bind out her sons James and William to Walter Edie [Orders 1762-4, 314]. In October 1764 James and William were called "Mulatto Children of Frances Cousins" when the Goochland County court ordered them bound to William Maddox [Orders 1761-65, 437]. Her children were

    i.   ?Cate, ordered bound out by the churchwardens of King William Parish in Cumberland County on 23 October 1758 [Orders 1758-62, 19].

    ii.   James[1], born say 1759, taxable in the upper district of Goochland County in 1790 [PPTL, 1782-1809, frame 235]. He was a free man of color who served as a substitute in the Revolution from Goochland County [NSDAR, *African American Patriots*, 148].

    iii.   William[1], born say 1761, head of a Prince Edward County household of 7 "other free" in 1810 [VA:651].

    iv.   Elizabeth[4], born say 1763, bound apprentice in Goochland County in July 1763. She was called the "mulattoe" daughter of Fanny Couzens on 28 March 1770 when the Cumberland County court ordered the churchwardens of King William Parish to bind her to George Smith [Orders 1770-2, 3]. She was head of a Goochland County household of 5 "other free" in 1810 [VA:686].

    v.   ?Phillis, a "poor orphan" ordered bound apprentice to Thomas Turpin, Jr., by the churchwardens of Southam Parish in Cumberland County, Virginia court on 27 February 1769 [Orders 1767-70, 279].

    vi.   ?Nathaniel, born say 1768, a "Mulatto" taxable in Chesterfield County from 1790 to 1793 [PPTL, 1786-1811, frames 60, 101, 138].

    vii.   ?Milley, a "poor orphan" ordered bound apprentice to Elizabeth Brooks by the churchwardens of Southam Parish in Cumberland County court on 27 February 1769 [Orders 1767-70, 279].

    viii.   ?Henry[1], a "mulattoe orphan" ordered bound apprentice to Francis Smith Couzens by the churchwardens of Southam Parish in Cumberland County court on 28 May 1770 [Orders 1770-2, 2]. He was a "M°" taxable in Powhatan County in 1793 [PPTL, 1787-1825, frame 90].

    ix.   ?Landy, born say 1773, taxable in Powhatan County from 1790 to 1798, called a "M°" in 1798 [PPTL, 1787-1825, frames 44, 104, 117, 130, 144, 160], called "Alexander Cousins Mulatto" in 1803 when he was taxable in the lower district of Goochland County in 1803 [PPTL, 1782-1809, frame 650].

6.   Margaret[1] Cousins, born say 1741, was an indented servant of John Woodson in June 1759 when her daughter Margaret (no race mentioned) was bound apprentice in Goochland County. She was called a "free Negro" in March 1770 when her son William was ordered bound out [Orders 1757-61, 218; 1767-70, 388]. She was the mother of ❧

    i.   Margaret[2], born say 1758, "an Infant of Margett Cousens an Indented Servant unto John Woodson," ordered bound apprentice by the churchwardens of St. James Northam Parish in June 1759 [Orders 1757-61, 218]. She or a daughter by the same name (no race indicated) was in adjoining Cumberland County on 29 March 1774 when the court ordered the churchwardens of Littleton Parish to bind her out to John Woodson [Orders 1774-8, 120].

8   ii.   Jacob[1], born say 1761.

iii. Sall[1], born say 1764, a child of Margaret Cousins apprenticed to John Woodson in May 1767.

iv. Charles, born say 1766, a child of Margaret Cousins bound to John Woodson in May 1767 [Orders 1767-70, 16], a "Free Black" head of a Nottoway County household of 4 "other free" in 1810 [VA:1020].

v. Shepherd, born say 1768, a child of Margaret Cousins bound to John Woodson in February 1769. He was called "Mulatto Shepherd" in 1788 when his tax was charged to John Woodson in the upper district of Goochland County in 1788, called Shepherd Cousins in 1790 [PPTL, 1782-1809, frame 184, 246].

vi. William[2], born say 1769, "a Child of Margaret Cousins (being a free Negro)" bound to Thomas Oliver in March 1770 [Orders 1767-70, 281, 388]. He may have been the William Cousins who was taxable in Charlotte County from 1787 to 1805: his tax charged to (his brother?) Jacob Cousins in 1787 [PPTL 1782-1813, frames 109, 141, 175, 204, 228, 252, 264, 301, 326, 353, 382, 621, 639, 654]. And he may have been the William Cousins who married Polly **Banks**, 4 October 1811 Goochland County bond, John **Banks** surety, 5 October marriage.

vii. Jane, born say 1770, a child of Margaret Cousins, "a free Mulatto," bound apprentice to Edward Redford in March 1772.

viii. Pat[2], born say 1772, a child of Margaret Cousins, "a free Mulatto," apprenticed to Edward Redford in March 1772 [Orders 1771-78, 115].

7. Elizabeth[3] Cousins, born say 1744, was a "Malatto Girl" (no parent named) apprenticed by the churchwardens of St. James Northam Parish in Goochland County in May 1754 [Orders 1750-57, 409]. She was the mother of Sall, John, and Celia who were ordered bound out as apprentices by the Goochland County court in November 1770 [Orders 1767-70, 497]. She was living in adjoining Cumberland County on 23 November 1767 when the court ordered the churchwardens of King William Parish to bind out her "mulatto" children Walter and Oyster Couzens to Jane Holeman [Orders 1767-70, 63]. She was taxable on a horse in the lower district of Goochland County in 1787, called a "free negroe Spinner" in 1801 when she was taxable on a free male tithable and a horse, taxable on a free male tithable in 1806 [PPTL, 1782-1809, frame 164, 579, 761]. Her children were

i. John[2], born about 1761, a child of Betty Cousins who was bound apprentice in Goochland County in November 1770. His tax was charged to Thomas Pleasants in the lower district of Goochland County in 1787 and 1788, charged with his own tax in 1790, called a "Mulatto" in 1793, a "freed Negroe" in 1794 and 1795, a "free negroe planter" in 1801 [PPTL, 1782-1809, frame 117, 195, 210, 251, 265, 325, 405, 579, 650]. He registered as a free Negro in Goochland County in 1806: *about five feet ten inches and three quarters high, about forty five years of age...short curled hair* [Register of Free Negroes, p.14, no.31]. He was head of a Fluvanna County household of 7 "other free" in 1810 [VA:689].

ii. Sall[2], born about 1767, child of Betty Cousins bound apprentice in November 1770. She may have been the Sally Cousins who was head of a Goochland County household of 2 "other free" in 1810 [VA:689]. She registered in Goochland County on 19 June 1815: *dark complexion about five feet four inches high, about forty eight years old, short curled hair* [Register of Free Negroes, p.87, no.166].

iii. Walter, bound apprentice in Cumberland County on 23 November 1767. He was taxable in Goochland County in 1782, a "Mulatto" taxable in 1783, taxable there from 1787 to 1789 and called a "free negroe wheelwright" in 1801 [PPTL, 1782-1809, frames 6, 34, 163, 190, 204, 579].

    iv. Oyster, bound apprentice in Cumberland County on 23 November 1767.

    v. Celia, born say 1770, child of Betty Cousins bound apprentice in Goochland County in November 1770.

    vi. Francis[2], born say 1772, a "bastard of Betty Cousins" bound to William Robards in Goochland County in September 1773. He may have been the Francis Cousins who was taxable in Charlotte County from 1790 to 1795 [PPTL 1782-1813, frames 204, 228, 314, 339]. He was taxable in the upper district of Goochland County on 2 horses in 1803, a "free Negroe" planter living near Thomas F. Bates in 1804, a "Freed Negro" cooper on Robert Pleasants' land in 1805, listed with wife Cloe in 1813 [PPTL, 1782-1809, frames 666, 738, 864; 1810-32, frames 5, 158].

    vii. Jesse, born say 1774, a son of Elizabeth Cousins bound to William Robards in Goochland County in August 1774 [Orders 1771-78, 360, 446].

8.   Jacob[1] Cousins, born say 1761, "Son of Margaret Cousens," was apprenticed by the churchwardens of St. James Northam Parish, Goochland County, in November 1762 [Orders 1761-65, 133]. He was taxable in Charlotte County from 1783 to 1812: taxable on a horse and 6 cattle in 1783, charged with the tax for (his brother?) William Cousins in 1787, taxable on 3 free males in 1804, 2 free males in 1805, His Charlotte County estate was taxable on 2 horses in 1813. (His widow) Suckey Cousins, Sr., was listed with 2 "free Negroes" in her household in 1813 [PPTL 1782-1813, frames 22, 109, 141, 175, 204, 252, 276, 300, 326, 353, 382, 484, 516, 550, 586, 621, 654, 688, 723, 756, 788, 821, 852, 894]. He was a "F.N." head of a Charlotte County household of 10 "other free" in 1810 [VA:1018]. He and his wife Sukey were the parents of

    i. ?John[3], a "fn" taxable in Charlotte County from 1804 to 1810: listed with wife Lucy, a male child, and a female child in 1805, 1806 and 1807; listed with Betty **Chavis** in 1811 and 1812 [PPTL 1782-1813, frames 604, 639, 648, 672, 682, 708, 717, 784, 814, 846].

    ii. Jacob[3], born about 1785, registered in Charlotte County on 10 February 1806: *son of Jacob Cozens, Black complexion, aged 21, born free* [Ailsworth, *Charlotte County--Rich Indeed*, 485]. He died about 1809 when his Charlotte County estate was taxable on a horse [PPTL 1782-1813, frame 756].

    iii. James, born about 1789, listed in Charlotte County with Nancy **Steward** in 1813 [PPTL 1782-1813, frames 894]. He registered in Charlotte County on 16 January 1819: *son of Jacob Cozens & Sukey his wife, free persons of Colour, Mulatto complexion, aged 30, born free* [Ailsworth, *Charlotte County--Rich Indeed*, 486].

    iv. Henry, born about 1791, registered in Charlotte County on 25 February 1811: *son of Jacob and Sukey Cozens his wife, Mulatto complexion, aged 20, born free* [Ailsworth, *Charlotte County--Rich Indeed*, 485]. He was taxable in Charlotte County to 1813 [PPTL 1782-1813, frames 894].

    v. Suckey **Bird**, born about 1805, registered in Charlotte County on 1 December 1828: *daughter of Susan Cozens, Dark complexion, aged 23, born free* [Ailsworth, *Charlotte County--Rich Indeed*, 488].

    vi. Nancy **Brogdon**, born about 1806, registered in Charlotte County on 1 December 1828: *daughter of Susan Cozens, Dark complexion, aged 22, born free* [Ailsworth, *Charlotte County--Rich Indeed*, 488].

Other Cousins families in Virginia were

9   i. Polly, born about 1773.

ii. Martin, born before 1776, married Jincey **Cole,** 31 December 1802 Mecklenburg County, Virginia bond, Robert **Cole** security. Martin was taxable on 1 poll in Country Line District of Granville County, North Carolina, in 1815 and was head of a household of 3 "free colored" in Country Line District in 1820 [NC:35].

iii. Henry[2], taxable in Goochland County from 1809 to 1813: a "Mulatto" farmer living on William Richardson's land in 1811, a "free negro" listed with wife Sally in 1813 [PPTL, 1782-1809, frames 844; 1810-32, frames 32, 52, 71, 120, 139]. He married Lydia **Pierce,** daughter of John **Pierce** ("a negro man of Dr. James Bryden's") and Milly **Pierce,** 30 May 1812 Goochland County bond. He was head of a Goochland County household of 5 "other free" in 1810 [VA:685].

iv. Josiah, taxable in the upper district of Goochland County, listed with Lewis Chaudoine in 1800 [PPTL, 1782-1809, frame 543]. He was head of a Buckingham County household of 10 "other free" in 1810 [VA:828].

v. Barbary, born about 1772, registered as a free Negro in Goochland County on 18 April 1815: *dark complexion, about five feet four inches high, about forty three years old...short curled hair* [Register of Free Negroes, p.86, no. 163].

vi. Louis, born about 1800, obtained "free papers" in Brunswick County on 24 November 1828: *the bearer hereof a free man of dark complexion about five feet five & an half Inches high ...about twenty eight years of age and was borne free as appears by the Evidence of James E. Webb.*

vii. Joshua, born about 1804, obtained "free papers" in Brunswick County on 24 November 1828: *the bearer hereof a free man of yellow complexion five feet five Inches high ...about twenty four years of age was born free as appears from the Evidence of James E. Webb* [Wynn, *Register of Free Negroes,* 101].

9. Mary[2]/Polly Cousins, born about 1773, was head of a Mecklenburg County, Virginia household of 5 "free colored" in 1820. She was called Molly Cousins on 19 June 1820 when she registered in Mecklenburg County: *five feet high, about forty seven Years old, of a light Complexion, free born* [Free Person of Color, no. 6, p.15]. She may have been the mother of

i. George I., born about 1793, paid poll tax in Country Line District, Granville County, in 1815. He was head of a Mecklenburg County household of 4 "free colored" in 1820. He registered in Mecklenburg County on 19 June 1820: *five feet Seven & 3/4 Inches high, about Twenty Seven years old, of a light Complexion* [Person of Color, no. 1, p.13].

ii. Robert/ Robin, born about 1795, registered in Mecklenburg County on 19 June 1820: *Robin Cousins, five feet Seven and 1/2 Inches high about twenty five years old...of a light Complexion* [Person of Color, no.3, p.14]. He was called Robert Cousins in 1820, head of a Mecklenburg County household of one "free colored." He was probably the same Robert Cousins who paid poll tax in Country Line District, Granville County, in 1817, and was taxed on 120 acres on Grassy Creek in 1820. He was head of a Country Line District, Granville County, household of 7 "free colored" in 1820 [NC:35], called "free Negro" in the 1823 Granville tax list, taxed on 60 acres on Grassy Creek adjacent to Asa Cousins who was taxed on 4 acres.

iii. Henry[3], born about 1797, registered in Mecklenburg County on 19 June 1820: *five feet Eight & 3/4 Inches high about twenty three years old...of a light Complexion* [Person of Color, no. 4, p.14]. He was head of a Mecklenburg County household of one "free colored" in 1820.

iv.   Nelson, taxable on one poll in Country Line District, Granville County, in 1815, head of a Mecklenburg County household of 1 "free colored" in 1820, perhaps the Nelson Cousins, born about 1797, who obtained a certificate of freedom in Chesterfield County on 13 July 1818: *twenty one years old, black complexion, born free* [Register of Free Negroes 1804-53, no. 321].

v.   Lewis, born about 1801, registered in Mecklenburg County on 17 July 1826: *a man of dark complexion 25 years of age five feet ten inches high... part of his left thumb Cut off by a whitlow, was born free in the County of Mecklenburg* [Person of Color, no. 15, p.20].

Other members of the Cousins family in North Carolina were

i.   John[4], born about 1783, paid poll tax in Country Line District, Granville County in 1815. He registered in Mecklenburg County, Virginia, on 19 June 1820: *about thirty Seven years old, dark complexion* [Register, no. 2, p.13].

ii.   Rebecca, "free born negro," bound an apprentice to Robert Davey by the July 1782 Caswell County court [A:205].

iii.   Grief, head of a Randolph County household of 6 "other free" in 1810 [NC:64].

iv.   Levina, "a woman of colour," presented in Granville County in November 1812 for moving to Granville from Virginia "without the necessary to entitle to be a citizen" [CR 044.928.25].

COX FAMILY

1.   Gilbert Cox, born say 1738, was taxable with (his brother?) Simon Cox in Bladen County in 1763, a "Molato" taxable in 1768, taxable with James **Percey** in 1770, a taxable "Mulato" in 1772 (also counted as a white taxable with James **Purcey** in 1772), a white taxable in 1774 with (his son?) John Cox, a "Molato" taxable in 1776, taxable on 100 acres of improved land and 300 acres unimproved in 1779, and counted in 1786 with 1 white male from 21-60 years old, 1 white male under 21 or over 60, 4 white females and 2 Blacks (slaves) from 12 to 50 and 3 over 50 or under 12 years of age [Byrd, *Bladen County Tax Lists,* I:8, 34, 78, 94, 104, 130; II:68, 76, 117, 183].[84] He was granted a patent on 11 March 1775 for 300 acres southwest of Drowning Creek in the part of Bladen County which became Robeson County in 1787 [Hoffman, *Land Patents,* II:602], and he was taxable on 600 acres, 1 free poll, and 2 slave polls in Captain Barnes' District of Bladen County in 1784 [1784 Bladen County Tax List]. He entered 150 acres bordering this land on Ten Mile Swamp on 25 April 1791 [Pruitt, *Land Entries: Robeson County,* I:45]. He purchased land in Robeson County by deed proved on 4 October 1797, purchased 340 acres on 2 January 1793, and sold land by deed proved 1 October 1798. He purchased "a Negro boy named Ned" by deed proved by his son Isham Cox on 3 October 1797, and sold this slave and 650 acres of land to Isham on 27 November 1809 [Minutes I:12, 15, 49; DB C:402; P:238-40, 263]. He was head of a Robeson County household of 6 "other free" and 8 slaves in 1790 [NC:49], 4 "other free" and 9 slaves in 1800 [NC:371], and he was counted as white in 1810, head of a Robeson County household of 1 male over 45 and 1 white female over 45 [NC:235]. By his 29 June 1810 Robeson County will he left 1,200 acres and twenty-three slaves to his wife Sarah and children: Isom (Isham), Mary **Britt**, Sarah Ivey, and Treacy **Ivey** [WB 1:119-20]. Gilbert was the father of

---

[84]James **Percey** was probably related to John **Purse**, head of a Beaufort County, South Carolina, household of 5 "other free" in 1800 [SC:104], and William **Pierse**, head of a Beaufort County, South Carolina, household of 10 "other free" in 1800 [SC:116].

   i. ?John, born say 1758, a white taxable in Gilbert Cox's Bladen County household in 1774, a "Molato" taxable in 1776, and counted in 1786 with 1 white male from 21 to 60 and 1 white male under 21 or over 60 years of age [Byrd, *Bladen County Tax Lists*, I:130; II:68, 76, 183].

   ii. Isham, born say 1775.

   iii. Mary, wife of John **Britt**.

   iv. Sarah **Ivey**.

   v. Treacey, wife of Silas **Ivey**.

2. Simon[1] Cox, born say 1742, was taxable with (his brother?) Gilbert in Bladen County in 1763, a "Mulato" taxable with Adam **Ivey** in 1768, a "Molato" taxable in 1769 and 1770, taxable with James Perry/ **Purcey** in 1771, a white taxable from 1772 to 1774, a "Molato" taxable in 1776, taxable on 400 acres of improved land and 300 acres unimproved in 1779, taxable on 500 acres and one free poll in Captain Barnes' District of Bladen County in 1784, and counted in 1786 with 1 white male 21-60 years old, 3 white males under 21 or over 60 and 4 white females [Byrd, *Bladen County Tax Lists*, I:4, 15, 33, 78, 94; II:68, 76, 116, 184; Bladen County Tax List (1763, 1784)]. He entered 40 acres between his two old surveys on both sides of Hog Swamp in Robeson County on 6 June 1788 and another 60 acres on 1 January 1789. On 8 October 1793 he entered 400 acres on "Gilbert Cox's meadow" and 200 acres bordering his own line [Pruitt, *Land Entries: Robeson County*, I:16, 20, 86]. He purchased land by deed proved in Robeson County court on 7 January 1799, 7 October 1806, and 1 January 1810; he sold land by deed proved on 2 April 1804, and transferred land to Levi Cox by deed proved on 6 January 1800 [Minutes I:55, 90; II:4, 172, 281]. He may have been the father of

   i. Levi, counted as white in Robeson County in 1800, head of a Robeson County household of 3 "other free" and a slave in 1810 [NC:233].

   ii. Simon[2], Jr., born say 1778, head of a Robeson County household of 2 "other free" in 1800 [NC:371] and 4 in 1810 [NC:233].

   iii. James, born say 1782, head of a Robeson County household of 3 "other free" in 1810 [NC:235] and 8 "free colored" in 1820 [NC:308].

   iv. Jesse, head of a Robeson County household of 3 "other free" in 1810 [NC:233], perhaps the Jesse Cox who was head of a Wythe County, Virginia household of 4 "other free" in 1810. He was head of a Robeson household of 3 "free colored" in 1820 [NC:308].

   v. Harmon, head of a Robeson County household of 1 "other free" in 1810 [NC:233].

Members of the Cox family in Virginia were

   i. William, born say 1750, a "mulattoe" examined by the Cumberland County court on 19 June 1775 on suspicion of breaking and entering the house of Henry Skipworth and stealing corn valued at 20 shillings. He denied the charge and was discharged because there was no evidence against him [Orders 1774-8, 333]. He was head of a Henrico County household of 3 "other free" in 1810 [VA:991].

   ii. Rachel, born about 1752, obtained a certificate of freedom in Chesterfield County on 14 May 1810: *fifty-eight years old, black complexioned, born free* [Register of Free Negroes 1804-53, no. 129].

   iii. Nancy, head of a Chesterfield County household of 7 "other free" in 1810 [VA:70/1062]. She married Manuel **Valentine** (free persons of colour), 13 September 1813 Chesterfield County bond, Jeremiah **Ligon** security [Marriage Register, 122]. She may have been the Nancy **Valentine** who obtained a certificate of freedom in Chesterfield County on 28 October 1816, the same day that members of the Cox family registered: *fifty-four years old, yellow complexioned, emancipated by will of John Brown, deced.* [Register of Free Negroes 1804-53, no. 279].

iv. Ann, head of a Norfolk County household of 1 "other free" in 1810 [VA:892].

COY FAMILY

Members of the Coy family were
    i. Thomas, born about 1760, taxable in Petersburg on a tithe and a horse in 1799 [PPTL B, p.3], registered in Petersburg on 13 June 1810: *a brown Mulatto man, five feet two 3/4 inches high, fifty years old, born free & raised in Fredericksburg* [Register of Free Negroes 1794-1819, no. 602].

1   ii. Sarah, born about 1767.
    iii. Anthony, head of an Amherst County household of 3 "other free" in 1810 [VA:307].

1. Sarah Coy, born about 1767, was a "M°" taxable on 2 horses in Powhatan County from 1799 to 1815: counted with 2 "free negroes & mulattoes over the age of 16" in 1813 [PPTL, 1787-1825, frames 182, 205, 222, 238, 254, 276, 292, 315, 361, 378, 397, 419, 437, 456, 479]. She registered in Powhatan County on 19 December 1822: *Age 55; Color: Dark yellow; Stature: 5'5"; Born Free* [Register of Free Negroes, 1820-65, no. 57]. She may have been the mother of
    i. Nancy, born about 1783, over the age of twenty-one when she married William **Armstrong**, "Free Negroes," 13 July 1809 Powhatan County bond, Charles **Coy** surety. She registered in Powhatan County on 19 December 1822: *Age: 39; Color: Dark yellow; Stature: 5'3-1/2"; Born Free* [Register of Free Negroes, no. 52].
    ii. Joe, born about 1785, registered in Powhatan County on 20 September 1821: *Age: 36, yellow complexion, 5'6" high, Born free* [Register of Free Negroes, no. 27].
    iii. Charles, born about 1786, married Patty **Hickman**, daughter of Tim **Mosby**, "free Negroes," 4 October 1809 Powhatan County bond. He was a "M°" taxable in Powhatan County from 1809 to 1815: a "F.B." taxable on 2 free tithes, 2 slaves and a horse in 1811; a "F.B." with 2 "free negroes & mulattoes over the age of 16" in 1813 [PPTL, 1787-1825, frames 361, 378, 397, 419, 437, 456, 479]. He was a "F.B." head of a Powhatan County household of 17 "other free" in 1810 [VA:13]. He registered in Powhatan County on 5 October 1840: *Age: 54; Color: brown; Stature: 5'9-1/2"; Born Free* [Register of Free Negroes, no. 477].
    iv. William, a "F.B." taxable in Powhatan County in 1815 [PPTL, 1787-1825, frame 479].

CRAIG/ CRAGG FAMILY

Members of the Craig/ Cragg family were
    i. George[1] Crag, born about 1730, certified to be born of a free white woman and that he was upwards of forty years old in Halifax County, Virginia court in April 1770 [Pleas 6:488].
    ii. Cattey (Catby?) Craig, born say 1780, mother of George[3] Craig who registered as a "free Negro" in Alleghany County and presented his papers to the Botetourt County court on 18 June 1836: *33 years of age; Bright Mulatto...Born free and son of Cattey* (Catby?) *Craig raised in the Town of Fincastle* [Free Negroes &c Registered in the Clerk's Office of Botetourt County, no. 95].
    iii. Thomas Craig, "F. Negroe" head of a Fauquier County household of 8 "other free" in 1810 [VA:386].

iv. Thomas Cragg, "F. N." head of a Culpeper County household of 1 "other free" in 1810 [VA:18].
v. Sally Craig, "F. Negroe" head of a Fauquier County household of 6 "other free" in 1810 [VA:386].
vi. Henry Craig, "F. Mo." head of a Culpeper County household of 4 "other free" in 1810 [VA:24].
vii. Betty Craig, a "Mulatto" spinster recorded in "A List of Free Negroes & Mulattoes within the District of James Trenor" in Botetourt County in 1803 and 1804 [Free Negroes &c Registered in the Clerk's Office of Botetourt County, 1803: no. 19, 1804: no. 27], head of a Botetourt County household of 2 "other free" in 1810 [VA:614].
viii. George[2] Cragg, born say 1780, a "Mulatto" laborer recorded in "A List of Free Negroes & Mulattoes within the District of James Trenor" near Salem in Botetourt County in 1802 [Free Negroes &c Registered in the Clerk's Office of Botetourt County, no. 16].

CRANE FAMILY

1. Elizabeth Crane, born say 1690, was the servant of Robert Allworthy of Cople Parish in Westmoreland County on 26 November 1712 when the court ordered her to be sold for five years for having a "Mulatto" child [Westmoreland Orders 1705-21, 203a]. She may have been the ancestor of
   i. Sarah Craney, "free negro" head of a Northumberland County household of 2 "other free" in 1810 [VA:996].

CUFF FAMILY

1. John Cuff, born say 1750, was head of a Gates County household of 1 male 21-60, 5 males under 21 or over 60, and 2 females in the 1786 North Carolina State Census, 9 "other free" in 1790 [NC:23], 8 in 1800 [NC:264], and 2 in 1810 [NC:835]. He may have been related to Will Cuff who was head of a Fluvanna County, Virginia household of 8 "other free" in 1810 [VA:474]. John Cuff's land adjoining White Pot Pocosin was mentioned in Gates County deeds of 28 December 1800 and 2 February 1801. He purchased 98 acres adjoining John Cuff, Jr., on 8 March 1805 [DB 5:222, 306; 9:278]. His children were most likely
   i. Smith, born before 1776, head of a Gates County household of 4 "other free" in 1800, 8 in 1810 [NC:849], and 12 "free colored" in 1820 [NC:146]. He married Mary **Knight**, 24 October 1799 Gates County bond.
   ii. Mason, born before 1776, head of a Gates County household of 8 "other free" in 1810 [NC:849] and 5 "free colored" in 1820 [NC:146].
   iii. John[2], born say 1780, owned land adjoining (his father?) John Cuff on 8 March 1805 [DB 9:278]. He may have been the John Cuff who was head of a Gates County household of 2 "other free" in 1810 [NC:835].
   iv. Malechiah, born say 1786, purchased 50 acres "whereon his father lived on Honey Pot" on 7 April 1807 [DB 7:44]. He was head of a Gates County household of 4 "free colored" in 1820 [NC:146].
   v. Isum, born say 1789, purchased 29 acres at the head of White Pot on 18 February 1810 [DB 8:97].
   vi. Levin, an insolvent taxpayer in 1819 [Minutes 1818-23, 1291]. He married Milley **Ellis**, 15 February 1823 Gates County bond with John Cuff bondsman.
   vii. Daniel, insolvent in Gates County in 1819 [Minutes 1818-23, 1291].

CUFFEE FAMILY

1. John[1] Coffee, born say 1690, was called "my Negro Coffee" in the 10 September 1716 Elizabeth City County will of James Burtell, recorded 10 days later. The following year on 17 July 1717 he appealed to the court for help in curing his ulcerated leg, and the court ordered Robert Taylor, one of the securities for Burtell's estate, to help him. Emanuel Alkin, a chirugeon, cared for his leg, but Alkin's suit against Taylor for payment was dismissed by the court. John Coffee was free the following year on 18 September 1718 when he was called "John Coffee a Negro" in a suit he brought against Robert Taylor for assault and battery. Taylor delayed the case each time it was called until it was dismissed on 19 August 1719 because of Taylor's death. Coffee then brought the suit on 18 November 1719 against the other administrators of Burtell's estate, John King and John Burtell, who also asked for a delay. When the suit was called again on 18 May 1720, it was restated as his suit for his freedom, but the case was dismissed because John Coffee was "gon" (left the county) [DW&O 1715-21, 49-50, 58-60, 73, 103, 129, 135, 145, 155, 166, 174, 184, 121]. His children may have been

       2   i.   Sarah[1], Sr., born say 1725.
       3   ii. Mary[1], born say 1738.

2. Sarah[1] Cuffee, Sr., born say 1725, was a "free Negro" taxable in Norfolk County in the district from Great Bridge to Edmond's Bridge from 1751 to 1768: charged with her own tithe from 1751 to 1756; her tax charged to John Curling in 1761; listed with John Cuffee in 1765; charged with her own tithe, Mary Cuffee's and Ann **Smith**'s tithe in 1767 [Wingo, *Norfolk County Tithables, 1751-65*, 25, 40, 47, 76, 97, 131, 176, 198; *1766-80*, 23, 52]. On 19 March 1763 the churchwardens of St. Brides Parish were ordered to bind out her children Rachel and Charles as apprentices [Orders 1763-65, 15]. She was taxable in Norfolk County from 1782 to 1811 (called Sarah Cuffee, Sr., or oldest): taxable on 4 cattle in 1782; taxable on a horse and 4 cattle in 1787; a slave over the age of sixteen in 1792 and 1793, 2 free tithes in 1796; 2 slaves in 1798; a slave from 1801 to 1811 [PPTL, 1782-91, frames 391, 414, 449, 494, 547, 589, 604; 1791-1812, frames 50, 65, 188, 271, 548, 609, 636, 674, 716]. She was the mother of

       4   i.   ?John[2], born say 1743.
       5   ii. ?Sarah[2], Jr., born say 1745.
               iii. ?Nan, born say 1747, taxable in the household of John Cuffee in the Norfolk County district from Great Bridge to Edmund's Bridge and New Mill Creek in 1765 and 1766, called Nan/ Nanny (no last name indicated) [Wingo, *Norfolk County Virginia Tithables, 1750-65*, 198; *1766-1780*, 1]. She was called "Nan Coffee, a free negro," on 18 March 1773 when she and Drew Halstead's slave named Roger were convicted of hog stealing [Orders 1771-3, 161]. She was taxable on a free male in St. Bride's Parish, Norfolk County, in 1791 [PPTL, 1791-1812, frame 5].
               iv. ?Dinah, taxable on 2 cattle in Norfolk County in 1787 [PPTL, 1782-91, frame 589].
               v.   Rachel, born say 1753, bound apprentice to Ruth Gamman in Norfolk County on 19 May 1763 [Orders 1763-65, 15].
       6   vi. Charles[1], born about 1755.

5. Sarah[2] Cuffee, Jr., born say 1745, was taxable in Norfolk County in the district from Great Bridge to Edmunds Bridge from 1761 to 1766: her tax charged to Frances Curling in 1761, charged to William Sikes, Jr., from 1765 to 1767 [Wingo, *Norfolk County Tithables, 1751-65*, 176, 198; *1766-80*, 3]. She was taxable in St. Bride's Parish from 1782 to 1817 (called Sarah Cuffee, Jr., or youngest): taxable on a horse and 4 cattle in 1782; a slave over the age

of sixteen and 4 horses in 1793; a free male and a horse in 1798; in the list of "free Negroes" which start in 1801; taxable on a slave over the age of sixteen from 1804 to 1810; taxable on 2 free male tithes, a horse and 12 cattle in 1815, 1 free male in 1817 [PPTL, 1782-1791, frames 391, 413, 494, 661; 1791-1812, frames 65, 272, 548, 609, 636, 674; 1813-24, frames 72, 205]. She may have been the mother of

    i.   Euphan, taxable in St. Bride's Parish on 2 cattle in 1783, a horse in 1785, 3 cattle in 1787, perhaps identical to Fan Cuffee who was taxable on 2 free tithes and a horse in 1812 [PPTL, 1782-91, frames 413, 494, 589; 1791-1812, frame 802].

    ii.   Rhoda, taxable on a horse in St. Bride's Parish, Norfolk County, in 1793 [PPTL, 1791-1812, frame 65].

3.   Mary[1] Cuffee, born say 1738, was a "free negro" taxable in Norfolk County in the district from Great Bridge to Edmond's Bridge and New Mill Creek from 1754 to 1768: charged with her own tithe in 1754 and 1768; her tax charged to Frances Curling in 1759; listed with John Cuffee in 1766; with Sarah Cuffee in 1767 [Wingo, *Norfolk County Tithables, 1751-65*, 76, 132; *1766-80*, 1, 23, 52]. She was living in Norfolk County on 19 May 1763 when her daughter Frances was ordered bound apprentice to John Gammon by the churchwardens of St. Brides Parish [Orders 1763-65, 15]. She was called Moll Cuffy in the 31 March 1774 issue of the *Virginia Gazette* when it reported that she was a "Negro woman" about thirty-five years old who claimed to be free but was jailed in Norfolk [*Virginia Gazette* (Purdie & Dixon edition)]. She was called Molly Cuffee when she was taxable in Norfolk County from 1782 to 1794: taxable on a horse in 1782; charged with her son Lemuel's tithe, a horse and 6 cattle in 1784; her sons Lemuel and John in 1785 and 1786; taxable on a horse in 1787; a free male and 3 horses in 1792; a free male and a slave over the age of sixteen in 1793; a slave and 2 horses in 1794 [PPTL, 1782-91, frames 390, 414, 449, 494, 547, 698; 1791-1812, frames 5, 50, 64, 120]. Her children were

    i.   ?Elijah, born say 1759, taxable in the Norfolk County household of Benjamin Butt in 1780 [Wingo, *Norfolk County Tithables 1766-80*]. He was charged with his own tax from 1784 to 1786, called "Elijah Cuffee Senior" in 1785 [PPTL, 1782-91, frames 449, 494, 547].

    ii.   Frances, born say 1762, bound apprentice on 19 May 1763. Fanny was taxable in St. Bride's Parish, Norfolk County, on 2 cattle in 1784 and 1786; 2 free males in 1798; a free male in 1814 [PPTL, 1782-91, frames 449, 547; 1791-1812, frames 272; 1813-24, frames 11, 67].

6   iii.   Lemuel, born say 1765.

7   iv.   John[3], born say 1769.

    v.   ?Aaron, taxable in St. Bride's Parish from 1795 to 1817: in the "List of Free Negroes" which start in 1801; charged with 3 "free Negro" tithables and a horse in 1815 [PPTL, 1791-1812, frames 155, 317, 400, 558, 609, 674, 716; 1813-24, frames 11, 72, 206], head of a household of 8 "other free" in 1810 [VA:794].

    vi.   ?George[1], taxable in St. Bride's Parish, Norfolk County, from 1799 to 1807: taxable on a horse in 1799, taxable on 2 free males in 1800 [PPTL, 1791-1812, frames 316, 337, 416, 456], a "Free Black" head of a Princess Anne County household of 5 "other free" in 1810 [VA:445].

4.   John[2] Cuffee, born say 1743, was taxable in Norfolk County in the district from Great Bridge to Edmunds Bridge from 1761 to 1766: his tax charged to John Curling in 1761; charged with his own tithe, Sarah Cuffee and Nan in 1765; a "free negro" taxable on his own tithe, Molly Cuffee, and Nanny Cuffee in 1766 [Wingo, *Norfolk County Virginia Tithables, 1750-65*, 176, 198; *1766-1780*, 1]. He may have been the father of

    i.   Courtney **Allen**, born about 1768, registered in Norfolk County on 18 October 1815: *Courtney Allen formerly Courtney Cuffee 5 feet 6 1/2 Inches 47 Years of age of a dark Complexion, Born free in the County of Norfolk* [Register of Free Negros & Mulattos, no.103].

    ii.   James, taxable in St. Bride's Parish of Norfolk County from 1797 to 1817: taxable on 2 tithes in 1815, 5 horses in 1817 [PPTL, 1791-1812, frames 205, 272, 400, 456, 548, 636, 802; 1813-24, frames 67, 72, 204]. He was head of a Norfolk County household of 11 "other free" and a slave in 1810 [VA:795].

    iii.   Lydia **Mitchell**, born about 1771, registered in Norfolk County on 18 October 1815: *Lydia Mitchell formerly Lydia Cuffee 5 feet 8 Inches 44 Years of age of a dark Complexion, Born free in the County of Norfolk* [Register of Free Negros & Mulattos, no.103]. She may have been the wife of Robert **Mitchell**, head of a Norfolk County household of 7 "other free" in 1810 [VA:794].

    iv.   Mary[2] **Mitchell**, born about 1774, registered in Norfolk County on 18 October 1815: *Mary Mitchell formerly Mary Cuffee 5 feet 2 Inches 41 Years of age of a Yellowish Complexion, Born free in the County of Norfolk* [Register of Free Negros & Mulattos, no.104].

5.   Charles[1] Cuffee, born about 1755, was called the son of "free Negro" Sarah Coffe when he was bound apprentice to Nathaniel Sikes in Norfolk County on 19 May 1763 [Orders 1763-65, 15]. He was taxable in St. Bride's Parish, Norfolk County, from 1797 to 1801 [PPTL, 1791-1812, frames 205, 315, 400; 1813-24, frame 72] and a "Free Black" head of a Princess Anne County household of 4 "other free" in 1810 [VA:445]. He enlisted in the Revolution in 1780 for eighteen months, and he applied for and was granted a pension while a resident of Princess Anne County on 7 June 1830 when he was seventy-five years old. He stated in court that he was living with his thirty-year-old wife Katy and his twelve or thirteen-year-old son Tom. His widow Catherine declared that she was about sixty years old when she applied for a survivor's pension on 28 August 1857. She further testified that her maiden name was Catherine **Fuller**, that they were married in Princess Anne County in 1815 by Samuel Brown, a Baptist Minister, and that her husband died on 1 Oct 1844. Her widow's pension was suspended during the Civil War, but it was reinstated based on her application of 3 June 1867 [National Archives Pension file W-9402]. One of their children was

    i.   Thomas, born about 1817.

6.   Lemuel Cuffee, born say 1765, was taxable in St. Bride's Parish, Norfolk County, from 1784 to 1817: charged with 2 tithes in 1788; taxable on a slave in 1798; in the "List of Free Negroes" which start in 1801; taxable on 2 "free Negro" tithes in 1815, a "B.M." (Black Man) living on Deep Creek in 1816 [PPTL, 1782-91, frames 547, 603, 661, 699; 1792-1812, frames 5, 50, 188, 271, 337, 456, 636; 1813-24, frames 73, 126, 242]. He was head of a Norfolk County household of 10 "other free" in 1810 [VA:804]. He was the father of

    i.   Charles[2], taxable in St. Bride's Parish from called "son of Lam" when he was counted as a "free Negro" in Norfolk County in 1813 and 1815 [PPTL, 1813-24, frames 11, 73]. He may have been the Charles Cuffee, born about 1789, who registered in Norfolk County on 15 March 1811: *5 feet 3 In. 22 Years of age of a light Complexion, born free in the County of Norfk.* [Register of Free Negros & Mulattos, no.47].

7.   John[3] Cuffee, born say 1769, taxable in St. Bride's Parish, Norfolk County, from 1785 to 1814: a 16-21-year-old taxable listed with his mother Molly Cuffee in 1785 and 1786, called John Cuffe, Sr., in 1800, in the "List of Free Negroes" which start in 1801, taxable on 2 free males and a horse in 1814

[PPTL, 1782-91, frames 494, 547, 603, 661; 1791-1812, frames 5, 64, 187, 316, 337, 416, 456, 548, 636, 802; 1813-24, frames 11, 67]. He married Sally **Shafer (Chavers?)**, 4 March 1790 Norfolk County bond, Lemuel Cuffee surety, with a note attached to the bond: *John Cuffee, a free man, made oath before me that Sally Shafer, orphan of John Shafer, is upwards of twenty-one years of age.* He was head of a Norfolk County household of 12 "other free" in 1810 [VA:794]. He was the father of

    i.   Charles³, called "son of John" when he was counted as a "Free Male Negro above the age of 16" in Norfolk County in 1813 [PPTL, 1813-24, frame 11].

Their descendants in Norfolk County were

    i.   William, head of a household 3 "other free" in 1810 [VA:794], a "free Negro" taxable in St. Bride's Parish in 1812 and 1813 [PPTL, 1791-1812, frame 802; 1813-24, frame 11]. He was a man of color from Norfolk County who was listed in the size roll of troops who enlisted at Chesterfield Courthouse [NSDAR, *African American Patriots*, 149].

    ii. Isaac, born say 1772, a "N."(Negro) gardener living near Norfolk who was taxable on a slave over the age of sixteen in 1801, taxable on 2 horses in 1802, a horse and 2 carriage wheels in 1802 [PPTL, 1791-1812, frames 373, 428, 461A].

    iii. Samuel, born say 1782, a "free Negro" taxable in St. Bride's Parish from 1799 to 1813: charged with 3 tithes in 1799 and 1800 [PPTL, 1791-1812, frames 316, 337, 456, 802; 1813-24, frame 11].

    iv. Caleb, born say 1784, a "free Negro" taxable in St. Bride's Parish from 1801 to 1817: taxable on a slave aged 12-16 and a horse in 1802 [PPTL, 1791-1812, frames 400, 416, 548, 716, 802; 1813-24, 67, 205].

    v.   Willis, born say 1784, a "free Negro" taxable in St. Bride's Parish from 1801 to 1817 [PPTL, 1791-1812, frames 400, 416, 456, 548, 716, 802; 1813-24, 67, 204], head of a Norfolk County household of 5 "other free" in 1810 [VA:795].

    vi. Patsy, head of a Norfolk County household 6 "other free" in 1810 [VA:795].

    vii. Nancy, head of a Norfolk County household 4 "other free" in 1810 [VA:795].

    viii. Nancy, head of a Norfolk County household 4 "other free" in 1810 [VA:802].

    ix. George², taxable in St. Bride's Parish from 1811 to 1817: called George Cuffee, Jr., in 1811, George D. Cuffee in 1812 [PPTL, 1791-1812, frame 802; 1813-24, frames 11, 67, 205], head of a Norfolk County household 3 "other free" in 1810 [VA:795].

    x.   Abram, a "free Negro" taxable in St. Bride's Parish in 1812 [PPTL, 1791-1812, frame 802].

    xi. Lovey, head of a household 2 "other free" in 1810 [VA:794].

    xii. John³, born about 1779, head of a Norfolk County household of 2 "other free" in 1810 [VA:795]. He registered in Norfolk County on 19 August 1811: *6 feet 2 In. 32 years of age of a light Complexion...Born free* [Register of Free Negros & Mulattos, no.56].

    xiii. Henry, born about 1790, registered in Norfolk County on 4 March 1811: *6 feet, 21 Years of age, of a Yellowish Complexion, Born free* [Register of Free Negros & Mulattos, no.46].

CUMBO FAMILY

1.   Emanuell¹ Cambow, "Negro," was granted a patent for 50 acres in James City County on 18 April 1667 [Patents 6:39]. He may have been the "Mulata named Manuel" who was adjudged to be a Christian servant by the Virginia

Assembly in September 1644. He was ordered to serve as other Christian servants and freed in September 1665 [*VMHB* XVII:232]. He was probably the father of

2   i.   Richard[1], born say 1667.

2.   Richard[1] Cumbo, born say 1667, was living in St. Peter's Parish, New Kent and James City counties, on 15 February 168_ when his daughter Elizabeth was baptized [NSCDA, *Parish Register of St. Peter's*, 3]. He was taxed on 80 acres in New Kent County in 1704 [Smith, *Virginia Quit Rent Rolls*, 218], and he and his wife Ann sold 100 acres where they were living in Westover Parish, Charles City County, on 2 February 1724/5 [W&D 1725-31, 8, 9]. In January 1737/8 the Charles City County court dismissed a grand jury presentment against him, and in April 1741 he was awarded 50 shillings in his suit against Benjamin Evans [Orders 1737-51, 32]. His children were

3   i.   Elizabeth[1], born 15 February 168_.
4   ii.   ?John[1], born say 1700.
5   iii. ?Gideon[1], born say 1702.
6   iv.   ?Richard[2], born say 1715.
         v.   ?David, born say 1722, sued James Nance in Charles City County in March 1744/5 [Orders 1737-51, 340, 352, 359]. He was a "Black" taxable in Brunswick County, North Carolina, in 1772 [G.A. 11.1].
         vi.   ?William, born say 1723, sued Hubbard Williams for trespass, assault and battery in Charles City County in January 1744/5 [Orders 1737-51, 329, 337, 341]. He was taxable on 2 white tithes in Cumberland County, North Carolina, in 1755 [T&C - Box 1], and he entered 181 acres in Granville County in January 1761.
         vii. ?Mary, born say 1724, mother of William **Bates** who was bound out by the Charles City County court in August 1744 [Orders 1737-51, 319].
         viii. ?Paul, born say 1726, presented by the Charles City County court in May 1742 for not going to church. He sued Lewis Delony in court in February 1748/9 [Orders 1737-51, 204, 213, 491, 497, 533, 561].

3.   Elizabeth[1] Cumbo, born say 1688, was baptized 15 February 168_ in St. Peter's Parish, New Kent County. She may have been the mother of
7   i.   Elizabeth[2], born say 1720.

4.   John[1] Cumbo, born say 1700, received a patent on 22 February 1724 for 150 acres in Surry County, Virginia, on both sides of the Rockey Run of Little Creek and the south side of Three Creeks [Patents 12:162]. He was a "Mul[o]" listed in Col. Nathaniel Harrison's account books which were recorded in the Surry County estate of his wife Mary Harrison in 1733, and he was listed in the account of sales of the 16 August 1738 Surry County estate of John Barlow [Deeds, Wills 8:318, 881]. He was in Brunswick County, Virginia, in 1738 [Orders 1732-41, 192] and was living in adjoining Northampton County, North Carolina, on 2 July 1746 when a deed mentioned land on Peahill Creek and John Cumbo (on the Brunswick County, Virginia line) [DB 1:260]. On 5 February 1747 Nathan Edwards sued him for a 6 pound, 9 shillings debt in Brunswick County claiming that he had absconded. William Pettway, who had 30 barrels of Indian corn and part of a crop of tobacco belonging to John Cumbo, paid the debt for him [Brunswick Orders 1743-49, 130]. He was witness to the 20 April 1750 Northampton County deed of John Avent to John Wood for land on Peahill Creek [DB 1:420]. There were four suits against him for debt in Brunswick County court between December 1753 and July 1756 [Orders 1753-6, 95, 191, 295, 370; 1756-7, 106]. James **Gowen** sued him in Brunswick County court on 27 December 1757 [Orders 1757-9, 143]. He sold 238 acres in Brunswick County on 6 August 1760 [DB 6:595]. His plantation was probably the Northampton County tract of land called "Cumboes" in the

19 February 1759 Granville will of William Eaton [Grimes, *Abstract of N.C. Wills,* 172]. On 7 August 1761 Major Tiller was granted a patent for land adjoining "Cumboes" in Brunswick County, Virginia, on the north side of Peahill Creek, up the Stoney Lick Branch [Patents 33:1066-7]. On 6 April 1764 he made a Northampton County deed of gift of his cattle and household goods to (his son?) Thomas Cumbo for maintaining him for his lifetime [DB 3:197]. Perhaps he was the father of

    i.   Cannon[1], born say 1730, living on land owned by John MacKinne when MacKinne made his 28 February 1753 Edgecombe County, North Carolina will. He allowed Cannon the use of the land until 1758 [Gammon, *Edgecombe County Will Abstracts,* 54]. Cannon was listed in the Edgecombe County Muster Roll of Captain William Haywood in the 1750s [Clark, *Colonial Soldiers of the South,* 677].

8   ii. Thomas[1], born say 1731.

  iii. Fortune, born say 1733, the mother of a poor soldier in the Continental Service on 17 December 1778, 20 May 1779 and 19 August 1779 when the Halifax County, Virginia court issued a certificate to the Treasurer that she had been provided with public assistance. She may have been the mother of Thomas Gimbo, a poor soldier whose wife and children received assistance in Halifax County on 21 August 1777 [Pleas 1774-9, 236, 384, 414; 1779-83, 65].

  iv. John[2], born say 1734, called John Cumbo, Jr., when he was sued for debt in Brunswick County, Virginia court on 22 April 1755 and 27 January 1756. On 28 July 1760 the court ordered that he be given fifteen lashes for breaking into the house of John Pearson Taylor and stealing goods of very little value [Orders 1753-6, 386, 520; 1760-84, 90]. He was paid 5 shillings by the Brunswick County estate of James Stewart on 23 September 1765 [DB 3:436]. He was a "Mulato" taxable in Bladen County, North Carolina, in 1772 and taxable with his wife Lucy in 1774 [Byrd, *Bladen County Tax Lists,* I:83, 124, 127]. He sold 100 acres in Bladen County east of the great Marsh on 11 January 1786 [DB 1:340].

   v. Charles[1], born say 1742, proved the 6 April 1764 deed of (his brother?) Thomas Cumbo in Northampton County, North Carolina court [DB 3:197]. He was one of the freeholders of Halifax County, Virginia, who were ordered to work on the road from the courthouse to Banister Upper Bridge in July 1770 [Pleas 6:510]. He was head of a Halifax County, Virginia household of 7 persons in 1782 [VA:22] and 7 in 1785 (Charles Kumbo) [VA:88]. He was taxable in the northern district of Halifax County from 1782 to 1801: taxable on 2 horses and 6 cattle in 1782 [PPTL, 1782-1799, frames 9, 21, 35, 66, 99, 158, 369, 559, 862; 1800-12, frames 9, 95]. He married Elizabeth Maskill, 17 April 1786 Halifax County bond, William Powell surety. He purchased property from James Maskill by deed proved in Halifax County court on 21 April 1780 [Pleas 1779-83, 129]. His 4 March 1802 Halifax County will, proved in April 1802, named his wife Elizabeth and children Molly, Sally, Elizabeth, Annis, Nancy, Elexander, William, Charles and Lucy C. Cumbo who were considered white [WB 6:347].

  vi. Jacob, born say 1750, counted as white in 1790, head of a Chatham County household of 4 persons [NC:84].

5.   Gideon[1] Cumbo, born say 1702, was a delinquent taxpayer reported at the vestry held for Blisland Parish, Virginia, on 11 October 1723 [Chamberlayne, *Vestry Book of Blisland Parish,* 7]. He was added to the list of tithables by order of the Brunswick County, Virginia court on 6 December 1733. His Brunswick County court petition against William Person was dismissed "on hearing both parties" on 2 June 1748 [Orders 1732-37, 41; 1743-49, 391, 427,

501]. He was called Gibeon Cumbo in Brunswick County court between 27 June 1750 and 28 January 1756 when a dozen suits were brought against him, most of them for debt [Orders 1749-50, 102; 1751-3, 213, 219, 438, 450, 512, 519; 1753-6, 94, 183, 221, 305, 309, 360, 417, 450, 529; 1756-7, 58, 70]. He was called "Gibeon Cumbo a Mallato" when he was sued for debt in Cumberland County, North Carolina, on 20 October 1758. His attorney asked for but was denied the right to claim insolvency. He was also sued for debt on 21 July 1759 by James Wright [Minutes 1755-59, 39, 41, 53, 60]. On 9 June 1762 Major Tiller entered a caveat against him for 222 acres on the south side of the Meherrin River in Brunswick County, Virginia, and Tiller was granted a patent for the land [Hillman, *Executive Journals of the Council*, VI:225]. Perhaps his children were

    i.   Peter[1], born say 1723, sued Joseph **Jeffries** in Brunswick County, Virginia court in June 1749. The case was dismissed when both parties failed to appear. John Williams obtained an attachment against his estate, including a rug, wallet, plats, handkerchief, thread, a knife, a meal bag, a pewter dish, 9 yards of sheeting linen, 3 ells of chex cloth, remnants of chex, serge, brown linen, drugget, a hank of silk and some thread which was returned to court on 1 and 2 January 1752 [Orders 1743-49, 523; 1751-3, 118, 125, 170]. He may have been the Peter Combon who was a taxable in the 1751 Lunenburg County list of Hugh Lawson [Bell, *Sunlight on the Southside*, 174] and the Peter Cumbo who was taxable in Nash District of Caswell County in 1780 [CR 020.701.10].

9   ii. Solomon[1], born say 1727.
10   iii. Elizabeth[3], born say 1728.
11   iv. Stephen[1], born say 1730.
      v. Mary, called "Mary Cumbo alias Morris" on 26 December 1753 when Francis Myrick sued her in Brunswick County, Virginia court for 47 shillings due by account [Orders 1753-6, 99].
12   vi. Cannon[2], born say 1735.

6.   Richard[2] Cumbo, born say 1715, was called Richard Cumbo, Jr., in June 1741 when the Charles City County court presented him for not going to church, and in February 1741/2 when he was fined 20 shillings for refusing to assist the sheriff in the pursuit of a runaway. He was probably the Richard Cumbo (no Jr.) who was fined 500 pounds of tobacco by the Charles City County court on 6 September 1758 for not listing his wife as a tithable [Orders 1737-51, 165, 180, 191; 1758-62, 57]. He was added to the list of tithables in York County on 17 August 1772. He sued Robert **Evans** in York County on 17 May 1773 and was awarded 1 shilling damages. Reuben and Peter **Gillett** were his witnesses [Orders 1772-4, 84, 272, 336]. He, or perhaps a son by the same name, was a soldier from Charles City County who served in the infantry during the Revolution [Gwathmey, *Historical Register of Virginians in the Revolution*, 198]. His widow may have been Sarah Cumbo whose deed to Simon **Gillett** was proved in York County court on 18 October 1784 by Lawrence **De Rozario**, a witness [Orders 1784-7, 86]. And a Sarah Cumbo was taxable on 53 acres in James City County in 1800 [1800 Land Tax List, p.3]. Richard may have been the father of

    i.   Edith, born say 1757, sued Adam White in York County court on 15 June 1778 for trespass, assault and battery [Orders 1774-84, 162]. She was head of a household of 2 persons in Williamsburg City in 1782 [VA:46]. She may have been the Edith Cumbo who was sued by the churchwardens of Antrim Parish, Halifax County, Virginia, in August 1769 (for having an illegitimate child?) in a case that was dismissed "for reasons appearing to the court" [Pleas 6:446].

7. Elizabeth[2] Cumbo, born say 1720, was living in New Kent County on 19
    November 1772 when St. Peter's Parish paid her son Turner for maintaining
    her [Chamberlayne, *Vestry Book of St. Peter's*, 181, 192, 206, 210]. She was
    the mother of
    i. Turner[1], born say 1750, paid by the churchwardens of St. Peter's
        Parish on 19 October 1772 for keeping his mother Elizabeth
        [Chamberlayne, *Vestry Book of St. Peter's*, 181, 192, 206, 210]. He
        was head of a New Kent County household of 3 whites in 1785
        [VA:92]. He was taxable in Blisland Parish, New Kent County, on the
        south side of Warrenny Road on 2 horses and 6 cattle from 1783 to
        1785. His widow was probably Mary Cumbo who was taxable on a
        horse and 8 cattle in New Kent County in 1786 and 1787 and taxable
        on a horse from 1793 to 1803. Their child was probably Nelson
        Cumbo who was taxable on a horse from 1805 to 1814 [PPTL, 1782-
        1800, frames 33, 37, 61, 80, 94, 205; 1791-1828, frames 355, 368,
        381, 405, 418, 429, 441, 453, 463, 474, 485, 497]. He and a woman
        over the age of forty-five (his mother Mary?) were counted as white in
        the 1810 New Kent County census [VA:748].

8. Thomas[1] Cumbo, born say 1731, was sued for debt in Brunswick County,
    Virginia court on 29 November 1752. He had left the county by June 1755
    when William Wyche brought suit against his estate [Orders 1751-3, 352;
    1753-56, 450; 1756-7, 58]. He bought 172 acres in Northampton County,
    North Carolina, near Ivy's Branch and Gilliam's Spring Branch bordering
    Brunswick County, Virginia, on 10 December 1761 and sold this land two
    years later on 23 January 1764 [DB 3:188, 274]. He was one of the
    freeholders of Halifax County, Virginia, who were ordered to work on the
    road from the courthouse to Milner's Ordinary in April 1769 and was called
    Thomas Cumbo, Sr., in September 1769 when he was sued in Halifax County
    court for a debt of 24 pounds [Pleas 6:332, 462]. He was head of a Halifax
    County, Virginia household of 12 persons in 1782 [VA:24] and 13 in 1785
    [VA:89]. He was taxable in the southern district of Halifax County from 1782
    to 1797: taxable on his unnamed son in 1789, listed with 3 tithables in 1792,
    1793, 1795 and 1796, 2 in 1797, called a "Mul°" in 1795, called Thomas
    Cumbee in 1797 [PPTL, 1782-1799, frames 7, 261, 413, 437, 535, 599, 673,
    697]. He and his wife Susannah sued John Franklin in Halifax County court
    on 19 September 1783. On 27 August 1789 he was paid as a witness for Sarah
    Jones in her suit for false imprisonment against James Johnson, Jr., James
    Johnson, Alexander Hillson, William Johnson and James Hammonds [Pleas
    1779-83, 400; 1788-9, 204; 1789-90, 46-47]. He was taxable from 1800 to
    1802, called Thomas Cumby, Sr., in Charlotte County where the family was
    considered white [PPTL, 1782-1815, frames 484, 516]. He was the father of
    i.   ?Peter[2], married Milly Ramsey, 28 December 1785 Halifax County,
          Virginia bond, Charles Cumbo surety; John Perkins and Thomas
          Cumbo witnesses. He was taxable on his own tithe and a horse in the
          southern district of Halifax County in 1789, called a "Mul°" in 1795,
          called Peter Cumbee, Jr., in 1797 [PPTL, 1782-1799, frames 296, 413,
          534, 599, 673, 697, 812].
    ii.   ?Patience, married Robert **Wilson**, 16 April 1787 Halifax County,
          Virginia bond, surety Robert Smith.
    iii. Molly, "daughter of Thomas Cumbo," married James **Matthews**, 20
          July 1790 Halifax County, Virginia bond, David **Gowing** surety, 29
          July marriage.
    iv.   ?Sarah, married Ezekiel **Matthews**, 23 April 1793 Halifax County,
          Virginia bond and 7 May 1793 Caswell County bond with Allen **Going**
          bondsman.
    v.   ?John[6], born say 1773, married Polly Jennings, 19 August 1794 Halifax
          County, Virginia bond, Bolling Hamlett surety. He was a "Mul°"

taxable in the southern district of Halifax County in 1795 [PPTL, 1782-1799, frame 599]. He died before 25 February 1797 when his Halifax County, Virginia estate was appraised at 20 pounds [WB 3:316].

vi.   ?Jeffrey, a "Mul°" taxable in the southern district of Halifax County in 1795 [PPTL, 1782-1799, frame 599].

vii.   ?Emanuel[2] Cumbee, taxable in the southern district of Halifax County in 1798 [PPTL, 1782-1799, frame 810], taxable in Charlotte County in 1799 and 1800 [PPTL, 1782-1813, frames 447, 484], taxable from 1801 in Campbell County where the family was considered white [PPTL, 1785-1814, frames 512, 593, 728, 873].

9.   Solomon[1] Cumbo, born say 1727, successfully brought suit in New Hanover County court against John **Potter** on 2 May 1759, William Wilkinson on 7 December 1764, and Thomas Watson on 5 April 1771 [Minutes 1738-69, 233; 1771-79, 8].[85] On 7 October 1768 the sheriff paid Thomas Lloyd, Esq., out of the county tax to attend to "Mrs. Cumbow while she was sick with the smallpox" [Minutes 1738-69, 377-378, 388]. He was called Solomon Cumbo "free Mulatto" when he was ordered to work on the streets of Wilmington [Wilmington Town Book cited by Crow, *Black Experience in Revolutionary North Carolina*, 29]. He was head of an Onslow County household of 6 "other free" in 1790 [NC:197], 5 in Brunswick County, North Carolina, in 1800 [NC:14], and 7 in Brunswick County in 1810 [NC:226]. His children may have been

i.   Reuben, head of an Onslow County household of 4 "other free" in 1790 [NC:197], 6 in Brunswick County in 1800 [NC:14], and 9 in Brunswick County in 1810 (R. Cumbo) [NC:226]. He entered 50 acres on the east side of Lewis Bridge in Brunswick County on 30 January 1801 and another 50 acres in this area on 5 November 1804 [Pruitt, *Land Entries: Brunswick County,* 69, 90].

ii.   Absalom, entered 100 acres in Brunswick County on both sides of Russell's Branch on 22 September 1800, 50 acres in the fork of Scraping Hole Branch on 22 March 1813, and 100 acres on the east side of Scraping Hole Branch on 16 August 1814. On 27 January 1819 John **Skipper**, Sr., entered this land, including "Absalom Cumbow's improvement" [Pruitt, *Land Entries: Brunswick County*, nos. 1074 2123, 2169, 2512]. Absalom was counted as white in Cumberland County in 1820 [NC:169].

iii.   Solomon[3], head of a Brunswick County household of 7 "other free" in 1810 [NC:226], entered 50 acres in Brunswick County on both sides of Russell's Branch bordering his own land on 16 November 1804 and 75 acres on the east side of Lewis' Branch and Cypress Branch on 26 January 1811 [Pruitt, *Land Entries: Brunswick County,* 90, 123].

10.   Elizabeth[3] Cumbo, born say 1728, was living in Surry County, Virginia, in July 1750 when the court ordered her "Natural-born" children: Darcus, Winifred and Hercules bound out by the churchwardens of Albemarle Parish [Orders 1749-51, 110]. She sued Charles Bass for debt in Brunswick County, Virginia court on 27 June 1758. On 24 April 1775 the Brunswick County court ordered the churchwardens of Meherrin Parish to bind out her orphan-son Cannon Cumbo [Orders 1757-9, 204; 1774-82, 73]. She may have been the Elizabeth Cumbo whose "mulattoe" son Solomon Cumbo was ordered bound out by the churchwardens of Southam Parish, Cumberland County, Virginia, on 27 March 1775 [Orders 1774-8, 321]. She was the mother of

i.   Dorcus, born say 1746.

---

[85]John **Potter** (6 "other free"), James **Potter** (7 "other free"), and Robert **Potter** (4 "other free") were heads of Brunswick County, North Carolina households in 1800 [NC:14].

 ii. Winifred, born say 1748.

 iii. Hercules, born say 1750.

13 iv. Cannon[3], born say 1758.

14 v. Solomon[2], born say 1765.

15 vi. ?Matthew, born say 1774.

11. Stephen[1] Cumbo, born say 1730, was taxable in Granville County, North Carolina, in 1750 in the list of Jonathan White [CR 44.401.23]. In 1769 he was taxed on 4 persons in Brunswick County, North Carolina:

 Cumbo, Stephen Moll° 3 Negro men, 1 Negro boy [SS 837],

and he was taxed in Brunswick County on 3 Black polls in 1772 [G.A. 11.1]. He was also taxable in 1772 with his son Jacob in Bladen County ("Molatoes") [Byrd, *Bladen County Tax Lists*, I:78]. He was head of an Onslow County household of 4 "other free" in 1790 [NC:197] and 7 in Edgefield District, South Carolina, in 1810 [SC:797]. He may have been identical to Stephen Cumbee, a taxable on 150 acres in Winton, South Carolina, in 1788 [S.C. Tax Returns 1783-1800, frame 34]. His children were

 i. Jacob, taxable in his father's Bladen County household in 1772.

 ii. ?Leroy, head of an Edgefield District, South Carolina household of 6 "other free" in 1810 [SC:777].

 iii. ?Thomas[2], called "Thomas Cumbee, overseer," when he married Charlotte **Collins**, "free persons of color," on 27 June 1805 at St. Philip's and Michael's Parish, Charleston.

12. Cannon[2] Cumbo, born say 1735, was taxable with his wife in Bladen County from 1768 to 1776 ("Molatoes"), taxable on a female slave and a male slave under 16, and head of a household of 8 white males under 21 or over 60, 4 white females, and 1 "Black" in 1786 [Byrd, *Bladen County Tax Lists*, I:5, /14, 34, 60, 78, 95, 123, 134; II:55, 74, 162]. He was granted a patent for 100 acres in Bladen County on the southwest side of Drowning Creek on 22 January 1773 [Hoffman, *Land Patents*, II:319]. He was taxable in Bladen County on this 100 acres and a free poll for himself and a slave poll in 1784 in Captain Regan's District. He entered two tracts of land of 100 acres each in what was then Robeson County on the north side of Jacob Swamp and Drowning Creek on 19 January 1789 [Pruitt, *Land Entries: Robeson County*, I:21] and sold 100 acres of this land to Horatio **Hammond** on 17 May 1804 [DB N:216]. He transferred land to his sons Aaron and Elisha by deeds proved on 8 July 1800. On 22 May 1801 his slave Caesar was convicted of stealing two pairs of shoe bolts and a trunk from John Peter Martin and was given thirty-nine lashes at the public whipping post. He purchased two tracts of land in Robeson by deeds proved on 5 April 1802 [Minutes 1797-1806, 112, 152, 191]. He was head of a Robeson County household of 11 "other free" in 1790 [NC:50] and 6 "other free" and a slave in 1800 [NC:372]. His children: John, Stephen, Gibion, Elijah, and Aaron were ordered to work on the road from Raft Swamp to Gibion **Gibson**'s Landing by the 6 October 1801 Robeson County court [Minutes 1797-1806, 173]. His 19 March 1817 Robeson County will, proved in November 1823, named his children [WB A:204]. They were

 i. Gideon[2]/ Gibion, born say 1755, called Gilbert Cumbo in 1784 when he was taxable in Captain Regan's District of Bladen County on 250 acres and one poll. He was head of a Bladen County household of 1 white male from 21 to 60 years old and 3 white females in 1786 [Byrd, *Bladen County Tax Lists*, II:162], head of a Robeson County household of 1 "other free" in 1790 [NC:50], 5 in 1800 (called Gibby) [NC:372], and 6 in 1810 (called Gibby) [NC:231]. He made a Robeson County nuncupative will on 1 November 1837, proved May 1838, leaving all his estate to Mary Cumbo. Elizabeth and Jemima Cumbo were witnesses [WB A:327].

ii. Stephen[2], born say 1758, head of a Robeson County household of 3 "other free" in 1800 and 4 "free colored" in New Hanover County in 1820 [NC:227]. He married Sarah Broom, 23 October 1799 Robeson County bond with (his brother) Aaron Cumbo bondsman. He was exempted from paying poll tax on 5 July 1808 [Minutes II:96]. He sold land by deed proved in Robeson County court in February 1827 [Minutes III:142].

iii. ?Nathaniel, born say 1761, not mentioned in his father's will, perhaps deceased or left the county before then. He was taxable on one poll in Captain Regan's District of Bladen County in 1784 and entered 100 acres on the east side of Drowning Creek on 5 May 1791 [Pruitt, *Land Entries: Robeson County*, I:45]. He was head of a Robeson County household of 4 "other free" in 1790 [NC:50].

iv. John[4], born say 1765, head of a Robeson County household of 3 "other free" in 1790 [NC:50], 4 in 1800 [NC:372], and 3 in 1810 [NC:231]. He made a nuncupative will witnessed by his brother Gibson in Robeson County on 20 May 1814 leaving all his estate to his wife Mary [WB A:153]. His father Cannon left "Daughter Mary Cumbo, widow of John Cumbo 200 acres where she now lives." Mary was head of a Robeson County household of 3 "free colored" in 1820 [NC:304].

v.   Aaron, born say 1775, head of a Robeson County household of 6 "other free" and 3 slaves in 1800 [NC:372]. The 6 July 1803 Robeson County court attached seven of his cattle for a debt to Mitchel Biggs [Minutes 1797-1806, 255]. He sold land to his brother Elisha by deed proved by their brother Stephen in Robeson on 27 August 1811 [Minutes 1806-13, 282]. Aaron was head of a Georgetown, South Carolina household of 6 "other free" in 1810 [SC:219].

vi. Elisha, born say 1777, head of a Robeson County household of 3 white males and 2 white females in 1800 and 8 "other free" in 1810 [NC:231]. In 1805 one of Elisha's brothers was convicted of larceny on complaint of a white man named William Townsend. Soon afterwards, Townsend's horse was shot dead. He felt certain that Elisha had done it but was unable to obtain a warrant because he had no evidence. He prevailed upon Major William Odom and five other whites to arrest Elisha without a warrant for which Elisha brought a bill of indictment against them. In October 1805 the Superior Court of Fayetteville District fined Major Odom 15 pounds and the other six 10 pounds each for riot. They appealed to the North Carolina General Assembly, describing the Cumbos as "Mulattoes who are well known as Infamous Characters," but their petition was rejected [Schweninger, *Southern Debate over Slavery, vol. 1: Petitions to Southern Legislatures*]. Elisha purchased land from his brother Aaron by deed proved by their brother Stephen in Robeson County on 27 August 1811 [Minutes 1806-13, 282].

vii. Elijah, born say 1780, head of a Robeson County household of 6 "other free" in 1810 [NC:231].

viii. Solomon[4].

ix. Moses.

13. Cannon[3] Cumbo, born say 1758, orphan son of Elizabeth Cumbo, was living in Brunswick County, Virginia, on 23 February 1778 when the court ordered the churchwardens of Meherrin Parish to bind him to Joseph Prince on the condition that he receive 15 pounds per annum during his apprenticeship and that he be taught the trade of shoemaker [Orders 1774-82, 73, 189]. He was living alone in 1783 when he was counted in the Greensville County, Virginia census [VA:54] and was taxable that year on a horse and 3 head of cattle

[PPTL 1782-1807, frame 17]. He was sued in Greensville County court on 23 March 1792 [Orders 1790-9, 122]. He was head of Northampton County, North Carolina household of 5 "other free" in 1790 [NC:73]. He was not mentioned again in Northampton County records, so he may have been identical to "Bird Cumbo" whose estate inventory was dated 3 August 1799. Tabitha Cumbo, his widow, was allotted a years support in December 1799 [Gammon, *Records of Estates, Northampton County*, I:33]. She died before 17 November 1805 when her father Moses **Newsom** gave "the heirs of my daughter Tabitha Cumbo decd" one dollar each by his Northampton County will [WB 2:297]. They were

    i.   Jinny, received a dollar by her grandfather's will.

    ii.   Henry, born 1794-1806, head of a Northampton County household of 1 "free colored" in 1820 [NC:222].

    iii.   John[8], born 1794-1806, head of a Northampton County household of 1 "free colored" in 1820 [NC:220].

Other members of the Cumbo family in Northampton County were

    i.   Phoebe, head of a Northampton County household of 4 "other free" in 1810 [NC:716].

    ii.   Polly, head of a Northampton County household of 5 "other free" in 1810 [NC:716].

    iii.   Britain, born 1776-1794, head of a Northampton County household of 5 "free colored" in 1820 [NC:222].

    iv.   Wyatt, deceased by 5 June 1820 when the Northampton County court granted administration of his estate to James Rowell [Minutes 1817-21, 274].

    v.   Fady, married Howell **Wade**, 17 May 1823 Northampton County bond. Howell **Wade**, born before 1776, was head of a Northampton County household of 6 "free colored" in 1830.

14. Solomon[2] Cumbo, born say 1765, was taxable on his own tithe and 3 horses in Williamsburg in 1788 [PPTL, p.1]. He was the father of three children whose births were registered in Bruton Parish, York and James City counties. He died before 20 May 1799 when William **Jarvis** sued the administrator of his estate in York County court for 14 pounds, 7 shillings. Perhaps his widow was Martha Cumbo who sued James **Cannady**, Jr., for trespass, assault and battery in York County court on 19 May 1801 [Orders 1795-1803, 317, 458, 539]. His children were

    i.   James Johnson, born 11 June 1786 [Bruton Parish Register, 36].

    ii.   Elizabeth[4], born 20 November 1787 [Bruton Parish Register, 36].

    iii.   Sarah, born 19 August 1790 [Bruton Parish Register, 36].

15. Matthew Cumbo, born say 1774, illegitimate child of ___ Cumbo, was ordered bound out by the churchwardens of Meherrin Parish, Brunswick County, Virginia, on 28 February 1780 [Orders 1774-82, 331]. He was head of a Hertford County, North Carolina household of 5 "free colored" in 1820 [NC:188] and 4 "free colored" in 1830 [NC:405]. He may have been the father of

    i.   David, born about 1798, head of a Hertford County household of 3 "free colored" females (males crossed out) in 1820 [NC:186], 2 in 1830 [NC:405], a "Mulatto" counted with twenty-eight-year-old Nancy Cumbo in 1850 [NC:667].

Other members of the Cumbo family from Charles City and James City counties were

    i.   Jethro, born say 1750, taxable in James City County on a tithe and a horse from 1782 to 1787 [PPTL, 1782-99].

16 ii.   Stephen[3], born say 1755.

    iii.   Daniel, born say 1760, a solider from Charles City County who served in the Revolution [Gwathmey, *Historical Register of Virginians in the Revolution*, 198]. George Harwell sued him in Greensville County, Virginia court on 22 August 1782, and the sheriff sold a bay mare of his to pay a 10 pound debt he owed Robert Stewart on 25 May 1786 [Orders 1781-9, 40, 277]. He was taxable in James City County on 2 slaves and 2 horses in 1788 and taxable there from 1794 to 1813: taxable on a slave and a horse in 1794, 1798 and 1801, a slave and 3 horses in 1807 and 1808, and counted with 1 male and 1 female in a list of "Free Persons of Colour above 16 years" in 1813 [PPTL, 1782-99; 1800-15].

    iv.   Michael, born say 1760, a Revolutionary soldier from Charles City County [Jackson, *Virginia Negro Soldiers*, 34]. He was taxable in York County from 1788 to 1793 [PPTL, 1782-1841, frames 139, 161, 191].

    v.   John[3], born say 1762, died before 26 July 1791 when the overseers of the poor of Charles City County bound his orphan daughter Mourning Cumbo to George Hubbard until the age of eighteen [DB 4:61]. He may have been the John Cumbo who served in the Revolution from Charles City County [Gwathmey, *Historical Register of Virginians in the Revolution*, 198].

    vi.   Peter, a soldier from Charles City County who served in the Revolution [Gwathmey, *Historical Register of Virginians in the Revolution*, 198]. He may have been the Peter Cumbo who was sued by the churchwardens of Meherrin Parish, Brunswick County, Virginia, on 24 January 1785 [Orders 1784-8, 59, 85].

    vii.   Fluellen, born say 1765, taxable in Charles City County from 1787 to 1802. Perhaps his widow was Nancy Cumbo who was taxable on a horse in 1809 [PPTL 1788-1814].

    viii.   Jesse, born say 1767, taxable in James City County from 1788 to 1795: taxable on a slave and 2 horses in 1790 and 1792. He apparently died before 1797 when his estate was taxable on 2 horses. His wife was probably Tabitha Cumbo who was taxable on a horse in 1798 and 1799, taxable on a free male tithe in 1803, 1804, and 1806, taxable on a horse in 1812 and a "mulatto" head of a household of a "Free Person of Colour above 16 years" in 1813 [PPTL, 1782-99; 1800-15]. On 22 November 1803 she was paid for travelling from James City County and attending York County court as a witness for Lucy **Harris** in her suit against William **Jarvis** [Orders 1795-1803, 602, 613].

    ix.   Abram **Thomas** (alias Cumbo), born say 1769, married Mary **Brown**, "daughter of Abram Brown deceased," by marriage agreement of 13 April 1791, proved in Charles City County court on 15 December 1791, by which he recognized her right to slaves Isaac and Jane, two feather beds, and some stock of cattle and hogs which were in her possession [DB 4:66]. He was taxable in Charles City County as Abraham Cumbo alias **Thomas** from 1790 to 1799 and called Abraham **Thomas** in 1800 and thereafter [PPTL, 1788-1814].

17   x.   John[5], born say 1771.

    xi.   James, born say 1772, taxable in Charles City County in 1793 [PPTL, 1788-1814], taxable in James City County in 1802 [PPTL, 1800-15] and head of a household of 2 "free Negroes & mulattos over 16" in Williamsburg in 1813 [Waldrep, *1813 Tax List*].

18   xii.   Anderson, born about 1773.

    xiii.   Turner[2], born say 1773, taxable in Charles City County in 1794, 1797, 1798, 1800, 1802, 1809 and 1813: called Turner Cumbo alias **Thomas** in 1794 and called "Turner Comboo Mulattoe" in 1813 [PPTL, 1788-1814]. He was probably the Turner Cumbo who was taxable in the lower district of Henrico County in 1799 and 1800: his tax charged to William **Thomas** in 1799 [PPTL 1782-1814, frames 420]. He was head of a Charles City County household of 3 "other free" in 1810 [VA:953]. On 19 December 1811 he was married to Rebecca **Cannady** when their son Walker Cumbo received a Charles City County deed of gift of a cow and two calves from his grandfather James **Cannady** of James City County [DB 5:405-6]. Turner was a "col^d" man taxable in James City County in 1814 [PPTL, 1800-15].

16. Stephen^3 Cumbo, born say 1755, was a soldier from James City County who served in the Revolution [Gwathmey, *Historical Register of Virginians in the Revolution*, 198]. He was taxable in James City County from 1782 to 1814: taxable on 3 horses and 4 cattle in 1782, a "Mulatto" taxable in 1785, taxable on 2 horses and 6 cattle in 1787 and 2 tithes and a horse in 1800. He was counted with a male and a female in a list of "Free Persons of Colour above 16 years" in James City County in 1813 [PPTL, 1782-99; 1800-15]. He may have been the father of

    i.   William, born say 1782, taxable in James City County from 1803 to 1812 and counted with a male and a female in a list of "Free Persons of Colour above 16 years" in 1813 [PPTL, 1800-15].
    ii. Robert, born say 1788, taxable in James City County from 1809 to 1814, a "col^d man" counted with a male and a female in a list of "Free Persons of Colour above 16 years" in James City County in 1813 [PPTL, 1800-15].
    iii. Kitty, counted in the list of "Free Persons of Colour above 16 years" in James City County in 1813 [PPTL, 1800-15].

17. John^6 Cumbo, born say 1771, was taxable in Charles City County from 1792 to 1814: a "Mulattoe" taxable in 1813 and 1814 [PPTL, 1788-1814] and head of a Charles City County household of 4 "other free" in 1810 [VA:958]. He may have been the John Comboe who married Sally Delaney, 10 August 1797 York County bond. John was the father of

    i.   Thomas, born about 1814, obtained a certificate of freedom in Charles City County on 20 August 1835: *son of John Cumbo, mulatto man, straight hair, almost twenty one years old* [Minutes 1830-7, 244].

18. Anderson Cumbo, born about 1773, was taxable in Charles City County from 1792 to 1812 and was counted as a "Mulattoe" in 1813 [PPTL, 1788-1814]. He obtained a certificate of freedom in Charles City County on 18 September 1823: *a mulatto man aged fifty years, five feet seven & 1/2 inches high, much pitted with the smallpox, was born in this county* [Minutes 1823-9, 8]. He was head of a Charles City County household of 6 "other free" in 1810 [VA:958]. He was the father of

    i.   John^9, born about 1807, obtained a certificate of freedom in Charles City County on 21 July 1831: *son of Anderson Cumbo, a bright mulatto man, about twenty four years old, is a free man of colour* [Minutes 1830-7, 65].
    ii. Warren, born 4 August 1810, obtained a certificate of freedom in Charles City County on 17 November 1831: *son of Anderson Cumbo, a bright mulatto, twenty one years old 4 August last* [Minutes 1830-7, 84].
    iii. Stanhope, born about 1815, obtained a certificate of freedom in Charles City County on 20 August 1835: *son of Anderson Cumbo, mulatto man, twenty years old* [Minutes 1830-7, 244].

CUNNINGHAM FAMILY

1. Mary Cunningham, born say 1730, was living at John Kinsman's on 13 November 1750 when the Charles County, Maryland court presented her for

bearing a "Mullatto Child" by information of Constable Alexander MacPherson [Court Record 1750, 140]. She may have been the ancestor of

    i. Waters, a "Mulatto" child bound apprentice to John Williams in Frederick County, Virginia, on 9 March 1753 [Orders 1751-3, 449].

    ii. John, head of a Washington County, Maryland household of 3 "other free" in 1800 [MD:570].

    iii. Benjamin[1], head of a Hampshire County, Virginia household of 10 "other free" in 1810 [VA:818].

    iv. Philip[1], head of a King George County, Virginia household of 8 "other free" in 1810 [VA:193].

    v. Benjamin[2], head of a King George County household of 5 "other free" in 1810 [VA:193].

    vi. Cyrus, born about 1777 when he was bound as an apprentice, registered in King George County on 28 May 1799: *of a dark yellow Colour aged about twenty two years and about five feet ten inches high is now a free man, has served William Hooe, Gent., of this County twenty one years* [Register of Free Persons, no.10].

    vii. Philip[2], Jr., head of a King George County household of 2 "other free" in 1810 [VA:195].

    viii. Nancy, head of a Goochland County household of 5 "other free" in 1810 [VA:688].

    ix. Jas.(?), head of a King George County household of 1 "other free" in 1810 [VA:195].

    x. Charity, head of a Northampton County, North Carolina household of 2 "other free" in 1790 [NC:76].

CURLE FAMILY

Members of the Curle family of North Carolina and Virginia were

    i. William, head of a Petersburg Town household of 9 "other free" and 2 slaves in 1810 [VA:119b].

    ii. Susan, head of a Petersburg Town household of 9 "other free" in 1810 [VA:125a].

1   iii. Nancy, born say 1765.

1. Nancy Curle, born say 1765, was living in Gates County, North Carolina, in May 1791 when the court ordered her four-year-old "Molatto" son Bryant Curle bound apprentice to Aaron Ellis. She was the mother of

    i. Noah, born about 1783, eight-year-old illegitimate child of Nancy Curle, no race indicated, bound apprentice to Michael Lawrence by the August 1791 Gates County court.

    ii. Bryant, born about 1787, bound apprentice in May 1791 [Fouts, *Minutes of County Court of Pleas and Quarter Sessions 1787-93*, 84, 84, 90].

CURTIS FAMILY

The Curtis family may have originated in St. Mary's County, Maryland, where there were five "other free" families in 1790. (See *Free African Americans of Maryland and Delaware* by this author). Jonathan Curtis was a "Free Negro" living in Spotsylvania County, Virginia, in June 1744. He was called "Jonathan Curtis late of Charles County, Planter," in March 1749/50 in Charles County, Maryland court when William Hunter and Company of Spotsylvania County sued him for debt, and he was called a "free Negroe" in Hunter's accounts which were copied into the court record. He may have been the father of Ignatius Curtis whose "Mulatto" son Henry was bound out in Fauquier County, Virginia, in 1769.

Members of the Curtis family in Virginia and North Carolina were

1   i.   Jonathan¹, born say 1715.
2   ii.   Richard, born say 1730.
3   iii.   Jonathan², born say 1755.
      iv.   James², born say 1755, an apprentice boy who ran away from William Row before 1 August 1771 when Row advertised for his return in the *Virginia Gazette*: *yellow complexion, has a sharp nose, and wears his own short hair* [*Virginia Gazette* (Rind edition)].
      v.   Chloe, a "free Negro" head of a Culpeper County household of 5 "other free" in 1810 [VA:24].

1.   Jonathan¹ Curtis, born say 1715, was indicted by the Spotsylvania County, Virginia court on 5 June 1744 (along with five other persons) for selling liquor without a license. He was called a "Free Negro" on 6 November 1744 when the court ordered him to post bond of twenty pounds for his good behavior because John Doncastle complained that he had broken open some of his locks. Doncastle sued him for a 1 pound, 9 shillings debt on 6 February 1744/5, but the court found in Jonathan's favor [Orders 1738-49, 265, 286, 308, 322, 335]. He was called "Jonathan Curtis late of Charles County, Planter," in March 1749/50 in Charles County, Maryland court when William Hunter and Company of Spotsylvania County sued him for a debt of 10 pounds, 12 shillings Maryland currency. He was called a "free Negroe" in Hunter's accounts which were copied into the court record. The accounts were from October 1746 to 18 November 1747 and included a pocket book, shoes, rum, cloth, sheeting, buttons, thread, handkerchiefs, and a padlock. Samuel Luckett was Jonathan's security [Charles County court Records 1748-50, 630-2]. He was also sued by William Hunter in Spotsylvania County court in July 1749, but the case was dismissed [Orders 1748-50, 521]. Jonathan may have been the father of

4   i.   Ignatius, born say 1737.

2.   Richard Curtis, born say 1730, received a patent for 158 acres in Onslow County, North Carolina, on 26 September 1751 [Hoffman, *Land Patents*, I:254]. He and his wife were "free Negro" taxables in Beaufort County in 1755 [SS 837]. On 9 November 1764 he received a patent for 400 acres in Beaufort County on the north side of the Bay River between Chapel Creek and Raccoon Creek and on the side of Whitehouse's Creek [Hoffman, *Land Patents*, I:519]. He was listed in the Beaufort County militia under command of Colonel William Brown prior to 1765 [Clark, *Colonial Soldiers of the South*, 782]. He was counted as white in 1764 with his son James (Cortis Richd & Son James) [SS 837]. His wife may have been Mary Cirtis who received land on Raccoon Creek by the 23 April 1773 Beaufort County will of her father James **Muckelroy**. Richard's children were
      i.   James¹, born say 1748, perhaps the husband of Ann Curtis, head of a Beaufort County household of 6 "other free" in 1790 [NC:125].
      ii.   ?John, taxed on an assessment of 247 pounds in Beaufort County in 1779 [LP.30.1 by *NCGSJ* XV:145]. His 3 August 1791 Beaufort County will loaned his wife Mary his plantation which was to go to his daughter Easter after her death and gave his son David 100 acres on Raccoon Creek. His son David and Adam **Mackelroy** were executors. James **Mackelroy** was a witness [Original at Archives].
      iii.   ?George, born say 1760, married Casiah **Johnston**, 20 May 1783 Craven County bond with George **Ransom** bondsman.[86]

3.   Jonathan² Curtis, born say 1755, was a "Mulatto" head of household in Buxton's list for Nansemond County in 1784 [VA:74], taxable on a tithe and

---

[86]George **Ransom** was head of a Craven County household of 5 "other free" in 1790 [NC:134].

a horse in Petersburg in 1799 [1799 PPTL B, p.3] and head of a Petersburg household of 9 "other free" and a slave in 1810 [VA:117b]. He may have been the father of

    i.   Simon, born about 1776, taxable in Petersburg on a slave and a horse in 1799 [PPTL B, p.3], registered in Petersburg on 16 August 1800: *a dark brown Mulatto man, five feet eleven inches high, twenty four years old, born free & raised in Nansemond County* [Register of Free Negroes 1794-1819, no. 185].

    ii. Isham, born about 1781, registered in Petersburg on 12 November 1801: *a dark brown Mulatto man, five feet ten inches high, short bushy hair, twenty years old, born free in Nansemond County* [Register of Free Negroes 1794-1819, no. 218].

4.   Ignatius Curtis, born say 1737, was a "free Negro" taken before the Spotsylvania County court on 21 March 1757 and accused of breaking open the storehouse of John Spotswood, Esq., and stealing several pieces of cloth. He was sent for further trial at the General Court [Orders 1755-65, 65]. He was called a "Criminal Free Negro" on 11 October 1759 when the sheriff of Henrico County was paid for putting him in jail [Orders 1755-62, 379-80]. He was living in Fauquier County on 28 August 1769 when the court bound out his "Mulatto" son Henry as an apprentice carpenter to George Henry [Minutes 1768-73, 132]. He was the father of

5   i.   Henry¹, born say 1760.
6   ii. ?Ann, born say 1770.

5.   Henry¹ Curtis, born say 1760, a "Mulatto," was ordered bound to George Henry as an apprentice carpenter by the Fauquier County court on 28 August 1769. He was called "Harry, a Mulatto" on 25 September 1769 when he complained to the court about George Henry [Minutes 1768-73, 132, 141]. He was taxed in Caswell County, North Carolina, in 1790 [NC:79], and was head of a Person County household of 4 "other free" in 1800 [NC:596] and 2 in Caswell County in 1810 [NC:468]. In 1797 he was one of the freeholders of Person County who were ordered to work on the road from the Caswell County line to Hyco. He was sued for a 27 pound debt in the June 1799 Person County court and was again ordered to work on a Person County road in June 1802 [Minutes 1797-1802, 17, 132, 350]. He was bondsman for the 18 May 1807 Caswell County marriage bond of Jesse **Hood** to Polly **Sawyer**. He (or perhaps Henry, Jr.) purchased two tracts in Person County on the waters of the South Hyco Creek on 3 March 1816, one of 41-1/2 acres and the other 40 acres [Deeds p.471]. This was land on the border of Caswell and Person Counties. He may have been the father of

    i.   Henry² Jr., born say 1785, head of a Caswell County household of 8 "other free" in 1810 [NC:468].

    ii. James J., head of a Caswell County household of 6 "other free" in 1810 [NC:468] and 8 "free colored" in 1820 [NC:50]. He married Nancey **Pendergrass** ("colored"), 19 February 1800 Person County bond with Byrd Rogers bondsman.

    iii. Elizabeth, born say 1780, married Richard **Pendergrass**, 6 December 1798 Person County bond, Richard **Pendergrass** (Sr.?) bondsman.

6.   Ann Curtis, born say 1770, was the wife of Austin Curtis **Jones** of Halifax County, North Carolina. He was called "Austin Curtis a Mulatto Slave belonging to Willie Jones" when the North Carolina General Assembly approved his manumission [Byrd, *In Full Force and Virtue*, 4]. He was the former servant of Willie Jones, Sr., who received $200 by Willie's 22 February 1798 Halifax County will, proved August 1801 [WB 3:355]. He may have been the "Austin" who was head of a Halifax County household of 6 "other free" in 1800 [NC:289]. He purchased 165 acres on Red Hill branch

of Quankey Creek in Halifax County for $600 on 19 August 1803 and another 145 acres nearby for $300 on 21 March 1808 [DB 19:147, 207]. In his 3 December 1808 Halifax County will, proved February 1809, Austin left 330 acres to his wife Nancy Curtis **Jones** and nine of his children who were free and mentioned his son William, whose freedom he had recently given him [WB 3:484]. His free children were probably children of Ann Curtis. She was called Ann Curtis **Jones** on 19 August 1810 when she received title to 110 acres on Quankey Creek adjoining John Hawson, her third part of the land mentioned in her husband's will. In November 1826 her children were called by the name Curtis when Henry, Joseph, Patsy, and Lucy sold their share of their father's land, and Betsy, Fanny, and Jackey divided the remainder [DB 21:469; 27:218]. Ann Curtis was head of a Halifax County household of 7 "other free" and 6 slaves in 1810 [NC:13], and 8 "free colored" in 1830 (born 1776-94). She was probably related to Lucy **Murray** who mentioned Fanny Curtis and Patsy **Jones**, mother of William **Jones**, in her 15 November 1815 Halifax County will [WB 3:587]. Austin Curtis **Jones**' children were

    i.   Henry[3].
    ii. Lucy **Bell**, whose husband, by her father's will, was to receive no part of her inheritance. He was probably Zadock **Bell**, head of a Halifax County household of 5 "other free" in 1800 [NC:290] and 5 in 1810 [NC:7].
    iii. Patsy.
    iv. Elizabeth.
    v. Joseph.
    vi. Frances.
    vii. Jacky.
    viii. Matilda.
    ix. Austin[2].
    x. William.

Other members of the Curtis family in Halifax County were

    i.   Rachel, born before 1776, head of a Halifax County household of 3 "free colored" in 1830.
    ii. Mary, born 1794-1806, head of a Halifax County household of 7 "free colored" in 1830.
    iii. Margaret, bound apprentice to Henry Curtis by order of the 17 November 1840 Halifax County court. Henry may have been the H.W. Curtis, living in household no. 1847 in the 1860 Halifax County census: 44 years old, "Mulatto," $250 personal estate.
    iv. Mary, bound apprentice to Melvin **Dempsey** by order of the 17 November 1840 Halifax County court.

CUSTALOW FAMILY

1. John Castellaw, born say 1730, a white man, was taxable in Bertie County, North Carolina on Martha **Butler**, a "Free Mulatto Female" in 1761 and 1763 and taxable on her tithe in the lists for 1766 through 1772 [CR 10.702.1]. In June 1768 he was security in Bertie County court for the maintenance of Martha's illegitimate child [Haun, *Bertie County Court Minutes*, III:831]. She was apparently his common-law wife since in 1771 William Castellaw was taxed in the Bertie County list of Humphrey Nichols as a "free Molattoe," and in 1771 John made a deed of gift to "William Castellaw son of Martha Butler." The deed was proved in Bertie County by the oath of Arthur Williams who was probably the common-law husband of Martha's sister Elizabeth **Butler** [DB L:283; CR 10.702.1]. Martha was head of a Gates County household of 10 "free colored" in 1820 [NC:143]. Her children were

2   i. William Castellaw, born say 1755.
3   ii. ?Agnes Custalow, born say 1768.

2. William Castellaw, born say 1755, was a "free Molattoe" taxable in Bertie
    County in 1771. He may have been the father of
    i.   James Custalow, born say 1781, a "free Mulatto" taxable in the lower
         district of Henrico County in 1803 [Land Tax List, 1799-1816 (includes
         Personal Property Tax lists)] and head of a Richmond City household
         of 3 "other free" in 1810 [VA:373].
    ii. Reuben Custiloe, born say 1783, a "free negro" taxable in St. Martin's
         Parish, Hanover County, Virginia, in 1800, a "Mul." taxable there in
         1801 and 1803 [PPTL, 1792-1803, pp. 177, 199, 229, 252], a "FN"
         taxable in the upper district of Henrico County in 1804 and 1805 [Land
         Tax List, 1799-1816].

3. Agnes Custalow, born say 1768, may have been the illegitimate child born to
    Martha **Butler** in Bertie County in 1768. She was a charter member of Lower
    College Baptist Church in King William County, Virginia, on the "coloured"
    roll" from 1791 [Colosse Baptist Church Minute Book, 1813-1834 cited by
    Rountree, *Pocahontas's People*, 342]. She may have been the mother of
    i.   Jack, born about 1790, a sixty-year-old "Black" man counted in the
         1850 King William County, Virginia census with thirty-nine-year-old
         "Black" woman Nancy [VA:243].
    ii. Caroline, born about 1790, a sixty-year-old "Mulatto" woman counted
         in the 1850 King William County, Virginia census [VA:243].

CUTTILLO FAMILY

1. Katherine Jewell, born about 1639, was the mother of a "Malato" boy William
    who was bound apprentice to William Boosh for thirty years in York County,
    Virginia, on 6 March 1670/1. By the terms of the indenture Boosh was
    required to give William a heifer when he reached the age of fourteen.
    Fourteen years later on 24 March 1684/5 Boosh confirmed in York County
    court that he had marked a heifer which William was to receive with its
    increase when he completed his indenture [DOW 7:61]. Katherine may have
    married Stephen Pond, a white man. Sixty-year-old Katherine Pond and her
    thirty-year-old daughter Mary Catilla made depositions in York County on 14
    December 1699 concerning Jane Merry's nuncupative will. Stephen Pond was
    one of the securities for administration of the will. Mary was probably
    identical to Mary Jewell, "a mollotto" whose fine for having an illegitimate
    child was paid by Stephen Pond on 24 May 1694 [DWO 9:341; 11:269-70,
    287; Richter, *A Community and its Neighborhoods*, 343]. She was the mother
    of
2   i.   Mary[1], born about 1669.
3   ii. William[1], born before 6 March 1670/1.
4   iii. Matthew[1], born say 1672.

2. Mary[1] Jewell/ Cattila, born about 1669, was called Mary Jewell, a "mollotto,"
    on 24 May 1694 when the churchwardens of the lower precincts of Poquoson
    Parish presented her for having a child by John Berry (a white man). Stephen
    Pond was security for her fine and for the maintenance of the child [DOW
    9:341]. She was called Mary Catilla, daughter of Katherine Pond, and was
    about thirty years old on 14 December 1699 when she made a deposition in
    York County court concerning Jane Merry's nuncupative will [DOW 11:269-
    70]. She was called Mary Qustilla on 20 May 1724 when the Elizabeth City
    County court excused her from paying levies [Orders 1723-9, 13]. Mary was
    the unmarried mother of several children born in Charles Parish, York County
    [Bell, *Charles Parish Registers*, 60-1]. Her children were
    i.   James Cattilla (**Berry**), born 16 September 1693, no father named in
         the register.

ii. Matthew[3] Cattilla, born 12 December 1700, no father named, apparently the illegitimate birth Mary was indicted for on 24 February 1700/1 [DOW 11:400, 444], perhaps the Matthew Cattila whose death (13 November 1748) was registered in Charles Parish.

iii. Catherine Cattilla, born 1 November 17(03) in Elizabeth City County, no father named, died 7 November 1718.

iv. Ann[1] Cattilla, born 31 March 1710, daughter of Mary Cattilla by Christopher Robinson [Bell, *Charles Parish Registers*, 60-1, 207].

3. William[1] Catillah, born before 6 March 1670/1, sued his mistress, Mrs. Margaret Booth, for his freedom in York County court on 6 April 1695, swearing that he was born of a free woman, was a baptized Christian, and had served his mistress to the full age of twenty-four years. The 24 May 1695 session of the court ordered her to release him and pay him his freedom dues. He was sued for debt by Stephen Pond on 24 February 1701/2 [DOW 10:137, 153; 12:553]. He gave evidence in Elizabeth City County court for Joshua Myhill in his suit against John **Sampson** on 20 January 1725/6 [Orders 1723-9, 148]. He and his wife Ann registered the birth and baptism of their children in Charles Parish, York County. In April 1725 the Elizabeth City County court granted Anne's petition to be levy free [Orders 1723-9, 94]. She may have been the Ann Cattilla whose death on 13 October 1729 was recorded in the Charles Parish Register [Bell, *Charles Parish Registers*, 207]. On 16 February 1729/30 he confessed to the York County court that his daughter Judith had delivered an illegitimate child in his house, and the court fined him for failing to give notice of the fact to the churchwardens. When he failed to give security for payment of the fine, the court ordered that he receive twenty-five lashes [DOW 17:29]. William and Ann's children were

5 i. Judith, born 20 December 17(03).

ii. William[2], baptized 12 April 1702, perhaps the William Cattilla who was married to Hannah on 10 December 1726 when their daughter Angelica was born [Bell, *Charles Parish Registers*, 60, 61]. He was called William Qustilla, Jr., on 20 May 1725 when the Elizabeth City County court dismissed a suit brought against him by John **Sampson** [Orders 1723-9, 103].

4. Matthew[1] Cattilla, born say 1669, was a witness for John Pond in his suit against Francis Callohill in York County court in January 1694/5. He owed money to the estate of Samuel Mackentosh in February 1697/8 [DOW 10:141, 514]. He and his wife Mary had two children whose births were recorded in the Charles Parish Register of York County. His death was recorded there on 15 March 1700 and Mary's death was recorded on 10 December 1703 [Bell, *Charles Parish Registers*, 61, 207]. Their children were

6 i. Edward[1], born 8 September 1693.

7 ii. Matthew[2], born 2 September 1697.

5. Judith Cuttillo, born 20 December 17(03), daughter of William and Ann Cattilla, was charged in York County on 15 December 1729 with bearing an illegitimate "mulatto" child [Bell, *Charles Parish Registers*, 61; DOW 17:12]. She may have been the mother of

8 i. Edward[3], born say 1729.

6. Edward[1] Cuttillo, born 8 September 1693, was married to Elizabeth on 26 June 1720 when their son Matthew was baptized in Charles Parish, York County [Bell, *Charles Parish Registers*, 61]. He was residing in Elizabeth City County on 1 October 1750 when he purchased for 20 pounds 293 acres in Lunenburg County bounded by Bears Element Creek [DB 2:117]. His suit against William Parsons, Jr., in Elizabeth City County court for trespass was dismissed on agreement of both parties on 2 June 1752 [Orders 1747-55, 258,

280]. In 1752 he was taxable in the Lunenburg County list of Richard Witton with (his sons) Matt. and Abrm. Cuttillo, and with Jas. Lowman [1748-52 Tithables]. In July 1761 the Lunenburg County court exempted him from paying personal tax [Orders 1761-2, 81]. The vestry of Cumberland Parish in Lunenburg County paid for the upkeep of his son William between 1 November 1762 and 11 November 1784 and for (his wife?) Elizabeth Cuttillo on 8 January 1784 [Bell, *Cumberland Parish*, 385, 415, 450, 456]. He sold 171-1/2 acres in Lunenburg County on Bears Element Creek to (his son) Abraham Cuttillo on 11 February 1779 [DB 13:185]. His 1 July 1771 Lunenburg County will, proved 11 April 1783, left his land to his son Abraham, mentioned his son William and mentioned his unnamed wife [WB 3:134]. His wife (apparently his second) was Elizabeth, daughter of John **Epps** according to the 1798 Lunenburg County chancery suit which settled the estate of John **Epps**. Edward was the father of

  i.   Matthew[4], born 30 May, baptized 26 June 1720 in Charles Parish [Bell, *Charles Parish Registers*, 61], made a 25 March 1754 Lunenburg County will, proved 3 September the same year, naming his wife Lucy and her unborn child, his brother Abraham Cuttillo, and his father Edward Cuttiller. He also mentioned but did not state his relationship to John Cuttiller, Edward Cuttiller, and Isaac Brown [WB 1:135]. Lucy and her brother Isaac Brown were named in the 22 August 1757 Lunenburg County will of their father Israel Brown [WB 2:21] (who was named in the 10 April 1727 Charles City County will of Edward **Gibson** [DW 1724-31, 167-8]). Lucy rented 200 acres in Lunenburg County on Flat Rock Creek from Isaac Brown during her life for an unstated amount on 12 November 1767 [DB 11:104]. She was a widow, taxable on 200 acres in Cumberland Parish of Lunenburg County in 1764 and 1769 [Bell, *Sunlight on the Southside*, 229, 273].

  ii. Elizabeth[1], born 31 March, baptized 23 May 1725 in Charles Parish [Bell, *Charles Parish Registers*, 61].

  iii. ?John, born say 1730, tithable "at Mr. Kerby's Quarter" in Lunenburg County in 1751 [Bell, *Sunlight on the Southside*, 173]. He and his two slaves were among the male tithables ordered to work on a road in Lunenburg County in June 1754 [Orders 1753-4, 110].

9 iv. Abraham[2], born say 1733.

  v.   William[3], born say 1749, perhaps an invalid, supported by the vestry of Cumberland Parish between 1 November 1762 and 11 November 1784 [Bell, *Cumberland Parish*, 385, 415, 456].

7. Matthew[2] Cattiler, born 2 September 1697, and his wife Judith baptized their children in Charles Parish, York County. Judith died 10 December 1735. He had married, second, Sarah, by 6 January 1737/8 when their son John was born [Bell, *Charles Parish Registers*, 60, 61, 207]. On 17 November 1740 he was presented by the York County court for not listing his "Mallatto" wife as a tithable, and he was called a "Molatto" on 19 June 1744 when he was presented for the same offence [W&I 18:667; 19:314, 332]. Perhaps Sarah's maiden name was **Combs** since Sarah's daughter Martha lived in Thomas **Combs'** household in 1763. Matthew died 13 November 1748 [Bell, *Charles Parish Registers*, 207]. On 19 November 1750 Sarah was presented by the York County court for failing to list herself and Ann **Berry** as tithables. The case was dismissed after she paid the levies and court costs. She was presented again on 18 May 1752 for not listing herself as a tithable and fined 1,000 pounds of tobacco [Judgments & Orders 1746-52, 364, 384, 393; 1752-4, 18, 58-9]. Matthew and Judith had

  i.   Edward[2], born 11 December, baptized 11 January 1724, died 6 November 1748 ("Edward Catilla, son of Matthew").

  ii. Sarah, born 20 September, baptized 29 October 1727.

10 iii. Abraham[1], born 18 March 1729/30.

iv. Matthew[5], born 20 September, baptized "private" 5 November 1732.
v. Rachel, born 18 January, baptized 16 February 1734 [Bell, *Charles Parish Registers*, 60, 61, 207].

Matthew and (his second wife) Sarah had
vi. John[1], born 6 January baptized 12 March 1737/8.
vii. Frances, born 15 March, baptized 27 March 1740/1.
viii. Martha, born 9 November 1743, baptized 8 January 1743/4, mother of Nancy, born __ September, baptized 12 October 1766, "bastard child of Martha Cattillow." She was a tithable in Thomas **Combs**' household in 1763. The York County court presented her on 21 May 1764 for having a bastard child and fined her 500 pounds of tobacco [Judgments & Orders 1763-5, 186, 254].
ix. William[4], born 14 September, baptized 21 September 1746.
x. Mary[2], born 22 October 1747, baptized 22 November 1747 [Bell, *Charles Parish Registers*, 61].

8. Edward[3] Cuttillo/ Cottillin, born say 1729, was married to Anne (**Berry**?) on 3 March 1771 when they recorded the birth and baptism of their daughter Ann and son John **Berry** Cottillow in Charles Parish, York County [Bell, *Charles Parish Registers*, 61, 72]. Edward's wife Anne may have been identical to the Ann **Berry** who was living in Sarah Cuttillo's household on 19 November 1750 when Sarah was presented by the court for failing to list her as a tithable. And she may have been the Ann Cottiler who was paid for attending three days as a witness for Frazier on 2 March 1762 in the Elizabeth City County suit of Armistead vs. Frazier et uxor [Court Records 1760-9, 66]. The vestry of Elizabeth City Parish paid Edward for boarding "Old" James **Berry** in 1765 [von Doenhoff, *Vestry Book of Elizabeth City Parish*, 163]. He was taxable on a free tithe in York County in 1784, 2 tithes in 1789 and exempt from personal tax in 1790 [PPTL, 1782-1841, frames 87, 95, 140, 149, 161]. He was the father of

11 i. ?Abraham[3], born say 1760.
12 ii. ?Edward[4], born say 1763.
iii. ?James[2], born say 1767, taxable in York County from 1790 to 1801 [PPTL, 1782-1841], perhaps the James Critillow who was taxable in Lunenburg County in 1804 and 1806 [PPTL 1782-1806].
iv. Anne[3], born 4 August 1770, baptized 3 March 1771.
v. John **Berry**, born 27 October 1773, baptized 23 January 1774 [Bell, *Charles Parish Registers*, 61], taxable in York County from 1794 to 1801 [PPTL, 1782-1814].

9. Abraham[2] Cuttillo, born say 1733, was taxable in the Lunenburg County household of (his father) Edward Cuttillo in 1752 [1748-52 Tithables]. He was witness to a Lunenburg County deed for land on Flat Rock Creek, bounded by John **Evans**, which James and Mary Loman sold on 12 October 1769 [DB 11:303]. In 1774 John **Drew** was taxable in his Lunenburg County household [Bell, *Sunlight on the Southside*, 330]. He purchased 171-1/2 acres in Lunenburg County on Bears Element Creek from (his father) Edward Cuttillo on 11 February 1779 [DB 13:185]. He was taxable in Lunenburg County on a slave over sixteen years of age named Suck, 4 slaves under 16, and 12 horses in 1782 and taxable on 3 slaves under 16, 9 horses and a head of cattle in 1785 [PPTL 1782-1841]. His 7 March 1790 Lunenburg County will named his wife Sarah as executrix and named his sons: John, Abraham, and Edward, and his daughters: Mary, Sally, Jane Lowman, and Betsy Cuttillo, who were to receive their share of his estate when they came of age. Mary Loman was a witness to the will [WB 3:365]. His children were
i. John[2], born say 1778, taxable in Lunenburg County from 1799 to 1804 [PPTL 1782-1806], head of a household in the Lunenburg County "List

of Free Negroes and Mulattoes" in 1802 [Lunenburg County Free Negro and Slave Records, 1802-3, LVA], a taxable "FN" in Halifax County in 1812 [PPTL, 1800-12, frame 1023].

ii.   Abraham[4], a "FN" taxable in Halifax County, Virginia, in 1812 [PPTL, 1800-12, frame 1023].

iii. Mary[3].

iv.   Sally/ Sary, married Thomas **Stewart**, 15 July 1800 Mecklenburg County bond, Richerson Farrar bondsman, or perhaps she was the Sally Curtiller who was listed as a "FN" over the age of sixteen in Halifax County in 1813 [Waldrep, *1813 Tax List*].

v.   Jance Loman, probably the daughter of James and Mary Lowman who sold 100 acres on Flat Rock Creek on 12 October 1769 [DB 11:303].

vi.   Elizabeth[2], married John **Epps**.

vii. Edward[4], a taxable "FN" in Halifax County in 1812 [PPTL, 1800-12, frame 1023].

10. Abraham[1] Cuttillo, born 18 March 1729/30, was baptized on 3 May 1730 in Charles Parish, York County. He and his wife Mary baptized their daughter Ann in Charles Parish on 25 April 1750. Mary, "wife of Abraham Cattilla," died 3 May 1750 [Bell, *Charles Parish Registers*, 60, 207]. Their child was

i.   Ann[2], born 26 March baptized 25 April 1750, perhaps the Nanny Cotillo who was listed in the account of Edward **Berry**'s York County estate in October 1790 [WI 23:450-2] and the Ann Cottillo who was taxable on a horse in York County in 1791 [PPTL, 1788-1814].

11. Abraham[3] Cuttillo, born say 1760, married Mary **Francis**, 10 November 1787 York County bond, Robert **Gillett** bondsman. In July 1791 they sold 16 acres in Elizabeth City County that Mary had inherited from her great-grandmother Hannah **Francis** [Deeds & Wills 34:118]. He was taxable in York County from 1784 to 1814 and head of a household of 5 "free Negroes & Mulattoes over the age of 16," one of whom was tithable in 1813 [PPTL, 1782-1814, frames 76, 95, 104, 149, 161, 200, 244, 285, 326, 352, 363, 387] and was head of a York County household of 6 "other free" in 1810 [VA:873]. He died before 1815 when his estate was taxable on a horse and 11 cattle [PPTL, 1782-1841, frame 421]. On 21 May 1838 Henry Buchanan, aged seventy-seven, of York County, deposed that Abraham Cottier, a "free man of color" from York County, enlisted in the Revolution in 1779, served at the Battle of Yorktown, and died about thirty years previous leaving children: Nancy Cottiler, Betsy Cottiller (wife of, first, John **Francis**, then James **Wallace**), and John Cottiller [Hopkins, *Virginia Revolutionary War Land Grant Claims*, 58]. He was the father of

i.   Nancy, perhaps the Nancy Cotillo who was head of a Warwick County household of 2 "free colored" in 1830.

ii.   Betsy, married John **Francis**, 25 January 1816 York County bond, the age of the bride attested to by Edward Cottiler. She married, second, Robert **Wallis/ Wallace**, 25 August 1838 bond, John **Wallis** bondsman.

iii. John[3], born about 1792, taxable in York County in 1814 [PPTL, 1782-1841, frame 404], registered in York County on 20 February 1815: *a bright Mulatto about 22 or 23 years of age 5 feet 6-3/4 Inches high - has very black fierce Eyes & long bushy hair* [Free Negro Register 1798-1831, no.84].

12. Edward[4] Cuttillo, born say 1763, was called Edward Jr., when he was first taxable in York County in 1785 [PPTL, 1782-1841, frame 95]. He married Elizabeth **Berry**, widow of Edward **Berry**, before 21 December 1791 when she returned the account of Edward **Berry**'s estate in York County court [WI 23:450-2]. He was taxable on a slave in York County from 1791 to 1819 and head of a household of 4 "free Negroes & Mulattoes over the age of 16," two

of whom were tithable in 1813 [PPTL, 1782-1814, frames 387, 404, 420, 468]. He was one of the inhabitants of York, Warwick, and Elizabeth City who signed a 19 November 1796 petition to the House of Delegates to establish a landing where Rose Warehouse formerly stood on Charles River near Charles Church (signing Edwd Cottilo) [*Magazine of Virginia Genealogy* 34:147]. He was bondsman for the 20 December 1799 York County marriage of Thomas **Eppes Hobson** and Martha **Hobson**. He was head of a York County household of 7 "other free" in 1810 [VA:872]. He was the father of

    i.   Mary, born say 1804, of Charles Parish, York County, married John **Hopson** ("Free Black"), 10 September 1822 marriage with the consent of her father Edward.

Other members of the Cuttillo family were

    i.   John Cotillo, born 1775-1794, head of a Person County, North Carolina household of 1 "free colored" in 1820 [NC:498].

    ii. Holland, born about 1806, registered as a "Free Negro" in York County on 19 September 1831: *a woman of very bright complexion, 5 feet 5-1/4 inches high about 25 years of age...long strait dark hair, grey eyes* [Free Negroes Register 1831-50, no.294].

CYPRESS FAMILY

1.   Tom^1 Cyprus, born say 1707, was listed among the "Negros &c At the Home House" in the 15 July 1728 inventory of the Surry County, Virginia estate of Nathaniel Harrison, Esq. [DW 1715-30, 843]. He may have been the husband of Judith Cypress who was described as an Indian when her children Tom and Frank Cypress were bound apprentices by the churchwardens of Southwarke Parish in Surry County on 16 April 1754 [Orders 1753-57, 64]. Judith was the mother of

2   i.   ?Eleanor, born say 1742.
3   ii. Thomas^2, born say 1748.
4   iii. Frank, born say 1750.

2.   Eleanor Cypress, born say 1742, was the mother of William Cyprus--called "Son of Eleoner Cyprus" when he was bound out in Surry County on 15 July 1766 and called a "poor Mulatto Boy" when he was bound out on 24 June 1772 [Orders 1764-74, 90, 310]. She was the mother of

5   i.   William^1, born say 1762.

3.   Thomas^2 Cypress, born say 1748, was bound apprentice in Surry County in 1754, and bound apprentice to Henry Deloney in Lunenburg County in November 1760 [Orders 1759-61, 191]. He was taxable in his own household in Mecklenburg County in 1783 [Personal Tax List, 1782-1805, frame 48]. William Rainey sued him in court on 10 Nov ember 1795, but the case was discontinued on agreement of the parties [Orders 1792-5, 517]. He was security for the 27 July 1801 Mecklenburg County marriage of John **Chavous** and Sally **Blair**. He may have been the father of

    i.   William^2, head of a Mecklenburg County household of 8 "free colored" in 1820, married Polly **Thomas**, 1816 Mecklenburg County bond. His widow and eight children are mentioned in a Mecklenburg County chancery case settled in 1846 [LVA, 1846-012].

4.   Frank Cypress, born say 1750, was bound apprentice in Surry County in 1754, bound apprentice to Henry Deloney in Lunenburg County in November 1760 [Orders 1759-61, 191] and listed in the Surry County account of the estate of Dr. Patrick Adams in 1771 [WB 12:248]. On 27 August 1782 the Surry

County court ordered Francis's son Zachariah bound out [Orders 1775-85, 160, 332]. Frank was the parent of

    i.   Zachariah, born say 1769, listed as Henry Gilbert's Surry County tithe in 1789 and 1790 [PPTL, 1782-90, frames 525, 572]. He was probably identical to Sacky Cypress who married John **Jones**, 12 February 1807 Sussex County marriage [Marriage Returns, 283].

    ii.   ?John, born about 1771, charged in the Court of Oyer & Terminer in Sussex County on 15 September 1798 with stealing a horse belonging to William Welborne of Sussex and selling it to Augustine Carseley. Carseley testified that he had checked with his brother, Hartwell Carseley, as to John Cyprus' character before purchasing the horse, but his brother assured him that Cyprus had "a pretty good" character when he had known him in Petersburg [Haun, *Sussex County Court Records*, 60-2]. He registered in Petersburg on 18 August 1794: *a brown Mulatto man, five feet six inches high, twenty three years old, born free in the County of Surry* [Register of Free Negroes 1794-1819, no. 18]. He was a "F.N." taxable in the upper district of Henrico County from 1803 to 1805 [Land Tax List, 1799-1816 (includes Personal Property Tax lists)] and head of a Norfolk County household of 2 "other free" and 4 slaves in 1810 [VA:799].

5.   William¹ Cypress, born say 1762, was bound out in Surry County on 15 July 1766 and was called a "poor Mulatto Boy" when the court ordered him bound out on 24 June 1772 [Orders 1764-74, 80, 310]. He married Rebecca **Walden**, daughter of William **Walden**, 30 December 1785 Surry County bond. He was taxable in Cabin Point district of Surry County from 1786 to 1795: taxable on slave Agga in 1787, taxable on slave Nanny in 1788, charged with Charles **Andrews**' tithe in 1789, charged with William **Charity**'s tax in 1793, William **Gilchrist**'s in 1794 and 1795. (His widow) Rebecca Cypress was taxable on a horse in 1797 and 1798 and taxable on a free male from 1806 to 1816: listed with 2 "free Negroes & Mulattoes above the age of 16" in 1813 [PPTL, 1782-90, frames 397, 450, 472, 548; 1791-1816, 7, 107, 158, 236, 256, 288, 611, 650, 733, 774, 851]. William's 18 January 1796 Surry County will, recorded 25 October the same year, mentioned his unnamed wife and children. Howell **Debereaux** was executor [WB 1:183]. Rebecca was head of a Surry County household of 5 "other free" in 1810 [VA:604]. William was the father of

    i.   David, born about 1785, taxable in Surry County from 1810 to 1816, a "free Negro & Mulatto" taxable in 1813 [PPTL, 1791-1816, frames 667, 706, 809, 851]. He married Elizabeth **Walden**, 28 July 1812 Surry County bond, Sillar **Walden** witness, David Sebrell surety, 6 August marriage. He registered in Surry County on 22 December 1831: *a bright mulatto man about 42 years of age, was born of free parents, is the son of Becky, has long bushy hair...5'5-1/4"* [Hudgins, *Surry County Register of Free Negroes*, 106].

    ii.   ?Hamblin, born say 1789, witness to the 23 March 1807 Surry County marriage of David Fulks and Sarah **Charity**, registered as a free Negro in Surry County on 22 July 1850: *aged 57 years and upwards, very bright complexion, 5 feet 9-1/4 inches high* [Register of Free Negroes, p.59, #1093].

    iii. ?Elizabeth, born say 1791, married John **Bruce**, 24 December 1812 Surry County bond, Benjamin **Banks** surety, Samuel **Blizzard** witness. Their son William **Bruce** registered in Surry County on 23 December 1842: *a mullatoe boy, son of Betsy Cypress...is a spare make, bushy hair...aged about 24 years and is 5'8-1/4" high* [Hudgins, *Surry County Register of Free Negroes*, 164].

    iv. ?James, born say 1795, married Rebecca **Bird**, 26 January 1818 Surry County bond, John **Charity** surety.

DALE/ DIAL FAMILY

1. Benjamin Dolls, born say 1620, "a Negro," was granted a patent for 300 acres in Surry County, Virginia, on the south side of the Reeded Marsh and the east side of Blackwater River adjoining Captain Jordan's line on 17 December 1656 for the importation of six persons [Patents 4:71-2]. On 26 December 1659 Judah Hide authorized him (called Benjamin Dawl) to act as her attorney, and on 19 July 1660 he witnessed a deed from William and Alice Lea to William Heath [Haun, *Surry County Court Records* I:146, 156]. He was probably the father of

2   i.   John¹, born say 1648.

2. John¹ Daule, born say 1648, and his wife Isabell were the "Negro" servants of Arthur Jordan on 10 March 1669 when they paid him to release them from any further service [Haun, *Surry County Court Records* I:146, 156]. John Doll purchased 162 acres in Newport Parish, Isle of Wight County, from John Sojourner sometime after 21 April 1689 [DB 7:217]. They may have been the ancestors of

3   i.   James¹ Doyal/ Dial, born say 1740.
4   ii. William Dales, born say 1743.

3. James¹ Doyal, born say 1740, purchased 100 acres near Ash Pole Swamp in Bladen County, North Carolina, on 19 July 1765 and sold this land on 20 February 1767 [DB 23:162]. He was taxable in Bladen County with his wife and Arthur **Evans** ("Mulatoes") in 1768 and taxable with his wife from 1769 to 1772 [Byrd, *Bladen County Tax Lists*, I:6, 15, 44, 61, 95]. He was granted land on the south side of Ash Pole Swamp in Bladen County on 23 October 1782 and was taxable in Bladen County on 100 acres in 1784 [DB 1:264; 1784 Tax List]. He was the father of

    i.   Tapley Dial, born before 1776, head of a Opelousas, Louisiana household of 6 "other free" in 1810 [LA:312] and 4 "free colored" in 1820 [LA:107]. He was called Tapley Dial "of North Carolina," son of James Dial and Elizabeth **Hill**, when he married Sarah **Johnson**, 24 January 1816 Opelousas, Louisiana marriage [License no.1].
    ii. ?Peter Dial, born before 1776, head of a Robeson County household of 6 "other free" in 1800 [NC:231], 6 in 1810 (Peter Deal) [NC:144] and 10 "free colored" in 1820 [NC:311], perhaps the father of Duncan Dial, head of a Robeson County household of 6 "free colored" in 1820 [NC:309].
    iii. ?Keziah Dial, born say 1775, married James **Ashworth** "of South Carolina" according to the 3 October 1810 Opelousas, Louisiana marriage license of their son Jesse **Ashworth** to Sarah **Perkins** [License nos.14, 17]. James **Ashworth** was head of an Opelousas household of 11 "other free" in 1810 [LA:306] and 6 "free colored" in 1820 [NC:101].

4. William Dales, born say 1743, and his wife Sarah sold 50 acres in Brunswick County, Virginia, on the south side of Fountain Creek on 14 July 1764 [DB 7:508]. He was sued for a two pound debt in Brunswick County in April 1765 [Orders 1765, 127]. He received a patent for 150 acres in Brunswick County on 14 July 1769 [Patents 38:658-9]. He and his wife Sarah and George Ledbetter and his wife Elizabeth sold 250 acres on Fountain Creek in Brunswick County on 8 November 1779 [DB 14:9]. He was called "father" of John Dale in Greensville County court on 25 July 1782 when they sued Julius Perry and Thomas Pair for trespass. He sold land by deed proved in Greensville County court on 23 October 1783 [Orders 1781-9, 40, 88]. He was head of a Northampton County, North Carolina household of 10 "other free"

in 1790 [NC:76] and 3 in Halifax County, North Carolina, in 1800 [NC:304]. He was the father of

 i. ?Mary Dole, born say 1767, married Andrew **Jeffries** of Greensville County, Virginia, according to the Greene County, Ohio, court suit of their grandson Parker Jeffries (son of Sally Jeffries) in 1841 [Parker Jeffries v. Ankeny].

 ii. John² Dale, head of a Halifax County household of 5 "other free" in 1800 [NC:304] and 4 in 1810 [NC:16].

 iii. ?Fanny Doles, head of a Halifax County household of 3 "other free" in 1810 [NC:17].

 iv. ?Bery Dale, head of a Rockingham County, North Carolina household of 5 "other free" in 1800 [NC:491].

 v. ?Charles Dale, head of a Rockingham County household of 3 "other free" in 1800 [NC:491].

Other members of the family were:

 i. Lucy Ann Deal, born in December 1819 in Brunswick County, North Carolina, of free parentage, was residing in Cumberland County, North Carolina, when the court issued her a certificate of freedom, describing her as: *a bright Mulatto about five feet three and one half inches high* [Minutes 1840-42, Wednesday, 9 September 1840].

DAVENPORT FAMILY

1. Ann Davenport, born say 1720, was living in Stratton Major Parish, King and Queen County, on 9 October 1738 when the churchwardens ordered her bastard children bound to Doctor John Strachey [Chamberlayne, *Vestry Book of Stratton Major Parish,* 33, 44, 59, 73, 119]. She was apparently the common-law wife of a slave or free African American since she had a number of "Mollatto" children bound out over a twenty year period. She was the mother of

 i. Amey, born say 1736, bound apprentice on 10 October 1744, head of a Williamsburg City household of 3 "Blacks" in 1782 [VA:46].

 ii. Anne, born say 1738, ordered bound apprentice to Dr. Strachey on 10 November 1741.

 iii. William¹, born say 1745, "Mollatto Baster'd of Ann Davonport," bound apprentice to Doctor John Strachey in Stratton Major Parish on 9 October 1747 [Chamberlayne, *Vestry Book of Stratton Major Parish,* 73].

 iv. George, born say 1753, ordered bound apprentice to Mary Strachey on 16 November 1757.

 v. Thomas, born say 1756, ordered bound apprentice to Thomas Metcalfe on 16 November 1757.

 vi. ?Stephen¹, a soldier in the Revolution from York County [Jackson, *Virginia Negro Soldiers,* 34].

Their descendants were

 i. William², born say 1771, married Elizabeth **Alvis**, 7 July 1796 York County bond. He was taxable in York County from 1792 to 1813: called a "Mulatto" in 1792, taxable on a slave in 1804 and 1809, and head of a household of 2 "free Negroes & mulattoes over 16" in 1813 [PPTL, 1782-1841, frames 182, 254, 276, 296, 315, 339, 364, 387]. He was taxable on 15 acres in 1800 [Land Tax List, p.2] and head of a York County household of 3 "other free" in 1810 [VA:873].

 ii. Henry, born say 1772, taxable in York County in 1793 and from 1801 to 1813 [PPTL, 1782-1841, frames 191, 264, 286, 305, 327, 353, 387] and head of a York County household of 6 "other free" in 1810 [VA:873].

iii. Stephen[2], born about 1778, registered as a free Negro in York County on 19 October 1802: *dark mulatto with woolly hair, large flat nose, wide mouth...5 feet 7 Inches high proved to be born of a free woman by the oath of John Crittenden* [Register 1798-1831, no.20]. He was taxable in York County from 1803 to 1813 [PPTL, 1782-1841, frames 286, 305, 327, 353, 387].

iv. Hannah, born about 1782, registered in York County on 16 December 1822: *a dark mulatto abut 40 years old, 4 feet 11-3/4 inches high - she has small feacears* (features)*...short woolly hair* [Register, no.187].

v. Anthony, born about 1785, head of a York County household of 5 "other free" in 1810 [VA:873]. He registered as a free Negro in York County on 20 January 1823: *a black fellow between 36 & 40 years of age 5 feet 11-1/2 Inches high has short hair, large whiskers...Born free* [Register 1798-1831, no. 201].

vi. Disy, born about 1789, registered in York County on 16 December 1822: *a Mulatto woman about 33 years of age...born free* [Register of Free Negroes 1798-1831, no. 148].

vii. John, born 1801, registered as a free Negro in York County on 17 October 1831: *a mulatto man about 30 years of age, 5 feet 10-1/2 inches high...large eyes & nose* [Free Negroes Register, no.322].

viii. Mary Ann, born about 1806, registered as a free Negro in York County on 17 October 1831: *dark complexion, about 24 or 25 years of age, 5 feet 5 inches high...large mouth, thick pouting lips & full head of hair* [Register, no.312].

DAVIS FAMILY

The Davis family may have descended from Hugh Davis who was ordered to be whipped "before an assembly of Negroes and others for abusing himself to the dishonor of God and shame of Christians, by defiling his body by lying with a negro" in 1630 [Hening, *Statutes at Large*, III:459-460].

1. Mary[1] Davis, born say 1700, was living in Surry County, Virginia, on 22 April 1742 when her daughters Mary and Isabella (no race indicated) appealed to the court that Richard Parker was detaining them as servants. The court ruled that they were free women and should be discharged from any further servitude. The same court bound out her children Jacob, David, and Lucy Davis [Orders 1741-42, 22]. She was the mother of

   2   i. Mary[2], born say 1721.
   3   ii. Isabella[1], born say 1723.
        iii. Jacob, born say 1730.
        iv. David, born say 1733.
        v. Lucy, born say 1735.

2. Mary[2] Davis, born say 1721, was a "free Mulatto" whose unnamed children were ordered bound out by the churchwardens of Southampton County on 14 September 1749. She was probably the Moll Davis whose "Mulatto" son Daniel was bound out in Southampton County ten years later on 11 May 1759 [Orders 1749-54, 19; 1754-59]. And she may have been the Mary Davis who was a taxable head of household in the eastern division of the Borough of Norfolk in 1765 [Wingo, *Norfolk County Tithables 1751-65*, 217]. Her children were

   i. ?John[3], born say 1746, "Mulatto" head of a Nansemond County household with no whites in 1784 [VA:74], head of a Norfolk County household of 5 "other free" in 1810 [VA:815], perhaps the husband of Nancy Davis who registered as a "free Negro" in Norfolk County on 16 August 1815: *5 feet 4 Inc, 22 Years of age, of a dark Complexion,*

Born free in Southampton County [Registry of Free Negros & Mulattos, no.101].

ii. Daniel, born say 1748, bound apprentice in Southampton County on 11 May 1759.

iii. ?Isabel[2], head of a Southampton County household of 3 "other free" in 1810 [VA:79].

3. Isabella[1] Davis, born say 1723, was living in Southampton County on 9 August 1759 when the court ordered the churchwardens of Nottoway Parish to bind out her "Mullatto" child Frank [Orders 1754-9, 527]. She was the mother of

i.   Frank, born say 1758.

Other members of the family in Virginia were

i.   Catherine, born say 1718, the (white) servant of Willoughby Newton of Cople Parish, Westmoreland County who confessed in court to having a child by "Akey a Negro Man Slave to her said Master." The court ordered that she serve her master an additional year and be sold by the churchwardens for five years after completing her indenture [Orders 1731-9, 173a].

ii. Sarah, born say 1719, the (white) servant of Captain John Elliott of Washington Parish, Westmoreland County on 29 July 1735 when she confessed in court to having a "Mulatto" child by her "Masters Negro man Fan." The court ordered that after her indenture was completed she should be sold by the churchwardens for five years [Orders 1731-9, 176a, 263, 270a].

iii. Daniel, "a mulatto," born in Lancaster County, who enlisted for the war and deserted from the ship *Gloucester* near Warwick with William **Smith**, a Creole born in Barbados, according to an advertisement in the 2 August 1780 issue of the *Virginia Gazette* [*Virginia Genealogist* 4:136].

iv. John, head of a Westmoreland County household of 4 "other free" in 1810.

v.   George, head of a Loudoun County household of 5 "other free" in 1810 [VA:268].

vi. Deborah, head of a Norfolk County household of 2 "other free" in 1810 [VA:894].

vii. Susan, head of an Isle of Wight County household of 3 "other free" and a slave in 1810 [VA:28].

viii. Toby, "Free Negro" head of an Isle of Wight County household of 4 "other free" in 1810 [VA:28].

ix. Sarah, head of an Accomack County household of 9 "other free" in 1810 [VA:91].

x.   David, head of a Frederick County household of 7 "other free" in 1810 [VA:549].

xi. Lucy, head of a Buckingham County household of 9 "other free" in 1810 [VA:338].

xii. Samuel, head of a Buckingham County household of 11 "other free" in 1810 [VA:816].

xiii. Betsy, head of a Lunenburg County household of 6 "other free" in 1810 [VA:338].

North Carolina

3. Robert Davis, born say 1715, was a "Black" taxable in 1753 in Osborn Jeffrey's Granville County list in 1753. In 1754 he was head of a household of four "Black" taxables including (his wife?) Margaret, (his children?) Ephraim, and Sarah Davis in Gideon Macon's list [CR 44.701.1]. He was listed as a "Mulatto" in the muster of Colonel William Eaton on 8 October 1754 [Clark, *Colonial Soldiers of the South*, 718]. His children may have been

    i.   John[1], born say 1733, a "Black" taxable in the 1754 list of Gideon Macon and a "mulatto" taxable with Margaret Davis in the 1761 list of James Paine for Cross Road District. He may have been the John Davis who purchased 400 acres in Granville County on both sides of Beaver Pond Creek on 5 March 1754 [DB B:294].

    ii.   Ephraim, born before 1743 since he was taxable in 1754.

    iii.   Sarah, born before 1743 since she was taxable in 1754.

    iv.   Simon, head of a Granville County household of 15 "free colored" in County Line District in 1820 [NC:35].

4.   William Davis, born say 1725, a "Molatto," was listed with 180 acres at the head of Chinquopin Creek in a 1753 Craven County list of landowners [Craven Wills, Deeds, Bonds, Inventories, Accounts of Sales, 306]. He was head of a Craven County household of one "Black" male taxable and three "Black" female taxables in 1769 [SS 837]. His descendants may have been

    i.   John[2], born say 1743, head of a Craven County household of one "Black" male and one "Black" female taxable in 1769 [SS 837]. He married Nancy **Godet**, another "Black" taxable in Craven County in 1769, by 12 November 1796 Craven County bond with William **Dove** bondsman.

    ii.   Richard, head of a Brunswick County, North Carolina household of 8 "other free" in 1800 [NC:13], probably the R. Davis who was head of a Brunswick County household of 5 "other free" in 1810 [NC:236]. In 1791 he petitioned the North Carolina General Assembly claiming that he had been an artilleryman in the Revolution, his wife had been emancipated by her master in 1784, and he asked that his children be also emancipated [Crow, *Black Experience in Revolutionary North Carolina*, 99].

    iii.   Ephram, head of a Jones County household of 6 "other free" in 1810 [NC:257].

    iv.   Michael, head of a Jones County household of 5 "other free" in 1810 [NC:257].

    v.   Luzana, married William **Godett**, 24 May 1805 Craven County bond with Peter **George** bondsman.

    vi.   George, head of a Pasquotank County household of 4 "other free" and 3 slaves in 1800 [NC:627], 5 "other free" in 1810 [NC:895], and 4 "free colored" in 1820 [NC:247].

DAY FAMILY

1.   Mary Day, born say 1671, was an indentured servant for whom Peter Cotanceau claimed transportation rights in Northumberland County court on 21 September 1699. On 22 November 1689 the Northumberland County court indicted her for having an illegitimate child. And on 21 December 1692 she was the servant of John Webb when the court indicted her for having twin "molatta" children John and Rachel who were born on 17 February 1692. On 22 November 1694 the court bound her "molatto" son Samuel **Webb** alias Day as an apprentice to William Yarratt. Samuel was probably the son of Daniel[2] **Webb** who was called the "molatto" son of an English woman servant in the Northumberland County court on 6 October 1687 when he was freed from his indenture to the orphans of Major John Mottron. Daniel had a child by another English servant woman named Margaret Lawson before 16 July 1701 when she confessed in court that the father of her illegitimate child was "a Negro called Daniell Webb." In May 1703 the court indicted Mary for having another child [Orders 1678-98, 405, 412, 494, 681; 1699-1713, part 1, 167, 247]. Mary was the mother of

    i.   John[1], born 17 February 1692, bound to John Webb until the age of thirty, called "Mulatto Jack" on 18 April 1716 when he was sued in

Northumberland County court by one of the executors of John Webb. He may have been identical to John Day who was the servant of William **Grinstead** on 18 June 1719 when the court ordered him to serve his master another six months for running away [Orders 1713-9, 153, 323].

2   ii.   Rachel[1], born 17 February 1692.

      iii. Samuel[1], born say 1694, called "Saml Webb als Day a Mulatto Servt. to Mrs. Jane Yarratt on 20 July 1715 when he sued for his freedom in Northumberland County court [Orders 1713-19, 126].

2. Rachel[1] Day, born 17 February 1692, was bound to John Webb until the age of thirty years. She was called "Rachell a Molatto Girle belonging to the estate of John Webb, deceased" on 22 September 1709 when she testified in Northumberland County court that Arthur Thomas was the father of her illegitimate child. On 17 December 1712 she was called "Rachel Day A Mulatto Servant to the Orph'ts of John Webb deceased" when she was presented by the court for having a child by a slave of Captain Kenner named "Negro Will." On 18 February 1712/3 she was called Rachel Webb alias Day when Sarah Webb, daughter of John Webb, deceased, reported to the court that Rachel had a child named Winnifred by "a Negro." The churchwardens of St. Stephen's Parish bound Winnefred to Sarah Webb until the age of thirty-one. She was probably identical to "___ Day als Webb Servt. to Sarah Webb" whose "Mulatto" child was ordered bound to Sarah Webb on 15 June 1715 [Orders 1699-1713, Part 2, 627, 803, 809, 815; Record Book 1710-3, 270; Orders 1713-19, 114]. Rachel was the mother of

      i.   Winnifred[1], born in June 1712.

Their descendants were probably the members of the Day family who were free in Virginia and North Carolina during the colonial period.[87] They were

      i.   David, born say 1745, a "Mulatto" who ran away from Augustine Smith of Middlesex County, Virginia, about 1766 according to the 27 July 1769 issue of the *Virginia Gazette* [Headley, *18th Century Newspapers*, 89].

3   ii.   George[1], born say 1753.

      iii. Elizabeth, born say 1755, "free Negro" mother of Reuben Day, an illegitimate child bound to Edward Lewis by the Orange County, Virginia court on 23 November 1775 [Orders 1769-77, 354].

4   iv.   Ann, born say 1759.

5   v.   Winnifred[2], born about 1759.

6   vi.   Rachel[2], born say 1760.

      vii. John[2], born say 1760, a "man of color" who enlisted in Granville County, North Carolina, in the 2nd North Carolina Regiment. He was said to have died in Valley Forge on 14 January 1778 [Crow, *Black Experience in Revolutionary North Carolina*, 99].

7   viii. Lucy[1], born say 1760.

8   ix.   Jesse[1], born say 1761.

9   x.   John[3], born say 1764.

      xi.   Joseph, born say 1765, taxable on one tithe and a horse in Westmoreland County in 1787 [Schreiner-Yantis, *1787 Census*, 1115].

      xii. Benjamin[2], born say 1766, his Northumberland County tax charged to Jesse Crowder in 1787 [Schreiner-Yantis, *1787 Census*, 1271].

10   xiii. Judith[1], born about 1766.

---

[87]There was also a Day family in Maryland. Elizabeth Day was the indentured servant of John Sanders on 13 March 1710/1 when she admitted to the Charles County, Maryland Court that she had an illegitimate "Malatto" child by a "Negro man named Quasey belonging to her master" and later admitted to having a second mixed-race child [Court Proceedings D-2:70; E-2:301, 304].

11	xiv.	Nancy[1], born say 1768.
12	xv.	Susannah, born say 1769.
13	xvi.	Stephen, born say 1770.
14	xvii.	Samuel[2], born say 1770.

3. George[1] Day, born say 1753, was a seaman from Northumberland County in the Revolution [Jackson, *Virginia Negro Soldiers*, 34]. He was taxable in Northumberland County in 1787 [Schreiner-Yantis, *1787 Census*, 1263] and a "free negro" head of a Northumberland County household of 5 "other free" in 1810 [VA:976]. He and his wife Nancy, no race indicated, registered the birth of their son Willoughby in St. Stephen's Parish, Northumberland County. They were the parents of

    i.   ?Jane, born about 1775, registered as a "free Negro" in Northumberland County on 11 March 1822: *Mulatto woman, about 47 yrs. 5 feet 3 Inches high, Born of free parents in N[d] County* [Register, no. 137].

    ii. Willoughby, born 13 November 1778 [Fleet, *Northumberland County Record of Births*].

4. Ann Day, born say 1759, was living in Caswell County, North Carolina, in 1780 when her children were bound apprentices [CR 20.101.1]. They were

    i.   George[3], born 1776, "of color, son of Nan Day," bound apprentice in Caswell County to Samuel Winstead on 20 June 1780 and then to J.S. Hutchinson on 12 July 1780. He was head of a Person County household of 8 "free colored" in 1820 [NC:498].

    ii. Lucy[2], born 1779, bound to Drury Allen in Caswell County on 20 March 1780 and to David Allen in March court 1783 [A:240].

5. Winnifred[2] Day, born about 1759, "a free Malatto," registered the birth of her children Judith, Isaac, and Winnie in St. Stephen's Parish, Northumberland County [Fleet, *Northumberland County Record of Births*, 42]. On 10 June 1799 the Northumberland County court certified that she, called Winney Day, Senr., and Judith Day, Nanny Day, and Winny Day, Jr., were free born "Mulattoes" [Orders 1793-1800, 80]. She registered as a "free Negro" on 1 August 1814: *Mulatto, about 55 years, 5 feet & 1/2 an inch high, Born of free parents in North[d] County* [Northumberland County Register, no. 78]. Her children were

    i.   Judith[2], born 3 September 1778, registered as a "free Negro" in Northumberland County on 10 May 1819: *Judy Day, jr., Black woman, about 40 years old, 5 feet 3-1/4 Inches hight, born of free parents in North[d] County, presented her children, James, Polly, Sally, & Betsy, between the ages of 9 & 2* [Register, no. 120]. Her daughter Harriet Day registered the same day: *Dark girl, about 12 years old, 5 feet 2-1/2 Inches high* [Register, no. 121].

    ii. Isaac, born 21 June 1780.

    iii. Winnie[3], born 11 January 1784, registered as a "free Negro" in Northumberland County on 1 August 1814: *Black woman, about 22 years old, 5 feet 2 & 1/4 Inches, Born of free parents in North[d] County* [Register, no. 82].

    iv. ?Samuel[3], born about 1791, registered as a "free Negro" in Northumberland County on 10 February 1806: *Black, nearly 15 years old, 5 feet 4 Inches high, Born free* [Register, no. 20].

    v. ?William[3], born about 1805, registered as a "free Negro" in Northumberland County on 11 March 1822: *Black man, 19 years old, 5 feet 7 & 1/2 Inches high, Born of free parents in North[d] County* [Register, no. 136].

6. Rachel[2] Day, born say 1760, was living in Caswell County, North Carolina, in 1780 when her children were bound as apprentices. They were
    i.   Thomas[1], born in 1777, "son of Rachel," bound apprentice to Samuel Winstead in Caswell County court on 20 June 1780 [CR 20.101.1]. He was head of a Person County household of 7 "free colored" in 1820 [NC:498].
    ii. Jesse[2], born in 1779, "son of Rachel," bound an apprentice to Drury Allen in Caswell County on 20 March 1780 and to David Allen in March court 1783 [Book A:240]. He married Love **Pettiford**, 27 January 1819 Orange County bond with William Day bondsman and was head of an Orange County household of 4 "free colored" in 1820 [NC:306].
    iii. ?Nancy[2], born January 1783, bound apprentice in Caswell County to David Allen in March court 1783, no parent named [A:240].

7. Lucy[1] Day, born say 1760 (before 1776), was bound apprentice in Southampton County on 12 March 1762 (no parent or race named) [Orders 1759-63, 196]. On 28 May 1789 the grand jury of Greensville County presented her for living in fornication with John Turner's slave Cudger. She was called only "Lucy" on 25 August 1791 when the court dismissed the presentment. The court discontinued her case against Drury and Dorothy Peebles for trespass, assault and battery at defendants' costs on 23 July 1789 after the parties reached agreement. James Binford was her witness [Orders 1781-9, 412, 422, 427; 1790-9, 88]. She was taxable in Meherrin Parish, Greensville County, from 1791 to 1799 and from 1804 to 1820: taxable on a slave above the age of sixteen and 2 horses in 1791, taxable on a slave and a free tithable aged 16-21 in 1793, called "Lucy Day & Cudger Day" from 1804 to 1812, "Lucy Day & Cudgoe Mulattos" in 1813, "Cudjoe & Lucy Day Free Negros" in 1814. She was not on the tax rolls from 1800 to 1803, so she may have been related to John Day who was taxable in Meherrin Parish, Greensville County, in the 1790s but not listed from 1800 to 1802 when he was in Dinwiddie County [PPTL 1782-1850, frames 126, 161, 178, 187, 200, 217, 230, 243, 320, 336, 352, 371, 386, 401, 414, 432, 446, 461, 481, 578, 602]. On 25 April 1793 the Greensville County court ordered the overseers of the poor to bind out her children Edmund, Cudger, and Lucy. She appealed the ruling, and on 25 July 1793 the court rescinded the order to bind Cudger to Stephen Ragland [Orders 1790-9, 195, 210, 212]. Her Greensville County land in the area between Great Swamp branch to Fountain's Creek up to Halifax Road adjoining Richard Sills was among those processioned in May 1800 [Processioners Returns 1796-1820, 27]. She was head of a Greensville County household of 3 "free colored" in 1820 with "Cudjoe" [VA:261]. Lucy was the mother of
    i.   Edmund, born say 1784.
    ii. Cudger, born say 1785.
    iii. Lucy[3], born say 1787.
    iv. ?Thena **Artis**, born about 1787, registered in Greensville County on 7 February 1832: *born free of a yellow complexion, about forty five years of age, five feet four & 1/2 inches high*. She was probably the wife of Willie **Artis** who registered the same day. Her son Henry **Day** also registered the same day: *son of Thena Artis, formerly Day, born free of a dark complexion, about twenty two years of age, five feet seven inches high...by occupation a farmer* [Register of Free Negroes, 1805-1832, nos. 192, 195].
    v.   Nathaniel, born in 1789, registered as a "free Negro" in Greensville County on 14 April 1821: *Son of Lucy Day, light dark Complexion, about 32 years of age, five feet 4 inches high (in Shoes)...a planter, & Shingle gator & coarse shoe maker* [Register of Free Negroes, no. 89]. He was head of a Greensville County household of 6 "free colored" in

1820 [VA:261]. He may have been the Nathaniel Day who was a "free Negro" taxable in Southampton County in 1812 [PPTL 1807-21, frame 289].

8. Jesse[1] Day, born say 1761, married Prissey **Bass**, 6 November 1782 Granville County, North Carolina bond with Solomon Walker bondsman. He applied for the Revolutionary War pension of his brother John [Crow, *Black Experience in Revolutionary North Carolina*, 99]. He was head of a Granville County household of 10 "other free" in 1810 [NC:916] and 5 "free colored" in Orange County, North Carolina, in 1820 [NC:312]. His children may have been

   i. John[4], born say 1785, head of a Granville County household of 2 "other free" in 1810 [NC:916].
   ii. Reuben, born say 1788, witness to the 4 October 1808 Granville County marriage bond of Rhoda Day and Dempsey **Bass**. He was head of an Orange County household of 8 "free colored" in 1820 [NC:288].
   iii. Rhoda, born say 1790, married Dempsey **Bass**, 4 October 1808 Granville County bond.
   iv. William[2], married Jinsey **Pettiford**, 6 October 1818 Orange County bond, James Hopkins bondsman. He was head of an Orange County household of 3 "free colored" in 1820 [NC:306].
   v. Benjamin[4], married Bedy **Pettiford**, 19 November 1819 Orange County bond, William **Pettiford** bondsman. He was head of an Orange County household of 8 "free colored" in 1820 [NC:354].

9. John[3] Day, born say 1764, married Mourning **Stewart**, daughter of Dr. Thomas **Stewart** of Dinwiddie County [Dinwiddie County Chancery Orders 1832-52, 1; Sneed & Westfall, *History of Thomas Day*, 6]. He was taxable in Dinwiddie County from 1800 to 1802: charged with the tax for his brothers-in-law Henry and Armstead **Stewart** in 1800, his brother-in-law Armstead **Stewart** in 1801, and his brothers-in-law Armstead and John **Stewart** in 1802 [PPTL, 1800-19 (1800B, p.4; 1801A, p.4; 1802A, p.4)]. He was apparently the John Day who was taxable in Meherrin Parish, Greensville County, from 1795 to 1799 and taxable in St. Andrew's Parish, Greensville County, in 1803 and 1804 since his son John Day was born in Greensville County in 1797. He was taxable in Greensville County on a slave in 1795 and 1796, taxable on 2 free tithes from 1797 to 1799, called a "workman" in 1798 and 1799 to differentiate him from another John Day who was taxable in Greensville County.[88] He was also called a "workman" when he was taxable in St. Andrew's Parish in 1803 [PPTL 1782-1850, frames 187, 200, 217, 230, 243, 296, 314]. According to the recollection of his son John, he purchased a small plantation in Sussex County near Edward Whitehorne's house in 1807, but later sold the land and moved back to Dinwiddie County, and then moved to North Carolina in 1817 [Sneed & Westfall, *History of Thomas Day*, 7]. The sale of his Sussex County land apparently took place in 1810 when the tax

---

[88]The other John Day, born say 1740, purchased 100 acres on both sides of Lick Creek in Meherrin Parish, Brunswick County, Virginia, from William and Lucy Robinson on 8 June 1769 [DB 9:505]. He was head of a Greensville County, Virginia household of 1 "white" (free) person in 1783 [VA:55] and was taxable in Greensville County from 1782 to 1802, called John Day, Sr., from 1795 to 1797 [Personal Property Tax List 1782-1850, frames 3, 14, 34, 41, 62, 81, 187, 200, 217, 230, 243, 258, 273, 286]. He married Agnes Sexton, 3 January 1787 Greensville County bond. She may have been the Agnes Sexton who was fined 500 pounds of tobacco in Brunswick County on 24 July 1765 [Orders 1765, 339; 1765-8, 267-8]. John voted in Greensville County in 1792, 1794, and 1795. He and his wife Agga Day sold 35 acres adjoining the road from Hicks Ford (Emporia) to Eaton's Ferry in Greensville County on 8 February 1797. His 12 October 1801 Greensville County will was proved in October 1802 and witnessed by Henry and William Wyche. He left his land and estate to his wife Agnes during her lifetime and then to Joseph Sexton [DB 1:450; 2:134, 192; 3:283-4; WB 1:471].

assessments on two parcels of land in Sussex County were transferred from John Day to George Dowden and William Parham [Sussex County Land Tax List, 1810; Dowden and Parham sold the land in 1813: DB L:249, 252]. John was listed as a cabinetmaker in the Dinwiddie County list of "Free Negroes and Their Occupations" between 1814 and 1817 [PPTL, 1800-19 (1814A, p.4; 1817A, p.23)]. In 1820 he was head of a Warren County, North Carolina household of 5 "free colored" [NC:808]. He died at the age of sixty-eight [Sneed & Westfall, *History of Thomas Day*, 10]. His wife Mourning was counted as an eighty-four-year-old woman living in the household of her son Thomas Day in the 1850 census for Caswell County [NC:193a]. John and Mourning were the parents of

    i.   John[6], born on 18 February 1797 in Hicksford (Emporia), Greensville County, Virginia. When his family moved to Sussex County, he boarded with his neighbor Edward Whitehorne and went to school with Whitehorne's children. In 1804 his grandfather Dr. Thomas **Stewart** gave him a slave named Thody by his Dinwiddie County will which was proved in 1810. In 1817 he was living with his family in a rented house in Dinwiddie County when his father moved to North Carolina. He remained in Dinwiddie and carried on a small cabinetmaking business, but "associating myself with ___ young white men, who were fond of playing cards, contracted that habit" [Rev. John Day Letters, 1847-59 by Sneed & Westfall, *History of Thomas Day*, 5-8; Chancery Orders 1832-52, 1]. He may have been the John Day who was a "F.N." taxable in Greensville County on 2 slaves in 1827 and a slave and a horse in 1830 [PPTL 1782-1850, frames 827, 851]. He became a Baptist minister and emigrated to Liberia in 1830 with his wife and four children. He was superintendent of the Baptist Mission and later chief justice of the Liberia Supreme Court [African Repository 35 (1859):158; and 37 (1861):154-58 by Wiley, *Slaves No More*].

    ii.   Thomas[2], born about 1801, operated the Yellow Tavern in Milton, Caswell County, the third largest furniture factory in the state, from 1823 to 1858. He married Acquilla **Wilson** in Virginia in 1829 but needed special dispensation from the legislature to allow her to migrate into North Carolina since a North Carolina law of 1827 made it illegal for free African Americans to enter the state. The Yellow Tavern is a National Historic Landmark. He was listed as a forty-nine-year-old in the 1850 census for Caswell County. His land near the main road from Milton to Yanceyville near County Line Creek was mentioned in a 3 April 1851 Caswell County land entry [Entry no. 1418].

10. Judith[1] Day, born about 1766, was living in Northumberland County on 10 June 1799 when the county court certified that she, Winney Day, Senr., Nanny Day, and Winny Day, Jr., were free born "Mulattoes" [Orders 1793-1800, 80]. She was a "free mulatto" head of a Northumberland County household of 5 "other free" in 1810 [VA:977]. She registered as a "free Negro" in Northumberland County on 17 April 1819: *Dark mulatto, about 53 years old, 5 feet three inches high, born of free parents in North[d] County* [Register, no. 119]. Her children were

    i.   ?Presly, born about 1788, registered as a "free Negro" in Northumberland County on 10 February 1806: *bright mulatto, about 18 years old, 5 feet 6-1/4 Inches high, Born free* [Register, no. 19].

    ii.   ?Sally, born about 1795, registered as a "free Negro" in Northumberland County on 16 May 1821: *Bright Mulatto, 26 years old, 5 feet 6 inches high, Born of free parents in North[d] County* [Register, no. 132].

    iii. ?Nancy Taylor, born about 1799, registered as a "free Negro" in Northumberland County on 6 June 1818: *Bright Mulatto, about 19 years old, 5 feet three Inches high* [Register, no. 111].

iv. Spencer, born about 1805, registered as a "free Negro" in Northumberland County on 16 May 1821: *son of Judy Day, Mulatto boy, 16 years of age, 5 feet one Inch high* [Register, no. 130].

v. James Stokely, born about 1809, registered as a "free Negro" in Northumberland County on 16 May 1821: *son of Judy Day, Mulatto, 4 feet 8 inches high* [Register, no. 131].

11. Nancy[1] Day, born say 1768, was living in Person County, North Carolina, on 3 December 1794 when she consented to the court binding her "Negro" sons Jesse and John to Charles Allen [Minutes 1792-6, 3 December 1794; 1796-7, 22]. Her children were

   i. Jesse[3], born 2 August 1786, head of a Person County household of one "other free" in 1810 [NC:629]. He obtained a certificate of freedom in Gallatin County, Illinois, on 25 November 1828: *a man of colour, forty years of age or near as can be recollected, five feet eleven inches and a quarter high, well made, dark Complection tho not Black...born free in Person County, North Carolina.* His wife Sina obtained a certificate in Giles County, Tennessee, on 31 May 1824: *Sina Day wife of Jesse Day, formerly Sina Jones, a mulatto woman now residing in the town of Pulaski, was born free.* She recorded the certificate in Gallatin County: *Sina Day enters her five children Arenna, 17 years of age five feet five inches high, light complexion of the black cast, rather small features; Nancy, 15 years of age, dark complexion, nearly black; John, 13 years of age, dark complexion, nearly Black; Wilson, 8 years old, light colour tho not quite light enough for a mulatto; Elizabeth, six years old of the Colour of Wilson* [Gallatin County Servitude Register 1815-39, 114, 122].

   ii. John[5], born 9 August 1788, head of a Person County household of one "free colored" in 1820 [NC:498].

   iii. ?Betty, born say 1792, no parent named when she was ordered bound out by the 5 June 1797 Person County court [Minutes 1797-1802, 1].

12. Susannah Day, born say 1769, was living in Southampton County on 11 December 1795 when the court ordered the overseers of the poor to bind out her son Solomon Day to Enos James. The court repeated the order on 14 July 1796 [Minutes 1793-9, 198, 225]. Susannah was the mother of

   i. Solomon, born about 1790, taxable in Southampton County with wife Julia on William Whitehead's land in 1813 and 1814 [PPTL 1807-21, frames 316, 416]. They registered in Southampton County on 29 March 1823: *Solomon Day, mulatto man, age 33, 5 feet 6 inches high, free born in So. Julia Day Mulatto woman, 26, 5 feet 6 1/2 inches high, born in So.* [Register of Free Negroes, nos. 1376, 1377].

   ii. ?Davis/ David, born about 1789, registered in Southampton County on 3 August 1810: *Davy Day, age 21, Blk, 5 feet 9 inches high, free born* [Register of Free Negroes, no. 824]. He was a "free Negro" taxable in Southampton County on Ben Whitfield's land in 1812, taxable on a horse in 1813 and 1814, living with his sisters Silvia and Cherry on Ben Whitfield's land in 1813 [PPTL 1807-21, frames 289, 316, 416].

13. Stephen Day, born say 1770, and his wife Jinney Day and children Naney, Suckey, and Lucy were listed among the "Free Mulattoes & Negroes in Westmoreland County" in 1801 [*Virginia Genealogist* 31:40]. He was a "free mulatto" head of a Northumberland County household of 7 "other free" in 1810. His children were

   i. Naney/ Nancy[3] married Joseph **Kelly**, 18 December 1812 Northumberland County bond, Stephen Day security.

   ii. Suckey.

   iii. Lucy[4], perhaps the Lucy Day, born about 1802, who registered as a "free Negro" in Northumberland County on 16 May 1821: *Bright Mulatto, 19 years old, 5 feet 3 Inches high* [Register, no. 133].

14. Samuel[2] Day, born say 1770, was a farmer living in Westmoreland County in 1801 when he and his wife Jinney Day were listed among the "Free Mulattoes & Negroes" living on James Rice's land [*Virginia Genealogist* 31:40]. He was head of a Westmoreland County household of 7 "other free" in 1810 [VA:770] and 5 "free colored" in 1830. He may have been the father of

   i. Samuel[4], Jr., born about 1793, a child listed in the 1801 list of "Free Molattoes in Westmoreland County" [*Virginia Genealogist* 31:40], married Lotty **Ashton**, 7 January 1818 Westmoreland County bond, Samuel **Tate** security. He was head of a Westmoreland County household of 6 "free colored" in 1830. He registered in Westmoreland County in May 1838: *a Mulatto man, five feet four and three fourths inches high, aged forty five, born free*. Charlotte Day registered in April 1838: *a woman of light complexion, five feet three & 3/4 inches high, aged forty years* [Register of Free Negroes, 1828-1849, pp.31-2, nos, 265, 269].

Other Virginia descendants were

   i. Simon Peter, "free negro" head of a Fairfax County household of 3 "other free" and 2 slaves in 1810 [VA:252].

   ii. Tempy, head of a Botetourt County household of 7 "other free" in 1810 [VA:617].

   iii. Benjamin[3], head of a Botetourt County household of 4 "other free" in 1810 [VA:618].

   iv. Judy[3], born about 1780, registered as a free Negro in Essex County on 8 December 1810: *born free by cert. of the clerk of Essex County, dark Mulattoe, about 30 years of age, 5 feet 1-3/4 inches high* [Register of Free Negroes 1810-43, p.7, no.13].

   v. George[2], head of a Middlesex County household of 4 "other free" in 1810 [VA:472].

   vi. Elijah, born about 1790, married Judith[2] **Banks**, twenty-one-year-old daughter of John **Banks**, 28 December 1815 Goochland County bond, Jacob **Martin** surety [Ministers' Returns, 127]. He registered as a free Negro in Goochland County on 2 September 1829: *yellowish complexion, about thirty nine years of age*, and his wife Judy registered on 17 September 1829: *yellow complexion, about thirty nine years of age, about five foot three & an half inches high* [Register of Free Negroes, pp.201, 204].

DEAN FAMILY

Members of the family in Virginia were

   i. Thornton[1], head of a King George County household of 13 "other free" in 1810 [VA:196].

   ii. Frances, born about 1751, registered in King George County on 3 August 1801: *a dark mulatto woman, aged about fifty years, about five feet high, was born free* [Register of Free Persons 1785-1799, no.27].

   iii. John, born about 1767, taxable in King George County from 1793 to 1813 [PPTL, 1782-1830, frames 117, 168, 303, 339], registered in King George County on 8 August 1801: *a bright mulatto man aged about thirty four years, five feet seven inches high having descended from a free woman.* His wife Betsy registered the same day [Register of Free Persons 1785-1799, nos.33, 34]. He was head of a King George County household of 6 "other free" in 1810 [VA:196].

iv. William, born about 1769, taxable in King George County from 1789 to 1807: called William, Sr., in 1791, 1792, 1795, and 1797 [PPTL, 1782-1830, frames 70, 87, 104, 135, 154, 228, 276], registered in King George County on 18 November 1799: *William Hall alias Dean a Mulattoe Man aged about Thirty Years & about five feet Seven Inches high, was born free* [Register of Free Persons 1785-1799, no.11]. He was indicted in King George County on 6 June 1799 for retailing liquor without a license [Orders 1790-9, 657].

v. Susan, head of a Richmond City household of 2 "other free" and 5 slaves in 1810 [VA:335].

vi. Philip, head of a Goochland County household of 1 "other free" and 1 slave in 18610 [VA:690].

vii. Jane, born about 1777, registered in King George County on 3 August 1801: *a light mulatto woman, aged about twenty four years, five feet & one inch high, was born in this County of a free woman* [Register of Free Persons 1785-1799, no.26].

viii. Elijah **Hall**, born about 1779, registered in King George County on 14 October 1800: *Elijah Hall alias Deen, a dark Mulatto man aged about twenty one years, & about five feet seven Inches high, was born in this County of a free Woman* [Register of Free Persons 1785-1799, no.15]. He may have been related to Reuben and Rapple **Hall**, both heads of Fairfax County households of 2 "other free" in 1810 [VA:261, 268].

ix. James **Hall**, born about 1781, registered in King George County on 4 December 1800: *James Hall alias Deen, a bright mulatto man aged about nineteen years and about five feet five inches high, was born in this County of a free woman* [Register of Free Persons 1785-1799, no.19].

x. Dicey, born about 1788, registered in King George County on 17 August 1801: *a bright mulatto woman aged about twenty three years, four feet ten inches high, having descended from a free woman* [Register of Free Persons 1785-1799, no.32].

xi. Thornton[2], born about 1790, a poor orphan bound by the overseers of the poor to Peter Hansbrough in King George County on 3 December 1795 [Orders 1790-9, 428]. He registered in King George County on 3 December 1807: *a dark mulatto man about sixteen or seventeen years old, five feet high, stout made...born free* [Register of Free Persons 1785-1799, no.42].

xii. Ceiley, a "poor orphan Molatto" bound by the overseers of the poor to Peter Hansbrough in King George County on 3 December 1795 [Orders 1790-9, 428].

DEAS FAMILY

Members of the Deas family were
1 i. William, born say 1740.
2 ii. Benjamin, born say 1745.

1. William Deas, born say 1748, and Mary (his wife or sister?), "two adult Negroes," were baptized on 9 August 1772 in St. Thomas and Dennis Parishes, South Carolina [Parochial Register of the Parishes of St. Thomas & St. Denis, n.p. (alphabetical listing under D)]. They may have been the parents of

i. Joseph, married Venus **Caunou**, "Blacks," at St. Philip's and Michael's Parish, Charleston on 13 June 1806.

ii. William, married Ann **Timothy**, "free people of color," at St. Philip's and Michael's Parish, Charleston on 7 October 1812.

iii. Lydia, married Joseph **Bull**, 6 April 1815, "Col'd persons, free," at St. Philip's and Michael's Parish, Charleston.

iv. Ann, paid the "free Negro" capitation tax while living at Jehu **Jones'** Inn at Broad Street in Charleston in 1821 [Free Negro Capitation Tax Book, 1821, p.7]. Ann was **Jones**'s stepdaughter. Jehu **Jones**, born about 1769, was a "Mulatto Man" who was manumitted by Christopher Rogers of Charleston on 22 January 1798. He worked as a tailor and was able to purchase a house on Broad Street behind St. Michael's Church for $2,000 in 1809. In 1815 he purchased the adjacent lot and house at 33 Broad Street for $13,000 and owned at least six slaves. The hotel became popular with Charleston's elite white society. Jehu was a trustee of the Brown Fellowship Society [S.C. Dept. of Archives & History, "Jehu Jones: Free Black Entrepreneur"]. Jehu's wife Abigail and Ann Deas visited New York about 1822 and were not allowed to return because of a law passed in 1823 barring the return of free African Americans who left the state. Jehu died in 1833 leaving an estate estimated at $40,000. Ann returned in 1835, bought the inn from the estate, received a pardon from the governor for entering the state without permission, and ran the inn for the next twelve years.

2. Benjamin Dees, born say 1745, purchased 200 acres in Anson County, North Carolina, on the north side of the Pee Dee River on the Falling Creek branch of Hitchcock's Creek from Jordan **Gibson** on 15 November 1768 by deed witnessed by Gideon **Gibson** [DB 7:224]. He was a white taxable in Bladen County in 1770 and 1772 when he had "Mulato" Benjamin **Sweat** in his household [Byrd, *Bladen County Tax Lists*, I:44, 78, 143]. On 13 October 1773 it was reported to the Governor of the colony that he was among a group of "free Negors and Mullatus" living on "the Kings land" in what was then Bladen County [G.A. 1773, box 7]. Other mixed-race families in the group were **Chavis**, **Grant**, **Groom**, **Ivey**, **Kersey**, **Locklear**, and **Sweat**. Many of these families had title to their land. He may have been the father of

    i. Nancy, living with Thomas **Lowry** on 24 November 1812 when the Robeson County court ordered her to bring two of her illegitimate children by James **Lowry** to the next court [Minutes 1806-13, 351].

DEBRIX FAMILY

Two members of the Debrix family, perhaps brothers, were living in Surry County, Virginia, about 1760. They were

1   i. John¹, born say 1725.
2   ii. David¹, born say 1740.

1. John¹ Deverix/ Debrix, born say 1725, was one of fourteen free African Americans in Surry County (called John Deverix) who were presented by the court on 21 November 1758 for failing to pay taxes on their "Mulatto wives."[89] The inventory of his Surry County estate was taken on 12 February 1772. On 25 March 1783 the court summoned the administrators of his estate, William Collins and Benjamin Putney, to give their account on motion of (his son?) John Debereaux [Orders 1757-64, 135; 1764-74, 211; 1775-85, 207]. He was probably the father of

3   i. John², born say 1745.
    ii. Burrell, born say 1766, taxable in Surry County from 1787 to 1805; his tax charged to John Debrix in 1787 [PPTL, 1782-90, frames 451; 1791-1816, frames 289, 326, 407, 560, 591].

---

[89] He may have been related to John Deberry who purchased 150 acres in Surry County adjoining Johnshehawkin Swamp at Turks Branch on 1 January 1724 [DW 7:557].

2. David[1] Debrix /Debricks, born say 1740, purchased 43 acres on the south side
of Cypress Swamp in Surry County, Virginia, from William **Walden** on 14
June 1762 [DB 8:129] and was taxable on 47 acres in Surry County in 1787
[Land Tax Lists, 1782-1820]. He was head of a Surry County household of 11
persons in 1782 [VA:43], 10 in 1784 (called David Debereaux) [VA:78] and
2 "other free" in 1810 [VA:605]. He was taxable in Surry County from 1782
to 1813: charged with Howell and David Debrix's tithes in 1787; charged with
David Debreaux, Jr.'s tithe from 1790 to 1792; charged with Richard
Deborix's tax in 1797; taxable on a slave named Isham, aged 12-16, in 1798
and 1799; taxable on a slave named Ratley in 1803; taxable on 2 free males
in 1807 and 1809; listed with 2 "free Negroes & Mulattoes" in 1813 (himself
and a female over the age of 16) [PPTL, 1782-90, frames 358, 398, 598;
1791-1816, frames 10, 108, 237, 326, 407, 446, 522, 591, 630, 650, 688,
735]. His will was proved in Surry County in 1816 [WB 3:95]. He was the
father of

   i.   ?Howell, born about 1770, taxable in Surry County from 1787 to 1796:
        his tax charged to David Debrix in 1787 [PPTL, 1782-90, frames 450,
        473, 551; 1791-1816, frames 10, 161, 257]. He purchased 75 acres in
        Surry County on 22 February 1790 from John **Banks**, Henry and Judy
        Charity, Susanna **Howell**, and Joseph and Hannah **Roberts**, being the
        land descended to them from Matthew **Banks** [DB 1792-9, 296].
        Howell was executor of the 18 December 1796 Surry County will of
        William **Cypress** and was mentioned in the 3 September 1796 Surry
        County will of Mary Andrews [WB 1:183, 186]. He was taxable in
        James City County on a slave from 1798 to 1809 and was a "mulato"
        taxable there in 1813 [PPTL, 1782-99; 1800-24].

   ii. ?David[2], born say 1771, taxable in Surry County from 1787 to 1794:
        listed with (his father?) David Debrix in 1787 (aged 16-21) and from
        1790 to 1792 [PPTL, 1782-90, frames 480, 598; 1791-1816, frames
        10, 59]. He was taxable in James City County from 1805 to 1812, a
        "cold." taxable in 1814 [PPTL, 1800-24].

   iii. Richard, born about 1776, registered as a "free Negro" in Surry
        County on 22 May 1798: *Richard Debereaux son of David Debereaux
        a mulatto resident yellowish complexion, straight made 5'10", 22 years
        of age, born of free parents* [Back of Guardian Accounts Book, 1783-
        1804, no.29]. He was taxable in Surry County from 1797 to 1816:
        listed in his father's household in 1797, counted as a "free Negro &
        Mulatto" in 1813 [PPTL, 1791-1816, frames 289, 369, 447, 812, 852].
        He married Anna **Peters**, 21 January 1817 Surry County bond, with
        the consent of her father Jesse **Peters**.

   iv. ?Edy, born say 1779, married Samuel **Thompson**, 18 September 1790
        Surry County bond, Howell Debrix surety.

   v.   ?Luran, married William **Gilchrist**, 20 December 1798 Surry County
        bond.

   vi. ?John[5], born about 1787, registered in Surry County on 11 June 1810:
        *a Mulatto man aged about 23 years is 5'5" high, pretty stout and well
        made, of a bright complexion* [Hudgins, *Surry County Register of Free
        Negroes*, 41].

3. John[2] Debrix, born say 1745, was head of a Surry County household of 13
persons in 1782 [VA:43] and was taxable on 280 acres in Surry County in
1782 [Land Tax Lists, 1782-1820]. He was taxable in Surry County from 1782
to 1816: called John Debereaux, Jr., in 1782; charged with Burrell and John
Debrix's tax in Cabin Point district in 1787; charged with Major Debreaux's
tax in 1790; charged with Major and Moses Debrix's tax in 1791; called John
Deborix, Sr., in 1794; charged with John Deborix, Jr.'s tax in 1795 [PPTL,
1782-90, frames 350, 398, 451, 472, 598; 1791-1816, frames 10, 60, 161,
237, 289, 326]. He was head of a Surry County household of 18 "other free"

in 1810 [VA:605] and 3 "free colored" in 1830. On 28 December 1790 he (called John Debereaux) sold 160 acres in Surry County to Armistead **Peters** [DB 1788-92, 236]. By his 1829 Surry County will, he left 50 acres to his son Major [WB 7:410]. He was the father of

4   i.   Major, born about 1766.

    ii.   John[4], born about 1774, taxable in John Debrix's Cabin Point, Surry County household in 1795, charged with his own tax in 1797, called "son of John" in 1802 [PPTL, 1782-90, frames; 1791-1816, frames 237, 289, 326, 481]. He registered in Petersburg on 3 July 1810: *a brown Mulatto man, five feet six inches high, thirty six years old, born of free parents in the County of Surry p. certificate* [Register of Free Negroes 1794-1819, no. 629]. He was head of a Petersburg household of 2 "other free" in 1810 (John Devereux) [VA:123b].

    iii. Sally, born about 1775, married Jesse **Peters**, 9 January 1796 Surry County bond, 15 January marriage. She registered as a "free Negro" in Surry county on 20 August 1804: *wife of Jesse, born of free parents (John Debrix and Lucy his wife); bright complexion, ca 30 yrs. old, 5'3/4" high* [Registry of Free Negroes, Surry County courthouse].

    iv.   Moses, born say 1779, taxable in Surry County from 1791 to 1816: listed with (his father?) John Debrix in 1791 and 1792; head of a household of 2 "free Negroes & Mulattoes" over the age of sixteen in 1813 [PPTL, 1791-1816, frames 10, 60, 237, 561, 612, 650, 688, 735, 812, 853]. He married Anne **Charity**, 30 December 1800 Surry County bond, Davis **Charity** surety. Anne may have been the Anny Debrix who was head of a Surry County household of 5 "free colored" in 1830.

    v.   Henry[1], born about 1782, registered in Surry County on 24 July 1805: *a mulatto man (son of John Debrix a free mulatto of the county of Surry) is of a bright complexion aged 23 years or thereabouts, 5'1/4" high, has a projecting mouth* [Hudgins, *Surry County Register of Free Negroes*, 27]. His will was proved in Surry County in 1810 [WB 2:351].

    vi.   Polly, born say 1784, "daughter of John Debrix," married Elick **Charity**, 12 June 1800 Surry County bond, Aaron **Taylor** surety.

    vii. David[3], taxable in Surry County from 1801 to 1809, called the son of John Debrix [PPTL, 1791-1816, frames 447, 523, 591, 630, 650]. He married Nancy **Scott**, 25 December 1802 Surry County bond, William **Scott**, surety, 26 December marriage.

    viii. ?Nancy, married Robert **Elliott**, 19 September 1798 Surry County bond, John Debereux surety, 20 September marriage.

    ix.   ?Pamelia, born about 1778, thirty-five years old on 6 November 1813 when she married James **Williams**, Surry County bond, Nicholas **Scott** surety.

4.   Major Debrix, born about 1766, registered in Surry County on 25 November 1822: *son of John and Lucy Debrix, free persons of this county aged about 56 is 5'6" high of yellow Complexion, has a large mouth and prominent teeth, and has hair rather long than otherwise* [Hudgins, *Surry County Register of Free Negroes*, 75]. He was taxable in Surry County from 1790 to 1816: listed in John Debrix's household in 1790; listed with Peter **Fagan**, Jr., in 1792; called Major Deborix, Sr., in 1797; listed with a slave named John, aged 12-16, in 1800; head of a household of 1 "free Negro & Mulatto" in 1813 [PPTL, 1782-90, frame 598; 1791-1816, frames 65, 161, 257, 289, 406, 481, 560, 612, 650, 688, 735, 853]. He married Silvey **Cannady**, 7 February 1797 Sussex County bond, Joseph **Cannady** surety; and second, Polly **Walden**, 18 March 1814 Surry County bond, Nicholas **Scott** surety. Major was head of a Surry County household of 6 "free colored" in 1830. By his 1837 Surry

County will he left his land to his wife Polly and after her death, to his son Thomas [WB 8:384]. His children were

    i.   David[4], born about 1797, registered in Surry County on 26 June 1820: *a Mulatto Man the son of Major Debrix of this County was born free of a bright Complexion aged about 23 years is 5'8" High Well made.*

    ii.   Betsy, born in June 1802, married Robert **Bailey**, 26 May 1823 Surry County bond, Isham Inman security, "Robert a free negro and Betsy a mulatto." She registered in Surry County on 28 February 1825: *Betsy alias Betsy Bailey, the Daughter of Major Debrix & Sylvia Debrix free Mulattoes of Surry County, the said Betsy was born free. She was 22 years old in June 1824 of a bright complexion is 5'6-3/4" high has pretty straight hair* [Hudgins, *Register of Free Negroes*, 80].

    iii.   John[6], born in August 1803, registered on 28 February 1825: *the Son of Major Debrix & Sylvia Debrix free Mulattoes of Surry County the said John Debrix was born free, he was 21 years old in August 1824 of a bright complexion rather down look, his Head projected forward, distended Nostrils, tho' not remarkably large...is 5'8-3/4 high, pretty straight and well proportioned.*

    iv.   Henry[2], born about 1807, registered in Surry County on 28 July 1828: *son of Major Debrix...about 21 years of age of a bright complexion, well made...5'8" high.*

    v.   Thomas, born about 1823, registered in Surry County on 28 July 1845: *son of Major Debrix and Polly his wife...of a bright complexion, bushy hair...aged about 22 years and is 5'8-3/4" high* [Hudgins, *Surry County Register of Free Negroes*, 72, 80, 87, 166].

Another member of the family was

    i.   John[3], born say 1760, a "Negro" taxable in James City County in 1786 who served in the Revolution [NSDAR, *African American Patriots*, 149].

DEMERY FAMILY

1.   John[1] Demerea, born say 1685, was called a "Negro belonging to John Lear of Nansemond County" when he was allowed to sue for his freedom in the General Court of Virginia. On 13 June 1711 he complained that, contrary to instructions from the court, Lear had severely beaten him. The Council of Colonial Virginia ordered the attorney general to prosecute Lear for his contempt of court [McIlwaine, Minutes of the Council, III:277-8]. He purchased 118 acres on the south side of Seacock Swamp in Isle of Wight County adjoining Bartholomew Andrews on 8 September 1732 (called John Demaris); he sold 43 acres on the south side of Blackwater Swamp adjoining John Warren and Randal Revel on 21 February 1742 (called John Dimrea); and on 28 October 1745 he and his wife Bridget Demmira sold 97 acres to John **Portis**. This was land on the south side of Lightwood Swamp which was part of the 118 acres he had purchased in 1732 [DB 4:233; 6:198; 7:205]. He was called John Demira on 12 November 1747 when the Isle of Wight County court exempted him from paying taxes due to his old age and infirmity [Orders 1746-52, 57]. On 13 June 1754 he was one of fourteen heads of household who were sued in Southampton County court by William Bynum (informer) for failing to pay the discriminatory tax on free African American and Indian women.[90] He pled not guilty at first but withdrew his plea and confessed when Francis **Locust**, James **Brooks**, James **Brooks**, Jr., John **Byrd** and John

---

[90]The other householders were John **Porteus**, Isaac **Young**, Thomas **Wilkins**, Francis **Locust**, James **Brooks**, Jr. and Sr., John **Byrd**, Jr. and Sr., Abraham **Artis**, Lewis **Artis**, William **Brooks**, Ann **Brooks**, and William **Tabor**.

Byrd, Jr., were found guilty. He was fined 1,000 pounds of tobacco, the fine for concealing two tithables, so he probably had two women in his household over the age of sixteen [Orders 1749-54, 501, 512; 1754-9, 25, 39]. He was called John Demaree of Northampton County in the 3 May 1758 session of the North Carolina Assembly when he was excused from paying taxes because he was old and disabled [Saunders, *Colonial Records of North Carolina*, V:1008]. He was probably the ancestor of

2   i.   John[2], born say 1735.
3   ii.   Frederick, born say 1738.
4   iii. Daniel, born say 1740.
       iv.   David[1], born say 1745, sued Moses Hasty in Southampton County court on 12 November 1773. His suit against William **Brooks** was dismissed on 12 August 1779 by agreement of the parties. He was executor of Frederick Demmery's 28 August 1780 Southampton County will. On 9 July 1784 he was a co-defendant with Abraham **Freeman** in a Southampton County suit brought by the administrator of Burwell Barnes, deceased, and he sued John and Britain Bowers for 2 pounds, 18 shillings on 13 August 1787 [Orders 1772-7, 302; 1778-84, 84, 439; 1784-9, 317]. He was executor of the 28 August 1780 Southampton County will of Frederick Demmery [WB 3:348]. He was taxable in St. Luke's Parish, Southampton County, from 1782 to 1788: taxable on 3 horses and 17 cattle in 1782, charged with Richard Demery's tax in 1787, charged with Micajah Demery's tax in 1788 [PPTL 1782-92, frames 504, 545, 569, 635, 658].
       v.   Lucy, born about 1757, head of a Northampton County household of 4 "free colored" in 1820 [NC:226]. She registered in Southampton County on 15 March 1827: *Lucy Dimmery, age 70, light complexion, 5 feet 4-3/4 inches, free born* [Register of Free Negroes 1794-1832, no. 1757].

2.   John[2] Demery, born say 1735, purchased 100 acres near Corduroy Swamp in Northampton County, North Carolina, on 8 January 1757 and another 100 acres adjoining this on 16 April 1771 [DB 2:345, 5:93]. He voted for Joseph Sikes in the Northampton County election of 1762 [SS 837 by *NCGSJ* XII:170]. He was one of the "Black" members of the undated colonial muster of Captain James Fason's Northampton County militia [Mil. T.R. 1-3]. He sold his Northampton County land on 15 February 1778 [DB 6:227], and was taxed on 350 acres and one Black Poll in Captain Dupree's District of Bladen County in 1784 [Bladen Co. Historical Soc., *1784 Tax List, Bladen County*, 13]. He was a taxable head of a Bladen County household of one "white" (free) male from 21-60 years old, six under 21 or over 60, and one white female in 1786 and taxable on 550 acres in 1779 and 450 acres in 1789 [Byrd, *Bladen County Tax Lists*, II:142, 171, 201]. He was head of a Bladen County household of 9 "other free" in 1790 [NC:188] and a Liberty County, South Carolina household of 5 "other free" in 1800 [SC:779]. His probable children were
       i.   Allen[1], born say 1758, a taxable "Black Male" in Matthew Moore's Bladen County household in 1770 and head of a "white" (free) household in 1786: one male 21-60 years old, two males under 21 or over 60, and three females [Byrd, *Bladen County Tax Lists*, I:50; II:174]. He was head of an Anson County household of 7 "other free" in 1790 [NC:35] and 5 in 1800 [NC:203]. He enlisted in the 10th North Carolina Regiment [Clark, *Colonial and State Records*, 16:1047]. He received an Anson County grant for land on Savannah Creek on 21 January 1800 and sold this land on 27 August 1806, 20 February 1807, and 2 April 1807 [DB 12:170, S:167, N&O:142, T:39, 90]. He was called a "Mulatto man" on 8 August 1800 when he and a white man named James Porter were charged in Southampton County

court with the murder of Jacob **Artis** at Jacob's house in Southampton County on 30 July that year. The court heard testimony from five white witnesses and Rebecca **Artis** and sent the prisoners to Suffolk for trial [Minutes 1799-1803, 109-10, 123, 213].

ii. Derinda, head of a Bladen County household of 3 "other free" in 1800 and 4 "free colored" women in 1820 [NC:132].

5 iii. John[3], born about 1774.

iv. Wiley, born say 1777, neglected to give in his list of tithables in Wake County in 1794 [MFCR 099.701.1, frame 212], head of an Anson County household of 3 "other free" in 1800 [NC:207], and counted a second time as Wiley **Young** [NC:203], called William Demery in 1810, head of a Marion District, South Carolina household of 3 "other free" in [SC:80].

3. Frederick Demmery, born say 1738, was living in Southampton County, Virginia, on 28 August 1780, when he made his will, proved 8 November 1781, David Demmery executor [WB 3:348]. He named the following beneficiaries but did not state his relationship to them:

i. Richard, born say 1762, sued in Southampton County court by Lewis **Artis** for a debt of 4,000 pounds of tobacco. On 9 December 1784 the court attached his goods which included two feather beds and furniture, two spinning wheels, a chest, table, frying pan, pot, 20 weight of cotton, 20 barrels of corn, 250 pounds of tobacco, a plow hoe, four weeding hoes, two tubs, three water pails, and two brandy barrels [Orders 1784-9, 7]. He was taxable in Southampton County in Jacob Newsum's household in 1784, charged with his own tax in 1785, taxable in David Dimmory's household in 1787, in Drew Powell's household in 1788 and 1789, and in Thomas Holladay's household in 1792 [PPTL 1782-92, frames 549, 563, 635, 667, 716, 876]. He was head of a Northampton County, North Carolina household of 6 "other free" in 1800 [NC:435].

ii. Tempy.

iii. Micajah[1], born say 1765, a "Black" person 12-50 years old living alone in Captain Dupree's District of Northampton County in 1786 for the North Carolina state census. He was taxable in St. Luke's Parish, Southampton County, in David Demery's household in 1788 and was called Micajah Y. Dimory when he was charged with his own tax in 1789 [PPTL 1782-92, frames 658, 708]. He called himself Micajah **Young** on 30 April 1794 when he married Elizabeth **Evans**, Wake County, North Carolina bond. He was head of a Wake County household of 2 "other free" in 1790 (abstracted as Micajah Dempsey) [NC:106]. He was head of an Anson County household of 5 "other free" in 1800, counted as Micajah **Young** [NC:203] and counted a second time as Micajah Demery [NC:207], 7 in 1810 (as Micajah Demery) [NC:44], and 11 "free colored" in 1820, called "Micajah Demery alias Young" [NC:12].

iv. Day, born say 1773, probably identical to David[2] Demery who was ordered bound out by the overseers of the poor in St. Luke's Parish, Southampton County, on 11 September 1789 [Minutes 1786-90, n.p.]. David was over the age of 16 when he was listed as a taxable in John Kindred's St. Luke's Parish, Southampton County household from 1794 to 1796 [PPTL 1792-1806, frame 84, 164, 194].

v. Collin, born say 1775, ordered bound out by the overseers of the poor in St. Luke's Parish, Southampton County, on 11 September 1789 [Minutes 1786-90, n.p.]. He was taxable in St. Luke's Parish, Southampton County, in Howell Vaughn's household in 1795 [PPTL 1792-1806, frame 172].

4.   Daniel Demery, born say 1740, may have been identical to Daniel Dunery of
      Southampton County whose wife (no race indicated) gave birth to triplets,
      Jemima, Kezia (who died a few days after birth), and Karenhappuch, in
      October 1768 according to the 3 November 1768 issue of the Virginia Gazette
      [Headley, *18th Century Newspapers*, 100]. He was living in Southampton
      County on 12 September 1771 when he was sued by Shadrack Kennebrough
      for 1 pound, 12 shillings, and he sued Simon Turner, executor of Exum
      Williamson, for a debt of 6 pounds, 19 shillings on 10 June 1773 [Orders
      1768-72, 449; 1772-7, 204, 221, 356]. He was taxable in Northampton
      County, North Carolina, in 1780 [G.A. 46.1] and head of a household of 7
      "Black" persons 12-50 years old and 8 "Black" persons less than 12 or over
      50 years old in Captain Dupree's District in 1786 for the state census for
      Northampton County. He was head of a Northampton County household of 10
      "other free" in 1790 [NC:74]. The administration of his Northampton County
      estate was granted to Edward Lawry on 1 June 1795 on security of 100 pounds
      [Minutes 1772-96, 172]. His children may have been
      i.   Shadrack, born say 1775, married Charlotte **Hicks**, 8 February 1794
            Southampton County, Virginia bond, Aaron **Heathcock (Haithcock)**
            surety. He was taxable in Southampton County in John Robertson's
            household in 1792 and in Thomas Taylor's household in 1795 [PPTL
            1782-92, frame 883; 1792-1806, frame 171]. He was head of a
            Northampton County household of 7 "other free" in 1810 [NC:718].
6   ii.   Wright, born say 1777.
      iii. James, head of a Halifax County, North Carolina household of 11
            "other free" in 1810. Perhaps his widow was Winny, born before 1776,
            head of a Halifax County household of 4 "free colored" females in
            1820 [NC:145].
      iv.   John[4], born about 1783, registered in Southampton County on 31
            February 1804: *age 21, yellow 5 feet 4 3/4 inches, Free born* [Register
            of Free Negroes 1794-1832, no. 303]. He married Rebecca **Stewart**,
            10 February 1806 Greensville County, Virginia bond, Frederick
            Shelton surety. He registered in Greensville County on 9 May 1807:
            *Born free as appears from a Certificate of Norfolk County, aged twenty
            four years...five feet five Inches & 3/4 high* [Register of Free Negroes,
            no.10]. He and his wife Rebecca were living in Northampton County,
            North Carolina, on 8 November 1806 when they sold 91 acres in
            Greensville County to Henry **Stewart** with Benjamin **Gowing** as
            witness [DB 3:523]. He was taxable in Meherrin Parish, Greensville
            County, in 1806. He apparently died before 1810 since Rebecca was
            taxable in Greensville County on a horse in 1810 and was listed by
            herself as a "Mulatto" in 1813 [PPTL 1782-1850, frames 352, 432,
            401, 446, 461, 487].
      v.   Beehy, head of a Greensville County household of 3 "free colored" in
            1820 [VA:261].

5.   John[3] Demery, born about 1774 in Charleston, South Carolina, married Sarah
      Robinson in Anson County, North Carolina, in 1801 according to his own
      recollection [*History of Randolph County, Indiana*, 137]. He was head of a
      Bladen County household of 4 "other free" in 1800, 3 in Marion District,
      South Carolina, in 1810 [SC:80, 84a], and 5 "free colored" in Anson County
      in 1820 [NC:12]. He was taxed on 300 acres and two free Negroes in Horry
      District, South Carolina, in 1824 [Comptroller General, Returns 1824,
      no.311]. He purchased land in Anson County on Island Creek that same year
      on 12 January and sold it three months later on 6 April 1824 [DB V:108,
      140]. He was the first African American to settle in the western part of
      Randolph County, Indiana. He came to Randolph County with Lemuel Vestal
      in 1825 and settled in Stony Creek. He had 80 acres of land and a house and
      lot in Winchester at the time of his death in 1860 [*History of Randolph*

County, Indiana, 137]. He was a sixty-nine-year-old head of a Washington Township, Randolph County, Indiana household with Polly (sixty years old) and son Maston (thirteen years old) in 1850. His children were

   i. Mary, married William **Weaver**.
   ii. Irvin.
   iii. John[5], born say 1805.
   iv. Hannah, married James **Scott**, son of Robert **Scott** who was emancipated in 1779 in North Carolina. They came to Randolph County from Wayne County in 1832. They had fourteen children.
   v. Robert, who lived in Cabin Creek settlement.
   vi. Charles.
   vii. Coleman.
   viii. William H., born say 1830, told his life story to the author of the *History of Randolph County* in 1888 as follows: He started life at sea in 1845 as servant to Commodore Perry aboard the James K. Polk which burned at the Strait of Gibraltar. In 1847 he worked as a steward on a steamer to Europe, the Middle East, and the West Indies. In 1852 he worked on several Mississippi steamboats and later returned to farm life in Randolph County [*History of Randolph County*, 137-138].
   ix. Zachary.
   x. Phebe Ann, married Jacob Felters.
   xi. Maston, born about 1837, thirteen years old in 1850.

6. Wright Demery, born say 1777, was head of a Northampton County household of 6 "other free" in 1810 [NC:718]. His children may have been
   i. William, born say 1798, married Tamer **Wilkins**, 31 January 1816 Northampton County marriage bond with Wright Demery bondsman. William and Tamer were found dead six years later on 5 March 1822 when a coroner's jury was appointed by the Northampton County court to determine the cause of death [Minutes 1821-25, 84].
   ii. Micajah[2], born 1814, married Nancy **Roberts**, 20 August 1833 Northampton County bond. They were counted in household no. 231 in the census for Jefferson Township, Logan County, Ohio, in 1850.

DEMPSEY FAMILY

1. Patience[1] Dempsey, born say 1700, purchased 50 acres on Salmon Creek in Bertie County on 6 May 1743 and another 50 acres adjoining this land on 23 April 1759. She may have been the daughter of Mary Dempsey who also purchased land on Salmon Creek in Bertie a few years earlier on 4 June 1739 [DB F:84, 425; I:224]. Mary died shortly after, before November that year, when George[1] Dempsey proved an inventory of her estate in Bertie County court [Haun, *Bertie County Court Minutes*, I:267]. George lived in the vicinity of Patience and her family but was taxed as white in all the extant Bertie tax lists. Patience was taxable on one tithe in the 1751 summary tax list for Bertie [CCR 190] and taxable in the 1756 list of Constable John Reddit adjacent to George and Joseph Dempsey [CR 10.702.1, Box 1]. She was probably a white woman who was taxable on her children. In 1759 she was listed in John Brickell's list, not taxed on herself, but taxable on her "sons Thorogood, James, Joshua," and "Negro Kate" (her daughter Catherine, named in her will). Her 12 February 1764 Bertie County will was proved in August 1764. The will mentions the gift of a horse to her daughter Amy "in trust for her father" [WB A:58]. However, there is no further record of him in the Bertie County records.

A June 1849 North Carolina court case provides a description of the family. A Dempsey descendant, accused of carrying his gun without a license, gave evidence of his parentage. A witness deposed that he heard "barncastle, a very old man now deceased," say that the defendant's great grandfather, Joseph Dempsey, alias Darby, was a "coal black negro;" his wife a white woman (Patience?); their child Joseph, a reddish copper colored man with curly red hair and blue eyes; his wife a white woman; their child William married a white woman; their son Whitmel married a white woman, and they were the parents of the defendant [Catterall, *Judicial Cases Concerning American Slavery*, II:132].

William, the defendant's grandfather, was taxed in Joseph Dempsey's household about 1772 [CR 10.702.1, box 3]. Barncastle may have been Richard Barnecaster, counted in the 1790 census for Bertie County [NC:11]. "Whitmel" may have been Whitand Demsey, head of a Bertie County household of 13 "free colored" in 1820 [NC:68]. Patience's children were

2	i.	Joseph, born say 1720, died after 1788.
3	ii.	Amy, born say 1724.
4	iii.	Catherine/ Kate, born say 1734.
5	iv.	Thoroughgood[1], born say 1740.
6	v.	James[1], born say 1742.
	vi.	Joshua, born say 1745, taxed as a single "free Mulatto" in the 1763 list of John Nichols, and in 1764 with wife, identified as Mary in the 1766 list of John Crickett. He purchased land on the south side of Salmon Creek on 1 October 1767 [DB L:101]. He was ordered to work on the road from Duckinfield's in May 1782, and his sons were ordered to work on the road from the "middle swamp to Hootins" in November 1787 along with the other freeholders of that district [Haun, *Bertie County Court Minutes*, V:680]. He purchased 75 acres near Duckinfield's line in December 1797 and sold land that same year [DB R:514; S:50]. He was head of a Bertie County household of 9 "other free" in 1790 [NC:12], 7 in 1800 [NC:40], and 12 in 1810 [NC:147].
7	vii.	Mary **Brantly**, born say 1744, married Peter **Brantly**.

2. Joseph Dempsey, born say 1720, was not named in Patience Dempsey's will but may have been the father of the "grandson Billy" mentioned in her will. William, though not identified as Joseph's son, was taxed in his household in the 1772 list of George Lockhart [CR 10.702.1, box 3]. Joseph bought 78 acres on the south side of Bucklesberry Pocosin in Bertie County on 10 August 1742, sold this land to Robert West on 11 May 1752, and repurchased it again on 5 April 1756 [DB F:377; G:527; I:242]. His wife Eleanor Dempsey signed the dower release for the 11 May 1752 sale. Since she was not tithed in any of the tax lists, she was probably white as claimed in the 1849 court case. He was taxed on two tithes in the 1754 summary list, and was a "Mul." insolvent taxpayer in 1758. He was taxable with his son George in 1759; with William, in 1770 and 1772, and with Keziah in 1774 and 1775. He sold the remainder of his land by a deed proved in the August 1788 Bertie County court [DB O:241]. His children were

	i.	George[2], born before 1748, taxed in his father's household in the list of William Gray in 1759: "Joseph Dempsey and George his son" 2 black tithes. He was head of a Bertie County household of 9 "other free" in 1790 [NC:12].
8	ii.	William[1], born about 1760.
	iii.	Keziah, born 1762, taxable in Joseph's household in 1774.
	iv.	?Johnson, born say 1770, among the freeholders ordered by the May 1792 Bertie court to work on the road from Luke Collins Ferry to Sprewell Road with William and George Dempsey [Haun, *Bertie County Court Minutes*, VI:942]. He was head of a Bertie County household of 7 in 1800 [NC:40], 5 in Halifax County, North Carolina, in 1810 [NC:16], and 8 "free colored" in Halifax County in 1830.

3. Amy Dempsey, born say 1724, was called "Amey Demsey of Bertie County Spinster" when she sued Samuel Ormes, agent for Nathaniel Duckingfield, for her freedom on 29 March 1745 in Chowan County General Court [General Court Dockets, 1742-45, 2nd and 3rd pages from the end of reel]. She may have been the "Ann Dempsey" who was taxed as a "free molato" in John Nichols' list for Bertie County in 1763. By her mother's Bertie County will, she was allowed to keep a cow, a calf, and a mare previously lent to her. In her will Patience also mentioned a granddaughter Patience[2] Dempsey, who was to receive the first calf from the cow she had given her unnamed mother. Both Amy and Catherine received cows, so one of them was Patience[2]'s mother. Amy's children were

    i. Jesse[1], born about 1748, the eight-year-old son of Amy Demsey a "Free Mullatoe," bound to Margaret Dukinfield to learn husbandry on 27 January 1756. He was taxable in 1767 in John Pearson's household in the list of William Nichols. He was listed in the 1778 Bertie tax summary list, assessment blank.

    ii. George[3], born about 1748, the eight-year-old son of Amy Demsey a "Free Mullattoe," bound to Margaret Dukinfield to learn husbandry on 27 January 1756.

    iii. Squire, born about 1750, the six-year-old son of Amy Demsey a "Free Mullattoe," bound to Margaret Dukinfield to learn husbandry on 27 January 1756 [CR 010.101.7 by *NCGSJ* XIII:168, 169, 170].

    iv. ?Patience[2], head of a Perquimans County household of 11 "other free" and 2 white women in 1810 [NC:948].

4. Catherine/ Kate Dempsey, born say 1734, was taxable in 1751 in Thomas Ashley's household in the summary list for Bertie County [CCR 190]. She was a "free Mulatto" taxable in her own household in the 1762 Constable's list of Benjamin Ashburn(?) and taxed for the last time in 1767 in the list of William Nichols. Her son was

    i. George[4], born about 1750, ordered by the August 1763 Bertie County court bound an apprentice to John Nichols, one of the executor's of his grandmother's will [Haun, *Bertie County Court Minutes*, III:631]. George was a taxable "free Mulatto" in John Nichols' household in the 1766 list of John Crickett.

5. Thoroughgood[1] Dempsey, born say 1740, was taxed in the 1763 list of John Nichols with Elizabeth Dempsey, identified as his wife in the 1764 summary and later Bertie tax lists. He received 50 acres by his mother's will. He probably left the county after 1770 since he and Elizabeth were last taxed in the 1770 list of Edward Rasor. He was head of a household of 5 free males and 5 free females in District 3 of Halifax County, North Carolina, in 1786 for the state census. He purchased 40 acres in Halifax County on Little Quankey Creek on 20 November 1792 [DB 17:465] and was head of a Halifax County household of 8 "other free" in 1790 [NC:61] and 5 in 1800 [NC:307]. He may have been the ancestor of the many Dempseys who were living in Halifax County in the early nineteenth century:

    i. James[2], head of a Halifax County household of 5 "other free" in 1800 [NC:306], 11 in 1810 [NC:16], and 10 "free colored" in 1820 [NC:145].

    ii. Melvin, head of a Halifax County household of 9 "other free" in 1810 [NC:16].

    iii. Uriah, born before 1776, head of a Halifax County household of 6 "other free" in 1810 [NC:16], 8 "free colored" in 1820 [NC:145], and 4 "free colored" in 1830.

    iv. William[2], head of a Halifax County household of 4 "other free" in 1810 [NC:17] and 11 "free colored" in Bertie County in 1820 [NC:68].

v.   John, head of a Halifax County household of 3 "other free" in 1810 [NC:17] and 8 "free colored" in 1820 [NC:145].

vi.   Eliza, head of a Halifax County household of 5 "other free" in 1810 [NC:17].

6.   James[1] Dempsey, born say 1742, was a "free molatto" taxed in the Bertie County list of John Nichols in 1763 with "free molatto" Rebecca Dempsey, identified as his wife in the 1764 summary and later Bertie lists. He purchased 75 acres on Sams Branch adjoining his land and George[1] Dempsey's on 13 October 1762 and sold this land to William **James** on 5 September 1772 [DB K:217; L:349]. He was taxed on a valuation of 513 pounds in the 1779 list of Ryan and Hardy. He moved to Halifax County where he was head of a household of 3 "other free" in 1790 [NC:12] and 7 in 1800 [NC:304]. His children may have been

i.   Thurogood[2], born say 1760, head of a Bertie County household of 7 "other free" in 1790 [NC:12], 10 in 1800 [NC:40], and 7 in Martin County in 1810 [NC:433].

ii.   Edmund, head of a Bertie County household of 14 "other free" in 1810 [NC:147].

iii.   Josiah, born 1776-94, head of a Bertie County household of 10 "free colored" in 1830 [NC:68].

7.   Mary **Brantly**, born say 1744, was probably the "daughter Mary" mentioned in Patience Dempsey's 1764 will. She was taxable with Patience's grandson Isaac in the 1764 summary list, and she was taxable in her own household in the 1766 summary list and the 1767 list of William Nichols. Her children and husband were identified in the Bertie County court and indenture records:

i.   Sarah, born about 1760, called orphan of Peter Brantly, deceased, in Mary's September 1771 Bertie County court petition to have her bound as an apprentice to John Pearson, the executor of Patience's will [Haun, *Bertie County Court Minutes*, III:982]. The indenture was signed the same month [*NCGSJ* XIV:34]. She received "one Motherless Calf" by the will of her grandmother Patience.

ii.   Darby, born about 1768, also called orphan of Peter Brantly, bound out with his sister Sarah. He was head of a Bertie County household of 4 "other free" in 1790 [NC:11].

iii.   ?Jeremiah, born 10 January 1774, (no parent named) bound to be a shoemaker on 16 May 1791 [*NCGSJ* XIV:165].

iv.   Rachel, daughter of Mary Brantly, born February 1776, bound an apprentice in May 1786 [Haun, *Bertie County Court Minutes*, V:582]. She married King **Sanderlin**, 21 December 1805 Bertie County bond, Richard Dempsey bondsman.

v.   Joshua, born January 1778, bound an apprentice cooper in May 1786 [Haun, *Bertie County Court Minutes*, V:582], head of a Bertie County household of 6 "other free" in 1810 [NC:147].

8.   William[1] Dempsey was born about 1760 since he was taxed in the household of (his father?) Joseph Dempsey in 1772. He was head of a Bertie County household of 8 "other free" in 1800 [NC:41] and 11 "free colored" in 1820 [NC:68]. According to the 1849 court case mentioned above, his son was probably

i.   Whitand/Whitmel, born 1776-94, called Whitand Demsey, head of a Bertie County household of 13 "free colored" in 1820 [NC:68]. He was called Whitmell Demsey when he married Anna Bowen (who was most likely white), 17 June 1801 Bertie County bond with Elisha Dempsey bondsman.

Other Demseys

9. Parthena Dempsey, born say 1760, had several of her children, "mulatto Bastards," indentured by the Bertie County court. They were
    i.   Dick, born 1775, ordered bound to Zedekiah Stone in November 1778.
    ii. Rendah, born 1777, ordered bound to Zedekiah Stone [Haun, *Bertie County Court Minutes*, IV:274].
    iii. Bristol, born 1779, bound to Zedekiah Stone to be a shoemaker, on 9 February 1780 [*NCGSJ* XIV:36].
    iv. ?Thomas, born about 1779, no parent named when he was ordered bound by the August Bertie court to David **James** to be a blacksmith [Haun, *Bertie County Court Minutes*, V:458]. He was head of a Bertie County household of 4 "other free" in 1800 [NC:40].

10. Ann Dempsey, born say 1770, was head of a Bertie County household of 5 "other free" in 1800 [NC:41] and 3 in Halifax County in 1810 [NC:17]. Her children were
    i.   Johnston, son of Ann, no age or race stated when he was bound to Jehu Nichols to be a blacksmith on 3 February 1794 [*NCGSJ* XV:34]. He was head of a Bertie County household of 2 "free colored" in 1820 [NC:68] and one "free colored" in Halifax County in 1830.
    ii. ?William[3], bound an apprentice on 3 February 1794, no parent named [*NCGSJ* XV:34]. He was head of a Bertie County household of 6 "free colored" in 1820 [NC:68].
    iii. ?Elisha, born before 1776, bound an apprentice on 3 February 1794, no age or parent named [*NCGSJ* XV:34]. He was head of a Bertie County household of 12 "free colored" in 1820 [NC:68].

11. Henry[1]/ Harry Dempsey, born circa 1770, was head of a Northampton County, North Carolina household of 2 "other free" in 1800 [NC:436]. He obtained free papers in Northampton County on 11 October 1839, and registered in Logan county, Ohio, on 1 October 1847. The papers described him and his wife as

    yellow complexion, 65 or 70, 5 foot nine and one half inches high, right leg missing, wife Tabitha, yellow complexion...[Turpin, *Register of Black, Mulatto, and Poor Persons*, 12].

    They were living in Urbana Township, Champaign County, Ohio, in 1850 [Census p.831]. Their children were
    i.   Wesley, born about 1817, married Sally **Anders**, 2 June 1838 Northampton County bond, Squire **Walden** bondsman. He obtained free papers in Northampton County on 9 October 1838: *son of Henry and Tabitha Dempsy...five feet nine or ten inches high of brown complexion well set...married to Sally Andus daughter of Archer Andus.* His wife Sally was born about 1820, *of free parentage...of bright complexion.* They recorded their free papers in Champaign County, Ohio, on 22 December 1841.
    ii. Henry[2], born 28 December 1821.
    iii. Eliza, born 28 May 1824.
    iv. Elisha, born 22 February 1827.
    v.   Harrison, born 4 January 1829.
    vi. Elizabeth, born 5 April 1832 [Turpin, *Register of Black, Mulatto, and Poor Persons*, 12].

12. Jesse[2] Dempsey, born about 1773, was head of a Northampton County household of 7 "free colored" in 1820 [NC:224]. He was counted in the 1850 Ohio census for Logan County in Monroe Township, household number 155, page 20: seventy-seven years old, Male Mulatto, with sixty-year-old Angeline, twenty-year-old Willis, seventeen-year-old Rachel, and seven-year-old Edward,

all born in North Carolina. Perhaps his other children were the Dempseys living in the nearby households:

    i.   James[3], born in North Carolina about 1823, counted with Kiturah Dempsey who was thirty years old.

    ii.   Dillard, born in North Carolina about 1825, counted with Anna Dempsey. Like many free African Americans he moved to Canada where his children were born. They were listed with him in his 1860 Logan County household: six-year-old Thomas, seven-year-old Angeline, and three-year-old Joseph. He had real estate worth $1,800 and personal estate of $300 in 1860.

DENNIS FAMILY

1.   Elizabeth Dennis, born say 1736, was living in Brunswick County, Virginia, on 24 June 1765 when she was sued for debt by the churchwardens of Meherrin Parish. She may have been the mother of Robert and Catherine Dennis, "mullata Bastard Children," who were bound out by the churchwardens of St. Andrew's Parish, Brunswick County on 23 July 1759 [Orders 1765, 270; 1757-9, 374]. And she may have been related to Diverz Dennis, head of a Bertie County household of 9 "other free" in 1800 [NC:42]. Perhaps she was the mother of

    i.   Robert, born say 1754, called "a Certain Molatto Boy, Bob," in Chatham County, North Carolina court on 14 February 1775 when he complained that Pritteman Berry was unlawfully detaining him as a servant. He was called Robert Dennis "molatto" when the court ordered him released from his indenture to Berry about a month later on 9 May. He died about May 1795 when an inquest on his dead body was returned to court by the coroner [Minutes 1774-9, 51, 54, 61; 1794-1800, 43b].

2   ii.   Catherine, born say 1756.

2.   Catherine Dennis, born say 1756, was living in Chatham County when her daughter Mary Dennis was bound to Joseph Griffin. She was the mother of

    i.   Mary, born about 1772, eleven years old when she was bound out by the Chatham County court on 13 May 1783 [Minutes 1781-5, 31b].

    ii.   ?Phillis, a "free woman of colour," living in Cumberland County on 10 June 1841 when the court gave her permission to use her gun in the county [Minutes 1840-2].

Another member of a Dennis family was

    i.   Andrew, born 22 February 1755, a sixteen-year-old "Mulatto" bound to Daniel Roberts in Norborne Parish, Frederick County, Virginia, on 7 August 1771 [Orders 1770-2, 239].

DENNUM FAMILY

1.   Hannah Dennam, born say 1690, received slaves Jack and Peter by the 2 March 1726/7 Charles City County will of (her father?) Gibson **Gibson** [DW 1724-31, 122, 161-2, 166-7]. She may have been the mother of

    i.   Philip, born say 1730, living in Halifax County, Virginia, when he and William **Donathan** were among those ordered to clear a road from Burches Creek to Mirey Creek. On 21 March 1765 his bill of sale to James Roberts, Jr., Gentleman, was proved, and on 16 May 1765 the court presented him, Shadrack **Gowin**, and Peter **Rickman** for concealing a tithable on information of John Bates, Gentleman. The tithables were probably their wives. Their cases were dismissed in August 1766, perhaps on payment of the tax. He was sued for debt seven times between June 1769 and 23 April 1774. In October 1770 the court awarded one of Philip's debtors 10 shillings for carpentry work that he had performed for Moses Echols [Pleas 1763-4, 303; 1764-7, 46, 358; 369, 415, 491, 528; 1770-2, 55, 86, 114, 147-8; 1774-9, 43].

DE ROSARIO FAMILY

1. Lawrence De Rosario, born say 1735, and his wife Susannah, "free Negros," were the parents of Mary De Rozaras who was born 30 August and baptized 6 October 1765 in Bruton Parish, James City County [Bruton Parish Register, 26]. He proved a deed from Sarah **Cumbo** to Simon **Gillett** in York County court on 18 October 1784 [Orders 1784-7, 86]. He was taxable in York County from 1782 to 1793 and taxable on 2 free tithes and a slave in 1794. His widow Susanna Derozario was taxable on a horse in 1796, a horse and a slave in 1797 and head of a household of a "free Negro & mulatto over 16" in 1813 [PPTL, 1782-1841, frames 69, 92, 107, 140, 191, 201, 220, 229, 387]. Lawrence was taxable on 20 acres in York County in 1791, and his estate was taxable on 30 acres in 1800 [1791 Land Tax List, p.2; 1800, p.2]. A report of the allotment of Susanna's dower in the lands of her late husband Lawrence was returned to court on 19 June 1797 [Orders 1795-1803, 180]. He was the father of

    i.   ?Elizabeth Rozario, born say 1760, head of a household of 3 "free" black persons in Williamsburg in 1782 [VA:45], probably the mother of Caroline and Suckey Rosara who were counted in a list of "Free Negroes and mulattoes" in Williamsburg in 1813 [Waldrep, *1813 Tax List*]. See also the Rosario family.
    ii. Mary, born 30 August 1765.
    iii. ?Clary Rozorro, born before 1776, head of a James City County household of 4 free colored" in 1820 [VA:119].
    iv. John W., born say 1776, taxable in York County in 1797 and head of a household of a "free Negro & mulatto over 16" in 1814 [PPTL, 1782-1841, frames 229, 296, 305, 405].

They may have been the ancestors of

    i.   Laurence Rosarran, born about 1804, obtained a certificate of freedom in Charles City County on 19 February 1824: *twenty years of age, 5 feet 4-1/2 inches, dark complexion* [Minutes 1823-9, 25].

DIXON FAMILY

Members of the Dixon family of Virginia were

    i.   Richard Dickson, born say 1760, a "Mul" head of household in Buxton's District of Nansemond County in 1784 [VA:74].
    ii. Francis, Sr., taxable on 30 acres on North Run in Charles City County from 1787 to 1817 [Land Tax List 1782-1830].
    iii. Francis, Jr., a "Mulattoe" taxable in Charles City County in 1813.
    iv. Henry, head of a Charles City County household of 1 "other free" in 1810 [VA:959].

DOBBINS FAMILY

1. George[1] Dobbins, born say 1710, and his wife Mary were the parents of Elizabeth and Mary Dobbins, "poor orphans" of Southam Parish, who were bound out by the Cumberland County, Virginia court on 26 August 1752 [Orders 1752-8, 37]. They were the parents of

2   i.   ?Sarah, born say 1730.
3   ii. ?Jane[1], born say 1740.
4   iii. Elizabeth, born say 1747.
        iv. Mary, born say 1749.

2. Sarah Dobbins, born say 1730, petitioned the Cumberland County court on 27 August 1751 for her freedom from Thomas Walker and was granted her petition on 26 August 1752. She was called Sarah Dobbins alias Young on 27 August 1751 when the court ordered the churchwardens of Southam Parish to bind out her son Will. On 23 March 1761 the court ordered the churchwardens to bind her son Charles Dobbyns to Philip Dunford, and on 27 July 1761 the court ordered the churchwardens to bind her children William and George Dobbyns to William Clarke [Orders 1749-51, 316; 1752-8, 40; 1758-62, 371]. She was the mother of

    i.   William[1], born say 1751, discharged from the service of William Clarke by the Cumberland County court on testimony of Joseph Robinson on 27 July 1772. On 23 November 1772 the court ordered William Clarke and his wife Martha to pay him his freedom dues [Orders 1770-2, 315].

    ii.   Charles, born say 1760, a "yellow" complexioned soldier born in Prince Edward County who enlisted as a substitute in the Revolution in Dinwiddie County [NSDAR, *African American Patriots*, 149]. He was taxable in Powhatan County in 1794, 1795 and a "M°" taxable there from 1802 to 1806 [PPTL, 1787-1825, frames 105, 117, 239, 255, 277, 293, 316].

    iii.   George[2], taxable in Powhatan County on 2 horses in 1787 and 1788 [PPTL, 1787-1825, frames 5, 18], head of a Nelson County household of 6 "other free" in 1810 [VA:689].

3. Jane[1] Dobbins, born say 1740, was mother of Benjamin **Branham** (no race indicated) who was bound by the Cumberland County court to Robert Moore on 24 August 1761. He was called Benjamin **Branum**, a "Mulattoe Boy," on 23 May 1763 when the court ordered the churchwardens of Southam Parish to bind him to Absalom Davenport [Orders 1758-62, 391, 477; 1762-4, 219]. She was the mother of

    i.   Benjamin **Branham**, a "Mulattoe" boy bound out in 1763.

    ii.   William[2], son of Jane Dobbins bound to Joseph Harris in Cumberland County on 27 August 1764, no race indicated [Orders 1764-7, 4].

4. Elizabeth Dobbins, born say 1747, was living in Cumberland County on 23 January 1769 when the court ordered the churchwardens of Southam Parish to bind out her son James Dobbins to James Bryden. On 28 August 1775 the court bound her "mulattoe" children Henry and John Dobbins to Hans Stegar [Orders 1774-8, 339]. She was the mother of

    i.   James, born say 1766, ordered bound to James Bryden on 23 January 1769 and a "poor orphan" bound to Francis Stegar on 26 April 1773 [Orders 1772-4, 178].

5   ii.   Richard, born about 1768.

    iii.   Henry, born say 1772, taxable in John Chitwood's Powhatan County household in 1791 [PPTL, 1787-1825, frame 58].

    iv.   John, born say 1774, taxable in Powhatan County in 1801, a "F.B." taxable there in 1812 [PPTL, 1787-1825, frame 222, 419].

5. Richard Dobbins, born about 1768, son of Betty Dobbyns, was bound by the churchwardens of Southam Parish to John Skip Harris on 23 September 1771 [Orders 1770-2, 320]. He was a "free Black" taxable in Powhatan County in 1792 [PPTL, 1787-1825, frame 76] and a "Mulatto" ditcher in the upper district of Goochland County in 1805 and 1806 [PPTL, 1782-1809, frames 739, 779]. He was a "free Negro" listed with a male and female (probably his wife) in Prince Edward County in 1813 [Waldrep, *1813 Tax List*]. He registered in Petersburg on 8 July 1818: *a free man of Colour, five feet seven and a half inches high, fifty years old, yellowish brown Complection, born free*

p. cert. of Registry from Prince Edward County [Register of Free Negroes 1794-1819, no. 920]. He may have been the father of

    i.   Jane², married Anthony **Jenkins**, 26 October 1815 Goochland County bond, Austin **Isaacs** surety.

DOLBY/ DOBY FAMILY

1. John¹ Daulby, born say 1740, and his wife Mary, were "F.N." taxables in St. Brides Parish, Edmonds Bridge District, Norfolk County, Virginia, in 1767 [Wingo, *Norfolk County Tithables, 1766-1780*, p.27]. They were probably the parents of

    i.   Jarrot Doby/ Dalbey/ Dolby, born say 1760, head of a Northampton County, North Carolina household of 7 "other free" in 1790 [NC:75], 10 in 1800 [NC:435] and 7 in 1810 [NC:719].

    ii. John² Dobby, head of a Northampton County household of 5 "other free" in 1810 [NC:718].

DONATHAN FAMILY

1. Catherine Donathan, born say 1685, the white servant of Major Robert Bristow, had a "bastard Child born of her body begotten by a negroe man" in Lancaster County, Virginia, on 10 March 1703/4 [Orders 1702-13, 23]. Her child was most likely

2   i.   William¹, born 28 February 1704.

2. William¹ Donathan, born 28 February 1704, a "Mullatto," petitioned the Spotsylvania County court for his freedom from his master, John Grayson, claiming that he was over thirty-one years of age. However, Grayson convinced the court that William would not be thirty-one until 28 February 1735 [Orders 1734-5, 285]. He was sued for debt in Orange County, Virginia court in May 1738, but the case was dismissed on agreement of both parties. In July 1741 he purchased land by deed recorded in Orange County court. On 27 May 1742 he was living in St. Thomas' Parish when the Orange County court presented him and Elizabeth Hawkins for committing fornication. The charges were dismissed on 28 August when it was reported that they had run away. And on 29 January 1742/3 the court ordered the sheriff to sell his estate which consisted of 57 acres of land to pay a debt of 68 pounds which he owed Joseph Morton, Gent. [Orders 1734-9, 324, 339; 1739-41, 429; 1741-3, 153, 223, 344]. He purchased 90 acres in Louisa County by deed proved on 26 March 1745, and he was living in Louisa County on 28 May 1745 when he was presented by the court for failing to list a tithable (probably his wife) [Orders 1742-8, 140, 152, 157, 172]. He was granted 200 acres in Louisa County on both sides of Gibby's Creek adjoining his own land and George **Gibson** on 7 August 1752 [Patents 31:183]. He was in Cumberland Parish, Lunenburg County, by 14 November 1753 when he purchased 227 acres on Fucking Creek. He sold this land on 31 July 1758 and purchased another tract of 200 acres in Lunenburg County on the head branches of Little Creek [DB 4:66; 6:82]. He purchased land in Halifax County, Virginia, by deed proved in August 1766 and was added to the list of tithables in September 1769 but exempted (due to old age) from paying taxes in June 1770. He was permitted to build a water grist mill on his property in July 1770 [Pleas 5:265; 6:461, 506, 512]. He was living in Halifax County on 16 July 1773 when he sold his 200 acre tract in Mecklenburg County to Jacob **Chavis** [DB 4:144]. He and his wife Betty sold 400 acres of land by deed proved in Halifax County on 17 February 1780 and 21 February 1782 [Pleas 1779-83, 114, 231]. He was taxable in Henry County on slaves Rose and Nance from 1782 to 1784 [PPTL, 1782-1830, frames 10, 33, 82]. He was probably the ancestor of

    i.   William², head of a Wilkes County, North Carolina household of one white male over 16, one under 16, and 4 slaves in 1790 [NC:124].

    ii.   Sarah, born say 1750, living in Halifax County, Virginia, on 15 July 1773 when the court bound her daughter Mary Ann to Jane Jones. On 17 March 1774 the court ordered the churchwardens to bind out her illegitimate son Frederick Donathan [Pleas 1772-4, 185, 393]. Frederick was counted as white in Wilkes County in 1790 [NC:124].

    iii.   Elijah, and Rachel Donathan sold for 100 pounds 80 acres in Henry County on the south fork of the Little Dan River on 13 December 1787 [DB 1:432].

    iv.   Nelson, sued jointly with William Donathan in Halifax County, Virginia court on 17 December 1773 for a debt of 2 pounds, 12 shillings [Pleas 1772-4, 322]. He was counted as white in Wilkes County, North Carolina, in 1790 [NC:122].

    v.   Benjamin, born say 1765, head of a Wilkes County household of one male over 16 and three females (counted as white along with the **Gibson, Collins, Wooten,** and **Underwood** families) [NC:124], 7 "other free" and 2 slaves in 1800 [NC:35] and 9 "other free," a white woman, and 3 slaves in 1810 [NC:886].

    vi.   Jacob, born before 1776, head of a Surry County, North Carolina household of 4 "other free" in 1810 [SC:654] and 12 "free colored" in 1820 [NC:740].

    vii.   Reuben, head of a Wilkes County household of one "free colored" in 1820 [NC:531].

DOUGLASS FAMILY

Members of the Douglass family in Virginia and Maryland were

1   i.   Gabriel, born say 1760.

    ii.   Adam, head of a Rockbridge County household of 11 "other free" in 1810 [MD:271].

    iii.   William, head of an Accomack County household of 6 "other free" in 1810 [VA:89], perhaps identical to William Douglas who was head of a Petersburg Town household of 6 "other free" in 1810 [VA:126a].

    iv.   Charles, "F.N." head of a Culpeper County household of 3 "other free" in 1810 [VA:26].

1.   Gabriel Douglass, born say 1760, was head of a Washington County, Maryland household of 7 "other free" in 1800 [MD:636]. He was the father of Thomas Douglass who registered as a free Negro in Washington, D.C., on 3 October 1821: *son of Gabriel Douglass, a free man, and his wife, who is also free. Douglass has passed as free in Harper's Ferry for some years past* [Provine, *District of Columbia Free Negro Registers*, 10]. He was the father of

    i.   Thomas, head of an Anne Arundel County household of 9 "other free" in 1810 [MD:63].

    ii.   ?James, head of a Prince George's County household of 9 "other free" in 1810 [MD:44].

DOVE FAMILY

The Dove family of Anne Arundel County, Maryland, may have been related to John Dove, the "Mallatto slave" of Doctor Gustavus Brown, who was brought before the Charles County, Maryland court on suspicion of burglary on 14 November 1727 [Court Records 1727-31, 42].

1.   Mary Dove, born say 1710, was a "Negro woman" slave listed in the Anne Arundel County, Maryland, inventory of the estate of Eleazer Birkhead on 28

April 1744 [Prerogative Court (inventories) 1744-5, 43]. Birkhead's widow married Leonard Thomas, and Mary Dove sued him in Anne Arundel County court for her freedom in June 1746 [Judgment Record 1746-8, 118]. The outcome of the suit is not recorded, apparently because Thomas took her with him when he moved to Craven County, North Carolina.

In September 1749 the Dove family was living in Craven County when William Smith complained to the court on their behalf that Leonard Thomas was detaining them as slaves:

> *Moll, Nell, Sue, Sall, & Will, Negroes Detained as Slaves by Leonard Thomas That they are free born Persons in the Province of Maryland and brought to this Province by the said Leonard Thomas*

William Smith travelled to Maryland to prove their claim, and they were free by November 1756 when James Dove, a "Negro Servant," complained to the Craven County court that Smith was mistreating him, Nelly, Sue, Sarah, Moll, and William Dove [Haun, *Craven County Court Minutes,* IV:11-12, 366].

A grandson of Mary Dove named William **Dowry** was still held in slavery in Anne Arundel County in 1791 when he sued for his freedom in the General Court of Maryland. In October 1791 a fifty-seven or fifty-eight-year-old woman named Ann Ridgely (born about 1734), who was the daughter-in-law of Leonard Thomas, testified in Anne Arundel County that Mary Dove was a tall, spare woman of brown complexion and was the granddaughter of a woman imported into the country by the deponent's great grandfather. The deponent always understood that the grandmother of Mary Dove was a "Yellow Woman," had long black hair, was reputed to be an East Indian or a Madagascarian, and was called "Malaga Moll." Ridgely testified that Mary Dove had a daughter named Fanny who was the mother of William **Dowry** who petitioned for his freedom in the General Court of Maryland in 1791. She also testified that Mary Dove sued Leonard Thomas for freedom in Maryland, but before the suit was decided he moved with his family about twenty miles from Newbern, North Carolina, and took with him Mary, her three children, and her grandchildren Will and Sal. A certain Alexander Sands, commonly called Indian Sawony, was a witness for Mary Dove in her suit in Craven County, North Carolina, in 1749 and testified that her grandmother was an East Indian woman [Craven County Miscellaneous Records, C.R. 28.928.10, cited by Byrd, *In Full Force and Virtue*, 37-8].

Mary died before 6 April 1763 when the Craven County court appointed her son James Dove administrator of her estate on security of 100 pounds. On 6 April 1765 the court appointed George Hays administrator as greatest creditor on security of 200 pounds [Minutes 1762-66, 13d, 21b]. Her descendants were

   i.   Fanny, born about 1734, mother of William **Dowry** according to testimony by Ann Ridgely.

   ii.   James, born say 1737, described as "~~a free negro~~ a Negro Servant" in Craven County court in November 1756 when he complained on behalf of himself, Nelly, Sue, Sarah, Moll, and William Dove for mistreatment by William Smith, their master [Haun, *Craven County Court Minutes,* IV:366]. He complained in court again on 17 February 1759 that he had not received his freedom dues [Minutes 1758-61, 22a].

2   iii.   Nelly, born say 1738.

   iv.   Lucy, born say 1742, a servant girl, no age or race mentioned, who was ordered by the Craven County court to serve her master, Thomas Hasline, Esquire, another five months more than her indenture in July

1763 - perhaps as punishment for having a child during her indenture [Minutes 1762-64, 28c].
- v.   Susan, born say 1746.
- vi. Sally, born say 1747.
3 - vii. William[1], born say 1748.

2. Nelly Dove, born say 1738, complained to the Craven County court on 17 February 1759 that she had not received her freedom dues, but the court ruled that she should not be freed since she had two children during her indenture [Minutes 1758-61, 22a]. She was head of a Craven County household of 2 "other free" in 1790 [NC:131]. One of her children may have been
4 - i.   Susan, born 25 December 1768.

3. William[1] Dove, born say 1748, was the grandson of Mary Dove according to testimony by Ann Ridgely of Anne Arundel County, Maryland, in 1791. He purchased 90 acres on the east side of Hancock's Creek on Cahoque Creek in Craven County from Martin **Black** on 6 February 1775 [DB 22:73]. He received 4 pounds pay for 40 days service in the Craven County Militia under Major John Tillman in an expedition to Wilmington [Haun, *Revolutionary Army Accounts, Journal "A"*, 141]. He was head of a Craven County household of 9 "other free" in 1790 [NC:131]. Perhaps his children were
- i.   Pompey, born say 1770, head of a Craven County household of 1 "other free" in 1790 [NC:131].
- ii.   John, born before 1776, head of a Craven County household of 2 "free colored" in 1820 [NC:69].
- iii. Isaac[1], born 5 May 1771, bound an apprentice tanner to Bartholomew Howard by the 14 March 1775 Craven County court [Minutes 1772-84, vol. 1, 29d].
- iv.   Jacob, head of a Craven County household of 9 "free colored" in 1820 [NC:67]. He married Charity **Carter**, 3 June 1815 Craven County bond with George **Carter** bondsman. On 4 November 1821 Jacob and Charity Dove sold land in Craven County which she inherited from her father, George **Carter** [DB 43:82].
- v.   Keziah, married Richard **Lewis**, 16 March 1798 Craven County bond with Thomas **Lewis** bondsman.
- vi.   William[2], married June **Moore**, 13 March 1805 Craven County bond with Isaac Dove bondsman. He was head of a Craven County household of 8 "free colored" in 1820 [NC:65]. He and his wife June were mentioned in the 1816 Craven County will of her father John **Moore**.
- vii. Simon, married Anna **Carter**, 16 January 1802 Craven County bond with Abel **Carter** and Isaac **Perkins** bondsmen. He was head of an Onslow County household of 4 "other free" in 1810 [NC:775] and 8 "free colored" in 1820 [NC:338].
- viii. Hester, head of a Craven County household of 3 "free colored" in 1820 [NC:70].

4. Susan Dove, born 25 December 1768, was a "Free Base Born Negroe Girl" bound to Bartholomew and Ruth Howard in Craven County on 14 March 1771 [Minutes 1767-75, 167b]. She was head of a Craven County household of 3 "free colored" in 1820 [NC:70]. On 20 July 1793 she was called "Susannah Dove, free Negro" when she bound out her sons to John Brown of Craven County [DB 31:97, 99]. They were
- i.   Isaac, born 4 April 1787, perhaps the Isaac Doves ("colored") who married Silvey **Richards** ("colored"), 24 September 1803 Carteret County bond. He was head of a Craven County household of 3 "free colored" in 1820 [NC:70]. Silvey was probably related to Silas **Richards**, head of a Carteret County household of 4 "other free" in

1810 [NC:450] and 7 "free colored" in Craven County in 1820 [NC:65].
ii. Thomas, born 4 May 1790.

DRAKE FAMILY

Members of the Drake family were
i. Aaron, born say 1747, a "Mulato" taxable in Bladen County, North Carolina, in 1768 and 1772 [Byrd, *Bladen County Tax Lists*, I:5, 82]. He was probably the ancestor of Aaron and Marie Rachel Drake. Aaron was head of a St. Landry Parish, Louisiana household of 3 "free colored" in 1830 [LA:26]. He married Sarah **Ashworth**, 26 November 1831 Opelousas marriage. Marie Rachel married John **Dial**, 30 August 1822 Opelousas marriage [Opelousas Courthouse License nos. 46, 79].
ii. Susanna, a "Mulatto" ordered bound by the churchwardens of Washington Parish, Westmoreland County, Virginia, to William Mitchell on 24 September 1776 [Orders 1776-86, 6].

DREW FAMILY

Members of the Drew family were
1 i. Ephraim[1], born say 1752.
2 ii. John, born say 1757.

1. Ephraim[1] Drew, born say 1752, was taxable in Lunenburg County, Virginia, in the household of William **Stewart** in 1772, was head of a household with George **Chavers** in 1775 [Bell, *Sunlight on the Southside*, 299, 351], and was head of a Mecklenburg County household of 4 "whites" and 2 "blacks" (slaves) in the 1782 Virginia census [VA:33]. On 12 May 1783 the Mecklenburg County court ordered his male laboring tithables to work on a road with William **Stewart** (shoemaker) and William **Stewart** (blacksmith) [Orders 1779-84, 300]. He was taxable on slaves Beck and Jim and 2 other slaves 12-16 years old in 1782, taxable on 2 horses in 1784, taxable on Titus **Stewart** in 1785, taxable on a slave named Charles in 1786. An exempt tithable named Alexander Williams was in his household in 1787. He was taxable on a 12-16-year-old slave named Jemima in 1788, taxable on Edward **Chavis** in 1789, taxable on an emancipated slave named Charles in 1790 and 1792 (probably Charles **Durham**), taxable on only his own tithe in 1791, and taxable on his own tithe and his son Pinson in 1799 [Personal Property Tax 1782-1805, frames 12, 61, 86, 99, 164, 213, 318, 442, 369]. James **Chavous** was security for him when he was sued for 23 pounds on 8 January 1798. William **Stewart** was security for him when Robert Birchett & Company sued him on 11 May 1801. Frederick **Ivy** sued him on 10 September 1804 for a 5 pound debt due by note of hand and on 8 April 1805 for a bond of 15 pounds [Orders 1795-8, 387; 1798-1801, 582; 1803-5, 267, 360]. He was security for the 20 December 1800 Mecklenburg County marriage of Nancy **Brandon** and Frederick **Graves**. He was taxable on his son James, Frederick Drew and Hutchins **Mayo** in 1805 [PPTL, 1782-1805, frame 1082]. His wife may have been identical to Caty Drew who deposed that Peggy **Going** came to her house after drawing water from a nearby spring on 3 August 1811 and complained to her daughter Polly Drew that Matthew **Flood** had raped her at the spring [Orders 1809-11, 7]. Ephraim was listed as "free Negro and Mulatto" in 1813 and 1814, with 2 females over the age of sixteen in his household in 1813 [PPTL, 1806-28, frame 307, 418]. He died about 1818 when his estate was settled in Mecklenburg County. He was the father of
i. Pinson, born say 1780, taxable in his father's Mecklenburg County household from 1796 to 1799, charged with his own tax in 1806 [PPTL, 1782-1805; 1806-28, frame 7]. Frederick **Ivy** was his security

when he was sued for debt in Mecklenburg County court on 10 March 1806 [Orders 1805-6, 104].

ii.   ?Priscilla, born say 1784, married William **Chavis**, 29 January 1806 Mecklenburg County bond.

iii. Claiborne, born say 1785, over the age of sixteen when he was taxable in his father's Mecklenburg County household from 1801 to 1803. He was taxable in his own household from 1804 to 1812 [PPTL, 1782-1805, 871, 971, 996; 1806-28, frames 7, 84, 108, 286].

iv.   James, born about 1786, registered in Mecklenburg County on 19 June 1820: *five feet two and a half Inches high, of a light Complexion about thirty four years old...born of a free woman* [Free Person of Colour, #5, p.15]. He was called the son of Ephraim when he was a taxable in his father's household from 1804 to 1806 [PPTL, 1782-1805, frames 996, 1082; 1806-28, frame 6]. He was indicted on 14 August 1814 for retailing spirituous liquors at Sarah Naish's house in Mecklenburg County, but the case was dismissed [Orders 1809-11, 10, 29]. He was taxable on a lot in Clarksville, Mecklenburg County, from 1819 to 1822 [Land Tax List 1811A-1824B, B lists].

v.   Frederick, born say 1789, over the age of sixteen in 1805 when he was taxable in his father's household [PPTL, 1782-1805, 1082].

vi.   Ephraim², Jr., born about 1793, registered in Mecklenburg County on 18 September 1814: *born in the County of Mecklenburg...free by birth, is five feet 11-1/2 Inches high of a yellow Complexion about Twenty one years old...has Supported good character from his youth up as I have been acquainted with him nearly all his life & never heard anything to the Contrary...a Shoemaker by Trade J. T. { Jos. Towers, Jun.* [Free Person of Colour, #9, p.5]. He was called the son of Ephraim when he was listed as a taxable in his father's household in 1812 [PPTL, 1806-28, frame 286]. He purchased 7 acres on the waters of Gum Branch adjoining William **Stewart** from William Avery in 1820 and was taxable on the land until 1824 [Land Tax List 1806B-1824A, A lists].

vii. ?Polly, born say 1795, probably a teenager in August 1811 when she testified with her mother Caty Drew in the Mecklenburg County trial of Matthew **Flood** [Orders 1809-11, 7].

2. John Drew, born say 1757, was taxable in Abraham **Cuttillo**'s Lunenburg County household in 1774 [Bell, *Sunlight on the Southside*, 299, 330]. He was taxable in Mecklenburg County on his own tithe and his son Benjamin in 1799 and was a "mulatto" taxable from 1806 to 1814 [PPTL, 1782-1805; 1806-28, frames 33, 60, 134, 258, 336, 387] and was taxable on 100 acres in the lower district of Mecklenburg County on Fox's Road near the Warren County line from 1804 to 1823 [Land Tax List 1782-1811A, 1811B-1824A, B lists]. His 8 May 1827 Warren County, North Carolina will was proved in August 1827. He named his wife Althew and children. He divided his land among his sons Hardaway and Anderson [DB 31:50]. He was the father of

i.   Nancy, born say 1780, married George **Guy**, 11 December 1799 Mecklenburg County bond.

ii.   Benjamin, born say 1783, over the age of sixteen when he was taxable in his father's Mecklenburg County household from 1799 to 1803 [PPTL, 1782-1805, frames 758, 795, 845, 944]. He married Mason **Griffiths**, 10 May 1804 Orange County, North Carolina bond.

iii. Kesiah, born say 1784, married Matthew **Stewart**, 20 June 1804 Warren County bond, Stanfield Drew security.

iv.   Stanfield, born say 1785, over the age of sixteen when he was taxable in his father's Mecklenburg County household from 1801 to 1803 [PPTL, 1782-1805, frames 845, 917, 944]. He was a "mulatto"

Mecklenburg County taxable from 1806 to 1815 [PPTL, 1806-28, frames 33, 134, 161, 258, 387, 504].

v. Elizabeth, born say 1787, married Bartlett **Stewart**, 21 October 1807 Mecklenburg County, Virginia bond, George **Guy** security.

vi. Hardaway, born say 1790, married Polly **Guy**, 1813 Mecklenburg County bond. He was head of a Mecklenburg County household of 5 "free colored" in 1820 [VA:159b]. In 1831 he sold the land he inherited from his father [DB 24:327].

vii. Anderson, born say 1795, head of a Mecklenburg County household of 3 "free colored" in 1820 [VA:159b].

viii. William, called Buck Drew when he married Betsy **Griffis**, 16 June 1812 Orange County, North Carolina bond. He was called "Buck Drew alias William Kersey" in his War of 1812 pension application.

ix. Didamy, called Daisy Drew when she married Philemon **Harris**, 22 January 1816 Warren County bond.

x. Parthenia, married Jesse **Brandom**, 2 July 1822 Warren County bond.

DRIGGERS FAMILY

1. Emmanuel Driggers, "Negroe," born say 1620, was the slave of Francis Pott on his plantation in Magotha Bay, Northampton County, Virginia. On 27 May 1645 when American slavery had not yet fully developed, he purchased a cow and calf from Pott and recorded the sale in the Northampton County court [DW 1645-51, 82]. He and his wife Frances were assigned as servants to Stephen Charlton in 1649 to pay Pott's debt to Charlton. On 30 December 1652 his former masters, Francis Pott and Stephen Charlton, clarified the status of the cattle he and Bashaw **Fernando** acquired while they were servants (slaves), declaring that

ye said cattle, etc. are ye proper goods of the sd Negroes [DW 1651-54, 28, 114].

In 1656 he gave a black heifer to a young slave on a nearby plantation. Pott died in 1658 and his widow married William Kendall. Kendall freed Driggers' companion, Bashaw **Fernando**, declaring in court that it was the verbal request of Pott before he died [DW 1657-66, fol. 106, 57]. There is no record of Emmanuel's manumission, but he was freed not long afterwards. On 16 September 1661 he sold a black heifer to Joan, daughter of Peter **George** [DW 1657-66, fol.123]. By 1 October 1661 he had married his second wife Elizabeth, with whom he made a deed of jointure in which he gave her a three-year-old mare and its increase [Orders 1664-74, fol.75, p.78]. Perhaps as the wife of a newly freed slave she was concerned about her property rights. She was probably white since she was not tithable.

The name Driggers was apparently short for the Portuguese or Spanish name, Rodriguez, since he was called "Manuell Rodriges" from 1660 to 1663 when he was on three tithes in Northampton County [Orders 1657-64, 102, 176]. In 1664 he was taxed on only himself, "Manuell Rodriggs." In 1665 he leased 245 acres for ninety-nine years from his former master, William Kendall, and in 1672 assigned the unexpired part of the lease to John Waterson [Whitelaw, *Virginia's Eastern Shore*, 151, 152]. In 1673 he gave a bay mare to Frances and Ann, his daughters who were still slaves, and a bay mare to Devorick and Mary, his free children, and mentioned his "loving son in Law William Harman, Negro" [D&c 1668-80, fol.59-60]. In 1677 he was taxable in his own household in John Michael's Division [Orders 1674-79 191]. He and John Isaac rented land from the estate of Southy Littleton from 1679 to 1685 [OW&c 1683-9, 150-1]. His children were

i. Elizabeth[1], born in 1637 since she was eight years old when she was bound to serve Francis Pott in 1645. She may not have been his natural daughter since her indenture stated that she was "given to my negro (Emmanuel Driggers) by one who brought her up by ye space of 8 years..." [DW 1645-51, 82].

ii. Frances[1], born say 1640, taxed in Thomas Poynter's household in 1666 and in John Eyre's household in 1675 [Orders 1664-74, fol.29; 1674-79, 75]. As mentioned above, she received a bay mare from her father in 1673, and in 1678 she recorded her livestock mark in court [DW 1651-54, 16 at the end of the volume].

iii. Jane, born in 1644, one year old on 27 May 1645 when Emmanuel bound her to Captain Francis Pott to serve him until the age of thirty-one. Like Elizabeth, she may not have been his natural daughter since her indenture stated that Emmanuel Driggers "bought and paid for to Capt. Robert Shepard." On 24 May 1652 when she was eight years old, Driggers paid Captain Pott for her freedom. In 1663 she had an illegitimate daughter, Sarah **Landum**, by an Irish freeman, Dennam Olandum [DW 1651-54, 82; Orders 1657-64, fol.179]. She married first, John **Gussal** about 1665. He died shortly afterwards and in April 1666 she was charged in court with failing to prove his will. She had married William **Harman** by June 1666 when he submitted letters of administration on her first husband's estate [Orders 1664-7, fol.24, p.24].

2 iv. Thomas[1], born about 1644.

v. Ann, born about 1648, ten years old in December 1657 when she was sold to another planter, John Pannell. He left her to his daughter Hannah Penuell by his 18 December 1660 Northampton County will [DW 1655-68, 78].

vi. Edward, born say 1650, sold to Henry Armitrading in 1657 when he was about three years old [DW 1655-68, 74].

vii. ?William[1], born say 1655. On 28 March 1679 the Northampton County court ordered that he receive twenty lashes, and his wife Alice fifteen, for killing a hog belonging to their neighbor [Orders 1678-83, 3]. On 3 June 1686 he and a white servant were accused of breaking into the cellar of Captain John Custis. He died, still a slave, before 5 February 1693/4 when Ralph Pigot reported to the Northampton County court that William was indebted to him for 800 pounds of tobacco and that Thomas Taylor was indebted to William for eight pairs of shoes [OW 1689-98, 261].

3 viii. Devorax[1]/ Deverick, born say 1656.

ix. ?Mary, born say 1658, bore an illegitimate child in 1674, and that year the parish paid her tax [Orders 1664-74, 254, 273-4]. She may have married Peter **George**.

2. Thomas[1] Driggers, born say 1644, remained a slave. He was taxable in Thomas Poynter's household from 1664 to 1667 [Orders 1657-64, fol. 198; 1664-74 fol. 29]. In 1666 he was presented by the Northampton County grand jury for the sin of fornication with Sarah **King**, who he married about a year later. In 1668 Lieutenant Colonel William Kendall complained to the court that Thomas was still a slave belonging to him and that he was neglecting his master. "Negroes" John **Francisco** and Francis **Payne** complained that he was abusing them. The court ordered that he be given twenty-one lashes and shortly afterwards ordered Thomas' child, who was then a slave of Kendall's, indentured to John **Francisco** until the age of twenty-one [Orders 1664-74, fol. 30, fol. 52, 53]. Apparently, Thomas did not pay much attention to the court or Kendall for that same year he was listed as head of a household:

Tho: Rodriggus Negro } 4
Sara Negro
Morgan Thomas
Walter Manington

In 1671 we find that "Sarah Negro" was his wife:

John Hayes   *} 6*
Tho: Driggus
Sarah his wife   [Orders 1664-7, 55, fol.114].

Sarah was the daughter of "Kinge Toney Negro" who named her in his Northampton County will which was proved 28 February 1677 [Orders 10:247]. In 1672 the court ordered that Sarah "shall not depart the house of Mr. John Eyres master of the said Rodrigus without the leave of both her husband and Mr. John Eyre. Sarah did not follow the court ruling since she and her husband were listed in separate households in John Michael's Division from 1675 to 1677 [Orders 1664-74, 122; 1674-79, 75, 191]. She was in Somerset County, Maryland, before 23 April 1688 when she, called "negroe Woman & wife to Thomas Griggers Negro," complained to the Somerset County court that Margaret Holder had stolen some of her goods. Peter **George**, "Negroe" of Wiccocomoco Hundred, posted five pounds sterling security for Sarah's appearance. The court heard testimony from Peter **George**, Mary **George**, Mary **Johnson**, and Sarah Driggers, Jr., and found in favor of Margaret Holder. By 14 August 1688 Sarah, Peter **George**, three unnamed women, and an unstated number of men petitioned the Somerset County court to stop taxing them as slaves since they were free born. The court ruled that for that year the women should be exempt, but the men should pay taxes. The court also ordered that they obtain certificates from where they formerly lived to prove that they were free born [*Archives of Maryland* 91:47; Judicial Record, 1687-89, 58]. In 1689 Sarah was back in Northampton County where she and "Sarah Landrun free Negroes" (her niece Sarah **Landrum**) were given twenty-five lashes on their bare backs for stealing some yarn from "a free Negro woman commonly called Black Nanny" [Orders 1679-89, 463]. She was about forty years old when she made a deposition in the case of Peter **George** in the 29 May 1691 session of the Northampton County court [Orders 1689-98 116]. She was called a widow in March 1694 when she recorded her livestock mark in court [DW 1651-4, p.28 at the end of the volume]. Judith Patrick left her a worsted gown by her 12 May 1697 Northampton County will. On 1 February 1698 Sarah won a suit against A. Westerhouse for 300 pounds of tobacco for curing his arm, and on 28 May 1700 Lieutenant Colonel Nathaniel Littleton won a suit against her for 83 pounds of tobacco per account of public dues and officers fees [Orders 1689-98, 521; OW&c 1698-1710, 39, 43]. Since Sarah was free, so also were her children. They were

    i.   Sarah[1], Jr., born say 1667, raised by John and Christian **Francisco** until she was twenty-one years old. She testified in Somerset County court on 13 June 1688. Her mother sued William Kenny, Jr., in Northampton County court on 28 July 1691 when she heard a report that Sarah Driggers, Jr., was bound "to go to the Southward with him" for two years [OW 1689-98, 121, 125]. He was probably the William Kening, Jr., who sued Sarah Driger for defamation in Sussex County, Delaware court on 3 June 1691 [Court Records 1680-99, 497]. She brought a successful suit against Edward Fadlooks(?) in Kent County, Delaware court on 14 November 1717 [Court Dockets 1680- February 1725, fol. 119].

    ii.   ?Thomas[2], born say 1670, living in Somerset County, Maryland in the late 1690s [Judicial Record, 1698-1701, index].

4	iii.	Frances², born about 1677.
5	iv.	?Elizabeth², born say 1678.
6	v.	?John¹, born say 1680.
7	vi.	?William², born say 1682.
8	vii.	?Johnson¹, born say 1686.

3. Devorick/ Devorax¹ Driggers, born say 1656, received a bay mare from his father Emmanuel Driggers by a 1673 Northampton County deed, and he was mentioned in the 9 May 1673 Northampton County will of Francis **Payne**, "Negro," proved 29 September 1763, which stated that Devrox **Dregushe** was to have nothing [D&c 1668-80, fol.59-60; Orders 1664-74, 220-1]. He moved to Somerset County, Maryland, about 1677 when he was one of the headrights claimed by Stephen Cosden in his patent [Maryland Provincial Patents, Liber 15:433]. In 1689 he signed a Somerset County address of loyalty to King William and Queen Mary [Torrence, *Old Somerset on the Eastern Shore*, 349]. On 12 January 1701/2 he provided security in Somerset County court for Deborah Wildgoose who had an illegitimate child by Samuel Webb. He was living in All Hollows Parish when he and several whites were presented for being drunk on the Sabbath. He was acquitted after paying court costs [Judicial Records 1702-5, Liber G-I, 21; 1707-17, 16]. He was renting a 300 acre plantation in Pasquadenorton Hundred of Somerset County in 1707 [Somerset County Rent Roll, 1707, Calvert Papers, ms. 174, MHS, cited by Davidson, *Free Blacks on the lower Eastern Shore of Maryland*]. He died in 1709 when his estate was valued at about 37 pounds [Inventories and Accounts, Liber 30:88]. He may have been the father of

    i.   Devorax², born about 1680, a "Molatto" Accomack County tithable in Jonathan Owen's household in 1696. He was sued in Accomack County court by Robert Houston on 7 August 1704 [Orders 1690-7, 222a, 224, 235; 1703-9, 30a]. He and (his wife?) Arendia Driggas were witnesses with Thomas Purnell to the 24 December 1720 Somerset County will of Henry Hudson, Sr., a wealthy planter [Maryland Wills 16:279; Baldwin, *Maryland Calendar of Wills*, 5:36]. He was taxable in Thomas Purnell's Bogerternorten Hundred, Somerset County household in 1724 [List of Taxables, 1724]. In 1731 he purchased 75 acres in Somerset County on St. Martins River in present-day Worcester County [Land Records, Liber SH:324]. He and his wife Ann sold this land in 1734 and were renting it in 1748 [Worcester County Debt Book, 1748, 190].

4. Frances² Driggers/ Drighouse, born about 1677, was presented by the Northampton County court for the sin of fornication on 28 May 1694 for which she received thirty lashes and an extension of her indenture by two years. On 28 May 1695 she was presented by the court for bastard bearing and named her master John Brewer as the father, but the court accepted his testimony that he had been over a hundred miles from home when the child had been conceived [OW 1689-98, 274, 279, 314, 322]. She was called the daughter of Thomas and Sarah Driggus on 18 September 1695 when she petitioned the Accomack County court for her freedom, stating that she had attained the age of eighteen, was free born, that John Brewer had sold her indenture to Thomas Mills, and that Mills intended to transport her where her freedom could not be proved. Brewer produced a letter from her mother Sarah, but the court ruled that it was not a formal indenture and set Frances free [Orders 1690-97, 158a, 169a-170]. On 28 February 1699/1700 she was "called Frances Driggus Negro" in Northampton County court when she was given thirty lashes for stealing goods from Arthur Roberts. She was also charged with stealing meat from Charles Trelfo. On 29 December 1702 she failed to answer a summons for bastard bearing [OW&c 1698-1710, 35, 36, 122, 129]. On 28 September 1703 she was called "ye daughter of Sarah

Drighouse decd., being a free born negro" when she indentured herself and her unnamed three-week-old daughter to Captain Isaac Foxcroft and his wife Bridget in Northampton County, herself for ten years and her daughter (and any children born during her indenture) until the age of twenty-five in consideration of Foxcroft paying a debt she owed Thomas Clark [DW 1692-1707, 348-9]. On 30 November 1703 she complained to the court that Foxcroft's widow had assigned her indenture to Thomas Ward. On 28 January 1703/4 the court ordered Sarah Drighouse, alias **Landman**, to pay her for attending four days as a witness in a case in which Sarah was sued by Colonel John Custis [OW&c 1698-1710, 176, 178, 182]. Her children may have been

    i.   Comfort, perhaps the illegitimate child born to Frances about 1695 in Accomack County [OW 1689-98, p.322]. Comfort was presented by the Accomack County court for bastardy on 4 March 1712/3 and on 8 April 1715. Francis **Johnson** paid her fine for the first child and John Watts was her security for the second [Orders 1710-4, 56a, 58; 1714-17, 7a, 9].

9   ii.   Thomas³, born say 1702.

5.   Elizabeth² Driggers, born say 1678, appeared before the Accomack County court on 19 November 1695 and identified John Pash as the father of her illegitimate child. On 5 April 1699 she was presented by the court for having another illegitimate child [Orders 1690-7, 169a; 1697-1703, 59a]. She may have been the mother of

10   i.   Azaricum, born say 1699.

6.   John¹ Drighouse, born say 1680, a "free Mullatto," was living in Accomack County on 3 December 1701 when an Indian named Protestant George accused him in court of beating an Indian named Will who died shortly afterwards [Orders 1697-1703, 122]. On 8 November 1702 the Northampton County court ordered that he, Johnson Driggus and Samuel **George** receive thirty-nine lashes for abusing and threatening Robert Gascoigne. Gascoigne sued John on 28 August 1707 but neither party appeared [OW&c 1693-1710, 106, 212, 306, 361]. On 20 June 1716 he posted bond to keep the parish harmless from an illegitimate child he had by Ann **Beckett** [Orders 1710-16, 252]. On 3 December 1717 he was called John Drigus "Mullatto" when he failed to appear in court to answer William Taylor's suit for a 500 pound debt. The sheriff reported that he had given the writ to John's wife. On 8 October 1718 the Accomack County court ruled in his favor in his suit against John Justice for 500 pounds of tobacco [Orders 1717-19, 5a, 17a, 22]. He was a "Negro" tithable in Northampton County in his own household in 1721, tithable on himself and Jacob **Carter** in 1722, and tithable in 1723. He was tithable with "Betty Drighous negro" from 1724 to 1725, tithable with Betty Drighouse and Beck **Beckett** "negro" in 1726, and tithable with Betty **Beckett** in 1727. By June 1728 he had married Lydia **Carter** who was tithable in his household as Lydia Drighouse in 1728 and 1729. Jacob Brown was tithable in his household in 1728, and Lydia Drighouse, Eliza **Beckett** and Thomas **Landum** were tithable in his household in 1729 [Bell, *Northampton County Tithables*, 15, 26, 40, 54, 78, 105, 127, 145, 161, 172, 190; OW&c 1698-1710, 504]. (Thomas **Landum** was probably his cousin, the one-year-old "negro" son of Sarah **Landrum**, alias Driggers, who was bound to Richard Jacob in 1710). John died in 1729 when his estate was valued at about 10 pounds [WD&c 1725-33, 216]. On 10 February 1729/30 his widow Lydia bound out her nine-year-old son Nathaniel and two-year-old son Johnson. She petitioned the court on 10 August 1730 to be allowed 150 pounds of tobacco out of her deceased husband's estate for funeral expenses [WD&c 1725-33, 216; Orders 1722-9, 394; 1729-32, 44]. Lydia Drighouse was taxable in the household of Thomas Savage in 1731 [Bell, *Northampton County Tithables*, 228]. He paid her fine

for the bastard child she was charged with on 11 May 1731 [Orders 1729-32, 84, 94, 97]. John's children were

11   i.   Nathaniel[1], born 1 July 1720.
      ii.   Johnson[3], born about August 1727, two and a half years old on 10 February 1729/30 when he was bound to Benjamin Dunton [Orders 1729-32, 4]. He was listed as one of John Paridise's Northampton County tithables in 1769 [Bell, *Northampton County Tithables*, 400] and was charged with his own tax from 1785 to 1797: called a "Mulatto" in 1787 [PPTL, 1782-1823, frames 43, 73, 115, 191, 226]. He registered as a "free Negro" in Northampton County on 12 June 1794 [Orders 1789-95, 358].
      iii. ?Solomon, born about June 1728, a "Negroe," aged fourteen years and six months on 14 December 1742 when the Northampton County court bound him to Stephen Whitehead. His petition to the court against Stephen Whitehead was dismissed on 13 September 1749 [Orders 1742-8, 36; 1748-51, 130, 147].

7.   William[2] Driggus, born say 1682, was called the "Maletto Servant" of Daniel Neech when he recorded his cattle mark in Northampton County court in 1698 [DW 1651-54, 30 at end of volume]. He was living in Somerset County, Maryland, in April 1708 when he was presented for having an illegitimate child by Mary Winslow. The court ordered that he receive twenty-five lashes when he told the justices that

they had no more to do with sd Woman than his Arse

Edward Winslow and David Hudson were security for him. (Mary also had a child by Daniel **Francisco**) [Judicial Records 1707-11, 95-6, 103; 1713-5, 5, 26]. William signed his 7 January 1720 Somerset County will which was proved 7 May 1722. He left his 100 acre plantation called "Drigus Adventure" to his son William and mentioned unnamed children under eighteen years old and his wife Jane. He specified that his children were to be cared for by their uncle, John Driggus of Accomack County, if his wife remarried. The inventory of his estate included a parcel of old books [Maryland Wills, Liber 17:285; Inventories 8:65]. Jane was called a "maleto widow" in 1724 when Winslow Driggus (William's son by Mary Winslow?) was taxable in her Baltimore Hundred, Somerset County household [List of Taxables]. William's children were

      i.   William[3], born about 1702.
12   ii.   ?Winslow[1], born say 1705.
      iii. ?John, taxable in Poquetenorton Hundred, Somerset County from 1734 to 1740.
      iv.   Sabra, born say 1722, presented by the Somerset County court on 17 November 1741 for having an illegitimate child [Judicial Record 1740-2, 175].

8.   Johnson[1] Driggers, born say 1686, appeared in Northampton County, Virginia court on 8 November 1702 when he, his brother John, and Samuel **George** were convicted of stealing a hog and then abusing and threatening several whites "in an insolent manner" [Orders 1698-1710, 102, 106]. He probably left the county shortly afterwards as he was not listed as a taxable in the 1720-29 Northampton County lists. He purchased 40 acres in Norfolk County on the north side of the Northwest River known by the name of Hoose Pool Point on 14 May 1718 [DB 10:34]. He was taxable in the Norfolk County district between Great Bridge and Sugg's Mill, called Johnson Drigus, Senr., and in the same district in 1731 with his son Johnson, taxed together as one tithe:

Johnson Drigus & his son Johnson Drigus - 1 tithe

and taxed separately as one tithe each in 1732, 1733 and 1734 [Wingo, *Norfolk County Tithables 1730-50*, 28, 55, 81, 131]. On 11 August 1752 he claimed head rights in the Craven County, North Carolina court: *Johnston Driggers Came into Court and made Oath that his family consisted of seven Black Persons* [Haun, *Craven County Court Minutes*, IV:103]. His children were

13 i. Johnson[2] Jr., born say 1716.
14 ii. ?Mark, born say 1723.
    iii. ?Thomas[4], born say 1724, sued in Chowan County March General Court in 1745 by Susannah Lister but "was not to be found" [Chowan County General Court Dockets, 1742-45, Actions Returnable to March 1745 General Court, Docket #102]. He purchased 100 acres in Craven County from Thomas Philips by deed proved in Craven County court in September 1748 [Haun, *Craven County Court Minutes*, III:660] and was a resident of Craven County on 18 December 1770 when he sold this land known by the name of "Braun Ridges" [DB 19:103]. He may have been the same Thomas Driggers who entered 100 acres in Bladen County south of Drowning Creek on 31 August 1759 [Philbeck, *Bladen County Land Entries*, no. 1147]. And a Thomas Driggers was in Bedford County, Virginia, on 27 July 1779 when he proved in court that he had served as a regular soldier among the new levies under the command of Col. Byrd in the Year 1760 (in the French and Indian War) [Minutes 1774-82, 241].
15 iv. ?Matthew, born say 1725.
    v. ?Caleb, born say 1730, number 43 in the 8 March 1754 muster roll of Captain Casson Brinson's Craven County Company, listed next to Johnston Drigers [Clark, *Colonial Soldiers of the South*, 701].
    vi. ?William[4], born say 1737, purchased land in Cumberland County, North Carolina, by deed proved on 17 October 1759 and sold land in Cumberland County by deed proved five years later in May count 1764 [Minutes 1759-65, 54, 103]. His improvements on Gum Swamp east of Drowning Creek were mentioned in a 22 July 1769 Bladen County deed [DB:91]. He may have been the William Driggers who was granted administration on the Marlboro County, South Carolina estate of Charles Kirby in December 1788. Perhaps his wife was Mary Driggers whose deed of gift from Sarah Kirby was recorded in March 1788 [Minutes 1785-1808, 52, 35].
    vii. ?Winslow[7], born say 1739, number 12 in the Muster Roll of Captain Alexander McKintosh's Company of Colonel George Gabriel Powell's Battalion of South Carolina Militia "Serving in the Late Expedition Against the Cherokees from October 11, 1759 to January 15, 1760, inclusive ..." [Clark, *Colonial Soldiers of the South*, 892]. He was a notorious leader of one of the outlaw, back-country communities which were said to accept free African Americans as equals. In the fall of 1770 he escaped from jail in Savannah, Georgia, and returned to the area of the Little Peedee River in North and South Carolina where he continued his outlaw career. He was described as: *about six Feet; Complexion, black; Visage, pale, being much reduced by Sickness; Hair, black and long, generally cued.* The following year a band of ex-Regulators captured him at his hideout near Drowning Creek and used the provisions of the Negro Act as an excuse to hang him on the spot [Brown, *South Carolina Regulators*, 29-31, 103; Saunders, *Colonial Records of North Carolina*, IX:725, 771].[91]

9. Thomas[3] Drighouse, born say 1702, may have been the illegitimate child born to Frances Driggers in 1702 [OW&c 1698-1710, 122, 129]. He was tithable

---

[91]Ironically, Gideon **Gibson** was one of the Regulators in that area.

in 1727 with his wife Jean **Beckett**, called Jane Drighouse in his household in 1728, and called Jane **Beckett** in 1729. She was called Jane Drighouse when she was tithable in his household from 1737 to 1744. Other tithables in their household were (her daughter) Sarah **Beckett** in 1737 and 1738, "Sarah and Comfort" in 1739, (her daughter) Comfort **Beckett** in 1740 and 1741, Nathaniel Drighouse in 1742 and 1743, and their daughter Esther Drighouse in 1744 [Bell, *Northampton County Tithables*, 127, 136, 163, 194, 198, 228, 266, 272, 285, 308, 317, 332, 353, 362]. Jane Drighouse was taken into custody in April 1740 as security for the court appearance of her daughter Sarah **Becket** to answer for having a bastard child [Mihalyka, *Loose Papers II:*124]. On 14 May 1751 Thomas he was security for Comfort **Morris**'s administration of the estate of her deceased husband Jacob **Morris** [Orders 1748-51, 377]. He called himself a "free Negro" in his 21 April 1757 Northampton County will which was proved 14 June 1757 [WB 21:281]. He mentioned (his wife) Jane **Beckett** and her three daughters: Hester, Betty, and Lydia **Beckett**. Their children were

    i.   Hester **Beckett**, born about 1728, taxable in her parents' household in 1744.
    ii.   Betty **Beckett**.
   iii.   Lydia **Beckett**.

10. Azaricum Drigghouse may have been the illegitimate child Elizabeth Driggers had by John Pash in Accomack County in 1699 [Orders 1697-1703, 59a]. He was bound apprentice in Northampton County to Richard Carver between 1715 and 1717 with the stipulation that he receive two months of schooling each fall [WD&c 1711-18, 83]. He was a "Negro" Northampton County tithable in Jonah Batson's household in 1721, in his own household in 1722, tithable with his wife Margaret Drighouse in 1724, tithable in 1725 and 1726 with his wife Margaret Drighouse and Tabitha **Copes**. On 8 June 1725 he paid Tabitha's fine and posted bond to keep the parish harmless from her bastard child [Orders 1722-9, 189]. This suggests that his wife may have been the daughter of Margaret **Copes** who had a "Maletto Barstard" child in 1699 [OW&c 1698-1710, 36]. He was a "negro" tithable with "malatto" wife Margaret Drighouse and "mallatos" Jacob and Tabitha **Carter** in 1727, tithable with wife Margaret in 1728, tithable with wife Margaret and a slave named Stephen in 1731, and tithable with his wife Margaret in 1737 [L.P 1721-1727; Bell, *Northampton County Tithables*, 16, 34, 47, 65, 92, 115, 127, 145, 165, 167, 202, 213, 221, 254]. He was committed to the stocks on 16 April 1726 for misbehavior before the court. He sued Jeremiah Townsend for assault and battery on 14 February 1726/7 and sued Thomas Downs for trespass and assault on 11 March 1731/2. His suit against Jacob **Carter** was agreed on 12 March 1728/9. He was presented for profane swearing on 10 December 1734 [Orders 1722-9, 240, 273, 279, 377; 1729-32, 138]. He had acquired a slave named Bridget by 13 July 1736 when her age was adjudged at nine years and a slave named Harry before 13 September 1737 when his age was adjudged at twelve years [Orders 1732-42, 142, 146, 222, 275]. He wrote his 2 June 1738 will which was proved 12 September the same year. He left two slaves to his son Isaiah and mentioned sons Jacob and Josiah [WB 18:279]. His two page inventory, including a bible, was presented in court on 14 December 1742 by "Mark Beckett who Intermarried with the said Decedent's Widow & Executrix" [Orders 1742-8, 33, 56]. Margaret Drighouse was tithable in Henry Japson's household in 1738 and in her own household with her son Isaiah Drighouse and William **Carter** in 1739. She had married Mark **Beckett** by June 1740 when she was taxable in his household [Bell, *Northampton County Tithables*, 277, 292, 305]. Azaricum's children were

16   i.   Isaiah, born say 1720.
    ii.   Jacob, born about 1728, fourteen years old in December 1742 when he chose Mark **Beckett** as his guardian [Orders 1742-48, 38], taxable in

Mark **Beckett**'s household in 1744. John Millard's suit against him was agreed in Northampton County court on 15 February 1748/9 [Orders 1748-51, 42-3].

iii. Josiah.

11. Nathaniel[1] Drighouse, born 1 July 1720, was bound to Benjamin Dunton in Northampton County, Virginia, on 10 February 1729/30 [Orders 1729-32, 4]. He was taxable in Northampton County in Thomas Westerhouse's household in 1739, in Thomas Drighouse's household in 1742, and in the household of John Custis Matthews in 1743 and 1744. Jonathan Tilney sued him for trespass on 12 June 1744, but the case was dismissed on agreement of the parties. Thomas Marshall, Gent., sued him for minor debts on 10 July 1750 and 10 June 1752 [Orders 1742-8, 162; 1748-51, 241; 1751-3, 243]. He was head of a household with (his wife?) Bridget Drighouse and Rebecca **Reed** in 1765, and with Bridget in 1769 [Bell, *Northampton County Tithables*, 354, 371, 399], and was taxable from 1782 to 1801: called Nathan, Sr., in 1794 and 1801 [PPTL, 1782-1823, frames 4. 95, 172, 193, 306]. Perhaps Bridget was the Bridget Drighouse who registered as a "free Negro" in Northampton County on 12 June 1794 [Orders 1789-95, 358]. Nathaniel may have been the ancestor of

i. Sarah, born 11 June 1743, a four-year-old orphan bound apprentice to William Holland on 13 October 1747 [Orders 1742-8, 463]. She was taxable in the household of Edmund Custis in 1765 [Bell, *Northampton County Tithables*, 379].

ii. Elizabeth, born say 1760, mother of Esther Drighouse who was nine years old the 15th August next when she was bound by the Northampton County court to William Simkins, Jr., on 9 June 1789 [Minutes[2], 1787-9, 285].

iii. Nathan[2], born 10 May 1768, two years old when he was bound apprentice to Francis Costen in Northampton County on 15 August 1770 [Minutes 1765-71, 382]. He was taxable in Northampton County from 1790 to 1813, called Nathan Driggers, Jr. [PPTL, 1782-1823, frames 115, 172, 191, 306, 533]. He married Elizabeth **Bingham**, 23 January 1794 Northampton County bond, Reubin **Reed** security; and second, Polly **Jeffry**, 24 July 1810 Northampton County bond, Abraham Lang security.

iv. Lear, registered as a "free Negro" in Northampton County on 12 June 1794 [Orders 1789-95, 358], married Lightly **Collins**, 3 January 1795 Northampton County bond, Thomas Lewis security.

v. George, born say 1777, registered as a "free Negro" in Northampton County on 13 June 1794 [Orders 1789-95, 364], married Peggy **Land** (**Lang**), 2 March 1798 Northampton county bond, Abraham **Lang** security. He was taxable in Northampton County from 1795 to 1798 [PPTL, 1782-1823, frames 193, 245].

vi. Jacob, registered as a "free Negro" in Northampton County on 13 June 1794 [Orders 1789-95, 364]. He was a "free Negro" taxable in Northampton County from 1796 to 1797 [PPTL, 1782-1823, frame 208].

vii. Dilly, registered as a "free Negro" in Northampton County on 12 June 1794 [Orders 1789-95, 358], married Revel **Morris**, 7 September 1801 Northampton County bond, James Smith security. She was still called Dilly Driggus when she was a "Negro" listed in the Indian town of Northampton County in 1813 [PPTL 1782-1823, frame 533] and head of a Northampton County household of 7 "free colored" in 1820 [VA:216A], called Dilly Drighouse on 22 June 1824 when she consented to the marriage of her daughter Sukey Drighouse to Littleton **Sample**.

    viii. Elishe, married Daniel **Liverpool**, 25 June 1799 Northampton County bond, Josias **Liverpool** security.

    ix. William[8], born say 1780, married Ann **Bingham**, 25 September 1802 Northampton County bond, Samuel **Beavans** security. He was taxable in Northampton County from 1796 to 1809, a "N"(egro) living in the Indian town in 1809 [PPTL, 1782-1823, frames 208, 469]. Ann Drighouse was a "Negro" living in the Indian town of Northampton County in 1813 [PPTL 1782-1823, frame 533].

12. Winslow[1] Driggers, born say 1705, was taxable in the Baltimore Hundred, Somerset County, Maryland household of Jane Drigus in 1724 and in the household of Isabee Parkins in 1725 [List of Taxables]. He may have been identical to ___ Drigers who was taxable in William Beckett's Little Creek Hundred, Kent County, Delaware household in 1727 and ___ Driggers who was taxable in the Murderkill Hundred, Kent County household of ___ Perkins (Isaac Perkins) in 1729 [Kent County Assessments, Film RG3535, reel 1, frame 354, 364]. He may have been the ancestor of

    i. Drake, taxable in Indian River and Angola Hundreds, Sussex County, Delaware from 1770 to 1787. Administration of his Sussex County will was granted to John Wiltbank on 2 September 1788. It mentioned his sister Rhoda **Hodgskin** [de Valinger, *Calendar of Sussex County Probate Records*, 195].

    ii. Rhoda, sister of Drake Driggers, married Jonas **Hodgskin**.

    iii. Richard, taxable in Kent County, Delaware, in 1773 [Kent County Assessments, frame 0183].

    iv. Luke, taxable in Lewes and Rehoboth Hundred, Sussex County, Delaware in 1774.

    v. Benjamin, taxable in Little Creek Hundred, Sussex County, Delaware, in 1777.

    vi. William[5], born say 1765, a delinquent taxpayer in Little Creek Hundred, Sussex County, Delaware, in 1787, taxable in Dover, Kent County in 1788, and head of a Sussex County, Delaware household of 6 "other free" in 1800 [DE:425].

    vii. Betty, married Peter **Beckett** on 27 November 1788 at Lewes and Coolspring Presbyterian Church [Wright, *Vital Records of Kent and Sussex Counties*, 132].

    viii. Noval, head of a Sussex County, Delaware household of 3 "other free" in 1800 [DE:425].

13. Johnson[2] Driggers, born say 1716, was taxable in 1732 in Norfolk County, Virginia [Wingo, *Norfolk County Tithables 1730-50*, 55].[92] He was listed in the 8 March 1754 muster roll of Captain Casson Brinson's Craven County, North Carolina Company [Clark, *Colonial Soldiers of the South*, 701]. On 21 December 1760 he was called "Johnson Driggers, free negro, son of Johnston Driggers" in the deed by which he bought 75 acres in Craven County on the east side of the head of Lower Broad Creek. In 1764 he was taxed in Beaufort County on himself and his wife:

    Driggott, John & wife 2 Black tithes [SS 837].

He was living near the Bay River when he sold 60 acres of his Lower Broad Creek land on 31 August 1793 [DB 32:301]. Since he was not living there

---

[92]He may have been the John Grigger (no age, race, or parent specified) who was bound an apprentice tailor to William Keeling in Princess Anne County on 3 January 1722 [Minutes 1717-28, 129].

when he sold it, he may have been the subscriber who placed the following ad in the 10 April 1778 edition of the North Carolina Gazette of New Bern:

Broad Creek on Neuse River, April 9. On Saturday night, April the 4th, broke into the house of the subscriber at the head of Green's Creek, where I had some small property under the care of Ann Driggus, a free negro woman, two men in disguise, with marks on their faces, and clubs in their hands, beat and wounded her terribly and carried away four of her children, three girls and a boy, the biggest of said girls got off in the dark and made her escape, one of the girls name is Becca, and other Charita, the boy is named Shadrack...[Fouts, *NC Gazette of New Bern*, I:65-66].

He was head of a Craven County household of 4 "other free" in 1790 [NC:134]. On 20 January 1800 he and (his son-in-law?) Joshua **Lindsey** sold his 40 acres on the south side of Bay River [DB 34:361], and he moved to Beaufort County where he was head of a household of 10 "other free" in 1800, called "Johnston Griggers Senr" [NC:8]. On 28 November 1801 he and his wife Mary sold 80 acres in Beaufort County on the north side of Bay River [DB 2-3:209]. His children may have been

17   i.   Elizabeth[3], born say 1745.
      ii. Eleanor, born say 1750, a "Black" taxable in Craven County in 1769 [SS 837].
18   iii. Ann, born say 1755.
     iv. William[6], born before 1776, head of a Buncombe County household of 3 "other free" in 1820 [NC:79].
     v. Johnston[3] Jr., born say 1775, head of a Beaufort County household of 4 "other free" in 1800 [NC:8]. He married Mary Driggers, 15 July 1801 Craven County bond with Shadrack Driggers bondsman.

14. Mark Driggers, born say 1723, received a grant for 100 acres in Craven County, North Carolina, joining a branch of Gum Swamp and Jumping Run on 11 October 1749 [Hoffman, *Land Patents*, II:256] and sold this land on 18 December 1760 [DB 2:126]. He moved to South Carolina where he was a landowner on the Little Pee Dee River [Brown, *The South Carolina Regulators*, 29]. He was counted as white in 1790, head of a Cheraw District household of one male over 16, one under 16, and one female [SC:49] and counted as white in Marlboro County in 1800, born before 1755, head of a household of 7 persons [SC:59]. He may have been the father of

    i. Ephraim, born before 1755, a "Molato" taxable in Bladen County in 1776 [Byrd, *Bladen County Tax Lists*, I:64, 77], head of a Liberty County, South Carolina household of 14 whites in 1800 [SC:798].
    ii. Matthew[2], counted as white in 1790, head of a Cheraw District household of one male over 16 and 4 females [SC:49] and head of a Marlboro County, South Carolina household of 12 "other free" in 1800 [SC:59].
   iii. Naomi, head of a Marlboro County household of 9 "other free" in 1800 [SC:59]. Administration on her estate was granted to Gilbert **Sweat** on 3 May 1815 in Marlboro County court on $250 bond, Benjamin and Solomon **Sweat** bondsmen [Minutes of the Court of Ordinary, 123].
    iv. Thomas[5], taxable on one "Mullators & free Negroes & other slaves" in Prince Frederick Parish, South Carolina in 1784 [S.C. Tax Returns 1783-1800, frame 45], counted as white in 1790, head of a Cheraw District household of 2 males over 16, 4 under 16, and 5 females [SC:49] and head of a Marlboro County household of 8 "other free" in 1800 [SC:59].
    v. John[2], head of a Marlboro County household of 7 "other free" in 1800 [SC:59].

15. Matthew[1] Driggers, born say 1725, went to South Carolina where he died in Prince George's Parish before 13 July 1765 when Gideon **Gibson**, his greatest creditor, was granted administration on his estate [*SCH&GM* 23, 35]. His wife may have been Catian Drigers who signed an affidavit in Marion County, South Carolina, on 7 May 1785 swearing that Pilisha **Bruinton** had always passed as a white woman and was "clar of any Negro blood Indian or Mulatto" [Marion DB C:156 by Henry, *Police Control of the Slave in South Carolina*].[93] Matthew's descendants may have been

    i. Corse, head of a Georgetown District, Prince George's Parish, household of 2 "other free" in 1790 [SC:54].

    ii. William[7] Driggus, born say 1777, purchased land in Charleston District by release proved between 1798-9 [Lucas, *Index to Deeds of South Carolina*, U-6:408]. He was head of a Sumpter District, South Carolina household of 5 "other free" in 1810 [SC:216a].

    iii. Lisha, born say 1780, purchased land by deed recorded in South Carolina in 1800 [Lucas, *Index to Deeds of South Carolina*, A-7:149].

16. Isaiah Drighouse, born say 1720, was executor of the Northampton County, Virginia will of his father Azaricum Drighouse. He married Sarah Drighouse (Jane **Beckett**'s daughter Sarah **Beckett**) soon after his mother's marriage to Mark **Beckett** and had a daughter named Leah. Isaiah died before 12 April 1743 when his widow Sarah Drigghouse asked the court to appoint someone to divide his estate. (His mother) Peggy **Beckett** returned the division of his estate to the court two months later on 14 June. On 13 July 1743 Mark and Margaret **Beckett** brought a bill in chancery against Jacob Drighouse (Isaiah's brother) and Leah Drighouse (Isaiah's orphan) petitioning for the sale and division of slave Bridget and her son Paul who descended to them by the will of Azaricum Drighouse [Orders 1742-8, 97, 101, 107-8, 112]. Isaiah's widow Sarah Drighouse was taxable in Mark and Margaret **Beckett**'s household from 1740 to 1743 and taxable in her own household in 1744 [Bell, *Northampton County Tithables*, 305, 328, 334, 350, 361]. Isaiah was probably identical to Isaac Draghouse who was listed among the soldiers who died on 9 June 1741 while serving aboard His Majesty's ship *Princess Caroline* [Clark, *Colonial Soldiers of the South*, 142]. Sarah Drighouse, a "free Negro," received five pounds on 21 September 1744 for the services of her unnamed husband who died in the expedition against the Spanish [McIlwaine, *Journals of the House of Burgesses*, 87, 101]. Sarah died before 10 July 1745 when the sheriff was ordered to pay Mark **Beckett** 1 pound, 8 shillings from the sale of her estate [Orders 1742-8, 230]. Isaiah and Sarah were the parents of

    i. Leah **Beckett**, born 31 August 1739, a nine-year-old orphan bound apprentice in Northampton County in 1748 to Richard Hanby, a neighbor of Mark and Margaret **Beckett**. She was probably the illegitimate child for which Sarah **Beckett** was whipped on 8 April 1740. She petitioned the court against Richard Hanby on 15 February 1758. She was called Leah Drighouse, orphan, when her guardian Mark Freshwater returned an account of her estate to court on 8 August 1749 [Orders 1732-42, 394; 1748-51, 3, 113, 120; 1753-8, 489]. A Leah **Beckett** was presented for bastard bearing on 13 May

---

[93]Several members of the Driggers family were counted as white in the South Carolina census in 1790 and 1800. Ephraim Driggers (11 whites) and Mark Driggers (3 whites and a slave) were heads of Prince George's Parish, Georgetown District households in 1790 [SC:54]. Ephraim Driggers (Liberty County), Elija Driggers (Charleston County), Elisha Driggers (Charleston County), John Driggers (Marlboro County) and Jordan Driggers (Marlboro County) were counted as white in 1800 [SC:52, 60, 61, 798]. Pilisha **Bruinton** was probably related to Amey and Ann **Brewington**, heads of "other free" households in Sampson County, North Carolina, in 1790 [NC:53], and Lewis and Joshua **Bruenton**, heads of "other free" New Hanover County households in 1800 [NC:311].

1766, but the case was dismissed--perhaps because she had left the county [Minutes 1765-71, 39, 59]. She was probably identical to Leah Drighouse who was a "free negro" tithable in Norfolk County in 1769. Isaky Drigshews, a Norfolk County tithable in 1778, was probably a close relation [Wingo, *Norfolk County Tithables 1766-80*, 269, 87].

17. Elizabeth Driggers, born say 1745, was a "Black" taxable in Craven County, North Carolina, in 1769 [SS 837]. She was head of a Craven County household of 5 "other free" in 1790, called Elizabeth "Griggers" [NC:134]. She may have been the mother of

   i. Joshua, born about 1771, a "Mollato Orphan Lad Aged 14 years," apprenticed as a blacksmith to Thomas Clayton by the 18 March 1785 Craven County court [Minutes 1784-86, 13a].

   ii. Makey, born say 1788, married Sarah **Kelly**, 24 December 1809 Craven County bond, Joshua **Lindsey** bondsman.

18. Ann Driggers, born say 1755, had four of her children stolen from her home on Green's Creek in Craven County, North Carolina, on 4 April 1778 [Fouts, *NC Gazette of New Bern*, I:65-66]. They were

   i. a daughter who escaped, perhaps the Elizabeth Gregers who married Benjamin **Mitchell**, 27 August 1788 Craven County bond, Benjamin **Moore** bondsman. Benjamin **Mitchell** was head of a Craven County household of 3 "other free" in 1790 [NC:130].

   ii. Becca.

   iii. Charita, born say 1771, married David **Johnston**, 20 December 1796 Craven County bond, Joshua **Lindsey** bondsman.

   iv. Shadrack, born about 1773, called "Shadrack Lindsay a free Molatto Boy of the Age of 10 son of Ann Driggos" in Craven County court on 9 December 1783 when he was bound apprentice to John Avery to learn the trade of House Carpenter [Minutes 1772-78, 62c]. He married Lucy Seat, 15 July 1801 Craven County bond with Johnston Driggers bondsman. She may have been the Lucy Grigus whose lease from William Farris was proved in Beaufort County court in June 1814 [Minutes 1809-14, n.p.].

DRING FAMILY

1. Mary Dring, born say 1700, was a "runaway Mulatto woman" who was the servant of Dorothy Price of York County before 16 April 1721 when the York County court approved Frederick Bryan's claim for taking her up [DOW 16:126]. She was probably the ancestor of

2   i. Percival, born say 1740.

2. Percival Dring, born say 1740, was a bachelor living in Prince George Parish, South Carolina, on 18 March 1761 when he married Elizabeth Crook of the same parish, spinster, in St. James Santee Parish with George and Ann MackDowll witnesses [St. James Santee Parish Register]. He purchased two tracts of land in Currituck County, North Carolina, one for 50 acres and another for 60 acres on the Cape Hatteras Banks on the Sound on 16 November 1797. About a year and a half later on 29 July 1799 he sold both tracts of land. Perhaps his wife was the Elizabeth Dring who sold 50 acres in Currituck County on Cape Hatteras and the Sound on 29 July 1799 [DB 7:265; 8:219-220]. He was head of a Currituck County household of 4 "other free" in 1790 [NC:20]. On 8 May 1804 he sold 50 acres adjoining his land on Hatteras Banks [DB 3:505]. His 12 March 1807 Currituck County will was

proved circa 1814. He named his brother Azariah; wife Amy; and friend Willoughby **Basnett**.[94] His children were probably,

    i.   Thomas, who served in Allen's Company in the Revolutionary War and died 11 September 1777 [Clark, *Colonial and State Records*, XVI:1040].

    ii.   Joseph, bondsman for the 16 April 1792 Craven County, North Carolina marriage of Jesse **Moore** and Keziah **George** (called Joseph Dering). He married Hannah **George**, 18 December 1794 Craven County bond with William **George** bondsman.

DRIVER FAMILY

1.   Susannah Driver, born say 1740, was head of a Gloucester County household of 4 free persons in 1783 [VA:53] and was taxable on 4 cattle in Gloucester County in 1787 [PPTL, 1782-99]. The births of her children Mary ("a mylatto bastard") and Richard ("Sp. son of Susanna Driver") were registered in Kingston Parish, Gloucester and Matthews Counties [Matheny, *Kingston Parish Register*, 46]. Susannah's children were

    i.   ?Emanuel, born say 1750, head of a Kingston Parish, Gloucester County household of 5 free persons in 1783 [VA:53], taxable in Kingston Parish on his own tithe and 2 horses in 1784, 4 cattle in 1787, taxable on his own tithe from 1788 to 1790 [PPTL, 1782-99]. In July 1835 his nephew John Driver, son of John Driver, testified that Emanuel enlisted in the 2nd Virginia Regiment in 1776 and was discharged in 1780 or 1781. He lived in Mathews County and died there in 1835 [Hopkins, *Virginia Revolutionary War Land Grant Claims*, 75].

    ii.   ?William, head of a Kingston Parish, Gloucester County household of 3 free persons in 1783 [VA:53], taxable in Kingston Parish from 1784 to 1790: on his own tithe and a horse in Kingston Parish from 1784 to 1789 [PPTL, 1782-99] and head of a Chatham County, North Carolina household of 2 "other free" in 1800. He (or perhaps a younger William Driver) was a "Mulatto" taxable in Gloucester County in 1809 and from 1812 to 1820 [PPTL 1800-20].

    iii.   ?John[1], born say 1758, the father of John[2] Driver who deposed that his father enlisted in the 2nd Virginia Regiment and resided in Mathews County. He was taxable in Kingston Parish, Gloucester County, from 1783 to 1790: taxable on 4 cattle in 1783, 3 in 1785, 5 in 1787 [PPTL 1782-99]. And he was a "Mulatto" taxable in Gloucester County from 1801 to 1803 [PPTL 1800-20].

    iv.   Mary, born April 1761, "a mylatto bastard, daughter of Susanna Driver." Mary Driver and Mary Driver, Jr. (who lived with James Purcell), were counted in a "List of Mulattoes and Free Negroes" above the age of sixteen" in Gloucester County in 1813 [PPTL 1800-20].

    v.   Richard, born 13 June 1773, "Sp. son of Susanna Driver." He was taxable in King William County on his own tithe and a slave in 1810, taxable on 1 "Free Negro" and 1 "Free Mulatto" in 1813, listed as a "Free Negro" with a free female "Free Negro" in his household in 1814, listed as a "Free Negro" taxable on 2 horses in 1815 [PPTL 1782-1811; 1812-50].

---

[94]Willoughby **Basnett** was the son of Robert **Basnett**, a Currituck County taxable in 1779 and head of a Currituck County household of 8 "other free" and one white male under sixteen years in 1790 [NC:20]. He was mentioned in his father's 27 September 1800 Currituck County will, proved 22 June 1806. Azariah Dring was witness to the 9 October 1782 will of Josiah Basnett, proved 10 October 1785.

vi. ?Edmund, born before 1776, head of a Mathews County household of 6 "other free" in 1810 [VA:453] and 2 "free colored" in Halifax County, North Carolina, in 1830.

vii. ?Thomas, head of a Loudoun County household of 3 "other free" in 1810 [VA:291].

DRURY FAMILY

1. Sam Drury, born say 1730, was called "Free Sam Overseer for Mr. Lowther," a "free molatto" taxable in the 1763 Bertie County summary list. He may have been related to a "Negro fellow named Thomas" who William Drury freed (after the death of his wife) by his 6 October 1723 will which was proved in York County, Virginia, on 18 July 1726 [OW 16:400]. Sam and his wife Jenny were "free molatto" taxables in the 1764 summary list for Bertie County [CR 10.702.1]. He was head of his own household in John Crickett's list for 1766 and listed in William Lowther's household in the 1768 list of Edward Rasor. He was again head of his own household in the 1774 list of George Lockhart, counted as a "free Mollato" with "Negro Women" Jenny and Milly in his household. In August 1774 the Bertie County court agreed to his petition that his daughter Milley, whom he purchased from Young Miller and Co., be set free [Haun, *Bertie County Court Minutes*, IV:98]. His will, proved in Bertie County in May 1782, mentioned his wife Jenny and daughter Milly. Two years later Jenny married Andrew **James**, 24 February 1784 Bertie County bond. Sam and Jenny's daughter was

   i. Milly, married Frederick **Wilkison**, 15 May 1780 Bertie County bond with William Griffin bondsman.

DUNCAN FAMILY

1. Elizabeth Dunkinton, born say 1693, was convicted by the Princess Anne County court on 1 June 1715 for having two "Molatto" children [Minutes 1709-17, 186]. She may have been the ancestor of

2   i. Sarah Duncan, born say 1732.
3   ii. Betty Duncan, born say 1735.
   iii. Nanny Duncan, born say 1759, a "free Mullatto" ordered bound by the Princess Anne County court to Sam **Nichols** on 20 November 1759 until the age of eighteen, to be taught to read, sew, and knit [Minutes 1753-62, 367].
   iv. Solomon[1] Duncan, "Free Black" head of a Princess Anne County household of 5 "other free" in 1810 [VA:450]. He was a yellow-complexioned blacksmith who was born in Pasquotank County, North Carolina, served in the Revolution, and was living in Princess Anne County when he was listed in the size roll of troops who joined at Chesterfield Courthouse [cited by NSDAR, *African American Patriots*, 149].

2. Sarah Duncan, born say 1732, was "a free Molatto" living in Norfolk County on 18 October 1754 when her children John and Luke were bound apprentices to Samuel Coverly and on 17 March 1763 when her son Thomas was bound out [Orders 1753-55, 90; 1759-63, 242]. She was a "free negro" taxable in Martha Scott's household on the south side of Western Branch in 1768 [Wingo, *Norfolk County Tithables, 1766-80*, 72]. Sarah was the mother of

   i. John, born say 1750, bound to Samuel Coverly in Norfolk County on 18 October 1754, taxable on the south side of Tanners Creek in Norfolk County in James Godfrey's household in 1773, called John Duncan, Jr. [Wingo, *Norfolk County Tithables, 1766-80*, 200]. He may have been the husband of Ann Dunkin, the daughter of William **Brooks** who mentioned her in his 9 May 1788 Southampton County will [WB 4:276].

ii.   Luke, born say 1752, taxable in Lemuel Coverly's Norfolk County household in the list for Tanner's Creek in 1765 [Wingo, *Norfolk County Tithables, 1751-65*, 185]. He was called a "free Mulatto" on 8 April 1782 when the Norfolk County court ordered him released from his indenture to Thomas Lowry. John Warren sued him, but the court dismissed the case on 16 May 1782 at the plaintiff's costs [Orders 1782-3, 9, 20, 31]. He was taxable in Norfolk County in 1782 and 1794 [PPTL, 1782-1791, frame 407; 1791-1812, frame 102]. He was a man of color from Norfolk County who enlisted in the Revolution between 1777 and 1783 [NSDAR, *African American Patriots*, 149].

iii.   Thomas, born say 1760, bound apprentice in Norfolk County on 17 March 1763 [Orders 1759-63, 242]. He was head of a Currituck County, North Carolina household of 5 "other free" and two slaves in 1800 [NC:168].

iv.   Ann, a "free Negro" washerwoman heading a family in Portsmouth, Norfolk County, with Betty and Sukey Duncan in 1801 [PPTL, 1791-1812, frame 383].

3.   Betty Duncan, born say 1735, was a taxable in Samuel Smith's Norfolk County household in the district from the Borough of Norfolk to the south side of Tanner's Creek in 1751 [Wingo, *Norfolk County Tithables, 1751-65*, 14]. She may have been identical to Elizabeth Dungin who was the servant of Mary Wood on 3 October 1765 when the Frederick County, Virginia court ordered her "Mulattoe" son Solomon Duncan bound to her mistress. She was called Elizabeth Duncan, a "Mulatto," on 8 November 1770 when Mary Wood came into Frederick County court and agreed to discharge her from the remainder of her service in consideration that she had not sufficiently taught her to read [Orders 1765-7, 21; 1770-2, 57]. She was the mother of

i.   Solomon[2], born say 1763, bound to Mary Wood on 3 October 1765.

ii.   ?Susannah, born 28 November 1768, a two-year-old "Mulatto" ordered bound to John Lawrence in Frederick County on 7 August 1771 [Orders 1770-2, 246].

Other members of the Duncan family were

i.   Alexander, born say 1770, consented to the 12 March 1813 Fredericksburg marriage of his son Alexander Duncan, Jr., who married Fanny **More**, *a Mulatto girl formerly the property of Edward More, deceased, of Stafford County who was legally emancipated in April 1806 as appears in Stafford Court.*

ii.   Mary, a "Mulatto" child bound by the Pittsylvania County court to Samuel Walker on 24 March 1774 [Court Records 1772-5, 324].

iii. Lucy, head of a Spotsylvania County household of 3 "other free" in 1810 [VA:110b].

iv.   Frank, head of an Accomack County household of 3 "other free" in 1810 [VA:89].

v.   Abey, head of a Southampton County household of 4 "other free" in 1810.

vi.   Nancy, born say 1780, mother of Jack Duncan, a poor boy of colour, bound to John Allen in Bourbon County, Kentucky, on 20 July 1815, recorded in Ross County, Ohio, on 3 July 1816 [Turpin, *Register of Black, Mulatto, and Poor Persons*, 20].

vii. Ridley, born about 1790, obtained a certificate of freedom in Chesterfield County on 10 November 1835: *forty five years old, Mulatto complexion, born free* [Register of Free Negroes 1804-53, no. 1083].

DUNGEE/ DUNGILL FAMILY

1. Frances[1] Dungee, born say 1707, a servant woman, was the mother of two_
    children, John and Millison Dungey, who were bound apprentice to John
    Douglass by the Brunswick County, Virginia court in December 1735 until
    they reached the age of twenty-one. Frances petitioned the Brunswick County
    court for her freedom from servitude to Douglass in October 1740, but her
    petition was denied in March 1741/2, and the same court session ordered the
    churchwardens of Saint Andrew's Parish to bind her children Rebecca and
    John to Douglass [Orders 1732-41, 115, 375, 428; 1741-83, 72, 104]. She was
    the mother of

2   i.   Rebecca, born say 1723.
3   ii.   ?William[1], born say 1727.
4   iii. John[1], born 23 June 1729.
    iv.   Millison, born 12 June 1731, discharged by the Brunswick County
          court from serving John Macklin in July 1752 when he could not
          produce an indenture.

2. Rebecca Dungee, born say 1723, was bound apprentice by the Brunswick
    County, Virginia court in March 1741/2. Her unnamed children were bound
    apprentice to John Douglass in April 1742 [Orders 1741-83, 108]. She was
    probably identical to Rebecca **Dungeon** who was maintained by the Brunswick
    County estate of John Maclin in January 1773. Maclin was ordered to let her,
    William **Blizzard**, and Thomas O'Riley out to the lowest bidder [Hopkins, *St.
    Andrew's Parish Vestry*, 93, 94]. She may have been the mother of

5   i.   John[1] Dungill, born say 1738.
6   ii.   William[1] Dungill, born about 1754.

3. William[1] Dungee, born say 1727, was living in Cumberland County, Virginia,
    on 28 September 1761 when a presentment against him for tending tobacco
    seconds was dismissed. He purchased 50 acres in Cumberland County
    adjoining Henry Scruggs from Henry Scruggs on 25 February 1764 [DB
    3:448]. He and his wife Mary registered the birth and baptism of their son
    Bartholomew in St. Peter's Parish, New Kent County, on 7 September 1767
    [NSCDA, *Parish Register of St. Peter's*, 152]. He was sued in Cumberland
    County on 25 June 1770, but the case was dismissed on agreement of the
    parties. He died before 25 January 1773 when his wife Mary was granted
    administration on his Cumberland County estate, and Mary died before 28
    February 1780 when Henry Scruggs was granted administration on William's
    unadministered estate [Orders 1770-2, 43; 1772-4, 85]. The inventory of the
    estate totalled about 30 pounds, and included: "1 old negro man named
    Barcas," two horses and other farm animals, a woman's saddle, a flax wheel,
    a parcel of books, carpenter's tools, a gun, two beds and other household
    furniture and goods [WB 2:92]. He was the father of

    i.   ?Nancy, mother of Polly Dungee who was ordered bound to John
          Creasy by the Cumberland County court on 22 January 1787 [Orders
          1786-8, 210].
    ii.   ?James, born say 1760, taxable in Cumberland County from 1787 to
          1793 [PPTL, 1782-1816, frames 88, 155, 202]. He married Elizabeth
          Fears, daughter of Absalom Fears, 2 March 1795 Prince Edward
          County bond, 5 March marriage. He was head of a Prince Edward
          County household of 7 "other free" in 1810 [VA:562].
    iii. Sherwood, born say 1762, "orphan of William Dungee" bound
          apprentice to Obediah Hendrick on 27 March 1780. Hendrick was
          presented by the court on 24 November 1783 for failing to list
          Sherwood as a tithable [Orders 1779-84, 110, 474]. He was taxable in
          Cumberland County from 1787 to 1799 [PPTL, 1782-1816, frames 88,
          174, 237, 313]. On 23 September 1799 the Cumberland County court

ordered him to appear at the next court to show cause why his son Reuben should not be bound out [Orders 1797-1801, 268].

7 iv. William[2], born say 1765.

  v. Bartholomew, born 3 August, baptized 7 September 1767 [NSCDA, *Parish Register of St. Peter's*, 152]. He sold (signing) 33 acres in Cumberland County on the north side of the main ridge road for 25 pounds on 25 August 1776 [DB 5:463-4]. He served in the Revolution according to a statement made by his older brother William [LVA chancery file 1803-002].

  vi. Burwell, "orphan of William Dungee" bound to Samuel Allen on 27 March 1780 [Orders 1779-84, 110]. He was taxable in the upper district of Cumberland County from 1794 to 1806, called a "fM" in 1804 [PPTL, 1782-1816, frames 226, 274, 396, 426, 522]. He was sued for debts totalling 31 pounds on 25 October 1801 [Orders 1797-1801, 465, 466].

4. John[1] Dungee, born 23 June 1729, was a "Mulatto" who was convicted of the attempted rape of Frances Kennon in Brunswick County, Virginia, in July 1755 for which he received thirty lashes [Orders 1753-56, 451, 498]. He may have been the John Dungee who was taxable in King William County from 1782 to 1785: taxable on a free tithe, 2 horses and 10 cattle and listed with 4 persons in his household in 1783, taxable on 3 horses in 1784 and 1785 [PPTL 1782-1811]. He was taxable on 2 horses and 5 cattle in the upper district of Cumberland County, Virginia, from 1787 to 1792, called "Sr." from 1789 [PPTL, 1782-1816, frames 88, 107, 122, 144, 155, 174]. He signed a promissory note in Cumberland County to Ford & Allen for 185 pounds, dated 9 November 1799, which was also signed by William Dungey and Burwell Dungee. To cover the note, on 17 June 1800 he executed a deed of trust for a wagon and five horses which was foreclosed by Ford & Allen in 1803 [LVA chancery file 1803-002]. His descendants may have been

8 i. John[2], born say 1758.

  ii. Joseph, born say 1760, taxable in King William County from 1782 to 1799 and from 1811 to 1820: taxable in St. John's Parish on a horse in 1782, listed as a "Mulatto" in 1813 [PPTL 1782-1811; 1812-50].

  iii. Frances[2], married John **Stewart**, 20 April 1797 Powhatan County marriage, Wade Woodson, Sr., surety [Marriage Register, 34].

  iv. Isabella, taxable in King William County on a free male tithable in 1802 [PPTL 1782-1811], a "M"(ulatto) taxable on a horse in New Kent County in 1807 [PPTL 1791-1828, frame 430], head of a New Kent County household of 4 "other free" in 1810 [VA:751].

  v. Reuben[1], taxable in King William County in 1798 and 1799 [PPTL 1782-1811], taxable in New Kent County from 1800 to 1814: listed as a "M"(ulatto) in 1806 and thereafter; listed with his unnamed wife in 1813 [PPTL 1791-1828, frames 342, 356, 368, 381, 393, 406, 418, 430, 463, 491, 503] and head of a New Kent Count household of 7 "other free" in 1810 [VA:751].

  vi. Gideon, head of a New Kent County household of 7 "other free" in 1810.

5. John[1] Dungill, born say 1738, was sued for a two pound debt in Brunswick County, Virginia court by Archibald Wager, assignee of William Daniel, on 22 May 1759. This suit was called Wager against **Dungeon** in the Execution Dockets [Orders 1757-9, 349; Dockets 1757-9, 12 (at the end of the court order book)]. He was called John Dungion on 8 July 1765 when he sold goods, furniture and a mare in Brunswick County to Henry Cock [DB 8:235].

He died before 24 January 1774 when Edmund **Wilkins** was granted administration of his Brunswick County estate on 200 pounds security [Orders 1772-4, 494, 495]. On 23 March 1778 his son John, "heir to John Dungill deceased," purchased 520 acres in Brunswick County. Perhaps his widow was Dicey Dungill who sued Burwell **Blizzard** for debt due by account in Greensville County, Virginia court on 22 March 1787 [Orders 1781-9, 317]. John was the father of

    i.   John[2] Dungill, born say 1760, called an infant and heir to John Dungill, deceased, of Meherrin Parish on 23 March 1778 when he purchased 520 acres adjoining John **Robinson** in Brunswick County for 30 pounds [DB 13:85].

6.   William[1] Dungill, born about 1754, was living in Brunswick County, Virginia, on 25 June 1770 when the court ordered him (and Mason **Blizzard**) bound apprentice by the churchwardens of St. Andrew's Parish [Orders 1768-72, 289]. He was head of a Greensville County, Virginia household of 7 persons in 1783 [VA:55] and taxable in Meherrin Parish, Greensville County, from 1783 to 1807: taxable on Drury Dungill's tithe in 1800 and taxable on William Dungill, Jr.'s tithe in 1806 and 1807 [PPTL 1782-1850, frames 13, 40, 62, 106, 126, 135, 161, 178, 187, 200, 217, 230, 243, 273, 302, 320, 336, 352, 371]. On 1 January 1801 he mortgaged 22 acres in Greensville County to pay a debt he owed Daniel **Robinson** and Company [DB 3:36]. He registered as a "free Negro" in Greensville County on 7 March 1807: *born free, black Complexion, aged about fifty three years...five feet six Inches high* [Register of Free Negroes, #14]. On 11 May 1807 the Greensville County court ordered the overseers of the poor to bind to him Dudley Dungil, "natural child of Molley Dungil" [Orders 1806-10, 98]. He was head of a Chatham County household of 8 "other free" in 1810 (called William **Dungeon**) [NC:195]. William and his family were called "the Dungill people of Colour" when they were among the freeholders ordered to work on the road from Boylan's Mill on Deep River to Little Lick Creek by the Tuesday, May 1823 session of the Chatham County, North Carolina court [Minutes 1822-27]. He was probably the father of

    i.   Drury, born about 1775, taxable in Greensville County from 1798 to 1803 [PPTL 1782-1850, frames 230, 259, 273, 302]. He registered in Greensville County on 10 October 1803: *born free of a dark colour, aged 28 years about 5 feet 7 inches high* [Register of Free Negroes, #1].

    ii.   William[2], Jr., born about 1781, registered in Greensville County on 9 March 1807: *born free of a darkish Complexion, aged Twenty six years about five feet nine & 1/4 Inches high* [Register of Free Negroes, #16].

    iii.   John/Jack, born about 1786, registered in Greensville County on 9 March 1807: *born free of a black Complexion aged twenty one years last Christmas, five feet seven Inches high* [Register of Free Negroes, #17]. He was granted administration on the 10 June 1831 Chatham County will of Anthony **Evans**, witnessed by Jarrel **Walden**. Perhaps John's wife was Noony Dungill whose daughter Sary Betty **Ledbetter** received all of **Evans'** property and his plantation [WB p.24].

    iv.   Fanny[1], born say 1800, married Daniel **Wadkins** (**Watkins**), 10 February 1824 Greensville County bond, David **Wadkins** surety, 12 February marriage by Rev. Nathaniel Chambliss [Ministers' Returns, 93].

7.   William[2] Dungee, born say 1765, was called the "orphan of William Dungee" by the Cumberland County court on 25 April 1780 when it appointed Henry Scruggs as his guardian [Orders 1779-84, 116]. He and his wife Nancy sold property by deed proved in Cumberland County court on 27 July 1790 [Orders 1788-92, 272]. On 30 January 1798 Charles **Williams** mortgaged slave

children David and Mourning to cover a debt of 96 pounds he owed Dungee. Williams failed to pay, so the court foreclosed and gave the children to William. On 31 October the court appointed commissioners to sell the children to satisfy the debt and court costs [Orders 1797-1801, 255, 296]. In April 1799 he sued Littleberry Scruggs declaring "that he is oldest brother and heir at law of Bartholomew Dungee who departed this life in the year [blank] being a soldier in the American Army in the late Revolutionary War...at which time the said Bartholomew Dungee had right and title to ten acres of land, which were bought and paid for by him from John Henry Scruggs--that the said Henry (who is now decd) made, in his lifetime, on the 24th day of August 1776, a good & sufficient deed of conveyance to the said Bartholomew"...which is recorded...that Littleberry Scruggs has taken possession of the land and will not relinquish it" [LVA chancery files 1799-003; 1803-002]. He was taxable in Cumberland County from 1785 to 1814: charged with 2 tithables in 1786, taxable on a slave in 1797, a wagoner living on his own land with wife Nancy and sons Anderson and Frank in 1810 when he was in a list of "free Negroes and Mulattoes," listed with Nancy, Sally and Richard Dungy in a list of "Free persons of Colour" in 1813 [PPTL, 1782-1816, frames 57, 68, 226, 274, 657, 764, 795], head of a Cumberland County household of 5 "other free" in 1810 [VA:114]. He was the father of

    i.   Anderson.
    ii.   Frank.
    iii. Sally.
    iv. ?Richard.

8.   John[2] Dungee, born say 1755, was taxable in Stratton Major Parish, King and Queen County from 1783 to 1786 and taxable in the lower district of the county from 1787 to 1802: counted with 5 persons in his household and taxable on a horse and 5 cattle in 1783; taxable on a horse and 4 cattle in 1787; taxable on a horse in 1791, 1794 and 1795; taxable on 2 free male tithes in 1801 [PPTL, 1782-1803; 1804-16]. He was taxable on 110 acres in 1790 and 1798 [1790 Land Tax List, p.4; 1798, p.5]. He may have been the father of

    i.   John[5], born say 1780, a "M"(ulatto) taxable on a slave aged 12-16 in New Kent County in 1807 [PPTL 1791-1828, frame 430] and a "Mulatto" taxable in King and Queen County in 1813 and 1814 [PPTL, 1782-1803; 1804-23]. He was a pilot on the Chesapeake Bay who was "descended from the aborigines of this Dominion" (a Pamunky Indian) according to the petition which he and his wife Lucy Ann made to the Virginia Legislature from King William County on 19 December 1825. They called themselves "free persons of colour" in this petition which asked the Legislature to allow her to remain in the state after she was freed by her master Edmund Littlepage who was her father by his slave, Sophia. In their testimony supporting his petition, seventy-two white persons from King William, New Kent, Richmond, Hanover, and King and Queen County certified that: *Capt. John Dungee...Commander of a Vessel, constantly employed in the navigation of the Chesapeake Bay and the Rivers of Virginia...his loss would be an evol seriously felt by those particularly who ship Grain or other articles from the shores of Pamonkey and Matapond Rivers* [King William County Legislative Petition of 19 December 1825].

Other members of the family were

    i.   John[4], born say 1775, taxable on a slave over the age of 16 in King William County in 1797 and from 1802 to 1809 [PPTL 1782-1811].
    ii.   John[3], called John, Jr., when he was taxable in Cumberland County from 1789 to 1793 and from 1800 to 1802 [PPTL, 1782-1816, frames 122, 155, 331, 352, 373]. He was a "Mulatto" taxable in Buckingham

County from 1805 to 1809: called John Dungeon in 1805 and 1806, called John Dungy from 1807 to 1809, taxable on 3 free males in 1806, 2 free males and 2 horses in 1807 [PPTL 1804-9].

iii. Reubin, a "FM" taxable in Cumberland County from 1813 to 1815 [PPTL, 1782-1816, frames 739, 773, 816].

iv. Reuben, taxable in the lower district of Henrico County in 1813 and 1814: in a list of "Blacks free" with his unnamed wife in 1813, listed as a "free Negro" in 1814 [PPTL 1782-1814, frames 757, 823]. Perhaps his wife was Agnes Dungy who registered in Henrico County on 7 September 1839: *about 45 years of age, a mulatto woman, 5 feet 2-1/2 inches, Born free as appears by a certificate of her register from the clerk of Richmond Hustings Court* [Register of Free Negroes and Mulattoes, 1831-1844, p.34, no. 936].

v. Polly Dungy, born about 1789, registered in Middlesex County on 23 July 1821: *born free; 32 years of age; 5'6"; yellow complexion* [Register of Free Negroes 1800-60, p.16].

vi. Harry Dungy, born about 1794, registered in Middlesex County on 21 July 1821: *born free; 27 years of age; 5'0"; yellow complexion* [Register of Free Negroes 1800-60, p.16].

vii. John and Fanny "Dungill or Dungron, children of color," ordered apprenticed as a blacksmith and spinster, respectively, to Beverly **Brown** in Northampton County, North Carolina, on 7 June 1813 with William **Walden** providing security [Minutes 1813-21].

DUNLOP FAMILY

1. Mary Dunlop, born say 1717, was living in St. Paul's Parish, King George County, Virginia, in 1735 when the birth and baptism of her son James was recorded (no race indicated). She was the mother of

    i. James, born 6 August 1735, baptized September 29, 1735 [St. Paul's Parish Register, 60].

    ii. ?Henry, born say 1740, a "Mulatto Boy" listed in the 1 June 1750 inventory of the King George County estate of Peter Nugent [Inventories 1745-65, 62].

2   iii. ?Lydia[1], born say 1745.

2. Lydia[1] Dunlop, born say 1745, registered the 18 April 1773 birth of her daughter Charlotte at St. Paul's Parish, King George County (no race indicated). She was taxable in King George County from 1787 to 1815: taxable on 2 cattle in 1787; a free male and a horse from 1788 to 1793; a free male, a slave and a horse in 1796; a free male, a slave and 2 horses in 1801; a retail license in 1802 [PPTL, 1782-1830, frames 48, 55, 94, 110, 144, 201, 216, 328, 339]. She was head of a King George County household of 4 "other free" in 1810 [VA:197]. She was the mother of

    i. Charlotte[1], born 18 April 1773.

3   ii. ?Joseph, born about 1768.

    iii. ?Gerard, taxable on a horse in King George County in 1794 and 1795 [PPTL, 1782-1830, frames 125, 136].

    iv. ?Augustavus, born about 1774, registered as a free Negro in King George County on 25 September 1798: *a "molatto man about twenty four years old about five feet eight inches high, was free born* [Register of Free Persons 1785-1799, no.8]. He was taxable in King George County from 1796 to 1814 [PPTL, 1782-1830, frames 144, 339, 451] and head of a King George County household of 6 "other free" in 1810 [VA:197].

4   v. ?Sarah, born say 1780.

    vi. ?Nathan[1], born about 1782, registered in King George County on 11 April 1801: *a bright mulatto lad, aged about nineteen years, five feet ten inches high, was born in this county of a free woman* [Register of Free Negroes, no.20].

3. Joseph[1] Dunlop, born about 1768, was taxable in King George County from 1794 to 1804: taxable on 3 horses and a retail license in 1800; 2 free males, 4 horses and a retail license in 1803; 2 slaves, 4 horses and a retail license in 1804 [PPTL, 1782-1830, frames 125, 238]. He registered as a free Negro in King George County on 25 September 1798: *a mulatto man about thirty years old and five feet three inches high was born free* [Register of Free Persons 1785-1799, no.9]. He moved to Prince George's County, Maryland, before 7 August 1817 when his son George registered there as a "free Negro." He was the father of

  i.   Winny, born say 1788, registered as a free Negro in Prince George County, Maryland, on 7 July 1819: *a black woman about 5 feet 2-1/2 inches tall, and about 51 (31?) years old...free and the daughter of Joseph Dunlap and Lydia his wife free people of color, born in Virginia King George County, who have been residing in Prince George's County for the last twelve months.*

  ii. George, born about 1796, registered as a free Negro in Prince George's County, Maryland, on 7 August 1817: *a dark mulatto man, 5 feet 8 inches tall, and 21 years old...the son of Joseph Dunlop Sr. of Prince George's County, a respectable colored freeman.*

  iii. Joseph[2], born about 1797, registered on 14 September 1818: *a colored man of dark complexion, about 21 years old, and 5 feet 8 inches tall. He is a free man, being the legitimate son of Joseph Dunlop Sr., a free man of color* [Provine, *Registrations of Free Negroes*, 23, 27, 29].

4. Sarah Dunlop, born say 1780, was taxable on a slave and a horse in King George County in 1809, taxable on 2 horses in 1810 and 1813 [PPTL, 1782-1830, frames 291, 303, 339]. head of a King George County household of 6 "other free" in 1810 [VA:197]. She was the mother of

  i.   ?Nathan[2], born about 1802, registered in King George County on 4 February 1819: *a dark mulatto lad about 17 years of age.*

  ii. Charlotte[2], born about 1803, registered in King George County on 6 October 1819: *a dark mulatto Girl about 16 years of age...born free in this County, a daughter of Sarah Dunlop.*

  iii. Trecy, born about 1807, registered in King George County on 6 October 1819: *a mulatto girl about 12 years old, born of a free woman, Sarah Dunlop, in this County.*

  iv. Lydia[2], born about 1815, registered in King George County in 1819: *an infant Girl 4 years old a dark mulatto...born of a free woman, Sarah Dunlop, in this County* [Register of Free Persons 1785-1799, nos.53-56].

Other members of the Dunlop family were

  i.   Mary, head of a Richmond City household of 10 "other free" in 1810 [VA:333].

  ii. Naney, head of a Richmond City household of 4 "other free" in 1810 [VA:333], perhaps the mother of Nancy Dunlap, born about 1799, registered as a free Negro in Prince George's County, Maryland, on 7 July 1819: *about 5 feet 3-1/4 inches tall, about 22 years old, and of a yellow complexion...daughter of Nancy Dunlap, a free woman of color...born in King George County, Virginia and has been residing in Prince George's County for about a year* [Provine, *Registrations of Free Negroes*, 29]

  iii. Patsey, born about 1804, registered in King George County on 1 August 1822: *a bright Mulatto Girl between 18 and 19 years of age, 5' 3-1/2 Inches high* [Register of Free Negroes, no.65].

iv. Harril, born about 1805, registered in King George County on 1 August 1822: *a bright Mulatto Girl between 17 and 18 years of age 5' 3-1/4 Inches high* [Register of Free Negroes, no.66].

v. Charlotte[3], born about 1807, registered in King George County on 1 August 1822: *a dark Mulatto between 15 and 16 Years of age, 5' 3-1/2 inches high* [Register of Free Negroes, no.67].

DUNN FAMILY

1. Elizabeth Dunn, born say 1730, was the servant of Sampson Darrell on 8 February 1752 when she confessed to the Fairfax County court that she had an illegitimate child. The court ordered that she receive twenty-five lashes. She was probably the mother of an illegitimate "Mullatto" child named Peter Dunn who the court ordered bound to Sampson Darrell on 26 March 1751 [Orders 1749-54, 128, 186]. She was the mother of

    i. Peter, born say 1751.

    ii. ?Stephen, head of a Robeson County, North Carolina household of 5 "other free" in 1800 [NC:375].

2   iii. ?Peggy, born say 1770, a seamstress counted in a list of "Free Negroes & Mulattoes" in Portsmouth and Elizabeth River Parishes, Norfolk County, in 1801, living near Norfolk with Mark, Tom, and James Dunn who were probably her sons [PPTL 1791-1812, frame 384].

    iv. ?James, a "free Negro" taxable in St. Bride's Parish, Norfolk County, from 1792 to 1809 [PPTL 1791-1812, frames 51, 120, 400, 456, 636, 674]. Perhaps his widow was Mary Dunn, head of Norfolk County household of 4 "other free" in 1810 [VA:806].

    v. ?Charles, born before 1776, head of a Mecklenburg County, Virginia household of 7 "free colored" in 1820.

    vi. ?Valentine, head of a Norfolk County household of 2 "other free" in 1810 [VA:802]. Balentine Dunn was a "free Negro" taxable in Norfolk County from 1807 to 1816 [PPTL 1791-1812, frames 636, 716; 1813-24, frame 172].

DUNSTAN FAMILY

The Dunstan family of Virginia was probably related to Ann Dunstan who confessed to having illegitimate "Mulatto" children in Piscataway Hundred, Prince George's County, Maryland, in 1746 and 1748 [Court Record 1746-7, 20; 1748-9, 47].

1. Patience Dunstan, born say 1734, was a "Mulatto" girl belonging to the estate of Peter Brewer of Brunswick County, Virginia, in May 1741 [Orders 1732-41, 444]. She was living in Lunenburg County when the churchwardens of Cumberland Parish were ordered to bind out her son Charles to John Howell in April 1751 and her daughter Lucy (no race indicated) in November 1753. In April 1754 the court bound her daughters Lucy and Amey to John Howell, and in October 1759 the court bound Alice, her "Molatto" child, to John Howell [Orders 1746-52, 391; 1753-4, 486, 623; 1755-57, 278; 1759-61, 32]. On 26 August 1766 the churchwardens of Meherrin Parish in adjoining Brunswick County were ordered to bind out her children Isaac and Pheby (no race indicated) [Orders 1765-68, 148]. She was called Patience Dunstal, a "mallatto," in Bute County, North Carolina, on 9 November 1778, when the court ordered her children James, Tom, Frank, and Isaac bound as apprentices. She was probably living in John Howell's household since her children were bound to him in Lunenburg County and her son James was bound to him in Bute County [Minutes 1777-79, 136]. She was head of a Franklin County, North Carolina household of 4 "other free" in 1810 [NC:826]. Her children were

2   i.   Charles[1], born say 1750.

3   ii.   Lucy, born say 1752.

       iii. Amy, born say 1753, "daughter of Patience Dunstan," bound by the churchwardens of Cumberland Parish, Lunenburg County, to John Howell, in April 1754 [Orders 1753-54, 623].

       iv. William, born about 1755, one of the "Molatto Children of Patience Dunstan," bound apprentice to John Howell by the April 1757 Lunenburg County court [Orders 1755-57, 278]. According to the militia returns for Bute County, he was born in Virginia about 1755, about 5'9" high, one of the Continental Soldiers from Bute County who volunteered for nine months [Militia Returns, *NCGSJ* XV:109]. He married Fanny **Bibby**, 11 July 1778 Bute County bond.

       v.   ?Wallace, born say 1757, a soldier from Halifax County, Virginia, who deserted Captain Shem Cook's Second Georgia State Battalion. On 27 October 1777 Cook placed an advertisement in the *Virginia Gazette* offering "mulattoes" Wallace Dunstan and James **Smith** of Halifax County (and 10 other soldiers, including a sergeant) a pardon if they returned [*Virginia Gazette*, Purdie edition, p.3, col. 1].

       vi. Alice, born say 1759, "a Mulatto Girl daughter of Patience Dunston," bound out to John Howell in Lunenburg County in October 1759 [Orders 1759-60]. Alcey was head of a Franklin County, North Carolina household of 3 "other free" in 1810 [NC:826].

       vii. Phebe, born say 1760, bound apprentice in Brunswick County in August 1766.

     viii. Isaac[1], born say 1762, ordered bound apprentice in Brunswick County in August 1766 [Orders 1765-68, 148].

       ix. James, born about 1764, fourteen-year-old son of Patience Dunstal, bound apprentice to John Howell in Bute County on 9 November 1778 [Minutes 1777-79, 136], head of a Franklin County, North Carolina household of 3 "other free" in 1810 [NC:826].

       x.   Tom, born about 1769, a seven-year-old bound apprentice to Peter Tatum in Bute County on 9 November 1778.

       xi. Frank, born about 1773, five-year-old bound apprentice to Peter Tatum in Bute County on 9 November 1778.

       xii. Isaac[2], born about 1776, a two-year-old bound apprentice to Peter Tatum in Bute County on 9 November 1778 [Minutes 1777-79, 136].

2.   Charles[1] Dunston, born say 1750, son of Patience Dunston, was bound apprentice in to John Howell in Cumberland Parish, Lunenburg County, in April 1751. He was called "a poor soldier in the service of the United States" on 8 May 1780 when the Mecklenburg County, Virginia court allowed his wife Elizabeth Dunston a barrel and a half of corn and 50 pounds of bacon for the support of herself and two children [Orders 1779-84, 34, 53]. He purchased 230 acres in Wake County, North Carolina, on both sides of Little Lick Creek on 21 September 1787 [DB H:221]. He sold 105 acres of this land to William **Evans**, Sr., before 21 June 1798 when **Evans** sold this land [Deeds, p.76]. He was counted as white in 1790, head of a Wake County household of one male over 16, two under 16 and six females [NC:105]. He was living in Orange County when he received his final settlement for his service in the Revolutionary War [*The North Carolinian* VI:755]. He may have been the father of

       i.   Phillis, born say 1800, married Solomon **Locklear**, 19 January 1818 Wake County bond, John Phillips bondsman.

3.   Lucy Dunston, born say 1752, daughter of Patience Dunstan, was bound apprentice to John Howell in Lunenburg County in April 1754, and she was one of the "Mollatto Children of Patience Dunstan" bound to John Howell in April 1757 [Orders 1753-54, 623; 1755-57, 278]. She was living in

Mecklenburg County, Virginia, on 13 April 1772 when her son Charles, no age or race mentioned, was bound an apprentice to William Murphy [Orders 1771-73, 184]. Her children were

   i.   Charles[2], born say 1771, married Sally **Bass**, 21 November 1814 Wake County bond, Mark Beasley bondsman.

   ii.   ?Winny, head of a Wake County household of 7 "other free" in 1800 [NC:760].

   iii.   ?Richard Miles, married Nancy **Stewart**, 18 February 1802 Mecklenburg County, Virginia bond, Thomas **Spence** security. He and Robert **Brannum**, Thomas **Spence**, William **Stewart**, Humphrey **Wilson**, Joseph **Stewart**, Frederick **Ivey**, Pompy **Mayo** were ordered to work on the road which Benjamin Edmundson was surveying in Mecklenburg County on 10 October 1803 [Orders 1803-5, 45].

Other members of the Dunston family were

   i.   Margaret Dunson, born say 1751, sued by her master Hugh Bartly in Botetourt County court on 12 November 1771 for having a "Mullato" bastard. The court ordered her to serve Bartly another twelve months and ordered her child bound to him until the age of twenty one [Orders 1770-1, 490].

   ii.   Joseph, born say 1760, a yellow complexioned man from James City County who was listed in the size roll of troops who joined at Chesterfield Courthouse [cited by NSDAR, *African American Patriots*, 149]. He was taxable in James City County from 1783 to 1812 [PPTL 1782-99; 1800-15].

   iii.   Mary, taxable on a free male tithe aged 16-21 in James City County in 1787 [PPTL 1782-99].

   iv.   John, born say 1770, taxable in James City County from 1797 to 1813: a "cold. man" who was head of a household of 2 tithables and 3 "free persons of color" in 1813 [PPTL 1782-99; 1800-15].

   v.   James, taxable in James City County from 1797 to 1813, a "cold. man" listed with 2 "free persons of color" (probably his wife) in 1813 [PPTL 1782-99; 1800-15].

   vi.   William, taxable in James City County from 1797 to 1803 [PPTL 1782-99; 1800-15].

   vii.   Nathaniel, taxable in James City County from 1800 to 1805 [PPTL 1800-15].

   viii.   Tarlton, taxable in James City County from 1801 to 1813: a "cold. man." taxable in 1813 [PPTL 1782-99; 1800-15].

   ix.   Stephen, born say 1782, a "cold. man." taxable in James City County in 1813 [PPTL 1782-99; 1800-15].

DURHAM FAMILY

The Durham family were not free during the colonial period, but their family history is included here because several family members had relations with free African Americans. Members of the Durham family were

1   i.   Hannah, born about 1746.
2   ii.   Squire, born about 1769.

1.   Hannah, born about 1746, a "Negro" slave, was thirty-six years old on 12 October 1782 when Thomas Durham Madkins freed her and nine "Negro" children by Mecklenburg County, Virginia deed, the boys at age twenty-one and the girls at age eighteen. They may have been her children or near relations [DB 6:256]. Perhaps she was the mother of

   i.   Charles, born 15 February 1765, called "Charles late the property of Thomas Durham Madkins" when he testified on 20 January 1787 in the trial of Dick who was also freed by Madkins by 12 October 1782 deed of emancipation. Charles testified that he was living at Billey **Stewart**'s when Dick asked him to accompany him to Mr. Joseph Royster's where Dick shot and killed a slave named Tom who belonged to James Hester. Dick was sent for trial at the General Court in Richmond [Orders 1784-7, 648]. He was probably the emancipated slave named Charles who was taxable in Ephraim **Drew**'s Mecklenburg County household in 1790 and 1792. He called himself Charles Durham when he witnessed (making his mark) the deed for 50 acres of land from John **Chavis Walden** to Susannah **Mayo** on 25 December 1797 [DB 9:431-2]. Charles Durham was a "Free Negro" taxable in Mecklenburg County from 1810 to 1820 [PPTL, 1782-1805, frames 318, 441; 1806-28, frames 161, 235, 259, 335, 386, 503, 702] and head of a Mecklenburg County household of 2 "free colored" in 1820 [VA:165a].

   ii.   Dick, born 15 November 1766, probably executed at Richmond City where he was sent for trial in 1787 for murdering a slave named Tom [Orders 1784-7, 648].

  iii.   Bett, born 7 July 1768.

  iv.   Beck, born 17 January 1771.

   v.   Peg, born 15 September 1773.

  vi.   Jacob[1], born 9 February 1776.

  vii.   Ben, born 25 May 1778.

 viii.   Ann, born 11 March 1779.

  ix.   Maria, born about 1779, a "Negro" woman about thirteen or fourteen years old on 3 November 1792 when Thomas Durham Madkins emancipated her by Mecklenburg County deed [DB 8:246-7]. She was probably the mother of Henry Durham who was bound by the Mecklenburg County court to Alexander Gillespie on 19 September 1814. On 20 February 1815 she complained that Gillespie was misusing Henry. She may also have been the mother of Hannah and Nancy Durham who were bound to Thomas Gillespie and his wife on 19 September 1814 [Orders 1813-15, 270, 281, 329].

2.   Squire Durham, born about 1769, was a "Negro" slave about twenty-three years old on 3 November 1792 when Thomas Durham Madkins emancipated him and Maria by Mecklenburg County, Virginia deed [DB 8:246-7]. He was taxable in Mecklenburg County from 1806 to 1820: taxable with his son Stephen in 1810, identified as a "Free Negro" from 1811 to 1820 [PPTL, 1806-28, frames 7, 109, 187, 235, 335, 386, 702]. He was head of a Mecklenburg County, Virginia household of 2 "free colored" in 1820 [VA:165a]. He was the father of

   i.   Stephen, born about 1794, head of a Mecklenburg County household of a "free colored" man with 3 female slaves in 1820 [VA:159b].

Other members of the Durham family were

   i.   ?Thomas, born say 1796, a "Free Negro" taxable in Mecklenburg County from 1813 to 1815 [PPTL, 1806-28, frames 335, 503].

  ii.   ?James, married Mary **Pettiford**, 31 December 1813 Granville County bond, head of a County Line, Granville County, North Carolina household of 5 "free colored" in 1820 [NC:35].

  iii.   ?Jacob[2], born 1794-1806, head of Halifax County, North Carolina household of 2 "free colored" in 1830.

  iv.   ?John, married Mary **Pettiford**, 30 December 1822 Granville County bond.

   v.   ?Rosa, married William **Pettiford**, 30 December 1822 Granville County bond.

DUTCHFIELD FAMILY

1. Elizabeth[1] Dutchfield, born say 1728, was the white servant of John Gibbon of Yorkhampton Parish on 1 November 1748 when the York County court presented her for having a "Mulatto" child. She confessed to the offense and the court ordered that she pay a fine of 15 pounds currency or be sold for five years [Judgments & Orders 1746-52, 141, 146, 157, 365]. She may have been the mother of

   i. Jane, born say 1748, a "poor orphan" living in Yorkhampton Parish on 21 February 1763 when the court ordered her bound as an apprentice [Judgments & Orders 1759-63, 470].

   ii. James, born say 1750, head of a Williamsburg household of 1 white person in 1782 [VA:46].

   iii. Elizabeth[2], born about 1767, bound out by the churchwardens of Yorkhampton Parish by order of the York County court on 21 December 1772 [Orders 1772-4, 171]. She registered in Petersburg on 18 August 1794: *a light brown Mulatto woman, five feet two inches high, about twenty seven years old, born free in York Town. re-recorded 13 June 1810 with her three children.* Her son John Majeville Dutchfield registered on 14 January 1802: *a light brown Free Mulatto man, son of Betty Dutchfield, a free Mulatto woman, five feet seven and a half inches high, twenty one Christmas last, born free & raised in the Town of Petersburg* [Register of Free Negroes 1794-1819, nos. 27, 221].

EADY FAMILY

1. Daniel Eady[1], born say 1740, received a grant for 100 acres in St. John's Parish, Berkeley County, South Carolina, on 31 August 1774 [S.C. Archives series S213019, vol. 32:572]. He may have been the ancestor of

   i. James, head of a St. John's Parish, Berkeley County household of 1 "other free" in 1790 and 4 "other free" in 1800 [SC:69].

2 ii. Daniel[2], born say 1760.

   iii. Jonathan, head of a Charleston County household of 9 "other free" in 1800 [SC:69], taxable on 680 acres, 4 slaves, and 1 "free Black" in St. Stephen's Parish, South Carolina, in 1824 [S.C. Archives series S126061, item 3176].

   iv. George, head of a St. John's Parish, Berkeley County household of 6 "other free" in 1790 and 3 in 1800 [SC:69]. He was sued by the executors of Andrew Kennedy's estate on 16 June 1804 [S.C. Archives series L10018, item 324A].

   v. John, head of a St. John's Parish, Charleston household of 1 "other free" in 1790 and 5 "other free" in 1800 [SC:69]. He paid tax on 1 "free Black" in Prince George Parish, South Carolina, in 1824 [S.C. Archives series S1260661, item 866].

   vi. Molly, head of a Liberty County household of 6 "other free" in 1800 [SC:805].

   vii. Nancy, head of a Liberty County household of 7 "other free" in 1800 [SC:805].

   viii. William, head of a St. John's Parish, Berkeley County household of 1 "other free" in 1790 and 9 in 1800 [SC:69]. His land in St. John's Parish was mentioned in an October 1825 plat [S.C. Archives series L10005, reel 9, plat 4833].

   ix. Judy, head of a Liberty County household of 9 "other free" in 1800 [SC:804] and 10 in Georgetown in 1810 [SC:219].

   x. Sarah, paid tax on 1 "free Black" in Prince George Parish, South Carolina, in 1825 [S.C. Archives series S126061, item 867].

     xi.   Thomas, paid tax on 1 "free Black" in Prince George Parish, Georgetown District, South Carolina, in 1824 [S.C. Archives series S126061, item 868].

2. Daniel[2] Eady, born say 1760, was head of a St. John's Parish, Charleston, Berkeley County household of 4 "other free" in 1790 and 3 "other free" in 1800 [SC:69]. He called himself a "free coloured man" on 10 September 1834 when he made his St. John's Parish, Charleston, Berkeley County will, proved 21 December 1834. He left his plantation and four slaves to his daughter Esther Bluit, two slaves to his granddaughter Elizabeth Peigler, and named his nephew Jonathan Eady his executor [WB 40:266]. His daughter was

     i.   Elizabeth Bluit.

Other members of the Eady family were

     i.   Ann, living on Wentworth Street in Charleston about 1811-1817 when she paid the "free Negro" capitation tax [Capitation Tax Book, p.5].

EASTER FAMILY

1. Frances Easter, born say 1730, was presented by Charles County, Maryland court on 13 March 1749/50 for bearing an illegitimate "Melato" child by information of John Franklin, constable for the lower part of Durham Parish. On 12 June 1750 she was convicted of the charge, and the court bound her four-month-old son John to Bayne Smallwood [Court Record 1748-50, 604, 720]. She was the mother of

     i.   John, born February 1749/50.
     ii. ?Wilcher, head of a Free Town, Brunswick County, Virginia household of 8 "other free" in 1810 [VA:769].
     iii. ?Harrison, a "Mulatto" boy bound to Ayres Hodrick by the Pittsylvania County, Virginia court on 25 April 1776 [Court Records 1776-91, 9].

EDGAR/ EDGE FAMILY

1. Mary Edgar, born say 1752, was the mother of a "Mulatto" girl named Betty who was ordered bound out by the churchwardens of Princess Anne County on 12 November 1772 [Orders 1770-3, 369]. Mary was the mother of

     i.   Betty Edgar, born say 1772.
     ii. ?Willis Edge, born before 1776, head of a Northampton County, North Carolina household of 6 "other free" in 1810 [NC:721] and 8 "free colored" in 1820 [NC:188].
     iii. ?Jack Edge, head of a Pasquotank County household of 6 "other free" in 1810 [NC:897].

EDWARDS FAMILY

1. Edward[1] Edwards, born say 1720, was the slave of Merritt Sweney of Elizabeth City County in 1746 when Ann **Ellston**, a "free Mulatto woman," purchased and married him. They had two children by 1758 when their case came before the Council of Virginia [Hillman, *Executive Journals of the Council* VI:111]. Their son Elston, "son of Ned Edwards, formerly Major Sweney's slave," was baptized in Bruton Parish, James City County, on 7 August 1748 [Bruton Parish Register, 5]. They were the parents of

     i.   Elston, baptized 7 August 1748.
2   ii. ?Edward[2], born about 1762.

2. Edward[2] B. Edwards, born about 1762, married Mary **Scott**, daughter of Robert **Scott**, 14 February 1789 Henrico County bond, John **Scott** and Edward **Bowman** sureties. He obtained a certificate of freedom in Chesterfield County

on 13 September 1813: *fifty one years old, bright yellow complexion, born free*. And Mary Ann Edwards (probably his wife) obtained a certificate of freedom on 13 March 1823: *fifty years old, bright yellow complexion, born free* [Register of Free Negroes 1804-53, no. 192, 482]. They were probably the parents of

    i.   Mary Ann, born about 1794, registered in Chesterfield County on 11 July 1814: *twenty years old, bright yellow complexion, born free*

    ii. John Brown, born about 1797, registered in Chesterfield County on 13 April 1818: *twenty one years old, mulatto complexion, born free*.

    iii. Lucy, born about 1800, registered on 14 July 1823: twenty three years old, Mulatto complexion, born free [Register of Free Negroes 1804-53, nos. 222, 317, 484, 492, 1174].

Other members of the Edwards family were

    i.   Isaac, born about January 1767, a "Mulatto boy" bound apprentice to Seth Pryor for nineteen years and nine months until the age of twenty one by the New Hanover County, North Carolina court in April 1768 [Minutes 1738-69, 336].

3   ii. Edward[3], born say 1770.

    iii. Hezekiel, head of a Stafford County household of 3 "other free" in 1810 [VA:127].

    iv. Lydda, head of a Fredericksburg, Spotsylvania County household of 3 "other free" in 1810 [VA:112a].

3. Edward[3] Edwards, born say 1770, was taxable in Louisa County on 3 horses from 1810 to 1814: called a "FN" in 1811, taxable on 2 free tithes in 1812, in a list of "free Negroes & Mulattoes" in 1814 [PPTL, 1782-1814]. He and his wife Dicy were the parents of

    i.   Edmund, born 3 June 1796, registered in Louisa County on 10 June 1831: *son of Edward and Dicy Edwards who was born free, yellow man, about 5'9" high, 35 years old the 3d inst.*

    ii. William, born 1 July 1801, registered in Louisa County on 12 November 1827 and 4 January 1846: *a person of colour, the son of Edward Edwards who was born free, about 5'11" high, light complexion, bushy head of hair...son of Edward and Dicy Edwards...will be 45 years old 1st July 1846.*

    iii. Dicy, born about 1804, registered in Louisa County on 7 September 1833: *daughter of Edward and Dicy Edwards who was free born, very bright mulatto woman 28-30 years* [Abercrombie, *Free Blacks of Louisa County*, 29, 37, 45, 66].

ELLIOTT FAMILY

Members of the Elliott family of Norfolk County may have been the descendants of Suzan Ellet, a white woman who was presented by the Norfolk County grand jury on 15 March 1691/2 for having a bastard child, no race stated [DB 5, pt. 2, 248, 252, 259]. They were

1   i.   Elizabeth, born say 1735.

2   ii. Ann, born say 1740.

3   iii. Rachel, born say 1742.

1. Elizabeth Elliott, born say 1735, was a "free Molatto" living in Norfolk County on 17 May 1753 when the court bound her daughter Dinah Ellet to Shadrack Wiat [Orders 1750-3, 153b]. Elizabeth was taxable in Portsmouth Parish on the west side of Western Branch District of Norfolk County in 1761, adjacent to Rachel Elett in a non-alphabetized list, and a "free negro" taxable in Western Branch District in 1768 and 1769 [Wingo, *Norfolk County Tithables* 1751-65, 168; 1766-80, 14, 87]. She was the mother of

      i.   ?Peter, born say 1751, taxable in Norfolk County in John Woodside's Elizabeth City Parish household in 1767 and 1768 and taxable in James Grimes's household in Western Branch Precinct in 1771 [Wingo, *Norfolk County Tithables* 1766-80, 36, 83, 152]. He married Peggy **Young** ("Free Negroes"), 20 August 1785 Norfolk County bond, Charles Conner surety. He was taxable on a horse in Norfolk County on the north side of the Western Branch in 1786 [PPTL, 1782-90, frame 520].

      ii.   Dinah, born say 1753, ordered bound apprentice to Shadrack Wiat on 17 May 1753.

4   iii.   ?Nancy, born say 1763.

2.   Ann[1] Elliott, born say 1740, was taxable in Norfolk County in the district from Portsmouth to Western Branch, living on Campbell's land in 1761 and taxable in 1765. She and (her sister) Rachel were probably identical to "Ann & Rachel, free negroes" who were taxable in Western Branch Precinct in 1759 [Wingo, *Norfolk County Tithables* 1751-65, 133, 170, 189]. She was taxable in Portsmouth & Elizabeth River Parish District of Norfolk County on 2 free males from 1796 to 1798, 1 free male and a horse in 1800; she was a labourer in Western Branch District of Norfolk County in a "List of Free Negroes and Mulattoes" with Absalom Elliott in her household in 1801; and was taxable on a horse in 1806 [PPTL, 1791-1812, frames 383, 574]. She was probably the mother of

      i.   David, born say 1777, taxable in Portsmouth and Elizabeth River Parishes, Norfolk County, from 1794 to 1813: a "M"(ulatto) butcher in Western Branch District in a "List of Free Negroes and Mulattoes" in 1801 [PPTL, 1791-1812, frames 103, 226, 298, 483, 577, 688, 740, 773].

      ii.   Edmond, born say 1782, a "M"(ulatto) Norfolk County taxable from 1799 to 1806: a labourer in Western Branch District of Norfolk County in a "List of Free Negroes and Mulattoes" in 1801, perhaps identical to Ned Elliott who was taxable in 1815 and 1817 [PPTL, 1791-1812, frames 298, 577; 1813-24, 101, 250].

      iii.   Absalom, born say 1785, a "N"(egro) Norfolk County taxable from 1802 to 1811 [PPTL 1791-1812, frames 430, 577, 463, 688, 740].

3.   Rachel Elliott, born say 1742, was a taxable head of a household in Norfolk County in Portsmouth Parish on the west side of Western Branch in 1761 (adjacent to Elizabeth Elet), in 1765, and in 1768 [Wingo, *Norfolk County Tithables* 1751-65, 168; 1766-80, 67]. She was called a "free negro" on 20 April 1775 when the Norfolk County court ordered the churchwardens of Portsmouth Parish to bind her sons Samuel and James Elliott to Willis Eastwood to learn the trade of cooper [Orders 1773-5, 71]. She was a labourer in Western Branch District of Norfolk County in 1801 in a "List of Free Negroes and Mulattoes" with William Elliott in her household [PPTL, 1791-1812, frame 383]. She was the mother of

5   i.   Ann[2], born say 1764.

6   i.   ?Sarah, born say 1765.

7   ii.   ?Keziah, born about 1766.

      iii.   Samuel, born say 1768, bound apprentice to Willis Eastwood in Norfolk County on 20 April 1775.

      iv.   James[1], born say 1770, bound apprentice to Willis Eastwood in Norfolk County on 20 April 1775.

4.   Nancy Elliott, born say 1763, was a labourer in Western Branch District of Norfolk County in 1801 in a "List of Free Negroes and Mulattoes" with males Jeremiah and Lewis Elliott and females Sally and Charlotte Elliott in her household [PPTL, 1791-1812, frame 383]. She was head of a Norfolk County

household of 7 "other free" in 1810 [VA:817]. She was probably the mother of

    i. ?James[2], born about 1782, twenty-eight years old when he registered in Norfolk County on 16 July 1810: *5 feet 3 1/2, of a Dark Complexion* [Register of Free Negros & Mulattos, Norfolk County courthouse, no.18].

    ii. Lewis, born say 1786, taxable in Portsmouth & Elizabeth River Parish of Norfolk County from 1803 to 1817 [PPTL, 1791-1812, frames 463, 559, 646, 723; 1813-24, frames 101, 250].

    iii. Sally.

    iv. Charlotte.

    v. Jeremiah, taxable in Portsmouth & Elizabeth River Parish of Norfolk County from 1815 to 1817 [PPTL, 1813-24, frames 101, 250].

5. Ann[2] Elliott, born say 1764, may have been identical to "Nanny daughter of Rachel a free Negro" (no last name mentioned) who was ordered bound by the churchwardens of Elizabeth River Parish, Norfolk County, to Rev. Thomas Davis on 19 April 1764 [Orders 1763-65, 97]. Nanny Elliott was a labourer in Western Branch District of Norfolk County in a "List of Free Negroes and Mulattoes" with males Lemuel and William Elliott and females Betsey, Patty, Jenny and Fanny Elliott in her household [PPTL, 1791-1812, frames 172, 226, 247, 374, 383]. She was probably the mother of

    i. Betsy, perhaps the Betty Elliott who was head of a Norfolk County household of 6 "other free" in 1810 [VA:815].

    ii. Lemuel.

    iii. Patty.

    iv. William.

    v. Jenny.

    vi. Fanny.

5. Sarah Elliott, born say 1765, was head of a Norfolk County household of 7 "other free" in 1810 [VA:815]. Her children registered as "free Negros" in Norfolk County. They were

    i. James[3], born about 1785, registered in Norfolk County on 27 June 1810: *son of Sarah Elliott, 5 feet 5 Inches, twenty five years of age, of a Black Complexion* [Register of Free Negroes, no.4]. He was a "N"(egro) taxable in Portsmouth & Elizabeth River Parish of Norfolk County in 1805 and 1806 [PPTL, 1791-1812, frames 559, 577] and a "Free Negro" taxable in Nansemond County in 1815 [Yantis, *A Supplement to the 1810 Census of Virginia*, S-14].

    ii. Israel, born about 1787, registered in Norfolk County on 27 June 1810: *son of Sarah Elliott, 5 feet 4 and a half Inches, twenty three years of age, of a light Complexion* [Register of Free Negroes, no.5]. He was a "free Negro" taxable in Portsmouth & Elizabeth River Parish of Norfolk County in 1810 and 1811, a "B.M." taxable on a slave over the age of twelve on Western Branch in 1815 [PPTL, 1791-1812, frames 723, 740; 1813-24, frames 101]. And there was an Israel Elliott who was a "Free Negro" taxable on a horse and a head of cattle in Nansemond County in 1815 [Yantis, *A Supplement to the 1810 Census of Virginia*, S-14].

6. Keziah Elliott, born about 1766, was forty-five years old when she registered in Norfolk County on 19 August 1811: *of a light Complexion & Pitted with the Small Pox, 5 feet 3 In., Born free* [Register of Free Negroes, no.60]. Her children may have been

    i. Daniel, born about 1782, twenty-eight years old when he registered in Norfolk County on 15 September 1810: *5 feet 8 3/4 Inc., of a yellow complexion, Born free* [Register of Free Negroes, no.39]. He was a "free Negro" or "M"(ulatto) taxable on Western Branch in Norfolk County from 1811 to 1817: taxable on 3 free males and 2 horses in 1812, taxable on 2 slaves over the age of twelve in 1814 and 1815 [PPTL, 1791-1812, frames 740, 773; 1813-24, frames 101, 133, 250].

ii. Jean, born about 1786, registered in Norfolk County on 16 July 1810: *5 feet 2 1/4 In, Twenty four Years of age, of a Yellowish Complexion* [Register of Free Negroes, no.19].

iii. Sukey, born about 1788, twenty-three years old when she registered in Norfolk County on 19 August 1811: *5 feet __ In, of a dark Complexion, Born free* [Register of Free Negroes, no.62].

iv. James[4], born about 1789, twenty-one years old when he registered in Norfolk County on 19 August 1811: *5 feet 4 In., of a dark Complexion, Born free* [Register of Free Negroes, no.61]. He was a "B.M." taxable on a slave over the age of twelve on Western Branch in 1815 and 1817 [PPTL, 1813-24, frames 101, 250].

Members of the family in nearby Virginia counties were

i. Mary, born about 1775, registered in Petersburg on 9 July 1805: *a light Mulatto woman, five feet high, thirty years old, born free & raised in Charles City County* [Register of Free Negroes 1794-1819, no. 302].

7   ii. Robert[1], born say 1777.

iii. Thomas, born about 1780, registered in Petersburg on 31 December 1808: *a light brown free Negro man, five feet seven and half inches high, grey Eyes, blacksmith, born free in the Town of Petersburg, twenty eight years old* [Register of Free Negroes 1794-1819, no. 442]. He was head of a Petersburg Town household of 6 "other free" in 1810 [VA:127a].

iv. Lucy, born say 1780, married Squire **Charity**, 25 April 1791 Surry County bond, Henry **Charity** surety, 26 April marriage by Rev. Samuel Butler, Rector of Southwark Parish Episcopal Church [Ministers' Returns, 32].

v. Stephen, "Free Negro" head of an Isle of Wight County household of 6 "other free" in 1810 [VA:43].

vi. Becky, head of a Petersburg household of 3 "other free" in 1810 [VA:122a].

vii. Edward, head of a Petersburg Town household of 3 "other free" and a slave in 1810 [V:122b].

7. Robert[1] Elliott, born say 1777, married Nancy **Debereux (Debrix)**, 19 September 1798 Surry County bond, John **Debereux** surety, 20 September marriage by Rev. Samuel Butler [Ministers' Returns, 51]. He was taxable in Surry County from 1787 to 1804: listed as Samuel Cocke's tithe in 1787 and 1788, charged with his own tithe in 1790 [PPTL, 1782-90, frames 449, 471, 599; 1791-1816, 60, 259, 524, 562]. He was the father of

i. ?Harler, born about 1785, registered in Surry County on 24 June 1816: *a Mulattoe Man, aged 21 years, is 5'3-7/8" high of light complexion, low forehead, distended nostrils large prominant lips, streight and well made and by profession a Ditcher, was born of Nancy Elliott a free woman.*

ii. Samuel G., born about 1797, registered in Surry County on 26 June 1820: *a Mulatto Man of a bright Complexion was born free and is the son of Bob Elliott decd: late of this county, aged about 23 years pretty well made is 5'5-1/2" high large Ears.*

iii. Henry A.B., born about 1799, registered in Surry County on 26 June 1820: *a Mulatto man of a bright Complexion was born free and is the son of Bob Elliott decd: late of this County aged about 21 years pretty well made and inclined to be bowledged is 5'2-3/4" high.*

iv. ?Hannah, born about 1804, registered in Surry County on 28 November 1831: *daughter of Nancy Elliott, was born free, a bright mulatto woman about 27 years of age, has a broad face large full eyes...and is 5'7-3/4" high.*

v. ?John, born about 1806, registered in Surry County on 26 February 1827: *a free black Man of this County, Son of Nancy alias Nancy Elliott a free Woman of this County...5'6-1/2" high, has coarse bushy hair* [Hudgins, *Surry County Register of Free Negroes*, 57, 72, 83, 104].

Members of the family in North Carolina were

i. John, head of a Moore County, North Carolina household of 2 "other free" in 1800 [NC:62].

ii. William, head of a Moore County, North Carolina household of 2 "other free" in 1800 [NC:62].

iii. Cloe, born before 1776, head of a Chowan County, North Carolina household of one "free colored" woman over 55 in 1820 [NC:114].

iv. Robert[2], head of an Anson County, North Carolina household of 3 "free colored" in 1820 [NC:12].

ELLIS FAMILY

Essex County

1. Jane Ellis, born say 1720, was a "Free Negro" woman living in Essex County, Virginia, on 18 April 1749 when the court ordered the churchwardens of South Farnham Parish to bind out her daughter Letty to James Jones until the age of twenty-one. On 21 August 1750 Jane petitioned the court stating that Rachel Young was mistreating her son James who was bound to her deceased husband Henry Young. On 21 March 1750/1 the court dismissed her suit and ordered the churchwardens of South Farnham Parish to bind her sons Will and James, "two free xxx born Indians," to Rachel Young [Orders 1747-9, 297; 1749-51, 150, 207, 292]. She was the mother of

i. James, born say 1740.

ii. Will, born say 1744.

iii. Letty, born say 1748.

Their descendants may have been

i. Eliza, head of a Richmond City household of 5 "other free" in 1810 [VA:363].

ii. Lucy, head of a Richmond City household of 2 other free" and 4 slaves in 1810 [VA:379].

iii. Joseph, born before 1776, head of a Surry County, Virginia household of 12 "free colored" in 1830.

iv. Patience, born before 1776, head of a Surry County, Virginia household of 5 "free colored" in 1830.

Halifax County, Virginia

1. Martha Ellis, born say 1735, was living in Halifax County, Virginia, in August 1759 when the churchwardens of Antrim Parish were ordered to bind out her children by "Daniel a Negroe formerly belonging to Peter Overby." Two of her children were bound to Abraham Maury in February 1760 [Pleas 2:478; 3:20]. Her descendants may have been

i. John, born about 1754 in Virginia, moved with his mother to Nutbush District in North Carolina when he was a child and later moved to Wake County where he enlisted in the 10th Regiment of the North Carolina Line on 27 April 1776. He was a "man of Colour" who made a declaration for a pension in Wake County court on 27 July 1820. He resided in Franklin County, Illinois, on 12 September 1837 when he made another declaration to obtain a pension. He died on 21 October 1850, and his only surviving heirs James Ellis, William Ellis, Polly Ellis, Mahalah Ellis and Henry Ellis received survivors' benefits in 1852 [M804-916, frame 0427]. He was head of a Wake County household of 3 "other free" in 1790 [NC:103]. He sold the land which was due him for his service to Thomas Henderson, Jr., of Raleigh for $114 [N.C. Archives, Wake County folder #339].

  ii.   Joanna, head of a Petersburg Town household of 5 "other free" and one slave in 1810 [VA:123b].
 iii.   Lewis, head of a Petersburg Town household of 2 "other free" in 1810 [VA:113a].
  iv.   Richard, head of a Campbell County household of 10 "other free" in 1810 [VA:880].
   v.   David, married Lucy **Hacket**, 12 February 1798 Campbell County bond. He was a "F.N." taxable in the northern district of Campbell County from 1797 to 1813 [PPTL, 1785-1814, frames 387, 892] and head of a Campbell County household of 9 "other free" in 1810 [VA:880].

ELMORE FAMILY

1. Joseph Elmore, born say 1754, was a free "mulatto" taxable in Bertie County, North Carolina, in his own household in the list of Peter Clifton for 1775 and taxable as a married man in 1779 [CR 10.702.1, Box 2]. He was a "Mulatto" head of a Nansemond County, Virginia household with no whites, one dwelling, and one other building in 1784 [VA:74]. He may have been the father of

  i.   Henry, head of a Hanover County household of 2 "other free" in 1810 [VA:874], in the list of "free Negroes and Mulattos" in St. Paul's Parish, Hanover County, from 1811 to 1814: taxable on a slave in 1812 and 1813, listed with wife Grace in 1813 [PPTL 1804-24].

EPPERSON FAMILY

Members of the Epperson family were

  i.   Jack Epesom, born say 1737, a "Molatoe fellow" who claimed his freedom from George Brack in Onslow County, North Carolina, in July 1758 [Minutes 1749-65, 43a].
1 ii.   Elizabeth, born say 1738.

1. Elizabeth Epperson, born say 1738, was the mother of a bastard child named Rod (no race indicated) who was bound out to Robert Bird by the Prince Edward County court in September 1758 [Orders 1754-8, 161]. She was the mother of
2   i.   Rod/ Rhoda, born say 1758.

2. Rhoda Epperson, born say 1758, was living in Prince Edward County on 15 February 1779 when the court ordered the churchwardens of St. Patrick's Parish to bind out her children James and Milly to Isham Chasten [Orders 1771-81, part 2, 18]. She was the mother of
  i.   ?Sam, born say 1775. He and his wife Leday were the parents of Sucky Epperson (Colored) who married George Guthrey (Colored), 27 December 1815 Prince Edward County bond, 28 December Halifax County, Virginia marriage. Lydia, born about 1780, registered in Halifax County on 21 December 1810: *aged about thirty years, Complection that of a dark mulatto...which appears from a certificate of the County Court of Prince Edward was born of a free mulatto Woman is hereby duly registered as a free negro* [Register of Free

Negroes, no. 29]. She consented to the 29 May 1828 Halifax County marriage of Nancy Epperson and Collin **Bomar**.

ii. James, born say 1776, bound apprentice in Prince Edward County in February 1779, head of a Prince Edward County household of 5 "other free" in 1810 [VA:564].

iii. Milly, born say 1778, bound apprentice in Prince Edward County in February 1779.

EPPS FAMILY

Members of the Epps family born about 1735 were
1   i.   John1, born say 1735.
2   ii.   Lucy, born say 1738.

1. John[1] Epps/ **Evans**, born say 1735, was apparently the illegitimate son of a member of the Epps and **Evans** families. He was called John **Evans** in 1751 and 1752 when he was taxable in the Lunenburg County household of (his half-brother?) Thomas **Evans** [Bell, *Sunlight on the Southside*, 166, 193]. He was called John Epps in September 1752 when he and Margaret Evans were called as witnesses in the trial of Peter, a slave of Edward Epps, but he was called John **Evans** in January 1753 when he was paid for his attendance at the trial [Orders 1748-52, 249; 1752-3, 456]. He was called John **Evans** on 6 October 1761 when he purchased 400 acres on Flat Rock Creek jointly with Thomas **Biddie** for 60 pounds and on 3 August 1762 when he and **Biddie** allowed Ann Mitchell the use of the plantation to raise stock and grow corn or other grains during her natural life as long as she and her sons Richard and Isaac remained single. He was called John Epps when he and his wife Martha sold 299 acres of this land for 115 pounds on 8 January 1771 [DB 6:473; 7:321; 11:433]. He was called John **Evans** on 10 December 1767 when the Lunenburg County court ordered the churchwardens of Cumberland Parish to bind Daniel **Redcross** to him and called "John Evans (alias Eppes)" on 13 April 1769 when the court ordered the churchwardens to bind Isham **Harris** (son of Martha **Stewart**) to him [Orders 1766-69, fol. 122, 202]. Isham **Harris** and Daniel **Redcross** were taxable in his Lunenburg County household in 1772 and 1773. Daniel was called Daniel Evans when he was taxable in his household in 1775 [Bell, *Sunlight on the Southside*, 304, 324, 354]. John Epps was executor of the 12 September 1777 Lunenburg County will of Daniel **Redcross**, proved 10 June 1779 [WB 3:26]. Daniel left him half his estate and the other half to Charles **Evans** who he called his brother, so perhaps Daniel was John Epps' step-son or nephew. He was taxable in 1782 on 2 slaves, 2 horses and 30 cattle and taxable in 1783 on slaves Cyrus, Susan, James, James, and Mary, 5 horses and 17 cattle [PPTL 1782-1806]. On 7 December 1784 he and his wife Martha Epps purchased an additional 200 acres adjoining his land for 70 pounds, and on 11 October 1787 they sold land on Flat Rock Creek adjoining Abraham **Cuttillo** and James Lowman [DB 14:139; 15:120]. He died before 10 June 1790 when the inventory of his Lunenburg County estate was recorded. The inventory included 20 pounds paid to Thomas Epps and debts owed by Edward, John and Thomas Epps. On 12 June 1800 his children Thomas Eppes, John Eppes, Edward Eppes, Elizabeth **Cuttillo** the wife of Edward **Cuttillo**, William Eppes, Sally Eppes, Joel Eppes, and Freeman Eppes, a minor by his guardian, sued the administrator of the estate, James Buford, in chancery for division of the land. On 11 July 1805 the administrator reported that he had sold 145 acres on Flat Rock Creek near Cocke's Road for 182 pounds, divided the money among the eight children, and allotted the widow Patty Eppes the remaining 70 acres [Orders 1799-1801, 82; 1802-5, fol. 209, p.209]. Martha was head of a household in a "List of Free Negroes & Mulattoes" in Lunenburg County in 1802 and 1803 with her children: Sally, Freeman, Betsy **Critillow**, and Suky Epes [Lunenburg County,

Free Negro, Slave Records, 1802-1830, p.1]. Martha died before 14 September 1809 when an inventory of her estate was returned to court by Thomas **Evans** [WB 4:106; WB 3:169, 377; WB 6:259]. Their children were

3   i.   Thomas[1], born say 1757.
4   ii.   John[2], born 23 December 1763.
     iii. Edward[1], born say 1767, taxable on 2 horses in Lunenburg County in 1790, granted a license by the Lunenburg County court on 11 April 1805 to keep an ordinary at his house [Orders 1802-5, 194].
5   iv.   William[1], born say 1769.
     v.   Elizabeth, married Edward **Cuttiloe**.
     vi.   Sally, born about 1770, registered as a free Negro in Lunenburg County on 12 September 1836: *about 66 years of age, 5 feet 2 Inches high bright Mulatto Complexion, rather freckled & inclined to Corpulent* [WB 5, after page 89, no. 82].
     vii. Joel, born say 1775, taxable in Lunenburg County from 1797 to 1804 [PPTL 1782-1806]. He and his wife Tabitha sold land by deed proved in Lunenburg County court on 13 June 1799 [Orders 1796-9, 24]. He purchased 200 acres on Sandy Creek in Mecklenburg County, Virginia, from his father-in-law, Thomas **Stewart** adjoining William **Stewart** on 5 November 1799 for 30 pounds [DB 10:177]. He and his wife Tabby were counted in the "List of Free Negroes & Mulattoes" on Bears Element Creek in Lunenburg County in 1802 with their children Rebecca and Wilkerson [Lunenburg County Free Negro & Slave Records, 1802-1803, LVA]. He married second, Polly **Bass**, 31 December 1804 Granville County bond. He was head of a Guilford County, North Carolina household of 7 "other free" in 1810 [NC:990] and 7 "free colored" in Abington Township, Wayne County, Indiana in 1840.
6   viii. Freeman, born say 1783.

2.   Lucy Epps, born say 1738, was the "Mulatto" servant of Andrew King of Sussex County in April 1758 when her illegitimate child was ordered bound to King [Orders 1757-9, 160]. She may have been the mother of
     i.   Ephraim, born before 1776, head of a Sussex County household of 7 "free colored" in 1830.
     ii.   Mary, head of a Prince George County household of 6 "other free" in 1810 [VA:538].

3.   Thomas[1] Epps, born say 1757, was taxable in Lunenburg County on a slave named Phillis from 1783 to 1787 and taxable there from 1794 to 1804: on 2 free tithes and a slave from 1794 to 1797, on 4 free tithes and a slave in 1798, 3 free tithes from 1799 to 1803, and 2 free tithes and 2 slaves in 1804. His widow Elizabeth was tithable on a free tithe and 2 slaves in 1806 [PPTL 1782-1806]. He was married to Elizabeth **Berry** by 20 November 1798 when they brought suit in York County court against the administrators of the estate of her brother Edward **Berry** to recover her share of the estate of her father James **Berry**. The administrators were Edward's widow Elizabeth and her husband Edward **Cuttillo** [Orders 1795-1803, 297]. Elizabeth **Berry** had probably been living in Lunenburg County about 1779 when her father's York County estate was settled. Thomas was counted in the "List of Free Negroes & Mulattoes" on Flatrock Creek in the lower district of Lunenburg County in 1802 and 1803 with his wife Betsy and children James, John, and Ned. The orphans of Abraham **Cuttillo** were also living with him: Abram, Ned, and Betsy **Critillow** [Lunenburg County Free Negro & Slave Records, 1802-1803, LVA]. On 8 September 1803 the Lunenburg County court granted him a license to keep an ordinary at his house [Orders 1802-5, 95]. He died before 23 September 1805 when his Lunenburg County estate was inventoried. The account of his estate included seven slaves, called him the guardian of the

orphans of Abraham **Cuttillo**, and found a balance in their favor of 117 pounds [WB 6:138-9]. Elizabeth was head of a Lunenburg County household of 4 "other free" and 4 slaves in 1810 [VA:339]. They were the parents of

    i. James, married Milley **Stewart**, 28 March 1804 Lunenburg County bond, Buckner **Valentine** surety.

    ii. John[3], married Elizabeth **Curtillar** (**Cuttillo**), 25 March 1803 Lunenburg County bond, Freeman Epps surety. He was listed as a "free Negro" in Lunenburg County in 1802. He and his wife Betsy and children: Franky, Thomas, Blanchy, and Martha Epes were counted in a list of "Free Negroes & Mulattoes" in Lunenburg County in 1814 [*Magazine of Virginia Genealogy* 33:267].

    iii. Edward[2], born about 1780, counted in a list of "Free Negroes & Mulattoes" in Lunenburg County in 1814 with his wife Elizabeth and children Mary and Betsy [*Magazine of Virginia Genealogy* 33:267], registered as a free Negro in Lunenburg County on 10 March 1835: *fifty five years of Age of Yellow Complexion, 5 feet 6 Inches high...his face wrinkled and his hair somewhat Grey* [WB 5, after page 89, no. 79].

4. John[2] Epps, born 23 December 1763, was taxable on a horse in Lunenburg County from 1786 [PPTL 1782-1806]. He was counted in the "List of Free Negroes & Mulattoes in the Lower District of Lunenburg County" in March 1802 with his wife Lucy and children: Nancy, Dolly, Allen, Sally, Peter, Patsy, and John [Lunenburg County, Free Negro, Slave Records, 1802-1830, p.1]. He was committed to jail in Lunenburg County on 30 January 1805 for "feloniously beating, maiming and wounding of Thomas Eppes" about two weeks previous but was found not guilty [Orders 1802-5, folio 183]. He was a "FN" taxable in Halifax County, Virginia, from 1809 to 1812 [PPTL, 1800-12, frames 798, 941, 1026]. He may have been identical to Jack Epps who was head of a Wilkes County, North Carolina household of 9 "free colored" in 1820 [NC:519]. He was seventy-one years old on 10 October 1834 when he made a declaration in Halifax County, Virginia court to apply for a pension for Revolutionary War service. He stated that he was born in Lunenburg County. He was granted a pension while residing in Person County on 8 February 1836 [M805-306]. He was the father of

    i. Nancy.

    ii. Dolly.

    iii. Allen, born 1776-1794, taxable in Halifax County, Virginia, in 1811 and 1812 [PPTL, 1800-12, frames 941, 1026], counted in a list of "Free Negroes & Mulattoes" in Lunenburg County in 1814 [*Magazine of Virginia Genealogy* 33:267], head of a Person County, North Carolina household of 3 "free colored" in 1820 [NC:498].

    iv. Sally.

    v. Peter, head of a Person County household of 2 "free colored" in 1820 [NC:498].

    vi. Patsy.

    vii. John.

5. William[1] Epps, born say 1769, was taxable on his own tithe in Lunenburg County from 1791 to 1798 and taxable on 2 tithes from 1799 to 1806 [PPTL 1782-1806]. He and Thomas Epps **Hobson** were sued by the assignee of Jacob **Chavis** in Lunenburg County court for a debt of 7 pounds on 13 November 1800 [Orders 1799-1801, 112]. He was counted in the "List of free Negroes & Mulattoes" in the lower District of Lunenburg near Flatrock Creek in 1802 and 1803 with his wife Caty and children: George, Priscilla, William, Thomas & James **Critillow**. He died before 14 September 1809 when the account of his Lunenburg County estate was taken by Thomas **Evans** [WB 6:260-1]. His children were

     i.   George.
    ii. Priscilla.
   iii. William³.
   iv. Thomas², counted in a list of "Free Negroes & Mulattoes" in Lunenburg County in 1814 with his wife Sally [*Magazine of Virginia Genealogy* 33:267].

6.   Freeman Epps, born say 1783, was a minor on 12 June 1800 when the children of John Epps, deceased, brought suit in Lunenburg County for division of their father's land [Orders 1799-1801, 82]. He was taxable in Lunenburg County on his own tithe, a slave and 2 horses in 1802 [PPTL 1782-1806]. He was counted in the "List of Free Negroes & Mulattoes" on Flat Rock Creek in the household of his mother Martha Epps in 1802 and in his own household in 1803 with his wife Rebecca and their daughter Polly. He was head of a Person County household of 9 "free colored" in 1820 [NC:498]. He was the father of
     i.   Polly, born about 1803.

Another member the Epps family was
     i.   William², listed as a "free Negro" shoemaker in Lunenburg County in 1802 [Lunenburg County Free Negro & Slave Records, 1802-1803, LVA].

EVANS FAMILY

1.   Eleanor Evans, born say 1660, was probably an African American since she was a taxable in Surry County, Virginia, in William Hancock's household in 1677, in the household of Robert Caufield in 1678, and in Joseph Rogers' household in 1679 [*Magazine of Virginia Genealogy*, vol.22, no.3, pp.57, 63, 67]. She may have been the ancestor of

2   i.   Morris¹, born say 1675.
3   ii. Ann¹, born say 1710.
4   iii. Thomas¹, born say 1710.
5   iv. James¹, born say 1720.
6   v. Thomas², born say 1723.
    vi. Ann², Sr., a "taxable free Female" with Ann Evans, Jr., in Bertie County, North Carolina, in 1751 [CCR 190].

2.   Morris¹ Evans, born say 1675, was living in York County on 15 May 1738 when the court presented him (or his son by that name) and Beck **Hulet** for not listing themselves as tithables. His 18 February 1739/40 York County will was proved 17 March 1739/40. He left his son Charles a shilling, left a mare and foal to Elizabeth **Hulet**, left his bed, furniture, and two cows to his "friend" Rebecca **Hulet**, and left furniture and three head of cattle to his son Morris. He also left a boat and cart for the use of Rebecca and his son Morris as long as they "live and agree together." He appointed Rebecca and Morris his executors and his friend and neighbor John Washer his trustee [W&I 18:414, 427, 558-9]. His children were

7   i.   Charles¹, born say 1696.
8   ii. Morris², born say 1710.

3.   Ann¹ Evans, born say 1710, died before 15 February 1748/9 when the Prince George County, Virginia court ordered the churchwardens of Bristol Parish to bind out her "Mulotto" children Philip and Elizabeth. The churchwardens bound them to the Rev. Robert Fergeson on 10 May 1749 [Chamberlayne, *Register of Bristol Parish*, 134]. She was the ancestor of

9   i.   ?Isaac¹, born say 1735.
     ii. ?John Evans/ **Epps**, born say 1735. See the **Epps** family history.

iii. ?Jacob, born say 1737, sued Edward Epps in Lunenburg County court in May 1753 for mistreating him and Isaac Evans. The court allowed them to go to Martin Brandon Parish in Prince George County to search the register for proof of their age. The court later ordered them bound instead to Abraham Martin [Orders 1753-4, 111, 165-6, 254].

10 iv. ?Robert[1], born say 1740.

11 v. Philip, born say 1745.

vi. Elizabeth, born say 1747.

vii. ?Daniel **Redcross**, born say 1752, bound to John Evans/ **Epps** by the churchwardens of Cumberland Parish, Lunenburg County, on 10 December 1767 [Orders 1766-69, fol.122]. He was taxable in the Lunenburg County household of John Evans in 1772 and 1773 and called Daniel Evans in John's household in 1775 [Bell, *Sunlight on the Southside*, 304, 324, 354]. He left a 12 September 1777 Lunenburg County will, proved 10 June 1779, leaving half his estate to his brother Charles Evans and the remainder to John **Epps** [WB 3:26].

viii. ?Morris[4], born about 1754, registered in Petersburg on 16 August 1794: *a light Mulatto man about five feet eight inches high, forty years old, born free, served an apprenticeship with Col. Wm Call. in Prince George County* [Register of Free Negroes 1794-1819, no. 8]. He may have been one of two Morris Evanses who were heads of Wake County, North Carolina households in 1800 [NC:761-2], perhaps the Morris Evans who was head of an Anson County household of 7 "other free" in 1810 [NC:55].

12 ix. Martha, born say 1756.

x. ?Thomas[7], born about 1756, a wagoner living at the head of "C. Run" in the lower district of Lunenburg County in 1802 and 1803 when he was counted in the "List of free Negroes & Mulattoes" [LVA, Lunenburg County, Free Negro & Slave Records, 1802-1803]. He returned an inventory of the estate of Martha **Epps** to the Lunenburg County court on 14 September 1809 [WB 6:259]. Sally **Epes** was living in his household in 1814 when he was counted in the "List of free Negroes and Mulattoes" as a planter on Susanna Moore's land [*Magazine of Virginia Genealogy* 33:267]. He was a "free man of Colour" about sixty-three years of age on 23 December 1819 when he applied for a pension in Lunenburg County for his services in the Revolution. He stated that he enlisted in September 1777 while resident in Mecklenburg County and served until 1780 [23 December 1819 Lunenburg County Legislative Petition, LVA]. He testified on behalf of Randall **Chavis** in his petition to obtain money due his father John **Chavis** and his uncle Anthony **Chavis** for their service as wagoners in the Revolution. He stated that he had been living in Petersburg Town about 1795 but moved to Lunenburg County where the clerk of the court issued a paper certifying that Thomas Evans was a respectable and credible person [Mecklenburg County Legislative Petition of 19 January 1836, LVA].

xi. ?Charles[4], born say 1760, underage on 12 September 1777 when Daniel **Redcross** called him his "brother" in his 10 June 1779 Lunenburg County will. He may have been the Charles Evans who was listed as a "yellow" complexioned soldier, born in Petersburg and living in Mecklenburg County when he enlisted in the Revolution [NSDAR, *African American Patriots*, 149].

xii. ?Polly, born about 1763, registered in Petersburg on 3 November 1803: *a light brown Mulatto woman, five feet one and a half inches high, forty years old, short bushy hair & holes in her ears, born free & raised in the County of Prince George* [Register of Free Negroes 1794-1819, no. 264].

xiii.   ?Robert[2], born about 1765, taxable in Thomas **Brandom**'s household in the upper district of Mecklenburg County in 1787 and taxable in his own household from 1797 to 1814, taxable on his son John in 1809, head of a household of a "free Negro" man and woman over the age of 16 in 1813, a "free Negro" taxable in 1814 [PPTL, 1782-1805, frames 158, 635, 657, 1082; 1806-28, frames 7, 109, 211, 307, 418], called Robin Evans when he married Amy **Stewart**, 13 February 1809 Mecklenburg County bond, James **Chavous** security. He received a certificate in Mecklenburg County on 7 September 1814: *born free and raised in the County of Mecklenburg...of a black complection and good Stature, he is five feet eight inches high, about forty nine years old, his head nearly half grey* [Free Person of Colour, # 6, p.4].

xiv.   ?Nancy, born about 1767, registered in Petersburg on 26 August 1805: *a yellow brown Mulatto woman, five feet one and a half inches high, thirty eight years old, holes in her ears, born free & raised in the County of Prince George* [Register of Free Negroes 1794-1819, no. 355].

xv.   ?Nancy, born about 1782, registered in Petersburg on 3 November 1803: *a light brown Mulatto woman, five feet four inches high, twenty one years old, short bushy hair, born free & raised in the Town of Petersburg* [Register of Free Negroes 1794-1819, no.263].

4. James[1] Evans, born say 1720, was living in Surry County, Virginia, on 16 April 1746 when he and Elizabeth **Walding** (**Walden**) were presented by the churchwardens for living in adultery [Orders 1744-49, 166]. He may have been the James Evans who was in Captain William West's muster of Edgecombe County, North Carolina Militia in the 1750s, listed next to Francis **Scott** and near John and Abraham **Scott** and Benjamin **Cheaves** (**Chavis**) [N.C. Archives, Militia Troop Returns, Box 1, folder 12, last page]. He may have been the father of

13   i.   James[2], born say 1750.

    ii. Thomas[6], born say 1752, taxable in Warren County as a married man in Smith Creek and Hawtree District in 1779, taxable on an assessment of 341 pounds in 1780, 58 pounds in Captain Shearing's District in 1782, 9 pounds in Hawtree District in 1783, a free poll and 80 acres in Captain Wyatt Hawkins' district in 1784, and taxable on 100 acres and a free poll in Hawtree District in 1785 and 1786 [1779 Assessments, p.13; Tax List 1781-1801, pp. 5, 45, 69, 80, 101, 121]. He was head of a Warren County household of 5 white (free) persons over 60 or less than 21 years of age and 3 white females in the 1785 North Carolina census (called Thomas Ivans), head of a Wake County household of 6 "other free" in 1790 [NC:104], 7 in 1800 [NC:762], and 7 in Anson County in 1810 [NC:29]. He and Morris Evans may have gone to Anson County with Micajah **Young**/ **Demery** who married Elizabeth Evans.

4. Thomas[1] Evans, born say 1710, was called "Thomas Evings (otherwise lately called &c)" in Amherst County court on 2 September 1766 when the sheriff attached a fork of his for a debt he owed Samuel Woods. He was added to Henry Bell's road gang on 7 December 1767. In December the court ordered his male laboring tithables to keep the road in repair from Buffaloe River to Stoval's Road and ordered that Thomas be surveyor thereof [Orders 1766-9, 74, 233; 1773-82]. By his 28 June 1774 Amherst County will, proved 5 September 1774, he left to his son Benjamin his land and a horse as well as cattle and hogs for the use of his daughters Mary and Hannah and grandson Thomas as long as they abided together and left a shilling each to sons Charles, Thomas, William and Stanup (Stanhope) and daughter Nelly [WB 1:264-5]. He was the father of

i. Charles, called son & heir-at-law of Thomas Evans, deceased, when he was summoned by the Amherst County court on 5 September 1774 to contest the will of his father [Orders 1773-82, 107].

ii. Thomas[4].

iii. William.

iv. Stanhope, born say 1740, granted 350 acres in Amherst County on both sides of Johns Branch, a north branch of Buffaloe River, on 14 July 1780 [Grants A, 1779-80, 634].

v. Nelly.

14 vi. Benjamin[1], born say 1749.

vii. Mary, born say 1751, perhaps the Mary Evans whose illegitimate daughter Sarah Evans was ordered bound by the churchwardens of Lexington Parish on 7 March 1785 [Orders 1784-7, 72], and perhaps identical to Molly Evans who was head of an Amherst County household of 2 "other free" in 1810 [VA:286].

15 viii. Hannah, born say 1753.

5. Thomas[2] Evans, born say 1723, was head of a household in Lunenburg County, taxable on his own tithe and Solomon **Harris** in 1748, taxable on his own tithe in 1749 and 1750, taxable on his own tithe and John Evans/ **Epps** in 1751 and 1752, and taxable on his own tithe in 1764 [Bell, *Sunlight on the Southside*, 68-9, 109, 166, 193, 250]. He was called "Thomas Evans (Negro)" on 14 May 1764 when he was sued in Lunenburg County court by Sterling Thornton and Company who attached his effects for a 5 pound debt [Orders 1764-5, 39]. His personal effects were ordered released to Matthew Marable for an 18 pound debt by the same court [Orders 1764-5, 39]. Morris Evans brought a suit against him in Mecklenburg County, Virginia court, but it was dismissed on 11 September 1769 when Morris failed to appear. On 10 May 1773 Thomas acknowledged in Mecklenburg County court that he owed a debt of 63 pounds to John Potter & Company [Orders 1768-71, 254; 1773-9, 2]. He mortgaged 13 cattle, 15 hogs, 2 horses, 2,000 weight of tobacco, and his household goods to Matthew Marable for about 50 pounds in Mecklenburg County on 12 February 1773 [DB 4:156]. Randolph **Locklear** sued him in Mecklenburg County court on 14 March 1774 for a debt of 2 pounds due by note of hand [Orders 1773-9, 185]. He sold by Mecklenburg County deed (signing) 2 horses, a colt, 9 cattle, 18 hogs, 6 sheep, 20 geese, 3 featherbeds, and other household items to James Anderson for 50 pounds on 15 May 1777, and purchased 50 acres of land on Little Bluestone Creek adjoining Charles Royster's line in Mecklenburg County from James Anderson for 6,000 pounds of tobacco on 11 March 1781 [DB 5:72; 6:123]. On 9 April 1782 the Mecklenburg County, Virginia court allowed his claim for providing 225 pounds of beef for the use of the Continental Army [Orders 1779-84, 134]. He was head of a Mecklenburg County household of 7 persons in 1782 [VA:34] and called Thomas Evans, Sr., when he was taxable in Mecklenburg County on 2 horses from 1782 to 1787: exempt from personal tax in 1783 and taxable on slave Phebe in 1786 [PPTL, 1782-1805, frames 12, 25, 69, 99, 152]. On 10 May 1784 the Mecklenburg County court exempted him from paying taxes due to his old age and infirmity and on 8 October 1787 the court exempted his sixty-year-old slave [Orders 1784-7, 2; 1787-92, 109]. His 22 May 1787 Mecklenburg County will, recorded 14 July 1788, listed his wife (unnamed), son Thomas and grandchildren: Evans **Chaves** (son of James and Jane Chaves), John **Chavous**, and Nancy **Brannom**. John **Chaves** and Ann Gregory were witnesses. James Anderson of North Carolina was executor [WB 2:250]. A Mecklenburg County suit for debt brought by Scottish merchants James & Robert Donald & Co. on 12 October 1796 and continued until 17 May 1798 named his heirs: Thomas Evans, Jacob **Chavous** and his wife Elizabeth, James **Chavous** and his wife Jane, Thomas **Brandom** and his wife Peggy, and

William **Caisey** (**Kersey**) and his wife Polly [Orders 1795-8, 160, 470]. His children were

    i.   Elizabeth, born say 1745, married Jacob **Chavis**.

   ii.   Thomas[5], born say 1750, called Thomas Evans, Jr., on 6 March 1787 when he purchased 50 acres in the upper district of Mecklenburg County on Little Bluestone Creek adjoining Charles Royster's line from Joshua Ivey of Prince George County. On 12 February 1789 he purchased for 50 pounds 2 horses, a colt, 9 cattle, 18 hogs, 6 sheep, 20 geese, 3 featherbeds, and other household items from James Anderson of Chatham County, North Carolina, the executor of his father's estate, who had purchased the items from Thomas Evans, Sr., in 1777 [DB 7:144; 470]. He was taxable on his land from 1787 to 1812 [Land Tax List 1782-1811A, 1811B-1824A, A lists]. He was taxable in Mecklenburg County from 1782 to 1798 and from 1803 to 1820: taxable on a slave named Harrison in 1785, taxable on a slave named Dick in 1789, taxable on D. Evans in 1792, taxable on slave Gloster in 1797, and head of a household of a "Free Negro" man and woman over the age of 16 in 1813 [PPTL, 1782-1805, frames 2, 25, 99, 165, 213, 265, 319, 442, 541, 712, 972, 1082; 1806-28, frames 7, 109, 211, 307, 576, 668, 685]. He was head of a Mecklenburg County household of 10 "free colored" in 1820 [VA:144a].

  iii.   Margaret/ Peggy, born about 1753, married Thomas **Brandom** on 3 January 1771. She gave her maiden name as **Walden** in her application for a survivor's pension in 1840, so she may have been his illegitimate child by a member of the **Walden** family or perhaps **Walden** was his wife's maiden name [Dorman, *Virginia Revolutionary Pension Applications*, 9:74-75]. Their daughter Nancy **Brannom** was born in 1771.

  iv.   Jane, born say 1755, married James **Chavis**.

   v.   Mary Carsey (**Kersey**), married William **Cazy** (**Kersey**), 23 December 1786 Mecklenburg County bond, Kinchen **Chavous** surety.

7.   Charles[1] Evans, born say 1696, was sued for debt in Brunswick County court by Littlebury Epes in December 1735 [Orders 1732-37, 68]. He was called "Charles Evans a mulatto" in December 1746 in Lunenburg County when the court dismissed charges brought against him by Andrew Bresslar [Orders 1746-48, 81]. He received a patent on 20 August 1747 for 120 acres on Stith's Creek in the part of Brunswick County which became Lunenburg County in 1748 and Mecklenburg County in 1765 [Patents 28:135]. He was taxable in Lunenburg County in the list of Lewis Deloney in 1748, taxable in the list of Field Jefferson in 1751 with his son Tom [Bell, *Sunlight on the Southside*, 68, 166] and taxable with Thomas and Major Evans in 1752 [Tax List 1748-52, 1]. He petitioned the Lunenburg County court in May 1753 to be exempt from personal taxes, but was rejected "for Reasons appearing to the Court" [Orders 1753-54, 113]. He was granted 38 acres in Lunenburg County in the fork of Miles Creek and Dockery's Creek on 23 July 1753 [Patents 31:337]. He left a 22 March 1760 Brunswick County, Virginia will (signing), proved 27 October 1760, leaving his "mannor" plantation on the south side of Dockery's Creek to his son Major Evans, left an equal quantity to his son Charles Evans and left the residue of his land on the southside of Dockery's Creek to son Dick Evans on condition they give twenty pounds or 100 acres of land to his youngest son Erasmus. He left a bed and furniture to his daughters Sarah and Joice, but left only a shilling to his "undutiful" son Thomas [WB 3:375-6]. He died before June 1760 when a suit against him in Lunenburg County court abated by his death [Orders 1759-61, 136]. On 18 October 1764 Sarah and Richard Evans sold about 39 acres in the fork of Miles and Dockery's Creek in Mecklenburg County which was land they had been given by Charles Evans [DB 1:514]. And on the same date Sarah, Charles and Major Evans sold 120

acres on Stith's Creek in Lunenburg County adjoining Philip Morgan [DB 8:356]. His children were

16   i.   Thomas[3], born say 1734.
17   ii.   Major[1], born say 1735.
18   iii.   Charles[2], born say 1737.
19   iv.   Richard[1], born say 1740.
      v.   Sarah.
    vi.   Joyce.
20   vii.   Erasmus, born say 1745.

8.   Morris[2] Evans, born say 1710, was sued by Joseph Makepeace in Charles City County in May 1738 for 40 shillings, 300 pounds of tobacco, and a hog due by bill. The sheriff reported that he had attached three beds, blankets, eighteen plates, seven dishes, two chests, a table, a mare and some tobacco hanging in the loft which were in the hands of Jane Evans, but the court ruled that the goods did not belong to Morris. In July 1747 William Gray's suit against him was dismissed at the plaintiff's cost, and in June 1749 John Pleasants sued him for 37 shillings due on account [Orders 1737-51, 3-4, 447, 495]. On 1 June 1750 Edward Eppes sued him for a 3 pound debt in Chesterfield County [Orders 1749-54, 53]. He was taxable in Field Jefferson's list for Lunenburg County in 1751 adjacent to Edward Epps and Solomon **Harris** [Bell, *Sunlight on the Southside*, 169]. He died before 3 December 1754 when his widow Amey Wright was named as his executrix. At the same court she obtained a peace bond against her husband John Wright, claiming that she feared he was going to kill her. She presented the inventory of Morris' estate on 2 June 1756. Morris was apparently the father of Richard Evans, son of Amy Wright, who was bound out by the Lunenburg County court to Richard Rodgers on 12 February 1767. Amy appears to have been a white woman [Orders 1754-5, 244; 1766-9, 25a; WB 1:155, 219]. Morris was the father of

      i.   ?Gilbert, born say 1730, taxable in Lunenburg County in 1751 [Bell, *Sunlight on the Southside*, 166], married Febey Lumbley, 20 June 1780 Wake County, North Carolina bond, John Ross bondsman. He was taxable in Wake County in Henry King's district on 500 acres, 2 horses and 12 cattle about 1782-1784, taxable on 481 acres and 1 poll in 1793, 944 acres and 1 poll in 1799, and taxable on 844 acres and no polls in 1802 [CR 99.701.1, frames 54, 96, 151, 227]. He was head of a Wake County household of 2 white males over 16, 6 under 16 and 3 white females in 1790 [NC:106].
    ii.   ?Arthur, born say 1745, over sixteen years old when he was taxable in Major Evans' Granville County household in 1764, a taxable in James **Doyal**'s Bladen County, North Carolina household in 1768 ("Mulatoes") [Byrd, *Bladen County Tax Lists*, I:6]. He was head of a Richland District, South Carolina household of 7 "other free" in 1810 [SC:171a]. He owned land near Big Crane and Little Crane Creeks in Richland District in 1814 [South Carolina Archives series S213192, 43:552].
21   iii.   Richard[2], born say 1750.

9.   Isaac Evans, born say 1735, was tithable in Edward Epps' Lunenburg County household in 1752: "Peter and Isaac" [Bell, *Sunlight on the Southside*, 194]. Isaac was probably one of the unnamed "Molatto Children" Edward Epps asked the Lunenburg County court to bind to him in July 1752 [Orders 1752-3, 69]. He and Jacob Evans were apprentices of Edward Epps in May 1753 when they sued him for mistreating them and holding them illegally. The court allowed them to go to Martin Brandon Parish in Prince George County to search the register for proof of their age. The court ordered them bound instead to Abraham Martin [Orders 1753-4, 111, 165-6, 254]. Isaac was head

of a Warren County household of 9 "other free" in 1790 [NC:77] and 5 in Randolph County in 1800 [NC:310]. He may have been the father of

22   i.   Matthew, born say 1760.

     ii.   Sally, born say 1770, married James **Stewart**, 2 May 1791 Warren County bond, Eaton **Walden** bondsman.

    iii.   Leven, born before 1776, residing in Warren County on 23 November 1797 when he purchased 122 acres in Halifax County, North Carolina, on the waters of Falling Creek. He was taxable in district 12 of Halifax County on 122 acres and a free poll in 1800 [Gammon, *Halifax County Tax Lists* I:34]. He sold 22 acres of this land to John **Richardson** on 9 December 1800 with Joel Evans and Joseph **Lantern** as witnesses [DB 18:269, 916]. He was head of a Warren County household of 7 "other free" in 1810 [NC:754] and 3 "free colored" in Halifax County in 1820 [NC:147], perhaps the Leaven Evans who married (second?) Hariot **Scott**, 18 December 1829 Warren County bond, Thomas Edwards bondsman. Harriet, a "Mulatto" farmer born about 1811, was listed in the 1860 Halifax County census with $85 real estate. She may have been identical to Harriet Richardson, daughter of Hardy Richardson.

    iv.   Susannah, married Benjamin **Stewart**, Warren County bond, no date, Eaton **Walden** bondsman.

     v.   Godfrey, married Polly **Walden**, 3 November 1818 Randolph County bond, Hugh Moffett bondsman.

    vi.   Pleasant, married Delilah **Walden**, 21 April 1819 Randolph County bond, Godfrey **Evins** bondsman.

10. Robert[1] Evans, born say 1740, was living in York County on 17 December 1764 when a presentment against him by the grand jury was dismissed [Judgments & Orders 1759-63, 320]. He and his wife Mary, "Both free Mulattas," registered the 16 October 1766 birth of their son Littlebury in Bruton Parish, James City County [Bruton Parish Register, 30]. On 21 July 1766 he and Thomas **Maclin** were securities for a 55 shilling debt William **Roberts** owed Lawson Burfoot in York County. On 19 November 1770 he was presented by the court for selling rum without a license and for failing to list himself as a tithable, and he appeared in court the same day in his suit against George **Jones** for trespass, assault and battery. Francis Peters and Elizabeth **Grymes** were his witnesses. Peter **Gillett** sued him for a 4 pound, 18 shilling debt on 17 December 1770. Richard **Cumbo** sued him for trespass, assault and battery on 17 May 1773 and was awarded 1 shilling damages on testimony of Reuben and Peter **Gillett** [Orders 1765-68, 91; Judgments & Orders 1770-2, 105, 124, 153, 170, 211, 336, 337; 1772-4, 272, 336]. He was the father of

     i.   Littleberry, born 16 October 1766, perhaps the Littleberry Evans who was taxable in Charles City County in 1784 and 1786 [PPTL, 1783-7].

    ii.   ?William, "alias **Redcross**," born say 1768, taxable in Charles City County from 1789 to 1791 [PPTL, 1788-1814].

    iii.   Richard, taxable on a horse in James City County from 1797 to 1814: listed as a "Mulatto" in 1809 when he was taxable on 2 tithes, listed as a "Mulatto" in 1813 with 4 "Free Persons of Colour above the age of 16" in his household (apparently himself and three women), listed as "col^d" in 1814 [PPTL 1782-99; 1800-15].

    iv.   ?Thomas[10], born say 1790, a "Mulattoe" taxable in Charles City County in 1813 [PPTL, 1788-1814]. His wife Sarah obtained a certificate of freedom in Charles City County on 19 January 1832: *Sarah Evans, wife of Thomas Evans, who was Sarah Stewart, daughter of Wm Stewart, a light mulato, twenty four years of age* [Minutes 1830-9, 89].

v. ?Sally, born say 1792, married Elijah **Crew**, 4 January 1813 Charles City County bond [*Wm & Mary Quarterly Historical Papers* Vol. 8, No.3, p.195]. Elijah was a "Mulattoe" taxable in Charles City County in 1813 [PPTL, 1788-1814].

11. Philip Evans, born say 1745, the "Mulotto" son of Ann Evans, was bound apprentice to the Rev. Robert Fergeson in Bristol Parish on 10 November 1748 [Chamberlayne, *Register of Bristol Parish*, 134]. He was taxable in Prince George County from 1782 to 1793: taxable on a horse and 2 cattle in 1782, 2 slaves in 1783, taxable on his own tithe and a free male tithable 16-21 years of age in 1786, taxable on John Evans and a slave in 1787, taxable on John and Jesse Evans in 1788, and taxable on a slave in 1792 and 1793 [PPTL, 1782-1811, frames 161, 171, 182, 210, 223, 244, 263, 283, 323, 356]. He was taxable on 140 acres in Prince George County in 1790. His widow was apparently Agnes Evans who was taxable on 140 acres in 1799 [1790 Land Tax List, p.5; 1799 Land Tax List, p.7]. Aggy was a "Mulatto" taxable on 2 free male tithes in 1804, 1806, 1810 and 1811 [PPTL, 1782-1811, frames 602, 652, 721, 742]. She was head of a Prince George County household of 11 "other free" in 1810 [VA:537]. They were probably the parents of

    i. John, born say 1766, taxable in the household of Philip Evans from 1787 to 1789.

    ii. Jesse, born say 1767, taxable in the Prince George County household of Philip Evans in 1788 and 1789, perhaps the Jesse Evans who was head of a Johnston County, North Carolina household of 6 "other free" in 1800 and 13 "free colored" in 1820 [NC:274].

    iii. Major[2], born say 1778, taxable in Prince George County from 1799 to 1806: called "a dark man" in 1800, a "Mulatto" in 1801 and 1802 [PPTL, 1782-1811, frames 487, 508, 533, 576, 627, 651]. Perhaps he was the Major Evans who was a peddlar, no race indicated, in Southampton County in 1794 [PPTL 1792-1806, frame 104].

    iv. Joseph, born say 1779, a "Mulatto" taxable in Prince George County from 1800 to 1806 [PPTL, 1782-1811, frames 532, 553, 576, 627, 651].

    v. Mason, head of a Prince George County household of 3 "other free" in 1810 [VA:537].

    vi. Charles[6], born say 1788 a "free" taxable in Prince George County in 1809 [PPTL, 1782-1811, frame 701].

12. Martha Evans, born say 1756, was "a free Mulatto woman" living in Lunenburg County on 14 August 1777 when the court ruled that she was entitled to her freedom from the service of Frizel McTeir. The same court bound out her children Thomas and Mary [Orders 1777-84, fol. 2]. She may have been the Martha Evans who was head of a Granville County household of 3 "other free" in 1800. Her children were

    i. Thomas[9], born say 1773, purchased land in Granville County, North Carolina, by deed acknowledged by James **Chavers** in August court 1794 [Minutes 1792-95, 191; DB P:90]. He was head of an Abrams Plains, Granville County household of a "free colored" man over the age of 45 in 1820 [NC:23].

    ii. Mary, born say 1775.

13. James[2] Evans, born say 1750, was taxable in Warren County on 40 acres and a free poll in 1784 and taxable on 245 acres and a free poll in 1792 [N.C. Archives L.P. 64.1, p.10; Pittman Papers PC 123.9]. He was counted as white in Warren County for the North Carolina state census in 1785 with a male aged 21-60, 3 males under 21 or over 60, and 3 females, head of a Warren County household of 9 "other free" in 1790 [NC:77], 5 "other free" with a white woman 26-45 years old and a white boy under ten years of age in 1800

[NC:802], and 7 "free colored" in 1820 [VA:10]. He was living in Warren County on 12 February 1787 when he purchased 107 acres in Halifax County, North Carolina. He was granted 100 acres on the south side of Buckskin Creek in Halifax County on 20 December 1791 and was living in Warren County on 20 November 1797 when he purchased 50 acres in Halifax County adjoining Timothy Matthews. He was taxable on 250 acres in district 12 of Halifax County in 1800, but not subject to poll tax [Gammon, *Halifax County Tax Lists* I:34]. He was living in Halifax County on 25 January 1805 when he sold two tracts, one of 50 acres on Hawtree Branch and the other of 100 acres on Haw Tree Swamp [DB 16:260; 17:567; 20:264, 378]. He may have been the father of

i.   Benjamin², born say 1775, head of a Halifax County household of 6 "other free" in 1800 [NC:306]. He received a grant for 35 acres in Halifax County on the north side of Falling Creek on 30 June 1797 [DB 18:330]. He was taxable in Halifax County on 2 free polls and 35 acres in 1800 [Gammon, *Halifax County Tax Lists* I:34]. He died before 16 February 1802 when Joel Evans was granted administration on his Halifax County estate on a bond of 100 pounds with Elijah **Richardson** security [Minutes 1799-1802, Tuesday session, n.p.].

ii. Joel, born about 1779, head of a Halifax County household of 4 "other free" in 1800, 2 in 1810 [NC:18], and 3 "free colored" in 1820 [NC:147], seventy one years old in 1850 when he was listed with (wife?) Polly who was the same age. He and Joseph **Lantern** were witnesses to John **Richardson**'s 7 February 1795 Halifax County deed of sale of 100 acres on the north side of Little Fishing Creek [DB 17:747]. He was taxable in district 12 of Halifax County on 2 free polls in 1800 and 1 in 1802 [Gammon, *Halifax County Tax Lists* I:34, 46].

iii. Elias, born before 1776, head of a Halifax County household of 8 "free colored" in 1820 [NC:147].

iv. Moses, born before 1776, head of a Halifax County household of 6 "free colored" in 1820 [NC:147].

v.   Charles, married Susanna **Chavis**, Franklin County, North Carolina bond, Nicholas Murphey bondsman, undated but between 12 December 1808 and 5 December 1810. He was head of a Warren County household of 4 "other free" in 1810 [NC:738].

vi. Archibald, born about 1790, married Anna **Mason**, 15 January 1815 Granville County bond, Lewis **Anderson** bondsman and second, Lucretia **Green**, daughter of Thomas and Priscilla **Green**, 29 December 1829 Warren County bond, Mims **Guy** bondsman. He was head of a Warren County household of 6 "free colored" in 1820 [NC:796], a sixty-year-old "Mulatto" farmer counted in the 1850 Warren County census with wife Creasy [NC:56].

14. Benjamin¹ Evans, born say 1750, received two patents for a total of 153 acres in Amherst County on the north branch of Buffuloe River on 7 December 1774 [Patents 42:791, 808]. He was one of the freeholders of Amherst County ordered to work on Stovall's Road from Buffuloe River to Tye River in May 1783 [Orders 1782-4, 118]. He was head of an Amherst County household of 6 free persons in 1783 [VA:48] and 6 "Mulattoes" in 1785 [VA:84]. He was taxable in Lexington Parish, Amherst County, in 1782, 1786 and 1787 [PPTL 1782-1803, frames 13, 69, 99]. He sold 100 acres where he was then living on the north side of Buffalo Creek, being all the land he owned in Amherst County, on 14 January 1789 [DB F:322]. And he sold property to John Christian by deed proved in Amherst County on 16 April 1792 with endorsement annexed of the claim of Samuel Megginson [Orders 1790-4, 391]. Perhaps his widow or sister-in-law was Jane Evans, head of an Amherst County household of a white woman over forty-five years of age and 4 "other

free" in 1810 [VA:287] and 6 "free colored" in 1820. He may have been the father of

    i.   Henry, born say 1775, taxable on a horse in Lexington Parish, Amherst County, in 1791 and from 1804 to 1810, called Henry A. Evans, a "man of color," in 1811 and 1812, a "Mulatto" in 1813 [PPTL 1782-1803, frame 226; 1804-23, frames 23, 64, 189, 211, 232]. He was head of an Amherst County household of 2 "other free" in 1810 [VA:302] and 2 "free colored" over forty-five years of age in 1820.

    ii.   John[3], born say 1776, head of an Amherst County household of 9 "other free" in 1810 [VA:392] and 5 "free colored" in 1820. He was a "man of color" taxable in Lexington Parish, Amherst County, in 1811 and 1812 [PPTL 1804-23, frames 189, 211, 232].

    iii.   Charles, taxable in Amherst County from 1798 to 1813, called a "man of color" in 1813 [PPTL 1783-1803, frame 406; 1804-23, frame 254]. He was head of an Amherst County household of 1 "other free" in 1810 [VA:289].

15. Hannah Evans born say 1753, was living in Lexington Parish, Amherst County, on 6 July 1789 when the court ordered the overseers of the poor to bind her illegitimate "Molatter" son Thomas Evans to Samuel Brown to learn the trade of blacksmith [Orders 1787-90, 499]. She was the mother of

    i.   ?Nancy[1], born say 1769, married Edward **Branham** (**Brandon**), 6 December 1790 Amherst County bond.

    ii.   Thomas[8], born say 1772, named in the Amherst County will of his grandfather Thomas Evans. He, a blacksmith, married Ann **Penn**, daughter of Rolly (Raleigh) and Sarah **Pinn**, 2 November 1795 Amherst County bond. Thomas was taxable in Amherst County from 1800 to 1810, called a "man of color" in 1811 [PPTL 1782-1803, frames 481, 553, 587; 1804-23, frames 23, 167, 189, 210] and head of an Amherst County household of 7 "other free" in 1810 [VA:268]. He was listed on South River in Rockbridge County in 1813 as a "Black" male with two "Black" females over the age of sixteen [Waldrep, *1813 Tax List*].

    iii.   Levisay, daughter of Hannah Evans, married George **Clark**, 13 May 1795 Amherst County bond, Leonard **Clark** security. She was called Loisa **Clark**, widow, when she married Charles **Johns** of Bedford County, 10 October 1805 Amherst County bond.

    iv.   ?Ambrose, taxable in the southern district of Campbell County in 1786, 1787, 1788 and 1792: called Ambrose Evans in 1786, Ambrose Ambrose alias Evans in 1787, Ambrose Ambrose in 1788 and 1792 [PPTL, 1785-1814, frames 20, 36, 64, 207], taxable in Buckingham County in 1790, 1791, 1797 and 1798: called a "Molatto" in 1797 and 1798 [PPTL 1782-97; 1798-1803]. He was taxable in Amherst County from 1803 to 1820: taxable on a horse in 1806 and 1807, 2 horses in 1810, probably identical to Anderson A. Evans, a "man of color" who was taxable on 2 horses in 1811, called "Ambrose A. Evans a M. of C." in 1812, a "Mulatto" in 1813, taxable with his unnamed son in a list of "Free Mulattoes & Negroes" in 1814 [PPTL 1782-1803, frame 587; 1804-23, frames 23, 106, 146, 167, 189, 211, 232, 284, 330, 538, 550]. He was head of an Amherst County household of 6 "other free" in 1810 [VA:302].

    v.   ?Pleasant, taxable in Amherst County from 1800 to 1812: a "man of color" in 1811 and 1812 [PPTL 1782-1803, frames 481, 516, 587; 1804-23, 23, 106, 211, 232].

    vi.   ?Richard[4], taxable in Amherst County from 1803 to 1812: a "man of color" in 1811 and 1812 [PPTL 1782-1803, frame 587; 1804-23, frames 23, 106, 189, 211, 232].

vii. ?Juriah, a "W. of C." (woman of color) who was taxable on a horse in Amherst County in 1812, called a "Mulatto" in 1813 [PPTL 1804-23, frames 232, 254].

viii. ?Anderson, born say 1783, taxable in Lexington Parish, Amherst County, on a horse from 1804 to 1821: taxable on a horse in 1804, a "man of color" in 1811 and 1812, a "Mulatto" in 1813, a "free Negro" taxable in 1815 [PPTL 1804-23, frames 23, 64, 106, 145, 189, 211 230, 254, 300, 537, 599]. He made a deed of trust for land in Amherst County acknowledged on 15 May 1820 to secure a debt he owed [Orders 1815-20, 607].

Other members of the Evans family in nearby Buckingham County were

i. Rhoday, taxable on William and Foster Evans' tithes and 2 horses in Buckingham County in 1798 [PPTL 1798-1803].

ii. Henry, born say 1765, a "Mulatto" taxable in Buckingham County from 1788 to 1807 [PPTL 1782-97; 1798-1803; 1804-9].

iii. Forster, a "Molatto" taxable in Buckingham County in 1797 and from 1802 to 1807 [PPTL 1782-97; 1798-1803; 1804-9].

iv. William, a "Molatto" taxable in Buckingham County in 1797 and from 1802 to 1807 [PPTL 1782-97; 1798-1803; 1804-9].

16. Thomas[3] Evans, born say 1734, was taxable in the Lunenburg County household of his father Charles Evans in 1751 [Bell, *Sunlight on the Southside*, 166]. He was living in Mecklenburg County on 10 March 1789 when the court described him as "so poor and Idle and dishonest that he cannot make the necessary provisions for his family and ought not to have the governing of them." The court ordered his children Elizabeth Evans, Olive Evans, Delilah Evans, Matthew **Stewart**, and Charles Evans bound out as apprentices [Orders 1787-92, 363]. Thomas was the father of

23   i. Elizabeth, born say 1769.

ii. Matthew **Stewart**, born say 1768.

iii. Olive, born say 1772, ordered bound to John Davis, Jr., on 10 March 1789. She married Austin **Pettiford**, 31 December 1814 Granville County bond.

iv. Delilah, born say 1774, ordered bound apprentice to Charles Evans on 10 March 1789. She married Thomas **McLin**, 23 December 1794 Mecklenburg County bond.

v. Charles[5], born say 1775, ordered bound apprentice to Charles Evans by the Mecklenburg County court on 10 March 1789 [Orders 1787-92, 363]. He married Martha **Jeffries**, 17 August 1796 Mecklenburg County, Virginia bond, Kinchen **Chavous** security. He was taxable in Mecklenburg County in 1798 [PPTL, 1782-1805, frame 684] and head of an "other free" Orange County, North Carolina household in 1800 (perhaps living near the **Jeffries** family) [NC:505].

vi. ?Penelope, married William **Jeffries**, 21 February 1800 Orange County bond, Rept **Stewart** bondsman.

vii. ?Thomas, married Lucy **Jeffers** (**Jeffries**), 26 September 1810 Orange County bond, Henry Shult bondsman.

17. Major[1] Evans, born say 1733, was taxable in Charles Evans' Lunenburg County household in 1752 [Tax List 1748-52, 1]. He was taxable in St. James Parish, Lunenburg County, in Edmund Taylor's list in 1764 [Bell, *Sunlight on the Southside*, 259], and he owned land on the south side of Taylor's Creek in Mecklenburg County on 6 July 1765 [DB 1:72]. In 1764 he was living across the state line in Granville County, North Carolina, taxable with his wife Martha and Arthur Evans in the list of Samuel Benton [CR 44.701.19]. His wife was called Ann in the 1768 list of Jonathan Kittrell. In 1769 he was taxable in Granville County with his unnamed wife on 2 black tithes, and in

1771 he was in the adjoining county of Bute, a taxable head of a household of five persons including his wife but taxed on 4 "Black" tithes:

Majer Eavens Wm Chavers overseer & Gordin & his Son Burrel Evins & wife   0 Whites / 4 Blacks [CR.015.70001, p.12 of pamphlet].

On 16 February 1780 he purchased 100 acres "near the Buffilow Race paths" in Granville County from Philip **Chavis**, and he purchased 100 acres near his own line on Buckhorn Branch of Newlight Creek in Granville near the Franklin County line on 19 July 1794 [Granville DB O:84; Franklin DB 1:140]. On 9 April 1782 the Mecklenburg County, Virginia court allowed his claim for providing 225 pounds of beef for the use of the Continental Army [Orders 1779-84, 127]. He was taxable in Mecklenburg County on a tithe, a horse, and 8 cattle from 1782 to 1787 and taxable on 101 acres in the upper district of Mecklenburg County in 1782. He sold his Mecklenburg County land to Anthony **Chavis** in 1787 [PPTL 1782-1805, frames 12, 99, 165; Land Tax List 1782-1811A]. And he was taxable on 2 polls in Granville County in 1785. His children were

24
- i. ?Morris[3], born say 1750.
- ii. Burwell, born say 1758, taxable in his father's Bute County household in 1771. He married Mary **Mitchell**, 22 July 1779 Granville County bond with William Roberson bondsman. He was taxable in Epping Forest District of Granville County on a horse and 3 cattle in 1782, taxable in the summary list for Granville County on poll tax from 1785 to 1791 and taxable in Beaver Dam district in 1800 and 1801. He was taxable in District 5 of Halifax County in 1783 [Gammon, *Halifax County Tax Lists* I:54], head of a Nash County household of 1 "other free" in 1790 [NC:70] and 2 "other free" in Halifax County in 1810 [NC:18].
- iii. ?Nelly, born say 1762, married William **Taborn**, 1 January 1778 Northampton County, North Carolina bond [recorded in his pension application].
- iv. William, born say 1764, head of a Wake County household of 2 white males over 16, 6 under 16 and 5 white females in 1790 [NC:106].
- v. ?John[2], born say 1767, taxable on a tithe and 4 horses in Mecklenburg County in 1788 [PPTL, 1782-1805, frame 213], taxable in Granville County on one poll in Goshen District in 1791, taxable in Tarr River District in 1800, taxable on 180 acres in Fort Creek District in 1801 and 230 acres in 1802 but taxable on only poll tax from 1803 to 1815 [Tax List 1797-1802, 272, 355; 1803-9, 189, 325]. He married Hannah **Anderson**, 22 February 1806 Granville County bond, Abel **Anderson** bondsman, and was head of a Granville County household of 5 "other free" in 1810 [VA:879].
- vi. ?Daniel, born say 1775, married Prissly **Jones** 10 September 1800 Granville County bond, Emmanuel **Jones** bondsman. He was head of a Granville County household of 2 "other free" in 1800 and was taxable in Beaver Dam District of Granville County in 1801.
- vii. ?Sarah, married George **Anderson**, 14 October 1800 Granville County bond, William **Pettiford** bondsman.
- viii. ?Elizabeth, married Isaac **Chavis**, 6 September 1800 Granville County bond, Peter **Chavis** bondsman.
- ix. ?Thomas, born 1776-1794, married Sally **Bass**, 20 February 1812 Granville County bond, Moses **Bass** bondsman. He was head of an Abrams Plains, Granville County household of 9 "free colored" in 1820 [NC:23].
- x. ?William, married Franky **Anderson**, 27 September 1812 Granville County bond, Abel **Anderson** bondsman.

18. Charles[2] Evans, born say 1737, was taxable in the Lunenburg County list of
     Edmund Taylor for St. James Parish in 1764, listed with 60 acres [Bell,
     Sunlight on the Southside, 248]. On 18 October 1764 he, Sarah Evans (his
     mother) and Major Evans (his brother) sold 120 acres on Stith's Creek in
     Lunenburg County adjoining Philip Morgan [DB 8:356]. On 9 April 1782 the
     Mecklenburg County, Virginia court allowed his claim for providing 275
     pounds of beef for the use of the Continental Army [Orders 1779-84, 124]. He
     was head of a Mecklenburg County, Virginia household of 6 persons in 1782
     [VA:34] and was taxable in Mecklenburg County from 1782 to 1794: taxable
     on slave named Ned, 9 cattle, and 4 horses in 1784 and taxable on slave Jack
     in 1786 [PPTL, 1782-1805, frames 2, 54, 107, 192, 291, 343, 401, 500], He
     sent a note to the Mecklenburg County clerk approving the 20 December 1788
     marriage bond of his daughter Nanny to Eaton **Walden**. His children were
     i.   Nanny, born about 1772, married Eaton **Walden**, 20 December 1788
           Mecklenburg County bond.

19. Richard[1] Evans, born say 1740, was taxable in Lunenburg County in 1764
     [Bell, *Sunlight on the Southside*, 250, 304, 333]. On 18 October 1764 he and
     his mother Sarah sold about 39 acres in the fork of Miles and Dockery's Creek
     in Mecklenburg County which was land they had been given by Charles Evans
     [DB 1:514]. He was called Richard Evans "Mallotto" when Dinwiddie,
     Crawford & Company sued him in Mecklenburg County court on 14 June
     1773 for a debt of 19 pounds. He was called the next friend of Isaac Evans in
     Mecklenburg County court on 8 May 1780 when they consented to the
     arbitration of their suit for trespass, assault and battery against Thomas
     Maclin. Robert **Corn** was his security when he was sued in Mecklenburg
     County court on 10 May 1784, and Charles Evans was his security when he
     was sued on 13 December 1784. His estate was attached for 1,136 pounds of
     tobacco on 9 January 1786 [Orders 1773-9, 24; 1784-7, 6, 107, 188, 440,
     442, 554]. He was head of a Mecklenburg County household of 9 persons in
     1782 [VA:34] and taxable in Mecklenburg County on a tithe, 2 horses, and
     about 8 cattle from 1783 to 1786 [PPTL, 1782-1805, frames 43, 66, 111,
     136]. He may have been the father of
     i.   Isaac, born say 1766, sued Thomas **Maclin** for trespass, assault and
           battery in Mecklenburg County court. He was taxable in his own
           Mecklenburg County household in 1787 and 1789, taxable with Richard
           Evans in 1790, and taxable in 1793 and 1798 [PPTL, 1782-1805,
           frames 192, 291, 343, 481, 685]. He married Dicey **Stewart**, 24
           December 1792 Mecklenburg County bond. On 29 July 1796 he made
           a Mecklenburg County deed of trust for 75 acres bounded by Samuel
           Young, Bartlett Cox and Sir Peyton Skipwith to secure a debt of 33
           pounds which he owed William Hendrick [DB 9:125].
     ii.   Richard[3], born about 1774, taxable in the Mecklenburg County
           household of Isaac Evans in 1790, perhaps the D. Evans who was
           taxable in the household of Thomas Evans in 1792 [PPTL, 1782-1805,
           frames 343, 442, 684]. He married Lucy Evans, 17 December 1793
           Warren County bond, Randolph **Rowe** bondsman. He was head of a
           Chatham County household of 6 "other free" in 1800, 8 in 1810
           [NC:201], 12 "free colored" in 1820 [NC:211] and a "Mulatto" farmer
           worth $480 in Chatham County in 1850 with "Mulatto" Lucy Evans
           who was aged seventy-three [NC:474b]. He purchased land in Chatham
           County by deeds proved in November 1818 and February 1820 [DB
           V:307, X:137]. His 21 June 1855 Chatham County will lent his land
           to his wife Lucy and named his children: Fildon (Fielding),
           Granderson, Ancel, Lucy **Byrd**, and John Evans [WB C:409].
     iii. Joshua, born say 1775, a poor orphan, son of Crecy Dinkins, bound to
           Benjamin Pennington in Mecklenburg County on 10 April 1780 [Orders
           1779-84, 29]. He sued Thomas **Epps** in Lunenburg County for

trespass, assault and battery on 9 March 1797, but the suit was dismissed on agreement of the parties [Orders 1796-9]. He was to marry Judah **Stewart**, 16 December 1797 Lunenburg County bond. He was taxable in Lunenburg County from 1794 to 1806, called Joshua E. **Dinkins** in 1795 [PPTL 1782-1806]. He was counted in a list of "free Negroes and Mulattoes" as a "Mulatto" in 1802 with his wife Celia, children Polly and John, and Matthew **Holmes**, farmers on Flat Rock Creek. He was listed as a ditcher on Cedar Creek in 1803 with his wife Celia and children Matthew, Polly and Sally. He was probably related to William **Dinkins** who was listed with his wife Lucretia in the lists for 1802 and 1803 and Thomas **Dinkins** who was listed in 1803 [LVA, Lunenburg County, Free Negro & Slave Records, 1802-1803]. William was taxable in Lunenburg County from 1789 to 1806, and Thomas was taxable from 1792 to 1806. They were called **Dickens** from 1799 to 1806 [PPTL 1782-1806].

iv. Charles, taxable in Nutbush District of Granville County, North Carolina, in 1801 [Tax List 1796-1802, 307]. He married Frances **Hunt**, 9 February 1806 Wake County bond, Charles **Hunt** bondsman. He was one of the freeholders of Chatham County who was ordered by the court to work on the road from Beaver Creek to the Wake County line in February 1806 [Minutes 1805-10, 73]. He was head of a Chatham County household of 7 "other free" in 1810 [NC:193].

20. Erasmus Evans, born say 1745, was taxable in Granville County in Benjamin Ragland's household with wife Mary in 1767 [CR 44.701.19]. His orphan Anthony was living in Mecklenburg County, Virginia, on 8 August 1774 when the court ordered the churchwardens to bind him to John Bozman. On 9 January 1775 the court bound his son Isham to Francis Lightfoot. Erasmus may have been married to a member of the **Chavis** family since his son Anthony was called Anthony **Chavis**, orphan of Erasmus Evans, deceased, when the Mecklenburg County court ordered the churchwardens to bind him out [Orders 1773-9, 291, 301; 1779-84, 435]. His children were

i. Anthony, born say 1771, ordered bound apprentice in Mecklenburg County on 8 August 1774, taxable in Thomas **Brandom**'s Mecklenburg County household in 1787 and 1788 and taxable in his own household from 1790 to 1798, called a "Mulatto" in 1790 (adjoining Isaac and Richard Evans) [PPTL, 1782-1805, frames 208, 343, 517, 684]. And there was an Anthony Evans who was a "melatto" taxable in the northern district of Campbell County from 1790 to 1792 [PPTL, 1785-1814, frame 148, 188, 231]. He was taxable in Nutbush District of Granville County, North Carolina, in 1800 and 1801 [Tax List 1796-1802, 249, 307] and head of a Chatham County household of 2 "other free" in 1810 [NC:193]. He purchased land in Chatham County by deed proved in August 1819 [DB W:95]. His 10 June 1831 Chatham County will, witnessed by Jarell **Walden**, was proved in August 1835. He left his plantation and all his other property to Sary Betty **Ledbetter**, daughter of Noony **Dungill**. He appointed Stephen **Walden** executor, but John **Dungill** was granted administration on the estate since Stephen had left the state when the will was offered for probate [WB p.24].

ii. Isham, born say 1773, bound apprentice to Francis Lightfoot on 9 January 1779. He was a "melatto" taxable in the northern district of Campbell County from 1789 to 1792 [PPTL, 1785-1814, frames 121, 148, 231].

21. Richard[2] Evans, born say 1750, son of Amy Wright, was bound by the Lunenburg County court to Richard Rodgers on 12 February 1767. On 13 April 1769 he was security for Mary Wright in John Maclin's Lunenburg

County suit against her for a debt of 11 pounds [Orders 1766-9, 25a, 205b]. He was taxable in Lunenburg County in 1772 and 1774 adjoining John Evans/ **Epps** [Bell, *Sunlight on the Southside*, 250, 304, 333]. He purchased 100 acres on White's branch of Flat Rock Creek in Lunenburg County for 10 pounds on 12 November 1772, made a deed of trust (signing) on 4 March 1773 to secure a loan he owed Buchanans Hastie & Company with Elijah Hathcock as witness, and sold the land on 2 November 1775 [DB 12:219, 278, 501]. He may have been the Richard Evans who was head of a Robeson County, North Carolina household of 4 "other free" in 1790 [NC:49], and he may have been the ancestor of

    i.   Nancy, married Wiley **Locklear**, 25 May 1817 Robeson County bond, Joseph **Locklear** bondsman.

22.   Matthew Evans, born say 1760, was head of a Warren County household of 6 "other free" in 1810 [NC:755] and 2 "free colored" and 5 slaves in 1830. He was taxable on 1 poll in Fishing Creek District of Warren County in 1811 [WB 16:152]. His Warren County estate was settled in 1845 and divided his 56 acre tract among his eight heirs who were probably his children [CR 100.508.17]. They were:

    i.   Lucretia/ Crecy (**Green**), probably identical to Fanny Evans who married Allen **Green**, 24 December 1809 Warren County bond, Kinchen **Toney** bondsman. Allen was head of a Warren County household of 4 "other free" in 1810 [NC:736a] and 6 "free colored" in 1820 [NC:798]. Crecy was called C. Green in the 1860 Warren County census. The **Green** family descended from Crease, Tom (apparently son of Crease) and his wife Priss and their children Allen, Charity, Byrna/ Breny, Willie and Crease **Green** who were freed by the 1791 Warren County will of Samuel Williams which did not take effect until 1798 when the North Carolina General Assembly passed an act to emancipate them [Byrd, *In Full Force*, 298]. Thomas **Green** was head of a Warren County household of 13 "other free" and 2 slaves in 1800 [NC:805], 11 "other free" in 1810 [NC:762], and 10 "free colored" in 1820 [NC:794].

    ii.   Fanny (**Toney**), probably wife of Kinchen **Toney**.

   iii.   Moses.

   iv.   Nancy, married James **Green**, born about 1778 according to the 1850 and 1860 Warren County census. James was freed by the May 1825 Warren County will of John C. Green [WB 27:261; 39:406; communication with **Green** descendant Deloris Williams].

    v.   Isaac, married Winifred **Dales**, 14 October 1825 Franklin County bond, Lewis C. Bobbit bondsman.

   vi.   Henry.

   vii.   Ceily (**Toney**), married Matthew **Toney**, 22 December 1808 Warren County bond, Allen **Green** bondsman.

  viii. Patience (**Martial**), married David **Marshall**, 25 June 1823 Warren County bond.

23.   Elizabeth Evans, born say 1769, was bound by the Mecklenburg County, Virginia court to John Kindrick on 10 March 1789. She was the mother of Jordan and Reuben Evans who were bound out by the court to John Kendrick on 14 April 1794 [Orders 1787-92, 363; 1792-5, 261]. She was probably the Elizabeth Evans who married Micajah **Young**, 30 April 1794 Wake County bond, Nathaniel Jones bondsman. She was the mother of

    i.   Reuben, born about 1785, a "Mulattoe" taxable in Mecklenburg County from 1812 to 1816 [PPTL, 1806-28, frames 258, 337, 388, 537]. He registered in Petersburg on 8 September 1804: *a dark brown Mulatto man, five feet six inches high, nineteen years old, born free & raised in the Town of Petersburg* [Register of Free Negroes 1794-1819, no. 281].

ii. Jordan[2], a "Mulattoe" taxable in Mecklenburg County from 1813 to 1816 [PPTL, 1806-28, frames 337, 388, 537]. He was head of a Mecklenburg County household of 9 "free colored" in 1820 [VA:153a].

24. Morris[3] Evans, born say 1750, brought suit against Thomas Evans in Mecklenburg County, Virginia court, but the suit was dismissed at his costs when he failed to appear on 11 September 1769 [Orders 1768-71, 254]. He married Liddy **Anderson**, 8 December 1784 Granville County bond with Burwell Evans bondsman. He was taxable in Granville County on one poll in the summary list for 1788-1790 and taxable in Beaverdam District in 1791. He and John Seegar were residents of Wake County on 10 February 1794 when they sold 300 acres on Great Lick Creek [DB F:21]. He was counted as white in 1790, head of a Wake County household of one male over 16, two under 16, and 8 females [NC:103] and 7 "other free" in 1800 [NC:761]. He was taxable on 180 acres in Henry King's district of Wake County in 1793 [CR 099.701.1, frame 54]. His death on 25 August 1834, supposedly at the age of 105 years, was reported in the Raleigh *Star* on 4 September 1834 and *Hillsborough Recorder* of 10 September 1834. He may have been the father of

i. Polly, married Hardy **Harris**, 22 October 1793 Wake County bond, John Reighley bondsman.

ii. Nancy[2], born say 1775, married Allen **Sweat**, 7 January 1792 Wake County bond, Reuben Evans bondsman.

iii. William, called son of Morris when he was taxable in Wake County in 1793 [CR 99.701.1, frame 54].

iv. Jordan[1], born say 1780, married Delilah Reynolds, 21 November 1805 Wake County bond, Curtis **Snelling** bondsman. He may have been one of two males under the age of sixteen in Morris's household in 1790. He was head of a Wake County household of 3 "free colored" in 1830.

v. Levina, born say 1790, married Curtis **Snelling**, 7 February 1811 Wake County bond, Richard Davis bondsman.

vi. Morris[5], born about 1790, married Elizabeth House, 1812 Wake County bond, Michael Evans bondsman. He was listed in the 1819 Wake County tax list as "of M." (probably meaning son of Morris). He was head of a Wake County household of 7 "free colored" in 1830.

vii. Elizabeth, married Robert **Walden**, 15 February 1813 Wake County bond, Andrew Peddy bondsman.

viii. Rody, married John **Locklear**, 26 December 1822 Wake County bond, Tyre **Locklear** bondsman.

ix. Patsy, married Thomas **Copeland**, 30 January 1821 Wake County bond, Edmund **Pettiford** bondsman.

Members of the Evans family from Southampton County were

25 i. Amy, born say 1755.

ii. Frances, born about 1761, registered in Southampton County on 4 October 1813: *age 52, Blk., 5 feet 7-3/4 inches, free born* [Register of Free Negroes 1794-1832, no. 826].

iii. Moses, born about 1769, registered in Southampton County on 16 December 1819: *age 50, Black, 5 feet 8 1/2 inches, free born* [Register of Free Negroes 1794-1832, no. 1197]. He was taxable in St. Luke's Parish, Southampton County, called a "Mulatto" in 1799 and a "Black" in 1800, a "Mulatto" taxable on 2 free male tithables in 1801, called a "free Negro" in 1802, a "Mulatto" from 1803 to 1806, taxable on 2 horses in 1810 and on 2 slaves and 3 horses in 1811, listed with wife Polly in 1813 and 1814 [PPTL 1792-1806, frames 378, 412, 589, 621, 690, 805, 841; 1807-21, frames 49, 71, 168, 191, 417].

iv.   Isaac, born say 1771, a "f. Negro" taxable in Nottoway Parish, Southampton County, from 1792 to 1809, taxable on 2 persons over the age of 16 in 1805 and 1806 [PPTL 1792-1806, frames 9, 128, 220, 242, 481, 589, 658, 728, 762, 877; 1807-21, frames 16, 98].

v.   Patty, born about 1773, registered in Southampton County on 26 November 1818: *age 45, 5 feet 4-1/2 inches high, rather of a bright complection free born.* She registered again on 21 March 1827 [Register of Free Negroes 1794-1832, nos. 1166, 1621].

vi.   Henry, born about 1783, ordered bound out by the overseers of the poor in the lower district of St. Lukes Parish, Southampton County, on 11 September 1789 [Minutes 1786-90, n.p.]. He was listed with his wife Nancy on John Barnes' land from 1812 to 1814 [PPTL 1807-21, frames 296, 316, 416]. He registered in Southampton County on 31 July 1810: *age 27, Blk., 5 feet 8-1/2 inches, free born.* He registered again on 22 October 1820 and 10 February 1832 [Register of Free Negroes 1794-1832, nos. 758 1238, 1963].

vii. Matthew, born about 1784, a "f.n." taxable in St. Luke's Parish, Southampton County, from 1805 to 1810 [PPTL 1792-1806, frame 805, 841; 1807-21, frames 49, 71, 168]. He registered in Southampton County on 21 July 1806: *age 22, Blk, 5 feet 7-1/2 inches, born of Free parents.* He registered again in Southampton County on 12 July 1810 and 8 June 1818 [Register of Free Negroes 1794-1832, nos. 392, 602, 1141] and registered in Petersburg on 24 June 1818: *a free man of Colour, dark near black Complection, five feet seven inches high, thirty four years old, born free p. cert. of Southampton County* [Register of Free Negroes 1794-1819, no. 915].

25. Amy Evans, born say 1755, was the mother of illegitimate children Charlotte and Nanny Evans who were bound out by the Southampton County court on 18 June 1782 [Orders 1778-84, 203]. She was the mother of

i.   Charlotte, born about 1780, registered in Southampton County on 30 July 1805: *age 25, blk, 5 feet 4 3/4 inches, free born* [Register of Free Negroes 1794-1832, no. 332].

ii.   Nanny, born say 1777, married Edmund **Artis**, 23 February 1796 Southampton County bond.

Other members of the Evans family were

i.   Claiborne, taxable in the lower district of Henrico County from 1783 to 1811: charged with Ben **Scott**'s tithe in 1791 and 1792, taxable on 2 tithes and 2 horses in 1799, taxable on a slave from 1793 to 1811, called a "free Negro" in 1806 and 1807, a "Mulatto" in 1809, a "F. negro" in 1810 and 1811, taxable on 25 acres from 1799 to 1812 [PPTL 1782-1814, frames 36, 77, 123, 160, 177, 234, 252, 291, 303, 316, 329, 342, 353, 421, 432, 462, 511, 531, 552, 574, 614, 680; Land Tax List 1799-1816]. Robert **Scott** was his security when Isaac Younghusband sued him in Henrico County court for a 2 pound, 17 shilling debt on 5 May 1790. He was sued by Andrew **Scott** on 6 December 1790 [Orders 1789-91, 288, 417, 430]. He purchased "a Negro woman named Aggy" who was probably his wife from James Shepherd of Richmond City on 18 December 1797 and emancipated her three days later by Henrico County deed [DB 5:383]. He was head of a Henrico County household of 10 "other free" and 2 slaves in 1810 [VA:999]. He may have been the father of Harry Evans who was head of a Henrico County household of 2 "other free" and a slave in 1810 [VA:979].

ii.   Charles[3], born say 1750, a "Mulatto man" taken up in Spotsylvania County together with two slaves on suspicion of stealing and killing a cow. He pled guilty on 17 August 1775 and chose to receive thirty-nine lashes rather than be sent for further trial [Orders 1774-82, 38].

iii. Britton, born about 1768, registered in Petersburg on 25 August 1796: *a brown Mulatto man, five feet five inches high, short bushy hair, twenty eight years old, born free & raised by Mr. Rowlet in Chesterfield County* [Register of Free Negroes 1794-1819, no. 114]. He was a "Mulatto" taxable in Mecklenburg County from 1813 to 1815, listed with Reuben and Jordan Evans [PPTL, 1782-1805, frames 337, 505].

iv. Charles, a "FN" taxable in the upper district of Henrico County from 1806 to 1809: in the same list as "FN" John **Epps** from 1807 to 1809 [PPTL 1782-1814, frames 485, 531, 593, 661].

Northumberland County
1. Mark Evans, born say 1747, was head of a Northumberland County household of 8 "Black" persons in 1782 [VA:37], head of a household with no whites in 1784 [VA:75], and was taxable on 2 tithes, 2 horses, and 7 cattle in 1787 [Schreiner-Yantis, *1787 Census*, 1264]. He was a "free negro" head of a Fairfax County household of 7 "other free" in 1810 [VA:253]. He and his wife Leanna were the parents of

   i. ?John, born say 1771, married Fannah **Sorrell**, 23 November 1792 Northumberland County bond, Thomas Pollard security. John was listed in "A List of Free Mulattoes & Negroes in Westmoreland County" in 1801 with his wife Judy Evins and Rockey **Tate**, a child [*Virginia Genealogist* 31:47]. He was head of a Westmoreland County household of 5 "other free" in 1810 [VA:772].

   ii. Salley Evens, born 27 August 1774, "Daughter of Mark & Leanna his wife [Fleet, *Northumberland County Record of Births*, 43]. She married Frank **Bee**, 21 February 1798 Westmoreland County bond, William Corbell security.

   iii. James, born 27 October 1778, "son to Mark Evins" [Fleet, *Northumberland County Record of Births*, 43].

   iv. ?Patty, married Lewis **Boyd**, 9 February 1802 Northumberland County bond, John Evans security.

   v. ?Fanny, married Moses **Blundon**, Spencer **Thomas** security. Moses registered as a free Negro in Northumberland County on 14 September 1807: *Moses, Mulatto, about 27 years old, 5 feet 11 Inches high, Emancipated by the will of John Blundon, recorded in North^d District court* [Register # 32, Northumberland County Courthouse]. He was called Moses **Blundel** in 1810, a "free mulatto" head of a Northumberland County household of 6 "other free" [VA:973].

   vi. ?Thornton, "mulatto," born say 1797, married Rebecca **Hudnall**, "mulatto," 27 December 1814 Northumberland County bond, Joseph Peters security.

   vii. ?Elizabeth, born say 1798, married Jesse **Spriddle**, 11 November 1818 Northumberland County bond, Moses **Blundon** security.

King George County, Virginia
1. Elizabeth Evans, born say 1706, was living in St. Paul's Parish, King George County, in 1733 when the births and baptisms of her "free Molatto" children were recorded [St. Paul's Parish Register, 54, 57, 70, 78, 86]. Her children were

   i. ?Mary, born say 1724, ordered by the King George County court on 3 June 1743 to serve John Tyler for two years over and above her convicted time for having two "Molatto Bastards" [Orders 1735-51, pt.1, 338].

   ii. Virgin, a free Molatto born 3 September, baptized 26 September (no year stated).

      iii. Katherine, born 12 April 1730.

2   iv. Jemima[1], born 2 May, baptized 1 June 1733, "a Molatto Daughter of Elizabeth Evans."

      v. Lawrence, born 18 November 1736.

      vi. Bathsheba, born 29 September, baptized 19 November 1738.

     vii. Evans, born 6 August, baptized 21 September 1740.

    viii. Bethia, born 25 May, baptized 17 July 1742.

     ix. Lettice, born 25 January 1744.

      x. Barbara, born 19 December 1745.

2. Jemima[1] Evans, born 2 May, baptized 1 June 1733, was "a Molatto Daughter of Elizabeth Evans." She was the mother of

      i. ?Thomas, born about 1766, registered in King George County on 30 March 1805: *aged about thirty nine years, five feet seven inches high, with bushy curled hair, dark complexion, tolerably well set...born in the...County of King George of a free woman* [Register of Free Persons 1785-1799, no.40].

3   ii. Rachel, born about 1772.

3. Rachel Evans, born about 1772, registered in King George County on 4 December 1817: *a dark mulatto woman about forty five years of age about four feet eleven inches and a half high, stout made...born of Mima Evans a free woman in this County* [Register, no.50]. She was the mother of

      i. Jemima[2]/ Mima, born about 1802, registered in King George County on 4 December 1817: *a dark Coloured Girl about fifteen years of age, about five feet and an half Inches high...born of Rachel Evans* [Register, no.51].

Other members of the family in King George County were

      i. Moses, born about 1786, registered in King George County on 3 December 1807: *a dark mulatto man aged about twenty one or twenty two years, stout made, five feet six and a quarter inches high, was born of a free woman in King George County* [Register, no.43].

     ii. John, born about 1787, registered in King George County on 5 February 1812: *a dark mulatto man, a resident of King George County, aged about twenty five years & three months, five feet five and a quarter Inches high...was born free* [Register, no.45].

FAGAN FAMILY

Members of the Fagan family, born about 1750 were

1   i. Peter[1], born say 1740.

     ii. William, born say 1746, a taxable head of a Bertie County, North Carolina household with his unnamed wife in the list of Samuel Granberry for 1774.

1. Peter[1] Fagan, born say 1740, was called "a Negro man late the slave of Frederick Parker" in Sussex County court on 19 September 1765 when he recorded an order of confirmation of his freedom from the Halifax County, North Carolina court [Sussex County Orders 1764-66, 301]. He was called "A Free Negro...a Dancing Master living in Halifax (North Carolina) or Southampton County, Virginia" when a British merchant made a claim for a debt Peter had owed him since 1776 [*NCGSJ* XI:247]. In 1787 he was paid by the Southampton County estate of Lucy Hunt for teaching Charles and Henry Briggs to dance [WB 2:212]. He brought a Greensville County suit against the executor of Daniel Fisher for 25 pounds currency on 23 March 1797 and against the executors of David Putney on 22 March 1798 [Orders 1790-9, 474, 528; 1799-1806, 400], and on 9 February 1801 he was paid 3 pounds by the

Greensville County estate of James Epps for teaching his daughter Polly Epps to dance during the year 1800 [WB 1:475]. He was taxable on a horse in St. Luke's Parish, Southampton County, from 1801 to 1811 [PPTL 1792-1806, frames 514, 552, 621, 691, 805, 841; 1807-21, frames 71, 163, 191]. His deed of emancipation to a member of his family was proved in Southampton County court on 15 November 1802. He sued a number of people for debt in Southampton County between 1793 and 1805. He won a Southampton County case against John Wright for failing to pay the dancing school fees for his two daughters. Wright brought a suit in chancery against Peter in August 1805 claiming that Peter had moved away and neglected the school, but Peter replied that the school was kept by his son Peter, Jr., who was equally qualified [Minutes 1793-99, 33; 1799-1803, 195; 1804-7, 82, 83; LVA chancery case 1814-003]. On 13 June 1808 the Greensville County court awarded him 21 pounds in his suit against Andrew Rhea [Orders 1806-10, 237]. He was head of a Petersburg Town household of 5 "other free" in 1810, and there was another who was head of a Petersburg household of 1 "other free" and 2 slaves [VA:126b, 125b]. Peter was the ancestor of

   i.   Peter^2, Jr., born about 1767, taxable in Cabin Point district of Surry County, Virginia, from 1791 to 1805: called Peter Phaygan, Junr., in 1791 when he was listed with Anne, "a slave now his wife;" taxable on Major **Debrix**'s tithe in 1792; taxable on a slave named Sarah in 1794; taxable on a slave and a two-wheeled carriage in 1796; taxable on 2 slaves in 1797; taxable on Tom **French**'s tithe, slaves Sarah and Cupid, and a carriage in 1798 and 1799 [PPTL, 1791-1816, frames 15, 65, 115, 166, 242, 292, 330, 371, 410, 485, 563, 593]. He was taxable on 60 acres in 1799 [1799 Land Tax List, p.7]. Anna registered in Surry County on 8 April 1807: *Anna alias Anna Fagan a Mulatto woman, who was emancipated by Benjamin Drew by his deed (of emancipation) bearing date the 20th day of December 1792 and carried to record in the County Court of Southampton the 10th January 1793 as appears by an attested copy of said deed...The said Anna is of a bright complexion, long but bushey Hair, small Eye-brows, 5'4" high rather delicately made, aged about 21 years* [Back of Guardian Accounts Book 1783-1804, no. 65]. And she registered in Petersburg on 9 June 1810: *a bright yellow brown Mulatto woman, five feet three and a half inches high, twenty five years old, long bushy hair, delicately made, emancipated by Benjamin Drew in Southampton County* [Register of Free Negroes 1794-1819, no. 584]. Peter registered in Southampton County on 14 July 1804: *age 37, blk, 5 feet 5 inches, emancipated by Peter Fagan, Sr.* [Register of Free Negroes 1794-1832, nos. 311, 412]. He was head of a Southampton County household of 2 "other free" in 1810. Ann Fagan was head of a Petersburg Town household of 3 "other free" in 1810 [VA:334b].

   ii. ?Thomas, a "Mulatto" taxable in Mecklenburg County from 1809 to 1818 [PPTL 1806-28, frames 134, 162, 235, 338, 388, 595, 654].

   iii. ?John, head of a Mecklenburg County household of 4 "free colored" in 1820.

   iv. ?Peter^3, born say 1786, taxable in Meherrin Parish, Brunswick County, Virginia, from 1804 to 1813, listed as a "Free Negro" from 1811 to 1813 [PPTL 1799-1815, frames 240, 343, 388, 433, 519, 559], head of a Free Town, Brunswick County, Virginia household of 1 "other free" in 1810 [VA:769].

FAGGOT FAMILY

1.   Mary Faggot, born say 1720, was living in Prince Edward County in May 1757 when the court ordered George Ewing, Sr., to appear in court to prove that he was holding (her son) Jethro Faggott, a "Molatto boy," under legal

indentures. In October 1757 the court ruled that the indentures were not legal and ordered Mary to pay her witness Charles Irby 103 pounds of tobacco for testifying for her and travelling twenty-six miles from his home (in Amelia County). The court also ordered the churchwardens of St. Patrick's Parish to bind Jethro to Ewing on condition that he post a bond of 300 pounds currency not to remove him out of the colony [Orders 1754-8, 112, 127, 129]. Mary may have been identical to Mary Taggat, a white woman, whose "Molatto" son Peter was bound out by the churchwardens of Lunenburg County to Hugh Lawson on 9 July 1752 [Lunenburg County Orders 1752-3, 69]. Mary Faggot was the mother of

    i.   ?Agnes, born say 1739, called "Agnes Foquett, a "Mulatto," in Rowan County, North Carolina, on 25 October 1760 when she successfully sued Hugh Lawson for her freedom [Minutes 1753-67, 76, 78]. She married Isaac **Freeman** 19 January 1762 Rowan County bond.

    ii.   Peter, born say 1750, bound to Hugh Lawson in Lunenburg County on 9 July 1752.

    iii.   Jethro, born say 1753, a "Malatto" boy bound to George Ewing of Prince Edward County in October 1757.

FARRAR/ FARROW FAMILY

Members of the Farrar family born about 1750 were

1   i.   Amy, born say 1746.

2   ii.   Drury[1], born say 1748.

    iii.   Joseph, born say 1750, married Mally **Gantlet**, "Molattoes in Goochland," on 23 September 1773.

    iv.   Molly[1], born say 1752, married Stephen **Scott**, "Molattoes," on 10 November 1773 [Jones, *The Douglas Register*, 347].

    v.   Amy, born say 1754.

    vi.   John[1], born say 1760, a "yellow" complexioned soldier who enlisted in the Revolution from Goochland County (called John Farrow) [NSDAR, *African American Patriots*, 149]. John Farrar was a "Mulatto" taxable in Powhatan County from 1788 to 1792 [PPTL, 1787-1825, frames 18, 32, 46, 60, 77].

    vii.   Benjamin, born say 1763, married Elizabeth **Cockrane**, 10 March 1784 Goochland County bond, Mary **Cockrane** surety, Fleming Payne witness. Benjamin Farrow was a "Free Negro" taxable in the northern district of Campbell County from 1800 to 1805 [PPTL, 1785-1814, frames 484, 544, 622].

    viii.   Lucy Farrow, a "FN" listed in Botetourt County in 1813 [PPTL, 1811-1822].

1.   Amy Farrow, born say 1746, was taxable in Fredericksville Parish, Albemarle County, from 1783 to 1797: taxable on 2 horses and 5 cattle in 1783; a free male tithable, 3 horses and 8 cattle in 1786, 1787 and 1789; taxable on 2 free males and 3 horses in 1790 and 1794 [PPTL, 1782-1799, frames 29, 75, 116, 201, 418, 480, 515]. She may have been the mother of

3   i.   Thomas, born say 1770.

    ii.   Molly[2], born say 1772, taxable on a horse in Fredericksville Parish, Albemarle County, in 1794 [PPTL, 1782-1799, frame 418].

    iii.   Reuben, born say 1776, taxable in Fredericksville Parish, Albemarle County, in 1794, 1795, 1798, and from 1801 to 1813: listed with 2 horses in 1801; called "or gardner" in 1805; called a "Mulatto" from 1810 to 1813 [PPTL, 1782-99, frames 418, 448, 554, 590; 1800-1813, frames 72, 118, 250, 296, 387, 434, 566]. He was called Reuben Farrar when he sued Minan Mills in Albemarle County court on 5 May 1797 for trespass, assault and battery. Mills pleaded not guilty and said the beating, if any there was, proceeded from an assault by the plaintiff. The jury found for Reuben and awarded him a penny [Orders 1795-8, 316, 355].

2. Drury[1] Ferrar, born say 1748, married "_____, Mulattoes both of Maniken Town," on 27 October 1769 [Jones, *The Douglas Register*, 347]. He was living in Cumberland County, Virginia, in November 1774 when he was presented for failing to list himself as a tithable but discharged (along with forty-two other persons) on 24 March 1778 for reasons appearing to the court [Orders 1774-8, 300, 441]. He was taxable on 3 horses and 7 cattle in Albemarle County in 1783, called "Drury Farrow free negroe" when he was taxable on his son Daniel in St. Ann's Parish, Albemarle County, in 1802 [PPTL, 1782-99, 29; 1800-1813, frame 96], a "M"(ulatto) taxable in Buckingham County in 1804 [PPTL 1804-9], and a "Free N." taxable in the northern district of Campbell County from 1805 to 1813: called "Sr." in 1809, listed with 2 free males and 4 free persons of color in 1813 [PPTL, 1785-1814, frames 622, 695, 730, 767, 803, 853]. He was the father of

    i. ?Drury[2], born say 1771, married Elizabeth **Banks**, "daughter of Jacob Banks," 2 December 1792 Goochland County bond, 3 December marriage by Rev. Lewis Chaudoin. He was taxable on 2 horses taxable in the upper district of Goochland County from 1790 to 1792 [PPTL, 1782-1809, frame 236, 280, 295]. He was taxable in Fluvanna County on his own tithe and a 16-21 year-old tithable in 1793 [PPTL 1782-1826, frame 154]. He was a "F.N." taxable in the northern district of Campbell County in 1809 [PPTL, 1785-1814, frame 730]. He may have been identical to Drury Farrow who was a "F.B." head of a Bedford County household of 6 "other free" in 1810 [VA:461] and a "Negr." taxable there on 2 persons in 1813 [PPTL, 1785-1814].

    ii. ?James, born about 1780, registered in Campbell County on 23 October 1834: *Age: 54; 5 feet 8 Inches, bright Complexion, Born free.* And his wife Charity Farrar, born about 1780, registered with him on the same day: *Age: 54; 5 feet 2-1/2 Inches, bright Complexion, Born free* [A Register of Free Negroes and Malattoes, p. 10]. He was called James Farrow in 1813 when he was a "free Negro" taxable on a female free person of color in Campbell County [PPTL, 1785-1814].

    iii. Betsy, born say 1781, head of a Nelson County household of 3 "other free" in 1810 [VA:691], perhaps the Betsy Farrar who was counted in a "List of free Negroes & Mulattoes" in St. Ann's Parish, Albemarle County, in 1813 [PPTL, 1800-1813, frame 553]. She was married to Benjamin **Whitesides** on 21 November 1831 when their daughter Judith Farrar, registered in Amherst County: *daughter of Benjamin and Betty Whitesides of dark complexion 5 feet 5 inches high about 34 years of age* [Register #50]. Benjamin **Whitesides** was head of an Amherst County household of 4 "other free" in 1810 [VA:297].

    iv. Daniel, born about 1791, registered in Campbell County on 29 October 1831: *Age: 40; 5 feet 10 Inches, Yellow Complexion, born free* [Register of Free Negroes, 1801-50, p. 9].

    v. Moses, a "Negr." taxable in Bedford County in 1813 [PPTL, 1785-1814].

    vi. Mary, head of a Nelson County household of 2 "other free" in 1810 [VA:691].

3. Thomas Farrow, born say 1770, was taxable in Fredericksville Parish, Albemarle County, in 1799, 1802, 1804, and from 1805 to 1810: taxable on 2 horses in 1799; called a "Mulatto" from 1805 to 1810 [PPTL, 1782-1799, frames 589; 1800-1813, frames 27, 117, 207, 250, 296, 343, 386]. He may have been identical to Thomas Farrar who was a "M"(ulatto) taxable in adjoining Buckingham County on a tithe and 2 horses in 1804 and taxable on a tithe in 1807 [PPTL 1804-9]. He and his wife Charity Farrer were living in

Campbell County on 1 November 1830 when their son John Pierce registered as a "free Negro." Thomas and Charity were the parents of

    i. ?John[2], born about 1797, registered in Campbell County on 3 October 1830: *Age: 34; 5 Feet 7 Inches; Colour: Yellow; born free* [Register p. 10].

    ii. ?Wilson, born about 1799, registered in Campbell County on 16 June 1831: *Age 32; 6 feet; Yellow Complexion, born free* [Register, p. 9].

    iii. John Pierce, born about 1801, registered in Campbell County on 1 November 1830: *Age: 29; 6 Feet 2-1/2 Inches, Bright Mallattoe, Born free and a son of Thomas and Charrity Farrer* [Register, p. 9].

    iv. ?Elijah, born about 1804, registered in Campbell County in November 1836: *Age: 32; 5 ft 7-1/2 in.; Bright complexion, Born free* [Register, p. 15].

FARTHING FAMILY

1. Ann Farthing, born say 1718, was living in Saint Paul's Parish, Kent County, Maryland, on 19 June 1739 when the court convicted her of having a "Mollatto" child by a "Negro" [Criminal Record 1738-9, 178-180]. She was probably the ancestor of

    i. Ann, head of a Kent County, Maryland household of 4 "other free" in 1810 [MD:844].

    ii. Henrietta, a "mulatto" child living in Fairfax County, Virginia, on 17 February 1761 when the court ordered the churchwardens of Truro Parish to bind her as an apprentice to James McKensy [Orders 1756-63, 553].

FARRELL/ FERRELL FAMILY

1. Mary Farrell, born say 1670, was the servant of Arthur Robins on 21 June 1687 when the Accomack County court ordered that she receive twenty-five lashes for having a bastard child. She was the servant of William Bradford on 18 February 1690/1 when she confessed to the Accomack County court that she had an illegitimate child named Thomas Farrell who was begotten by "Spindolz, Negro Slave to ye Said Bradford." On 15 September 1691 she bound her son Thomas to William Bradford until the age of twenty-four years. On 21 March 1693 she won a suit against her master, Richard Bally, for her freedom dues stating that she had served Arthur Robins and William Bradford before completing her indenture with Bally. The court found in her favor [W&Co 1682-97, 115; Orders 1690-7, 20a, 38, 99]. She was the mother of

2   i. Thomas[1], born 1690-1691.

2. Thomas[1] Ferrell, born before 18 February 1690/1, was a "Mulatto" who petitioned the Accomack County court on 6 July 1715 for release from his indenture to William Bradford. He testified that he had completed twenty-four years of service as stipulated in his indenture, and the court ordered that he be released after verifying his age from the register of births [Orders 1714-7, 10]. However, he was still a servant on 14 December 1722 when he petitioned the Northampton County, Virginia court stating that he was born of a white woman and had completed thirty-one years of service. On 13 March 1722/3 the court allowed him three days liberty to get his indenture, and on 9 April 1723 the case was dismissed on agreement of the parties [Orders 1722-9, 41, 45, 55, 60; Mihalyka, *Loose Papers I:*52]. Thomas was taxable in the Northampton County household of Thomas Marshall from 1723 to 1725 and was head of his own household with (his wife?) Ann Ferrell in 1726 and 1727. Ann was taxable by herself in 1728 and 1729 in Jacob Stringer's household [Bell, *Northampton County Tithables*, 43, 60, 85, 109, 122, 171]. Ann was the mother of

    i.   Peter, bound to John Lowry with the consent of his mother Ann Ferrell on 15 May 1728 [Orders 1722-9, 327].

    ii. Thomas[2], bound to John Lowry with the consent of hie mother Ann Ferrell on 15 May 1728 [Orders 1722-9, 327].

    iii. Moses, born in August 1730, bound to Abraham Collins with the consent of his mother Ann Ferril on 8 June 1736 [Orders 1732-42, 218].

    iv. Sisley, born in the Spring of 1734, bound apprentice to Savage Bloxam with the consent of her mother Ann Ferrill on 10 February 1735/6 [Orders 1732-42, 197].

Other members of the Ferrell family were

    i.   Adam Farrell, head of a Baltimore City, Maryland household of 7 "other free" in 1800 [MD:202].

    ii. Charity, head of a Beaufort County, South Carolina household of 4 "other free" in 1800 [SC:88].

    iii. John, head of a Colleton District, South Carolina household of 6 "other free" in 1810 [SC:603].

    iv. Watson, head of a Colleton District, South Carolina household of 5 "other free" in 1810 [SC:603].

    v.   William, head of a Colleton District, South Carolina household of 5 "other free" in 1810 [SC:603].

FIELDING FAMILY

1. Eleanor Fielding, born say 1732, was the mother of William Fielding, a "Mulatto" boy bound out by order of the York County court on 18 June 1753. She was the mother of

    i.   William, born say 1752, the "Mulatto" son of Eleanor Fielding bound to Rev. John Camm of Yorkhampton Parish by order of the York County court on 18 June 1753 [Judgments & Orders 1752-4, 232].

FIELDS FAMILY

Members of the Fields family were

1   i.   Joyce, born say 1747.
2   ii. John[1], born say 1753.
3   iii. Sarah, born say 1770.
4   iv. John[2], born say 1775.

1. Joyce Fields, born say 1747, was living in Amherst County on 7 September 1767 when the court bound her "Molatto" child Mink to Henry Bell. In July 1784 she complained to the court that Bell had sold his apprentice named Moses Thomas, but the court dismissed the case after a hearing [Orders 1766-9, 200; 1782-4, 344]. Joyce was head of an Amherst County household of 8 "whites" (free persons) in 1783 [VA:48]. She was the mother of

    i.   Mink, born say 1767.

2. John[1] Fields, born say 1753, was a "Mulatto" taxable in Buckingham County in 1774 [Woodson, *Virginia Tithables From Burned Counties*, 39]. He was a "free person of color" from Charles City County who enlisted in the Revolution in Amherst County [Register at Chesterfield Courthouse, cited by NSDAR, *African American Patriots*, 149]. On 5 October 1785 the Amherst County court ordered the overseers of the poor to bind out his "Molatto" child Joice Fields [Orders 1787-90, 538]. He was head of a Buckingham County household of 4 "other free" in 1810 [VA:806] and was a taxable "man of color" in Amherst County in 1811 and 1812 [PPTL 1804-23, frames 211, 233]. He was the father of

    i.   ?John[3], born say 1776, a "melatto" taxable in the northern district of Campbell County from 1792 to 1813 [PPTL, 1785-1814, frames 231, 268, 302, 730, 696, 892].

    ii.   ?David, born about 1781, taxable in Campbell County from 1800 to 1813 [PPTL, 1785-1814, frames 484, 730, 696, 892], head of a Campbell County household of 2 "other free" in 1810 [VA:849]. He registered in Campbell County on 11 October 1831: *age 50, 5 feet 9 inches, dark Complexion, born free and formerly bound to John McCallister* [Register of Free Negroes and Mulattoes, p.9].

    iii.   Joyce[2], born say 1785.

3.   Sarah Fields, born say 1770, was head of a Buckingham County household of 19 "other free" in 1810 [VA:799]. She was the mother of

    i.   Miles, born about 1807, registered in Campbell County on 11 October 1831: *age 24, 5 feet 10 inches, dark complexion, born free, straight hair & bushy, and a son of Sarah Fields* [Register of Free Negroes and Mulattoes, p.9].

    ii.   Rixey, born about 1811, registered in Campbell County on 11 October 1831: *age 20, 5 feet 7 inches, light complexion, born free, straight hair, daughter of Sarah* [Register of Free Negroes and Mulattoes, p.9].

    iii.   Sarah, Jr., born about 1814, registered in Campbell County on 11 October 1831: *age 17, 5 feet 7 inches, Bright complexion, daughter of Sarah* [Register of Free Negroes and Mulattoes, p.9].

4.   John[2] Fields, born say 1775, was head of a New Kent County household of 4 "other free" in 1810 [VA:752]. In 1802 he received 9 pounds as his wife's part of the Charles City County estate of her father Edward **Bradby** [WB 1:591, 601]. He was probably the father of

    i.   Edna, born about 1796, registered in Charles City County on 16 September 1824: *a bright mulatto woman, aged 28 years, born free in this county* [Minutes 1823-9, 77].

    ii.   Littleberry, born say 1805, married Elizabeth **Thomas** before 16 February 1826 when he received her legacy due from the Charles City County estate of her father William **Thomas** [WB 3:158]. She obtained a certificate of freedom in Charles City County on 17 November 1831: *(testimony of Peter Crew) wife of Littleberry Fields who was Elizabeth Thomas, bright mulatto, was twenty three years old 23 March last* [Minutes 1830-7, 84].

Other members of the Fields family were

    i.   Betty, head of a Buckingham County household of 10 "other free" in 1810 [VA:799].

    ii.   Thomas, "F. Mo." head of a Culpeper County household of 7 "other free" in 1810 [VA:31].

    iii.   Nancy, "m." head of a Buckingham County household of 7 "other free" in 1810 [VA:806].

    iv.   William, head of a Washington, D.C. household of 4 "other free" in 1800.

    v.   Adam, born before 1776, head of Rockingham County, North Carolina household of 6 "free colored" in 1820 [NC:641].

FINDLEY FAMILY

1.   James, born about 1704, and Chance, born about 1706, were the Indian slaves of Henry Clay who had their ages adjudged in Henrico County court in August 1712:

*James an Indian belonging to Henry Clay is judged to be Eight years of Age
& Chance a Girle also belonging to him is adjudged to be six years of Age*
[Orders 1710-4, 161].

Henry Clay left a 8 March 1749 Chesterfield County will dividing his slaves
among his children William, Henry, Charles and John Clay. John Clay's
inventory was returned to Chesterfield County court on 19 August 1763:

> *one Negro Bowser, one Negro Peter, one Indian Peter, one Mulato James,
> one Mulato Sam, Negro Combo, Mulato woman Nann, Indian woman Jude,
> Indian girl Chance, Mulato girl Anica, Mulato Boy Frank* [WB 1:344;
> Orders 1759-67, 459].

The division of his slaves was recorded on 7 February 1772 [Orders 1771-4,
63]. About two months later on 29 April 1772 depositions were taken in
Chesterfield County at the direction of the General Court in the suit of Ned,
Lucy, Silvia, Bristol, Chance, Ned, Frank, Peter, Sam, Rachel and her
children against Charles Clay, Millie Clay, Thomas Clay and Richard Newman
for holding them in slavery. Henry Clay's eighty-five-year-old widow Mary
Clay, Clay's seventy-three-year-old neighbor Bartholomew Stovall, Clay's
eighty-five-year-old neighbor Elizabeth Blankenship and thirty-year-old
grandson John Clay testified that Henry Clay had brought home two Choctaw
Indians, one a boy and the other a girl named Chance, from a trip beyond
Carolina in 1712 and that the plaintiffs Ned, Peter, Sam and Rachel were
Chance's grandchildren. The plaintiffs Chance and Frank were apparently
identical to "Indian Chance and Frank," children of Jude, who were bound out
by the churchwardens of Manchester Parish in Chesterfield County on 2 July
1773 [Orders 1771-4, 294]. In November 1785 Hannah Fender/ Fendley
brought a Henry County suit for her freedom which relied on the Chesterfield
County depositions as well a deposition taken in Powhatan County in 1786
which stated that she was the grandchild of James and Chance [Fender vs.
Marr, Henry Co. Va. Loose papers, Determined Cases 1788-1789, folder 66,
LVA, published in the *Virginia Genealogist*]. Chance was the ancestor of

    i.   Judy[1], born say 1730, an Indian slave listed in the inventory of John
        Clay's Chesterfield County estate on 19 August 1763 [WB 1:344;
        Orders 1759-67, 459]. She was free by 2 July 1773 when the
        Chesterfield County court ordered the churchwardens of Manchester
        Parish to bind out her Indian children Chance and Frank [Orders 1771-
        4, 294].

2   ii. Hannah, born say 1745.

   iii. Samuel Findley, born say 1750, guardian of Phoebe **Ligon** on 10 May
        1788 when he gave his consent to her Henrico County marriage to
        Thomas Findley. He was taxable in Chesterfield County in 1792, 1795,
        and a "free Negroe" taxable in 1802 [PPTL, 1786-1811, frames 140,
        248]. He died before 16 January 1802 when a coroner's inquest
        reported to the Chesterfield County court that he had been found dead
        at Manchester Warehouse with no marks of violence on his body [WB
        5:492].

   iv. Rachel Findley, born about 1750, registered in Powhatan County on 17
        August 1820: *Age: 70; Color: Brown; Stature: 5'5"; Recovered her
        freedom in the Superior Court of Powhatan County May 1820* [Register
        of Free Negroes, no. 10].

   v. James Findley, born about 1759, registered in Powhatan County on 19
        December 1822: *Age: 63; Color: Dark yellowish; Stature: 5'10";
        Emancipated by order of Powhatan Court 18 August 1786* [Register of
        Free Negroes, no. 54]. He was a M°" taxable on a horse in Powhatan
        County from 1792 to 1800 [PPTL, 1787-1825, frames 77, 92, 184,
        206].

3   vi.   Thomas, born say 1765.
      vii.   Effey Findley, born about 1784, obtained a certificate of freedom in
             Chesterfield County on 11 October 1819: *thirty five years old, dark*
             complexion, born free [Register of Free Negroes 1804-53, no. 364].
      viii. Fanny Findley, born about 1788, head of a Chesterfield County
             household of 1 "other free" in 1810 [VA:70/1062]. She registered as
             a free Negro in Botetourt County on 13 June 1823: *35 years of age;*
             Brown colour; born free as per Certificate from Court Powhatan
             County [Free Negroes &c Registered in the Clerk's Office of Botetourt
             County, no. 38].

2.   Hannah Fender/ Fendley, born say 1745, "suppose to be an Igeon," sued John
       Marr, Esquire, for her freedom in Henry County court on 25 November 1785.
       The court allowed her to take the depositions of Lucy Marshall, Thomas Clay
       and Samuel Clay on her posting security for her return. On 13 August 1788
       the court found in her favor and awarded her 40 shillings damages. Marr
       appealed to the General Court, but on 31 March 1789 he reached agreement
       with Hannah that he would not prosecute his appeal, would pay all costs, and
       that he would immediately free her children Sally, Judy, Prudence and Ned
       and free her other children Jeany, Alias, Peter, Patty, and Billy when they
       came of age, the boys at twenty-one and the girls at eighteen [Orders 1785-8,
       62, 96, 279, 281]. Hannah was taxable on a horse in Patrick County in 1804
       [PPTL, 1791-1823, frame 396]. On 29 October 1807 the Patrick County court
       bound to her (her granddaughter?) three-year-old Ruth Findley, child of
       Susannah Findley [Orders 1800-10, n.p.]. She was the mother of
      i.   Sally, married Nicholas **Rickman**, 28 March 1799 Stokes County,
             North Carolina bond.
      ii.   Judy[2].
      iii.   Prudence.
      iv.   Ned.
      v.   Jeany.
      vi.   Alias, married Polly **Gowen**, 1802 Grayson County bond.
      vii.   Peter, born say 1770, married Rebecca **Gowens**, 28 September 1797
             Patrick County bond, John Cameron security.[95] He purchased land in
             Patrick County in 1805 and sold it in 1810 [DB 2:475; 3:354]. He was
             taxable in Patrick County from 1800 to 1804 [PPTL, 1791-1823,
             frames 286, 342, 395] and head of a Grayson County, Virginia
             household of 7 "free colored" in 1830.
      viii. Patty.
      ix.   William, married Susannah **Rickman**, 1802 Patrick County bond, John
             Going surety. Suckey registered in Patrick County in June 1832: *aged*
             about 45 or 50 years, of dark complexion...with black eyes and
             somewhat a round face and 5 feet 3 inches and 3 quarters high...Free
             born in the County of Patrick [Pilson and Baughan, *Alphabetical List*
             of Lands Taxed in Patrick County, 11].

3.   Thomas Findley, born say 1765, married Phoebe **Ligon**, 10 May 1788 Henrico
       County bond, Hannah **Liggon**, Jerry **Liggon**, and William **Logon** witnesses.
       Samuel **Findley**, guardian of Phobe, gave his consent. He was taxable in
       Chesterfield County in 1792, 1801, a "free Negroe" taxable in 1802 and 1804,
       a "Mulatto" taxable in 1805, 1806, 1807 and 1809 [PPTL, 1786-1811, frames
       140, 467, 503, 579, 658, 717, 753]. He was a "Mullatto" taxable in
       Chesterfield County from 1800 to 1813 on a lot he purchased in 1800 [Land
       Tax List, 1791-1822, B lists]. He was head of a Chesterfield County

---

[95]John Cameron appeared in Patrick County court on 27 December 1804 and emancipated his slave
Ceasar who was to be called Ceasar Fendly [Orders 1800-10, n.p.].

household of one "other free" in 1810 [VA:70/1062]. He may have been the father of

   i. Betsey, born about 1796, obtained a certificate of freedom in Chesterfield County on 14 July 1823: *twenty seven years old, light brown complexion, born free* [Register of Free Negroes 1804-53, no. 490].

   ii. Washington, born about 1803, obtained a certificate of freedom in Chesterfield County on 10 September 1827: *twenty four years old, brown complexion, born free* [Register of Free Negroes 1804-53, no. 591].

FINNIE FAMILY

1. Margaret Finnie, born say 1730, was living in Westmoreland County, Virginia, on 29 January 1750/1 when the court agreed to William Fitzhugh's motion that she be taken into custody by the sheriff because she was "Dealing with peoples Slaves & other ill Compy. in the Dead time of Night." The court ordered that her "Mulatto" son John be bound out as an apprentice by the churchwardens of Cople Parish [Orders 1750-2, 26-26a]. Her children were

   i. John, born say 1750.

   ii. ?Daniel, born say 1752, head of an Accomack County household of 7 "other free" in 1800 [*Virginia Genealogist* 1:107].

   iii. ?Abraham[1], born say 1755, head of an Accomack County household of 8 "other free" in 1810 [VA:94], perhaps the father of Abraham[2] Finnie, head of an Accomack County household of 5 "other free" in 1810 [VA:23].

   iv. ?Phillip, head of an Accomack County household of 6 "other free" in 1810 [VA:23].

FLETCHER FAMILY

1. Polly Fletcher, born say 1745, was an Irish servant who was indentured to Matthew Whiting, Esq., of Prince William County, Virginia. Whiting's executor, E. Brooke, Sr., certified in the court of the District of Columbia in Alexandria that Polly was the mother of Betsy, Mary, and Alice Fletcher, "Mulatto" women [Arlington County Register of Free Negroes, 1797-1861, nos. 57, 59, 61, 62, pp.51-3]. Her children were

2   i. ?Ann, born say 1764.

   ii. Betsy, born about 1775, registered in Alexandria on 2 May 1820: *a forty-five-year-old "bright Mulatto" woman born on the Prince William County estate of Matthew Whiting.*

   iii. Mary, born about 1780, registered in Alexandria on 8 December 1820: *a forty-year-old "bright Mulatto" woman born on the Prince William County estate of Matthew Whiting.*

   iv. Alice, born about 1795, registered in Alexandria on 2 May 1820: *a twenty-five-year-old "bright Mulatto" woman born on the Prince William County estate of Matthew Whiting.*

   v. ?Peter, head of an Accomack County household of 7 "other free" in 1810 [VA:94].

   vi. ?John, "F. Negroe" head of a Fauquier County household of 7 "other free" in 1810 [VA:398].

   vii. ?Cloe, head of a Petersburg Town household of 2 "other free" in 1810 [VA:125b].

2. Ann Fletcher, born say 1764, was head of a St. Mary's County, Maryland household of 3 "other free" in 1790. She may have been the mother of

   i. Jane, born about 1784, a thirty-seven-year-old "stout negro woman" who obtained a certificate of freedom in Alexandria, Virginia, on 6

August 1821 and registered in Washington, D.C., on 3 November 1834. Sarah Harper swore that Jane was born free in St. Mary's County and was bound to Sarah's mother Catherine Cheveller to serve until she came of age. Harper testified that she and Jane "grew up and were girls together" and that Jane's parents were free as were her several brothers and sisters [Provine, *District of Columbia Free Negro Registers*, 254].

FLOOD FAMILY

Members of the Flood family born before 1750 were

1   i.   Mary[1] born say 1725.
2   ii. Absalom, born say 1727.
     iii. John[1], born say 1730, head of an Amelia County household of 3 free persons in 1782 [VA:13]. He was taxable in Charlotte County on his own tithe and 3 horses in 1787, levy free from 1790 to 1804 when he was called a "fm" [PPTL 1782-1813, frames 94, 177, 205, 229, 253, 302, 383, 399, 448, 466, 517, 551, 606].
3   iv. Pat, born say 1738.

1.   Mary[1] Flood, born say 1725, was living in Henrico County on 3 September 1764 when the court ordered the churchwardens of Henrico Parish to bind out her "Mulatto" children: Fanny, Lucy, Dick, and Charles [Orders 1763-67, 328]. Her children were

4   i.   ?William[1], born say 1752.
5   ii. ?Mary[2], born say 1754.
     iii. Fanny, born say 1755.
     iv. Lucy, born say 1757.
     v.   Dick, born say 1760.
     vi. Charles, born say 1763, "Free Negro" head of an Isle of Wight County household of one "other free" in 1810 [VA:37].

2.   Absalom Flood, born say 1727, was taxed with his unnamed wife in the 1757 and 1758 tax summary for Bertie County, North Carolina [CR 10.702.1, box 1]. He was probably living in the part of Bertie which became Hertford County. Few Hertford County records have survived, but he is listed in the Sheriff's tax receipt book in 1768 and 1770, taxable on two tithes [Fouts, *Tax Receipt Book*, 8], and taxable in the 1779 Hertford Property Tax list filed with the state government, taxed on a horse in District 2 [GA 30.1]. There is no record of his children, but they may have been those counted in the census for Hertford and Halifax County, North Carolina:
     i.   Jesse, born say 1748, taxable in Hertford County on two tithes in 1770 [Fouts, *Tax Receipt Book*, 42], head of a Halifax County household of 6 "other free" in 1800 [NC:308] and 6 in 1810 [NC:19].
     ii. Ann/ Nanny, born say 1750, taxable on one tithe in Hertford County in 1768 [Fouts, *Tax Receipt Book*, 48].
     iii. Josiah, born say 1760, head of a Hertford County household of 11 "other free" in 1800. He was a labourer in a "List of Free Negroes and Mulattoes" on Western Branch in Norfolk in 1801, head of a household with W. **Turner** and Willoughby **Weaver** [PPTL, 1791-1812, frame 383].
     iv. Benjamin, born say 1762, living in Halifax County on 4 August 1789 when he deposed that he had served as an eighteen months soldier in the North Carolina Continental line and assigned all that was due to him for the service to John Eaton [*NCGSJ* IX:153]. He purchased 40 acres in Halifax County on the north side of Beech Swamp on 4 January 1792 [DB 17:503]. He married Lackey **Underdue**, 1790 Halifax County bond [CR 047.928.2]. He sold 640 acres in Davidson

County, Tennessee on the south side of the Cumberland River, a grant for his services in the Revolution, by Halifax County deed on 31 August 1801 [DB 18:806 & Franklin County DB 6:89]. He was head of a Halifax County household of 7 "other free" in 1800 [NC:308], 6 in 1810 [NC:19], and 7 "free colored" in 1820 [NC:148]. Lackey **Underdue** was probably the daughter of Dempsy **Underdew/Underdue** who purchased 85 acres in Halifax County joining Hunter on 15 September 1783 [DB 15:101]. He was counted as white in 1790, head of a Halifax County household of 1 male over 16, two under 16, and four females [NC:63]. He was a private in the Continental Line who assigned his right to 640 acres in Tennessee to Nicholas Long in Halifax County on 25 July 1795 [DB 17:810]. His widow may have been Polly **Underdew**, head of a Halifax County household of 5 "other free" in 1800 [NC:346], perhaps the Mary **Underwood** who was head of a Halifax County household of 4 "other free" in 1810 [NC:52]. They were probably related to Underdue **Austin**, head of a Halifax County household of 6 "other free" in 1810 [NC:3].

v. William[2], born say 1775, head of a Hertford County household of 3 "other free" in 1800, 2 in Halifax County in 1810 [NC:19] and 7 "free colored" in Halifax County in 1830.

vi. John[2], born before 1776, head of a Hertford County household of 4 "other free" in 1810 [NC:99] and 10 "free colored" in 1820 [NC:182]. John, Demsey, Jesse, and Samuel Flood were among "Sundry persons of Colour of Hertford County" who petitioned the General Assembly in 1822 to repeal the act which declared slaves to be competent witnesses against free African Americans [*NCGSJ* XI:252].

vii. James, born before 1776, head of a Hertford County household of 6 "free colored" in 1830.

viii. Lovet, born before 1776, head of a Halifax County household of 8 "free colored" in 1820 [NC:148] and 6 in 1830. He married Polly **Amis**, 2 March 1822 Halifax County bond.

ix. Demsey, born 1776-94, head of a Hertford County household of 4 "free colored" in 1820 [NC:190]. He married Kitty **Morgan**, 30 December 1819 Halifax County bond with Hansel **Dempsy** bondsman.

3. Pat Flood, born say 1738, was living in Raleigh Parish, Amelia County, on 26 November 1767 when the court ordered the churchwardens to bind out her children: Tom, Frederick, Stephen, and Sawney (no race indicated). She was called a "free Mulatto" on 26 October 1769 when the court ordered the churchwardens of Raleigh Parish to bind out her unnamed children [Orders 1767-8, 113; 1768-9, 265]. She was the mother of

i. Burwell, born about 1756, registered in Petersburg on 19 August 1794: *a brown Mulatto man, five feet seven and a half inches high, thirty eight years old, born free & raised in Mecklenburg County* [Register of Free Negroes 1794-1819, no. 49].

ii. Thomas, born about 1757, registered in Petersburg on 25 August 1794: *a dark brown Mulatto man, five feet eight inches high, thirty seven years old, born free & raised in Amelia County* [Register of Free Negroes 1794-1819, no. 87].

iii. Frederick.

iv. Stephen.

v. Alexander, born about 1765, taxable in Charlotte County, Virginia, from 1789 to 1799, called Sawney Flood in 1793 [PPTL 1782-1813, frames 159, 205, 179, 253, 277, 302, 328, 383, 448]. He married Levina **Lawrence**, 4 April 1792 Charlotte County bond. He registered as a "free Negro" in Charlotte County on 7 October 1806: *Mulatto complexion, aged 41, born free.* His wife Levina registered on 26 November 1806 with their children Coleman and Charity [Ailsworth,

Charlotte County--Rich Indeed, 485]. He registered again in Pittsylvania County using the Charlotte County registration papers, stating that he was born in Amelia County and his wife was born in Brunswick County.

4. William[1] Flood, born say 1752, a "Free Negro," was living on land in Amelia County near Rowling's Church when James Farley placed an advertisement in the 31 October 1777 issue of the *Virginia Gazette* cautioning the subscribers not to purchase William's land since Farley had already received part of the purchase price [*Virginia Gazette*, Dixon's edition, p.2, col. 2]. He married Molly Harris **Brogdon**, 12 November 1785 Mecklenburg County bond, William **Brogdon** consenting. He was taxable in Charlotte County, Virginia, from 1782 to 1805: taxable on a slave named Dick, 4 horses and 12 cattle in 1782, taxable on a horse and 6 cattle in 1785, taxable on 2 free males and a slave in 1789, taxable on a slave in 1794, 2 slaves in 1795, 2 horses in 1796 and 1800, called a "f. Mulattoe" in 1801, a shoemaker counted in a list of "free Negroes & Mulatters" from 1802 to 1805 with his wife Molly and children Betsey, Polly, Patsey, William and John. He apparently died about 1806 when Molly was taxable on a horse and listed with 2 male and 2 female children in her household. She was listed as a weaver with 2 males and 3 females in her household in 1811 and 1812, 2 males and 2 females in 1813 [PPTL 1782-1813, frames 10, 15, 52, 128, 191, 217, 242, 265, 290, 316, 340, 399, 434, 466, 503, 542, 580, 606, 648, 673, 682, 709, 717, 751, 806, 814, 886]. She was a "Free Negro" head of a Charlotte County household of 9 "other free" [VA:1010]. His children were

    i.   Betsey, "dau of William Flood who is surety," married Joshua **Gallimore**, 29 February 1803 Charlotte County bond.
    ii. Polly.
    iii. Patsey, married George **Gallimore**, 9 May 1813 Charlotte County bond, John Flood surety.
    iv. William[3], born about 1788, registered in Charlotte County on 28 December 1812: *son of William Flood, Mulatto complexion, aged 24, born free* [Ailsworth, *Charlotte County--Rich Indeed*, 485].
    v.   John[3].

5. Mary[2] Flood, born say 1754, was living in Chesterfield County on 2 July 1784 when the court ordered the churchwardens of Dale Parish to bind her daughter Nancy Flood to Abner Jackson [Orders 1774-84, 555]. She was the mother of

6   i.   ?Jenny, born about 1770.
    ii. Nancy, born about 1774, ordered bound apprentice to Abner Jackson in Dale Parish, Chesterfield County, on 2 July 1784 [Orders 1774-84, 555]. She registered in Petersburg on 15 August 1800: *a brown Mulatto woman, five feet and one half inches high, twenty six years old, thick bushy hair, born free in the County of Mecklenburg as appears by the affidavit of Thomas Drumwright* [Register of Free Negroes 1794-1819, no. 172].
    iii. Betsy, daughter of Mary Flood, bound apprentice to Edward Eanes by order of the Chesterfield County court on 2 July 1784 [Orders 1774-84, 555].
    iv. ?Edia, child of Mary **Banks**, bound apprentice to Edward Eanes, Jr., by order of the Chesterfield County court on 2 July 1784 [Orders 1774-84, 555].
    v.   Polly **Banks**, daughter of Mary Flood, bound apprentice to Edward Eanes by order of the Chesterfield County court on 2 July 1784 [Orders 1774-84, 555].

6. Jenny Flood, born about 1770, registered in Petersburg on 19 August 1794: *Jenny Floyd, a brown Mulatto woman, slender made, five feet four inches*

high, twenty four years old, born free & raised in Mecklenburg County. She registered again on 9 July 1805 as Jenny Flood [Register of Free Negroes 1794-1819, nos. 50, 305]. She may have been the mother of

    i. ?Mark, born about 1792, living in Mecklenburg County on 13 June 1796 when the court ordered the overseers of the poor to bind him to William Pulliam [Orders 1795-8, 94]. He received a certificate in Mecklenburg County, Virginia, on 10 December 1817: *a man of Colour, twenty five years of age, five feet five inches high, yellow complexion, Slender made...his front under teeth placed in two rows, was born free* [Free Person of Color, #17, p. 9].

    ii. ?Matthew, born say 1794, living in Mecklenburg County on 13 June 1796 when the court ordered the overseers of the poor to bind him (no race indicated) to William Pulliam [Orders 1795-8, 94]. He and Mark Flood were listed as "free Negroes and Mulattoes" in Mecklenburg County from 1813 to 1817 [PPTL, 1806-28, frames, 307, 419, 576].

FLORA FAMILY

1. Mary Floro, born say 1700, was the servant of Lewis Delony on 18 January 1718/9 when the York County court ordered that she serve him an additional year for having a bastard child [OW 15, pt. 2, 536]. She was probably the mother of

    i. Peter Flora, called "Peater Flura, ye Spanard," head of a Norfolk County household in the Southern Branch District near Batcheldor's Mill in 1753 and 1754 and taxable in Western Branch District in Alice Forrester's household in 1767 and 1768. He was taxable in his own household in 1769 and 1770 [Wingo, *Norfolk County Tithables, 1751-1765*, 55, 89; *1766-1780*, 14, 71, 87, 105]. The Norfolk County court declared him to be levy free on 21 June 1771 [Orders 1771-3, 6].

2   ii. Mary Flora, born say 1730.

2. Mary Flora, born say 1730, was the mother of a "free Negro" son bound apprentice to Joshua Gammon in Norfolk County in April 1763 [Orders 1763-5, 15]. Mary's child was

    i. William, born about 1755, bound to Joshua Gammon in Norfolk County in April 1763 [Orders 1763-5, 15]. He was taxable in Norfolk County in 1771 in the Edmond's Bridge District in John Fentress' household and in William Bressie's household in 1773 [Wingo, *Norfolk County Tithables, 1766-1780*, 128]. He was taxable in Portsmouth and Elizabeth River Parishes, Norfolk County, from 1782 to 1817: taxable on a slave and a horse in 1787; taxable on 6 horses from 1795 to 1799; taxable on 2 free males; a slave under 16, 5 horses and 4 carriage wheels in 1800; counted in a list of "free Negroes" as a pedlar living in Portsmouth with (wife?) Gracy Flora in 1801; taxable on 3 riding chairs and 6 horses in 1802, 8 horses from 1804 to 1806; a stage wagon, 6 chairs and 6 horses in 1807 [PPTL, 1782-91, frames 392, 485, 567, 613, 643, 682; 1791-1812, frames 22, 82, 138, 172, 248, 354, 383, 463, 560, 646, 689, 742; 1813-24, frames 101, 251]. He fought in the battle at Great Bridge, Norfolk County, in the Revolution, prying loose the last board in the bridge to prevent the British from attacking his retreating comrades [Jackson, *Virginia Negro Soldiers*, 34; WPA, *The Negro in Virginia*, 23].

FLOWERS FAMILY

Members of the Flowers family were

1   i. Sarah, born say 1745.

2   ii. Mary, born say 1748.

1. Sarah Flowers, born say 1745, was a "Mulatto" woman living in Sussex
    County, Virginia, on 19 June 1777 when the court ordered the churchwardens
    of Albemarle Parish to bind out her children Ben, Lucy, and Cealy Flowers
    to Isaac Robertson [Orders 1777-82, 17]. She was the mother of
3   i.   Benjamin¹, born say 1768.
       ii.   Lucy, born say 1771.
      iii.   Cealy¹, born say 1773, married Joseph **Lewis**, 3 November 1797
             Sussex County bond. Joseph was a "FN" taxable in Sussex County in
             1807 [PPTL 1782-1812, frame 705]. He registered in Sussex County
             on 25 July 1818: *dark complexion, 5 feet 8-1/2 inches high, age 45,
             free born* [Register of Free Negroes, 1800-50, no. 333]
       iv.   ?Isham², born say 1776, a "FN" taxable in Sussex County from 1797
             to 1813 [PPTL 1782-1814, frames 444, 598, 677, 701, 749, 782, 815,
             836].

2. Mary Flowers, born say 1748, "a free mulatto," registered the birth of her
    daughter Nancy in Bruton Parish, James City County on 27 July 1766. On 16
    May 1785 the York County court charged her with failing to list her taxable
    property [Orders 1784-7, 150]. Her children were
        i.   Nancy, born 27 July 1766 [Bruton Parish Register, 30].

3. Benjamin¹ Flowers, born say 1768, married Anne **Owen**, 5 August 1790
    Sussex County bond. Anne was probably related to James and Nathan **Owen**
    who were "FN" taxables in Sussex County in 1806 and 1807 [PPTL 1782-
    1812, frames 683, 707]. Benjamin was taxable in Sussex County from 1789
    to 1813: taxable on 2 tithes and a horse in 1803; called a "FN" starting in
    1806; taxable on 2 tithes in 1807 and 1809; 3 tithes in 1811; 4 tithes and 2
    horses in 1812 [PPTL 1782-1814, frames 251, 286, 344, 407, 444, 458, 500,
    550, 598, 515, 611, 647, 677, 701, 749, 782, 815, 836]. He may have been
    the father of
        i.   Sally, born about 1790, obtained a certificate of freedom in Sussex
             County on 21 April 1817: *light complexion, 5 feet 4 inches high, age
             27, free born* [Register of Free Negroes, 1800-50, no. 302].
       ii.   John, born about 1791, obtained a certificate of freedom in Sussex
             County on 9 September 1814: *light complexion, 5 feet 6-3/4 inches
             high, age 23, free born* [Register of Free Negroes, 1800-50, no. 242].
      iii.   Betsy, born about 1792, obtained a certificate of freedom in Sussex
             County on 21 April 1817: *light complexion, 5 feet 2 inches high, age
             25, free born* [Register of Free Negroes, 1800-50, no. 301].
       iv.   Ben², born about 1793, obtained a certificate of freedom in Sussex
             County on 9 September 1814: *bright complexion, 5 feet 8 inches high,
             age 21, free born* [Register of Free Negroes, 1800-50, no. 246].
        v.   Celia², born about 1796, obtained a certificate of freedom in Sussex
             County on 21 April 1817: *light complexion, 5 feet 2 inches high, age
             21, free born* [Register of Free Negroes, 1800-50, no. 303].

Other Flowers family members were
        i.   John, head of a Sampson County, North Carolina household of 1 "other
             free" in 1790 [NC:52], perhaps the father of Thomas² Flowers, head
             of a New Hanover County household of 3 "free colored" in 1820
             [NC:222].
       ii.   Isham¹, born say 1770, a "free" (Negro) taxable in Dinwiddie County
             in 1799 and 1800 [PPTL 1799, B, p. 5; 1800, B, p. 5].
      iii.   Thomas, born before 1776, head of a Cumberland County, North
             Carolina household of 2 "free colored" in 1820 [NC:191].

FORTUNE FAMILY

Members of the Fortune family in Virginia and North Carolina were
1   i.   Humphrey, born say 1745.
2   ii.   William, born say 1747.
3   iii.   James², born say 1750.
        iv.   John, a free man of color who enlisted as a substitute in the Revolution from Amherst County [NSDAR, *African American Patriots*, 149].
        v.   Lewis, a free man of color born in Caroline County but living in Essex County when he was listed in the size roll of troops who enlisted at Chesterfield Courthouse [The Chesterfield Supplement cited by NSDAR, *African American Patriots*, 149]. He was taxable in St. Paul's Parish, Hanover County, on a horse in 1786 (no race indicated) [PPTL, 1782-1803, p. 145], was taxable in the upper district of Henrico County in the same household as William **Maxfield** in 1787 [PPTL 1782-1814, frame 128] and a "Mᵒ" or "free Black" taxable in Powhatan County from 1792 to 1813: taxable on a slave and 2 horses in 1809 [PPTL, 1787-1825, frames 76, 92, 105, 118, 132, 162, 184, 206, 239, 256, 294, 341, 362, 438].
        vi.   Samuel, a free man of color born in Caroline County but living in Powhatan County when he enlisted in the Revolution [NSDAR, *African American Patriots*, 149].

1. Humphrey Fortune, born say 1745, was a "Mulatto" head of an Essex County, Virginia household of 8 persons in 1783 [VA:52]. He was presented by the grand jury in Essex County on 17 May 1784 and 16 May 1785 for failing to list his tithables, and on 21 August 1786 the court ordered his list to be added to the list of William Waring, Gentleman. He and Andrew **Kee** were sued for debt in Essex County on 20 December 1785 [Orders 1784-7, 9, 174, 185]. He was taxable in St. Ann's Parish, Essex County, from 1783 to 1816: taxable on a tithe; 3 horses and 5 cattle in 1783; taxable on a slave over the age of 16 in 1787 and 1788; taxable on 2 free tithes and a horse in 1794, 1796, 1798-1800, 1809 and 1810, taxable on a male and female "Free Negro & Mulatto" above the age of sixteen in 1813 [PPTL, 1782-1819, frames 42, 64, 99, 156, 171, 185, 199, 213, 225, 237, 249, 275, 310, 371, 396, 428, 460, 625]. He left a 29 January 1820 Essex County will, offered for proof by Thornton **Chandler** but opposed by John **Bird** (**Byrd**) and Daniel **Johnson**, and proved on 20 March 1820. He left all his estate to his wife Jarusy during her lifetime or widowhood. He left to son John Fortune that part of a tract of land whereon his son Thomas Fortune was then living on the south side of the branch in B.H. Munday's line, and gave the remaining part of the land to son Thomas Fortune and daughter Caty **Chandler**. He divided the remainder of his estate between his daughters Polly and Anny Fortune and left a shilling to daughters Sally **Bird** and Patsy **Johnson**. He also asked his sons to take care of their unnamed mother [WB 19:92]. He was the father of
        i.   John, born say 1778, taxable in St. Ann's Parish, Essex County, from 1804 to 1814 when he was listed as a "free Negro & Mulato" [PPTL, 1782-1819, frames 371, 384, 413, 460, 538].
        ii.   Anna, born about 1785, listed as a "free Negro" in St. Ann's Parish, Essex County, in 1813 [PPTL, 1782-1819, frame 510]. She registered as a free Negro in Essex County on 4 August 1829: *sister of Thomas Fortune, born free, bright Mulattoe, 44 years of age, 5 feet 6 inches* [Register of Free Negroes 1810-43, p.65, no.114].
4   iii.   Polly, born about 1786.
        iv.   Thomas, born about 1792, taxable in St. Ann's Parish, Essex County, from 1811 to 1816: listed as a "free Negro" from 1813 to 1815 [PPTL, 1782-1819, frames 538, 625]. He married Judith **Kay** (**Kee**), 23 December 1813 Essex County bond. He registered as a free Negro in

Essex County on 4 August 1829: *born free by certificate of Richard Rowzee, very bright Mulattoe almost white, 37 years of age, 5 feet 9-3/4 inches.* His wife Judith registered the same day: *wife of Thomas Fortune who was Judith Johnson, born free by certificate of Richard Gouldman, tawny, 30 years of age, 5 feet 6 inches* [Register of Free Negroes 1810-43, p.64, nos.147-8].

    v.   Catherine **Chandler**, born about 1795, registered as a free Negro in Essex County on 15 August 1829: *wife of Thornton Chandler who was Catherine Fortune, born free by statement of Col. Richard Rowzee, bright Mulatto, about 34 years of age, 5 feet 5 inches* [Register 1810-43, p.94, no. 192].

    vi.   Patsy, wife of Daniel **Johnson**.

    vii. Sally, wife of John **Bird**.

2.   William Fortune, born say 1747, was a "Mulatto" head of an Essex County, Virginia household of 8 persons in 1783 [VA:52]. He was presented by the grand jury in Essex County on 17 May 1784 for failing to list his tithables. His suit against Taylor Noell for debt was dismissed by the court on 21 August 1786 [Orders 1784-7, 9, 222]. He was taxable on a horse in St. Ann's Parish, Essex County, from 1783 to 1785 [PPTL, 1782-1819, frames 42, 99, 145], was a taxable in St. Paul's Parish, Hanover County, in 1787 and 1790 [PPTL, 1782-91, pp. 179, 249] and head of a Martin County, North Carolina household of 1 "other free" in 1790 [NC:68]. He was taxable in Hanover County again in 1809 [PPTL, 1804-23]. He may have been the father of

    i.   Hannah, head of a Martin County, North Carolina household of 2 "other free" in 1790 [NC:68] and 2 in Henrico County, Virginia, in 1810 [VA:980].

    ii. Jesse, born say 1785, head of a Martin County, North Carolina household of 3 "other free" in 1810 [NC:444], and a "Free Negro" taxable on a slave, a horse, and 2 cattle in Hanover County in 1815 [PPTL, 1804-23].

3.   James[2] Fortune, born say 1750, was a "free Negro" or "Mulatto" taxable in St. Paul's Parish, Hanover County, Virginia, from 1782 to 1814: taxable on 3 horses and 6 cattle in 1782; taxable on his own tithe and a free male aged 16-21 in 1785; taxable on 2 free males from 1792 to 1798 and from 1800 to 1810; paid for a merchant's license in 1804 [PPTL, 1782-91, pp.15, 35, 70, 114, 178, 209, 219, 249, 262; 1792-1803, pp. 12, 44, 65, 95, 108, 130, 149, 189, 210, 226, 249; 1804-18]. And he was taxable in Hanover County on 291 acres from 1782 to 1801 [Land Tax List, 1782-1801]. He was head of a Hanover County household of 3 "other free" in 1810 [VA:845]. He may have been the father of

    i.   James[3], Jr., born say 1784, a "Free Negro" taxable in Hanover County from 1805 to 1807 [PPTL, 1804-23] and a "free Negro" taxable in the upper district of Henrico County from 1807 to 1814, his tax charged to John Harvie's estate in 1807 [PPTL 1782-1814, frames 533, 661, 758, 823].

    ii. Curtis, born say 1791, a "Free Negro" taxable in Hanover County in 1803 and from 1811 to 1814 [PPTL, 1792-1803, p. 249; 1804-23].

    iii. Milley, head of a Hanover County household of 2 "other free" in 1810 [VA:901].

4.   Polly Fortune, born about 1786, registered as a free Negro in Essex County on 10 August 1829: *born free by cert. of Richard Rowzee, dark Mulattoe, 43 years of age, 4 feet 5-1/8 inches* [Register of Free Negroes 1810-43, p.71, no. 161]. She was the mother of

    i.   Susan, born about 1803, registered as a free Negro in Essex County on 10 August 1829: *daughter of Polly Fortune, born free by cert. of*

Richard Rowzee, bright Mulattoe, 26 years of age, 5 feet 4-5/8 inches
[Register of Free Negroes 1810-43, p.71, no.162].

Accomack County
The Fortune family of Accomack County may have been related to James Fortune, born say 1745, the "Mulatto" son of Sarah **Game**, who bound himself as an apprentice in Somerset County, Maryland court to James Laws until the age of twenty-one in March 1761 to learn the trade of light cooper [Judicial Records 1760-3, 63b]. Members of the family in Accomack County were

i. Shadrack, a free man of color who enlisted as a substitute in the Revolution from Accomack County [NSDAR, *African American Patriots*, 149].

ii. Major, head of an Accomack County household of 5 "other free" in 1810 [VA:95]. He was taxable in Accomack County in 1798, called a "B.M." (Black Man) in 1807. His daughter Jane was listed as a "free Negro" in Accomack County in 1813 [PPTL 1782-1814, frames 377, 677, 855].

FOX FAMILY

Members of the Fox family of Virginia were

i. Judith, born say 1753, mother of Rhoda **Martin** who married Edward **Fuzmore**, 22 September 1794 Goochland County bond. She may also have been the mother of James **Fox**, a "Mulatto" farmer living at Samuel **Martin**'s in Goochland County in 1814 [PPTL, 1810-32, frame 192].

ii. James, born say 1760, taxable in New Kent County from 1791 to 1815: taxable on 2 tithables and 2 horses in 1799, 1800, 1802, 1804 and 1805; listed as a "M"(ulatto) in 1804, 1807 and 1809; a "Mul." taxable on his wife, son and daughter in 1813; charged with his son William's tithe in 1814. He may have been the father of Joseph Fox, a "F.N." New Kent County taxable in 1806 and 1807 [PPTL 1782-1800, frames 164, 184, 207; 1791-1828, frames 267, 295, 306, 319, 330, 343, 369, 394, 406, 419, 431, 442, 464, 474, 491, 503]. He was head of a New Kent County household of 12 "other free" in 1810 [VA:752].

iii. James, a "Mulatto" living in Loudoun County on 12 June 1780 when the court ordered the churchwardens of Cameron parish to bind him to James Oram [Orders 1776-83, 247]. He was a "free negro" head of a Fairfax County household of 6 "other free" in 1810 [VA:255].

iv. Toby, head of a Stafford County household of 8 "other free" in 1810 [VA:127].

FRANCIS FAMILY

1. Hannah[1] Francis, born say 1664, petitioned the Elizabeth City County, Virginia court to be levy free (not have to pay the discriminatory tax on free African American women). Her petition was granted on 20 May 1724 (as was the petition of Mary **Pickett** and Elizabeth **George** [DWO 1724-30, 15]. Her brother Francis **Savoy** left her and her two sisters 50 acres on the Poquosin River bounded by the land of Thomas Wythe and John **George** by his Elizabeth City County estate. Hannah exchanged her third part of the land on 7 March 1740/1 for 16 acres adjoining the land of William Mallory on the south side of the King's gaol and 6 pounds, 10 shillings and twenty hogsheads of cider [DW 1737-56, 101]. Her descendant Mary **Cuttillo** sold this land in July 1791 [DW 34:118; Richter, *A Community and its Neighborhoods*, 362]. Hannah was probably the ancestor of

2   i.   John, born say 1728.
3   ii.   Abraham[1], born say 1740.

4   iii.   Hannah[2], born say 1740.
5   iv.   Thomas[1], born say 1745.
      v.   William[1], born about 1757, paid by Anthony Robinson's York County
             estate for currying leather in November 1779 [WI 22:483].
             He was taxable on one tithe and 6 cattle in York County in 1784 [PPTL, 1782-
             1841, frames 89, 97, 112, 140] and head of a York County household
             of 4 "other free" in 1810 [VA:872a]. He registered in York County on
             18 June 1810: *a Mul[o] man ab[l] 53 yrs. of age 5 feet 10 Inches
             high...Born of free parents* [Free Negro Register 1798-1831, no. 40].
      vi.   Christopher, born say 1758, a soldier in the Revolution from York
             County [Jackson, *Virginia Negro Soldiers,* 34], taxable in York County
             on a free tithe and a slave in 1784, taxable on slave Nanny in 1786
             [PPTL, 1782-1841, frames 78, 122].
      vii.   Elizabeth, born about 1793, registered in York County on 18
             November 1833: *a bright mulatto about 40 years of age, 5 feet 3
             inches high, long straight hair* [Free Negro Register, no.354].

2.   John Francis, born say 1728, acknowledged a debt to John Holt of 4 pounds,
      8 shillings in York County on 17 July 1749. He was indicted by the York
      County court on 19 November 1750 for not listing his wife as a tithable for
      which he was fined 1,000 pounds of tobacco [Judgments & Orders 1746-52,
      226, 364, 384, 393]. He and his wife Susanna registered the birth of their
      daughter Elizabeth in Charles Parish, York County in 1750. Susanna died soon
      after on 24 January 1750/1. On 15 June 1752 the court fined him 1,000
      pounds for not listing himself as a tithable in Charles Parish, and on 17
      September 1753 the court ordered that he and his wife be added to the list of
      tithables in Mr. Moore's precinct (the upper precinct of Charles Parish)
      [Judgment & Orders 1752-4, 59, 303]. By 22 May 1756 he had married Sarah
      when their son Thomas died [Bell, *Charles Parish Registers,* 216]. On 19
      September 1763 the court ordered that he and his "Mulatto" wife be added to
      the list of tithables for the upper precinct of Charles Parish. He died before
      May 1765 when three white men were acquitted of his murder in York County
      court. His estate was ordered to be appraised on 15 July 1765. His wife Sarah
      was the administratrix of the estate [Judgments & Orders 1763-5, 83, 87, 372,
      439, 450]. John was the father of
      i.   Elizabeth[1], born 15 September 1750 [Bell, *Charles Parish Registers,*
             91, 91].
      ii.   Thomas[2], died 22 May 1756.
      iii.   ?Mary[2], born say 1762, married Abraham **Cuttillo**, 10 November 1787
             York County bond, Robert **Gillett** bondsman. In July 1791 they sold
             16 acres in Elizabeth City County that Mary had inherited from her
             ancestor, Hannah Francis [DW 34:118].

3.   Abraham[1] Francis, born say 1740, was presented by the York County court on
      20 May 1765 for not attending Charles Parish Church [Judgments & Orders
      1763-5, 374, 448]. He and his wife Mary baptized several of their children in
      Charles Parish, York County. He was taxable in York County on a horse and
      14 cattle in 1784, taxable in York County in 1788, 1790, 1796 and 1797,
      1804, 1805 [PPTL, 1782-1841, frames 89, 140], a "Mulatto" taxable on
      himself and 2 horses in Warwick County in 1798 [1798 PPTL, p.2] and head
      of a York County household of 6 "other free" in 1810 [VA:872a]. His children
      were
      i.   Elizabeth[2], born 26 May 1761, baptized 7 June.
6   ii.   ?Mary[3], born say 1763.
      iii.   John, born 20 February 1766, died November 1782 [Bell, *Charles
             Parish Registers,* 91, 216].
7   iv.   Abraham[2], born 30 May 1769.

5. Hannah[2] Francis, born say 1740, was the mother of an illegitimate child by Philip **Chavis** who was bound out by the Johnston County, North Carolina court. She may have been the Hannah **Chavis** whose son Charles was bound out in Orange County, North Carolina, in May 1763. Her children were

    i.   Philip, born about 1758, ordered by the January Johnston County court bound as an apprentice to William Calvet in January 1762 [Haun, *Johnston County Court Minutes*, I:86, 89].

   ii.   Charles, born about October 1760, son of Hannah **Chavis** ordered bound an apprentice shoemaker to William Mebane by the May 1763 Orange County court.

8   iii.   ?Burrell, born say 1773.

   iv.   ?Levy, born say 1775, head of a Halifax County, North Carolina household of 11 "free colored" in 1820 [NC:148].

5. Thomas[1] Francis, born say 1745, and his wife Mary registered the birth of their child in Charles Parish, York County [Bell, *Charles Parish Registers*, 91]. On 20 October 1766 the York County court presented him for not listing himself as a tithable [Orders 1765-8, 161]. He was a "M"(ulatto) taxable in Warwick County on his own tithe, a slave and a horse in 1798 [1798 PPTL, p.2]. His child was

9   i.   Betty[3], born September 1767.

6. Mary[3] Francis, born say 1763, was the mother of several children baptized in Charles Parish, York County, no father named [Bell, *Charles Parish Registers*, 91]. They were

    i.   Sarah, born 28 October 1780, baptized 25 February 1781.

   ii.   Mary[4], born 20 January, baptized 23 March 1783.

   iii.   Molly, born 15 November, baptized 30 April 1786, probably the Polly Francis who registered in York County on 21 November 1831: *a bright mulatto about 40 years of age, five feet two inches high...flat face, long straight hair which she wears plaited* [Free Negroes Register 1831-50, no.334].

7. Abraham[2] Francis, born 30 May 1769, was baptized 25 June in Charles Parish, York County [Bell, *Charles Parish Registers*, 91, 216]. He was a "M"(ulatto) taxable above the age of sixteen in Warwick County in 1798, taxable on a slave and a horse (called Abraham Francis, Jr.) [1798 PPTL, p.2]. He was head of a Warwick County household of 10 "other free" in 1810 [VA:678]. He was living in Warwick County on 25 January 1816 when he consented to the York County marriage of his minor son John. One of his children was

    i.   John, born say 1798, married Elizabeth **Ketiller (Cuttillo)**, 25 January 1816 York County bond.

8. Burrell Francis, born say 1773, was head of a Halifax County, North Carolina household of 7 "other free in 1810 [NC:20], 9 "free colored in 1820 [NC:147], and 3 "free colored" in 1830. There is no record of his children, but they may have been those members of the Francis family counted in the census for Halifax County:

    i.   Burck, born say 1795, head of a Halifax County household of 7 "free colored" in 1820 [NC:148] and 8 in 1830.

   ii.   Willis, born say 1800, married Temperance **Price**, 29 December 1821 Halifax County bond, Edmund Francis bondsman. He was head of a Halifax County household of 7 "free colored" in 1830.

   iii.   Daniel, born say 1802, head of a Halifax County household of 5 "free colored" in 1830.

   iv.   John, born say 1805, head of a Halifax County household of 5 "other free" in 1830.

    v. Beb, born say 1807, married Nancy **Jones**, 27 May 1828 Halifax County bond, James Brewer bondsman. He was head of a Halifax County household of 4 "free colored" in 1830. He was fined $1 for a petty offence in the 20 May 1834 Halifax County court. On 25 February 1842 the court included him among several: *persons of color of good character allowed to use their guns*...And on 17 August 1846 he renewed his permit: *allowed to carry shot gun they having produced a certificate of good character signed by 5 or more of their respective neighbors of good character:...Beverly Francis, Willis Francis* [Minutes 1732-46].

9.   Betty[3] Francis, born September 1767, baptized 15 November the same year, registered the birth of her daughter Sukey Francis in Charles Parish [Bell, *Charles Parish Registers*, 91]. She was the mother of

    i. Sukey, daughter of Betty Francis, born Feb _, baptized 10 April 1768.

    ii. Rebecca, born about 1772, registered in York County on 16 December 1822: *a bright Mulatto about 50 years of age 5 feet 2-1/2 Inches high...born free* [Free Negro Register 1798-1831, no.150].

Members of the Francis family on the Eastern Shore of Virginia were

    i. John, born say 1750, married Ibby **Shepherd**, widow, 28 December 1792 Northampton County, Virginia bond, Abraham Lang security. He registered as a "free Negro" in Northampton County on 12 June 1794 [Orders 1789-95, 358]. He was taxable on a horse in Northampton County in 1794 [PPTL 1782-1823, frame 173].

    ii. William, born say 1770, married Polly **Jacob**, 30 December 1791 Northampton County, Virginia bond, Abraham Lang security.

    iii. Thomas, born say 1775, married Tabby **Press**, 26 December 1796 Northampton County, Virginia bond, Edmund **Press** security.

    iv. Betty, born say 1783, "free negro," married Thomas **Stephens**, 13 July 1804 Accomack County bond, Babel **Major**, "free negro," surety.

    v. Thomas, born 24 March 1796, registered in Accomack County on 29 September 1807: *Yellow Colour, 5 feet 1-3/4 Inches...Born free* [Register of Free Negroes 1785-1863, no.82].

Other members of the Francis family were

    i. John, born say 1760, head of a Beaufort District, South Carolina household of 5 "other free" in 1790.

    ii. Nathl., "f. negro" head of a Fairfax County household of 6 "other free" in 1810.

FRANKLIN FAMILY

Charles, Ambrose[1], and Noah Franklin were sons of Martha **Walden**, wife of Micajah **Walden** of Northampton County, North Carolina. Martha was the heir of her sons Charles and Ambrose Franklin who died while serving in the Revolutionary War. According to the testimony of Micajah **Walden**, administrator of their estate, their heirs were granted land warrants for 228 acres. They were also granted an additional 412 acres to be released when there was additional proof of their death. The additional land was released on 13 December 1805 when Micajah **Walden** presented the testimony of Samuel Parker, Henry Parker, and James Bradley, Captain of the North Carolina Regiment of Halifax [*NCGSJ* III].

1.   Noah Franklin, born say 1760, another son of Martha **Walden**, was not counted in the census, so he may have been living with Micajah and Martha **Walden**. He was a buyer at the Northampton County, North Carolina estate sale of Solomon Pace on 20 December 1798 [Gammon, *Record of Estates, Northampton County*, 101]. He was identified as Martha's son in Micajah

Walden's 6 November 1806 Northampton County will and Martha's 18 August 1807 will, proved March 1808. He received $50 from his foster father and furniture from his mother [WB 2:575, 597]. His children were not identified but may have been

    i.   Archibald, an orphan (no race indicated) bound apprentice in Granville County to Richard Inse and then bound instead to John Owen in November 1794 [Minutes 1792-5, 205-6], head of a Halifax County household of 3 "other free" in 1810 [NC:19], perhaps the Archer Franklin, born 1776-94, who was head of a Northampton County household of 11 "free colored" in 1830. He married Celia **Evans**, 15 January 1820 Halifax County bond with Randolph **Morgan** bondsman.

    ii. Zebulon, born 1776-94, head of a Northampton County household of 9 "free colored" in 1830.

    iii. Ezekiel, born about 1792, apprenticed as a carpenter to Isaac Ross of Franklin County, North Carolina, in 1804 [*NCGSJ* XI:12]. He was head of a Northampton County household of 9 "free colored" in 1820 [NC:230].

    iv. Ambrose², born about 1790, married Hicksey **Jones**, 3 October 1814 Wake County bond with (her father?) Francis **Jones** bondsman. Francis **Jones** was head of a Wake County household of 5 "other free" in 1790 [NC:103]. Ambrose was a "Negro" head of a Guilford County household of 7 "free colored" in 1830 and was living in household #110, New Garden Township, Wayne County, Indiana, in 1850.

2.   Elizabeth Franklin, born say 1754, was the mother of Delilar Franklin, a nine-year-old "Mullato" girl ordered bound to Drury Jackson in Warren County, North Carolina, in September 1780 [Minutes 1780-3, 50]. Her child was

    i.   Delilah, born 22 February 1771, but called a twelve-year-old "base born mulatto" when she was bound by the Warren County court to John Mayfield on 2 March 1792 [WB 6:79 by Kerr, *Warren County Records*].

FRAZIER FAMILY

1.   Caty Frazier was head of a King George County household of 4 "other free" in 1810 [VA:199]. She may have been the mother of

    i.   James Fraser, born about 1777, registered in King George County on 6 June 1802: *a black man, aged about twenty five years, about five feet five inches high, rather stout made about the body and shoulders, who has been deprived of the left leg and greater part of the thigh by amputation...was born in this county of a free negro woman...served Thomas Jordan formerly of this county...the term of twenty one years, for which he was bound by his said mother* [Register of Free Persons, no.37].

FREEMAN FAMILY

1.   Abraham¹ Freeman, born say 1721, was the servant of Thomas Jerrell of Southampton County on 9 April 1752 when he petitioned the court to sue for his freedom in forma pauperis. His lawyer Richard Baker, Gent., sued Jarrell for trespass, assault and battery and false imprisonment, but the case was dismissed on 11 June that year when he and Jarrell reached agreement. He sued Arthur Washington in court on 10 July 1755. Richard Vick sued Abraham on 14 August the same year but he was found not guilty. He was paid by the county for maintaining Flower's Bridge each year from 1759 to 1762. On 10 July 1761 the court excused his wife from paying taxes for the year 1761. On 20 November 1769 he was paid by the county for guarding a prisoner named Richard Harris alias Chapman for six days, and on 10 January

1771 he was paid for guarding a slave named Will for seven days. He was added to Nicholas Maget's list of tithables on 12 September 1771. He died before 9 July 1784 when a suit for debt brought against him in Southampton County court abated by his death. The suit, brought by the administrator of Burwell Barnes, deceased, continued against his co-defendant David **Demery** [Orders 1749-54, 216-7, 235, 238; 1754-9, 105, 125, 221; Orders 1759-63, 11, 123, 171, 253; 1768-72, 220, 341, 442; 1778-84, 439]. He was probably the ancestor of

2 i. Nathaniel, born about 1747.
3 ii. Jacob¹, born say 1768.
   iii. Benjamin, born say 1777, a "f. Negro." taxable in Nottoway Parish, Southampton County in 1794 and 1795 [PPTL 1792-1806, frames 104, 128].
   iv. James, born say 1778, a "f.N." taxable in Nottoway Parish, Southampton County in 1794, listed in the St. Luke's Parish household of John Simmons in 1796 [PPTL 1792-1806, frames 104, 202].
   v. Thomas, born about 1794, registered in Southampton County on 20 December 1815: *age 21, light Complected, 5 feet 9-1/4 inches, free born* [Register of Free Negroes 1794-1832, no. 990]. He was listed in Southampton County with his wife Tempty on Thomas Newsum's land in 1812 [PPTL 1807-21, frame 290].

2. Nathaniel Freeman, born about 1747, registered in Southampton County on 30 January 1807: *age 60, yellow (Colour), 5 feet 7-1/4 inches, free born* [Register of Free Negroes 1794-1832, no. 405]. He was taxable in Southampton County from 1782 to 1807: taxable on a horse in 1782, 1792 and 1794, called a "Mulatto" in 1802 and thereafter, charged with Jacob Freeman, Jr.'s tithe in 1805, taxable on 2 persons in 1807 [PPTL 1782-92, frames 507, 546, 622, 660, 760, 874; 1792-1806, frames 80, 189, 317, 553, 806, 841; 1807-21, frame 50]. He may have been the father of
   i. Jacob², born about 1787, registered in Southampton County on 31 July 1810: *age 23, Mulatto, 5 feet 8-1/2 inches, free born* [Register of Free Negroes 1794-1832, no. 763].

3. Jacob¹ Freeman, born say 1768, married Sally **Artis**, 4 February 1789 Southampton County bond. Sarah was the mother of Benjamin **Artis** who was ordered bound apprentice in Southampton County on 13 June 1793 [Minutes 1793-9, 20]. Jacob was taxable in Southampton County from 1787 to 1814: called a "M"(ulatto) in 1802 and thereafter, taxable on 2 free male tithables in 1806 and 1807, listed without a wife in 1813 and 1814 [PPTL 1782-92, frames 267, 379, 622, 691, 760, 874; 1792-1807, frames 80, 161, 553, 806, 841; 1807-21, frames 50, 168, 317, 417]. He may have been the father of
   i. Abraham³, born about 1787, registered in Southampton County on 30 July 1810: *age 23, Blk, 5 feet 11 inches, born free* [Register of Free Negroes 1794-1832, no. 754]. He was listed in Southampton County with his wife Elitha on Ann Hunt's land in 1812, listed with his wife Delilah on Mac Bryant's land in 1813 and 1814 [PPTL 1807-21, frames 290, 317, 417].

Other members of the Freeman family in Virginia were
4 i. Margaret, born say 1740.
5 ii. Ann, born say 1744.
   iii. Richard, born say 1746, taxable in Gloucester County in 1770 [Tax List 1770-1, 51] and in 1784, listed as a "Mulatto" in Gloucester County in 1803 [PPTL, 1782-99; 1800-20].
6 iv. James, born say 1748.
7 v. Thomas, born say 1750.

vi. Robert, born say 1763, taxable in Gloucester County from 1784 to 1811, called a "Mulatto" after 1800 [PPTL, 1782-99; 1800-20]. He was head of a Gloucester County household of 3 "other free" and a white woman in 1810 [VA:403b].

4. Margaret Freeman, born say 1740, was a "Free Negro" living in Nottoway Parish, Amelia County, on 22 May 1766 when the grand jury presented her for not listing herself as a tithable. On 29 May 1767 the churchwardens of Nottoway Parish were ordered to bind out her "free Negro" children Isham and David to John Marshall [Orders 1765-7, 90, 101]. She was the mother of

i. ?Charles, born say 1758, a "Mulatto Boy" living in Nottoway Parish, Amelia County, on 28 June 1759 when the court ordered the churchwardens to bind him as an apprentice to John Howsing [Orders 1757-60, 224]. He was a free man of color from Amelia County who enlisted in the Revolution [NSDAR, *African American Patriots*, 149].

ii. ?Matthew, born say 1759, a Free Mulatto" boy living in Nottoway Parish, Amelia County, on 28 February 1760 when the court ordered the churchwardens to bind him as an apprentice to John Howsing [Orders 1757-60, 271].

iii. Isham, born say 1763, bound to John Marshall in Amelia County on 29 May 1767 [Orders 1766-9, 58].

iv. David, born say 1765, bound to John Marshall in Amelia County on 29 May 1767 [Orders 1766-9, 58], a "M°" taxable in Powhatan County in 1790 [PPTL 1790, p.6].

5. Ann Freeman, born say 1744, "a free mulatta," was the mother of Joseph Freeman who was baptized in Bruton Parish, James City County. Her son was

i. Joseph, baptized 4 July 1762 [Bruton Parish Register, 20].

6. James Freeman, born say 1748, was taxable in Gloucester County in 1770 [Tax List 1770-1, 51] and head of a Petsworth Parish, Gloucester County household of 7 free persons in 1784 [VA:69]. He was taxable on 34 acres in Gloucester County from 1787 to 1813, called a "Mulatta" from 1805 to 1813, listed with the notation "Mul° decd." in 1814 [Land Tax List 1782-1820]. He, his unnamed wife and daughters Betsey and Lucy were counted in a list of "Mulattoes and Free Negroes" in Gloucester County in 1813 [PPTL, 1800-20]. He was head of a Gloucester County household of 6 "other free" in 1810 [VA:403b]. He was the father of

i. Betsey, over the age of sixteen in 1813 when she was counted in a list of "Mulattoes and Free Negroes" in Gloucester County.

ii. Lucy, over the age of sixteen in 1813.

iii. ?Jasper, born say 1774, taxable in Gloucester County from 1796 to 1800 [PPTL, 1782-99; 1800-20]. He was taxable on 7-1/2 acres in Gloucester County from 1795 to 1814 and another plot of 6 acres in 1813 and 1814. His widow Rachel held a life estate on this land from 1815 to 1819 [Land Tax List 1782-1820].

iv. ?John, born say 1775, taxable in Gloucester County from 1796 to 1819, head of a Gloucester County household of 3 "other free" and a white woman in 1810 [VA:403b]. He was a bricklayer, taxable on 30 acres in Gloucester County from 1806 to 1819, called a "Mulatto" from 1814 to 1819. In 1820 his widow Frances Freeman was taxable on the land with the notation "Transferred to her by John Freeman, decd., mulattoe, see his will recorded in Gloucester Court office" [Land Tax List 1782-1820].

7. Thomas Freeman, born say 1750, was taxable in Gloucester County in 1769 and 1770, called Thomas Freeman, Jr. [Tax List 1770-1, 206]. He was head of an Abingdon Parish, Gloucester County household of 4 free persons in 1784

[VA:68]. He was taxable on 25 acres in Gloucester County in 1791 to 1805. From 1806 to 1812 the land was taxable with the notation "deceased Mul°." In 1813 Thomas and William Freeman were taxable on 12-1/2 acres of this land and Mary Freeman was taxable on the other 12-1/2 acres [Land Tax List 1782-1820]. Mary was called the widow of Thomas Freeman when she was counted in a Gloucester County list of "Mulattoes and Free Negroes" in 1813 [PPTL, 1800-20]. He was apparently the father of

    i.   Thomas, taxable in Gloucester County in 1812, called Thomas, Jr. [PPTL, 1800-20], jointly taxed with William Freeman on 12-1/2 acres in 1813.

    ii. William.

North Carolina
1.   Abraham[2] Freeman, born say 1730, was a "free Negro" taxable in Bladen County with (his wife?) Sue and (daughter?) Rachel in 1763 (called "Abrm. Sue Rachal free Negroes"). He was a "Negro" man taxable in Bladen County from 1768 to 1779 (called Abraham Freeman from 1768 to 1770 and called "free Abe" in 1771), taxable on three males and one female in 1774, taxable on three males in 1775, and taxable on 300 acres, five horses and fifteen head of cattle in 1779 [Byrd, *Bladen County Tax Lists*, I:12, 40, 51, 53, 124; II:36, 141]. His wife may have been Susanna Freeman who was taxable with him in Bladen County from 1763 to 1771, called Susannah Freeman in 1770 when she was listed with (their daughter?) Rachel Freeman [Byrd, *Bladen County Tax Lists*, I:12, 40, 51]. He and Abigail **Chavis** were named as executors of the 21 May 1793 Bladen County will of James **Moore** [Campbell, *Abstracts of Wills, Bladen County*, 54]. He sold 600 acres in Bladen County on Platt Swamp on 20 July 1799 [DB 1:261]. He was head of a Brunswick County household of 10 "other free" in 1800 [NC:13] and 5 "other free" in Bladen County in 1810 (called Abraham Freeman, Senr.) [NC:196]. He may have been the father of

    i.   Rachel, born say 1748, taxable in Bladen County with Abraham and Susanna from 1763 to 1771.

2   ii. Samuel, born say 1751.
3   iii. Roger, born say 1753.

    iv. William, born say 1754, a "Black" taxable in Bladen County, called "free Will" in 1771 and called William Freeman when he was a "Mixt Blood" taxable on one male and one female in 1774. He was taxable on two males in 1775, and taxable on 100 acres, two horses, and three head of cattle in 1779 [Byrd, *Bladen County Tax Lists*, I:53, 124; II:36, 141]. He was taxable in Bladen County on 100 acres and one black poll in Captain Dupree's District in 1784 [*1784 Bladen County Tax List,* 13]. He was head of a New Hanover County household of 2 "other free" in 1790 [NC:194].

2.   Samuel Freeman, born say 1751, was a "Negro" man taxable in Bladen County in 1768 and 1770, taxable in the household of Isaac **Hays** in 1771 and 1772, listed with the "Mixt Blood" taxables in one list for 1774 and called a "free Negro" taxable in John Smith's list for 1774 when he was taxable on one male and one female, and taxable on a horse in 1779 [Byrd, *Bladen County Tax Lists*, I:12, 40, 51, 76, 91, 124, 125; II:141]. He was head of an Onslow County household of 8 "other free" in 1790 [NC:197], 14 in Brunswick County in 1800 [NC:13], and 9 in Bladen County in 1810 [NC:196]. There is no record of his children, but they may have been

    i.   James, head of a Brunswick County household of 5 "other free" in 1800 [NC:13] and as J. Freeman, head of a Brunswick County household of 4 in 1810 [NC:234].

    ii. B., head of a Brunswick County household of 2 "other free" in 1810 [NC:234].

iii. Isaac, born before 1776, head of a Columbus County household of 8 "free colored" in 1820 [NC:55]. He entered 100 acres in Brunswick County on Bear Pen Branch on 17 January 1799 [Pruitt, *Land Entries: Brunswick County,* 52].

3. Roger Freeman, born say 1753, was a "Negro" man taxable in Bladen County in 1768 and 1770, taxable on 50 acres, a horse and three head of cattle in 1779, and taxable on 150 acres and one black poll in Captain Dupree's District of Bladen County in 1784. He was head of a Bladen County household of two Blacks from 12 to 50 years old and six Blacks over 50 or under 12 years in 1786 [Byrd, *Bladen County Tax Lists,* I:12, 40, 51; II:169; *1784 Bladen County Tax List,* 13]. He was head of an Onslow County household of 7 "other free" in 1790 [NC:197], and 8 in 1800 [NC:14]. His widow may have been Elizabeth Freeman, head of a Brunswick County household of 7 "other free" in 1810 [NC:228]. He may have been the father of
   i. Abraham², Jr., head of a Bladen County household of 5 "other free" in 1810 [NC:196].

Members of the Freeman family in Rowan County, North Carolina, were
1   i. Isaac, born say 1740.
   ii. Ruth, born say 1762, mother of a molatto" child who was taken from Samuel Cooper by the Rowan County court on 5 February 1784 and returned to his mother because he was born free and not subject to be dealt with as a poor orphan [Minutes 1753-95, II:377 (original p. 140)].

1. Isaac Freeman, born say 1740, married Agnes **Faggott**, 19 January 1762 Rowan County bond. He was called a "free Negro" on 9 August 1786 when administration on his Rowan County estate was granted to his widow Agnes Freeman on 100 pounds bond [Minutes 1753-1795, II:416]. His children John, William, Leonard and Mary petitioned for division of his land [C.R. 085.508.58 cited by Mosher, Merrill Hill, *John Freeman of Norfolk County, Va.*]. His children were
   i. John.
   ii. William.
   iii. Leonard, married Love Birth, 17 August 1808 Rowan County bond.
   iv. Mary.

FROST FAMILY

Members of the Frost family in South Carolina were
   i. John, head of a Bartholomew's Parish, Charleston District household of 6 "other free" in 1790 and 4 in Colleton County in 1800 [SC:178]. He was a "free" taxable on himself, his wife, and daughter ("Free Negroes & Mulattoes") in St. Bartholomew's Parish, Charleston District in 1798.
   ii. Cyrus, head of a Charleston District household of 3 "other free" in 1790 and a "Free" taxable on himself and his wife in St. Bartholomew's Parish, Charleston District in 1798 [S.C. Archives microfilm AD 942, frame 248].
   iii. Benjamin, head of a Richland District household of 6 "other free" in 1810 [SC:178].
   iv. William, head of a Richland District household of 5 "other free" in 1810 [SC:177a].
   v. Lydia, a slaveowner from Charleston whose son Florian H. Frost was elected to the state house of representatives in 1870 [Koger, *Black Slaveowners,* 198].

FRY FAMILY

1. Jane Fry, born say 1690, was living in Washington Parish, Westmoreland County, on 9 February 1713/4 when she bound her one-year-old "mulatto" son William Fry to Jonas Williams [DW 1716-20, 66]. She was the "Mulatto" servant of William Bridges on 26 June 1723 when she was summoned before the Westmoreland County court to answer the presentment of the grand jury. On 28 February 1723/4 she was ordered to serve her master an additional year and a half for having an illegitimate child [Orders 1721-31, 41-2, 45a]. Jane was the mother of

    i.   ?John, born say 1711, petitioned the Westmoreland County court against William Bridges for his freedom and freedom dues on 28 July 1732. The suit was agreed by both parties [Orders 1731-9, 35]. He sued Thomas Finch in Westmoreland County court on 28 May 1751 [Orders 1750-2, 56a].

    ii.   William, born 31 March 1713.

    iii. ?Joanna, born say 1721, a servant to the estate of Daniel McCarty, deceased, in February 1744/5 when she and Ketany Fry sued for their freedom. The court ordered that they be freed and paid their freedom dues [Orders 1743-7, 57, 64a].

    iv.   ?Ketany, born say 1723, a servant to the estate of Daniel McCarty, deceased. The Westmoreland County court ordered that she be freed and paid her freedom dues in February 1744/5 [Orders 1743-7, 57, 64a].

    v.   ?George, born say 1725, called a "Free Mulatto" when he came into Westmoreland County court on 29 January 1750/1 and agreed to serve Lawrence Butler for four years in exchange for payment of 2,000 pounds of tobacco [Orders 1750-2, 26]. He may have been the George Fry who was head of a Fredericksburg household of 5 "other free" and 7 whites in 1810 [VA:113a].

Other descendants were

    i.   Alice, a "Mulatto" child ordered bound to Sarah Martin by the churchwardens of Washington Parish, Westmoreland County, on 27 November 1751 [Orders 1750-2, 86a].

    ii.   Andrew, a "Mulatto" head of an Essex County, Virginia household of 6 persons in 1783 [VA:52].

    iii. Nathan, born say 1755, a man of color born free in Westmoreland County, enlisted in the Minute Service of the Revolutionary War in Henrico County, served as a drummer against the Creek Indians in Georgia and applied for a pension in Henrico County [National Archives pension file S39545 cited by NSDAR, *African American Patriots*, 177-8]. He was a "F.N." taxable in the upper district of Henrico County from 1790 to 1813: charged with Jeffry **Golding**'s tithe in 1806, listed with his unnamed wife in 1813. Perhaps his son was Jeffry Fry who was listed there as a "free Negro" in 1814 [PPTL 1782-1814, frames 376, 402, 444, 486, 532, 593, 636, 661, 757, 823; Land Tax Lists 1799-1816]. Nathan, Will **Anthony** and Angelica **Barnett** were in the Henrico County jail on 7 February 1791 for a breach of the peace and were ordered to remain there until they gave security of 40 pounds each for their good behavior for a year. William **Anthony** was a Negro slave emancipated by William Duval by deed proved in Henrico County court on 8 August 1789. On 10 October 1798 Nathan posted bond of 10 pounds for his good behavior for twelve months on the complaint of Patty **Cole** for a breach of the peace [Orders 1789-91, 67, 428; 1798-9, 256]. He was head of a Henrico County household of 3 "other free" and a white woman aged 26-45 in 1810 [VA:978].

iv. Thomas, head of a Spotsylvania County household of 5 "other free" in 1810 [VA:107a].

FULLAM FAMILY

1   Mary Fullam, born say 1700, was the white servant woman of Henry Ashton of Cople Parish, Westmoreland County, on 27 July 1720 when the county court convicted her of having a "Mulatto" child and ordered that she be sold for five years at the completion of her indenture. On 25 March 1724 the court ordered her arrested to answer the churchwardens, and she was still Henry Ashton's servant on 30 July 1729 when the churchwardens of Cople Parish informed the court that she had had another "Mulatto" child [Orders 1705-21, 392a; 1721-31, 61, 72a]. She was probably the mother of
2   i.   Martha, born say 1729.

2. Martha Fullam, born say 1729, was the mother of two "Mulatto" children bound apprentice in Prince William County. They were
        i.   Alexander, born 3 March 1748, bound to Richard Blackburn on 22 January 1751.
        ii. Baker, born 3 March 1748, bound to Richard Blackburn on 22 January 1751 [Dettington Parish Vestry Book 1748-85, 3, 4]. He ran away from Thomas Blackburn of Prince William County near Dumfries in September 1775 according to an ad Blackburn placed in the 1 December 1775 issue of the *Virginia Gazette*: *a 31 years servant...a likely well set fellow, about 27 years old, 5 feet 7 or 8 inches high, is of a light colour, with hazle eyes, and wears his hair, which is short, and of a dark brown colour* [*Virginia Gazette* (Purdie edition)].

FULLER FAMILY

1. Shadrack Fuller, born say 1710, was a "Mullatto Boy" bound by the Princess Anne County court to John Bryan on 7 December 1715 until the age of thirty-one to learn the trade of weaver [Minutes 1709-17, 198]. He may have been the father or uncle of
        i.   Abby Fullard, born 11 October 1739. On 16 October 1753 the Princess Anne County court ordered her, Jane, and William Fullard, "Mullattos," bound to James Moore. On 21 June 1756 the court ordered Moore to provide land and security not to remove or sell Joanah and Abby Fullard ("two free Mulattos bound to him by this Court") out of the county [Minutes 1753-62, 62, 242].
        ii. Jane Fullard, born in May 1742, twelve years old when she was bound to James Moore.
2   iii. William[1], born in February 1743.
3   iv. Mary, born say 1748.
4   v.   Robert, born say 1750.
        vi. Savinah Fullard, a "Mullatto" bound by the Princess Anne County court on 21 July 1756 to Mrs. Mary Walke. On 18 July 1758 the court bound her to Miss Mary Anne Walke and stated that she should teach her to read and sew [Minutes 1753-62, 242, 323].
        vii. Sall Fullard, a "Mullatto" bound by the Princess Anne County court on 21 July 1756 to Mary Walke, daughter of Major Thomas Walke [Minutes 1753-62, 242].
        viii. Plymouth Fuller, born say 1764, a "Mulatto" ordered bound to Charles Williamson by the Princess Anne County court on 19 February 1765 [Orders 1762-9, 157], perhaps identical to Plumb Fuller, "Free Black" head of a Princess Anne County household of 3 "other free" in 1810 [VA:453].

2.   William[1] Fuller, born in February 1743, was an eleven-year-old "Mullatto" when he (called William Fullard) was bound to James Moore by the Princess Anne County court on 16 October 1753 [Minutes 1753-62, 62]. He (called William Fuller) was taxable in 1767 and 1768 on the north side of Tanners Creek in Norfolk County with his wife Sarah **Anderson** [Wingo, *Norfolk County Tithables, 1766-80*, 49, 73]. Sarah was head of a Princess Anne County household of 7 "Blacks" in 1783 [VA:61]. They may have been the parents of

    i.   Hannah, born say 1770, married Meshack **Africa**, 4 April 1789 Princess Anne County bond, Beriah Butt surety, 19 April marriage. He may have been identical to Meshack Fuller who was taxable in Norfolk County in 1794 and a "free Negro" taxable in St. Brides Parish from 1803 to 1811 [PPTL, 1791-1812, frames 103, 456, 548, 609, 674].

    ii. Nancy, born say 1772, married Samuel **Anderson**, 26 December 1792 Princess Anne County bond, Charles Whitehurst surety, 27 December marriage.

    iii. Fanny, head of a Norfolk County household of 9 "other free" and a slave in 1810 [VA:800], a "free Negro" listed in St. Brides Parish in 1813 [PPTL, 1813-24, frame 11].

    iv. Diana, born about 1781, head of a Norfolk County household of 2 "other free" in 1810 [VA:802]. She registered in Norfolk County on 19 August 1811: *5 feet 5 In., 30 years of age light Complexion, Born free* [Register of Free Negros & Mulattos, #57].

    v.   Africa, "Free Black" head of a Princess Anne County household of 8 "other free" in 1810 [VA:453], married (second?) Nancy **Davis**, "persons of colour," 6 January 1821 Norfolk County bond, Robert **Armistead** surety.

3.   Mary Fuller, born say 1748, complained to the Princess Anne County court on 8 November 1771 on behalf of her son William **Bullard** that his master William Barker was mistreating him [Minutes 1770-3, 210]. She may have been identical to Molly Fuller, "Free Black" head of a Princess Anne County household of 3 "other free" in 1810 [VA:452]. She was the mother of

    i.   William **Bullard**, a "free Negro" bound by the Princess Anne County court to William Barker on 4 April 1771 [Minutes 1770-3, 99].

4.   Robert Fuller, born say 1750, was living in Northampton County, North Carolina, between 1772 and 1784 when money was received from him by the estate of Benjamin Roberts [Gammon, *Records of Estates, Northampton County*, I:46]. He purchased 100 acres on Middle Branch in Northampton County adjoining John and David Futrell on 15 January 1789 [DB 9:88]. He was head of a Northampton County household of 4 "other free" in 1790 [NC:74] and 3 in 1800 [NC:443]. His 10 July 1803 will, proved in September 1803, left his land to his wife Mary during her lifetime and then to his daughter Cidney [WB 2:248]. Mary was head of a Northampton County household of 3 "other free" and 1 slave in 1810 [NC:722]. Their daughter was

    i.   Cidney Fuller.

Other Fuller descendants were

    i.   Edom, head of a Currituck County, North Carolina household of 1 "other free" in 1790 [NC:21].

    ii. Anthony, born say 1771, bound by the Princess Anne County court to Nicholas Griffin on 1 August 1771 to learn the trade of millwright [Minutes 1770-3, 162]. He and Thomas Fuller, infant "Free Negroes," were bound to Thomas Walker to be planters on 10 February 1780 [Minutes 1773-82, 460].

    iii. Peter, born say 1772, a "free negro" living in Norfolk County on 21 May 1774 when the court ordered the churchwardens of Elizabeth

River Parish to bind him to John Guy [Orders 1773-5, 54]. He was a "Free Mulatto" bound by the Princess Anne County court to William Nimmo, Gent., to be a planter on 11 September 1778 [Minutes 1773-82, 310].

iv. Thomas, an infant "Free Negro" bound by the Princess Anne County court on 10 February 1780 to Thomas Walker to be a planter [Minutes 1782-4, 2]. He was a "Free Black" head of a Princess Anne County household of 3 "other free" and 2 slaves in 1810 [VA:453].

v. William[2], an infant "free Negro" bound by the Princess Anne County court to Malbone Shelton to be a shipwright on 11 March 1779 [Minutes 1773-82, 369]. He married Nancy **Moss**, "free persons of colour born free," 27 June 1818 Norfolk County bond, Henry Oatest surety. He may have been the William Fuller, born before 1776, who was head of a Halifax County, North Carolina household of 10 "free colored" in 1820 [NC:148].

vi. Judy, a "free negro" ordered bound out by the churchwardens of Elizabeth River Parish, Norfolk County, to Malbone Sheldon on 16 October 1783 [Orders 1782-3, n.p.].

vii. Catherine, born about 1797, a sixty-year-old resident of Norfolk County on 28 August 1857 when she applied for the Revolutionary War pension of her husband Charles **Cuffee** [W-9402].

viii. Betsy, "free Negro" huckstress of Norfolk County who owned her husband before the Civil War [Lower Norfolk County Virginia Antiquary, IV:177].

FUZMORE FAMILY

The Fuzmore family were slaves freed after 1782. They are included here because they often had relations with families that were free during the colonial period. Members of the Fuzmore family were

1   i.   Isaac, born say 1760.
2   ii. Edward, born say 1765.
     iii. Benjamin, taxable in Goochland County from 1783: a "free Negro" in 1783 to 1794, taxable on a horse and 6 cattle in 1787 [PPTL, 1782-1809, frames 35, 70, 87, 151, 177, 237, 280, 296, 340, 359].
     iv. Toby, taxable in the upper district of Goochland County from 1783 to 1786, a "free Negro" taxable on a "Negro" tithe in 1783 [PPTL, 1782-1809, frames 36, 70, 123].

1.   Isaac Fuzmore, born say 1760, was taxable in the upper district of Goochland County from 1783 to 1791: a "free Negro" taxable on a "Negro" tithe, 2 horses and 2 cattle in 1783 [PPTL, 1782-1809, frames 36, 87, 131, 151, 219, 280]. He was taxable in Louisa County from 1793 to 1805, listed with 2 tithables in 1803 and 1805 [PPTL, 1782-1814]. He was a farmer living near Foster's Creek in Louisa County about 1802-1803 when he, his wife Patty, and their children were counted in the list of free Negroes in the district of Peter Crawford [Abercrombie, *Free Blacks of Louisa County*, 19]. He was taxable on 2 free male tithes and a horse in Fluvanna County in 1806 and 1807 [PPTL 1782-1826, frames 365, 385]. He was taxable in the upper district of Goochland County from 1809 to 1815: a "Freed Negroe" planter on Dabney Wade's land in 1809, living on Francis **Cousins'** land in 1812, listed with wife Amey and (daughters) Nancy, Betty and Fanny Fuzmore on John Hicks' land in 1813, over the age of forty-five in 1815 [PPTL, 1782-1809, frames 866; 1810-32, frames 21, 73, 98, 160, 192, 260]. He was head of a Goochland County household of 1 "other free" in 1810 [VA:692]. He had married the mother of Amey **Bennett** before 1 January 1814 when he gave his consent for

her Goochland County marriage to James **Scott**. Isaac and Patty's children were

   i.   Martha, born say 1780.

   ii. Agnes, born say 1782.

  iii. Lucy, born about 1784, registered as a free Negro in Louisa County on 29 July 1817: *a free woman of colour, born in sd. county, 5'1" high, dark complexion about 33 years.* Her daughter Betsey registered on 28 February 1839: *(daughter of Lucy Fuzemore) who was free born, black complexion, about 25 years of age* [Abercrombie, *Free Blacks of Louisa County*, 24, 56].

  iv. Tabitha, born about 1786, registered in Goochland County on 13 May 1813: *a free woman of colour aged about twenty seven years, dark complexion, short black hair* [Register, p.60, no.119].

   v. Isaac², Jr., born say 1787, taxable in the upper district of Goochland County from 1809 to 1814: a "Freed Negroe" planter at Thomas Herndon's in 1809, a waterman at Isaac Fuzmore's in 1814 [PPTL, 1782-1809, frame 866; 1810-32, frames 7, 192].

  vi. Nancy.

 vii. Betty.

viii. Judith.

  ix. Fanny.

   x. Sarah.

2.   Edward Fuzmore, born say 1765, was taxable on a horse in the upper district of Goochland County from 1790 to 1814: a "free negroe" farmer living near Thomas F. Bates in 1804, a "Freed negroe" farmer on Robert Pleasants' land in 1805, taxable on Billy **Martin**'s tithe in 1806 and 1807, charged with George Fuzmore's tithe in 1811 and 1812, living near Licking Hole Church in 1812, listed with wife Roda and (children?) George and Judy Fuzmore in 1813 [PPTL, 1782-1809, frames 237, 296, 359, 465, 527, 617, 688, 740, 823; 1810-32, frames 7, 98, 160]. He married Rhoda **Martin**, "of age daughter of Judith Fox," 22 September 1794 Goochland County bond. Edward was surety for the 16 April 1801 Goochland County marriage of Frank **Cousins** and Chloe **Cousins**, the 29 July 1801 marriage of Thomas **Lynch** and Sally **Banks**, and the 3 January 1810 marriage of James **Shelton** and Charity **Coons**. He was head of a Goochland County household of 12 "other free" in 1810 [VA:691]. He was probably the father of

   i. George, taxable in the upper district of Goochland County from 1811 to 1814, a "freed negro" sawyer at Edward Fuzmore's in 1814 [PPTL, 1810-32, frame 192].

  ii. Judy, born say 1797, over the age of sixteen in 1813 when she was listed in Edward Fuzmore's household.

Another member of the family was

   i. Harriet **Dickinson**, born about 1805, registered in Louisa County on 1 October 1832: *wife of Garland Dickinson who was Harriet Fuzzamore a free woman of colour, about 5'2" high, light complexion, hair inclined to be straight...about 27 years old* [Abercrombie, *Free Blacks of Louisa County*, 42].

GALLIMORE FAMILY

1.   Elizabeth¹ Gallimore, born say 1720, was living in Amelia County in September 1746 when her son William (no race indicated) was ordered bound apprentice. She was summoned before the Amelia County court to answer the complaint of the churchwardens in June 1750, but she did not appear, the sheriff reporting that she was no longer an inhabitant. On 25 May 1759 she was presented by the Amelia County court for "unlawfully Cohabiting with a

Negro Slave belonging to Henry Jones and having Several Mulatto Children" [Orders 1746-51, 21, 250; 1757-60, 218]. Her children were

2 i. William[1], born say 1737.
3 ii. ?Elizabeth[2], born say 1748.
4 iii. George[1], born about 1757.
 iv. ?Joan, born say 1759, a "Free Mulatto," ordered bound to Henry Jones of Raleigh Parish, Amelia County, on 28 June 1759 [Orders 1757-60, 229].
 v. ?David, born say 1761, a "Free Mulatto," ordered bound apprentice in Nottoway Parish, Amelia County, on 27 June 1771. He was a "Mulatto" taxable in Charlotte County from 1809 to 1811 [PPTL 1782-1813, frames 757, 790, 823].
 vi. ?Anna, born say 1763, a "Free Mulatto," ordered bound apprentice in Nottoway Parish, Amelia County, on 27 June 1771.
 vii. ?John, born say 1765, a "Free Mulatto," ordered bound apprentice in Nottoway Parish, Amelia County, on 27 June 1771 [Orders 1769-72, n.p].

2. William[1] Gallimore, born say 1737, was bound apprentice in Amelia County in September 1746. He was called the son of Elizabeth Gallimore on 22 January 1756 when the court bound him as an apprentice to John Flynn [Orders 1746-51, 21; 1751-5, 10; 1755-7, 25]. He was taxable in Charlotte County in John Fuqua's household in 1782, taxable on a horse and 3 cattle in 1785, levy free from 1788 to 1796 when he was taxable on 2 horses [PPTL 1782-1813, frames 6, 59, 95, 129, 161, 191, 217, 265, 290, 316, 341]. He was the father of

 i. Sarah, born say 1772, "dau. of William Gallimore," married Acquila **Hailey**, 13 December 1790 Charlotte County bond, Thomas Hayes surety, 16 December marriage.
 ii. Polly[1], born say 1778, "dau of William Gallimore," married John **Smith**, 31 October 1796 Charlotte County bond, 3 November marriage. John was head of a Charlotte County household of 8 "other free" in 1810 [VA:64].

3. Elizabeth[2] Gallimore, born say 1748, a "Free Mulatto," was ordered bound to Henry Jones of Raleigh Parish, Amelia County, on 28 June 1759 [Orders 1757-60, 218]. She was the mother of

 i. Ritta, born say 1770, "daughter of Elizabeth Gallimore," ordered bound to Zachariah Vaughan of Raleigh Parish, Amelia County, on 25 July 1771 [Orders 1769-72, n.p.].
 ii. ?James, head of a Chester County, South Carolina household of 1 "other free" in 1800 [SC:94].

4. George[1] Gallimore, born about 1757, was taxable in Charlotte County from 1797 to 1799: taxable on 2 free males and 3 horses in 1797 and 1798, and 3 free males and 2 horses in 1799, levy free in 1807 and 1811 when he was taxable on a horse [PPTL 1782-1813, frames 368, 400, 435, 724]. He registered in Charlotte County on 7 January 1812: *son of Betty Gallimore, born free, Mulatto complexion, aged 54-55* [Ailsworth, *Charlotte County--Rich Indeed*, 485]. He was the father of

 i. ?Joshua, born about 1779, married Betsey **Flood**, "dau. of William Flood who is surety," 29 February 1803 Charlotte County bond. Joshua, a "free Mulatto" planter, was taxable in Charlotte County from 1802 to 1811: taxable on a horse in 1807, listed with 4 males and 2 females in his household in 1811, 3 males and 2 females in 1812 and 1813 [PPTL 1782-1813, frames 542, 580, 673, 710, 743, 775, 807, 846, 886]. He was a "free Negro" head of a Charlotte County household in 1810 [VA:50] and a seventy-year-old "Black" man counted in the 1850 census with Betsy Gallimore who was born about 1783 [VA:12b]. Joshua registered in Charlotte County on 7 November 1831: *Yellow complexion, aged 52, born free* [Ailsworth, *Charlotte County--Rich Indeed*, 490].

ii. ?Polly[2], born say 1785, a "free Mulatto" weaver listed with 3 females in her Charlotte County household in 1812 and 1813 [PPTL 1782-1813, frames 846, 886].

iii. ?George[2], born about 1786, called George Gallimore, Jr., when he was a "Mulatto" taxable in Charlotte County in 1809 [PPTL 1782-1813, frames 757, 790]. He was a "free Negro" head of a Charlotte County household of 3 "other free" in 1810 [VA:50]. He married Patsey **Flood**, daughter of William **Flood**, 9 May 1813 Charlotte County bond, John **Flood** surety, 10 May marriage. George registered in Charlotte County on 7 November 1831: *Yellow complexion, aged 45, born free*. Patsey registered the same day: *Dark complexion, aged 32, born free* [Ailsworth, *Charlotte County--Rich Indeed*, 490].

iv. ?William[2], a "Mulatto" taxable in Charlotte County from 1809 to 1811 [PPTL 1782-1813, frames 757, 790, 823], a "free Negro" head of a Charlotte County household of 1 "other free" in 1810 [VA:50].

v. James, born about 1793, taxable in Charlotte County in 1811 [PPTL 1782-1813, frames 823]. He registered in Charlotte County on 7 January 1812: *son of George Gallimore, Mulatto complexion, aged 19, born free* [Ailsworth, *Charlotte County--Rich Indeed*, 485].

GAMBY/ GUMBY FAMILY

1. Martha Gamby, born say 1675, was an (East) Indian woman living in England on 5 January 1701/2 when Henry Conyers made an agreement with her that she would serve him in Virginia on condition that he would pay her passage back to England if she wished to return within the following four years. The agreement was recorded in Stafford County court about 1704 [WB, Liber Z:194]. She may have been the ancestor of

i. John Gumby, head of a Frederick County household of 9 "other free" in 1810 [VA:562].

ii. Rachel Gumby, head of a Frederick County household of 5 "other free" in 1810 [VA:595].

GARDEN FAMILY

The Garden family of South Carolina may have been identical to the Gordon family. Members of the Garden/ Gordon family of South Carolina were

i. William[1] Gordon, born say 1744, head of a Beaufort District, South Carolina household of 7 "other free" and a slave in 1790 and 6 "other free" in 1800 [SC:104].

ii. William[2] Gordon, head of a Newberry District, South Carolina household of 3 "other free" in 1800 [SC:77].

iii. Melia Gordon, head of a Beaufort County household of 3 "other free" in 1800 [SC:104].

iv. Penelope Gordon, born say 1746, "free" head of a St. Philip's & Michael's Parish, Charleston, South Carolina household of 7 "other free" in 1790.

1 v. Flora Garden, born say 1753.

vi. James Gordon, head of a Camden District, Lancaster County, South Carolina household of 1 "other free" in 1790, perhaps the James Gordon who married Teresa **Roberts**, "col'd persons," on 2 February 1814 in St. Philip's Parish, Charleston, South Carolina.

1. Flora Garden, born say 1753, was called a "free Mustee" when she married Robert **Baldwin**, "a free Blackman" and house carpenter, in Charleston, South Carolina, on 5 September 1801. Before her marriage to **Baldwin**, she had
   i. John, born about 1772, married Elizabeth Susan **Gardner** who inherited nine slaves by the 1788 will of her grandfather William **Raper**. John applied for membership in the Brown Fellowship Society of Charleston in 1795 [Koger, *Black Slaveowners*, 16, 17, 141-2]. He was head of a "free colored" St. Paul's Parish, Charleston District household with 26 slaves in 1820.
   ii. ?Martha, married Robert **Wells**, "colored persons," in St. Philip's and Michael's Parish, Charleston on 12 October 1815.

GARDNER FAMILY

Members of the Gardner family of South Carolina were
1 i. George, born say 1750.
   ii. John, born say 1752, head of a Georgetown District, South Carolina household of 4 "other free" and 40 slaves in 1810 [SC:219].

1. George Gardner, born say 1750, married Ruth **Raper**. He was head of a St. Philip's and Michael's Parish, Charleston, South Carolina household of 4 "other free" and 9 slaves in 1790. The slaves were the property of his daughter Elizabeth Susan who received them by the 1788 will of her grandfather William **Raper**. George died in 1797. His children were
   i. Elizabeth Susan, still a minor in 1788 when her grandfather left her nine slaves. She married John **Garden**, a "free mestizo" [Koger, *Black Slaveowners*, 16, 17, 141-2].
   ii. Rachel.

GARNER FAMILY

Members of the Garner family were
1 i. Ann, born say 1733.
2 ii. Sarah, born say 1735.
   iii. Mary Gardner, born say 1750, a "Mulatto" woman held as a servant by John Richmond in Louisa County on 11 February 1771 when the court ordered that she be set at liberty, "the said Richmond failing to appear when called and it appearing she is no servant" [Order 1762-72, 438].

1. Ann Gardner/ Garner, born say 1733, was the servant of Isaac Mason of Southampton County on 11 October 1753 when the court ordered the churchwardens of Nottoway Parish to bind out her unnamed "Mulatto" child. On 11 April 1754 the court ordered Mason to deliver a "Mulatto" child in his possession to Henry Blunt and bound the child to Blunt. The churchwardens sued Ann for debt (probably for bastardy) on 12 August 1756. On 8 December 1757 the court charged her with being a person of lewd life and conversation and ordered her to post a total of 60 pounds bond for her good behavior and ordered her "mulatto" daughter Peggy bound out. On 13 April 1759 the court fined her 15 pounds for bastardy [Orders 1749-54, 420, 478; 1754-9, 291, 296, 402, 430]. Her children were
   i. Margaret[1]/ Peggy, born say 1754.
   ii. William[1], born say 1756, a "Mullatto" son of Ann Garner, ordered bound by the Southampton County court on 10 May 1759 [Orders 1754-59, 498].
   iii. Priss, born say 1758, a "Mullato" child of Ann Gardner ordered bound out in Southampton County on 12 July 1759. On 13 April 1775 the court ordered the churchwardens of Nottoway Parish to bind her to

John Scott, noting that she had formerly been bound to John Bradley until the age of thirty-one but that Bradley had not been able to perform the covenants of the indenture [Orders 1754-9, 516; 1772-7, 405].

iv.   ?Anthony, born say 1760, head of a Hertford County household of 2 "other free" in 1790 [NC:26]. He served in the Revolution from Hertford County (called Anthony Garnes) [National Archives pension file S38723 cited by NSDAR, *African American Patriots*, 165].

v.   ?Burwell Gardner, born about 1767, taxable in Nottoway Parish, Southampton County, from 1794 to 1811: called a "free Negro" in 1796, 1801 and 1802, a "Mulatto" in 1792, 1795, and 1797, taxable on 2 free males and 2 horses in 1811 [PPTL 1792-1806, frames 10, 31, 105, 129, 221, 245, 294, 414, 483, 659; 1807-21, frames 17, 99, 137, 220]. He registered in Southampton County on 29 July 1815: *age 48, Mulatto, 5 feet 7 1/4 inches, free born* [Register of Free Negroes 1794-1832, nos. 422, 969]. He was head of a Southampton County household of 10 "other free" in 1810 [VA:60].

vi.   ?Sylvia Gardner, born about 1778, registered in Southampton County on 8 November 1808: *age 30, Mulatto, born free*. She was about 40 when she registered again on 10 February 1819 [Register of Free Negroes 1794-1832, nos. 433, 1170]. She was head of a Southampton County household of 6 "other free" in 1810 [VA:56].

vii.   ?Pherebe Gardner, born about 1781, registered in Southampton County on 8 November 1808: *age 27, Mulatto, 5 feet 2-1/2 inches high, free born*. She registered again on 18 May 1815 [Register of Free Negroes 1794-1832, nos. 434, 953].

viii. ?Smith, born 1776-1794, head of a Caswell County, North Carolina household of 8 "free colored" in 1820 [NC:86].

2. Sarah Garner, born say 1735, was living in Isle of Wight County on 1 May 1760 when she was presented for having a "Molatto" child. She pleaded not guilty, but the court ordered her sold for five years. On 4 December 1760 the court ordered the churchwardens of Newport Parish to bind out her "_l tt _" children Fanny, Betty and Abell; on 5 July 1765 the court ordered the churchwardens to bind out her "Bastard" children John Randolph Garner and Sarah Garner; and on 5 August 1773 the court ordered the churchwardens to bind out Randall Garner and Miles Garner, "poore Mulatoes" [Orders 1759-63, 145, 186, 191, 195; 1764-8, 204; 1772-80, 164]. She was the mother of

i.   Urina, born say 1754, "Molatto" daughter of ___ Garner living in Isle of Wight County on 5 June 1760 when the court ordered the churchwardens of Newport Parish to bind her out [Orders 1759-63, 152].

ii.   Fanny, born say 1756, ordered bound apprentice on 4 December 1760.

iii.   Betty, born say 1758, ordered bound apprentice on 4 December 1760.

iv.   Abel, born say 1759, ordered bound apprentice on 4 December 1760.

v.   ?Dennis, born say 1760, a "yellow" complexioned soldier from Isle of Wight County listed in the size roll of troops who enlisted at Chesterfield Courthouse [The Chesterfield Supplement cited by NSDAR, *African American Patriots*, 149].

vi.   Randall/ Randolph, born say 1762, "Bastard" child of Sarah bound out in Isle of Wight County on 5 July 1765, a "poor Mulatto" ordered bound out on 5 August 1773. He was ordered bound out to someone else on 7 May 1778 when he complained that John Murphey was misusing him [Orders 1764-8, 204; 1772-80, 164, 421]. He was head of a Hertford County household of 3 "other free" in Captain Lewis' District in 1800, 6 in 1810 [NC:725], and 9 "free colored" in Northampton County in 1820 [NC:230].

vii.   Drucilla, born say 1764, bound apprentice in Isle of Wight County in 1765.

viii.   Miles, born say 1767, a "poore Mulatto" ordered bound out in Isle of Wight County on 5 August 1773, called son of Sarah Garner when he was ordered bound out on 1 May 1777 [Orders 1772-80, 164, 385].

GARNES FAMILY

1.   Elizabeth[1] Garns, born say 1720, and Lucy, Janey, David, Martha, and Lydia Garns complained to the Surry County, Virginia court in August 1751 that Sarah Edwards, John Powell, and Lucas Powell were holding them in servitude. Sarah Edwards refused to allow them to appear in court, so on 19 December 1752 the court ordered her committed to the custody of the sheriff until she posted bond of 300 pounds that she would produce them. On 17 January 1753 the court ruled that they were free. Martha was called "Daughter of Elizabeth Gerns" when she was bound apprentice by the same session of the court [Orders 1749-51, 278, 299; 1751-3, 118, 170, 296-7, 312-3, 318]. On 23 January 1753 the Brunswick County, Virginia court ordered the churchwardens of St. Andrew's Parish to bind out her "natural" children Lucy, David, Lydia, and Jane to Lucas Powell [Orders 1751-3, 366]. She was the mother of

2   i.   Lucy[1], born say 1740.
3   ii.   Martha, born say 1742.
4   iii.   Janey/ Jenny, born about 1747.
     iv.   David[1], born say 1748.
5   v.   Lydia[1], born say 1749.

2.   Lucy[1] Garnes, born say 1740, was living in Lunenburg County, Virginia, on 13 December 1764 when the court ordered the churchwardens of Cumberland Parish to bind out her children: Jeffrey, Thomas, Edward, and Elizabeth Garnes to William Cocke. She was sued by William Cocke in Lunenburg County court on 13 April 1765 [Orders 1764-5, fol.200; 1765-66, 59]. Jeffry was six years old and Thomas was four years on 8 May 1765 when they were bound to William Cocke in Granville County, North Carolina (no parent named) [N.C. Archives Indentures, CR 044.101.2]. The Mecklenburg County, Virginia court bound out her son Gaby Garnes (on 14 July 1766) and her son William (on 10 August 1767) to John Lynch. On 8 November 1773 the court ordered her children David and Elijah bound out to the Rev. Mr. John Cameron, and 14 April 1777 the court ordered the churchwardens to bind her children Gaby and William Garnes to William Bridgewater with the consent of their master John Lynch. On 8 June 1778 Lucy complained to the court that Bridgewater had disposed of Billy and Gaby, but the court dismissed the complaint after a hearing on 15 September 1778. On 12 February 1781 the court ordered the churchwardens to bind out her children Isaac and Lucy. On 9 September 1782 she complained to the court on behalf of her daughter Nancy Garnes against her master James Hughes, and the court cancelled the indentures and instead bound Nancy to William Randolph, Gentleman [Orders 1765-8, 173, 380; 1773-9, 127, 251, 413, 437; 1779-84, 89, 208]. She was granted administration of the Granville County, North Carolina estate of her deceased sons Thomas and Jesse Garnes in August 1791 [Minutes 1789-91]. She was head of a Mecklenburg County, Virginia household of 4 "free colored" in 1820 [VA:153b]. Her children were

     i.   Jeffrey, born about 1759, a six-year-old bound by the Lunenburg County court to William Cocke to be a planter on 8 May 1765. In the 1778 Militia Returns for Captain Richard Taylor's Company of Granville County, North Carolina, he was listed as "a black man," twenty years old, (serving) in place of William Edwards Cock [Mil. T.R. 4-40 by Granville County Genealogical Society, *Granville Connections*, vol.1, no.1, 10].

    ii.   Thomas, born about 1761, a four-year-old bound to William Cocke on 8 May 1765 to be a planter, died before August court 1791 when his mother Lucy was granted administration on his Granville County estate [Minutes 1789-91].

    iii. Edward, born say 1762.

    iv. Elizabeth[2], born say 1764.

    v.   Gabriel[1]/ Gaby, born say 1765.

6   vi. Nancy, born say 1765.

    vii. William[1], born say 1766, ordered bound to John Lynch on 10 August 1767 [Orders 1765-8, 380].

    viii. Moses[1], born say 1768, child of Lucy Garnes, ordered bound apprentice to Samuel Wooton in Mecklenburg County on 12 October 1772 [Orders 1771-3, 337].

    ix. David, born say 1770, bound to the Rev. John Cameron in Mecklenburg County on 8 November 1773.

    x.   ?Catherine, born about 1772, a seventy-eight-year-old "Black" woman living with sixty-five-year-old Lucy Garnes in the 1850 Mecklenburg County census [VA:65b].

7   xi. Elijah[1], born say 1772.

    xii. Isaac[1], born say 1775, son of Lucy Garnes, ordered bound out by the Mecklenburg County court on 12 February 1781 [Orders 1779-84, 89]. He married Fanny **Mayhaw (Mayo)**, 17 February 1797 Warren County, North Carolina bond, Elijah Garnes bondsman. He was head of a Mecklenburg County household of 5 "free colored" in 1820 [VA:153b].

    xiii. Lucy, born say 1777, child of Lucy Garnes, ordered bound out in Mecklenburg County on 12 February 1781.

    xiv. Margaret[2], born say 1785, "bastard Child of Lucy Garnes" bound to Samuel Wooton, Sr., in Mecklenburg County on 9 June 1788 [Orders 1787-92, 237]. She married Henry **Mayo**, 17 October 1809 Warren County bond, Richard Russell bondsman.

3.   Martha Garnes, born say 1742, "Daughter of Elizabeth Gerns," was bound apprentice by the Surry County court on 17 January 1753 [Orders 1751-3, 318]. She may have been the mother of

    i.   Anthony, born about 1761, head of a Hertford County, North Carolina household of 2 "other free" in 1790 (called Anthony Garner) [NC:26]. He applied for a pension at the age of fifty-nine while residing in Wilson County, Tennessee, on 27 October 1820 with his thirty-eight-year-old wife and three step children. He stated that he enlisted in the 7th North Carolina Regiment in 1778 and served until 1782 [M804-1050, frame 940].

8   ii. Lucy[2], born say 1765.

    iii. Daniel, born before 1776, head of a Hertford County household of 2 "other free" in 1800, 3 in 1810 [NC:98], and 12 "free colored" in 1820 [NC:192].

    iv. Doll, born before 1776, head of a Hertford County household of 2 "other free" in 1810 [NC:99] and one "free colored" over forty-five years old in 1820 [NC:190].

4.   Jenny Garnes, born about 1747, was called Jenny Guarnes in Surry County, Virginia, on 20 September 1797 when her son Drury registered as a "free Negro." She registered herself on 25 March 1805: *a bright complexion aged about 58 years, 5'2-1/2" high...born of a free woman* [Hudgins, *Surry County Register of Free Negroes*, 25]. Her Children were

    i.   David[2], born about 1777, taxable in Surry County from 1792 to 1804: listed as Robert McIntosh's tithable in 1792 [PPTL, 1791-1816, frames 89, 372, 411, 450, 486, 526, 563]. He registered as a "free Negro" in

Surry County on 29 June 1803: *son of Jenny Garns a free mulatto woman, of a yellowish complexion, 5'3" high, square and pretty stout made aged about 26 years and by profession a waterman* [Hudgins, *Surry County Register of Free Negroes*, 21].

ii. Drury, born about 1778, registered on 20 September 1797: *son of Jenny Guarnes a free mulato woman resident of this county, 19 years old, yellowish complexion, 5'2-1/2 inches tall, square & pretty stout made by profession a waterman* [Back of Guardian & Accounts Book 1783-1804, no.21].

iii. Caty, born about 1779, registered in Surry County on 23 July 1808: *(daughter of Jenny Garnes a free Mullatto Woman late of Surry county) is of a yellow complexion, 4'11-1/4" high, about 29 years of age.*

iv. ?Lydia[2], born about 1782, listed as a "free Negro & Mulatto" in Surry County in 1813 [PPTL, 1791-1816, frame 738]. She registered as a free Negro in Surry County on 22 November 1847: *dark complexion; born of free parents; about 65 years of age, 4 feet 11-1/2 inches tall* [Register of Free Negroes, p.8, no.945].

v. ?Patsey, born 30 September 1784, registered in Surry County on 31 December 1804: *a free woman of this county is of a bright complexion aged 20 years the 30th day of September 1804, she is 5'4-3/4" high, has a small nose, was born of a free woman of this county* [Hudgins, *Surry County Register of Free Negroes*, 37, 24].

5. Lydia[1] Guarnes, born say 1749, was freed from the service of Sarah Edwards in Surry County, Virginia, on 17 January 1753. On 23 January 1782 the court bound out her "Molatto" children Betty, James, David and Lucy [Orders 1751-3, 312-3; 1775-85, 135]. She was the mother of

9   i. Elizabeth[3], born say 1766

     ii. James, born before 1774, head of a Lenoir County, North Carolina household of 3 "free colored" in 1820.

     iii. David[3], born say 1774.

     iv. Lucy[3], an "other free" woman living alone in Lenoir County in 1810 [NC:293].

6. Nancy Garnes, born say 1765, "a bastard Child of Lucy Garns," was bound apprentice to John Lynch in Mecklenburg County on 10 September 1770 (no race mentioned), probably identical to Nan Garnes, child of Lucy Garnes who was ordered bound apprentice to Samuel Wooton on 12 October 1772, called "Nanney Garnes, Bastard of Lucy Garnes," on 8 March 1773 when she was released from John Lynch and bound to James Hughes. She was removed from James Hughes' service and bound to William Randolph on 9 September 1782 [Orders 1768-71, 465; 1771-73, 337, 479; 1779-84, 208]. She was the mother of

     i. William[2], born say 1783, ordered bound apprentice by the Mecklenburg County court on 9 June 1788 (no parent named), child of Nancy Garnes bound to Francis Moody by order of the court on 10 September 1792. On 11 January 1802 he was charged in Mecklenburg County court with stealing articles from Benjamin Heulin but was found not guilty. On 13 October 1806 he was charged with breaking and entering the house of James Johnson, tavern keeper, and stealing about $30 worth of goods. A witness named Henry Wilson testified that he had seen Lewis **Cousins** return some of the goods to Johnson and that **Cousins** had said the property had been left with him by William. He was sent for trial at the district court in Brunswick County [Orders 1787-92, 240; 1792-5, 60; 1801-3, 137; 1805-6, 334]. He may have been the Billy Garns who was head of a Henrico County household of 4 "other free" in 1810 [VA:996].

10   ii. Lucy[3], born about 1785.

    iii.   David², born say 1787, ordered bound apprentice by the Mecklenburg County court on 9 June 1788, bound to Richard Thompson on 10 July 1797 and bound to Francis Lett, hatter, on 9 July 1804. He and Henry Mason were licensed by the Mecklenburg County court as hawkers and peddlers from 16 June 1806 to 16 June 1807 [Orders 1787-92, 240; 1795-8, 289; 1803-5, 190; 1805-6, 294].

    iv.   Lewis, born say 1789, child of Nancy Garnes, bound to Edward Holloway by order of the court on 10 September 1792 [Orders 1792-5, 60, 226].

    v.   Letty, born say 1792, child of Nancy Garnes, bound to Edward Holloway by order of the court on 10 February 1794 [Orders 1792-5, 226].

    vi.   ?Moses², born say 1795, a "Mullatto" bound by the Mecklenburg County court as an apprentice to Jacob Garrot, millwright, on 13 June 1806 [Orders 1805-6, 63].

    vii.   ?Sally, born say 1800, a "Mullatto" bound by the Mecklenburg County court as an apprentice to Jacob Garrot and his wife on 13 June 1806 [Orders 1805-6, 63].

    viii.   Gabriel², born say 1803, illegitimate son of Nancy Garnes, bound to Isaac Watson, carpenter, on 8 August 1808 and bound instead to Lewis Smith, blacksmith, on 14 November 1808 [Orders 1807-9, 437, 486].

7.   Elijah¹ Garnes, born say 1772, was ordered bound apprentice to the Reverend John Cameron in Mecklenburg County, Virginia, on 8 November 1773. He married Rhoda **Mayhoe/Mayo**, 5 February 1797 Warren County, North Carolina bond, Charles **Durham** bondsman. He was in Mecklenburg County, Virginia, on 14 August 1797 when his suit against Adam Loving and Major Butler for trespass, assault and battery was submitted to arbitration [Orders 1795-8, 297]. He was head of a Mecklenburg County, Virginia household of 5 "free colored" in 1820 [VA:165a]. He may have been the father of

    i.   John, married Peggy **Brannum** (**Brandon**), 8 September 1823 Warren County bond, Benjamin **Durom** (**Durham**) bondsman.

    ii.   David⁵, born about 1800, registered in Mecklenburg County in August court 1824: *about 24 years of age about five feet Eight 1/2 inches high...of black complexion* [Free Person of Color, no.13].

    iii.   Elijah², Jr., head of a Mecklenburg County household of one "free colored" in 1820 [VA:150a].

8.   Lucy² Garnes, born say 1764, "a Free Mullatto Woman," moved from Hertford to Bertie County by 29 December 1783 when James Jones of Hertford agreed to transfer the indentures of her children Sarah and Benjamin to James Fleetwood of Bertie County [CR 10.101.7 by *NCGSJ* XIV:159]. Her children were

    i.   Sarah, born say 1780, bound to James Jones of Hertford and then bound to James Fleetwood of Bertie on 29 December 1783.

    ii.   Benjamin, born say 1782, bound to James Jones of Hertford and then bound to James Fleetwood of Bertie on 29 December 1783.

9.   Elizabeth³ Garnes, born say 1766, was living in Surry County on 5 January 1804 when her son Henry Garns registered as a "free Negro." She was the mother of

    i.   Henry, born about 1784, registered in Surry County on 5 January 1804: *a negro man of dark complexion who is 5'5-1/4", is the son of Betty Garns a free woman of this county* [Hudgins, *Surry County Register of Free Negroes*, 22]. He was listed as Robert Watkins' Surry County tithable in 1801, listed with Samuel Butler in 1802 [PPTL, 1791-1816, frames 466, 473].

10. Lucy[3] Garnes, born about 1785, child of Nancy Garnes, was bound to Edward Holloway by order of the Mecklenburg County court on 10 September 1792 [Orders 1792-5, 60, 226]. She head of a Mecklenburg County household of 4 "free colored" females in 1820 [VA:155a] and was sixty-five years old when she was counted in the 1850 Mecklenburg County census [VA:133b]. She was the mother of

    i. Isaac[2], born about 1793, "son of Lucy Garnes," bound apprentice to Richard Brown, carpenter, on 14 May 1805 and bound instead to Jacob Garrot, millwright, the following day [Orders 1803-5, 376, 389]. He registered in Mecklenburg County in July 1820: *a man of dark complexion, five feet Seven and one fourth Inches high, twenty Seven Years old* [Free Person of Color, no.7].

GEORGE FAMILY

1. Peter[1] George, "Negro," born say 1630, was imported as a slave by Nathaniel Littleton in 1640. He, "the Negro carpenter," and his daughter Jane were mentioned without surnames in the 1656 Northampton County, Virginia will of Littleton's wife Anne who left them to her son Edward [*VMHB* 75:17-21]. Edward Littleton mentioned Peter, his wife Joan, and their daughters Jane and Susan with their surnames in his 1663 will to his wife Frances who later married Francis Pigot [DW 1657-66, 174-5]. Peter was taxable in 1664 in Frances Littleton's household in Northampton County:

> *Mr. Littletons Family*
> *Wm Clements*
> *peter George Negro*
> *Paull Carter & wife*
> *Ould Jack Negro   5*   [Orders 1657-64, fol.198].

He and his wife "Jone" were taxable in Captain Francis Pigott's household with Thomas **Carter** "Negro" in 1667, 1668, 1671, and 1675. Joan probably died about 1677 since she was not listed with him in Pigot's household that year [Orders 1664-74 fol. 42, p.55, fol.114; 1674-79, 75, 191]. About 1676 he received his freedom from Pigot on the promise to pay 10,000 pounds of tobacco. He completed the last payment in 1682 [DW&c 1680-92, 53 by Deal, *Race and Class*, 444]. He must have been a free man when he was a witness to the will of King Tony, "Negro," proved 28 February 1677/8 [Orders 1674-79, 247]. He rented land on the estate of Southy Littleton for 2,400 pounds of tobacco for the years 1679 to 1685 (near Emmanuel **Driggers**) [OW 1683-9, 150-151]. In March 1687/8 he was duped into thinking that "free Negroes should be slaves againe" by one of his white neighbors, Robert Candlin. He left all his household goods and livestock with Candlin and fled to Somerset County, Maryland, with his neighbor, Sarah **Driggers**, and several other unidentified free African Americans. He was called Peter George of Wiccocomoco Hundred Negro" on 23 April 1688 when he posted 5 pounds surety, and he and (his wife?) Mary George were witnesses in a Somerset County court case for "Sarah Driggers Negro woman wife of Thomas Driggers Negro" [*Archives of Maryland* 91:47]. Perhaps his wife Mary was Mary **Rodriggus** whose Northampton County tax was paid by the parish in 1674 [DW 1664-74, 273]. Peter George and Sarah **Driggers** had returned to Northampton County by 29 May 1691 when they successfully sued Candlin's widow for the recovery of Peter's livestock. On 19 September 1698 Peter was charged with being in possession of a silver spoon stolen from Henry Harmonson's house. He testified that he had bought the spoon from King Tom Indian who stated that he had gotten it from Living Denwood of Somerset County. The court found King Tom guilty and ordered that he receive twenty lashes [OW 1689-98, 106, 115-116, 510]. Peter's children were

       i.   Jane, born say 1653.
       ii. Susan, born say 1655.
2   iii. Anthony¹, born about 1660.
       iv. Peter², born about 1666, a thirty-nine-year-old man listed in the 20
            August 1705 inventory of Ralph Pigot's estate on Hog Island [DW
            1692-1707, 417].
3   v.   Peter³, born say 1678.
       vi. ?Samuel, born say 1680, a "Negro" who, in company with John and
            Johnson **Driggers** on 8 November 1702, was convicted of killing a hog
            belonging to Samuel French and then "in an insolent manner" abusing
            several white persons. On 28 January 1703/4 the court ordered Sarah
            Drighouse, alias Landman, to pay him for appearing as her witness in
            the suit of Colonel John Custis [OW&c 1698-1710, 106, 182].

2.   Anthony¹ George, born about 1660, remained a slave and was forty-five years
     old when he was listed in the inventory of Ralph Pigot's Northampton County
     estate in 1705 [DW 1692-1707, 417]. He married Frances **Harman** in 1693
     when she recorded her livestock mark in Northampton County court [DW
     1651-4, 26]. He, or perhaps a son by the same name, was taxable in Ralph
     Pigot's household in 1720 [Bell, *Northampton County Tithables*, 1]. Since his
     wife was free, so were their children. They may have been
       i.   William¹, born say 1688, perhaps the illegitimate child born to Frances
            Harman before May 1688 [OW 1683-89, 202]. He was tithable in his
            own household in 1720, tithable with his brother Anthony in 1721, a
            "negro" tithable by himself in 1723, with his wife Elizabeth in
            Anthony's household in 1724, and in his own household with Elizabeth
            from 1725 to 1731 [Bell, *Northampton County Tithables*, 1, 18, 36, 53,
            76, 101, 119, 147, 168, 222]. He was sued by William Mills on 11
            March 1730/1 but did not appear when the case came to trial on 11
            May 1731 [Orders 1729-32, 77, 85].
4   ii. Anthony², born say 1690.
       iii. Joannah, born say 1695, tithable in Anthony George's household from
            1724 to 1726.

3.   Peter³ George, born say 1678, may have been the Peter George, "free Negro"
     who was sued by Thomas Harmonson, Sr., in Northampton County on 28
     November 1700 for 700 pounds of tobacco [OW&c 1698-1710, 53]. On 2
     March 1705/6 he and his wife Mary bound their one-year-old "mallato or
     negro child" Amarrica to George and Susannah Corbin until the age of twenty-
     one [OW 1698-1710, 448-9]. Perhaps Mary was identical to Mary **Carter** who
     was presented for bastard bearing on 30 May 1699 (for a child she had by
     Daniel Benthall's slave Daniel) and in 1703 [OW&c 1698-1710, 8, 18, 165].
     Peter and Mary's child was
5   i.   America, born about January 1704/5.

4.   Anthony² George, born say 1690, may have been the unnamed illegitimate
     child born to Frances **Harman** before May 1690 [DW 1689-98, 35, 58]. He
     was tithable in Ralph Pigot's Northampton County household in 1720, in the
     household of (his brother?) William George from 1721 to 1723, head of a
     household with William, Joannah, Ann, and Elizabeth George in 1724, with
     Joannah and Ann George in 1725 and 1726, not counted in 1727, and head of
     a household with (his wife?) Ann from 1728 to 1731 [Bell, *Northampton
     County Tithables*, 1, 18, 36, 53, 76, 101, 119, 147, 168, 222]. Ann made a
     deed of gift of 150 acres in Craven County, North Carolina, on the Neuse
     River at the head of a long creek to (her son?) Elijah George in 1757 [DB
     9:425]. She may have been the "Nanney George" who was head of a Craven
     County household of 1 "Black female" in 1769 [SS 837]. Anthony and Ann's
     children may have been

i. Peter[4], born say 1720, listed in the 4 October 1754 muster of Abner Neale's Craven County, North Carolina Company between the head of Slocomb's Creek and the head of Turnagain Bay. In Neale's 4 October 1755 muster he was among five "free Negroes" including John and Abel **Carter** [Clark, *Colonial Soldiers of the South*, 708]. In 1757 he witnessed the Craven County deed of Ann George to Elijah George [DB 9:425]. His will, proved in 1763, named his brother William and sisters Susanny and Deborah [DB 8:220].

ii. Elijah, born say 1722, received 150 acres on the Neuse River by deed of gift from Ann George in 1757. He probably died before 20 September 1765 when his brother William sold this land [DB 9:425; 17:290].

iii. Susan, born say 1725, mentioned in the 1760 will of her brother Peter taxable in her own Craven County household in 1769 [SS 837].

iv. Deborah, born say 1728, mentioned in the 1760 will of her brother Peter George. She may have married George **Godett**.

6 v. William[2], born say 1730.

5. America George, born about January 1705/6, was one year and two months old when she was bound out by her parents Peter and Mary George in Northampton County, Virginia. She was presented by the churchwardens of Accomack County for having a bastard child in 1728 [Orders 1724-31, 99]. She probably moved to Maryland where a George America was head of a Worcester County household of 6 "other free" in 1790 [MD:124]. One of her children was most likely

7 i. Sabra, born say 1728.

6. William[2] George, born say 1730, was mentioned in the 1760 Craven County will of his brother Peter George. As "William George Free Negroe" he sold 100 acres of Peter's land on the south side of the Neuse River in Craven County on 20 September 1765, and on the same day he sold 150 acres which his brother Elijah received by deed of gift from Ann George [DB 14:286; 17:290]. He was tithable in Craven County in 1769 [SS 837]. In 1779 he was taxable in the District of Captain Adam Tooley & Captain John Carney on an assessment of 196 pounds [LP 30.1]. He sold 100 acres on the south side of the Neuse River in Craven County to Mingo **Stringer** in 1782 [DB 24:284]. He was head of a Craven County household of 10 "other free" in 1790 [NC:130] and 4 "other free" in Wake County in 1800 [NC:764]. In 1801 he sold Craven County land [DB 36:96]. His children may have been

i. John, born say 1769, a "negro fellow" wanted on 5 April 1794 for breaking jail in New Bern District where he was indicted for burglary [Fouts, *NC Gazette of New Bern*, II:39]. 9, no.430]. He may have been the same Jonathan George who married Pheraby **Locus** 27 January 1802 Orange County bond with Lawrence **Pettiford** bondsman. He married, second, Anna **Manuel**, 23 August 1815 Wake County bond with Jesse **Manuel** bondsman.

ii. Kezia, born say 1775, married Jesse **Moore**, 16 April 1792 Craven County bond with Joseph **Dring** bondsman.

iii. Hannah, married Joseph **Dring**, 18 December 1794 Craven County bond with William George bondsman.

iv. Ned, head of a Pasquotank County household of 5 "other free" in 1810 [NC:900].

v. Peter[5], married Hannah **Carter**, 9 April 1795 Carteret County bond with George **Carter**, bondsman. He was head of a Craven County household of 5 "free colored" in 1820 [NC:65]. On 4 November 1821 he and Hannah sold land in Craven County which Hannah inherited from her father George **Carter**. He purchased land from the **Martin** family in 1825 [DB 43:82; 45:428].

vi.   William³, married Charity **Carter**, 16 February 1804 Craven County bond with Peter George bondsman.

vii. Elijah, married Nancy **Carter**, 24 September 1803 Craven County bond with Samuel **Moore** bondsman.

viii. Betsy, married Theophilus **Carter**, 16 November 1804 Craven County bond with George **Carter** bondsman.

ix.   Polly, married Peter **Godet**, 10 January 1805 Craven County bond with Peter George bondsman.

7.   Sabra George, born say 1728, was presented on 27 January 1746 by the churchwardens of Accomack Parish for having a bastard child. She was ordered to serve Covinton Corbin an additional year because he paid her fine [Orders 1744-53, 182]. She was probably the mother of

8   i.   Joshua¹, born say 1744.

         ii. Bridget, born say 1746, bound to Samuel Toddiman of Accomack County on 31 March 1747 [Orders 1744-53, 182].

8.   Joshua¹ George, born say 1744, was bound as an apprentice cooper to Samuel Toddiman of Accomack County on 31 March 1747 [Orders 1744-53, 195]. On 22 February 1774 Robert Martin sued him in Accomack County court for a 4 pound, 17 shilling debt due by account [Orders 1774-7, 100]. He was taxable in Accomack County from 1783 to 1812: taxable in 1789 on 2 free males and a slave over the age of sixteen who may have been his wife [PPTL, 1782-1814, frames 48, 314, 343, 414, 512, 678, 743, 807]. He was head of an Accomack Parish household of 5 "other free" in 1800 [*Virginia Genealogist* 1:108] and 7 in 1810 [VA:26]. He was the father of

         i.   Parker, taxable in Accomack County from 1799 to 1813: called a "Blackman" in 1799, with the notation "by Forman" in 1800, "of Joshua" in 1810 [PPTL, 1782-1814, frames 415, 446, 546, 677, 743, 855]. He was head of an Accomack Parish household of 3 "other free" in 1800 [*Virginia Genealogist* 1:107] and 7 in 1810 [VA:97].

         ii. ?Jacob, head of an Accomack Parish household of 1 "other free" and a white woman (Sally Jarvis) in 1800 [*Virginia Genealogist* 1:108], taxable in Accomack County in 1802, called a "B.M." in 1807 [PPTL, 1782-1814, frames 512, 678].

         iii. ?Joshua, Jr., taxable in Accomack County from 1807 to 1812 [PPTL, 1782-1814, frames 678, 807].

Other members of the George family were

         i.   Scotch and Bess George, "2 F.N.," were "Black" taxables in Perquimans County, North Carolina, in 1771. In 1772 Scotch George was head of a Hertford District, Perquimans County household of 4 taxables, including himself, Bess, Dinea, and Juda George [CR 077.701.1].

         ii. Zachariah, a "Mulatto" bound by the churchwardens of Accomack Parish to John Matthews, Jr., on 22 February 1774 to be a shoemaker [Orders 1774-7, 43]. He was head of an Accomack Parish, Accomack County household of 8 "other free" in 1800 [*Virginia Genealogist* 1:107].

         iii. Jemima/Jesemine, head of an Accomack Parish household of 5 "other free" in 1800 [*Virginia Genealogist* 1:107] and 5 in 1810 [VA:97].

         iv. Esther, registered in Accomack County about 1832: *born about 1780, a Black, 5'6-1/2" high, born free in Accomack County* [Register of Free Negroes, 1785-1863, no. 554].

         v.   Sarah, head of an Accomack County household of 4 "other free" in 1810 [VA:19]. She registered in Accomack County: *born about 1789, a light Black, 5'6" high, born free in Accomack County* [Register of Free Negroes, 1785-1863, no. 392].

GIBSON FAMILY

The Gibson family probably descended from Elizabeth **Chavis**. On 28 March 1672 she made a successful petition to the General Court of Virginia to release her son Gibson Gibson who had been unlawfully bound by Berr. Mercer to Thomas Barber, who had gone to England leaving the boy with Samuel Austin [Minutes of the Council 1670-76, 106, Virginia Historical Society Mss 4V81935a2; McIlwaine, *Minutes of the Council*, 302-3]. Her children were

1   i.   Gibson[1] Gibson, born say 1660.
2   ii.   ?Hubbard Gibson, born say 1670.

1.   Gibson[1] Gibson, born say 1660, was released from his unlawful apprenticeship to Thomas Barber on 28 March 1672. He was called Gibey Gibson in 1704 when he was listed in the Quit Rent Rolls for James City County with 150 acres [*VHM* 31:156]. He called himself Gibby Gibson, planter, on 7 September 1726 when he made a Charles City County deed of gift to his daughter Mary Smith by which he gave her two "Negro" boys named Simon and Civility during her lifetime and at her death to her children Tom, Lightfoot, Sarah, Mary, Elizabeth, Rebecca and Ann. He left a 2 March 1726/7 Charles City County will, proved 3 May 1727, by which he gave Hannah Dennam cattle and a boy slave named Jack during her lifetime and then to his son Gibby Gibson, also gave Hannah Dennam a boy named Peter during her lifetime and then to his son George Gibson, gave his wife Frances Gibson a girl slave named Verity(?) during her lifetime and then to his daughter Frances Smith, gave his son Edward a "Negro wench" named Judy and his carpenter's and cooper's tools, gave a slave girl named Nanny to Tabitha **Rollinson**, gave his son-in-law George Smith two boys named Sovillaty and Simon and named him as his executor [DW 1724-31, 122, 161-2, 166-7]. He was the father of

    i.   Mary Smith, born say 1684, mother of Tom, Lightfoot, Sarah, Mary, Elizabeth, Rebecca and Ann Smith.
3   ii.   Gibby/ Gilbert[1], born say 1686.
    iii.   Edward[1], born say 1688, received a slave named Judy by his father's will. He left a 10 April 1727 Charles City County will, proved 7 June 1727, by which he left Israel Brown his carpenter's and cooper's tools, his slave Judy to his wife Anna Gibson, and named his daughters Rebecca Gibson and Tabitha Ellet. His wife was executor [DW 1724-31, 167-8].[96]
    iv.   ?Hannah Dennam, born say 1690, received two slaves by the will of (her father?) Gibby Gibson.
    v.   George[1], born say 1695, sued William Drinkard in Charles City County in January 1737/8 but failed to prosecute Orders 1737-51, 29]. He was granted a patent for 62 acres on Pease Hill Swamp in Charles City County on 25 July 1741 [Patents 19:1085]. In November 1741 the court presented him and George Gibson, Jr., for not going to church. In July 1745 Phillis **Goeing (Gowen)** petitioned him concerning her children, but he failed to answer the petition so the court ordered the churchwardens to bind them out. In December 1745 he and Captain Samuel Harwood posted 20 pounds security for his good behavior for a year. In February 1745/6 he, William Witherspoon, and John Atkinson provided a total of 80 pounds security for his good behavior, and he and his son Randolph Gibson and his wife Elizabeth posted bond of 20 pounds each for the good behavior of Randolph and

---

[96]Israel Brown left a 22 August 1757 Lunenburg County will naming his wife Anne Brown and daughter Lucy **Cuttillo** [WB 2:21].

Elizabeth. The court fined him 5 shillings for not going to church in 1746, 1748, 1749, 1755 and 1756 [Orders 1737-51, 185, 196, 371, 383, 391, 392, 394, 417, 474, 499; 1751-7, 194, 298, 419].

vi. Frances Smith, wife of George Smith. She probably married William **Chavis** of Granville County, North Carolina, who named his son Gibby. His wife Frances had a son named John Smith who settled her Granville County estate in May 1781. In the account of the estate he claimed his right to six slaves which were due him from his father [WB 1:303].

vii. ?Tabitha **Rollinson**, received a girl slave named Nanny by the will of (her father?) Gibby Gibson. She was apparently the wife of George **Rollinson** (**Rawlinson** of York County) who received a girl slave named Nanny by the 6 May 1727 distribution of the estate [DW 1724-31, 167].

4   viii. ?John², born say 1700.

2. Hubbard¹ Gibson, born say 1670, was living in Charles City County on 24 March 1691/2 when he appeared in court and on 3 August 1693 when he sued John Hardiman for riding his horse to its death [Orders 1687-95, 394, 454, 463]. He purchased 200 acres on the north side of the Blackwater Swamp in Prince George County from John Poythres on 11 December 1704. He and his wife (making their mark) and their son Edward (signing) sold this land by lease and release for 32 pounds while residing in North Carolina on 11 and 12 December 1721 [Deeds, Etc. 1713-28, 508-9]. He may have left Prince George County by 12 February 1716/7 when the court ordered that the appraisement of his estate (on an attachment by James Thweatt) be continued to the next court [Orders 1714-20, 104]. In 1721 he was taxed on 370 acres and one poll in Chowan County, North Carolina [Haun, *Old Albemarle County NC Miscellaneous Records*, 331]. On 13 November 1727 he bought an additional 100 acres on the north side of the Roanoke River in what was then Bertie County. His daughter Mary co-signed this deed with him [DB B:324]. The land was situated on the south side of Cypress Swamp in what became Northampton County in 1741. A little over six months later on 11 July 1728 he and his sons Edward Gibson and Hubbard Gibson, Jr., sold 370 acres in Bertie County on the north side of the Roanoke River, explaining in the deed that the land had been granted to Hubbard's deceased son John by patent of 10 August 1720 [DB C:37]. The family probably moved to South Carolina with Gideon Gibson in 1731. Hubbard probably died before 1742 when Mary Gibson of Amelia County, South Carolina, sold the 100 acres she and Hubbard purchased in Northampton County [DB 1:58]. His children were

5   i. John¹, born say 1690.
6   ii. ?Thomas¹, born say 1692.
7   iii. ?Gideon¹, born say 1695.
    iv. Edward², born say 1697, signed his father's 11 December 1721 Prince George County, Virginia deed while residing in North Carolina. He was taxable in 1721 in the same Chowan County district as his father and witness to the 15 October 1732 Edgecombe County, North Carolina deed of William Sims to James Millikin for land on the south side of Quankey Creek [DB 1:20]. He may have been related to another Edward Gibson, "(a Mulatto) a stout well-set Man, with short black curly Hair," who escaped prison in South Carolina according to the 19 May 1767 issue of the South Carolina Gazette [Jordan, *White Over Black*, 174].
    v. Hubbard², Jr., born before 1706, taxed in 1721 in the same district as his father.
    vi. Mary, born say 1705, cosigner of a Bertie County deed with her father on 13 November 1727 [DB B:324]. She was living in Amelia County, South Carolina, in 1742 when she sold this land in what was by then

Northampton County [DB 1:58]. She recorded a plat for 200 acres on
Flat Creek in Craven County, South Carolina, on 27 January 1756
[Colonial Plats 6:389]. She made a Craven County deed of gift of
slaves named Owen and Carolina to her son Samuel Gibson on 25
October 1768 [Miscellaneous Record Book NN:401].

3. Gilbert [1] Gibson, born say 1686, was sued in Henrico County court on 1 June
1709 by John Ellis for a debt of 2 pounds currency due by account. He sued
Joseph Watson in court in July 1710, and he was sued by Allenson Clarke for
a 4 pound currency debt in September the same year [Orders 1707-9, 153,
163; 1710-4, 15, 25]. He was granted two patents for land in what was then
New Kent County on 11 July 1719: one for 224 acres adjoining Stephen
Sunter's patent and Captain Dangerfield's line and another for 125 acres
adjoining John Macon and Matthew and Thomas Anderson. And he received
a patent for 400 acres on both sides of the South Anna River on 28 September
1728 in Hanover County, 400 acres in Hanover County adjoining John
Woodey on 28 January 1733, and 200 acres on both sides of Ballenger's Creek
in Albemarle County on 20 August 1747 [Land Office Patents 10:437; 14:3;
15:146; 23:138]. On 10 October 1743 Agnes **Goin** sued him in Louisa County
court for 3 pounds due for services performed. On 26 August 1746 the court
approved his request to make a bridle path through Captain Holland's land at
Green Spring. He married Sarah Lemay sometime before 24 February 1746/7
when the court ordered the churchwardens of Fredericksville Parish to bind
her children out because she was not educating them. On 23 February 1747/8
the court found Gilbert guilty of selling liquor without a license and ordered
that he receive twenty-one lashes if he refused to pay the fine [Orders 1742-8,
82, 91, 190, 200, 220, 252]. He made an 18 December 1756 Louisa County
deed by which he gave his son Gilbert 200 acres and a slave named Peter,
gave his son Jordan 200 acres and a slave named Jack, gave his daughters
Tabitha and Mary 100 acres each, gave John Lemay 200 acres and a slave
named Kate, gave Samuel and Sarah Lemay a cow each when they came of
age, lent 200 acres to George Gibson and his wife Susannah and Benjamin
Brannum and his wife Frances the plantations they were then living on during
their lifetimes, and made his wife his executrix. However, he stated that the
deed was to be void if he returned from a planned trip to South Carolina [DB
B:140-2]. Gibson Jones of South Carolina made a deposition in May 1767
stating that he had been living with Gilbert in Louisa County about 20 August
1758 when Gilbert packed up all his household goods and left for South
Carolina. The sheriff stopped him about a quarter of a mile from his home and
executed a judgment for 10 pounds against a mare and some of the household
goods, delaying him until the following morning [Abercrombie, *Louisa County
Judgments*, 46]. Gilbert made a 7 June 1760 Louisa County will, proved 15
October 1764, by which he gave all his estate to his wife Sarah during her
lifetime and then divided the estate as follows: to (her son) John Lemay 200
acres on Ballanger's Creek in Albemarle County, to his sons Gideon and
Jordan Gibson land on Pamunkey River, to his son William Gibson land on
South Anna River, to his sons Gilbert and David one shilling each, to
daughters Tabitha, Mary, and Jane Gibson household items and farm animals,
and lent to his son George Gibson and daughter Frances Gibson the land where
they were then living during their lifetimes provided they paid ten shillings.
Feeba Bunch was a witness to the will [WB 1:78]. His children George and
Frances sued his widow Sarah and his children by her in 1766. The court took
depositions from a number of people including Agnes **Going**, and on 12
September 1770 the court awarded George Gibson 200 acres and awarded
Benjamin and his wife Frances **Branham** a tract of land between Peter's Creek
and Little Creek [Orders 1766-74, 6, 20, 27; 1766-72, 412-3]. Among the
depositions was one by Mrs. Ann Moore who stated that Gilbert Gibson's
mother had been living with him until he "turned her out" because she would

not make over a slave ("Negro wench") that she had for her maintenance [Abercrombie, *Louisa County Judgments*, 21]. This slave was probably identical to or the daughter of Verity(?) who was lent to her by Gibby Gibson's 1727 Charles City County will. Gilbert's children were

    i.   George[2], born about 1711. He purchased 320 acres in Louisa County and he and his wife Susanna sold 90 acres in Louisa County to William **Donathan** by deeds proved on 26 March 1745. He was presented by the court on 28 May 1745 for concealing a tithable who was probably his wife. On 14 August 1769 he and Nathan Gibson were brought into court for riotous behavior. George was found not guilty, but Nathan was required to give security for his good behavior for one year. George posted bond as executor of the last will of James Haggard on 8 October 1770 [Orders 1742-8, 140, 152; 1766-72, 335, 418].

   ii.   Gilbert[2], born about 1714, about fifty-three years old on 2 May 1767 when he made a deposition regarding 200 acres of land given by his father to his brother George [Abercrombie, *Louisa County Judgments*, 46-7]. He was sued for a debt of 1 pound, 14 shillings in Louisa County court on 27 May 1746 [Orders 1742-8, 192].

  iii. Frances, wife of Benjamin **Branham**.

   iv. William.

    v. Gideon[4], born say 1730, a defendant with Jordan Gibson in Sally **Going**'s suit for trespass, assault and battery which was dismissed by the Louisa County court by agreement of the parties on 11 April 1774. On 10 July 1775 Gideon provided security of 25 pounds for Moses **Going** in Louisa County court. On 11 September 1775 Colonel Robert Anderson made a motion in Louisa County court charging that Gideon, being a "Mulatto," had beaten him. The court ruled that Gideon was not a "Mulatto" and granted Anderson an appeal to the General Court. Gideon and his wife Milly sold land by deed proved in Louisa County court on 11 December 1780 [Orders 1774-82, 10, 42, 127, 130, 318].

   vi. Mary, born say 1735, pregnant with a child when her father made his 18 December 1756 deed.

  vii. Jordan[2], born say 1738, not yet of age when his father deeded him two hundred acres and a slave named Jack on 18 December 1756.

 viii. David.

   ix. Tabitha.

    x. Jane.

4.   John[2] Gibson, born say 1700, received a grant for 328 acres on the south side of the Roanoke in Bertie County, North Carolina, joining John Lowe, Jackson, and the swamp on 1 December 1727 [Patent 3:249, #2552]. He was a witness to the 12 August 1728 Bertie County deed of William Whitehead to Edward **Bass** for land near Urahaw Swamp [DB C:135]. He purchased 335 acres in Bertie County on the north side of Cashie River and Wahton Swamp near the Northampton County line on 28 October 1728 [DB C:52] and was a resident of Bertie on 28 October 1731 when he sold 250 acres on Elk Marsh in Bertie County by an Edgecombe County deed [DB 1:7]. On 5 February 1756 he made a deed of gift of his household goods in Northampton County to his son George Gibson [WB 2:251]. His children were

8   i.   George[3], born say 1730.

   ii. ?William, born say 1732, a resident of Northampton County on 18 February 1755 when he purchased 100 acres on Burnt Coat Swamp in the part of Edgecombe County which became Halifax County in 1758 [DB 2:186].

  iii. ?Charles, born before 1739 since he was taxable in 1750 in John Wade's list for Granville County [CR 44.701.23]. This part of Granville County became Orange County in 1752 and Charles was "a Molata" taxable there in 1755 [T&C Box 1, p.19]. He received a grant for 190 acres on the south side of Bear Swamp in Northampton County on 9 August 1786 and sold it two years later on 31 December 1788 [DB 8:169]. He was head of a Northampton County household of 7 free males and 2 free females in Captain Winborne's District for the state census in 1786 [Census p.29]. He was living in Wayne County, North Carolina, in August 1818 when he made a declaration to obtain a pension for Revolutionary War service. He claimed that he enlisted for nine months in the Tenth Regiment at the courthouse in Northampton County, North Carolina. However, there was no record of his discharge or service. Perhaps he was the same Charles Gibson who applied for a pension from Hawkins County, Tennessee, at the age of ninety-two on 19 January 1839. He claimed to have been born in Louisa County, Virginia, on 19 January 1739 and entered into the service in Salisbury, North Carolina.[97] His neighbors, Jordan and Jonathan Gibson and Benjamin **Collins**, testified on his behalf [M805-355, frames 55, 62].

5. John[1] Gibson, born say 1690, was a joint plaintiff with Adam Cockburn in a Chowan County suit for a debt against Thomas Crank in October 1718 [DB B-#1:45]. He was granted 370 acres on 5 April 1720 on a bank of Falling Run in the part of Chowan County which later became Northampton County, but was not listed in the Chowan County Tax list with his father who was taxable on this land in 1721 [Patent 3:15, #1601]. He was said to have been deceased in his father's deed of sale of this land on 11 July 1728 [Bertie DB C:37]. However, he may have been the John Gibson who recorded a plat for 300 acres and a town lot in Berkeley County, South Carolina, on 31 February 1735 and received a grant for the land on 17 September 1736 [South Carolina Archives Series S213184, Vol. 4:43; S213019, vol. 34:527]. He was deceased by 4 January 1744 when his wife Elizabeth, son Gilbert, and daughters Sarah, Thene, Hannah, and Jane were living in Saxagotha Township when Gilbert recorded a plat of 300 acres [South Carolina Archives Series S213184, Vol. 4:43; S213019, vol. 34:527; *Petitions for Land from South Carolina Council Journals*, 145-6, 480-1]. John was the father of

    i.   Gilbert[3], born say 1721, living in Saxagotha Township when he recorded a plat for 300 acres in Craven County, South Carolina, on 4 January 1744 based on his petition that his family consisted of his mother Elizabeth and his younger sisters Sarah, Thene, Hannah and Jane. Thomas Wallexelleson petitioned for the same land saying that Gilbert's deceased father John Gibson had already been granted land based on those rights [South Carolina Archives series S213184, vol. 4:272; vol 6:211; *Petitions for Land from South Carolina Council Journals*, 145-6, 480-1].
    ii. Sarah.
    iii. Thene.
    iv. Hannah.
    v.   Jane.

6. Thomas[1] Gibson, born say 1692, left a 29 October 1734 Hanover County will, proved that year on 7 November, by which he gave his sons Thomas and John Gibson 50 acres each, gave daughter Vine Nicks, wife of Edward Nicks, Frances Humphrey, and Mary Brock a shilling each. He gave his house and cattle to his son-in-law Edward Nicks who he named as executor and directed

---

[97]George and Thomas **Gibson** were living in Louisa County on 28 May 1745 when they, William **Hall**, Thomas **Collins**, Samuel **Collins**, William **Collins**, William **Donathan**, Benjamin **Branham**, and Samuel **Bunch** were presented by the court for failing to list a tithable (probably their wives) [Orders 1742-8, 152, 157, 172].

that Edward should bring up his children John and Valentine Gibson and also
William Roberson [Court Records 1733-5, 151]. He was the father of

9   i.   Thomas[2], born say 1712.
      ii.   Vine, born say 1714, wife of Edward Nicks/ Nix.
      iii. John, born say 1716.
      iv.   Valentine.

7. Gideon[1] Gibson, born say 1695, settled near the Roanoke River in North
    Carolina about 1720. He purchased 200 acres in what was then Chowan
    County on the south side of the Roanoke River on 24 July 1721 [DB C-1:142].
    He acquired over one thousand acres of land in present-day Halifax County,
    North Carolina, and on the north side of the Roanoke River in Northampton
    County.[98] He married Mary Brown sometime before 22 October 1728 when
    they sold 150 acres "bounded according to the Will of William Brown Gentl
    decd..." [Bertie DB C:36]. She was under the age of eighteen when her father
    made his 15 December 1718 Chowan County will, proved July 1719, by which
    he gave her and each of her six siblings 150 acres [N.C. Archives File SS
    841]. Gideon, or (his uncle?) Gibby Gibson, must have impressed the other
    prosperous free African Americans in that area of North Carolina because
    three of them named their children after him: Gideon/Gibby **Chavis**, Gideon/
    Gibby **Bunch**, and Gibson **Cumbo**. Many of the well-to-do Gibson and **Bunch**
    families married whites and were considered white after a few generations.

    He sold 108 acres of his land on the south side of the Roanoke River in the
    first few months of 1730 in what was then Bertie County before moving to
    South Carolina with several of his relatives who were living on the other side
    of the Roanoke River in present-day Northampton County [DB C:276]. They
    came to the attention of the South Carolina Commons House of Assembly in
    1731 when a member announced in chamber that several "free colored men
    with their white wives" had immigrated from Virginia with the intention of
    settling on the Santee River" [Jordan, *White Over Black*, 171]. Governor
    Robert Johnson of South Carolina summoned Gideon Gibson and his family
    to explain their presence there and after meeting them reported,

> *I have had them before me in Council and upon Examination find that
> they are not Negroes nor Slaves but Free people, That the Father of them
> here is named Gideon Gibson and his Father was also free, I have been
> informed by a person who has lived in Virginia that this Gibson has lived
> there Several Years in good Repute and by his papers that he has
> produced before me that his transactions there have been very regular,
> That he has for several years paid Taxes for two tracts of Land and had
> seven Negroes of his own, That he is a Carpenter by Trade and is come
> hither for the support of his Family. ...I have in Consideration of his
> Wifes being a white woman and several White women Capable of working
> and being Serviceable in the Country permitted him to Settle in this
> Country* [Box 2, bundle: S.C., Minutes of House of Burgesses (1730-35),
> 9, Parish Transcripts, N.Y. Hist. Soc. by Jordan, *White over Black*, 172].

Like the early settlers of the North Carolina frontier Governor Johnson was
more concerned with the Gibsons' social class than their race.

---

[98]Gideon Gibson's purchases:

24 Jul 1721 200 acres south side of Roanoke River [Chowan DB C-1:142].

3 May 1722 540 acres southwest side of Quankey Creek [Chowan DB C-1:227].

7 Aug 1727 300 acres north side of Roanoke River [Bertie DB B:289].

8 Aug 1727 300 acres south side of Roanoke River [Bertie DB B:293].

Both Gideon **Bunch** and Gideon Gibson were in South Carolina when they sold their adjoining Halifax County land to Montfort Eelbeck of Halifax, and both families were taxed in 1755 as "free Molatas" in Orange County, North Carolina [N.C. Archives File T&C, box 1].

Gideon and his wife Mary recorded the birth of their child William in the Parish Register of Prince Frederick Winyaw on 9 October 1743. As "Gideon Gibson of Pe De South Carolina" he sold part of his Northampton County land on 16 November 1746 and the remainder on 15 February 1749 [DB 1:280, 383]. In South Carolina he recorded a plat for 200 acres on the northwest side of the Pee Dee River in Craven County on 13 April 1736 and 200 acres on the south side of the Pee Dee on 1 January 1746/7 [Colonial Plats 4:320, 4:397]. He petitioned the South Carolina Council on 12 November 1747 stating that he had been granted a warrant for 650 acres in the Welch Tract where he had settled fifteen years previous and had kept it as a cow pen with a servant on it for about two years. He had since settled in Persimmon Grove and had nine persons in his household: a wife, seven children and a slave [Holcomb, *Petitions for Land from the South Carolina Council Journals*, I:266]. On 29 November 1750 he received a grant for 450 acres in Persimmon Grove on the Little Pee Dee River in Craven County [Royal Grants 4:296]. He was granted 300 acres on the upper end of Marrs Bluff based on his petition of 4 August 1752 which stated that he had begun to cultivate land there and had two children and four slaves for which he had not been assigned any land [Holcomb, *Petitions for Land* III:56]. Land which had been surveyed for him in North Carolina on the north side of the Little Pee Dee River was mentioned in a 17 November 1753 Bladen County land entry [Philbeck, *Land Entries: Bladen County*, no. 904]. On 13 July 1755 he was granted administration on the estate of James Rowe, "late of Prince George's parish planter as greatest creditor," and on the same day he was granted administration on the estate of Matthew **Driggers**, also as greatest creditor [Record of Court Proceedings, 35, 97, 127]. He purchased two slaves (a boy named An[s?]lls and a girl named Hannah) from Sarah **Sweat** of North Carolina for 500 pounds on 28 November 1764, purchased seven slaves (Rillis, Benjamin, Lucey, Pleasants, Cander, Hannah and Nell) from John and Agnes Gibson (his son and daughter) on 7 April 1766, made a deed of gift of three slaves (Achilles, Pleasant, and Pleasant's youngest daughter Judith) to John and Agnes Gibson's children on 24 August 1767, and made a deed of gift to Mary Holland (his daughter?), wife of Joseph Holland, for 50 head of cattle, 50 hogs, 8 horses, and 10 sheep on his plantation at Marrs Bluff Ferry on 8 January 1770 [Miscellaneous Record Books MM:302-3, 371-2; OO:91-2, 222-3]. He was the father of

10   i.   Gideon², born say 1721.
11   ii. John³, born say 1723.
     iii. ?Jordan¹, born say 1724. He was listed in the accounts of the Public Treasurer on 29 October 1759 for supplying the expedition against the Cherokees with 18 horses which he apparently failed to deliver [Clark, *Colonial Soldiers of the South*, 937]. He was granted land in what was then Bladen County, North Carolina, on the east side of Mitchel's Creek in present-day Robeson County near the South Carolina border which he sold on 25 September 1761 [Bladen DB 23:85]. He may have been the father of Jordan Gibson, Jr., who recorded a plat for 150 acres adjoining Jordan Gibson, Sr., on the southwest side of the Pee Dee River in Craven County, South Carolina, on 26 January 1765 [Colonial Plats 8:20]. He sold 200 acres in Anson County, North Carolina, on the north side of the Pee Dee River on the Falling Creek branch of Hitchcock's Creek to Benjamin **Deas** on 15 November 1768 by deed witnessed by Gideon Gibson, and he sold another 300 acres in Anson County in the same area on 2 May 1777 [DB 7:224, 320]. Perhaps he was related to Thomas Gibson who purchased land in this

same area of Anson County on 18 August 1761 [DB 6:190]. According to Gregg, Jordan went to the West as a companion of Daniel Boone. He or perhaps a son by the same name was among those "killed by Indians" in North Carolina on 7 January 1788 [*NCGSJ* IX:236].

iv.   ?Mary, wife of Joseph Holland.

v.   Agnes, born say 1730, identified as Gideon's daughter in his Craven County, South Carolina deed of gift for the sale of three slaves for the benefit of her unnamed children [Miscellaneous Record Book OO:91-2].

vi.   ?Luke, listed in the accounts of the Public Treasurer of South Carolina, paid 4.17.6 pounds on 31 October 1759 for unspecified services to the battalion in the expedition against the Cherokees [Clark, *Colonial Soldiers of the South*, 936].

vii.   ?Daniel, taxable on 100 acres in Marrs Bluff, Liberty County (Prince Frederick Parish) in 1786 [S.C. Tax Returns 1783-1800, frame 119], head of a Georgetown District, Prince Fredericks Parish, household of 6 "other free" in 1790.

viii.   William, born 15 September 1743, son of Gideon and Mary, baptized 9 October 1743 [NSCDA, *Parish Register of Prince Frederick Winyaw*, 15].

8.   George³ Gibson, born say 1730, was a taxable in 1750 in John Wade's list for Granville County [CR 44.701.23]. This part of Granville became Orange County in 1752, and George was a "Molata" taxable in 1755 [T&C Box 1, p.19]. By 19 November 1757 he had married Elizabeth Lowe, a white woman of Northampton County, daughter of John and Sarah Lowe. She was mentioned in her father's will of that date. By the terms of this will his wife received a slave and he was allowed to continue to live on 150 acres of land in Northampton County [WB 1:41]. While resident in Northampton County he purchased 439 acres on Quankey Creek in Halifax County on 5 June 1761 and sold it for the same price two years later on 17 January 1763 [DB 7:318; 8:209]. While residing in Orange County on 18 July the same year, he sold two slaves and sixteen head of cattle (which he received from his mother-in-law's estate) to his brother-in-law, Thomas Lowe, of Northampton County [DB 3:622]. On 26 May 1770 he purchased 150 acres on the west side of Flat River in Orange County from (his uncle?) Thomas Gibson. His 5 November 1775 Orange County will was proved in May 1776 [WB A:195]. He named his (then) wife Mary, and mentioned but did not name his "Sons and Daughters now living in the County" and provided for the schooling of his unnamed younger children. Joel Gibson and Lucrecy **Collins** were witnesses; Thomas Gibson, Sr., was executor. After his death Mary entered 300 acres on Greens Creek and Rutledges Creek in Caswell County on 13 January 1779 on a line agreed between William Hog and Julius Gibson, and she entered 200 acres in Caswell County on the South Hyco Creek bordering Orange County on 26 July 1779 [Pruitt, *Land Entries: Caswell County*, I:75, 89].[99] She was taxable in Caswell in 1790 [NC:79]. The inventory of her Caswell County estate was recorded by Joel Gibson in 1795. The inventory mentioned James, John, and Richard Gibson [WB C:118]. Perhaps George Gibson's children were

i.   Andrew, born say 1755, a Caswell County taxable in 1777. He entered 100 acres on both sides of Kilgore's Bridge in Caswell County on 25 August 1778 [Pruitt, *Land Entries: Caswell County*, 47]. He may have been the Andrew Gibson who was appointed Tax Collector for Chatham District of Orange County at the 29 August 1782 session of the County court of Pleas and Quarter Sessions. He was a juror on 26

---

[99]Caswell County was formed from Orange County in 1777.

November 1783. In 1790 he was counted as white in the Tenth Company of Wilkes County, head of a household of one male over 16, 3 males under 16, and 6 females [NC:123]. He was head of an Ashe County household of 7 "other free" in 1800 [NC:79].[100]

ii. George[4], born say 1757, a Randolph County taxable in 1779.

iii. John[6], born in Orange County, North Carolina, on 16 September 1760 according to his father's family bible. He grew up in Guilford County, North Carolina, where he entered the service. He moved to Tennessee in 1805, and was living there on 16 July 1833 when he made his pension application. He was a horseman employed in collecting cattle for the use of the army [M805-355, frame 0197].

iv. Thomas[2], born in Randolph County, North Carolina, on 15 November 1763. When he was eighteen years old, he volunteered in Guilford County and served for two years. He was allowed a pension while a resident of Randolph County. He died 15 October 1850 leaving his children David, Joseph, Hannah (wife of P.M. Nixon), Mary (wife of John H. Hill), and George Gibson [M805-355, frame 0409].

v. Wilbourne, born in Guilford County in 1763 according to his father's family bible. He was drafted into the service in Randolph County in 1781. He applied for a pension while residing in Ripley County, Indiana, on 15 May 1838. His wife Rebecca died 3 March 1839, and he died on 4 April 1843. His only heirs were his daughter Mary Ann Lewis and her husband George W. Lewis who were living in Ripley County, Indiana, on 19 October 1852 when they applied for a survivor's pension [M805-355, frame 0411]. There is a marriage bond recorded for him in Stokes County on 20 November 1797 with Thomas Hill bondsman, but the bride's name was not recorded. His sixteen-year-old son Hezekiah was bound to James Reed in Burke County in October 1804 "due to abandonment" [Wills, Administrations, & Orphans, 1791-1810, 511 by *N.C. Genealogy* XIX:2827].

vi. Julius, a Wilkes County taxable in 1784.

vii. Lucrecy **Collins**.[101]

9. Thomas[2] Gibson, born say 1712, was presented by the Louisa County court on 28 May 1745 for failing to list a tithable who was probably his wife. A suit against him was dismissed by the court on 24 September the same year because he was not an inhabitant of the county [Orders 1742-8, 152, 157, 167, 171]. He was taxable in Granville County with Charles and George Gibson in John Wade's list in 1750 [CR 44.701.23]. He received two patents for a total of 250 acres in Granville County on Flat River on 2 May 1752 [Hoffman, *Granville Land Grants*, 31-2]. Orange County was formed from this part of Granville County in 1752, and he was head of an Orange County household of 3 taxable "Molatas" in 1755 [T&C, box 1, p.19]. This land was on Flat River adjoining Charles Gibson, Moses **Ridley**, and Thomas **Collins** [Bennett, *Abstract of Loose Papers in Granville Proprietary Office*, 34, 43]. On 26 May 1770 he sold three tracts of land on the west side of Flat River "part of 606 acres which the sd. Thos. Gibson purchased of Earl Granville:" 100 acres to James Williams, 150 acres to George Gibson, and land to Joel Gibson [DB 3:471, 468, 622]. He received a grant for 150 acres in Wilkes County on the north side of Obed's Creek on the South Fork of New River on 3 November

---

[100]Ashe County was formed from Wilkes County in 1799.

[101]Like the Gibsons, the **Collins** family were taxable "Molattos" in Orange County in 1755 [T&C, Box 1, pp.15,19], were counted as white in the Tenth Company of Wilkes County in 1790 [NC:123], and were counted as "other free" in Ashe County in 1800 [NC:74,75,76].

1796 and sold 100 acres of this land on 18 January 1800 [DB A:142, 147].[102] He probably died about 1802 when (his son?) Joel sold land in this same area. His children may have been

i. Major, born before 1746, "a Molata" taxable in 1755 in Orange County [T&C Box 1, p.19], and a taxable in Randolph County in 1779. He was counted as white in the 1790 Burke County census, head of a household of 2 males and 3 females in the Eighth company [NC:109]. He was taxable in Burke County on 55 acres and no polls in 1794 (since he was over fifty years old) [Huggins, *Burke County, N.C. Records*, IV:110].

ii. Joel, born about 1750, purchased land in Orange County from (his father?) on 26 May 1770. He was a Caswell County taxable in 1777 and 1786. He was counted as white in Tenth Company of Burke County in 1790, head of a household of one male over 16 and one female [NC:123]. He sold 200 acres in Ashe County on Obed's Creek on 29 January 1802 and another 100 acres on 6 March 1804. He bought 50 acres on the north bank of the South Fork of New River in Ashe County on 13 July 1804 and sold it a year later on 5 March 1805 [DB A:213; B:311, 339]. He was head of an Ashe County household of 2 "other free" in 1800 [NC:78] and was counted as white in Wilkes County in 1810 [NC:853]. He may have been the Joel Gibson who applied for a pension in Henderson County, Kentucky, on 25 April 1825 at the age of seventy-five for service in the First North Carolina Regiment. His wife was deceased at the time and all his children but one were married and away from home. He was supported by his son Bailey Gibson who had numerous small children to support [M805-355, frame 0162].

iii. John[5]/Jack Gibson, born say 1756, a Caswell County taxable in 1777, 1784, and 1786. He was head of a Wilkes County household of 2 "other free" and 1 white woman over forty-five years of age in 1810 [NC:853]. The white woman was probably Milley Gibson who made a Wilkes County deed of gift of 2 tracts of land in Burke County on 27 February 1818. The land was to be held by her son Drury in trust for her son Isom when he came of age [DB I:138].

iv. Nathan, born before 1776, head of a Burke County household of 6 "other free" in 1800 and 12 "free colored" in Haywood County in 1830.

v. Archibald, who was counted as white in the Tenth Company of Wilkes County, head of a household of one male over 16, one under 16, and 9 females in 1790 [NC:123] but counted as "other free" in 1800, head of an Ashe County household of 7 [NC:78].

vi. Jordan[3], head of a Tenth Company, Wilkes County household of one white over 16, 3 under 16 and one white female in 1790 [NC:123].

vii. Dorothy, head of a Tenth Company, Wilkes County household of two males over 16, two males under 16, and two females in 1790 [NC:123].

viii. Ezekiel, born say 1763, head of a household of one white male over sixteen years in the Tenth Company of Wilkes county in 1790 [NC:123] and head of an Ashe County household of 3 "other free" in 1800 [NC:78].

10. Gideon[2] Gibson, born say 1721, had been a resident of South Carolina for fifteen years on 12 December 1746 when he was granted a warrant for 50 acres at a place called Duck Pond on the south side of the Pee Dee River where he was then residing. He called himself Gideon Gibson, Jr., on the

---

[102]Obed's Creek is near the present day county line of Wilkes and Ashe Counties.

same day when he petitioned the South Carolina Council for 200 acres at Duck Pond for himself, his wife and two children [Holcomb, *Petitions for Land from the South Carolina Council Journals*, I:266]. He and his wife Martha were the parents of Sarah Gibson whose birth (on 29 July 1745) and baptism were registered in the parish of Prince Frederick Winyaw [NSCDA, *Parish Register of Prince Frederick Winyaw*, 15, 20]. On 2 September 1755 he recorded a plat for 200 acres on the southwest side of the Pee Dee River adjoining Jordan Gibson [Colonial Plats 6:45]. On 15 January 1760 he was paid 343 pounds by the Public Treasurer for supplying the militia in the campaign against the Cherokees [Clark, *Colonial Soldiers of the South*, 936]. On 15 February 1765 he was granted administration on the estate of John Herring and appointed guardian to John, Peter, Mary, and Hester G___eys of Prince George's Parish [Record of Court Proceedings, 97]. On 25 July 1767 as a leader of the Regulators, Gideon was involved in a skirmish with a constable's party near Marrs Bluff on the Pee Dee River. The incident brought matters between the Governor and the Regulators to a head. The *South Carolina Gazette*, which like the government was far removed from the location, reported in the 15 August 1768 edition that there were two parties of Regulators. One was made up of people of good principle and property, and the other made up of a

> *gang of banditi, a numerous collection of outcast Mulattos, Mustees, Free Negroes, etc. all horse thieves from the borders of Virginia and other Northern Colonies...headed by one Gideon Gibson...*

Perhaps in a move to divide the two parties Governor Bull pardoned all those involved except

> *those persons concerned with the outrages and daring violences committed by Gideon Gibson and others upon George Thompson, a lawful constable, and his party, in the actual execution of a legal warrant, at or near Mars Bluff, in Craven County, upon the 25th day of July last....6 August 1768*
> [Council Journal, no. 34, 208-211].

Colonel Gabriel Powell, sent to arrest Gideon, arrived with 300 men, but to his utter humiliation, his men sided with Gideon saying he was "one of them" [Hooker, *The Carolina Backcountry on the Eve of the Revolution*, 177]. Powell resigned his commission and made a racist attack on Gideon Gibson in a discussion of the incident on the floor of Commons. Apparently, he fared little better amongst his colleagues of the Commons than he had in the back country. There are no minutes of the session, but a prominent Charleston merchant, Henry Laurens, was present and described the discussion years later in a letter to England:

> *Reasoning from the colour carries no conviction...Gideon Gibson escaped the penalties of the negro law by producing upon comparison more red and white in his face than could be discovered in the faces of half the descendants of the French refugees in our House of Assembly...* [Wallace, David Duncan, *The Life of Henry Laurens*, (N.Y. and London, 1915) by Jordan, *White over Black*].

Gideon was described by Gregg as

> *a man of very marked character, of commanding influence, and prominently connected with the leading events of the region in which he lived.*

He was shot dead by his nephew, Colonel Maurice Murphy, during an argument over Murphy's mistreatment of an elderly Tory during the

Revolutionary War [Gregg, *History of the Old Cheraws*, 354]. His children were

    i.   Sarah, born 29 July 1745, daughter of Gideon and Martha, baptized 20 October 1745 [NSCDA, *Parish Register of Prince Frederick Winyaw*, 20].

    ii. Gideon[5], born 12 March 1750, son of Gideon and Martha, baptized 2 June 1753 [NSCDA, *Parish Register of Prince Frederick Winyaw*, 34]. On 21 September 1773 he was accused before the court in Charleston of having assaulted James McCasey the previous month in Georgetown [Judgment Roll 1774, Box 99B, 23A]. He received about 39 pounds for providing provisions to the militia between 1780 and 1782 [Accounts Audited, no.2786].

    iii. Reuben, born 29 November 1751, son of Gideon and Martha, baptized 29 May 1753 [NSCDA, *Parish Register of Prince Frederick Winyaw*, 32].

    iv. ?Stephen. According to Gregg, Gideon had three sons, one of whom was Stephen who became wealthy and moved to Georgia about the year 1800. The Hon. Thomas Butler King married his daughter [Gregg, *History of the Old Cheraws*, 74].

    v. ?Roger, another son of Gideon who, according to Gregg, went West before the Revolution.

11. John[3] Gibson, born say 1723, and his wife Jemima registered the birth and baptism of their son Gibson in Prince Frederick Winyaw Parish. On 7 April 1766 he and his sister Agnes Gibson of Craven County sold seven slaves to Gideon Gibson, and on 3 September 1767 Gideon sold three slaves for their benefit [Miscellaneous Records MM:371-2; OO:91-2]. John and Jemima were the parents of

    i.   Gibson[2], born 25 February 1749, baptized 29 May 1753.

    ii. John[4], born 6 January 1753, baptized 29 May 1753 [NSCDA, *Parish Register of Prince Frederick Winyaw*, 33]. Perhaps he was the John Gibson who was head of a Charleston District, St. Bartholomew's Parish, household of 7 "other free" in 1790 [SC:36].

GILBERT FAMILY

Members of the Gilbert family were

    i.   Thomas, born about 1727, a seventeen-year-old "Mustee" apprentice who ran away from John Brown, a wheelwright, on 9 March 1744 according to an ad placed by his master in the *Virginia Gazette*: *has a broad Face, and full Set of Teeth, is of low Stature, pretty well-set, of a dark Complexion, being a Mustee, and has a thick bushy Head of Hair* [*Virginia Gazette* (Parks), March 14 to March 21, 1744/5].

    ii. Lewis, "Negro" head of a Kent County, Maryland household of 7 "other free" and a white woman in 1790.

    iii. Sukey, born before 1776, head of a Stokes County, North Carolina household of 5 "free colored" in 1820 [NC:345].

    iv. William, head of a Robeson County, North Carolina household of 3 "other free" in 1800 [NC:380].

    v. Betsey, head of a Hanover County, Virginia household of 2 "other free" in 1810 [VA:863].

GILLETT FAMILY

The Gillett family apparently descended from Simon and Peter (no last name indicated), "Mulatto" men, who sued for their freedom from Sir Grey Skipwith and his wife Dorothy on 5 July 1743 in Middlesex County court, claiming that they were entitled to their freedom because they had served until the age of twenty-one.

They were probably children of a white woman because the court ordered that they serve until the age of thirty-one [Orders 1740-4, 227, 229-32, 235-6]. Members of the Gillett family were

        i.   Rebecca, married William **Chaver** on 8 July 1730 in Christ Church Parish, Middlesex County [NSCDA, *Parish Register of Christ Church*, 167].

1   ii. Simon[1], born say 1720.

2   iii. Peter[1], born say 1722.

1.   Simon[1] Gillett, born say 1720, was sued by John Holt for a debt of 6 pounds in York County on 21 May 1750 [Judgments & Orders 1746-52, 313]. He may have been the Simon Gillett who sued John Tilman in Brunswick County, Virginia court for a 4 pound, 10 shilling debt due by note of hand [Orders 1760-84, 43]. He was the "erect and dignified" body servant to Lord Botetourt, governor-in-chief in Williamsburg from 1768 to 1770. During the first decade of the nineteenth century he was official violinist at state balls in Richmond, described by contemporaries as wearing "an embroidered silk coat and vest of faded lilac, silk stockings, terminated in shoes decorated with large buckles...and a brown wig." His wardrobe consisted of fifty suits, "his manner as courtly as his dress." He was appointed to the office of sexton by the churchwardens of the Church of England in Richmond [Mordecai, *Richmond in By-gone Days*, 310-11]. Lawrence **DeRozario** proved a deed to him from Sarah **Cumbo** in York County court on 18 October 1784. His York County suit against Anne **Carter** was dismissed on 16 October 1786, and he won a suit against Sarah **Carter** for a featherbed on 21 November the same year [Orders 1784-7, 86, 368, 375]. He was taxable in York County on his own tithe, Anthony **Peters**, a slave named Phil, 9 horses and 3 cattle from 1784 to 1786 (called Simon Gillett, Sr., in 1785), exempt from personal tax by 18 January 1790 but taxable on 2 horses from 1790 to 1796 and taxable on a slave in 1794 and 1795. His estate was taxable on a horse in 1797. Perhaps his widow was Hannah Gillett, Sr., who was taxable on a horse and a slave in 1798 and 1799 and taxable on a horse in 1800 [PPTL, 1782-1841, frames 69, 91, 107, 130, 162, 172, 182, 192, 201, 210, 229, 237, 244, 255; Orders 1788-95, 198]. He may have been the father of

        i.   Simon[2], Jr., born say 1757, presented in York County on 15 November 1779 for failing to list his tithables [Orders 1774-84, 240], head of a Richmond City household of 3 "other free" and 2 slaves in 1810 [VA:379].

2.   Peter[1] Gillett, born say 1722, a "free Negro," registered the birth of his son Reuben in Bruton Parish, James City County in 1747 [Bruton Parish Register, 8]. He sued Daniel **Armfield** in a suit that was dismissed in York County court on 22 September 1747 because both parties were in agreement, and he was paid as a witness for Thomas Cowles when he was sued by Daniel **Armfield** on 16 January 1748/9. Thomas **Poe** sued him on 16 September 1751 for a debt due by account, but the case was dismissed. On 17 December 1764 he was presented by the court for failing to list his daughters Patience and Nanny as tithables. Peter and (his son) Reuben were sued for a 35 shilling debt on 18 January 1769, and Peter and Sarah Gillett were paid as witnesses on 15 January 1770 in Sarah Freeman's suit against George Jones [Judgments & Orders 1746-52, 39, 159, 313, 473; 1763-5, 321, 362; 1768-70, 174, 407]. He was taxable in York County on himself, slaves Charles and Eve, 8 cattle and 4 horses in 1784, taxable on slaves Charles and Eleanor, 4 horses and 9 cattle in 1785 and 1786, taxable on 2 slaves and 4 horses in 1788 and 1789 (called Peter Gillet, Sr.), exempt from personal tax by 1 June 1790, taxable on a slave in 1790 and 1793, and taxable on 2-3 horses from 1790 to 1795 [PPTL, 1782-1841, frames 69, 91, 107, 128, 162, 172, 182, 192, 201, 210; Orders 1788-95, 283]. His children were

  i.   Patience, born say 1745, tithable in 1764.
3 ii.   Reuben[1], born 6 November 1747.
 iii.   Nanny, born say 1748, tithable in 1764.
 iv.   ?Robert, security for the 11 July 1792 York County marriage bond of
       Reuben Gillett and Winneford **Maclin**. Peter Gillett and he sued James
       Lyons in York County court on 18 March 1788. He died before 18
       August 1789 when his suit against James **Lyons** abated by his death
       [Orders 1788-95, 7-8, 171].
  v.   ?Peter[2], Jr., born say 1755, presented by the York County court on 15
       November 1779 for failing to list his tithables [Orders 1774-84, 240].
       He was taxable in York County on slaves Pat and Hannah, 9 cattle and
       9 horses in 1784, taxable on 2 horses and a head of cattle in 1785,
       taxable on a slave named Jack, 2 horses and 2 cattle in 1786, taxable
       on a slave and 3-4 horses in 1788 and 1789. His estate was taxable on
       two horses in 1793 (called Peter Gillet, Jr.) [PPTL, 1782-1841, frames
       69, 91, 128, 140, 151, 192]. On 16 September 1793 his unnamed
       widow applied to the sheriff for any estate which belonged to her
       deceased husband, but the sheriff reported that Peter had mortgaged all
       his property to the trustees of Samuel Beall [W&I 23:388]. Perhaps his
       widow was Hannah Gillett who was taxable on a horse in 1795, taxable
       on a horse and slave in 1796 and 1797, probably the Hannah Gillett,
       Jr., who was taxable on a slave and horse from 1798 to 1800 [PPTL,
       1782-1841, frame 210, 220, 229, 237, 244, 255]. Hannah was head of
       a York County household of 3 "other free" and 2 slaves in 1810
       [VA:889].

3.   Reuben[1] Gillet, born 6 November 1747, was taxable in York County from
     1782 to 1812 and taxable on two tithes in 1794 and 1812 [PPTL, 1782-1841,
     frames 96, 91, 107, 128, 162, 182, 201, 237, 255, 375]. He and his wife
     Mary, "Free Mulattoes," baptized their son Reuben in Bruton Parish, James
     City County on 1 June 1784 [Bruton Parish Register, 35]. He married, second,
     Winneford **Maclin**, 11 July 1792 York County bond, Robert Gillett security.
     Reuben's children were
   i.   Reuben[2], baptized on 1 June 1784.
  ii.   ?Simon[3], born about 1797, registered in York County on 16 December
        1822: ~~a dark man~~ *a person of tawny complexion, is about 25 years old*.
        His wife Polly **Lyons** registered on 18 June 1832: *Polly Lyons (now the
        wife of Simon Gilliat) a bright mulatto about 33 years of age...long
        straight hair - Born free* [Free Negro Register 1798-183, no. 161;
        1831-1850, no. 342].

A member of the family probably married or had children by Sarah Gillett, a slave
of Mary Stith:

4.   Sarah Gillett, born say 1770, was the slave of Mary Stith until 2 October 1793
     when Stith emancipated her and her children Jane and Peter Gillett by York
     County deed [Orders 1788-95, 597]. Her children were
   i.   Jane, born about 1789, registered in York County on 19 August 1811:
        *a bright Mulatto ab[t] 22 or 23 years of age 5 feet 1-1/2 Inches
        high...black Eyes...Ears perforated for Earrings. Small regular features
        & good countenance. Emancipated by deed from Mary Stith recorded
        in York Ct.* [Register of Free Negroes 1798-1831, no.62].
  ii.   Peter[3], born about 1791, registered in York County on 15 February
        1813: *Peter alias Peter Gillett is a Mulatto of bright complexion about
        22 years of age, 5 feet 6-1/2 Inches high - has long bushy
        hair...Emancipated by a deed from Mary Stith dated the 2[d] of Oct[r] 1793
        & recorded in York Court* [Free Negro Register 1798-1831, no.70]. He
        had moved to Lunenburg County by 7 October 1818 when he registered

as a free Negro, using his York County registry papers [WB 5, after page 89, no.1].

iii. Martha, born about 1794, registered in York County on 20 February 1815: *Patty alias Martha Gillett is a short black woman ab[l] 21 years of age 5 feet 1-1/4 Inches high - long hair which she usually wears platted before - flat nose...Daughter of Sarah Gillett who was set free by deed from Mary Stith dated 2 Oct[r] 1793 since which period the sd Martha was born* [Register of Free Negroes 1798-1831, no.87].

GILMORE FAMILY

1. Margaret Gilmore, born say 1725, was apparently the mixed-race child of a white woman bound by indenture for thirty-one years. On 16 October 1777 her descendant Patty Gilmour brought suit for freedom from her master Thomas Tunstall in Halifax County, Virginia. Tunstall maintained that Patty should serve until the age of thirty-one since she was the descendant of a woman bound until the age of thirty-one. But the court ruled that Patty was twenty-one, had never been bound by any indenture, and was free from any further service. Tunstall appealed [Pleas 1774-9, 259]. He was the son of Richard Tunstall of King and Queen County [Morris, *The First Tunstalls in Virginia and Some of Their Descendants*]. Margaret was the mother of

    i. ?Isaac, born in February 1742/3, registered in Petersburg on 17 May 1796: *a brown Mulatto man, five feet five inches high, fifty three in Feby. last, born free in King & Queen County* [Register of Free Negroes 1794-1819, no. 112].

    ii. Sabra, born say 1752, complained to the Halifax County, Virginia court against her master Thomas Tunstall on 20 August 1773. The court ordered her to return to his service until she arrived to the age of thirty-one years [Pleas 1773-4, 226, 251].

    iii. Patty, born about 1756, over the age of twenty-one when she was released from Thomas Tunstall's service on 16 October 1777.

2   iv. ?Richard[1], born say 1760.

2. Richard[1] Gilmore, born say 1760, was taxable in the lower district of King and Queen County form 1782 to 1815: his tax charged to John Kauffman from 1782 to 1791; taxable on his own tithe and a horse in 1792; taxable on 2 free tithes and 2-4 slaves over the age of sixteen from 1793 to 1797; taxable on a free male in 1798; 3 free males in 1799 and 1800; 4 in 1801 and 1802; 2 free males; a slave and a horse in 1803; head of a household of 4 "Mulattoes" (male and female) above the age of sixteen in 1813; a "free Negro" over the age of forty-five in 1815 when he was taxable on 7 cattle [PPTL, 1782-1803; 1804-23]. He was head of a King and Queen County household of 9 "other free" in 1810 [VA:219a]. He may have been the father of

    i. Mourning, a "free Negro" taxable on a free male tithe in King and Queen County in 1813 [PPTL, 1804-23].

    ii. Richard[2], Jr., a "Mulatto" taxable in the lower district of King and Queen County in 1813 and 1814 [PPTL, 1804-23], a "free mulatto" head of a Gloucester County household of 1 "other free" and 3 slaves in 1810 [VA:656].

    iii. Delpha, a "Mulatto" taxable in King and Queen County in 1813 [PPTL, 1804-23].

    iv. Fanny, a "Mulatto" taxable in King and Queen County in 1813, taxable on a horse in 1823 [PPTL, 1804-16], perhaps identical to the Fanny Gilmore who was a "free Negro" taxable in Middlesex County in 1813.

    v. Benjamin, a "free Negro" taxable in King and Queen County in 1815 [PPTL, 1804-23].

GODETT FAMILY

1. George[1] Godett, born say 1730, was excused from paying tax by the 14 September 1780 Craven County, North Carolina court because he was a cripple [Minutes 1772-84, 2:22a]. He was not taxed in the 1769 Craven County tax list nor was he counted in the 1790 Craven County census. His 29 March 1802 Craven County will was proved September 1803. His son-in-law, Isaac **Perkins**, was one of the witnesses to the will. George left all his land to his son William and divided his other property among his children [CR 28.508.24]. He may have married Deborah **George** since he named his daughter Deborah and his son Peter (after Peter **George**). His children were
    2   i.   William[1], born say 1750.
    3   ii.   John[1], born say 1755.
        iii. Deborah, born about 1763, married Isaac **Perkins**, 24 March 1784 Craven County bond.
        iv.   Susanna.
        v.   Mary **Moore**.
        vi.   Peter, head of a Craven County household of one "other free" in 1790 [NC:130] and 5 "free colored" in 1820 [NC:67]. He married Sarah **Barber**, 26 April 1797 Craven County bond, William Tignor bondsman. He purchased 100 acres in Craven County on the south side of the Neuse River and the east side of Kings Creek on 26 August 1802 [DB 36:247]. He married second, Polly **George**, 10 January 1805 Craven County bond, Peter **George** bondsman. He mortgaged his land adjoining Isaac **Perkins** on Cahooque Creek and six head of cattle for $50 to Peter **George** on 12 June 1819 (acreage not stated). Peter **George** signed a release for this land and cattle on 18 July 1832 [DB 41:245; 49:279].

2. William[1] Godett, born say 1750, was taxable on one black tithe in Craven County in 1769 [SS 837]. He married Suckey **Drigg** (**Driggers**), 25 May 1806 Craven County bond, Elijah **George** bondsman. By his 26 March 1815 Craven County will he left all his real and personal property to his wife Susanna and mentioned her child Charlotte and an unnamed child his wife was pregnant with. Elijah **George** proved the will in March 1816 [CR 28.508.24]. One of William's children was
        i.   Charlotte, married William **Martin**, 24 January 1828 Craven County bond, Samuel **Martin** bondsman.

3. John[1] Godett, born say 1755, purchased 50 acres in Craven County on the west side of Adams Creek near Brook's Run on 23 January 1781 and 40 acres joining this land on 8 January 1785 [DB 24:163; 26:77]. He was head of a Craven County household of 2 "other free" in 1790 [NC:130]. On 15 October 1801 he purchased 100 acres on the south side of Neuse River and west side of Clubfoot Creek adjacent to land formerly owned by William **George**. His heirs may have been George **Lewis** and Stephen, Nancy, Annanias, and Eliza Godett who sold 80 acres at the head of Clubfoot Creek adjoining Gideon Jones on 13 June 1826 [DB 35:247; 45:417]. His children may have been
        i.   Stephen, born before 1776, married Mary **Martin**, 12 June 1817 Craven County bond, Jacob **Moore** bondsman. Stephen was head of a Craven County household of 3 "free colored" in 1820 [NC:65].
        ii.   a daughter, married George **Lewis**.
        iii. Nancy.
        iv.   Annanias.
        v.   Eliza.

4. George[2] Godett, born say 1765, received a patent for 300 acres on the south side of the Neuse River at the head of Clubfoot Creek joining Elijah Gibson

on 23 August 1813 [Land Patents, N.C. Archives, C.028.48002, IV:175]. He made a deed of gift of 50 acres of this land (adjoining the land of John Godett) to his daughter Deborah **Morris** on 13 June 1818 [DB 41:188]. He was head of a Craven County household of 12 "free colored" in 1820 [NC:65]. He was living on Clubfoot Creek on 14 May 1825 when he wrote his will, proved May 1827. He named his wife Leurainah, children, and his grandchildren Jeremiah and Jesse who were sons of Betsy **Powers**. His grandson Jeremiah Godett, his daughter Betsy **Powers**, and his son-in-law Joshua **Lewis** were executors [CR 28.508.24]. He named his children:

5   i.   Betsy **Powers**, born say 1785.

       ii. James A., born say 1789, purchased 200 acres at the head of Clubfoot Creek on 16 May 1810 [37:837]. He married Hepsey **Parker**, 24 February 1816 Craven County bond, Shadrack **Morris** bondsman. James was head of a Craven County household of 5 "free colored" in 1820 [NC:65]. He made a deed of gift of 200 acres on the east side of Clubfoot Creek to (his brother) John Godett for $1 on 10 February 1825, and on the same day he made a deed of gift of 200 acres near the head of Clubfoot Creek to (his brother) George Godett, Jr., for $1 [DB 44:338-9].

    iii. John[2], married Ann Holly, 22 October 1812 Craven County bond. He was head of a Craven County household of 3 "free colored" in 1820 [NC:65]. He may have been the same John Godett who married Clarissa **Jackson**, 4 January 1825 Craven County bond, with Theophilus **George** bondsman. John and Clary purchased for $5 from William and Eady Jones their rights to land belonging to the heirs of Hody Jackson on the east side of Vandimere Creek on 16 August 1827 [DB 51:164].

    iv. George[3], Jr., married Julia **Lewis**, 29 October 1813 Craven County bond, George **Goddett** bondsman. He was head of a Craven County household of 7 "free colored" in 1820 [NC:65].

     v. Deborah, married Manuel **Morris** 30 November 1804 Craven County bond, George Godett bondsman. Manuel was head of a Pasquotank County household of 2 "other free" and 5 slaves in 1810 [NC:912] and 7 "free colored" in Craven County in 1820 [NC:65].

    vi. Peter, married Mary **Lewis**, 12 May 1813 Craven county bond, Stephen Gaudett bondsman. Peter was head of a Craven County household of 3 "free colored" in 1820 [NC:62].

   vii. Leurainah, whose two children William **Dempcey** and Peter were mentioned in her father's will.

5. Betsy Godett, born say 1785, was called Betsy **Powers** in her father's 1825 will. Her sons Jeremiah and Jesse Godett were also mentioned in the will. Betsy was called Betsy Godett when she married Joshua **Lewis**, 30 June 1809 Craven County bond, James **Goddett** bondsman. Joshua **Lewis** was the son-in-law who was one of the executors of George Godett's will. Betsy's children mentioned in her father's will were

     i. Jeremiah Godett, born say 1804, who received by his grandfather's will one tract for 40 acres and another for 2 acres which his grandfather purchased from Manuel **Morris**.

     ii. Jesse Godett, born say 1806. On 11 March 1833 the sheriff sold 100 acres of his land at the head of Clubfoot Creek adjoining Manuel **Morris** and Elijah Gibson for a debt he and Francis Mason owed [DB 50:426].

Other members of the family were

     i. Nancy, born say 1750, head of a Craven County household of one "Black" female in 1769 [SS 837] and called Ann Godet in 1790, head of a Craven County household of 6 white females [NC:130]. This was probably an error and should be 6 "other free." She married John **Davis**, another "Black" Craven County taxable in 1769, by 12 November 1796 Craven County bond, William Godett bondsman.

    ii.   Abraham, born say 1760, head of an Anson County household of 5 "other free" in 1800 and 2 in 1810 [NC:16].

    iii.   William², born say 1775, married Luzana **Davis**, 24 May 1805 Craven County bond, Peter **George** bondsman. William was head of a Hyde County household of one "other free" and a slave in 1800 [NC:368].

GOFF FAMILY

1.   Samuel Goff, born say 1720, was sued for debt in Cumberland County, Virginia, on 22 May 1758. He and his wife Diana sold 127 acres in Cumberland County on 23 June 1762 [Orders 1752-8, 526; 1762-4, 60, 356]. He was the father of Samuel and Abram Gauf who were ordered bound out by the Chesterfield County court on 4 June 1762 [Orders 1759-67, 225]. He was living in Pittsylvania County on 24 June 1768 when he was summoned to appear in court to show cause why his children should not be bound out [Orders 1767-72, 63]. He had moved back to Cumberland County by 28 November 1774 when he was added to the list of tithables. He was called an "aged person" with four sons in the continental service on 27 April 1779 when the court certified to the board of auditors that he depended on them for subsistence. On 28 February 1780 he was exempted from payment of levies. A suit brought against him by Joseph Callend, assignee of Carter Henry Harrison, Gent., was dismissed on 28 September 1783 when the plaintiff failed to prosecute [Orders 1774-8, 294; 1779-84, 20, 106, 435]. He was the father of

2   i.   Abraham, born about 1743.

    ii.   Samuel, enlisted in the Virginia Continental Line on 15 September 1777 and was killed at Powles Hook on 16 August 1779 according to a certificate presented by his brother Abraham Goff in Cumberland County court [Orders 1779-84, 496].

    iii.   Daniel, born in June 1754, made a declaration in Boone County, Kentucky, on 4 February 1833 in order to obtain a pension for his services in the Revolution. He was living in Chesterfield County when he enlisted in the 15th Virginia Regiment for three years. James Taylor testified that Daniel, a "poor colored man," came to live with him in Campbell County, Virginia, in 1793 as a gardener and laborer [M805-362, frame 97].

    iv.   Zachariah, born before 1759, added to the list of tithables in Cumberland County, Virginia, on 28 November 1774 [Orders 1774-8, 294]. He was a "Melatto" taxable in Campbell County from 1788 to 1792 [PPTL, 1785-1814, frames 84, 150, 212]. He was called a "free mulatto" on 19 August 1793 when the Campbell County court found him not guilty of poisoning Micajah Moorman. Ned **Jenkins** was Zachariah's witness [Orders 1791-7, 219]. On 28 February 1796 the Cumberland County court ordered the clerk to issue a certificate of freedom "it appearing to the court that the said Zachariah by birth and parentage is intitled to the same" [Orders 1792-7, 613]. He was a Revolutionary War pensioner from Bedford County. He enlisted in Cumberland County in 1777 and served for three years. On 25 September 1851 his widow Betsy Goff, a "free Negroe," testified that they were married in June 1796, that her maiden name was Betsy **Moss**, and that her husband died in 1823 [M805-362, frames 288-295].

3   v.   Moses, born say 1760.

2.   Abraham Goff, born about 1743, was living in Pittsylvania County on 28 May 1768 when an attachment on his estate was dismissed [Orders 1767-72, 52].

He sued Edmund Vaughan for trespass, assault and battery in Cumberland County, Virginia, on 27 January 1777. The suit was dismissed on agreement of the parties. On 23 February 1784 he produced in court the certificate of Captain Samuel Baskerville of the First Virginia Regiment, certifying that Samuel Goff enlisted in the Virginia Continental Line on 15 September 1777 and was killed at Powles Hook on 16 August 1779. Abraham testified that he was eldest brother and heir to Samuel [Orders 1774-8, 391, 500; 1779-84, 496]. He was a "Mulatto" taxable in Buckingham County in 1790 [PPTL 1782-97]. He appeared as the next friend of Charles Goff in his suit against Charles Howle and Anthony Christian for trespass viet armis and imprisonment in Cumberland County court on 26 April 1796 [Orders 1792-7, 507]. He married Sally **Ruff**, 25 July 1798 Bedford County bond, John **Mann** and Richard **Moss** bondsmen. He was head of a Botetourt County household of 5 "other free" in 1810 [VA:625]. He was counted in the list of "Free Negroes and Mulattoes" for Botetourt County in 1813 with (his wife?) Rhoda Goff [Waldrep, *1813 Tax List*]. He was a "free man of Colour," about seventy-seven years old on 28 August 1820 when he testified in Bedford County, Virginia court to obtain a pension for his service in the Revolution. He stated that he enlisted in Cumberland County, Virginia, in 1778 and served for four years. He had four children living with him: Matilda aged fourteen years, Ely aged twelve years, Samuel aged six years, and Mary aged three years [M805-362, frames 56-65]. He registered in Bedford County on 26 October 1820: *aged 77, Mulatto, 5 feet 11 inches, Born free* [Register of Free Negroes 1820-60, p.3]. Four of his children were

   i.   Matilda, born about 1806, registered the same day as her father: *aged 15, Bright Mulatto, 5'6", Born free* [Register of Free Negroes 1820-60, p.3].

   ii.   Ely, born about 1808.

   iii.   Samuel, born about 1814.

   iv.   Mary, born about 1817.

3.   Moses Goff, born say 1760, was a soldier in the Revolution from Cumberland County [Jackson, *Virginia Negro Soldiers*, 34]. He was taxable in the upper district of Cumberland County, Virginia from 1783 to 1807: a "f. M°" taxable on Henry and Thomas Goff's tithe in 1804, taxable on Thomas Goff's tithe in 1806, 3 tithes in 1807 [PPTL, 1782-1816, frames 33, 89, 122, 155, 257, 294, 353, 428, 486, 523, 559]. He and his unnamed son were "M"(ulatto) taxables in Buckingham County in 1813 [Waldrep, *1813 Tax List*]. He may have been the father of

   i.   Henry[2], born say 1782, taxable in Cumberland County in 1804, a shoemaker living with wife Cate on John Seay's land in a list of "free Negroes & Mulattoes" in the upper district of Cumberland County in 1810 [PPTL, 1782-1816, frame 658].

   ii.   Thomas, born say 1786, taxable in Cumberland County in 1804, listed with William Goff as jobbers in 1810 [PPTL, 1782-1816, frame 658].

   iii.   William, say 1790, taxable in Cumberland County in 1810 and 1813 [PPTL, 1782-1816, frames 658, 764].

   iv.   David, a "M"(ulatto) taxable in Buckingham County in 1813 [Waldrep, *1813 Tax List*].

Other members of the Goff family were

   i.   Sarah Gauf, born say 1725, petitioned the Chesterfield County court on 6 April 1759 to order Richard Locket to show cause why (her son?) Isham **Joiner** should not be bound to some other person. Her petition was dismissed [Orders 1754-9, 506, 522].

   ii.   Lewis Gauf, born about 1757, a twenty-year-old "negro man" jailed in Louisa County according to the 31 October 1777 issue of the *Virginia*

Gazette. He was bound to the widow Netherland of Hanover County, late of Halifax County.

iii. Henry[1] (Harry), born about 1765, a "Negro claims to be free, about 30 years old," who was jailed in Fredericksburg according to the 14 July 1795 issue of the Virginia Herald and Fredericksburg Advertiser [Headley, *18th Century Virginia Newspapers*, 137].

iv. Joney, head of a Bertie County, North Carolina household of 1 "other free" in 1790 [NC:12].

v. Alice, married Thornton **Pettiford**, 31 March 1804 Petersburg Town, Virginia bond [Hustings Court Records].

GOLDMAN/ GOULDMAN FAMILY

Members of the Goldman family were

1   i. Martin, born say 1750.

ii. George, born say 1763, taxable in the lower district of King and Queen County from 1784 to 1820, head of a household of 4 "free Negroes" (male and female) above the age of sixteen in 1813 [PPTL, 1782-1803; 1804-23].

iii. James, born say 1765, taxable in the lower district of King and Queen County from 1783 to 1820, aged 16-21 in 1783 [PPTL, 1782-1803; 1804-23].

1. Martin Goldman, born say 1750, was taxable in the lower district of King and Queen County from 1782 to 1815: taxable on 1 "black" tithe, 0 whites, 2 horses and 13 cattle in 1782; a "white" tithable with 0 "black" tithables but with George, James, Ben, Milly (his wife?), Keasar (Kesiah), Willis and James (no last name) in his household in 1783; taxable on James and George Goldman and 10 cattle in 1784; taxable on 3 free males and a horse in 1791; 4 free males in 1792 and 1794, 2 in 1795, 3 in 1796, 2 from 1797 to 1801; called a "free Negro" in 1807; head of a household of 2 "free Negroes" over the age of sixteen (male and female) in 1813; over the age of forty-five in 1815 [PPTL, 1782-1803; 1804-23]. He may have been the father of

i. Kesiah, listed in Martin Goldman's household in 1783 [PPTL, 1782-1803].

ii. Ralph, born say 1776, taxable in the lower district of King and Queen County from 1792 to 1813, head of a household of 3 "free Negroes" (male and female) above the age of sixteen in 1813 [PPTL, 1782-1803; 1804-23].

iii. Benjamin, born say 1780, taxable in King and Queen County from 1795 to 1815, head of a household of 3 "free Negroes" (male and female) above the age of sixteen in 1813 called a "free Negro" in 1813 [PPTL, 1782-1803; 1804-23].

iv. Willis, born say 1782, taxable in the lower district of King and Queen County from 1802 to 1821: called a "Mulatto" in 1813 when he was taxable on a gig [PPTL, 1782-1803; 1804-23].

v. Martin, Jr., a "free Negro" taxable in King and Queen County in 1815 [PPTL, 1804-23].

GORDON FAMILY

Members of the Gordon family born before 1750 were

1   i. Peter, born say 1740.

ii. Motley, born say 1747, a "mulatto" tithable in Buckingham County in 1774 [Woodson, *Virginia Tithables from Burned Counties*, 47].

1. Peter Gordon, born say 1740, was a "free negro" head of household in Norfolk County, Virginia, on the south side of Western Branch District in

1770 [Wingo, *Norfolk County Tithables, 1766-80*, 105]. He was taxable in Currituck County in 1779 and was head of a Currituck County household of 10 "other free" in 1790 [NC:21] and 3 in 1800 [NC:88]. Perhaps his widow was Hannah Gorden, head of a Currituck County household of 4 "other free" in 1810 [NC:91]. Peter may have been the father of

  i.   Solomon, head of a household of 4 "other free" in Raleigh, Wake County in 1800 [NC:809].
  ii. Betsy, head of a Pasquotank County household of 2 "other free" in 1810 [NC:899].
  iii. Luke, head of a Currituck County household of one "other free" in 1810 [NC:92].
  iv. Louis, head of a Norfolk County household of 2 "other free" in 1810 [VA:900].

GOWEN/ GOING FAMILY

Members of the Gowen family in Virginia were

1   i.   Michael[1], born say 1635.
    ii. Philip[1], born say 1650, called "Phillip Cowen a Negro" when he petitioned the Governor and Council of State for his freedom. He was the servant of Amye Beazleye whose 9 April 1664 will stated that he was to be free and receive three barrels of corn and a suit of clothes after serving her cousin, Humphrey Stafford, for eight years. Stafford sold the remaining years of his indenture to Charles Lucas who forced Philip to acknowledge an indenture for twenty years before the Warwick County court [Colonial Papers, Library of Virginia microfilm, p.19, fol. 2]. On 16 June 1675 he was called "Philip Gowen negro Serving Mr. Jno Lucas" when the court ordered that his indenture in Warwick County was invalid, that Philip was free, and that he should be paid three barrels of corn according to Mrs. Amye Beazleye's will [McIlwaine, *Minutes of the Council,* 411]. He may have been identical to Philip Gawen who was listed in the quit rent roll for James City County with 50 acres in 1704 [*VMHB* XXI:220].

1. Michael[1] Gowen, born say 1635, was the "negro" servant of Christopher Stafford who gave him his freedom by his 18 January 1654 York County will after four years of service. Accordingly, Stafford's sister, Anne Barnehouse, discharged "Mihill Gowen" from her service on 25 October 1657, and she gave him his child William, born of her "negro Prossa" [DWO 3:16]. Since nothing further is said of Prossa, she probably remained a slave. If she and Michael had any more children, they too would have been slaves. Perhaps Michael married a free woman - most likely white since most branches of the family were very light skinned. Also, there may not have been any eligible free African American women in York County at that time.

He patented "30 or 40 acres" in Merchants Hundred Parish in James City County on 8 February 1668 and died before 11 September 1717 when this land was mentioned again in James City County records:

It appears that Mihil Goen late of the said County of Jas. City dyed seized of 30 or 40 acres [Duvall, *James City County*, 42, 78].[103]

His children were

2   i.   William[1], born 25 August 1655.

---

[103]The name appears like Mihill Gowree in the 1668 patent, but the 11 September 1717 inquisition refers to the same land as belonging to Mihil Goen / Michael Gowen.

3   ii.   ?Daniel[1], born say 1657.
4   iii.   ?Christopher[1], born say 1658.
5   iv.   ?Thomas[1], born say 1660.

2.   William[1] Gowen (Michael[1]), born 25 August 1655, son of Prossa, was baptized by Mr. Edward Johnson on 25 September 1655 [York County DWO 3:16]. He received a grant for land in Charles City County on 20 April 1687 [Patents 7:58]. He may have been the father of
6   i.   Edward[1], born say 1681.

3.   Daniel[1] Gowen (Michael[1]), born say 1657, received a patent for 100 acres in Kingston Parish, Gloucester County, adjoining his own land on 1 May 1679 and another 52 acres in Gloucester County adjoining Henry Preston, Ambrose Dudley, and Captain Ranson on 26 April 1698 [Patents 6:679; 9:147]. He may have been the ancestor of
         i.   James[3], born say 1728, taxable in Gloucester County in 1770. Perhaps his widow was Mary Gowen, taxable on 120 acres in 1784. He and his unnamed wife were the parents of Sarah Gowen, born 16 January 1759 [Mason, *Records of Colonial Gloucester,* 33, 95].

4.   Christopher[1] Gowen (Michael[1]), born say 1658, may have been named for Christopher Stafford, Michael[1] Gowen's master. Christopher and his wife Anne Gowen were living in Abingdon Parish, Gloucester County, in January 1679 when their son Michael was born [Wynn, *Abingdon Parish, Gloucester County, Register,* 319].[104] Their children were
7   i.   Michael[2], born in January 1679.
8   ii.   ?Philip[2], born say 1685.
         iii.   ?Christopher[2], purchased 150 acres on the north side of the Roanoke River in Bertie County, North Carolina, on 25 March 1728 [DB C:23].

5.   Thomas[1] Gowen (Michael[1]), born say 1660, was living in Westmoreland County between 1693 and 1702 when he was involved in several minor court cases, both as defendant and plaintiff, for debts.[105] In 1703 he provided security of 2,000 pounds of tobacco for Chapman Dark that he would return to the county after travelling to Maryland to get testimony that he was a free man. On 1 March 1704/5 the court ordered him to pay Edward Barrow 1,200 pounds of tobacco which Thomas lost to him in a horse race [Orders 1690-98, 90, 244a, 250a; 1698-1705, 33, 39a, 56a, 109, 174, 190a, 190, 238a, 254a]. He was called Thomas Goin of Westmoreland County on 8 June 1707 when he was granted 653 acres in Stafford County below the falls of the Potomac River. This land was adjoining Robert Alexander's land according to a 29 May 1739 Prince William County deed [Gray, *Virginia Northern Neck Land Grants,* 39, 125]. In an 8 May 1767 land dispute a seventy-year-old deponent, Charles Griffith, related a conversation which he had with Major Robert Alexander forty-three years previously in 1724. Major Robert Alexander, who owned land adjoining the Gowens, supposedly said of them,

---

[104]Few other Gloucester County records have survived.

[105]An Easer Goeing, born say 1662, was also mentioned in Westmoreland County records. He had left the county by 31 May 1693 when the court seized his horse for a debt he owed Gawen Corbin [Orders 1690-8, 97]. He may have been identical to Eser Gorin(?), a "free Negro" who with "divers Others Negroes & Molattoes to the number of nine in Company" left Maryland by boat and were apprehended as runaways in Norfolk County. On 16 August 1692 the Norfolk County Court held the boat as security for the owner, Thomas Cook of Maryland, to pay the charges for apprehending them. The same court reported that Ezar Goren had left a crop growing on the ground of Lewis Conner's land which was claimed by Conner for rent and claimed by John Wakefield for debt [DB 5, pt. 2, 265, 268].

he had a great mind to turn the Molatto rascals (who were then his tenants) of[f] his land.

Griffith further stated that

he was at a Race in the same year where the Goings were (who then had running horses) and that the old people were talking about the Goings taking up Alexanders land and selling it to Thomas and Todd which land the old people then said was in Alexanders back line or at least the greatest part of it...and if it were not for the Alexanders land...the Goings would not be so lavish of their money of which they seemed to have plenty at that time...[Sparacio, *Land Records of Long Standing, Fairfax County,* 89].

"Thomas and Todd," mentioned in the abstract, owned 1,215 acres in Stafford County on Four Mile Creek adjoining Robert Alexander on 3 August 1719 which was land formerly surveyed for Thomas, John, William, and James Goins [Gray, *Virginia Northern Neck Land Grants,* 69]. Later in his testimony Griffith mentioned conversations with Thomas and James Gowen. Thomas' children may have been

9   i.   William², born say 1680.
10   ii.   James¹, born say 1683.
       iii.   Peter Goeing, born say 1690, granted 187 acres in King George and Stafford counties adjoining Alexander Clements and Shrines' land on 7 October 1724, but the deed was canceled and the land granted to John Mercer [Northern Neck Grants A:86].

6.   Edward¹ Gowen (William¹, Michael¹), born say 1681, was taxable on 150 acres in Kingston Parish, Gloucester County, in 1704 [Smith, *Quit Rents of Virginia, 1704,* 37]. He may have been the father of

11   i.   Edward², born say 1700.

7.   Michael² Gowen (Christopher¹, Michael¹) was born in January 1679 in Abingdon Parish, Gloucester County [Wynn, *Abingdon Parish, Gloucester County, Register,* 319] and was living in New Kent County on 4 July 1702 [Bockstruck, *Virginia's Colonial Soldiers,* 218]. He was probably living near the New Kent - Hanover County line on 14 July 1720 when the New Kent County court ordered the vestry of St. Paul's Parish, Hanover County, to take "Michl Gowing's Male Tithables" [Chamberlayne, *Vestry Book of St. Paul's Parish,* 93]. His children may have been

       i.   John², born say 1705, purchased 170 acres including a plantation in St. Martin's Parish, Hanover County, from Shirley Whatley on 7 June 1734 [Court Records 1733-8, 71-3].[106] Perhaps John Gowen was the ancestor of Henry Going who was head of a Hanover County household of 8 persons in 1782 [VA:27].
12   ii.   Mary¹, born say 1708.
13   iii.   Ann¹, born say 1719.

8.   Philip² Gowen (Christopher¹, Michael¹), born say 1685, was living in New Kent County on 4 July 1702 [Bockstruck, *Virginia's Colonial Soldiers,* 218]. He may have been the ancestor of

14   i.   George¹, born say 1715.
       ii.   William, born say 1720, sued for trespass in Goochland County in July 1741. Job Thomas sued him in May 1742 but failed to prosecute. He

---

[106]Shirley Whatley was living in Shocco District of Granville County, North Carolina, in the 1762 list of Constable John Gibbs [*NCGSJ* XIII:107].

and his wife Anutoice brought an action of trespass upon the case against William Harris which was dismissed in August 1752. In September 1755 the sheriff attached a horse belonging to Henry Adkins for a 7 pounds, 10 shilling debt he owed William. In July 1757 he acknowledged his deed to Jeremiah Rach. William Harris sued him for trespass in a case that was dismissed by agreement in August 1752. John Pleasants, Sr., sued him for 15 pounds damages in December 1763 [Orders 1735-41, 580; 1741-4, 36; 1750-7, 155, 170, 189; 1761-5, 250, 417, 573].

iii.   Edward, born say 1722, sued by Mary Sutton in Goochland County in May 1745. She failed to prosecute and the case was dismissed in July 1746. Samuel Jordan sued him for debt in February 1746/7, but he also failed to prosecute [Orders 1747-9, 67, 176, 212].

15   iv.   Agnes[1], born say 1725.
16   v.   David[1], born say 1727.

vi.   Philip[3], born say 1740, married Judith Potter and had a daughter named Molly who was born 4 March 1770, baptized 27 May [Jones, *The Douglas Register*, 87]. He was head of an Amherst County household of 13 persons in 1783 [VA:48] and 12 in 1785 [VA:83]. He and his descendants were counted as white in the 1810 Virginia census.

vii.   Mary Anne, born say 1742, bound out by the churchwardens of Southam Parish, Goochland County, to David Thomas in January 1747/8 [Orders 1744-9].

9.   William[2] Gowen (Thomas[1], Michael[1]) was probably born about 1680. He and Evan Thomas were granted 124 acres in Stafford County on Jonathan's Creek of Occaquan River on 10 September 1713, and he was granted 180 acres on the main run of Accotinck Creek on 28 February 1719 [Gray, *Virginia Northern Neck Land Grants*, 54, 70]. He sold the land on Jonathan's Creek on 6 May 1724. His wife Katherine Gowing was called a widow in a 6 March 1726 Stafford County deed by which she purchased 112 acres in Overwharton Parish near Rattlesnake Branch of Pope's Head Run from her son Ambrose, which Ambrose's father, William Gowing, was granted by patent of 12 November 1725 [DB J:121, 353]. She was called Catherine **Padderson** (**Patterson**) in her 21 May 1739 Prince William County will which was proved 23 July 1739 by her son John Going. She left slaves and land to her children Alexander and Susanna Going [WB C:180-181]. Thomas Ford, a neighbor of William[2] Gowen [Joyner, *Virginia's Northern Neck Warrants,* 156], was a witness to the will. William and Katherine's children were

17   i.   John[1], born say 1702.
ii.   Ambrose, born say 1704, who sold William[2]'s land to his mother.
iii. Susanna, who received a slave by her mother's will.
18   iv.   ?William[3], born say 1710.
v.   Alexander, who may have been named for their neighbor, Major Robert Alexander. He received 66 acres by his mother's will, and sold it on 14 August 1747 [Fairfax DB B:253]. He was in North Carolina by 15 July 1760 when he received a patent for 600 acres in Orange County in St. Matthew's Parish on both sides of Hogan's Creek [Hoffman, *Granville District Land Grants*, 273].

10.   James[1] Gowen (Thomas[1], Michael[1]), born say 1683, sold 652 acres in Stafford County on Four Mile Run adjoining Thomas Pearson on 4 March 1730 [DB C:118]. He may have been the ancestor of

i.   Daniel[2], born about 1730, a 5'4", twenty-seven-year-old planter from Stafford County who was listed in the 13 July 1756 size roll of Captain Thomas Cocke's Company of the Virginia Militia. He was called a hatter in the July 1757 size roll of Captain Joshua Lewis' Seventh

Company of the Virginia Regiment [Clark, *Colonial Soldiers of the South*, 385, 449].

19   ii.   Luke, born say 1740.

       iii.   Michael⁵, born say 1742, head of a Shenandoah County household of 7 persons in 1785 [VA:105].

       iv.   Joseph, taxable in Loudoun County in 1769 [Sparacio, *Loudoun County Tithables*, 80], head of a Fairfax County household of 7 persons in 1782 [VA:17].

       v.   George², born say 1750, "free Negro" head of a Fairfax County household of 8 "other free" in 1810 [VA:257].

       vi.   Jason, born before 1762, taxable in Loudoun County in 1782 [Fothergill, *Virginia Tax Payers*, 50]. He was called the "brother of Luke Goins" on 23 December 1795 when they obtained certificates as "free Negroes" in Loudoun County. The certificate stated that Jason had been living in the neighborhood of John Littleton for upward of twenty years [Certificates of Free Negroes at the Loudoun County courthouse, transcribed by Townsend Lucas].

11. Edward² Goeing (Edward¹, William¹, Michael¹), born say 1700, was sued by Francis Tyree for a debt of 450 pounds of tobacco in Charles City County in August 1737. He sold land by deed he acknowledged in court in Charles City County in May 1746 [Orders 1737-51, 16, 409]. He may have been the father of

       i.   Phillis Goeing, born say 1720, presented by the grand jury in Charles City in November 1739 for having a bastard child. She petitioned the court in July 1745, apparently asking that her children be bound to George **Gibson**, but the court ordered the churchwardens to bind them out because **Gibson** failed to answer her petition. On 7 August 1754 the churchwardens of Westover Parish sued her for debt, probably for having an illegitimate child [Orders 1737-51, 105, 117, 371, 383; 1751-7, 112, 142, 251].

20   ii.   Michael³, born say 1722.

21   iii.   James², born say 1725.

22   iv.   Edward³, born say 1727.

23   v.   Joseph¹, born say 1730.

24   vi.   David², born say 1735.

25   vii.   Shadrack¹, born say 1737,

       viii.   Suffiah, born say 1739, head of a Pittsylvania County household of 12 persons in 1785 [VA:100].

26   ix.   John⁷, born say 1740.

       x.   Moses³, born say 1743, testified in Henry County court on 27 April 1780 that he had served as a soldier in Captain James Gunn's Company in Colonel Byrd's Regiment in 1760 (in the French and Indian War) but had not received bounty land. On 28 March 1783 he owned land on both sides of the North Mayo River when the Henry County court allowed him to build a water grist mill on it [Orders 1778-82, 86; 1782-5, 75]. He was taxable in Henry County from 1782 to 1786, charged with 2 tithes in 1785 and 1786 [PPTL, 1782-1830, frames 18, 38, 87, 152, 217].

12. Mary¹ Going (Michael², Christopher¹, Michael¹), born say 1708, was living in Brunswick County, Virginia, in April 1740 when the court ordered her children Drury and Eleanor bound to Ralph Jackson. She may also have been the mother of Cave Gowen, a seven-year-old boy who was bound to James Vaughan by the 6 June 1734 Brunswick County court and Thomas and John Going who were bound out by the court in May 1739, no parent named [Orders 1737-41, 254, 302]. Her children were

       i.   ?Cave, born about 1727.

      ii. ?Thomas[3], born say 1734, sued in Brunswick County, Virginia court by James House on 27 November 1759. He sued Joseph King in Brunswick County court on 23 January 1760 [Orders 1757-9, 426; 1760-84, 75].

27   iii. ?James[4] Gowen, born say 1735.

      iv. ?John[4], born say 1736.

28   v. Drury[1], born say 1738.

      vi. Eleanor, born say 1740.

     vii. ?Frederick[1], born say 1745, living in New Hanover County, North Carolina, in December 1767 when there was a warrant for his arrest for contempt and aiding the escape from jail of Richard Burbage who was held on suspicion of horse stealing [Minutes 1738-69, 331]. He and his wife were taxable "Molatoes" in Bladen County in 1770 and 1772 [Byrd, *Bladen County Tax Lists*, I:34, 95].

13. Ann[1] Going (Michael[2], Christopher[1], Michael[1]), born say 1719, sued John Magoffe and his wife Jane in Brunswick County, Virginia, in September 1740 [Orders 1737-41, 353, 379]. Ann was living in Granville County, North Carolina, on 5 September 1753 when the court ordered her "Mulatto" child Cooper bound to John Parnall [Owen, *Granville County Notes*, vol. I]. She was in Cumberland County, North Carolina, in November 1761 when the court ordered her to "keep in her possession a Mulatto Boy which she now has in order that she may have him here next court" [Minutes 1759-65, 75]. She may have been the Ann Goin who was granted 100 acres on Broad River and both sides of Fannin's Creek in what later became Union County, South Carolina [Lucas, *Some South Carolina County Records*, 2:524]. On 3 April 1799 the Robeson County court ordered John Ford, Esquire, in South Carolina to take her deposition on behalf of James Terry vs. Willis Barfield [Minutes 1797-1803, 69]. Her children may have been

      i. Cooper, born say 1752.

29   ii. John[6], born say 1758.

     iii. Olive, born say 1780, head of a Robeson County household of 2 "other free" in 1800 [NC:381] and 2 "free colored" in 1840 [NC:222].

     iv. William[9], born about 1787, eleven years old when he was ordered by the 3 April 1798 Robeson County court bound apprentice to James Alford [Minutes 1797-1803, 37]. He was head of a Robeson County household of 3 "other free" in 1810 [NC:232] and 6 "free colored" in 1840 (55-100 years old) [NC:222]. On 23 November 1841 the Robeson County court granted him permission to carry his gun in the county [Minutes 1839-43, 240].

14. George[1] Gowen (Philip[2], Christopher[1], Michael[1]), born say 1715, and his wife Sarah Gowan were the parents of Aaron, born 9 June, baptized 3 September 1737 in St. Peter's Parish, New Kent County [NSCDA, *Parish Register of St. Peter's*, 134]. He sued William Chamberlayne for trespass in Goochland County in May 1748. Job Pleasants sued him for debt in February 1748/9 and he sued William Chamberlayne in August 1752 [Orders 1744-9, 436, 476, 506]. In July 1760 William Winston "Essex," who "as well in behalf of Us as for himself" sued Sarah Going, perhaps for failing to list herself as a tithable. He failed to prosecute and was ordered to pay her costs in July 1761 [Orders 1757-61, 318, 429]. George was added to the list of tithables in Goochland County in August 1761. Thomas Whitlock sued him and Sarah Going in a case which was agreed between the parties in July 1764. George and Sarah sued Thomas Whitlock for trespass, assault and battery in February 1765, and Whitlock sued Sarah for debt in the same court. To satisfy the debt, the court ordered the sheriff to sell nine pigs belonging to Sarah in the hands of garnishee William French [Orders 1761-5, 15, 404, 468, 470, 507-8]. They were the ancestors of

i. Aaron[1], born 9 June, baptized 3 September 1737 in St. Peter's Parish, New Kent County [NSCDA, *Parish Register of St. Peter's*, 134]. He sued John Winston for trespass assault and battery in Goochland County in June 1760. Winston testified that he only touched the plaintiff gently, but Aaron was awarded 5 shillings [Orders 1757-61, 303, 328-9, 353; 1761-5, 8, 104]. He mortgaged several goods to Thomas Underwood by deed proved in Goochland County in September 1764 [Orders 1750-57, 84; 1757-61, 429; 1761-65, 429]. He was taxable in Powhatan County in John Chitwood's household in 1791, charged with his own tax in 1792, 1796 and 1797 [PPTL, 1787-1825, frames 58, 77, 132, 146].

ii. ?Moses[2], born say 1742, sued in Goochland County by William Hudnell in April 1763. Thomas Riddle posted his bail. The suit was dismissed on agreement between the parties. He sued James Moseley in April 1763 but the case was also dismissed on agreement. He sued Charles Murler for a 16 pound, 12 shilling debt in August 1763; he was sued by Robert Smith for 30 shillings in May 1764; he acknowledged a debt of 14 pounds, 10 shillings to Messrs. William Pryor and William Merriwether in June 1764 and acknowledged a debt of 15 pounds, 12 shillings to Adams and Thomas Underwood in September 1764 [Orders 1761-5, 145, 151, 158, 228-9, 327, 334, 369, 424]. He was a taxable in Powhatan County from 1792 to 1797 and from 1801 to 1817: called a "M°" from 1793 to 1795 and from 1801 to 1814; listed with 1 "free negroes & mulattoes" above the age of 16 in his household in 1813 [PPTL, 1787-1825, frames 77, 92, 106, 118, 132, 146, 223, 257, 278, 295, 317, 342, 363, 380, 399, 421, 438, 458, 482, 533].

iii. ?Shadrack[3], taxable in Powhatan County from 1791 to 1797: his tax charged to Judith Bingley in 1791, called a "M°" from 1793 to 1795 [PPTL, 1787-1825, frames 57, 92, 106, 118, 132, 146].

15. Agnes[1] Going (Philip[2], Christopher[1], Michael[1]), born say 1725, was living in Louisa County on 10 October 1743 when she sued Gilbert **Gibson** for 3 pounds currency for services done on a contract. On 9 January 1743/4 the court ordered that she receive twenty-five lashes on her bare back for having an illegitimate child. She bound her son Joseph and daughter Sarah Going to James Bunch by 28 November 1759 Fredericksville Parish indenture [Davis, *Fredericksville Parish Vestry Book*, 29]. On 9 September 1766 she made a deposition in George **Gibson**'s suit against his step-mother Sarah Gibson. On 14 May 1770 the court ordered the churchwardens of Trinity Parish to bind out all her children under twenty-one years except the youngest. On 12 February 1776 she complained to the court about the treatment her son Sherod was receiving from his master William Phillips [Orders 1742-8, 82, 91, 92, 95; 1766-74, 20; 1766-72, 379; 1774-82, 140, 142]. She was taxable in Fredericksville Parish, Albemarle County, from 1787 to 1794: taxable on a free male tithe in 1787 and 1788; taxable on a horse from 1791 to 1794 [PPTL, 1782-1799, frames 116, 153, 203, 347, 419]. She was the mother of

i. ?Moses[1], born say 1742, possibly the unnamed child born to Agnes Gowen in Louisa County before January 1743. He was called "Moses Going, mulatto" in his February 1761 to March 1762 account with Archibald Ingram, George Kipper, & Co. of Albemarle County [Weisiger, *Albemarle County Court Papers*, 23]. He was a taxable in the Trinity Parish, Louisa County household of John Fox in 1770 and in his own household in 1772 [Davis, *Louisa County Tithables*, 25, 34]. He was required to post a bond of 50 pounds and his security George **Gibson** posted 25 pounds on 10 July 1775 when Joseph Cooper swore the peace against him in Louisa County court [Orders 1774-82, 126-7]. He purchased 353 acres in Louisa County from Michael

Ailstock on 13 January 1777, and he and his wife Agnes sold this land six months later on 9 June 1777 [DB E:14, 156]. On 14 July 1777 he, Joshua Going and Charles Sprouse, Sr., were charged by the Louisa County court with hog stealing, but the sheriff was unable to arrest them because they were in hiding. The court ordered the sheriff to summon a posse to arrest them [Orders 1774-82, 171]. He was taxable in Louisa County on a horse in 1783 and 1785 [PPTL, 1782-1814].

30   ii.   Joseph[3], born about 1747.

iii.   Sarah, born about 1751, eight years old when she was bound to James Bunch as an apprentice planter on 28 November 1759 [Davis, *Fredericksville Parish Vestry Book*, 29]. Her suit against Gideon and Jordan **Gibson** for trespass, assault and battery was dismissed by the consent of the parties on 11 April 1774. She was the mother of Amey Going who was bound apprentice by the churchwardens of Trinity Parish, Louisa County, on 9 January 1775 [Orders 1774-82, 42, 113]. She registered as a "Free Negro" in Campbell County on 12 May 1802: *5 feet 8 Inches, 45 years old, Malattoe, born free in Louisa County*. Her daughter Amey, born about 1768, registered in Campbell County on 20 January 1802: *5'2-3/4", 34 years old, yellow complection, born free* [A Register of Free Negroes and Mulattoes, 1, 3].

iv.   ?David[3], born say 1751, taxable in Fredericksville Parish, Louisa County, in his own household in 1772, taxable in Moses Going's household in 1775, taxable in the Trinity Parish household of Pouncy Bunch in 1774 and taxable in Joseph Bunch's household in 1778 [Davis, *Louisa County Tithables*, 133, 45, 73]. His suit against Robert Anderson for trespass, assault and battery was dismissed by the Louisa County court on 13 July 1773 at Anderson's costs [Orders 1766-74]. He was taxable in Fredericksville Parish, Albemarle County, from 1782 to 1809, called a "Mulatto" in 1812, called "David Going Senr. Mula" in 1813 [PPTL 1782-1799, frames 12, 29, 44, 76, 116, 153, 202, 252, 300, 386, 419, 459, 481, 516, 555, 591; 1800-1813, frames 161, 207, 250, 297, 344, 388, 434, 478, 522, 566] and head of an Albemarle County household of 8 "other free" in 1810 [VA:195].

31   v.   ?Benjamin[1], born say 1753.
32   vi.   ?Joshua, born say 1755.

vii.   ?Elizabeth, born say 1760, sued James Usher in Albemarle County court for failing to pay for a gown, an apron, a quilted petticoat, and three linen handkerchiefs. Hannah Witheral was her witness. The court awarded her 2 pounds currency on 7 December 1786 [Orders 1795-8, 229-30].

33   viii.   Sherrod[1], born say 1762.

ix.   ?Archibald, born say 1763, taxable on 2 horses and 5 cattle in Fredericksville Parish, Albemarle County, in 1784 [PPTL, 1782-1799, frame 44].

x.   ?Milly, born say 1763, of Louisa County, married Charles **Croucher**, 22 June 1785 in Fredericksville Parish, Albemarle County. He was head of an Albemarle County household of 1 "other free" in 1810 [VA:153].

xi.   ?Usly, born say 1765, married Jonathan **Tyre**, 21 October 1786 Albemarle County bond, Shadrack **Battles** bondsman.

16.   David[1] Going (Philip[2], Christopher[1], Michael[1]), born say 1727, was indicted by the Henrico County court on 6 November 1752 for not going to church and for failing to list his "Mulatto" wife as a tithable. He paid a 5 shilling fine for not going to church but pleaded not guilty to the other charge. He failed to appear when the case came to trial in April 1753 and was fined 1,000 pounds of tobacco [Minutes 1752-5, 19, 26, 27, 52]. He may have been the David

Going who sued Richard Farris for trespass, assault and battery in Goochland County but discontinued the suit on 21 May 1754 [Orders 1750-7, 387]. He purchased 400 acres adjoining William Harlow's land in Henrico County from Michael Gawin (Gowen) of Bute County, North Carolina, on 20 March 1765 with John Gawin as witness [Miscellaneous Court Records 6:1943-4]. He and his wife Elizabeth sold 100 acres of this land in the fork of Farrar's Branch adjoining John Harlow, Nathan Dunaway and his own land to David Barnett on 25 October 1770 [Deeds 1767-74, 260]. He was taxable in the upper district of Henrico County from 1784 to 1790: taxable on a horse and 7 cattle in 1785, exempt from tax on his person in 1787 [PPTL 1782-1814, frames 57, 73, 124, 143, 195, 217; Orders 1784-7, 568]. He was taxable on 100 acres on the headwaters of Chickahominy Swamp in the upper district of Henrico County from 1799 to 1805 [Land Tax List 1799-1816]. He left a 17 March 1803 Henrico County will which was proved on 8 March 1805. He left all to his grandson David Going, reserving to Agatha Going peaceful possession where she was then living during her lifetime. He also named grandson John Harlace 4 pounds, left Meredith Childress a bed and furniture, and named his grandson David Going and Meredith Childress his executors. His estate was valued at 55 pounds [WB 3:183-4]. He was probably the father of

34   i.   Agnes², born say 1748.

17. John¹ Gowen (William², Thomas¹, Michael¹), born say 1702, and wife Mary sold land, "...part of a tract granted William Gowen, deceased, father to said Gowen..." on Pope's Head Run in Fairfax County on 5 March 1744. John's wife Mary, probably a white woman, was identified as the daughter of Cornelius Keife in a 9 June 1746 Fairfax deed by which he and his wife sold 112 acres on Occoquan Run which had belonged to her father [DB A-1:551; A-2:349]. John and his wife Mary moved to Lunenburg County where he was taxable on two tithables in the list of Lewis Deloney in 1748 [Tax List 1748-52]. He may have been the John Going who was tithable in Granville County in the list of Jonathan White circa 1748 [CR 44.701.19]. On 14 February 1761 he patented 400 acres in Lunenburg County on Reedy Branch [Patents 34:809]. He and wife Mary made a deed of gift of 100 acres of this patent to two of their sons, William and John, on 10 June 1761 [DB 6:378-9]. Their children were

35   i.   William⁴, born say 1725.
       ii.   John³, born say 1730, who sold the 100 acres of land his father gave him while a resident of Lunenburg County on 1 December 1761 [DB 7:151]. He was probably the John Going who was living in Orange County, North Carolina, in May 1764 when he was a defendant in a court case [Haun, *Orange County Court Minutes*, 185, 383]. It was reported that Colonel John Hogan of Orange County said he knew him well in 1765 and that he was: *a trifling, contemptible fellow, a gambler, and a mulatto...was then insolvent and probably is so still if alive* [*NCGSJ* IV:157 (Claims of British Merchants after the Revolutionary War)]. He may have been the John Gowen who was granted 100 acres on Tiger River in South Carolina on 19 August 1774 [DB 32:205].
36   iii.   ?Thomas², born say 1732.

18. William³ Gowen (William², Thomas¹, Michael¹), born say 1710, was a planter in Brunswick County, Virginia, on 4 June 1747 when he was fined and had to post security for his good behavior, "having behaved himself in a very disorderly indecent and contemptuous manner to this court" [Orders 1743-49, 204]. He purchased 910 acres on Grassy Creek in Granville County, North Carolina, near the border with Lunenburg County, Virginia, on 5 March 1751 [DB A:343]. He and his family were counted as white taxables in the early Granville Tax lists. He was taxed on two tithes in the 1751 Granville County

list of Samuel Henderson. He was in the 8 October 1754 muster of Captain John Sallis' Company in the Granville County Regiment of Colonel William Eaton [Clark, *Colonial Soldiers of the South,* 722]. He was fined for trespass in the Granville County court on 3 December 1754, 5 March 1755, 1 March 1757, and again on 6 September 1757 [Minutes 1754-70, 11, 43, 46]. In the 1755 Summary Tax List he was taxable on two white tithes for himself and son Joseph [CR 44.701.19]. In 1758 he was taxable on two white polls for himself and son William in the list of James Yancey. On 2 December 1760 he patented two tracts of land in St. John's Parish, Granville County, near the head of Dogwood Branch, one for 650 acres and the other for 667 acres. In 1761 he was taxed on two tithes for himself and James Gowen in Country Line District in the list of Larkin Thompson. He sold 640 acres of his land in Granville on 4 October 1762, made a deed of gift of 350 acres to his son Joseph on 7 August 1765, and the sheriff sold 350 acres of his land for debt on 5 February 1767 [DB E:440-448; F:382; H:28, 226]. He may have been the William Gowen, Sr., who was granted 396 acres on Sink Hole Fork of Middle Tiger River in South Carolina [Pruitt, *Spartanburg County Deed Abstracts* (DB A:109)]. His children who were taxable in North Carolina were

    i.   Joseph[2], born circa 1740, taxable in his father's household in the 1757 Granville County list of Richard Harris. He received a deed of gift of land in Granville County from his father on 7 August 1765 [DB H:28]. He was taxed in Granville County for the last time in 1767 when he had 3 "white" males in his household in the list of Philips Pryor: Presley Harrison, John Cunningham, and Minor Cockram. By 1771 he was in South Carolina where he received a grant for land in the northwest part called the Tiger River tract [DB 23:539].

   ii.   William[5], born circa 1742, taxable in Granville County in 1758. He may have been the William Gowen, Jr., who was granted 116 acres on Mill Creek in South Carolina [Owens, *Patent Land Survey*, 15].

  iii.   James[5], born circa 1745 since he was taxable in 1761 in his father's Country Line District household.

19. Luke Gowen (James[1], Thomas[1], Michael[1]), born say 1740, was taxable in Loudoun County in 1768 with William Allin in his household and on two tithes in 1782 [Sparacio, *Loudoun County Tithables 1758-1769*, 68; Fothergill, *Virginia Tax Payers*, 49]. He was head of a Loudoun County household of 10 "other free" in 1810 [VA:288]. He and his wife Margaret were certified to be "free Negroes" in Loudoun County on 23 December 1795. The certificate stated that they had been living in the neighborhood of John Littleton for above thirty years [Certificates of Free Negroes at the Loudoun County courthouse, transcribed by Townsend Lucas]. He may have been the father of

    i.   Joseph[4], born say 1780, head of a Loudoun County household of 4 "other free" and 1 white woman in 1810 [VA:292].

   ii.   Leonard, father of Elihu Goins who was born 15 April 1788. Elihu married Susannah, the daughter of Anthony **Lucas**. Susannah was born 25 April 1785 [Certificates of Free Negroes at the Loudoun County courthouse, transcribed by Townsend Lucas].

20. Michael[3] Gowen (Edward[2], Edward[1], William[1], Michael[1]), born say 1722, was sued for debt in Henrico County in June 1744 [Orders 1737-46, 267]. He was called Micahael Gawin when he was granted 400 acres in Henrico County on 30 June 1743 adjoining William Harlow. Land adjoining Michael Going, Farrar's Branch and Orphant's line was patented in Henrico County on 15 September 1752 [Patents 21:424; 31:193]. He was living in Bute County, North Carolina, on 20 March 1765 when he sold this land to David Gawin [Miscellaneous Court Records 6:1943-4]. He was taxable in John MacKisick's household in the 1750 Granville County, North Carolina tax list of Edward Jones [CR 44.701.23]. On 3 May 1752 he purchased 225 acres on both sides

of Taylors Creek in Granville County [DB B:73]. He was taxed as a "Black" tithe in 1753 in the list of Osborn Jeffreys, as a "white" tithe in Jeffreys' 1754 list, and as a "black" tithe in the 1755 tax summary. He was in the 8 October 1754 Muster Roll of the Granville County Regiment of Colonel William Eaton, Captain Osborne Jeffrey's Company:

> *Thomas Gowen   Mulatto*
> *Mickael Gowen   Mulatto*
> *Edward Gowen   Mulatto*   [Clark, *Colonial Soldiers of the South*, 718].

He was taxed in 1759 in the list of John Pope with John **Wilson**, both called "Mulattoe," and he was taxed in Pope's 1761 list with the notation, "Refuses to list his wife," probably claiming that he was white. He was taxed in the Bute County List of Philemon Hawkins in 1771:

> *Michle Gowine & Wife & Sons Michile & David Doughter Elizebeath*
> *Wm Wilson   0 white/ 6 black/ 6 total* [1771 List of Taxables, p.11].

He was in Prince George Parish, Craven County, South Carolina, on 3 June 1778 when he made a deed of gift of 80 acres on the south side of Taylor's Creek on the border of Bute and Granville Counties to Jenkins Gowen, no relationship stated. Jenkins (his nephew?) was to take title to the land at the death of Michael's brother Edward and his wife who were given permission to live on the land [Granville County WB 1:193]. His children were

    i.   Michael[4], Jr., born say 1738, a defendant in a 3 September 1755 Granville County court case.

    ii.   Elizabeth, born before 1760 since she was taxable in Michael Gowen's household in 1771.

    iii. David[5], born before 1760 since he was taxable in Michael Gowen's household in 1771. He may have been the _avid Gowen who received thirty nine lashes in Granville County for petty larceny in 1773 [Minutes 1773-83, 1].

21.   James[2] Gowen (Edward[2], Edward[1], William[1], Michael[1]), born say 1725, was not mentioned in Granville County, North Carolina records until 1756, so he may have been living in Virginia before then. He received a patent for 529 acres in St. John's Parish, Granville County on Wharton's Branch on 29 November 1756 [DB E:439]. He and his son William, "Mulattoes," were taxable in the 1759 Granville County list of John Pope and were delinquent taxpayers that year. In 1762 he was taxable in Fishing Creek District with his son William, with the notation "Refs. to list his wife," and he was an insolvent taxpayer from 1762 to 1764. He was the father of

37   i.   William[6], born before 1748.

22.   Edward[3] Gowen (Edward[2], Edward[1], William[1], Michael[1]), born say 1727, purchased 100 acres on the south side of Mill Creek in Brunswick County, Virginia, on 2 June 1748 [DB 3:444]. He was sued in Brunswick County court in September 1753 [Orders 1753-56, 65]. He was taxable in 1753 in Osborn Jeffrey's Granville County tax list, and he was a "Mulatto" listed in the 8 October 1754 muster roll of Captain Osborne Jeffreys' Granville County Company [Clark, *Colonial Soldiers of the South*, 718]. He was prosecuted in Edgecombe County by the Attorney General for concealing his tithables in August 1756 [Haun, *Edgecombe County Court Minutes*, I:131], but he still refused to list his wife in the Granville County Tax List for 1765 [CR 44.601.20]. He and his wife were two "Black" taxables in Bute County in the list of Philemon Hawkins in 1771 [1771 List of Taxables, p.6]. On 3 June 1778 his brother Michael, while a resident of South Carolina, allowed him to remain on 80 acres on Taylor's Creek [WB 1:193-4]. The sheriff sold this land

shortly afterwards on 3 August 1779 [DB M:179], and Edward was taxed on 90 acres in nearby Ford Creek District, Granville County, in 1782. He was probably related to Elizabeth **Bass** since he made over all his interest in her estate to his nephew Thomas Gowen on 14 October 1788 [WB 2:79]. He was head of a Granville County household of 2 free males and 3 free females in the 1786 state census and head of a Granville County household of 5 "other free" in 1810 [NC:905]. His children were

  i.   Edward[4], born circa 1744 in Virginia, taxable in 1761 in his father's household in the list of Robert Harris. In 1767 he was head of his own household, one Black male, in John Pope's list. In 1779 he was listed among the continental soldiers from Bute County who served for nine months: *Edward Going private, born Virginia, 5'7", 35 years old Black Fair; black eyes* [*NCGSJ* XV:109]. On 3 August 1779 he entered 75 acres on the South Hyco Creek in Caswell County (called Edward Gains) [Pruitt, *Land Entries: Caswell County*, 89] and in 1784 he was taxed on one poll and 100 acres on Hyco Creek in St. Luke's District, Caswell County. This part of Caswell County became Person County in 1791, and he was taxed on 245 acres and one poll in Person County in 1793 [*N.C. Genealogy* XVII:2678, abstracted as Edward Gains]. He was head of a Person County household of 6 "other free" in 1800 [NC:599]. He and Jenkins Goins sold their claims for Revolutionary War pay to John Hall of Hyco, Caswell County, on 27 April 1791 [*NCGSJ* IX:224]. Perhaps he was the Edward Goins who was the great grandfather of Daniel Goins, born about 1816, who made an affidavit in Randolph County, North Carolina, in 1882 that he was the son of William, grandson of William, and great grandson of Edward Goins, who was "Slitly mixt about an eight" [Randolph County Genealogical Society, *The Genealogical Journal*, Winter (1980): 21].

  ii. Reeps, born circa 1749, taxable in his father's Granville County household in the 1761 list of Robert Harris. He was called Rapes Going when he enlisted in the Second South Carolina Regiment under Captain Thomas Hall on 1 July 1779 [Moss, *Roster of S.C. Patriots in the American Revolution*, 367].

  iii. ?Jenkins, born about 1761, a seventeen-year-old "mullato" in 1778 when he enlisted in Captain John Rust's Company of Granville County militia [*The North Carolinian* VI:726 (Mil. TR 4-40)]. He received 30 acres by a Granville County deed of gift from Michael Gowen (his uncle?) on 3 June 1778 [WB 1:193]. He was taxable in Granville County in 1790.

  iv. ?Jesse[1], born say 1762, married Sealey Bairding, 9 June 1784 Caswell County bond, John Going bondsman.

Other members of the family in Person County were

  i.   Goodrich, born say 1764, purchased 175 acres on Cane Creek in Caswell County on 1 November 1784 and sold it five years later on 4 January 1798 [DB C:3; F:163]. He was taxed on this 175 acres and one poll in St. Lawrence District, Caswell County, in 1784. On 6 September 1791 he married Betsey **Matthews**, Caswell County bond with Allen Going bondsman. He was head of a Person County household of 7 "other free" in 1800 [NC:612] and 5 in 1810 when his name was interlined [NC:702]. Gutrige Goin was a "Mulatto" taxable in the southern district of Halifax County, Virginia, from 1802 to 1804, perhaps identical to Birbridge Goin, a "Mulatto" taxable there in 1805 and 1806 [PPTL, 1800-12, frames 186, 317, 372, 517, 626] and called Berridge/ Burbage Goin in Patrick County from 1809 to 1813: listed as a Mulatto" in 1812 and 1813 [PPTL, 1791-1823, frames 515, 537, 553, 569, 598]. Beveridge Going, born before 1776, was head of a Patrick County household of 3 "free colored" in 1820 [VA:106].

Burbridge Gowing was taxable in Person County in 1793. He married Agnes **Harris**, daughter of James **Harris**, 26 July 1810 Patrick County bond.

ii. Isham, born say 1770, married Fanny Going, 26 November 1792 Person County bond, with Patrick **Mason** bondsman. He was head of an Orange County household of 4 "other free" in 1800 [NC:565] and 6 in 1810 [NC:876].

iii. Patsy, born say 1772, married Patrick **Mason**, 3 December 1790 Caswell County bond, Zachariah **Hill** bondsman.

iv. Sherwood[2], born say 1772, married Ruth Bennett, 30 April 1793 Caswell County bond, James Gillaspy bondsman.

v. Allen, born say 1774, married Rebecca Goins, 7 April 1795 Person County bond. He was head of a Person County household of 7 "other free" in 1800 [NC:621] and 10 in 1810 [NC:625].

23. Joseph[1] Gowen (Edward[2], Edward[1], William[1], Michael[1]), born say 1730, was taxable in his own Lunenburg County household in the 1752 list of Field Jefferson [Tax List 1748-52, 1]. He was a "Black" taxable in the 1755 Granville County summary list and a "Mulattoe" in John Pope's 1759 tax list. On 1 December 1760 he received a patent for 680 acres on both sides of Taylor's Creek, but sold this land less than one year later on 11 August 1761 [DB E:143; D:253]. In 1761 he was taxable in John Pope's list with the notation, "Refuses to list his wife." In 1765 he was listed by John Pope with the notation, "Mullattoe, has a wife and other Family not listed." He was taxed (with his son Nathaniel or a slave by that name?) in John Pope's 1768 list as "Joseph Gowin his Nat 2 tithes." He was last taxed in Granville County in 1771. One of his children may have been

i. Nathaniel, born say 1755. He was brought to Granville County court in 1773 with Robert **Locklear** on an unspecified charge, but they were released on payment of their prison charges when no one appeared against them [Minutes 1773-83, 1].

24. David[2] Going (Edward[2], Edward[1], William[1], Michael[1]), born say 1735, purchased land by deed proved in Halifax County, Virginia, in August 1765 [Pleas 1764-7, 122]. He was sued in Pittsylvania County in July 1768 for a debt of 84 pounds he owed from 1 August 1764 of which he had paid 27 pounds in October 1767. He sold land by deed proved in Pittsylvania County in May 1773, and he sued Peter **Rickman** on 25 June 1773 for a 3 pound debt due by account [Court Records 1767-72, 219; 1772-5, 158, 211-2]. On 17 August 1778 he owned land on both sides of Spoon Creek when the Henry County court allowed him to build a water grist mill the creek [Orders 1778-82, 15]. He was taxable in Henry County from 1782 to 1790: taxable on William, Charles and Jacob Going in 1783 and 1784; listed with 3 unnamed sons in 1785; 4 unnamed sons, 10 horses and 17 cattle in 1786; listed with William and Jacob in 1787; 5 tithes in 1788 [PPTL, 1782-1830, frames 8, 37, 88, 218, 301, 352]. He received a grant for 94 acres on Spoon Creek in Henry County on 30 March 1789 [Grants 19:297]. He was taxable in Patrick County from 1791 to 1800: listed with 6 horses in 1791, 2 tithes from 1792 to 1795, 3 in 1797 [PPTL, 1791-1823, frames 150, 207, 251, 288]. He sold land by deed proved in Patrick County on 29 May 1794 [Orders 1791-1800]. He was the father of

i. William, taxable in Henry County from 1783 to 1790 [PPTL, 1782-1830, frames 314, 352] and taxable in Patrick County from 1791 to 1814: listed with 2 tithes in 1791, called "Sr." in 1803, listed on the Dan River in 1806, listed with 2 tithes in 1809 and 1811, in a list of "free Negroes & Mulattoes" in 1813 and 1814 [PPTL, 1782-1830, frames 150, 177, 207, 234, 288, 343, 369, 396, 455, 515, 553, 598, 616]. His land on the west side of Little Dan River in Patrick County adjoining Shadrack Going's land was mentioned in a 19 August 1805 grant [Grants 54:212].

ii. Jacob, born about 1762, married Nancy Smith, 18 January 1792 Patrick County bond, John Camron surety. He was taxable in Henry County from 1784 to 1787 [PPTL, 1782-1830, frames 88, 253], taxable in Patrick County in 1791, 1792, 1798 and 1800 [PPTL, 1791-1823, frames 151, 251, 288], and head of a Stokes County household of 6 "other free" in 1800 [NC:495]. He was about seventy years of age and living in Vermillion County, Illinois, on 7 June 1832 when applied for a Revolutionary War pension, stating that he was born in Henry County, Virginia, that he lived in Kentucky for about thirty years, then lived for seven years in Vincennes, Indiana [M805, reel 368, frame 0115, reel 368].

iii. Charles, born about 1763, taxable in Henry County from 1783 to 1790 [PPTL, 1782-1830, frames 302, 352], taxable in Patrick County from 1791 to 1795 [PPTL, 1791-1823, frames 151, 177, 207]. He was about seventy years old on 22 October 1833 when he applied for a Revolutionary War pension, stating that he had been born in Henry County, lived there until 1797, then moved to Kentucky and moved to Gallatin in 1815 [M805, reel 368, frame 0144].

iv. Martha, born say 1779, married Peter Burress, 7 June 1797 Patrick County bond with the consent of David Going.

25. Shadrack^1 Gowen (Edward^2, Edward^1, William^1, Michael^1) born say 1737, listed his tithables in Halifax County, Virginia on 15 September 1763. He was presented by the court in May 1765 for concealing a tithable who may have been his wife. The case against him was dismissed in August 1766, perhaps on his payment of the tax. He won a suit against John Bates in Halifax County court for about 2 pounds in July 1767. He purchased land by deed proved in Halifax County court in August 1768 [Pleas 1764-7, 46, 358, 454; 6:221]. He was head of a Halifax County household of 12 persons in 1782 [VA:23] and 10 in 1785 [VA:89]. He was taxable in Halifax County from 1782 to 1785 [PPTL, 1782-1799, frames 7, 25, 35, 63]. His land on the west side of Little Dan River in Patrick County adjoining William Going's land was mentioned in a 19 August 1805 grant [Grants 54:212]. He sold land by deed proved in Halifax County on 17 November 1785 [Pleas 1783-6, 242]. He was taxable in Patrick County from 1791 to 1805: listed with 2 tithables from 1791 to 1794, 3 in 1795 and 1796, 2 in 1798, taxed on 5 horses but not tithable from 1800 to 1805 [PPTL, 1791-1823, frames 150, 193, 220, 251, 288, 343, 396, 425], exempted by the court on 31 May 1798 from paying tax on his person [Orders 1791-1800, n.p.]. He made a Patrick County deed of gift to his grandson Shadrack Beasley in 1803 [DB 2:268]. He left a 4 June 1805 Patrick County will which was returned to court in December 1805, leaving his wife Hannah furniture and the use of his house during her lifetime, to be divided between Jerushe and Keziah Going at her death. He left his plantation on both sides of the Little Dan River to his son Obediah, left a cow to Rebecca Going, daughter of Fanny Going and wife of Edmond Bowlin, left 5 shillings each to sons John Going, David Smith Going, James, Claiborn, Solomon, Shadrack, and Caleb Going; left 5 shillings to daughter Fanny Bowling, wife of Edmund Bowling and Hannah Beazley, wife of Thomas Beazley [WB 1:80-1]. On 24 July 1806 his children Jerusha, John, David Smith, James, Fanny, Claiborne, Shadrick and Leaborne Gowing were in Grainger County, Tennessee, when they appointed Henry Howell to sue Obediah Gowing for settling the property unfairly and submitting a will which was not Shadrack Gowing's [Patrick DB 3:87]. Shadrack was the father of

i. David^4, born about 1754, head of a Halifax County, Virginia household of 2 persons in 1782 [VA:24] and 4 in 1785 [VA:89]. He was taxable in Halifax County from 1782 to 1793 and from 1796 to 1806: called a

"Mul°" from 1792 to 1806, living at Walne's in 1796 and 1797, a planter in the list of "free Negroes & Mulattoes" who was living on "D.C." (Difficult Creek?) with wife and two daughters over the age of sixteen in 1801. He may have been the father of John and William Going who were listed as "Mul°" in 1794 and 1795 [PPTL, 1782-1799, frames 7, 71, 302, 417, 442, 732, 819; 1800-12, frames 59, 187, 517, 676]. He registered in Halifax County on 11 October 1802: *aged about forty eight years, six feet and a half inch high, light yellow Colour, inclining to white, straight hair...born free* [Register of Free Negroes, no.20]. He was head of a Wythe County household of 8 "other free" in 1810. He was about seventy-six years old on 26 February 1834 when he appeared in Hamilton County, Tennessee court to apply for a pension for his services in the Revolution. He testified that he entered the service in Halifax County, Virginia, moved to Grayson County, Virginia, for three years, then to Wythe County for ten years, then to Grainger County, Tennessee, for fourteen years and lived in Hamilton County for one year. His younger brother Laban Goens testified on his behalf [M805-362, frames 27-30].

38   ii.   James, born say 1758.

     iii.   Jerusha, born about 1760, head of a Stokes County household of 3 "free colored" in 1820. On 12 April 1821 she obtained a Patrick County, Virginia, Certificate of Freedom: *Jarussa Going, dark, aged about 62; Polly Going, light complexion, aged 28; son Andrew Going 9, all residing on Little Dan River.* The certificate was recorded about twenty years later in Highland County, Ohio [Turpin, *Register of Black, Mulatto, and Poor Persons,* 8].

     iv.   John[7], born say 1760, head of a Halifax County, Virginia household of 2 persons in 1782 [VA:23] and 4 in 1785 [VA:89], perhaps the John Going who was taxable on the Dan River in Patrick County from 1791 to 1814: taxable on 2 tithes in 1802, 1804, 1805, and 1810; called John Going Sr. "Molatto" in 1812, in a list of "free Negroes & Mulattoes" in 1813 and 1814 [PPTL, 1791-1823, frames 150, 343, 396, 537, 598, 614]. Administration on his estate was granted Lindy P. Stovall on 12 October 1820 [Orders 1810-21, n.p.].

     v.   Nathaniel, born say 1766, taxable in Henry County from 1787 to 1790 [PPTL, 1782-1830, frame 253, 352], taxable in Patrick County from 1791 to 1793 [PPTL, 1791-1823, frames 150, 177]. He died on 21 September 1793 after being struck in the head with a weeding hoe by Robert Hall according to the coroner and a 9 November 1793 Patrick County jury of inquest held at Shadrack Going's plantation. Robert Hall was examined for the murder but not charged, perhaps because his accusers could not legally testify against him. Shadrack Going was granted administration on his estate on 10 December 1793 [WB 1:6, 53].

     vi.   Hannah, married Thomas Beasley of Patrick County, Virginia.

     vii.   Claiborn[2], taxable in Henry County from 1788 to 1790 (with the notation "Dan River") [PPTL, 1782-1830, frames 301, 314, 352], taxable on the Dan River in Patrick County from 1791 to 1794 [PPTL, 1791-1823, frames 150, 177, 193].

     viii.   Fanny, wife of Edmund Bowlin, and mother of Rebecca Going who received a cow by her grandfather Shadrack's will.

     ix.   Laban, born about 1764, taxable in Henry County in 1790 [PPTL, 1782-1830, frame 352] and taxable in Patrick County from 1791 to 1803 [PPTL, 1791-1831, frames 150, 207, 250, 370]. He was about seventy years old on 26 February 1734 when he testified in support of the pension application of his brother David in Hamilton County, Tennessee court [M805-362, frames 27-30].

    x.   Shadrack[2], born say 1772, taxable in Patrick County from 1793 to 1798 [PPTL, 1791-1831, frames 177, 207, 234, 250], head of a Grainger County Tennessee household of "other free" in 1810.

    xi.   Caleb, married Polly Duncan, 9 June 1802 Patrick County bond, Harden Dunham surety. He was taxable in Patrick County from 1800 to 1802 [PPTL, 1791-1823, frames 288, 342] and taxable in Henry County in 1803 [PPTL, 1782-1830, frame 517].

    xii.   Obediah, born say 1777, taxable in Patrick County from 1798 to 1807 [PPTL, 1782-1830, frames 250, 288, 396, 487].

26. John[7] (Edward[2], Edward[1], William[1], Michael[1]), born say 1740, owned land on both sides of Blackberry Creek on 17 February 1777 when the Henry County, Virginia court allowed him to build a water grist mill over the creek. The Henry County court appointed him surveyor of the road from Cogar's path to John Cox's from 27 May 1784 to 25 May 1789 [Orders 1777-8, 5; 1782-5, 149; 1788-91, 44]. He was taxable in Henry County from 1782 to 1801: taxable on 4 horses and 13 cattle in 1782; charged with Zephaniah, Claiborn and James Going's tithe in 1783, listed with 2 unnamed sons in 1784; listed with Claiborn and Asaiah Going in 1785; listed with 4 unnamed sons in 1786; listed with John and Zephaniah Going in 1787; listed with the notation "Black Berry" when he was taxable on 4 tithes in 1788, 6 in 1789 and 5 in 1790 [PPTL, 1782-1830, frames 15, 37, 86, 150, 158, 302, 315]. He received a grant for 156 acres on both sides of Blackberry Creek adjoining his own land in Henry County on 14 April 1796 [Grants 35:153]. He left a 17 March 1801 Henry County will, proved 27 July 1801, by which he lent his wife Elizabeth his stock and household goods and directed that his land in Patrick and Henry counties be sold and divided among his children Zephaniah, Nancy, Susanna, Zedekiah, Simeon, John, Isaiah, Zachariah, Clabourn, and Littleberry Going and Elizabeth Minor, wife of Hezekiah Minor. He named John Stone and John Cox, Jr., his executors [WB 2:37-9]. His estate was taxable on a free male tithable in 1802, 3 free males in 1803, 4 free males in 1804 [PPTL 1782-1830, frames 504, 517, 531. Elizabeth Going was administratrix of an estate on 24 November 1803 when she sued Joseph Newman in Patrick County court [Orders 1800-10, n.p.]. She was taxable in Henry County on 3 free tithes in 1805 and 2 in 1806 and 1807 [PPTL, 1782-1830, frames 553, 578]. The inventory of her estate totaled $546 and was proved in March 1814 [WB 2:205-6]. John was the father of

    i.   Simeon, taxable in Henry County in 1807 and 1810 [PPTL, 1782-1830, frames 578, 591].

    ii.   Zephaniah, born say 1762, taxable in Henry County from 1783 to 1796 and in 1802: listed with 2 tithables in 1794 [PPTL, 1782-1830, frames 159, 302, 402, 428, 504], taxable in Patrick County from 1797 to 1799 [PPTL, 1791-1823, frames 234, 268]. He was about seventy-six years old and living in Hawkins County, Tennessee on 18 December 1834 when he applied for a Revolutionary War pension, stating that he had entered the service in Henry County [M805, reel 368, frame 0134].

    iii.   Zedekiah, taxable in Patrick County in 1811, in a list of "free Negroes and Mulattoes" in 1813 and 1814, probably identical to Hezekiah Going who was taxable in Henry County in 1803 and in Patrick County from 1804 to 1809, called a "Mulatto" in 1812 [PPTL, 1791-1823, frames 396, 487, 553, 569, 598, 616, 664, 679, 696, 713]. Zedekiah was head of a Patrick County household of 7 "free colored" in 1820 [VA:116A], and Hezekiah was head of a household of 9 "free colored" in 1830 [VA:154].

    iv.   Claiborn[1], born say 1764, taxable in Henry County from 1783 to 1787 [PPTL, 1782-1830, frames 253].

    v.   Isaiah, born say 1768, taxable in Henry County in 1785 and 1791 [PPTL, 1782-1830, frames 315, 364].

vi. Littleberry, taxable in Henry County from 1807 to 1814: in a list of "free Negroes & Mulattoes" in 1813 and 1814 [PPTL, 1782-1830, frames 578, 591, 603, 641, 656].

vii. John, in a list of "free Negroes & Mulattoes" in Henry County in 1813 and 1814 [PPTL, 1782-1830, frames 641, 656], perhaps the John Going who was about forty-eight years old on 15 November 1824 when he registered as a free Negro in Pittsylvania County.

viii. Elizabeth Minor, wife of Hezekiah Minor who was taxable in Henry County in 1802 [PPTL, 1782-1830, frame 506].

ix. Nancy.

x. Susanna.

xi. Zachariah.

27. James[4] Gowen (Mary[1], Michael[2], Christopher[1], Michael[1]), born say 1735, was living in Brunswick County, Virginia, on 27 December 1757 when he sued John **Cumbo** for trespass [Orders 1757-9, 143]. He received a grant for 376 acres adjoining Brewer, Perry, and Cook on Carter's Creek in Brunswick County on 23 May 1763 [Patents 35:137]. He and his wife Amy sold 150 acres of this land in Meherrin Parish on the south side of the Meherrin River on 22 September 1765 [DB 8:359]. Greensville County was formed from Brunswick County in 1781, and James was head of a Greensville County household of 7 persons in 1783 [VA:54]. James, Henry Going, and Avent Massey posted bond in Greensville County on 24 August 1786 for the illegitimate child Henry Going had by Mary Hill [DB 1:173]. He voted in Greensville County in 1792, 1794, and 1795 [DB 1:451; 2:24, 135, 190]. He was taxable in Greensville County from 1782 to 1811: taxable on Edmund, Henry and James Going's tithes in 1782; 3 tithes in 1783, 2 in 1784; 1 in 1785; 2 slaves from 1787 to 1792; 3 in 1794; 4 from 1799 to 1802; 6 from 1806 to 1811 [PPTL 1782-1850, frames 4, 17, 22, 28, 42, 63, 107, 126, 136, 179, 244, 259, 273, 287, 302, 321, 336, 353, 372, 402] and head of a Greensville County household of 2 whites and 7 slaves in 1810 [VA:735]. He was probably the father of

i. Edmund, born say 1770, taxable in Greensville County in James Going's household in 1782, charged with his own tax in 1790 [PPTL 1782-1850, frames 4, 107]. He married Mary **Stewart**, daughter of Dr. Thomas **Stewart**, in Dinwiddie County [Chancery Orders 1832-52, 12]. He purchased 200 acres on Sandy Creek in Mecklenburg County, Virginia, from his father-in-law on 5 November 1799, and he and his wife Polly sold 242 acres on Sandy Creek to Frederick **Ivey** while resident in Person County, North Carolina [DB 10:176, 188-9]. He purchased 124 acres in Person County from (his cousin) Frederick Going, and sold this land by deeds proved in June 1801 Person County court. On 5 June 1804 he mortgaged a slave named Patty and his farm animals in Person County for 90 pounds [DB C:453].

ii. Henry, born say 1764, taxable in Greensville County from 1782 to 1811: taxable in James Going's household in 1782 and 1791; taxable on 3 slaves in 1800 [PPTL 1782-1850, frames 63, 107, 179, 273, 287, 353, 372, 402, 415].

iii. James, Jr., born say 1766, taxable in Greensville County from 1782 to 1806: underage in 1782; taxed in his own household in 1784 and 1785; taxable in John Turner's household in 1788; taxable on a slave from 1800 to 1804; 2 slaves in 1806 [PPTL 1782-1850, frames 4, 22, 28, 63, 88, 259, 287, 321, 336, 353].

iv. Benjamin, born say 1773, taxable in Greensville County from 1794 to 1811 [PPTL 1782-1850, frames 179, 231, 259, 287, 321, 353, 415]. He took the oath of deputy sheriff in Greensville County on 11 May 1801 [Orders 1799-1806, 125].

28.   Drury¹ Going (Mary¹, Michael², Christopher¹, Michael¹), born say 1738, was
paid 5 pounds for a year's work according to the account of the Brunswick
County, Virginia estate of Sampson Lanier which was returned 23 July 1759
[WB 3:297]. He purchased 50 acres in Meherrin Parish, Brunswick County,
on the south side of the Meherrin River on 28 November 1766 and purchased
223 acres on the north side of Fountains Creek on 4 February 1779.
Greensville County was formed from this part of Brunswick County in 1781
[DB 8:505; 13:347]. He was head of a Greensville County household of 4
persons in 1783 [VA:55] and was taxable in Meherrin Parish, Greensville
County from 1782 to 1801: taxable on an under-age tithable, 2 horses and 11
cattle in 1783; 1 tithe in 1784 and 1785; 4 in 1786; his own tithe and Thomas
Going's in 1787 [PPTL 1782-1850, frames 3, 13, 22, 28, 34, 42, 108, 217,
273]. On 12 March 1782 the Greensville County court credited him with the
value of a gun impressed for the public use (during the Revolution) [Orders
1781-9, 13-14]. He sold 200 acres in Greensville County for 40 pounds on 15
May 1785 [DB 1:106-7]. He was called Drury Going of Greensville County
on 1 October 1787 when he sold 50 acres on the south side of the Meherrin
River in Brunswick County adjoining Rebecca **Stewart**'s line [DB 14:366]. He
may have been the father of

  i.   Frederick², born about 1760, listed in the Greensville County household
        of William Powell in 1787 [PPTL 1782-1850, frame 45] and listed in
        the Mecklenburg County, Virginia household of Dr. Thomas **Stewart**
        in 1788. He was taxable in his own Mecklenburg County household
        from 1790 to 1802: taxable on slave Phillis in 1796 and taxable on
        slave Patsy in 1800 [PPTL, 1782-1805, frames 223, 372, 544, 613,
        713, 822, 873, 899]. He married Suckee **Chavous**, 9 March 1789
        Mecklenburg County, Virginia bond, with a note from the bride's
        father, Henry **Chavous**, Sr. Frederick **Ivey** was security, James
        Stewart, Robert Singleton, and Belar **Chavous** witnesses. He
        purchased 250 acres on the east side of Blue Wing Creek in Person
        County, North Carolina, on 16 September 1793 and sold 124 acres of
        this land while a resident of Mecklenburg County, Virginia, on 6 July
        1801 [DB A:147; C:290]. On 14 April 1800 the Mecklenburg County,
        Virginia court granted him a license to keep an ordinary at his house
        [Orders 1798-1801, 331]. He was a "free man of Color" who stated
        that he was about seventy-eight years old on 21 March 1838 when he
        appeared in Lawrence County, Alabama court to apply for a pension
        for services in the militia during the Revolution. He stated that he was
        born on the Meherrin River in the part of Brunswick County, Virginia,
        from which Greensville was formed after the war, and he was about
        sixteen years old when drafted. He was in Illinois on 2 December 1842
        when Daniel Hay wrote a letter enquiring about the status of his
        application [M805-362, frames 14-24].

39 ii.   Thomas⁴, born say 1761.

  iii.   Marcus/ Mark, born before 1776, probably one of Drury Going's
        tithables when he and Thomas Going were ordered to work on the road
        in Greensville County from the Falling Run to the county line on 25
        June 1789 [Orders 1781-9, 416]. He married Sarah **Jones**, 29
        September 1794 Greensville County bond, Robert Brooks **Corn**
        bondsman. On 23 September 1799 Mark and his wife Sally sold 35
        acres adjoining Robert **Watkins**, and he and his wife, together with
        Robert and Sally **Watkins**, sold 9 acres which their wives had inherited
        from their father Thomas **Jones** [DB 2:576, 577]. On 24 August 1799
        he was paid as a witness for William Lanier in the Greensville County
        suit of William Stewart [Orders 1790-9, 635]. He was taxable in
        Greensville County from 1788 to 1803 and from 1810 to 1815: taxable
        in Drury Going's household in 1791; listed with Michael and Sally
        Gowing as "Mulattos" in 1813 [PPTL 1782-1850, frames 63, 126, 136,

179, 188, 201, 217, 244, 259, 273, 287, 302, 402, 415, 446, 482]. He was a "M"(ulatto) taxable on a horse in St. Luke's Parish, Southampton County, in 1805 and 1806 [PPTL 1792-1806, frames 807, 843] and head of a Greensville County household of 3 "free colored" in 1820 [VA:261].

29. John⁶ Gowen (Ann¹, Michael², Christopher¹, Michael¹), born say 1758, made his Robeson County will on 19 February 1800. He gave his unnamed wife the right to use his plantation which was to revert to his son John who was not yet twenty-one years of age when he wrote the will [WB 1:60]. His wife was probably Sarah Gowen who was granted administration on his estate by the 6 April 1802 Robeson County court [Minutes 1797-1803, 193]. She conveyed land to Elizabeth Gowen by deed proved in Robeson County court on 26 May 1812 [Minutes 1806-13]. His son was
    i. John¹⁰, born say 1785, appeared in Robeson County court for an unnamed offence on 2 July 1805 [Minutes 1803-06, 329]. He was one of three John Goines counted as white in Robeson County in 1810 [NC:232, 239].

30. Joseph³ Going, born about 1747, was twelve years old when he was bound as an apprentice planter to James Bunch in Louisa County on 28 November 1759 [Davis, *Fredericksville Parish Vestry Book*, 29]. He was taxable in James Bunch's Trinity Parish, Louisa County household in 1767 [Davis, *Louisa County Tithables*, 10] and taxable in Fredericksville Parish, Albemarle County, from 1783 to 1792: taxable on 2 tithes from 1788 to 1792 [PPTL, 1782-1799, frames 29, 44, 76, 116, 202, 300, 346]. He may have been the father of
    i. Thomas, born say 1772, taxable in Fredericksville Parish, Albemarle County, from 1789 to 1796 and from 1811 to 1813: listed with "Jos. S" (either Joshua or Joseph's son) after his name in 1811 and 1812; called "J.S. a Mula" in 1813 [PPTL, 1782-1799, frames 202, 251, 300, 386, 419, 459, 481; 1800-1813, frames 477, 521, 566].
    ii. Anthony, born say 1776, taxable in Fredericksville Parish, Albemarle County, in 1793 [PPTL, 1782-1799, frame 386].

31. Benjamin¹ Going, born say 1753, was taxable in Fredericksville Parish, Albemarle County, from 1782 to 1800: taxable on 2 tithes from 1788 to 1790, 3 in 1791, 2 in 1792, 3 in 1793, 2 in 1794 and 1795, 3 in 1796 and 1797, 2 from 1798 to 1801; 3 from 1802 to 1807; 2 in 1809; 1 from 1810 to 1813: called a "Mula" in 1813 [PPTL, 1782-1799, frames 12, 44, 116, 201, 300, 386, 459, 515, 590; 1800-1813, frames 28, 118, 208, 297, 388, 478, 567]. He was head of an Albemarle County household of 4 "other free" in 1810 [VA:195]. He was the father of
    i. Mary, born say 1773, daughter of Benjamin Goin who consented, married Richard Broke (**Brock**), 3 January 1791 Albemarle County bond, Charles **Barnett** bondsman.
    ii. James⁶, born say 1776, taxable in Fredericksville Parish, Albemarle County, from 1792 to 1813: called "B.S." (Benjamin's son) starting in 1806; called a "Mula" in 1813 [PPTL, 1782-1799, frames 347, 419, 459, 555, 590; 1800-1813, frames 28, 160, 251, 344, 435, 522, 567]. He married Jenny **Ailstock**, 2 December 1799 Albemarle County bond, Michael **Ailstock** bondsman. On 7 May 1801 the Albemarle County court ordered James and Benjamin Gowin to pay their debt of $23 to William Frailey, subject to a credit of $14.50 paid on 10 July 1800 [Orders 1800-1, 362]. He was head of a Albemarle County household of 8 "other free" in 1810 [VA:196].
    iii. Jesse, born say 1778, called Ben's son when he was taxable in Fredericksville Parish, Albemarle County, from 1798 to 1811 [PPTL,

1782-1799, frames 555, 590; 1800-1813, frames 28, 117, 208, 297, 388, 478].

iv. Anderson, born say 1791, taxable in Fredericksville Parish, Albemarle County, from 1801 to 1810: called "B.S." (Benjamin's son) from 1805 to 1807; called "J.S." (Joshua's son) in 1809 and 1810 [PPTL, 1800-1813, frames 74, 118, 160, 208, 251, 297, 344, 435, 478].

v. ?Agnes/ Aggy, married Richard Newman, 7 September 1793 Albemarle County bond, Benjamin Going bondsman.

vi. Daniel[4], born say 1783, taxable in Fredericksville Parish, Albemarle County, in 1801 and 1802 from 1810 to 1813: called B.S. (Benjamin's son); called a "Mula" in 1813 [PPTL, 1800-1813, frames 28, 73, 435, 479, 522, 567].

32. Joshua Going, born say 1755, was a "yellow" complexioned soldier from Louisa County who was drafted in the Revolutionary War [NSDAR, *African American Patriots*, 150]. He was taxable in Fredericksville Parish, Albemarle County, from 1783 to 1813: taxable on 2 tithes in 1792, 1793, and 1796; 3 tithes in 1797; 2 from 1798 to 1800; 2 from 1802 to 1804; and 2 in 1809; called a "Mula" in 1813 [PPTL, 1782-1799, frames 29, 59, 116, 202, 300, 386, 459, 516, 591; 1800-1813, frames 29, 117, 208, 297, 435, 522, 567]. He was the father of

i. John, born say 1777, taxable in Fredericksville Parish, Albemarle County, from 1793 to 1796 and called "Jos. S." (either Joshua or Joseph's son) from 1805 to 1813; called a "Mula" in 1813 [PPTL, 1782-1799, frames 386, 459, 481; 1800-13, 252, 344, 434, 522, 567].

ii. Jesse, born say 1776, taxable in Fredericksville Parish, Albemarle County, from 1794 to 1813: called Joshua's son; called a "Mula" in 1813 [PPTL, 1782-1799, frames 419, 459, 516, 590; 1800-1813, frames 29, 118, 208, 297, 522, 567]. He married Becky **Ailstock**, 2 December 1799 Albemarle County bond, Michael **Ailstock** bondsman, and was head of a Albemarle County household of 6 "other free" in 1810 [VA:196].

iii. David[5], born say 1780, taxable in Fredericksville Parish, Albemarle County, from 1802 to 1813: called Joshua's son in 1810; called "little David" in 1812 and 1813; a Mula" in 1813 [PPTL, 1800-1813, frames 118, 435, 479, 522, 567]. He was head of an Albemarle County household of 3 "other free" in 1810 [VA:196].

iv. Caty, born say 1788, married James **Tyree**, 21 December 1807 Albemarle County bond, Joshua Gowen bondsman and father of the bride.

v. ?Hezekiah, born say 1790, taxable in Fredericksville Parish, Albemarle County, from 1810 to 1813 [PPTL, 1800-1813, frames 435, 567].

vi. ?Jonathan, born say 1795, taxable in Fredericksville Parish, Albemarle County, in 1812 and 1813: listed with "Jos. S." (Joshua's son) after his name in 1812; called "J.S. a Mula" in 1813 [PPTL, 1800-1813, frames 521, 566].

33. Sherrod[1] Going, born say 1762, was a "yellow" complexioned soldier born in Louisa County [NSDAR, *African American Patriots*, 150]. He received a grant for 196 acres on the waters of Buck Mountain Creek in Albemarle County on 30 September 1783 and 31 acres on the north side of the Green Mountain on 1 June 1798 [Grants H:575; 40:215]. He was taxable in Fredericksville Parish, Albemarle County, from 1783 to 1813: listed with 2 tithables from 1810 to 1812; 3 in 1813 when he was called a "Mula" [PPTL, 1782-1799, frames 29, 59, 116, 251, 386, 459, 516, 591; 1800-1813, frames 28, 118, 207, 297, 388, 478, 566]. He married Susannah **Simmons**, 5 June 1791 Albemarle County bond. He sued Joseph Hicks for assault and battery in Albemarle County court on 12 August 1797, but the jury found for the defendant. On 18 August 1797

he was accused of stealing a quantity of corn from Absolem Clarkson and was ordered to be tried at the district court in Charlottesville [Orders 1795-8, 378, 381-2]. He was head of an Albemarle County household of 12 "other free" in 1810 [VA:196] and 9 "free colored" in 1820. He received a pension for his service in the 14th Virginia Regiment during the Revolution. He owned 217 acres in Albemarle County when he made his pension application, describing himself to the court at Charlottesville as "a colored man and very illiterate" [National Archives pension file W7545; Jackson, *Virginia Negro Soldiers*, 35]. He was the father of

   i.   Ann, daughter of Sherod Gowen, married John Gowen, 3 January 1810 Albemarle County bond, Sherod Gowen surety.

   ii.   Jincy, married Noah **Tate**. On 22 November 1844 Noah and his wife Jincy made an Albemarle County deed of trust for land they inherited from her parents Sherod and Susan Goings [DB 42:444-5].

Other members of the family in Albemarle County were

   i.   Rhoda, listed as a "Mula" in Fredericksville Parish, Albemarle County, in 1813 [PPTL, 1800-1813, frame 566].

   ii.   Sally, listed as a "Mula" in Fredericksville Parish, Albemarle County, in 1813 [PPTL, 1800-1813, frame 567].

   iii.   Elizabeth, head of a Albemarle County household of 6 "other free" in 1810 [VA:196].

34. Agnes² Going, born say 1748, was taxable on (her son?) John Going's tithe and 2 horses in the upper district of Henrico County from 1787 to 1791 [PPTL 1782-1814, frames 124, 143, 195, 217, 271]. She was taxable on 97 acres in the upper district of Henrico County from 1799 to 1807 [Land Tax List 1799-1816]. Her children married white and were considered white. She was apparently the mother of

   i.   David, Jr., born say 1764, taxable in the upper district of Henrico County from 1785 to 1791 and taxable on a slave from 1806 to 1813 when he was listed as a white man [PPTL 1782-1814, frames 73, 90, 195, 271, 487, 532, 636, 662, 722, 744]. He married Clawey Webb, 17 July 1789 Henrico County bond, surety John Geoine, who testified that Clawey was over twenty-one years of age, Anne Going witness. He was taxable on 100 acres from 1805 to 1815 and taxable on 193 acres adjoining John Harlow in 1816 [Land Tax List 1799-1816].

   ii.   Mary, born say 1769, gave her own consent to her marriage to Meredith Childers, 23 December 1791 Henrico County bond, surety John Goyne, witness Aggy Goyne.

   iii.   John, born say 1770, his tax charged to Agnes Going in 1787.

   iv.   Milly, married John Harlow, 21 September 1792 Henrico County bond, consent of Agness Goyne, David Going surety, John Geoine witness.

   v.   Ann, of lawful age, daughter of Agnes Goine, married Dudley Miner, 22 December 1795 Henrico County bond, Meredith Childers surety.

   vi.   Nancy, married Patrick Childers, 12 December 1797 Henrico County bond.

35. William⁴ Gowen (John¹, William², Thomas¹, Michael¹), born say 1725, received a deed of gift of 100 acres in Lunenburg from his parents, John² and Mary Gowen, on 10 June 1761 and sold this land while resident in Lunenburg County on 30 December the same year. He was residing in Orange County, North Carolina, six months later on 6 July 1762 when he sold a further 100 acres adjoining this land in Lunenburg County [DB 7:153, 302]. In November 1763 (his uncle?) Alexander Going had a petition against him in Orange County court [Minutes I:232]. He may have been the William Gowen who received a patent for 300 acres in Cumberland County, North Carolina, on both sides of Pocket Creek on 9 November 1764 and was taxable on one white

tithe in 1767 [*N.C. Genealogy*, XXI:3132]. He was head of a Moore County household of 10 whites in 1790, 1 white male over 16, 4 under 16, and 5 white females [NC:44]. He may have been the same William Gowen who was head of a Moore County household of 10 "other free" in 1790 [NC:43], 9 in 1800 [NC:60], and 6 in 1810 [NC:615]. Moore County records were destroyed in a courthouse fire, so there is no further record of him. His children were probably those counted as "other free" in Moore County:

  i.   Henry, head of a Moore County household of 5 "other free" in 1800 [NC:60] and 9 in 1810 [NC:615].
  ii.   Levy, head of a Moore County household of 5 "other free" in 1800 [NC:62], 8 in 1810 [NC:615], and he may have been the ive Goins counted in Moore County with 10 "free colored" in 1820 [NC:307].
  iii. Edward[5], head of a Moore County household of 2 "other free" in 1810 [NC:615] and 7 "free colored" in 1820 [NC:308].
  iv.   lin, head of a Moore County household of 3 "free colored" in 1820 [NC:317].

36. Thomas[2] Gowen (John[1], William[2], Thomas[1], Michael[1]) born say 1732, was taxable in the 1751 Lunenburg County household of (his father?) John[2] Gowen in the list of Richard Witton [Tax List 1748-52]. On 30 May 1752 he purchased 150 acres in Granville County on both sides of Taylors Creek at the mouth of Spring Branch [DB B:53]. He was in the Granville County list of Osborn Jeffreys, adjoining Michael and Edward Going, taxable on one white and one black poll in 1753 and one black poll in 1754. He was called a "Mulatto" in Captain Osborne Jeffreys' Company in the 8 October 1754 Muster Roll of the Granville County Regiment of Colonel William Eaton [Clark, *Colonial Soldiers of the South*, 718]. In the 1761 list of John Pope he had Moses Gowen in his household with the notation "Refuses to List his wife," and in 1764 he and Moses were taxed in John Pope's list for St. John's Parish as two white polls. In 1768 he was tithable on three persons: himself, John Gowin, and Alston Hopkins who was white. In 1780, called Thomas Gowen Sr., he was taxed on an assessment of 997 pounds, and he was taxed on 150 acres in 1785. He was head of a Granville County household of 4 free males and 5 free females in the 1786 state census in Dutch District. On 25 January 1788 he sold his land in Granville [DB O:555], and he may have moved to Montgomery County where Thomas Gain was counted in the 1790 census with 3 white males and 5 white females in his household [NC:164]. His 7 February 1797 Montgomery County will named only his five youngest children. His children were

  i.   Moses[4], born circa 1749 since he was taxable in 1761 in the list of John Pope. He may have been the Moses Jewil, alias Gowin, who purchased 100 acres on the south side of the Tarr River on both sides of Middle Creek in Granville County on 2 February 1768 [DB H:481].
  ii.   John[5], born circa 1756, not identified as Thomas' son but taxed in his 1768 household.
  iii. Vini, married ____ Hardister.
  iv.   Burgess, born 1780/4, died in Montgomery County in 1849.
  v.   Burton, counted as white in the Randolph County census through 1830.
  vi.   Hali.
  vii. Elizabeth.

37. William[6] Gowen (James[2], Edward[2], Edward[1], William[1], Michael[1]) was born before 1748 since he was taxable in the Granville County household of his father James[2] Gowen in 1759. He may have been the William Going who was deceased by 10 November 1783 when his thirteen-year-old daughter Nancy was ordered bound apprentice to William Cope by the Chatham County court. His children (no race mentioned) bound apprentice in Chatham County were

i. Nancy, born about 1770, ordered bound apprentice to William Cope by the 10 November 1783 Chatham County court [Minutes 1781-85, 26].

ii. John[9], born about 1771, about twelve years old on 10 November 1783 when he was ordered bound an apprentice farmer to William Riddle by the Chatham County court and bound to James Sutter in May 1785 [Minutes 1781-85, 55].

iii. Elizabeth, born about 1772, about twelve years old on 8 November 1784 when she was bound apprentice to William Douglass by the Chatham County court [Minutes 1781-85, 45].

iv. Ann[3], born about 1774, about ten years old on 8 November 1784 when she was bound apprentice to James Howard [Minutes 1781-85, 45].

v. William[7], born about 1775, bound an apprentice farmer to George Desmukes on 10 November 1783. He was and insolvent taxpayer in Chatham County in 1806 [Minutes 1781-85, 26, 157].

vi. Mary[3], born say 1777, no age mentioned when she was removed from William Cope's care in Chatham County [Minutes 1781-85, 45].

38. James Going, born say 1758, was taxable in Henry County from 1783 to 1790 [PPTL, 1782-1830, frames 38, 88, 301, 352]. He purchased for 5 pounds 201 acres on both sides of the Dan River on 21 October 1784 [DB 1:62]. He was taxable on the Dan River in Patrick County from 1791 to 1807: called "Sr." starting in 1793, listed with 2 tithables in 1797, 3 in 1801 [PPTL, 1791-1823, frames 150, 234, 251, 268, 315, 487]. He left a 24 August 1807 Patrick County will, administration on which was granted to his widow Nancy Going on 29 October 1807, leaving $25 to his daughter Peggy Adams, 5 shillings to his daughter Prudence Goin, 5 shillings to his son Stephen, $55 to his son William Goin, $150 to his daughter Betsy Goin when his youngest children came to age and the remaining to be equally divided between the youngest Arthur, Isaac and Nancy Goin. And his widow was to have an equal child's part. His estate was valued at $520 [WB 1:106, 247]. On 28 April 1809 the Patrick County court appointed Benjamin Going guardian for Arther, Isaac and Nancy Going, heirs of James Going, deceased [Orders 1800-10, n.p.]. On 11 January 1810 his widow Nancy Goins appointed Benjamin Goins of adjoining Surry County, North Carolina, as her attorney to sue Harman Bowman of Surry County [Surry DB 3:351] and she sued Harmon Bowman in Patrick County on 27 April 1810 [Orders 1810-21, n.p.]. James was the father of

i. Peggy, born say 1778, married Bartholomew Adams, 8 July 1796, with the consent of her father Jesse James Going, Caleb Going surety.

ii. Prudence, a witness with Nancy Going, Margaret Adams, and William Going on 26 April 1811 in the Patrick County suit of the Commonwealth v. Thomas Beazley and Elizabeth Bellar for the crime of bigamy. The court dismissed the suit when it met for adjournment on 30 May 1811 on the grounds that the adjournment of the last examining court had been illegal and the court had not cognizance over them [Orders 1810-21, n.p.].

iii. Stephen, born say 1785, married Nancy Going, daughter of John Going, 24 February 1807 Patrick County bond, Obediah Going surety. Stephen was taxable in Patrick County from 1806 to 1814: in a list of "free Negroes & Mulattos" in 1813 and 1814 [PPTL, 1782-1830, frames 455, 537, 598, 616]. He was head of a Patrick County household of 6 whites in 1820 and 9 "free colored" in 1830.

iv. William.

v. Betsy.

vi. Arthur, born say 1795, taxable in Patrick County in a list of "free Negroes & Mulattos" in 1813 [PPTL, 1782-1830, frames 587, 598], counted as white in Patrick County in 1820 [VA:121A], head of a Patrick County household of 6 "free colored" in 1830 [VA:154].

vii. Isaac, underage in 1807.

viii.   Nancy, married Robert **Harris**, 1816 Patrick County bond.

39.   Thomas[4] Going (Drury[1], Mary[1], Michael[2], Christopher[1], Michael[1]) born say 1761, head of a Greensville County, Virginia household of 1 person in 1783 [VA:55]. He was taxable in Greensville County from 1783 to 1803 [PPTL 1782-1850, frames 13, 126, 162, 231, 259, 302]. He married Sarah **Jones**, 24 July 1794 Greensville County bond, William **Dungill** surety. He was probably the Thomas Gowen who was head of a Halifax County, North Carolina household of 6 "other free" in 1810 [NC:21]. His children may have been

> i.   Frederick[3], born in Virginia about 1794, head of a Halifax County household of 9 "free colored" in 1820 [NC:148], still living in Halifax County when he was counted in the 1860 census: *Frederick Going, 66 yrs, Male, Mulatto, farmer, $100 real estate/$148 personal estate, b. Va. Roda, 70 years, Female, Mulatto, b. N.C.* He sold land in Halifax to Isham **Mills** by a deed proved 21 November 1836 and purchased land by deed proved 19 February 1838. He was permitted to carry his gun by order of the Halifax County court on 17 August 1841 [Minutes 1832-46].
>
> ii.   Drury[2], head of a Halifax County household of 11 "free colored" in 1820 [NC:148] and 6 in 1830.
>
> iii.   Heartwell, permitted to carry his gun by order of the Halifax County court on 17 August 1841.
>
> iv.   Jerry, born in North Carolina circa 1803, permitted to carry his gun by order of the Halifax County court on 17 August 1841. He was still living in Halifax County in 1860 at age fifty-seven with Louvenia, age fifty. He had $264 real and $328 personal estate.

Others counted in South Carolina in 1810 were

> i.   Sarah, head of a Greenville District household of 4 "other free" [SC:567].
>
> ii.   Catherine, head of a Colleton District household of 7 "other free" [SC:626].

Others in Virginia were

> i.   John Goings, born say 1695, a "negro" servant of Roodolphus Malbone on 5 September 1716 when the Princess Anne County court ordered that he receive forty lashes on the complaint of Tully Smyth [Minutes 1709-17, 222].
>
> ii.   Amy, mother of an illegitimate son Lewis Goings who was bound out by the Essex County court on 21 June 1784 [Orders 1784-7, 12].
>
> iii.   Nancy, issued a certificate of freedom by the Essex County court on 20 March 1787 [Orders 1784-7, 311]. She may have been the Nancy Going who registered in Middlesex County on 2 June 1802: *born free; 46 years of age; 5'2-1/4"; yellow complexion* [Register of Free Negroes 1800-60, p.15].
>
> iv.   William[8], head of a Montgomery County household of 7 "other free" in 1810 [VA:661].
>
> v.   Fanny, born about 1785, registered in Botetourt County on 3 February 1806: *a Dark Mulatto, 5 feet four Inches, Born free, by 14th Augt. Certificate from Clk of Henrico* [Free Negroes &c Registered in the Clerks Office of Botetourt County, no.7].

Those counted in Louisiana in 1810 were

> i.   Benjamin[2], head of a household of 4 "other free" in Opelousas [LA:316].
>
> ii.   Philip[4], head of a household of 3 "other free" in Opelousas [LA:305].
>
> iii.   James[7], head of a household of 3 "other free" in Opelousas [LA:305].

GRACE FAMILY

1. Joan Grace, born say 1714, an indentured servant to William Penn, admitted in Charles County, Maryland court on 8 June 1731 that she had a "Mullatto" child "by a Negroe." And she admitted to a second mixed-race child on 13 March 1732/3. Her son William Grace, born 6 November 1732, was bound to serve Penn until the age of thirty-one. On 10 June 1735 her "Mullatto" son Thomas was bound to serve Penn for thirty-one years and on 10 August 1736 the court ordered that she be sold for twenty-one years as punishment for having three "Mullatto" children [Court Record 1727-31, 521; 1731-4, 297-8; 1734-9, 2, 37-38, 220]. She may have been the ancestor of

    i.   Amie², head of a Stafford County household of 6 "other free" in 1810 [VA:130].
    ii. Thomas², head of a Stafford County household of 4 "other free" in 1810 [VA:136].
    iii. Rachel, head of a Stafford County household of 4 "other free" in 1810 [VA:136].
    iv. William², head of a Stafford County household of 3 "other free" in 1810 [VA:135].
    v.   Polly, born about 1767, registered in Stafford County on 13 August 1804: *a black woman aged about thirty seven years...appearing to the satisfaction of the Court to have been born free* and registered a copy in King George County [King George County Register of Free Persons, no.39].

GRAHAM FAMILY

1. Elizabeth Graham, born say 1696, appeared in Prince George's County, Maryland court on 26 June 1716 with her child who was adjudged to be a "Mallato." She was ordered to serve Thomas Wells, Sr., until November court. Later that year on 27 November the court sold her and her child to Thomas Clagett for 3,000 pounds of tobacco. She was called the "Servant woman of Thomas Wells" (no last name) on 25 November 1718 when the court bound her seventeen-month-old daughter Margaret to Edward Marlow. On 24 March 1718/9 she confessed to having another illegitimate child [Court Record 1715-20, 87, 143; 1715-20, 721, 814]. She was the ancestor of

    i. Sandy, born in 1765, head of a Frederick County, Virginia household of 4 "other free" in 1810 [VA:511].
    ii. ?Lethy, head of a Wilkes County, North Carolina household of 3 "free colored" in 1820 [NC:524].

GRANT FAMILY

1. Elizabeth Grant, born say 1700, was the servant of Ann Fitzhugh of King George County, Virginia, on 1 December 1721 when she was presented for having a "mulatto" child within the previous six months. And she had a second "mulatto" child before 4 September 1725 [Orders 1721-34, 27, 277, 280]. She may have been the ancestor of

    i. John, born say 1739, living in Fairfax County on 17 July 1760 when (his master?) John Dalton acknowledged a certificate of his age and that of Elizabeth Grant, "two Mulatto servants," which was recorded by the court on motion of John Grant [Orders 1756-63, pt. 2, 502]. He was a "molatto" who was taxable with his wife Joan in the Loudoun County tax list for 1762, 1769 and 1771 [Sparacio, *Loudoun County Tithables 1758-1769*, 23, 88; *Virginia Genealogist*, v.17, no.1, p.10], perhaps the John Grant who was head of a Talbot County, Maryland household of 1 "other free" in 1790.

ii.   Elizabeth, born say 1740, a "Mulatto" servant living in Fairfax County on 17 July 1760 when John Dalton acknowledged a certificate of her age [Orders 1756-63, pt. 2, 502].

iii. Margaret, born about 1750, a twenty-year-old "mulatto" who ran away from her master in Baltimore with an English convict servant man named John Chambers. Her master advertised a reward for her return in the 5 April 1770 issue of the *Virginia Gazette* stating that she had been in Barbados, Antigua, Granada, and Philadelphia and that she said she was born in Carolina [*Virginia Gazette* (Purdie & Dixon)].

iv.   Gideon, a "Mulato" taxable with James **Ivey** in Bladen County, North Carolina, in 1772, one of the "free Negors and Mullatus living upon the Kings Land" in Bladen County on 13 October 1773 [Byrd, *Bladen County Tax Lists*, I:79; G.A. 1773, Box 7], taxable in Bladen County in 1784, perhaps the father of J. Grant who was head of a Brunswick County, North Carolina household of 4 "other free" in 1810 [NC:234].

v.   Hugh, head of a Bohemia Manor, Cecil County, Maryland household of 1 "other free" in 1790.

GRANTUM/ GRANTHAM FAMILY

1.   David[1] Grantum, born say 1700, petitioned James Christian in Goochland County court on 3 December 1731 but failed to prosecute when the case came to trial in March 1731/2 [Orders 1728-31, 21, 56]. He may have been the father of

2   i.   David[2], born say 1725.

ii. William, born say 1730, taxable in Goochland County in 1755.

iii. Samuel, born say 1732, taxable in Goochland County in 1755.

2.   David[2] Grantum/ Grantham, born say 1725, was a tithable overseer on John Christian's Goochland County estate from 1746 to 1755 [List of Tithables]. He attached household items of Edmund Daniel for a 3 pound debt due by account in March 1747/8 and sued Obediah Patterson for 3 pounds, 12 shillings in May 1752. And he brought suit against William Christian, executor of John Christian, deceased, in chancery in February 1765 claiming that Charles Christian of Charles City County was indebted to him for 30 pounds in payment for which he agreed to convey to him a tract of 100 acres on Wild Boar Creek in Goochland but died before completing the agreement. John Christian, Charles's oldest son, at first agreed to transfer the land but later refused to sign the deed unless his brothers would give security not to challenge it. For seventeen to eighteen years up to this time David had lived on John Christian's land as overseer in a profit-sharing arrangement [Orders 1741-4, 409; 1750-7, 132; 1761-5, 466; LVA chancery case 1782-004]. He married Elizabeth, "Mulattoes," in Goochland County on 2 October 1778 [Jones, *Douglas Register*, 18]. He was taxable in the upper district of Goochland County from 1782 to 1799: taxable on 3 horses and 6 cattle in 1782, levy free by 1790, charged with Samuel **Mealey**'s tithe in 1797, with James **Mealey**'s tithe in 1798 [PPTL, 1782-1809, frames 17, 151, 177, 237, 281, 296, 341, 422, 477, 481, 527]. By his 17 October 1801 Goochland County will, proved 18 June 1804, he lent most of his property to his wife Elizabeth and mentioned his son David, other unnamed children, and his granddaughter Jenny **Mealy**. His land was to revert to his wife's son James **Mealy**, after her decease [DB 19, part 1, 64]. Elizabeth was a "Mulatto" midwife taxable on a horse and living near Joseph Shelton's in the upper district of Goochland County from 1806 to 1814 [PPTL, 1782-1809, frames 782, 824, 867; 1810-32, frames 8, 73, 99, 193]. She was head of Goochland County household of 2 "other free" in 1810 [VA:693]. David was the father of

i.   David[3].

William or Samuel Grantum may have had a common-law marriage with a slave. A slave named Kate received her freedom and the use of her master's land during her lifetime by the 17 July 1797 Goochland County will of Gideon Cawthon [DB 17:515]. Kate called herself Catherine Grantham on 17 February 1800 when she manumitted her son Woodson Grantham [DB 17:553]. On 13 March 1802 she sold land in Goochland County to James Holman for seventy-five pounds and set free her husband Phil Grantham, who she purchased from Holman [DB 18:356, 374]. Catherine left a will in 1802 which mentioned her sons Gideon and Woodson and left her land to her husband as long as he remained single [DB 20, pt. 1, 53]. Philip Grantum was head of a Goochland County household of 3 "other free" in 1810 [VA:693], a "Freed Negroe" living near Licking Hole Church from 1804 to 1810, living on William M. Holman's land in 1813 [PPTL 1782-1809, frame 689; 1810-32, frames 7, 161]. Gideon Grantum, born about 1798, registered as a free Negro in Goochland County on 11 October 1821: *twenty three years of age, five feet seven inches high...free born* [Register of Free Negroes, p.126].

GRAVES/ GROVES FAMILY

1. Sarah Graves, born say 1728, was presented by the churchwardens of St. Andrew's Parish in Brunswick County, Virginia court in November 1747 for having a bastard child, and in January 1747/8 her son Ezekiel was ordered bound out [Orders 1745-49, 303, 323]. Her son was

2   i.   Ezekiel, born about 1747.

2. Ezekiel Graves, born about 1747, was sued for debt by Thomas Wallton in Brunswick County, Virginia court on 30 September 1767 [Orders 1765-8, 500]. He was taxable on a horse in Greensville County, Virginia, in 1787 [Schreiner-Yantis, *1787 Census*, 778] and head of a Northampton County household of 6 "other free" in 1790 [NC:72] and 3 in 1800 (called Ezekiel Graves) [NC:447]. On 22 November 1787 he applied for compensation for twelve months service as a soldier in Captain Troughton's North Carolina Company [*NCGSJ* V:161]. He may have been the father of

    i.   Sally Greaves, born say 1775, head of a Franklin County, North Carolina household of 2 "other free" in 1800.

    ii.   James[3] Groves, born 22 March 1780 in North Carolina, traveled to Natchez, Mississippi with the **Dial** family.[107] He married Mary **Nash**, born 6 June 1781, daughter of Thomas **Nash**.

    iii.   B. Graves, born say 1785, head of a Brunswick County, North Carolina household of 2 "other free" in 1810 [NC:228].

    iv.   Mary Graves, head of a Cumberland County, North Carolina household of 4 "free colored" in 1820 [NC:222].

<u>South Carolina</u>
1. John Graves, born say 1745, may have been the John Graves who was listed in the Muster Roll of Captain Alexander McKintosh's Company in Gabriel Powell's South Carolina Battalion in the expedition against the Cherokees from 11 October 1759 to 15 January 1760, in the same list as Thomas **Sweat** [Clark, *Colonial Soldiers of the South*, 893]. According to the 1858 Johnson County, Tennessee trial of his great-grandson, Jacob F. **Perkins**, his wife's name was Susan [The Perkins File in the T.A.R. Nelson Papers in the Calvin M. McClung Collection at the East Tennessee Historical Center, deposition of Elizabeth Perkins]. In 1787 he was taxable on 92 acres and one free poll in Washington County, North Carolina (which became Tennessee in 1796) [Creekmore, "East Tennessee Taxpayers," *East Tennessee Historical Society's*

---

[107]Perhaps the families became acquainted when Ezekiel Groves and William **Dales** were "other free" heads of Northampton County, North Carolina households in 1790 [NC:72; 76].

Publications, (1963): 108], 192 acres and one free poll in Washington County in 1788, 75 acres and one free poll in Washington County in 1789 [Creekmore, *Tennessee Ancestors,* 5:38, 82] and 60 acres in Carter County, Tennessee, in 1798 but not subject to poll tax since he was over fifty years old [Carter County Tax List]. In the previously mentioned Johnson County, Tennessee trial, several persons deposed that John Graves had been a constable.[108] Mary Wilson described him as a dark-skinned white man and his wife Susan as a dark white woman [The Perkins File, depositions of Elizabeth Cook, John J. Wilson]. They were the parents of

    i.   Ann, born say 1763, married Jacob **Perkins** about 1790.

   ii.   Benjamin[2], born about 1765, an eighty-eight-year-old resident of Monroe County, Tennessee, on 12 May 1853 when he testified on behalf of Jacob **Perkins** to obtain a pension. He testified that his sister Ann was married by Parson Mulkey [Pension File R-8105]. He was taxable in Carter County, Tennessee, on one poll in 1798, 1799, and 1805 [Carter County Tax List].

  iii. ?James[2], born say 1771, taxable on one free poll in Washington County, Tennessee, between 1792 and 1795 [Creekmore, *Tennessee Ancestors,* 5:95, 100, 132, 149] and taxable in Carter County in 1796 [Carter County Tax List].

   iv. ?Thomas, born say 1772, taxable in Washington County in 1793 [Creekmore, *Tennessee Ancestors,* 5:115].

    v. ?William, born say 1784, purchased 50 acres in Carter County on Roan's Creek from his father-in-law, George **Perkins,** on 26 August 1805 and another 50 acres in the same area on 10 April 1807 [DB B:16, 108].

   vi. ?Peter[2] Graves, born say 1780, married Sarah **Tann,** 15 September 1801 in South Carolina [Holcolm, *South Carolina Marriages].*

  vii. ?Hardy, born about 1794, sixty-four years old in 1858, living in Kentucky when he made a deposition for Jacob F. **Perkins'** Johnson County, Tennessee trial.

GRAY FAMILY

The Gray family of Virginia may have descended from Priscilla Gray, a "Mollatto Woman born of a white Woman," who had seven illegitimate children in Prince George's County, Maryland, between 1727 and 1745 [Court Records 1726-7, 626; 1730-2, 2, 5; 1732-4, 118; 1734-5, 357; 1738-40, 199; 1744-6, 298-9; 1749-50, 244].

1.   Winney Gray, born say 1746, a "mulatto," was living in Fauquier County, Virginia, on 25 November 1766 when the court ordered the churchwardens of Hamilton Parish to bind her to Elizabeth Tennill [Orders 1764-8, 239]. She may have been the mother of

    i.   Forester, "f. negro" head of a Fairfax County household of 5 "other free" in 1810 [VA:258].

   ii.   Davey, head of a Fairfax County household of 4 "other free" in 1810 [VA:257].

  iii. James, "other free" head of a Frederick County, Virginia household in 1810 [VA:507].

   iv. Rachel, head of a Lenoir County, North Carolina household of 4 "other free" in 1800 [NC:35].

---

[108]John J. Wilson's statement, "John Graves ... Was a constable. Sent to South Carolina for certificate," may indicate that he was born there.

GRAYSON FAMILY

1. Ann Grayson, born say 1700, the servant of William Harris, confessed to the Prince George's County, Maryland court on 23 August 1720 that she had a "Mallatoe" child by Clement Brooke's "Negro man" John. John confessed to the charge when he appeared in court on 28 March 1720/1, and the court ordered that he receive twenty-five lashes [Court Record 1715-20, 1032, 1040-1; 1720-2, 91-2]. She was probably the ancestor of
   i. William, head of a Stafford County, Virginia household of 7 "other free" in 1810 [VA:128].
   ii. Matilda, head of a Stafford County household of 3 "other free" in 1810 [VA:127].
   iii. Winney, "F. Negroe" head of a Fauquier County, Virginia household of 4 "other free" in 1810 [VA:355].
   iv. Nice, head of a Fredericksburg, Spotsylvania County household of 2 "other free" in 1810 [VA:113b].
   v. David, head of a Prince William County, Virginia household of 1 "other free" in 1810 [VA:498].

GREGORY FAMILY

1. Elizabeth Gregory, born say 1670, was called "my Christian Negro Elizabeth" in William Thornbury's 5 November 1697 Essex County will by which he left her his estate consisting of farm animals and household goods to be divided amongst herself, her daughter Sarah, son William, her "Irish Girle" Katherine, and a motherless child named Ann. He called William his godson. Elizabeth was his executrix [DB 9:158]. She was called Elizabeth Christian on 13 July 1698 when her petition for probate on the will was granted after being delayed from the 10 March 1697/8 court [Orders 1695-9, 99, 110]. She was called "Elizabeth Gregory Exec'x of William Thornbury" on 23 June 1699 when she sued John Jones for 930 pounds of tobacco in Northumberland County court and called "Elizabeth a Christian Negro Exec'x of Wm Thornbury" on 25 September 1699 when the case was dismissed [Hamrick, *Northumberland County Court Order Book 1699-1713*, 34, 57, 47, 72]. She was called "Eliza a Christian Negro" on 20 June 1699 and 11 August 1699 and called "Eliz. Gregory Negro" on 11 June 1701 when her assignees brought suit in Essex County court [Orders 1695-99, 157; 1699-1702, 4, 93]. She may have been the Elizabeth Gregory who made an Essex County deed of gift of a cow, calf, and mare to her grandson Benjamin, son of John Acres, on 10 October 1700 [D&W 10:59]. She was the mother of
   i. Sarah.
   ii. William, godson of William Thornbury.
   iii. Katherine, "her Irish Girle."

Another Gregory family:
1. Christian Gregory, born say 1738, a white servant woman of John Hooe, was living in Prince William County on 27 October 1755 when the court ordered her to serve her master additional time for running away for sixteen days. On 24 November the same year she agreed to serve Hooe an additional two years and to forego her freedom dues in exchange for his curing her of "the French Disease" [Sparacio, *Prince William County Orders 1753-57*, 81, 83]. She was the mother of Thomas and Presley Gregory, "mulatto" bastard children born in Prince William County, Virginia [Historic Dumfries, *Records of Dettingen Parish*, 112, 114]. Her children were
   i. Thomas, born 21 September 1762, bound to John Hooe on 5 September 1763.

ii. Presley, born about September 1763, bound to John Hooe on 3 September 1763. He was head of a Frederick County household of 9 "other free" in 1810 [VA:555].

iii. ?John, born about 1758, head of a Craven County, North Carolina household of 2 "other free" in 1790 [NC:130] and 2 "free colored" in 1820 [NC:65]. He was seventy-four years old on 15 August 1832 when he made a declaration in Craven County court to obtain a pension for his services in the Revolution. He stated that he was living in Brunswick County, North Carolina, when he was drafted, and had two severe cuts from a sword which extended from his eyelid to the crown of his head [*NCGSJ* XII:186 (CR 28.301.29)].

iv. ?Adam, born say 1768, head of a Philadelphia County, Pennsylvania household of 2 "other free" in 1790 [PA:199].

v. ?Charles, born say 1785, head of a Charles City County household of 3 "other free" in 1810 [VA:939].

vi. ?Ann, born say 1780, married James **Ligon**, 14 November 1798 Mecklenburg County, Virginia bond.

GRICE FAMILY

1. Moses Grice sold 180 acres in Halifax County, North Carolina, joining Elk Marsh by a deed registered in October 1767 [DB 10:44] and moved to Bladen County where he was a white taxable from 1768 to 1772 [Byrd, *Bladen County Tax Lists*, I:9, 59, 95]. On 27 April 1770 he purchased 300 acres in Bladen County which he and his wife Mary sold by deeds of 8 January and 15 January 1774 [DB 23:126, 359, 360]. He purchased 100 acres in Robeson County on the south side of Drowning Creek in 1784 [DB 1:246]. His 1789 Robeson County will named his wife Mary, and children: Benjamin, Patty, Tabby, Fathey, John, and Jonathan Grice. Mary was head of a Robeson County household of 4 "other free" in 1790 [NC:49].

GRIFFIN FAMILY

1. Catherine Griffin, born say 1704, was a white woman living in Henrico County in November 1722 when she was presented by the court for having an illegitimate child by a "mulatto man" [Orders 1719-24, 220]. She may have been the mother of

  2 i. John, born say 1722.

    ii. Elizabeth, born say 1725, living in Goochland County in November 1747 when the court ordered the churchwardens of King William Parish to bind out her "Mulatto" child [Orders 1744-9, 392].

2. John Griffin, born say 1722, was taxable in Fishing Creek District, Granville County, North Carolina, in 1761 with his wife Miles and Fanny **Bunch** (one Black male and two black females over sixteen years of age) and taxable with Miles in 1762. Miles may have been related to Fanny **Bunch**. He may have been the John Griffin who recorded a plat for 250 acres on the Santee River near the Wateree River in South Carolina on 19 September 1764 [S.C. Archives series S213184, vol. 7:413]. He was head of a Camden District, Richland County, South Carolina household of 4 white males and 4 females in 1790 [SC:26]. Perhaps John and Miles were the parents of

    i. Patty, married Council **Bass**, 4 May 1782 Bertie County, North Carolina bond, Cader **Bass** witness.

    ii. Gideon, recorded a plat for on Spears Creek in Camden District, South Carolina, on 28 November 1785 [S.C. Archives series S213019, vol. 12:543]. He married Patience **Rawlinson** and was head of a Camden District, Richland County, South Carolina household of a white male and a white female in 1790 [SC:26] and 7 "other free" in 1810

[SC:175a]. He was living in Richland District on 29 November 1826 when he petitioned the legislature for a pension for his services in the Revolution. His petition mentioned the services of Morgan Griffin [S.C. Archives S108092, reel 61, frame 18].

iii. Morgan, recorded a plat for 200 acres on Horse Range Swamp in Orangeburgh District, South Carolina, on 20 September 1785. He was head of a white household of 4 males and 4 females in the north part of Orangeburg District in 1790 [SC:96]. In 1816 he petitioned the legislature for compensation his service in the Revolution [S.C. Archives S213190, vol. 14, p.250; series S108; series S108092, reel 61, frame 104].

Pasquotank County, North Carolina

1. Jemima Griffin, born say 1730, (no race indicated) was living in Pasquotank County, North Carolina, on 22 March 1757 when the court ordered her "Mallatto" daughter Patience bound to James Hodges until the age of thirty-one. On 26 March 1759 the court bound Patience to Hodges' widow Merriam Hodges. And on 14 October 1766 the court ordered that her orphan children be bound to Daniel Bray as apprentice coopers until the age of twenty-one, the children being about seven at the time [Minutes 1755-77, March Court 1757, n.p., March Court 1759, n.p.; 1765-8, 34]. She was the mother of

    i. Patience, born say 1757.

    ii. ?Sam, born say 1759, head of a Pasquotank County household of 19 "other free" in 1810 [NC:901].

    iii. ?Ned, head of a Pasquotank County household of 3 "other free" in 1810 [NC:900].

Other members of the Griffin family were

    i. Aaron, born about 1748, a twenty-two-year-old "Mulatto" slave who brought suit for his freedom from Henry Randolph of Chesterfield County in the General Court under the name Aaron Griffin in October 1770. He lost his suit and ran away, but "many of his Colour got their Freedom that Court" according to an advertisement placed in the *Virginia Gazette* by John Randolph, son of Henry [*Virginia Gazette* (Purdie & Dixon edition)].

    ii. Edward, a man of "mixed blood" who was promised his freedom when he was sold to William Kitchen to serve in his place in the Revolution. The North Carolina General Assembly passed a bill to give him his freedom on 15 May 1784 [NC Archives GASR Apr-June 1784, Box 3, location 3A-464]. He was a "Mulatto" head of an Edgecombe County household of 1 "other free" in 1790 and 1800 [NC:202].

GRIMES FAMILY

1. Susanna[1] Grimes, born say 1670, ran away from Prince George's County, Maryland, to Anne Arundel County with her "Malatta" child Elizabeth in 1704 after the death of her master, Colonel Hollyday. She was arrested and returned to Prince George's County court on 23 August 1704 when the court sold her and her four-year-old daughter to Edward Willett [Court Record 1699-1705, 321a]. She may have been the ancestor of

2   i. Charity, born say 1700.

3   ii. Benjamin[1], born say 1742.

4   iii. George, born say 1746.

    iv. ?Nace, head of a Loudoun County, Virginia household of 11 "other free" in 1810 [VA:258].

    v. Andrew, married Molley **Goins**, 11 April 1810 Loudoun County, Virginia bond. He was head of a Loudoun County household of 3 "other free" in 1810 [VA:258].

vi. Juda, married James **Lucas**, 12 September 1814 Loudoun County bond.

2. Charity Grymes, born say 1700, was set levy free in King George County on 7 July 1763. She may have been identical to Charity **Boyd** whose grandsons William and Moses Grimes were bound out by the King George County court on 5 July 1759 [Orders 1751-65, 586, 1073]. She was probably the Charity Grymes who petitioned the Spotsylvania County court for the freedom of (her daughter?) Averilla Grymes in September 1747. She may have been the ancestor of

5   i.   Averilla, born say 1726.

  ii. Moses, born say 1740, ordered bound as an apprentice carpenter to Charles Carter, Jr., in King George County until the age of twenty-one on 5 July 1759. He was a "mulatto" who served in the Virginia Regiment commanded by Colonel Gibson and waited on Colonel Brent during the Revolution. He was married to a forty-five-year-old "mulatto" woman named Jane **Wilson** on 2 October 1779 when Cuthbert Bullitt of Dumfries, Virginia, placed an ad in the *Maryland Journal and Baltimore Advertiser* which stated that she had run away, perhaps to her husband or to the plantation of her former master Colonel George Mason or to Mrs. Page, among whose slaves she had a number of relations [Windley, *Runaway Slave Advertisements*, II:232-3].

  iii. Nancy, born say 1775, niece of David **Pinn**, married David **Pinn**, Jr.

3. Benjamin[1] Grimes, born say 1742, was sued for debt by Francis Willis, Jr., in York County court on 19 March 1764. John Robinson, Gentleman, of Middlesex County was his security [Judgments & Orders 1763-5, 184]. He and his wife Elizabeth Grymes, "free Mulattas," registered the birth of their daughter Frances in Bruton Parish, James City County, Virginia, on 11 February 1765 [Bruton Parish Register, 26]. Benjamin's children were

  i.   Frances, born 11 February 1765.

  ii. ?John, born say 1767, taxable in York County from 1788 to 1804, taxable on a slave in 1800 and 1801. Perhaps his widow was Peggy Grimes who was taxable on a free male tithable in York County in 1812 and head of a household of two "free Negroes & mulattoes over 16," one of whom was tithable in 1813 [PPTL, 1782-1841, frames 140, 182, 220, 244, 265, 375, 388]. She was head of a York County household of 6 "other free" in 1810 [VA:889].

  iii. ?Daniel, born about 1777, taxable in York County from 1801 to 1813 [PPTL, 1782-1841, frames 265, 286, 327, 339, 364, 389], head of a York County household of 7 "other free" in 1810 [VA:889], registered in York County on 21 September 1812: *a person of light complexion about 35 years of age...short hair, large nostrils & very fierce Eyes...Born of free parents on Queens Creek in the parish of Bruton* [Free Negro Register 1798-1831, no.67]. He may have been identical to the Daniel Grimes who was head of a Norfolk County, Virginia household of 8 "other free" in 1810 [VA:814].

  iv. ?Benjamin[2], born 1776-94, head of an Ash County, North Carolina household of one "other free" in 1800 [NC:79] and 3 "free colored" in Salisbury, Rowan County, in 1820 [NC:283].

  v.   ?Thomas, head of a Cumberland County, North Carolina household of 2 "other free" in 1810 [NC:625] and 3 "free colored" in 1820 [NC:224].

4. George Grymes, born say 1746, and his wife Elizabeth, "Boath free mulattoes," were the parents of Philip whose birth and baptism were recorded in Bruton Parish, James City County. They were the parents of

    i.   Philip, born 7 April 1769, baptized 14 August [Bruton Parish Register, 33].

    ii. ?James, a "free man of colour" who purchased a lot on South Street in the Borough of Norfolk for $120 in 1818 [DB 48:332-3].

5. Averilla Grimes, born say 1726, petitioned the Spotsylvania County court for her freedom from James Steven and wife Alice, executrix of Ambrose Grayson, deceased, on 2 June 1747. When the case was called for trial in September 1747 it was styled "Charity Grymes & others vs. James Stevens &c." And the plaintiffs were called Averilla Grymes, William Grymes and Elizabeth Grymes when the court dismissed their petition in February 1747/8 [Orders 1738-49, 420, 430, 439, 453]. The court dismissed their petition in February 1747/8 [Orders 1738-49, 420, 430, 439, 453]. She may have been the mother of

    i.   William, born say 1742, petitioned the Spotsylvania County court in February 1747/8, perhaps the William Grimes who was ordered bound as an apprentice carpenter to Charles Carter, Esq., in King George County on 5 July 1759 [Orders 1751-65, 586].

    ii. Elizabeth, petitioned the Spotsylvania County court in February 1747/8.

GROOM FAMILY

1. John Groom, born say 1720, entered 200 acres in Bladen County, North Carolina, on Drowning Creek near a place called Errington's Cowpen on 3 October 1748 [Philbeck, *Bladen County Land Entries*, no. 448]. He was probably related to Thomas Groom who was granted 200 acres on the Peedee River in Craven County, South Carolina, on 29 May 1745 [South Carolina Archives, Royal Grants 24:23]. And he was probably related to Recher Groom who was one of the "Harbourers" of the "free Negors and Mulattus" who were "Raitously Assembled together in Bladen County on 13 October 1773": Richard Groom, William Groom, William Groom, Jr., Thomas Groom, and members of the **Locklear, Sweat, Chavis,** and **Ivey** families [G.A. 1773, Box 7]. John was a "mulatto" taxable in New Hanover County in 1763 [SS 837] and head of a household of 7 "other free" in Marlboro County, South Carolina, in 1800 [SC:59]. John was probably the father of

2   i.   Richard, born say 1745.

    ii. William[1], Sr., listed among the "free Negors and Mulattus" in Bladen County in 1773. He recorded a memorial for 100 acres in Craven County, South Carolina, on 4 January 1771 [South Carolina Archives, Memorials 10:300]. Perhaps his widow was Charity Groom, head of an Orangeburgh District, South Carolina household of 3 white females and 1 white male under 16 in 1790 [SC:96].

    iii. Isaac, a "Molato" taxable in Bladen County from 1772 to 1774 and listed with a female "Mixt Blood/ free Negro" taxable in 1776 [Byrd, *Bladen County Tax Lists*, I:79, 107, 135; II:64, 80], head of an Orangeburgh District household of 1 white male over 16 and 2 white females in 1790 [SC:96].

    iv. Thomas, taxable in Bladen County as white in 1769 and a "Mulato" taxable in 1770 and 1771 [Byrd, *Bladen County Tax Lists*, I:14, 45, 61].

2. Richard Groom, born say 1745, was living on land on the southwest side of the Little Peedee River in Craven County, South Carolina, on 6 April 1762 when the area was surveyed for a memorial of Hugh Thompson [South Carolina Archives, Memorials 6:24]. This area is located just across the border with Robeson County, North Carolina. He was in present-day Robeson County on 13 October 1773 when he was among the "free Negors and Mulattus" who were "Raitously Assembled together in Bladen County" [G.A.

1773, Box 7]. Richard was head of a household of 3 white males over 16, 2 under 16, and 4 white women in the north part of Orangeburgh District, South Carolina, in 1790 [SC:96] and 8 "other free" in 1800 [SC:935].[109] He may have been the father of

    i.   Richard[2], head of an Orangeburgh District household of 6 "other free" in 1800 [SC:935].

    ii. William[2], ("Jr."), a white taxable in Bladen County in 1774 [Byrd, *Bladen County Tax Lists*, I:107], head of an Orangeburgh District household of 1 white male over 16, 1 under 16, and 2 white females in 1790 [SC:96].

    iii. Nancy, a resident of Richland District who petitioned the South Carolina legislature in 1806 asking to be exempted from the tax on free Negro women [S.C. Archives series S.165015, item 01885].

GUY FAMILY

1.   Daniel[1] Guy, born say 1725, was sued by John Underwood in a Brunswick County, Virginia chancery case on 27 January 1767. He was paid 6 pounds, 17 shillings by the Brunswick County court for Adam Sims, Jr.'s building a bridge over Fountain Creek at Proctor's Ford on 23 February 1767 [Orders 1765-8, 207, 212, 340, 493]. On 13 March 1769 he and his wife Sarah sold 100 acres where they were then living on Fountain Creek in Meherrin Parish (present-day Greensville County), and he sold 220 acres bounded on the north by Fountain Creek on 27 January 1773, explaining in the deed that it was land he had purchased from Katherine Gusses [DB 9:459; 11:39]. He was sued in Brunswick County court for a 10 pound debt on 26 July 1773 [Orders 1772-4, 235, 334]. He was in Mecklenburg County, Virginia, by 14 September 1778 when the court ordered that he, William and John Guy be added to the list of tithables. On 12 May 1783 the court ordered that he be exempt from paying taxes, "he being old and infirm" [Orders 1773-9, 425; 1779-84, 308]. He was head of a Mecklenburg County, Virginia household of 8 white (free) persons in 1782 [VA:34]. He was taxable in Mecklenburg County on his own tithe, a horse and 7 head of cattle in 1782 and 1783. His estate was taxable on a horse and 8 cattle from 1784 to 1787 [PPTL, 1782-1805, frames 15, 46, 137, 193]. He and John Guy were sued in Mecklenburg County for 14 pounds by Charles Gilmour on 14 July 1783, and on 10 May 1790 the court ordered that he have taxes on 2 horses and 4 head of cattle remitted for the year 1786 [Orders 1779-84, 388; 1787-92, 220, 231, 496]. He was probably the father of

2   i.   John[1], born say 1758.

3   ii. William, born about 1763.

      iii. Lucy, born say 1768, mother of Betsy Guy who married Robert **Jones**, 6 August 1809 Mecklenburg County bond, with a note from her mother Lucy. Perhaps she was also the mother of Susan Guy and four-year-old Lewis Guy who were bound apprentices by the Mecklenburg County court to Samuel Holmes and his wife on 8 January 1810. On 21 September 1812 James and David **Thomas** and Susan and Lewis Guy complained that Holmes was illegally detaining them in slavery, but the court found that their indentures were legal. They complained again on 15 November 1813 that they were being held in slavery, and the court ordered the overseers of the poor to bind them to Holmes, giving Susanna's age as twelve and Lewis' age as eight on 21 March 1814 [Orders 1809-11, 114; 1811-13, 317, 328; 1813-15, 116].

4   iv. Christopher, born say 1766.

---

[109]Benjamin **Sweat**, Gideon **Bunch**, Jr., and Gutridge **Locklear** were also counted as white in the Orangeburgh census in 1790 [SC:96].

2. John[1] Guy, born say 1758, was added to the list of tithables in Mecklenburg County, Virginia, on 14 September 1778 [Orders 1774-9, 425]. He was bondsman for the 23 December 1794 Mecklenburg County marriage of Thomas **Maclin** and Delilah **Evans**. He purchased 130 acres on Flat Creek for 156 pounds by deed proved in Mecklenburg County on 11 September 1797 [DB 9:425]. On 14 July 1783 the Mecklenburg County court ordered that a slave over the age of 16 named Israel be added to his list of taxables [Orders 1779-84, 387]. He was taxable in Mecklenburg County on his own tithe and 6 horses and 3 cattle in 1783, taxable on a slave named Hannah in 1784, and a slave named Phillis in 1791 and 1792. He was a "Mulattoe" taxable from 1806 to 1820: taxable on a slave and 4 horses in 1806, counted with 4 free "Mulattoes" and 2 slaves in his household in the list of "Free Negroes and Mulattoes" in 1813, over the age of 45 in 1815 and exempt from personal tax in 1819 [PPTL, 1782-1805, frames 42, 137, 204, 345, 425; 1806-28, frames 340, 506, 596, 654, 703] and head of a Mecklenburg County household of 5 "free colored" in 1820 [VA:154b]. He purchased land in Mecklenburg County by deed proved in 1797. This land was sold by his estate in 1843 [DB 9:245; 30:168]. He died before 1827 when his sons Spencer and Asa Guy executed a deed of trust on their father's estate. A Mecklenburg County chancery suit in 1844 named his children [LVA chancery file 1844-023]. He was the father of

   i. George, born say 1778, over the age of 16 years when he was listed as a tithable in his father's Mecklenburg County household from 1795 to 1798. He was head of his own household in 1799 when he was taxable on a horse [PPTL, 1782-1805, frames 573, 659, 686, 762]. He married Nancy **Drew**, 11 December 1799 Mecklenburg County, Virginia bond. He was a "Mulatto" taxable in Mecklenburg County from 1806 to 1814: listed with 2 "Mulattoes" over the age of 16 (probably himself and his wife) and a slave in 1813 [PPTL, 1806-28, frames 35, 62, 136, 235, 260, 390]. He may have been identical to the George W. Guy who married Nancy **Hailstock** (**Ailstock**), 20 July 1815 Warren County bond. He was head of a Mecklenburg County household of 4 "free colored" and 3 slaves over 45 years of age in 1820 [VA:162b].

   ii. Spencer, born say 1785, over the age of 16 years when he was listed as a taxable in his father's Mecklenburg County household from 1802 to 1805 [PPTL, 1782-1805, frames 919, 946, 1025, 1056]. He was a "Mulatto" taxable in Mecklenburg County from 1809 to 1820: counted in the list of "Free Negroes and Mulattoes" in 1813 [PPTL, 1806-28, frames 135, 163, 235, 340, 537, 596, 703]. He married Sally Barnard, 1815 Mecklenburg County bond and was head of a Mecklenburg County household of 3 "free colored" in 1820 [VA:154b].

   iii. Polly, born about 1786, married Hardaway **Drew**, 1813 Mecklenburg County bond.

   iv. Asa, a "Mulatto" taxable in Mecklenburg County from 1813 to 1820 [PPTL, 1806-28, frames 340, 389, 537, 703]. He married Nancy **Robards**, 9 February 1824 Warren County bond, Hardaway **Drew** surety.

   v. Lucinda, born say 1795, married Willis Guy, 1815 Mecklenburg County bond. Willis was a "Mulattoe" taxable in Mecklenburg County from 1818 to 1820 [PPTL, 1806-28, frames 637, 654, 703].

3. William Guy, born about 1763, was added to the list of tithables in Mecklenburg County, Virginia, on 14 September 1778 [Orders 1773-9, 425]. He was head of a Mecklenburg County household of 4 white (free) persons in 1782 [VA:34] and taxable there from 1782 to 1791 [PPTL, 1782-1805, frames 15, 46, 117, 193, 292, 403]. He was sued in Mecklenburg County court on 13 September 1784 for debt due by account, and on 14 November 1803 he was charged with retailing liquor without a license at the house of Thomas Booth,

but the presentment was dismissed when the witness against him failed to appear [Orders 1784-7, 119; 1803-5, 53, 128, 165-6]. He was head of a Granville County, North Carolina household of 7 "other free," one white woman over forty-five years of age, and one white woman 16-26 years old in 1810 [NC:890]. He called himself "a free man of Color" on 5 February 1833 when he made a declaration in Granville County court in order to obtain a pension for his services in the Revolution. He testified that he was about seventy years old, was born in Brunswick County, Virginia, and lived in Mecklenburg County, Virginia, when he enlisted as a substitute for Jack Goode at Mecklenburg courthouse. He moved to Granville County about 1803. On 8 November 1842 his widow Abigail Guy, aged eighty years, testified in Granville County in order to obtain a widow's pension. She stated that she and William Guy were married on 12 June 1780, and her husband died on 30 January 1837. Her application included a copy of their 10 January 1780 Halifax County, North Carolina marriage bond: William Guy to Abigail **Chavers (Chavis)**. It stated that William Guy and Charles **Chavers** provided the bond, but it was signed William Guy and Samuel **Chavers** (by mark) [M804-1149]. They may have been the parents of

    i.   Daniel^2, born say 1784, taxable in Mecklenburg County from 1802 to 1805 [PPTL, 1782-1805, frames 919, 1056]. He married Nancy **Erle**, 26 February 1806 Mecklenburg County bond, William **Chandler** security. Nancy **Erle** may have been identical to Nancy Bigers **Earl** who received land by the 19 January 1789 Henry County will of her father Menoah **Chavis** [WB 1:180]. Daniel was taxable in Mecklenburg County from 1806 to 1814, listed as a "Mulatto" in 1813 and 1814. The second "Mulatto over the age of 16" in his household in 1813 was probably his wife [PPTL, 1806-28, frames 35, 235, 340, 389]. He was taxable in Hawtree District of Warren County, North Carolina, in 1815 [Tax List Papers, Vols TC 8, 1795-1815] and head of a Warren County household of 4 "free colored" in 1820 [NC:804].

    ii. Vines, married Elizabeth **Jeffries**, 8 January 1805 Orange County, North Carolina bond, Jesse Blalock bondsman. Vines was head of an Orange County household of 5 "other free" in 1810 [NC:795] and 7 "free colored" in 1820 [NC:61].

4.   Christopher Guy, born say 1766, was taxable in Mecklenburg County in 1783 [PPTL, 1782-1805, frame 46] taxable in Meherrin Parish, Greensville County, in 1787, 1792 and 1793 [PPTL 1782-1807, frames 63, 136, 162], taxable in Mecklenburg County on his son John in 1804, and taxable on sons John and Buck in 1805 [PPTL, 1782-1805, frames 137, 685, 798, 919, 1025, 1056]. Richard **Evans** was his security in Mecklenburg County court when he was sued for a debt of 5 pounds on 13 May 1783, and Daniel Guy was his security on 14 August 1786 when he was sued for a debt of 10 pounds [Orders 1779-84, 315, 343; 1784-7]. He was a "Mulatto" taxable in Mecklenburg County from 1806 to 1817 [PPTL, 1806-28, frames 35, 135, 163, 235, 341, 390, 596] and head of a household of 2 "free colored" in 1820 [VA:159b]. He was the father of

    i.   John^2, born say 1787, over the age of 16 years when he was listed in his father's Mecklenburg County household in 1804. He married Aggy **Whitmore**, 21 February 1814 Orange County bond. Aggy was probably the daughter of Charles **Whitmore**, born before 1776, head of an Orange County household of 4 "free colored" in 1820 [NC:A:412]. Charles was deposed in Orange County on 22 November 1832 and 27 May 1833 for the Revolutionary War pension application of John **Jeffries**. He stated that he was born in Brunswick County, Virginia, in 1765, moved to North Carolina about 1798, and was acquainted with John **Jeffries** in 1780 when he left home to serve in the war [M804-1409, frames 0406, 0425]. Charles was called the "natural son of Agathy Whitmore" on 22 December 1777 when the Brunswick County court ordered the churchwardens of Meherrin Parish to bind him out as an apprentice [Orders 1774-82, 177]. He was taxable in Mecklenburg County, Virginia, in the same district as the Guy family in 1795 [PPTL, 1782-1805, frame 585] and taxable in Nutbush District of Warren County in 1798 [Tax List 1781-1801, 364].

  ii. Buck/ Buckner, born say 1789, over the age of 16 years when he was listed in his father's Mecklenburg County household in 1805. Buckner married Sylvia **Jeffries**, 16 July 1810 Orange County bond.

  iii. Fanny, married Benjamin **Manning**, 5 May 1796 Mecklenburg County bond. And a Frances Guy was counted as a "Mulatto" in Mecklenburg County in 1813 [PPTL, 1806-28, frame 340].

  iv. Miles, head of a Caswell County, North Carolina household of 3 "free colored" in 1820 [NC:61].

  v. Wilson E., head of a Caswell County household of 6 "free colored" in 1820 [NC:352].

  vi. Jesse, head of an Orange County, North Carolina household of 5 "free colored" in 1820 [NC:342].

GWINN FAMILY

1. Mary Gwinn, born say 1686, was the "Covenant Servant" of Joseph Pleasants on 21 August 1704 when the Henrico County court bound her illegitimate "Mulatto" child named Beck to her master [Oprhans Court 1677-1739, 46]. Her children were

2   i. Rebecca, born about February 1704.

    ii. ?Thomas Quinn, born say 1710, presented by the York County court on 21 August 1738 for failing to list his wife Betty as a tithable [OW 18:440].

    iii. ?Edward[1], born about 1715, "a Negro," petitioned the Henrico County court for his freedom from Martha Bennett in April 1746, but the court ruled that he had to serve until December that year. He was called a "free negroe" on 7 April 1789 when the court exempted him from payment of taxes [Orders 1737-46, 367; Orders 1787-9, 569].

3   iv. ?Joseph, born say 1720.

2. Rebecca Gwinn, born about February 1704, was about six months old when she was bound to Joseph Pleasants in Henrico County on 21 August 1704 [Orphans Court 1677-1739, 46]. Her children may have been

    i. John, born say 1722, a "Mulatto" brought before the Chesterfield County court on 4 December 1767 on suspicion of burning the house of Joseph Bass. He was sent for further trial at the General Court [Orders 1767-71, 156].

    ii. William, born say 1727, presented by the court in Henrico County on 6 November 1752 for failing to list his "Mulatto" wife as a tithable. He was fined 500 pounds of tobacco [Minutes 1752-5, 19, 27].

4   iii. Ann[1], born say 1730.

3. Joseph Gwinn, born say 1720, was presented by the York County court on 19 January 1746/7 for not listing his wife as a tithable [W&I 19:486]. Perhaps his wife was identical to Jane Gwinn who sued William Lyon, Jr., in York County court on 17 May 1762. The case was dismissed because neither party appeared [Judgments & Orders 1759-63, 361]. Joseph may have been the father of

    i. Anne[2], an infant on 16 May 1763 when she, by her "next friend" Jane **Savy** (**Savoy**), sued Elizabeth and Martha **Armfield** in York County court for trespass, assault and battery. Martha was found not guilty, but Elizabeth was ordered to pay her 20 shillings [Judgments & Orders 1763-5, 14, 37].

ii. Nancy, born about 1777, registered in York County on 16 December 1822: *a mulatto about 45 years old 5 feet 1-1/4 inch high...Born free* [Free Negro Register 1798-1831, no.172].

4. Ann¹ Guin, born say 1730, was the mother of Hannah, a child bound out by the Henrico County court on 1 December 1766, no race indicated [Orders 1763-67, 644]. She was the mother of

i. ?Obedience, a "Mulatto" bound out by the Henrico County court on 1 November 1756, no parent named [Orders 1755-62, 53].

ii. ?Phil, a "Mulatto" bound by the churchwardens of Henrico County in December 1763, no parent named [Orders 1763-67, 171]. He was a "F.N." taxable in the upper district of Henrico County from 1801 to 1807 [PPTL 1782-1814, frames 446, 487, 532; Land Tax List 1799-1816].

iii. Hannah, bound out on 1 December 1766 [Orders 1763-67, 644].

iv. ?Edward², born say 1755, taxable in the lower district of Goochland County from 1787 to 1815: taxable on 2 horses in 1790, called a "Mulatto" in 1793, exempt from taxation in 1815 [PPTL, 1782-1809, frames 165, 253, 281, 327, 451, 509, 581, 636, 723, 805; 1810-32, frames 53, 121, 240].

One of their descendants may have been

i. Edward³/ Ned, born about 1759, a "Mᵒ" taxable on a horse in Powhatan County from 1801 to 1815: taxable on 2 slaves in 1807, 3 horses in 1809, and 2 "free negroes & mulattoes over the age of 16" in 1813 [PPTL, 1787-1825, frames 223, 257, 295, 342, 380, 421, 483]. He was a "Free Black" head of a Powhatan County household of 5 "other free" in 1810 [VA:11]. He may have been identical to or the father of Ned Gwinn who married Chloe Gwinn, 25 January 1811 Powhatan County bond. He registered in Powhatan County on 19 December 1822: *Age: 63; Color: Dark yellow; Stature: 5'6"; Emancipated by decree of the Court of Appeals in virtue of the wills of John & Jonathan Pleasants* [Register of Free Negroes, no. 49].

HACKET FAMILY

Members of the Hacket family were

i. Peter, born say 1760, a Revolutionary soldier from Campbell County [Jackson, *Virginia Negro Soldiers*, 36]. He may have been the father of Peter Hacket, a slave emancipated by Micajah Teawell by deed proved in Campbell County on 5 September 1782. He was one of the hands ordered by the Campbell County court to work on the road from Lynches Ferry on the James River to the main road near the water lick on 4 August 1785 [Orders 1782-5, 89; 1785-6, 137; 1782-5, 89]. He was a "Free Negro" taxable in the northern district of Campbell County from 1787 to 1807, listed the same day as Peter Hacket, Jr., in 1807 [PPTL, 1785-1814, frames 85, 119, 331, 459, 697]. He was head of a Campbell County household of 11 "other free" in 1810 [VA:869].

ii. Joseph, born say 1764, married Winney **Roberts**, "fn's," 4 December 1785 Campbell County bond, consent of John Lynch. He was a "free Negro" taxable in the northern district of Campbell County from 1787 to 1795 [PPTL, 1785-1814, frames 85, 120, 331].

iii. Isaac, born say 1770, married Lucy **Napier**, "daughter of Charles who consents," 4 January 1792 Campbell County bond. He was a "f. negro" taxable in the northern district of Campbell County from 1790 to 1791 [PPTL, 1785-1814, frames 150, 190].

iv. Lucy, born say 1777, married David **Ellis**, "f.n's," 12 February 1798 Campbell County bond.

HAGINS FAMILY

The Hagins family probably came from Hanover County, Virginia, where the "Widow Hagin & son Zachariah" were listed in a merchant's account book for 6 April 1744 [*Magazine of Virginia Genealogy* 34:196].

Three mixed-race Hagin/ Hagins children, "Base Born Malatas," were bound apprentice to Arthur Due in October 1760 by the Johnston County, North Carolina court [Haun, *Johnston County Court Minutes*, I:46]. They were

1   i.   Obediah, born say 1754.
2   ii.   Zachariah, born say 1756.
     iii.   Malachiah, born say 1758, head of a Sumter County, South Carolina household of 11 "other free" in 1800 [SC:935].

1.   Obediah Hagins, born say 1754, was bound apprentice in Johnston County in 1760. He was head of a Wayne County household of 4 "other free" in 1800 [NC:245] and apparently moved to Sumter County, South Carolina, that same year when he was head of a household of 4 "other free" [SC:935] and 6 in 1810 [SC:217a]. He may have been the father of
     i.   Flavd, head of a Sumter District household of one "other free" in 1810 [SC:217a].

2.   Zachariah Hagins, born say 1756, may have been the Rias Heagin, a "Malatto," who was in Cumberland County, North Carolina, on 14 January 1797 when the court ordered that he receive thirty-nine lashes [Minutes 1791-97, n.p.]. He was taxable on 100 acres in Prince Frederick Parish, South Carolina, in 1786 [S.C. Tax Returns 1783-1800, frame 119]. His son Thomas Hagans was living in Marion District, South Carolina, on 14 August 1809 when he refused to pay the levy "upon all Free Negros Mulatoes and Mestizos," claiming that he was a white man. Robert Coleman and John Regan testified at the October 1812 session of the Marion District Court of Common Pleas that Thomas was the son of Zachariah Hagans and his wife Kesiah **Ivey**, who was the daughter of Thomas and Elizabeth **Ivey** of Drowning Creek, Bladen (Robeson) County. The court ruled that Thomas Hagans was of Portuguese descent and acquitted him [*NCGSJ* IX:259]. Zachariah and Kesiah were the parents of
     i.   Thomas, born say 1785.

Other members of the family in North Carolina were
     i.   Amy, head of a Martin County household of 3 "other free" in 1790 [NC:67] and 3 in 1800 [NC:395].
     ii.   Mary, head of a Wayne County household of 1 "other free" in 1790 [NC:150].
     iii.   Penny, head of a Martin County household of 4 "other free" in 1810 [NC:437].
     iv.   Priscilla, head of an Edgecombe County household of 3 "other free" in 1810 [NC:764].

HAILEY FAMILY

1.   John Hayly, born say 1670, was living in York Parish when he made his 5 February 1702/3 York County will, proved 24 May 1703, by which he gave fifteen pounds to an eight-year-old "Mullatta" boy named William who had been given to him by Major Buckner. Hayly left William the sum of fifteen pounds sterling when he reached the age of twenty-one for transporting himself out of the colony. He indicated that William was to live with Major Buckner

who was to care for his schooling [DOW 12:136]. He was probably the father of

2   i.   William, born December 1694.

2.   William Hayly, born December 1694, may have taken the name Haley and been the husband of Mary Haley who was presented by the York County court on 20 November 1727 for not listing herself as a tithable [OW 16:489]. She was probably the ancestor of

3   i.   Peter, born about 1757.

    ii. Acquila, married Sarah **Gallimore**, "dau. of William Gallimore," 13 December 1790 Charlotte County bond, Thomas Hayes surety, 16 December marriage.

3.   Peter Haley, born about 1757, registered as a "free Negro" in York County on 28 April 1802: *a bright mulatto with woolly hair high forehead...5 feet 6-1/2 Inches high...about 45 years of age...addicted to the intemperate use of ardent Spirits* [Register of Free Negroes 1798-1831, no.19]. He was taxable in York County on 2 tithes and 2 horses in 1782, a slave named Jack in 1784, slaves Jack and Naney, 3 horses and 2 cattle in 1786, and taxable on a slave in 1788, 1789, 1794 to 1802, 1805, and 1807 to 1810 [PPTL, 1782-1841, frames 69, 91, 128, 141, 162, 193, 227, 276, 297, 327, 340, 354]. On 22 November 1796 the York County court awarded him 25 pounds in his suit against Daniel **Lyons** for trespass, assault and battery. Daniel then brought a suit in chancery to stay the execution of the judgment and this case was continued until 19 November 1798 when Daniel was again found guilty [Orders 1795-1803, 138, 144, 192, 239, 249, 250, 292-3]. He was head of a York County household of 4 "other free" and a slave in 1810 [VA:875]. (His widow?) Rebecca Hailey was tithable on two free males over the age of 21 in 1811 and one in 1812 [PPTL, 1782-1841, frames 354, 364]. Peter was the father of

    i.   ?Fanny, born about 1776, registered in York County on 16 December 1822: *a bright Mulatto about 46 years of age 5 feet 4-1/4 inches high* [Register of Free Negroes 1798-1831, no.185].

    ii. Sarah **Scott**, born about 1781, registered in York County on 17 June 1805: *late Sarah Haley Daughter of Peter Haley a free Woman of a dark complexion about 24 years of age 5 feet 3-3/4 Inches high her hair resembling long Wooll* [Register of Free Negroes 1798-1831, no.29].

    iii. ?Richard, born about 1783, registered in York County on 18 February 1805: *yellow complexion about 22 years of age 5 feet 4-1/4 Inches high has long woolly Hair...born of free parents on Queens Creek in the Parish of Bruton* [Register of Free Negroes 1798-1831, no.30]. He was taxable in York County from 1805 to 1813 [PPTL, 1782-1841, frames 307, 327, 354, 365, 390] and head of a York County household of 4 "other free" in 1810 [VA:876].

    iv. ?Thomas, born about 1795, registered in York County on 18 November 1822: *a mulatto fellow about 27 years of age 5 feet 9-3/4 Inches high...high forehead, tolerable long hair* [Register of Free Negroes 1798-1831, no.135]. He was taxable in York County in 1814 [PPTL, 1782-1841, frame 406]. He registered in Henrico County on 5 December 1831: *age 45, a dark mulatto man, 5 feet 9-3/4 inches, Born free as per register of York County Court and identified by George W. Banks.* His wife may have been Sally Hailey who registered the same day: *age 49, bright mullatto woman, 5 feet 1-1/2 inches* [Register of Free Negroes and Mulattoes, 1831-1844, p.12, nos. 691, 692].

HAITHCOCK/ HATHCOCK FAMILY

The Haithcock family may have descended from Edward Heathcot, a resident of Henrico County in November 1712 when the court noted that Elizabeth Sproson had lately come out of New Kent County and had delivered a bastard child at his house. The court called him Edward Heathcocke in November 1721 [Orders 1710-4, 85, 198; Minutes 1719-24, 142]. Members of the Haithcock family were

1   i.   Joseph[1], born say 1708.
2   ii.   Edward[1], born say 1710.
3   iii.   Mary[2], born say 1740.

1.   Joseph[1] Heathcock, born say 1708, received three patents for land in Brunswick County, Virginia: 200 acres on the south side of Galling Run on 28 September 1732, 254 acres on the north side of Fountain Creek on 12 January 1747, and 269 acres on the south side of Fountain Creek on 7 July 1763 [Patents 14:506; 26:165; 35:216]. On 13 June 1748 he voted in the Brunswick County election. In December 1753 his Brunswick County case against John Willis was dismissed because it was agreed to by both parties [DB 1:168; 3:510; Orders 1753-56, 94]. And he was a resident of Brunswick County on 23 June 1763 when he sold 50 acres in Northampton County, North Carolina, adjacent to Drury Jordan, a former neighbor of Edward Haithcock [DB 3:303]. His 11 October 1782 Meherrin Parish, Brunswick County will was proved 26 April 1784, John Haithcock, executor. He lent 116 acres to his wife Elizabeth during her lifetime and then to his son John, gave 100 acres to his grandson David Haithcock adjoining 35 acres which he gave to his granddaughter Elizabeth Haithcock, gave furniture to his grandson Howell Haithcock, gave a total of 216 acres to his son Charles, gave 100 acres to his son Jesse Haithcock, gave 100 acres to his son William, and mentioned his daughter Mary Haithcock [WB 2:295]. His wife Elizabeth was a widow in Brunswick County in 1787, taxable on a free male tithe and a horse [Property Tax List 1782-1807, frame 203]. Joseph's children were

4   i.   Mary[1], born say 1730.
      ii.   Charles, born say 1736, received 216 acres by his father's will. He had 6 persons in his Greensville County household in 1783 [VA:55]. On 28 October 1784 the Greensville County court appointed him to appraise the estate of Nathaniel Mitchell [Orders 1781-9, 166]. He purchased 34 acres adjoining his land on the southside of Fountain Creek on 20 September 1801 [DB 3:248]. By his 23 October 1806 Greensville County will, proved in December 1806, he left his land and four slaves to his wife Frances and sons Roland and Charles when they came of age and named his daughters Anny, Patsy, Julia and Lucy Heathcock [DB 2:26]. Frances was one of the heirs of her brother Robert Hill on 8 March 1807 when she sold 11 acres in Greensville County [DB 4:229]. Her son Charles was head of a Greensville County household of 2 whites and 3 slaves in 1820 [VA:262].
5   iii.   Jesse, born say 1738.
     iv.   William[1], born say 1740, received 100 acres by the Greensville County will of his father Joseph Heathcock. He had 5 persons in his Greensville County household in 1783 [VA:55]. He and James **Going** were sued in Greensville County court for a debt of 10 pounds on 28 October 1784. He sold land to Ann Heathcock by deed proved in court on 25 August 1785 [Orders 1781-9, 170, 231]. He was taxable in Greensville County in 1782 and 1783 and from 1790 to 1793 [PPTL 1782-1807, frames 3, 13, 108, 127, 137, 161]. He was probably identical to William Hathcock, Sr., who was head of a Northampton County household of 2 white males and 2 white females in the Captain Williams' district for the 1786 North Carolina state census.

    v.   John[2], born say 1746, and his wife Peggy sold 164 acres on Fountain Creek in Greensville County for $410 on 15 February 1805 while residing in Warren County, North Carolina [DB 3:436]. He was head Warren County household of 8 whites and 2 slaves in 1790 [NC:77].

    vi. ?Jemima, born say 1750, chosen in Greensville County court by David Heathcock as his guardian to rent out his plantation and to maintain him until he came of age, so she may have been his mother [Orders 1781-9, 389-90]. She was taxable on a free male tithable and a horse in Greensville County from 1788 to 1790; taxable on a slave and a horse in 1791 [PPTL 1782-1807, frames 64, 83, 108, 127]. David was taxable on a horse in Greensville County from 1792 to 1806 [PPTL 1782-1807, frames 137, 179, 202, 232, 260, 353]. He and his wife Patsey sold 53 acres in Greensville County to Henry **Stewart** for 53 pounds on 16 January 1807 [DB 4:49].

2.   Edward[1] Hathcock, born say 1710, sold 100 acres of the land he patented near Arthur's Creek in Northampton County, North Carolina, to his son-in-law, James Norton, on 26 November 1753. On 2 April 1757 he sold another 100 acres on the north side of Ragland's Road to Drury Jordan of Brunswick County, Virginia. On 15 May 1758 he made a Northampton County deed of gift of 100 acres on Turbyfield's Run near Ragland's Ferry Road to his son Thomas, and two days later on 17 May 1758 he sold 20 acres on Turbafield's Run for 2 pounds 10 shillings to (his son?) John Heathcock [DB 2:129, 387, 475-6]. He was co-defendant in a suit with John **Brooks**, probably as his security, for a debt of 4 pounds, 2 shillings which the Southampton County court ordered him to pay Samuel Sands on 13 May 1762 [Orders 1759-63, 219]. He entered 400 acres on both sides of Black Creek below the mouth of Mirey Branch in Johnston County on 11 August 1778 [Haun, *Johnston County Land Entries*]. His plantation where he formerly lived on Little Crooked Creek in Franklin County was mentioned in a Franklin County deed on 29 October 1779 [DB 1:52, 124, 360]. In May 1782 Edward, Holiday, and Joseph Hathcock were ordered to work on the road from the head of Gum Swamp in Johnston County to the Cumberland County line. He may have been living on land of (his son?) Isam Hathcock when he was counted in Halifax County, head of a household of 4 free males and 7 free females in district 3 for the 1786 North Carolina state census. He died before November 1786 when the Johnston County court ordered his orphans Stephen, Amos, and Mary brought to court to be bound out [Haun, *Johnston County Court Minutes*, III:206, 336]. And on 22 August and 21 November 1786 the Halifax County court bound out Hathcock "base born children," no race mentioned: David (nine years), Nancy, and Mark (eight years old) [Minutes 1784-87, 154, 164, 177]. Perhaps Edward's wife was Elizabeth Hathcock, head of a Johnston County household of 2 free males and 4 free females in the 1787 State Census. His children were

    i.   Thomas[1], born say 1735, received a deed of gift of 100 acres in Northampton County from his father on 15 May 1758 [DB 2:476]. He sold this land on 30 January 1763 [DB 3:240]. He was an insolvent Bute County taxpayer in 1769 [*NCGSJ* XV:2431] and head of a household of 3 white males and 3 white females in Richmond County, North Carolina in 1790 [NC:46].

6   ii. ?John[1], born say 1736.

    iii. Martha, born say 1737, married James Norton before 26 November 1753 when James received a deed of gift from his father-in-law. He and his wife Martha sold this land on 2 April 1757. They were still in Northampton County on 23 August 1779 when James Norton, Sr., Martha, and (their children?) James, Jr., and Keziah Norton sold their remaining 250 acres in Northampton County [DB 2:129, 392; 6:363]. James Norton, Sr., was head of a Richmond County, North Carolina household of 4 white males and 3 white females in 1790 living nearby Thomas Hathcock [NC:46].

iv. ?Aney, born say 1743, purchased 50 acres on Arthur's Creek in Northampton County from James Norton on 22 June 1762 and sold it on 9 February 1787 [DB 3:202; 7:422].

v. ?James[1], born say 1750, purchased 100 acres on Rocky Branch in Northampton County on 28 January 1778 [DB 6:320] and was taxed on an assessment of 590 pounds in 1780 [GA 46.1]. On 6 April 1787 he sold 100 acres on Jack Swamp as administrator of the estate of James Seaton [DB 11:184]. He was an insolvent Northampton County taxpayer in 1789 [Minutes 1792-96, 13] and sold his 100 acres on Rocky Branch on 2 January 1790 [DB 11:299].

vi. ?Joseph[2], born say 1751, ordered to work on the road in Johnston County on May 1782 with Edward Hathcock so he may have been his son [Haun, *Johnston County Court Minutes*, III:206]. On 27 January 1779 he entered 150 acres in Johnston County on the north side of Black Creek [Haun, *Johnston County Land Entries*, no. 692] and was taxed on this land in 1784 [GA 64.1]. His wife may have been Sarah Haithcock who received $1 by the 20 December 1780 Johnston County will of her father Stephen **Powell**.

7 vii. ?Isham, born say 1754.

8 viii. ?Holiday, born about 1760.

ix. ?Lucy, born say 1766, mother of a ten-year-old "base born child" John Hathcock who was bound to John Eason by Johnston County court in February 1792 [Haun, *Johnston County Court Minutes*, III:190]. She was head of a Sumter District, South Carolina household of 3 "other free" in 1810 [SC:222a].

x. Stephen[2], born say 1768, one of the orphans of Edward Hathcock ordered brought before the May 1786 session of the Johnston County court [Haun, *Johnston County Court Minutes*, III:336]. He paid a bond of 250 pounds security in the September 1789 Johnston County court for begetting a bastard child by Nancy **Powell**. He married Sally **Jones**, 30 July 1799 Wake County bond, and was head of a Wake County household of 3 "other free" in 1800 [NC:767] and 7 in Chatham County in 1810 [NC:201]. He was a resident of Wake County on 4 September 1805 when he purchased 100 acres in Chatham County on the north side of Big Beaver Creek [DB O:262]. He died before August 1818 when the Chatham County court granted administration of his estate to Jordan Holleman on $500 security [Minutes 1811-18, 139].

xi. Amos, born say 1770, one of the orphans of Edward Hathcock ordered brought before the May 1786 session of the Johnston County court. He was ordered bound an apprentice farmer to John Dodd [Haun, *Johnston County Court Minutes*, III:336]. He was head of a Northampton County household of 4 "other free" in 1810 [NC:728].

xii. Mary[3], born say 1772, one of the orphans of Edward Hathcock ordered brought before the May 1786 session of the Johnston County court, perhaps the Mary Heathcock who married James **Maclin**, 5 October 1799 Wake County bond.

3. Mary[2] Heathcock, born say 1740, may have been the mother of John and Aaron Heathcock, poor children, who were called "orphans of ____ Heathcocke" when the Southampton County court ordered their indenture to John Powell vacated and bound them instead to Arthur **Byrd** because their mother had indentured them to him. The indenture was indexed in the court order book as "Heathcocke Mary & Jno." [Orders 1772-7, 134, 213; Index in front of book]. She may have been the Mary Hathcock who was head of a Halifax County household of 9 "other free" in 1800 [NC:318]. And she may have been the mother of

   i.   John[3], born say 1758, living in Southampton County on 11 March 1773
        when the court ordered the churchwardens of St. Luke's Parish to bind
        him and Aaron Heathcock, "poor children." On 11 June 1773 the court
        ordered the churchwardens to bind him to Arthur **Byrd** [Orders 1772-7,
        134, 213]. He was living in Southampton County in 1779 when he
        enlisted in the Revolution [Jackson, *Virginia Negro Soldiers*, 37]. He
        was head of a Halifax County household of 1 free white person in
        District 2 for the 1786 North Carolina census, 4 "other free" in 1810
        [NC:27] and 7 "free colored" in 1820 [NC:151].
   ii. Aaron, born say 1760, bound apprentice to Arthur **Byrd** in
        Southampton County on 11 June 1773 [Orders 1772-7, 213]. He sued
        Elijah **Hunt** for a debt of 16 pounds, 4 shillings and obtained an
        attachment on his estate on 14 October 1784 [Orders 1778-84, 505]. He
        was taxable in St. Luke's Parish, Southampton County, from 1784 to
        1796: taxable on a horse and 3 cattle in 1784, taxable in Samuel
        Mecum's household in 1789, taxable on 2 horses in 1793 [PPTL 1782-
        92, frames 548, 635, 632, 710, 762, 818, 876; 1792-1806, frames 54,
        82, 163, 190]. He was surety for the 8 February 1794 Southampton
        County marriage bond of Shadrack **Demery** and Charlotte **Hicks**. On
        1 January 1796 he and Batt **Chavis** sold their household goods to John
        Walden by Northampton County, North Carolina deed [DB 11:42]. He
        was allowed pay until 5 June 1781 for his services in the Revolution
        [Haun, *Revolutionary Army Accounts*, vol. II, Book 1, 273]. He was
        head of a Northampton County household of 5 "other free" in 1800
        [NC:449].
   iii. Sarah, born say 1768, married James **Byrd**, 30 August 1789
        Southampton County marriage [Ministers' Returns, 646]. She was
        called Sarah **Bird** on 12 October 1786 when the court bound out her
        "poor child" Michael **Heathcock** [Orders 1784-9, 215].
9 iv. Dorcas, born about 1770.
10 v.   Reuben[2], born about 1772.

4. Mary[1] Heathcock, born say 1730, was taxable on her son Howell Hathcock's
    tithe in Brunswick County in 1784 [PPTL 1782-1807, frame 90]. She was "old
    and weak" when she made her 18 July 1785 Brunswick County will, proved
    24 April 1788. She gave all her estate to her son Howell Heathcock and made
    her brother John Heathcock her executor [WB 1:118]. Her son was
    i.   Howell, born say 1767, married Mary Woodal/ Woodle, daughter of
         Sally Woodal, 30 January 1788 Greensville County bond, George
         Collier surety, married by Rev. William Garner [Ministers' Returns,
         13].[110] He was taxable in Greensville County in 1788 and 1789,
         taxable on a horse from 1790 to 1794 [PPTL 1782-1807, frames 64,
         108, 137, 179]. He may have been identical to Hall Heathcock who
         was head of a Halifax County, North Carolina household of 9 "free
         colored" in 1820 [NC:151] and 5 in 1830 [NC:296].

5. Jesse, born say 1738, received 100 acres by his father's will. He had 6 persons
    in his Meherrin Parish, Greensville County household in 1783 [VA:55], and
    was taxable there from 1783 to 1796: taxable on 4 slaves in 1784; taxable on
    (son?) Daniel in 1789, taxable on (sons?) Daniel and Reuben Hathcock in 1792
    [PPTL 1782-1850, frames 13, 27, 42, 83, 127, 161, 202]. He and his wife
    Molly sold 100 acres in Greensville County where they were then living for
    60 pounds on 19 July 1796 [DB 3:5]. He was probably the Jesse Hathcock,

---

[110]Mark **Woodle** was head of a Richmond County, North Carolina household of one "other free"
in 1800 [NC:257].

over 45 years of age, who was head of a Halifax County, North Carolina household of 5 whites in 1800 [NC:312]. He may have been the father of

    i.   Daniel, born say 1768, taxable in Jesse Hathcock's Greensville County household in 1789 [PPTL 1791-1828, frame 83].

    ii. Reuben[1], born say 1771, taxable in Jesse Hathcock's Greensville County household in 1792, charged with his own tax from 1793 to 1796 [PPTL 1782-1807, frames 162, 179, 188, 202]. He married Mary **Jones**, 6 August 1793 Greensville County bond, Braxton Robinson surety [Marriage Bonds, 28] and was head of a Northampton County household of 2 white males and 1 white female in 1790 [NC:75], 1 white male and 4 white females in Halifax County in 1800 [NC:312], and 9 "other free" in Halifax County in 1810 [NC:24].

    iii. ?Colby, born say 1774, married Grief **Jeffries**, daughter of Andrew **Jeffries**, 24 July 1794 Greensville County bond, Shadrach **Jeffries** surety [Ministers Returns, 147]. He was taxable in Greensville County from 1795 to 1800 and from 1804 to 1814 [PPTL 1782-1807, frames 189, 218, 245, 321, 462]. He was head of a Greensville County census of 8 whites in 1810 [VA:738]. Grief Haithcock, apparently his widow, was head of a Greensville County census of 8 "free colored" in 1820 [VA:262].

    iv. ?Silvey, married Thomas **Jeffries**, 8 October 1789 Greensville County bond, Rev. William Garner minister [Ministers Returns, 30]. Thomas **Jeffries** was head of an Orange County, North Carolina household of 9 "other free" in 1810 [NC:817] and 7 "free colored" in 1820 [NC:406].

6.   John[1] Haithcock, born say 1736, purchased 20 acres in Northampton County from Edward Haithcock for 2 pounds, 10 shillings on 17 May 1758. This was two days after Edward made a deed of gift to his son Thomas, so perhaps John was also Edward's son. John sold this land on 2 June 1761 for 5 pounds [DB 2:475; 3:132]. He paid 330 pounds for 160 acres on Jack Swamp in Northampton County on 18 November 1778, and he and wife Martha sold this land for 375 pounds on 4 January 1779 [DB 6:344, 339]. He was taxed in Northampton County in 1780 on 172 pounds cash and a total assessment of 1,737 pounds [GA 46.1]. He was head of a Northampton County household of 3 free males and 8 free females in Captain William's District for the 1786 state census, 4 "other free" in 1790 [NC:74] and 9 "other free" in 1800 [NC:449]. His children may have been

    i.   Meshack, born say 1757, taxable in 1780 in Northampton County on an assessment of 161 pounds [GA 46.1]. He married Elizabeth **Jones**, 26 December 1789 Greensville County, Virginia bond.

    ii. William[2], Jr., born say 1758, head of a Northampton County household of 4 free males and 2 free females in Captain Williams' district for the 1786 state census, perhaps the William Hathcock who was head of a Halifax County household of 5 "other free" in 1790 [NC:61] and 6 "other free" in 1810 [NC:26].

11 iii. Frederick[1], born say 1758.

    iv. Newman, born say 1763, head of a Northampton County household of 1 free male and 2 free females in Captain William's District for the 1786 state census and 4 "other free" in 1790 [NC:73].

    v.   James, born 1776-1794, head of a Northampton County household of 6 "free colored" in 1820 [NC:234].

7.   Isham Hathcock, born say 1754, was taxable on 10 pounds valuation in District 4 of Halifax County, North Carolina, in 1782 [Tax List, 1:12] and taxable on 193 acres and one poll in 1790. He was head of a Halifax County household of 4 free males and 3 free females in the 1786 state census. He was a buyer at the sale of the estate of Jordan Stafford in Northampton County on

29 October 1787 [Gammon, *Record of Estates Northampton County*, I:56]. He was head of a Halifax County household of 5 "other free" and a white woman in 1790 [NC:61]. Perhaps his wife was Lucy Mason. She and Thomas Mason may have been co-heirs when Isham and his wife Lucy and Thomas Mason sold land on Dogwood Branch in Halifax County in September 1790 [DB 17:333]. He may have been the father of

    i.   Surry, born before 1776, head of a Halifax County household of 5 "other free" in 1800 [NC:318], 8 "other free" in 1810 [NC:24], and 2 "free colored" in 1830 [NC:293].

    ii. Curtis, head of a Halifax County household of 4 "other free" in 1800 [NC:316].

   iii. Jeffrey, born before 1776, head of a Halifax County household of 3 "other free" in 1810 [NC:24] and 6 "free colored" in 1820 [NC:151].

    iv. Rachel, head of a Halifax County household of 6 "other free" in 1810 [NC:26].

    v. Henry, head of a Halifax County household of 6 "other free" in 1810 [NC:26].

8.   Holiday Haithcock, born about 1760, may have been Edward Haithcock's son since he was ordered by the May 1782 Johnston County court to work on the road with him. According to his application for a Revolutionary War pension he was born about 1760 in Northampton County, Virginia, but this is probably an error and should read Northampton County, North Carolina. In November 1782 he was charged in the Johnston County court with begetting a bastard child [Haun, *Johnston County Court Minutes,* III:206, 230], and he was an insolvent Sampson County taxpayer in 1785 [Minutes 1784-1800, 39]. He was head of a Johnston County household of 6 "other free" in 1790 [NC:142] and 6 in Orange County in 1800 [NC:569]. He had returned to Johnston County on 23 February 1836 when he made his application for a pension for his Revolutionary War service. He gave an account of his service in his application before the court and stated that he volunteered in Johnston County, spent about a year in Fayetteville, and spent about twenty years in Orange County. His application was not approved, but several prominent Johnston County citizens did their best for him. William Bryan, a Justice of the Peace, testified for him and Thompson Venable wrote to the Commissioner of Pensions in Washington,

> *On examining the case of Holliday Hethcock of N.C. for pension under act of June 7, 1832, we find that his services and identity are fully proven by three witnesses, and that his case has been suspended merely because he was a free man of color. As we understand that several cases of this sort have been admitted, you will oblige us by having it admitted.*

He may have been the father of

    i.   Pattie, married Jesse **Archer**, 24 October 1807 Orange County bond, Holiday **Heathcock** bondsman.

    ii. M., head of an Orange County household of 6 "other free" in 1810 [NC:876].

   iii. Tattom, head of a Chatham County household of 3 "other free" in 1810 [NC:201].

9.   Dorcas Hathcock, born about 1770, was living in Southampton County on 17 March 1792 when the court ordered the churchwardens of St. Luke's Parish to bind out her illegitimate son John [Minutes 1793-9, 251]. She registered in Southampton County on 16 August 1810: *age 40, Mulatto, 5 feet 1 inch, free born* and registered there again on 13 June 1832: *age 60, Yellow, 5 feet 1/2 inch, free born* [Register of Free Negroes 1794-1832, nos. 836, 2003]. She was the mother of

i. John[4], born about 1788, head of a Northampton County household of 8 "free colored" in 1820 [NC:234]. He may have been identical to John Hathcock who registered as a "Free Negro" in Greensville County on 10 October 1814: *born free of a yellowish Complexion, about twenty six years old...5' 2-1/2 Inches high in Shoes* [Register of Free Negroes, no. 48]. And he may have been the husband of Jane Hathcock who received a bed and furniture by the 27 January 1816 Greensville County will of her father Francis **Stewart** [WB 3:41].

ii. ?Thomas[2], born about 1792, registered in Southampton County on 13 June 1832: *age 40, Bright, 5 feet 6-1/4 inches, free born* [Register of Free Negroes 1794-1832, no. 2002].

iii. ?Hezekiah, born about 1792, registered in Southampton County on 22 January 1823: *age 31, dark mulatto man, 5 feet 2-3/4 inches, free born* [Register of Free Negroes 1794-1832, no. 1353]. He registered in Sussex County on 2 November 1826 at the age of 35 [Certificates Granted to Free Negroes & Mulattoes 1800-50, no. 532].

iv. ?Bartlet, born about 1793, registered in Southampton County on 11 February 1822: *age 29, Mulatto of Brown complection, 5 feet 11-3/4 inches, free born* [Register of Free Negroes 1794-1832, no. 1310]. He was head of a Northampton County household of 2 "other free" in 1810 [NC:727].

v. Elijah, son of Dorcas Hethcocke, ordered bound out in St. Luke's Parish, Southampton County, on 23 November 1803 [Minutes 1803-4, unpaged].

10. Reuben Hathcock, born about 1772, married Miriam **Artis**, 10 February 1791 Southampton County bond. He registered in Southampton County on 31 July 1810: *age 38, Mulatto, 5 feet 5-1/2 inches, free born.* (His wife) Miriam Hathcock registered the same day: *age 40, Dark Mulatto, 5 feet 3-1/2 inches, free born* [Register of Free Negroes 1794-1832, no. 772, 773]. He was head of a Southampton County household of 9 "other free" in 1810 [VA:58]. He was taxable in Southampton County in Charles Birdsong's household in 1792, in James Edwards' household in 1794, in William Newton's household in 1795 and 1796, charged with his own tax from 1799 to 1803, a "Mulatto" taxable on a horse in 1804, taxable on 3 free male tithables in 1807, listed with his wife Mariam on Jacob Bailey's land in 1812 and 1813. Lemuel **Archer** was listed in his household in 1812 and Viney **Archer** was listed there in 1813 [PPTL 1782-92, frame 870; 1792-1806, frames 78, 198, 415, 556, 694; 1807-21, frames 73, 293, 319, 419]. Administration of his Northampton County estate was granted to Sterling Haithcock on a bond of 500 pounds on 6 September 1815. Later that year on 7 December, his widow Miriam successfully sued Sterling for one year's provisions [Minutes 1813-21]. Miriam was head of a Northampton County household of 5 "free colored" in 1820 [NC:234]. Their children were

12   i. Sterling, born about 1792.

ii. ?Mills, born about 1800, head of a Northampton County household of 3 "free colored" in 1820 [NC:234]. He and his wife sold land in Northampton County to Sterling Haithcock by deed proved on 1 December 1823 [Minutes 1821-25, 230]. He was counted in the Logan County, Ohio census in 1850 in District 87, Jefferson Township, household #283, a "Black" man born in Virginia about 1800, with Sarah Heathcock who was born in North Carolina about 1810. Their five children were all born in North Carolina.

11. Frederick[1] Haithcock, born say 1758, served in the Revolution from Halifax County, North Carolina [NSDAR, *African American Patriots*, 165]. He was head of a Northampton County household of 4 free males and 4 free females in Captain Winborn's District for the North Carolina state census in 1786

[Census p.29], head of a Halifax county household of 7 "other free" in 1790 [NC:61] and 5 "free colored" in 1820 [NC:151]. Perhaps he was the father of

    i.   Fed[2], born 1776-94, head of a Halifax County household of 4 "free colored" in 1830 [NC:349]. He was found guilty of a minor offense and ordered to receive twenty-five lashes by the Halifax County court on 21 February 1833. The 16 November 1841 Halifax County court allowed him to carry his gun.

12.   Sterling Haithcock, born about 1792, married Charlotte **Newsom**, 24 November 1813 Northampton County bond. He was head of a Northampton County household of 4 "free colored" in 1820 [NC:234]. He was surety for Drury **Walden**'s Northampton County bond as guardian to David **Byrd**, orphan of Jesse **Byrd**, on 6 June 1822, and he was fined five cents on a charge of assault and battery on 6 June 1822. He purchased land in Northampton County from Mills Haithcock and his wife by deed registered on 1 December 1823 [Minutes 1821-25, 105, 111, 230]. His wife Charlotte was mentioned in the 31 July 1835 Northampton County will of her father Nathaniel **Newsom** [WB 4:137]. Sterling obtained free papers in Northampton County on 23 March 1830 and registered them in Logan County, Ohio [Turpin, *Register of Black, Mulatto, and Poor Persons*, 12]. His papers stated that he was thirty-eight years old, the son of Reuben Heathcock, dark complexion, husband of Charlotte, and father of eight children: Edwin, Mary, Reuben, Starling, Nathaniel, Joshua, William, and Ethelred Haithcock. He was head of a Rush Creek, Logan County, Ohio household in 1850 with his wife Charlotte and (his mother) ninety-five-year-old Mariam Heathcock. He was born in Virginia and his estate was worth $3,500 [Census p.245].

Other members of the family in North Carolina were

    i.   Young, head of a Halifax County household of 2 free males and 3 females for the 1786 North Carolina census.

   ii. Ptolemy, born say 1763, head of a Halifax County household of 5 "other free" in 1790 [NC:61], an insolvent taxpayer in district 4, Halifax County in 1798 [Minutes 1799-1802, 25 August 1799], perhaps identical to Toliver Hathcock who was head of a Halifax County household of 8 "other free" in 1800 [NC:318].

  iii. Celah, head of a Halifax County household of 10 "other free" in 1800 [NC:318].

   iv. Absalom Heathcock, born before 1776, brought suit for his freedom against Robert Paulen in Halifax County court on 20 February 1801. The jury ruled that Absalom was not a slave but a free man. He was head of a Halifax County household of 5 "free colored" in 1830 [NC:530].

HALL FAMILY

1.   Elizabeth Hall, born say 1675, appeared in York County court on 25 June 1694 and confessed to having an illegitimate child. Samuel Snignall and Richard Nickson were security for the payment of her fine. She was Richard Nickson's servant on 26 August 1695 when she confessed to the York County court that she had borne a child by a "Negroe" [DOW 10:9, 195]. She was probably the mother of

2   i.   William[1], born say 1694.

3   ii. Jane, born say 1695.

   iii. Margaret[1], born say 1706, presented by the Elizabeth City County court on 20 January 1726/7 for having a "Mulato Bastard" child. She did not deny the fact and was ordered to pay a fine of 15 pounds or serve for five years after the completion of her former servitude. She was presented again for a "Mulatto Bastard" on 16 November 1727 [Orders 1724-30, 191, 200, 211, 220].

2. William[1] Hall, born say 1694, a "negro," ran away from Christ Church Parish, Lancaster County, between 8 May and 12 June 1728 when the court charged him with "keeping a white woman and having children by her" [Orders 1721-29, 270, 278]. He was probably the William Hall who was living in Louisa County on 28 May 1745 when he, Thomas **Collins**, Samuel **Collins**, William **Collins**, George **Gibson**, Thomas **Gibson**, William **Donathan**, Benjamin **Branham**, and Samuel **Bunch** were presented by the court for failing to list a tithable (probably their wives) [Orders 1742-8, 152, 157, 172]. He may have been the father of

4   i.   Joseph[1], born say 1710.

3. Jane Hall, born say 1695, was a "negro" living in Christ Church Parish, Lancaster County, on 8 May 1728 when the grand jury presented her for having an illegitimate child. She was called a "free negro Woman" on 11 June 1729 when the court bound her daughter Ann as an apprentice to Ruth Sydnor in Lancaster County until the age of eighteen years at her daughter's request. On 14 October 1730 she complained to the Lancaster County court that her son Caleb was illegally bound to his master, Andrew Donalson. The court agreed that the indenture was illegal but ordered Caleb to serve Donalson until the age of twenty-one years in consideration of his taking care of him since his birth. The court ordered Donalson to teach him to read and pay him freedom dues at the end of his indenture [Orders 1721-9, 270, 278, 326; 1729-43, 21]. Her children were

    i.   Caleb, born say 1718, an apprentice of Andrew Donalson of Lancaster County in 1730.
    ii.   ?Abraham, born say 1720, sued in Westmoreland County, Virginia court on 28 February 1743/4. He appeared in Westmoreland County court a number of times as plaintiff and defendant between 1744 and 1750. He was identified as a "free Molatto" on 24 February 1747/8 in his suit against John Crabb for which he was awarded 15 pounds damages by a jury and on 30 November 1749 when he sued William Cox [Orders 1743-7, 14a, 23a, 66a, 67; 1747-50, 57, 95a, 113a, 133, 174a, 198; 1750-2, 8a].
    iii.   Ann, born 16 July 1722.

4. Joseph[1] Hall, born say 1710, was taxable with his wife Peg in Norfolk County, Virginia, in 1735 and taxable by himself in William Sivels' household in 1736 [Wingo, *Norfolk County Tithables 1730-50*, 157, 169]. His wife may have been identical to the Margaret Hall who was presented by the Elizabeth City County, Virginia court on 20 July 1727 for having a "Mulatto Bastard" child, "She appearing and not denying the fact" [DWO 1724-30, 211]. Joseph and his wife were in Bertie County, North Carolina, by 6 August 1748 when "Joseph Hall yeoman" purchased 200 acres at Chinkapin Neck on Wiccacon Creek. He sold this land six years later on 7 December 1754 [DB G:194; H:175]. Joseph, Mary, and Thomas Hall were "free mulato" taxables in the 1751 Bertie County summary tax list filed with the central government [CCR 190]. In 1757 he, his wife Margaret, and 3 children were taxables in the Bertie County list of Henry Hunter along with Gabriel **Manly**, who had been a neighbor of theirs in Norfolk County in 1735 [Wingo, *Norfolk County Tithables 1730-50*, 158]. In 1758 Joseph and his family were taxables in the list of John Brickell along with Thomas **Archer** who had also been one of their Norfolk County neighbors in 1735 [CR 10.702.1, box 1]. The family was not taxed in Bertie County after 1759 when Hertford County was separated from Bertie County. Joseph died before 22 January 1760 when his wife "Margaret Hall, Widow of Joseph Hall Deced.,....resigned her right of Admn. of Joseph

Hall" in Bertie County court [Haun, *Bertie County Court Minutes*, II:503-4].
Their children were

5   i.   Thomas, born say 1738.

ii.   ?Ebenezer, born say 1740, purchased two tracts of land from John and
Elizabeth **Bass** near the head of Deep Creek in the Southern Branch of
the Elizabeth River in the Parish of Portsmouth in Norfolk County, one
of 90 acres on 19 October 1763 and another of 50 acres on 14 May
1764. He sold the 90 acre tract on 18 March 1765 [DB 21:200A, 86B;
22:78 A&B]. He was taxable on himself and (his wife?) Mary Hall,
"Muls" (Mulattos), and 50 acres of land in Western Branch District of
Norfolk County from 1766 to 1769, with Joseph **Bass** in his household
in 1770, and taxable by himself from 1771 to 1780, called a "Mulatto"
in 1774 [Wingo, *Norfolk County Tithables, 1766-80*, 8, 45, 76, 87,
105, 149, 228, 267, 285].

iii.   Stephen, born before 1746, taxable in 1757 in his father's Bertie
County household in the list of Henry Hunter and taxable in Hertford
County on two persons from 1768 to 1770 [Fouts, *Tax Receipt Book*,
55]. He may have been the Stephen Hall was taxable in Norfolk
County in 1785 [PPTL, 1782-90, frame 485].

iv.   ?Absalom, taxable on one person in Hertford County from 1768 to
1770 [Fouts, *Tax Receipt Book*, 9].

v.   Naomi, born before 1746, taxable in 1757 in her father's Bertie County
household in Henry Hunter's list, perhaps the Amy Hall who was
taxable there in 1758. She may have been the Naomy **Bass** who was
taxable in Norfolk County in 1765 with her husband William[4] **Bass**
[Wingo, *Norfolk County Tithables, 1751-65*, 205].

vi.   ?Jemima, born say 1750, taxable on the south side of Western Branch
in Norfolk County in 1769 in the same district as Ebenezer Hall
[Wingo, *Norfolk County Tithables, 1751-65*, 87].

vii.   ?Isaac, probably born after 1746 since he was not taxable in Bertie
County in 1758. He was taxable in Hertford County on one person in
1769 [Fouts, *Tax Receipt Book*, 39], was head of a Hertford County
household of 5 "other free" in 1800, and he was over 45 and had 7
"free colored" in his Hertford County household in 1820 [NC:190].
Isaac, Allen, and Harvey Washington Hall were among "Sundry
persons of Colour of Hertford County" who petitioned the General
Assembly in November- December 1822 to repeal the act which
declared slaves to be competent witnesses against free African
Americans [*NCGSJ* XI:252].

viii.   ?Mary, head of a Hertford County household of 6 "other free" in 1790
[NC:27], 12 In 1810 [NC:106], and in 1820 as Polly Hall, an over
forty-five-year-old head of a household of 3 "free colored" [NC:186].

5.   Thomas Hall, born say 1738, was a taxable "free mulato" in his father's Bertie
County household from 1751 to 1757 but not in 1758. He was probably the
Thomas Hall who indentured himself to James Wood of Norfolk County for
four years (until the age of twenty-one years?) to learn the trade of bricklayer
on 20 May 1757 [DB 18:40]. He was taxable in Norfolk County on 53 acres
of land in 1763, taxable in Hertford County on two persons in 1770 [Fouts,
Tax Receipt Book, 58], and was taxable in Norfolk County on the north side
of the Western Branch District in 1773 [Wingo, *Norfolk County Tithables
1751-65*, 190; 1766-80, 197]. He was taxable on 2 horses in District 3 of
Hertford County in 1779 [GA 30.1] and head of a Hertford County household
of 7 "other free" in Captain Louis' District in 1800. Perhaps his wife was

Rachel Hall, the daughter of Richard **Nickens** who mentioned her in his 1774 Currituck County will.[111] Their children may have been

6   i.   Joseph², born say 1764.

7   ii.   Lemuel, born say 1768.

     iii.   Margaret², born about 1770, head of a Hertford County household of 12 "free colored" in 1820 [NC:190], an eighty-year-old "Mulatto" woman counted in the 1850 Hertford County census [NC:651].

     iv.   David, head of a Camden County household of 2 "other free" and one white woman in 1790 [NC:16].

     v.   Anthony, a "free colored" man over forty-five years of age who was living alone in New Hanover County in 1820 [NC:222].

6.   Joseph² Hall, born say 1764, married Elizabeth **Bass**, 7 May 1792 Norfolk County bond. He was taxable in Norfolk County from 1784 to 1817: not listed there in 1800; a planter in a "List of Free Negroes and Mulattoes" on Deep Creek with George Hall, Betsy, Sally and Mary Hall in his household in 1801; called a "M"(ulatto) in 1802 and 1804; a "B.M." (Black Man) taxable on Western Branch in 1815 [PPTL, 1782-1791, frames 485, 626; 1791-1812, frames 106, 251, 383, 484, 743; 1813-24, frame 105]. He was head of a Hertford County household of 1 "other free" in 1800 and a Norfolk County household of 9 "other free" in 1810 [VA:815]. Joseph and Elizabeth were probably the parents of

     i.   Sally, listed in Joseph Hall's household in 1801.

     ii.   George, a "B.M." (Black Man) taxable in Norfolk County from 1815 to 1817 [PPTL, 1813-24, frames 105, 139, 256].

     iii.   Mary, listed in Joseph Hall's household in 1801.

     iv.   Priscilla, a "free woman of colour," married James **Ash**, a free man of colour, 31 December 1814 Norfolk County bond, Nathan Mathews security.

7.   Lemuel Hall, born say 1768, was head of a Pasquotank County household of 9 "other free" in 1810 [NC:902]. He was called "a free man of mixed blood" in 1795 when the North Carolina General Assembly passed an act to allow him to free his wife, a slave named Jenny, and their three children: Seth, Milley and Tabitha [Byrd, *In Full Force and Virtue*, 297]. His heirs sold 29-8/10 acres in Pasquotank County on Great Flatty Creek adjoining Lemuel **Overton** for $268 on 3 July 1822. The land adjoined one acre which Phillis, (a slave?) who belonged to the estate, was allowed to live on [DB W:273]. Lemuel's heirs were

     i.   Milley, married Burdock **Overton**.

     ii.   Rhody, married Robert **Bow**.

     iii.   Ephraim, who was underage on 3 July 1822.

     iv.   Mary, who was underage on 3 July 1822.

     v.   Rachel, who was underage on 3 July 1822.

Other Hall families in Virginia were

     i.   Sally, head of a Petersburg Town household of 5 "other free" in 1810 [VA:125a].

     ii.   Reuben, "f. negro" head of a Fairfax County household of 2 "other free" in 1810 [VA:268].

     iii.   Rapple, "f. negro" head of a Fairfax County household of 2 "other free" in 1810 [VA:261].

---

[111]The **Nickens** family were also from Lancaster County.

HAMILTON FAMILY

1. Isabell Hambleton, born say 1718, was living at Colonel George Dent's when the Charles County, Maryland court presented her for bearing a "Molatto" child by information of George Thomas, the constable for William and Mary Parish [Court Record 1734-9, 263]. She may have been the ancestor of
    i.   Charles, head of a Hampshire County, Virginia household of 4 "other free" in 1810 [VA:805].
    ii. Dido, head of a Hampshire County household of 5 "other free" in 1810 [VA:793].

Norfolk County
1. Elizabeth Hamilton, born say 1745, was living in Norfolk County on 16 November 1758 when the court ordered the churchwardens of Elizabeth River Parish to bind her illegitimate "Molatto" daughter Lydia Hamilton to George Chamberlain [Orders 1755-9, 209]. She was the mother of
    i.   Lydia, born say 1758, ordered bound apprentice to George Chamberlain on 16 November 1758 and ordered bound to Philip Carbery on 15 September 1768 [Orders 1768-71, 18].

HAMLIN FAMILY

1. William Hamlin, born say 1728, and his wife Lucy were living in Henrico County on 1 November 1756 when the court ordered the churchwardens to bind out their "Mulatto" son Arthur [Minutes 1752-5, 52]. They were the parents of
    i.   Arthur, born say 1750.
    ii. ?Joseph, born before 1776, head of a Charles City County household of 3 "other free" in 1810 [VA:957].

HAMMOND FAMILY

1. Margaret[1] Hammond, born about 1667, was a twenty-two-year-old white servant living in Northampton County, Virginia, on 28 March 1689 when she was deposed in a suit brought against her master John Baron [OW 1683-1689, 422-3]. She was called "Margaret late servant to Mr. John Barons" on 28 May 1690 when she was presented by the court for having an illegitimate child. The same court ordered that she receive thirty-nine lashes for uttering scandalous words against Colonel John Custis and Mr. Thomas Harmonson by information of Joane, the wife of John Brewer [OW&c 1689-98, 35, 45, 53]. She was a servant living in the home of Captain William Kendall on 29 September 1692 when he reported to the churchwardens that she bore a "maletto bastard" child in his house. She was apparently the first white woman in Northampton County charged with having a mixed-race child since the churchwardens asked the court for its opinion about the "late law the year 1691." The court ordered the churchwardens to dispose of her (sell her for five years) [OW&c 1698-1710, 190-1]. She and her "Mulatto" child Elizabeth were bound to Captain Robins in Northampton County court, and this indenture was transferred to Drummond Hill of Accomack County [Accomack County Orders 1724-31, 30]. Margaret was the mother of
    2   i.   Elizabeth[1], born about 1694.

2. Elizabeth[1] Hammon, born about 1694, was called "Betty a mulatto" on 6 July 1714 when her master, Hill Drummond, complained to the Accomack County court that she had run away and been absent from his service for sixty-two days. She was presented by the churchwardens of Accomack County for having a bastard child on 2 May 1721 and testified on 6 June 1721 that the child was "begott...by one Negro Slave named Robin belonging to Hill

Drummond." She was presented for having other children on 6 April 1725, 7 November 1727, 7 May 1728, 8 August 1729, and on 22 December 1731 [Orders 1714-7, 10; 1719-24, 30, 32; 1724-31, 26, 88a, 102, 107; 1731-36, 10, 29, 38]. On 4 February 1724/5 she petitioned the Accomack County court for her freedom from her indenture to Drummond Hill, but the court ruled on 2 June 1725 that

Whereas Elizabeth Hammon a Mullatto woman late Servant to Mr. Hill Drummond petitioned in February Court for her discharge...Elizabeth was duly bound with her mother, She being an Infant, a Servant for thirty one years by the Churchwardens of Hungar Parish in Northampton County Court...Mr. Hill Drummond produced to this Court Several Accts for Running Away and fines...for which she was to Serve for as ye Law in Such Cases Directs. Said Elizabeth hath not fully completed with All.

Elizabeth continued to enter petitions against Hill on 7 December 1726 and 8 March 1726/7 and against Drummond Hill's administrator, George Douglas, on 8 January 1728/9. Finally, on 2 July 1729 she reached agreement with Douglas that she released him from all claims she had against Drummond's estate (her freedom dues?) and on account of her mother Margaret Hammond, deceased, in exchange for her own release. At least one of her children was probably by a white man since on 5 August 1729 Rev. Mr. William Black appeared in Accomack County court and made oath that he was not "concerned with a Certain Mullatoe Woman name Elizabeth Hammond" as he had been "scandalously aspersed." On 7 March 1737/8 a petition by her (or a daughter by the same name) against Thomas Watson was dismissed, and on 2 August 1738 Watson entered a petition against her, a "Mulatto his Servant," in court for running away. Later that year he added himself and Elizabeth to the list of tithables for the county. On 30 November 1742 she was accused of stealing a hog; on 29 November 1744 her complaint against Comfort Jenkinson was dismissed, and her complaint against William Arbuckle dismissed on 30 May 1745 [Orders 1724-31, 20, 31, 68, 131a, 163, 164; 1737-44, 6, 91, 100, 435; 1744-53, 15, 57]. Elizabeth was a "fr. mulato" who was taxable in Bertie County, North Carolina, in 1751 [CCR 190] but not mentioned again in Bertie County records. Her children were

3   i.   ?Ann, born say 1720.

     ii.   James, born say 1721, "Mulatto Bastard Child" of Elizabeth Hammon, bound to Henry Bazwell to the age of thirty-one on 8 December 1725 in Accomack County [Orders 1724-31, 42].

     iii.   ?Robert, born say 1725, purchased 50 acres on the west side of Bridger's Creek in Northampton County, North Carolina, on 1 December 1750 [DB 1:454]. His Northampton County estate was administered by Elijah Boddie on 100 pounds in November 1760 (Robert Himmons) [*NCGSJ* XIV:154].

     iv.   ?John[1], born about 1728, a five-year-old bound as an apprentice shoemaker to David Sparrow in Accomack County court on 6 June 1732 (no parent named) [Orders 1731-36, 29].

4   v.   ?Jemima, born say 1730.

5   vi.   Isaac[1], born say 1732.

     vii.   ?Drummond, born about 1734, probably named for Drummond Hill, his mother's master, twenty-four years old when his two-year apprenticeship agreement with Alexander Brodie was proved in the 15 March 1758 Edgecombe County, North Carolina court (no race stated) [Minutes 1757-59, 19].

6   viii.   ?Margaret[2]/ Peggy, born about March 1735.

7   ix.   ?Mary, born say 1737.

x. ?Josiah, born about December 1739, "Orphan aged 4 years next Christmas," bound to Caleb Broadwest in Accomack County on 28 December 1742 [Orders 1737-44, 449].

3. Ann Hammond, born say 1720, acknowledged in Bertie County court in February 1739 that she had two bastard children, race not mentioned, while indentured to John Pratt, the keeper of the ferry across the Roanoke River at Gideon **Gibson**'s landing [Haun, *Bertie County Court Minutes*, I:52, 265]. She may have been the same Ann Hammon who was reported to have delivered a bastard child during her service to Mary Wilson, widow, of Chowan County in July 1737 [Chowan Minutes 1735-48, 73]. She was the mother of

    i. ?Catherine, born say 1739, the "free Mulatto" wife of James **McDaniel** [CCR 190]. See the **McDaniel** history.

8   ii. ?Horatio, born say 1744.

    iii. ?Richard, born say 1745, a taxable "Molato" in Bladen County, North Carolina, from 1769 to 1776, head of a household of one white male and seven white females in 1786 [Byrd, *Bladen County Tax Lists*, I:16, 33, 89, 109; II:66, 81, 183].

9   iv. ?John², born say 1747.

    v. Sarah, born about 1750, the seven-year-old daughter of Nann Hammond, a "Free Mullatoe," bound to Cornelius Campbell of Bertie County on 29 July 1757 [*NCGSJ* XIII:168]. In 1767 she was in Christopher Clark's household in the list of William Nichols. She may have been the Sally Hammond who was head of a Lenoir County household of 12 "other free" in 1800 [NC:12].

    vi. Elizabeth², born about 1753, ten years old on 23 February 1763, "Daughter of Ann Hammond," bound to Thomas Ashburn in Bertie County [*NCGSJ* XIV:30]. In 1768 she was a "Free Mullato" Bertie County taxable in Thomas Mason's household in the list of Edward Rasor [CR 10.702.1].

4. Jemima Hammons (Ammons), born say 1730, was living in Accomack County on 27 November 1750 when the court ordered her daughter Sarah bound out. She was the mother of

    i. Sarah Ammons, born about 1747, three-year-old orphan of Jemima Ammons, bound to Peter Watson on 27 November 1750 [Orders 1744-53, 450], perhaps the same Sarah Hammond who was an orphan bound to Robert Baley on 26 August 1755 [Orders 1753-63, 105].

    ii. ?Anthony, born say 1755, head of a Halifax County, North Carolina household of 7 "other free" in 1790 [NC:66]. He married Isaac Hammond's widow, Dicey, in 1827 and died the same year according to Dicey's application for Isaac's pension.

5. Isaac¹ Hammond, born say 1732, was married to Margaret **Akin**, "free Negroes," between 21 September 1755 and 22 June 1764 when their children were baptized at St. Thomas and St. Dennis Parish, South Carolina [Parochial Register of the Parishes of St. Thomas & St. Denis, n.p. (alphabetical listing under H)]. Margaret **Akin** was probably related to Carter **Akins**, head of a Charleston County, South Carolina household of 7 "other free" in 1800 [SC:36]. Isaac and Margaret were the "free Negro" parents of

10   i. Isaac², baptized 21 September 1755.

    ii. Joseph, baptized 15 November 1761.

    iii. Abraham, baptized 22 June 1764.

6. Margaret²/ Peggy Hammons, born about March 1735, was "8 years old next March" when she was bound apprentice to Peter Delastations on 28 December 1742 in Accomack County court [Orders 1737-44, 449]. On 29 July 1754 she

was found guilty by the Accomack County court of having an unnamed bastard child [Orders 1753-63, 16]. She may have been the mother of

    i.   Mary **Hammond**, head of an Octararo, Cecil County, Maryland, household of 9 "other free" in 1790.

    ii. Elizabeth, born say 1767, ordered bound out to Samuel Matthews in Accomack County court on 29 August 1769 [Orders 1769-70, 219].

7.   Mary **Hammons**, born say 1737, was living in Edgecombe County in 1779 when the 25 May session of the Court of Pleas & Quarter Sessions ordered her "base begotten child" Jordan Hammons bound to Willis Hyatt (no race stated) [Minutes 1772-84, 2nd page of May Minutes]. Her children were

11   i.   ?Shadrack, born say 1757.

    ii. Jordan, born say 1767, no age or race stated when he was ordered bound out by the May 1779 Session of the Edgecombe County court. He was head of an Edgecombe County household of 4 "other free" in 1790 [NC:57], 4 in Chatham County in 1800, and 6 "free colored" in Chatham in 1820 [NC:211].

    iii. ?Frederick, born circa 1778, "Mullatto," ordered bound to Dempsey Odam by the Edgecombe County court on 24 July 1787, no parent named. He was removed from Odam's care and ordered bound to James Coker by the 28 May 1793 Edgecombe County court. He married Nancy **Pettiford**, 19 May 1802 Granville County bond with George **Anderson** bondsman. He may also have been the Frederick Hammond who married Polly **Stewart**, 14 August 1807 Mecklenburg County, Virginia bond, Frederick Dyson security.

8.   Horatio **Hammond**, born say 1744, purchased 100 acres in Bladen County on the east side of Drowning Creek on Jacobs Swamp on 7 November 1784 (called Rhesa Hammons) [DB 1:262]. He and his wife Patience sold 100 acres on Saddletree Swamp in Robeson County to John Hammons on 6 May 1789 [DB B:142]. His wife was probably the daughter of David **Braveboy** who named his daughter Patience Hammons in his 20 October 1787 Robeson County will [WB 1:10]. He made a deed of gift to (his son?) James Hammond proved in Cumberland County on 9 October 1792 [Minutes 1791-97; the deed has not survived] and made a quit claim deed for 100 acres on the east side of Jacob Swamp by deed recorded in Robeson in 1793 [DB C:149]. He was living in Robeson County on 12 January 1797 when the Cumberland County court issued an execution against him for twelve pounds [Minutes 1791-7]. He was called Ratia Hammond in 1790, head of a white Cumberland County household of 2 males over 16, 1 under 16, and 4 females [NC:39] and was head of a Robeson County household of 6 "other free" in 1800 [NC:384]. He sold 100 acres in Robeson County on the north side of Jacob Swamp to Cannon **Cumbo** on 17 May 1804 and sold 100 acres on the south side of Drowning Creek by deed recorded in 1808 [DB N:216; P:25]. John **Braveboy**, a five-year-old "boy of colour," was ordered bound as an apprentice to him by the 5 October 1802 Robeson County court [Minutes I:219]. His children were

    i.   James, born say 1771, received land in Cumberland County by deed of gift from his father in 1792.

    ii. ?Willis, born say 1773, entered 100 acres east of Drowning Creek in Robeson County on 18 January 1794 [Pruitt, *Land Grants: Robeson County*, no. 1460] and received a grant for this land [DB H:17]. He purchased 80 acres in Robeson west of the Great Swamp in 1811 and sold 100 acres on the west side of the Great Swamp in 1828 [DB P:330; U:168]. He was head of a Robeson County household in 1810 [NC:220]. He died before March term 1837 when James Hammond proved his handwriting on a deed in Robeson County court [Minutes 1829-39].

12   iii. ?Elsey, born before 1776.

13   iv.   ?Ephraim, born say 1776.

9.   John² Hammond, born say 1747, was a "free molato" taxable in the 1763
Bertie County list of John Nichols [CR 010.702.1, box 2]. He purchased 100
acres on the north side of Saddle Tree Swamp in Bladen County on 26
February 1768 [DB 23:137] and received a patent for 100 acres northeast of
Drowning Creek on Saddle Tree Swamp on 22 December the same year
[Hoffman, *Land Patents*, II:526]. He was a "Molato" taxable in Bladen County
from 1770 to 1776, taxable on his wife in 1772 [Byrd, *Bladen County Tax
Lists*, I:45, 70, 80, 124, 135; II:65, 81]. He purchased 100 acres on
Saddletree Swamp on 29 October 1774 [DB 23:465], and on 22 January 1793
he entered another 100 acres adjoining this land in what was then Robeson
County [Pruitt, *Land Entries: Robeson County*, I:70]. He sold 100 acres of this
land on the west side of the swamp to his son Samuel Hammons on 14
November 1800; made a deed of gift of 100 acres on the east side of the
swamp to his grandson Lewis Hammons, son of John, Jr., on 2 October 1804,
another 25 acres to Samuel Hammons on 21 December 1805, and 50 acres to
his son Elisha Hammons, by a deed recorded in 1811 [DB K:88; N:240;
O:254; Q:85]. The 1 January 1798 Robeson County court ordered James
Whitley, a white boy about seventeen years old, bound apprentice to him
[Minutes I:21]. He was head of a Robeson County household of 9 "other free"
in 1790 [NC:48], 4 in 1800 [NC:384], and 7 in 1810 [NC:220 & 241]. His 1
March 1811 will was proved in Robeson County on 25 November 1811
[Minutes II:287]. He named his wife Christian, his children: Enoch, Elijah,
Harvey, Arenith Jackson (wife of Thomas Jackson), Samuel, Jacob, John,
Christian, Norfleet, Elias, Stradford, and Helen; and his grandchildren:
William Hammond (Harvey's son) and Cornelius Jackson (Arenith's son) [WB
1:125]. His first wife was probably the daughter of Elias Stradford since
Stradford's 6 August 1800 Robeson County nuncupative will left John
Hammon, Sr., his crop and left all the remainder of his estate to sons of John
Hammon: Jacob, Samuel, Enoch, John, and Harvey. Ann Hammon and Dicy
Hammon (John³ Hammon's wife) were witnesses to the will [WB 1:60]. John
Hammond's second wife was Christian Norfleet according to a letter dated
about 1900. His children mentioned in his will were

14   i.   Jacob, born say 1767.
15   ii.   Samuel¹, born say 1770.
    iii.   Enoch, sold 100 acres on the east side of Poplar Pole Branch in
Robeson County to Samuel Hammons on 1 July 1797 [DB G:140]. He
was counted as white in 1800, head of a Robeson County household of
3 males [NC:384], called Enoch Eammins in 1810, head of a Robeson
County household of 2 "other free" [NC:233].
    iv.   Elijah, who received 100 acres on the west side of Saddle Tree Swamp
which he was then in possession of by his father's will. He was head
of a Robeson County household of 3 "other free" in 1810 [NC:241].
He sold 250 acres on the west side of Drowning Creek in 1795. He
purchased 50 acres from John Hammond, Senior, on 21 December
1805 and sold this land by a deed recorded in 1814. He sold 75 acres
on Mussels Branch by deed recorded in 1816, and sold two tracts, one
for 75 acres and one for 30 acres, on Saddletree Swamp by deeds
recorded in 1826 [DB E:244; Q:85, 415; R:195; T:478, 479].
    v.   Harvey, who received 150 acres which he had in his possession, to
pass to his son William at his death. He was head of a Robeson County
household of 5 in 1800 [NC:384]. He sold 30 acres on the west side of
Saddletree Swamp to Elijah Hammons on 12 March 1813 [DB R:24].
    vi.   Arenith, who married Thomas Jackson. Their son Cornelius Jackson
received 50 acres on the Poplar Pole Branch including Lovec **Bunche**'s
old field by the will of her grandfather John² Hammond.
16   vii.   John⁴, born 1776-94.

    viii. Norfleet.
     ix. Elias[1].
      x. Stradford.
     xi. Helen.

10. Isaac[2] Hammond, baptized 21 September 1755, "a man of color," was a fifer in the 10th North Carolina Regiment for twelve months. He married Dicey _____ in Fayetteville in 1787 [M805, reel 393, S.8654]. He was found guilty of assault and battery on Lucretia **Bass** by the 16 March 1809 Cumberland County court and ordered to post bond of 50 pounds to keep the peace with her for twelve months [Minutes 1808-10]. He died in 1822. Dicey, born about 1772, remarried in 1827 to Anthony Hammonds who died that same year [M805, reel 393]. She sold a lot on the south edge of Franklin Street in Fayetteville on 15 May 1841 [DB 44:189]. She filed a pension application in September 1849 which stated that Isaac was the son of a barber, both his parents being "Mulattoes or Mustees having no African blood in them" [Crow, *Black Experience in Revolutionary North Carolina*, 66]. He was head of a Fayetteville, Cumberland County, household of 5 "other free" in 1790 [NC:42]. Dicey's 3 October 1852 Cumberland County will was proved December the same year. She named only her daughter Rachel **Lomack**, wife of Enoch **Lomack** [WB C:229]. Their children were

      i. ?John[3], head of a Cumberland County household of 5 "other free" in 1800.
     ii. ?Jerusha, head of a Cumberland County household of 4 "other free" in 1800.
    iii. ?Jane, head of a Cumberland County household of 3 "other free" in 1800.
     iv. ?Theophilus, head of a Cumberland County household of 8 "free colored" in 1820 [NC:141]. He married Delila **Pettiford**, 25 February 1811 Wake County bond, Absalom **Locust** bondsman.
      v. ?Isaac[3], head of a Cumberland County household of 5 "free colored" in 1820 [NC:191].
     vi. ?Albert, born say 1790, sold a lot in Fayetteville by deed recorded in 1834 [DB 41:17], took the oath of an insolvent debtor in the 5 September 1842 Cumberland County court and was allowed to keep a shotgun by the 5 June 1843 court [Minutes, 1835-44].
    vii. Rachel **Lomack**, born about 1794, married Enoch **Lomack**, 17 June 1813 Cumberland County bond. Enoch was the son of William **Lomack**, another Revolutionary War veteran who was head of a Robeson County household of 10 "other free" in 1810 [*NCGSJ* XIV:45; NC:240]. She applied for her father's pension on 22 July 1854 stating that she was the only living child of Isaac and Dicey [M805, reel 393, frame 0499]. Her children were probably the "free children of colour" bound out by the Cumberland County court: Albert **Lomack** (born about 1827, bound out on 8 March 1844), George **Lomack** (born about 1827, bound out on 5 June 1843), and Hybart **Lomack** (bound out on 8 March 1844) [Minutes 1835-44].

11. Shadrack Hammond, born say 1757, was "a free Mulatto boy" ordered bound to William Speir by the September 1760 Edgecombe County court (no parent named) [Minutes 1759-64, 6]. He was head of an Edgecombe County household of 8 "other free" in 1790 [NC:57], 9 "other free" and 1 white woman in 1800 [NC:209], 8 "other free" in 1810 [NC:748], and 6 "free colored" in 1820 [NC:126]. His children may have been
17   i. Burrell, born about 1775.
     ii. Willis[2], born 1776-94, head of an Edgecombe County household of 3 "other free" in 1810 [NC:748] and 6 "free colored" in 1820 [NC:126].

iii. Elijah, head of an Edgecombe County household of 5 "other free" in 1810 [NC:748].

iv. James, head of an Edgecombe County household of 3 "other free" in 1810 [NC:748] and 5 "free colored" in 1820 [NC:148].

v. Oliff, head of an Edgecombe County household of 6 "other free" in 1810 [NC:746].

vi. Levy, born 1776-94, perhaps the Levi Hammonds who married Lydia **Bass**, 3 November 1813 Cumberland County bond, Leven Jones bondsman. He was head of an Edgecombe County household of 2 "free colored" in 1820 [NC:111].

12. Elsey Hammons, born before 1776, was head of a Cumberland County household of 7 "free colored" in 1820 [NC:214]. She was called Alsey Hammons on 7 December 1818 when she and John **Sampson** sold a lot in Fayetteville on the south edge of Mumford Street, 230 feet from Winslow Street, for $750 [DB 31:48]. She was probably the Eliza Hammons whose 13 February 1838 Cumberland County will, proved date not mentioned, left her lot on Mumford and Winslow Streets to her children, cautioning that it was not to be sold for her husband's debts [WB B:290]. Her children named in the will were

i. Martha, who received half her mother's lot in Fayetteville. Her son George was mentioned in Eliza's will.

ii. Henry, who was to receive the lot in Fayetteville after Martha's death.

iii. James **Sampson**, who received half the lot in Fayetteville.

13. Ephraim Hammons, born say 1776, may have been the son of Horatio Hammons since they were both barbers. He was bound an apprentice in Cumberland County to Dr. John Sibly and then bound to James Howat for the remaining part of his indenture on 14 April 1796 [Minutes 1791-7]. On Saturday, 14 March 1807, the Cumberland County court ordered James **Patterson**, a fourteen-year-old "Boy of Colour," bound as an apprentice to him, and the 8 September 1810 Cumberland County court bound William **Scott**, a five-year-old "boy of Colour" to him [Minutes 1805-08; 1808-10]. He was head of a Cumberland County household of 2 "other free" in 1800, 4 "other free" in 1810 (E. Hammons) [NC:622], and 6 "free colored" and 5 slaves in 1820 (Ephraim Hammons) [NC:191]. He purchased land by deed proved in Cumberland County court on 9 March 1810 [Minutes 1808-10]. He married Rebecca **Bell**, 26 February 1812 Cumberland County bond with Thomas **Sampson** bondsman. He was bondsman for the 12 November 1818 Cumberland County marriage of Harry **Mitchell** and Betsy **Jones**.[112] Ephraim was called a barber when he purchased a lot in Fayetteville on Cold Spring Street on 3 November 1819 and an additional two lots in Fayetteville by deeds proved in Cumberland County in 1819. The lot on Cold Spring Street was sold by the sheriff for debt by a deed recorded in 1823. On 13 September 1832 he sold 100 acres in Cumberland County on the west side of Black River Swamp [DB 31:521; 32:142-3; 35:56; 40:453]. The 8 June 1837 Cumberland County court bound Elsey **Parker**, a "free girl of colour," to him [Minutes 1836-38]. Perhaps one of his children was

i. Lydia, married Timothy **Bass**, 28 May Cumberland County bond.

14. Jacob Hammon, born say 1767, entered 100 acres in Robeson County on the southwest side of Saddle Tree Swamp on 21 February 1788 [Pruitt, *Land Entries: Robeson County*, I:14] and sold this land to Samuel Hammons on 8 September 1800. The sheriff sold another 49-1/2 acres of his land on Ten Mile

---

[112]Harry **Mitchell**, born before 1776, was head of a Cumberland County household of 5 "free colored" in 1820 [NC:152].

Swamp for debt in 1802 [DB K:46; L:194]. He was head of a Robeson County household of 4 "other free" in 1790 [NC:48] and 3 in Anson County in 1800 [NC:198]. He was absent from Robeson County on 5 October 1802 when the court ruled that the indenture of his daughter Phereby was illegal and that she should be returned to her mother [Minutes I:216]. His children were

    i.   Pheraby, born about 1790, twelve years old when the Robeson County court ordered her bound to Reuben Rozar on 6 July 1802 [Minutes I:207].

    ii. ?Sarah, head of a Robeson County household of 1 in 1800 [NC:384].

15. Samuel[1] Hammond, born say 1770, entered 100 acres in Robeson County on the east side of Saddletree Swamp bordering his father's land on 21 February 1788 [Pruitt, *Land Entries: Robeson County*, I:14]. He deeded 1 acre of land and "Hammons' Meeting house," to be used "to hold Divine Worship," to the trustees of the Methodist Episcopal Church for 10 shillings on 3 October 1792. He purchased 100 acres on the east side of Poplar Pole Branch on 1 July 1797 from Enoch Hammons and sold this land to Nathaniel **Revell** on 4 May 1801. He purchased 100 acres on Saddletree Swamp from his brother Jacob on 8 September 1800 and 100 acres from his father on 21 December 180_ [DB C:160; K:46; M:355; O:254]. He was head of a Robeson County household of 10 "other free" in 1810 [NC:241]. His 28 June 1812 Robeson County will, proved February 1815, named his wife Deborah; his daughters Anna, Dorcas, Delilah, Mary, and Rebecca; and left 225 acres to his three sons: Elias, Samuel, and James [WB 1:158]. His daughters' married names were listed in a 2 May 1829 deed of gift they made to their mother for three tracts of land totalling 225 acres [DB U:317]. Deborah's 9 February 1832 Robeson County will mentioned all their children except Samuel and mentioned her granddaughter Mariah [WB 1:266]. Their children were

    i.   Elias.[2]

    ii. Sally, married Bryant **Bowen**.[113]

    iii. Nancy, married Guilford **Best**.

    iv. Samuel[2].

    v. Mary, married James **Jacobs**.

    vi. Rebecca, married James **Paul**, who was probably the son of George **Paul**, head of a Robeson County household of 5 "other free" in 1800 [NC:409].

    vii. James.

    viii Delilah, married Wright **Ivey**.

    ix. Dorcas Hammond.

16. John[4] Hammond, born 1776-94, was head of a Robeson County household of 4 in 1810 [NC:220] and 6 "free colored" in 1820 [NC:325]. His wife was identified as Dicy Hammond in the 23 October 1800 deed of gift of 100 acres from John[2] Hammond to his grandson Lewis [DB U:37]. One of John[4]'s children was

    i.   Lewis, who was given title to 100 acres where his father was living from John Hammons, Sr., on 23 October 1800 and was given another deed of gift from his grandfather of 100 acres on the east side of Saddletree Swamp on 2 October 1804 [DB U:37; N:240]. He was not counted in Robeson County so he may have been the Lewis Hammon who was head of a Halifax County, North Carolina household of 5 "other free" in 1810 [NC:27].

---

[113]Other members of the **Bowen** family were Lucy **Bowen** (head of a Lenoir County household of 3 "other free" in 1810 [NC:303]), James **Bowen** (head of a Bladen County household of 6 "free colored" and 2 slaves in 1820 [NC:130]), and William **Bowen** (head of a Bladen County household of 4 "free colored" in 1820 [NC:132]).

17. Burrell Hammond, born say 1775, was ordered by the 30 August 1796 Edgecombe County court to pay Nancy Adkins for maintaining her child begotten by him. He married Betsey **Jenkins**, 11 September 1811 Edgecombe County bond. He was head of an Edgecombe County household of 3 "other free" in 1800 [NC:209], 3 in 1810 [NC:745], and 6 "free colored" in 1820 [NC:128]. His children were

    i. Willie Hammons, born say 1796, wrote his 24 September 1814 Nash County will before leaving to serve in the militia as a substitute for Sam Vick. He mentioned his brother John, not yet twenty-one years old, and his father Burwell Hammons. The will was proved in August 1815 [WB 1:308].

    ii. John[5].

Others who remained in Virginia were

    i. Larry Hammons, born about 1785, registered in Norfolk County on 17 July 1810: *5 feet 1/2 Inc, 25 years of age, of a light Complexion, Born free.*

    ii. Margaret[3]/ Peggy Hammon, born about 1788, registered in Norfolk County on 17 July 1810: *4 feet 11 1/2 In., twenty two years of age, of a light Complexion, Born free* [Registry of Free Negros & Mulattos, nos. 24, 25].

HANSON/ HENSON FAMILY

1. Mary Hanson, born say 1686, was presented by the York County court on 24 May 1706 for having a "Mulatto" child on information of her master Robert Read. She appeared in court on 2 July 1706 and declared that the father of her child was "Dick Broo_ a Malatto slave belonging to said Robert Read. Robert Read received Dick by his mother's 10 February 1685/6 York County will: "one Negro woman named Black Betty with her child a Mollatto boy named Dick." Dick was probably the son of Richard Brooks a (white) servant of Madame Reade whose age was adjudged as sixteen years on 26 February 1677/8 when the York County court ordered that he serve her until the age of twenty-four. Robert Read left a York County will by which he gave "a Malatto Man named Dick Brookes" to his son Thomas Reade, gave a servant named James Hanson, "bound by the Churchwardens to serve to ye age of one and thirty," to his daughter Mildred Reade and gave a servant boy named Richard Hanson, "bound by the Churchwardens to serve to ye age of one and thirty," to his son Francis Reade. Mary's children were listed in the 7 April 1713 inventory of Read's estate: "James & Richard Hanson indented Mulattoes" [DOW 6:35; 7:257; 12:414, 424; 14:241, 251-3]. Mary was the mother of

    i. James, born say 1706, complained to the York County court against his master John Goodwin on 15 June 1730. The court ordered that he return to Goodwin's service and ordered Goodwin to treat him well and allow him "cloathing and victuals suitable to a servant of his degree [DOW 17:75].

    ii. Richard, born say 1707.

They may have been the ancestors of

2   i. William Henson, born say 1730.

    ii. Rebecca Hanson, born about 1778, registered in Petersburg on 7 July 1818: *a free woman of colour, five feet two inches high, forty years old, brown Complection, rather light, born free in Dinwiddie County* [Register of Free Negroes 1794-1819, no. 919].

    iii. Milley Hanson, born say 1775, mother of three children who obtained certificates of freedom in Prince George's County, Maryland from 14 July 1814 to 18 April 1825 [Provine, *Registrations of Free Negroes*, 19, 50].

2. William Henson, born say 1730, was the father of "poor children" Elizabeth, Shad, John, and Margaret Henson who were bound out in Bedford County in July 1766 [Orders 1763-71, 262]. He was the father of
3   i.   Elizabeth, born say 1754.
        ii. Shadrick, born say 1758, head of a Petersburg Town household of 7 "other free" in 1810 [VA:118a].
        iii. John, perhaps the John Henson who was bound apprentice to Christopher Slinker in Bedford County on 24 June 1782 [Orders 1774-82, 360].
        iv. Margaret.

3. Elizabeth Henson, born say 1754, was the mother of a "Mulattoe" child named Aggy Henson who was ordered bound out in Bedford County in October 1774. She was ordered to serve her master Joseph Akins an additional year for having a bastard child [Orders 1774-82, 81]. She was the mother of
        i.   Aggy, born say 1774.

HARDEN FAMILY

Members of the Harden family of North Carolina were
        i.   Solomon, born say 1760, taxable on one poll in the 1784 Sampson County tax list [L.P. 64.1 by *N.C. Genealogy* XIV:2172]. He was head of a Robeson County household of 6 "other free" in 1790 [NC:49], 10 in 1800 [NC:383] and 10 in 1810 [NC:239]. He was called a "yeoman of Richmond County, North Carolina, Husband of Delaney Order (alias Harden), wife of Peter Order, Deceased," on 25 October 1791 when he and his wife gave power of attorney to Robert Webb to receive the final settlement for Revolutionary War service of his wife's deceased husband [*NCGSJ* XIV:114].
        ii. David Harden, head of a Sampson County household of 12 "other free" in 1800 [NC:501].
        iii. Benjamin, one of the freeholders of Sampson County who were ordered to work on the road from the courthouse to Drew's Ford on 15 February 1797 with (his brother?) Sion Harden, Henry Harden, John **Manuel**, and Larry **Manuel** [Minutes 1784-1800, 225]. He was head of a Sampson County household of 9 "other free" in 1800 [NC:510] and was counted as head of a household of 5 white males and 5 white females in 1810 [NC:486].
        iv. Sion, head of Sampson County household of 4 white males and 3 white females in 1810 [NC:486] and 11 "free colored" in 1820 [NC:308].
        v.   Abraham, charged in Sampson County court on 13 August 1799 with begetting a bastard child by Loretta Odum [Minutes 1784-1800, 272]. He was head of a Sampson County household of 4 "other free" in 1800 [NC:501] and 9 "free colored" in 1820 [NC:308].
1   vi. Lucy, born say 1770.

1. Lucy Harden, born say 1770, delivered a bastard child but refused to identify the father in Sampson County court on 14 August 1787 [Minutes 1784-1800, 65]. She was head of an Anson County household of 5 "free colored" in 1820 (called Lucy Harding) [NC:12]. She may have been the mother of the members of the Harding family counted as "free colored" in Anson County in 1820:
        i.   Jacob, head of a household of 3 males and __ females [NC:12].
        ii. John, head of a household of one "free colored" man and 2 white women [NC:12].

HARMAN FAMILY

1. William[1] Harman, born about 1632, was about forty years old when he made
    a deposition in Northampton County, Virginia court in 1672 [Orders 1664-74,
    fol.156a-f]. He arrived in Virginia as a slave sometime before 1648 when he
    was claimed as one of the headrights of planters Lewis Burwell and Thomas
    Vause [Nugent, *Cavaliers & Pioneers*, I:171-2]. In 1654 he was called the
    slave of William Andrews when he recorded his purchase of a calf in
    Northampton County court [DW 1654-55, 38]. William Andrews died about
    this time and his widow Mary married William Smart [DW 1654-55, p.85,
    fol.85]. In 1660 Smart sold William Harman to William Kendall who, on the
    same day he purchased Harman, agreed to sell him his freedom if he could
    provide sufficient security for the payment of 5,000 pounds of tobacco within
    two years [DW 1657-66, 70, 74 by Deal, *Race and Class*, 398-412]. This was
    1,000 pounds more than his purchase price. He was still listed in Kendall's
    household in 1664 and 1665 [Orders 1657-64, 198; 1664-74, 15].

    In March 1666 he sold a colt to Jane **Gossall**, the twenty-two-year-old
    daughter of Emmanuel **Driggers**, and stated in the deed that he intended to
    make her his wife, promising that the colt would be her sole property as long
    as she lived [DW 1655-68, pt.2, fol.12]. He had married Jane by June 1666
    when he submitted the letters of administration on her first husband's estate to
    the court [Orders 1664-7, fol.24, p.24]. He was head of his own household
    with his wife Jane in the Northampton County list of tithables from 1667 to
    1677 [Orders 1664-74, 42; 1674-79, 190].

    He appeared to have been equally friendly with slaves, free African
    Americans, and whites. According to the court deposition of a neighbor, he
    spent New Years Eve of 1672 drinking rum and sugar with the slaves on John
    Michael's plantation [Orders 1664-74, fol.125]. He made a deposition in court
    about an argument he had witnessed while at the home of John **Francisco**
    [Orders 1664-74, fol.138, fol.143, fol.146, fol.156a-f, fol.157]. And in the
    summer of 1683 there was a court hearing about an argument among six white
    neighbors of his who were gathered at his house to help him harvest his crop
    [OW 1683-9, 15-16].

    In the summer of 1675 he was involved in a dispute with William Gray over
    the possession of a gun that once belonged to Francis **Payne**. **Payne**'s widow
    Amey had delivered the gun to Harman, perhaps as a gift, and her second
    husband William Gray, white like her, protested and took it back. The court
    ordered the gun returned to Harman [OW 1674-79, 58-59].

    In September 1673 Jane Harman was the wet nurse for the illegitimate child
    of Nicholas Silvedo, a Portuguese servant, and English maidservant Mary Gale
    [Deal, *Race and Class*, 405]. William and Jane were tithables in their own
    Northampton County household in 1677. He was about fifty years old on 30
    December 1686, called "William Harmon Negro," when he made a deposition
    about a gun said to be a part of the estate of Edward Jessop, "Maletto" [OW
    1674-9, 190; OW 1683-9, 258, 262-3]. William was still living in April 1699
    when he recorded the livestock mark of his son Manuel Harman [DW 1651-4,
    31 at end of volume]. Jane may have been the Jane Harman who bought a
    "parcel of cloathes" in the 15 June 1700 sale of the estate of Philip **Mongon**,
    deceased [Orders 1692-1707, 262]. William and Jane's children were

        i.   Frances, born say 1667, mother of an illegitimate child by a white
    man, Samuel Johnson, in 1685, another in 1686 by Jarvis Cutler,
    another before 28 May 1688, and another before 1692 [OW 1683-9,
    112, 358, 386; OW 1689-98, 160-1]. In May 1690 Thomas **Carter** was
    security for her fine of fornication [OW 1689-98, 35, 58]. She married

a slave, Anthony **George**, by 1693 when she recorded her livestock mark in Northampton County court [DW 1651-4, 26 at end of volume].

    ii. Manuel[1], born say 1670, recorded his livestock mark in court with his father in April 1699 [DW 1651-4, 31 at end of volume]. He was a tenant on land in Accomack County on 7 December 1714 [Orders 1714-1ʳ, 2].

2   iii. Edward[1], born say 1672.

    iv. John[1], born say 1674.

3   v. William[2], born say 1676.

2. **Edward**[1] Harman, born say 1672, was living in Northampton County on 8 November 1702 when he and (his brother?) John Harman, Johnson **Driggus**, John **Driggus**, and Samuel **George**, "Free Negroes," were convicted of stealing a hog and then abusing and threatening several whites "in an insolent manner" [Orders 1698-1710, 102, 106]. He purchased 100 acres in Accomack County a few miles from Chincoteague in the northeastern part of the county in 1711. He and his wife Patience sold this land twenty-five years later [DW 1729-37, fol. 235-p.236; Whitelaw, *Virginia's Eastern Shore*, 1333]. On 10 August 1719 he admitted in Accomack County court that he owed William **Johnson** 7-1/2 bushels of Indian corn [Orders 1717-19, 1]. He may have been identical to Edward Harman who was taxable in Bogerternorten Hundred, Somerset County, Maryland, from 1738 to 1740. Edward and Patience may have been the ancestors of some of the family members who were in Maryland and Delaware:

    i. Zachariah, taxable in Bogerternorten Hundred, Somerset County, in William Smith's household in 1733, in Ursley Greer's household (with William Harman) in 1734, in Presgrave William's household in 1735, in Edward Franklin's household in 1737, in Edward Harman's household in 1738, and in Edward Franklin's household in 1739.

4   ii. William[3], born say 1715.

    iii. John[2], born say 1718, taxable in Bogerternorten Hundred, Somerset County, in Edward Franklin's household in 1737 and taxable in 1740 in his own household with his unnamed "melotto" wife in Baltimore Hundred, Somerset County.

    iv. Edward, born say 1720, taxable in Bogerternorten Hundred, Somerset County, in the household of (his brother?) William Harman in 1739 and the household of (his father?) Edward Harman in 1740.

    v. Jane, born say 1722, living in All Hollow's Parish, Somerset County, in June 1738 when she was indicted for having an illegitimate child. She was found not guilty. Edward Harmon, planter, was her security for the payment of court fees [Judicial Record 1738-40, 43]. She was a taxable "mulato" in the Bogerternorten Hundred household of Robert Warren in 1740 [1740 Tax List]. On 18 November 1740 she was again indicted for having an illegitimate child, but this time confessed that John Jackson was the father. Robert Warren was her security [Judicial Record 1740-2, 59-60, 310].

5   vi. Daniel[1], born say 1725.

6   vii. Job, born say 1726.

3. **William**[2] Harman, born say 1676, was a "Negro" tithable head of his own Northampton County household from 1720 to 1725 [Bell, *Northampton County Tithables*, 2, 13, 24, 36, 51, 68, 73]. He was called William Harmon "Negro" in December 1721 when he paid Hannah **Carter**'s fine of 500 pounds of tobacco and indemnified the parish from any charge from her illegitimate child [Orders 1719-22, 144, 146]. He died without making a will before 12 January 1725/6 when his children Jane and Edward Harman chose Philip **Mongon** as their guardian. His estate was valued at 32 pounds [Orders 1722-9, 226; DW 1725-33, 32]. His children were

7

   i.   ?Dinah **Mongon**, wife of Philip **Mongon**.

   ii.   Jane, born about 1706.

   iii.   Edward[2], born say 1707, a "Negro" tithable in his father's Northampton County household in 1723 and 1724. He was tithable in Philip **Mongon**'s household in 1726, a "negro" tithable in Matthew Welch's household from 1727 to 1731, and tithable in the household of Henry Speakman from 1737 to 1744 [Bell, *Northampton County Tithables*, 36, 51, 73, 102, 118, 170, 212, 221, 255, 276, 292, 304, 361]. He sued Philip **Mongon** for his part of his father's estate on 11 July 1727, and he was sued by Daniel **Jacob** on 11 October 1727 [Orders 1722-9, 285, 299].

   iv.   ?Nan, born say 1710, a "negro" taxable in Thomas Moor's Northampton County household from 1726 to 1728 [Bell, *Northampton County Tithables*, 107, 132].

   v.   ?George[1], born about 1717, a ten-year-old "orphan Mulatto" bound apprentice in Accomack County on 5 March 1727 to Jeptha Perry and then bound instead to Benjamin Salmon on 3 August 1736 when Salmon complained to the court that Perry neither taught him a trade nor "put him to School" [Orders 1724-31, 95a; 1731-36, 190]. On 30 September 1766 the Accomack County court ordered that he be added to the list of tithables [Orders 1765-67, 235].

4.   William[3] Harman, born say 1715, was taxable in Bogerternorten Hundred, Somerset County, in Ursley Greer's household in 1734, in Robert Warren's household in 1737, in his own household from 1738 to 1739 (with his brother? Edward Harman), and taxable in Baltimore Hundred with his wife Betty in 1740 "by order of Court" [List of Taxables]. Worcester County was formed from this part of Somerset County in 1742, so his descendants may have been those members of the family counted as "other free" in Worcester County:

   i.   Jeremiah, head of a Worcester County, Maryland household of 6 "other free" in 1790 [MD:124].

   ii.   Abel, head of a Worcester County, Maryland household of 10 "other free" in 1800 [DE:744].

   iii.   Sophia, head of a Worcester County, Maryland household of 7 "other free" in 1800 [MD:830].

   iv.   Sally, head of a Worcester County, Maryland household of 5 "other free" in 1800 [MD:745].

   v.   Lazarus, born about 1758, served in the 6th Company of the 1st Maryland Regiment from 1 August 1780 to 15 November 1783 [*Archives of Maryland* 18:356, 539]. He was head of a Worcester County, Maryland household of 6 "other free" in 1790 [MD:124], 9 in 1800 [MD:745] and 7 "other free" and a slave in 1810 [MD:623]. He made a declaration in Worcester County court on 10 April 1818 to obtain a pension for his service in the Revolution. On 28 July 1821 he stated that he was about sixty years old and was living with his wife Betty and their sons John, aged eighteen years, and Joseph, aged twelve years [M805-399].

5.   Daniel[1] Harman, born say 1725, was a Little Creek Hundred, Kent County, Delaware taxable from 1766 to 1773. He died before 10 May 1774 when his widow Elizabeth was granted administration of his Kent County, Delaware estate. She married Joseph **Lantern** [de Valinger, *Kent County, Delaware Probate Records*, 289]. Daniel may have been the father of

   i.   Daniel[2], a "Mulatto" taxable in the Kent County Levy Assessments circa 1820.

   ii.   Gabriel, born say 1760, married Rhoda **Hanser**. She assigned her right to the estate of her father William **Handsor** to Gabriel on 16 February 1790 [Estate Accounts, by Heite]. He was a "free Negro" taxable in

Murderkill Hundred in 1787 and in Little Creek Hundred in 1798, head of a St. Jones Hundred, Kent County household of 3 "other free" in 1800 [DE:45] and 3 "free colored" in Dover in 1820 [DE:36].

6. Job Harman, born say 1726, and his wife Comfort registered the 16 April 1750 birth of their "mulatto" son Shepherd at St. George's Protestant Episcopal Church, Indian River, Delaware [Wright, *Vital Records of Kent and Sussex Counties*, 101]. They were the parents of

   i. Jemima, daughter of Job Harmon baptized same day (16 April 1750) at St. George's Protestant Episcopal Church, Indian River [Wright, *Vital Records of Kent and Sussex Counties*, 95].

   ii. ?Eunice, born say 1752, married Southy **Pride**, "mulattoes," on 13 May 1772 at Lewes and Coolsprings Presbyterian Church [Wright, *Vital Records of Kent and Sussex Counties*, 126].

   iii. ?Edward, born about 1758, married Agnes **Jackson** on 27 November 1788 at Lewes and Coolspring Presbyterian Church [Wright, *Vital Records of Kent and Sussex Counties*, 132]. He was head of an Indian River, Sussex County household of 6 "other free" in 1800 [DE:438], 8 in 1810 [DE:437] and 5 "free colored" in Lewis and Rehoboth Hundred in 1820 [DE:308]. He was a resident of Lewes and Rehoboth Hundred, Sussex County, on 20 April 1818 when he applied for a pension for his service in the Revolutionary War. He enlisted under Captain Kirkwood in the First Company of the Delaware Regiment in 1777. Mitchell Kirkwood, Lieutenant Colonel of the Ninth Delaware Regiment testified in his favor. Hezekiah Lacey testified that Edward worked for his father when he enlisted [M805-399].

   iv. William[4], born say 1770, married Mary **Hanser** "Free mulattoes" on 11 May 1795 at Lewes and Coolspring Presbyterian Church [Wright, *Vital Records of Kent and Sussex Counties*, 135]. He was a "Negro" taxable in St. Jones Hundred, Kent County in 1798 and head of an Indian River, Sussex County, Delaware household of 3 "other free" in 1800 [DE:437], 5 "other free" in Cedar Creek Hundred in 1810 [DE:303], and 9 "free colored" in Indian River Hundred, Sussex County in 1820 [DE:220].

   v. Shepherd, born 15 April 177_ (probably 1771 or 1772), "mulatto" son of Job and Comfort ___. He was head of a Sussex County household of 7 "other free" in 1810 [DE:458]

7. Jane Harmon, born about 1706, was a "Negro" tithable in Philip **Mongon**'s Northampton County household in 1726 and 1727 [Bell, *Northampton County Tithables*, 102, 119]. She was twenty-one years old in February 1727/8 when she petitioned the Northampton County court to allow her to take control of the remaining part of her father's estate which was then in the hands of her guardian Dinah **Mongong**, widow and executrix of Philip **Mongong**. The court ordered Dinah to pay Jane her share of her deceased father's estate [L.P Pk#12, February 1727/8; Orders 1722-9, 316, 317]. Jane was tithable in the household of Richard **Malavery** (Dinah's second husband) from 1728 to 1731 [Bell, *Northampton County Tithables*, 135, 148, 169, 221]. She had an illegitimate child before 11 December 1733. She petitioned the court for her estate which was in the hands of Richard **Malavery**, and on 9 January 1733/4 the court appointed Colonel John Robins and Mr. William Stott to inspect the appraisement of the estate and to be present when Richard **Munlavery** delivered it to her, "that she may not be wronged" [Orders 1732-42, 87, 88, 89]. She may have been the Jane Harmon who was living in Accomack County on 25 April 1749 when several of her children: Elijah, Harman, Solomon, and Nimrod were bound as apprentice shoemakers [Orders 1744-53, 327]. She was called "Jane Harmon free Negro" in April 1758 when the Northampton County

court released her from paying taxes in the future [Minutes 1754-61, 156]. Her children were

i.   ?John[3], born say 1732, head of a Halifax County, North Carolina household of 4 "other free" and one white man over sixteen years of age in 1790 [NC:63] and 9 "other free" in 1800 [NC:316]. On 30 October 1795 he sold 100 acres, tools, furniture, cattle, and hogs in Halifax County to Joseph **Lantern**, Moses Matthews, and John Kelly and sold 100 acres near the road from Halifax Town to Enfield old courthouse to Joseph **Lantern** on 3 December 1795 [DB 17:920; DB 18:130]. (Joseph **Lantern** was taxable in Dover Hundred, Kent County, Delaware, from 1776 to 1785).

ii. Elijah, born about 1735, a fourteen-year-old bound to Hezekiel Purnoll on 25 April 1749.

iii. Harman, born about 1738, an eleven-year-old bound to Hezekiel Purnoll on 25 April 1749.

iv. Solomon, born about 1743, a six-year-old bound out on 25 April 1749.

v.   Nimrod, born about 1747, a two-year-old bound out in Accomack County on 25 April 1749, head of a Worcester County, Maryland household of 6 "other free" in 1790 [MD:124].

vi. ?Jemima, born say 1749, a "free Negro" living in Accomack County on 4 July 1768 when the court presented her for not listing herself as a tithable [Orders 1768-9, 227].

8.   Emanuel[2] Harmon, born say 1733, was sued in Northampton County by John Wilkins, Sr., on 15 May 1754. He was called a free Negro on 10 June 1760 when the court ordered him sent to the General Court to be tried for receiving stolen goods from a slave named Will who belonged to the estate of Benjamin Stratton [Orders 1753-8, 100; Minutes 1754-61, 223]. He was head of an Accomack County household of 6 "other free" in 1800 [*Virginia Genealogist* 2:153] and 8 i.ı 1810 [VA:29]. He was the father of

i.   George[2], born say 1755, taxable in Accomack County from 1782 to 1813: taxable on 2 free males, 2 slaves and 5 horses in 1782; 2 free males in 1798; called a "fn" in 1806 and 1812; called "Geo: Harmon (of Emawell)" in a list of "free Negroes & Mulattoes" in 1813. His son George was called "of George" in 1812 [PPTL, 1782-1814, frames 8, 149, 248, 314, 378, 447, 630, 791, 835]. He was head of an Accomack County household of 9 "other free" in 1800 [*Virginia Genealogist* 2:153] and 5 "other free" in 1810 [VA:29]. He served as a soldier in the Revolution. His only heirs Betsy, Comfort, Leah and Sarah Harmon applied for a pension for his service in Accomack County court on 25 September 1832 [Orders 1832-36, 16].

Other descendants of the Harmon family were

i.   James, born say 1755, a "Mulatto" bound as an apprentice house carpenter to George Chappel until the age of twenty-one in Princess Anne County, Virginia, on 17 July 1759, no age or parent named [Minutes 1753-62, 357]. He and his son James were mentioned in the 30 December 1792 Princess Anne County will of his father-in-law, William **Shoecraft** [WB 1:210]. He was taxable in St. Bride's Parish, Norfolk County, from 1783 to 1811: in the list of "free Negroes and Mulattoes" from 1801 to 1811 [PPTL, 1782-91, frames 415, 450, 592; 1791-1812, frames 8, 191, 400, 548, 636, 716]. He may have been the father of Craftshoe Harmon, head of a Liberty County, South Carolina household of 3 "other free" in 1800 [SC:806].

ii. Eleanor, bound to George Chappel to read, sew, and knit in Princess Anne County, Virginia, on 17 July 1759, no age or parent named [Minutes 1753-62, 357].

iii. Thomas, a "Negro" taxable on 130 acres and 5 "Negroes" in Prince Frederick Parish, South Carolina, in 1786 [S.C. Tax Returns 1783-1800, frame 119], head of a Georgetown District, Prince Frederick's Parish, South Carolina household of 5 "other free" in 1790 [SC:51].

iv. Abraham, head of a South Orangeburgh District, South Carolina household of 3 "other free" in 1790 [SC:101].

v. Southey, head of an Accomack County household of 5 "other free" in 1800 [*Virginia Genealogist* 1:108].

vi. Stephen, head of an Accomack County household of 9 "other free" in 1810 [VA:100].

vii. Ann, head of an Accomack County household of 5 "other free" in 1800 [*Virginia Genealogist* 1:108].

viii. Scarburgh, head of an Accomack County household of 4 "other free" and a slave in 1810 [VA:101].

ix. Molly/ Mary, head of an Accomack County household of 4 "other free" in 1800 [*Virginia Genealogist* 1:157] and 7 in 1810 [VA:102].

x. Easter, head of an Accomack County household of 4 "other free" in 1810 [VA:30].

xi. Emanuel[3], born about 1789, registered in Accomack County on 29 September 1807: *a light Black, 5 feet 7-1/2 Inches...Born free* [Free Negro Register, #5].

HARRIS FAMILY

1. John[1] Harris, born say 1635, may have been identical to "my Negro man John" named in Thomas Whitehead's 6 April 1660 York County will by which he set John free, gave him all his wearing apparel and two cows, lent him as much land as he could tend himself, and appointed him guardian of his (Whitehead's) daughter if the court would permit it. On 11 September 1660 the court declared that John was a free man and ordered that the cattle and other things be delivered to him according to the will. On 28 October 1667 "John Harris, Negro" purchased from Robert Jones of Queen's Creek 50 acres in New Kent County adjoining Mr. Baker's and the main swamp by deed recorded in York County on 12 April 1669 [DWO 3:82, 89; 4:237].

Members of the Harris family who may have been descendants of John Harris were

2   i. Martha[1], born say 1720.
3   ii. Solomon[1], born say 1722.
4   iii. James[1], born say 1723.
5   iv. Mary[1], born say 1729.
6   v. Edward[1], born say 1730.
7   vi. Martha[2], born say 1730.
8   vii. George[1], born say 1740.
     viii. Eleanor, born say 1732, living in Brunswick County, Virginia, on 23 January 1753 when the court ordered the churchwardens of St. Andrew's Parish to bind her "Mullatto" son Moses to Drury Stith, Gentleman [Orders 1751-3, 366].
     ix. Martha[3], born say 1733, married Joseph **Hawley** of Granville County, North Carolina.
9   x. Phebe[1], born about 1734.
10   xi. Nathan[1], born say 1735.

2. Martha[1] Harris, born say 1720, was the mother of "a mulatto boy" named Charles Harris who was bound to Lewellin Eppes in Charles City County, Virginia, in August 1746 [Orders 1737-51, 420]. She was the ancestor of

     i. Charles[1], born say 1740, bound apprentice in August 1746.
11   ii. ?___, born say 1744.
12   iii. ?Joan, born say 1752.

iv.   ?Willia:n, born say 1755, a deserter from Captain Thomas Massie's new recruits for the sixth Virginia Regiment. The 21 November 1777 issue of the *Virginia Gazette* offered a reward for his return, describing him as: *a mulatto fellow about five feet eleven inches high, the veins in his leg much broke, appear in knots, he was enlisted in New Kent, but expect he is lurking about Charles City* [*Virginia Gazette*, Purdie's edition, p.3, col. 3].

v.   ?Betty, born about 1760, registered in Petersburg on 13 July 1805: *a yellow brown Mulatto woman, five feet and a half inches high, forty five years old, born free in Charles City County* [Register of Free Negroes 1794-1819, no. 336].

13   vi.   ?Edward[3], born say 1760.

vii.   ?Richard, born say 1775, taxable on one tithe and a horse in Charles City County in 1800 [1800 PPTL, p.11], head of a Charles City County household of 6 "other free" in 1810 [VA:959].

3.   Solomon[1] Harris, born say 1722, sued Abraham Morris in Charles City County court in July 1744 but failed to prosecute [Orders 1737-51, 311]. He was a tithable in Lunenburg County in the list of Lewis Deloney in the household of Thomas **Evans** in 1748 [Tax List 1748-52].[114] He was tithable in his own household in William Howard's list for 1749 and 1750, the 1751 list of Field Jefferson, and the 1764 list of Edmund Taylor [Bell, *Sunlight on the Southside*, 109, 142, 169, 252]. He and his wife Sarah and son William were 3 "Black" tithables in the 1765 Granville County, North Carolina list of Wm. Bullock. He was the father of

14   i.   ?Mary[2], born say 1750.

ii.   William, born about 1753, taxable in his parents' household in Wm. Bullock's Granville County list in 1765. He was married to Eady **Stewart** by 11 September 1780 when the Mecklenburg County court ordered Zachariah Mallett to deliver up the will of her mother Patty **Stewart**, deceased, on the motion of William Harris and Eady his wife [Orders 1779-84, 76].

15   iii.   ?John, born say 1755.

16   iv.   ?Phebe[2], born say 1755.

4.   James[1] Harris,, born say 1723, a "free Negro," was given fifteen lashes when he confessed in Charles City County court in February 1743/4 that he stole a small quantity of sugar from the store of James Rae. George Minge paid his court fees [Orders 1737-51, 289]. He was taxable in Charles City County from 1784 to 1787, called "James Harris, Sr." in 1787 when he was not tithable on his person [PPTL 1783-7]. He made a 29 July 1784 Charles City County will by which he directed that his stock of sheep should be sold, his crop delivered to Abraham **Brown**, and the rest of his estate divided among his children, his son John Harris excepted. He named Abraham **Brown** executor (who died before him). The will was proved on 21 May 1791 by oath of Dixon **Brown**, a witness (making his mark). James Harris was granted administration on the estate on 50 pounds security [WB 1:55]. James, Sr.'s widow was apparently Frances Harris who was a witness to the 15 December 1791 Charles City County will of Sarah **Brown** (widow of Abraham). Frances left a 12 November 1803 Charles City County will, proved 19 June 1806. She left a bed and furniture to her grandson George Hunt Harris (son of Haly Harris) left son Chavis Harris and his wife Susanna all the rest of her estate excluding her wearing apparel, left grand daughter Rebecca **Brown** (daughter of John **Brown**) a spinning wheel and cards, left her wearing apparel to be divided among her daughter Susanna **Brown** (wife of Dixon **Brown**), Susanna's

---

[114]Mecklenburg County was formed from this part of Lunenburg County in 1765.

daughter, her granddaughter Celia **Harris** and Rebecca **Brown** (wife of Edward **Brown**). She named her son-in-law John **Brown**, Abraham **Brown** and William **Brown** executors. She made a codicil stipulating that her sons John and James Harris and her daughter Priscilla were to receive no more than one penny each [WB 1:650]. She was the mother of

    i.   John⁴, born say 1758, taxable in Charles City County from 1783 to 1814, listed as a "Mulattoe" in 1813 [PPTL 1783-7; 1788-1814] and head of a Charles City County household of 4 "other free" in 1810 [VA:958].

17   ii.   James², born say 1760.

    iii.   Priscilla, born say 1765, wife of John **Brown** and mother of Rebecca **Brown**.

    iv.   Haly, born say 1770, father of George Hunt Harris who was called Hunt Harris when he was a "Mulattoe" taxable in Charles City County in 1813 [Waldrep, *1813 Tax List*].

18   v.   Chavis, born say 1780.

    vi.   Susanna, wife of Dixon **Brown**.

    vii.   ?Rebecca, wife of Edward **Brown**.

5.   Mary¹ Harris, born say 1729, a "mullato orphan," was living with Willing Wynne on 4 October 1734 when the vestry of St. Andrews Parish in Brunswick County, Virginia, paid him to keep her until she reached the age of twenty-one [Hopkins, *St. Andrew Parish Vestry Book*, 41]. She may have been the daughter of Katherine Harris, (no race indicated), who was presented by the Prince George County court on 13 November 1739 for having a bastard child [Orders 1737-40, 362], perhaps the Katherine Harris who died before 10 October 1741 when Thomas Neuse was paid by the St. Andrew Parish Vestry of Brunswick County for making her coffin [Hopkins, *St. Andrew Parish Vestry Book*, 48]. Mary was called a "free Mulatto" on 15 December 1767 when the Mecklenburg County, Virginia court ordered the churchwardens to bind out her sons Nimrod and William to Peter Field Jefferson [Orders 1765-8, 450]. She was the mother of

    i.   Nimrod, born say 1764, bound apprentice on 15 December 1767.

    ii.   William, born say 1766, bound apprentice on 15 December 1767.

    iii.   Catherine², born say 1767, bound to Peter Field Jefferson in Mecklenburg County, Virginia, on 11 November 1771 [Orders 1771-73, 84].

    iv.   James³, born about 1769, ordered bound apprentice to Benjamin Ferrell in Mecklenburg County on 9 December 1771 [Orders 1771-73, 135]. He received a certificate in Mecklenburg County on 29 June 1812: *This is to Certify that James Harris who was born & raised in the County of Mecklenburg & Commonwealth of Virginia, is a free man, he is five feet seven inches high, of a Colour but little removed from black, is about forty years old & has lost his upper fore teeth. The said James Harris was bound to, and Served his apprenticeship with Benjamin Ferrell, late of this County & Commonwealth aforesaid decd. where he has resided ever since, and has uniformly, as far as I recollect ever to have heard, supported a good Character* [Register of Free Negroes, 1809-41, no. 4].

6.   Edward¹ Harris, born say 1730, had two taxables in his Granville County, North Carolina household in the list of Jonathan White in 1750 [CR 44.702.19]. He was called "negro" in the 1752-54 tax lists and in the 8 October 1754 Muster Roll of the Granville County Regiment of Colonel William Eaton [Clark, *Colonial Soldiers of the South*, 716]. In 1753 he was tithable but refused to pay tax for his wife, perhaps claiming she was white. She was the light-skinned daughter of William **Chavis** who made a deed of gift of 340 acres in Granville on the north side of Tabbs Creek to his "daughter

Sarah Harris wife of Edward Harris" on 6 September 1756 [DB C:73]. Edward and Sarah were taxables with their children in all the extant Granville County colonial tax lists [CR 044.701.19]. In 1782 he was taxed on 190 acres, 4 horses, and 6 cattle in Fishing Creek District. His wife Sarah died in January 1785 according to the deeds of her oldest sons Gibson and Sherwood who sold their interest in her dower lands to John Penn, administrator of her estate [DB O:408, 423]. Penn divided the remaining 192 acres among her other two sons Jesse and Solomon on 13 March 1789 [WB 2:233]. In 1785 Edward or his son by that name was a buyer at the sale of an estate in Northampton County [Gammon, *Record of Estates, Northampton County*, I:50], and he was head of a Northampton County household of 10 "other free" in 1790 [NC:72]. Edward and Sarah's children named in the tax lists and Sarah's 1789 Granville County bequest were

   i.   Amey, born about 1749, taxable in her parents' Epping Forest District household in 1761.

   ii.   Lucy, born about 1752, taxable in her parents household in Samuel Benton's list for Epping Forest District in 1764.

  iii. Nancy, born about 1752, taxable in her parents household in Samuel Benton's list for Epping Forest District in 1764.

  iv. Nelly, born about 1754, taxable in her parents household in the list of Stephen Jett in 1766.

   v.   Edward[2]/ Ned, born about 1756, taxable in the list of Jonathan Kittrell in 1768. He died before 14 July 1792 when his brother Gibson, as "Eldest Brother & heir at law to Edward Harris decd.," gave power of attorney to Philemon Hodges to receive his pay for service in the Revolution. His brothers, Sherwood and Solomon Harris, made a similar deposition confirming Gibson's statement on 22 July 1792 [*NCGSJ* X:111].

  vi. Gibson, born about 1760, not mentioned in the tax lists but sold his share of land to John Penn on 5 July 1785, identifying it as the land which "William Chavers gave to his daughter Sarah, wife of Edward Harris" [DB O:408]. In the 1778 Granville County Militia Returns for Captain Abraham Potter's Company he was listed as a seventeen-year-old "black man," occupation: planter [*The North Carolinian* VI:726 (Mil. TR 4-40)]. He was head of a Surry County, North Carolina household of 12 "other free" in 1810 [NC:684].

 vii. Sherwood, born say 1761, not mentioned in the tax lists but sold his share of his mother's land to John Penn on 24 December 1785 [DB O:423]. He was head of a Wake County household of 6 "other free" in 1800 [NC:770] and 10 in Granville County in 1810 [NC:864].

viii. Jesse, born say 1762, not taxed in his father's household, but named as Edward and Sarah's son in his brothers' 1785 deeds [DB O:408, 423]. He received half of his mother's land by the 1789 division of her estate [WB 2:233]. He was taxable in Granville County on 50 acres in 1789 and sold his farm animals in Granville County on 10 March 1791 [WB 2:225]. He married Elizabeth **Ivey**, 29 November 1790 Wake County bond. He was taxable on 100 acres in 1798 and was head of a Granville County household of 2 "other free" in 1800 and 4 in 1810 [NC:864]. He was taxable on 200 acres in Beaverdam District of Granville County in 1805 (called "Jessee Harris of Colour") but was assessed only poll tax in 1808 (called F. Negro) [Tax List, 1803-09, 130, 271]. He may have been the Jesse Harris, about sixty years old on 21 February 1821, who made a declaration in Wake County court to obtain a pension for service in the Revolution. He stated that by his first wife he had four children, one named Fennell (seventeen years old) living with him, and by his second wife a child Billy who was also living with him [*NCGSJ* XIII:34]. Perhaps his second marriage was to

Julia **Tabon** (**Taborn**), 23 February 1820 Wake County bond, Thomas Roycroft bondsman.

 ix. Solomon[2], born say 1767, named in his brothers' 1785 Granville County deeds [DB O:408, 423]. He received half his mother's remaining land by the 1789 division of her estate. He was taxable in Fishing Creek District of Granville County in 1796 on 103 acres and one poll and on 73 acres in 1798 [Tax List 1796-1802, 12, 73]. He was head of a Granville County household of 4 "other free" in 1800.

7. Martha[2] Harris, born say 1730, was the mother of Isham Harris who was bound by the Lunenburg County court to Amos Tims, Jr. on 13 October 1763. She married John **Stewart** who died before 14 February 1765 when the Lunenburg County court ordered the churchwardens of St. James Parish to bind his orphan daughter Eleanor **Steward** to William Taylor [Orders 1763-4, 257; 1764-5, 2, 203]. Mecklenburg County was formed from St. James Parish later that year, and in September 1772 the Mecklenburg County court bound Eleanor to Molly Taylor [Orders 1771-73, 318]. On 27 April 1777 Martha's son Moses **Stewart** purchased 100 acres from Henry Jackson in Mecklenburg County on the south side of Allen's Creek adjoining Stephen Mallett, with Stephen and Zachariah Mallett as witnesses [DB 5:56]. She apparently purchased this land in his name since he was only ten years old at the time. Her 17 January 1779 Mecklenburg County, Virginia will, witnessed by Zachariah Mallett, was proved 9 October 1780 on motion of her executor, Henry Jackson. By her will she left her land to her son Moses and left livestock and money to her children Isham, Nelly, Edy, Fanny, Moses, Sinai, and Disea [WB 1:341]. She was counted as head of a Mecklenburg County household of 7 persons in 1782, but this was probably the listing for her estate [VA:32]. Her estate included 54 acres of land which was sold for taxes in 1793 [DB 8:407-8]. Martha was the mother of

 i. Isham Harris, born say 1756, called "Isham Harris, Son of Patty Stewart" on 13 October 1763 when he was ordered bound to Amos Tims, Jr., by the Lunenburg County court. On 13 April 1769 the court ordered Isham bound instead to John **Evans** (alias **Eppes**) [Orders 1763-64, 257; 1766-69, folio 202]. He was taxable in John Evans' Lunenburg County household in 1772 [Bell, *Sunlight on the Southside*, 304]. He applied for a pension for services in the Revolution at the age of eighty-four years on 8 August 1843 in Rutherford County, North Carolina, stating that he was born in Charlotte County, Virginia, in 1759 and that he was drafted in Lunenburg County.

10. George[1] Harris, born say 1730, was head of a household with his wife Catherine in the Oxford District of Granville County, North Carolina, in 1761. On 6 February 1775 he purchased 144-1/2 acres in Granville County near John Tatom's line for 105 pounds [DB K:249]. In 1782 he was taxable in Granville County on 145 acres, 3 horses, and 12 cattle in Ragland's District. He was head of a Granville County household of 7 persons in the 1786 state census, and he was taxable in Granville on his land for the last time in 1789. His children were

 i. Mary, born say 1750, taxable in the Granville County household of her father George Harris in Samuel Benton's list for 1762 and 1764.

 ii. ?Claiborn, born about 1766, head of a Wake County household of 5 "other free" in 1800 [NC:770], 11 in Stokes County in 1810 [NC:573], and 12 "free colored" in Stokes County in 1820 [NC:346]. He entered the NW:NW part of Section 34, Town 10, Range 5 in Marion Township, Owen County, Indiana, on 10 August 1836 and SW:SE of Section 28 on 8 February 1845 [Land Entry Book #1]. He sold the SW:SE part of Section 28 a month later on 4 March 1845 [DB 8:285]. He was head of an Owen County, Indiana, household of 3 "free colored," one of them a woman over one hundred years of age, in 1830 [IN:22] and 5 "free colored" in 1840 [IN:42]. In 1850 he was in household #167 of Marion Township, Owen County, Indiana. Perhaps one of his children was Hardin Harris, born about 1797, living next door to him in household # 168 in Marion Township.

 iii. ?Hardy, born say 1772, married Polly **Evans**, 22 October 1793 Wake County bond, John Reighley bondsman. He was head of a Wake County household of 3 "other free" in 1800 [NC:767]. He may have been the Hardy Harris who was head of a Abbeville District, South Carolina household in 1810 [SC:82].

 iv. ?Edward[5]/ Ned, born say 1780, head of a Richland District, South Carolina household of 6 "other free" in 1810 [SC:175a]. Eleanor, Keziah, Lydney and Elizabeth Harris were residents of Richland District in 1806 when they petitioned the South Carolina legislature to be exempted from the tax on free Negro women [S.C. Archives series S.165015, item 01885].

9. Phebe[1] Harris, born about 1734, registered in Petersburg on 20 August 1794: *a brown Mulatto woman, five feet two inches high, supposed sixty years old, born free in County of Prince George* [Register of Free Negroes 1794-1819, no. 75]. She may have been the mother of

19 i. James, born about 1748.

 ii. John[2], born about 1752, a "yellow" complexioned soldier born in Prince George County who enlisted as a substitute in the Revolution in Dinwiddie County [NSDAR, *African American Patriots*, 150]. He was a "Mulatto" taxable in Dinwiddie County in 1790 and 1792 and a "free" taxable from 1794 to 1801 when he was listed as a cooper in the same district (Braddock Goodwyn's) as another "free" John Harris and a "free" Andrew Harris [PPTL 1801 B, p.7]. He was called a "free man of Colour" on 27 April 1818 when he made a declaration in Prince George County to obtain a pension for his services, stating that he enlisted in 1777 in the 15th Virginia Regiment. He was taken from the regiment and made a servant to President Monroe who was then the major of horse and aide-de-camp to Lord Sterling. He made a second declaration on 18 May 1821 in Petersburg court, stating that he was about sixty-nine years old and residing in Dinwiddie County in the immediate vicinity of Petersburg. He was a cooper by trade and his family consisted of himself and four children: three boys and a girl [M805-401, frame 0640].

 iii. Aggy, born about 1769, registered in Petersburg on 20 August 1794: *a brown Mulatto woman, five feet two inches high, twenty five years old, born free & raised in Prince George County near Petersburg*. Her son Thomas registered on 10 June 1805: *a dark brown Negro man, feet inches five high, twenty years old 10 Aug. next, son of Agga Harris a free Negroe woman* [Register of Free Negroes 1794-1819, nos. 76, 291].

 iv. Betty, born about 1770, registered in Petersburg on 20 August 1794: *a brown Mulatto woman, five feet four inches high, twenty four years old, born free & raised in Prince George County near Petersburg* [Register of Free Negroes 1794-1819, no. 77].

10. Nathan[1] Harris, born say 1735, was taxable in his own household with his wife Amey in the 1758 Granville County, North Carolina list of Nathaniel Harris. He entered 200 acres on the waters of Beaverdam Creek in Granville County on 22 March 1780 and another 350 acres in 1779 [Pruitt, *Land Entries, Granville County*, 49]. He was assessed tax on 737 pounds in Beaverdam in 1780, but by 1785 he was in Northampton County where he was a buyer at the sale of an estate [Gammon, *Record of Estates, Northampton County*, I:51]. In

1800 he was head of a Northampton County household of 6 "other free" [NC:449] where he was renting the estate of Edward Capell [Gammon, *Record of Estates, Northampton County*, I:111] and 7 "other free" in Franklin County in 1810 [NC:826]. Nathan and Amey may have been the parents of

   i.   Ephraim, head of a Franklin County household of 8 "other free" in 1810 [NC:826].

   ii.   Elizabeth, born say 1762, married Drury **Walden** in Northampton County in 1780 according to his pension records.

   iii.   Henry, born before 1776, head of a Halifax County, North Carolina household of 4 "other free" in 1800 [NC:316] and 9 "free colored" in 1820 [NC:151].

   iv.   Mary, head of a Northampton County household of 3 "other free" in 1800 [NC:451].

   v.   Hamilton, born 1776-94, head of a Halifax County household of 4 "other free" in 1810 [NC:26], and 2 "free colored" in Wilkes County in 1820 [NC:505].

   vi.   Ary, head of a Halifax County household of 3 "other free" in 1810 [NC:26].

   vii.   Ruthen, head of a Halifax County household of 3 "other free" in 1810 [NC:26].

   viii.   William, head of a Halifax County household of 2 "other free" in 1810 [NC:27].

11. ____ Harris, born say 1743, was the mother of several illegitimate children by Dixon **Brown**. Dixon made a 24 January 1811 Charles City County will, proved 18 January 1821, by which he left 30 acres to his illegitimate children Polly Harris, Susannah Harris (wife of James Harris), and Peggy **Bowman** which was the land they were then living on [WB 2:471]. Susannah Harris died intestate without a living child before October 1826 when Polly Harris, Morris Harris and Patsy his wife, Pegg **Bowman**, James **Brown**, Jr., (son of Dixon) and his wife Sally (nee **Stewart**), and Peter **Brown** and his wife Susan appointed James **Brown** to sell the 10 acres she received by her father's will. Edward **Brown** was the highest bidder at $32 [DB 7:371]. ____ was the mother of

   i.   Polly Harris, born say 1760, died before 26 May 1832 when her estate was sold. Edward **Bowman**, Abraham **Brown** and John **Bowman** were buyers at the sale [WB 4:29-30].

   ii.   Susannah, born about 1762, fifty-eight years old in 1820 when her husband James Harris applied for a pension [Jackson, *Virginia Negro Soldiers*, 36]. She died before October 1826 when her heirs appointed James **Brown** to sell her land [DB 7:371].

   iii.   Pegg **Bowman**.

20   iv.   ?Morris, born say 1784.

12. Joan Harris, born say 1752, was a "Mulatto" servant who was discharged from the service of Benjamin Abbot by the Halifax County, Virginia court on 17 June 1773 because he had no indentures for her [Orders 1772-3, 155]. On 16 January 1777 the court ordered the churchwardens to bind out Mill Harris, daughter of Johannah Harris to Benjamin Abbott, and on 18 March 1784 the court ordered the churchwardens to bind Jean's "bastard Mulattoe boy" Micajah Harris to Edward Akin but rescinded the order on 17 June that year and ordered him returned to his mother [Pleas 1774-9, 185; 1783-6, 35, 75]. She was the mother of

   i.   Mill, born say 1776.

   ii.   Micajah, born say 1780.

13. Edward[4] Harris, born say 1762, was a soldier from Chesterfield County who enlisted in the Revolution while a resident of Amelia County [Jackson,

Virginia Negro Soldiers, 36]. He may have been the Edward Harris who was head of a Charles City household of 5 "other free" in 1810 [VA:959] and a "Mulattoe" taxable in Chesterfield County 2 tithes and 3 horses in 1810, 1811 and 1813, living on James Scott's land with his 6 children in 1811 [PPTL, 1786-1811, frame 824; Waldrep, *1813 Tax List*]. He was the father of

    i.   Archer[2], born 18 August 1812, obtained a certificate of freedom in Charles City County on 16 June 1836: *son of Ned Harris, mulatto man, twenty three the 18th August last* [Minutes 1830-9, 281].

14. Mary Harris, born say 1738, was living in Brunswick County on 24 November 1756 when the court ordered the churchwardens to bind out her "natural child" Isham Harris [Orders 1756-7, 174]. She was apparently identical to "Mary Haris now Stuart" whose son Isham Harris was ordered bound out by the churchwardens of St. James Parish in Mecklenburg County court on 8 November 1766 [Orders 1765-8, 231]. She was married to William **Stewart** when they sold 200 acres on Little Creek in Mecklenburg County on 11 February 1788 [DB 7:253]. William **Stewart** was head of a Wake County household of 11 "other free" in 1790 [NC:105] and 11 "other free" and 2 slaves in 1800 [NC:798]. She was the mother of

    i.   Isham, born say 1756, bound out in Mecklenburg County on 8 November 1766 [Orders 1765-8, 231]. He sued Frederick Collier and Samuel Lark for trespass, assault and battery in Mecklenburg County court on 13 July 1784. Lucy Poole was deposed as his witness. Both suits were dismissed [Orders 1784-7, 95, 141, 169, 261, 263]. He married Mary **Dobey** (**Dolby**), 11 January 1792 Wake County bond and was head of a Wake County household of 7 "other free" in 1800 [NC:769].

15. John[3] Harris, born say 1755, was head of a Warren County, North Carolina household of 6 "other free" in 1790 [NC:77]. He was married to the widow of Stephen **Walden** by May 1791 when he settled Stephen's Warren County estate [Gammon, *Records of Estates, Warren County*, I:21]. Solomon Harris, John **Walden**, and Jesse Cunningham were buyers at the sale of the estate [WB:6:82].[115] John's children may have been

    i.   Kizee, born before 1776, head of a Warren County household of 3 "other free" in 1810 [NC:754] and one "free colored" in 1820 (Casiri Harris) [NC:816].

   ii. Phil, born say 1778, head of a Warren County household of 4 "other free" in 1800 [NC:808], 3 in 1810 [NC:758] and called Philemon Harris when he was head of an Orange County household of 3 "free colored" in 1820 [NC:290].

16. Phebe[2] Harris, born say 1755, was living in Mecklenburg County, Virginia, on 12 June 1780 when the churchwardens were ordered to bind out her daughter Elizabeth, "a poor orphan" [Orders 1779-84, 53]. On 11 February 1782 the churchwardens were ordered to bind her "Bastards" Milley and Jeremiah (no race mentioned) to Edward McDaniel [Orders 1779-84, 119]. Her children were

    i.   Elizabeth, born say 1772.

   ii. Milley, born say 1773.

  iii. Jeremiah, born say 1775, married Lydia **Chavous**, 13 November 1797 Mecklenburg County bond, James **Chavis** security.

  iv. ?John, married Rittah **Stewart**, 27 December 1802 Mecklenburg County bond, Jere Harris security.

---

[115]Jesse Cunningham may have been related to Charity **Cunningham**, head of a Northampton County household of 2 "other free" in 1790 [NC:76].

17. James[2] Harris, born say 1760, was taxable in Charles City County in 1783, called James Harris, Jr. He was taxable on a horse in 1790 and 1800, charged with 2 tithes in 1806, called James, Sr., in 1810, listed as a "Mulattoe" in 1813 [PPTL, 1783-7; 1788-1814] and head of a household of 5 "other free" in 1810 (called James Harris, Sr.) [VA:958]. He was a resident of Charles City County when he enlisted in the 2nd Virginia Regiment. He applied for a pension in 1820 stating that he was a farmer with a fifty-eight-year-old wife who was sickly [Jackson, *Virginia Negro Soldiers*, 36]. His wife Susannah **Harris**, illegitimate daughter of Dixon **Brown**, received 10 acres of land by the 24 January 1811 Charles City County will of her father. She died intestate without a living child before October 1826 when (her sister) Polly Harris, Morris Harris and Patsy his wife, (her sister) Pegg **Bowman**, James **Brown**, Jr., (son of Dixon) and his wife Sally, and Peter **Brown** and his wife Susan appointed James **Brown** to sell the land [DB 7:371]. James Harris died before 15 March 1834 when his estate was sold and divided between James **Brown**, Peter **Brown**, Burwell Harris, and James Harris. Peter **Brown** was executor [WB 4:72]. James and Susannah may have been the parents of

    i.   James[4], Jr., born say 1782, head of a Charles City County household of 6 "other free" in 1810 [VA:958]. The inventory of his Charles City County estate, taken on 2 June 1826, included a sheep, a sow and a bedstead and totalled $13.92 [WB 3:181].

18. Chavis Harris, born say 1780, and his wife Susanna were named in the 12 November 1803 Charles City County will of his mother Frances Harris [WB 1:650]. He was head of a Charles City County household of 8 "other free" in 1810 [VA:958]. His father-in-law Dixon **Brown** made a 24 January 1811 Charles City County will, proved 18 January 1821, by which he gave Chavis and his wife Susannah and (her brother) Dixon **Brown**, Jr., 40 acres where they were then living. He was called Henry C. Harris when he proved Dixon **Brown**, Sr.'s will on 18 January 1821 [WB 2:471]. On 4 January 1825 he was called Chavis Harris when he purchased 1/3 acres in Charles City County known as "Binns" adjoining his land and bounded by Henry Adams [DB 7:41]. But he was called Henry C. Chavis when he purchased 75 acres adjoining his land and bounded by Henry Adams and Morris Harris from David and his wife Lockey **Goin** on 8 November 1830 [DB 7:476]. His wife Sally Harris (apparently his second, born about 1795) obtained a certificate of freedom in Charles City County on 21 June 1832: *a woman of color aged thirty seven years (wife of Henry C. Harris), born free in this county* [Minutes 1830-7, 109]. He was called Henry C. Harris in his 24 December 1832 Charles City County will, proved 21 February 1833. He gave a bed to his son Benjamin, gave 3-1/3 acres of land which he had purchased from Cornelius and Lockey **Brown** to his sons Burwell and Benjamin Harris, gave grandchildren Zebedie and Julian Ann Harris a cow, daughter Patsey a bed, sons Thomas, William and Burwell Harris 20 shillings each and divided the remainder between all his children. He named Peter **Brown** and his son Burwell Harris executors. Francis **Bowman** dug his grave and James **Brown** made his coffin [WB 3:513-4; 4:116]. His children were

    i.   Thomas, born say 1805.

    ii. William, born say 1807.

   iii. Burwell, born 3 July 1810, obtained a certificate of freedom in Charles City County on 17 November 1831: *son of Henry C. Harris, twenty one years of age 3d July last, born free in this county* [Minutes 1830-7, 83].

   iv. Benjamin Hampton, born in February 1812, obtained a certificate of freedom in Charles City County on 17 November 1831: *son of Henry C. Harris, a boy of brown complexion, nineteen years in February last, born free in this county* [Minutes 1830-7, 83].

19. James Harris, born about 1748 in Dinwiddie County according to his Revolutionary War pension file, enlisted in the service while resident in Orange County, North Carolina, in 1775. In 1781 he moved to the part of Henry County which later became Patrick County and applied for a pension from there in 1835. He was a "Mulatto" taxable in Patrick County in 1799, listed with 2 tithes in 1799, 1804 and 1805 [PPTL, 1791-1823, frames 269, 398, 428, 460, 538, 598] and head of a Patrick County household of 6 "free colored" in 1830. His widow Keziah was head of a Patrick County household of 4 "free colored" in 1840 and was an eighty-year-old "Mulatto" woman, born in Virginia, counted in the 1850 census [VA:389]. She applied for a survivor's Revolutionary War pension in 1855 stating that her maiden name was Keziah Minor and that she and James had married in Rockingham County, North Carolina, in 1801. James was apparently the father of

    i.   Agnes, daughter of James Harris, married Burbage **Goin**, 26 July 1810 Patrick County bond. Beveridge **Going**, born before 1776, was head of a Patrick County household of 3 "free colored" in 1820 [VA:106].

    ii. James, Jr., a "Mulatto" taxable in Patrick County in 1806 [PPTL, 1791-1823, frame 460].

    iii. Alexander, a "Mulatto" taxable in Patrick County from 1807 to 1813 [PPTL, 1791-1823, frame 571]. He married Judith **Fendley**, 1807 Patrick County bond.

    iv. Tabitha, married John **Rickman**, 1805 Patrick County bond.

    v. Nancy, married Cam **Loggins**, 1817 Patrick County bond.

    vi. Robert, married Nancy **Goins**, daughter of James and Nancy, 1816 Patrick County bond.

20. Morris Harris, born say 1784, was head of a Charles City County household of 5 "other free" in 1810 [VA:939]. In October 1826 he and his wife Patsy appointed James **Brown** to sell 10 acres which (his aunt?) Susannah Harris, deceased, received by the will of Dixon **Brown** [DB 7:371]. Morris was the father of

    i.   Sandy, born 2 July 1808, obtained a certificate of freedom in Charles City County on 16 December 1830: *son of Morris Harris, a bright mulatto man, twenty two years of age 2 July last* [Minutes 1830-7, 35].

    ii. Mitchel, born 11 September 1811, obtained a certificate of freedom in Charles City County on 21 February 1833: *son of Morris Harris, a bright mulattoe man, aged twenty one years 11 September last* [Minutes 1830-7, 142].

    iii. Pamelia, born 4 June 1820, obtained a certificate of freedom in Charles City County on 21 August 1834: *daughter of Morris Harris, aged fourteen last June 4, bright mulatto* [Minutes 1830-7, 158].

    iv. Matthew, born June 1822, obtained a certificate of freedom in Charles City County on 21 August 1834: *son of Morris Harris, aged twelve in June last, a mulatto boy* [Minutes 1830-7, 142].

    v. Susan, born July 1824, obtained a certificate of freedom in Charles City County on 21 August 1834: *daughter of Morris Harris, aged ten in July last, a mulatto girl* [Minutes 1830-7, 142].

    vi. Abby, born April 1827, obtained a certificate of freedom in Charles City County on 21 August 1834: *daughter of Morris Harris, aged seven in April last, a mulatto girl* [Minutes 1830-7, 142].

    vii. Peter, born 20 January 1814, obtained a certificate of freedom in Charles City County on 18 June 1835: *son of Morris Harris, mulatto man, twenty one 20 January last* [Minutes 1830-7, 238[.

Other members of the Harris family from the Petersburg area were

    i.   Fanny, born say 1756, mother of Nancy **Braughton** (**Brogdon**?) (born about 1775) who registered in Petersburg on 8 July 1805: *Nancy Braughton, a very light Mulatto woman, five feet two inches high, thirty* *years old, long curled hair, holes in her ears, born free and raised in the County of Chesterfield, daughter of Fanny Harris* [Register of Free Negroes 1794-1819, no. 294].

ii. Rebecca, born about 1760, registered in Petersburg on 18 August 1794: *a light brown Mulatto woman, five feet one inches high, about thirty four years old, born free in Chesterfield County* [Register of Free Negroes 1794-1819, no. 24].

21 iii. John⁵, born say 1761.

iv. David, born about 1765, registered in Petersburg on 14 June 1810: *a brown Mulatto man, five feet six inches high, forty five years old, born free and raised in the County of Chesterfield* [Register of Free Negroes 1794-1819, no. 599].

v. Paterson, born about 1774, registered in Petersburg on 7 December 1796: *a light brown Mulatto man, five feet ten and a half inches high, twenty two years old, with short bushy hair, his eyes rather dark yellowish grey, born free & raised in the County of Dinwiddie* [Register of Free Negroes 1794-1819, no. 118].

vi. Patsy, born about 1775, registered in Petersburg on 9 June 1810: *a light yellow brown Mulatto woman, five feet five inches high, thirty five years old, born free in Dinwiddie County* [Register of Free Negroes 1794-1819, no. 579].

vii. William, born about 1783, registered in Petersburg on 24 June 1805: *a brown Mulatto man, five feet five inches high, twenty two years old, born free in Chesterfield County* [Register of Free Negroes 1794-1819, no. 293]. He was a "Mulatto" taxable in Chesterfield County from 1806 to 1809 [PPTL, 1786-1811, frames 660, 704, 753].

viii. Archer¹, born say 1788, a "Mulatto" taxable in Chesterfield County in 1809 living on Mrs. Hamblin's hire land [PPTL, 1786-1811, frame 738].

21. John⁵ Harris, born say 1761, was a soldier who enlisted in the Revolution in Petersburg. His children were living in Wilkes County, North Carolina, on 3 July 1852 when they applied for a pension for his services as a drummer. They declared that he and their mother Mary **Walker** were married by the Episcopal Minister in Dinwiddie County in October or November 1785. They moved to Randolph County, North Carolina, near the old courthouse, called Randolph Cross Roads, and lived there for five or six years, and then moved to Rowan County near Lexington (Davidson County) where their father died on 20 April 1806. John may have been the "free" John Harris who was taxable in Dinwiddie County in Braddock Goodwyn's district adjoining "free" Andrew Harris in 1801 [PPTL 1801 B, p.7]. Their mother married Drury **Mitchell**, head of a Wilkes County household of 8 "other free" in 1810 [NC:867]. Their father had a record of the marriage and the births of his children, but the record was "taken off" by Drury **Mitchell** [CR 104.923.2 by *NCGSJ* V:251-2]. Mary purchased 85 acres in Wilkes County from Jordan **Chavis** in 1829 [DB M:206]. Her 20 August 1833 Wilkes County will, proved February 1834, named her seven children: Nancy, Lucy, Jehu, Isaac, Polly **Baley**, John, and Ibby [WB 4:169]. Their children were

i. Nancy, born about 1786, married William **Ferguson**, 27 October 1802 Rowan County bond. She was the oldest child of John and Mary Harris according to William **Ferguson**'s deposition in support of the Harris family pension application. William **Ferguson** was head of a Wilkes County household of 8 "free colored" in 1820 [NC:543].

ii. Lucy, born say 1792, married Jordan **Chavis** as his second wife.

iii. Jehu, born about 1794, married Clarissy **Chavis**, 1 June 1821 Wilkes County bond. She was fifty-eight years old in 1852.

iv. Isaac, born about 1800, married Icy **Wooten** 22 September 1832 Wilkes County bond. He was fifty-two years old in 1852.

  v.   Polly **Baley**, probably the wife of Jesse **Bailey**, "free colored" head of
       a Wilkes County household of 4 in 1820.
  vi. John⁶, deceased by the time his mother made her will.
  vii. Iby **Anderson**, born about 1807, forty-five years old in 1852.

Other Harris family members in Virginia were
  i.   John, born say 1710, a "Mullatto" fined by the Accomack County court
       on 4 January 1736/7 for swearing six profane oaths [Orders 1731-36,
       201].
  ii. George², born say 1752, a "negroe" tithable in Gloucester County in
       1770 [Mason, *Records of Gloucester County*, 52]. He was a "Free
       Negro" in St. Paul's Parish, Hanover County, where he was tithable
       from 1807 to 1812 and tithable on a horse in 1815 [Cocke, *Hanover
       County Taxables, St. Paul's Parish*, 57].

Craven County, North Carolina
1. Thomas Harris, born about 1747, was a twelve-year-old "Mulatto" orphan
    ordered bound to Thomas Haline to be a tanner by the 11 May 1759 Craven
    County court [Minutes 1758-62, 32b]. He was head of a Craven County
    household of 10 "other free" in 1790 [NC:134]. He was probably the Thomas
    Harris who was taxed on 100 acres in District 3 of Craven County in 1779
    [LP 30.1]. And he may have been the brother of John Harris who was head
    of a Craven County household of 6 "other free," 3 slaves, and a white woman
    in 1790 [NC:130]. John was taxable on 335 acres in District 3 of Craven
    County in 1779 [LP 30.1]. Thomas was probably the father of
  i.   Isaac, head of a Craven County household of 7 "free colored" in 1820
       [NC:76].
  ii. Mary, head of a Craven County household of 6 "free colored" in 1820
       [NC:71].

HARRISON FAMILY

1. Susan Harrison, born say 1690, was the mother of a "Mullatto Bastard Child
    named John" who was about seven years old on 6 October 1703 when Henry
    Armitrading testified in Accomack County court that his mother had left the
    boy with him. The court bound the boy as an apprentice to Armitrading
    [Orders 1703-9, 13]. She may have been the ancestor of
2   i.   Ann, born say 1730.
3   ii. Sarah, born say 1733.

2. Ann Harrison, born say 1730, was sued by the churchwardens in Southampton
    County on 9 November 1749, but the charges were dismissed when they failed
    to prosecute. On 13 November 1755 the court presented her for having a
    bastard child, but on 9 April 1756 the sheriff reported that she was not an
    inhabitant of the county and the court ordered her "mulatto" daughter Hannah
    bound out [Orders 1749-54, 26, 31; 1754-9, 149, 170, 221, 230]. Her children
    were
  i.   ?James, born say 1750, a taxable "mulatto" in Joseph **Gowen**'s 1764
       Granville County household in the list of John Pope, perhaps the James
       Harrison who was head of a Colleton District, South Carolina
       household of 5 "other free" and a slave in 1810 [SC:591].
  ii. Hannah, born say 1755, ordered bound an apprentice in Southampton
       County on 8 April 1756, no age or master named.
  iii. ?Charles, born say 1770, married Martha **Eppes**, 3 November 1791
       Sussex County bond; and he married second, Rebecca **Johnson**, 13
       September 1792 Southampton County bond. He was a "free Negro"
       head of an Isle of Wight County household of 4 "other free" in 1810
       [VA:37].

iv. ?Patience, head of a Free Town, Brunswick County, Virginia household of 6 "other free" in 1810 [VA:770].

v. ?Carter, born before 1776, head of a Halifax County, North Carolina household of 7 "free colored" in 1820 [NC:151]. Perhaps his widow was Martha Harrison, head of a Halifax County household of 7 "free colored" in 1830.

vi. ?Nathan, head of a Currituck County, North Carolina household of 3 "other free" in 1810 [VA:88].

3. Sarah Harrison, born say 1733, was the mother of Anselum, a "mulatto child who the Southampton County court ordered bound on 9 April 1756 [Orders 1754-9, 221]. She was the mother of
   i. Anselm, born say 1755.

Other members of the Harrison family in Virginia were
   i. Henry, a "free Molatto" farmer living alone on Need's Old Field in Westmoreland County in 1801 [*Virginia Genealogist* 31:43], head of a Westmoreland County household of 4 "other free" in 1810 [VA:774] and 5 "free colored" in 1830.
   ii. Samuel, a "free Molatto" farmer living with (his wife?) Judy Harrison and (their?) children Sally and Emelia Harrison on Need's Old Field in Westmoreland County in 1801 [*Virginia Genealogist* 31:43]. Judy was head of a Westmoreland County household of 2 "other free" in 1810 [VA:774].

HARTLESS FAMILY

1. Henry[1] Hartless, born say 1730, a "mulatto," was presented by the Spotsylvania County court on 4 May 1761 for cohabiting with a white woman [Orders 1755-65, 208]. He was head of an Amherst County household of 9 whites (free persons) and a slave in 1783 [VA:48] and 9 "whites" in 1785 [VA:85]. He was taxable in Amherst County from 1783 to 1803: taxable on 2 slaves, 6 horses and 17 cattle in 1783, 4 free tithables and a slave in 1788, 3 tithables, 3 slaves and 5 horses in 1791 [PPTL 1782-1803, frames 23, 53, 137, 167, 227, 291, 349, 395, 482, 589]. He purchased 215 acres in Amherst County on a branch of the south fork of Buffalo and on Long Mountain on 28 February 1778 and 330 acres in Amherst County on Horsley Creek on 6 January 1797 [DB E:47; H:219]. On 2 April 1782 the Amherst County court ordered that he be paid for providing 20 pounds of bacon and 275 pounds of beef to the Revolution [Orders 1773-82, 281]. He was called Henry Hartlas, Sr., on 16 July 1798 when he received a grant for 72 acres on Swaping Creek [Grants 1797-98, 311]. He proved the will of John Jarvis in Amherst County court on 17 June 1799 [Orders 1799-1801, 1]. He died intestate on 9 July 1802, and on 17 September 1803 his widow Isabella Hartless made a deed appointing four of her sons Henry, James, William, and Richard administrators [DB I:582]. The inventory of his estate, recorded on 19 December 1803, totaled 777 pounds [WB 4:140]. His heirs sold 523 acres on the north fork of the Pedlar River to William Hartless on 8 August 1818 and sold other land to John **Clark**, Joseph Jarvis, Reuben **Peters** and Nathaniel **Cooper** by deed proved in court on 18 October 1819. They were William Hartless and his wife Nancy, Henry Hartless and his wife Jane, Richard and his wife Mary, William Wilson and his wife Nancy, Mariant Hartless, Annis Hartless, James Graham and his wife Isbell, Joseph Jarvis and his wife Nancy, John **Clark** and his wife Mary, Reuben **Peters** and his wife Susannah, and Nathaniel **Cooper** and his wife Patsy [DB O:293, 295, 331; Orders 1815-20, 434, 438-9]. His children were most likely

2 i. James, born say 1750.

ii.   Peter, born about 1752, about eighty years old on 1 November 1832 when he made a declaration in Amherst County court to obtain a pension for his services in the Revolution. He was born in Caroline County, enrolled in the militia in 1777 or 1778, drafted in 1781, and returned to Caroline County until 1787 when he moved to Amherst County. Bounty land was issued to Lawrence **Mason** for his services in the North Carolina Militia during the War of 1812 [M804-1210, frame 0249]. He was one of the freeholders ordered to work on the road from the Blue Ridge at Irish Creek Gap to the three forks of the Pedlar River in Amherst County on 4 November 1789 [Orders 1787-90, 590]. He married Jean **Mason**, 2 January 1792 Amherst County bond, with the consent of Thomas and Jane **Mason**. Peter was taxable in Caroline County in 1783 [Fothergill, *Virginia Tax Payers*, 56], taxable in Lexington Parish, Amherst County, from 1787 to 1821: called a "man of color" in 1811 and 1812, a "Mulatto" in 1813, in a list of "Free Mulattoes & Negroes" in 1814, 1816, and 1818 [PPTL 1782-1803, frames 101, 167, 227, 349, 395, 452, 510, 588; 1804-23, frames 25, 108, 168, 213, 234, 256, 284, 403, 503, 539, 601]. He was head of an Amherst County household of 3 "other free" in 1810 [VA:288]. His 16 March 1828 Amherst County will, proved 17 September 1835 named his wife Jane, Nancy **Mason** (daughter of Larsons **Mason**) and Peter **Mason** [WB 9:124].

3   iii.   William[1], born about 1754.

iv.   Richard[1], born say 1771, an infant over the age of fourteen in November 1791 when his guardian Henry Hartless sued Bartholomew Staton for trespass, assault and battery [Orders 1790-4, 303]. He was taxable in Amherst County from 1792 to 1812: taxable on a slave from 1798 to 1811 and listed as a "man of color" in 1811 and 1812 [PPTL 1783-1803, frames 259, 327, 349, 395, 421, 482; 1804-23, frames 24, 107, 191, 213, 234]. He was head of an Amherst County household of 5 "other free" and 5 slaves in 1810 [VA:284]. He purchased 180 acres in Amherst County bordering the middle fork of the Pedlar River and the south side of Mount Pleasant on 15 February 1808 [DB L:70].

v.   Henry[2], born say 1777, married Jane **Clark**, 25 June 1798 Amherst County bond, William **Clark** surety. Henry was head of an Amherst County household of 12 "free colored" in 1820.

vi.   Nancy, born say 1780, married William Wilson, 8 October 1798 Amherst County bond.

vii.   Susanna, born say 1785, "a free mulatto," married Reuben **Peters**, "a free Negro," in Amherst County on 8 January 1812 [Marriage Register, 229].

viii.   Isabel, married James Graham, apparently a white man.

ix.   Mariant, in a Rockbridge County list of "Free Negroes and Mulattoes" above the age of sixteen in James McClug's district in 1813 [Waldrep, *1813 Tax List*].

x.   Annis, in a Rockbridge County list of "Free Negroes and Mulattoes" above the age of sixteen in James McClug's district in 1813 [Waldrep, *1813 Tax List*].

xi.   Mary, married John **Clark**.

xii.   Patsy, married Nathaniel **Cooper**.

2.   James Hartless, born say 1750, was one of the freeholders of Amherst County ordered to work on a new road from Irish Creek Gap down the Pedlar River to Campbell Road on 5 January 1778, listed next to Michael **Ailstock**. On 4 March 1783 the Amherst County court dismissed his suit against Hugh McCabe [Orders 1773-82, 211-2; 1782-4, 84]. He was taxable in Amherst County on 3 horses and 2 cattle in 1782 but not taxable there again until 1800. His estate was taxable on 3 horses in 1805 [PPTL 1782-1803, frames 9, 482;

1804-23, 67]. His estate was inventoried on 16 September 1805 at 71 pounds [WB 4:190]. His administrator paid board and schooling for his sons Richard and Henry Hartless [WB 5:64; 6:223, 306]. He was the father of

  i. ?Nancy, married Joseph Jarvis (apparently a white man), a taxable in Amherst County in 1804. She was one of the heirs of Henry Hartless who sold land in Amherst County in 1819 [Orders 1815-20, 438-9].

  ii. Richard, Jr., born say 1796, taxable in Amherst County in 1817 and 1820 [PPTL 1804-23, frames 447, 539, 551].

  iii. Henry, Jr., born say 1798, taxable in Amherst County in 1819 and 1820 [PPTL 1804-23, frames 539, 551].

3. William[1] Hartless, born about 1754, made a declaration in Amherst County court on 17 September 1832 to obtain a pension for his services in the Revolution. He stated that he was born in Caroline County, moved to Amherst County when he was twenty-three years old, entered the militia in Albemarle County in 1779, and was drafted from Amherst County in 1781 [M804-1210, frame 0260]. He was taxable in Lexington Parish, Amherst County, from 1782 to 1821: taxable on 3 horses in 1782, 2 tithables in 1803, 3 tithables in 1804, 4 in 1805 and 1807, 3 slaves in 1809, called a "man of color" in 1811 and 1812, a "Mulatto" in 1813 [PPTL 1782-1803, frames 9, 54, 101, 137, 197, 259, 327, 372, 421, 482, 555, 588; 1804-23, frames 24, 67, 147, 169, 213, 234, 255, 503, 600]. He was head of an Amherst County household of 1 white (free) person in 1783 [VA:48] and 1785 [VA:85], 13 "other free" in 1810, and 6 "free colored" and a 26-44 year old white woman in 1820. He married Nancy Staton, 7 February 1785 Amherst County bond, John Jarvis surety, with the consent of her mother Ann Staton [Orders 1784-87, 111]. In February 1811 the Amherst County court appointed him and Peter Hartless as commissioners to view a way for a road through the lands of John Martin [Orders 1811-4]. He purchased 523 acres on the north fork of the Pedlar River from Henry Hartless' heirs on 8 August 1818 [DB O:293, 295, 331]. He was probably the father of

  i. William[2], Jr., a "M. of C." (man of color) taxable in Amherst County in 1812, a "Mulatto" in 1813 [PPTL 1804-23, frame 234, 256].

HARVEY FAMILY

1. Mary Harvey, born say 1740, was living in Cumberland County, Virginia, on 27 July 1761 when the court ordered the churchwardens of King William Parish to bind her "Mulatto" daughter Phebe Harvy to John Bilbo [Orders 1758-62, 372]. Mary was head of a Loudoun County household of 3 "other free" in 1810 [VA:396]. She was the mother of

2   i. Phebe, born say 1761.

2. Phebe Harvey, born say 1761, was a "Mulatto" bound out by the Cumberland County, Virginia court on 27 July 1761. She was living in Mecklenburg County, Virginia, (no race indicated) on 11 August 1783 when the court dismissed her complaint against her master John Bilbo for misusage. The court bound her daughter Nelly Harvey to Bennett Sandifer with the consent of her master [Orders 1779-84, 400]. She was the mother of

  i. Nelly, born say 1780.

  ii. ?Martha, born about 1789, a six-year-old "Mullatto" girl bound to Richard Moss by the Warren County, North Carolina court in August 1795 [Minutes 1793-1800, 71].

  iii. ?Nancy, born about 1791, a four-year-old "Mullatto" girl bound to Richard Moss by the Warren County, North Carolina court in August 1795 [Minutes 1793-1800, 71].

  iv. ?Thomas, born 1794-1806, head of a Halifax County, North Carolina household of 4 "free colored" in 1830 [NC:314].

HATCHER FAMILY

1. Jack Hatcher, born say 1729, "alias Indian Jack," petitioned John Parish, Sr., in Goochland County, Virginia court on 19 September 1750. Parish died before November court 1751, and Jack sued his widow and administrator Judith Parish for trespass in May 1752. The deposition of Robert Napier, Sr., an "aged and infirm person" of Albemarle County was taken on Jack's behalf. In July 1764 the court found in Jack's favor for 40 shillings damages. In July 1759 Bouth Napier sued him for debt, but Jack delayed the case until September 1762 when judgment was entered against him [Orders 1750-57, 36, 47, 94, 128, 204, 409, 594; 1757-61, 227, 252; 1761-5, 99]. He may have been the father of
    i.   David, born about 1762, a sixteen-year-old "half Indian" planter who enlisted in the Granville County, North Carolina Militia during the Revolution [*The North Carolinian*, 726 (N.C. Archives Troop Returns File TR 4-40)]. He was head of a Chesterfield County, South Carolina household of 9 "other free" in 1800 [SC:103] and 8 in 1810 [SC:550].
    ii. William, born say 1770, "Negroe" head of a Cheraw District, South Carolina household of 3 "other free" in 1790 [SC:49], and 5 in Chesterfield County in 1800 [SC:103].
    iii. Nancy, head of a Fairfield County, South Carolina household of 3 "other free" in 1800 [SC:227].

HATFIELD/ HATTER FAMILY

1. Richard[1] Hatfield, born say 1680, was an "Indian man" who bound himself as an apprentice to Burr Harrison for seven years by indenture proved in Stafford County on 9 April 1706, "to be dealt with when absent or runaway" the same as an imported servant [WB Liber Z, 1699-1709, 315-6]. He was probably the ancestor of
    i.   Richard[2], born say 1748, a free-born man who was indentured to Samuel Lambuth of Smithtown. He ran away before 18 May 1769 when an ad appeared in the *Virginia Gazette* describing him as: *a Negro man named Richard Hatfield, though he goes by the name of Hatter...a very yellow Negro...I imagine he has gone to Norfolk or Hampton, as he has a brother at Col. Cary's, and another at Mr. Balfour's* [*Virginia Gazette* (Purdie & Dixon edition, page 3, column 3].
2   ii. Jacob Hatter, born say 1750.
    iii. Patty Hatter, head of a Frederick County household of 4 "other free" in 1810 [VA:516].
    iv. Peter Hatfield, born 1776-1794, head of a Duck Creek Hundred, Kent County, Delaware household of 4 "free colored" in 1820 [DE:55].

2. Jacob Hatter, born say 1750, married Milly **Walden**, 14 June 1806 Petersburg Hustings Court marriage. He may have been the father of
    i.   Jack Hatter, born about 1771, registered in Petersburg on 14 June 1806: *a dark brown Negro man, five feet six and a half inches high, thirty five years old, born free & brought from raised Maryland by Jas. French late of Dinwiddie County* [Register of Free Negroes 1794-1819, no. 382].

HAWKINS FAMILY

Members of the Hawkins family born before 1750 were
1   i.   Solomon[1], born say 1720.

ii. David[1], born say 1730, purchased 100 acres on Quankey Creek in North Carolina on June 1755 from Solomon Hawkins for 5 pounds [Edgecombe County DB 2:329].

iii. Stephen, born say 1738, a "free negro" taxable on the north side of Tanners Creek in Norfolk County in 1754 [Wingo, *Norfolk County Tithables, 1751-65*, 91].

iv. Hannah, born say 1746, a "free Negro" living in Norfolk County on 18 February 1763 when her son Thomas was bound as an apprentice [Orders 1759-63, 238] and a taxable "negro" in Elizabeth River Parish in 1768 [Wingo, *Norfolk County Tithables, 1766-80*, 81].

1. Solomon[1] Hawkins, born say 1720, was witness (signing) to the 16 February 1742 Edgecombe County, North Carolina deed of John Inman and Edward Pore [DB 5:21], Gideon **Gibson**'s 15 February 1749 Northampton County, North Carolina deed [DB 1:383], and the 3 January 1758 Halifax County, North Carolina will of William Jones [WB 1:65]. He purchased 220 acres of land in Edgecombe County joining James Carter for 7 pounds on 20 November 1752 and sold it about nine months later on 23 August 1753 for 15 pounds [DB 3:345; 4:491]. He was called Solomon Hawkins, shoemaker, on 21 August 1754 when he purchased for 30 pounds 210 acres on Quankey Creek in the part of Edgecombe County which became Halifax County in 1758. About a year later on 3 June 1755 he sold 100 acres of this land to (his brother?) David[1] Hawkins for 5 pounds. He and David were called cordwainers when they jointly sold their land on 10 January 1756 for 40 pounds [DB 2:245, 329, 425]. He was head of a household of one "mulatto," 3 black males, and one black female tithable in the Bertie County tax list of James Moore in 1769 and 1770 [CR 10.702.1]. He may have been the father of

2   i. Solomon[2], born say 1745, died in 1816.
3   ii. Joseph[1], born say 1755, died 1817-18.

2. Solomon[2] Hawkins, born say 1745, purchased 100 acres in Halifax County, North Carolina, on 9 January 1775 [DB 13:277]. He was head of a Halifax County household of 14 "other free" in 1790 [NC:61], 9 "other free" in 1800 [NC:318], and 14 "other free" in 1810 [NC:26]. By his 4 April 1815 will, proved August 1816, he lent 100 acres to his unnamed wife during her lifetime, and named his children [WB 3:589]:

i. Henry, born say 1765, served in the Revolution from Halifax County [NSDAR, *African American Patriots*, 165]. He purchased 60 acres in Halifax County on 26 October 1793 [DB 17:673]. He was head of a Halifax County household of 3 "other free" in 1790 [NC:61], 7 in 1800 [NC:318], 8 in 1810 [NC:23], and 9 "free colored" in 1820 [NC:151]. He was probably the Henry Hawkins of Halifax County who made a deposition on 23 November 1812 that he was in the service with Nathan **Scott** and that **Scott** died in the hospital in Philadelphia [LP 262, by *NCGSJ* VI:15].

ii. David[2], born say 1770, head of a Halifax County household of 4 "other free" in 1800 [NC:314].

iii. Hannah **Jones**.

iv. Betty **Rudd**, perhaps the wife of John **Rudd**, head of a Halifax County household of 6 "other free" in 1800 [NC:338]. He was probably a son of William **Rudd**, head of a Halifax County household of 8 "other free" in 1790 [NC:62]. He may have been the William **Rudd** who purchased 150 acres joining Jumping Run in Halifax County on 2 December 1789 [DB 17:20].

v. Polly **Carter**.

vi. Betty **Scott**.

vii. Patty Hawkins.

    viii. Prissy Hawkins.

    ix. Nancy, married Exum **James**, 18 January 1826 Halifax County bond.

3. Joseph[1] Hawkins, born say 1755, was called a shoemaker when he purchased 70 acres from William Bozeman joining the Marsh Swamp in Halifax County on 11 December 1779 [DB 17:316]. He was head of a Halifax County household of 9 "other free" in 1790 [NC:64], 5 in 1800, and 5 "other free" and 1 slave in 1810 [NC:27]. His 23 April 1817 Halifax County will, proved February 1818, mentioned his children [WB 3:611]:

    i. Elizabeth Hawkins.

    ii. Mary Hawkins.

    iii. Nancy Bozeman, mother of John Bozeman who received $100 for his education by the will of his grandfather Joseph Hawkins.

    iv. Samuel, living alone in Halifax County in 1790 [NC:63], head of a household of 7 "other free" in 1800 [NC:314] and 9 "other free" in 1810 [NC:27]. He may have been the Samuel Hawkins who purchased 100 acres on Haw Tree Creek in Halifax County on 12 April 1783 and purchased a further 15 acres on the north side of Little Fishing Creek which he sold on 10 May 1795 [DB 17:383, 673, 677].

    v. Joseph[2], Jr. (J.J.), executor of his father's will, living alone in Halifax County in 1810 [NC:26] and head of a household of 7 "free colored" in 1820 [NC:150].

Another member of a Hawkins family was

    i. James, born about 1763, about fifty-seven years old with no family living with him on 14 October 1820 when he made a declaration in Fluvanna County to obtain a pension for his service in the Revolution. He stated that "being a Coloured man," he was taken as a waiter to Major Chrogham. He received a land warrant for three years service [M804-1227, frame 0576].

HAWLEY FAMILY

1. Micajah/ Michael Hawley, born say 1700, may have been related to Mary Haley who was presented by the York County court on 20 November 1727 for not listing herself as a tithable [OW 16:489]. On 17 May 1731 he received a patent for 640 acres in Bertie County, North Carolina, on the south side of the Meherrin River [Northampton County DB 3:422 & 4:10].[116] He and his wife Sarah sold 300 acres of this land on 7 August 1738 [Bertie DB E:313]. His 1 March 1752 will was proved in the August 1752 Northampton County court. He gave sons: Joseph, William, and Christopher, only one shilling each and left the bulk of his estate to son Benjamin, who may have been the youngest since he was mentioned last. And he left his grandson William **Mitchell** 60 acres at the mouth of Flat Branch near Cypress Branch. He also mentioned his three daughters: Ann, Elizabeth, and Mary (no last names) [SS original]. His children were

2   i. Joseph, born say 1725.

3   ii. William, born say 1728.

    iii. Christopher, born say 1730, tithable in Granville County in the list of Jonathan White circa 1748.

    iv. Ann, born say 1732, perhaps the one who married ____ **Mitchell** and was the mother of Benjamin's grandchild William **Mitchell**. He may have been identical to William **Shoecraft**, son of Ann **Mitchell**, "a free Mulattoe," who was bound an apprentice by the Bertie County court on 24 October 1758 [Haun, *Bertie County Court Minutes*, II:452].

---

[116]Northampton County was formed from this part of Bertie County in 1741.

4 v. Benjamin¹, born say 1735.
   vi. Elizabeth, born say 1737.
   vii. Mary, born say 1739.

2. Joseph Hawley, born about 1725, and his wife were taxables in Granville County in 1750 in the list of Jonathan White, and in 1754 he and his wife "Marthew" (Martha) were taxables in John Sallis' list [CR 44.701.19]. He was in the 8 October 1754 Granville County colonial muster of Colonel Eaton, called Joseph Halley, next to Lawrence **Pettiford** [Clark, *Colonial Soldiers of the South*, 728]. He was an insolvent taxpayer in 1757 and 1758 in the list of Sheriff William Johnson. In the 1767 list of Stephen Jett he was in Fishing Creek District with wife and children, and in 1767 the constable provided his wife's maiden name: Martha **Harris**. She was probably the sister of Edward and George **Harris** of Granville County. On 4 November 1778 Joseph entered 602 acres in Granville County adjoining **Chavis** and **Snelling** including the plantation where he was then living [Pruitt, *Land Entries: Granville County*, 32]. In 1785 he was taxable on 624 acres and 1 head of cattle. He had 6 persons in his household in Beaver Dam District in 1786 in the North Carolina State Census. On 25 May 1791 he gave Thomas Bevan his power of attorney to receive the wages due him for three years service as a Continental soldier [*NCGSJ* X:112]. Joseph and Martha's children were

5 i. Sarah, born about 1748.
   ii. Mary, born about 1749, first taxed in 1761 in her father's household in Fishing Creek District.
   iii. Martha, born about 1750, first taxable in 1762.
6 iv. Jacob, born about 1751.
   v. Nathan, born about 1755, first taxable in 1767. He was taxable on 1 poll in 1788 in Abraham's Plain District. On 26 December 1793 he entered 20 acres on the waters of Grassy Creek [Pruitt, *Land Entries: Granville County*, 61]. In 1796 he was taxable on 15 acres and 1 poll in Abrams Plains District, and in 1799 he was taxable on 110 acres and 1 poll. In 1805 he was taxable on only 15 acres in Goshen District [Tax List 1796-1802, 41, 188; 1803-09, 118], and in 1808 he entered 400 acres in Granville County on the waters of "Bannets" Creek [Pruitt, *Land Entries: Granville County*, 81]. He was head of a Granville County household of 7 "other free" in 1800, 10 in 1810 [NC:913] and 6 "free colored" in Caswell County in 1820 [NC:65].
   vi. Joan, born about 1755, first taxable in 1767.
7 vii. ?Jesse, born say 1760.
   viii. Benjamin², born say 1765, underage when he enlisted for nine months in the Continental Line according to the deposition of his father Joseph Hawley who was living in Granville County on 7 June 1791 when he gave Thomas Beavan his power of attorney to collect wages due to Benjamin for service in the Revolution [*NCGSJ* X:112].
   ix. ?Pearson, born about 1770, taxable in Granville County in 1791. In 1793 he was in Fort Creek District in the list of John Pope taxable on 1 poll. He was head of a Granville County household of 5 "other free" in 1800 and was taxable on 1 poll in Country Line District in 1803 [Tax List 1803-09, 37].

3. William Hawley, born say 1728, may have been the William Hawly who was taxable on a white tithe in Granville County in 1751 and a white tithe in 1762 in Goodwins District, Granville County [CR 44.702.19]. He may have been the husband of Amy Hawley, daughter of John **Scott**, "free Negro" of Berkeley County, South Carolina, whose complaint was entered in Orange County, North Carolina court on 12 March 1754:

Joseph Deevit Wm. Deevit & Zachariah Martin, entered by force, the house of his daughter, Amy Hawley, and carried her off, by force, with her six children, and he thinks they are taking them north to sell as slaves.[117]

One of the children, "a mulatto boy Busby, alias John Scott," was recovered in Orange County, North Carolina, and on 12 March 1754 the county court appointed Thomas **Chavis** to return the child to South Carolina [Haun, *Orange County Court Minutes*, I:70, 71]. William recorded a plat for 250 acres in Craven County, South Carolina, near the Tiger River and Fair Forest Creek on 15 June 1772 [S.C. Archives series S213190, vol. 19:484]. The child of Amy (and William?) was

   i.   Busby, born say 1745-50.

Other South Carolina descendants were probably:

   i.   Elizabeth Holly, head of a Richland District household of 4 "other free" in 1810 [SC:175a].

   ii.   Sarah Holly, a resident of Richland District in 1806 when she petitioned the South Carolina legislature to be exempted from the tax on free Negro women [S.C. Archives series S.165015, item 01885].

   iii.   Isham Holley, a taxable "free negro" in the district between Broad and Catawba River in South Carolina in 1784 [South Carolina Tax List 1783-1800, frame 37].

   iv.   Benjamin Holley, a taxable "free negro" in the district between Broad and Catawba River in South Carolina in 1784 [South Carolina Tax List 1783-1800, frame 37].

   v.   Charles Holly, head of an Edgefield District household of 7 "other free" in 1810 [SC:813].

   vi.   Milly Holly, head of an Edgefield District household of 2 "other free" in 1810 [SC:766].

4.   Benjamin[1] Hawley, born say 1735, was the executor and main beneficiary of his father's estate. He voted for Joseph Sikes in the Northampton County election of 1762 [SS 837 by *NCGSJ* XII:170]. He sold the estate which included 4 slaves, 15 head of cattle, 50 hogs, and his household furniture in Northampton County on 29 March 1766 for 330 pounds. He mortgaged 600 acres of his father's land for 100 pounds on 12 May 1766 and repaid the mortgage on 1 September that same year [DB 3:422, 429; 4:10]. On 4 February 1767 he and his wife Mary sold 580 acres of their land for 325 pounds, and he bought 200 acres on Batty's Delight Swamp in Northampton County on 3 March 1769 [DB 4:36, 204]. He was taxed in Northampton County on an assessment of 667 pounds in 1780 [GA 46.1]. He was head of a Northampton County household of 3 "other free" in 1790 [NC:75]. His 7 July 1797 will was proved in March 1805 [WB 2:276]. He named his children:

   i.   William, executor of his father's estate, received his father's land, plantation, and carpenter and blacksmith tools. He was head of a Northampton County household of 3 "other free" in 1800 [NC:447] and 12 "free colored" in 1820 [NC:236]. He bought land by deed proved in Northampton County court on 6 March 1820 [Minutes 1817-21, 240].

   ii.   Eady, married Nathaniel **Newsom**. Her child Charlotte received 10 pounds by the will of her grandfather Benjamin Hawley.

---

[117]Francis **Scott** had a case against a member of the Hawley family in Edgecombe County court in November 1746 [Haun, *Edgecombe County Court Minutes*, I:115].

5. Sarah Hawley, born about 1748, was first taxed in 1761 in her father's household in Fishing Creek District. Her bastard children were bound apprentices to William Wilkerson by the Granville County court on 7 August 1786 [Minutes 1786-87, n.p.]. They were

    i. Obediah, born about 1776, perhaps the O. Holly who was head of a Greensville District household of 3 "other free" in 1810 [SC:528].
    ii. Zedekiah, born about 1776.

6. Jacob Hawley, born about 1751, was first listed in his father's Granville county household in 1764 in the list of Samuel Benton, but he was probably taxable earlier in 1762 when his father was a delinquent taxpayer on 5 tithes. He was taxable as a married man in Granville County in 1780, and he had 6 persons in his Beaver Dam District household in Granville County in the state census. He was taxable on 1 poll in Granville County until 1793 after which he is not listed until 1805 when he was taxable on 1 poll in Oxford District [Tax List 1803-09, 104]. He married, second, Liddy ___, 9 July 1804 Granville County bond with Benton **Taborn** bondsman. He was head of a Granville County household of 8 "other free" in 1810 [NC:893]. He was called Jacob Holley on 11 March 1806 when the Greensville County, Virginia court ordered him to deliver his son Joseph Holley to his son's master Henry **Stewart** [Orders 1799-1806, 540]. He was the father of

    i. ?Ezekiel Holley, born about 1777, registered in Greensville County, Virginia, on 7 October 1805: *born free of a yellowish complexion, aged about 28 years* [Register of Free Negroes, no.4].
    ii. Joseph Holley, born say 1785, charged by the Greensville County, Virginia court on 14 January 1805 with having an illegitimate child by Jane **Stewart**. Henry and Peyton **Stewart** provided security for the payment of 10 pounds per year for seven years for the maintenance of the child. In exchange Joseph bound himself to serve Henry **Stewart** for seven years. On 13 January 1806 the court ordered the child Lindsey **Stewart** bound as an apprentice to Francis **Stewart** but rescinded the order the following month for reasons appearing to the court. On 10 February 1806 the court summoned Jacob and Joseph Holley to show cause why Joseph did not return to the service of his master Henry **Stewart**, and the following month on 11 March the court ordered Joseph to return to the service of his master Henry **Stewart**, serve an additional four months and continue in his service until Jane **Stewart**'s child Lindsey was bound out by the overseers of the poor. Asa **Byrd** was Henry's witness, and Patsey **Jones** and Peyton **Stewart** were witnesses for Jacob and Joseph [Orders 1799-1806, 439, 532, 535, 540, 541].

7. Jesse Hawley, born about 1760, was taxable in Granville County in 1789 and in 1793. He was head of a Halifax County, North Carolina household of 3 "other free" in 1800 and 2 in 1810 [NC:22]. He was an insolvent taxpayer in Halifax County in 1800 [Minutes 1799-1802, 19 August 1801]. On 19 May 1823 he took the oath of insolvent debtor in Halifax County court. He was over fifty-five years of age with 4 "free colored" in his Halifax County household in 1830. Perhaps his wife was Winnefred Holley who was eighty-eight years old on 20 May 1844 when she made a deposition for the Revolutionary War pension application of Drury **Walden**. His children were

    i. Labon **Taborn**, born about 1782, Jesse's two-year-old "Free Malater" son, bound to David Bradford by the 3 November 1784 Granville County court [Owen, *Granville County Notes*, vol. VI].

8   ii. ?Henry, born say 1785.

8. Henry Hawley, born say 1785, was head of a Halifax County, North Carolina household of 5 "other free" in 1810 [NC:24]. On 16 August 1841 he was in

a list of "free persons of color" who were allowed by the Halifax County court to use their guns in the county. He may have been the father of

    i.   Washington Haley, born 1806 to 1820, a "free colored" man living alone in Halifax County in 1830.

HAWS FAMILY

1.   Winefred Haws, born say 1700, the servant of John Welsh, confessed to the Anne Arundel County, Maryland court in March 1720/1 that she had a child by her master's "Negroe" Jack. She was ordered to serve her master seven years, Jack was given twenty-five lashes, and their child was bound to their master until the age of thirty-one [Judgment Record 1720-1, 88-9]. They were probably the ancestors of

 2   i.   Peter, born say 1750.

    ii.   William[1], born say 1752, died in Revolutionary War service aboard the ship Dragon [Hopkins, *Virginia Revolutionary War Land Grant Claims*, 104].

   iii.   Amy Haw, head of a St. Mary's County, Maryland household of 3 "other free" in 1790.

2.   Peter Haw(s)/How, born say 1750, was head of a Lancaster County, Virginia household of 9 "Blacks" in 1783 [VA:56] and 6 "other free" in 1810 [VA:349]. He was taxable on a horse in Lancaster County from 1783 to 1814: not charged on his own tithe after 1785, in the list of "free Negroes & Mulattoes" in 1813 and 1814 [PPTL, 1782-1839, frames 15, 30, 44, 72, 119, 187, 385, 399]. He and his brother William[1] Haw were seamen from Lancaster County in the Revolution. On 1 November 1834 Peter's four children: Rachel Haw, Peter Haw, Alice Haw, and Betsy Haw applied for bounty land for his services [Hopkins, *Virginia Revolutionary War Land Grant Claims*, 104]. He was the father of

    i.   Rachel Howe, "daughter of Peter Howe," married Daniel **Jones**, 13 June 1794 Lancaster County bond.

    ii.   ?Nancy Howe, spinster over 21, married Robert **Nickens**, 5 March 1793 Lancaster County bond.

   iii.   ?Jane Haws, married Holland **Wood**, 15 October 1821 Lancaster County bond.

   iv.   Sally, born about 1771-6, a nineteen-year-old "free light mulatto woman" who ran away with a "Negro man named Syphax" from Lancaster County according to the 30 September 1795 issue of the *Virginia Gazette* [Headley, *18th Century Newspapers*, 156]. She registered as a "free Negro" in Lancaster County on 18 June 1805: *Age 34, Color yellow...born free* [Burkett, *Lancaster County Register of Free Negroes*, 2].

    v.   Peter[2], born about 1785, called Peter Haw, Jr., when he registered as a "free Negro" in Lancaster County on 16 January 1809: *Age 23, Color yellow...born free* [Burkett, *Lancaster County Register of Free Negroes*, 5].

   vi.   Alice, born about 1782, called Alice Harrison Haw when she registered as a "free Negro" in Lancaster County on 16 January 1809: *Age 27, Color yellow...born free* [Burkett, *Lancaster County Register of Free Negroes*, 5].

  vii.   Betsy, born about 1780, registered as a "free Negro" in Lancaster County on 18 June 1805: *Age 25, Color yellow...born free* [Burkett, *Lancaster County Register of Free Negroes*, 2]. She was the mother of William[2] and Milley Haw (wife of William **Jones**). William[2] Haw married Fanny **Toulson**, 8 January 1827 Northumberland County bond, William **Toulson** security.

HAYNES/ HINES FAMILY

1. Anne Haynes, born say 1682, was living in Middlesex County, Virginia, on 6 March 1703/4 when Lt. Col. John Grymes, churchwarden of Christ Church Parish, informed the court that she had two "Mulatto bastard Children." She did not deny the fact, and the court ordered that she receive forty lashes [Orders 1694-1705, 545]. She may have been the ancestor of

   i. William Hines, one of the "Chief Men" of the Nottoway Indians who were living in present-day Southampton County, Virginia, on 6 August 1735 when they sold 400 acres of their land on the north side of the Nottoway River [Surry County DB 8:550].

   ii. Solomon, born say 1745, a "Mulatto man" who ran from James Srosby in October 1768 according to an ad placed by his master in the 3 November 1768 issue of the *Virginia Gazette* [Windley, Runaway Slave Advertisements, 1:66].

   iii. Patsy Haynes, married Absalom **Bass**, 15 January 1794 Granville County bond with Benjamin Bass surety. He was head of a Granville County household of 7 "other free" in 1800.

   iv. Melethan Hines, married Isaac **Anderson**, 28 September 1800 Granville County bond, Peter **Chaves** bondsman. Isaac was head of a Granville County household of 4 "other free" in 1800 [NC:545], 4 in 1810 [NC:904], 4 "free colored" in 1820 [NC:3], and 3 in 1830 [NC:29]. His wife Melethan was living at the age of seventy-five in the household of William **Evans** in 1850 [NC:104].

   v. Nancy Hines, married Hardy **Bass**, 23 December 1788 Granville County bond, Reuben **Bass** bondsman. Hardy was head of a Granville County household of 4 "other free" in 1800.

   vi. Polly Hines, married Reuben **Bass**, 23 December 1788 Granville County bond, Hardy Bass bondsman. Reuben was head of a Wake County household of 7 "other free" in 1800 [NC:753].

   vii. Daniel Hines, head of a Duplin County, North Carolina household of 9 "other free" in 1810 [NC:644].

   viii. Isam Hains, head of a Rowan County, North Carolina household of 1 "other free" and 3 slaves in 1810 [NC:336].

   ix. Charles Hines, "free negro" head of a Fairfax County household of 8 "other free" in 1810 [VA:263].

HAYS FAMILY

Members of the Hays family in North Carolina were

1 i. Isaac, born say 1730.

   ii. Jacob, born 17 November 1736 if he was the "Mulatto" boy named Jacob (no last name recorded) who was bound apprentice to John Todd by the Onslow County court on 6 April 1743 [Minutes 1734-49, fol. 38]. He was taxable in Bladen County on 9 head of cattle and 3 horses in 1778 [Byrd, *Bladen County Tax Lists*, II:102] and head of an Onslow County household of 6 "other free" in 1790 [NC:197] and 7 in 1800 [NC:14].

   iii. Samuel, born say 1740, taxable with his wife Susannah in Constable Daniel Harris' list for Fishing Creek District of Granville County, North Carolina, in 1761 [CR. 044.701.19].

1. Isaac Hayes, born say 1730, was a "Molato" taxable on himself, John Hayes, (his wife?) Eliza Hayes and Hannah Hayes in Bladen County in 1770. In 1771 and 1772 Samuel **Freeman** was also a taxable in his household. Isaac was a "Free Negro" taxable on two adults, one Boy and two females in 1774; taxable on himself, one Black male and one Black female in 1776; and taxable on 160

acres, four horses and two cows in 1778 [Byrd, *Bladen County Tax Lists*, I:24, 76, 91, 124; II:51, 81, 102, 105]. He may have been the father of

    i.   John, born say 1755, taxable in the household of (his father?) Isaac Hayes in Bladen County from 1770 to 1772. Perhaps his wife was Hannah Hayes, another taxable in Isaac's Bladen County household [Byrd, *Bladen County Tax Lists*, I:24, 76, 91]. He was head of a Brunswick County household of 1 white male 16 or over, 3 under 16, and 4 white females in 1790 [NC:189], 7 "other free" in 1800 [NC:14] and 7 "other free" and 1 white woman in 1810 [NC:222].

    ii.   William, born before 1776, head of a Sampson County household of 2 "free colored" persons, a man and woman over forty-five years of age in 1820 [NC:282].

    iii.   Charles, born say 1797, head of a Brunswick County household of 3 "other free" in 1810 [NC:236], and 3 "free colored" in Cumberland County in 1820 [NC:168].

    iv.   Peter, head of a Pendleton District, South Carolina household of 1 "other free" in 1800 [SC:43].

    v.   Esther, born 1776-1794, head of a New Hanover County household of 8 "free colored" in 1820 [NC:221].

Members of the Hays family in Virginia were

    i.   Delphia, head of an Essex County household of 8 "other free" in 1810 [VA:198].

    ii.   David, head of a Pendleton County household of 8 "other free" in 1810 [VA:1111].

HEARN FAMILY

Members of the Hearn family were

1   i.   Ephraim, born about 1745.

    ii.   James Harn, alias Harringham, a "Negro or Mulatto" indentured to the Peachey family of Richmond County in July 1763 when he ran away according to an ad William Peachey placed in the 4 November 1763 issue of the *Virginia Gazette* [*Virginia Gazette* (Royle edition)].

    iii.   Francis, a "Mulatto" bound as an apprentice cabinet maker to James Tyrie in York County on 19 July 1785 [Deeds 1777-91, 274].

1.   Ephraim Hearn, born about 1745, was a "man of colour" about eighty-four years old on 8 August 1829 when he made a declaration in Gloucester County court to obtain a pension for his services in the Revolution. He was a weaver living with his wife Molly (more than sixty years old) and a twenty-year-old daughter Betsy [M804-1242, frame 0662]. He was taxable in Gloucester County in 1787, taxable on a horse in 1789, a "mulatto" taxable on 2 tithes in 1806, 1811, and 1812, a "negroe" taxable with his unnamed wife in 1813 [PPTL, 1782-1799; 1800-20], and head of a Gloucester County household of 6 "other free" in 1810 [VA:657]. He was the father of

    i.   Peter, born say 1785, "son of Ephraim," a taxable "negroe" in Gloucester County from 1815 to 1820 [PPTL, 1800-20].

    ii.   ?Jane, a "free negro" taxable on a 2-wheeled chair in Middlesex County in 1810 [PPTL, 1800-20, frames 244, 272].

    iii.   Betsy, born about 1809, twenty years old in 1829.

HEATH FAMILY

1.   Sarah Heath, born say 1715, was a white woman living in Washington Parish, Westmoreland County, Virginia, on 1 April 1741 when the grand jury presented her and William **Kayton (Caton)**, a "Mulatto," for "Cohabiting

Together (and having Sundry Children) under pretence of man and wife"
[Orders 1739-43, 100, 114a]. They may have been the ancestors of
    i.   Aggy, head of a Petersburg Town household of 3 "other free" and a
         slave in 1810 [VA:128a].
    ii. Lewis, head of a Petersburg Town household of 2 "other free" in 1810
         [VA:122b].

HEDGEPETH FAMILY

Members of the Hedgepeth family were
1   i.   Peter, born say 1755.
    ii. Hulin, head of a Wake County, North Carolina household of 4 "other
         free" in 1800 [NC:768]. He may have been named for the **Huelin**
         family.
    iii. James, head of a Wake County household of 4 "other free" in 1800
         [NC:768]. He married Delilah **Tabourn**, 15 July 1797 Granville
         County, North Carolina marriage, William Mitchell bondsman.

1. Peter Hedgepeth, born say 1755, was head of a Wake County, North Carolina
    household of 5 "other free" in 1790. He was living in Wake County on 21
    March when he gave William Fearel power of attorney to collect his final
    settlement for his service in the Revolution [*NCGSJ* X:235]. He purchased
    land in Wake County from Thomas **Tabourn** by deed proved in September
    1791 Wake County court [Haun, *Wake County Court Minutes*, II:535]. He may
    have been the father of
    i.   Bythea, married William **Mitchell**, 11 August 1796 Granville County
         bond, Darling **Bass** bondsman.
    ii. Patty, married Pomphrey **Taborn**, 24 December 1801 Wake County
         bond, Peter Hedspeth bondsman.
    iii. Bartlett, born before 1776, head of a Halifax County, North Carolina
         household of 8 "free colored" in 1820 [NC:150] and 12 in 1830
         [NC:340].
    iv. Robert, born 1776-1794, head of a Halifax County household of 8
         "free colored" in 1820 [NC:151].
    v.   Stephen, born 1776-1794, head of a Halifax County household of 7
         "free colored" in 1830 [NC:314].

HEWLETT FAMILY

1. Rebecca Hulet, born say 1717, was presented by the York County court in
    June 1738 for not listing herself as a tithable. She was called the "friend" of
    Morris **Evans** in his 18 February 1739/40 York County will by which he left
    a mare and foal to Elizabeth Hulet, left his bed, furniture, and two cows to
    Rebecca and left furniture and three head of cattle to his son Morris. He also
    left a boat and cart for the use of Rebecca and his son Morris as long as they
    "live and agree together." He appointed Rebecca and Morris his executors.
    She was living in York County on 15 November 1742 when a suit brought
    against her by John **Sampson** was dismissed. Sarah **Hopson (Hobson)** testified
    on Rebecca's behalf [W&I 18:414, 427, 558-9; 19:131, 132]. She was
    probably the ancestor of
    i.   Elizabeth, who was mentioned in the York County will of Morris
         Evans.
    ii. James Hewlett, head of a Chesterfield County household of 1 "Black"
         person in 1783 [VA:49].
    iii. Miguiel Hewlett, head of a Richmond City household of 2 "other free"
         and a slave in 1810 [VA:367].
    iv. George Hewlett, head of a Chesterfield County household of 4 "other
         free" in 1810 [VA:70/1062].

HEWSON/ HUSON FAMILY

1. William Hewson, born say 1750, and his wife Mary were living in Charles
    Parish, Elizabeth City County, Virginia, on 6 September 1772 when their son
    Charles was baptized [Bell, *Charles Parish Registers*, 105]. In March 1777
    William was paid by the York County estate of Anthony Robinson for weaving
    thirteen yards of material [WI 22:482]. He was taxable on one tithe in
    Elizabeth City in 1782, presented in York County for failing to list himself as
    a tithable in 1783 [Orders 1774-84, 334] and taxable in York County from
    1784 to 1799 [PPTL, 1782-1841, frames 83, 95, 14, 192, 220, 244]. His
    widow may have been the Mary Huson who was head of a York County
    household of 7 "other free" in 1810 [VA:876]. William was the father of
    i.   Charles, born 4 August, baptized 6 September 1772, taxable in York
          County from 1800 to 1812 and a "free Negro" tithable in 1814 [PPTL,
          1782-1841, frames 256, 297, 354, 390, 407].
    ii.   Anne, born 17 January, baptized 12 March 1775 in Charles Parish.
    iii. John, born 22 August 1777, baptized 8 March 1778 in Charles Parish.
    iv.   Elizabeth, born say 1780, "daughter of William Hughson," married
          John **Combs**, 22 December 1800 York County bond, Charles and John
          Hughson securities.
    v.   Mary, born 14 February, baptized 28 April 1782.
    vi.   Sarah, born 10 July, "Mulatto" dau. of William and Mary, baptized 22
          August 1784 [Bell, *Charles Parish Registers*, 105].
    vii. ?Nancy, head of a Petersburg household of 1 "other free" in 1810
          [VA:123a].

HICKMAN FAMILY

1. Cloe Hickman, born say 1750, was living in Cumberland County, Virginia,
    on 24 October 1774 when the court ordered the churchwardens of Southam
    Parish to bind her "mulattoe" children Betty, Alce, and Hannah to Robert
    Biscoe [Orders 1774-8, 288]. Cloe was a "F.B." head of a Powhatan County
    household of 5 "other free" in 1810 [VA:5] and a "M°" listed in Powhatan
    County in 1813 [PPTL 1787-1825, frame 440]. She was the mother of
2   i.   Betty, born say 1770.
    ii.   Alce, born say 1772.
    iii. Hannah, born say 1774.
    iv.   ?Polly, born about 1778, a "F. B." listed in Powhatan County in 1813
          [PPTL 1787-1825, frame 440]. She registered in Powhatan County on
          16 January 1823: *Age: 45; Color: Dark Brown; Stature: 5'4-1/2"; Born
          Free* [Register of Free Negroes, no. 100].
    v.   ?Jesse, born about 1780, a "Molatto" taxable in Chesterfield County
          from 1805 to 1810 [Personal Property Tax List, 1786-1811, frames
          618, 660, 717, 753, 799], security for the 17 December 1812
          Powhatan County marriage of "free Negroes" James **Henderson** and
          Anna Maria **Holt**. Jesse registered in Powhatan County on 16 June
          1830: *Age: 50; Color: yellow; Stature: 5'8-1/3"; Born Free in
          Powhatan County* [Register of Free Negroes, no. 237].

2. Betty Hickman, born say 1770, "mulattoe" daughter of Cloe Hickman, was
    bound to Robert Biscoe of Cumberland County on 24 October 1774. She
    apparently married Tim **Mosby** who she emancipated on 21 July 1803. He
    registered in Powhatan County on 7 September 1835: *Age: 70; Color: black;
    'tature: 5'10"; Emancipated by Elizth Hickman by deed dated 21 July 1803*
    owhatan County Free Negro Register, no.369]. They were probably the
    'ents of

    i.   Patty[1] Hickman, daughter of Tim **Mosby**, married Charles **Coy**, "free Negroes," 4 October 1809 Powhatan County bond.

Other members of the family were
    i.   Charles, born say 1788, taxable in Chesterfield County from 1809 to 1813 [Personal Property Tax List, 1786-1811, frames 753, 799; [Waldrep, *1813 Tax List*].
    ii.   Narcissa, counted in the list of "free Negroes" for Chesterfield County in 1813 [Waldrep, *1813 Tax List*].
    iii.   Patsy[2], born about 1807, a seventeen-year-old "free Girl of Colour" bound to Mrs. Eleanor McIntyre until the age of eighteen by the Cumberland County, North Carolina court on 12 June 1824 [Minutes 1823-35].

HICKS FAMILY

Members of the Hicks family were
    i.   Micajah, born 4 July 1754 according to his 27 May 1829 declaration for a Revolutionary War pension in Orange County, North Carolina. His apprentice indenture was canceled in Sussex County on 18 October 1770, and the court ordered the churchwardens of Albemarle Parish to bind him out to another master (no race or parent indicated) [Orders 1770-76, n.p.]. He may have been the son of Sarah Hicks who was presented by the grand jury of Sussex County on 16 May 1760 for having an illegitimate child [Orders 1757-61, 326]. In Micajah's pension declaration he claimed to have been in the battles of Gilford and Eutaw Springs, and he stated that he was a farmer with no family [*NCGSJ* XIII:38]. He was head of a Chatham County household of 4 "other free" in 1800. His wife Mary, aged eighty-six years old, was living in Wilkes County on 12 September 1843 when she made a declaration to obtain his pension. She stated that they were married 10 December 1780 in Chatham County on the Tar River. Her husband died on 30 December 1837 [File W-7738, by *N.C. Genealogy* XVIII:2715].

1   ii.   Jemima, born say 1768.
    iii.   Lewis, born about 1769, received one of the "Certificates Granted to free Negroes & Mulattoes" in Sussex County, Virginia, on 3 November 1824: *free born, dark brown complexion, 5'9" tall, aged 55* [Certificates Granted to Free Negroes & Mulattoes 1800-50, no. 494].
2   iv.   Winnie, born say 1772.
    v.   Charlotte, born say 1773, married Shadrack **Demery**, 8 February 1794 Southampton County bond, Aaron **Heathcock** (**Haithcock**) surety.
    vi.   Lurany, born say 1773, married Charles **Haithcock**, 13 December 1794 Greensville County bond.
    vii.   Herbert, head of a Halifax County, North Carolina household of 6 "free colored" in 1820 [NC:150] and 3 in 1830. John **Toney** was ordered bound apprentice to him by the 20 May 1822 Halifax County court.
    viii.   Sally, a poor child living in Sussex County on 15 June 1786 when the court ordered the overseers of the poor on the southside of the Nottoway River in district 3 to bind her to John Speris [Orders 1786-91, 31].
    ix.   James, born about 1784, a "FN" taxable in Sussex County from 1809 to 1813 [PPTL 1782-1812, frames 750, 782, 816, 838]. He registered in Petersburg on 6 January 1818: *James Hix a free man of Color, brown Complection, thirty four years old, born free of Indian mother p. cert. from Sussex County* [Register of Free Negroes 1794-1819, no. 891].

    x.   Jesse, born say 1784, head of a Petersburg Town household of 4 "other free" in 1810 [VA:124b].

    xi.   Amy, born about 1790, registered in Sussex County on 4 March 1820: *brown complexion, 5'4", free born, 30 years old* [Certificates granted to Free negroes & mulattoes, no.386].

    xii.   Isham, a "FN" taxable in Sussex County in 1810 [PPTL 1782-1812, frame 782].

1.   Jemima Hicks, born say 1762, was the mother of Littleberry Hicks, a "poor child" (no race indicated) who was bound out in Southampton County on 11 March 1784 [Orders 1778-84, 383]. She was the mother of

    i.   Littleberry, born say 1782.

    ii.   ?Phoeby, born about 1783, registered in Southampton County on 30 July 1810: *age 27, Dark Mulatto, 5'4", free born in Southampton County.* She registered again on 29 October 1824 [Register of Free Negroes 1794-1832, nos. 750, 1515].

    iii.   ?Kinchen, born about 1789, registered in Southampton County on 30 July 1810: *age 21, Mulatto, 5 feet 7 1/4, free born* [Register of Free Negroes 1794-1832, no. 735]. He was a "free Negro" taxable in Southampton County on Lewis Worrell's land in 1812, listed with his wife Sally on Jesse Holt's land in 1813, living on B. Whitfield, Jr.'s land in 1817, living on Jonas **Cosby**'s land in 1820 [PPTL 1807-21, frames 292, 419, 671, 695, 794].

    iv.   ?Jason, born about 1795, a "free Negro" living in Southampton County on William Cutler's land in 1819 and 1820 [PPTL 1807-21, frames 689, 792]. He registered in Southampton County on 14 December 1821: *age 26, mulatto man, 5'6" high, free born in Southampton County.* He registered again on 19 January 1826 and 13 March 1835 and used the Southampton County certificate to register in Logan County, Ohio, in 1837 [Register of Free Negroes 1794-1832, nos. 1299, 1552; Turpin, *Register of Black, Mulatto, and Poor Persons,* 11].

2.   Winnie Hicks, born say 1772, was living in Warren County, North Carolina, when the court bound her "mulatto" children as apprentices [Minutes 1787-93, 188; WB 5:208, 6:14, 6:153; Kerr, *Abstracts of Warren County Will Books*]. Her children were

    i.   Fathey, born about 1786, four-year-old "base born child of Winney Hicks" apprenticed to George Allen in May 1790 [Minutes 1787-93, 130; WB 5:208].

    ii.   ?Benjamin, born about 1788, no parent or race given, a three-year-old apprenticed to Ralph Neal on 25 August 1791 to be a planter [Minutes 1787-93, 191; WB 6:14].

    iii.   Winnie, born in February 1792, nine-month-old "mulatto girl" of Winnie Hicks, apprenticed to William Clark on 30 November 1792 [Minutes 1787-93, 247; WB 6:153].

    iv.   Lizzie, born in February 1792, nine-month-old "mulatto girl" of Winnie Hicks, apprenticed to William Clark on 30 November 1792 [Minutes 1787-93, 247; WB 6:153].

    v.   Sterling, born 1794, "base born child of Winnie Hicks," bound apprentice to Tabitha Marshall on 27 February 1804 [WB 12:188].

    vi.   Lewis, born 1792, "8 year old of Winnie Hicks," bound to Tabitha Marshall on 27 February 1804 [WB 12:189].

    vii.   Parthena, born about 1800, "base born child of color of Winnifred Hicks," bound to Edmond Kimbell on 27 February 1804 [WB 12:215].

    viii.   Nancy, born in June 1801, "base born child of colour" of Winniford Hicks, bound to Richard Tinstall on 27 February 1804 [WB 12:207].

HILL FAMILY

Two members of the Hill family born before 1750 were
1   i.   Hannah, born say 1736.
2   ii.   Susanna, born say 1743.

1.   Hannah Hill, born say 1736, a "free mulatto," was living in Culpeper County
     on 18 May 1758 when her son Zachariah was bound out. Her son was
3   i.   Zachariah¹, born about 1753.

2.   Susanna Hill, born say 1743, was the mother of twin "mulatto" boys, Thomas
     and James, who came to the house of Joseph Wooling of Albemarle County
     according to the 29 June 1776 issue of the *Virginia Gazette*. According to the
     gazette their mother lived with one Thomas Mitchell, a Scottish merchant, and
     went away with him to Scotland or Lord Dunmore [Headley, *18th Century
     Newspapers*, 164]. Her children were
     i.   Thomas, born about 1763.
     ii.   James, born about 1763, perhaps the Jimmy Hill who was a "free
           Black" head of a Nottoway County household of 9 "other free" in 1810
           [VA:1018].
     iii. ?Zachariah², born about 1766, registered in Bedford County on 27
           January 1824: *aged 58, Dark Mulatto, 5 feet 9 inches high, Born free*.
           Perhaps his wife was Sally Mason who registered the same day: *aged
           50, Dark Mulatto, 4 feet 11 inches high, Born free* [Register of Free
           Negroes 1820-60, p.6].
     iv.   ?Charles, a "Mulatto" taxable in the upper district of Halifax County,
           Virginia, from 1793 to 1795 [PPTL 1782-1799, frames 469, 507, 570].
4   v.   ?Jemima, born about 1767.

3.   Zachariah¹ Hill, born about 1753, was bound to John Rossan in Culpeper
     County on 18 May 1758. He was twenty-four years old in 1777 when he
     complained to the Halifax County, Virginia court that he had been treated as
     a slave. The court ordered him released [Pleas 9:194]. He married Sally
     Mason, "daughter of Thomas Mason," 20 July 1788 Halifax County, Virginia
     bond, John Jones surety, 31 July marriage by Rev. James Watkins [Minister's
     Returns, 14]. David **Pinn** attached his effects in Halifax County but the
     attachment was dismissed on 22 September 1788 [Pleas 1788-9, 1]. Zachariah
     was bondsman for the 3 December 1790 Caswell County marriage bond of
     Patrick **Mason** and Patsy **Going**. He was a "Mulatto" taxable in the southern
     district of Halifax County, Virginia, from 1806 to 1812 [PPTL, 1800-12,
     frames 521, 629, 682, 804, 949, 1032] and a "FN" taxable in the northern
     district of Campbell County in 1814 [PPTL, 1785-1814, frame 928]. His
     children may have been
     i.   William, born 1776-94, head of a Halifax County, North Carolina
           household of 2 "free colored" males in 1820 [NC:150].
     ii.   Samuel, born 1794-1806, head of a Caswell County household of 3
           "free colored" in 1820 [NC:62].

4.   Jemima Hill, born about 1767, "free Black" head of a Bedford County
     household of 4 "other free" in 1810 [VA:464]. She registered in Bedford
     County on 25 August 1812: *Mima Hill, aged 45, Mima Hill, Dark Mulatto,
     5'2", Born free* [Register of Free Negroes 1820-60, p.11]. She was the mother
     of
     i.   Harry, born about 1796, registered in Bedford County on 28 June
           1824: *son of Mima, Light Mulatto, 5 feet 7-1/2 inches high, Born free*
           [Register of Free Negroes 1820-60, p.6].

Members of a Hill family in Isle of Wight County were

    i.   Elizabeth, born about 1740, registered in Petersburg on 5 August 1805: *a light coulourd Mulatto woman, five feet two inches high, supposed sixty to seventy years old, born free in Isle of Wight County* [Register of Free Negroes 1794-1819, no. 351]. She may have been the mother of

    ii. Charles, Sr., born say 1744, a "free Negro" taxable in Isle of Wight County from 1783 to 1805: taxable on a slave named Cate over the age of sixteen in 1783; taxable on 3 horses and 5 cattle in 1786; exempt from tax on his person in 1804 and 1805 [PPTL 1782-1810, frames 33, 65, 79, 103, 121, 198, 215, 261, 316, 408, 512, 601, 638, 698] and a "free Negro" head of an Isle of Wight household of 8 "other free" in 1810 [VA:5].

    iii. Charles, Jr., a "free Negro" head of an Isle of Wight household of 8 "other free" in 1810 [VA:5].

Other members of the family were

    i.   Caleb, a "yellow" complexioned soldier born in King & Queen County who lived in King William County when he was listed in the size roll of troops who enlisted at Chesterfield Courthouse [The Chesterfield Supplement cited by NSDAR, *African American Patriots*, 150].

    ii. Henry, born about 1756, obtained a certificate of freedom in Orange County, Virginia court on 24 May 1802: *a Mulatto man forty six years old, about five feet eight or nine inches, is free* [Orders 1801-3, 290]. He may have been the Henry Hill who was a "melatto" taxable in Campbell County from 1792 to 1813 [PPTL, 1785-1814, frames 233, 268, 332, 892] and head of a Campbell County household of 7 "other free" in 1810 [VA:854].

    iii. Jack, born about 1776, obtained a certificate of freedom in Chesterfield County on 12 December 1808: *thirty two years old, yellow complexion, born free* [Register of Free Negroes 1804-53, nos. 78, 209, 318].

    iv. Peter, "free Negro" head of a Sussex County household of 15 "other free" in 1810.

    v.   Charles, head of a Loudoun County household of 8 "other free" in 1810 [VA:238].

    vi. Goodwin, head of a Charles City household of 4 "other free" in 1810 [VA:959].

    vii. Thomas, head of a Westmoreland County household of 3 "other free" in 1810 [VA:696].

Rowan County, North Carolina

1.   Elizabeth Hill, born say 1753, was the mother of an unnamed female child (one year and three months old) who was bound to Samuel Woods by the Rowan County court on 4 August 1774 until the age of thirty-one [Minutes 1773-77, 14].

HILLIARD FAMILY

1.   Lydia Hilliard, born say 1685, was the white woman servant of the Reverend St. John Shropshire on 25 April 1705 when she was convicted by the Westmoreland County court of having a "mulatto" child by a "Negro man." She was the servant of William Munro of Washington Parish on 8 March 1706 when he complained to the court that he had maintained her "Mulatto" child for two years and that the Reverend St. John Shropshire refused to release the child to him [Orders 1698-1705, 257; 1705-21, 22, 27a]. Lydia was probably the ancestor of

2   i.   Ann, born say 1730.

ii. Sarah, a "mullato" listed in the inventory of the Westmoreland County estate of William Monroe taken on 30 May 1737 [Estate Settlements, Records, Inventories 1723-46, 177].

iii. Daniel, head of a Southampton County, Virginia household of 6 "other free" in 1810 [VA:61].

iv. Jacob, head of a Southampton County household of 5 "other free" in 1810 [VA:79].

v. James, head of a Halifax County, North Carolina household of 3 "other free" in 1810 [NC:26], 7 "free colored" in 1820 [NC:150] and 9 in 1830.

vi. Samuel, head of a Sussex County, Virginia household of 2 "free colored" in 1830.

2. Ann Hilliard, born say 1735, was the servant of Benjamin Ryan on 43 December 1754 when her unnamed son was bound to her master until the age of twenty-one. On 4 March 1756 when the court also bound her son Peter Hilliard to her master until the age of twenty-one [Owen, *Granville County Notes*]. She was the mother of

i. Peter, born 10 December 1755 [Owen, *Granville County Notes*], a "Malatto" head of a Ninety-Six District, Edgefield County, South Carolina household of 6 "other free" in 1790, with his unnamed wife and four children [SC:66].

HITCHENS FAMILY

1. Major[1] Hitchens, born say 1700, was head of a Northampton County, Virginia household of 4 tithables in 1733 and 1744 and head of a household of 4 free tithables and 2 slaves, Nan and Sue, from 1737 to 1744 [Bell, *Northampton County Tithables*, 232, 237, 262, 274, 280, 312, 325, 330, 362]:

Master of family	tithable names nubr.
Major Hitchens :	*Tamar, Edward and Anne Hutchins*
nann & Sue negros	*6*

Major may have been the son of Mary Hitchens, "Mr. Robinson's wench," who was presented by the churchwardens in Accomack County for having a bastard child about 1700 [Orders 1697-1703, 96]. On 12 May 1747 the Northampton County court presented him for intermarrying or cohabiting with a "mulatoe" woman and presented Siner Bennett alias Hitchens for cohabiting with Major Hitchens, a "mulatoe man." The King's attorney discontinued the suit against Major on 10 June 1747 and discontinued the suit against Siner on 9 September 1747 [Orders 1742-8, 402-3, 422, 429, 445, 457]. He was probably the father of

i. Edward, born say 1716, tithable in Major's household in 1737. He married Tamer Smith, a white woman, before 10 October 1738 when the sheriff was ordered to take her into custody, keep her in the county jail for six months without bail, and to discharge her after she paid a fine of 10 pounds currency as punishment for marrying Edward Hitchens, a "Mulatto man" [Orders 1732-42, 334; Deal, *Race and Class*, 216].

ii. Anne, born say 1720, tithable in Major's household from 1737 to 1744, presented on 8 November 1737 for bastard bearing. Major Hitchens paid her fine [Orders 1732-42, 284, 291].

iii. James, born say 1722, tithable in Major's household in 1738 and 1743.

iv. Major[2], Jr., born say 1724, tithable in Major's household in 1740 and 1741 and in Edward Hitchen's household in 1743.

v. Jared, born say 1726, tithable in Major's household in 1743 and 1744. He was called Garret Hitchens, a "mulato," on 12 May 1747 when the court presented Mary Filby for intermarrying and cohabiting with him. The case was dismissed by the King's attorney on 12 August 1747 [Orders 1742-8, 402-3, 429, 444].

Northumberland County

1. Sarah Hutchins, born say 1690, was the servant of Madam Elizabeth Rawls on 21 June 1710 when she was presented by the Northumberland County court for having a "Molatto" child who was called a "Negro bastard" on 18 August 1710 when she failed to appear in court [Orders 1699-1713, pt. 2, 703]. She may have been the ancestor of

2   i. Nancy, born about 1769.

2. Nancy Hitchens, born about 1769, was called Nancy Hickings on 13 June 1805 when the Lunenburg County court ordered that her children Nancy, Betty and Polly be bound to John H. Craddock. The court rescinded the order the following month [Orders 1802-5, fol. 200, 206]. She was called Nancy Hitchens when she registered as a free Negro in Lunenburg County on 9 June 1823: *about 54 years, bright Mulatto Complexion, about five feet high...tolerable straight hair, rather grey, born free.* Her children were

    i.   Nancy **Kelly**, born about 1796, registered in Lunenburg County on 9 June 1823: *daughter of Nancy Hitchens about 27 years of Age, about five feet three inches high, dark complexion.*

    ii. Betsy **Holmes**, born about 1797, registered on 9 June 1823: *daughter of Nancy Hitchens, about 26 years of age, about 5 feet 3 inches high, dark Complexion.*

    iii. Colley **Thomas**, born about 1798, registered on 9 June 1823: *daughter of Nancy Hitchens, about twenty five years old, light brown Complexion, about five feet 3 inches high.*

    iv. Jesse, born about 1801, called son of Nancy Hickings on 11 February 1802 when the Lunenburg County court ordered the overseers of the poor to bind him to John Robertson [Orders 1802-5, fol. 6]. He registered in Lunenburg County on 11 November 1822: *about 21 years of age, 5 feet 7 inches high, dark brown Complexion.*

    v.   Rebecca **Lawson** Hitchings, born about 1808, registered on 14 August 1827: *a daughter of Nancy Hitchings, about 5 feet high, about 19 years of age, brown complexion, bushy head* [WB 5, after page 89, nos. 20-23, 51].

HITER FAMILY

1. Thomas Hiter/ Hoyter, born say 1700, was one of the "Chief men of the Chowan Indians" who sold thousands of acres in Chowan County by a total of thirteen deeds signed between 9 January 1733 and 22 November 1734 [Chowan DB W-1, 215-216, 237-239, 247-253]. Another member of the tribe, James Bennett, petitioned the General Assembly on 14 March 1745 complaining that Thomas Hoyter and John Robin sold land they had no right to sell [Saunders, *Colonial Records of North Carolina*, IV:802]. Thomas Hiter's descendants, perhaps grandchildren were

    i.   Elizabeth, head of a Currituck County household of 5 "other free" in 1790 [NC:21] and 4 in 1810 [NC:89].

    ii. Abraham, head of a Currituck County household of 6 "other free" in 1800 [NC:149] and 3 in 1810 [NC:89]. He leased 15 acres in Currituck County from John Lindsey for one ear of corn per year on 13 February 1796 [Deed Book 8].

    iii. John, head of a Currituck County household of 3 "other free" in 1810 [NC:84].

    iv. Asa, head of a Pasquotank County household of 8 "other free" in 1810 [NC:902].

v. John, called "John Haul Hiters" in December 1780 when the Pasquotank County court allowed him to be bound as an apprentice to Robert Pendleton to learn the trade of shoemaker. He was probably related to Hezekiah Haul who was bound out the same day and Elisha Hawll who was bound out in March 1781 [Minutes 1777-81, fol. 52b, 54b]. He was head of a Pasquotank County household of 6 "other free" in 1810 [NC:902].

vi. Thomas, born before 1776, head of a Pasquotank County household of 3 "other free" in 1810 [NC:902] and 4 "free colored" in Camden County in 1820 [NC:38].

HOBSON FAMILY

1. Ann Hobson, born say 1670, was living in Elizabeth City County, Virginia, when she registered the 9 August 1688 birth of her daughter Mary in Charles Parish, York County. Her son William Hobson was called "son of Ann a mulatto" when his birth was registered in Charles Parish in 1696. She was probably related to Richard Hobson whose son Charles Hobson was born in Charles Parish in 1684 and Robert Hobson whose son Armager was born there in 1696 [Bell, *Charles Parish Registers*, 105]. Ann was the mother of

    i. Mary, born 9 August 1688, "daughter of Ann of Elizabeth City County."

2   ii. William[1], born about 1696.

2. William[1] Hobson, born about 1696, was called the son of Ann a "mullatto" when his birth was registered in Charles Parish [Bell, *Charles Parish Registers*, 106; no date but the entry occurs between one dated 18 May 1696 and 13 August 1696]. He may have been the father of

3   i. Charles[1], born say 1722.

3. Charles[1] Hobson, born say 1722, may have been the Charles Hobson who sued William **Teemer** in Elizabeth City County court in 1743. His suit against William Smelt for trespass, assault, and battery was dismissed by the court with the agreement of both parties on 20 February 1744/5. On 21 November 1744 he was presented by the court for being a "common Drunkard" [Orders 1731-47, 341, 403, 414, 419, 422]. Perhaps his wife was the Sarah Hobson who was sued in York County for trespass upon the case by John **Sampson** in a suit which was dismissed on 16 August 1742 when the parties reached agreement. She testified for Rebecca **Hulet** in John **Sampson**'s case against Rebecca [W&I 19:121, 132]. Charles was the owner of a bag of meal, valued at 15 shillings, which was stolen from the mill house of John Howard in Charles Parish by a slave belonging to Miles Cary, Gentleman. The trial was held in York County on 29 August 1763 [Judgments & Orders 1763-5, 69]. He was living in James **Berry**'s household on 16 November 1772 when the York County court presented James for not listing him as a tithable [Judgments & Orders 1772-4, 151]. He leased land from John Hay by deed acknowledged in York County court on 18 September 1780. On 19 May 1783 the court presented him for not listing himself and his son Amicher (Armager) as tithables and presented him and John Hay for having barbecues and selling liquor. He paid Amicher's tax but was not required to pay tax on himself, probably because he was elderly. And on 17 May 1784 the court presented him and Charles Hopson, Jr., for failing to list their taxable property [Orders 1774-84, 287, 324-5, 334; 1784-7, 1]. He was taxable in York County on 3 horses and a slave in 1789 and 2 horses in 1790 but not subject to personal tax [PPTL, 1782-1841, frames 152, 162]. He was the father of

4   i. ?Charles[2], born say 1755.

5   ii. ?John[1], born say 1761.

6   iii. Armager, born say 1763.

4.   Charles[2] Hobson, born say 1755, and his wife Sarah were the parents of five
      children baptized in Charles Parish, York County: John, Mary, Martha,
      Edward and Charles [Bell, *Charles Parish Registers*, 106, 109]. He was called
      Charles Hopson, Jr., on 17 May 1784 when the York County court presented
      him and Charles Hopson, Sr., for failing to list their taxable property [Orders
      1774-84; 1784-7, 1]. He was taxable in York County from 1785 to 1813:
      taxable on a slave in 1788, on 2 free male tithes in 1796, 2 from 1801 to
      1804, 2 in 1811 and 1812, and 4 "free Negroes & mulattoes over 16" in 1813
      [PPTL, 1782-1841, frames 95, 141, 152, 265, 297, 365, 390]. His children
      were
        i.   John[2], born 23 September 1777, baptized 25 January 1778, "son of
              Charles Junr. and Sarah." He was taxable in York County in 1799,
              called John Hopson, Jr. [PPTL, 1782-1841, frame 244].
       ii.   Mary, born 4 November 1779, baptized 5 March 1780, "dau. of
              Charles Junr., and Sarah."
      iii.   Martha, born 4 November 1779, "twin with Mary," baptized 5 March
              1780, "dau. of Charles Junr. and Sarah." She married Thomas **Epps**
              Hobson.
       iv.   ?Abraham, born say 1782, taxable in York County from 1803 to 1813
              [PPTL, 1782-1841, frames 287, 307, 327, 340, 365, 390] and head of
              a York County household of 4 "other free" in 1810 [VA:876].
        v.   Edward, born 20 November 1783, baptized 28 March 1784, "son of
              Charles and Sarah." He was taxable in York County from 1805 to 1807
              [PPTL, 1782-1841, frames 307, 316, 328].
       vi.   Charles[3], born 4 November 1785, baptized 12 March 1786, "Mulatto
              son of Charles and Sally." He married Betsy **Berry**, 20 June 1808
              York County bond, Abraham Hopson, bondsman. He was head of a
              York County household of 3 "other free" in 1810 [VA:876]. His wife
              was probably the Elizabeth Hobson, born about 1789, who registered
              in York County on 21 September 1835: *a light mulatto about forty Six
              Years of age, five feet one & half Inches high, has long black hair,
              dark Eyes* [Register of Free Negroes, 1831-50, no.391].

5.   John[2] Hobson, born say 1761, was a soldier in the Revolution from York
      County [Jackson, *Virginia Negro Soldiers*, 38]. He was taxable in York
      County from 1784 to 1799: taxable on a slave named Sarah in 1785, taxable
      on a slave in 1788 and 1789, called John Hopson, Sr., in 1799 [PPTL, 1782-
      1841, frames 89, 141, 172, 192, 220, 244]. He and his wife Mary were living
      in Charles Parish, York County, when their children James, Nancy and Polly
      were baptized. Mary was probably the Mary Hopson who was taxable on 1-2
      horses in York County from 1800 to 1805 and taxable on a free male tithable
      in 1803 and 1804 [PPTL, 1782-1841, frames 256, 287, 297, 307]. Their
      children were
        i.   James, born 1 August 1783, baptized 14 September 1783, "son of John
              and Mary" [Bell, *Charles Parish Registers*, 106]. He registered as a
              "free Negro" in York County on 21 October 1805: *a bright Mulatto
              about 22 years of age 5 feet 7-3/4 Inches high, long curly black Hair,
              Hazle eyes, thick Eye brows* [Register of Free Negroes, 1798-1831, no.
              32]. He was head of a York County household of 6 "other free" in
              1810 [VA:876] and a James Hopson was head of an Elizabeth City
              County household of 8 "other free" in 1810 [VA:185]. He married
              Elizabeth, the widow of Edward **Berry**, before 1852 [LVA, York
              County chancery file 1852-004].
       ii.   Nancy, born 24 March 1785, baptized 8 May 1785 "Mulatto daughter
              of John and Mary" [Bell, *Charles Parish Registers*, 106].
      iii.   Polly, born 10 April 1787, baptized 20 May 1787 in Charles Parish,
              "Mulatto daughter of John and Mary" [Bell, *Charles Parish Registers*,
              106].

6. Armager Hobson, born say 1763, was taxable in John Sclater's York County household in 1785 and taxable in his own household from 1789 to 1792 [PPTL, 1782-1841, frames 97, 152, 162, 182]. He was married to Mary on 14 November 1785 when their "mulatto" daughter Anne Hopson was born in Charles Parish [Bell, *Charles Parish Registers*, 109]. They were the parents of
    i. Anne, born 14 November 1785, baptized 12 March 1786.

7. Thomas **Epps** Hobson, born about 1768, married Martha Hobson, 20 December 1799 York County bond, Edward **Cuttillo** bondsman. He and William **Epps** were sued by the assignee of Jacob **Chavis** in Lunenburg County court for a debt of 7 pounds on 13 November 1800 [Orders 1799-1801, 112]. In 1802 he was listed as a ditcher with his wife Patsy in a "List of Free Negroes & Mulattoes" on Flat Rock Creek in Lunenburg County [Lunenburg County Free Negro & Slave Records, 1802-1803, LVA]. He was taxable in York County from 1804 to 1812: taxable on a slave in 1811 [PPTL, 1782-1841, frames 297, 307, 327, 340, 354, 365] and head of a York County household of 5 "other free" and a slave in 1810 [VA:890]. He registered in York County on 19 September 1831: *a bright mulatto about 63 years of age 5 feet 7 inches high, black straight hair, very little grey considering his age...a little freckled, his teeth decayed, he is very loquacious and fond of ardent liquors. Born free* [Register of Free Negroes, 1831-50, no.301]. Their children were
    i. Thomas, born about 1807, registered in York County on 19 September 1831: *(son of Thos. Eppes Hopson) bright mulatto 24 years old, 5 feet 10-3/4 inches high, wide face, black eyes, straight hair, large eyebrows, very small beard and walks a little lame* [Register of Free Negroes, 1831-50, no.303].
    ii. John[3], born about 1808, registered in York County on 19 September 1831: *(son of Thos. Eppes Hopson) a bright mulatto 5 feet 9-1/2 inches high twenty three years old, has long curly hair* [Register of Free Negroes, 1831-50, no.302].

Their descendants in North Carolina were
    i. Ginny Hopston, born say 1790, head of a Jones County household of 3 "other free" in 1810 [NC:262].
    ii. William[2] Hopston, born say 1785, head of a Jones County household of 4 "other free" in 1810 [NC:261].

HODGES FAMILY

1. Mary Hodges, born say 1725, was living in Henrico County, Virginia, in March 1743/4 when the churchwardens of Henrico Parish were ordered to bind out her "Mulatto" child Aggy. She the mother of
    i. Aggy, bound apprentice in March 1743/4. She was discharged from further servitude to Thomas Baker by the Chesterfield County court in August 1767 [Orders 1767-71, 90].

Other members of the Hodges family were
    ii. Sam, head of a Norfolk County household of 2 "other free" in 1810 [VA:793].
    iii. Charles, head of a Princess Ann County household of 7 "other free" in 1810 [VA:458].
    iv. Airz/ Isaiah(?), head of a Beaufort County, North Carolina household of 4 "other free" in 1800 [NC:9] and 10 "other free" and a slave in 1810 [NC:118].
    v. Peter, head of a Beaufort County, North Carolina household of 4 "other free" in 1810 [NC:118].

HOGG FAMILY

1. Hannah Hogg, born say 1750, the servant of Stephen Phillips, was the mother of "Mulatto" children: Tom, Cary, Bill, and Leah who were ordered brought to court in April 1775 so they could be bound apprentice in Cumberland County, North Carolina [Minutes 1772-76, 41; 1777-82, 79]. Her children were

    i.   Thomas, born 27 April 1766, head of a Cumberland County household of 4 "other free" in 1800, and 11 in 1810 [NC:607]. He purchased land by deed proved in Cumberland County on 12 April 1805 [Minutes 1805-08]. On 18 June 1808 the court bound Elizabeth **Campbell**, a two-year-old "orphan of Colour," to him as an apprentice. His heir was probably Lam(?) Hogg, head of a Cumberland County household of 9 "free colored" in 1820 [NC:155].
    ii. Cary, 23 September 1769.
    iii. ?Cader, born say 1772, a "mulatto man" who was released from Angus and William Philips' service in Cumberland County on 16 January 1794 when he proved that the was born free of a white woman [Minutes 1791-97].
    iv. Chloe, born say 1773, "daughter to Hannah Hogg," bound to Flora Phillips on 27 July 1786 until October 1791 [Minutes 1784-87], head of a Robeson County household of 2 "other free" in 1800 [NC:384]. The 8 October 1799 Robeson County court bound Elizabeth Hogg, a three-year-old girl, to her. She purchased land by deed proved in Robeson County court on 6 October 1802 [Minutes 1797-1806, 84, 221].
    v.   William, born 15 July 1776.
    vi. Leah, born 20 February 1779, mistakenly called daughter of Chloe Hogg on 16 October 1794 when she was set free from her indenture [Minutes 1791-97].
    vii. Betsy, born say 1781, head of a Cumberland County household of 8 "free colored" in 1820 [NC:202]. Her property at 1 Ramsey Street, Fayetteville was ordered to be sold for taxes in 1837 [Minutes 1836-8].

HOLLINGER FAMILY

1. Sally Hollinger, born about 1750, registered as a free Negro in Essex County on 8 December 1810: *born free by certificate of her enrollment by the Com[r] of the Revenue, dark Mulattoe, about sixty years of age, five feet two and one quarter inch* [Register of Free Negroes 1810-43, p.5, no.9]. She was head of an Essex County household of 3 "other free" in 1810 [VA:208]. She, Susan, and Judy Hollinger were listed as "free Negroes" in South Farnham Parish, Essex County, in 1813 [PPTL, 1782-1819, frame 522]. She may have been the mother of

2   i.   Judy, born about 1766.
    ii. Edmund, head of a Spotsylvania County household of 9 "other free" in 1810 [VA:113b].
3   iii. Suckey, born about 1775.

2. Judy Hollinger, born about 1766, registered as a free Negro in Essex County on 8 December 1810: *born free by certificate of her enrollment by the Commissioner of Revenue, a bright Mulattoe, about 44 years of age, five feet two and one quarter Inches* [Register of Free Negroes 1810-43, p.6, no. 10]. She was head of an Essex County household of 2 "other free" in 1810 [VA:208]. She was the mother of

i. Sally, Jr., registered on 8 December 1810: *daughter of Judy Hollinger, by affidavit of Sally Hollinger to be born free, dark Mulattoe, 9 years of age, four feet five & 1/4 inches* [Register p.6, no.11].

3. Suckey Hollinger, born about 1775, registered as a free Negro in Essex County on 8 December 1810: *free born by statement of Thos. Brockenbrough, always passed as a free person, dark Mulattoe, 35 years of age, five feet 5 & 1/2 inches* [Register of Free Negroes 1810-43, p.12, no.26]. She was head of an Essex County household of 6 "other free" in 1810 [VA:208]. She was the mother of

    i. William, born about 1797, registered in Essex County on 8 December 1810: *born free, Sucky Hollinger his mother has always passed as a free person, bright Mulattoe, 13 years of age, four feet 3 & 1/2 inches* [Register of Free Negroes 1810-43, p.12].

    ii. Smith, born about 1800, registered in Essex County on 8 December 1810: *born free...son of Sucky Hollinger, dark Mulattoe, ten years of age* [Register of Free Negroes 1810-43, p. 13, no. 28].

    iii. Henry, born about 1802, registered on 8 September 1810: *son of Sucky Hollinger, bright Mulatto, 8 years of age, four feet high* [Register of Free Negroes 1810-43, p.13, no.28].

    iv. Mary, born about 1805, registered on 8 September 1810: *daughter of Sucky Hollinger, bright Mulatto, 5 years, 3 feet 3 & 1/4 inches* [Register of Free Negroes 1810-43, p. 13, no. 29].

HOLMAN FAMILY

1. John[1] Holman, born say 1740, an Englishman, established himself as a slave trader and merchant on the Rio Pongo River in present-day Guinea about 1764. He had an African mistress named Elizabeth by whom he had five children: John, Samuel, Esther, Elizabeth, and Margaret. He sent his son John, Jr., to school in Liverpool. John, Sr., left West Africa with his family and slaves for Charleston, South Carolina, in January 1790 but had to stay in Georgia until February 1791 until the legislature approved the importation of his slaves into the state. He established a plantation in St. Thomas & St. Dennis Parish in Charleston District where he made his will, proved in July 1792. He freed his mistress Elizabeth and their children and also freed John Cameron and Richard and William Holman who were his children by another African woman. He divided his estate which included fifty-seven slaves, among his children and charged his sons John and Samuel with supporting their mother [Koger, *Black Slaveowners*, 110-115]. He was the father of

2   i. John[2], born about 1768.

    ii. Samuel, born say 1770, perhaps the Samuel Holman who married Agnes **Mitchel**, "free persons of color," on 25 September 1805 in St. Philip's and Michael's Parish, Charleston.

    iii. Esther, married James **Anderson**.

    iv. Elizabeth, married Elias **Collins**.

    v. Margaret, married Robert **Collins**.

    vi. William, remained in West Africa where he continued his slave trading operations.

    vii. Richard.

    viii. John Cameron.

2. John[2] Holman, born about 1768, was about sixteen years old in 1784 when he began assisting his father as a slave trader. Within a few years he owned thirteen slaves who he used in his slave-trading operations on the Dambia River. He moved with his father to South Carolina in 1790 and received thirty-seven slaves by his father's will. He operated his father's plantation on the Cooper River in Charleston District until 1798 when he moved to Georgetown

District. He rented a plantation in Georgetown District on the Santee River until 1804 when he purchased it for $15,000. He returned to his homeland in Rio Pongo, West Africa in May 1805, leaving his brother Samuel in charge of his plantation which by then consisted of 128 slaves. Samuel mismanaged his brother's estate as well as his own, and they were lost to creditors by 1819 when Samuel joined his brother John in Rio Pongo. John left a will in 1821, calling himself "a Native of Africa" in which he divided his estate between his wife Sally and his nephew Samuel, "both of whom are Natives of Africa" [Koger, *Black Slaveowners*, 111-118].

HOLMES/ HOMES/ HOOMES FAMILY

Members of the Holmes/ Homes/ Hoomes family were

i. William[1] Holmes, born about 1710, a "Mulatto" living in Henrico County in August 1744 when he complained to the court that he had not received payment for taking up a runaway Negro slave who belonged to Nicholas Davies of Goochland County [Orders 1737-46, 277]. On 28 February 1755 he was listed as a soldier from King William County in the French and Indian War who had deserted: *a mulatto, age 45 years, 5'11"* [*Magazine of Virginia Genealogy* 31:93].

ii. John[1] Holmes, born say 1714, a "free Negro" wheelwright and carpenter who indentured himself to Judge Nicholas Trott in South Carolina. Trott sold John Holmes' services to a resident of Savannah Town, but Holmes ran away from him according to the 13 November 1736 edition of the *South Carolina Gazette* [Wood, *Black Majority*, 101].

1   iii. Elizabeth Homes/ Hoomes, born say 1717.

iv. Moses Hoomes, a "Negro" who still had time to serve when Patrick Belsches gave the remaining time to his wife Judy Belsches by his 29 December 1763 Louisa County will, proved 10 April 1764 [WB 1:59-62].

v. Duncan, born say 1750, taxable in Louisa County from 1782 to 1806: taxable on 2 horses and 3 cattle in 1782, 2 free males from 1797 to 1799, 2 slaves in 1801, a slave in 1805 and 1806, deceased by 1807 when his estate was taxable on 7 horses [PPTL, 1782-1814]. He sued Joseph **Ailstock** in Albemarle County court for trespass, assault and battery on 7 May 1799. The suit was dismissed on agreement of the parties on 6 August 1800 [Orders 1798-1800, 215; 1800-1, 116]. He and his wife Sally were counted in a list of free "Mulattoes" in Louisa County about 1802 [Abercrombie, *Free Blacks of Louisa County*, 20].

2   vi. Milley Homes/ Hoomes, born say 1752.

vii. Polley Homes, head of a Richmond City household of 3 "other free" in 1810 [VA:350].

viii. Amos Hoomes, head of a New Kent County household of 1 "other free" and a slave in 1810 [VA:757].

ix. Sarah Hoomez, head of a Henrico County household of 4 "other free" in 1810 [VA:1015].

x. Betsy Hoomez, head of a Henrico County household of 4 "other free" in 1810 [VA:1015].

xi. John[3], born say 1770, head of a Buckingham County, Virginia household of 9 "other free" in 1810 [VA:804].

xii. Polley, born say 1785, head of a Richmond City household of 3 "other free" in 1810 [VA:350].

1.   Elizabeth Homes/ Hoomes, born say 1717, was a "Molatto" presented by the York County court for not listing herself as a tithable on 15 November 1735 and 15 May 1738 [W&I 18:237, 245, 414, 434]. She may have been the ancestor of

4   i.   Stephen, born say 1745.

      ii.   Richard, born say 1751, taxable in King William County on his own tithe and a horse in 1794 (called Richard Hoomes, adjoining Stephen and William Hoomes) [Land Tax List 1782-1832]. He was taxable in Charles City County from 1797 to 1814: taxable on his own tithe and a horse in 1797, on two tithes in 1809, exempt from personal tax in 1811, a "Mulattoe" taxable in 1813 and 1814 [PPTL, 1788-1814].

     iii.   William, taxable in King William County on his own tithe and a horse in 1794 and taxable on his own tithe from 1800 to 1812, listed as a "mulatto" in 1813 [Land Tax List 1782-1832; PPTL 1812-50].

     iv.   Bartholomew, a "yellow" complexioned soldier born in James City County who was living in King William County when he was listed in a register of soldiers who enlisted in the Revolution [NSDAR, *African American Patriots*, 150].

2.   Milley Holmes, born say 1752, was the mother of Tempie Homes who was bound to George Walton by the Prince Edward County court on 18 May 1778. She was probably identical to _____ Hoomes who complained to the court against Walton on 18 March 1781. On 16 December 1782 the court ordered the churchwardens to bind out her daughter Suckey Hoomes [Orders 1771-81, part 2, 528, 94; 1782-5, 24]. She was living in Charlotte County on 6 September 1786 when she complained to the court that Thomas Tombs was holding her "Mulatto" child Sally in servitude [Orders 1784-86, 138]. Milley Homes was head of a Prince Edward County, Virginia household of 6 "other free" in 1810 [VA:572]. Her children were

      i.   Tempy, born say 1772.

     ii.   Suckey, born say 1775.

3   iii.   Sally[1], born about 1777.

3.   Sally[1] Holmes, born about 1777, registered as a free Negro in Lunenburg County on 8 September 1828: *about 51 years of age, black complexion, flat nose, large lips...five feet 8 inches high.* She was probably the mother of

      i.   William[2], born about 1793, registered in Lunenburg County on 14 August 1823: *aged about 30 years, dark Complexion, about 5 feet 3 inches.*

     ii.   Sally[2], born about 1795, registered in Lunenburg County on 8 September 1828: *black Complexion, thick lips, 5 feet 8 inches high* [WB 5, after page 89, nos. 28, 56, 57].

     iii.   George, apprenticed to Jesse Moore in 1802 and 1803 when he was counted in the "List of free Negroes & Mulattoes" in the lower district of Lunenburg County [LVA, Lunenburg County, Free Negro & Slave Records, 1802-1803].

     iv.   Matthew, living in the household of Joshua and Celia **Evans** in 1802 and 1803 when he was counted in the "List of free Negroes & Mulattoes" in the lower district of Lunenburg County [LVA, Lunenburg County, Free Negro & Slave Records, 1802-1803].

4.   Stephen Hoomes/ Homes, born say 1745, was taxable on his own tithe and a horse in King William County in 1794 (called Stephen Hoomes, adjoining Richard and William Hoomes) [Land Tax List 1782-1832]. He was taxable in Charles City County from 1797 to 1814: exempted from personal tax in 1805 and thereafter, taxable on 2 free tithes and a horse in 1809, and taxable on a horse in 1810 [PPTL, 1788-1814]. He was the father of

      i.   ?Burnett, born say 1790, taxable in Charles City County in 1811 and a "Mulattoe" taxable there in 1813 and 1814 [PPTL, 1788-1814].

     ii.   Mary, born about 1809, obtained a certificate of freedom in Charles City County on 18 May 1826: *daughter of the late Stephen Homes,*

> *bright mulatto girl, about 17 years of age, 5 feet 2-1/4 inches high, born free in this county* [Minutes 1823-9, 167].

   iii. Susanna, born about 1812, obtained a certificate of freedom in Charles City County on 19 July 1827: *daughter of Stephen Homes, brown mulatto girl 15 years of age* [Minutes 1823-9, 239].

Members of the Holmes family in North Carolina were

   i. John[2], born say 1760, head of a Beaufort County, North Carolina household of 6 "other free" in 1790 [NC:126] and 7 in 1800 [NC:9].

   ii. Edward, born say 1765, head of a Beaufort County household of one "other free" in 1790 [NC:126].

   iii. David, born say 1772, head of a Pasquotank County household of 2 "free colored" in 1820 [NC:275].

   iv. James, born say 1775, a "Mulatto" boy bound as an apprentice shoemaker to Baker Bowden in New Hanover County, North Carolina, on 8 July 1783 [Minutes 1779-92, 100].

HOLT FAMILY

1. Mary Holt, born 10 January 1698, was the daughter "of a white woman and a mulatto man" at Captain Alexander Walker's according to a certificate attested by the clerk of Wilmington Parish, New Kent County. She died on 24 December 1718, called "a mulatto belonging to Mr. Allin" [NSCDA, *Parish Register of St. Peter's*, 16, 53]. She was probably the mother of

2   i. Ann[1], born say 1716.

2. Ann[1] Holt, born say 1716, was the "free Mulatto" mother of Ann and George Holt whose birth and baptism were registered in St. Peter's Parish, New Kent County [NSCDA, *Parish Register of St. Peter's*, 117, 134]. Her children were

   i. Ann[2], "Daughter of Ann Holt a free Mulatto woman," born 20 December 1734, baptized 27 June 1735.

3   ii. George, born 20 October 1736.

3. George Holt, born 20 October 1736, the "Bastard Son of Ann Holt a free mulatto woman," was baptized 23 July 1737 in St. Peter's Parish, New Kent County [NSCDA, *Parish Register of St. Peter's*, 117]. He was taxable on a horse and 3 cattle in the Pamunkey Indian town in King William County in 1787 [PPTL 1782-1811]. He was probably the father of

   i. Richard, born say 1771, taxable in New Kent County from 1792 to 1797: a "Negroe" taxable in 1791 and 1792, a "F.N." in 1795, taxable on a horse from 1795 to 1797 [PPTL 1791-1828, frames 229, 240, 296, 307]. He was taxable in the Pamunkey Indian town of King William County on his own tithe and a horse in 1798, and he was taxable on his own tithe in King William County from 1803 until 1813, the year he was listed as a "Mulatto" taxable on a horse [PPTL 1782-1811; 1812-50]. He was probably the husband of Molly Holt who was said to have been over eighty years of age in the early 1840s when Reverend Edwin Dalrymple of St. Peter's Parish, New Kent County, interviewed her on the Pamunkey reservation. (She was one of the last members of her tribe who could still remember a few words of their language). Richard and Molly were probably the parents of Anderson, William and Ben Holt who were adults living on the Pamunkey reservation when they signed a legislative petition in the early 1840s [Rountree, *Pocahantas's People*, 341, 344].

HONESTY FAMILY

1. Elizabeth Honest, born say 1725, was a servant woman valued at 1 pound currency in the 24 January 1749/50 inventory of the Westmoreland County, Virginia estate of Presley Neale with (her children?) a "Malatto Boy" named John Honest, valued at 2 pounds, and a "Malatto Girl" named Jane Honest who was valued at 5 pounds [Records & Inventories 1746-52, 101b]. She was probably the mother of
    i.   Jane, born say 1745.
    ii. John, born say 1747, perhaps the John Honesty who was head of a Fairfax County household of 9 "other free" in 1810 [VA:267].
    iii. Hannah Honesty, head of a Fairfax County household of 5 "other free" in 1810 [VA:267].

HOOD FAMILY

1. Mary Hood, born say 1740, was living in Charles City County, Virginia, in July 1758 when her "mulatto" son William was ordered bound out by the churchwardens of Westover Parish [Orders 1758-62, 24]. She was the mother of
    i.   William, born about 1753, a "remarkably smart" sixteen-year-old "Mulatto boy" who had been on two voyages to sea, ran away from Henry Minson of Charles City County on 23 September 1769 and was taken up in Halifax County, North Carolina, according to the 21 December 1769 issue of the *Virginia Gazette* [Windley, *Runaway Slave Advertisements*, 1:301; Headley, *18th Century Newspapers*, 169]. He was a "Mulatto" counted in the 1786 North Carolina State Census for the Caswell District of Caswell County adjacent to "Mulattoes" Arthur **Toney** and John **Wright** and head of a Rockingham County, North Carolina household of 7 "other free" in 1800 [NC:491]. He was about sixty-five years old in 1818 and living in Jefferson County, Indiana, when he applied for a pension. His children residing with him were Hannibal, Jesse, Sally, and Eleanor. He died on 8 April 1829, and his wife Catherine Frances or Kitty Dephens, was awarded a survivor's pension at the age of seventy in July 1855 [M804-1320, frame 644-672].
    ii. ?Charles, born about 1755, married Patsey **Johnston**, 26 July 1805 Orange County, North Carolina bond, a sixty-five-year-old "Man of Colour" living with his forty-year-old wife when he made a declaration in Orange County court to obtain a pension on 27 May 1820 [M804-1320, frame 70-78].
    iii. ?Jesse, an "orphan" bound out in Caswell County in March 1783. He married Polly **Sawyer**, 18 May 1807 Caswell County bond, Henry **Curtis** bondsman. He was head of a Caswell County household of 10 "other free" in 1810 [NC:481]. He purchased 120 acres in Caswell County in 1816 [DB R:354]. His 30 April 1818 Caswell County will, proved July 1818, left all his property to his wife Mary. Polly was head of a Caswell County household of 11 "other free" in 1820 [NC:65].

HORN FAMILY

1. Mary Horn, born say 1735, was the mother of a "base born mulatto" child named Charity who was bound by the Granville County, North Carolina court to Thomas Bradford on 18 January 1769 [Owens, *Granville County Notes*]. She was the mother of
    i.   Charity, born about 1754, about fourteen or fifteen years old when she was bound as an apprentice in Granville County on 18 January 1769.

She may have been the ancestor of James Horn, an eight-year-old "boy of colour" who was bound apprentice to James Anderson by the Cumberland County, North Carolina court on 5 December 1810 [Minutes 1808-10, n.p.].

ii. ?William, a taxable "Molato" in the Bladen County household of John **Carsey/ Kersey** in 1771 [Byrd, *Bladen County Tax Lists*, I:61], head of a Beaufort County, North Carolina household of 1 "other free" in 1790 [NC:127].

iii. ?Meshack, head of a Wayne County, North Carolina household of 6 "other free" in 1810 [NC:827].

HOWARD FAMILY

1. Frances Haward, born say 1672, was the servant of Captain William Taylor on 5 October 1692 when she confessed to the Richmond County, Virginia court that she had committed the sin of "fornication with a Negro." Her master paid her fine of 1,000 pounds of tobacco and she agreed to serve him an additional year after the completion of her service [Orders 1692-4, 40]. She may have been the mother of

    i. Barbara, born say 1718, (no race indicated) the mother of a five-year-old "Mulatto" child named Sarah Howard who was bound by the Anne Arundel County, Maryland court in June 1737 to serve Robert Perry until the age of thirty-one [Judgment Record 1736-8, 171].

2   ii. Ann, born say 1720.

2. Ann Howard, born say 1720, was a "free Mulatto" living in Spotsylvania County on 6 December 1758 when the court ordered the churchwardens to bind out her children Benjamin, Simon, Rebecca, Peter, Alexander, Eliza, William, John and Rachel Howard (all "born in her freedom") to serve Richard Tutt, Gent. About twelve years later on 24 May 1771 Peter and Betty sued James Tutt for detaining them in servitude [Orders 1755-65, 129; 1768-74, 165]. She was the mother of

    i. Benjamin, born say 1743.

    ii. Simon, born say 1745.

    iii. Rebecca, born say 1747, probably identical to Becky Hoard, head of a Fredericksburg, Spotsylvania County household of 10 "other free" in 1810 [VA:107b].

    iv. Peter, born say 1749, sued James Tutt on 24 May 1771 for detaining him as a servant.

    v. Alexander.

    vi. Eliza, sued James Tutt on 24 May 1771 for detaining her as a servant.

    vii. William.

    viii. John.

    ix. Rachel, "free" head of a Botetourt County household of 7 "other free" in 1810 [VA:628].

Their descendants in Virginia were

    i. Elizabeth, born about 1775, registered in Middlesex County on 24 May 1832: *born free; 57 years of age; 5'2"; Mulatto complexion* [Register of Free Negroes 1827-60, p.5].

    ii. Jane, head of a Stafford County household of 4 "other free" in 1810 [VA:136].

    iii. Mary, head of a Stafford County household of 3 "other free" in 1810 [VA:128].

    iv. Polly, head of a Stafford County household of 2 "other free" in 1810 [VA:127].

    v. Susan Hoard, head of a Fredericksburg, Spotsylvania County household of 2 "other free" in 1810 [VA:109b].

vi. Reuben, head of a Campbell County household of 1 "other free" in 1810 [VA:852, 853].

Members of a Howard family in North Carolina were

i. William, born say 1784, married Tabitha **Carter**, 9 June 1807 Craven County bond, James **Godett** bondsman. He was head of a Craven County household of 6 "free colored" in 1820 [NC:65].

ii. Joseph, head of a Craven County household of 9 "free colored" in 1820 [NC:67].

Members of a Howard family in South Carolina were

i. David, head of a Beaufort District household of 4 "other free" in 1790 [SC:11] and 4 in 1800 [SC:122].

ii. James, head of a Beaufort District household of 3 "other free" in 1790 [SC:11].

HOWELL FAMILY

1. Elizabeth Owell, born say 1678, was the servant of Mrs. Mary Timson in York County in 1695 when she admitted to having a bastard child by a "Negro" for which she had to serve her mistress an additional two years. She also agreed to serve her mistress an additional two and one-half years for paying her fine [DOW 10:107, 121, 152]. (And a woman named Martha Howell confessed to the Princess Anne County court on 2 November 1699 that she had a "Molatto" child. She received twenty-five lashes and was ordered to serve her master Robert Thorowgood an additional year [Minutes 1691-1709, 225].) Elizabeth was probably the ancestor of

2   i. Dorothy, born say 1707.

ii. John[1], born say 1740, presented by the York County court on 15 November 1762 for failing to list his wife as a tithable. The case was dismissed after he paid her taxes and court costs. He was presented on 20 May 1765 for not attending Charles Parish Church [Judgments & Orders 1759-63, 437, 453, 480; 1763-5, 374, 448].

iii. Charles[1], born say 1735, said to be living in Gloucester County and the father of a "Mulatto Boy" of the same name who was about twelve or fourteen years old on 24 February 1774 when he was taken up in Chesterfield County. The boy told the jailer that he had been stolen three years previous by some sailors who took him to Warwick County where they sold him to a Mr. John Scott of Albemarle [*Virginia Gazette* (Purdie & Dixon)].

3   iv. Mary, born say 1740.

v. Elizabeth, born say 1744, (no race indicated) presented by the York County court on 20 May 1765 for having a bastard child [Judgments & Orders 1763-5, 374, 447].

vi. _____, husband of Susanna Howell, nee **Banks**, who was a widow by 22 February 1796 when she was named as one of the heirs of Matthew **Banks** who left her one fourth of 75 acres in Surry County, Virginia [Deeds 1792-99, 344].

2. Dorothy Howell, born say 1707, a "mulatto Servt to Mr. Sherwood Lightfoot, was living in St. Peter's Parish, New Kent and James City counties, in 1725 when the birth of her daughter Judith was recorded [NSCDA, *Parish Register of St. Peter's*, 91]. She was the mother of

4   i. Lucy, born about 1723.

5   ii. Judith[1], born in 1725.

iii. ?Samuel[1], born about 1732, 5 feet 10 inches tall, a twenty-five year old "mulatto" sawyer from Charles City County, Virginia, listed in the

1757 size roll of Captain Robert Spotswood's Company in Fort Young [Clark, *Colonial Soldiers of the South,* 570].

    iv.   Robin, born 18 March 1739, "mulatto son of Dorothy Howel" [NSCDA, *Parish Register of St. Peter's,* 87].

3.   Mary Howell, born say 1740, was presented by the York County court on 17 May 1762 for having a bastard child. She was called a "Poor Mulatto" on 19 March 1764 when the York County court ordered the churchwardens of Charles Parish to bind out her son John Howell to Starkey Robinson. Six months later on 27 September the court ordered the churchwardens of Charles Parish to bind her unnamed daughter to Starkey Robinson [Judgments & Orders 1759-63, 358; 1763-5, 166, 284]. She was the mother of

    i.   John[2], born say 1762, son of Mary Howell ordered bound to Starkey Robinson on 19 March 1764.

    ii.   an unnamed daughter who the York County court ordered the churchwardens of Charles Parish to bind to Starkey Robinson on 27 September 1764 [Judgments & Orders 1763-5, 166, 284].

4.   Lucy Howell, born about 1723, was a "free Mulattoe" living in Goochland County on 7 March 1756 when her daughter Elizabeth was baptized [Jones, *The Douglas Register,* 348]. She was called a "Mulatto...bound until the age of thirty one years" on 28 February 1757 when the Cumberland County, Virginia court bound her sons Sam and Simon, "Born during her Servitude," to Wade Netherland, and on 28 March 1757 the court bound her children Charles, Betty and Isaac to John Fleming [Orders 1752-8, 447, 462]. On 27 August 1770 the court ordered the churchwardens of Southam Parish to bind her "mulattoe" children Robin, Doll, and Matthew Howell to Thomas and William Fleming, executors of John Fleming, deceased. She complained to the court about the treatment of her son Isaac Howell, and on 28 April 1772 his masters Thomas and William Fleming agreed to teach him the trade of blacksmith and carpenter. And the court ordered that her other children be removed from their care unless they agreed to teach her other children a trade [Orders 1770-2, 77, 429, 481]. Lucy was head of a Henrico County household of 7 "other free" in 1810 [VA:1015]. Her children were

6   i.   Samuel[2], born about 1742.

    ii.   Simon, born say 1744, described as "5 feet 8 or 9 inches high, thin visage, and sharp chin" in the August 1770 issue of the *Virginia Gazette* which also identified him as the brother of Samuel Howell [Purdie & Dixon's edition, p. 3, col. 3]. Simeon was a "Mulatto" taxable in the lower district of Henrico County in 1811 [PPTL 1782-1814, frame 684].

    iii.   Elizabeth, born October 1748.

7   iv.   Charles[2], born say 1753.

    v.   Judith[2] (Judah), born 10 June 1755, daughter of Lucy Howell, baptized 7 March 1756 in Goochland County [Jones, *The Douglas Register,* 348]. She registered there as a free Negro on 17 September 1804: *a free born Black person aged about fifty three years, about five feet seven inches high* [Register of Free Negroes, p.1, no.2]. She was a "Mulatto" taxable on a horse, doing housework and living on William M. Richardson's land in the upper district of Goochland County from 1805 to 1807 [PPTL, 1782-1809, frames 743, 782, 826].

8   vi.   Isaac, born say 1757.

9   vii.   ?David, born about 1763.

5.   Judith[1] Howell, born in 1725 in St. Peter's Parish, New Kent and James City counties, complained to the Amelia County court on 26 March 1752 that she was "kept and detained as a slave" by John Thomas. On 25 May 1753 the court ordered the churchwardens of Nottoway Parish to bind out her son

Matthew Howell. She was taxable that year in the Nottoway Parish, Amelia County household of Abraham Cocke [Orders 1751-55, 29, 47; 95-96, 98; List of Tithables, 1753] and was taxable on a horse in Nottoway County in 1791 and 1801 [PPTL, 1791, p.13; 1801, p.10]. She was the mother of

10   i.   Matthew[1], born say 1752.
11   ii.   ?Thomas, born say 1760.
      iii.   John[3], born say 1765, taxable in New Kent County from 1790 to 1809: listed as a "M"(ulatto) in 1806, 1807 and 1809 [PPTL 1782-1800, frame 147; 1791-1828, frames 229, 240, 268, 330, 344, 357, 370, 382, 407, 420, 431, 443].

6.   Samuel[2] Howell, born about 1742, and his brother Simon (no surnames) were bound as apprentices to Wade Netherland in Goochland County on 18 October 1748 [Orders 1744-49, 496]. They were bound again to Netherland in Cumberland County in February 1757 [Orders 1752-8, 447]. Samuel ran away in October 1765 according to an ad placed by Netherland in the 2 May 1766 issue of the *Virginia Gazette*: *a likely young Mulatto man named SAM HOWEL, 23 years old, about 5 feet 9 inches high...He was bound for 31 years, according to the condition of his mother, who was to serve until that time; his pretence for going away was to apply to some lawyer at Williamsburg to try to get his freedom, though he had a trial in the county court, and was adjudged to serve his full time* [Windley, *Runaway Slave Advertisements*, 1:39]. He appeared in Cumberland County court on 27 October 1766 and agreed to serve Netherland an additional year for absenting himself from his master's service for six months [Orders 1764-7, 351]. In the August 1770 edition of the *Virginia Gazette* he was called Samuel Howell, a "mulatto servant man," who had run away from Wade Netherland of Cumberland County, the master to whom he was indentured until the age of thirty-one. He was described as twenty-eight years old, well set, 5 feet 8 or 9 inches high, and his brother Simon Howell, who ran away with him, was described as 5 feet 8 or 9 inches high, thin visage, and sharp chin. Samuel had brought an unsuccessful suit in the General Court for his freedom just prior to running away [*Virginia Gazette* (Purdie & Dixon's edition), p. 3, col. 3]. In this case held in April 1770 he had claimed that his grandmother was a "mulatto begotten on a white woman by a negro man after the year 1705." His mother was born in 1723, and he was born in 1742. Thomas Jefferson was his lawyer [Catterall, *Judicial Cases Concerning American Slavery*, I.90-91]. He was a "Mulatto" taxable in Chesterfield County from 1796 to 1798 [PPTL, 1786-1811, frames 283, 357] and a "M°" taxable in Powhatan County in 1798 [PPTL, 1787-1825, frame 163].

7.   Charles[2] Howell, born say 1753, was bound to John Fleming in Cumberland County on 28 March 1757 [Orders 1752-8, 462]. He sued Benjamin Russell in Cumberland County court for a 4 pound, 10 shilling debt on 28 September 1773. On 28 November 1774 Frank **Couzens** was presented by the Cumberland County court for not listing him as a tithable [Orders 1772-4, 403; 1774-8, 300]. He married Abbie **Scott**, "Mulattoes both," on 18 June 1775 in Goochland County [Jones, *The Douglas Register*, 347]. He was taxable in Powhatan County from 1787 to 1805: taxable on 2 horses and 10 cattle in 1787, called a "M°" from 1790 to 1805, taxable on John Howell's tithe in 1793 [PPTL, 1787-1825, frames 7, 19, 34, 47, 61, 78, 93, 106, 119, 132, 186, 224, 259, 296]. He was a "Mulatto" taxable in Goochland County from 1806 to 1815: taxable on a free tithe aged 16-21 in 1806; taxable on Bennett Howell from 1807 to 1809; taxable on a free tithe aged 16-21 in 1810 and 1812; listed with his wife Abba and children Billy & Polly who were over 16 & under 21 years old in 1813; taxable on Wilson and Bennett Howell in 1815 [PPTL, 1782-1809, frames 762, 806, 847; 1810-32, frames 35, 54, 141, 241]. He was the father of

i.   Sally, born say 1780, daughter of Charles Howell, married Francis **James** of Buckingham County, 26 March 1799 Powhatan County bond, Charles **Scott** security. Francis **James** may have been the son of "Mrs. Lucy James, a "Mulatto" taxable on a free male tithe, 2 horses and 5 cattle in Buckingham County in 1784 and 1785. Her husband may have been James **James** a "Mulatto" taxable in Buckingham County from 1786 to 1806: called "Cannon's" to differentiate him from another "Mulatto" James **James** who was called "Ayre's." Cannon's James was taxable on a slave, 3 horses and 9 cattle in 1786; 2 horses and 12 cattle in 1787, taxable on 3 tithables in 1795, and taxable on Francis and James **James**, Jr.'s tithe in 1796 and 1797.

ii. Betsy Ann, "daughter of Charles Howell," married Martin **Banks**, 11 March 1812 Goochland County bond, William Howell surety.

iii. ?Bennett, born say 1790, taxable in Charles Howell's household in 1807, a "F.B." taxable in Powhatan County in 1813 [PPTL, 1782-1825, frame 440].

iv. Polly, born 1791-1795, 16-21 years old in 1813.

v.   Wilson, born say 1796, taxable in Charles Howell's household in 1813 and 1815.

8. Isaac Howell, born say 1757, was a man of color born in Powhatan County who later lived in Goochland County. He enlisted as a substitute and served as a waiter in the Revolution [NSDAR, *African American Patriots*, 150; Jackson, *Virginia Negro Soldiers*, 38]. He was taxable in the upper district of Goochland County from 1786 to 1802: taxable on John Howell's tithe in 1795, taxable on Junior Howell's tithe from 1798 to 1802 [PPTL, 1782-1809, frames 129, 152, 221, 238, 282, 342, 483, 619]. He was head of a Buckingham County household 6 "other free" in 1810 [VA:810] and a "M"(Mulatto) taxable with his unnamed son in Buckingham County in 1813 [Waldrep, *1813 Tax List*]. His children were

i.   ?John[4], born about 1779, registered in Goochland County on 15 August 1808: *about 29 years of age...yellow complexion* [Register of Free Negroes, p.22, no.47]. He was head of a Goochland County household of 4 "other free" in 1810 [VA:694].

ii. Junior, born about 1781, registered in Goochland County on 15 August 1808: *about twenty seven years old, light complexion...free born* [Register of Free Negroes, p.22, no.46].

iii. Betsy, born say 1782, "daughter of Isaac Howell," married Charles **Scott**, 3 June 1800 Goochland County bond, consent for Betsy by (her aunt?) Judith Howell, Junior Howell surety.

iv. Judith[3], born say 1784, "daughter of Aise (Isaac) Howell," 6 November 1800 Goochland County bond, Junior Howell surety, 7 November marriage [Ministers Returns, 76].

9. David Howell, born about 1763, was a Revolutionary War soldier from Powhatan County [Jackson, *Virginia Negro Soldiers*, 38]. He married Nancy **Moss**, 24 April 1786 Powhatan County bond, John **Moss** surety; and second, Patsy **Moss**, daughter of Richard **Moss**, 30 May 1793 Powhatan County bond. He was taxable in Powhatan County from 1788 to 1817: called a "M°" from 1790 to 1810, a "F.B." taxable on 2 tithes in 1811 [PPTL, 1782-1825, frames 19, 46, 78, 106, 133, 186, 224, 259, 296, 342, 381, 422, 459, 535]. He registered in Powhatan County on 19 December 1822: *Age: 59; Color: Dark Brown; Stature: 5'6-1/2"; Born Free.* (His wife) Patsy Howell registered the same day: *Age: 47; Color: Yellow; Stature: 5'6"; Born Free* [Register of Free Negroes, nos. 64, 65]. He may have been the father of

i.   Charles[3], born about 1785, a "F.B." taxable in Powhatan County from 1811 to 1815 [PPTL, 1782-1825, frames 400, 440, 460, 484]. He registered in Powhatan County on 20 February 1833: *Age: 48; Color:*

dark; Stature: 5'9-1/2"; *Born Free* [Register of Free Negroes, no. 302].

ii. Samuel[3], born say 1796, a "F.B." taxable in Powhatan County from 1813 to 1815 [PPTL, 1782-1825, frames 440, 460, 484].

10. Matthew[1] Howell, born say 1752, son of Judith Howell, was bound an apprentice by the Amelia County court in 1753 and was bound out by the court again on 25 February 1762 [Orders 3:29, 95-96, 98; 1760-3, 223]. He may have been the Matthew Howell, no age, race or parent named, who complained to the Mecklenburg County, Virginia court on 13 May 1765 against his master Robert Rowland for misusage. Matthew was ordered to continue with Richard Epperson, to whom he was hired, until the next court on 10 June 1765 when he was ordered bound instead to Abram Martin [Orders 1765-68, 21, 34]. He may have been the widower of Peggy Howell whose son Zachariah was called "son of Matt Howell and Peggy his wife" when he registered in Charlotte County on 18 June 1814 [Ailsworth, *Charlotte County-- Rich Indeed*, 485]. Peggy Howell was taxable in Charlotte County on 2 free male tithables and a horse in 1793 [PPTL 1782-1813, frame 266]. She was called a "Mulatto" on 7 April 1794 when the Charlotte County court ordered her daughter Peggy Howell bound to William Childrey [Orders 1792-94, 174], and she was a midwife counted in a list of "free Negroes and Mulattos" in Stephen Bedford's district of Charlotte County in 1802 with her children Peggy, Betty, Zachariah and Drewry, counted with Betsy and Peggy Howell in 1803, listed with 3 male children and 4 female children in 1805, 5 males and 7 females (including herself) in 1806, 3 males and 6 females in 1809 [PPTL 1782-1813, frames 542, 607, 641, 648, 674, 682, 751, 814, 876, 886]. She was a "Free Negro" head of a Charlotte County household of 8 "other free" in 1810 [VA:1002]. She was the mother of

    i. ?Freeman, born say 1777, taxable in Charlotte County from 1794 to 1797 [PPTL 1782-1813, frames 291, 317, 369], a "FN" taxable in Mecklenburg County, Virginia, from 1806 to 1820 [PPTL 1806-28, frames 11, 89, 190, 310, 420, 561, 687], head of a Mecklenburg County household of 8 "free colored" in 1820 [VA:164b].

12   ii. Peggy, born about 1781.

    iii. John[4], born say 1782, a "free Negroe" taxable in Charlotte County from 1798 to 1807: taxable on a horse in 1801, listed in Peggy Howell's household in 1803 [PPTL 1782-1813, frames 401, 504, 573, 580, 607, 642, 711].

13   iv. Elizabeth, born say 1783.

    v. Matthew[2], born about 1784, married Mildred **Byrd**, 25 December 1808 Charlotte County marriage by Rev. Joseph Jenkins [Minsters' Returns p.37]. He was taxable in Charlotte County in the same household as John Howell in 1803, a "fm" ditcher taxable in 1809 and 1810, living with "fm" planter Rose and family of 4 males and 2 females in 1811, listed with a female above the age of 16 and a horse in 1813 [PPTL 1782-1813, frames 573, 744, 777, 814, 876]. He registered in Charlotte County on 30 August 1815: *son of Peggy Howell, a free Mulatto, Mulatto complexion, aged 31, born free* [Ailsworth, *Charlotte County--Rich Indeed*, 485]. He registered in Mecklenburg County, Virginia, on 19 June 1820: *a Man of dark Complexion, five feet Eleven and 3/4 Inches high about thirty six Years old, a ditcher by trade* [Free Person of Colour, no.7, p.16] and was head of a Mecklenburg County household of 12 "free colored" in 1820 [VA:164b]. He registered in Halifax County, Virginia, on 20 June 1831: *Matthew B. Howell, a dark mulatto, aged 49 years the 15 December next, six feet high...born free* [Registers of Free Negroes, 1802-1831, no. 194].

    vi. ?Charles[4], born say 1790, a "fm" ditcher taxable in Charlotte County from 1807 to 1813: listed with a woman in his household from 1811 to 1813 [PPTL 1782-1813, frames 710, 744, 777, 807, 814, 839, 846, 875].

vii. Zachariah, born about 1791, listed in Peggy Howell's household in 1802, registered in Charlotte County on 18 June 1814: *son of Mat Howell & his wife Peggy Howell, Mulattos born free, Mulato complexion, aged 23* [Ailsworth, *Charlotte County--Rich Indeed*, 485].

viii. Drury, born about 1799, registered in Charlotte County on 7 June 1831: *son of Peggy Howell, a free woman, Bright complexion, aged 32* [Ailsworth, *Charlotte County--Rich Indeed*, 485].

11. Thomas Howell, born say 1760, and his wife Lucy Howell were the parents of several children whose births were recorded in St. Peter's Parish, New Kent County, Virginia [NSCDA, *Parish Register of St. Peter's*, 163]. He was taxable in New Kent County from 1790 to 1807: taxable on 2 tithes from 1803 to 1805, listed as a "M"(ulatto) in 1806 and 1807 [PPTL 1782-1800, frame 146; 1791-1828, frames 229, 268, 307, 344, 370, 395, 420, 431]. He was a "free Negro" taxable in the upper district of Henrico County from 1811 to 1814: listed with his unnamed wife in 1813 [PPTL 1782-1814, frames 664, 758, 823]. He was head of a Richmond City household of 6 "other free" in 1810 [VA:345]. Thomas and Lucy were the parents of

i. Robert, born 20 February 1785, son to Thomas and Lucy Howel. He was a "M"(ulatto) taxable in New Kent County in 1809 [PPTL 1791-1828, frame 443] and head of a Henrico County household of 2 "other free" in 1810 [VA:1013].

ii. Susannah, born 17 April 1787, daughter of Thomas and Lucy Howel.

iii. Rebecca, born 27 April 1790, daughter of Thomas and Lucy Howel. She was listed as a "Black" person over the age of sixteen in Henrico County in 1813 [PPTL 1782-1814, frame 758].

iv. Elizabeth, born 12 March 1794, daughter of Thomas and Lucy Howel [NSCDA, *Parish Register of St. Peter's*, 163].

12. Peggy Howell, born about 1781, was taxable in Charlotte County from 1807 to 1813, called Peggy Howell, the younger: a "fm." planter listed with a male child in her household in 1807, a "fm." spinner with 2 males in 1810 [PPTL 1782-1813, frames 717, 751, 783, 876]. She registered in Charlotte County on 7 November 1831: *Bright complexion, aged 50, born free* [Ailsworth, *Charlotte County--Rich Indeed*, 490]. She was the mother of

i. Matthew³, born about 1798, registered in Charlotte County on 21 December 1819: *son of Peggy Howell, a free woman, Mulatto complexion, aged 23, born free* [Ailsworth, *Charlotte County--Rich Indeed*, 486].

ii. ?Charles⁵, born about 1802, registered in Charlotte County on 9 May 1833: *Bright complexion, aged 31, born free* [Ailsworth, *Charlotte County--Rich Indeed*, 490].

iii. Peter, born about 1808, registered in Charlotte County on 2 May 1831: *son of Peggy Howell, a free woman, Dark complexion, aged 23* [Ailsworth, *Charlotte County--Rich Indeed*, 488].

13. Elizabeth Howell, born say 1784, was counted in the Charlotte County household of her mother Peggy Howell in a list of "free Negroes and Mulattoes" in 1802, a weaver with 4 female children in her family in 1807 and 1809, a "fn" taxable on a horse in 1812 and 1813 [PPTL 1782-1813, frames 542, 717, 751, 876]. She was the mother of

i. Polly, born about 1804, registered in Charlotte County on 6 June 1831: *daughter of Betsey Howell, a free woman, Bright complexion, aged 27, born free* [Ailsworth, *Charlotte County--Rich Indeed*, 488].

  ii. Nancy, born about 1805, registered in Charlotte County on 6 June 1831: *daughter of Betsey Howell, a free woman, Bright complexion, aged 26, born free* [Ailsworth, *Charlotte County--Rich Indeed*, 488].

  iii. John[5], born about 1807, registered in Charlotte County on 2 May 1831: *son of Betsey Howell, Dark complexion, aged 24, born free* [Ailsworth, *Charlotte County--Rich Indeed*, 488].

  iv. Lizzy, born about 1811, registered in Charlotte County on 6 June 1831: *daughter of Betsey Howell, a free woman, Bright complexion, aged 26, born free* [Ailsworth, *Charlotte County--Rich Indeed*, 488].

Other members of the Howell family in North Carolina and Virginia were

14   i. Aaron, born say 1749.

  ii. Jacob, born about 1769, registered in Petersburg on 22 September 1806: *a brown free Negro man, five feet nine inches high, born free in Powhatan County & raised in the Town of Petersburg, by trade a sadler & harness maker, thirty seven years old* [Register of Free Negroes 1794-1819, no. 396]. He was head of a Petersburg Town household of 3 "other free" and a white woman in 1810 [VA:122a].

  iii. Nancy, born about 1772, registered in Petersburg on 7 June 1810: *a light yellow brown Mulatto woman, five feet one inches high, thirty eight years old, born free and raised in the County of Chesterfield* [Register of Free Negroes 1794-1819, no. 517(?)].

14. Aaron Howell, born say 1749, purchased 100 acres in Northampton County, North Carolina, near the "old Line" and a spring branch on 6 March 1770 from Hopkin Howell and his wife Elizabeth [DB 5:11]. Later that year on 21 September, his mother Elizabeth Howell made a deed of gift to him of 100 acres near the Spring Branch of Cypress Swamp [DB 5:58]. He was taxable in Northampton County on an assessment of 877 pounds in 1780 [GA 46.1]. On 1 December 1785 Aaron and his wife Martha sold 85 acres of the land he purchased from Hopkin Howell and sold the remaining 15 acres on 26 February 1798 without a dower release. On 31 May 1787 Sarah Howell, perhaps Aaron's aunt, gave to "Martha wife of Aaron Howell" furniture and to Aaron a cow and yearling. On 2 June 1792 Aaron and Martha mortgaged 50 acres of the land he received from his mother and sold the remainder to John Boykin for 50 pounds without a dower release on 24 December 1794. He repaid the mortgage a year later on 1 January 1796 and sold 15 acres on 26 February 1798 [DB 7:356; 9:175; 10:237, 238, 360]. Aaron was head of a Northampton County household of 6 "other free" in 1790 [NC:75] and 6 in 1800 [NC:449]. He may have been the father of

  i. Joseph, head of a Halifax County, North Carolina household of 2 "other free" in 1800 [NC:316].

HUBBARD FAMILY

1. Jane Hubbard/ Hubbart, born say 1675, was the white servant of John Jordan on 6 February 1693 when he left her nine pounds sterling by his Westmoreland County will to be delivered to her on the day of her marriage [DW 1707-9, 86a]. She was the servant of Charles Ashton, Gent., on 25 July 1705 when the Westmoreland County court convicted her of having a "mulatto" child. The court ordered the churchwardens of Washington Parish to sell her for five years. She was the mother of a "Mulatto" daughter named Elizabeth who was bound out by the churchwardens of Washington Parish until the age of thirty years on 26 September 1705 [Orders 1698-1705, 257, 262, 268; 1705-21, 3; DW 3:370-1]. They were probably the ancestors of

  i. Ruth, born about 1722, a fifty-four-year-old "mulato" head of Broad Creek Hundred, Harford County, Maryland household with (her children?) Belt (thirteen years old), Joe (ten), and Hanna (six) in 1776 [Carothers, *1776 Census of Maryland*, 88].

2   ii.   William, born say 1750.

       iii.   Abraham, counted with his wife Dorcas and children Amos, Polly, Abraham and Eley in a "List of Free Mullatoes and Negroes" living in Westmoreland County in 1801 [*Virginia Genealogist* 31:41]. He was head of a Westmoreland County household of 11 "other free" 1810 (called Abram Herbert) and 12 "free colored" in 1830, perhaps the father of Talbert Hubbard, head of a Westmoreland household of 3 "free colored" in 1830.

2.   William Hubbard/ Hubert, born say 1750, was mentioned in a 30 April 1795 entry in the account book of Benjamin **Banneker** [Bedini, *The Life of Benjamin Banneker*, 249]. He was head of a Patapsco Upper Hundred, Baltimore County, Maryland household of 5 "other free" in 1810 [MD:639]. He married a daughter of Robert and Molly **Banneker**. He and his wife were the parents of

       i.   Henry, born say 1770, obtained a certificate of freedom in Loudoun County, Virginia, on 24 December 1795 on testimony of Henry Jarvis that: *he was the son of a free woman and grandson of Robert Banneker, whose wife was also a free woman. Robert Banneker lived in Baltimore County about two and a half miles from Ellicott's Mills.*

       ii.   Charles, born say 1772, called brother of Henry Hubbard on 24 December 1795 when he obtained a certificate of freedom in Loudoun County [Certificates of Freedom in Loudoun County courthouse, cited by *Journal of the AAHGS* 11:123]. He (called Charles Hubbert) was head of a Loudoun County household of 8 "other free" in 1810 [VA:288].

Other likely descendants were

       i.   Isaac Hubbert, "negro" head of a Caroline County, Maryland household of 5 "other free" in 1810 [MD:165].

       ii.   Isaac, head of a Halifax County, North Carolina household of 5 "other free" in 1810 [NC:26].

       iii.   ?Anthony Herbert, head of a New Kent County, Virginia household of 6 "other free" in 1810 [VA:755].

       iv.   Nancy Herbert, head of a Norfolk County, Virginia household of 3 "other free" and 2 slaves in 1810 [VA:832].

       v.   Mary, married John **Butler**, 13 February 1802 Bertie County, North Carolina bond, Buffin Harrison bondsman.

HUGHES FAMILY

1.   Rosamond Hughes, born say 1720, was the servant of William McMachen, Gentleman, on 3 October 1745 when the Frederick County, Virginia court ordered the churchwardens of Frederick Parish to bind her "Mulatto" daughter Elizabeth to her master [Orders 1743-5, 467; 1745-8, 3]. She was the mother of

2   i.   ?Luke, born about 1740.

       ii.   Elizabeth, born say 1745.

2.   Luke Hughes, born about 1740, was listed among the slaves in Cadwelder Dade's estate inventory which was proved in Stafford County on 14 July 1761 "Luke...to serve till 31" [Wills, Liber O, 1748-63, 400]. He married Behethland **Kennedy**, 10 July 1779 at St. Paul's Parish, King George County [St. Paul's Parish Register, 223]. He was a Revolutionary War soldier who was born in King George County and later lived in Culpeper County [Jackson, *Virginia Negro Soldiers*, 38]. He registered in King George County on 27

October 1800: *a dark molatto man with long grey hair, about sixty years, was born in this County, served Cadwellder Dade untill he was thirty one years of age* [Register of Free Persons, no.16]. He was a "Mulatto" taxable on one tithe and two horses in Culpeper County in 1800 [*Virginia Genealogist* 16:188] and a "free Mulatto" head of a Culpeper County household of 3 "other free" in 1810 [VA:40]. His children were most likely:

    i.   William, born say 1760, a "yellow" complexioned man who enlisted in the Revolution in Caroline County [NSDAR, *African American Patriots*, 150]. He was head of a Spotsylvania County household of 2 "other free" and a slave in 1810 [VA:113b].

    ii.   Luke, Jr., "free Mulatto" head of a Culpeper County household of 2 "other free" in 1810 [VA:40].

    iii.   John, head of a Spotsylvania County household of 3 "other free" in 1810 [VA:112b].

    iv.   Samuel, head of a Rockingham County household of 5 "other free" in 1810 [VA:13].

HULIN FAMILY

Two members of the Hulin family born about 1720 were

1   i.   Thomas, born say 1720.
2   ii.   John[1], born say 1722.
3   iii.   Edward, born say 1725.

1.   Thomas[1] Hulin, born say 1720, purchased 200 acres on Corduroy Swamp in Northampton County, North Carolina, on 13 February 1742. He sold this land while resident in Granville County on 6 February 1748 [Northampton County DB 1:25, 396]. He was taxable in Aquilla **Snelling**'s Granville County household in 1764. He purchased 100 acres on the south side of Cedar Creek in St. John's Parish, Granville County, on 16 February 1759 and a further 613 acres adjoining this on 28 November 1760 [DB C:596; F:35]. He was taxable in Granville County in 1762 in John Pope's list for St. John's Parish [CR 044.702.19]. He sold 200 acres of his land to William **Bass** on 19 November 1762 [DB F:441]. He was listed among the "Black" members of the undated colonial muster roll of Captain James Fason's Northampton County Militia [Mil. T.R. 1-3]. His children may have been

    i.   William, born before 1750, taxable in the Granville County list of John Pope in 1761.
4   ii.   Thomas[2], born say 1745.

2.   John[1] Hulin, born say 1722, may have been identical to John Huins a "black" taxable in William **Chavis**' Granville County household in 1755 and called John Hewens when he was taxable in **Chavis**' household in 1762. On 6 March 1753 his "orphan" five-year-old son John was bound to James Paine of Granville County [CR 044.101.2]. His children were

    i.   ?Sarah, born 1742, no parent or race indicated, bound an apprentice to Sarah Sims on 4 December 1751 [CR 044.101.2].
    ii.   John[2], born about 1748.

3.   Edward Hulin/ Huling, born say 1725, and his wife Mary sold for 30 pounds 200 acres in Brunswick County, Virginia, on the Meherrin River on 30 May 1758, being part of a patent granted to him for 404 acres dated 24 April 1758 [DB 6:310]. He and his wife Mary were "Mulattoe" taxables in John Pope's Granville County list of 1759. He purchased 318 acres in Granville on both sides of Brandy Creek on 18 November 1760. He sold this land in two parcels while a resident of Brunswick County, Virginia, on 28 December 1763 and 14 March 1764 [DB D:133; F:490, 509]. He later moved to Northampton

County, North Carolina, where he was listed as a "Black" member of Fason's Muster [Mil. T.R. 1-3]. He may have been the ancestor of

    i.   Peggy, head of a Halifax County, North Carolina household of 9 "free colored" in 1820 [NC:150].

4.   Thomas[2] Hulin, born say 1745, was head of a Georgetown District, Prince George's Parish, South Carolina household of 8 "other free" in 1790, 9 in Liberty County in 1800 [SC:806], and 5 in Marion District in 1810 [SC:83]. (Other "black" families in Fason's Northampton County Company who went to South Carolina were the **Demerys**, the **Shoemakers**, and the **Sweats**). Thomas may have been the father of

    i.   James, born before 1776, head of a Wilmington, New Hanover County, North Carolina household of 8 "free colored" in 1820 [NC:214].

   ii. Zachariah, born before 1776, head of a Wilmington household of 5 "free colored" in 1820 [NC:214].

HUMBLES FAMILY

The Humbles family was probably related to Richard Humbles who successfully petitioned his master Charles Christian for his freedom dues in Charles City County court in April 1746 and to Eliza Humbles whose children Jesse and Obediah were bound out by the court in April 1748 [Orders 1737-51, 405, 471].

Members of the Humbles family were

1   i.   Jeremiah[1], born say 1740.
2   ii. Richard[1], born say 1748.
3   iii. Martha, born say 1750.
4   iv. Amy, born say 1752.

1.   Jeremiah[1] Humbles, born say 1740, was taxable in Charles City County in 1785 and an exempt taxable who was tithable on a horse in 1800 and 1801 [PPTL, 1783-7; 1788-1814]. He may have been the father of

    i.   Isaac, born say 1778, taxable in Charles City County in 1801 [PPTL, 1788-1814].

5   ii. Jeremiah[2], born say 1780.

   iii. David, born say 1783, taxable in Charles City County in 1807 [PPTL, 1788-1814].

   iv. John, born say 1786, taxable in Charles City County in 1807 [PPTL, 1788-1814].

2.   Richard[1] Humbles, born say 1748, was a "black man" taxable in Amherst County in 1803 [PPTL 1782-1803, frame 589] and head of a Buckingham County household of 19 "other free" in 1810 [VA:715a]. He may have been the father of

    i.   Richard[2], head of Buckingham County household of 1 "other free" in 1810 [VA:821].

   ii. Samuel, head of a Buckingham County household of 1 "other free" in 1810 [VA:821].

3.   Martha Humbles, born say 1750, was head of an Amherst County household of 3 "whites" (free persons) in 1783 [VA:49]. She may have been the mother of

    i.   Joyce, born about 1783, married Turner **Pinn**, 13 August 1807 Amherst County bond, William Solle security. She registered in Amherst County on 20 October 1828: *wife of Turner Pinn a free woman of color, rather light complexion, about five feet in hight, stout* *built, about forty five, was born free* [McLeRoy, *Strangers in Their Midst*, 56].

ii. Susanna **Thomas**, alias Humbles, born about 1790, married John **Redcross**, 13 February 1807 Amherst County bond, William Bryant security.

iii. Taba, born about 1796, registered in Amherst County on 22 June 1841: *dark complexion - about 45 years of age - 5 feet & 3 Inches high...born free* [McLeRoy, *Strangers in Their Midst*, 63].

iv. Joe, a "man of color" taxable in Amherst County in 1817 [PPTL 1804-20, frames 418, 436].

4. Amy Humbles, born say 1752, gave her consent for the 13 August 1793 Amherst County marriage bond of her daughter Betsy. She was the mother of

i. Betsy, born say 1775, married Abraham **Camp**, 13 August 1793 Amherst County bond with the consent of Amy Humbles. Abraham **Camp** was head of a Rockbridge County household of 2 "other free" in 1810 [VA:298].

5. Jeremiah Humbles, born say 1780, was taxable on one tithe in Charles City County in 1807 and 1809 [PPTL, 1788-1814]. He was the father of

i. Parkey **Miles**, registered in Charles City County on 17 November 1831: *daughter of the late Jeremiah Umbles, a bright mulatto woman, about 5 feet 5 inches, born free in this county* [Minutes 1830-9, 83].

HUNT FAMILY

Members of the Hunt family born before 1750 were

1 i. Joshua, born say 1730.

ii. William, born say 1733, a "mulatto servant" who ran away from John Hardyman of Charles City County according to the 24 May 1751 issue of the *Virginia Gazette*.

iii. Ann, born say 1735, a taxable "Mollatto" in John Miller's Norfolk County household in the Borough of Norfolk and the south side of Tanner's Creek to Spratt's Bridge in 1753 [Wingo, *Norfolk County Tithables, 1751-65*, 68].

iv. David, born about 1738, "a black man" listed in the Militia Returns of Captain Samuel Walker of Granville County in 1778 [*The North Carolinian* VI:726 (Mil. TR 4-40)].

2 v. Charles, born say 1745.

vi. Harry, born about 1765, registered in Petersburg on 29 June 1795: *a brown Mulatto man, five feet eight inches high, thirty years old, born free in Chesterfield County & raised in the Town of Petersburg* [Register of Free Negroes 1794-1819, no. 101].

1. Joshua Hunt, born say 1730, was living in Southampton County on 11 March 1763 when he and John **Byrd** were sued for a 2 pound debt [Orders 1759-63, 290]. He received a cow and a calf by the undated Southampton County will of (his father-in-law?) John **Byrd**, proved on 12 April 1781 [WB 3:322]. He was taxable in St. Luke's Parish, Southampton County, on 2 horses and 2 cattle in 1782, taxable on John Hunt in 1787, taxable on Will Hunt in 1789, on Will Hunt and Drury Hunt in 1791 [PPTL 1782-92, frames 508, 661, 711, 761, 817]. He may have been the ancestor of

i. Elijah, born say 1755, sued in Southampton County by Aaron **Haithcock** for a debt of 16 pounds, 4 shillings. The returned a list of his property to the court on 14 October 1784: a feather bed bolster, a sheet, a saddle, a pepper box, two brushes, 12 hogs, two waistcoats, a coat, and a shirt [Orders 1778-84, 505]. He was head of a Northampton County household of 10 "other free" in 1800 [NC:449].

ii. Hardy[1], born say 1760, a "Negro" from Southampton County listed in the size roll of troops who enlisted in the Revolution at Chesterfield Courthouse [The Chesterfield Supplement cited by NSDAR, *African American Patriots*, 150]. He enlisted in the service in Southampton County with John **Hathcock** and petitioned the Legislature for compensation in 1792 [Jackson, *Virginia Negro Soldiers*, 38]. He was taxable in Southampton County in 1787, taxable in the household of Sheriff Howell Edmund from 1788 to 1790, taxable in Nathaniel Edwards' household in 1792, in William Turner's household from 1793 to 1795, taxable in his own household from 1799 to 1805, called a "F.N." in 1803, a "M"(ulatto) in 1806 [PPTL 1782-92, frames 639, 658, 710, 758, 873; 1792-1806, frames 63, 91, 171, 382, 415, 518, 625, 694, 809, 844]. He was a witness to the 23 August 1790 Southampton County will of John **Reed** [WB 1:395].

iii. John[2], taxable in Southampton County in the household of Mary Grizzard in 1788 [PPTL 1782-92, frame 660], head of a Hertford County household of 3 "other free" in 1800 in Captain Lewis' District and head of a Northampton County household of 4 "other free" in 1810 [NC:727].

iv. Patt, head of a Southampton County household of 6 "other free" in 1810 [VA:87].

v. Drury, taxable in St. Luke's Parish, Southampton County, in Joshua Hunt's household in 1791, taxable in William Davis's household in 1793 [PPTL 1782-92, frame 817; 1792-1806, frame 50], head of a Hertford County, North Carolina household of 5 "other free" in 1800 in Captain Lewis' district, and head of a Northampton County household of 11 "free colored" in 1820 [NC:236].

vi. Charlotte, born about 1773, registered in Southampton County on 24 June 1810: *age 35, Mulatto, 5 feet 2 inches, free born* [Register of Free Negroes 1794-1832, no. 427]. She registered in Petersburg 3 July 1810: *a light brown Mulatto woman, five feet two inches high, thirty seven years old, born free & raised in Southampton County* [Register of Free Negroes 1794-1819, no. 644]. She was head of a Petersburg Town household of 3 [VA:124b].

vii. William, born say 1781, a "F.N." taxable in St. Luke's Parish, Southampton County, from 1802 to 1811, called a "M"(ulatto) in 1805 and 1806 [PPTL 1792-1806, frames 554, 693, 808, 843; 1807-21, frames 50, 73, 169, 193].

viii. Solomon, born about 1781, registered in Southampton County on 3 July 1802: *age 21, Black, 6 feet 2 inches, free born* [Register of Free Negroes 1794-1832, no. 230].

2. Charles Hunt, born say 1745, was taxable on 4 pounds, 2 shillings in the 1779 Currituck County tax list. He was head of a Currituck County household of 6 "other free" in 1790 [NC:20] and 5 "other free" in 1800 [NC:149]. He was also counted in Pasquotank County in 1790, head of a household of 5 "other free" [NC:28]. His 11 January 1804 Currituck County will was proved 11 September the same year. He named only his wife Lucy and "three small daughters" Lena, Susanna, and Deby [WB 2:87]. His children were

i. Lena.

ii. Susanna.

iii. Deby.

Other members of the Hunt family in North Carolina were

i. James, head of a Robeson County household of 4 "other free" in 1790 [NC:49], 7 in 1800 [NC:382], and 10 "free colored" in 1820 [NC:125].

ii. Lewis, head of a Robeson County household of 3 "other free" in 1790 [NC:49] and 6 "other free" in 1800 [NC:382].

iii. Elisha, a "Coloured Man" who lost his right arm at the siege of Charleston and was awarded a pension of $5 in 1789 while a resident of Lenoir County, North Carolina. On 5 October 1821 he applied for a pension in Cumberland County, North Carolina [M804-1370, frame 0091].

iv. John[1], a "Molatto" head of New Hanover County household of 1 male 21-60 years of age, and 2 female "Molattos" in 1786 in John Erwin's list for the North Carolina state census.

v. Isum, head of a Currituck County household of 2 "other free" in 1810 [NC:88].

vi. Dempsey, head of a Currituck County household of 2 "other free" in 1790 [NC:21] and 1 in 1800 [NC:141].

vii. Hyram, head of a Currituck County household of 2 "other free" in 1790 [NC:21].

viii. Service(?), head of a Currituck County household of 2 "other free" in 1810 [NC:88].

ix. Curria, born before 1776, head of a Pasquotank County household of 4 "free colored" in 1820 [NC:249].

x. Patience, head of a Northampton County household of 1 "other free" in 1810 [NC:728].

Members of the family in South Carolina were

i. Fanny, head of a Marlboro County household of 9 "other free" in 1800 [SC:60].

ii. James, born about 1764, a "Molatto Boy" about eighteen years old on 3 August 1782 when the vestry of Saint David's Parish ordered him bound to William Lankford.

iii. Lewis, born about 1768, a "Molatto Boy" about thirteen years old on 3 August 1782 when the vestry of Saint David's Parish ordered him bound to William Lankford.

iv. Saul, born about 1771, about eleven years old on 3 August 1782 when the vestry of Saint David's Parish ordered him bound to William Lankford [Holcomb, *Saint David's Parish, South Carolina, Minutes of the Vestry 1768-1832*, 24]. He was head of a Lancaster District household of 6 "other free" in 1800 [SC:8].

v. Samuel, head of a Sumter District household of 6 "other free" in 1800 [SC:8].

HUNTER FAMILY

1. Penelope Hunter, born say 1765, was a "free Negro" bound to Thomas Thompson by the churchwardens of Elizabeth River Parish by order of the Norfolk County court on 20 June 1771 [Orders 1771-3, 1]. She may have been the ancestor of

i. Sally, head of a Norfolk County household of 3 "other free" in 1810 [VA:904].

ii. Thomas, born 1776-1794, head of a Halifax County, North Carolina household of 4 "free colored" in 1830.

iii. Peter, a boy of color bound to Jesse H. Simmons by the Halifax County, North Carolina court on 16 February 1824 [Minutes 1822-4].

HURLEY FAMILY

Members of the Hurley family were

i. Mary, "Mo." head of a Culpeper County household of 7 "other free" in 1810 [VA:41].

ii.   Ruth, "Mo." head of a Culpeper County household of 6 "other free"
      in 1810 [VA:41].
iii. Henry/ Harry, born about 1779, registered in Culpeper County on 20
      October 1800: *a dark Mulatto, 21 years of age, 5 feet 10 Inches
      high...born free* [Minutes 1798-1800, 254]. He was head of a
      Rockingham County household of 4 "other free" in 1810 [VA:33].
iv.   John, head of a Bohemia, Cecil County, Maryland household of 1
      "other free" in 1790.

HURST FAMILY

The Hurst family may have descended from Richard Hurst, an eight-month-old
"Mulatto" valued at 4 pounds on 2 September 1724 when he was listed in the
inventory of the York County estate of Joseph Walker, Esq. [DOW 16, pt. 2, 329].
Members of the Hurst family were

1   i.   Faithy, born about 1757.
      ii.   Angey, born say 1762, married Burwell **Artis**, 21 August 1783
            Southampton County bond.
      iii. Robert, born say 1765, taxable in St. Luke's Parish, Southampton
            County, from 1790 to 1805: taxable on 2 horses in 1790, called a "free
            Negro" in 1801, a "FN" in 1803 and 1804, a "M" taxable with Henry
            Hix (Hicks) in 1805 [PPTL 1782-92, frame 762; 1792-1806, frames
            55, 82, 163, 192, 517, 555, 624, 694, 808].
      iv.   Mima, head of a Southampton County household of 9 "other free" and
            a slave in 1810 [VA:54].
      v.   Hannah, a "M" taxable on a horse in Southampton County in 1806,
            1807 and 1809, taxable on 2 free males and 2 horses in 1810 [PPTL
            1792-1806, frame 844; 1807-21, frames 73, 170]. She was head of a
            Southampton County household of 4 "other free" in 1810 [VA:75].
      vi.   Isabel, born about 1780, registered in Southampton County on 30 July
            1810: *age 30, Blk., 5 feet 3 inches, free born.* She registered again on
            12 March 1828 [Register of Free Negroes 1794-1832, nos. 733, 1694].
      vii. Milly, born about 1785, registered in Southampton County on 30 July
            1810: *age 25, Mulatto, 5 feet 3-1/2 inches, free born* [Register of Free
            Negroes 1794-1832, nos. 738, 1689]
      viii. Drury, born about 1786, registered in Southampton County on 28 July
            1810: *age 24, 5 feet 11 inches, Blk., free born* [Register of Free
            Negroes 1794-1832, nos. 705, 1690]. He was head of a Southampton
            County household of 2 "other free" in 1810 [VA:54].

1.   Faithy Hurst, born about 1757, was a "Mulatto" taxable in St. Luke's Parish,
      Southampton County, from 1802 to 1804: taxable on a free male tithable, a
      slave aged 12-16 and a horse in 1802; on 2 free males, a slave and 2 horses
      in 1804 [PPTL 1792-1806, frames 554, 623, 693]. She registered in
      Southampton County on 28 July 1810: *age 53, blk., 5 feet 4-3/4 inches high,
      free born.* She registered again on 12 March 1828: *age 71, Black, 5 feet 4-1/2
      inches high, born free.* She emancipated (her husband?) London **Williams** by
      deed acknowledged in Southampton County court on 21 April 1806 [Minutes
      1804-7, 158]. He registered in Southampton County on 15 September 1806:
      age 50, Blk., 5 feet 6-1/4 inches high, emancipated by Faithy Hurst deed
      [Register of Free Negroes 1794-1832, nos. 398, 707, 1691]. They may have
      been the parents of
      i.   Solomon, born about 1781, required to post bond on 19 March 1804
            for maintenance of an illegitimate child he had by Amey **Artis** [Minutes
            1803-4, unpaged]. He registered in Southampton County on 23 May
            1805: *age 35, 6 feet 1 inch high, blk., born free.* He registered again
            on 24 May 1817: *age 35, 6 feet 1-1/2 inches, blk., free born* [Register
            of Free Negroes 1794-1832, nos. 325, 1090]. He was head of a

Southampton County household of 6 "other free" in 1810, and there were two other Solomon Hursts who were heads of Southampton County households with 3 "other free" in 1810 [VA:54, 70, 74]. He was listed with his wife Milly in 1812 and 1814 [PPTL 1807-21, frames 291, 419].

IVEY FAMILY

George Ivie of Norfolk County petitioned the Assembly against the passage of the law against racial intermarriage in 1699 [McIlwaine, *Legislative Journals of the Council*, I:262]. Perhaps he petitioned on behalf of another member of the Ivey family. He was the son of a planter of the same name from whom he inherited 100 acres in 1689 [Norfolk Deeds 5-2:86a; 6:94, 105, 181, 188]. He died before 31 December 1710 when the inventory of his estate was recorded in Norfolk County court. The inventory was signed by his wife Elizabeth Ivey and included a note that seven sheep were given to his son William by his grandmother Elizabeth Thelaball [DB 9:36, 267, 384]. She may have been related to Margaret Theloball who paid a fine for having a "Mulatto" child in Princess Anne County on 2 July 1735 [Minutes 1728-37, 272].

1. Adam[1] Ivey, born say 1675, was the son of Adam Ivey of Prince George County, Virginia. He was the executor of the 26 April 1718 Prince George County will of his mother Elizabeth Ivey [Deeds, Etc. 1713-28, part 2, 443].[118] He received two patents on 21 February 1720/1 for land in the part of Isle of Wight County which is present-day Greensville County: one for 150 acres on the south side of the Meherrin River and another for 100 acres in the same area [Patents 11:56]. On 24 December 1725 he posted bond to Nicholas Hatch of Prince George County, Virginia, recorded in Isle of Wight County on 6 April 1725 for one Negro woman named Phillis and 100 acres where he then lived [Isle of Wight Deeds, Wills - Great Book vol. 2, 704]. He was living in Onslow Precinct, North Carolina, in 1736 when he sold land this land by Brunswick County, Virginia deed [Deeds, Wills, etc., #1, 303]. The Onslow County court listed him among thirteen people to lay out a new road from the King's Road to Chapel Spring in April 1734 [Onslow County Minutes 1732-43, 4]. He was the father of

    i. Elizabeth[1], named in the Prince George County will of her grandmother Elizabeth Ivey.
2   ii. ?Adam[2], born say 1710.
3   iii. ?Thomas[1], born say 1715.
4   iv. ?Joseph[1], born say 1717.

2. Adam[2] Ivey, born say 1710, was called "Adam Ivie melottoe" in July 1741 when he was presented by the Onslow County, North Carolina court for an unstated offense [Onslow County Minutes 1732-43, 25]. He was listed in the Edgecombe County, North Carolina militia in the 1750s [Clark, *Colonial Soldiers of the South*, 672]. He received a grant for 285 acres in Edgecombe County on 23 October 1754 [referred to in DB 2:154]. His 10 June 1762 Edgecombe County will was proved in September 1762. He named his sons Francis and Adam Ivey, daughters Elizabeth, Sarah, and Martha Ivey, left his son Lewis a plantation of 200 acres which he had purchased from William Register when he reached the age of twenty-one, left the use of his house and land for five years to his unnamed wife, left twenty-five pounds each to his son George and daughter Mary Ivey when they reached the age of twenty-one and left son Benjamin his 285 acre plantation [WB A:107]. When Benjamin

---

[118]See Robert Baird's article on this branch of the Ivey family: http://home.nc.rr.com/rwbaird/ivey/AdamIvey.htm

sold his land, he identified it as a Granville grant to Adam Ivey of 23 October 1754 [DB 2:154]. He was the father of

  i.   Francis, born say 1733, sold his land in Edgecombe County while resident in Bladen County in 1763. He purchased 300 acres on the south side of Drowning Creek on 15 June 1784 and sold it on 27 February 1786 [DB 1:151]. He was a white Bladen County taxable in 1776 [Byrd, *Bladen County Tax Lists*, II:69, 82, 118, 182].

  ii. Adam³, born say 1735, a "Mulato" taxable in Simon **Cox**'s Bladen County household in 1768 and a "Molato" taxable head of his own Bladen County household from 1770 to 1774 when he was taxable on his unnamed brother. He was a white taxable with his brother George in 1776 and was counted as white in 1786, head of a household of one male 21-60 years old, two under 21 or over 60, and eight females [Byrd, *Bladen County Tax Lists*, I:4, 34, 78, 124, 135; II:68, 82, 184]. He purchased 200 acres on Hog Swamp on 4 April 1772, sold 200 acres on Indian Swamp east of Ashpole Swamp on 31 July 1775 and was taxable on 450 acres in Bladen County in 1784 [DB 23:286, 509]. He was head of a Robeson County household of 12 whites in 1790 [NC:49]. He purchased land from Josiah Ivey by deed proved in Robeson County court on 1 July 1805 [Minutes I:329].

  iii. Elizabeth².

  iv. Benjamin, received 285 acres by the Edgecombe County will of his father. He and his wife Edey sold this land while resident in Bladen County in 1773 [Edgecombe County DB 2:154]. He was a white taxable in Bladen County from 1768 to 1772 (taxable on "Mulato" John **Phillips** in 1770), a "Mixt Blood" taxable in 1774 and a white taxable in 1776 [Byrd, *Bladen County Tax Lists*, I:4, 34, 81, 110, 124, 136; II:69, 82]. Edey was counted as white in 1790 with four females and one male over sixteen years [NC:49]. She was head of a Lumberton, Robeson County, household of 5 "other free" in 1810 [NC:218].

  v.   Sarah.

  vi. Martha.

  vii. Lewis, who was to inherit a plantation of 200 acres in Edgecombe County when he reached the age of twenty-one. He sold this land while resident in Bladen County in 1775 [Edgecombe County DB 3:232].

  viii. George, taxable in the Bladen County household of his brother Adam in 1776.

  ix. Mary.

3. Thomas¹ Ivey, born say 1715, entered 150 acres including his own improvements on the Five Mile Branch in Bladen County, North Carolina, on 20 February 1754 and another 300 acres on Drowning Creek where James Roberts formerly lived on 26 September 1755 [Philbeck, *Bladen County Land Entries*, nos. 974, 1048]. He was taxable with his two unnamed sons in Bladen County in 1763. He may have been the father of

5   i.   Thomas², Jr., born say 1738.

  ii. James, born say 1740, purchased 200 acres in Bladen County in the fork of the Little Peedee on the east side of Mitchell's Creek on 26 July 1766 and sold this land on 15 September 1769. It had originally been patented by Jordan **Gibson** (a relative of Gideon **Gibson**) on 1 July 1758 and sold by Jordan on 25 September 1761 [DB 23:85]. James was a white taxable in Bladen County in 1770 and taxable on himself and Gideon **Grant** in 1772 ("Mulatoes") [Byrd, *Bladen County Tax Lists*, I:45, 79]. He was called Captain James Ivey in a list of "free Negors and Mullatus" living in Bladen County on 13 October 1773 [G.A. 1773, Box 7].

  iii. Joseph², born say 1742, a "Mulato" taxable in Bladen County in 1768, taxable as white in 1770, and a "Mulato" taxable in 1772 [Byrd,

Bladen County Tax Lists, I:7, 45, 79]. He was in a list of "free Negors and Mullatus" living in Bladen County on 13 October 1773 [G.A. 1773, Box 7]. He patented 100 acres on the south side of Cow Branch west of the Great Shoe Heel in Bladen County and sold this land on 26 February 1785 [DB 1:129, 175]. He was a "Mulatoe" head of a Cheraws District, South Carolina household of 3 "other free" males over the age of 16 and 3 "other free" females in 1790 [SC:376], perhaps identical to Joseph Ivery, head of a Greenville County household of 6 "other free" in 1800 [SC:31].

    iv. Isham, a white taxable in Robeson county in 1772, 1774 and 1776 [Byrd, *Bladen County Tax Lists*, I:78, 110, 130; II:65, 82]. He made gifted 300 acres to Jesse Ivey by deed proved in Robeson County court on 7 January 1801 [Minutes 1797-1806, 136].

    v. David[1], born about 1760, "man of color," a musician and waggoner who enlisted in the 10th North Carolina Regiment for a three-year term. He married Nancy **Kelly** in November 1814 in Anderson County, Tennessee, and died in Davidson County, Tennessee, on 27 November 1828. Nancy, born about 1764, applied for a widow's pension and bounty land from Perry County, Tennessee, in September 1855 at the age of ninety-one. She had a daughter Lydia **Kelly**, born about 1795 [M804-1396, frame 0486].

4. Joseph[1] Ivey, born say 1717, died before 28 March 1750 when the Brunswick County, Virginia court ordered the churchwardens of St. Andrew's Parish to bind out his orphans Frederick and John Ivey [Orders 1749-50, 55]. He was the father of

6   i. Frederick[1], born say 1745.
      ii. John[1], born say 1748.

5. Thomas[2] Ivey, Junior, born say 1738, was granted a patent for 208 acres in Bladen County on the east side of Saddletree Swamp on 23 October 1761 [Hoffman, *Land Patents*, I:416]. He was a white taxable in Bladen County from 1768 to 1772, a "Mixt Blood" taxable in 1774, and a white taxable in 1776 [Byrd, *Bladen County Tax Lists*, I:6, 16, 45, 71, 78, 110, 124, 130; II:65, 82]. In 1784 he was assessed tax on 640 acres and one poll in Captain Regan's District of Bladen County. This part of Bladen County became Robeson County in 1787. He sold land in Robeson County by deeds proved on 4 October 1797, 1 July 1799, and 2 April 1804 (called Thomas Ivey, Senr.) [Minutes I:16, 76, 280]. He was counted as white in 1790 with 4 males over 16, 2 under 16, and 5 females in his Robeson County household [NC:50]. On 14 August 1809 his grandson Thomas **Hagans** refused to pay the tax on "all Free Negros Mulatoes and Mestizos," claiming that he was white. Two white men, Robert Coleman and John Regan, who were acquainted with Thomas Ivey when he had been living on Drowning Creek in Bladen (Robeson) County, testified before the Marion District, South Carolina court that he was *of Portuguese descent, that his complexion was swarthy, his hair black and strait - that his wife Elizabeth was a free white woman, very clear complection.* They testified further that his daughter Kesiah Ivey married Zachariah **Hagans**, and they were the parents of Thomas **Hagans** [*NCGSJ* IX:259]. He was called Thomas Ivey, Sr., on 26 August 1811 when he appeared in Robeson County court and proved by the oath of Joseph Wood, Esq., that he had "sometime ago" proved in Bladen County court that he was a white man [Minutes II:270]. Thomas Ivey's children were

     i. Kesiah, married Zachariah **Hagins**.
     ii. ?Josiah, head of a Robeson County household of 9 "other free" in 1810 [NC:238]. He sold land in Robeson County to Adam Ivey by deed proved on 1 July 1805 [Minutes I:329].

iii.   ?Joshua, head of a Robeson County household of 8 "other free" in 1810 [NC:237].

iv.   ?Jesse, head of a Robeson County household of 4 "other free" in 1810 [NC:241]. He purchased land by deed proved in Robeson County on 6 January 1806 [Minutes I:347].

v.   ?Thomas³, head of a Robeson County household of 4 "other free" in 1810 [NC:219].

vi.   ?Mary, head of a Robeson County household of 5 "other free" in 1810 [NC:238].

vii.   ?Sarabl, head of a Cumberland County household of 2 "other free" in 1800.

6.   Frederick¹ Ivey, born say 1745, was taxable on 175 acres in Lunenburg County in 1769 [Bell, *Sunlight on the Southside*, 275] and had removed from the county by November 1770 when he was listed among Anthony Street's list of insolvents for 1769 [*Magazine of Virginia Genealogy* 34:24-5]. He was head of a Mecklenburg County household of 6 free persons in 1782 [VA:34]. He may have been related to Rebecca Ivey who was ordered by the Lunenburg County court on 9 July 1773 to be paid as a witness for Anthony Gresham in his suit against John Hightower for 5 days attendance and coming and going 30 miles [Orders 1769-77, 339]. On 8 June 1776 the Mecklenburg County court ordered him to work on the road leading from the courthouse to the fork of Cook's old road [Orders 1773-9, 414]. He was taxable in Mecklenburg County from 1782 to 1820: taxable on a slave in 1785, 1786, 1794-1797, and from 1801 to 1820. His sons Jordan and Henry were taxable in his household from 1791 to 1795; Miles **Dunson** was taxable there in 1797, John **Chavis** in 1798 and Henry **Avery** in 1811. He was issued a retail merchant's license in 1806 and 1813 and was head of a Mecklenburg County household of a "free Negro" man and woman in 1813 [PPTL 1782-1805, frames 12, 76, 100, 124, 170, 376, 446, 521, 548, 616, 639, 851, 891, 977, 1002, 1082; 1806-28, frames 11, 22, 310, 319, 579, 687]. He purchased 60 acres at the head of Mayes Branch in Mecklenburg County on 13 December 1783, 96 acres in 1795, and 242 acres on Sandy Creek from Edmund **Gowen** on 9 December 1799. He was taxable on 666 acres in 1801, 941 acres on Sandy Creek in 1812, 1,041 acres in 1813, 1,187 acres in 1813, and 1,364 acres in 1816 [DB 5:388; 10:188-9; Land Tax List 1782-1811A, 1811B-1824A, A lists]. He married (second) Prissy **Stewart**, 14 December 1795 Mecklenburg County bond, William Willis security. Frederick was security for the 9 March 1789 Mecklenburg County marriage of Frederick **Goen** and Suckee **Chavous**. His estate was taxable on 1,284 acres in 1821 and his widow Priscilla was taxable on a life estate of 1,304 acres in 1822 [Land Tax List 1811B-1824A, A lists]. Frederick's estate was the subject of four chancery cases from 1830 to 1893 [LVA Chancery Cases 1830-018; 1834-048; 1869-050; 1893-005]. Priscilla was a seventy-year-old "Black" woman counted in the 1850 Mecklenburg County census [VA:137b]. She left an 1856 Mecklenburg County will. Frederick was the father of

i.   Jordan, born say 1774, over the age of 16 years from 1791 to 1794, called the son of Frederick when he was listed as a taxable with his father from 1791 to 1794. He was charged with his own tax in 1795 but was not listed again in the county [PPTL, 1782-1805, frames 376, 446, 466, 521, 548].

ii.   Henry, born say 1776, over the age of 16 years from 1793 to 1795 when he was listed as a taxable with his father from 1793 to 1795 but was not mentioned again in Mecklenburg County records [PPTL, 1782-1805, frames 466, 521, 548].

iii.   ?John², born say 1780, taxable in Mecklenburg County in the same district as Frederick Ivey in 1801 [PPTL, 1782-1805, frame 851].

iv. Elizabeth[3], born say 1800, married William **Chavous**, 6 March 1819 Mecklenburg County bond, Edward **Brandom** security.

v. Olive, born say 1801, married John **Naish**, 18 December 1823 Mecklenburg County bond.

vi. Margaret, born say 1803, daughter of Frederick and Priscilla Ivey, married William H. **Kersey**, 5 December 1822 Mecklenburg County bond.

vii. George, left a Mecklenburg County will in 1839.

viii. William, born about 1815.

ix. Frederick[2], born about 1820, a thirty-year-old "Black" man counted in the household of Priscilla Ivey in 1850 [VA:137b].

x. Catherine, born about 1820, married William H. **Mitchell**, 1836 Mecklenburg County bond.

Other members of the Ivey family were

i. Adam[4], head of a Sumter District, South Carolina household of 8 "other free" in 1800 [SC:605] and 10 "free colored" in 1820 [SC:211].

ii. Amos, head of a Marlboro District, South Carolina household of 7 "other free" in 1800 [SC:54a].

iii. Elizabeth, born say 1769, married Jesse **Harris**, 29 November 1790 Wake County, North Carolina bond, Reuben Embry bondsman.

iv. Molly, head of a Norfolk County household of 2 "other free" in 1810 [VA:905].

Lightning Source UK Ltd.
Milton Keynes UK
UKOW06f2316130217
294338UK00001B/39/P